LYTTON STRACHEY

———

A Critical Biography

Volume II

THE YEARS OF ACHIEVEMENT (1910–1932)

BOOKS BY MICHAEL HOLROYD

Hugh Kingsmill: A Critical Biography (John Baker)
Lytton Strachey: A Critical Biography

LYTTON STRACHEY

A Critical Biography

by

MICHAEL HOLROYD

Volume II
THE YEARS OF ACHIEVEMENT
(1910–1932)

HOLT, RINEHART AND WINSTON
NEW YORK   CHICAGO   SAN FRANCISCO

8656852
Printed in Great Britain

For Jennifer
with love

Contents

A*

Illustrations

Frontispiece: *Lytton Strachey, 1913, by Vanessa Bell*
(reproduced by courtesy of Mr Richard Carline)

PART I

'I suppose I ought to feel . . . a general sense of lamentation – but somehow I don't. My spirit refuses to be put down.'

Lytton Strachey to David Garnett (23 June 1915)

CHAPTER I

The Changing Past

'In or about December, 1910, human character changed.'
Virginia Woolf –
Mr Bennett and Mrs Brown (1924)

1

'CHÈRE MARQUISE' AND 'CHER SERPENT'

During the autumn of 1910, two people, who between them were to dominate the next few years of Lytton's life, emerge for the first time into prominence. Lady Ottoline Morrell he had encountered casually some time earlier at Haslemere, where his mother had taken him to see the Berensons. Their initial response to each other had been amiable, but lukewarm. 'His tall, bending figure and a rather long, cadaverous face, with long nose and a drooping moustache, made him then a not very attractive figure,' recalled Ottoline, who was on a visit to Logan Pearsall Smith at the time, 'but I found him most sympathetic and everything he said was of interest.'

In Lytton's correspondence there are occasional references to Ottoline after this meeting which suggest a latent curiosity about her. But it was not until about 1908, when they met as fellow guests of C. P. Sanger and his wife Dora, that the real beginning to their long and unusual friendship was formed. The Sangers were then living near the Strand, high up above the noise of the traffic in a flat where, once a week, they would give a party for their friends. Amid this intellectual group of young people – many of them from Cambridge – Ottoline felt rather inadequate; but her timidity was soon dispelled by Lytton, who was in his most animated and forthcoming mood. 'I see him now,' Ottoline wrote of that evening, 'sitting in a long basket-chair by the Sangers's gas fire leaning forward as he would still do, holding out his long, thin hands to warm. I think he had just come from one of Bernard Shaw's plays. Altogether I enjoyed my first evening at the Sangers immensely and came home quite excited.'

Lady Ottoline Morrell had felt herself to be something of a misfit, and in the plush and sunless land of late Victorian and Edwardian society, her prodigal, Gothic figure always stood out as a curious anomaly. Some seven years older than Lytton, she was the daughter of General Arthur Cavendish-Bentinck and his wife, Lady Bolsover. Her childhood had been lonely, lavish and discontented, and even before the age of eighteen she had shown herself to be deeply unconventional in her determination to escape from her upper-class, philistine background of material comfort and débutante dullness. The progress of this struggle was erratic: first she plunged into evangelical religion; next she persuaded her embarrassed family to allow her to travel to Italy, absorbing the beauties of art and nature; and finally she had fallen hopelessly in love with Axel Munthe. Returning to England, she determined briefly on a career of academic study at the University of St Andrews, but soon secured her freedom through marrying Philip Morrell, the Liberal member of Parliament – a man of fine aspirations, whose handsome features betrayed little potency behind them and whose kindly, fastidious temperament, lacking intellectual toughness, seemed somehow defeated and ineffective beside his wife's far more spectacular personality.

It was only now, as a married woman, that she was able to find a satisfying outlet for her egregious energies – in the political activities of her husband, and, more completely, in those realms of art and intellect that represented everything antagonistic to her prim, uneducated and aristocratic upbringing. Her entrée into this exciting world came largely through Virginia Stephen, whose Thursday evenings in Fitzroy Square she now began to frequent. Here she would regularly come across Lytton, and though she did not yet get to know him well, the impressions of him which she carried away from these gatherings and which she subsequently put down in her memoirs, are exact and acute. 'Of Lytton Strachey I used to feel most shy,' she wrote, 'for he said so little and he seemed to live far away in an atmosphere of rarefied thought. His voice so small and faint, but with definite accentuations and stresses of tone, giving a sense of certainty and distinction, appeared to come from very far away, for his delicate body was raised on legs so immensely long that they seemed endless, and his fingers equally long, like antennae. It was not till I knew him better that I found how agile those long legs could be, and what passion and feeling lay in that delicate body, and how rapidly those long and beautiful antennae could find passages in Racine or Dryden, and the strength and vigour of his voice when he read these passages aloud to me.'

It was not long before Ottoline constituted herself as the fashionable

London hostess to a wide and varied circle of writers and artists. Once a week she would invite a select company of them to her home at 44 Bedford Square. Here, in a great double room on the first floor, decked with modernistic pictures, pale grey walls, yellow taffeta curtains, soft lights and banks of flowers, they would talk over their coffee and cigarettes, listen to chamber music or dance in their pullovers and corduroy trousers. During the four or five years before the war, Lytton was among the most frequent of her guests at these functions, and also at the more formal and distinguished dinner-parties which she gave.

Ottoline Morrell has been described as an impresario rather than a creator, but her submerged creative instincts did come to the surface as a genuine flair for spotting original artists before they had made their reputations. In Lytton she rightly detected a figure destined to make his mark on the literature of the day, and she took him up as part of a determined effort to gate-crash her way into the secret world of the artist – a world with which, so her intuition proclaimed, she possessed more affinity than with her own unenlightened background. The dilemma in which she now found herself was unenviable. Without being able to command enough natural talent or intelligence to develop into a creative artist in her own right, she was nevertheless of too wilful and individual a nature to remain content with the inert traditions of her past. Her exertions to absorb vicarious nourishment from the intellectual milieu of which she had made her home the vortex took a curiously literal form in their unorthodoxy and directness. Loudly sucking and crunching between her prominent equine teeth a succession of bull's-eye peppermints, she would subject some of the shyer poets and more inarticulate painters to a series of searching and insistent questions concerning their work and the specific details of their love-affairs. 'M–m–m. Does your friend have *no* love-life?' she once complained in her drawling, deep, resonant voice to a poet who had brought some particularly reticent friend to tea. Frustrated, almost inevitably, in these attempts to find full satisfaction from literary gossip, she sometimes despaired of ever achieving fulfilment by such ruthless questionnaire tactics. Many of her friendships exploded into violent terminating quarrels, in the aftermath of which she could expect to see herself savagely caricatured in her late friend's next novel – as Priscilla Wimbush in Aldous Huxley's *Crome Yellow*, for example, or as Hermione Roddice in D. H. Lawrence's *Women in Love*.[1]

---

[1] Most of the spiteful stories about Ottoline emanated from her old friend turned enemy, Logan Pearsall Smith. He believed, incorrectly, that she had been responsible for seducing Bertrand Russell away from Alys Russell, his, Logan Pearsall Smith's, sister,

Though her sensibilities were undisciplined and over-elaborate, and she was not always very sensible, something of the extraordinary qualities of those people she mixed with did rub off on her. She had, too, the power to make artists and writers feel that their ideas were immensely exciting and important to her. She was therefore, in some respects, particularly well-suited to act as Lytton's confidante and to give him the literary encouragement he needed. 'Ottoline has moved men's imaginations,' wrote D. H. Lawrence, 'and that's perhaps the most a woman can do.' Certainly she moved Lytton's imagination. He found her alternately stimulating and embarrassing, sometimes gloriously larger-than-life, on other occasions unendurably trivial. But the quality that appealed most to men's imaginations was the homeless pathos which underlay her baroque and flamboyant personality. Her eccentricities were the practical means by which she tried to unify and assert an essentially heterogeneous character. For the fantastic side of her temperament found expression not only in the striking décor of Bedford Square, but also in her own appearance, which seemed to have been artificially grafted on to the rest of her nature, and which at once tickled Lytton's sense of the ridiculous. Beside her outlandish get-up, his own elongated oddity almost faded into conventional insignificance. 'She was a character of Elizabethan extravagance and force,' wrote Lord David Cecil, 'at once mystical and possessive, quixotic and tempestuous.' Many other writers have testified to the bizarre impression she made upon them. David Garnett describes her as 'extremely handsome: tall and lean, with a large head, masses of dark Venetian red hair, . . . glacier blue-green eyes, a long straight nose, a proud mouth and a long jutting-out chin made up her lovely, haggard face.' Peter Quennell, who got to know her several years later, was particularly struck by the lines of her features which 'had a mediaeval strength, a boldly baronial, high-arched nose being accompanied by a prominent prognathous jaw. Her hair, arranged in seventeenth-century curls, was darkened to a deep mahogany red, which the pallor of her face and neck made at first sight all the more surprising; and from this strangely impressive mask proceeded a sonorous nasal voice, which drawled and rumbled, and rustily hummed and hawed, but might subside, if she were amused or curious, to an insinuating confidential murmur.' Less sympathetically, Osbert Sitwell described her as resembling 'a rather oversize Infanta of Spain or Austria', while her chameleon-like

---

and a woman of pedagogic saintliness. He also resented her marriage to his close friend Philip Morrell. 'Ottoline likes to eat people up,' he complained. And with sly insinuations and fantastic distortions of the truth he proceeded to blow up around her personality a mist of pernicious wickedness.

luminescence reminded Virginia Woolf of nothing more colourful than a mackerel swimming in an aquarium tank. In her later years, by which time she had become a literary legend, Stephen Spender used to observe her sporting a shepherd's crook with a number of Pekinese dogs attached to it by ribbons. Her dress, too, was at least as unpredictable as her behaviour or the colour of her hair. George Santayana, arriving at Garsington for the first time, came across his hostess attired in bright yellow stockings crossgartered, like Malvolio; while Siegfried Sassoon saw her as grotesquely overpainted and powdered, with her hair dyed purple.

It was at these parties in Bedford Square that Lytton now renewed his acquaintance and began to develop a close friendship with another of Ottoline's protégés, Henry Lamb. Lamb came from a family of mathematicians, and had been educated at Manchester where his father was professor of mathematics at the university. He himself was without any trace of mathematical ability and wished fervently to be an artist. His father, however, would not hear of this, and a compromise had been reached whereby Henry agreed to study at medical school. Encouraged by his friend Francis Dodd,[1] he had nevertheless persisted in drawing in his spare time, and when in 1905 he unexpectedly won an art competition, he at once threw up his studies – though he had by then almost completed his time as a medical student – and travelled south to London, where he was introduced into the Bloomsbury world by his elder brother Walter. It was now, at the Stephen home in Gordon Square, that Lytton first set eyes on him. 'He's run away from Manchester, become an artist, and grown side-whiskers,' he reported to Leonard Woolf (October 1905). 'I didn't speak to him, but wanted to, because he really looked amazing, though of course very very bad.'

But at that stage Lytton had had no opportunity of getting to know him, since Lamb suddenly married his first wife, Euphemia, a wild, unshy art student at Manchester; and together they eloped to Paris. Here Henry had embarked upon his serious artistic training in company with Augustus John. These were crucial years in his life, and Lytton used occasionally to hear something of them from Duncan Grant, who was also, of course, studying in Paris. Now, as later, Lamb was largely overshadowed by the figure of John, modelling much of his work and behaviour after John's style. A superb if rather clinical draftsman, his partial failure to match or excel his master's high standard of achievement often vexed his spirit, making him a touchy

[1] Francis Dodd (1874–1949), the etcher and painter of landscapes, who, in 1895, had gone to live in Manchester, and nine years later moved to London where he eventually became a Royal Academician and a trustee of the Tate Gallery (1928–35).

and irritable companion. Under John's exotic influence, he also clothed himself in gipsy fashion and increased his womanizing, a first conquest being one of John's own girl friends. Their liaison so alienated Euphemia that she never forgave her husband and separated from him there and then, though their actual divorce was not arranged for another twenty years.[1]

It was the whimsical, divergent element in both Ottoline and Henry that at first roused Lytton's curiosity, and for a while he appears to have been unable to distinguish clearly between the very different attractions that each held for him. 'Ottoline has vanished to her cottage, but tomorrow she begins her parties again, and I shall drag myself there if I can,' he wrote to Duncan Grant (4 April 1910). 'My last view of her was at a dim evening party full of virgins given by the Russells in a furnished flat. I was feeling dreadfully bored when I suddenly looked up and saw her entering with Henry. I was never so astonished, and didn't know which I was in love with most. As to *her*, though, there seems very little doubt. She carried him off to the country with her under my very nose, and I was left wishing that Dutch William and his friends had never come to England.'[2]

Eight months later Lytton himself was invited to stay at Peppard, Ottoline's cottage near Henley-on-Thames. One Sunday in October, they had met at a tea-party given at Newnham by Jane Harrison. Ottoline, half-laughingly, suggested that Lytton should come and

---

[1] In later life Euphemia took up with the painter James Dickson Innes (1887–1914). John Rothenstein, in his *Modern English Painters, Volume 2: Innes to Moore* (revised edition 1962, pp. 29–30) writes: 'But his [Innes's] last and deepest attachment was to Euphemia Lamb. They met in a Paris café, and Innes at once responded to the beauty of her pale oval face, classical in feature yet animated by a spirit passionate, reckless and witty, and the heavy honey-hued hair: a beauty preserved in many paintings and drawings by her artist friends, most notably, perhaps, in a tiny drawing in pen and ink by John, but even now not extinct. Together Innes and Euphemia made their way, largely on foot, to his favourite resorts on the foothills of the Pyrenees, and back to London, he contributing to their support by making drawings in cafés and she by dancing. Their attachment lasted until his death.' When he was dying in a nursing-home at Swanley in Kent, Horace Cole and Augustus John took Euphemia to see him. 'The meeting of these two was painful,' John records in *Chiaroscuro* (1962 edition, p. 180). 'We left them alone together: it was the last time I saw him. Under the cairn on the summit of Arenig, Dick Innes had buried a silver casket containing certain correspondence. I think he always associated Euphemia with this mountain and would have liked at the last to lie beside the cairn.'

[2] Ottoline's ancestor, Hans William Bentinck, first Earl of Portland (1649–1709), had entered William of Orange's household at the age of fifteen, becoming the Prince's loyal companion of a lifetime, his catamite, and his confidential agent. At William and Mary's coronation he was deluged with honours and rewards, but remained rather an unpopular figure in international politics. He married three times, his numerous children settling partly in Holland, partly in England. He himself died at his seat of Bulstrode, near Beaconsfield, following an attack of pleurisy.

visit her in the country, adding that Henry Lamb would be the other guest. Lytton appeared to ponder this suggestion very deeply, drifted away for a few minutes, then came back to ask: 'Do you really mean me to come to Peppard?' 'Of course I do,' replied Ottoline without hesitation, all at once doubting her sincerity, and dreading the responsibility of entertaining him at her home. And so it was settled.

Ottoline's fears over providing for Lytton's well-being soon proved to have been groundless. Away from the fogs of London and the noisy General Election fever that autumn, enjoyment came quite spontaneously to him, and he remained there for over three consecutive weeks. Peppard was extraordinarily comfortable, the country charming, the climate bracing. He could find no fault with anything. He ate enormous meals, went for enormous walks through the near-by beech-woods, and had his portrait painted by Henry, who had set up his studio in the stables. 'This is altogether exquisite,' he wrote rhapsodically to James Strachey (18 November 1910). 'Such comforts and cushions as you never saw! Henry, too, more divine than ever, plump now (but not bald) and mellowed in the radiance of Ottoline. The ménage is strange. Fortunately Philip is absent, electioneering in Burnley. Henry sleeps at a pub on the other side of the green, and paints in a coach-house rigged up by Ottoline with silks and stoves, a little further along the road. She seems quite gone – quite! And on the whole I don't wonder. But his attitude is rather more cranky. No doubt it's a convenience, and a pleasure even – but then – Meanwhile Philip electioneers at Burnley.

'. . . I'm afraid I have now been permanently spoilt for country cottage life. How does the woman do it? Every other ménage must now seem sordid . . .

'Ah! She is a strange tragic figure. (And such mysteries!)'

It was during these happy, exciting weeks at Peppard that the future pattern of a complicated triangular relationship was finally fixed and defined. Briefly stated, both Ottoline and Lytton had fallen uncompetitively in love with Henry Lamb, who returned their attentions with a mixture of affection and callousness. Lytton's infatuation is easily enough accounted for: Lamb had now come to occupy in his scheme of things that position recently vacated by Duncan Grant. He offered him the same humble accolade, showered on him the same lavish praise of his artistic accomplishments – 'that he's a genius', he wrote to his brother James (30 November 1911), 'there can be no doubt, but whether a good or an evil one?' This romantic speculation held its appeal for Lytton, who, half-cherishing the role of unrequited lover, was still drawn to people whom he instinctively felt might use him badly. Lamb was exclusively heterosexual, and of a charming, highly-strung, volatile disposition, a prey to feelings of morbid insecurity that were constantly being inflamed by his pessimistic, one-sided rivalry with Augustus John. All this made him a tricky and unpredictable inamorato: 'He is the most delightful companion in the world', Lytton once confessed to James (November 1911), '– and the most unpleasant.' Above all, Lamb resented any suspicion that he was being imposed upon. The intense possessiveness of both Lytton and Ottoline, which his own mercurial temperament did much to stimulate, often irritated him immeasurably, hardening his heart and making him behave in a deliberately unfeeling manner. Nor did he attach the same high priority to human relationships as did the Bloomsbury Group or the Cambridge Apostles, and his egocentricity caused Lytton much misery and bewilderment. 'His [Lamb's] state of mind baffles me,' he admitted to James (August 1911). 'He seems to be completely indifferent to every-thing that concerns me, and yet expects me to be interested in every trifle of his life.'

Despite these formidable disadvantages, Lamb's appeal was very potent. He offered both Ottoline and Lytton admission into an un-known, superbly bohemian set – the world of all-night Chelsea parties, gay and easy-going, and of dedicated exotic artists such as Augustus John and the Russian mosaicist Boris Anrep,[1] both of whom rapidly assumed in Lytton's mind the proportions of myths. He was, too, a man of salamander-like good looks, rather dashing and debonair, pale, slim, with long flowing hair, a sylphic physiognomy, evil and bewitch-ing goat's eyes and long thin lips that curved into the kind of grin one sees transfixed on the skeleton faces of some prehistoric monsters. Lamb's sinister, Pan-like beauty entranced and captivated Lytton. Ottoline, so close to the pair of them, was able to observe their friend-ship at first hand. The description of it which she gives in her memoirs catches perfectly the mood and spirit of Lytton's romantic fascination.

---

[1] After studying law at St Petersburg and travelling widely through Europe, Boris von Anrep (b. 1883) had gone to Paris where he studied Byzantine art. In 1910–11, when Lytton first encountered him, he had moved to the Edinburgh College of Art. In 1914, he joined the Imperial Guard and appeared, a terrific figure, in full Russian Guard uniform, claiming that a battle at the Front wasn't nearly so alarming as one of Ottoline's parties. After the war he was to live for a time in Hampstead, but returned to Paris in 1926 and devoted himself to the revival of mosaic as an independent art. His chief public commissions in Britain include the mosaic pavement at the Tate Gallery, the floor, vestibule landing and pavement at the National Gallery (which depicts, among others, Virginia Woolf, Mary Hutchinson, Clive Bell, Osbert and Edith Sitwell, T. S. Eliot and Bertrand Russell), and mosaics for Westminster Cathedral, the Bank of England and the Royal Military College chapel, Sandhurst. In 1918 he married Helen Maitland, who later left him to live with Roger Fry, whose wife had become incurably ill with a mental disease in 1910 and died in 1937.

'At this time his [Lytton's] devotion to Henry Lamb was very great, and tossing him about on a sea of emotion. Lamb enjoyed leading him forth into new fields of experience. They would sit in pubs and mix with "the lower orders", as Lytton called them, picking up strange friends. And so great is the imitative instinct in the human breast that he even altered his appearance to please Lamb, wearing his hair very long, like Augustus John, and having his ears pierced and wearing ear-rings. He discarded collars and wore only a rich purple silk scarf round his neck, fastened with an intaglio pin. They were a surprising pair as they walked the streets of London, as Lamb wore clothes of the 1860 period with a square brown hat, Lytton a large black Carlyle felt hat and a black Italian cape.'

Lytton's relationship with Ottoline was at least as picturesque, but psychologically less straightforward. A rumour had spread through Bloomsbury that he was romantically inclined towards her – a piece of gossip which Virginia Woolf, who had pictured the great hostess when absent from Lytton as 'languishing like a sick and yellow alligator', may well have helped to popularize. There were, too, scraps of prima facie evidence to lend credence to this oversimple diagnosis. Lamb once came upon them unawares, fixed in a fierce embrace from which they abruptly sprang free, so that he could witness blood trickling down Lytton's lip. Yet the basis of their intimacy was never really sexual or aggressive, and though romantic in the imaginative sense, it remained purely platonic. The flirtation at which they played was all good pseudo-robust Elizabethan stuff, flighty and rollicking and always more stagy than real. But that they did feel some affinity for each other is beyond question. 'Elizabethanism' was not all they held in common. Outcasts from their conventional family backgrounds, and eccentrics within the uniform world of formal society, they were both prone to persistent ill health, yet retained something of the same stubborn ambition mixed with vague transcendental overtones and a deep and abiding veneration for art. Ottoline belonged also to that breed of overruling, imperious women – a breed which included Florence Nightingale, Lady Hester Stanhope, Queen Victoria and Queen Elizabeth – that invariably fired Lytton's imagination. Her personality was so expansive, so spontaneous and affectionate that it would frequently sweep him off his feet. Beside her, everyone else seemed only half awake. He admired intensely her undaunted, indiscreet courage, her resolution in supporting enlightened causes, her incontestable disregard for colourless, unthinking conventions.

'What a pity one can't now and then change sexes!' Lytton had once written to Clive Bell (21 October 1909). 'I should love to be a dowager

Countess.' In the company of Ottoline, such a desire was partly gratified. Her unquenchable, aristocratic air appealed immensely to his eighteenth-century respect for noble birth; and left to themselves they carried on like a couple of high-spirited, teenage girls – all giggling and high heels and titillating gossip. Occasionally they would step outside the drawing-room to play at tennis in Bedford Square Gardens, their slow, huge lobs over the net being accompanied by such convulsive shrieks of laughter that a large crowd of passers-by and residents would quickly assemble to behold these hysterical performances.

Each seemed to fulfil a real need in the other; one hungering after secret confidences, the other so eager to impart them. By themselves they were natural and gay; but introduce a third person into the room and their friendship was immediately made subject to an uneasy strain. To Lytton's eyes, Ottoline would then shed her charmingly unaffected demeanour, and change from a beautiful, stately woman of genuine artistic sensibility into a fancifully bespangled and festooned monstrosity, embarrassingly effusive and artificial. This metamorphosis was partly a hallucination. Once, coming from a particularly sportive tête-à-tête with Ottoline, he began to extol her virtues in the most extravagant language to Duncan Grant and Vanessa Bell. 'She was majestic!' he cried. 'She was splendid! Magnificent! Sublime!' But when Duncan Grant and Vanessa Bell demurred at so excessive praise, he quickly amended his sentiments, adding a string of well-considered qualifications that in due course far outweighed the opening eulogy. Owing to his quite justified mistrust of Ottoline's malicious tongue, Lytton did not use her at any time as his sole confidante, apportioning the part equally between her and his brother James, who was less encouraging but more reliable.

Lytton had gone to Peppard expecting to stay on there only a few days; but the days dissolved into weeks, November slipped by and December came – and still he lingered on. Every day was delightfully lazy, comfortable, refreshing. Some of this time he spent reading up for *Landmarks in French Literature*, and also, in French, the novels of Dostoievsky, to which he had been introduced by Lamb.[1] In spare moments he would diligently transcribe his poems in a manuscript

[1] As a matter of speculation, the recommendation of Dostoievsky may have come originally or indirectly from Augustus John. In August 1909, John dined with James Strachey, and in the course of their conversation made a long speech in favour of the Russian novelist, about whose work only a few intellectuals knew at this time. Lytton sent Lamb his essays on both Dostoievsky and Stendhal, and Nicolette Devas records that Lamb used to mark them in the margin with the initials F.R., meaning Foreign Rot, or C.E., meaning Child's Essay.

book, beautifully bound in orange-vermilion vellum, with which Ottoline had specially presented him. Towards the end of November she went off to help her husband's electioneering in Lancashire, and Lytton was left with Lamb, dressed in Cossack boots and an amazing maroon suit, as his sole companion. Almost daily they wrote charming and affectionate letters to her, telling her of all they were doing. 'I felt he [Lytton] came more to see Henry Lamb than to see me,' she wrote afterwards. 'In my journal I say that "he terrified me" at first, but I found him more sympathetic than I had imagined, but there is something wanting in him: a perfect Epicurean without large or generous instincts, but from his exceedingly fine brain he sees light and has appreciation of nobility, but shrinks back, partly from pose, and from prejudice and nervousness. He is indeed delicate in his health and that helps to encourage self-indulgence. He too is one of those in whom feminine characteristics are strong.

'He and Lamb sat up until very late at night in the little sitting-room underneath my bedroom, and I heard the duet of their voices underneath, laughing and joking, Lytton playing with him like a cat with a mouse, enjoying having his own sensations tickled by Lamb's beauty, while his contrariness adds spice to the contact. I call him the Polish count, for he seemed to me as if he was a character out of a Russian novel.'

For his part, Lytton realized that he had entered upon a distinctly new and invigorating phase of his life. He was aware of a fresh confidence, stemming partly from his ripening friendship with Ottoline, that he could now at last establish himself independently of his mother and family. 'Extraordinary,' he exclaimed in a letter to James (30 November 1910). 'My existence here is something new. I tremble to think of what an "idyll" it might be, if only – and even as it is – in fact I really have no notion *what* it is. It seems to me more like Country House Life in the thirties than anything else. I feel like George Sand – shall I write an Indiana?'

2

MUMPS AND A BEARD

Shortly before Christmas, Lytton left England and set off for the South of France to stay with the Bussys, where he was to remain for the next four months. At Roquebrune he hoped to avoid the illnesses and hardships of the English winter, and, in the more amenable climate, to forge ahead with his writing of *Landmarks in French Literature*. But no sooner had he arrived at La Souco than he was prostrated by 'une légère attaque de cholerine', from which he seemed incapable of recovering. Unable to digest anything but vile and noxious slops, he grew every day weaker and thinner and more despondent. 'I've been having chills and general ruin for the last three weeks or so,' he complained to Maynard Keynes (6 February 1911). 'I hope I may now be recovering, but I'm rather shattered and in a very bad temper – at my having come all the way to escape getting ill, without any result.' A month later he could only report: 'My condition is wobbly still.' But at last the state of affairs seemed a little more hopeful. The weather, which for two months had been arctic and far colder than in England, grew milder; and though still very weak Lytton enrolled at the Zander Institute in Nice,[1] where he practised gentle isometric exercises to regain his stamina. At the same time, a sympathetic French doctor took him in charge, assuring him that the one thing absolutely essential for his health was 'suralimentation' – so in place of the unpalatable slops he began a new régime consisting of a square meal every few hours, which, if not entirely successful, was at least more appetizing.

To many of his friends he would write off, begging for some news with which to fill the vacuity of 'this lugubre exile'. Now that he was in France, England seemed infinitely desirable. 'You can imagine how I long to be at Peppard,' he assured Lamb (21 February 1911), 'and rejoice in the honest warmth of an English winter – it all sounds so heavenly that I hardly dare to think of it.' One of his few consolations were the French translations of Dostoievsky. He read *L'Idiot, Le Crime et Le Châtiment* and *Les Possédés*, which he liked best of all. 'I'm as converted as you could wish about Dostoievsky,' he declared in another letter to Lamb (5 January 1911). 'The last half of Vol 2 of the Possédés quite knocked me over. Colossal! Colossal! It's mere ramping and soaring genius, and all possible objections are reduced to absurdity. I shudder to think that I might never have read it, and I never should if it hadn't been for you. . . . As for my objections, some of them do remain – mitigatedly.' In due course, even this solitary comfort was exhausted – 'I'm now reduced to the Bible, which I find has a good deal of merit, in one way or another.'

At the beginning of March the Bussys left for Sicily, and Lytton's sister Marjorie came down to look after him and his child niece, Jane Simone. This reorganization hardly affected Lytton. His life went on much as before, 'a mere blank of utter nothingness punctuated by a few horrors and rages here and there'. In spite of this evergreen lassitude,

[1] Founded by Dr Emile Zander, under whose care Lytton had come at Saltsjöbaden.

he had been pressing doggedly on with his book, and completed what amounts, perhaps, to its best chapters, those on 'Louis XIV' and 'The Eighteenth Century' – though this was rather less than he had originally hoped to achieve in his four months of exile. 'I am in an almost complete stupor,' he admitted to James. 'Have been trying to write the history of French Literature without much success.' This estimate of his progress, infected by a kind of Mediterranean despondency, did himself less than justice. Out of the grim struggle to advance with his work was born a greater spiritual resilience and sense of freedom. 'I feel quite reckless,' he wrote to James, '– more I think than I ever have before. It came to me quite suddenly the other day – how little anything matters . . . and then that really, after all, one has a confidence.'

Early that April, Lytton returned to Hampstead 'in rather a low state' for a week's convalescence with his family. Sanatogen, which he seems to have swallowed nearly every half-hour, had apparently once more saved his life – aided on this occasion by Dr Gregory's noisome manipulation of rhubarb – and he soon felt strong enough to start away on his wanderings again. 'I should like to go on a sailing voyage for fourteen months,' he told Henry Lamb (9 April 1911). Three days later he travelled down by train to the Dog Inn, near Henley, for a week with Lamb. 'Order several beef-steaks,' he exhorted him before setting off (10 April 1911), 'and light all the fires. I am (at present) not ill, but cowardly.'

After eight pleasant days among these so-called 'lower orders',[1] Lytton left Lamb's lodgings at the Dog Inn, and went down with James to Corfe Castle in Dorset, putting up at the Greyhound Inn. The evening of their arrival, a Friday, he complained of being ill. James took his temperature with the thermometer he always carried about with him and saw that it was 104. Next day, to the general relief, an attack of mumps declared itself. James looked after him to start with, but had to go back to the *Spectator* on Tuesday morning. So Oliver was ordered to take his place at Corfe. He was furious. He had just arrived in England from India on short leave, and was longing to rush around in the social life he so much enjoyed. For some reason, possibly expense, they were obliged to transmigrate from the relatively comfortable Greyhound to the poky little Castle Inn. The two of them crammed themselves into a small closed carriage piled high and wide with luggage, balancing every sort of treasured object in their arms – oil cans, ink bottles, safety-razors and the novels of Dostoievsky – and arrived there on the afternoon of 21 April. Because

[1] James Strachey advised that although Ottoline referred to 'lower orders', Lytton in fact never did. The phrase he always used was 'lower classes'.

of the risk of infection, Lytton was entombed in his bedroom at the Castle Inn for almost three weeks, attended by Oliver who, very kind and very incompetent, endeavoured to look after him without succumbing to the disease himself. The boredom and defatigation of these weeks were intense. While Oliver sat downstairs writing love-letters to his fiancée Ray Costelloe, upstairs in his bed Lytton lay composing affectionate epistles to his '*très-cher* serpent' Henry Lamb, who had gone off to stay with Boris Anrep in Paris. During all this time the only book he had to read was a French edition of Dostoievsky's letters which, in spite of a certain number of good things, disappointed him and tended to deepen the gloom of his quarantine. 'For one thing his [Dostoievsky's] portrait – most infinitely abattu – with eyes – oh! – but almost, I thought, as if he had been too much crushed – which was also the effect of the letters,' he reported to Henry Lamb (4 May 1911). 'His life was perfect hell till six years before he died; and his letters are almost entirely occupied with begging for money – always "pour l'amour du Christ". At last whenever you see Christ on a page you skip it because you know that an appeal for 125 roubles will follow. It's deplorable and it's impossible not to have rather a lower opinion of the man. He was not at all souterrain – very simple and at all times silly. On Christianity he writes the most hopeless stuff.'

The tedium of these bed-ridden weeks was occasionally relieved by a visit from one of his friends. Clive Bell came for a day and waved up cautiously towards the invalid's window; and Ottoline Morrell blew an elaborate kiss at him from the roadway as she motored from Studland *en route* for London. 'It was very touching,' he commented, 'but insubstantial.'

It was now, during these weeks of illness at Corfe, that Lytton grew his beard – that most striking token of the metamorphosis which was changing him into a mature personality, in due course to grow famous throughout Britain, America and the Continent. At first he was doubtful as to its merits. Did it, for example, make him appear too ridiculous? 'The beard question is becoming rather dubious – but you shall judge,' he wrote to Ottoline. She, and all his other friends, begged him to keep it, since it made him look so well; and soon enough he agreed to do so. 'The chief news is that I have grown a beard,' he informed his mother (9 May 1911). 'Its colour is much admired, and it is generally considered extremely effective, though some ill-bred persons have been observed to laugh. It is a red-brown of the most approved tint, and makes me look like a French decadent poet – or something equally distinguished.'

The growing of this celebrated beard may be regarded as an outward manifestation of Lytton's newly reinvigorated attitude towards the world. Though he still remained outwardly shy and diffident, and tended to exaggerate his set-backs almost to the point of invention, a hard, inner kernel of self-assurance was expanding. In the past he too often allowed his heart to rule his head; now, for the first time, his intellect was beginning to take over control. Under the influence of his brother James he had, since leaving Cambridge, grown more interested in politics, and was in the gradual process of rejecting his vague, high-bred Conservatism in favour of a more combative, left-wing position, mildly socialistic and violently anti upper-class.

Something of this changing attitude, its immanence and scope, is already implicit in a most interesting paper which Lytton delivered to the Apostles (20 May 1911) at Cambridge, where he and Oliver had gone after leaving Corfe Castle. Near the opening of this paper, Lytton confesses his idyllic sentimentalism and the rather conservative form which it took: 'I even have a secret admiration for the typical English-man – the strong silent man with the deep emotions – too deep – oh! far too deep ever to come to the surface; I can't help being impressed.' Against this high emotional susceptibility he sets a more objective mental estimate of such a man's worth. The strict, Victorian conventions seemed to have slipped in the seven years since he had come down from Trinity; but with the new, dawning freedom, there was emerging a somewhat prosaic, matter-of-fact world. He deprecated the earnest pomposity with which it had become the fashion to treat matters serious and laughable. For instance, now that the bishops had started going to the music halls the community seemed to be faced not, un-fortunately, with a growing sense of humour among the clergy, but an increasing solemnity on the variety stage. The managers of those places had taken to writing to newspapers to assure everyone that no *risqués* jokes were to be heard in their establishments – one could only hope they were not telling the truth. Again, eminent literary critics would pull long faces over the more outspoken classics, wondering how, to take the case of Boccaccio for example, a book of such merit could also be so scandalously immoral. Soon one would not be able to dip into *Tristram Shandy* without being arraigned for impurity by the National Council of Public Morals. In Lytton's view it was high time that some light-hearted jester shook his cap and bells a little in the faces of such intruding Malvolios. Did they think that because they were virtuous there should be no more cakes and ale? In short, Lytton's comic and romantic sensibilities warmed to the exaggeration, the fantasy and the rhetoric of the more outspoken picturesque past; but his intelligence applauded that sober, slowly developing social justice and enlighten-ment which releases confidences of a more intimate humane kind – those voices which had lain pathetically inarticulate under all the Victorian gush of words. And so, rather regretfully, he comes down on balance in favour of the more colourless, unpoetical Age of Criticism:

'With us, at any rate, the old rule of the curt Englishman, who feels (so he says) that his emotions are too sacred for him to dare to do anything but hint at them – that old rule has broken down. Even in my memory there has been a change. Five years ago – the things that *didn't* happen! That's what, from the modern standpoint, strikes me now. And then – five years hence! – what a subject for a poem! – but no, we've given up poetry – we've reduced ourselves to prose.

'To prose? A queer sort of prose, I think. But really, in this so-called universe, what else can one expect? To be sure, to be sensible, to view things from the ordinary standpoint of the educated man – I've tried that, and found it really rather painful. For a moment, under the pressure of *The Times* newspaper, of the Home University Library, of the Ladies, and the rest of the phenomenal world, I've succeeded in feeling sensible, and then, looking back on my previous reflections I have seen quite clearly that they were simply the crude and crazy vaporizing of an eccentric in a dream. Perhaps that's what they are. So I think for a moment; but, opening the biography of our brother Maitland, I have a revulsion. Oh dear! the grey horror of those letters to our brothers Pollock, Verrall, and Jackson! The brave concealment of tragedy! The profound affection just showing, now and then, with such a delicacy – between the lines – "I am sorry indeed that the part of your letter to which I looked so anxiously contained such bad news – and having said that I think I won't say more – it is so useless." – "I feel good reason for hoping that long before now you have become reasonably comfortable. What I wish you know." – "I do very earnestly hope that things go fairly well with you and that you have not much pain." – What a world, what a life, passing in these dimnesses! I see once more the bleak and barren plain, and the dreadful solitary castles, with their blinds drawn down.'

Lytton's manner, too, as well as his appearance and his political opinions, was undergoing some change. The long and elastic body, which had for years proved such an embarrassment to him was to be co-ordinated by this expanding confidence, his natural ungainliness stylized and welded into part of an elegantly synthetic, physical personality. And that curious scarecrow figure, too, was in the process of being shaped and transformed by the same alchemy into strange, symmetrical proportions that radiated a spidery fascination and beauty. Of course, some people – Angelica Homere and Topsy Lucas among them – would always find his looks pleasing and remarkable; others –

Wyndham Lewis and Dorothy Brett, for example – were constantly revolted by the sight of him. Lytton himself, from the beginning, had sadly accepted this second view. Now, for the first time, he began to do so less readily. To some extent, his external appearance *had* changed; but there were also crucial internal changes to account for his more optimistic attitude and to influence the way in which others regarded him. Among his friends he began to speak and act with more than his old assurance. Like all sensitive egocentrics, he seemed timid among strangers, easily bored and only intermittently sociable. To avoid the risk of being spoken to in trains, he always, even when most badly off, travelled first class (though probably a more important reason for this luxury was his piles). And Harold Nicolson remembers seeing him later on, hiding in agony behind a door on the other side of which a party was in progress. But though still prone to boredom and acutely subject to outbursts of shyness, he was better able to retaliate and reflect embarrassment back on others. Shortly after his beard had grown to its full magnificent length, a lady came up and asked him: 'Oh, Mr Strachey, tell me, when you go to bed, do you keep that beard of yours inside or outside the blankets?' Adopting his most insinuating tone – which always reminded Desmond MacCarthy of the gnat in *Alice in Wonderland* – he piped: 'Won't you come and see?' At another party, the conversation turned to the question of which great historical character the people there would most have liked to go to bed with. The men voted for Cleopatra, Kitty Fisher and so on, but when it came to Lytton's turn he declared shrilly: 'Julius Caesar!'

Ottoline Morrell, whom he visited at Peppard for a few days that June, also observed some change in him. 'He was franker with me than he used to be,' she wrote, 'and I was less timid and nervous with him than I had been. . . .

'It is hard to realize that this tall, solemn, lanky, cadaverous man, with his rather unpleasant appearance, looking indeed far older than he is, is a combination of frivolity, love of indecency, mixed up with rigid intellectual integrity. . . .

'The steeds that draw the chariot of his life seem to be curiously ill-matched: one so dignified and serious, and so high-stepping, and of the old English breed, so well versed in the manners and traditions of the last four centuries; the other so feminine, nervous, hysterical, shying at imaginary obstacles, delighting in being patted and flattered and fed with sugar.

'In general he takes little part, rather lying in wait than giving himself away – only occasionally interrupting, throwing in a rational and often surprisingly witty remark. But tête-à-tête he is a charming companion –

his feminine quality making him sympathetic and interested in the small things of life, and with those who know him well he is very affectionate.'

Leaving Peppard early in June, Lytton returned once more to Cambridge, where he installed himself, with Oliver, in lodgings at 12 King's Parade. He had arranged to have sent on to him a trunk full of extra clothes so that there was no need to go back to Hampstead, and he was able to make Cambridge his headquarters for some time longer. Oliver soon left to marry Ray Costelloe, Gerald Shove took his place as Lytton's chief companion, and life jogged on along its amiable, enchanted course. He hardly knew why he felt so happy. The greater part of every day he spent lying in a punt near King's, 'propped up by innumerable cushions, and surrounded by innumerable books which we never read'. From this vantage point he held a sort of pastoral court among the undergraduates floating down to the bank while he passed – smoking cigarettes, talking, and eating *langues-de-chat* as they sat, row upon row, on the grass in the sunshine. The willows, the parasols, the blue skies, the white flannels – everything conspired to make these months into an elysium. At week-ends he would tear himself away to visit Lady Lytton at Knebworth, or George Mallory at Charterhouse, or, once again, his 'Chère Marquise' Ottoline Morrell at Peppard, 'where it was all very idyllic, dining out in the moonlight with purple candle-sticks'.

But Cambridge, though delightful, was not conducive to hard work. At the beginning of July, Lytton reluctantly decided to leave King's Parade, and travelled down, via Hampstead for reinforcements of clothes, to Becky House, near Manaton in Devon, which Rupert Brooke had recommended for its peace, inexpensiveness and comfort. A largish country cottage, primitive and remote, set by itself in a desolate rocky Dartmoor valley next to a waterfall and a small rushing stream, it was lived in by a working-class man and his family, who let lodgings – a large sitting-room and a few bedrooms. 'It is very agreeable,' he told Maynard Keynes,' – incredibly hot and exhilarating.' He now settled down to write the final chapters of *Landmarks in French Literature*, working not less than four hours every day, and describing himself as 'extraordinarily healthy and industrious'. His good health and general competence during this month proved to him what he had always instinctively believed: that the country was the one place for him in which to live if he wished to create some enduring work of literature. Open air, fresh food and strict, regular hours propped up his fleeting vitality and made possible his best and most sustained literary compositions.

While at Becky House he was joined for a week by two old friends,

G. E. Moore and Leonard Woolf – recently returned from Ceylon, his ascetic features burnt up by the tropical sun. 'He has a long, drawn, weather-beaten face,' Lytton rather morosely observed in a letter to James (15 June 1911), 'and speaks (when he does) very slowly, like one re-risen from the tomb – or rather on the other side of it.' As the time approached for their arrival he began to dread the prospect of their company. Why had he ever asked them? So much had happened in the six or seven years since they had been really close; he was a different, even an unrecognizable person now. Apprehensively he wrote off to Henry Lamb (5 July 1911): 'My heart quails at the thought of their conversation. Oh dear! How things must have changed since the days when I thought it was the absolute height of pleasure and glory! But now there is something cold and dry – I don't know what – the curiosity of existence seems to vanish with them: it's not that I don't like them – only that they are under the sea.' Then he had a brainwave – leading on to a very typical denouement. He invited Lamb to come and stay, at the same time apologizing to Moore and Woolf that another, possibly incompatible guest appeared to be arriving. He had invited him, he went on to explain, in a moment of unaccountable frenzy, thinking that he would certainly refuse, and had been astonished to receive a reply saying that he would be delighted to accept. But then, to his genuine surprise, Lamb cancelled this acceptance because of a trip to France; and Lytton was obliged to face his friends alone.

The visit of Moore and Woolf, however, turned out to be less submarine than Lytton had predicted. While his life and personality had been changing, theirs had not remained entirely static. 'I find them – oh! quite extraordinarily nice – but . . . if they are no longer under the sea, perhaps it's I who am somewhere else now – in the clouds, perhaps,' he told Lamb (14 July 1911); 'at any rate I find myself dreaming of more congenial company. However we are very happy, and go out for walks, and discuss this and that, and do a great deal of work. My health is a great success . . . fatness increasing and peevishness at breakfast almost unknown.' It was, in fact, Leonard Woolf to whom this old Apostolic atmosphere seemed most foreign. After his unintellectual, colonial career in Ceylon, the uncommunicative company of Moore and Lytton at Becky House was pretty astringent. 'In the morning Lytton used to sit in one part of the garden, with a panama on his head, groaning from time to time over his literary constipation as he wrote *Landmarks in French Literature* for the Home University Library,' he recalled, describing the everyday scene there; 'in another part of the garden sat Moore, a panama hat on his head, his forehead wet with

B

perspiration, sighing from time to time over his literary constipation as he wrote *Ethics* for the Home University Library. Lytton used to complain that he was mentally constipated because nothing at all came into his mind, which remained as blank as the paper on his knees. Moore on the contrary said that his mental constipation came from the fact that as soon as he had written down a sentence, he saw that it was just false or that it required a sentence to qualify the qualification.' In the afternoons the three of them would set off for long walks across Dartmoor, and Moore, who had a passion for bathing, would strip off his clothes whenever they came to one of the cold, black, rock pools, and plunge in. 'Nothing would induce Lytton to get into water in the open air,' Leonard Woolf records, 'and so I felt I must follow Moore's example. It nearly killed me.' Later on, in the evenings, 'Moore sang Adelaide, Schubert songs, or the Dichterliebe, or he played Beethoven sonatas. It was good to see again the sweat pour down his face and hear his passion in the music as he played the Waldstein or the Hammer-klavier sonata.'

After five satisfactory weeks, Lytton left Becky House to spend August at 82 Woodstock Road, Gilbert Murray's house in Oxford, which Lady Strachey had taken for the month. While Pippa typed out the previous chapters, he pressed on with his writing of *Landmarks in French Literature*. 'The book has become rather distasteful to me,' he confessed to James (22 August 1911), 'but it's drawing to a close. I've only seven more centuries to do.' The dankness and oppression of family life and of Oxford in August, however, proved almost too much for him; and his work slowed. He was now in terror lest he should fall seriously ill at the last moment, overrun his contract date and see all his formidable efforts wasted. The fifty pounds he was to be paid on receipt of the typescript had already been almost all spent in advance. 'I'm told the series is a great success,' he wrote to Maynard Keynes (24 August 1911), 'and that so long as there isn't a Crippen Case this winter, I ought to net at least £100.'

He had hoped to complete *Landmarks in French Literature* by the end of the month, but having failed to do this, he fled back to the solitude of Becky House for another fortnight during which he was to finish off Chapter VII – 'The Age of Criticism' – and his short 'Con-clusion'. Every morning here was given over to writing; the afternoons to scrambling among the rocks in company with his brother James, Rupert Brooke and Gerald Shove (who put in a rather sombre appear-ance for a day or two) until the muscles of his legs hardened into iron, causing him acute pain; and the warm evenings to sitting out in a somewhat indecisive garden overlooking the moor. He felt rejuvenated;

and by 10 September he was able to report to Maynard Keynes: 'I am feeling very lazy, as I've just this minute finished my poor book, after a solid two months of perpetual labour; and the thought of more such inventions is not attractive.'

A few days later, he set off from Becky House for a week's holiday at Harbour View, Clive and Vanessa Bell's house at Studland. In spite of the sunshine, the beach, the general salubriousness and relaxation, he did not altogether relish this visit. Virginia Stephen was very nice, but so shrivelled up internally that she had hardly any real being at all; Roger Fry was also there, like some mediaeval saint in attendance upon Vanessa Bell, who seemed quite unconscious of him and everyone else around her. The atmosphere was made worse by the presence of Julian, her son, since Lytton found most children tedious and impossible to get on with – 'When Lytton comes,' Desmond MacCarthy used to tell his wife, 'the children must go.' And then of course, as if all this were not enough, there was Clive Bell. 'Clive presents a fearful study in decomposing psychology,' he wrote off to James (24 September 1911). 'The fellow is much worse – fallen into fatness and a fermenting self-assurance – burgeoning out into inconceivable theories on art and life – a corpse puffed up with worms and gases. It all seems to be the result of Roger, who is also here, in love with Vanessa. She is stark blind and deaf. And Virginia (in dreadful lodgings) rattles her accustomed nut. Julian is half-witted.'

Not wishing to return immediately to Hampstead, Lytton decided on the spur of the moment to make a mad dash to see Henry Lamb in Brittany. He wrote off at once to Pippa in order to borrow five pounds, and then, on receiving it, started out on his adventure, travelling by G.W.R. boat from Plymouth to Brest, and the following day from Brest by train to Quimperlé. From the very first this impetuous and ill-judged expedition was marked by disaster. Almost at once he fell sick. The food turned out to be infinitely worse, the discomforts infinitely greater than he could have dreamed possible. Not alone this, but the countryside and Henry's models were far less beautiful than he had been led to expect. 'I felt', he told Ottoline (15 October 1911), 'like a white man among savages in Central Africa.' Although Henry struggled to be kind and patient with him, he was obviously put out by his guest's invalid querulousness, so that Lytton judged it best to escape after only three or four days there, and head for Paris. At the end of a night journey through Nantes he arrived at the Hôtel des Saints-Pères. After breakfast he walked, in an ecstasy of wonder, through the lovely Luxembourg Gardens. Here, in the brilliant morning light, was the very essence of France and all that he loved best in France – crowded, happy, well-ordered. The trees were beginning to turn; it seemed he had never known a scene more vivid and alive, and his spirits soared again to unprecedented heights. After the vicissitudes of his Brittany trip, the hardship, illness and emotional failure, an extraordinary sense of excitement came upon him; a spring of self-confidence gushed up; he felt able to face, to outface, the world – it was delightful and astonishing. He had finished his book on French Literature, he was thirty-one, and the best years of his life were still before him.

3

THE STRANGE CASE OF RUPERT BROOKE

While waiting for the publication of his book, Lytton spent the next three months with his family at Belsize Park Gardens. His finances were by this time so depleted that, except for one brief week-end at Cambridge with Maynard Keynes, and another with Gerald Shove at the Le Strange Arms in Hunstanton, he was unable to escape from the fogs of darkest Hampstead. 'My days pass (so far) in infinite idleness,' he wrote to Henry Lamb (15 October 1911). 'I'm engaged in refurnishing my room, and arranging my books and imagining where pictures can go – as if I was going to stay in the poor old shooting-gallery for the next forty years or so. Perhaps I am. Perhaps at the age of 71, I shall still be marching up there after the bed's made, and looking out of the window through the fog, and sitting down pen in hand to begin my masterpiece, every morning.'

London that winter was grim and misshapen after the invigorating glory of Paris, but life there still had its pleasures. He passed these weeks idly wandering from cocoa parties in Fitzroy Square to the more effulgent hospitality of Bedford Square. Much of this time, too, was spent with Henry Lamb, who in November had returned from France to work at the Vale Hotel Studios in Hampstead. And there were other friends, other activities: 'I have been having an exhausting day with Woolf looking for lodgings in Bloomsbury. Like everyone else he doesn't know where to live; but the rooms we saw to-day were enough to make one despair of all human habitations. Filth, darkness, and hideousness combined – I quite sink back with a sigh of relief among the new cretonnes of the poor old shooting-gallery. Otherwise I've been correcting my proof-sheets, which I find a very soothing occupation. But the printers seem to sniff vice everywhere. As there's so much talk about "literature", I sometimes use the phrase "letters" as a

variation – "men of letters" and so on. And once or twice I refer to
"French letters" – So and so "inaugurated a new era in French letters" –
and the words are underlined and queried. My innocent mind failed at
first to grasp the meaning of it. So you see there are singular pitfalls for
unwary authors.'

Towards the end of December, Lytton did at last succeed in leaving
Hampstead, and went down for two weeks to a reading party which
was being held at Lulworth in Dorset. Other friends who came and
went during the fortnight included Henry Lamb, Maynard Keynes,
Justin Brooke, Harry Norton, Gerald Shove, Rupert Brooke and
Katharine Cox, or Ka as she was known.[1] The weather was marvellous,
so hot that some people bathed, Lamb and Ka vanishing for most of
one Sunday together. The events of these few days, which led directly
to Rupert Brooke's estrangement from Lytton and, through him, from
the entire Bloomsbury Group including Virginia Stephen and even
Ottoline Morrell, were later to become the subject of much scandalous
rumour and speculation. One author, for example, repeats in his recently
published memoirs a story which, it seems, he picked up third-hand by
way of Stanley Spencer, to the effect that Lamb, as a callous practical
joke, persuaded Katharine Cox to spend an allegedly platonic night in
his room and, for the next day's amusement of Lytton and his friends,
teased the hopelessly love-sick Rupert Brooke. 'Naturally he [Brooke]
was very upset, but Lamb thought it was a splendid joke and pretended
he was saving Rupert Brooke and bringing the two of them to a sense
of reality.'

Ka was the orphan daughter of a gentleman-stockbroker of radical
opinions, a hefty young woman and a robust Fabian, fond of
tweeds and riding, whose large squashy appearance had once been
likened by Brooke himself to that of a vegetable.[2] Like practically
everyone else, she had been in love with Rupert, but he was not, it
seems, more than mildly flattered by her attentions until she went off
with Lamb. Suddenly he felt attracted irresistibly by her indifference to
himself. Bored by the endless adulation with which he had become so
familiar, he was only excited by other people's lack of interest; and
Ka's sudden unaccountable unconcern soon convinced him that he was
seriously in love with her. At Lulworth that winter, her obvious
preference for Lamb inflamed this illusory love into a pathological
jealousy, and he went into a paranoiac episode. He implored her to
marry him then and there; she refused; and in the irrational ferocity of

[1] Afterwards Mrs Will Arnold-Forster.

[2] This joke was evidently intended partly to describe her mental appearance. To many
– even to James Strachey – she was an attractive person to look at.

his humiliation he looked round for someone on whom to pin the blame – and selected Lytton. Had he selected Lamb – a more logical choice – his vanity would have been subjected to further injury; but by fixing on a homosexual as the chief culprit he was able to give vent to all his submerged puritanical horror and disgust. He saw Lytton as Lamb's evil genius, the instigator of all his own misfortunes; and the far-fetched stories he concocted out of the delirium of his fantasy were accepted by many at their face value.

From the private correspondence that passed between Lytton and Lamb immediately following these dramatic events, a rather different picture comes to light. Lamb, who had arrived at Lulworth after a few days at Parkstone with Augustus John, did, it appears, make some rather tepid advances towards Ka – little more than an automatic reflex in his determined role as a womanizer – but she, to the surprise of all and to the mortification of Brooke, whose own repulsed advances were to be far more desperate and intense, at once fell passionately in love with him – 'like a fish fascinated by the glitter of some strange bait'.

By the time her feelings had developed and become obvious to all, Lamb had already left for London, unaware that he had occasioned any quite such grand passion. It was, in fact, to Lytton that Ka first confessed her infatuation; and it was Lytton who immediately wrote off to inform Lamb (4 January 1912): 'Ka came and talked to me yesterday, between tea and dinner. It was rather a difficult conversation, but she was very nice and very sensible. It seemed to me clear that she was what is called "in love" with you – not with extreme violence so far, but quite distinctly. She is longing to marry you. She thinks you may agree, but fears, with great conscientiousness, that it might not be good for you. I felt at moments, while she was with me – so good and pink and agreeable, – that there was more hope in that scheme than I'd thought before. But the more I consider, the more doubtful it grows. I can't believe that you're a well-assorted couple – can you? If she was really your wife, with a home and children, it would mean a great change in your way of living, a lessening of independence – among other things a much dimmer relationship with Ottoline. This might be worth while – probably would be – if she was an eminent creature, who'd give you a great deal; but I don't think she is that. There seems no touch of inspiration in her; it's as if she was made somehow or other on rather a small scale (didn't you say that?). I feel it's unkind to write this about Ka, and it's too definite, but I must try and say what I think. . . . Henry, I almost believe the best thing she could do now would be to marry Rupert straight off. He is much nicer than I had thought him.

Last night he was there and was really charming – especially with her. Affliction seems to have chastened him, and he did feel – it was evident . . . they seemed to fit together so naturally – even the Garden-City-ishness.'

This letter patently exonerates Lytton himself from any charge of plotting against Brooke or encouraging Lamb's flirtation with Ka. Though he evidently felt rather double-faced about receiving her confidences and then making use of them to dissuade Lamb from marriage, and though it is just possible – if unlikely – that this advice was partly coloured by his own feeling of attraction for Lamb, there can be no doubt that he was endeavouring to act honourably, and to state in an objective manner what he thought to be the truth. One fact which appears to have been forgotten by everyone was that Lamb was himself still married. Ka certainly seems to have believed that she would marry Lamb, since, she explained, he had the same Christian name as her father. Surely here was a clear omen? But Lytton, far from recommending marriage, strongly advised both of them against even having an affair, on the grounds that it might break up Ka's much more suitable relationship with Brooke. Somehow he managed to prevent Ka from following Lamb up to London; while to Lamb himself he wrote (6 January 1912); 'If you're not going to marry her, I think you ought to reflect a good deal before letting her become your mistress. I've now seen her fairly often and on an intimate footing, and I can hardly believe that she's suited to the post. I don't see what either of you could really get out of it except the pleasures of the obelisk. With you even these would very likely not last long, while with her they'ld probably become more and more of a necessity, and also be mixed up with all sorts of romantic desires which I don't think you'ld ever satisfy. If this is true it would be worth while making an effort to put things on a merely affectionate basis, wouldn't it? I think there's quite a chance that . . . everything might blow over, and that she might even sink into Rupert's arms. Can you manage this?'

Although Lytton's intellectual assessment of Brooke had evidently not risen, he felt far closer to him in his present misery and frustration. 'The situation, though, seems to be getting slightly grim,' he told Lamb in another letter (5 January 1912). '. . . Rupert is besieging her – I gather with tears and desperation – and sinking down in the intervals pale and shattered. I wish I could recommend her to console him . . .

'As for Rupert – it's like something in a play. But you know his niceness is now certain – poor thing! I never saw anyone so different from you – in caractère. "Did He who made the Lamb make thee?" I sometimes want to murmur to him, but I fear the jest would not be well received.'

Ironically, now that Brooke was turning so violently against him, Lytton had begun to soften, to experience some genuine sympathy and fellow-feeling for him. Consumed by an insane jealousy, Brooke had convinced himself that Lytton was secretly scheming to discredit him in the eyes of Ka, and to bring about her marriage to the satanic Henry Lamb.[1] No one was able to persuade him otherwise; he refused to speak to Lytton, and, one by one, cut dead all his old Bloomsbury friends, who, he began to suspect, were abetting this Machiavellian plot. This condition persisted in an acute form for several months, but was cleared up manifestly by a complete change in character. The melo-dramatic climax in this process of alienation was staged in July 1914 in the crowded foyer at Drury Lane, where, coming unexpectedly upon Lytton, he refused the proffered hand, executed the movement known as 'turning on one's heel', and strode away. With Lytton at the time were several other old friends including Ottoline, and Brooke's im-petuous and irrational behaviour caused something of a sensation. 'The number of beastly people at Drury Lane is the only good reason for going there,' Brooke later wrote to a friend. 'One can be offensive to them.'[2] The late Christopher Hassall, Rupert Brooke's definitive biographer, told the author: 'The thing to bear in mind is that R.B. was easily jealous, and at that time he was under a very great strain from overwork (on his Fellowship Dissertation for King's) and in a state where he could well allow a petty grievance to develop into an irrational obsession.'

This irrational obsession was in fact a symptom of Brooke's worsen-ing paranoiac condition. The world of his youthful ideals had turned sour and neurotic. Suffering from insomnia, dejection and nervous exhaustion, he succumbed to the sick fever of his delusions, and underwent a complete volte-face from the Fabian intellectual to the chauvinistic fugleman of 1914. The obverse of his exaggerated, school-boy wish that everyone should love him was a curiously inverted form

[1] After the Lamb episode was over, Ka's real love for Rupert Brooke re-emerged. And when that happened he had another revulsion of feeling and backed away.

[2] About this incident at Drury Lane, James Strachey told the author: 'It was the first time I had met him [Rupert] since he came back [from America] and he talked to me in a perfectly friendly way. I then noticed that Lytton was standing just beside me, and I said jocosely to Rupert "I believe you know my brother Lytton." That was when he said "No" and "turned on his heel". It was decidedly awkward because it happened in an extremely visible place, with everyone one knew standing round. I believe it was a performance of Diaghilev's version of the Coq d'Or – a marvellous show. But this showed very plainly Rupert's paranoia, though I was so ignorant then that I had no notion of it.'

of vanity – the uneasy suspicion that people were planning his downfall. It was from this sickness that he had convalesced partly in the
South Seas, to re-emerge an apparently changed personality, the author
of a series of War Sonnets that stand oddly segregated from the earlier,
main body of his work.

4

LANDMARKS IN FRENCH LITERATURE

Landmarks in French Literature was published on 12 January 1912, as
No. 35 in the Home University Library. Lytton's dedication of the
book to 'J.M.S.', his mother, was particularly appropriate; for it was
she of course who had initially fostered his interest in French writing
and had provided him with something of an Anglo-French education.
Despite his timid disinclination to speak the language, he had grown up
to be 'one of those rare Englishmen', to use H. A. L. Fisher's words,
'who knew French from the inside'. Like his mother he was a true
francophil. André Maurois, in a letter to the present author, emphasizes
the relevance of this special twofold understanding in Lytton's interpretation to English audiences of typically French authors. *Landmarks
in French Literature*, he writes, 'is a book I greatly admired because it
said so much in so few pages. No other Englishman would have been
able to write about Racine and, more generally, about French poets as
Strachey did. As a rule French poetry is very little known in England
because French, as a language, is not accentuated and therefore the rules
of English prosody do not apply to French poets. Strachey had the
mysterious power, and probably the taste, that enabled him to judge
Racine, as a good French critic would. Of course, he was also a
very good judge in French prose and had learned quite a lot from
Voltaire.'

Lytton's deep and passionate enjoyment of the best French writing
pulses through every page of this book, forming its most potent and
appealing distinction. There are passages where his personal nostalgia
swells up and sweeps away the balanced critical and documentary framework in which they are set. His sense of crude historical realism is
buried beneath a layer of sweet and undismayed prejudice. He was, for
example, well aware of the terrifying atrocities committed in eighteenth-
century France, but for him they were smoothed out and transfigured
by the passing of time into a beautifully blended pattern in the rich and
colourful tapestry of the era. The same process of idealization is applied

B*

to the age of Louis XIV; and, remembering his own few halcyon days at Versailles with Duncan Grant, he depicts the palace as a memorial and grave of what had been the embodiment of a superhuman ideal – a strange, haunting cemetery, the majesty of which could still fill his imagination and stimulate his sentimental fancy. Envisaged thus, Versailles took on for him a personal significance, symbolizing the supernal aspirations and desolations of his own loves. Though he knew well enough the squalid intrigues and manifold shortcomings of those times, he preferred to treat Versailles not as the emblem of foolish and degraded snobbery, but as a splendid and spiritual *tour de force*. Across the centuries he felt the thrill of old, untold adventures:

'The fact that the conception of society which made Versailles possible was narrow and unjust must not blind us to the real nobility and the real glory which it brought into being. It is true that behind and beyond the radiance of Louis and his courtiers lay the dark abyss of an impoverished France, a ruined peasantry, a whole system of intolerance, and privilege, and maladministration; yet it is none the less true that the radiance was a genuine radiance – no false and feeble glitter, but the warm, brilliant, intense illumination thrown out by the glow of a nation's life. That life, with all it meant to those who lived it, has long since vanished from the earth – preserved to us now only in the pages of its poets, or strangely shadowed forth to the traveller in the illimitable desolation of Versailles. That it has gone so utterly is no doubt, on the whole, a cause for rejoicing; but, as we look back upon it, we may still feel something of the old enchantment, and feel it, perhaps, the more keenly for its strangeness – its dissimilarity to the experiences of our own days. We shall catch glimpses of a world of pomp and brilliance, of ceremony and decoration, a small, vital passionate world which has clothed itself in ordered beauty, learnt a fine way of easy, splendid living, and come under the spell of a devotion to what is, to us, no more than the gorgeous phantom of high imaginations – the divinity of a king. When the morning sun was up and the horn was sounding down the long avenues, who would not wish, if only in fancy, to join the glittering cavalcade where the young Louis led the hunt in the days of his opening glory? Later, we might linger on the endless terrace, to watch the great monarch, with his red heels and his golden snuff-box and his towering periwig, come out among his courtiers, or in some elaborate grotto applaud a ballet by Molière. When night fell there would be dancing and music in the gallery blazing with a thousand looking-glasses, or masquerades and feasting in the gardens, with the torches throwing strange shadows among the trees trimmed into artificial figures, and gay lords and proud ladies conversing together under the stars.'[1]

Landmarks in French Literature is disposed in seven chapters, each one scoring the crescendo and diminuendo of a separate epoch and literary movement. As he charts each individual landmark, pin-points it and, with exquisite neatness and economy, connects it with what is destined to succeed, Lytton weaves a graceful series of literary-historical contours that give the book its elegant, cohesive texture. The pattern is simple but immediately effective. In every chapter he erects a temple at which to worship; and then, after the architectural climax has been reached, introduces a figure who opposes the foregoing *Zeitgeist* and heralds the new emergent spirit of creation. By these means the link between one literary age and the next is drawn with fluency and eloquence. In the full blossoming of each flower one can detect that seed of decay, which, when transplanted under a fresh climate of thought and feeling, will burst into new, vigorous efflorescence. Of every writer he has something pregnant and appreciative to say. The 'potent and melancholy voice' of Villon, which 'gave utterance in language of poignant beauty to the deepest sentiments' of the Middle Ages, gives way to the glamour of the Renaissance. 'The poems of Villon', Lytton explains, effecting a characteristically ornate transition between two chapters, 'produce the impression of some bleak, desolate landscape of snow-covered roofs and frozen streets, shut in by mists, and with a menacing shiver in the air. . . . Then all at once the grey gloom lifts, and we are among the colours, the sunshine, and the bursting vitality of spring.'

To reduce and illustrate fairly the entire literature of a country within the compass of a short dissertation is a notoriously difficult undertaking. Closely following H. A. L. Fisher's preliminary advice, Lytton used J. W. Mackail's manual on *Latin Literature* as a model, his style being somewhat similar to Mackail's impressionistic prose – in those days much copied by students and, for that reason, much disparaged by academic teachers. The structure of his criticism makes no pretentions to originality, but it imposed a convenient neatness and unity of tone upon the book and conveyed the impression of constant development. The many merits which this skilful organization helps to bring out are freely displayed on almost every page. Above all else, his compression

[1] Logan Pearsall Smith, who had a great admiration for Lytton's writing – especially his critical writing – used to recall this passage as being especially fine. But when in 1944 he looked it up again, his admiration wilted a little. 'What intolerable clichés!' he exclaimed to Robert Gathorne-Hardy. 'Let's rewrite the passage.' After a few minutes, however, of removing the worn-out expressions, they decided that the task was too formidable, and gave it up.

and terse, though never austere, economy of verbal description is, in many passages, quite masterly. At his best, Lytton conveys in the briefest possible space the peculiar charm of each author whom he discusses, the unique flavour of his work, the literary influences which he first inherited and later exerted, the teachings of the various critic-philosophers, the obsessive themes of the novelists, poets, dramatists. On the more academic side he also elucidates the particular prose style into which each successive movement infused its thoughts and emotions, the historical background from which it naturally evolved and against which it must be set, and the quality of enjoyment which its chief exponents can liberate in the sensitive twentieth-century reader. Although, inevitably, no one will find himself in exact agreement with all Lytton's canons – his contention, for example, that the pen portraits of Saint-Simon are never caricatures because 'his most malevolent exaggerations are yet so realistic that they carry conviction' is surely an unnecessary piece of special pleading – or applaud the omission of some French writers – the exclusion of Prosper Mérimée and Gérard de Nerval are certainly controversial – yet as an example of pure literary craftsmanship, *Landmarks in French Literature* could hardly be bettered.

Lingering over the writers whom he really loves, Lytton's style is at its most opulent. Though his criticism is never inept, his appreciation does occasionally become rather too fulsome. In places the writing grows overripe, loaded down with a profusion of high-sounding, ornamental adjectives and adverbs, not always very originally chosen. There are fewer obvious clichés than in the biographies, fewer calculated extravagances, and less straining after dramatic effect. Yet these characteristics are present, and tend to stand out more conspicuously in the less intimate, conversational tone of his literary criticism. The luxurious abundance of praise sometimes gets out of control, too, as when he writes of Voltaire that his 'prose is the final embodiment of the most characteristic qualities of the French genius. If all that that great nation had ever done or thought were abolished from the world, except a single sentence of Voltaire's, the essence of their achievement would have survived.' The reader profits little, also, on being informed that 'still waters run deep' or that 'it is so difficult to take the measure of a soul!'

Apart from several such blemishes, there is little really indiscriminate eulogy and no awkward exposition. The narrative contains not a single obscure sentence from beginning to end – a rare achievement. Perhaps the most fitting tribute to the book as a work of fine aesthetic analysis came from the Cambridge critic A. Y. Campbell, who summed up his opinion thus: 'In general style and conception it is the model of what a book in this kind of series should be; showing a sense of proportion both in its entire design and in the author's selection of what to discuss and what to discard; maintaining, on the whole, a singular freedom from prejudice; written (unlike many modern works) in excellent English; and above all absolutely clear.'

Amid so much that is near-perfect, it may seem a little ungracious to complain at the general impact, which is surprisingly tame and muted. Despite the marvellous skill of presentation, something solid is lacking in the book, something to get one's teeth into. Its leaves reflect the rich, profuse colouring of tropical flowers no longer in their natural place of growth under the wind and rain and the hot glare of the sun, but removed and tastefully arranged as window-dressing in an over-heated exhibition room, where they are kept extant by phosphorescent lighting and artificial fertilizer. The real world is shut out; from behind the glass, the salesman gesticulates, and one receives the queer impression of being exhorted by a rhetorician without lungs. The book is supremely tidy and self-contained, and has the air of being almost embalmed. In scene after scene, the men of letters whom Lytton outlines pass before us like illuminated phantoms. They are not dead; nor are they quite alive; but something in between: they are asleep. Or perhaps it is we, the readers, who are sleeping, lulled by the seductive charm of Lytton's tranquil, nostalgic imagination. The impression which this dreamlike panorama leaves upon the mind is of an elysium, serene and undisturbed.

In his essay upon Racine, Lytton had written: 'It is the business of a poet to break rules and to baffle expectation; and all the masterpieces in the world cannot make a precedent.' *Landmarks in French Literature* is a very good but not a great book, since it achieves the difficult feat of obeying all the rules all the time. This was partly the result of following Mackail's *Latin Literature*, where he might equally have been guided by another volume brought out in the same series at the same time – Gilbert Murray's review of Greek literature. It does not possess anything like the same aesthetic balance and precision, but by its very imcompleteness, by the positive assertions of dislikes and prejudices, even by its imperfections, Murray's book does in some respects gain. It is a more individual work, for the author's mind overflowed the mould in which it worked and touched life too closely to attain absolute flawlessness of form.

Lytton interpreted the development of literature through the ages as a constant struggle waged between the divergent traditions of the Classical and Romantic schools, and between the opposing forces of scepticism and mysticism. By means of this interpretation, which separated artificially these variously intermingled tendencies, he sought to achieve a complete synthesis within his book. But in his determination to steer a middle course, he sometimes sacrifices matter for shape. Something of this preference for 'significant form' is here and there reflected within his own criticism, as, for example, in the lengthy comparison between Racine's *Bérénice* and Shakespeare's *Antony and Cleopatra*. He admits the general superiority of *Antony and Cleopatra* – the principal characters are more interesting and more proud, and the whole catastrophe is more inevitable and complete – but at the same time he considers it inferior 'as a play'; that is to say, less distinguished by unity of tone and concentration of development. To A. Y. Campbell, who objected to this eclipsing preference for the classical structure, Lytton replied by letter (27 October 1913): 'The comparison with A & C was rather too dashing, I dare say. . . . What good tragedies are there in English, outside the Elizabethan drama? – I mean tragedies that are fit to act? – I can hardly think of any. The Wild Duck is a good tragedy, and is successful on the stage in England, but then of course it belongs to the Racine tradition (as far as form goes). Also it seems to support my case that the only really successful Shakespeare play is Othello – the only play of his which is almost classical in form.'

Elsewhere, though his fondness for classical writing is detectable, he is scrupulously impartial, putting one in mind of Oscar Wilde's observation that the only person who can appreciate all schools of art is an auctioneer. After generously conferring accolades of praise upon the Romantic writers, he is obliged to excel himself when turning his attention to the classicists, so that as this alternating sequence proceeds, the crescendo of applause at times grows deafening. This excess of approbation, which often does no more than roundly assert what he hopes the reaction of his reader will be to his more sober and measured analysis, becomes increasingly exuberant when he deals with such favourites as Racine and Voltaire. He presents a superlatively good idea of the distinctive qualities of Racine's tragedy, but then weakens his argument by adducing an English parallel which, though apparently to Racine's advantage, is really quite misleading:

'Now and then, however, even in English literature, instances arise of the opposite – the Racinesque – method. In these lines of Wordsworth, for example:

> *The silence that is in the starry sky*
> *The sleep that is among the lonely hills –*

there is no violent appeal, nothing surprising, nothing odd – only a direct and inevitable beauty; and such is the kind of effect which Racine is constantly producing.'

But Wordsworth's lines do not achieve a typical Racinesque effect; his virtues are of an altogether different quality. Indeed, the difference between the two poets is fundamental. Wordsworth was a visual writer, as the above lines show; whereas a simile or metaphor in Racine is never meant to be visualized – it is purely dramatic.

Later, when he comes to examine the novels of Victor Hugo and Balzac – to whose sonorous harmonies he seems a little unresponsive – Lytton must strain every nerve to be fair, and more than fair, so that they will not be put in the shade by the greater luminaries who have preceded them. The estimate of Victor Hugo is, in fact, far nearer the truth than were the unbalanced encomiums of Swinburne, to which it acted as a wholesome corrective. Even so, his partial dislike of Victor Hugo is evident. He is out of sympathy with his bombastic egotism and false pathos, his rodomontade and journalistic cant, his lack of humour and overplus of vanity, all of which were qualities essential to Hugo's whole spirit and to the very substance of his literary output. Lytton's letters reveal that he used occasionally to enjoy brief seasons of enthusiasm for Hugo at Cambridge, yet his appreciation in *Landmarks in French Literature* does not seem quite spontaneous – more a succession of carefully chosen compliments, as if he were writing out of season. In the case of Balzac, he appears to suspend his powers of penetrative critical detachment, allowing himself to be swept off his feet by a sense of splendid masculine vitality. 'The whole of France is crammed into his pages,' he exclaims in rapture. Yet if this were really so, there would be only two types of person thriving in French civilization – frenzied demoniacs based on Balzac's idea of Napoleon, and village simpletons founded on Balzac's conception of Christ. By surrendering himself unconditionally to the passionate energy of Balzac's genius, Lytton temporarily discarded the faculty for distinguishing between vitality and variety.

Where Lytton's comparisons grow more reckless, his language becomes correspondingly luscious and repetitive. One sees not a vision of the author fixed in the composition of his work, but a picture of Lytton himself absorbing it; and it is this echo rather than any vibrations set up by the original inspiration which chiefly communicates itself to us. On every page one is presented with an invitation to sensitive enjoyment as a fellow reader, but is given little clue as to the source and urgency of the personal creative process. And, since the personality of the authors whose work Lytton discusses is largely excluded from his criticism, several of the passages which express in a general way his own enjoyment of their writing are so similar that they could be exchanged without doing much violence to the sense. He delights, for instance, in the plays of Molière; and he delights equally in the fables of La Fontaine. Technically, both were masters of their art – though as writers they were, of course, quite dissimilar. Yet since Lytton admires them both, since his criticism of their workmanship is almost entirely impressionistic, since the praise he bestows on each of them is mainly conditioned by a vague and imprecise pleasure in something perfectly executed, his writing is formalized into a kind of valueless metaphorical jargon. Of La Fontaine he writes: 'He is like one of those accomplished cooks in whose dishes, though the actual secret of their making remains a mystery, one can trace the ingredients which have gone to the concoction of the delicious whole. As one swallows the rare morsel, one can just perceive how, behind the scenes, the oil, the vinegar, the olive, the sprinkling of salt, the drop of lemon were successively added, and, at the critical moment, the simmering delicacy served up, done to a turn.' So much for La Fontaine. Previously, in a *Spectator* review of A. R. Waller's translation, *The Plays of Molière*, Lytton had expressed something of the fascination and appeal which the French dramatist held for English audiences in the following words: 'To read one of his scenes is to watch some wonderful cook at work over a delicious dish – keeping it on the simmer while each savoury ingredient is dropped in: the oil, the olive, the salt – and then at the psychological moment whipping it off the fire, and setting it before you done to a turn.' In the intervening two or three years the style had grown more polished and the formula was exploited more thoroughly. Yet, it remains little more than a long-winded manner of saying something which could be said – could almost be taken for granted – when considering very many of the finest creative writers.

It is only when he curtails these stereotyped metaphorical flights, and mixes in some intellectual interpretation of his emotional response that the true individuality of La Fontaine and Molière emerges. 'La Fontaine's creatures', he writes, 'partake both of the nature of real animals and of human beings, and it is precisely in this dual character of theirs that their fascination lies. . . . The creatures of La Fontaine's fantasy are not simple animals with the minds of human beings: they are something more complicated and amusing; they are animals with the minds which human beings would certainly have, if one could suppose them transformed into animals.' This is charming and acute comment, and probably as far as literary criticism can go without actual reference to La Fontaine himself. Lytton, however, sees him as little more than an ideal embodiment of the influence and character of the age in which he happened to live. 'In the nineteenth century,' he writes, 'one can imagine him drifting among Paris cafés, pouring out his soul in a random lyric or two, and dying before his time.' Yet surely it was by his unique nature and not by contemporary influence that La Fontaine was spared from 'pouring out his soul'? It is difficult to believe that he was as malleable and feckless as Lytton makes out, for his peculiar literary gifts, his pervading sense of humour, were certainly quite foreign to the genius of Verlaine or Baudelaire.

In contrast to La Fontaine, Lytton sees Molière as a more universal than national figure, and his treatment is correspondingly freer. Equally unsentimental, Molière is presented as a darker, more substantial personality than La Fontaine, holding an exact balance between the egotisms of solitude and society. 'It is the more remote quality of his mind – his brooding melancholy, shot through with bitterness and doubt – that may at first sight escape the notice of the reader, and that will repay the deepest attention. His greatest works come near to tragedy.'

To achieve the aesthetic unity at which he is aiming, Lytton everywhere ties in his literary panorama with its historical background. It was the obvious method to adopt for a generic book of this kind, yet it has severe drawbacks. He provides us with a series of set-pieces, eloquent, dignified disquisitions, informative, notably well-balanced and neatly ironed out. The chapters are all admirably constructed, and interspersed with some very good critical passages. But though the words are so elegantly spun about, there is no live centre to them, since Lytton fails to relate his criticism to the lives and natures of the authors concerned. One is left to deduce from his treatment that their writing emanated from the social, cultural and political cross-currents of the day. Amid all the talk of literary technique, of influences, effects and tendencies, the real character and impulse behind any poem or novel is lost from sight. He presents and discusses almost every work as if it were a direct or indirect symptom of the times in which it was produced, not the fruit of certain individuals' experiences within those times; and in failing to explain this, he ignores the quintessential quality of all literature.

For this weakness, the blame must partly be laid, of course, on the Home University Library. *Landmarks in French Literature* was, after all, intended as a textbook for students. Although it includes a large amount of material that was meant and felt very seriously, the volume was to some extent written as a pot-boiler. At the same time, Lytton's rather preconceived aesthetic theories were partly responsible for its limitations. Though, naturally, any work of art must by definition have form, this form should be engendered organically from within, not artificially applied like a strait-jacket. Nor need all artistic form be simple. The unblemished unity of *Landmarks in French Literature* is the result of a measured dilution of realism. The various works of literature as Lytton depicts them are not the creations of flesh-and-blood human beings, but magnificent appendages of some dressed-up props which are moved regularly across a shifting background of historical pageantry. Seen thus, they are deployed as convenient representations of the chameleon-like characteristics of the French national genius. Only now and then does some superabundant figure resist being assimilated into the overall pattern – Voltaire, for instance, to whom more pages are devoted than to anyone else. Here, as an exception to the general rule, we are given some extraneous biographical colouring. But Lytton is more eager to project a vivid surface-personality – 'curious', 'amazing', 'extraordinary', 'singular' – than to reconcile the diverse elements of his temperament; and the effect is one of para-doxical and striking dissonance. 'His character', Lytton writes, 'was composed of a strange amalgam of all the most contradictory elements in human nature, and it would be difficult to name a single virtue or a single vice which he did not possess. He was the most egotistical of mortals, and the most disinterested; he was graspingly avaricious, and profusely generous; he was treacherous, mischievous, frivolous, and mean, yet he was a firm friend and a true benefactor, yet he was pro-foundly serious and inspired by the noblest enthusiasms.'

Lytton knew well enough that if a man belongs altogether to his own epoch, then he can not speak with the greatest literary significance to later generations; he knew, too, that only the mannerisms of genius, in whatever sphere, can be inherited and passed on. But the pattern im-posed, perhaps inevitably, upon this study of French literature forced him to emphasize these more ephemeral matters. Throughout the book Lytton frequently uses – and with evident relish – the word 'psycho-logical'. Yet he employs little psychology himself, little of the ex-pansiveness and subjective complexity of his new literary hero, Dostoievsky. The connexions which he draws between one writer and the next are more often ornamental or dramatic than analytical or really imaginative. This method of association could sometimes appear rather self-contradictory when set against the more matter-of-fact survey which he conducts. The charm and delight of Versailles, viewed retro-spectively from the distance of the eighteenth century, seems moribund, autocratic and hypercritical. The Age of Reason is then extolled, but only to be seen, even in its prime, as having been a dry, shrivelled-up husk, 'something thin, cold and insignificant', from the succeeding Age of Romance.

In his essay on Stendhal (January 1914) Lytton wrote: 'Perhaps the

best test of a man's intelligence is his capacity for making a summary.'
Judged by this standard, Lytton's own intelligence is paramount. But,
perhaps also, the best test of a man's imagination is his capacity for
seeing connexions between elements that at first sight appear to be
unrelated. It is when evaluated by this standard that Lytton disappoints
– a disappointment in this case largely due to the cramped and restrictive
nature of the series for which he was writing. His criticism is of a kind
which is constantly making the reader reflect that its author is exceedingly cultivated and skilful, but only comparatively seldom does it discover some unobvious truth. Like Sainte-Beuve, he did not set himself
up as a judge but as an interpreter between the writer and his unknown
public. They were really biographical essayists rather than critics or
thinkers, and, in playing all sides successively in the Classical–Romantic
war, found imperfect sympathy with only the most extreme Romantics
– such as Victor Hugo. Both, too, lived lives in which melancholy
played an unusually large part. Since they showed greater interest in
personality than ideas and, though never tedious or obtuse, tended at
their worst to dwindle into the gossipy, the trivial and the 'feminine',
both gained something of a reputation – only remotely justified – for
being rather catty old women-of-letters. But Sainte-Beuve always
insisted that it was possible to understand a writer solely through knowing the man, a belief which Lytton himself put into practice only after
Landmarks in French Literature.

Round the central unreality of this biographical void the more
brilliant stars in his firmament cluster surely, serenely. *Landmarks in
French Literature* teems with rewarding observations which bring us
directly and easily in contact with an alert and ingenious mind. Today
its distinction seems to lie less with Lytton's skill in phrasing – though
this is charming and impressive – than with his strain of perceptive and
discriminating good sense. The most valuable passages are those in
which the intellectual content of his sentences is not dwarfed into insignificance by the effusive impressionistic framework surrounding it, when
the two divergent elements in his own nature hold an even balance.

5

A SPIRITUAL REVOLUTION

Landmarks in French Literature, when it came out, was reviewed not
widely but well. By April 1914 some twelve thousand copies of it had
been sold in the British Empire and America, and after Lytton became
famous at the end of the war it took on a new lease of life: four more

impressions were printed between 1923 and 1927, and the demand has continued steadily up to the present day.[1] A number of critics, among them Guy Boas, Nancy Mitford, Harold Nicolson and H. A. L. Fisher himself, regarded it as Lytton's finest book, his critical *tour de force*. The most severe disparagement that can legitimately be levelled against it was indicated in a letter which D. H. Lawrence sent to Ottoline Morrell in the summer of 1915: 'I still don't like Strachey,' he wrote, '– French literature neither – words – literature – bore.' Beneath the unaffected finesse and facility, the significant form, the cultivated refinement of taste, there was little cogent involvement with the condition of the human soul. At another level, the best that may fairly be said of it has been eloquently put by John Lehmann, who praised it as a 'luminous little masterpiece of interpretative criticism'. In *The Whispering Gallery*, the first volume of his autobiography, he recounts a conversation which he had during a train journey from France to England with an unknown travelling companion who identified herself on reaching Calais as Dorothy Bussy. 'It taught me, as no other book could have,' he told her, 'how to find excellence in the French tradition even if one were a devoted believer in the English tradition, and why Racine was a great poet and dramatist even though his greatness was so totally different from Shakespeare's.'

Among Lytton's personal friends the response to his book seems to have varied widely – even allowing for his own exaggerations. To Dorothy Bussy, who thought highly of its merits, he wrote (6 February 1912): 'James of course says that it's rubbish, Ottoline that it is a work of supreme genius, Virginia that it's merely brilliant, Woolf that it is bluff carried a little too far for decency, and Clive that it is almost as bad as "Sainte Beuve" (I haven't heard him say so, but I'm sure he must have).'

The writing and publication of *Landmarks in French Literature* marks a major point of transition in Lytton's career. Later in the same letter to his sister he observes: 'For the last year I have been going through a Spiritual Revolution – which has been exciting and on the whole pleasant. I had feared that after 30 one didn't have these things. Ah! – But now I shall be glad of a little recueillement – though it's rather doubtful whether I shall get it between Bloomsbury and Hampstead.' He was determined, he added, to do some real 'creative work', and this he still believed would be in the field of poetic drama.

---

[1] There are two editions now in print in Britain, the original one in the Home University Library series, and another in the uniform Collected Works of Lytton Strachey which, with the permission of the Oxford University Press, Chatto and Windus first brought out in 1948.

This phrase, Spiritual Revolution, was intended by Lytton as a joke –
but a joke with a serious meaning behind it. Over the last twelve to
fifteen months, he had found himself pitched into a fresh and entirely
unfamiliar environment that represented a total break with Cambridge
and was far less respectable than Bloomsbury. This was the world of
Chelsea, of Augustus John and Boris Anrep – artists of a type utterly
dissimilar to Roger Fry and all he stood for. It was like a transformation
scene at a pantomime. Precipitated by Henry Lamb and Ottoline, this
change was also influenced by a number of other events. His brother
Oliver, for instance, who had always led a knock-about sort of life –
travelling round the world, studying under Leschetizky in Vienna,
starting an Anglo-Indian career in India, marrying, divorcing and so
on – had returned to England in the spring of 1911. He was constantly
badgering Lytton for being too cooped up: 'You spend all your life
between Cambridge and the Reading Room of the British Museum,'
he used to complain. And then, there was the effect of Dostoievsky,
whose novels presented Lytton with a completely new attitude to
human beings and opened his mind to some things going on in
himself.

This new liberation enabled Lytton to experience something he had
always wanted to experience, something that had probably lain unconscious within him before – a firm belief in the writer's essential worth
within the hierarchy of the world's values; a creed essentially opposed
to that morbid, sentimental view expressed in the *Spectator* subleader
of 1908, 'The Prose Style of Men of Action', and implicit in so much of
his earlier work from the Warren Hastings dissertation to 'The Guides'.
He had now entered upon a period of his literary development which,
beginning with a rhapsodic acclamation of men of letters, would lead
up to his flank and rear attack on the legendary reputation of men of
action and affairs. It was a time of self-justification and gathering
confidence in the successful application of his own powers, a time when
he would turn the tables on that type of wilful person who set out to
govern the world, and by intolerance and prejudice added unnecessarily
to the world's stock of avoidable inhumanity.

Scattered throughout the pages of *Landmarks in French Literature*
are several signs and assurances of this new emergent faith. In a passage,
for example, describing the formation and influence of the French
Academy, he goes out of his way to explain his opposition to that
official and popular indifference, even contempt, shown by England
towards the arts – an attitude which deprived the writer particularly of
his rightful status in society. 'On the whole, perhaps the most important function performed by the Academy has been a more indirect one.

The mere existence of a body of writers officially recognised by the authorities of the State has undoubtedly given a peculiar prestige to the profession of letters in France. It has emphasised that tendency to take the art of writing seriously – to regard it as a fit object for the most conscientious craftsmanship and deliberate care – which is so characteristic of French writers. The amateur is very rare in French literature – as rare as he is common in our own. How many of the greatest English writers have denied that they were men of letters! – Scott, Byron, Gray, Sir Thomas Browne, perhaps even Shakespeare himself. When Congreve begged Voltaire not to talk of literature, but to regard him merely as an English gentleman, the French writer, who, in all his multifarious activities, never forgot for a moment that he was first and foremost a follower of the profession of letters, was overcome with astonishment and disgust. The difference is typical of the attitude of the two nations towards literature. . . .'

Throughout this book, too, Lytton seldom misses an opportunity for asserting that literature can express more richly than any form of transitory action the characteristic and abiding genius of a nation. The sword, he is repeatedly avowing, is less mighty than the pen. 'Montesquieu's great reputation', he writes, 'led to his view of the constitution of England being widely accepted as the true one; as such it was adopted by the American leaders after the War of Independence; and its influence is plainly visible in the present Constitution of the United States. Such is the strange power of good writing over the affairs of men!'

Elsewhere, he takes a surprising dip into the biography of Voltaire to recount, with evident satisfaction, the great wave of general popularity which greeted his sudden last appearance in Paris, the like of which is reserved in England for military and political figures. Lytton presents this scene as gloriously dramatic, a fitting curtain-call to Voltaire's incredible career. 'One day, quite suddenly, he appeared in Paris, which he had not visited for nearly thirty years. His arrival was the signal for one of the most extraordinary manifestations of enthusiasm that the world has ever seen. For some weeks he reigned in the capital, visible and glorious, the undisputed lord of the civilized universe. The climax came when he appeared in a box at the Théâtre Français, to witness a performance of the latest of his tragedies, and the whole house rose as one man to greet him. His triumph seemed to be something more than the mere personal triumph of a frail old mortal; it seemed to be the triumph of all that was noblest in the aspirations of the human race. But the fatigue and excitement of those weeks proved too much even for Voltaire in the full flush of his eighty-fourth year.

An overdose of opium completed what Nature had begun; and the amazing being rested at last.'

The gradual preparation for Lytton's Spiritual Revolution had been going on since he came down from Cambridge. Now almost complete, it was to be hurried to its full flowering by the war. But already he was filled and elated by a new assurance in his ultimate success. Like Voltaire he would live to be eighty-four, and devote most of his years to a humane and polemical art. His destiny was not, he felt sure, to be an unobtrusive Donne, penning tiny volumes of exquisite, unpublished verse for the delight of a few discriminating friends; it was more practical, and in its attainments more resounding and contentious. He felt, too, the need to expound this sense of vocation which underlay his mis-leadingly flippant and languid manner, to disabuse his friends of any possible misconception. 'You understand a great deal, and very wonder-fully,' he wrote to Ottoline (24 February 1912). 'But perhaps there's one thing that you don't quite realise about me – I mean what I feel about my work. Perhaps you don't see that the idea of my really not working is simply an impossibility. Sometimes you have admonished me on the subject, and I think I have been rather curt in my answers; it was because I felt so absolutely sure of myself – that you might as well talk of my not breathing as not writing. It's so happened that just the last month or two, when we've been getting to know each other, I've been having a time of transition and hesitation. . . . And then my health has been a vile nuisance – You see I'm making quite a case for myself! But I want you to understand this. From my earliest days I've always con-sidered myself as a writer, and for the last ten years writing has been almost perpetually in my thoughts.'

In the past Lytton had tended to equate writing with obscurity when-ever he thought of it in relation to himself. Writers, he sometimes felt, were men of action *manqués*, second-class heroes at best. Now, for the first time, he sensed that his appetite for success could be satisfied in a practical manner by means of his natural literary gifts – a kind of will to power, through the imagination. In the seventeenth century he might have found some sort of fulfilment as a Caroline mystic; but the religious motive had quietly dropped out of the modern world. If only one could still live for the glory of God, and find eternal crowns and reconciliations hereafter! But that type of thing was no longer done. Crowns were never worn, and heaven itself was out of fashion. To court success one had to be either in, or ahead of fashion.

In an address which he delivered to the Apostles that spring (11 May 1912), entitled 'Godfrey, Cornbury or Candide', Lytton makes the clearest and most explicit statement of his newly developed beliefs, defining in some detail the position to which this period of transition had brought him. Essentially, the new faith was a method of eradicating his past sense of morbid self-abomination. He had failed, in the love of men, imaginatively to reincarnate himself in the body of some heaven-born hero; now he sought to transform his own being into the sort of person he could admire, or at least respect, for his courage and achievements. In the course of his paper he points to three main motives which shape our ends – the thirst for pleasure, the desire to do good, and the need for self-development. Though sensitive to the force of these first two impulses, Lytton places himself in the third category of human being, those whose chief aim is self-development, adding that the mainspring of his life is really ambition. 'It seems to me that I live neither for happiness nor for duty,' he told the Apostles. 'I like being happy. I scheme to be happy; I want to do my duty, and I sometimes even do it. But such considerations seem to affect me only sporadically and vaguely; there is something else which underlies my actions more fundamentally, which guides, controls, and animates the whole. It is ambition. I want to excel, to triumph, to be powerful, and to glorify in myself. I do not want a vulgar triumph, a vulgar power; fame and riches attract me only as subsidiary ornaments of my desire. What I want is the attainment of a true excellence, the development of noble qualities, and the full expression of them – the splendour of a spiritual success. It is true that this is an egotistical conception of life; but I see no harm in such an egotism. After all, each of us is the only person who can cultivate himself; we may help on our neighbour here and there – throw him a bulb or two over the garden wall, or lend a hand with the roller; but we shall never understand the ins and outs – the complication of the soils and subsoils – in any garden but our own.'

Something of this revolutionary new creed was reflected in Lytton's presence which, always striking, had by this time grown positively challenging. With the possible exception of William Empson, he developed into the most photogenic and preposterous-looking figure in twentieth-century English literature. In May 1912, Max Beerbohm, who had recently returned to England after a two-years stay in Italy, was lunching at the Savile Club when he caught sight of Lytton for the first time, seated at a table with Duncan Grant. Even allowing for the looking-glass quality to the description which Max later wrote of this first visual impression, Lytton's appearance must obviously have riveted his attention to the exclusion of all the other unknown faces in the club – 'an emaciated face of ivory whiteness', he recalled, 'above a long square-cut auburn beard, and below a head of very long sleek dark brown hair. The nose was nothing if not aquiline, and Nature had chiselled it with great delicacy. The eyes, behind a pair of gold-rimmed spectacles, eyes of an inquirer and cogitator, were large and brown and luminous. The man to whom they belonged must, I judged, though he sat stooping low down over his table, be extremely tall. He wore a jacket of brown velveteen,[1] a soft shirt, and a dark red tie. I greatly wondered who he was. He looked rather like one of the Twelve Apostles, and I decided that he resembled especially the doubting one, Thomas, who was also called Didymus. I learned from a friend who came in and joined me at my table that he was one of the Stracheys; Lytton Strachey; a Cambridge man; rather an authority on French literature: had written a book on French Literature in some series or other; book said to be very good. "But why," my friend asked, "should he dress like that?" Well, we members of the Savile, Civil Servants, men of letters, clergymen, scientists, doctors and so on, were clad respectably, passably, decently, but no more than that. And "Hang it all," I said, "why *shouldn't* he dress like that? He's the best-dressed man in the room!'"

These clothes – no less than the beard – were worn partly as a token of his new liberation, partly for the joy of provoking the too hidebound and conformable. In time his presence grew still more commanding. During these early winter and spring months of 1912, Henry Lamb embarked on a series of portraits.[2] It is interesting to compare two of

[1] Max's memory or observation was faulty. James Strachey has pointed out that Lytton never in his life wore gold-rimmed spectacles and never a velveteen coat – unless this is meant to include corduroy, which he did go in for during his Augustus John period.

[2] Lamb was obviously fascinated by Lytton and did a great number of portraits of him. The best-known one (oil, 90 × 70 in.), for many years in the collection of Mr and Mrs Behrend, was bought in 1958 by the Tate Gallery under the terms of the Chantrey Bequest. A painting of the background of this portrait, 'Hampstead Heath from the Vale of Health', belongs to Mr Richard Carline. An earlier version, painted in 1912 (oil, 20 × 15½ in.), was bought in 1923 by Siegfried Sassoon who wrote to Sydney Cockerell (24 November 1923): 'The other day I committed an extravagance and bought Henry Lamb's first small oil picture of Lytton Strachey (the study for the big one). It is delightful, and, I think, of historic value. (I gave £60). Some day I will transfer it to the Fitzwilliam (L.S. being a Cambridge man it should be there). You can take this as a promise.' In fact Siegfried Sassoon gave this portrait to Lady Ottoline Morrell; it was exhibited at the Leicester Galleries in 1956 ('Pictures from Garsington', No. 32 in the Catalogue) and bought by Lord Cottesloe, who has shown it recently in Leningrad at a British Council Exhibition of British Painting. The Fitzwilliam Museum, Cambridge, have a bust, painted in 1913 (20½ × 16 in.) in which the head and shoulders exactly correspond to the Tate Gallery portrait. This was formerly owned by C. K. Ogden, and by J. E. Vulliamy, who presented it to the Fitzwilliam in 1945. The Ashmolean Museum, Oxford, have a 'Study for Portrait of Lytton Strachey', a preliminary drawing for the canvas now owned by Lord Cottesloe and purchased in 1961; and the Victoria and Albert Museum acquired in 1962 a pencil drawing of Strachey seated in a chair. A red chalk drawing was sold at Christie's on 4 July 1958. Mrs Gilbert Russell has another early portrait similar to that in the Fitzwilliam Museum and Mrs Julian Vinogradoff, daughter

these, both painted at Hampstead, the first in 1912, the second more celebrated one – now owned by the Tate – two years later. In both pictures there are many familiar, almost identical characteristics – the same boneless, inert, interminable legs, with their look of having been made of malleable wax which has somehow elongated extraordinarily; the same exotic slippers of brown felt; the same spade-like beard; the same astonished eyebrows; the same furled umbrella and Homburg hat, insignia of upper-middle-class respectability, pushed to one side but still in the picture. But there are differences, too, not just attributable to the less impressionistic treatment of the later famous portrait. The face has become less thin and wasted; the figure appears a little less enfeebled; the eyes, though not so sad, are more alarming; the pince-nez has been replaced by a pair of spectacles. Lytton still reclines, apparently without an ounce of energy in his fragile body, on the edge of a basket-chair, a green and black plaid rug over its arm, against a view of ordered parkland. But he is no longer quite alone. Outside, in the background, two figures have emerged from behind a tree and are wandering along a path away from the house – perhaps Mrs Humphry Ward and St Loe Strachey, having called to inquire after his well-sounding new book, *Eminent Victorians.* In both portraits Lamb displays that mingling of respect, affection and irony which several of his acquaintances felt for Lytton and which he mirrored back to the world at large. This second picture especially is sharp but subjective, and in the opinion of James Strachey too vulgarly and superficially caricatured. The lofty room and the unusual landscape seen through the vast window gives the impression of a cage in which Lytton is preserved for us as a rare specimen of the species *homo sapiens* – an amiable and bizarre botanist or an eccentric ecclesiastic. Several other people, however, who met Lytton during this period of his life but did not know him so intimately as his brother, have testified to the verisimilitude of Lamb's likeness, among them Osbert Sitwell, who stressed the individual and unorthodox effect which this recently manufactured personality produced upon his contemporaries. In 'an age when people tended to look the same,' he wrote, 'his [Lytton's] emergence into any scene, whether street or drawing-room, lifted it to a new plane, investing it with a kind of caricatural Victorian interest'.

---

of Lady Ottoline Morrell, a painting of the head and shoulders (recently exhibited at the Café Royal Centenary Exhibition, 1965, and at the Arts Council Gallery, 1966, 'Vision and Design', commemorating the life, work and influence of Roger Fry).

Lamb's earliest known portrait, a drawing done before Lytton grew his beard, is owned by Lamb's sister-in-law, Lady Lamb. And in rather a different vein, Lamb also did a caricature sketch of Lytton and Clive Bell, shown at the Henry Lamb Memorial Exhibition in 1961 at the Leicester Galleries, and now owned by Mr Roger Senhouse.

The affection and malice in Lamb's painting catches something of his own peculiar relationship with Lytton, who, though violently attracted sexually, sometimes disapproved of him on ethical and intellectual grounds. He saw Lamb without much self-deception, the ambience of his tough, mercurial and slightly satanic vitality infected him with a dark zest. He was stimulated at times – and by the most trivial happenings – to a state of ecstasy bordering on coma. Lamb's tantalizing smile, his expression in profile of complacent and intensified mockery, could almost make him faint with pleasure. Just so arrogantly self-willed might an angel look in repose – *an angel of the devil!* In his delirium of heightened fantasy, he began to see Lamb as a demon, a mythical creature of the woods, a satyr. His slyness and cleverness made him all the more attractive. He was inaccessible, too, yet the strain and paradox imposed by this impossible situation sharpened the excitement, preserved undimmed its illusory aura of beauty and romance. In his company Lytton was customarily quiet, docile, serviceable and, of course, chaste. It was often incomprehensible to him how he could go on desiring Henry, how the magnetism and tension between them did not slacken, rather that it approached snapping-point only to ease slightly and then agonizingly expand again. In all Henry's humours, whether grave or mellow, he was such a touchy, testy, pleasant fellow, so amusing, so irritable, there seemed no living with him, none without him. Sometimes the luxurious enjoyment of Lytton's indulged frustration changed to genuine misery, for heated altercations regularly broke out between them. Yet, because his new creed and confidence lent him an extra reserve of strength, Lytton was never so prostrated and totally oppressed as he had been during the most bitter moments of his relationship with Duncan Grant. He still desperately wanted true companionship and affection, but this longing was partly mitigated by his paramount desire for power, for an honourable prestige which, he felt, would somehow bring with it the ideal love of his dreams. Before the Spiritual Revolution, his dependence upon those few whom he loved and admired had been absolute. Now he was less wholly vulnerable. A new facet of his character had grown up which was unaffected by this volatile susceptibility. As his intellectual assurance in his own abilities and potential attainments developed, so correspondingly his quixotic enhaloment of the artist gradually diminished. And so, after the terrors and quarrels between them came, not the abject, cringing apologies he addressed to Duncan Grant, but explanations and excuses that tended to place their emotional dissensions in a less hysterical context.

'I know I'm exaggerated and maladif in these affairs,' he wrote to Henry Lamb after one early reconciliation (19 February 1912). 'I wish

I could say how I hate my wretched faiblesses. But I think perhaps you don't realise how horribly I've suffered during the last 6 or 7 years from loneliness, and what a difference your friendship has made for me. It has been a gushing of new life through my veins – enfin. I sometimes get into a panic and a fever, and a black cloud comes down, and it seems as if, after all, it was too good to be true. . . .'

And, similarly, he would write off to his confidante, Ottoline Morrell (25 January 1912): 'He [Henry Lamb] has been charming, and I am much happier. I'm afraid I may have exaggerated his asperities; his affection I often feel to be miraculous. It was my sense of the value of our relationship, and my fear that it might come to an end, that made me cry out so loudly the very minute I was hurt.'

These letters to Ottoline are not so full of violent perdition and panting recrimination as those to Maynard Keynes. While they eloquently celebrate the value of Lamb's affection, which Lytton was never absolutely sure of retaining for long, yet one is made aware of a feeling – as one seldom was in the Duncan Grant affair – that, when the final separation comes, life will not altogether cease; that, however inevitable it may be that things will turn out unhappily, Lytton was still young, and every kind of fresh and unexpected development lay in wait for him.

CHAPTER II

Town versus the Country

'Why is London the only place to live in . . .?'

Lytton Strachey to Virginia Woolf (8 November 1912)

'My theory is that if only I could get a cottage on these Downs, and furnish it comfortably, I could live and work in comparative happiness.'

Lytton Strachey to James Strachey (September 1912)

I

THE ANGEL, THE DEVIL AND *THE SON OF HEAVEN*

It was during the spring and summer months of 1912 that Lytton wrote his only play to be performed on the London stage. *The Son of Heaven*, as it was called, was a full-length tragic melodrama, the action of which passes on two August days in 1900 at the Imperial Palace, Peking. After a month of plotting and planning the first act, he reported his progress in rather dismal terms to Ottoline Morrell (18 March 1912): 'I'm proceeding with my play, but rather slowly and rather gloomily. The difficulties are too horribly great; and about half the time I feel simply incompetent. Well! Racine wrote two bad plays before Andromaque – so I suppose there's some hope.'

He attributed the chief cause of these difficulties to his lack of *recueillement* shuttling back and forth between Bloomsbury and Hampstead. To try and remedy this condition, he left Belsize Park Gardens late in April, spending the next six weeks in Cambridge, this time at number 10 King's Parade, Sydney Waterlow's rooms on the second floor front.[1] The main advantage of this place was its peacefulness – the absence of London tubes and traffic was in itself very remarkable. Despite his many

[1] Sir Sydney Philip Waterlow (1878–1944), diplomat and author. A prodigy at Eton and a brilliant classical scholar at Trinity, his career, which took him as British Minister to Bangkok, Addis Ababa, Sofia and Athens, was 'in some ways stranger than fiction' (Leonard Woolf). Among his books are a biography of Shelley (1912) and a translation of the *Medea* and *Hippolytus* of Euripides (1906).

friends there – Maynard Keynes, Walter Lamb, Harry Norton, Gerald Shove – he felt rather out of the swim. 'You should see my solitude!' he wrote plaintively to Ottoline (30 April 1912). 'It is only equalled by my insensibility. The most ravishing creatures (or at least so I'm told) pass by me all day, and I remain icy. Well! I came for peace and I have found it.'

He was now able to work at his play with unbroken concentration. Before the end of May he had completed the first act and almost finished the second. When not writing, he passed much of his solitude in reading – Flaubert's letters, Maupassant's *Bel-Ami* ('a profoundly depressing book') and in particular *The Brothers Karamazov*, which, he liked to tell the severely atheistic James, nearly converted him to Christianity. After his first rush of enthusiasm for Dostoievsky in French, he had begun to take Russian lessons; but it was the recently issued Constance Garnett translation into English which now absorbed him. 'It's been very exciting,' he told Henry Lamb (30 April 1912), 'but on the whole I was – disappointed! I don't think it's better than the other great ones – I hardly think it as good . . . I think it's the *ablest* – the mass and the supremacy of the detail, and the concatenation of the whole thing – the mastery of the material is complete. But the material itself – those tremendous overwhelming floods of unloosed genius that pour out of Les Possédés and L'Idiot – that was what I missed. Of course there are great heights, but only once, at the very end, did I feel the knife really in between my ribs, and turning. For one thing, I think there's too much of the detective-story apparatus. The Christianity also is slightly trying at times.'

In the last week of May, Lytton left Cambridge and started off with Henry Lamb on a ten-days walking holiday up to Cumberland. After a final tremendous trek of thirty miles across mountains and moors from Carlisle to the country town of Alston, they settled down together for a few days of rest and relaxation at Handy House, a comfortable inexpensive lodging house 'with a Scotch mist out of the window, plush brackets on the walls, furniture draped à la Roger [Fry] and Henry in the middle of it all, fuming over a picture'.

The Alston trip did them both good; but despite brilliant weather, good food and delightful country ('hills are ranged round on every side; and various streams rush by') its success was always precarious. Lytton, invariably affected by illness in other people, was distressed by Henry's erratic health, and the low spiritual state which, he believed, was directly associated with it. His position was in consequence always tricky. He longed to help Henry, to try and assuage his angry melancholy; but, knowing so well how he resented interference, dreaded bringing down on his own head his friend's fierce castigation and scorn. 'At times,' he confessed to Ottoline (7 June 1912), 'I feel terrified when I think of him – he seems like some desperate proud fallen angel, plunging into darkness and fate. Oh why? Why? He nourishes himself in bitterness, and wraps himself up in his torments as if he loved them.'

Rather unrealistically, Lytton believed that the horrors which tormented Henry would dissolve, and his temperament grow more placid and relaxed, once they could set up house together, preferably somewhere in the country. He had little real confidence of bringing this about, but on his arrival back in London he launched a new drive to set himself up on some permanent basis away from his family. Several schemes were considered. For a while he thought of moving to Milton Cottage in Rothiemurchus, with both Henry and James; and at various other times that summer he inspected houses in Gordon Square, Mecklenburgh Square and Woburn Square. But in every case there was some overriding objection – either the unsuitable location combining too close a proximity of relations and too great a remoteness of friends, or else simply the noise, the expense and the hopeless gloom. Once again his endeavours seemed to lead nowhere.

From his northern trip, Lytton appears to have accumulated such a store of energy that he was able to work at Belsize Park Gardens with unusual resolution, forging well into the third act of *The Son of Heaven* by the end of June. Nor were his spirits unduly dampened down by the failure of any new *ménage* to materialize. Wearing a great deer-stalker hat, tortoiseshell spectacles, a carnation in his button-hole, he would stroll down Piccadilly with his nimble, elastic tread, swinging his cloak and imagining himself a gay London spark, whirling along in taxis, drinking tea at Rumpelmayer's, striding through picture galleries with the best of them. Perhaps London was the most satisfactory place in which to live after all . . .

Certainly it was the most exciting. Extraordinary things were always happening there. A lady by the name of Marzials had got in touch with him asking whether he would write a life of St-Évremond, with the aid of material collected by her late husband. 'I don't think I shall,' he told Ottoline (12 June 1912), '– unless the materials turn out to be very exciting; and that is unlikely. St Evremond was a pleasant gentleman; but that was all, I fancy. If I must write somebody's life, it had better be Voltaire.'[1]

---

[1] Among other non-fiction books that he considered writing was one on the work of Augustus John. He was approached in the early summer of 1913 by J. C. Squire and John himself about this project, but replied that he thought such a volume would be premature and that, in any case, he was not the right man to do it.

More exciting still was the news that his friend Leonard Woolf was engaged to be married to Virginia Stephen, who some people had thought would end up as the wife of Walter Lamb. Such a curious event occasioned the sort of gossip which Lytton always particularly relished, full of improbable conjecture, and enlivened with humorous malice. 'I am *very* glad,' he wrote to Ottoline (12 June 1912). 'I've not seen either of them yet; but I know that he's in ecstasies of happiness. He had to besiege her a good deal before she accepted him. I feel rather a fool because I kept on urging him to propose, while he was doing it all the time; but why didn't he tell me? I suppose he thought I wouldn't be discreet enough. There's a story that a week or two before the engagement he proposed in a train, and she accepted him, but owing to the rattling of the carriage he didn't hear, and took up a newspaper, saying "What?" On which she had a violent revulsion and replied "Oh, nothing!" – She was very much disappointed at everyone taking the news so calmly. She hoped that everyone would be thunderstruck. Duncan alone came up to her expectations – he fell right over on the floor when she told him: and of course really he had been told all about it by Adrian before.'

By the beginning of July his unexpected bonus of London energy had at last been used up, and he hurried off back to Becky House for a month's enforced exile. The solitude here was very salutary, and his play progressed well. Every day he rose at seven, worked all morning, dozed, dreamed and read in the afternoon, walked during the evening, and read a little more at night, absorbing himself in Peking politics. 'My brain seethes like a witch's cauldron,' he wrote to Henry Lamb (13 July 1912), '– I keep ladling out the contents into my Chinese, but it continues to boil and bubble and sometimes I hardly know whether I'm on my head or my heels . . . I see that I should have been ruined if I hadn't come here. As it is, I've now finished my 3rd Act, and so only have one more to do. It ought to be the most exciting and therefore the easiest, and I hope to reel it off in a week, and then proceed to the grand revision.'

For relaxation he read Anatole France, Gray, *La Maison des Morts* (not yet translated into English), Van Gogh's letters, and Lanfrey's life of Napoleon, which drew from him a spirited tirade in one of his letters to Ottoline (6 July 1912). 'I think he [Napoleon] was the embodiment of all that is vilest in the character of man – selfishness, vulgarity, meanness, and falseness of every kind pushed to the furthest possible point. The *lowness* of him! If he had had one touch of the eminence of vice that Milton's Satan had, he would not have been utterly damnable; but the wretch was base all through. That so many people should have admired him so much seems to me one of the bitterest satires on humanity. It is the ape adoring its own image in the looking-glass.'

After two weeks of unrelieved solitude, G. E. Moore came down to stay – a soothing companion, not very enthralling, but, since they spent most of the time separately over their own respective works, ideal for the circumstances. On fine days in the afternoons they would go off for terrific walks together along deep, narrow, aromatic Devonshire lanes, thick with summer flowers, and then up high on to the moor, bowling away into far horizons, with the heather under their feet and great piled-up rocks on the tops of the hills. In the evenings they read aloud to each other from Froude's *Short Studies on Great Subjects* and Mahan's *Influence of Sea Power upon the French Revolution and Empire*; and sometimes Moore would warble Beethoven songs at the piano.

Some of Lytton's time during these weeks was occupied in devising and drafting a petition on behalf of the sculptor, Jacob Epstein. Early the previous year Epstein had been commissioned to carve the tomb of Oscar Wilde. For over nine months he had laboured in his London studio at an immense monolith weighing some twenty tons. Eventually this work was transported to Paris, and had recently been erected over Wilde's remains in the Père Lachaise cemetery. The Préfecture of the Seine, however, had considered the tombstone indecent, and immediately ordered it to be covered with a tarpaulin. In an effort to reach some compromise, Robert Ross, the trustee for the monument and Wilde's literary executor, had, without consulting Epstein (who, in any case, would never have sanctioned his action) arranged for a large plaque to be modelled and cast in bronze; and this was then applied to the offending regions of the sculpture in the manner of a fig-leaf. But one night, soon after its appearance, the plaque was removed by a marauding band of artists and poets; whereupon the tarpaulin had been quickly replaced over the tomb by the authorities, and a gendarme stationed on duty near by.

At once a protest went up in the French newspapers – a protest supported by many famous artists and men of letters. Lytton had been drawn into the affair by Francis Dodd and Ada Leverson.[1] It was the kind of situation that would always incite his most combative qualities – the fight against philistinism and prudery. About the Préfecture of the Seine there was little enough that a relatively unknown Englishman could do; but there were other ways in which he thought that he might help Epstein. His efforts and the language in which they were expressed,

---

[1] Ada Beddington (1862–1933), author of six epigrammatic novels, who had married Ernest Leverson, the son of a diamond merchant. She became one of the closest and most loyal friends of Oscar Wilde, who always called her 'the Sphinx'.

like those of most effective crusaders, were commendably reasonable.
The actual petition that he composed took the form of a modest proposal to the French Government, asking them to refund the money
which Epstein had been obliged to expend on the customs duties in
order to take the monument to France. It comprised little more than a
formal statement of facts. One copy was then sent to Dorothy Bussy
who translated it into French and forwarded it on to Auguste Bréal
with an informal letter explaining the circumstances of Epstein's
poverty, and asking him to get up a small committee to see the thing
through. The second copy was presented from the English side. It was
hoped to obtain some official representation from the Foreign Office,
but this failed. Many names were considered by Lytton to act as
signatures for his statement, names which were well-known in France
and which, he thought, might impress the Government – among others
Henry James, W. B. Yeats, Charles Ricketts and C. H. Shannon: 'As to
the English signatures,' he very properly concluded, 'Holroyd would of
course be the very thing.'[1] But in the end none of these people were to
be associated with the venture. The final version, which Lytton completed early in August, reads as follows:[2]

'Mr. Epstein, the sculptor, has now completed the tomb of Oscar
Wilde, which will shortly be placed in the Père Lachaise cemetery. It
is estimated that the duty, levied by the French customs on the im-
portation from England of the large blocks of stone composing the
tomb, will amount to at least £120. The monument is a serious and
interesting work of art, it is to be erected in a public place in Paris and
it is dedicated to the memory of an English poet and littérateur of high
distinction. In consideration of these facts, it has been suggested to us
that the French Government might be approached with a view to the
remission of the customs duty. The aesthetic merit of Mr. Epstein's
sculpture and the public interest attaching to it lead us to hope that he
may be relieved from a considerable financial burden, which falls upon
him owing simply to the commercial value of the mere stone of which
his work is composed. The granting of the proposed remission of duty
would, we feel, be in accordance with those traditions of enlightened
munificence in all matters connected with the arts, for which the French
Nation is so justly famed. George Bernard Shaw, H. G. Wells, John
Lavery, Robert Ross, Léon Bakst.'

[1] Sir Charles Holroyd (1861–1917), Director of the National Gallery and first Keeper
of the Tate Gallery, had four years previously lent his support in favour of Epstein's
Strand statues. He is no relation of the present author.
[2] A slightly different and shorter version of this statement appears in Jacob Epstein's
An Autobiography (revised edition, 1963, pp. 53–54).

The French Government, however, was unmoved by this piece of rhetorical flattery, and showed itself to be no different from the bureaucracy of any other country. The petition failed; but two years later, at the outbreak of war, the tarpaulin was removed from the tomb without remark, and has never been replaced.

By the end of July, Lytton had finished and completely revised his Chinese play. All that remained to be added were the numerous and elaborate stage directions for the benefit of actor-managers, and then it would be ready for typing. In style it owes something to the dramatic and psychological methods of Racine, and although Lytton did not take it altogether seriously, he had intended it as a possible spectacular production in the manner of Beerbohm Tree. Meanwhile, he put the manuscript to one side and left Becky House to embark on an ambitious holiday with Henry Lamb, whose vicious torments of the spirit would, he promised himself, simply melt away with the open air, the light of day, and his own congenial companionship.

With the highest expectations – 'a map, a hat, a pair of pants' – they set off for Scotland, spending a couple of days in Edinburgh with the Ainsworths. From here they travelled north into Inverness-shire, where they put up with some tenants of the laird, the Glasses, in the small cottage near Loch an Eilan where Lytton and James had stayed in August 1908. And here, at this famous beauty spot, they encountered the first of a disastrous and culminating series of misfortunes. The weather was cold and wet, and Henry's health at once took a turn for the worse. In sickness, his bad-temper and selfishness deepened, and under the stress of his sullen inattentiveness, his undeviating and contagious invalidism, Lytton, too, grew irritable and then ill. Nor was this all. The discomforts of the cottage soon proved beyond their endurance. Early each morning, they had to light the kitchen fire and make their own breakfast; but this they were happy to do, since they had already been woken at four o'clock by solos on the violin. 'Willie Glass would play the violin outside our bedroom from 4 to 5 a.m. in the morning,' Lytton complained in a letter to his mother (24 August 1912), 'and Annie never by any chance had a meal ready within 2 hours of the appointed time. . . . Willie told endless stories dated usually 1450, and was otherwise very cultured and agreeable – but the horrors were too great in the long run – especially as the weather was disgusting also.'[1]

[1] James Strachey remembered that Willie Glass was little more than a gillie, though, like all highlanders, exceedingly cultured. He was also mad, and said to be, like so many others, a descendant of an illegitimate son of Laird William, Lytton's great-uncle, a notorious loose liver. 'Glass' in fact is another version of 'Grant'.

The vagueness and hardships of this cottage life were not to be borne for long, and after a few enervating days they departed for the Alexandra Hotel in Inverness. 'So far the journey has not been a great success,' Lytton admitted to Ottoline (7 August 1912). But already he was cheered by a new brainwave – they would go to a fishing village called Helmsdale on the east coast of Caithness. This was sure to be amusing, and on the bracing North Sea shores Henry's state of mind should improve rapidly. 'We shall probably be there', he informed Ottoline, 'for a few days at least.' Twenty-four hours later they set off, arrived at Helmsdale in the evening – and, by the first train next morning, they fled! Lytton had imagined a romantic little village between the mountains and the sea, filled no doubt with young fishermen in earrings; but what he found was a place not merely desolate and gloomy, but imaginably hideous – nothing but a squalid street or two with equally squalid scenery round about: and not an earring in sight! His disappointment and distress mounted as Henry at last broke silence to claim that this was precisely what he had expected all along.

Amid terrible agitations they hurried off from Helmsdale together on an appalling journey via Glasgow, Belfast and Londonderry to Middletown, on the north-west coast of Ireland. For four mortal days they were perpetually on the move, their money pouring out in bucketfuls, their tempers badly fretted and frayed. Absolutely exhausted, they at last came to rest at a small detached house, McBride's Hotel, which seemed a satisfactory habitation. At any rate they could go no farther. 'At present I am almost killed with various fatigues,' Lytton lamented to his brother James (12 August 1912). He expected to stay on at Middletown, he added, for a minimum of two or three weeks – he doubted whether he would be up to travelling again any earlier. But once more his hopes were reviving. Perhaps, their tribulations over, the holiday would have a long and glorious conclusion. After all, they were comfortably housed, and the countryside was wonderfully beautiful, facing the Atlantic and of a kind to which Henry was particularly responsive – vast stretches of desolate, treeless, peaty land covered with multitudes of small cottages, remote mountains in the background, and, on the other side, the sea, with island upon island, sand-dunes and shores and bays and creeks innumerable; the unified impression was huge, full of complexity and coloured in those vivid browns and greens that Henry was so fond of using in his pictures. Surely he must now be happy.

And, at first, it must have seemed as though Lytton's recurring optimism was finally to be justified. Henry, in ecstasies over the country, had started to regain his spirits. But not for long. Within two days, the clouds of his expiring animosity had reassembled and grown darker. The brief truce was over, and with it their joint afflictions redoubled soon and multiplied. The rain, it rained every day and the wind, it blew; Lytton, who seldom needed much encouragement in this direction, fell ill with a severe chill; and tempers once more grew strained – Henry relapsing into iciness and the blackest sulks, while Lytton, tired, miserable and bewildered, took to his bed and in despair read through the complete works of Tennyson. 'Henry I suspect is daft,' he wrote to Ottoline (14 August 1912), '– that's the only explanation I can see for his goings on. . . . And then, of course, when he's not a devil, he's an angel – oh dear, what a muddle of a world we drag ourselves along in, to be sure! I sit here brooding over the various people – Woolf and Virginia, Duncan and Adrian, Vanessa and Clive and Roger, and James and Rupert and Ka – and the wildest Dostoievsky novel seems to grow dim and ordinary in comparison.'

In the course of the same long letter, he warned Ottoline: 'Don't be surprised if I suddenly arrive at Broughton pale and trembling – I should send a telegram first.' Yet even now he had not given up all hope of effecting some miraculous transformation to the holiday. It was, of course, rash to be too confident, but perhaps Henry was at long last really settling down more peacefully, ascending from devil to angel again. He thought he saw signs of it. And if their turmoils were in fact over and past, then there was no reason why they should not stay on in Ireland together until the end of August, until September. . . . Four days later the final embers of this hope had been ruthlessly extinguished, and he telegraphed to Ottoline:

Shall arrive tomorrow wire train later in need of your corraggio as well as my own.

What then happened has been described by Ottoline herself. 'He arrived soon after the telegram and fell into my arms,' she recounted, 'an emotional, nervous and physical wreck, ill and bruised in spirit, haunted and shocked. I comforted him and diverted him as much as I could. It was difficult to contend with the appalling weather; we gave him a sitting-room to write in, and he stayed some time. I had many an enchanting talk with him and we grew very intimate. He read aloud to me, poetry – Shakespeare, Racine and Crashaw (who carried me away by his intense passion). We took long walks together and went to see Broughton Castle where Lady Algernon Lennox was living. . . .

'At night Lytton would become gay and we would laugh and giggle and be foolish; sometimes he would put on a pair of my smart high-heeled shoes, which made him look like an Aubrey Beardsley drawing, very wicked. I love to see him in my memory tottering and pirouetting round the room with feet looking so absurdly small, peeping in and out of his trousers, both of us so excited and happy, getting more fantastic and gay.'

The atmosphere at Broughton, lively, soothing, comfortable, supremely civilized, was all that Lytton could have wished for in the way of convalescence. His recuperation was gradual, however, for he was full of vain and painful regrets. 'I seem to have been moving ceaselessly and quite pointlessly for the last 3 weeks,' he confessed to James (21 August 1912). 'Among other things I am almost ruined financially.' During the next fortnight with Ottoline he did no work in the sitting-room which had been set aside for him, feeling altogether too sick and exhausted. 'I am constantly relapsing into indigestions and internal disorders which, though not acute, are enough while they last to make work almost impossible,' he wrote in a letter to his mother (3 September 1912). 'I think that I am not in a really healthy and competent state for more than half my days.'

In this state of mental and physical prostration, he ruminated long hours over the miserable débâcle with Lamb, gradually working himself round to a more equable frame of mind. Poor Henry had not been to blame. Lytton knew only too well what a tiresome and objectionable companion he himself could be when sunk in a depressed mood. Really it was quite natural that Henry should have got so cross with him – even so, the extent of his rage and enmity, the virulence and vile brutality of his expression of feeling still bit deep into Lytton's memory, defying all the analgesics with which he nursed his wounds. Yet, under all that ferocity and desire to hurt there had still been something divine, he reasoned, something which proved that he, Lytton, was not merely in love with Henry's intermittent charm of manner, but with his *very self*. In future he resolved that, if this love were to be worth anything, he must try to retain more self-command, more strength for both of them. He must never again let his outward conduct fail. He must try harder: for the griefs and afflictions of mortal men were as nothing beside their loves.

Almost every day he wrote agonized letters to Lamb which did little to endorse this new striving after self-command. What had gone wrong between them? he asked. Perhaps he might return to Ireland and try again? Was it possible that, depressed by his cold, he had exaggerated the whole wretched business? Next time, in any event, they might sleep in separate bedrooms – how would Henry like that? Undoubtedly everything had been his own infernal fault. And so the correspondence drifted on, page after apologetic page. Shamelessly submissive, Lytton took upon himself the entire responsibility for the failure of their holiday. His letters intersperse passages of excruciating self-immolation with others of affected and effete cajolery, that pass into sexual fantasy and sexual infantilism, and are added as saccharine to Henry's bitter tantrums: 'Won't you take me back under your charge again, and cure me with the severest of your régimes? . . . I feel like a naughty child. Am I one? – At any rate a whipped one. Perhaps one who has been flogged hard for some mysterious naughtiness he hasn't understood, and then been shut up in a dark room to repent – Well, there is no trace of rancour in my heart now. Won't my papa come and open the door, and take me into his arms again?'

But in the hard core of his mind Lytton could not and did not believe that Henry was entirely blameless – despite all the pathetic, little-me flummery and coyness of these letters. The most moving sentences are always those which state quite simply his deep and bewildered sense of failure in the whole field of human relationships, a failure bound up with some intrinsic and ineradicable part of his being, cutting him off from the intimate conviviality of his friends: 'The longer I live the more plainly I perceive that I was not made for this world. I think I must belong to some other solar system altogether.'

By the time he returned to London, Lytton felt greatly re-invigorated; and, denuded of the self-pity that he had poured out in his letters, he was able to take some interest again in the general run of human activity – the people in the streets, the respectability of the Savile, the amenities of Bloomsbury. A fortnight earlier his whole future had seemed blank; now it began to fill up again with various new schemes and propositions. He was composing a 'solid and stiff' review of Constance Garnett's translation of *The Brothers Karamazov* for the *Spectator* – his first published piece of writing since *Landmarks in French Literature* and his first book review after an interval of nearly two and a half years. Then Constable, the publishing company, had also approached him with an offer to write an integrated history of French social life and literature, a work that would attempt to define what France means and has meant in the history of European civilization. Though assured that he might make three hundred pounds out of this venture, Lytton was not particularly anxious to undertake it – the subject struck him as rather dreary and too similar to his other book. With nothing to lose, he felt able in the publisher's office to play the part of the Great Author. He employed, so he told Ottoline, 'all the signs of genius – a rolling eye, a melancholy abstractedness, no notion of business', a charade that went down so well that the publisher begged him to send along any other of his works, completed or incomplete. But Lytton would not commit himself. He still wanted some day to write a life of Voltaire; in the meantime, he might send them, he told his mother (9 September 1912), 'the old Hastings lucubration which I should be glad to get off my hands'. More productive was an invitation from Harold Cox to write for the *Edinburgh Review*. Lytton at once accepted this offer, and in the course of the next three years contributed to the paper four of his most interesting and elaborate biographical essays.

'I *am* happy, excited, delighted, prancing, optimistic, impudent, and youthful, now I'm in London again,' he assured Ottoline only forty-eight hours after leaving her at Broughton. The next day he left town with James to spend a fortnight at Van Bridge, a cottage near Haslemere in Sussex, which Alys Russell had put at their disposal. 'James is a delightful companion,' he wrote off happily once again to Ottoline. 'It all seems a sort of Paradise – incredibly provided at the critical moment, like a conjuring trick.' Since there was a housekeeper to look after them, they were afforded almost every luxury of comfortable living, down to the last hot-water bottle at night. 'This is a very nice cottage,' Lytton informed his mother (9 September 1912), 'with only one flaw – the extreme lowness of the rooms. Most of the ceilings come down to the level of our shoulders, and we have to creep about on all fours.'

It was now that Lytton decided to put the final touches to his Chinese play. At first he had rather scoffed at the custom of appending long stage directions, a fashion which had been introduced by Shaw and developed by Harley Granville-Barker to the point where playwrights would give not only descriptions of the scenery and action but even some account of the characters and their feelings. He used to say that on this system, Shakespeare would have written: 'Lear (*angrily*): Blow, winds, and crack your cheeks.' However, James persuaded him that managers and others were so half-witted that they would never be able to make out what was going on unless he stuck in more explanations and directions; and so, under protest, he made the necessary additions.

In the next two years there were to be many attempts to get *The Son of Heaven* produced. The agent to whom Lytton sent it thought very highly of its chances. It was an excellent play, he said, exciting and picturesque, full of dramatic appeal, certain to make money. James Barrie and John Masefield, who also read it, echoed this favourable verdict. And the long list of actor-managers to whom it was in turn submitted – Oscar Asche, Harley Granville-Barker, Frederick Harrison, Norman Wilkinson and others – cordially agreed. He had written, they all maintained, a very good and interesting play. However, it was not precisely what was *needed* – not just then. The previous year might have provided a more propitious occasion on which to stage this particular type of tragic melodrama. But the fashion was always changing. They would continue rigorously to bear it in mind; perhaps later that year ... perhaps next year ... perhaps sometime ... perhaps. ... In desperation, Lytton finally, in January 1914, gave the typescript to his brother James, then on his way to Moscow, and he handed it on to Dudley Ward who was the *Manchester Guardian* correspondent in Berlin and had connexions with Max Reinhardt. Max Reinhardt liked *The Son of Heaven*. He declared it to be an excellent play, most exciting and picturesque. Not alone that, it was, he added, full of dramatic appeal, certain to make money. Unfortunately he was already committed for some time, and it would not be fair to the author under such circumstances to hold on to his work. He therefore returned it. After a while, Lytton grew resigned. It seemed, if one were to believe all that these distinguished and experienced men had written about his melodrama, that *The Son of Heaven* was fated to be the finest play never performed: and with that he would have to be content. He put it in a drawer and for several years forgot about it.

Meanwhile, acting on what he called an 'inspiration', Lytton shouldered a knapsack and marched off alone to Salisbury. The next few weeks he spent trudging obstinately over the Wiltshire and Berkshire downs, to Amesbury, Marlborough and Wantage. 'It was really a heavenly experience,' he afterwards enthused in a letter to Henry Lamb (9 November 1912). 'I recovered my health and spirits – but not only that: I found that there were joys in solitude that I'd hitherto hardly dreamt of.'

He was by this time sporting a conspicuous, bright yellow coat worn over a beautiful new suit of 'mouse-coloured corduroys' and an orange waistcoat; and his outlandish, heavily-haversacked figure caused some stir among the local populace as he stepped out gaily along the roads and fields, especially since he was also wearing golden earrings. These, he told James, were a great solace to him, though evidently outraging the good citizens of Wiltshire. 'They eyed me with the greatest severity,' he wrote from Amesbury (21 September 1912), 'but I bearded them.' He soon, however, elected to compromise on this outfit, skilfully arranging his long locks so as to conceal from the vulgar gaze all signs of his flashing *bijouterie*. One of the highlights of this journey – certainly the most exotic spectacle that it provided – was Lytton's raid on Stonehenge. From his hotel at Amesbury he stole out at dusk, and with the moon bright and rising behind him, approached the monument – a dark cluster of awkward shapes standing isolated in the empty

c*

plain, as if they had somehow been forgotten and left behind there. At a distance it all looked disappointingly small and squat; but then, drawing nearer, he realized that in this peculiar compactness lay its unique power and beauty. He thought of the fallen gods in *Hyperion* – the great old stones seemed to have come huddling together in a melancholy little group, like the last fragment of an army. They had that ominous look of blackness and contraction which extreme old age alone can give. The barbed wire fence was easy to negotiate, and on entering the ring, Lytton discovered that the effect from within, under the gathering twilight, was altogether different, inexplicably awe-inspiring. Each stone was in reality a gigantic bulk dwarfing him into insignificance, while, in the darkness which stretched away beyond the pillared circle, the twentieth century appeared all at once immeasurably remote.

After inspecting the Wiltshire Downs, Lytton turned north towards Churn where Ottoline, having temporarily taken up water-colour painting, was residing at a little farmhouse lent to her by her brother Henry. He had already warned her at the start of his tour that he might be travelling in this direction. 'So if one fine morning,' he had written (18 September 1912), 'you perceive a dishevelled tramp, with melancholy marked upon every limb, wearing a small black hat, a ragged beard, a pair of odd-looking spectacles, and for all I know fisherman's earrings – if you see such a figure come creeping upon a stick over your airy down – it may be . . . a certain eminent young literary gentleman.' Ten days later Lytton did make a flying descent upon Churn. Ottoline noted his hurried arrival and departure in her diary, like the first brief entrance and exit of some character from a classical novel.

September 28th

'Lytton arrived from Wantage with a huge pack on his back, young and gay and debonair, after two or three days' walking. He was as excited as a boy, for he had had his ears pierced and was wearing gold earrings, which he kept hid under his long hair, and he was wearing his new suit of corduroys, which were very short in the legs. What squeals of laughter and giggles and fun we had about it all.

'. . . Lytton stayed some days and fell so much in love with the little house that he wanted to take it. I was sad when he left, he was so well and full of fun and life and youth, adorable; and he and I and Philip had such delightful talks together. I watched his tall, thin back striding off with its rather quick nervous walk, vanishing into the distance. What a solitary figure he seemed then, seeking rather timidly and nervously for human adventures. I stood and waved to him and quite felt hurt that he didn't turn back.'

From Churn Lytton retreated to a temperance hotel in Wantage. He had enjoyed his unscheduled pilgrimage across Berkshire and Wiltshire so much that he feared something must be very wrong. Happiness was so inexplicable, the way it came and went, like the wind. All one could ever do was to seize it when it did come, and hold it as close as possible. All August he had actively pursued it over England, Scotland and Ireland, emerging bruised and broken; now, in September, when he had almost grown resigned to failure, when his plans and movements were completely haphazard, happiness had come bubbling up, catching him unawares. These last two months presented a kind of microcosm of all his years since Cambridge – an illogical mixture of boredom, pain, and enthralling excitement. So much of his life had been spent rushing around in a void, escaping from or chasing after something. He was a wanderer on the face of the earth, and had come increasingly to feel the need of some permanent habitation and society to substitute for Belsize Park Gardens and fulfil the past role of Cambridge. Ottoline had suggested marriage, recommending Ethel Sands as the most eligible partner. She was rich, sociable, lesbian, and owned a lovely house in Chelsea.[1] But could one really marry a house? On the whole, Lytton thought not. Sometimes, however, as a respite from the chaos and uncertainty of his bachelor life, he did toy with the idea of marriage. 'Is this a fearful muddle?' he asked James from his temperance hotel. 'It's too sickening to be trammelled up in these wretched material circumstances to the extent I am. I suppose a wife would settle such affairs for one – oh dear! the length of time this wobble has been going on – five years at least, I believe. I suppose I'm extraordinarily incompetent. . . . Oh for a little rest! – A little home life, and comfort, and some soothing woman! Supposing one married Ka? —'

Such moments of weakness, however, were comparatively rare. If he had been irretrievably middle aged, then he might have settled for marriage with hardly a qualm. It was, he felt, his unassuageable youthfulness that held him back from surrendering to such a second-rate solution – his youthful craving for ideal companionship, for affection

[1] Ethel Sands, painter and 'rich ugly elder spinster' (Mark Gertler), had migrated to Paris to live with her inseparable companion Nan Hudson, and only returned on the death of her mother. For a time she lived at Newington, a square grey stone house inaccurately attributed to Inigo Jones, with exquisitely decorated rooms, a forecourt, formal garden and great stone gates. By the time Lytton got to know her she was living at 15 The Vale, Chelsea. The dining-room here had mural decorations by Duncan Grant and paintings by Sickert, and in the hallway there were mosaics by Boris Anrep, one of which showed Lytton looking out from a cottage window towards Carrington, depicted from another fanciful mosaic window, looking up at him.

and the sharing of joys. And there was something else, too, that now gave him an added determination and stamina – his ambition. The universe might cavort like a wild horse, but he would not be thrown – not just yet. For at times, the vision of some splendid achievement, still a little way off, would rise up and mantle his brain. If he could but seize it, firmly possess himself of it, and stand strong and secure, then all those miserable weaknesses and futilities would melt away for ever. 'Do you know how passionately I desire to do this?' he wrote to Ottoline (6 September 1912). 'To achieve something – not unworthy of my hopes, my imaginations, and the spirit that I feel to be mine? Only the difficulties and terrors are so great – overwhelming sometimes. Oh, to bound forward and triumph!'

2

THE CHESTNUTS

Tired of temperance, Lytton departed from Wantage at the beginning of October and marched on the Bear Inn, some fifteen miles away at Hungerford. His perambulations about the countryside now took on a more definite purpose. The old nomadic life, which so quickly drained away his reserves of energy, could no longer go on, he had decided; at the same time he was in terror of being forced back, *faute de mieux*, into the bosom of his family. There was only one practical solution. He would avail himself of a standing offer from Harry Norton of a hundred pounds, and settle down for a time in some modest farmhouse in Berkshire or Wiltshire – like the one where Ottoline was living at Churn. 'My theory is that if only I could get a cottage on these Downs,' he explained to James, 'and furnish it comfortably, I could live and work in comparative happiness. I believe it would cost very little, and I should be able to afford another rat-hole in Hampstead, to fly to when the solitude became oppressive. . . . It seems to me my health *must* get all right in this air, which is amazing; and if I was really settled down properly with my books, etc. etc. I believe I should be able to work – and then people would come down for week-ends, and I could go up from time to time and gallivant – oh! it strikes me as a paradise.'

After several disappointments, Lytton's choice fell on The Chestnuts, a small farmhouse in the village of East Ilsley, set high up on the edge of the Berkshire Downs, and owned by a racehorse trainer and his Norwegian wife, Mr and Mrs Lowe. He moved in on 10 October, and remained there for the next three months.

Cut off from the pleasures and distractions of London, he was now able to concentrate wholly on writing. His published output during this time was not large – a Spectatorial review of H. J. C. Grierson's *The Poems of John Donne*, and his long essay on Madame du Deffand for the *Edinburgh Review*. These months, however, do form a particular landmark in his literary career. 'Madame du Deffand' heralds the opening of a new phase in his development as a writer – the transition from the critical to the biographical essay – and one symbolized by his use of a new combination of names. No longer was he to contribute anonymously or as 'G. L. Strachey'. From this time onwards he was 'Lytton Strachey', a name – 'rather theatrical, I think' – soon to grow more famous than he could have dared to hope.

This change, trivial in itself, was another indication of the new personality he wished to assume, supported by a new treatment and attitude towards his work. He wanted to write with more force and with less superficial emphasis than before – less reliance on the adjective and more on the verb. Already he felt a greater exhilaration at tackling the problems and complexities thrown up by his subject-matter, and at sorting out the maze of disordered rubble into a satisfying, coherent, literary pattern. When Henry Lamb asked him whether he was pleased with the Deffand essay, he replied (9 November 1912) that he was neither pleased nor displeased – 'but I notice with relief that I rather like writing it, which is something quite new'.

He expended much time and trouble on 'Madame du Deffand', reading everything about her that he could lay his hands on – far more than the three volumes of letters on which his paper was ostensibly based – before settling down to his own composition. 'I shall soon have to begin on the Deffand article – which I rather dread,' he told Ottoline (17 October 1912). 'So difficult to do well – and such a formality about it.' The more he read, the more 'difficult and alarming' his task appeared. 'I am appalled', he confessed after five days, more preliminary research, 'by the mass of matter to be digested, and by the small number of remarks that occur to me to say about it.' He almost wished now that he had never agreed to undertake the essay. No one would notice it, he thought, and the twenty pounds he was to be paid were little enough compensation for all the worry and exertion which would go into it.

Once he had started to write, however, all these subsidiary complaints were forgotten. He became completely absorbed in his subject. 'It is a dreadful story,' he wrote to Ottoline (31 October 1912), 'and on the whole very gloomy, though wit, cold wit, plays over it almost unceasingly. There are the most déchirant moments, and as for Horace

Walpole a more callous fiend never stepped the earth. It is impossible to forgive him – quite impossible. His brutality reminds one of – Henry! But he had none of the redeeming qualities; he was a thoroughly selfish and also a rather stupid man. She, au fond, was not much better; but anyway she loved much. It is a disillusioning spectacle – a woman with nearly everything that life can give – wealth, consideration, intellectual brilliance, experience of the world – reduced to such a pitch of cynicism, pessimism and despair. But it is also terribly pathetic. The last letter of all is ghastly.'

'Madame du Deffand' was completed by the end of November, and the proofs were corrected the following month in collaboration with the latter-day Horace Walpole – Henry Lamb. 'I meant to suggest', Lytton wrote to his mother when he had read the whole piece through again (20 December 1912), 'the kind of nasty turn that the easy-going optimism of everyday life gets, when it comes face to face with her sort of disillusionment.'

Of even greater interest and significance was another literary work which he was meditating while living at The Chestnuts. For it was here, in the autumn of 1912, that the first idea of *Eminent Victorians* was conceived. The scale and pattern of his original scheme were quite different from the completed work. The first title which suggested itself to him was *Victorian Silhouettes*, a book which, as he envisaged it, was to contain highly condensed biographies of about a dozen eminent Victorians – some (mostly scientists) were to be admired, others (mostly non-scientists) to be exposed. Preserved among his papers is a list of the twelve most likely candidates for this volume: Cardinal Manning, Florence Nightingale (whose official biography he had once been asked to write), General Gordon, Professor Sidgwick, Watts, the Duke of Devonshire, Charles Darwin, J. S. Mill, Jowett, Carlyle, Lord Dalhousie (who laid the foundations of modern India) and Thomas Arnold. The urgency of Lytton's feelings, greatly to be aroused by the coming war – which he interpreted as a natural climax to all the false complacency and repressed fear in the nineteenth century – later obliterated the balance of his initial plan, and the theme became a sifting of Victorian prejudice. Already something of this feeling was churning about within him. 'Is it prejudice, do you think, or is it the truth of the case?' he asked Virginia Woolf (8 November 1912) after reading through Meredith's letters. 'They seem to me a set of mouthing bungling hypocrites; but perhaps really there is a baroque charm about them which will be discovered by our great-great-grandchildren, as we have discovered the charm of Donne, who seemed intolerable to the 18th century. Only I don't believe it.' And later, as the war got under way, his indignation mounted, and the illustrious Victorians whom he had elected to portray grew more and more to resemble 'those queer fishes that one sees behind glass at an aquarium, before whose grotesque proportions and sombre menacing agilities one hardly knows whether to laugh or shudder'.

For the time being, however, his gallery of Victorian notables was to include a select number painted in attractive colours – men like his father, apostles of common sense and noble, unobtrusive achievement. The first of all, as a matter of fact, just happened to be drawn in satirical vein. 'I am . . . beginning a new experiment in the way of a short condensed biography of Cardinal Manning – written from a slightly cynical standpoint,' he explained to Ottoline in his first week at The Chestnuts (17 October 1912). 'My notion is to do a series of short lives of eminent persons of that kind. It might be entertaining, if it was properly pulled off. But it will take a very long time.' The writing of 'Cardinal Manning', which is the longest of the four finished portraits in *Eminent Victorians*, proved to him that he would have drastically to reduce the number of proposed biographies, if the work were not to occupy an entire lifetime. The amount of material to be compressed together was encyclopaedic. Round him at The Chestnuts he gathered the formidable engines of his new project – a suffocating assortment of treatises upon the English and Roman Church, various fat studies on Manning, Newman, Keble, Pusey and other divines. 'I can't make out what Mrs Lowe thinks me,' he wrote (17 October 1912), 'but I expect she judges that I am going into the Church – from the number of books on Cardinals, the Oxford Movement, etc. etc., that I have brought with me.'

Whatever her secret thoughts, Mrs Lowe – who claimed to be an intimate of Björnson and Grieg – looked after Lytton very well; while her husband, during the afternoons, endeavoured to teach him riding. 'To-day I had my first riding-lesson with Mr. Lowe,' he wrote excitedly to Ottoline (31 October 1912). 'He is infinitely gentle and sympathetic – just what I wanted. I circled round the paddock in the mildest way, and got hardly at all tired. I shall gradually increase the dose until – hunting, steeple-chasing, polo. No Spanish Cavalier will be in it.' This was a fine and spirited beginning, but the subsequent stages in his progress were less meteoric than he had foreseen. Three times a week Mr Lowe would take him out, shaking with terror, on a small, very well-behaved black cob. Together they would proceed unsteadily across the fields, walking, and occasionally trotting. For some weeks Lytton continued to feel hopeless and apprehensive. Then, one afternoon, he suddenly seemed to get the hang of it, and knew that he would be able to master this new art. His first action to celebrate this access of self-confidence was to order a peaked cap and a fine pair of striped gentleman's breeches to be made for him. His letters to Ottoline, James and Henry are full of his new equestrian prowess and exploits: 'I can sometimes trot for several minutes together with absolute equanimity,' he boasted (25 November 1912). 'The joys of cantering make me turn pale with ecstasy merely to think of. . . . Mr. Lowe does not say much either in approval or disapproval – except that my legs are perfect! I should never have suspected it. Full many a leg is born to blush unseen.' By the end of December he was going for frantic gallops along the Downs, his long hair and pendent *boucle d'oreilles* streaming wind behind in the him.

Despite a personal belief that 'my breeches and "leggings" are much admired', he was in fact regarded with the gravest, the most hostile terror and suspicion in the village of East Ilsley. Whether viewed whirling like some mythical, four-hoofed beast across the long line of the Downs, or encountered as a pedestrian when he descended into the village itself, a bearded man, like the tall Agrippa, 'so tall he almost touched the sky', Lytton presented an intimidating spectacle, and one from which the villagers instinctively shied away. And he, too, paled with fear, as he walked the streets among these staring, unfriendly strangers. He wished fervently that he possessed some capacity for making friends with people. 'I am quite tongue-tied,' he admitted unhappily to Ottoline (17 October 1912). 'I think it is caused by something in the blood – some sluggish element; but oh! I do desire to expand – I really do.'

This unrelieved solitude was the chief, perhaps the only disadvantage of living far off in the country. On some days he spoke to no one at all. His only connexion with the world at large, he told Maynard Keynes, was via *The Times*, which arrived just after lunch and soothed him into a *post meridiem* slumber. 'Why is London the only place to live in,' he asked Virginia Woolf, 'and why must one have the strength of a cart-horse, or you, to be able to manage it? You are not to suppose from this that I am unhappy here. No, my hours pass in such a floating stream of purely self-regarding comfort that that's impossible, only one does have regrets.' Such regrets grew most oppressive in the evenings when the day's work was done and he dearly felt the want of some companion. On the whole, however, solitude seemed to suit him both physically and spiritually. His health was good; he was nearly always contented; and he was working steadily and with enthusiasm.

Sometimes, to help banish this old Adam of loneliness, he would invite a friend down to stay – his sister Marjorie, or Henry Lamb, over whose indiscretions an act of oblivion had now been passed.[1] But more often at week-ends he would arrange to leave The Chestnuts and visit his friends elsewhere. Many of these excursions were to London, where the Second Post-Impressionist Exhibition was being held at the Grafton Galleries. On the first of several visits there he arrived rather late, and on asking the porter whether Leonard Woolf – the exhibition's secretary – was still within, was urged to 'pass through, Mr. Augustus John, pass through and see!'

Once inside, there was no chance of further misidentification, since one of the major exhibits was Lamb's first large portrait. Collected round it, more often than not, was a ring of irate old gentlemen delivering tirades of abuse on Lytton's moral character, based mainly, so far as he could overhear, upon the fact that he did not wear a linen collar. 'I suppose he does it to save his laundress's bills,' was the inspired guess of one lady. 'No, madam, no!' she was speedily corrected by an enraged white-haired escort. 'I am told that he is quite well off. It is affectation – mere affectation!' One Dublin newspaper, after describing the portrait, went on to say that even more extraordinary than any of the pictures were the people who went to look at them: 'There may be seen the autumn poet, in his long overcoat, his large Quaker hat, and his strange black tie, gazing in rapt admiration at his own portrait!'

In a different sense, Lytton, too, was more interested in the effect produced by Post-Impressionism than in the pictures themselves. The Matisses he did find interesting, and their colour thrilled him; otherwise the Post-Impressionists and the others appeared to him painfully anxious to paint only what was dull. Picasso was merely Futuristic and incomprehensible; Duncan a fish out of water; Vanessa rather pathetic; Wyndham Lewis execrable, utterly dreary; Bonnard and Marchand not worth a mention. What really did hold his attention, however, were the irritable buffooneries of the spectators. For, to an ever-increasing extent, his mind was becoming preoccupied by the ingredients of successful publicity, by the ways and means of animating public feeling, and by the methods – in his own craft – of amalgamating literature and journalism, art and polemics, the imagination and the will. 'Why do people get so excited about art? It made me feel very cold and cynical. I must say I should be pleased with myself, if I were Matisse or Picasso – to be able, a humble Frenchman, to perform by means of a canvas and a little paint, the extraordinary feat of making some dozen country

---

[1] 'A smoothing-over of the late crisis has taken place by means of long and amicable letters,' Lytton wrote to Virginia Woolf (1 December 1912), 'so if the dear fellow should go and see you, I hope you will be discreet and refrain from pouring salt on the wounds by injudicious repetitions of long-cancelled abuse. I'm longing to see him again, but I have the greatest fears that he's cut his hair short, which would be a severe blow.'

gentlemen in England, every day for two months, grow purple in the face!'

But the main feeling left by these week-ends in London, and especially at the Grafton, was that he had been wise and fortunate to settle down so comfortably in the country, away from his old friends. He no longer felt quite the same towards Bloomsbury. Roger Fry, for example – 'a most shifty and wormy character' – had quarrelled outrageously with Ottoline and with Simon Bussy. Then, when Henry Lamb had injured his right hand and was prevented from painting, Fry had commiserated with him by expressing a hope that it would not handicap his . . . piano-playing! And, so often, where Fry led, Clive Bell and the others hotly pursued. It was significant that Augustus John had thought so little of their absurdities as to send nothing at all to the Grafton. Besides which, their collective reaction to the divine Boris Anrep, on whom Lytton now had a rather schoolgirlish crush, was beyond forgiveness.[1] 'The Bloomsbury Gang have been most vile about him – including I'm sorry to say Duncan,' he told Lamb (20 November 1912). 'Their lack of prescience seems to be infectious.' Individually he still got on well with them all, especially the Woolfs, who had recently established themselves in small cosy rooms in Clifford's Inn, off the north side of Fleet Street. They seemed singularly unchanged – and it was, as always, delightful talking to Virginia, who had just completed her first novel, *The Voyage Out*. Leonard, too, had written a novel, *The Village in the Jungle*, that had been welcomed rhapsodically by a publisher, though not by Lytton himself, who had read it in typescript. 'Can you imagine what it's like?' he asked Henry Lamb (20 November 1912). 'It's painful to see how completely he seems at home on the niveau of that Bloomsbury gang.'

But the full horror of Bloomsbury was to be experienced at the Grafton itself, where the crowds of his friends and enemies were so overflowing that Lytton felt himself in danger of being entirely submerged. 'When last I went it was most painful,' he wrote to Ottoline (18 October 1912). 'Clive was strutting round in dreadful style, without a hat, as if he owned the place. It was impossible not to talk to him, and of course he would shout his comments, so that crowds collected – all so ridiculous and unnecessary. At last, when he began to explain the merits and demerits of the [Eric] Gill statue, and positively patted it with his fat little hand, I had to disown him, and became absorbed in a Matisse drawing. Poor Woolf sits at his table and sustains the bombardments of the enraged public – how he keeps his temper I can't think.

---

[1] Boris Anrep had written an introduction to the catalogue of the Second Post-Impressionist Exhibition.

Irate country gentlemen and their wives rush up to him purple in the face, as if *he* had painted all the pictures with the deliberate intention of annoying them.'[1]

The delirium of London was a good antidote to Lytton's solitude at The Chestnuts. Some week-ends, however, he would travel up to Cambridge instead, and stay with Maynard Keynes, or G. E. Moore, or Harry Norton. Here, too, there was much complicated bustle and activity, and Lytton soon found himself being drawn into the whirlpool of Apostolic politics. The chief excitement during these months centred round the election of the Austrian philosopher, Ludwig Wittgenstein, and another undergraduate named Bliss. Having studied engineering for a period at Manchester, Wittgenstein had come to Cambridge, where he was greatly impressed by Bertrand Russell's lectures on Mathematical Logic. A friendship had quickly sprung up between the two men – a friendship that, in the opinion of G. E. Moore, Desmond MacCarthy and others, Russell had tried to make exclusive of the rest of Cambridge. But then Maynard Keynes had interceded, and it was mainly through his efforts that Wittgenstein was elected to the Society. 'The poor man [Russell] is in a sad state,' Lytton reported to Saxon Sydney-Turner (20 November 1912) in a letter that conveys very well the flavour of these proceedings. 'He looks about 96 – with long snow-white hair and an infinitely haggard countenance. The election of Wittgenstein has been a great blow to him.[2] He clearly hoped to keep him all to himself, and indeed succeeded wonderfully, until Keynes at last insisted on meeting him, and saw at once that he was a genius and that it was essential to elect him. The other people (after a slight wobble from [Ferenc] Békássy[3]) also became violently in favour. Their decision was suddenly announced to Bertie, who nearly swooned. Of course he

[1] Leonard Woolf has given his own account of these experiences in *Beginning Again. An Autobiography of the Years 1911 to 1918* (1964), pp. 93–5.

[2] Bertrand Russell, in a letter to the author (14 September 1966), makes it clear that, to the best of his recollection, he was never worried about Wittgenstein and the Apostles. Lytton's account of this episode, he writes, 'completely surprised me, and I know nothing whatever about the matter concerning which you write. I knew nothing at the time about Wittgenstein's relations with the Society, nor had I any strong views as to whether he should be elected or not. I was interested in his intellectual potentialities, but I should have been glad of any outside influences that distracted him from the long monologues, lasting sometimes through the night, well into morning, during which he examined his own mind and motives. I do not think that I ever "worked myself into a frenzy" or "got quite ill" with any private worry, and, though I had anxieties at that time which were severe, they had nothing to do with the Society. I cannot imagine how the people whom you cite got these impressions of me, unless they thought the affairs of the Society were more important than I did at that time. I never felt any "mortification" at Wittgenstein being elected, nor can I think why I should have felt any such emotion.'

[3] Ferenc Békássy, the Hungarian poet, educated at Bedales, who had recently come from Budapest and made his mark as a Cambridge undergraduate.

could produce no reason against the election – except the remarkable one that the Society was so degraded that his Austrian would certainly refuse to belong to it. He worked himself up into such a frenzy over this that no doubt he got himself into a state of believing it:– but it wasn't any good. Wittgenstein shows no signs of objecting to the Society, though he detests Bliss, who in return loathes him. I think on the whole the prospects are of the brightest. Békássy is such a pleasant fellow that, while he is in love with Bliss, he yet manages to love Wittgenstein. The three of them ought to manage very well, I think. Bertie is really a tragic figure, and I am very sorry for him; but he is most deluded too. Moore is an amazing contrast – fat, rubicund, youthful, and optimistic. He read an old paper – on Conversion – very good and characteristic. Hardy[1] was there – p.p. and quite dumb. Sheppard was of course complaining that nobody liked him . . .'

Wittgenstein, however, had not fully appreciated the complex human reaction that would be set off by his election, and a few days later offered to resign from the Society. Lytton was at once sent for and succeeded in persuading him to remain an Apostle. It was thus partly owing to him and Keynes that Wittgenstein widened his circle of friends and eventually found his home at Cambridge. After the war, during which he did duty in Austria as a soldier and school-teacher, he was to return to the university, becoming a Fellow of Trinity and eventually professor of philosophy, and exercising a potent influence on the younger generation of philosophers.

3

OSCILLATIONS

The Chestnuts had never been anything more than a temporary solution to Lytton's domestic problems – for one thing, living there was too expensive. But it was also, of course, very pleasant, and gave him a permanent taste for country-cottage life. Without disrupting the flow of his work he was able to see quite a lot of his friends, especially Henry

---

[1] Godfrey Harold Hardy (1877–1947), Fellow of the Royal Society and later Sadleirian professor of pure mathematics at Cambridge. Lytton had first met him when an undergraduate at Trinity. 'I played bowls on the Fellows' Bowling Green which is behind the chapel and most charming,' he wrote to his mother (2 May 1901). 'Only fellows and their friends are allowed there – ours was Hardy, who got the Smith's Prize last year – he is *the* mathematical genius and looks a babe of three.' In 1940 he published a short book, *A Mathematician's Apology*, that is generally voted a masterpiece stylistically as well as in content.

Lamb, who came down to ride with him on the Downs, and who, as an especial mark of favour, allowed Lytton to cut his hair; and Ottoline, who was now encamped some ten miles off at Breach House, Cholsey, and who plied him with a continuous stream of letters and bewildering, upper-class gifts: a massive bottle of hair water ('I haven't yet dared to use it, as I've no notion how to. . . . A tooth-brush. But how does one apply a tooth-brush to the head?'); a garish stock ('How on earth does one put it on?'), a tortoiseshell snuff-box to match his spectacles ('I shall have to take to snuff, in order to be able to produce it with a rap and astound the world'); a voluminous embroidered red handkerchief ('I haven't yet dared to use it – it seems a profanation'); or simply a batch of sweet-smelling leaves to act as book-markers, which he put to use with more courage.

All this was very agreeable, and Lytton soon determined to find a furnished cottage or farmhouse somewhere in the neighbourhood, where he could settle down permanently in reasonable comfort and with less expense. The practical business of arranging such a move left him feeling weak with helplessness. 'I perceive that the path of the cottage-finder is not strewn with roses,' he wrote to Hilton Young (24 October 1912), who was helping him to clear away some of the thorns and who had invited him down for a few days to his own cottage, The Lacket, Lockeridge, near Marlborough. Here, Lytton was told, there existed the most propitious centre in the whole county for discovering what he wanted, something small, cheap and attractive. The Lacket was situated on a large estate belonging to a horse-trainer who took little interest in the property value of his land and was ready to let his houses without complex and protracted negotiations.

Lytton did not look forward to his stay at The Lacket. He hated the drudgery of house-hunting with its fearful dislodgement of his quiet mode of living; but, at the same time, it had been borne home to him that if he wished to perpetuate his amiable, sequestered existence, then all this introductory disturbance was unavoidable. Besides, Hilton Young was so kind and obliging that he could not find it in his heart to refuse the invitation. There were, too, as he soon saw, many pretty cottages in the vicinity that made his mouth water. As for The Lacket itself, this was disappointing, chiefly because of the staid manner in which Hilton Young had done it up. 'Dear me! the poor fellow has not been brilliantly successful,' he wrote to Ottoline (22 October 1912). 'It is all so correct – so scrupulously in the dullest and flattest taste – and, mon dieu! the drab dullness – the lack of inspiration – of colour even. I find myself feasting my eyes on my orange waistcoat. And in the country what gay clean and bright colours one might have. He himself was here for the week-end – exactly like his cottage. Is it Cambridge, or is it England that makes some of one's friends so spiritually anaemic? The bounce has quite gone – if they ever had any. I felt like a Spanish bull-fighter, prancing round him, and sticking darts into his hide. And the good-natured old bull came up mooing, and positively liked having them put in. His kindness was extraordinary – showing me round everywhere, and making endless enquiries. He begged me to stay on here as long as I liked. I am longing to be off, but it is difficult to move. . . . I don't see why I shouldn't stay here for the rest of my life; I'm sure Hilton wouldn't venture to raise any objections. I might begin re-decorating. It would be a nice surprise for him when he next came down, to find the place done up in orange and magenta!'

Though Lytton could not have guessed it then, The Lacket was to play a considerable role in the next few years of his life. But at this time, the few days he spent there seemed wasted, a complete wash-out. The estate agents whom he consulted in Marlborough were unhelpful; the rain came down in a way that looked eternal; he caught a chill which he tried unsuccessfully to quell with whisky; he did no writing; and he was bored. The only surprising item of his visit was the discovery of an article by Wyndham Lewis among some back numbers of the *English Review*, which Hilton Young very properly took in and preserved. By an odd coincidence this article contained an elaborate description of the innkeeper with whom he and Henry Lamb had stayed during those few, disastrous days in Brittany. This was, too, the first piece of writing by that arch-enemy of Bloomsbury that Lytton had come across. 'It was cleverly done – I could no more have written it than flown – fiendish observation, and very original ideas,' he told Ottoline (22 October 1912). 'Yet the whole thing was most disagreeable; the subtlety was curiously crude, and the tone all through more mesquin than can be described. . . . It seemed to me that Henry had picked up some of his beastly mean notions from that source. Ugh! the total effect was affreux. Living in the company of such a person would certainly have a deleterious influence on one's moral being. All the same I should like to see more of his work – though not his paintings . . .'

Lytton's intention had been to vacate The Chestnuts just as soon as he had fixed up some alternative accommodation near by. But in the second week of January, his landlady, Mrs Lowe, suddenly collapsed and was taken to a nursing-home, suffering from consumption. For some weeks Lytton had been eyeing the poor woman with mounting apprehension. Could it be dangerous, he nervously inquired of James, to remain in the house with her? Was consumption (which he already suspected) contagious? Now, after three leisurely months there, he fled hurriedly away, and having found no other suitable cottage, was forced to return to Belsize Park Gardens.

'My vision of the future is dim,' he admitted to Henry Lamb. He could see not a single ray of hope on any horizon, and he wanted, so he said, to bury himself 'under fifty oceans'. For a week he cut himself off in Hampstead from all his friends, feeling too diseased and gloomy to communicate with anyone. His new confidence temporarily faded. He was once again ill, once again in the bosom of his family, still having achieved practically nothing of what he knew himself to be capable. *Victorian Silhouettes*, on which he had built up such lofty aspirations, would take him years to complete – even now he had hardly begun the Manning biography. It would be a colossal undertaking – just how colossal he had only come to appreciate since beginning to get to grips with it. He was under no illusions: the work was arduous, the prospects remote – could he ever stay the course? Of one thing he was certain: he would achieve nothing so long as he stayed at Belsize Park Gardens. But, all of a sudden and quite unexpectedly, the clouds lifted, when Harry Norton promised to make over to him some sort of quarterly allowance pending his literary stability and success. With this support he should be able to find some cottage after all, he reasoned, and there, slowly and to the best of his ability, realize his ambitions. 'At the present moment,' he wrote to Ottoline (18 January 1913), 'you may be glad to hear that I'm almost ready to believe there may be something in me after all.'

He was also ready now to face the world again, to see his friends. For a few days he went down to visit Ottoline at Breach House, but the recovery of his spirits, she discovered, was only partial and intermittent. He was still oppressed by the obstacles which he saw between his present miserable state and the triumphs for which his spirit yearned. Yet, for him, there was no possible alternative to writing. 'I had a long talk with Lytton last night as I was on my way to bed,' Ottoline noted in her diary (24 January 1913). 'I sat on my bed and he stood beside me, looking so dejected and despondent, for he seems to feel baulked in his life, doubtful about his writing; he says that he is no good at conversation so that he could never be a social success, that his small voice would prevent his going into politics, which he would rather like to do, but how could he ever make speeches with his thin tiny voice? I did my best to encourage him with his writing, as I am sure that is his real *métier*. Poor Lytton, how dejected he becomes, and yet he is really very ambitious.'

His spirits and moods continued to oscillate violently. Back in London again, he was greatly cheered by Henry Lamb's good temper and sweet reasonableness. He was 'angelic'; he was 'divine'; not a trace of those inanities and animosities that had marred so many of their previous encounters. Since they were both living in Hampstead, they met frequently, though Lytton felt himself to be under no illusions as to Henry much wanting to see him. But that, he told Ottoline, 'makes me feel more grateful for his friendliness. I do really feel it intensely.' Part of this nobleness on Lamb's part may be traced to his celebrated portrait of Lytton, for which, by early March, he had begun to make his preliminary sketches. 'The last two days have been spent almost solid in sitting for Henry for the big portrait,' Lytton wrote plaintively (13 March 1913), '– the result is rather shattering.'

There were other activities and events, too, that helped to disburden Lytton while he was living with his family. His letters during these two months show him caught up in a round of sociality – theatres, parties, interviews and meetings of all kinds. There were 'hilarious' lunches at Simpson's with James, Harry Norton, Gerald Shove and others; teas in solitary pomp at the Savile, or in overcrowded Bloomsbury, or again with Ethel Sands in her magnificent Chelsea house where (13 February 1913) 'I found George Moore . . . Miss [Gertrude] Stein and others. I spent most of the time talking to a Spanish-Jew-American lady[1] – a friend of Miss Stein . . . and I gleaned a certain amount of information about Picasso, which interested me; but I wanted to listen to George Moore, and couldn't manage it, which was vexing. . . . G.M. I rather liked. He reminded me of one of those very overgrown tabbies that haunt some London kitchens.' And finally, in the evening, there were dinners with Henry Lamb and his patrons, J.L. and Mary Behrend – 'mostly very dull – but with amusing moments from the psychological point of view. They move in a queer stratum – I think rather like the sort of world that Wells describes in some of his novels – Fabian, and cultured, and oddly aimless and unsatisfactory. But the personal shades are many, and I think Mrs. Behrend is really nice.'

Among the highlights of these weeks was an announcement that the Russian Ballet was due to arrive in the country, and that they would be dancing *Petrushka*. Was there any chance of seeing the gorgeous Nijinski? Lytton asked Ottoline (13 March 1913), who had met him in

[1] Evidently Alice B. Toklas. Describing Lytton as 'a thin sallow man with a silky beard and faint high voice', Gertrude Stein wrote of this meeting in her *Autobiography of Alice B. Toklas*: '. . . we had been invited to meet George Moore at the house of Miss Ethel Sands. Gertrude Stein and George Moore who looked like a very prosperous Mellon's Food baby, had not been interested in each other. Lytton Strachey and I talked together about Picasso and the russian ballet.'

Paris and promised to introduce them. In eager preparation for this encounter he bought a new suit of dark purple ('no frills') and a fine orange stock. Meanwhile, between meals and visits to his tailor, there were plenty of other distractions. With Leonard and Virginia Woolf – she 'looking very pink and very attractive', he, in a yellow beard, somewhat less so – he went to Shaw's *John Bull's Other Island* 'and was positively rather amused. But I console myself with the reflection that, after all, the play was second rate.' With James he went to the first performance in England of Richard Strauss's *Der Rosenkavalier* and then, to James's indignation, walked out after the first act, complaining there were no tunes in it. 'I was bored to . . . death,' he told Henry Lamb the next day (30 January 1913). 'There seemed so many points, and so little point, as Zarathustra might have observed. . . . The discomfort of my seat, and the heat, which was far greater than any Turkish bath, contributed to my agony – Also a side view of Adrian. . . . Oh mon dieu! the interminability of it all!'

Almost equally interminable, though only intermittently dull, was a visit to the Aristotelian Society, where Karin Costelloe was reading a paper. It was an odd affair – Karin rather too feminine and boring; Bertrand Russell very brilliant; Moore supreme; Ethel Sands, having come for the sake of Karin's *beaux yeux*, silent and watchful. The atmosphere was stifling; the scene, a saturated mixture of the eccentric and the sublime in proportions that particularly appealed to Lytton's fancy, united his intellect and sense of comedy in an amusing, reverential description. 'There was the strangest collection of people,' he wrote to Lamb (4 February 1913), '– sitting round a long table with Bertie in the middle, presiding, like some Inquisitor, and Moore opposite him, bursting with fat and heat, and me next to Moore, and Waterlow next to me, and Woolf and Virginia crouching, and a strange crew of old cranky Metaphysicians ranged along like half-melted wax dolls in a shop window and – suddenly observed in the extreme distance, dressed in white satin and pearls and thickly powdered and completely haggard . . . Miss Sands! – the incorrigible old Sapphist – and Karin herself, next to Bertie, exaggeratedly the woman, with a mouth forty feet long and lascivious in proportion. All the interstices were filled with antique faded spinsters, taking notes. . . . Bertie, no longer the Grand Inquisitor, but the Joconde, with eyelids a little weary, delivered some pungent criticisms, but the excitement came with Moore. I wish you'd been there. I think you would have been converted. As for me I became (for the first time for ages) his captive slave. The excitement was extraordinary, and the intellectual display terrific. But display isn't the right word. Of course it was the very opposite of brilliant – appallingly sensible, and so easy to understand that you wondered why on earth no one else had thought of it. The simplicity of genius! But the way it came out – like some half-stifled geyser, throbbing and convulsed, and then bursting into a towering gush – the poor fellow purple in the face, and beating his podgy hands on the table in desperation. The old spinsters in the background tittered and gasped at the imprévu spectacle. He is really really a grand maître.'

At week-ends Lytton would desert London to press on with his quest for a rustic sanctuary somewhere near Marlborough. Often he went to stay at The Lacket with Hilton Young whom he described (27 February 1913) as 'my main prop in life. . . . The good fellow has again offered me his cottage, and is making all sorts of efforts towards getting me one.' And a fortnight later he told Ottoline: 'My plans for a cottage are developing, and Hilton is becoming more and more of a guardian angel.' But despite all Hilton Young's efforts, these house-hunting excursions were never successful, and the prospect of finding some place to suit his fastidious if modest requirements grew increasingly dark. When not staying at The Lacket, Lytton would usually put up near by at Lockeridge Farm, a very draughty and primitive farm-house, considerably less comfortable than Hilton Young's place. His search was impeded, too, by a multitude of minor inconveniences – among them the attentions of a housekeeper who turned out to be an ex-cook of Desmond MacCarthy's, and who had picked up from her past employment something of Desmond's style. 'The lady in charge', Lytton wrote to Ottoline during one week-end at Lockeridge (17 February 1913), 'is exceedingly vague, and can only remember occasionally that I'm staying here. When she does, she brings in a few wet sticks which she places on the fire. The result is not encouraging. . . . My chief fear, however, is that she's got – consumption!'

In his leisure hours between house-hunting expeditions, Lytton was reading the works of Strindberg, and also his old friend G. M. Trevelyan's three-volume life of Garibaldi. About the latter work his feelings were mixed. The story itself was wonderfully thrilling, and Garibaldi's tempestuous career made his own problems shrink drastically in size until they appeared altogether trivial; yet he did not really enjoy this biography. 'There is much interest in it,' he informed Henry Lamb (15 February 1913), 'but tiresomely told.'

His own literary plans were preoccupying him now for much of the time. But with so many distractions, social and domestic, he made little practical headway with them. At times this inactivity would profoundly depress him, but, significantly, his periodic fits of pessimism were of a different order from those that had afflicted him earlier. Then he used to wonder whether he was cut out to be a writer at all, whether he would ever be remotely capable of achieving something worth while; now he was seldom racked by such fundamental doubts, but rather weighed down in contemplation of the overwhelming difficulties, the vitality, the patience, the meticulous skill and concentration needed to bring to full fruit that talent which he recognized lying within him. 'My travail occasionally worries me horribly,' he confessed to Lamb (13 April 1913), 'but I do think I'm making a little progress. I sometimes feel – I can't say what. It is disgusting to *know* that there are things in one, but to see hardly a glimmer of a way of getting them out. . . . The thought of your encouragement is a great help.'

The urge to write was ever with him, though he shrank from making a full, irrevocable assault upon *Victorian Silhouettes* until the conditions of work were more favourable, until the summer had begun, by which time he hoped to be comfortably installed in the country. Meanwhile, during the months of February and March, he composed a highly successful and amusing *conte drolatique* entitled 'Ermyntrude and Esmeralda'. 'Will you believe me when I tell you that I have begun and got well under way with a new facétie?' he asked Henry Lamb, to whom the piece was dedicated (18 February 1913). 'Don't I deserve at least a lead medal for this? I'm actually enjoying it; but I see all too clearly that it's a mere putting off of the worst moment – but enough!'

'Ermyntrude and Esmeralda' was written as an exchange of letters between two fancifully naïve, nubile and inquisitive seventeen-year-old girls, one – Ermyntrude – living in the country, the other in town. At school they had both pledged themselves to discover as much as possible about the untold and manifold mysteries of sex, and in their holiday correspondence they report to each other the dramatic results of their investigations.

Everything from babies to homosexuality is ingeniously touched upon with an amusing air of innocence, piquancy and wonderment. But soon their investigations take a more practical turn, leading to some remarkable experiences that culminate for one – Esmeralda – in a proposal of marriage from a fifty-year-old general, and for the other in nightly copulation with the footman. Implicit throughout this lightly-written story is a scathing criticism of those prim, ignorant and repressive procedures and taboos that govern the upbringing of most adolescents, especially young girls. Though 'Ermyntrude and Esmeralda' was not intended for immediate publication, it is Lytton's most entertaining and accomplished work of fiction, and since the passing of the Obscene Publications Act (1959) should certainly find some publisher, even if no bishop might come forward to attest to its portrayal of the sex relationship as something essentially sacred, or acclaim it a work that all Christians should read.

4

GRAND TOUR

'Ermyntrude and Esmeralda' was completed in March, by which time Lytton had decided upon a further means of 'putting off the worst moment', that is, of postponing his serious, concentrated assault on *Victorian Silhouettes*. To avoid unnecessary disappointments, he liked to return for his holidays to places which he had already visited, which held all the allure of past associations, and which he knew beforehand were to his taste. But for several years he had dreamed of travelling through Europe, and through Italy especially, visiting many of the famous towns and cities of which he had read and heard but never seen for himself. Now he determined to make this dream a reality, to spend two months on his grand tour and then return in the late spring or early summer, bursting with health and buoyancy, and straining to be at his work again. This trip, he realized, might prove immoderately expensive, but he had made up his mind to go whatever the cost, and to live, if need be, on crusts and water for the rest of the year. He hoped also to persuade someone to accompany him – his brother Oliver, or Henry Lamb, or even Maynard Keynes – but no one was free to come, and he was obliged to plan his itinerary alone. He intended to spend a day or two in Paris, and then travel south to Marseilles, Turin, Palermo and Syracuse where he hoped to remain a few weeks before returning via Naples and Rome. It was an ambitious solo programme, but he made careful preparations. He wrote to E. M. Forster to find out about *pension* life in Italy, and received a favourably discreet reply; he also sent off for information about Sicily to Maynard Keynes who, a little less discreetly, provided him with the names of the cheapest comfortable hotels, and recommended him to go on to Tunis where 'bed and boy' were also not expensive.

On the morning of 15 March, Lytton set off from Hampstead to Folkestone, where he was put on a boat sailing to Boulogne. To amuse himself during this solitary voyage – and also on the train between Boulogne and Paris – he wrote up an account of the trip, describing in particular the fellow passengers who caught his fancy. This fragment of diary, full of entertaining observations and comments of feminine sartorial interest, records primarily his fastidious wondering preoccupation with the British upper classes, whom he regarded now, and for most of the remainder of his life, in much the same equivocal spirit as he had the Cambridge 'bloods'. His incredulous attention was taken especially by two young men from Eton, aged about seventeen or eighteen, both of whom were wearing single eyeglasses.

'Their faces', he wrote, 'were like joints of mutton – so full-blooded and fleshy. . . . A casual observer might have thought they were dressed shabbily . . . but really everything they had on – their cloth caps, their short waterproofs, their old flannel trousers, their old brown shoes – were impregnated with expensiveness. There was a look in their faces which showed both that they were born to command and that none of their commands would ever be of any good to anybody.'

Apart from these two Etonians there was a 'plutocrat' on board – possibly Sir James Mackay[1] – followed everywhere by four or five women in furs, for whom he took cabin after cabin, into which they eventually retired one after the other, while he himself, spied on by the ever-attentive Lytton, stood stonily on the deck outside, in a yachting cap, 'looking like an old sea-cock with his hens in the background'.

To Lytton's eyes there were still other eccentrics on board, notably two aristocrats remarkable for their overcoats. 'The first was perhaps a baronet,' he noted, 'about 35, with ginger hair and high colouring, and a blonde wife with ineffectual diamond earrings, who no doubt was considered pretty. He fussed a great deal as we were getting near Boulogne, about his luggage, walking to and fro, and instructing stewards – with that queer, pointed, almost German-goose-step walk which must be the right thing when one's travelling, because James and I saw Lord Portsmouth doing it in exactly the same way, on the platform at Inverness in his tailcoat of grey flannel. But what was particularly striking about the Baronet was his very big and very thick and very brilliant ultramarine overcoat, which one had to look at as much as one could whenever he passed, so that it was only after he'd passed several times that one noticed that he was wearing spats and that his brown boots were almost incredibly polished. At the buffet at Boulogne afterwards, sitting with his wife next to him and the maid opposite, he seemed to be quite frightened by the foreign language.

'The second man was no doubt a Lord – tall, dark and angular – rather like Victor Lytton; and *he* had on an immense *white* overcoat. The odd thing about both overcoats was that they had evidently been got for effect, and yet there was only one thing about them over which any care had been taken – and that was the quality of the material. The

[1] Sir James Mackay, first Earl of Inchcape (1852–1932), the shipowner; director and chairman of numerous shipping companies.

blue one was a bad blue, and the white one was a poor white; and neither had any shape; and each was provided with the vulgar strap and button at the back that happens to be common now. . . . Perhaps it is this inability to be interested in anything but the mere quality of materials that has made the English what they are. One sees it every-where – in their substantial food with its abominable cooking, in their magnificent literature with its neglect of form, in their successful govern-ment with its disregard of principle.'

There were many other classes and other nations represented among the passengers on the boat – a number of very sea-sick Polish young ladies, some pedantic French youths, a young don from Oxford and, on the upper deck, an academician (or possibly a Russian prince) retching systematically into a basin – but none of these roused Lytton's curiosity for long. It was a rough and windy crossing. By the time the boat had reached mid-channel Lytton, too, felt a little sea-sick, and as his soul began faintly to grow disembodied, so all these lesser breeds without the titles, spats and overcoats seemed to suffer a strange diminution.

But the British Upper Classes remained life-size to the end.

Lytton stayed only one full day in Paris, during which he went to *King Lear* at the Odéon – a bad translation, feebly acted, which seemed to fill the French audience with amazement. 'C'est d'un romantisme!' they repeated incredulously to each other. He also found time to see an exhibition of Renoir's pictures. 'Some of the early things were ex-quisite,' he wrote to Ottoline (17 March 1913), 'but the late ones are too horrid for words. I gather the poor old man's hand has grown very shaky. It seems a shame to show them.'

From Paris he travelled by train to Dijon. He had planned to move more quickly farther south, but the thick snow and the cold intimidated him, and he decided to make his journey in shorter hops until the skies had cleared, the temperature risen. There was, he noted, a kind of dis-honesty about *foreign* bad weather that particularly dismayed one. Sometimes, too, he felt lonely. 'I wish I had a companion,' he confessed to Ottoline (17 March 1913). 'It's slightly grim to be wandering all alone. But there are compensations.' He remained in Dijon for two days, at the very modern Grand Hôtel de la Cloche in the Place Darcy, which he described (19 March 1913) as 'splendid – with masses of food and wine, and such delightful rotund Burgundian fellow-guests – all with hooked noses and light eyes'. As for the town itself, Lytton was charmed by it and went everywhere with a Kodak camera which Henry Lamb had lent him, snapping old buildings and young boys. 'I felt', he wrote to Henry (19 March 1913), 'as if one could well live and die in one of those heavenly "hôtels", in some street off the tramline, wrapped in infinite repose. Probably one could get one for the cost of a country cottage! – They are not large, but the proportions are perfect and the feeling of space supreme. But I suppose one would really have to be a 17th Century Magistrate to carry it off properly – and on the whole I don't think I am.'

The next stage of his journey took him through Avignon to Marseilles, a bright and bustling town, whose whole population seemed to be continually passing and re-passing him in an endless, frantic hurry as he sat, with Kodak uncertainly poised, inspecting them all from a café table outside the Grand Hôtel de Noailles et Métropole in the rue Noailles-Canebière. 'I've tried some snapshots,' he reported back to Henry, 'but I find it very difficult to manage. It's such a business getting the machine into play. I've wasted several plates already.' In the evenings he would retire up to his bedroom and read Samuel Butler's *The Way of All Flesh*: 'To my surprise I find it cheering.'

As his expenses had already mounted far above the original conservative estimates he had made back in Hampstead, he decided to miss out Tunis and sail, via Toulon, to Naples. From Marseilles he set sail on Thursday 20 March, and arrived in Naples after 'a very painful sea passage' on Easter Saturday. Although by this time utterly weary of travelling, he had made up his mind during the voyage that Naples would not suit him and that he would have to hurry on almost immediately to Palermo. But within twenty-four hours of landing there, he thought that he would never be able to tear himself away. The exhilaration of the town was *sans pareille*, being far more spacious than he had envisaged, on all sorts of different levels, and overflowing with children and young people. As for the atmosphere, it was pure romance – infinitely long streets; sudden vistas solid with flowers; and over everything the beaming sun. During the daytime he would rattle about the place in taxi cabs, 'with my eyes bursting out of my head and my brain in a whirl of ecstasy', he told Ottoline (24 March 1913). 'I try to take snapshots, but my hands shake so with excitement that no doubt they're all failures.' In the evening he would return, fatigued but happy, to Parkers Hotel which, to his constant surprise, was crowded with *bourgeois* English majors and their ladies, all in evening dress and all listening stonily to Italian love-songs warbled by smiling Italian minstrels with mandolins.

'Everything is extraordinarily large,' he wrote to James shortly after his arrival, 'especially the town, which is infinite, and packed with wonders – people, not things. In spite of my deathly exhaustion I took

two excursions through it to-day in cabs – the rattling and the surrounding hubbub and general remuement are indeed intoxicating. Then you
look up at Vesuvius – (not erupting! I had fully expected a tuft of
smoke). . . . One of the oddities is this hotel, quite filled with English
of the most English – what on earth are they doing here? I look at them,
and look at them, but it remains an impenetrable mystery.'

For the most part Lytton was content simply to ride or wander about
the town itself. He did practically none of the proper things on the
sightseer's itinerary – scarcely stepped into a church, never went to
Capri, and only hurriedly visited the museum. The mere effort of
existing in those astonishing streets among that wonderful population
of people was enough for him. But one excursion he eventually did
make to Pompeii. 'It was an enchanting experience,' he eulogized in a
letter to Ottoline (26 March 1913). 'The heat of an English July – can
you imagine it – and the hills all round – and that incredible fossilisation
of the past to wander in. What a life it must have been! Why didn't we
live in those days? Oh! I longed to stay there for ever – in one of those
little inner gardens, among the pillars and busts, with the fountain
dropping in the court, and all the exquisite repose! Why not? Some
wonderful slave boy would come out from under the shady rooms, and
pick you some irises, and then to drift off to the baths as the sun was
setting – and the night! What nights those must have been!'

In spite of a good deal of bad taste, Lytton concluded that there
must have been much beauty in the houses at Pompeii – walls of deep
reds, yellows and blacks seen between white pillars in the brilliant sunshine, green-blue figures round square fountains, flowers of all colours
in the courtyards, and a vision of Vesuvius at the end of a street. Most
disappointing to him were the bawdy pictures, so feeble and anaemic,
on some of the walls. These were concealed from the public and only
unlocked by winking custodians for the benefit of respectable bachelors
such as himself. Some, however, they would not unlock, even in the
face of Lytton's most eager imprecations; after which his interest palled.
The heat was so intense during this expedition that he drank off several
pint bottles of beer, and while drinking them, was persuaded by his
guide to make a further excursion some way up Vesuvius. This climb
drained him of his last drop of energy, all the more so since politeness
obliged him to follow up his beer with several glasses of Lachryma
Christi in a village inn. 'If I were a carthorse,' he commented to
Ottoline, 'existence here would be perfect.'

As it was, he felt glad after a week to get away from Naples in search
of some rest. His plans had by this time grown vague and unsystematic;
the original route was finally abandoned, and since he had heard alarm-

ing reports of overcrowding in Sicily, he proposed instead to go off for some days to Ravello, which Hilton Young had recommended to him as being quiet and sequestered.

On the morning of Sunday 30 March, after a drive of three-and-a-half hours along the shores of the Mediterranean, he arrived at Ravello, set in the precipitous high hills above Amalfi and over a thousand feet above the sea, which lay, almost directly below his *pension*, perfectly blue and smooth. Hilton Young had not misled him. Ravello turned out to be a fairly small village, wonderfully peaceful and unsophisticated. Beyond the sea, looking south over the Gulf of Salerno, lay distant misty mountains with Paestum at their foot; and inland, steep cliffs covered with chestnut woods and fruit trees in full bloom; and in the foreground, Norman and Saracen church towers, terraced gardens and wild flowers of every colour and variety – hyacinths and freesias, wall-flowers and red roses. What adventures he might have had in this divine place if only he had spoken the language!

In another letter to Ottoline (4 April 1913) he describes Ravello as 'a heavenly spot', and continues in a vein reminiscent of his earlier letter (11 March 1906) to Maynard Keynes depicting 'My Castle in Spain' – the dream, now revised in the light of seven years' further experience, of a newly constituted Bloomsbury Group, rejuvenated and removed to Ravello. 'Why not come here?' he asked. 'We could collect a société choisie in this pleasant place – and dream away 2 years delightfully. Henry would be given a studio in the extreme end of the village. Desmond and Molly would have an apartment in the very centre. Duncan would lie out among the fruit-trees. Virginia would prance in after dinner. And even John might occasionally appear. I should insist on having James, but not Henry James – except for a week-end once a year. Don't you think it would do very well?'

The Pension Palumbo, where Lytton put up, was a plain lodging-house without any of the pretensions of a large city hotel. Originally it had been built as a Bishop's palace. Lytton's room was in the annexe, opening on to a spacious platform with views in every direction, and reached by a marble staircase. Since he had this annexe practically to himself, there seemed an admirable opportunity for settling down to some not too arduous work. He had brought with him several books on Cardinal Manning, but no sooner had he started to write than his health gave way. The cause of this collapse was the weather. He had arrived in intense heat, 'a blazing sun,' he told Henry Lamb (31 March 1913), 'and such a mass of light reflecting and refracting – and one can sit for indefinite hours with one's head in the shade and the rest of one grilling'. His health was barometrically dependent to an extraordinary degree

D

upon the climate. When the skies were open and blue, the sun hot, he was sprightly and well; but the passing of a single cloud could bring on internal apprehensions, indigestions, or even worse. And so, when the rain began to fall in Ravello and the temperature suddenly dropped, Lytton was at once reduced to his bed. After a week of this, he decided that, since there seemed no prospect of a return to summer conditions, he must leave for Rome. 'I hope Rome may improve me,' he wrote to Lamb (5 April 1913). 'It's very annoying to have such a futile inside.'

He arrived in Rome on Monday, 7 April under a clear, warm sky, and feeling quite revitalized. For three days he stayed at a small hotel which did not offer many facilities for repose. 'One's fellow-travellers are death indeed,' he complained to James, 'the human race at its lowest ebb – mon dieu! Fit only for Forster's novels, but he hasn't got them. Oh!' On Thursday he moved to the Pension Hayden, in the Piazza Poli, which was more comfortable but 'pretty thick with Americans'. He was nursing a certain grudge by now against E. M. Forster, who, he felt, had completely misinformed him about Italian accommodation. 'My experience of Pension life is most painful,' he grumbled in a letter to Saxon Sydney-Turner (14 April 1913), 'and I find that Forster has quite misrepresented it – whitewashed it absurdly. For sheer, stark ignorance, imbecility, and folly the conversations here can't be beaten. I'm rapidly becoming a second Flaubert under these influences. I can think of nothing but la Bêtise Humaine.'

Yet his stay at the Pension Hayden was comparatively a happy one. Despite the deplorable influence of Bernini, Rome offered, so he discovered, all the allures of Cambridge – the same sort of surprises in the street, and an air of fancy-dress. The Forum and the Palatine seemed like capricious college gardens thrown about among the wild enormities of ancient magnanimity. The town itself continually astonished and delighted him; the variety of attractions was so vast that he could not help being cheerful. For years he had imagined the architectural beauties of Rome, and now at last he could stare his fill at them. He went to the Pantheon; to the Castle of St Angelo (a Piranesi engraving of which had hung on the wall of his nursery at Lancaster Gate, and which he had always longed to see); to the Janiculum to look at the exquisite Bramante Tempietto; to St Peter's, the huge exterior of which took his breath away; to Hadrian's Villa; to the Colosseum; to the Medici Gardens, and the lake of Nemi and the Baths of Caracalla, 'like some strange impossible dream materialised'. He also went to the Sistine Chapel which, he told Henry Lamb, 'quite désorienté me at first. In the end I think I liked it – but it's very queer. As an effort of constructive skill the ceiling is terrific, but it seems rather thrown away. I believe if each morceau could be taken away separately and framed, it would be better. The difficulty of seeing any of it is very great. There are some lovely other frescoes round the walls, by Perugino, Botticelli, etc.' Most of the show pictures and statues, however, displeased him, and he began to sympathize with Roger Fry, who had once declared that Old Masters made him sick. But of all the wonders that he beheld, the most marvellous was the Forum, so very large, covered with green trees and shrubs, with lilac and wistaria, and whole choruses of singing birds – altogether different from anything he had expected.

Every morning and afternoon Lytton busied himself inspecting the curiosities of the town. And then he would repair to an appalling English tea shop to read the Continental edition of the *Daily Mail*. Between tea and dinner he usually wandered over to the Pincio and after listening to the band playing Rossini, strolled in the Borghese Gardens and meditated on Cardinal Manning. After dinner, and with the utmost regularity, he dashed off to the cinema. One afternoon, by way of a change, he went to hear Beethoven's Pastoral Symphony, conducted by Richard Strauss, and described it (13 April 1913) as 'dreadfully dull. Strauss looked like a prematurely-aged diplomat, and I thought did his best to add somnolence to an already somnolent affair. After that came his own things – Hero etc., but I didn't stop.'

When not off seeing a particular building or monument, he was quite happy to wander at will, looking in on an art gallery, or, like a decadent poet, sipping fatal drinks from café tables as the youths ambled by in squadrons, or just floating up some fascinating street or other past so many lovely small piazzas and splendid palace façades in the general direction of an obelisk or a church. There was a peculiar luxury in having only oneself to please, and being able to savour one's own sensations by degrees and to the heart's content. Yet unremitting solitude carried its disadvantages, too. 'I feel that I shall have left a multitude of things unseen,' he wrote to Ottoline (17 April 1913). 'I should like to linger on for weeks and weeks – but the expense is really getting too great, and also the silence! I haven't spoken one word to an intelligent human being for a month, and I'm beginning to feel it.'

Lytton had hoped to go on to Florence for a few days, but a financial seal was set on this scheme when he purchased a large and expensive Piranesi print – 'I think it's rather magnificent,' he concluded in his last letter from Rome to Ottoline. 'Well, someday we *must* come here together, that's certain, isn't it? What fun it'll be! . . . The Pope is dying. Shall I apply for the post? Then you could come and stay with me at the Vatican.'

After two happy weeks there, Lytton left Rome, spent one night in Milan and another in Paris before arriving back in the quiet, sophisticated groves of Hampstead, 'feeling infinitely content with the world', his grand, unco-ordinated tour triumphantly concluded.

5

PEREGRINATIONS AND ANGOISSES

Because his finances had 'been reduced to chaos by the voyage', Lytton resigned himself to spending most of the remaining spring and the summer with his family. His days, however, despite this penury, seem to have been far from monastic; and he plunged back almost immediately into the gyrations of London life – theatres, music-halls, parties. To assist in the cure of a chill that he had caught on stepping ashore in England, James dragged him off to a performance of *Tristan and Isolde* which, to his own surprise, he enjoyed and which effectively killed off his diseases. He also went, under James's direction, to *Ariadne on Naxos*, which bored him, and to hear Paderewski play the Emperor Concerto, and Nikisch conduct the Eroica. But by far the most exciting musical experience during these months was *The Magic Flute*, which he had not heard before and which he went to twice. The first time, he told Henry Lamb (5 May 1913), 'I went quite vaguely thinking it was a short light affair of no great importance – and I was overwhelmed. . . . I think it gives a new conception of Music itself. It seemed to me Perfection made manifest – an intarnishable vein of beauty, and a grandeur before which one fell prostrate. It is too abominable that it has not been done in London for years and years, and it is now only done by the poor Carl Rosa Company at the Coronet with all the drawbacks of bad scenery and poor singing and feeble acting. How can the English pretend to care for music? I go again on Friday.'

Most of the social entertainment in these first few weeks was provided by 'Our Lady of Bedford Square' as he now called Ottoline, at 'Throne Hall'. The turns within her flower-decked drawing-room were even more varied and numerous than usual, and of all the principal stars there, the one to interest Lytton most was the novelist, Gilbert Cannan. 'The poor fellow must have a dim time of it with his wife, who's 20 years older than him, and very distressing,' he remarked after their first meeting. Mary Cannan had formerly been married to J. M. Barrie, who still gave her an annual allowance of money on which the couple largely subsisted and which was handed over each year at a tête-à-tête dinner held, at Barrie's whimsical suggestion, on the divorced pair's wedding anniversary. Lytton at first confessed himself to be 'furiously prejudiced against G.C.', mainly, it appears, on account of a certain coolness which had temporarily sprung up between Ottoline and himself, and which he diagnosed as being due to her recent patronage of Cannan. When, early in May, Ottoline left England with her family for Lausanne, a whole month passed without the exchange of a single letter between them – an unprecedented silence. Meanwhile, Lytton declared himself to be quite converted to Cannan, owing partly to his honesty and openness of mind, but chiefly to his attractive statuesque appearance. Tall and handsome, Cannan had known Henry Lamb at school in Manchester, had gone to Cambridge after Lytton had come down, and was dramatic critic of the *Star*. He had also written several plays and three novels, the last and best of which – *Round the Corner* – Lytton now attempted to read. 'Perhaps it would have been wiser not to,' he confided to Henry Lamb (5 May 1913), 'as it would be difficult to conceive anything duller and more completely lacking in the joie de vivre. I stuck to it, and read every word of the blasted thing, but while I was doing so I felt a cloud over my life. The poor fellow is so modern and broad-minded too! But oh! the taste! – and the pointlessness.' He still hoped, however, that Cannan would appeal to him personally and 'in a moment of épanchement' invited him over to tea at Belsize Park Gardens. At that time the megalomania which was to drive Cannan into a mental home had not fully asserted itself, though already he was moody and disdainful, his embittered humour – a verbal assuagement of this latent desire for power – reminding some of his literary-minded friends of Hamlet. His visit to Lytton's home went off fairly well, though it was quite evidently not the preliminary to a really close friendship. 'He is very very dull,' Lytton informed Lamb after Cannan had left (17 May 1913), 'though good – an empty bucket, which has been filled up to the brim with modern ideas – simply because it happened to be standing near that tap. The good thing about him is a substratum of honest serviceableness – but that is not enough in my line to excite me. *He* no doubt found me far too rarefied for him. I daresay if I took the trouble I could induce in him a culte for me which would replace the one he at present has for Rupert [Brooke]. But of course I shan't.'

After Ottoline had departed for Switzerland, most of Lytton's social entertainment came in the form of Bloomsbury evening parties. These were very wild, unprincipled affairs, if one may judge from Lytton's description of a typical one given by his brother Oliver. All the guests

were in fancy-dress – among them Saxon Sydney-Turner got up as a
eunuch. 'Karin [Costelloe] was the leading figure,' Lytton wrote to
Lamb (16 June 1913), '– in white flannel cricketing trousers and shirt.
Duncan was appalling as a whore great with child, and Marjorie incredible as a post-impressionist sphinx. Oliver was a Harlequin, Roger
a Brahmin, and I Sarastro. The gambols were extraordinary and in the
middle of them Gerald [Shove] appeared, drunk, in evening dress and
a top-hat. He and Karin sang a Vesta Tilley song together and carried
on a good deal. I was considerably in love with both.'

Such parties were invigorating to Lytton, but sometimes, when he
was in his more fastidious and fragile moods, their rowdiness jarred
upon him. 'The dissipations of our circle are approaching a vertige,' he
reported to Lamb the week following Oliver's entertainment (23 June
1913). 'The last party was at Adrian's. Owing to an accident I couldn't
bring myself to go – further than the door in the square – whence I
heard such a Comus uproar that I slipped away again. I had been having
dinner with the Sangers, and felt that my condition was too hopelessly
inadequate. The accounts of the proceedings made me glad I didn't
venture. The nudity reached a pitch – Duncan in bathing-drawers, and
Marjorie with nothing on but a miniature of the Prince Consort. Next
time – next time is on Thursday, at Karin's, 10 o'clock. If you started at
once, couldn't you be there?'[1]

Lytton himself was very much there at Karin's party, during the
course of which a one-act farcette that he had written called *The
Unfortunate Lovers* or *Truth Will Out* – fashioned rather in the slight,
fantastic manner of a Chekhovian burlesque – was given its première.
Set at a country inn during the year 1840, the fun of the piece resides in
the suggestive and improbable inter-relationships assumed by the
Bloomsbury actor-guests, the entire cast comprising two pairs of
elopers – Duncan Grant playing a young boy disguised as a woman (a
part originally intended for Molly MacCarthy), Clive Bell apparently
his homosexual lover and dressed initially as a male, Marjorie Strachey
as a girl wearing the clothes of a man, and Vanessa Bell attired simply,
but misleadingly, as a woman. In the final scene, most of the characters
were revealed to have been in double-disguise, men originally got up as
men later assuming women's clothes and vice versa, and so complicated
were the metamorphoses, the sequence of split-second accidents uncovering one layer of masquerade after another, that before the end no
one could remember who was what.

To win a little recuperation from frenzies such as these, Lytton now
made the first of many agreeable week-end visits to Asheham, a lonely

---

[1] Henry Lamb was then staying in Ireland.

Sussex farmhouse which Leonard and Virginia Woolf had lately rented, and which lay among great trees in a meadow near the north-west corner of the South Downs. The other guest on this occasion was Desmond MacCarthy, 'with his eternal dispatch-box, from which he produced the first chapter of a novel on school life – not very inspiring. He can't make up his mind, he says, "how far to go"!'[1]

Lytton's own literary plans were equally indecisive. On his arrival back from the Continent the entire scheme of *Victorian Silhouettes* had presented itself clearly to his mind. 'An idée has suddenly crystallised,' he told Henry Lamb (5 May 1913), 'and I mean to attack it immediately.' But once again his programme was disrupted, the scheme faded, and he blamed his lethargy and unproductiveness on the irritations of *la vie de famille*. 'As to work,' he reported only twelve days later (17 May 1913), 'the crystal that formed itself so suddenly and beautifully has melted into a sticky little puddle at the bottom of my brain.' He dreaded having to pen some hasty, uncongenial hack work for money, and quickly devised a compromise solution which he put up to Constable. This was a book on Racine – a subject which appealed to him for several reasons. Because of his familiarity and understanding of Racine's work, and his previous writings on it in the *Spectator* and in *Landmarks in French Literature*, such a project might be completed with considerable speed and ease. He also believed in his own ability to produce an original and worthwhile volume of criticism that might command a very fair sale. The Constable directors, however, were more doubtful, and at a meeting held in the last week of May vetoed the proposition on the grounds that Racine was too unpopular in England for a book about him, however meritorious, to make money. Several other subjects were suggested as alternatives, but none of them sympathetic to Lytton, who left the office without any agreement having been reached.

He now resigned himself to the drudge of literary journalism, and wrote off to Harold Cox proposing an article in the *Edinburgh Review* on Samuel Butler. But Harold Cox was dubious about so untopical a contribution, and, in the manner of editors, succeeded, without ever rejecting the idea, in postponing a definite decision about it *sine die*. And so, between January and November of this year, Lytton published nothing, not even a review, though of course he composed a few unpublished pieces and contemplated several more. One of these latter

---

[1] MacCarthy in fact never completed this novel on school life. But a short story, *The Mark on the Shutter or A Small Boy's Conscience* – 'for me, the best short story ever written about a school' (Lord David Cecil) – may have been a distillation of his original idea. It is included in *Humanities* (1953).

was a satire on Roger Fry's Omega Workshops[1] and the whole fashionable, exclusive nonsense, as he saw it, talked about Post-Impressionism – a sketch to be thrown off quickly and light-heartedly in the Molière vein. 'A crank always wanting to be up to date – in the hands of a pseudo-impostor who would put him through all sorts of paces, and try to have his daughter', was how he explained it in a letter (28 July 1913) to Henry Lamb, whose work had recently been criticized by Boris Anrep for being too far removed from Post-Impressionism. 'The 2 Academicians, always coming in together and talking in unison – and all sorts of other cranks – Miss Stein, Rupert perhaps, and others – A General whom it was important not to offend, because of legacies, coming in at the critical moment while all the queer creatures were parading about, reciting poems, painting pictures, etc. – in the midst of a room newly furnished in the P-I manner – they in desperation having to dash into the said furniture, to conceal themselves from his wrath – Rupert into a commode, and Miss Stein into the Grand Piano. Then perhaps after all the General himself getting impressed and converted by the arch-impostor – and so on.'

The barrenness of these spring and summer months was intimately bound up with the overall uncertainty of his life. Leonard and Virginia Woolf's success in finding Asheham had stimulated once again his own desire for an agreeable country cottage. 'My existence is chiefly dominated just now by the housing question,' he told Henry Lamb (5 May 1913). To escape from Hampstead he had hoped to spend a week or two with Lamb, who was now occupying Cashelnagor, his friend George Kennedy's house in County Donegal; and, later in the year, he thought of travelling to Germany with James, to listen to Mozart and drink beer in Munich. Both these plans, however, had to be put off because of 'the housing question', which looked like using up all his time and available money, and which every day grew more involved.

What had happened was this: since it appeared that there was not a

---

[1] The Omega Workshops had officially opened in July 1913 at 33 Fitzroy Square, these premises serving as showroom, design studios and actual workshops. The driving force behind the scheme was Roger Fry, who was helped by two directors, Vanessa Bell and Duncan Grant. Among the young artists they employed part-time at thirty shillings a week to design and produce textiles, dress fashions, furniture and pottery were Wyndham Lewis, Edward Wadsworth, William Roberts and Gaudier-Brzeska. Several of their fabrics were hand-painted with dyes. In some cases local carpenters were employed to do basic joinery in white wood which the artists would then decorate; in others, designs were placed in the hands of large firms – furnishing fabrics sometimes printed in France, carpets sometimes woven by Royal Wilton, stained glass produced in Fulham. Amateur and experimental in execution, their products – which could be bought or made to order – aimed at educating the public taste to radically new aesthetic ideas. It was not wholly a success. In June 1919, Fry closed the workshops and the company was forced into voluntary liquidation.

single unoccupied farmhouse ready to be rented in the whole of
Wiltshire, Hilton Young had recommended Lytton to build a small
cottage to his own requirements and pay for it gradually over the years.
Lytton at once took up this idea and developed it. His plan was to
establish this place as a week-end retreat for his friends, who would all
contribute some amount towards its cost. After a great deal of cautious
reconnaissance, Hilton Young had spied out a likely plot of land, and
Lytton persuaded George Kennedy, the architect, to come down, inspect the ground and examine local conditions. Apart from the price,
which was steep, everything seemed set fair: the situation was excellent;
Kennedy agreed to design the building himself; and to celebrate the
new venture they all three drank warm champagne at eleven o'clock
one May morning on the platform of Marlborough railway station.
But then, when Lytton had finally nerved himself for every risk and
effort, a surprising discovery was made: the land in question, so carefully selected, happened to belong to the National Trust and was
therefore not for sale. This was a severe blow, and for several weeks
Lytton was reduced to 'a trance of slothful désespoir'. Rallied once
more by the miraculous Hilton – 'I shall have to write him a poem in
Heroic Couplets' – he then resumed his quixotic search for land. Soon
a new, rather inferior site was located, but this time Kennedy only
sent down his second-in-command, William Park, who in due course
produced a plan which struck Lytton as mediocre. By now everyone's
enthusiasm had waned, and, since it was obviously a mistake to proceed
with anything so permanent as actual construction work in this half-
hearted mood, it was generally agreed, with a sigh of relief, to let
matters drop.

To superintend all these fruitless negotiations Lytton had spent
much of May, June and July down at The Lacket, during which time he
read almost every book there and evinced a particular appreciation for
the gay absurdity of Chekhov, which seemed to catch so much of the
wry, comical futility of his own life. 'The more I think of them
[Chekhov's plays],' he wrote to Lamb (23 June 1913), 'the more eminent they seem.' Gradually, too, the internal atmosphere of The Lacket
came to appeal to him rather more. 'I find myself quite beginning to
like the matting on the walls,' he admitted (1 June 1913), 'and in a day
or two I foresee that I shall be seeing some merit in Arnold-Forster's
water-colours.' This change of mood was all the more fortunate since,
towards the end of July, Hilton Young suddenly announced that he
was not going to use his cottage for a year, and that, from the end of
September, Lytton was free to move into it and remain there till the
following autumn at a rent of thirty pounds. For an extra sum, the

D*

housekeeper, the excellent Mrs Templeman, would also stay on and look after him. This was tremendously good news and Lytton joyfully accepted the offer. 'I was in the greatest doubt as to how I could conveniently dispose of myself in the coming year,' he wrote to Hilton Young (28 July 1913), 'and I never dreamed that such a piece of good luck would come my way. It ought really to save my life, I think – temporarily if not permanently; and the most distinguished life-saving apparatuses can do no more. Of course Mrs. Templeman must be included. Is she frightfully expensive? But it doesn't matter – I would sell out all my East India Stocks to keep her.' Although, inevitably, his first six winter months would be rather ice-bound, their solitude would give him a perfect opportunity for some consecutive literary effort – the most vital consideration of all. 'I'm rather terrified by the prospect,' he confessed to Ottoline (16 August 1913), 'but I think on the whole it's a good thing. I ought to be able to do some work there, and get up a good dose of health. But I dread the bleakness of the wintry downs, and shall have to rush up from time to time and fling myself into the arms of the yellow drawing-room.'

Released from the pressure of endless doubt and indecisiveness, Lytton could spend the intervening weeks in a gregarious, holiday spirit. In mid-July he again visited Asheham, this time for a full week, feeling 'infinitely more cheerful – in fact altogether perky and insouciant'. The only cloud in the sky was the illness of Virginia Woolf, who, shortly after his departure, was struck down by violent headaches, sleeplessness, and an acute fit of despondency, and had to be removed to a nursing-home.

Back in London, Ottoline was again the focal point of all Lytton's entertainments, having returned from Switzerland and quickly resumed her succession of Bedford Square parties. These, as always, were crowded with celebrities, and carried off with a panache which, to Lytton's eyes, made the lamentable old Bloomsbury milieu appear like a subterranean world of fishes. At one of these fine parties he at last met the legendary Nijinski who, he told Henry Lamb (24 July 1913), 'was very nice, though you won't believe it, and much more attractive than I'd expected – in fact very much so, I thought. . . . Otherwise he did not seem particularly interesting – as the poor fellow cannot speak more than 2 words of any human language it's difficult to get very far with him. As it was, there was another Russian who acted as interpreter and the conversation was mainly conducted by Granville Barker.' The previous week, before retiring down to Asheham, Lytton had gone to see Nijinski's latest ballet, *Le Sacre du Printemps*,[1] 'one of the most

[1] Nijinski was the choreographer of *Le Sacre du Printemps*. He did not dance in it.

painful experiences of my life', he described it. 'I couldn't have imagined that boredom and sheer anguish could have been combined together at such a pitch. Stravinsky was responsible for this.' Yet at moments he still found the performance pleasing, and Nijinski dazzled and delighted him: 'I sent him a great basket of magnissime flowers, which was brought on to the stage and presented to him by a flunkey.'

After a week-end in Manchester with Henry, who had been commissioned to paint an official portrait of his father, Professor Lamb, Lytton hurriedly fled to the remoter country, fearing that Henry's struggles and tribulations over trying to combine filial sentiments, municipal expectations and the call of high art, all on one small canvas, might easily result in a mood of irritability directed, for want of any better target, against himself. On Wednesday, 23 July, he arrived at the Plough Inn, Holford, a lovely little village at the foot of the Quantock hills, and here he put up for almost three weeks. He had not intended at first to remain for more than a few days, but Henry's portrait occupied him longer than had been anticipated, and the Plough Inn was so *soigné*, the weather so radiantly hot and fine, the food so sumptuous ('Sir Walter Scott alone could describe it properly, and even my greed finds itself nonplussed'[1]), the country so green and undulating, that he seemed to fall into a kind of trance where time slipped by unnoticed. During the mornings he would go for walks, often to Alfoxton House which Wordsworth had rented for seven pounds a year less than The Lacket, and where he and Coleridge first collogued together until, suspected of being secret agents of the French Revolution, they were obliged to quit the place and go and live in the Lake District. Then, after returning to a lunch of smoked ham, mountains of fresh green peas, raspberries and Devonshire cream, he slumbered contentedly throughout the afternoon over a somniferous copy of *The Times*, roused himself for tea, wrote a few crepuscular letters to his friends – including Clive Bell, who had recently been appointed buyer for the Contemporary Arts Society and whom Lytton was now urging to purchase some pictures by Stanley Spencer and, after dinner, finished up the day with a little light reading of Dutch history and an early bed 'dreaming of Nijinski'.

At last Henry successfully completed his portrait and Lytton was able to join him down at Poole, in Dorset. After a week-end here, the two of them travelled north to the Lake District – a destination probably determined by Lytton's recent reflections on Wordsworth. For a week they stayed at an inn at Brampton, in Westmorland, and every day

---

[1] A fine description of this food, and of the inn itself, is given by Leonard Woolf in *Beginning Again. An Autobiography of the Years 1911 to 1918* (1964), pp. 153–4.

went off for fifteen-mile walks, sweating and toiling in the August haze, in their pockets sandwiches which they would eat under a hedge, talking and sketching until by the afternoon they had arrived at some place for tea; then home again over the mountains, Henry generally barefoot.

For the most part they were both in the best of humour, and though by the end of the week Lytton was completely walked off his feet, he had succeeded in enjoying himself immensely. 'I have practically no money left,' he confessed complacently to James (18 August 1913), 'and I shall be ruined by these absurd journeys backwards and forwards across England, but it can't be helped.'

On Monday, 19 August, Lamb returned again to Ireland, and two days later Lytton set off to join James, Pippa and Pernel at a farmhouse near Wiveton in Norfolk, sleeping one night at Leeds *en route*. He was not sorry now to sink down into a life of amiable lassitude after the open-air exertions of Brampton, and stayed on there for a quiet, comatose fortnight, reading a history of the Spanish Inquisition, writing innumerable letters, spending every fine day on the beach a mile away from their farmhouse, and generally, he told Clive Bell, 'leading a life of the most exemplary domestic quietude'.

His 'absurd journeys backwards and forwards across England' were, however, not yet at an end; and, having once more gathered up his strength, he travelled south in the first week of September to spend several days with Clive and Vanessa Bell at Asheham. Many of the Bloomsbury Group were also down there, including Adrian Stephen – who turned up from Dieppe where he had been staying with Wyndham Lewis and Frederick Etchells – Duncan Grant, Saxon Sydney-Turner – rather eerie with his rheumatic silences and indecisive flittings to and fro – Roger Fry, encamped with his children in a field, and Maynard Keynes, who tended to dominate the party. Despite this, and despite catching a heavy cold on his very first day, Lytton managed to distil a good deal of amusement out of his visit. He sat for portraits to Roger Fry, Duncan Grant and Vanessa Bell,[1] and in the intervals played, with great vigour, at badminton – a far more agreeable game, he thought, than tennis, which was merely a matter of brute agility. In the evenings they would all sit about and talk. 'Conversation, as you may imagine, eddied and swirled unceasingly,' he wrote to Ottoline (14 September 1913), 'so that even if my head hadn't been obfuscated

---

[1] The Vanessa Bell portrait – 'a more truly *fauve* Strachey than Henry Lamb's now canonical image of 1914' (Ronald Pickvance) – is now in the collection of Mr Richard Carline. Mrs Barbara Bagenal owns the Duncan Grant portrait. The Roger Fry painting was until recently in the Strachey house at Gordon Square.

it would hardly have kept its equilibrium. I was reminded of that verse in the Apocrypha about "a roaring voice of most savage wild beasts, or a rebounding echo from the hollow mountains" – but I managed to survive, and actually at the last moment succeeded in winning 30/- from them all at poker – which has come in very conveniently!'

Suddenly the gaiety and entertainment of this week were extinguished by the shocking news that Virginia Woolf had attempted to commit suicide. 'There has been a horrible occurrence,' Lytton wrote to Lamb (13 September 1913). 'Virginia tried to kill herself last Tuesday, and was only saved by a series of accidents. She took 100 grains of veronal and also an immense quantity of an even more dangerous drug – medinal. The doctors at one time thought there was very little hope. But she recovered, and is apparently not seriously the worse for it. Woolf has been having a most dreadful time for the last month or so, culminating in this. . . . The doctors all agree that the only thing required is feeding and rest, so really now the prospect seems to be pretty hopeful. George Duckworth has lent them his country home in Sussex, and they intend to go there in about a week.'

Remembering, perhaps, his own proposal of marriage to Virginia, Lytton felt an acute commiseration for Leonard Woolf, whom he visited briefly after leaving Asheham on his way north to Redcar in Yorkshire for a week-end with his old Liverpool friend Lumsden Barkway, now a vegetarian and fully-fledged Presbyterian clergyman. After a couple of days of cold vegetable fare, he struggled on farther northwards to Milton Cottage, Rothiemurchus, where James had set up house with two of the Olivier sisters, Noel and Brynhild,[1] together with the latter's husband, Hugh Popham. No sooner had he joined them than he subsided into a dismal decrepitude – indigestion, weakness and all sorts of nervous wreckage. Scotch rain pelted down outside; discomfort hounded him within. 'The arrival was worst of all,' he reported to Lamb (24 September 1913). 'A DOG! – One of those dreadful vast ones, standing higher than a table – ugh – belonging to the young woman – imagine my anguish, cooped up in the pouring rain in the tiny sitting-room with four other persons, and IT coiled about my ankles – day after day – Splitting headaches, nerves racked, yellow eyes revolving wildly in despair – and then at night having to make my way through the mist to a dark wooden outhouse where a bed had been rigged up for me, and where my agonised soles were pierced with icy oilcloths.'

Luckily the four others were not oppressed by Lytton's infirmities,

[1] Daughters of Sir Sydney (Lord) Olivier (1859–1943), civil servant, statesman, and at that time governor of Jamaica.

and once James had prescribed a quantity of Dr Gregory's malodorous rhubarb tabloids, he soon recovered and was able to take some interest in the Oliviers. 'I liked the Popham couple,' he told Henry. 'Noel is of course more interesting, but difficult to make out: very youthful, incredibly firm of flesh, agreeably bouncing and cheerful – and with some sort of prestige.'

At the end of the month the party broke up, and Lytton returned to London. 'Of course I've done not a stroke of work in these peregrinations and angoisses,' he admitted to Henry Lamb (24 September 1913). 'It's very annoying. I shall make for Lockeridge as soon as possible and sit down steadily there.' After a few days in Hampstead collecting together his belongings, he moved down to install himself at The Lacket where, feeling that his wanderings were now to be left behind, his long-cherished ambitions would at last be submitted to some practical test, and all his dreams of true eminence either made good or extinguished altogether.

CHAPTER III

The Lacket

This is an age whose like has never been
Since Jahveh made the world, and lo! 'twas green.
Through all the mouldy chronicle of Time
Scribbled in prose, or furbished up in rhyme,
Or in the pomp of monuments expressed
(Like some plain woman who is over-dressed),
Where shall we find, ye grim and dreary Powers
Of Human Folly, folly such as ours?
The bronze age and the iron age, we're told,
Were once; and was there once an age of gold?
Perhaps: but now no learning of the schools
Need we to know this age the Age of Fools.

Lytton Strachey (1915)

1

ALONE WITH A WIDOW

The Lacket was a compact, romantic-looking, thatched cottage, rather isolated, and sheltering behind a huge box hedge, with a boulder-strewn hillside rising directly behind it.[1] A few hundred yards away lived the philosopher and mathematician A. N. Whitehead and his wife, with both of whom Lytton became very friendly. Although his tenancy was to last for one year only, he eventually stayed on until the end of 1915; and it was here that he wrote, besides a number of his best-known literary and biographical essays, two of the four portraits which make up *Eminent Victorians*.

After moving in during the first week of October, he was immediately taken charge of by Mrs Templeman – a 'discreet old lady', as Virginia Woolf described her, 'who is as noiseless as an elephantine kind of mouse'. To his relief this formidable old woman seemed entirely to comprehend all his wishes, and was especially reassuring on the matter

[1] 'Small' was the epithet Lytton used when describing the cottage. Maire Lynd, who stayed there, remembers it as having at least five bedrooms.

of economy. He still had a little of the hundred pounds that Harry Norton had given him, and to this sum his mother had added a further hundred. With what he could earn from contributions to periodicals, he hoped to pay for sufficient free time in which to complete his *Eminent Victorians*. The solitude was, of course, comfortless at times – especially in the evenings; and Mrs Templeman, for all her massive qualities of discretion and practical competence, could be appallingly severe. 'She places the vegetables upon the table with a grimness . . . an exactitude . . . ,' he complained to James (April 1914). 'When she calls me in the morning she announces the horrors of the day in a tone of triumph:– "Rain, as usual, sir." – "Oh, Mrs. Templeman, Mrs. Templeman!" – "Yes sir; old fashioned weather; that's what I call it."' Otherwise the two of them got on very well, though Mrs Templeman evidently believed that the 'darkness' was bad for Lytton. 'When I observed that the darkness in London was worse,' he wrote to Hilton Young (9 January 1914), 'she said "Yes, sir, but then in London you have the noise" – to which no reply seemed possible.'

Yet despite the severities and non-sequiturs of his housekeeper, the bleakness and isolation of this winter in the country, and the recurrent colds and minor incapacities which came upon him, Lytton was content. 'I wish the place were mine,' he told Henry Lamb (27 October 1913), 'that I might mould it nearer to my eyes' desire.' And he implored Hilton Young to have an 'owl stuffed with wings outspread, so that I may hang it up over my bed and confuse it with the Holy Ghost in my last moments'. To Duncan Grant he wrote (28 October 1913) explaining that 'I lead a singularly egotistical life here, surrounded by every luxury, waited on by an aged female, and absorbed completely in Eternal-Peace. In the intervals of my satisfaction I struggle to justify my existence by means of literary composition, but so far the justification has not been so convincing as might be wished.'

The main literary composition during these first winter months was not 'Cardinal Manning', but some minor pieces for the *New Statesman*, and, for the *Edinburgh Review*, his long literary essay on Stendhal. 'Henri Beyle', as this paper was called, had been commissioned by Harold Cox early in October as a reply to Lytton's previous application to write on Samuel Butler. The subject was not altogether agreeable to Lytton, since it necessitated, he felt, a return to the adjectival, flamboyant style of *Landmarks in French Literature*, as opposed to his new, more incisive biographical approach (which he nevertheless managed partly to incorporate). He feared that the contrived emphasis of his treatment might not retrieve the essay from ultimate tedium, but he had no hesitation about taking it on, and, having assembled his library at The Lacket, began in the third week of October reading through the whole of Stendhal's work. 'I am beginning to gird up my loins for the wrestling bout with Stendhal,' he announced (27 October 1913) after ten days of intensive reading; and by 10 November he was able to report that 'I have plunged into the writing of the Stendhal affair and find it far less unpleasant than I'd expected – in fact I'm so far enjoying doing it very much.'

Concurrently with this he had also dashed off a much shorter, lighter composition on the subject of toleration entitled 'Avons-nous changé tout cela?' His first notion had been to send it off to A. R. Orage of the *New Age*, but because he did not have that paper's address readily to hand, he dispatched it instead to J. C. Squire at the *New Statesman*. Somewhat to his surprise, his mingled pleasure and alarm, the article was immediately accepted for the sum of three guineas. 'As for the New Statesman,' he wrote to Lamb (17 November 1913), 'I am getting to loathe it; and the worst of it is I now seem to be in imminent danger of becoming a regular contributor to its pages. The fellow Jack Squire, who is its editor or sub-editor, is most unpleasant, and I am trying hard to pick a quarrel with him, so as to escape having anything further to do either with him or it.' In fact the quarrel between Lytton and Squire was not to break out for almost another five years, and in the meantime Lytton continued to contribute infrequent articles, totalling about a dozen in all. In a number of these he is evidently spoiling for a fight, especially in his various pieces on toleration and enlightenment, which carry references to the Bible, for instance, that he felt sure *must* prove too strong for the editor, who, by demanding their excision, would show up his paper's fundamental spirit of intolerance and unenlightenment, and provide him with a legitimate excuse to sever his connexions with it. What actually happened was, for Lytton, far less satisfactory. His contributions appeared with all their more audacious comments and implications perfectly intact, but marred by many smaller changes, omissions of quite trivial words or insertions of Squire's own, almost always fractionally inferior to the original text, and, though intensely irritating, never drastic or important enough to supply Lytton with a sufficiently high-principled reason for cutting off this small but valuable source of income.

Lytton's life at The Lacket was strictly regulated. Every morning, when not overpowered by illness, he wrote at his desk; every afternoon, when it was not raining, he would set off in a thick overcoat, gloves, scarf and earrings, to trudge through the desolate idyllic woods, whose gamekeeper, 'a grimy old fellow with a nice bare breast', would engage him at great length in talk about football; every evening he would either

read – usually books involving the subject on which he was then working – or study manuals on the Italian language, or perform various
muscular exercises designed to regulate his digestive system.

At week-ends he sometimes went up to London, staying either at
Belsize Park Gardens or with the Bells in Gordon Square, and timing his
visits to coincide with some interesting concert, art exhibition, lecture
or theatre. One more irregular week-end he spent with the St Loe
Stracheys at a spectacular house-party in Surrey, full of reactionary
ambassadors and their ladies, of superior journalists and distinguished
K.C.s, and garnished with immense meals of the choicest kind, and an
exquisite footman. There was plenty of 'copy' for his letters, but, he
decided, no discoverable intelligence or romance. It was difficult to
understand how the inhabitants of that miasmal world managed to get
along in such a total flux of ignorance – and so preposterously bright
about it all, too! The ambassador and his wife were, he told Pippa, 'the
acme of unimportance'; and much of the conversation was taken in
charge by Leo Maxse, 'a mere spider in mind and body', who was still
raving obsessionally on about the Marconi scandal and discharging his
venom against the cabinet.[1] Among the guests was a couple whom he
was to get to know better once he himself was better known – the
Colefaxes.[2] 'He is a dreadful pompous lawyer and politician with a very
dull large face pétri with insincerity,' he wrote to Lamb (4 November
1913). '. . . She too is a thoroughly stupid woman.'

The unmitigated hostility of these observations indicates clearly
what an awkward and unsuccessful figure Lytton still cut socially. In
the fashionable, phoney world of the upper classes he was a complete
nonentity. People who, a mere half-dozen years later, would entreat
him to lunch or dine with them, now viewed him with unconcealed distaste or overlooked him altogether. And he returned their air of
contemptuous, empty-headed superiority with scathing disdain.

Yet he could not suppress a growing desire to enter this extraordinary
world, and be courted by it. These mediocre performances in society
tended to disrupt his peace of mind, and 'the result of it all is that I'm

[1] Leonard James Maxse, editor and proprietor of the *National Review*, was drawn into
the Marconi affair through some articles written in his paper by W. R. Lawson which
suggested that certain ministers in the Government were guilty of corruption. Maxse's
statement before the Select Committee of the House of Commons was largely responsible
for flushing out those ministers concerned and making them face public opinion. In due
course he became the butt of the Liberal press, and himself highly excited and obsessional
about the whole matter. See *The Marconi Scandal* by Frances Donaldson (1962).

[2] Lady (Sybil) Colefax, a middle-class fashionable hostess and camp-follower of the
arts, who managed an ambitious social career with military self-discipline. Her husband,
Sir Arthur Colefax, a pillar of the law, haunted her splendid entertainments like a smiling
but silent spectre.

now feeling singularly solitary,' he confessed to Ottoline (6 November 1913) on his return to The Lacket. 'But as I'm trying to work, it's so much the better.' At such hangover moments, the lack of human distractions deepened his gloom and the voice of duty would sound with particular asperity in his ear. Less disturbing in their after-effects were the week-ends when, instead of going off himself, he invited down one or two of his friends. His guests during these first four months at The Lacket included James, Pippa and Pernel, Duncan Grant, Maynard Keynes and Henry Lamb, whose arrival exactly coincided with one of Lytton's more severe attacks of flu, so that 'he [Lamb] had to perform the functions of sick-nurse – which pleased neither of us'. Leonard Woolf also came down a couple of times, with reports that, though Virginia's condition was still so serious as to warrant constant attendance by a team of four nurses, the doctors were confident that in time she would fully recover. 'Poor Woolf!' Lytton wrote to Ottoline (4 October 1913). 'Nearly all the horror of it has been and still is on his shoulders. Ka gave great assistance at the worst crisis, but she is now in London. Apparently what started this attack was anxiety about her novel coming on top of the physical weakness. The Doctors say that all depends upon rest and feeding-up.' Leonard himself had by this time finished a second novel, the typescript of which he sent to Lytton early in the New Year. After carefully going over every page, Lytton came to the conclusion that he could not with sincerity recommend his friend to publish it. By nature, he felt sure, Woolf was not a novelist. Probably he ought to have been an administrator, in a fairly subordinate position – or possibly even a member of the Stock Exchange like the rest of his family. He was wonderfully nice, but a trifle lost, which made matters all the more difficult when he arrived down at The Lacket asking for a candid opinion on his typescript. 'He was very sympathique, as ever, but there were some thorny moments during the discussion of his novel,' Lytton admitted to Lamb (19 January 1914). 'I don't think the poor fellow is in his right assiette – though what the right one is I can't imagine. Perhaps he should be a camel merchant, slowly driving his beasts to market over the vast plains of Baluchistan. Something like that would I'm sure be more appropriate than his present occupations of Fabianising and novel-writing, and even than his past one of ruling blacks.'

So frequent were these guests to The Lacket that Mrs Templeman soon began to display alarming symptoms of disintegration. Before each new arrival, her conscience would totally lose its head and she would insist on sweeping all the chimneys, scrubbing all the floors and spreading a general air of ruin throughout the house. For a few weeks it looked as if she might succumb to a fit of apoplexy, and sink altogether under her load of self-imposed, unnecessary duties. But Lytton's tact and resourcefulness – qualities not popularly credited to him in his dealings with *hoi polloi* – eventually carried the day, and after several confidential chats, the handsome tip of a golden sovereign at Christmas, and the promise that whenever he was away her sister might come over from Newbury and stay at The Lacket, she seemed to muster new strength and a very real disaster was averted.

'I am enjoying myself very much here,' he wrote to his mother, summing up his life at The Lacket after two months (7 December 1913), 'and feel as if I should like never to move away. The solitude is complete and the weather (just now) appalling, but it doesn't seem to matter. My old woman looks after me very well and very economically. I try to write a certain amount every day, and the rest of the time is spent in eating, sleeping, walking and reading. In the evenings I struggle with Italian. My occasional wish is for a wife – but it is not easy to be suited in that matter.'

So many of his best laid schemes had previously come to nothing that he could now scarcely believe his good fortune. Daily he waited for some calamity to descend and wreck everything, but to his mild surprise 'it continues very idyllic here', he informed Ottoline (9 October 1913). 'Whoever thought that I should end my days alone with a widow?'

2

SCENES FROM POST-EDWARDIAN ENGLAND

For the first seven months of 1914, Lytton's life continued to conform to the same simple pattern of daily work at The Lacket, surrounded by his books and his detestable medicines, and interspersed with frequent stimulating sallies up to town. One unlooked-for effect of residing in this rustic chastity was the change of attitude it engendered within him towards London itself. Only recently it had been somewhere from which to escape, a stale and unprofitable place that devitalized its inhabitants and impeded their ambitions. When, some years later, David Cecil asked him how he had spent his time in the metropolis, Lytton replied blankly: 'I walked about the streets, and sometimes I took a taxi.' This pointlessness and vacuity, he believed, had been symptoms of his premature middle age. But now, in the seclusion of emptiest Wiltshire, he was at times submerged by the most abject melancholia – a regurgitation, as he saw it, of the green-sickness of his youth. And with the onset once more of this shocking, but divine discontent, London became transformed from a flat, ugly and oppressive muddle, into a warm and exciting centre where no encounter was impossible and every adventure was for the asking.

Such adventures as did come his way were inconclusive. 'After I left you I went to the Tube,' he recounted one incident to Lamb (20 February 1914), 'and saw there a very nice red-cheeked black-haired youth of the lower classes – nothing remarkable in that – *but* he was wearing a heavenly shirt, which transported me. It was dark blue with a yellow edge at the top, and it was done up with laces (straw coloured) which tied at the neck. I thought it so exactly your goût that I longed to get one for you. At last on the platform I made it an épreuve to go up to him and ask him where he got it. Pretty courageous, wasn't it? You see he was not alone, but accompanied by two rather higher-class youths in billycock hats, whom I had to brush aside in order to reach him. I adopted the well-known John style – with great success. It turned out (as I might have guessed) that it was simply a football jersey – he belonged to the Express Dairy team. I was so surprised by that that I couldn't think what other enquiries I could make, and then he vanished.'

Fragmentary encounters of this kind helped, in some sense, to strengthen his resolve to excel at writing; for it was only on paper, he reflected, that he could carry things through to a successful conclusion. When it came to a platform, a black-haired youth and a football jersey, he failed manifestly to exhibit the sterling qualities of a man of action. London, however, continued to radiate an illusory aura, and if it provided no rhapsodical, consummating romances, there was always during his visits there plenty of breathless activity of a more humdrum sort. In January he went up and stayed with his family, who were then making preliminary arrangements to move from No. 67 to No. 6 Belsize Park Gardens. When not in conclave over this affair 'I flew from Square to Square, from Chelsea to Hampstead Heath with infinite alacrity,' he told Duncan Grant (6 February 1914). 'I even went to the Alpine Club.[1] I could not look much at the pictures there, as I found myself alone with [Nina] Hamnett,[2] and became a prey to the desire to

[1] The Second Grafton Group exhibition was being held at the Alpine Club Gallery, where Duncan Grant, Vanessa Bell and others were showing pictures.

[2] As an art student Nina Hamnett (1890–1956) had been encouraged by Sickert who spotted in her drawings a fine talent that she later never quite succeeded in developing. Instead of becoming a great artist, she set herself up as a great cicerone to the art world of Paris and London and a leader of the *vie de bohème* which she described in her two volumes of autobiography, *Laughing Torso* (1935) and *Is She a Lady?* (1955). Among

pass my hand lightly over her mane of black hair. I knew that if I did she'd strike me in the face – but that, on reflection, only sharpened my desire, and eventually I was just on the point of taking the plunge when Fanny Stanley[1] came in and put an end to the tête-à-tête.'

Early in February he again went up to London, 'my excuse being that Swithin has just returned from Burmah,' he explained to Duncan Grant (6 February 1914), 'but the truth is that I can't resist Piccadilly – though how it's spelt I've never been able to discover'. Swithinbank, however, gave him a magnificent lunch at Simpson's, with such quantities of Burgundy that he was ill for a week afterwards. He had not seen Swithin for nearly five years, and the change in his friend was very remarkable. They behaved at lunch almost like two strangers, and were quite unable to recapture their old intimacy. Was this the young man whom he, Lytton, had once thought so handsome, and with whom he had seriously contemplated falling in love? It seemed scarcely possible to him as he now sat regarding the 'very benevolent, medical man' lunching opposite him, so quiet, so respectable, so dazed. 'All youth gone,' he lamented in a letter to James (14 February 1914), '– and so sad – so infinitely sad and gentle: I suspect some tragedy – or would suspect one if there was anything in his character to allow of such a thing. Perhaps he's simply become a Buddhist. As for talking to him, it was quite impossible, and he was pained by my get-up.'

Another old friend whom he met by chance that same week at the Savile Club was E. M. Forster, whom he seems to have found just as unsatisfactory as Swithinbank. 'We went all over London together,' he told James (3 February 1914), 'wrapped in incredible intimacy – but it was all hollow, hollow. He's a mediocre man – and knows it, or suspects it, which is worse; he will come to no good, and in the meantime he's treated rudely by waiters and is not really admired even by middle-class dowagers.'

Not all his engagements up in town were social. On the same day as he encountered Forster, Desmond MacCarthy had fixed up for him to lunch with a Mr Kenneth Bell 'half-wit and publisher',[2] at the Devon-

---

[1] 'Aunt Fanny Stanley', though not really an aunt, was a proverbial figure of a faithful elderly female relative, on the Grant side of the family.

[2] Kenneth Bell (1884–1951), Fellow of All Souls and of Balliol, who five years before his death was ordained a priest in the Church of England.

---

her many friends were Modigliani, Gaudier-Brzeska, who did a sculpture of her body (now in the Victoria and Albert Museum), and Roger Fry, who employed her – together with her husband de Bergen – in the Omega Workshops, and who painted her portrait (in the collection of Mrs Roger Diamond). Among her enemies was Aleister Crowley, the Beast No. 666, against whom she successfully defended herself in 'one of the most extraordinary trials of the first half of the 20th century' (John Symonds). She died in poverty.

shire Club in St James's Street. 'It was a singular function,' he observed to James (3 February 1914), 'chiefly in my honour, as Mr. Bell, the young and advanced partner of the old-fashioned firm of Bell, wished especially to get in touch with me. I accordingly thought it would please if I appeared in a fairly outré style – cord coat, etc. – and the result was an extreme nervousness on the part of Kenneth. However, he suggested that I should write one of a new series of biographies of modern persons, to be written in a non-official manner; I suggested Cardinal Manning as a good subject; he appeared to be enthusiastic at the notion; but now I don't know (a) whether he really wanted it done by me, or (b) whether I really want to do it. I hope to find out when I interview him in a few days' time – if possible at his office; these club lunches with claret and kummel flowing through them in all directions don't make for lucidity.'

The second discussion took place ten days later at the Savile Club, and was really hardly more conclusive than the first. On both occasions, though subjected to great salesmanship pressure, Lytton could only be induced to propose schemes that amounted to slight variations of what he was already writing or planning to write. By this time he had been ruminating too long over his Victorian portraits to abandon them altogether; and he felt, in any case, too mentally exhausted to tackle some entirely fresh scheme of work. His real idea was to persuade Bell to forget his own project and fix up a contract for *Eminent Victorians*. For this second meeting he decided to adopt a very peevish, arrogant tone, in the hope that this would impress the publisher; but he was soon disarmed by the almost reverential manner in which he was received, and which brought to the surface his natural modesty. 'It's very queer how they're all after me so frantically,' he remarked to James (14 February 1914). 'I interviewed Mr. Basil Williams at the Savile (he's the editor of the new Biographical Series) and he fairly crouched.[1] It was plain that the series – "Creators of the 19th Century" – would not suit me, so I was firm and resisted all his pleadings. He begged me to write on Victor Hugo, Pius IX, Ibsen, and I really forget how many others, but I only smiled mysteriously, and a great deal, and so left him. However, at tea, Mr. Bell appeared and pretty well bowled me over with his bonhomie (B. Williams is a sad, cheerful, compact and strangely uninspired little man, I forgot to mention.) The result is that I was led to suggest a series of 19th century essays on great men, in one volume,

---

[1] Professor A. F. B. Williams (1867–1950), historian and barrister. He was the biographer of Cecil Rhodes and William Pitt, author of Volume XI of the Oxford History of England, *The Whig Supremacy 1714–60*, and editor of 'Makers of the 19th Century'.

which he (K.B.) eagerly seized upon – though so far the financial arrangements are in the vague.'

For some weeks these negotiations dwindled on, then finally broke off altogether; and Lytton was left still working at his volume of Victorian essays, but without a definite contract or a publisher. Would his *Eminent Victorians* ever attract *any* publisher? His doubts multiplied and stirred up a growing fear within him that the book might not appear in print for many years.

On the whole, Lytton's visits to London were made purely for pleasure and amusement. He would hurry off to the usual run of theatres, concerts and operas, and whenever possible went to hear the music of Mozart who, he declared after a performance of *Don Giovanni*, was 'the greatest artist that ever lived'. Some entertainment of a more unusual kind was provided by a meeting which he attended of *New Statesman* subscribers. This was held towards the end of April at the Kingsway Hall, and since he happened to be in town at that time Lytton turned up there out of simple curiosity. 'The so-called editor was "in the chair",' he told James, 'a most nauseous creature,[1] I thought – with Mr. and Mrs. Webb and B. Shaw on each side of him. I've no notion of what the point of the meeting was – no information of any kind was given, and I could only gather from some wails and complaints of the Webbs that it wasn't paying. B. Shaw made a quite amusing speech about nothing on earth. I'd no idea that the Webb fellow was so utterly without pretentions of being a gentleman. *She* was lachrymose and white-haired. Altogether they made a sordid little group. At the end there were "questions" from the audience – supposed to be addressed to the Editor qua Chairman, but the poor man was never allowed to get in a word. The three Gorgons surrounding him kept leaping to their feet with most crushing replies.'

Most of Lytton's entertainment came in the form of evening parties. The spring and early summer months of 1914 were unusually gay and active, as if the atmosphere had been charged with something electric, imbuing all that went on with a miraculous lightness. Distinguished foreigners flocked to London, which seemed to be enjoying a season such as it had not known for many years. The new Russian ballets, the operas at Covent Garden, the social and sporting calendar appeared more spectacular than ever before. Everything moved with an odd

---

[1] The first editor of the *New Statesman* was Clifford Sharp, the other permanent members of the staff at this stage being Desmond MacCarthy (dramatic critic), J. C. Squire (literary editor) and Emil Davies (City correspondent). The paper, a brain-child of the Webbs, had been founded in 1913. Shaw, a part-proprietor, was expected to be the star contributor, his articles, the Webbs estimated, being likely to attract up to a thousand new readers.

ease and brilliance, gorgeously illuminated like the dying moments of a fine day before the sun sinks finally from sight.

Although there were many wild and extravagant Bloomsbury parties in Gordon Square and elsewhere, Lytton tended to dissociate himself from them in the belief that he now belonged to a world outside the Bloomsbury Group. Yet the dislike that he often expressed for these gatherings was partly an extension of his own personal self-dislike, and pointed to his real affiliation there. For the time being, however, he found more enjoyment in other social intercourse – at the Bohemian celebrations, for example, provided by the Augustus John set. That May, John had moved into the vast square studio in Chelsea which he had had specially constructed for him; and it was here that he gave a magnificent all-night house-warming party in fancy dress, to which Lytton was invited. 'The company was very charming and sympathetic, I thought,' he wrote to James, '– so easy-going and taking everything for granted; and really I think it's the proper milieu for me – if only the wretches had a trifle more brain. . . . John was a superb figure. There was dancing – two-steps and such things – so much nicer than the waltzes – and at last I danced with him – it seemed an opportunity not to be missed. (I forget to say I was dressed as a pirate). Nina Lamb was there, and made effréné love to me. We came out in broad daylight.'

But undoubtedly the most eminent and urbane sociality of these months was to be found at the *salon* in Bedford Square, which by this time had reached the height of its fame as a centre for artists and writers. Among the most frequent *habitués* besides Lytton himself were the Gilbert Cannans; the handsome, volatile, Jewish painter Mark Gertler; Stanley Spencer, tiny and uncivilized; Desmond MacCarthy, soporific, reclining quite comatose on a peripheral sofa; Bertrand Russell, rather priggish and uncomfortable; Harry Norton, now pink and fat, but very bright; and, of course, Nijinski ('that cretinous lackey') with whom Lytton had become thoroughly disenchanted, but who still enthralled Ottoline 'gaping and gurgling like a hooked fish'. Her pointless advances were by this time causing much merriment and gossip among her friends. For though she plied him constantly with her most senti-mental attentions, Nijinski remained inexorably unresponsive and un-comprehending. On one occasion the two of them were sitting together in a tiny inner room when Lytton entered the house. As he advanced down the drawing-room he overheard Ottoline's husky voice, with its infinitely modulated intonations, utter the words: 'Quand vous dansez, vous n'êtes pas un homme – vous 'êtes une idée. C'est ça, n'est-ce pas, qui est l'Art? . . . Vous avez lu Platon, sans doute?' – The reply was a grunt.

The principal guest at the largest, most glittering of these Bedford Square receptions was Asquith, the prime minister. This party, held early in May, represented Ottoline's last bid to secure an under-secretaryship for her husband, and might ultimately have proved successful had they not both embraced militantly pacifist convictions at the outbreak of the war three months later. The gathering itself was brilliantly successful. Lytton's head spun alarmingly round and round at finding himself pressed cheek by jowl with so many celebrated per-sonages. Ottoline had warned him in advance that the prime minister was to be there, 'but I was rather surprised', he told James, 'to be rushed, the very minute I arrived into the dear man's arms. It was most marked; someone else whom he was talking to was scattered to the winds, and we were then planted together on a central sofa. He was considerably less pompous than I'd expected, and exceedingly gracious – talked about Parnell and such reminiscent matters at considerable length. I could see no sign of the faintest spark of anything out of the common in cet estimable Perrier Jouet. He seemed a pebble worn smooth by rubbings – even his face had a somewhat sand-papered effect. He enquired about my next book, and I gave him a sketch of it. At the end he said with slight pomp "Well, you have a difficult and interesting task before you." I said "*You* have a difficult and interesting task before *you*!" He grinned and said, "Ah, we do what we can, we do what we can," on which we parted, and I found myself involved in a tête-à-tête with the Lady Howard de Walden.[1] The company was most distinguished and the whole affair decidedly brilliant. Henry James of course loomed in the most disgusting way. The Raleighs were also there, and – very extraordinary – Sir M. Nathan. . . .[2] Ottoline was in a vast gold brocade dress, and seemed remarkably at her ease, and in fact at moments almost tête-montée. In the middle of it all she fell upon me, and charged me with infidelity, breaking her heart, etc.'

In the political sphere it was then the height of the Ulster crisis, and Asquith had just dramatically taken over the War Office. His gracious-ness on this occasion struck Lytton as being partly that of a genuine good humour, and partly the professional manner of a man whose business in life it was at all times to create a favourable impression. Apart from discussing Lytton's biographies they also talked about various public figures – Lord Randolph Churchill among others – and Asquith then turned the conversation back to Parnell who, he declared,

[1] Margerita Dorothy van Raulte, who had married Lord Howard de Walden, the professional amateur sportsman and patron of the arts, the previous year.

[2] Sir Matthew Nathan (1862–1939), civil servant and soldier, at this time chairman of the Board of Inland Revenue. He was later appointed governor of Queensland. In pristine days, he had been one of Dorothy Strachey's unsuccessful suitors.

was the most remarkable man he had known. Lytton wished later he had suggested that Gladstone was surely even more remarkable; then, after Asquith recounted how he had met Parnell in the Temple one morning when the divorce proceedings had just become public and how Parnell had shown that he had no notion of the hubbub this would produce, the talk pausing a moment with a slight embarrassment, he got up, cordially shook Lytton's hand, and walked off into another room. The entire meeting had lasted about ten minutes. 'If I hadn't known who he was,' Lytton afterwards wrote of this encounter in an un-published essay (May 1918), 'I should have guessed him to be one of those Oxford dons who have a smattering of the world – one of those clever, cautious, mediocre intelligences, who made one thank heaven one was at Cambridge. Two particulars only suggested a difference. His manner was a little nervous – it was really almost as if he was the whole time conscious, with a slight uneasiness, that he was the Prime Minister. And then, though his appearance on the whole was decidedly donnish – small and sleek and not too well made in the details – his hands were different. Small and plump they were too; but there was a masterfulness in them and a mobility which made them remarkable.'

Because Lytton could only feel relaxed and free with a single individual – and was therefore incomparably more eloquent in his correspondence than in his general conversation – it is easy to forget that in full company, however enjoyable and distinguished, he could still be refractory. His presence was felt by many acquaintances – even those he quite liked – to be coldly, suspiciously, watchful. 'He doesn't say anything, except tête-à-tête,' Walter Raleigh wrote to Logan Pearsall Smith describing the personal impression he had received after seeing Lytton that June at Newington. 'I wish he would write a book called *Life Among the Man-haters*, or *Out Against God*.'

In fact, during these weeks and months, Lytton was busy distilling some of this simmering animosity against God and man into his 'Cardinal Manning'. He laboured steadily and meticulously at this long essay, and his letters reveal something of the progress of his work, its complexities and amusements.

Lytton Strachey to Clive Bell, 22 February 1914

'I'm at present devoting 3 hours a day to Cardinal Manning, and as I'm not yet Voltaire I find there's precious little time left over for extraneous philanthropy.'

Lytton Strachey to Henry Lamb, 22 February 1914

'I sit here buried in books on Cardinals and Theologians, and am rapidly becoming an expert on ecclesiastical questions. For instance, I now know what Papal Infallibility means – or rather what it doesn't – the distinction is highly important. I think that dogmatic theology would make a much better subject for a Tripos than most. Fine examination papers I could set. – Discuss the difference between "definitionists" and "inopportunists". – Explain with examples the various meanings of "minimism". – Give a brief account of *either* Newman's attitude towards the Syllabus *or* Dollinger's relations with the Vatican Council. State clearly the interpretations put by (a) W. G. Ward, (b) Veuillot, (c) Dupanloup, upon the words "Ex cathedrâ". Doesn't it sound entrancing?'

Lytton Strachey to Henry Lamb, 14 March 1914

'I'm enjoying my Manning a good deal so far; the chief drawback seems to be that it's such a slow business. And of course I'm quite prepared to find when it's done that it's all a fantasia; but the only way of knowing that is to go through with it to the bitter end, and hope for the best.'

Lytton Strachey to Ottoline Morrell, 27 March 1914

'I'm trying to work, and even succeeding to some extent. My task is rather a strange one. I think it may have some vestiges of amusement in it – but it's difficult to say as yet. I won't, I fear, be quite as bright as the Chartreuse de Parme, though, in any case!'

When immersed in the actual process of writing, which stimulated his mind both imaginatively to construct cohesive literary patterns and journalistically to sharpen up interviews and conflicts and to embroider background settings, Lytton was happy at his work. But whenever he tried to evaluate Cardinal Manning more dispassionately as a vehicle of his personal ambitions, to look at it as a fraction of the long journey he had undertaken in search of an uncertain Holy Grail, his vision dimmed and he grew depressed and impatient. The whole enterprise looked too improbable. Writing was such a solitary business; it was impossible for him to relate his work to the outside world, to judge its effect on other people, and it assumed at times an illusion of unreality. Besides, this exacting project might, in any case, lie beyond his physical powers. 'If one had the thews of a bull,' he wrote to James that April, 'and the pen of a ready writer, one might get something done. As it is everything takes such a devil of a time. One has to sleep, eat, digest, take exercise – and after all that, one has to squeeze out one's carefully moulded sentences.'

His rate of progress on 'Cardinal Manning' was further decelerated by several other literary commitments over these months. At the beginning of the year he had applied again to Harold Cox asking whether he might write for him two articles, one on Dryden and the other on Byron. The reply was flattering but unspecific. His 'Henri Beyle' had been generously praised, and he was now asked to become a regular contributor to the *Edinburgh Review*; but no mention was made of Dryden and none of Byron. Six months later, however, he published in that paper the first of two long essays on Voltaire. Meanwhile he composed a couple of shorter pieces for the *New Statesman* – one of them a highly controversial reassessment of Matthew Arnold – and, as his very last contribution to the *Spectator*, a leading review of Constance Garnett's translation of *The Possessed*.

'A Russian Humorist', as this review was called, provides an eloquent testimony to the veneration in which he still held Dostoievsky at this time. Not being the work of a writer of great linguistic subtlety like Chekhov or Gogol, Dostoievsky's novels were all the easier to appreciate in translation, and had lately been gaining wide popularity in England. Lytton disapproved of the Constance Garnett versions. The first impact of Dostoievsky had, of course, come to him some three years earlier, when he had read the novels in French. That first impact had lasted, possibly even strengthened, as the less well-known books came his way. He was particularly fascinated by the inspired psychological effects that were grafted on to a conventional, clumsily constructed plot. With their complex 'feel' of life, their fondness for the abnormal, these novels embodied a peculiar strangeness of form and spirit that greatly excited him. Beforehand he had believed, as he wrote in a *Spectator* review of 1908, that 'those writers succeed best who are least anxious to combine the conflicting elements in their material'. Dostoievsky's example proved to Lytton the falsity of this earlier dictum, and had converted him to a more catholic and comprehensive point of view. So taken was he by Dostoievsky's 'strong psychology' that he attributed concealed virtues to the often careless and conservative method of narration. The apparent lack of balance which characterized the Russian novelist's work was, he reasoned, an illusion produced by his unbounded genius, the interior presence of which gave each book a unique, if concealed, aesthetic coherence. 'The strange vast wandering conversations, the extraordinary characters rushing helter-skelter through the pages, the far-fetched immense

digressions, the unexplained obscurities, the sudden, almost inconceivable incidents, the macabre humour with its extravagant exaggerations – all these things, which seem at first little more than a confused jumble of disconnected entities, gradually take shape, group
themselves, and grow at last impressive and significant.'

A number of critics in recent times have alluded to what Professor
C. R. Sanders calls 'the extremely important influence' of Dostoievsky
on Lytton's work, and especially on *Eminent Victorians*. There can be
no doubt that, at the time of writing this book, he was greatly impressed by Dostoievsky's originality in combining so many heterogeneous elements. But essentially the appeal was more emotional than
technical. 'The frenzy of Dostoievsky', his abandonment of all tasteful
artistic restraint and careful symmetry, acted upon him as upon other
writers of the age with whom he had little in common, T. S. Eliot and
James Joyce, as a release from the calm sobriety, the limiting, predict-
able common sense of the great tradition of English literature.
Dostoievsky commanded an unparalleled insight, Lytton believed,
into the workings of the human mind. At first sight it might appear
that the actual tenor of his own personality had little enough in common
with the tortured spirit of the great Russian novelist. But these novels
showed the unconscious processes at work in all human beings and
came to Lytton as a revelation. It was precisely because the events in
Lytton's mind were, in fact, underneath, very similar to Dostoievsky
that the novels produced such an effect on him – and on his writing of
Eminent Victorians. On the surface, the well-balanced arrangement of
his colloquial romantic style with its compact classical construction
owes nothing to the digressions and prolixities of *The Idiot* or *The
Possessed*. But Dostoievsky's extravagance, his exaggeration and comic
fantasy (which Lytton was the first critic to recognize), his untraditional
complexity and indifference to the commonplace, undoubtedly em-
boldened Lytton to experiment with the forms of traditional biography,
to mix the ingredients of drama, irony and psychological innuendo after
a fashion never previously attempted.

On the sixth and seventh days of each week Lytton rested from his
labours, and turned his attention to entertaining and being entertained
by his friends. One of his first week-end visitors to the country was his
landlord Hilton Young, bringing with him Desmond MacCarthy who,
a few years earlier, had himself rented The Lacket. 'Desmond is a
great study,' Lytton wrote to James (9 February 1914). 'I've never
seen anyone so extraordinarily incapable of pulling himself together.
He'll never write anything, I'm afraid, in that hopeless miasma. He
rode eighteen miles yesterday with Hilton, came back almost dead, and

stretched his now vast bulk on a chair in a stertorous coma. At last we somehow got him to bed. He rose at 11.30 this morning, refused to have anything for breakfast, and then ate the whole of a pot of marmalade with extreme deliberation. He's wonderfully good-natured, affable, and amusing, but there are moments when dullness seems to exude from him in concentrated streams.'

Other friends continued to besiege him at The Lacket throughout the spring and summer, including his brothers James and Oliver, Henry Lamb, Swithinbank, Harry Norton, and Leonard Woolf who stayed a full week. 'He has been having a nervous breakdown in a mild way,' Lytton told Lamb (12 March 1914), 'and seemed to want repose. He says he's now much better, and goes away on Saturday. Virginia is apparently all right now, and there are no nurses any more. I've been able to work in spite of his presence: but it's I fear going to be rather a long job.'

And so Lytton's life at The Lacket ambled amiably on – supported by his friends on Saturdays and Sundays, and by Cardinal Manning, Dostoievsky, Voltaire and others during the rest of the week. It was not an entirely smooth or easy existence: cold, illness and the pangs of temporary solitude constantly confronted him. Yet he was never unhappy, since his work now gave this existence some sense of progress and direction. Of course he still had a long way to go, but there seemed no reason why this present, settled mode of living should not continue on its quiet passage indefinitely. After all those wandering, disordered years since Cambridge, what could possibly disturb the calm, sensibly variegated flow of his days, the simple pattern of dedicated labour and civilized entertainment?

But on 4 August, war was declared with Germany, and the last brilliant afterglow of Edwardian England flickered out for ever.

3

TWO TYPES OF PATRIOTISM

Much that is fundamentally misleading has been written of Lytton's attitude to the First World War. It is assumed by some that he was almost totally unaffected by the outbreak of hostilities, and this view is *prima facie* sustained by previous synopses of his career. 'His activities', wrote Lord David Cecil in the *Dictionary of National Biography*, 'were not interrupted by the war of 1914–1918, for he was a conscientious objector.' For much of this time he remained living in the country,

Cecil goes on to recount, preserved in a state of financial independence by his family and friends, who, together, sedulously subscribed to foster his delicate literary talent.

The implications of such telescopic sketches are very far removed from the truth. Besides affecting his literary work, war cast over his private life a deep shadow that coloured much of his writing, both published and unpublished. With his invalid health, there was absolutely no question at any stage of the war of Lytton being called up for active service, or even participation of a more subsidiary kind. Logically, therefore, the wisest course he could take would have been to cut himself off entirely from political and military affairs. Yet this he could not do. Painfully and unwillingly he found himself involved in the whole wretched business. It filled the horizon wherever he went, blighting his days and troubling his nights.

> *Last night I dreamt that I had gone to Hell.*
> *I seemed to know the* milieu *pretty well.*
> *The place was crammed as tight as it would hold*
> *With men and hatred, folly, lust and gold.*
> *And lies? Ah, I'd forgotten: without fail*
> *Red hot for breakfast came* The Daily Mail.
> *Well, thought, they say, is free. I wish it were!*
> *Can you think freely in a dentist's chair?*
> *Then so can I, when, willing or unwilling,*
> *All Europe on my nerves comes drilling, drilling.*
> *I do my best; I shut my eyes and ears,*
> *Try to forget my furies and my fears,*
> *Banish the newspapers, go out of town,*
> *And in a country cottage settle down,*
> *Far from the world, its sorrow and its shame;*
> *But, though skies alter, still the mind's the same.*[1]
> *What comfort, when in every lovely hour*
> *Lurks horror, like a spider in a flower?*

The inescapable anguish of this time was not the symptom of a restrictive, bellicose form of patriotism. Far from it. Most patriots, while paying polite lip-service to the excellence of peace, welcomed the

---

[1] '*Coelum non animum*', the Strachey family's motto, comes from Horace – '*Coelum non animum mutant qui trans mare currunt*' – which Lytton translated for this line of his poem. This motto was subject to some variation. In the eighteenth century, when it was the fashion to get dinner services made in China, the Stracheys at Sutton Court sent orders to the East for a set to be made with the motto on each plate. The whole dinner service arrived eventually, inscribed COBLUM NON ANIMUM. Pieces of Coblum china still survive at Sutton Court.

Henry Lamb

Lytton Strachey: the
Augustus John period

Lytton Strachey, 1914: portrait by Henry Lamb
(*The Tate Gallery*)

outbreak of war with chauvinistic rejoicing. Lytton's hatred of it was never assumed, but deeply felt; he was not excited, only dismayed, by the fighting. Though he loved the English countryside dearly, feeling that he could never be happy living anywhere else in the world, he was not tempted to inflate this fondness into a fulsome national prejudice, an exclusive pride. 'On the whole I don't care much about England's being victorious (apart from personal questions),' he wrote to James (27 September 1914), '– but I should object to France being crushed. Mightn't it be a good plan to become a Frenchman?'

This preference for France on Lytton's part represents an avowal of his highly developed brand of humanism. France, to his mind, was the most civilized country in the world and therefore the one least likely to originate or provoke a war. All war was a return to barbarism, and, in a modern world all wars should be – *were* – avoidable. They plunged civilization back overnight into dark mediaevalism, away from the bright new age of enlightenment and detached toleration for which he had been quietly working, and whose dawn, not very long ago, he had so confidently proclaimed. In place now of these emergent virtues, warfare substituted insensitivity, injustice, cruelty, hypocrisy – vices that always flourished with much more frenzy and unreasonableness at home than at the front. And by this substitution, too, it disrupted at a blow all that made life worth living: art degenerated into infantile propaganda; friendships were callously wrenched apart.

Several of Lytton's friends were quickly infected by the mounting war fever. Throughout the country an immediate, unashamed howl went up for conscription, but the Liberal Government remained firm and in an official statement in *The Times* of 15 August, Kitchener, newly appointed as Secretary of State for War, announced that voluntary territorials were to be divided into two categories – those serving abroad and those at home. This announcement stressed the importance of home defence and made it clear that the Government 'does not desire that those who cannot, on account of their affairs, volunteer for foreign service, should by any means be induced to do so'.

Lytton himself seems to have believed that all physically fit intellectuals should be prepared to defend the shores of England, but with this reservation: no intellectuals were in fact physically fit. His highly personal views on military service were frankly set out in a letter which he wrote to James early that September. 'I think one must resist,' he explained, 'if it comes to a push. But I admit it's a difficult question. One solution is to go and live in the United States of America. As for our personal position, it seems to me quite sound and coherent. We're

E

all far too weak physically to be of any use at all. If we weren't we'd still be too intelligent to be thrown away in some really not essential expedition, and our proper place would be – the National Reserve, I suppose. God has put us on an island, and Winston has given us a navy, and it would be absurd to neglect those advantages – which I consider exactly apply to able-bodied intellectuals. It's no good pretending one isn't a special case.'

At this stage of the war Bloomsbury was less resolutely pacifist than is popularly supposed. That September, Clive Bell, whose *Peace at Once* (1915) was to be publicly burnt by order of the Lord Mayor, wrote to James Strachey asking for information as to how to join the Army Service Corps or some other non-fighting unit, since his health prevented him from going into the fully combative forces. Duncan Grant immediately entered the National Reserve. Rupert Brooke spoke unceasingly of his intention to go to Belgium. 'I cannot see the use of intellectual persons doing tl is,' Lytton commented on hearing the news, 'as long as there are enough men in any case, and the country is not in danger. Home defence is another matter, and I think I should certainly train if I had the strength.' But of all his friends the one most violently caught up by the call to arms was, to his great grief, Henry Lamb. For weeks he had repeatedly threatened to join up, and then, after prolonged hesitation, enrolled as an assistant at Guy's Hospital – an odd result, Lytton reflected, of Austria declaring war on Serbia. 'He's so fearfully undependable,' he sorrowfully complained to James (27 August 1914). 'Also his words have no connection with his feelings, nor his acts with anything; and he's constitutionally incapable of constancy. . . . It seems to me that really – from any point of view – it's grotesque for a person of his health to go into the army: and I don't think this has been sufficiently emphasised. I hope to goodness he'll get fixed into something fairly harmless before long, as otherwise there'll always be this terror.'

Despite the columns of militant journalism that were every day being poured out in the Press, Lytton did not believe that the feeling among ordinary men and women in the country was especially warlike. He blamed the newspapers – particularly those of Lord Northcliffe – for deluding credulous people like Henry Lamb who did not know their own mind, and for trying to whip up a blind, evil animosity against the Germans. Disregarding the Press, the condition of things seemed perfectly calm during these first weeks. In the remoteness of the country there was no detectable change at all, but within London it was obvious from the grave faces of the people in the streets that something grim and dreadful was happening. Their expressions denoted no intoxication or excitement, no lust for national conflict, but sorrow and despondency. 'So far as I can make out there isn't the slightest enthusiasm for the war,' Lytton reported to Dorothy Bussy (21 August 1914). 'I think the public are partly feeling simple horror and partly that it's a dreadful necessity. But I think there will be a change when the casualties begin – both in the direction of greater hostility to the Germans and also more active disgust at the whole thing. Though of course a great deal will depend on the actual turn of events.'

Lytton tended at this stage to dissociate himself from the more belligerent pacifists, not so much because he disagreed with what they said, but because he believed their general fulminations, directed for the most part against the Foreign Secretary, Sir Edward Grey, to be a bad error of tactics. 'Those anti-Grey people are really too senseless,' he wrote to James (18 August 1914). 'Can't they see that they do nothing at this moment if they appear as pro-Germans? The only hope is to appear anti-German and also pro-peace. The more they worry Grey the more rigid he'll become. I agree that the Japanese and Polish affairs are very bad – especially the latter, it seems to me. I didn't expect those Muscovites would show their hand so soon. That manifesto was a wonderful piece of blatant hypocrisy. Is it possible that the Poles will be such fools as to put their faith in the Tsar? Also won't it be plain pretty soon even to E. Grey that the war's being run for the aggrandisement of Russia? I don't believe the English public would stand that.'

The English public, Lytton considered, should be stirred up about peace. Instead of wasting energy blaming the Government, as Bertrand Russell was busy doing in the *Nation*, intelligent people ought to institute a Stop the War party in the cabinet, backed by public opinion. Far from canvassing this support, Russell's passionate denunciations were, in Lytton's view, wantonly alienating the populace. Nevertheless, there remained a residuum of fundamental good sense about people's attitude to the war which he found heartening. 'I haven't seen anyone,' he wrote to James (16 August 1914), 'who hasn't agreed on the main lines – viz: that we should take nothing for ourselves, and insist on ending it at the earliest possible moment.'

There seems little doubt that in his interpretation of the public's feeling at large Lytton was being too optimistic, amplifying those fairly faint echoes that answered his own spoken opinions, and recognizing too readily his own sentiments in other people's ambiguous expressions. In the early days of most international wars, the word 'peace' is likely to fall on deaf ears, and certainly never stimulates the popular imagination. Before the carnage gets under way, the idea of war is simple and inspiriting, not horrific. Though it is true that Bertrand Russell's activities resulted in more personal hardship than public good, Lytton's orderly, democratic schemes were equally ineffectual, for in order to change the *status quo* you must unfortunately break the laws that barricade it. The House of Commons would have had no debate at all on the question of England entering the war had not Philip Morrell courageously got to his feet and made a protest. His speech, by all accounts the finest he ever made, did no good and put an end to his political career – though nothing had so become that career as his leaving of it. 'I can never forget seeing him standing alone,' Ottoline noted in her diary (3 August 1914), 'with nearly all the House against him, shouting at him to "Sit down!"'

Momentarily, even Lytton himself would feel the faint vibration of war fever, instantly to be checked and objectified by his intelligence. Yet feeling it, he understood something of its power and appeal, and the force with which it was soon surging through the country, unerringly picking upon the female sex and those whom age exempted from service. 'I walked into Marlborough to-day,' he wrote to James (18 August 1914), 'and found there the news of the continued French advance in the Vosges, and the "confusion" of the German army. Is this possibly the beginning of a great turning movement? It is appalling to have to *wish* for such horrors – but now it's the only way.

'. . . Yesterday I felt for the first time a desire to go out and fight myself. I can understand some people being overcome by it. At any rate one would not have to think any more.'

For the most part, however, the war affected him as a personal tragedy. One of his sisters was in Germany and he was worried about getting her out. But when Evelyn Whitehead advised him to appeal to the British ambassador in Germany, he was nonplussed. 'But how can I?' he protested in his most penetrating voice. 'I have never met him.'

On a more public level he was equally incredulous. He followed the news carefully, growing more amazed and disgusted at each new communiqué and report. His political attitude in these early days of the war is nicely caught and summed up in a letter he wrote (21 August 1914) to Dorothy Bussy, after reading through a macabre White Paper that reproduced the official dispatches which had passed between Sir Edward Grey and the ambassadors. 'It's like a puppet-show, with the poor little official dolls dancing and squeaking their official phrases, while the strings are being pulled by some devilish Unseen Power. One naturally wants to blame somebody – the Kaiser for choice – but the tragic irony, it seems to me, really is that everyone was helpless. Even the Austrians were no doubt genuinely in terror of the whole régime being undermined by Slavism, and the Russians couldn't allow the Austrians to get hold of the Balkans; the crisis finally came when the Germans found out that the Russians were secretly mobilizing – that frightened them so much that the war party became supreme, and all was over. The real horror is that Europe is not yet half-civilized, and the peaceful countries aren't strong enough to keep the others quiet.'

4

POLEMICS AND PROPAGANDA

The war altered fractionally the direction in which Lytton's writing had been developing, and hastened the speed of that development. By inciting as never before his anger, sorrow and contempt, it lent him a sort of Dutch courage that helped to transform the academic quietist into a subtle literary propagandist. The war also changed, if not his values, the immediate priority of those values. Friendship and aesthetic beauty might still be more important to him than political ethics, but, for the time being, the latter were more urgent.

This rearranged scale of precedence led to some apparent contradictions in his ideas, especially between those expressed in his published and in his private writings. He had always disliked, as we already know, the Post-Impressionism which infiltrated Bloomsbury; but he now nourished a far greater dislike for the principal calumniators of Post-Impressionism, the type of people who in peacetime had so often been spoiling for a fight, and who were now united in a lustful hymn to battle. In order to present an equally united body of opinion opposed to this heedless militarism, it was necessary, Lytton considered, to join up with people he did not readily like, and to associate himself with ideas that were not his own.

What had chiefly impressed him about Post-Impressionism was its capacity for angering the opposition – mostly men and women of little intelligence who were unable to formulate their objections into coherent speech or account rationally for their inflamed sense of outrage. 'Pure pornography', 'admirably indecent' – such were some of the more appreciative comments which Lytton had overheard at the Second Post-Impressionist Exhibition. A year earlier, at the first exhibition (November 1910) organized by Roger Fry and Desmond MacCarthy at the Grafton Gallery and entitled *Manet and the Post-Impressionists*, the public reaction had been even stronger. 'The exhibition is either an extremely bad joke,' wrote Wilfrid Blunt in his diary, 'or a swindle. I

am inclined to think the latter, for there is no trace of humour in it.'
Other visitors, however, saw it as purely humorous; and one gentleman
laughed so loud that 'he had to be taken out and walked up and down
in the fresh air for five minutes'. Never less than four hundred spectators
turned up each day to be diverted, bemused or exasperated. As the
storm of blustering abuse grew in volume so its tone became more
vindictive. Respectable country gentlemen loudly reminded each other
that Roger Fry's wife was in an asylum and predicted that it would not
be long before he joined her. They prayed anxiously that he might be
confined before too much irreparable mischief had been done to the
country through subverting the morals of the young.

In the ordinary course of events Lytton never took to the extraordinarily chimerical views of Fry, who was a family friend, considerably older than most other members of the Bloomsbury Group,
and in appearance even older than his age. The bushy black eyebrows,
the spectacles through which he projected such magnified visual organs,
his magnificent full deep bass voice, his invariable dull Jaeger suit – a
homespun loosely cut jacket and shapeless trousers which gave him the
aspect of a fasting friar in brown habit with a rope around his waist –
all this endeared Fry to Lytton. But he sometimes felt irritated by
Fry's extreme credulity that found expression through the most
weighty, judicial manner. Speaking with grave deliberation, he was
given to enunciating highflown aesthetic theories that amounted to little
more than unpractical jokes. The most far-fetched manifestation of this
bigoted naïvety was, to Lytton's mind, the Omega Workshops, whose
textiles, dress fashions, precarious furniture and pottery, continued to fill
him with a kind of wonderment. At the same time he appreciated that
Fry was genuinely on the side of the artists. The Omega Workshops,
however extraordinary and amateur their productions, did provide a
number of impoverished painters with the security of part-time employment which could act as a sympathetic extension to their real function as artists. And, conversely, another of Fry's principal aims was to
launch a fresh attack on the firmly implanted philistinism of the British
towards the visual arts in general.

The British public, however, had not welcomed Fry's efforts to
educate them. The overall hubbub, hysteria and ridicule provoked by
the two Post-Impressionist Exhibitions and now by the Omega Workshops, increased Fry's natural indignation against their arrogant
insensitivity; and it was this indignation, comprising a violent repugnance against sentimental morality and a determination to overcome
the abject indifference officially and traditionally shown to all art by
Britain, that, above all else, attracted Lytton. Art, in his view, was a

civilizing and peaceful influence. Both he and Fry were strong in their hatred of social hypocrisy; they wanted to shatter this and all other loathsome aspects of what they considered to be the British way of life and remould it nearer to the pattern of enlightened French society.

In times of emergency and crisis it is necessary to oversimplify one's thoughts if they are to be heard and heard effectively. For Lytton, the feud which sprang up after the Post-Impressionist Exhibitions between the new artist and the art critics of established reputation acting as spokesmen for the public at large, came to represent a fierce and ex-hilarating encounter in the age-long struggle between light and dark-ness. He elected to see Fry impersonally, symbolically, as a lieutenant on the side of human moderation and liberality campaigning against the forces of human folly and barbarism.

And so, though the references in his private correspondence to Fry, the man, are frequently unflattering, in public he was now impelled into the combat beside Fry's banner. In the manner of Voltaire, he did not believe in what Fry was doing in the arts, but he strenuously defended his right to do it. His sense of purpose was sustained by a belief that the world's spirit of toleration had not advanced all that far since Galileo was imprisoned for blasphemously asserting that the earth went round the sun. Nobody, it was true, was going to put Dr McTaggart on the rack for writing a book which destroyed the legend of the Trinity, but, Lytton declared, 'after the late fulminations of Sir William Richmond[1] against Post-Impressionism, nobody could be very much surprised if a stake was set up to-morrow for Mr. Roger Fry in the courtyard of Burlington House'. And in his opening article for J. C. Squire in the *New Statesman* Lytton makes the nature of his allegiance to Fry quite explicit: 'It seems clear that the change which has come over us is not so much a change in our attitude towards persecution in general as a change in the class of subjects which raise our zeal to persecute.'

By 1914 the everlasting spirit of intolerance had been hunted out of metaphysics, had been transferred to the field of ethics, and gave signs of moving in the direction of aesthetics. It was partly because of this last transition that Lytton chose to wear odd clothing; in the absence of anything else, clothes were as good a means as any of signifying revolt. And he was seldom unsuccessful, too, in deliberately stimulating stupid remarks from stupid, narrowly conventional people who, in their

---

[1] Sir William Blake Richmond (1842–1921), Slade Professor of Fine Art at Oxford (1879–83) and a Royal Academician. He was a highly successful portrait painter, though perhaps his best-known work is the rather indifferent mosaic decorations for St Paul's Cathedral.

sartorial opinions, incoherently confused ethics with aesthetics. If a man looked out of place, wore an eccentric long red beard and black Quaker cloak, then automatically, the uniformly grey, respectable, bowler-hatted population knew what deductions to make concerning his *moral* behaviour. It stood to prejudice. 'What is known as bad taste', Lytton wrote, 'is certainly persecuted at the present day. The milder transgressions of this nature are punished by private society with extreme severity; the more serious are rigorously dealt with by the State. Again, the conventions connected with apparel fill our minds with feelings of awe and sanctity which our ancestors of the Middle Ages reserved for articles of their faith. If a man wears unusual clothes, we hate him with the hatred of a Franciscan for a Dominican in the fourteenth century. If he goes so far as not to wear black clothes at dinner, we are quite certain that he is doomed to eternal perdition; while if he actually ventures to wear no clothes when he bathes, we can stand it no longer and punish him by law.'

In another *New Statesman* article, 'Bonga-Bonga in Whitehall', the idea of which, cast in the form of a dialogue between a certain African chief named Bonga-Bonga and a minister of the British Government, was suggested to him by Adrian Stephen and Horace Cole's escapade on board H.M.S. *Dreadnought*, Lytton again sharply ridicules the naïve but popular assumption that the Liberal Party stood for genuinely liberal principles. The satire, however, is not really successful because he is over-anxious, within the limits of a meagre two thousand words, to hit too many targets–the Government's attitude towards suffragettes, its illogical arguments in favour of corporal and capital punishment, and the notion that they encouraged Freedom of Speech or Liberty of the Press.

With the possible exception of four pieces which he wrote in 1918 for Leonard Woolf's *War and Peace*, this small but detached body of his work for the *New Statesman* is unique in the number of its references to topical events. These papers also convey a tone of unusually determined self-assurance. In a critical appraisal of John Palmer's *The Comedy of Manners*, he casts an amused glance over his shoulder at the apprehension which in earlier days had afflicted him over the danger of making a fool of himself before the public as a critic. The awe-inspiring prestige of literary reputation, which had previously impressed him as being retrospectively unchanging, now strikes him as flexible; even, in part, ephemeral. He likens its rise and fall, as many have done, to the fluctuations of a stock market, with its accidental cross-currents of luck and prevailing sentiment. 'What are the subtle causes which led, quite lately, to the rise in Donne, after he had lain for two hundred years a drug on the market?' he asks at one point. 'He is still rising, and share-holders who picked him up for next to nothing – an old song, one might say – fifteen years ago, are now congratulating themselves.' Looking to the future, he recommends for those who enjoy the occasional flutter, an investment in the Restoration comedy, at that time being quoted well below par.

This attempt to promote the popularity of the Restoration play-wrights was for Lytton an oblique way of enhancing the esteem and status of English men of letters within their own country. Perhaps, his argument seems to have run, the English would treat their literature with greater respect were it seen to embody the easily recognized and popularly admired Anglo-Saxon virtues. At present, English literature stuck out as a mere adjunct to the country itself, some freak growth, an architectural peninsula whose most celebrated pinnacles and spires stood curiously dissociated from the firm, undulating terrain of the British mind. Admittedly there were Fielding and Scott, but what could be less British, in any accepted meaning of the word, than the intellectual subtleties of Donne and Browning, the high fantasies of Shelley and Swinburne, the precocious artistry of Keats and the peculiarly independent qualities of writers such as Sir Thomas Browne, Sterne, Lamb, and George Meredith? Yet there existed another side to the coin. In the solid, rough-and-tumble comedies of Wycherley, with their breath and bustle of common life, one was constantly being brought into contact with 'the confused and crowded atmosphere of an English inn'; and in the works of the talented but unjustly disregarded Sir John Vanbrugh one found 'the jovial, high-hearted gaiety of English outdoor life'. Even Congreve, notwithstanding his marvellous verbal felicity and the nimbleness of his wit, had his feet squarely planted upon good English earth. The quintessence of the extrovert English genius was embedded in the dramatic compositions of such men; the effect of their plays was Hogarthian; their air of 'solid British beef, thick British beer, stout British bodies, and . . . stolid British moralising' was unmistakable.

Sustaining the propaganda of this essay there lies the schoolboy's prostration before the familiar heroic figure of the man of action. If only, Lytton seems regretfully to have sighed, writers were inherently as attractive as ploughboys or soldiers, then writing might be a more honoured and more exciting profession. Of course it was not so, it could never be so – yet the Restoration playwrights, with their bawdy humour, their full and native masculine vigour, were imbued with something of the same virile and athletic glamour. Unfortunately they were largely ignored, while the best-known literary oracles of the past

E*

were, in comparison, very queer fish indeed. Matthew Arnold, for instance. What spectacle could be more unaesthetic, more uninvitingly pompous than this earnest inspector of schools, with his high-toned fleerings and erudite self-righteousness, when contrasted with the natural graces of the ordinary man of action? Yet, almost wantonly, Arnold prompted such damaging comparison by his repeated assertion that literature should act as a criticism of and a corollary to the one serious matter in the world – the living of an active, useful life. To be burdened in his propaganda efforts with this type of totally unprepossessing paternal figure was insupportable. If only Arnold had been on the other side! But 'unfortunately,' Lytton complained, adopting one of his favourite forms of comic speculation, 'he mistook his vocation. He might, no doubt, if he had chosen, have done some excellent and lasting work upon the movements of glaciers or the fertilization of plants, or have been quite a satisfactory collector in an up-country district in India. But no; he *would* be a critic.'

In these doleful circumstances Lytton, almost unconsciously, set about changing the past by means of a new type of vigorous polemic. Between the lines of his essays he put over what amounted to a lack-of-confidence trick, acting as the eloquent and persuasive public relations officer for a select number of the more stimulating, attractive men of letters. Concurrently, he undermined the reputations of well-established leaders in the world of affairs, statesmen, clerics, and bureaucrats of letters, whom he depicted as being slightly crazy, and, though incidentally diverting, without a trace of redeeming humour or humanity. The author of *Landmarks in French Literature* and *Eminent Victorians* had thus cast himself in the dual role of a Dr Jekyll and Mr Hyde, a twofold part that suited his divided nature so neatly that, at his most forceful and adroit, he rose to become what he himself called Voltaire – a journalist of genius.

In deliberate contravention of the revered literary canons of Matthew Arnold, Lytton considered it best to divorce literature from day-to-day affairs, presenting the former as an alluring fantasy world, the latter as more mundane. Otherwise there was the risk that he might succumb to temptation, begin to despise the whole business of criticism, and, like Macaulay or Leslie Stephen, make use of it mainly as a vehicle for propounding views on other matters. At the same time he wanted to stress the compensations and rewards which attached to writing – the coruscating lustre and prestige that permanently illuminated the craft of letters. In extreme cases it could light up and confer immortality on even the most eccentric or obscure relatives of the poets – Shelley's father, for example, 'an unwilling ghost caught up in everlasting glory'.

The kind of posthumous reputation enjoyed by a great writer depended largely upon the temper and personality of later critics – and here lay the real trouble in the organization responsible for renovating literary façades and images. In 'Rabelais', the last of his articles to appear in the *New Statesman*, Lytton places the blame squarely on the shoulders of the dons, who, in his opinion, had achieved the almost impossible task of making great writing seem dull and commonplace. To commemorate their own inaccessible superiority they wanted literature to be distinguished by reason of its exclusiveness – *and few there be who may comprehend it.* Lytton's aims were precisely the opposite of this. He wished to purge literary criticism of all restrictive, puritan influence, and develop the widest possible appeal and popularity of literature – to throw open its many mansions to universal delight. And so, at the end of 'Rabelais', he concludes by poking fun at the methods by which dons and teachers tended to impoverish the majesty of literature and limit its multifarious attractions. 'He [Rabelais] is read by many as a great humanist and moral teacher; by many more, probably, as a teller of stories, and in particular of improper stories; others are fascinated by his language, and others by the curious problems – literary, biographical, allegorical – which his book suggests. Mr. W. F. Smith, of St. John's College, Cambridge, belongs to another class – and it is a larger one than might have been expected – the class of those who read Rabelais for the sake of making notes. . . . Rabelais, so extraordinary in his nature, was no less extraordinary in his posthumous fate. Of this, the mysterious Fifth Book was the earliest manifestation; the latest is Mr. Smith's volume; but no doubt it will not be the last.'

Landmarks in French Literature marks the culmination of Lytton's pure literary criticism, after which his writing moved further and further towards biography. The four major essays which he produced between January 1913 and October 1915 for the *Edinburgh Review* each take for their subject some figure from the French literary world; and together they form a continuation of the main flow of those literary and biographical essays which first appeared in the *Independent Review* and the *New Quarterly*.

'Madame du Deffand' invites favourable comparison with the essay which Lytton had written a little over six years earlier on her protégée, Mademoiselle de Lespinasse. The latter glitters with all the spontaneous brilliance and enthusiasm of a born raconteur; the former has the more studied ease and flow of a practised conversationalist. Though packed with information, the tone is polished, the pace even and unhurried. The balanced classical style and structure exert, too, a more disciplinarian control over Lytton's romantic excesses, so that the residue of histrionic and rhetorical asides, which were sprinkled through the pages of 'Mademoiselle de Lespinasse', has here been dissolved without any obtrusive, visual trace into the central narrative stream. 'Madame du Deffand' is also composed of a more intricate texture – a measure of the greater detail with which it had been charted in advance. In the opening paragraph Lytton presents the historical frame within which the finished miniature of his subject will be placed. When Napoleon, he tells us, set off for his Russian campaign he ordered the proof sheets of a forthcoming book, Madame du Deffand's correspondence with Horace Walpole, to be put in his carriage, so that he might decide what suppressions ought to be made for the published edition. Shortly afterwards the book (which had appeared in England two years previously) came out for the first time in France. 'The sensation in Paris was immense,' Lytton wrote; and evoking the spell that this correspondence cast, and can still cast, over its readers, he carefully underlines his own desire to promote imaginative literature as a subject at least as worthy of public attention as the discordant, topical problems of politics.

The accent which he places on the glamour and consequence of letters is reasserted in the other three essays that he contributed to the *Edinburgh Review*, and constitutes an extension to his policy of popularizing literary personalities in this country. In *Landmarks in French Literature* he had successfully applied a beauty treatment to the changing face of writing in France, pointedly stressing the high favour in which the supreme artist was held in that country. Now he set out to spread that esteem over to this side of the Channel.

At the end of his study of Madame du Deffand, as a means of indicating the emergence of a new and vital generation, Lytton had introduced the personality of Voltaire, who reappears as the leading character in two of his other Edinburgh essays. The first of these, 'Voltaire and England', has as its theme the Frenchman's direct and significant connexion with English influences. This note is struck at once:

'The visit of Voltaire to England marks a turning-point in the history of civilization. It was the first step in a long process of interaction – big with momentous consequences – between the French and English cultures. For centuries the combined forces of mutual ignorance and political hostility had kept the two nations apart: Voltaire planted a small seed of friendship which, in spite of a thousand hostile influences, grew and flourished mightily. The seed, no doubt, fell on good ground, and no doubt, if Voltaire had never left his native country, some chance wind would have carried it over the narrow seas, so that history in the main would have been unaltered. But actually his was the hand which did the work.'

The metaphorical vagueness of this opening passage makes plausible and even impressive the rather mythical *entente cordiale* that forms the basis of Lytton's advocacy. Well aware that if he were to advertise French culture as being wholly superior to English he would run the risk of alienating his audience and thus, at the very outset, defeating his own purpose, he recommends a compromise between the two. This idea is never stated flatly, but is everywhere implied, and like all the best methods of persuasion, leads the reader to the very brink of a certain conclusion which, since he must actually formulate it himself, exerts a far more potent and lasting impression on his mind.

At first we are shown Voltaire in 1726 as the pet of the aristocratic *élite* which then governed France, a position of distinction unknown to equivalent English writers. Then we are told the story of how he insulted the Chevalier de Rohan-Chabot, of the celebrated and powerful family of the Rohans, how he was beaten up by the Chevalier's gang of lackeys, and finally, how the high-born company with whom Voltaire had always supposed himself to be so popular and intimate, 'now only displayed signs of frigid indifference. The caste-feeling had suddenly asserted itself.' The law, too, was eaten up with social prejudice. Although no police action was taken against Rohan, Voltaire himself was subsequently arrested on suspicion of taking duelling lessons, and conducted to the Bastille. Lytton deals at unusual length with this incident, the bitter realism of which is used to qualify his adulation of the French aristocracy, and to demonstrate that, for all their many admirable qualities, they possessed none of the fresh congeniality of English high society. The reverse side of their greater sophistication is in these episodes depicted as the hidebound, callous stupidity of a still half-barbarous nation.

After a fortnight's solitary detention, the authorities acceded to Voltaire's petition begging them to substitute exile for imprisonment, and he was released on the condition that he remained at a distance of not less than fifty leagues from Versailles. Little is known of the two or three years he then spent in England, but Lytton sketches in the meagre and tantalizing details, and recounts his various adventures, notably the occasion when, surrounded by a hostile crowd of pedestrians, he turned their jeers of 'French dog!' into a clamour of enthusiasm 'by jumping upon a milestone, and delivering a harangue beginning – "Brave Englishmen! Am I not sufficiently unhappy in not having been born among you?"'

Despite the lack of precise and well-authenticated information concerning Voltaire's life in England, Lytton confidently rejects as impossible the theory that he acted as a spy in the pay of Walpole, and that he eventually left the country under a cloud. On the contrary, he maintains that during the period of his exile he became highly popular and that these two or three years were extremely beneficial to his typically French genius. The most powerful stimulus that England exercised upon his vivid imagination can be seen in his *Lettres Philosophiques*, that epoch-making book which could only have been written after the more cosmopolitan and polyglot Voltaire had returned to France. It was not a work of literature, Lytton explains, but something *more substantial and important* – 'a work of propaganda and a declaration of faith'. For, like Lytton himself, Voltaire had gone through a spiritual revolution. No longer was he a mere literary butterfly, feeding on the condescension of a narrow, prejudiced, wholly French aristocracy. He was a true anglophil; 'whatever quips and follies, whatever flouts and mockeries might play upon that surface, he was to be in deadly earnest at heart. He was to live and die a fighter in the ranks of progress, a champion in the mighty struggle which he was now beginning against the powers of darkness in France.' In short, the moral of this long essay is that England had made Voltaire into a fighter in the noble cause of humanity, that same cause for which an admixture of French culture had made Lytton and Roger Fry such staunch combatants two centuries later. After Voltaire's return, England became the fashion in France in much the same way as Lytton now wished to see France become the fashion in England. The 'whispered message of tolerance, of free enquiry, of enlightened curiosity, was carried over the land. The success of Voltaire's work was complete.' Lytton's work lay along a parallel course, and in the enriching cross-fertilization of French and English ways of life he saw the final destruction of those 'powers of darkness' which still held sway in both countries disunited.

And in conclusion, after Voltaire's direct association with English influences had ceased, Lytton likes to picture him as what almost seems like a kind of nostalgic and benevolent eighteenth-century André Maurois. 'For the rest of his life, indeed, he never lost his interest in England; he was never tired of reading English books, of being polite to English travellers, and of doing his best, in the intervals of more serious labours, to destroy the reputation of that deplorable English buffoon, whom, unfortunately, he himself had been so foolish as first to introduce to the attention of his countrymen.'

And so the pattern of the essay is rounded off. Voltaire rejected only the timid and pompous conservatism of the English mind. His mature attitude to the world was not exclusively of either country, for he took a midway path which no insular Englishman or cynical Frenchman could ever tread. Lytton concludes his essay on a fitting military note, a rousing call to the newly allied populations on both sides of the Channel. The real fight – not with Germany but with the enemy in their midst – was in danger of being forgotten, swamped by the international conflict. The only way in which he felt that he could still be heard was to appeal to this prevailing spirit of warfare, to mobilize it to the cause of humanity, and remind people that such a cause was more, not less, urgent in times of political and military crisis. 'With what reckless audacity, what a fierce uncompromising passion he charged and fought and charged again! He had no time for the nice discriminations of an elaborate philosophy, and no desire for the careful balance of a judicial mind; his creed was simple and explicit, and it also possessed the supreme merit of brevity: "Ecrasez l'infâme!" was enough for him.'

This is a stirring motto, but like most propaganda, however passionately felt, it facilitates only a single, acutely-angled vision of the objective truth. That Voltaire developed to maturity by virtue of his trip to England during the late 1720s is partly contradicted by Lytton himself in another of his Edinburgh essays, 'Voltaire and Frederick the Great', where he makes it clear that Voltaire only became conscious of the true nature of his genius and the real work for which it was suited once he had reached the threshold of old age.

Lytton starts off this essay with a determined effort to woo the reader's sympathetic attention. In time of war it was natural, though ultimately tedious, that everyone's attention should be fixed upon the soldiers and statesmen of the day. Setting out to redress the balance of this attention and publicity, Lytton puts forward a modest yet seductive plea for the solace, and for the expediency, of reflecting upon other, less immediate matters. There might be valuable advantages to be won, he suggests, by turning one's mind away from current uncertainty to the settled tranquillity of the past. In recollecting afresh the familiar intercourse between the leading man of letters and the leading politician of the eighteenth century, and in recapturing something of a life intimately connected with several of the most agitated events in European history, one could hardly fail to find respite from present suffering, as well as some harmless entertainment, and perhaps even a little instruction also.

The ensuing account which he gives of the 'curious drama' that took place between Voltaire and Frederick the Great is certainly entertaining. The instruction which it contains is skilfully unfolded as the essay proceeds and expressly stated at the end – that in the cut and thrust of human diplomacy, Voltaire, the most celebrated writer of his day, could match and outwit Frederick the Great, the most powerful man of action, whose twentieth-century counterparts now so filled and be-mused everyone's minds. 'But their relationship was no longer that of master and pupil, courtier and king,' Lytton concludes; 'it was that of two independent and equal powers. Even Frederick the Great was forced to see at last in the Patriarch of Ferney something more than a monkey with a genius for French versification. He actually came to respect the author of *Akakia*, and to cherish his memory. "Je lui fais tous les matins ma prière," he told d'Alembert, when Voltaire had been two years in the grave; "je lui dis, Divin Voltaire, *ora pro nobis*".'

Yet it is not as equals that these two are really presented in the main body of the essay. As a literary and philosophical pupil Frederick was inept; as a courtier Voltaire was flagrantly rebellious. We are shown all Frederick's faults and all Voltaire's, but at the same time we are constantly being made aware that only Voltaire possessed the consum-mate genius to compensate for his shortcomings. Not for long did he remain under any delusion about the king's poetic talent; whereas Frederick all the time persisted in his mistaken belief that he could tame the Frenchman and transform him into the brightest ornament at his court. Among the blind masses of the world Frederick was the one-eyed man, whose cold gaze observed with absolute clarity all that was close at hand. He noted each defect in his rival, yet was still manifestly blind to his prevailing merits. And so, though he could measure to a nicety all the complicated components in the diplomatic game, he was limited in the perspective that Voltaire, with both his eyes open, could com-mand. Both were astute, but Voltaire's shrewdness was deepened by the greater dimension of his vision into profundity. For this reason he was, by and large, a realist; whereas Frederick remained a typical cynic, callous in action, lachrymose in sentiment. Despite his natural cunning, he was baffled by Voltaire's inexplicable superiority, which neutralized so much of his cleverness and made him seem to act in a manner, for him, highly ingenuous. Thus, in Lytton's interpretation of their rela-tionship – which some critics, notably James Pope-Hennessy, have disputed – it is evidently not the King of Prussia but his Court Chamberlain who deserved the epithet 'great'. And the instruction implicit in this story points to a moral: that it was, even in 1915, not the statesmen who saw things wholly and effectually, but the philosopher – not Lloyd George, say, but Bertrand Russell.

The subject of Lytton's fourth Edinburgh essay was, significantly, another rebel – Stendhal. 'In his blood,' he wrote, analysing his dis-similarity to the Patriarch of Ferney, 'there was a virus which had never tingled the veins of Voltaire. It was the virus of modern life – that new sensibility, that new passionateness, which Rousseau had first made known to the world and which had won its way over Europe behind the thunder of Napoleon's artillery.'

In the full flood of the Romantic revival, Stendhal represented the spirit of the eighteenth century without, perhaps, some of its elegance and artificial neatness. There existed in him, as in Lytton himself, a mingling of the Classical and Romantic strains. 'In his novels this characteristic cohabitation of opposites is responsible both for what is best and what is worst.' Both had a natural flair for narrative; and at their finest, when these two usually conflicting forces pulled in unison, when their prose was at its least emphatic and most controlled, then 'the procedure is almost mathematical: a proposition is established, the inference is drawn, the next proposition follows, and so on until the demonstration is complete. Here the influence of the eighteenth century is strongly marked.'

The particular occasion of this essay was Stendhal's sudden upsurge of current popularity in France. André Gide had recently named him as the best French novelist of all time, and his literary reputation, confined until then to a small distinguished circle, had all at once begun to expand enormously. Lytton now hoped further to extend the circumference of this popularity so that it encompassed Britain. Many Englishmen, of course, had read *Le Rouge et le Noir* and *La Chartreuse de Parme*, but how few had any further knowledge of 'a man whose works are at the present moment appearing in Paris in all the pomp of an elaborate and complete edition, every scrap of whose manuscripts is being collected and deciphered with enthusiastic care, and in honour of whose genius the literary periodicals of the hour are filling entire numbers with exegesis and appreciation'!

Having thus in his first paragraph shamed the British reader with this accusation of unfashionable ignorance, Lytton then proceeds to pique his curiosity by establishing the unknown Stendhal as a bewitching and controversial character. First he treats us to a brief biography in which he is careful to point out that the creator of one of the most magnificent battle scenes in the whole of literature possessed only the scantiest military experience; for, as the example of Stephen Crane confirms, it is unnecessary for an imaginative writer to undergo the personal experience of warfare in order to understand it and describe it with psychological exactitude. Stendhal, in fact, was a lieutenant of dragoons for hardly more than a year during the Italian campaign, and was present at only one great battle – Bautzen.

From this introductory sketch, Stendhal emerges as a highly fascinating personality, almost the ideal embodiment of the life of letters with 'his adoration of Italy and Milan, his eccentricity, his scorn of the conventions of society and the limits of nationality, his adventurous life, his devotion to literature, and, lastly, the fact that, through all the varieties of his experience – in the earliest years of his childhood, in his agitated manhood, in his calm old age – there had never been a moment when he was not in love.'

Lytton follows up this biographical résumé with an appraisal of the novels and miscellaneous writings. He notes with approval Stendhal's attempt to reach a real precision and detachment in his prose, and describes his literary style in words which apply equally well to his own writing at its most restrained. 'In fact, Beyle's method is the classical method – the method of selection, of omission, of unification. . . . His pen could call up pictorial images of startling vividness, when he wished. But he very rarely did wish: it was apt to involve a tiresome insistence. In his narratives he is like a brilliant talker in a sympathetic circle. . . .'

It is to this sympathetic circle of friends that Lytton returns at the end of his essay. In the penultimate section we are shown Stendhal as a public figure, a born rebel, with his enlightened 'hatred for the proudest and most insidious of all authorities – the Roman Catholic Church', whose fulminations against all authoritarian forces gives 'a surprising foretaste of the fiery potion of Zarathrustra'. But it is as Henri Beyle, the private man, whose character seemed almost to give the lie outright to all his autocratic prophecies, that we finally take leave of him. The dramatic emphasis which Lytton extracts from this dichotomy, suggests that he recognized in Stendhal's double role some parallel to his own – to that equivocal juxtaposition between the stern, revolutionary message which, in a disguised form, he wished to put over to the modern reading public, and the more diffident, amiable composition of his shy and peace-loving nature.

To Lytton the world appeared as a circus, full of gaudy colours and unnecessary cruelty, fascinating yet repellent. But he did not really want to have the animals liberated and returned to their native wilds, only transferred to the more comfortable amenities of a well-run zoo. The boredom and bestiality of life could be eliminated solely through love and the intimate pursuits of friendship. Therefore he appreciated the apparent inconsistency in Henri Beyle, whose 'wayward, capricious and eccentric' personality stood out in such vivid contrast to Stendhal's uncompromising, anarchic outlook. If men like Henri Beyle were to continue flourishing, then they would need their Stendhals to fight for them against the encroachments of the barbaric universe. Beyle's world of civilized intercourse and communion comprised the ends that vindicated all Stendhal's most bitter denunciations. And so the final, nostalgic valediction is addressed to the real, inner man, the private individual, in his ideal environment. 'And in such a Paradise of Frenchmen we may leave Henri Beyle.'

5

BUSINESS AS USUAL

Outwardly, Lytton's way of life was not shaken up very much by the war. For the time being he continued his quiet existence at The Lacket, 'living the life of a complete St. Anthony', as he described it to Ottoline (24 October 1914), 'with Mrs. Templeman in the role of the Queen of Sheba – and I can't say she plays the part with conviction'. On most evenings now he would spend a solitary hour or two, crouched over the fire 'knitting mufflers for our soldier and sailor lads,' he informed Clive Bell, 'but I expect that by the time I've finished them the war will be over, and they'll be given to Henry and Duncan'. Acknowledging the possibility of the country being overrun by the enemy, and feeling that at all costs it was essential to be ready with words of propitiation, he gave up Italian and began to take lessons in German.

For the next four years, of course, there was to be no more travelling abroad to France, or Italy, or even Sweden; but his perpetual oscillation between Wiltshire and the metropolis went on much as before. In London, there were still the Thursday evening parties at Bedford Square, where the pressure of worry and unhappiness could be relieved for a few hours in the company of other sympathetic artists and writers. To assist in the pretence that things were otherwise than they were, to liberate them from themselves and from their cares, the guests at these parties would robe up in fancy dress and, while Philip Morrell played Hungarian dances or fiery Russian ballet music at his pianola, throw themselves into wild and fantastic dances. 'Now and then,' recalled Ottoline, 'Lytton Strachey exquisitely stepped out with his brother James and his sister Marjorie, in a delicate and courtly minuet of his own invention, his thin long legs and arms gracefully keeping perfect time to Mozart – the vision of this exquisite dance always haunts me with its half-serious, half-mocking, yet beautiful quality.'

And there were also the Bloomsbury parties to which Lytton had now started going once again. One of the most spectacular of these affairs, which conveys the peculiar flavour of them all, was arranged at 46

Gordon Square by Clive and Vanessa Bell. After listening to some Mozart played by Adila and Jelly D'Arányi (who, as Hungarians, were looked upon with hostile suspicion by most Englishmen, but to whom Bloomsbury, for this reason, was now particularly hospitable) the guests all went upstairs to witness a performance of the last scene from Racine's *Bérénice*, acted by three huge puppets eight feet tall, painted and cut out of cardboard by Duncan Grant.[1] The words of the play were declaimed solely by members of the Strachey family, whose fearful Gallic mouthings before 'several eminent frogs' were as remarkable in their way as the puppets themselves.[2]

At moments the whirl of London gaiety was almost too extreme, the ingenuity needed to conjure forth these high spirits too preposterously far-fetched. Practical jokes abounded. One of the most skilful was successfully played by Duncan Grant on Lytton himself. At breakfast one morning, while he was staying with his family in Hampstead, he received through the post a poem in French purporting to come from a rather taciturn French actor named Delacre, a man whom he had met at several of Ottoline's parties and whose conversation seemed to consist entirely of long, sombre stories, usually beginning: 'Figurez-vous, mon cher . . .' This poem, composed in rhymed couplets, implied that the writer had recently seen Lytton in some extremely compromising situation. It was inscribed on a single sheet of paper, in ominous, anonymous capital letters.

> *SI UN VIEUX*
> *VEUT BAISER DANS LA RUE*
> *UN JEUNE HOMME*
> *VAUT MIEUX*
> *PRENDRE UN FIACRE*
> *AVANT QU' APRES*
> *TON AMI DELACRE*
> *DEMEURE TOUT PRES*
> *DE KNIGHTSBRIDGE CHER MAITRE?*
> *CA BIEN PEUT ETRE.*

Although he was quite honestly at a loss at to what indiscretion Delacre was claiming to have observed, Lytton felt terrified that the story might gain currency with his friends and that he would quickly

---

[1] 'We like Duncan Grant very much,' D. H. Lawrence wrote to Ottoline Morrell (27 January 1915). 'I *really* like him. Tell him not to make silly experiments in the futuristic line, with bits of colour on a moving paper. Other Johnnies can do that. Neither to bother making marionettes – even titanic ones. But to seek out the terms in which he shall state his whole. . . .'

[2] A rather different account of a second showing of this play, performed before an English audience, is given by David Garnett in *The Flowers of the Forest* (1955), pp. 22–23.

become the butt of their slanderous humour. His imagination began to run away with him. Perhaps, once started, the rumour would spread far beyond the immediate circle of Bloomsbury. Already he could see the garish newspaper headlines – '*Astonishing Accusation!*' In panic he rushed round at once to Delacre's hotel, and implored him not to show it to anyone.

What subsequently took place Lytton confided to David Garnett at tea that same afternoon. 'Delacre had then behaved in a most extra-ordinary and alarming manner,' David Garnett recounts. 'He had listened to Lytton's little speech without making any comment what-ever. He had then excused himself and left the room. After waiting three-quarters of an hour Lytton had asked a waiter to find Delacre and had been told that he had left the hotel. Lytton was completely baffled by this behaviour and felt that he had not improved matters by his *démarche*.'

After listening with great amusement to Lytton's account of this strange imbroglio, David Garnett read the lines again and pointed out that it was highly improbable that M. Delacre, who was presumably a vain as well as a serious actor, should select the word *fiacre* as a rhyme to his own name. 'You don't think that Duncan wrote it by any chance?' he hazarded.

Lytton stared in dismay. The notion had briefly occurred to him, but he had dismissed it, being unable to believe that Duncan was capable of such fiendish cleverness. The French seemed so idiomatic; and it rhymed, too, so ingeniously. But now, hearing the very same suspicion voiced by David Garnett, he suddenly recognized it as the obvious explanation.

'What, that monster!' he exclaimed. 'Of course! He's a devil! I believe if the truth were known all the preposterous predicaments in the Universe might be traced back to him.'

To all appearances therefore the Bloomsbury milieu was the same as ever; but appearances were misleading. Beneath the forced-up gaiety and manufactured high spirits there lay a darker side. According to Dr Johnson, every man thinks meanly of himself for not having been a soldier or not having been at sea. 'The profession of soldiers and sailors has the dignity of danger,' he once declared. 'Mankind reverences those who have got over fear, which is so general a weak-ness.' With his precocious invalidism, his ambition and romanticism, Lytton was occasionally, during these first few months of the war, a prey to this unreasonable feeling of inferiority. For although he believed that, in some circumstances at least, it was more courageous to refuse complicity in a largely lunatic and avoidable holocaust, this belief could not at all times hold its own against a horrid, resurgent sense of his inadequacy.

This gloom was soon deepened by news of the first fatalities. 'For myself I am absolutely and completely desolated,' Maynard Keynes wrote to him from King's (27 November 1914). 'It is utterly unbearable to see day by day the youths going away first to boredom and discomfort and then to slaughter. Five of this College, who are undergraduates or who have just gone down, are already killed, including to my great grief Freddie Hardman, as you may have seen from the papers.' Lytton had seen Hardman only a month or two earlier at one of Ottoline's parties. 'I think what the Greeks meant by that remark of theirs about those who die young was that they escape the deterioration of growing old; and perhaps if Freddie had gone on living he could hardly have gone on being so nice,' he wrote in his reply to Keynes (1 December 1914). 'But I'm afraid this reflection isn't much of a consolation to you.'

The war also put an end to Lytton's intimacy with Henry Lamb, who, after joining the R.A.M.C., was sent abroad to serve in France – where he was awarded a Military Cross – then to Macedonia and Palestine. For a while their flow of correspondence trickled on, but by the end of 1915 it had ceased altogether; and after the war they met only occasionally as casual acquaintances. There was no one, during these war years, who really commandeered Lamb's special place in Lytton's affections. Of course, with his restless emotional susceptibility, he was always entering into trivial romantic affairs – 'a violent, short, quite fruitless passion' for the twenty-one-year-old painter Geoffrey Nelson, for example, and a romantic affection for Ted Roussell, a young ploughboy from Sussex, who enlisted in 1917 and was killed in the last weeks of the war[1] – but these attachments, though sometimes highly-charged, were of little lasting significance and merely reproduced on a greatly reduced scale the lineaments of his more serious intimacies, those that created in themselves some precedent, some extension to the emotional pattern of his life.

Something of a new variation in this pattern did gradually come about, however, at this time. This was the emergence of a dual, half-reciprocated relationship that comprised in part ordinary affectionate friendship, and in part homosexual flirtation. On the whole, it was a happy development for Lytton. Two men in particular of whom he

---

[1] 'Dear Ted,' Lytton wrote to him on 13 November 1918, 'I wonder how you are. I haven't heard from you for a long time – and I hope you are well and flourishing. Now that the war's over, I expect you'll be coming back quite soon – which I daresay you won't be sorry for. Let me hear from you when you have time to write. Always your friend, L Strachey.' This letter was returned to Lytton, its envelope marked 'Deceased'.

soon grew especially fond were Francis Birrell and David ('Bunny')
Garnett, themselves very close friends. Both were younger than himself, but he did not idolize them as he had Thoby Stephen, Duncan
Grant, Henry Lamb or even Sheppard. He rejoiced in their company,
and with each of them felt a warm affinity, though his fondness was
seldom without some austere qualifications. 'I think he's a nice fellow
at bottom,' he wrote of Francis Birrell to James (21 January 1915), 'but
the overlaying paraphernalia are distinctly trying. He seems a sort of
secondary Clive – and in the Dostoievsky style, half knows it.' While
the innocent, bumptious Birrell chattered on so inexhaustibly, Garnett
would remain exasperatingly taciturn. In contrast to Birrell's sparkling
quickness and ever-ready tongue, he enunciated his thoughts with a
sort of rustic slowness and deliberation, his speech being pock-marked
with 'ghastly pauses', as Lytton once complained to Roger Senhouse
(2 February 1929), '– each long enough to contain Big Ben striking
midnight – between every two . . . words.' Nevertheless, Lytton quickly
developed an even closer friendship with him than with Birrell, a
friendship which did much to lighten the burden of these war years.
'No, the world is not agreeable,' he wrote to James six months after
meeting Garnett (11 June 1915). 'And then again I think of dear Bunny –
and the fact that such a person should exist in it fills me with delight.
Charming!'

It was Francis Birrell who in December 1914 had introduced Lytton
to David Garnett. That Christmas, Lytton held a large party at The
Lacket. Daphne and Noel Olivier, James Strachey and Duncan Grant
came down to stay with him in the cottage, while Birrell and Garnett
took rooms at a local inn. David Garnett has given a description of this
first meeting with Lytton and of his impressions over this holiday,
which vividly evokes the peculiar atmosphere of the place. 'Lytton was
tall and rather emaciated,' he recalled, 'with a reddish beard and lank
dark hair which hung in a long lock over his forehead and was cut off
squarely, in pudding-basin fashion, at the back of his head. His nose
was large with a high bridge; he wore spectacles and was obviously
rather short-sighted. I was struck first of all by his gentleness and his
hospitality. Then I could see he was very much alive and very responsive. That evening the response may sometimes have concealed
boredom, for Lytton was easily bored and the prospect of Christmas
with two young women in the house – one of whom often spoke in
tones of indignant emotional idealism – may have seemed rather appalling. James had let him in for them, and his curiosity and affection for
Frankie [Birrell] had let him in for the shy, but good-looking hobblede-
hoy he had brought with him.'

On Christmas Day, David Garnett continues, the animal spirits of the low-brow members of the party got out of hand, and he and Daphne Olivier, after exchanging a wild glance, dived into the soft, round, springy box hedge which encircled the garden. Noel Olivier, Francis Birrell and eventually Duncan Grant followed them. But their sport was checked, then abruptly terminated by the sudden appearance of their disconcerted host, who, in high-pitched and despairing tones, forbade them to continue. 'We realised', wrote Garnett, 'that Lytton was really a little upset and, sorrowfully, we desisted and for the rest of the day accepted Strachey canons of behaviour, though some of us passed up our plates for second helpings of turkey and plum pudding.

'Once again I was struck by the rigidity of the Strachey outlook. We had to conform to Strachey views and Strachey habits: the Stracheys would not even try to pretend to adapt themselves to manners or customs which were not their own.'[1]

This brand of forbidding, kill-joy severity, Garnett soon discovered, was only one side of Lytton's moral attitude, which, on a plane less rowdy and athletic, expressly sanctioned certain tentative deviations and serious experimentations in human intercourse. Garnett, whose career was perhaps remarkable for the multitude and ambivalence of its emotional experiences rather than the depth of feeling that these experiences engendered, was fascinated by this unusual blending of strictness and unorthodox condonation, and soon made Lytton into something of a moral mentor.

That evening, after his intervention over the box-hedge incident, Lytton read out to his guests, assembled round the fire after tea, 'Ermyntrude and Esmeralda'. The witty, rather scandalous manner of this story reminded Garnett of Laclos's *Les Liaisons Dangereuses*. It was the kind of *risqué* theme which Lytton enjoyed exploring in various unpublished dialogues, narratives, poems and short stories, and which, though intended specifically for the amusement of his friends, occasionally came near to compromising his friendly relations with a few of them, notably Clive Bell. But on this occasion he was surrounded by an entirely appreciative audience, and David Garnett was so especially receptive to the message contained in this particular story that he proclaimed himself to be there and then converted for the rest of his potent life into a confirmed and industrious *libertine* – 'that is a man whose sexual life is free of the restraints imposed by religion and conventional morality'.

---

[1] David Garnett appears to have misinterpreted Lytton's attitude on this occasion. He was not being old-maidish over their behaviour, but was concerned by the damage they were doing to a fine box hedge over two hundred years old.

6

UNDERTONES OF WAR

The war, though it sharpened up Lytton's critical faculties, acted as a giant encumbrance to the everyday, practical business of writing. The magnitude of world events burst through and disrupted his concentration, and, with its cargo of painful emotional disentanglements, seemed at first to threaten the realization of all his carefully laid literary plans. 'Namur is terrible,' he wrote to James (August 1914). 'I suppose it's certain now it will be a long business. As for my private hopes, they're almost gone.'

When he did manage to settle down to some literary composition, such as 'Voltaire and England', he found it, as he told Henry Lamb (5 September 1914), 'a considerable sedative'. But by and large he felt in no mood for writing, and the Manning biography, which should have been finished by the end of August, gave him great difficulty. Thirty-five foolscap pages of it had to be entirely rewritten, and it was not in fact completed until shortly before Christmas. His letters to his friends and family during this autumn contain repeated avowals of his determination to 're-attack the Cardinal', but it was only in the New Year that he could actually show them the fruit of his labours. Their response was immediately gratifying – all the more so because he had not expected everyone to care for it. 'I have seldom enjoyed myself more than I did last night, reading Manning,' Virginia Woolf wrote to him (January 1915). 'In fact I couldn't stop, and preserved some pages by force of will to read after dinner. It is quite superb – It is far the best thing you have ever written, I believe – To begin with, what a miracle it is that such a group should have existed – and then how divinely amusing and exciting and alive you make it. I command you to complete a whole series: you can't think how I enjoy your writing.'

Much fortified and encouraged by this and other similar letters of appreciation, Lytton now embarked on the second of his eminent Victorians.[1] Exactly one year ago he had read Sir Edward Cook's official biography of Florence Nightingale, telling his mother at the time (15 January 1914) that although the lady with the lamp was certainly a fascinating woman, he did not really like her, and that, in his opinion, her stature was not truly great. Having turned down the offer

[1] 'Send me your life of Manning at once or I shall go mad,' E. M. Forster wrote to him (17 May 1915). 'I will disinfect it.' A fortnight later he wrote again. 'I will return the Cardinal when I have read him again – a habit you censured some 12 years back. Meanwhile I wish you would send me Mademoiselle Nightingale and some short witty stories. I am certain you have some – they will be quite safe.'

of writing this book himself, he was particularly interested to see the kind of woman whom Edward Cook had depicted. 'I have just been reading the book I might have written – the Life of F. Nightingale,' he informed James (16 January 1914). 'I'm glad I didn't, as I couldn't have satisfied anybody. She was a terrible woman – though powerful. And certainly a wonderful book might have been made out of her, from the cynical point of view. Of course the Victorian Age is fairly reeking all over it. What a crew they were!'

From the cynical point of view, he now believed that he might make a wonderful short biography of Florence Nightingale, compressing the mass of diluted information in the official Life into a closely wrought solid and dramatic unity. 'I'm beginning to attack Florence Nightingale,' he announced to Henry Lamb (3 January 1915). 'I want it to be very much shorter than the Cardinal, which will involve rather a different method, I think. I'm not quite sure whether the damned thing will be possible, but I hope for the best.'

The preparation and actual writing of 'Florence Nightingale' occupied Lytton for almost six months. His correspondence over the first half of 1915 is sprinkled with references to this work which tell of the arduous growing pains of its composition and his own changing moods and difficulties.

Lytton Strachey to Henry Lamb, 12 January 1915

'Florence Nightingale is progressing. I wish I didn't dislike hard work quite so much. But of course it might be worse – I think it's chiefly the starting that is so unpleasant.'

Lytton Strachey to Ottoline Morrell, 11 February 1915

'I find Florence N. rather a hard nut to crack, but I'm struggling with extraordinary persistence. Don't you think I've become wonderfully industrious lately?'

Lytton Strachey to Virginia Woolf, 28 February 1915

'I am in rather a state just now with Miss Nightingale, who is proving distinctly indigestible. It's a fearful business – putting pen to paper – almost inconceivable. What happens? And how on earth does one ever manage to pull through in the end?'

From this time on there was no question of the 'possibility' of writing on Florence Nightingale, only of the difficulty. For six weeks of the spring he was laid up with 'influenza and its consequent dilapidations', and wrote nothing. Then, in the early summer, he re-applied himself to the biography with a desperate and concentrated energy.

Lytton Strachey to Ottoline Morrell, 8 June 1915

'It is very agreeable here – not *too* hot (it never is!) – a cool breeze perpetually blowing. I spend all day sitting out writing my étude of Florence Nightingale, in which I'm at present completely involved – I hope to get the wretched thing done before very long though.'

Lytton Strachey to James Strachey, 11 June 1915

'I've been getting into a frantic state with F. Nightingale – working incessantly until my brain spun round and round, and then in its usual dim unexplained way my health went groggy, and yesterday Lady S. arrived.

'. . . The F.N. affair has been much more terrific than I could have expected. I imagined originally that I'd be able to do the whole thing in a fortnight. It's still not nearly done; and I'm in terror lest after all it should turn out quite illegible – I imagine Eddie Marsh trying to read it and saying afterwards, "It bored me stiff." I feel there would be no appeal from that.'

Lytton Strachey to Henry Lamb, 13 June 1915

'I am submerged by Nightingale, which has turned out a fearful task. I'm now within sight of the end, though, I hope.'

Lytton Strachey to Ottoline Morrell, 23 June 1915

'F. Nightingale has at last been polished off, I'm glad to say. So I'm feeling very gay and chirpy —'

Illness and the dramatic events of the war continued to undermine his progress, the first making him 'feel as if my brain was lying perdu somewhere far away under the dustheaps of accumulated generations', the second giving him the sense of living on a perpetual volcano. Yet both, while depriving him of much of the initial urge and impetus to write, also helped to pin-point his concentration once he had embarked on his work. At times, however, the political and military calamities would still split through and shatter this literary concentration. He was

amazed and appalled by the lurid suggestions he read in some newspapers, notably *The Times*, about the possibility of forming a coalition
Government. His head buzzed with unanswered questions. Could the
rumours be true? And if they were, what did it all mean? Why should
the cabinet contemplate such a move? Had they made some ghastly
blunder, for which they were being coerced to pay this price in order
to preserve the Opposition's silence? Or had they come to the conclusion that the war was hopeless without conscription? If *that* were
true, then all was lost, and the country would be engulfed in a jungle
of militarism. The prospect was really frightful. Already there had been
a sinister augury of the rising mood in recent disgraceful riots directed
against civilians of Germanic extraction still living in England. The
most alarming feature of these incidents had been, perhaps, the conduct
of the authorities who, in effect, encouraged them and then made use of
them as an excuse for further maltreatment of those miserable people.
If matters continued to deteriorate there would soon be nothing decent
left in the whole wretched country. 'Doesn't it all make one want to go
and bury oneself somewhere far, far away – somewhere so far away that
even the Times will never get to one?' he asked Ottoline. '"Où me
cacherai? Fuyons dans la nuit infernale!"'

But more terrible than the political uncertainty at home was the
awful, unbelievable finality of the news from the front. The death of his
friends made him feel more than ever the horrible insignificance of
humanity. So much seemed, abruptly, to have come to an end. In June,
his fellow Apostle Ferenc Békássy was killed in the Bukovina after only
two days' fighting. Two months earlier Rupert Brooke had died. Owing
to his failure to maintain amicable relations with Brooke, the news of
this particular tragedy affected him more deeply than any other. So
much of his past was raked up by it. After their pointless estrangement,
the thought of Brooke had haunted Lytton. 'I feel his state is deplorable,' he had written to Ottoline (22 October 1912), 'and something
ought to be done to bring him back to ordinary cheerful ways of living.
I hope to see James next week-end, and talk about it. I feel it particularly
because once when I was very low – in health and spirits – Rupert
helped me a great deal, and was very charming. And then besides, how
wretched all those quarrels and fatigues are! Such opportunities for
delightful intercourse ruined by sheer absurdities! It is too stupid.
"My children, love one another" – didn't Somebody, once upon a
time, say that?'

That Rupert should have ended his life on such an unsatisfactory
note, with all the old quarrels and intrigues still unresolved, struck
Lytton with deep pathos, and brought home to him with added force

the tragic, the monstrous, the *unaesthetic* futility of human affairs. 'I suppose by the time you get this you will have seen about Rupert's death,' he wrote to Duncan Grant (25 April 1915). 'The news came yesterday: apparently it was owing to some illness or other. He was put into a French ship, and taken to Lemnos, where he died. James is a good deal shattered, and altogether it's a grim affair. It was impossible not to like him, impossible not to hope that he might like one again; and now ... The meaninglessness of Fate is intolerable; it's all muddle and futility. After all the pother of those years of living, to effect – simply nothing. It is like a confused tale, just beginning and then broken off for no reason, and for ever. One hardly knows whether to be sorry even. One is just left with a few odd memories – until they too vanish.

'Poor Eddie [Marsh] is quite wrecked – and busy writing an obituary notice for the Times.'

He now felt so strongly about the international situation that it was most sensible, he reasoned, not to discuss it with anyone, and if possible not to think of it himself. He opened *The Times* every morning with dread; and in the evenings tried to immerse himself in books which had little or no association with the war – the *Memoirs of Lady Hester Stanhope*, H. G. Wells's *Boon*, and *The Voyage Out* by Virginia Woolf. It seemed to him that as the years went by he was growing increasingly sensitive, instead of gradually turning, as he had once half-humorously predicted, into a solid and heartless rock of a man. At the same time he remained constitutionally incapable of wearing his heart on his sleeve for daws to peck at, and so had to seek solace from the ferment of this vulnerable inner sensitivity in hard work. The pains and anxieties of writing could obliterate for a time the greater horrors of public outrage and catastrophe. But the pace of such work was often agonizingly tedious. 'The slowness of my work is alarming,' he had written to Henry Lamb while still struggling with 'Florence Nightingale' (2 February 1915). 'I fully intend to do another play when this affair is finished, and after that I daresay a novel – by which time, at the present rate of progress, I shall be 75.'

The novel he never attempted, but a Chekhovian *jeu d'esprit*, *Old Lyttoff*, the scene of which was set at a farmhouse which Clive and Vanessa Bell had recently taken near West Wittering, he began later that year. It was, he told David Garnett (18 May 1915), 'a horribly melancholy story, ending with a pistol-shot, of course'. On the whole, however, he was unable to concentrate on work that was so entirely removed from the military crisis. He had been approached again during February by H. A. L. Fisher who asked him to contribute another

volume to the Home University Library, this one to be entitled *France*.
There were several good reasons why he might have accepted. It
seemed on the whole a bright journalistic notion; a mere pot-boiling
job occupying some three months in all, and providing him with a useful fifty pounds in advance of royalties. But he refused. At such a time,
when it was so difficult to think of anything but what actually was and
what might be, the degradation, irrelevance and triviality of penning
such a dainty manual for the leisured readership of the upper classes
would have been insupportable.

In the intervals between literary polemics, meals and sleep, he was
now re-reading *War and Peace* (in Constance Garnett's translation)
with ever-increasing admiration and wonder. 'It is an amazing
work,' he told Ottoline (21 August 1915), 'and I really think the best
chance of putting a stop to the War would be to make it obligatory
for everyone to read it at least once a year. In the meantime I
think it ought to be circulated broadcast, though to be sure it would
make rather a bulky pamphlet! But, oh dear me! in between whiles,
what an ass the poor man makes of himself! "Matter and impertinency mixed," but luckily there's a good deal more matter than
impertinency.'

Here then was a subject that could be turned to fine anti-war propaganda, a subject that made *France* seem vague and insubstantial. Perhaps the *Edinburgh Review* would be interested; before he was half-way
through the novel, he had sounded out the editor. 'In a moment of
rashness I wrote to Harold Cox, suggesting that I write an article on
him [Tolstoy],' he told David Garnett (7 August 1915). 'I don't know
whether he'll accept, but if he does it'll be a fearful job – rather like
writing on God. Have you read "Family Happiness" – in the Ivan
Ilytch book? After that, one's left wondering how anyone can dare to
write anything else ever again. And then – one remembers – Dostoievsky!'

As usual, Harold Cox countered Lytton's proposal with one of his
own. Tolstoy, he declared, was out of date. And Lytton, who in the
meantime had been reading Aylmer Maude's biography, experienced
some relief at this preposterous decision. Tolstoy was too mediaeval,
too earnest, too anti-intellectual to suit his kind of neat, Procrustean
treatment. The matter and impertinency were more mixed, too, than he
had originally thought, and a sense of exasperation perpetually mingled
with and confused his admiration. 'I have no patience with a man who
decides to commit suicide because he can't see the object of existence,'
he confided to David Garnett (23 August 1915), 'and then decides not
to because everything becomes clear to him after reading the Gospel

according to St. Mark. But I suppose one may forgive a good deal to the author of War and Peace.'

The immediate outcome of his negotiations with Harold Cox was 'Voltaire and Frederick the Great', which appeared in the *Edinburgh Review* that October. And as so often when he was productively employed, the nightmare of the war temporarily receded. 'My Voltaire-Frederick article occupies me to the exclusion of all else,' he wrote to Ottoline (21 August 1915), 'it is a fearful task, and must be finished by the end of the month. I feel like a negro slave; whenever I look up from my writing table, I seem to see Mr. Harold Cox over my shoulder whirling a cat-o'-nine-tails. Lord have mercy upon us.'

When not involved in writing, and especially at week-ends, Lytton would arrange for himself various social distractions. He visited the Behrends, Ottoline Morrell, and Clive and Vanessa Bell at Eleanor, a small farmhouse standing some fifty yards off from the shore of Chichester Harbour, which had been rented by Professor Tonks of the Slade from his friends St John ('Jack') and Mary Hutchinson.[1] Occasionally, too, he would go up to spend a few days with his family in Hampstead. After his rustic seclusion at The Lacket, the 'Temptations of London' were very hard for him to resist, and in spite of the very best resolutions he seldom got to bed before one o'clock each morning. 'Life here seems to continue in an agreeable manner,' he wrote to David Garnett from Belsize Park Gardens (14 July 1915), 'one can't help feeling rather guilty about it, with these surrounding horrors; but there it is. It's so nice and hot for one thing, and there are so many occupations in this town. One can go from Hampstead Heath to the British Museum, from the British Museum to Gordon Square, from Gordon Square to Treviglio's, from Treviglio's to the Palace to the Café Royal, from the Café Royal to . . . in fact a beneficent Deity appears to have provided suitably for every moment of the day and night. You need not suppose that I am idling: far from it. I am working hard. . . .'

Back at The Lacket there were fewer diversions so that, paradoxically, it was only in the deep peace of the country that he seemed fully vulnerable to fits of acute war pessimism. Paradoxically, too, he found himself becoming more, not less, susceptible to minor domestic inconveniences. The Lacket appeared now to incorporate drawbacks to which he had never been properly alive during the previous year. In the winter, the cold, the wind and the rain were so extreme and incessant that he felt he

[1] Mary Barnes, daughter of Winifred Strachey (who married Sir Hugh Barnes), the fourth child of John Strachey (1823–1907). Her grandfather, Sir John Strachey, was a younger brother of Lytton's father.

might as well be living on the coast of Alaska. The spring of 1914 had been idyllic – 'peonies and poppies in the garden, feathered songsters on every bough, and flannelled Marlborough boys in the middle distance'. But this year it was all very different, full of unforeseen terrors. 'The Spring has set in with all its hatefulness,' he announced to Henry Lamb (6 March 1915). 'It's cold, dank and stuffy at the same time: the birds wake one up at three o'clock in the morning with their incomplete repertories; and Mrs Templeman's fancy turns to thoughts of – I don't know what, but certainly something pretty astringent.' Even the summer came as a total disillusionment. Each week dragged by like seven years of utter desolation, with nothing but a few dismal books to amuse him, and nobody but Mrs Templeman to administer consolation. And to top it all there was the unnatural weather, plunging his already sinking heart down to the very soles of his boots – so hot, so damp, so costively thunderous it was that he felt as if he were living inside a conservatory. Whether or not he had as yet been transformed into a cactus, he couldn't be sure – but after all, what matter did it make if there were no one to admire him? And then, to add to his distress, they did nothing but fire off guns on Salisbury Plain – heavy, massive guns that boomed and boomed, though one knew, of course, all along that this could only be imitation artillery, cardboard cannons that acted as uncomfortable reminders of what, in any case, one could never forget. Slowly, in nervy, inconceivable dreariness, his life seemed to be ebbing past. 'It is fearful – I see that I have muddled the summer completely,' he wrote to Francis Birrell (August 1915). 'I am alone – desolate and destitute – in a country of overhanging thunder clouds and heavy emptiness. I've got so low that I can hardly bear the thought of anything else, like the prisoners who beg not to be let out of their sentence.'

The last few weeks of Lytton's tenancy at The Lacket were, however, crowded with visitors. Pippa and Pernel came down, and so did James with a new girl friend, Alix Sargant-Florence, an ex-Newnham student. Other week-end guests included Roger Fry, E. M. Forster and Clive Bell. Perhaps the most unexpected visitor of all was G. E. Moore. 'I feel that in my present state he'll reduce me to tears with his incredible reasonableness,' Lytton admitted to Francis Birrell (August 1915). 'When I last saw him I asked him whether the war had made any difference to him. He paused for thought, and then said – "None. Why should it?" I asked whether he wasn't horrified by it – at any rate at the beginning. But no; he had never felt anything about it at all.'

Lytton had originally planned to stay on at The Lacket until the beginning of October, thus completing exactly two years there. But

The Lacket

The Mill House, Tidmarsh: painting by Carrington

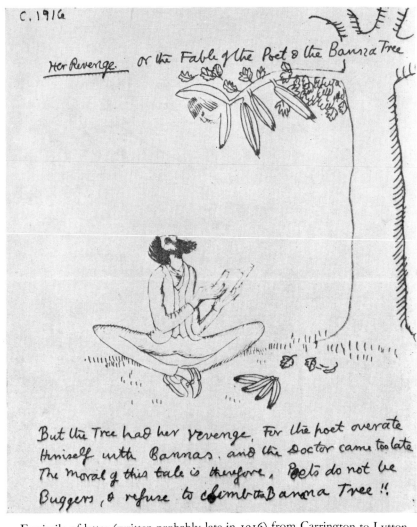

C.1916

Her Revenge.   or the Fable of the Poet & the Banna Tree

But the Tree had her revenge, For the poet overate Himself with Bannas, and the Doctor came too late The moral of this tale is therefore, Poets do not be Buggers, & refuse to climb the Banna Tree !!

Facsimile of letter (written probably late in 1916) from Carrington to Lytton

when an opportunity arose for sub-letting the cottage for the last three weeks of his tenancy, being at this time severely worried by money troubles, he eagerly seized upon it, moving out and back to London in the second week of September. 'By a stroke of genius I got Forster to do my packing up at The Lacket,' he gleefully told James (17 September 1915), 'and actually to transport the 10 million packages to B.P.G. for me!'

While E. M. Forster was humping his two years' accumulation of books and belongings back to Hampstead, Lytton, with a lingering touch of nostalgia, took himself off to a succession of country house parties. 'I'm feeling some twinges of regret, too, at leaving these remote regions,' he confessed to Ottoline (21 August 1915), 'but on the whole I'm not sorry – and anyhow it must be done. Adieu, adieu, adieu, remember me

Your

Lytton.'

CHAPTER IV

War and Peace

'The country is certainly the place for peaceful happiness –
if that's what one wants! I think one wants it about half the
time; and the other half *un*peaceful happiness. But happiness
all the time.'

Lytton Strachey to Lady Ottoline Morrell (24 February 1916)

I

GARSINGTON

Over the spring, summer and autumn months of 1912, Lady Ottoline
Morrell in company with a maid, her six-year-old daughter, and
Bertrand Russell, made a number of trips to Lausanne to consult a
Swiss 'faith doctor' by the name of Combe about her steadily worsen-
ing health. He had prescribed a new and drastic course of treatment out
there, and made other strong recommendations governing her future
life back in England – recommendations that seemed at first even more
devastating to her friends than to Ottoline herself. 'I had a sad blow this
morning from Ottoline (who is returning from Lausanne) to say that
the Combe man has ordered her to retire to the country, and not to
spend more than a week in London for the next 2 years!' Lytton wrote
from The Chestnuts to Henry Lamb in Ireland (9 November 1912).
'I suppose it won't make much difference to you; to me it will be desolating. It was the one centre where I had some chance of seeing amusing
and fresh people – my only non-Cambridge point of rapport in London.
I was looking forward to rushing up from time to time and mingling
with the beau monde! – All dashed. But I'm sure it's the only thing for
her health, and I don't think she'll much mind.'

In a reply to Ottoline herself written the same day, Lytton was
equally frank about the effect this move would have on him. 'I am
altogether écrasé by your new regime,' he declared, '– chiefly from a
selfish point of view – for I am sure it is the one thing to do you real
good, and I think you'll probably on the whole enjoy the country. I

had counted so enormously on Bedford Square for the future that I feel quite shattered. London will be almost a perfect blank now.'

From the depths of the Berkshire countryside, Bedford Square had beckoned to him as the one supremely civilized and illuminated focal point in a grey metropolis. He had only recently established himself there as one of Ottoline's most welcome visitors when now, out of the blue, it would all evaporate into thin air. He felt like a child cheated of some promised treat. The overcrowded and amorphous *salon*, which had offered so much romantic adventure, was to peter out into a mere episode, leading nowhere. For others who lived all their lives in London, this development could not, of course, seem so calamitous – might even appear beneficial. But Lytton felt utterly crushed by the news. 'I am écrasé by the loss of Bedford Square,' he admitted to Virginia Woolf (1 December 1912), 'but I suppose you hardly feel it. I think you've never taken to the caviare.'

This immediate uprush of regret, however, soon abated. Ottoline's imminent move to the country was continually being postponed, until altogether some two and a half years had elapsed, by which time Lytton was returning to his old life in London – a change round that, as it turned out, suited him perfectly. From the very first, Ottoline had had her eye on a certain house which she and Philip Morrell used to pass when they drove out to political meetings from Oxford. 'The vision of this house as we passed it one night touched some spot of desire,' she narrates, 'and I exclaimed, "That is the only country house I could live in." It had a wonderful beauty and mystery.' Accordingly, when this house happened to come up for sale in March 1913, Philip Morrell had gone down and bought it there and then – though he and Ottoline were not allowed to take possession of it until early in 1915. 'So this day our die was cast – for better or worse,' wrote Ottoline in her *Memoirs*. 'That which had been a misty castle was now a solid possession.'

Garsington Manor, as their new home was named, was a Tudor house built in Cotswold stone and set in five hundred acres of ground. Here Ottoline was to live for twelve years, forming her famous Arcadian colony where she resolutely acted out the part of evangelical patroness to the writers and artists of her choice. It was Bedford Square all over again, but on a far more spacious, crazy and spectacular scale. The early months of 1915 she spent supervising the painting and redecoration of the house itself, and the planting of the garden, both of which she re-fashioned after her own inimitable style. By June everything was more or less ready. 'I imagine wonder,' Lytton wrote to her with excitement (June 8 1915), '– ponds, statues, yew hedges, gold paint. . . . I'm sure you needn't be afraid of my Critical Eye – for the simple reason that it won't be able to find anything to criticize!'

Ottoline, however, remained apprehensive over the reaction of her friends to this bold new venture – and with some reason. The mark of her erratic personality was soon stamped firmly and unforgettably on these surroundings, which were of great natural beauty and symmetry. Situated on the slope of a hill, Garsington was screened by farm buildings, and though of noble, even grand proportions with its mullioned windows and steep-pitched roof, the front façade suggested a smaller house than it really was. Only from the ornamental garden which fell away to a converted swimming-pool, scattered with leaves and sheltered by dark yew hedges in which were set galleries of plaster casts, could the full imposing dimensions of the building be properly appreciated. 'Garden-statues lined the terraces; ancient trees surrounded the house,' wrote Peter Quennell describing its splendid and eccentric environs. 'From under the dusty shadow of an ilex would come wandering a dishevelled peacock – like all peacocks, except when they are in love and the quills of the tail, stiffly extended, rattle together with a staccato vibration, it appeared despondent and a little lost; and, after the trailing bird, the hostess might herself emerge. She seemed to trail, as did the bird she followed – in a dress of bottle-green that swept the lawn, trimmed with bands of thick white swansdown bordering the square-cut neck. The large feathered hat that she often assumed was both regal and pleasantly proletarian; for it suggested a portrait of Queen Henrietta Maria but also recalled an Edwardian photograph of a Cockney *élegante* on Hampstead Heath.'

The influence of Ottoline's demonic personality had also permeated the sumptuous decorations of the house. All the available space was littered with strange boxes of incense, cabinets, oriental china, coloured and patterned hangings. The large, low, panelled rooms, formerly a mixture of seventeenth-century and Victorian baronial styles, had undergone glaring alteration. Instead of staining or pickling the wood, she had daubed it with vivid coats of paint, blue and green to match the colour of her eyes, and, in the case of the sitting-room (from the central beam of which was suspended a cardinal bird in a lacquer cage) Chinese scarlet, which occasionally matched her hair. 'The oak panelling', David Garnett records, 'had been painted a dark peacock blue-green; the bare and sombre dignity of Elizabethan wood and stone had been overwhelmed with an almost oriental magnificence: the luxuries of silk curtains and Persian carpets, cushions and pouffes. Ottoline's pack of pug dogs trotted everywhere and added to the Beardsley quality, which was one half of her natural taste. The characteristic of every house in which Ottoline lived was its smell and the smell of Garsington was stronger than that of Bedford Square. It reeked of the bowls of pot-pourri and orris-root which stood on every mantelpiece, side table and window-sill and of the desiccated oranges, studied with cloves, which Ottoline loved making. The walls were covered with a variety of pictures. Italian pictures and bric-à-brac, drawings by John, water-colours for fans by Conder, who was rumoured to have been one of Ottoline's first conquests, paintings by Duncan and [Mark] Gertler and a dozen other of the younger artists.'

The celebrated Renaissance court over which Ottoline presided amid this ornate, other-worldly environment was soon the Mecca of all aspiring young writers and artists. And from being a highly fashionable meeting-place, Garsington was quickly transformed into a cultural legend. During the war years, and for some considerable time after-wards, Lytton was one of the most frequent guests here. At week-ends especially, he and other members of the Bloomsbury Group could with-draw from the ugly turbulence of London or emerge from the natural solitude of the country into the artificially rustic atmosphere which Ottoline cultivated. And here, by way of relaxation, they threw them-selves into the plays and *tableaux vivants* which formed a regular feature of Garsington entertainment. For Lytton such pastimes held a nostalgic appeal, and in the community at Garsington he hoped to dis-cover what he had failed to make permanent at Cambridge, a congenial home from home.

As a weird and flamboyant extension to Ottoline's odd temperament, Garsington both disconcerted and fascinated him. From the first, its garish novelty took his breath away. It was splendid and ridiculous, admirable and exasperating; and he continued to feel half-captivated by it, half-embarrassed. Though he appreciated a degree of sophistication in human relationships, he also responded to the simple, vegetable things of the universe, the trees, the open fields and the wild flowers of the country. Behind the silvery-grey stone front, the lofty elms and tall iron gates of Garsington, he entered an improbable world where sophistication and simplicity were incoherently mixed up. 'Only is the sunlight ever normal at Garsington?' Virginia Woolf once wrote to Barbara Bagenal. 'No I think even the sky is done up in pale yellow silk, and certainly the cabbages are scented.'

Max Beerbohm once likened Lytton's ageing mother to Madame du Deffand in the last period of her life; blind, still vivacious – though unable to understand young people – still a very fount of wit – yet profoundly sceptical – set fast in her literary prejudices and enthusiasms, and out of touch with the movement of contemporary life. In Ottoline,

Lytton himself thought he recognized an approximation to Madame du Deffand at the prime of her life. In Bedford Square he had looked to find re-created the atmosphere of unparalleled amenity which reigned in the drawing-room of the Convent of St Joseph. At Garsington he pictured another Sceaux 'with its endless succession of entertainments and conversations – supper-parties and water-parties, concerts and masked balls, plays in the little theatre and picnics under the great trees of the park'. It was here especially that Lytton wished to see Ottoline come to her full maturity and establish her pre-eminent position as one of the great leaders of contemporary English society. It was here –where Asquith (then prime minister), entering on one occasion with Maynard Keynes, was announced as 'Mr Keynes and another gentleman' – that literature and the arts could secure their true level of importance. It was here that Bloomsbury could mingle with the floating company of diplomats and aristocrats, fine ladies and their distinguished escorts, as in eighteenth-century France. And together, this *élite* of the nation could practise 'those difficult arts which make the wheels of human intercourse run smoothly – the arts of tact and temper, of frankness and sympathy, of delicate compliment and exquisite self-abnegation'. Through their literature, their art, their polished manners, they would be an example and an inspiration to the civilized world. Their gay company should even now hold its own as a subject for conversation with the battle of the Somme or the rout of the Germans at Jutland. At last the artist would rise to his rightful place in society. But though honoured by this world of high birth and aristocratic urbanity, he must never be its minion, so that his creations, while reflecting the finest social ideals of the times, would escape the worst faults of persons of rank – superficiality and amateurishness. His literature would be remarkable for precisely the contrary qualities – for the solidity of its psychological foundations and for the supreme excellence of its craftsmanship. Like the court of Louis XIV, Garsington was to bring into prominence the work of the profound and subtle artist who, while beneficently encircled by a select, leisured, illustrious and critical audience, yet retained the larger outlook and sense of proportion that had come to him from his own restless experience of life. This perhaps was Lytton's dream.

The reality turned out to be rather different. Long before it had moved back to London again, the company which met at Garsington seemed to have the hand of death upon it. The radiant atmosphere of Sceaux was only parodied. The arts of tact and temper proved far beyond the placatory powers of Lady Ottoline. Her exalted devotion to the arts was too indiscriminate, too unrestrained; her humour, seldom exercised at her own expense, was too malicious; her love of power, her possessiveness, embroiled at one time or another almost everyone, and grew into a poisonous obsession that hung over Garsington like a storm cloud. Instead of recapturing the graceful, easy motions of Madame du Deffand's *salon* – like those of 'dancers balanced on skates, gliding, twirling, interlacing, over the thinnest ice' – they floundered and pushed and pulled in a bedlam of conflicting egotisms, released as sudden tempests of altercation, as the cold wind of spiteful gossip or the blustering, dismal rain of envious bickering. Even in the calmer moments, it was not delicate compliment, exquisite self-abnegation that were practised, but the perpetual rumour of machination and intrigue, which bubbled and boiled below the surface of their gatherings.

Lytton first visited Garsington with Duncan Grant and Vanessa Bell in the second week of July. His Critical Eye soon found much to fix upon. 'It was not particularly enchanting,' he wrote to David Garnett (14 July 1915). 'Such fussifications going on all the time – material, mental, spiritual – and at the same time quite indefinite. *Dona nobis pacem, dona nobis pacem*, was all I could murmur. The house is a regular galanty-show, whatever that may be; very like Ottoline herself, in fact – very remarkable, very impressive, patched, gilded and preposterous. The Bedford Square interior does not suit an Elizabethan Manor house in the wilds of Oxfordshire. It has all been reproduced, and indeed redoubled. The pianola, too, with Philip, infinitely Philipine, performing, and acrobatic dances on the lawn. In despair I went to bed, and was woken up by a procession circumnavigating my bed, candles in hand . . . the rear brought up by the Witch of Endor. Oh! *Dona nobis pacem*!'

To Ottoline herself Lytton sent off a letter by the same post telling her how much he had enjoyed Garsington. He felt, he said, rejuvenated by the delightful company, the pleasing ambience of her new house. And to prove that this was not just formal politeness, he invited himself back there a fortnight later.

The other guests on this second visit were Clive Bell and Mary Hutchinson, a young Slade student, Barbara Hiles, and an ex-Newnham undergraduate, Faith Bagenal. The two latter were encouraged to scamper off together for most of the time, leaving their elders to discourse learnedly among themselves on life and literature. The hurly-burly, jamboree atmosphere swirled about them even more preposterously than before, and was given full throat by Clive Bell's raucous high-spirits. 'Somehow I feel horribly lonely on this occasion: a sort of eighteenth century grim gaiety comes upon me, and I can hardly distinguish people from pugs,' Lytton confided to David Garnett (25 July 1915). 'I wish they'd all turn into embroidered parrots, neatly framed and hanging on the wall – but they won't; they will keep prancing round, snorting, and (one after another) trying to jump up into one's lap. It's most tiresome – one pushes them down in vain – the wriggling wretches! . . .

'Since beginning this I've already had three visitations from the pug-world – and now I must go down on to the lawn, and have tea with them all, and practise my grim gaiety again with them, as if I were a M. le Marquis circa 1770. What fun it would be to be one really! – Or at least infinitely convenient. But I'm not. I'm circa 1915 or nothing. . . .'

To Ottoline he then (31 July 1915) wrote off to express the 'gratitude and delight' with which her hospitality had overwhelmed him. His short stay had been exhilarating. 'I find even my vigorous health taking on new forces, so that I am seen bounding along the glades of Hampstead like a gazelle or a Special Constable.' He was looking forward, so he assured her, to many more adventurous week-ends at Garsington. 'I shall come again,' the letter concluded.

In the following years he did go there again, very often, and almost always left behind him the same backwash of alternating flattery and complaint. Many of these complaints, which were perfectly genuine if sometimes exaggerated, arose from invitations which he himself had sponsored quite voluntarily. For he seems to have felt that by ridiculing Ottoline as a perpetual hostess, he would avert ridicule from himself as an inexplicably persistent guest. Virginia Woolf, who was the recipient of so many of Lytton's lampoons on Ottoline, was puzzled by this behaviour. Why ever did he continue to visit Garsington? Were his feelings really so bitter and uninvolved as he liked to make out? Or was this blasé attitude merely put on so as to cover up other, more romantic feelings of which he was ashamed? Perhaps he went on turning up there out of an excess of politeness, a superficial show of kindness to someone who seemed on the verge of spiritual and physical disintegration. 'I suppose the danger lies in becoming too kind,' she wrote to him inquisitively (14 September 1919). 'I think you're a little inclined that way already – take the case of Ottoline. It seems to me a dark one.'

But really it was less dark than she liked to imagine. Part of the fascination of Garsington lay in never knowing whom you would find there. The prolongation of Lytton's visits, with their sheer, inevitable boredom and troughs of acute anti-climax, represented a triumph of that wistful, fanciful strain within him over the more common-sense, down-to-earth side of his nature. 'Mr. Strachey is the eighteenth century grown up,' Aldous Huxley once wrote in a review of *Books and*

Characters, 'he is Voltaire at two hundred and thirty.' But if he was a superannuated Voltaire, then Ottoline should be cast as a would-be, reincarnated Madame de Châtelet. Lytton had dreamed of resurrecting the past as it appeared to him through the magic lens of retrospect. His sustained and incessant trips to this apogee of Garsington reveal the tenacity with which he clung to these impossible dreams, to the scenes of such imagined graces and delights.

On leaving The Lacket, Lytton went off to stay with the St John Hutchinsons at Eleanor, their house at West Wittering near Chichester, where he enjoyed himself a good deal doing nothing in particular and no writing whatsoever except a single letter to Ottoline asking himself back again to Garsington. He arrived there, from Eleanor, on 16 September, 'and shall probably stay about a week,' he notified Pippa (17 September 1915). 'It is deliciously hot, and it is nice sitting out on the lawn; but there are still too many pugs in the house, and Iris Tree is at the present moment reading her poems aloud to Bertrand Russell, and I feel that my turn will come next.'

To record the joys of this latest Garsington sojourn, Lytton told Ottoline, were a task beyond even 'the tongues of angels', and it was 'amid inward lamentations' that he left for the desolate regions of Ledbury. 'I wish I could rush back to Garsington helter-skelter,' he protested (28 September 1915). 'If you ever hear a faint sigh or an unusual creak when you open the door, you will know that it is my departed spirit still fluttering about, and revisiting the haunts of its youth.'

Life at Park Cottage with his mother and his aunt, the ever-vigorous Lady Colvile, was a startling change from Garsington. After Bertrand Russell, pacifism, poetry and *tout ce qu'il-y-a de plus moderne*, he was plunged into the strange antique world of county ladies and important gentry, who looked on him considerably askance, asked him whether he didn't think Russell a crank, pronounced Mrs Asquith to be in the pay of the Germans, and roundly declared that the country was going to the dogs. At the same time they fussed continuously over him with hot water bottles and second helpings and inquiries as to whether the buttered toast was done *exactly* to his taste, and were at once so kind, and so militant, that he sensed their happiness would be made complete only when they could persuade him to have an extra egg at breakfast and be certain that all the inhabitants of Germany would shortly be massacred in torment. 'Deans, Dowagers and retired Admirals reign supreme,' he wrote to James (3 October 1915), 'with various curates, organists, and female toadies filling up the interstices. It's all very very

F*

wicked of course, and how I keep silent I hardly know – except that nobody ever dreams of imagining that I might say anything. Lady C. is indomitable – dashing for miles in motors – and the food is very good – and there are several nice dull *books* to read . . . otherwise . . .'

Now that he had given up The Lacket, those restless, post-Cambridge years of wandering seemed to be reasserting themselves once more. He had no home but Hampstead, and his antipathy to communal family life was as strong as ever. From Ledbury he travelled on for a few days to Lyndhurst, and from here he went to stay with Augustus and Dorelia John at Alderney Manor, not very far from Henry Forde's school in Parkstone. He had hoped after this to return yet again to Garsington, but was suddenly struck down by illness and obliged to limp back to Belsize Park Gardens, 'apparently for the rest of my unnatural life', as he put it to Keynes (4 November 1915). 'The fog has descended in force and the shadow of Death reigns,' he wrote gloomily to James on his arrival there (19 October 1915). '. . . The comble was reached last night, when very nearly all the lights were put out, which combined with the fog produced complete darkness. In the streets of Soho one might have been on a Yorkshire Moor for all one could see to the contrary. How the human spirit manages to flicker even as faintly as it does is a mystery.'

2

SEX, CENSORSHIP AND D. H. LAWRENCE

During the autumn and late winter of 1915, the war hysteria had grown palpably more fanatical, and was being ventilated throughout London in a manner that recalled to Lytton the most septic hypocrisies of Victorian England. Truth, it has been said, is invariably the first casualty of war, and humour the second. In their place there now flourished a false, pugnacious sentimentality which had its root in repressed fear. Popular bigotry and fervour, widely championed by the patrio-sadistic reporting of the Press, was quickly fanned to a new intensity by the engines of official war propaganda. Everywhere were pasted up posters depicting alleged and mythical German atrocities, and these had lately been reinforced by others which were designed to stimulate the patriotic militancy of civilians, and which succeeded in arousing the unmitigated scorn of the front line troops. 'Women of Britain say – GO!' one caption read; but it was hardly the sort of call to inspire Lytton. He was astonished, almost awed by the sentimental ingenuity of mottoes such as 'Go! It's your Duty, Lad' (illustrated by a proud white-haired little old lady ushering her equally proud, debonair son into the ranks of the army); or the classic 'Daddy, what did YOU do in the Great War?' (a plainly guilt-ridden, civilian paterfamilias being interrogated by his young daughter perched trustingly on his knee, while his son plays innocently at soldiers on the floor near by).

It was the autumn of the Gallipoli failure, of the first large Zeppelin air raids, of the collapse of the Asquith Cabinet. The bishop of London, referring to the war as the greatest fight ever made for the Christian religion – 'the choice between the nailed hand and the mailed fist' – went on to state that 'there must be a kind of glorying in London at being allowed to take our little share of danger in the Zeppelin raids'. In the sphere of literature, the most dramatic event of these months was the successful prosecution and suppression of D. H. Lawrence's novel, *The Rainbow*, ostensibly on the grounds of obscenity but actually because of its denunciation of war. In times of national crisis the film of imbecility upon the ocean of life thickens appreciably, and the sentiments expressed by established men of letters does nothing to suggest that the incidence of fools among writers is any less high than in other professions. A good idea of the swollen confusion of mind now fashionable among the authorities may be gained from statements made by some notable literary figures. J. C. Squire, writing under the pseudonym of 'Solomon Eagle' in the *New Statesman*, suggested that D. H. Lawrence might be 'under the spell of German psychologists'. Augustine Birrell, the belletrist, in private conversation at Garsington, expressed surprise at so much fuss over the soldiery: 'After all,' he pointed out, 'the men out there will be returning some day.' In a public speech, however, delivered in his capacity as Chief Secretary for Ireland and a cabinet minister, his attitude was less casual, and he roundly declared that he, for one, would 'forbid the use, during the war, of poetry'. The belligerent zealotry of those proponents of war safely behind the lines – symbolized by the giving of white feathers to men in civilian clothes – and the unctuous Christian philosophizing extended to those who were risking their lives at the front, sickened Lytton. He felt himself to be more of a misfit and outsider than at any time since going up to Cambridge, and his attitude reverted to its most hostile and embittered.

The principal target for his rancour at this time was Scotland Yard's confiscation of *The Rainbow*. Though Lytton felt little affinity for Lawrence, and did not like his novel, he was compelled to support his cause. He interpreted the court case as yet another pitched battle between the powers of darkness and light, and many of his pacifist friends appeared to share this belief. Philip Morrell raised questions about the book's suppression in Parliament; and Lytton himself wrote off to the *New Statesman* an ironic letter in favour of the suppression, which was itself suppressed by the editor. 'It seems strange that they [the police] should have the leisure and energy for that sort of activity at the present moment,' he commented in a letter to David Garnett (10 November 1915). 'But no doubt the authorities want to show us that England stands for Liberty. Clive is trying to get up an agitation about it in the newspapers but I doubt if he'll have much success. We interviewed that little worm Jack Squire, who quite failed to see the point: he thought that as in his opinion the book wasn't a good one it was difficult for him to complain about its suppression. Damn his eyes! In vain we pointed out that it was a question of principle, and that whether that particular book was good or mediocre was irrelevant – he couldn't see it. At last, however, he agreed to say a few words about it in his blasted paper – on one condition – that the book had not been suppressed because it mentioned sapphism – he had heard that that was the reason – and in that case, well, of course, it was quite impossible for the *New Statesman* to defend perversity.'

Earlier that year David Garnett had introduced Lawrence to his Bloomsbury friends, and with disastrous consequences. 'To hear these young people talk', Lawrence complained to Ottoline, 'fills me with black fury: they talk endlessly – and never, never a good thing said. They are cased each in a hard little shell of his own and out of this they talk words.' And to Garnett himself Lawrence confessed that these friends of his 'sent me mad with misery and hostility and rage'. Garnett had then decided that, since he could not continue to see Lawrence and still count Francis Birrell, Duncan Grant, Maynard Keynes and Lytton among his companions, he had better have nothing more to do with Lawrence. This decision was hardly surprising. For although, at first sight, he might not appear to be a very typical member of Bloomsbury, Garnett had more in common with some of this group than he could ever have had with Lawrence. His animal spirits were strong and surprisingly various, while Lawrence's doubtful claim to be *'grand animal'* was little more than an expression of his wish to cut free from the strangulated, back-to-the-womb atrophy of his relationship with women. The Lawrentian cult of the dark primeval wild beast, involving a loss of responsible human identity, seemed far more rhapsodically unrestrained than Garnett's humanized and domesticated animal world, which represented for him an extension, not an abandonment, of the physical province of human beings. Lawrence, had he taken Garnett's woman-into-animal metamorphosis seriously, would have found it stifling and unendurable. As it was, he later dismissed *Lady into Fox* as 'mere playboy stuff', or, in other words, more Bloomsbury verbiage, empty and meaningless.

Although Lawrence had met his brother James and two of his sisters at Cambridge, he had never in fact seen Lytton himself until, by an unexpected coincidence, they encountered each other one Friday night early that November at a party held just off the Earls Court Road, in the studio of Dorothy Brett, the painter.[1] Lytton had been invited only indirectly as the dinner-guest of the St John Hutchinsons. Arriving there late, he was immediately thrust into the centre of a large and very miscellaneous crowd – Brett herself, looking, with her *retroussé* nose and childish hands, about seventeen (less than half her age), and spoken of as the 'virgin aunt' of her two constant companions, the wild and energetic painter Mark Gertler, who rushed about the room acting as assistant-host, and Dora Carrington 'like a wild moorland pony', as Ottoline once described her, 'with a shock of fair hair, uncertain and elusive eyes, rather awkward in her movements', standing speechless next to a large silent dog. While poor Brett, terribly deaf, laboured energetically at the pianola, her drunken guests disported themselves round the studio. 'Some seemed strangely vulgar,' Lytton afterwards told James (8 November 1915), 'dreadful women on divans trying to persuade dreadful men to kiss them, in foreign accents (apparently put on for the occasion).'

Among this jumble of humanity one couple claimed Lytton's particular attention – D. H. Lawrence and his German wife Frieda, who spent most of the time dancing with Clive Bell. 'There were a great many people I didn't know at all,' Lytton wrote to David Garnett (10 November 1915), 'and others whom I only knew by repute, among the latter, the Lawrences, whom I examined carefully and closely for several hours, though I didn't venture to have myself introduced. I was surprised to find that I liked her looks very much – she actually seemed

[1] 'I really did not like Lytton Strachey,' Dorothy Brett told the author (9 March 1966). 'First of all he was so unpleasant to look at, to put it mildly, and he was secretively obscene. I did not know him intimately, I used to meet him at week-end parties at Garsington, at parties in London. He was of delicate health, but as far as I could make out not delicate minded . . . I can remember an amusing incident at Garsington, when Lytton complained that Ottoline was stingy with the food. So the next morning, as a sort of ironical swatt at him, Ottoline had a breakfast sent up, consisting of eggs, sausages, bacon, mounds of toast, etc. To her chagrin he ate it all!! From that day he was stuffed with food. . . . The Bloomsburies scared me to death. I was much closer to Lawrence, Murry, Katherine, Gertler, who were not Bloomsburies. Virginia Woolf was the only one at all nice to me. I was a great nuisance with my deafness. I missed so much which irritated everybody. . . . There was something to me creepy about Lytton. I have no objection to homosexuals, no prejudices whatsoever, maybe it was just his looks, I don't know.'

(there's no other word for it) a lady: as for him I've rarely seen anyone so pathetic, miserable, ill, and obviously devoured by internal distresses. He behaved to everyone with the greatest cordiality, but I noticed for a second a look of intense disgust and hatred flash into his face ... caused by – ah! – whom? Katherine Mansfield was also there, and took my fancy a good deal.'

Lawrence's and Lytton's mutual aversion seems to have been aggravated by their many points of apparent similarity. With their reddish beards and their puny bodies, their crippling physical infirmities, their irritated contempt for ordinary men and women and intense internal envy of those vaulted up into high positions, their love of travelling – of 'moving on' – and their years of struggle to disburden themselves from the very different but pervasive influence of their mothers, each one seemed to stand as a painful caricature of the other's least admirable qualities. But it was their wide dissimilarity, especially of background, which cast their work into such opposing, incompatible forms, and which has posthumously led to the see-saw of their literary reputations. At any point in time, when one is venerated, the other, as if by some natural law of physics, will always be underrated. 'The poetic inspiration of an age', Lytton wrote in one of his *Spectator* reviews, 'seems to follow what may be called, for want of a better term, a nation's "centre of gravity". With the Elizabethans the centre of gravity was among the middle classes – the country gentleman like Drake or Raleigh, the country yeoman like Shakespeare, and the university scholars like Marlowe and Ben Jonson. After the Restoration the centre of gravity moved more and more rapidly towards the aristocracy, until at the beginning of the eighteenth century it became fixed in the great Whig families who had achieved the Revolution. And simultaneously literature took on the qualities of aristocracy, grew refined, brilliant, and ordered, and concerned itself exclusively with the life of London drawing-rooms.'

It is in just such an atmosphere of ordered refinement and aristocratic glitter that the main body of Lytton's work has been most readily appreciated. His natural medium as a writer was the essay, that drawing-room form of literature quaintly supposed these days to have been accompanied by a tinkle of tea-cups and the titter of well-bred amusement. The centre of gravity since and even during Lytton's time has moved away again from the drawing-rooms of the aristocracy, and taken new root in the industrial surroundings of the lower-middle and working classes. The democracy of Dickens, considered so vulgar in his own life, was made acceptable, even popular, by the inspired advocacy of G. K. Chesterton. The social 'message' of Lawrence himself has been disseminated through the schools and universities by the overwrought punditry of Dr Leavis and his educationalist disciples, and has culminated in a mood of fashionable and strident, left-wing 'moral' attitudinizing that would probably have been unpleasing to Lawrence and pure anathema certainly to Lytton.

The war, which crumbled the cement of Victorian standards into disused rubble and opened up unmendable fissures in the gilded Edwardian way of life, had the effect of quickening and distorting an inevitable upheaval of existing habits and traditions. A new dispensation slowly emerged. The political emancipation of women, the equalizing tax structure, the consolidation of the working class, the rise of collectivism and State control, the growth of the Labour Party, the changes in dress, manners and public attitudes to questions of morality, all helped to reform the fabric of class-relationships. These were the raw materials, so chaotically thrown together, for the architecture of a reorganized system of society. Yet in the immediate aftermath of the war, during the early 1920s, it seemed as if the poetic inspiration might again reside with the upper-middle class. The old order began to re-establish itself – but only briefly. The restoration of the aristocracy was never accomplished. Instead, an enormous, shapeless social transformation gradually came about, and history became increasingly a matter controlled by a heterogeneous group of men – the so-called meritocracy. By the time of his death, Lytton had already lost some of his high literary prestige, for he had gained his brilliant success by those very qualities that were to ensure his equally swift downfall. Marx and Freud, the two chief opposing influences on the humanities over the next thirty years, were both really inimical to Lytton's talent, and his belated endeavour to align himself with the latter in his *Elizabeth and Essex* may partly account for the comparative failure of that book.

Under such conditions the reputation of Lawrence has swollen disproportionately; that of Lytton shrivelled away too far. For Lawrence was like a man digging up with careless frenzy huge trenches of black useless earth, but every so often coming across a whole, rough nugget of gold. While the meticulous and skilful Lytton, crouched over a near-by stream, pans with methodical precision his few ounces of precious metal, peering all the time through his spectacles to assure himself that not even the faintest yellow speck has escaped his vigilance.

It was appropriate, however, that Lawrence and Lytton should meet during the war, the artificial conditions of which had temporarily made them into wary and grudging allies. In reaction from their smashed-up hopes and ideals, both sought to promote the same sort of revolution – a fierce, undismayed assertion of social and personal liberty – and subscribed to a short-lived, scatter-brained venture in the form of a fortnightly periodical entitled *The Signature* – fathered on the luckless and quixotic Middleton Murry. It was fitting, too, that as fellow guests at Brett's party they should never speak to each other or be formally introduced. They had come, momentarily and coincidentally, to the same point from two altogether different directions, and after this intersection the graph of their careers was again to veer off on two totally divergent courses. And so, though he carefully observed Lawrence, Lytton had nothing to do with him personally, and left the party surrounded by his own gay set. 'When it was time to go, we went with Iris [Tree],' he wrote to James (8 November 1915), 'and emerged upon the pitchblack Cromwell Road at half past one, Iris wildly whistling with her fingers in her mouth for taxis, rushing in front of them to stop them, and then, when they turned out to be full, leaping on to the footboard, and whirling off . . . it was a wild scene.'

3

CONSCRIPTION

'My life here has been rather dissipated of late,' Lytton wrote to David Garnett from Belsize Park Gardens (8 November 1915), '– and very idle.' One of his chief dissipations during these doldrum days was the reopening of his German lessons, now under the supervision of an astringent English spinster in Mecklenburgh Square, whom he called on once a week. In the intervals he would struggle with Heine; but it proved uphill work. He was too indolent and naturally inept at speaking languages to make much headway – besides which, German was a horribly difficult tongue to master. Apart from this 'I am also engaged on a short life of Dr. Arnold (of Rugby),' he wrote to his mother (12 December 1915), who was spending the winter in Menton, 'which is a distinctly lugubrious business, though my hope is to produce something out of it which may be entertaining. He was a self-righteous blockhead, but unlike most of his kind, with enough energy and determination in him to do a good deal of damage – as our blessed Public Schools bear witness!'

His progress with 'Dr Arnold' during this winter was scarcely more spectacular than his German tuition, and except for two *New Statesman* reviews he wrote little for publication. Yet it was an active, if unproductive winter. Political worries agitated and exhausted him, and his moods of melancholy were further deepened by various pestilential diseases which crowded in upon him – indigestions, coughs and colds – and an unfortunate accident when, in a moment of distraction, he walked straight into a lamp post, crashing his forehead against it with maximum velocity. 'I have been in such a sluggish, deathly state for the last – I don't know how many months!' he complained to Virginia Woolf (25 February 1916). 'Malebolge,[1] I think it must be. And the worst of it is that these torpors do not entirely overcome one – if they did one would at any rate be unaware of one's horrid state; but they leave one conscious – hideously conscious – of one's utter damnation.'

To shake off this feeling of apathy and damnation he now embarked on a wild life of entertainment, hurrying from party to party, his late hours growing ever later night by night. Soon, this social life had become almost too exigent – but he could not resist it. 'The London whirlpool is, as usual, very trifling when looked at in detail, but none the less absorbing on the whole,' he told Francis Birrell (November 1915). 'I rush from Hampstead to Bloomsbury, from Bloomsbury to Chelsea. I go to concerts, Music Halls, and the Café Royal. I attend lectures by Maynard and Mr. Shaw. The latter function was an odd one. Bertie in the chair, and a large audience eager for a pacifist oration and all that's most advanced – and poor dear Mr. Shaw talking about "England" with trembling lips and gleaming eyes, and declaring that his one wish was that we should first beat the Germans, and then fight them again, and then beat them again, and again, and again! He was more like a nice old-fashioned Admiral on a quarter-deck than anything else. And the newspapers are so stupid that, simply because he's Mr. Shaw, they won't report him – instead of running him as our leading patriot.'

The murky streets of London, so invitingly blacked out now at night, had grown extraordinarily attractive to him. 'How I adore the romance and agitation of them!' he exclaimed in a letter to Ottoline (21 January 1916). 'Almost too much I fear!' Periodically he would feel the need for the more peaceful enjoyments of the country, and he spent several week-ends with Clive and Vanessa Bell at Eleanor, and with Leonard and Virginia Woolf down at Asheham. But most of his country visitations were to Garsington. Although he seldom stayed for longer than a single week, his retreats there at this time were particularly frequent. The fresh country air, the luxurious living, good food and sympathetic quietude (at least during the weekdays) were, so he apologetically informed his friends, beneficial to his health.

It came as no surprise, then, that it was with Ottoline that he chose to spend the Christmas holidays. 'There has been a nice party here,

[1] The Eighth Circle of Dante's *Inferno*.

including the Bells and Keynes,' he wrote from Garsington to his mother (28 December 1915); 'it is a comfortable house, and the country round about is most beautiful – very hilly and romantic – and very unlike the dull flat expanses in the immediate neighbourhood of Oxford. On Christmas day there was a grand festivity in one of the barns, which was rigged up with decorations on a Christmas tree, and all the children in the village came and had tea there. It was really a wonderful affair. There were over a hundred children, and each one had a present from the tree; they were of course delighted – especially as they had never known anything of the kind before, since hitherto there haven't been any "gentry" in the village. Every detail was arranged by Ottoline, whose energy and good-nature are astonishing. Then in the evening there was a little dance here, with the servants and some of the farmers' daughters, etc. which was great fun, her Ladyship throwing herself into it with tremendous brio. It takes a daughter of a thousand Earls to carry things off in that manner.'

'How very kind Lady Ottoline is,' Lady Strachey replied. 'I am most grateful to her.'

Much of the talk during these winter weeks centred around conscription. To solve the difficult task of bringing enough men to the colours, within a country the bulk of whose population was still believed to be hostile to the idea of universal military service, the Government had, in October 1915, started the notorious Derby Scheme. This was a voluntary plan, on the continental pattern, the purpose of which was to persuade men of serviceable age to 'attest' – that is, to undertake to join up whenever called upon to do so – by means of a moral and not a legal obligation. At Asheham and Garsington, the Bloomsbury Group would assemble at week-ends to debate the situation, the nucleus of these gatherings consisting, besides Lytton himself, of Clive Bell, Vanessa Bell and Duncan Grant and Maynard Keynes, David Garnett, and Harry Norton. Almost all of them were opposed to the type of blandishment and blackmail on which the Derby Scheme operated, and felt alarmed by the compulsory conscription that was threatened if this scheme failed. 'The conscription crisis has been agitating these quarters considerably,' Lytton wrote to James from Garsington as early as 23 September; 'but the comments have not been particularly illuminating. Some say that Lloyd George is verging towards the madhouse cell. Others affirm that E. Grey is "immovable" against conscription. Personally I feel despondent – about that and most other things.'

By December, the Derby Scheme had failed, and, in the first week of January, the Government introduced their Military Service Bill, under which all single men were automatically deemed to have enlisted and been transferred to the Reserve, from which they could be called up when needed. The Labour members of the Coalition Government threatened resignation – then withdrew their threat. Nothing then stood in the way of the Bill – yet Lytton still hoped for some last-minute miracle, some nationwide uprising against it. 'Philip [Morrell] now seems to think that it may take a fortnight or even 3 weeks getting through the Committee stage,' he informed James; 'and in that case isn't it still possible that something should be done? Surely there ought to be a continual stream of leaflets and pamphlets. Also if possible meetings all over the country, and signatures collected against the Bill.'

To help disseminate this type of anti-conscription propaganda, Lytton at once joined the No Conscription Fellowship or N.C.F. as it was usually called, and the National Council against Conscription, or N.C.C. – the two societies that had been formed to resist the Act, to campaign for pacifism, and, subsequently, to urge that out-and-out conscientious objectors, or 'absolutists', should be given unconditional exemption from participating in the war, instead of being forced either into prison or into government occupations. Several other members of Bloomsbury, among them David Garnett, Duncan Grant, Vanessa Bell, Adrian Stephen, R. C. Trevelyan and James Strachey – recently sacked from the *Spectator* by the militaristic St Loe – assisted at the N.C.C. offices in Bride Lane, addressing envelopes, sticking on stamps, and writing leaflets. One of these, which stated that the Government's motive for bringing in compulsory service was to prevent strikes and crush labour, created a considerable stir. This was Leaflet No. 3, drawn up by Lytton, who, as so often when dealing with an immediate practical situation, resorted to allegory.

CONSCRIPTION

WHY they want it, and why they say they want it.

THEY SAY THEY WANT IT to punish the slackers
THEY WANT IT to punish the strikers.

THEY SAY THEY WANT IT to crush Germany
THEY WANT IT to crush labour.

THEY SAY THEY WANT IT to free Europe
THEY WANT IT to enslave England.

DON'T LET THEM GET WHAT THEY WANT
BECAUSE THEY KEEP SAYING THEY WANT
SOMETHING DIFFERENT.

The Cat kept saying to the Mouse that she was a high-minded person, and if the Mouse would only come a little nearer they could both get the cheese.

The Mouse said 'Thank you Pussy, it's not the cheese you want; it's my skin!'

Shortly after this leaflet had been printed, H. W. Massingham[1] saw it, decided it was seditious, and rushed round to the Bride Lane office to get it withdrawn from circulation. Sir John Simon, who had resigned from the Cabinet to lead the opposition to the Military Service Bill, and who, according to Maynard Keynes, was rather regretting his hasty and unpopular decision, also disapproved very violently of this piece of propaganda. And so it was agreed to send out no further copies, though, since half a million had by then been distributed, this decision came rather late in the day. *The Morning Post*, in any case, had already got hold of a copy and blazoned a long, angry article about pacifist propaganda in general. After quoting some sentences from Lytton's leaflet, the paper demanded: 'Would it be possible to imagine a more wanton and malicious indulgence in false witness?' There seemed no intelligible point of contact between the two sides. On reading the article Lytton commented with quiet indulgence to Ottoline: 'Queer fellows they are.'

Amid all the infuriate pessimism of this losing campaign, it was a great comfort for Lytton to find himself in a solid phalanx of agreement with his friends. Bloomsbury, as a whole, believed that the war had been started to refute militarism, and that to establish it now in England expressly contradicted our original and honourable intentions. Distrusting deeply the political management of the war, they favoured, from 1916 onwards, the policy of a negotiated peace settlement.

Lytton's own views, which surreptitiously found their way into much of what he wrote during these years, were strong and uncompromising. In his prepared statement as a conscientious objector, he explained his attitude in language that is unusually well-defined and explicit. Before 1914, he declared, 'I was principally concerned with literary and speculative matters; but, with the war, the supreme importance of international questions has been forced upon my attention. My opinions have been for many years strongly critical of the whole structure of society; and after a study of the diplomatic situation, and of the literature, both controversial and philosophic, arising out of the war, they developed naturally into those I now hold. My convictions as to my duty with regard to the war have not been formed either

[1] H. W. Massingham (1860–1924), the famous editor of the *Nation*.

rashly or lightly; and I shall not act against these convictions whatever the consequences may be.'

Among the men in command of political operations, none were any longer moved by philosophical ideals towards noble aims. Woodrow Wilson meant well, but was a simpleton; Clemenceau appeared to be no more than a worldly and ambitious cynic; and as for Lloyd George, Lytton's one ardent desire, he told Francis Birrell, was that, once the war had ended, the prime minister should be publicly castrated – if possible at the foot of Nurse Cavell's statue. Nor did Churchill inspire him with any confidence – a fact which he recorded in a Blakean epigram:

> *Though Time from History's pages much may blot,*
> *Some things there are can never be forgot;*
> *And in Gallipoli's delicious name,*
> *Wxxxxxx, your own shall find eternal fame.*

Asquith, too, though in some ways more appealing than Churchill, was equally unprincipled, and, Lytton had come to feel, of even greater incompetence. 'Nothing is more damning than his [Asquith's] having told Maynard (who told me of it at the time) that "the Conscriptionists were fools", and that he was giving them "enough rope to hang themselves by", three weeks before he was himself forced by them to bring in a bill for Conscription,' Lytton later commented in an unpublished biographical portrait of Asquith (May 1918). 'If it was true (as Maynard assured me it was, on what I gathered was the best authority) that in December 1916, after he had been turned out with ignominy and treachery by Lloyd George and Bonar Law, he was willing and in fact anxious to act under them as Lord Chancellor, his wits must have sunk even lower than his sense of decency. I think eventually he must have grown too positively fuddled – with too much food and drink, too much power, too much orotund speechifying, too many of those jovial adventures of the "lugubre individu".'

Ultimately, Lytton believed, the world was governed not by extremists, not by flagrantly unreasonable fanatics, but by moderate men. And the sight of these men, with their seductive plausibility, in full control of events, posed for him a profoundly menacing spectacle. For their inflated sentiments and headstrong actions presented a terrifying revelation of what the multitudes of ordinary, solid, humdrum and respectable men and women were thinking. By invoking the lowest common denominator within society, such leaders were able to exert a powerful brake upon the natural advancement of civilization, and to give dominion to the basest, most egotistical elements in human nature.

Amid the fevered bigotry and hysteria of war, people on both sides, Lytton felt, relinquished their individual detachment and with it their humanity, so that, as hostilities were prolonged, the opponents came to resemble each other ever more exactly. The British Government, for example, had, even before conscription, undertaken to improve recruitment by means just as inglorious and discreditable as the Germans themselves. 'Is your "best boy" wearing Khaki? ... If your young man neglects his duty to his King and Country, the time may come when he will NEGLECT YOU!' This was the type of advocacy, 'limited neither by the meagre bounds of the actual nor by the tiresome dictates of common sense', that Lytton particularly abhorred. He did not believe that everything should be sacrificed to the safety of the State; he did not believe that truth should be sacrificed. This twisted, repellent form of patriotism, which justified mendacity and tyranny to ensure national unity, spread like a rampant disease caused not by too much love of one's country, but by too little. A propagandist now himself, bent on persuading others not just by personal example but public exhortation, he employed methods similar to those used by the authorities to popularize his own convictions. In 'The Claims of Patriotism', an article published towards the end of the war in *War and Peace*, he wrote: 'The lover who loved his mistress with such passionate ecstasy that he would feed her on nothing but moonshine, with disastrous consequences – did he, perhaps, in reality, not love her quite enough? That, certainly, is a possible reading of the story. And it might be as well for patriots ... to reflect occasionally on that sad little apologue, and to remember that nothing sweetens love – even love of one's country – so much as a little common sense – and, one might add, even a little cynicism.'

To Lytton's common-sense and cynical mind, the passing that spring of the new universal Conscription Bill for compulsory National Service made Britain as ardent a supporter of the principle of militarism as Germany herself. 'What difference', he used to ask, 'would it make if the Germans *were* here?' Human beings had a value that was independent of any national or temporal processes, and individual human standards must never therefore be jettisoned to make room for the requirements of empirical transactions and passing circumstances. His own quarrel was with the whole militarist point of view, whether expressed by allied or enemy officialdom. 'L[loyd] G[eorge] is a sharper,' he wrote to Pippa. The prime minister's refusal to 'explore every avenue of peace' exposed him, and others in his Cabinet, as militarists pure and simple, who believed that eternal peace was just a sentimentalist's dream. For such men the actuality of peace

held no excitement or romantic appeal; it was attractive only as an
illusory concept which paradoxically justified the pursuit of war to
attain it.

Lytton saw himself as one in a long line of crusaders. During the
eighteenth century Voltaire had waged a constant fight against religion
– then the dominating factor in human affairs. Stendhal had continued
this struggle into the nineteenth century with his attacks upon the
powerful forces of Roman Catholicism. But by the end of that century,
with the sudden tremendous upsurge of scientific interest and discovery,
the social power of organized religion had slumped, until it now ceased
to represent any vital part of the national consciousness. The 'powers of
darkness' were no longer led by theologians, but by their modern
counterparts, the secular and political warmongers. It was with this
breed of men that the Voltaire of the twentieth century had to do
battle. Yet, despite the wartime rash of inhumanity, of hypocrisy and
intolerance, Lytton believed that the odds were not set quite so heavily
against him as they had been against his prototype two hundred years
back. War did not obsess or unnerve the human mind so ceaselessly as
the age-long, pernicious hocus-pocus of religious superstition. The
powers of light were gradually advancing; for human nature, Lytton
considered, had changed and was still changing for the better. To
moderate men with their limitations of average passions and average
thoughts, it might still appear that 'militarism and the implications of
militarism – the struggles and ambitions of opposing States, the desire
for national power, the terror of national ruin, the armed organisation
of humanity – that all this seems inevitable with the inevitability of a
part of the world's very structure; and yet it may well be, too, that they
are wrong, that is not so, that it is the "fabric of a vision" which will
melt suddenly and be seen no more'.

If, as Lytton believed, war were justifiable only as a means, the last
means, of defence, and never as an assertion of nationalism, then the
days of this pristine and aggressive type of patriotism, on which the
wilful politician and ambitious diplomat so abundantly thrived, were
already numbered. Lloyd George stalked the political arena like some
prehistoric monster, doomed to extinction. At the end of the war
Lytton wrote to Keynes: 'To my mind the ideal thing would be to
abolish reparations altogether – but of course that is not practical
politics – at any rate just yet; perhaps in the end it will become
so.'

These were opinions on which nearly all Bloomsbury, from Keynes
to Bertrand Russell, were in general agreement. But it was not so on all
matters connected with the military operations. 'Bertie was most

sympathetic,' Lytton wrote to Ottoline (31 December 1915) on the
eve of the introduction of the first Military Service Bill. 'I went to see
him this morning and we had lunch with Maynard in an extraordinary
underground tunnel, with city gents sitting on high stools like parrots
on perches, somewhere near Trafalgar Square. Maynard is certainly a
wonder. He has not attested, and says he has no intention of doing so.
He couldn't tell us much – except that McKenna is still wobbling; but he
seemed to think it not unlikely that he and Runciman[1] would resign –
in which case he would resign too, and help them to fight it.'

But after compulsory military service had been introduced Reginald
McKenna, chancellor of the exchequer, made no move to resign; nor
did Walter Runciman; and nor did Keynes. Maynard, it seemed, was
rather less of a wonder after all. Certainly both Lytton and Russell felt
that he had 'ratted', and, individually, they both pressed him to quit
the Treasury, reasoning that it must be impossible to reconcile his
avowed sympathy for conscientious objectors with the job of demonstrating how to kill Germans as cheaply as possible: 'the maximum
slaughter at the minimum expense'. Keynes now found himself situated awkwardly, midway between his Bloomsbury friends and his
friends at the Treasury. But there was no chance of resignation. 'He
obviously enjoyed the way the war had brought him up in the world,'
observed Alan Wood, 'and had given him friends among important
people, including Asquith when he was Prime Minister.' This opinion
is supported by the letters which Keynes wrote to his family during
these years. He did not, however, feel entirely easy over his decision,
and to appease Lytton and Russell made a token gesture of support. 'He
announced for their benefit that, although he was not a Conscientious
Objector, he would conscientiously object to compulsory service,'
Roy Harrod explains. 'Accordingly, when he received his calling-up
notice, he replied on Treasury writing-paper that he was too busy to
attend the summons. This appears to have quelled the authorities, for
he was troubled by them no more. On the other hand, he did not carry
this policy through to its final conclusion, for a year or two later the
Treasury discovered a gap in its records. In the file there was no notice
of exemption against his name. And so, to placate the Treasury
Establishment Officer, he walked quietly round and went through the
formalities of obtaining exemption.' In the meantime, however, he had
interceded to support, with great effectiveness, several of those conscientious objectors among his friends – notably James Strachey,

[1] First Baron Runciman (1847–1937), the prosperous shipowner and ardent Methodist
lay preacher, who had been in Asquith's Liberal cabinet. He was the author of several
books on the sea, and an autobiography, *Before the Mast and After* (1924).

Duncan Grant and David Garnett – on whose behalf he gave telling evidence before the Military and Appeal Tribunals.

Although at one in their repudiation of Keynes's quibbling, his sophistry and vacillation, Lytton and Bertrand Russell harboured differences of temperament and of opinion that became increasingly obvious as the year 1916 progressed. The passing of the Military Service Bill, which took the wind out of Lytton's sails as a political crusader, redoubled the force of Russell's pacifist propaganda. Even by the third week of January, Lytton was confessing to Ottoline (21 January 1916) that 'the anti-Conscription movement has been rather fading out as far as I'm concerned'. Russell, by contrast, was embarking on a series of pacifist lectures, later published under the title *Principles of Social Reconstruction*. These turned out to be a great success, crowded with ladies of fashion and intellectual young men attending earnestly to his every word. Lytton, too, went to all of them and was unstinted in his praise. They were, he told Ottoline, full of interest, courage and originality. 'Bertie's lectures help one,' he wrote (16 February 1916). 'They are a wonderful solace and refreshment. One hangs upon his words, and looks forward to them from week to week, and I can't bear the idea of missing one – I dragged myself to that ghastly Caxton Hall yesterday, though I was rather nearer the grave than usual, and it was well worth it. It is splendid the way he sticks at nothing – Governments, religions, laws, property, even Good Form itself – down they go like ninepins – it is a charming sight! And then his constructive ideas are very grand; one feels one had always thought something like that – but vaguely and inconclusively; and he puts it all together, and builds it up, and plants it down solid and shining before one's mind. I don't believe there's anyone quite so formidable to be found just now upon this earth.'

Two months later, Russell's campaigning reached a crisis over the Everett affair. On 10 April, Ernest F. Everett, a conscientious objector and member of the N.C.F., was sentenced to two years' hard labour for disobedience to military orders. Nine days afterwards the N.C.F. issued a leaflet protesting against this sentence, whereupon six men were arrested and imprisoned for distributing it. On learning this Russell immediately wrote off a letter to *The Times* declaring that he was the author of the leaflet and that, if anyone should be prosecuted, it ought to be himself as the person primarily responsible. This letter, of course, made prosecution unavoidable and Russell duly appeared before the Lord Mayor, Sir Charles Wakefield, at the Mansion House on 5 June 1916, charged with making, in a printed publication, 'statements likely to prejudice the recruiting discipline of His Majesty's forces'. A. H.

Bodkin[1] appeared for the prosecution; Russell defended himself; and the proceedings were brightened by the startling arrival of Lytton, and Ottoline Morrell dressed in a brilliant hat and cashmere coat of many colours. 'B.R. spoke for about an hour,' Lytton recorded, '– quite well – but simply a propaganda speech. The Lord Mayor looked like a stuck pig. Counsel for the prosecution was an incredible Daumier caricature of a creature – and positively turned out to be Mr. Bodkin. I felt rather nervous in that Brigand's cave.' Russell was found guilty and fined £100 (with £10 costs and the alternative of 61 days' imprisonment), a sentence that was confirmed on appeal.[2]

Disgusted by what he considered to be Lytton's defeatist attitude, Russell despised his inability to persevere with the cause of pacifism, to stick at nothing. But Lytton suspected that Russell, like so many professional reformers, wanted bad conditions of one sort or another, so that he might have the personal joy of altering them. Conscription filled Lytton with no such joy. 'It's all about as bad as it could be,' he wrote to Vanessa Bell from Garsington (17 April 1916). 'Bertie has been here for the week-end. He is working day and night with the N.C.F., and is at last perfectly happy – gloating over all the horrors and the moral lessons of the situation. The tales he tells make one's blood run cold; but certainly the N.C.F. people do sound a remarkable lot – Britannia's One Hope, I firmly believe – all so bright and cheery, he says, with pink cheeks and blithe young voice – oh mon dieu! mon dieu! The worst of it is that I don't see how they can really make themselves effective unless a large number of them do go through actual martyrdom: and even then what is there to make the governing classes climb down? It is all most dark in every direction.' Towards the end of 1917 Russell himself decided to withdraw from active pacifist agitation, believing – as did Lytton – that it was by then more important to wait and work for a constructive post-war peace. Yet he could point to some solid achievements as a propagandist. In the Everett case, for example, his own leaflet and the ensuing trial had caused the Government to commute the original sentence to a hundred and twelve days' detention.

Lytton had no triumphs of this sort to his credit. He much preferred to campaign indirectly, behind the scenes, even anonymously, rather

[1] Later Sir Archibald Henry Bodkin (1862–1957) who between 1920 and 1930 was Director of Public Prosecutions.

[2] This appeal was heard before the City Quarter Sessions, at the Guildhall, on 29 June 1916. Russell declined to pay the fine, but there was never any question of imprisonment since he owned valuable books that could be seized and sold. These books were saved by the action of Russell's friends, who subscribed the necessary hundred pounds and bid that sum for the first volume put up for sale at the auction.

than expose himself to the vulgar brawling of wind-and-winter combat. At first the various limitations imposed by the new Act appear to have released his mind from its baleful absorption in his own ill-health, and to have conferred upon him once more that simulacrum of vitality and bubbling humour that sparkles so brightly through the pages of *Eminent Victorians*. 'I seem to be rising a little out of them [low spirits] now,' he told Virginia Woolf (25 February 1916). 'I don't know why – perhaps because the horrors of the outer world are beginning to assert themselves – local tribunals, and such things – and one really can't lie still under *that*.' And to Ottoline Morrell he wrote (16 February 1916): 'At moments I'm quite surprised how, with these horrors around one, one goes on living as one does – and even manages to execute an occasional pirouette on the edge of the precipice!'

The view from the precipice, however, did not fire and enliven him as it did Russell, but increasingly filled out his thoughts with a cumulus of dread and worry. After the two Military Service Acts had been passed he at once appealed for absolute exemption on the grounds of health and conscience, expecting that, after a medical examination and an interview with the tribunal, he would be placed in Class IVb, and made liable for clerical work. Once this had happened he intended to appeal, and, in the eventuality of this appeal failing, he was prepared to be sent to prison – though with little confidence in his capacity to resist prolonged hardship. 'The conscience question is very difficult and complicated,' he wrote to James who was in a similar predicament to himself (28 February 1916), 'and no doubt I have many feelings against joining the army which are not conscientious; but *one* of my feelings is that if I were to find myself doing clerical work in Class IVb – i.e. devoting all my working energy to helping on the war – I should be convinced that I was doing wrong the whole time; and if that isn't a conscientious objection I don't know what is. . . . I'm willing to go to prison rather than do that work.'

Lytton was subject to much nervous strain while waiting for the Hampstead Tribunal. To combat this he came under the supervision of a new medicine man recommended this time by Mary Hutchinson, Dr Becket-Overy, who prescribed complete rest and feeding up. 'He seemed quite intelligent, and has relieved my mind a good deal,' Lytton reported to David Garnett (10 March 1916), 'but I am still in a most half and half state – with a brain like porridge, and a constant abject feeling of exhaustion. However, I am now on a diet, and drink petroleum o'nights, and even try now and then to do a Swedish exercise or two – so I hope I shall really soon begin to recover. I wish I could go away from this bloody town and its bloodier tribunals – I should like to go to sleep for a month; but it's no good thinking of moving till the first stage of the affair, at any rate, is over.'

His depression was deepened by a number of visits he made, as an ordinary member of the public, to watch the proceedings of the Hampstead Tribunal. 'It was horrible, and efficient in a deadly way,' he told Ottoline (March 1916). 'Very polite too. But clearly they had decided beforehand to grant *no* exemptions, and all the proceedings were really a farce. It made one's flesh creep to see victim after victim led off to ruin or slaughter.' And to Dorothy Bussy he declared (25 March 1916): 'I believe the name of the tribunals will go down to History with the Star Chamber.'

The Hampstead Tribunal, as he afterwards came to realize, was in fact an exceptionally congenial one. The atmosphere remained at all times fairly calm and restrained, and the attitude shown towards educated members of the upper and upper-middle classes was unusually lenient. But the amount of suppressed ill-feeling these tribunals were raising by this time all over the country was very considerable. Made up of ageing local worthies, they had become a means of venting public horror at the mounting slaughter on the Western Front, vicariously, upon the 'shirkers' who came up before them. Very few of the papers – except the *Manchester Guardian* – dared to refer to them, and the debates in the House of Commons were scarcely reported at all. It was really only by reading Hansard assiduously that one could discover what was going on. Perhaps it was not surprising that such scratch bodies, composed of miscellaneous Borough Councillors, without any judicial training, without any defined procedure, armed with immense powers and subject to the most violent animus, should find it difficult to interpret the conscience clauses of a fairly complicated Act of Parliament. Yet it was not just with conscientious objectors that they abused their powers; they were almost as unrelenting with cases of hardship. The accounts which Lytton got to hear from his friends of other tribunals were sometimes hair-raising. 'I don't think that even if you had mentioned God in your application it would have had much effect,' he wrote to Francis Birrell (March 1916), '– he is quite out of fashion; and as for Jesus he's publicly laughed at. Odd that one should have lived to find oneself positively on that fellow's side.'

On 7 March, Lytton appeared as a claimant for exemption before the local Advisory Committee. These Advisory Committees had no legal basis, though in effect they controlled the administration of the law, at the same time shrugging off admitted responsibility. When an applicant appeared before one of these bodies, he was not allowed to argue his case, since the Committee maintained that it existed for advice, not decision. Yet the Tribunal almost invariably carried out the recommendation of the Committee, so that, when each applicant subsequently came up before it, he would find its mind already made up on the motion of a body that had refused to consider his case judicially. Lytton at once stated that he had an ineradicable conscientious objection to assisting in the war:

'I have', he said, 'a conscientious objection to assisting, by any deliberate action of mine, in carrying on the war. This objection is not based upon religious belief, but upon moral considerations, at which I have arrived after long and painful thought. I do not wish to assert the extremely general proposition that I should never, in any circumstances, be justified in taking part in any conceivable war; to dogmatize so absolutely upon a point so abstract would appear to me to be unreasonable. At the same time, my feeling is directed not simply against the present war: I am convinced that the whole system by which it is sought to settle international disputes by force is profoundly evil; and that, so far as I am concerned, I should be doing wrong to take part in it.

'These conclusions have crystallised in my mind and I shall not act against those convictions whatever the consequences may be.'

To all this the Committee listened politely and patiently. At the end, they made no comment whatever. They did not attempt to dispute what Lytton had said, but they at once informed him that they would recommend the Tribunal to grant him 'no relief'. The only logical assumption he could make was that they had spontaneously decided, for reasons unexplained, that his objection was fraudulent. He bowed coldly and left the room, certain that the Tribunal later the same month would follow their eminently impartial advice.

Between these court appearances, his social life billowed on much as before, helping to drown the depression and apprehension that had settled on him. 'Ottoline has been up this week, receiving a series of visitors in her bedroom at Bedford Square, in a constant stream of exactly-timed tête-à-têtes – like a dentist,' he wrote to David Garnett (10 March 1916). 'Yesterday there was a curious little party at Maynard's, consisting of her ladyship, Duncan with a cold, Sheppard with a beard, James and me. There she sat, thickly encrusted with pearls and diamonds, crocheting a pseudo-omega quilt, and murmuring on buggery.

'I have also met Mr. Ramsay MacDonald lately – not I thought a very brilliant figure, though no doubt a very worthy one. He struck me as one of Nature's darlings, whom at the last moment she'd suddenly turned against, dashing a little fatuity into all her gifts.'

Nourished by special foods, fortified by Swedish exercises, Lytton prepared for his examination before the Hampstead Tribunal with all the thoroughness of a general laying plans for some military offensive. The exaggerated conduct of the Advisory Committee had given him an opening, he felt, for saying something really scathing, and he spent his days, so he told James, drawing up imaginary cross-examinations of Military Representatives. But although, as he wrote to Ottoline (11 March 1916), 'I am beginning to tighten my belt, roll up my sleeves and grind my teeth', he at no time relished the idea of putting his case without the aid of Counsel, and without any real hope of justice being done or even the elementary rules of fairness kept. 'I don't care much for the prospect,' he admitted to Francis Birrell (March 1916). 'I don't feel as if I had sufficient powers of repartee, and sufficient control of my voice, or my temper; and public appearances of any kind are odious to me.'

However he steeled himself for the ordeal. It was to be another pitched battle between reason and that purblind chauvinism defined by Dr Johnson as 'the last refuge of the scoundrel'. The spectacle he presented was even odder than his appearances at previous oral examinations, for entry to Balliol and to the Civil Service. For his eccentricity was now far more deliberate and assertive, and he was out to vindicate himself before an acknowledged enemy. The proceedings, especially in view of his unfitness for soldiering or even manual work in a farm or factory, soon grew farcical, as each side endeavoured with all possible ingenuity to make his opponent feel acutely silly and uncomfortable.

'There was a vast crowd of my supporters surging through the corridors of the Town Hall, and pouring into the council chamber,' Lytton described the scene in a letter to Pippa (17 March 1916). 'My case was the very last on the list. They began at about 5, and I appeared about 7.30, infinitely prepared with documents, legal points, conscientious declarations etc.' His friends and family now put in a strong appearance. First there entered Lytton's character witness, Philip Morrell, bearing a light blue air cushion. Following him innumerable brothers and sisters including James, Elinor, Marjorie, Pernel and Oliver, trailed in and lined themselves up opposite the eight members of the Tribunal, seated at a long table. Meanwhile, in other parts of the small courtroom, some fifteen attendant spirits, Bloomsbury painters and pacifists, took their seats amid a miscellaneous sprinkling of the general public. Finally, the applicant himself, suffering, among other disorders, from piles, and carrying a tartan travelling rug, made his entrance. Philip Morrell gravely handed him the air cushion which, to the astonishment of the chairman, he applied to the aperture in his beard and solemnly inflated. Then he deposited this cushion upon the wooden bench, lowered himself gingerly down upon it facing the mayor, and arranged the rug carefully about his knees.

The examination could now commence. In the course of it the military representative attempted to cause him some embarrassment by firing a volley of awkward questions from the bench.

'I understand, Mr Strachey, that you have a conscientious objection to all wars?'

'Oh no,' came the piercing, high-pitched reply, 'not at all. Only this one.'

'Then tell me, Mr Strachey, what would you do if you saw a German soldier attempting to rape your sister?'

Lytton turned and forlornly regarded each of his sisters in turn. Then he confronted the Board once more and answered with gravity: 'I should try and interpose my own body.'

His sense of the dramatic and the absurd had carried the day. The Tribunal, however, were not amused, and his application for absolute exemption on the grounds of conscience was adjourned pending an examination by the military doctors. This examination was held only a few days later at the White City, where Lytton turned up, this time equipped with sheaves of doctors' certificates and an inventory of his medical symptoms. From eleven in the morning until half-past three in the afternoon he sat among a crowd of rowdy and promiscuous young men, silently perusing Gardner's *History of England*. But for once, in compensation for past trials, his disabilities stood him in good stead. He was rejected as medically unfit for any kind of service and formally pronounced a free man. 'It's a great relief,' he confessed to Ottoline that same evening. '. . . Everyone was very polite and even sympathetic – except one fellow – a subordinate doctor, who began by being grossly rude, but grew more polite under my treatment. It was queer finding oneself with four members of the lower classes – two of them simply roughs out of the streets – filthy dirty – crammed behind a screen in the corner of a room, and told to undress. For a few moments I realised what it was like to *be* one of the lower classes – the appalling indignity of it! To come out after it was all over, and find myself being called "sir" by policemen and ticket collectors was a distinct satisfaction.'

Now that there was no call to return to the Tribunal, Lytton was at liberty to follow his doctor's instructions – rest and a special diet. He straightway set off for Garsington, where he spent the next three weeks recuperating. 'I am still infinitely délabré,' he declared in a letter to Virginia Woolf (15 April 1916), 'in spite of the infinite solicitudes of her Ladyship. It is a great bore. I lie about in a limp state, reading the Republic, which I find a surprisingly interesting work. I should like to have a chat with the Author.'

A few days later he left Garsington to spend Easter at Asheham with the Woolfs. 'Do you think I might have either rice or macaroni with the meat course at lunch & dinner?' he tentatively inquired. 'Dr. Overy insists on it, so if it could be managed without too much bother I should be much obliged.' At Asheham Lytton managed to enjoy himself a good deal in spite of, as it now seemed to him, the general lack of romance in his companions. 'Virginia is most sympathetic, and even larger than usual, I think,' he wrote back to Ottoline (23 April 1916); 'she rolls along over the Downs like some strange amphibious monster. Sanger trots beside her, in a very short pair of white flannel trousers with blue lines, rattling out his unending stream of brightness. Woolf and I bring up the rear – with a couple of curious dogs, whose attentions really almost oblige me to regret the charms of Socrates.'[1]

Lytton returned to Belsize Park Gardens at the end of the month. He had by now laid up such a store of bucolic health that he felt ready to face the constant *brusquerie* of London without flinching. There was the National Book Sale – a quiet affair – a performance of *The Magic Flute*, James's appearance before the Appeal Tribunal, and – a delightful novelty – a ringside seat at a boxing match featuring the handsome and legendary Jimmy Wilde, the 'Tigerstown Terror'; all of which he took in his stride.

This month, too, his mother returned from wintering in Menton. Lady Strachey was now in her seventy-fifth year and had recently lost the sight of one eye. 'The news of Mama is very appalling,' Lytton had written to Pippa (10 February 1916). 'The only hope is that in spite of everything it will be possible to read with the other eye. The whole thing is the most sickening piece of bad luck.' For the time being this other eye remained quite all right, and the light of Lady Strachey's vigorous spirit continued to shine out unimpaired. 'I have now passed the "mezzo del cammin di nostra vita",' Lytton announced to her on his thirty-sixth birthday, 'and am rather surprised to find that existence continues to be highly interesting in spite of that fact. I used to think in early youth that one's development would come to an end in one's thirties – but I don't find it so – on the contrary, things if anything seem to grow more interesting instead of less. Also, they grow more satisfactory. One seems, as one goes on, to acquire a more complete grasp of life – of what one wants and what one can get – and of the

[1] Ottoline's chief pug dog.

materials of one's work, which give a greater sense of security and power. I think I now see where my path lies, and I feel fairly confident that, with decent luck and if my health can go on keeping its head above water, I ought to be able to get somewhere worth getting to. Really I consider, apart from illness, and apart from the present disgusting state of the world, that I'm an extraordinarily happy person. One other reflection is this – that if I ever *do* do anything worth doing I'm sure it will be owing to you much more than to anyone else.'

Shortly after his return to London, Lytton took his mother down to Durbins, Roger Fry's house at Guildford, which Oliver and Ray Strachey had rented, and where Lady Strachey was to pass most of the next eighteen months. Before very long, the odd distinctive Strachey régime was in full swing. 'Several members of the Strachey family were staying there,' wrote Nina Hamnett, another guest that summer. 'In the evening Lady Strachey would read us restoration plays and we would play games. Everyone would choose a book from the library and hide the cover. They read a passage from their books and the others had to guess who had written it.'

After a few days at Durbins, Lytton left for another long spell at Garsington, which had recently been converted into a reserve for pacifist intellectuals, dons *manqués* turned farm labourers who, after digging in the fields during the day, would withdraw into the Manor House by night to 'puff churchwarden pipes by the fire', as Siegfried Sassoon put it, 'and talk cleverly in cultured and earnest tones about significant form in the Arts and the misdeeds of the Militants'. These nightly goings-on quickly excited the suspicions of the authorities, and the local police, taking it into their heads that the Member of Parliament for Burnley and the Duke of Portland's sister were German spies, spent much of their time nosing around the midnight shrubbery and trying to detect signals to Zeppelins.

Lytton did not greatly relish being incorporated into this flock of shaggily attired, argumentative critics and artists over which Lady Ottoline moodily presided as pastoral shepherdess. But amid this 'assemblage of Bloomsbury and Crankdom' he did come across a few interesting and attractive personalities – Katherine Mansfield 'very amusing and sufficiently mysterious'; Aldous Huxley 'young and peculiarly Oxford'; and the beautiful Maria Nys, later (1919) to become Huxley's wife, a niece of Ottoline's who had fled to England as a refugee from Belgium and whom Lytton was now coaching in Latin for her entrance examination to Newnham.[1] Both Katherine Mansfield

---

[1] Also living at Garsington was Sir Julian Huxley's future wife, Juliette Baillot, to whom Lytton was giving instruction in English verse.

G

and Maria Nys, with her vulnerable and defenceless look of a child with a mature body, stirred in him some indecisive, easily quenchable feelings of sexual attraction which exercised his imagination for a while before rapidly coming to nothing. 'Why on earth *had* I been so chaste during those Latin lessons?' he asked himself in an autobiographical essay written later that year (26 June 1916). 'I saw how easily I could have been otherwise – how I might have put my hand on her bare neck, and even up her legs, with considerable enjoyment; and probably she would have been on the whole rather pleased. I became certain that the solution was that I was restrained by my knowledge that she would certainly inform "Auntie" of every detail of what had happened at the earliest opportunity.'

When the week-end parties and entertainments broke up, the days between slipped by calmly and serenely. Lytton continued to lead a tolerably lazy and agreeable existence, eating hugely but with caution, taking a constitutional every afternoon and reading to her Ladyship and Mademoiselle of an evening. All over the country there were rumours of conscientious objectors being shut up in underground cells, fed on bread and water, and transported as cannon fodder to the front line. But in the early summer stillness, from behind those high yew hedges and the placid aloofness of that grey stone façade, these rumours dwindled into distant echoes that hung in the air, vague and im-probable. 'It's been unusually peaceful,' Lytton wrote to Maynard Keynes (10 May 1916), 'and I'm lying out under my quilt of many colours in the sun. I hope soon to have accumulated enough health to face London again for a little. It is horrid to sit helpless while those poor creatures are going through such things. But really one would have to be God Almighty to be of any effective use.'

4

THE VIRGIN AND THE GIPSY

During the autumn of 1915, Lytton had spent with the Bells at Asheham a certain week-end which set in motion seismic repercussions that were to reshape the entire story of the last sixteen years of his life.

Besides various Bloomsbury guests, including Duncan Grant and Lytton's cousin Mary Hutchinson, two ex-Slade student girls, Barbara Hiles and Dora Carrington, had been invited down. Barbara Hiles, 'a nice springing and gay girl', as Ottoline described her, was pretty and lively, considered by many of the Bloomsberries to be rather tire-some but kind.[1] Her friend Carrington was altogether different, and far more difficult to describe. She was not really pretty, and certainly not beautiful – her body being made for action, like a boy's. But she radiated an extraordinary aura of attractiveness. Her mind was intuitive rather than intelligent, and she had not been well educated. Nor did she talk particularly well, her voice being unusually flat and only in moments of emotion taking on a more expressive melodious tone. Although not erudite herself, she had the charming gift of making others feel clever, drawing them out and listening with rapt attention to every syllable they spoke. Her manner was naturally flattering; she had a dazzling smile; and she invariably made up to – almost flirted with – everyone she liked. The strong emotions she provoked in many men – among them Mark Gertler, Ralph Partridge and Gerald Brenan – were chiefly aroused by her strange and enchanting vivacity. She was alive at every point, consumed by the most vivid feelings about people, places, even things. One way or another she cared about everything, and the strength and variety of her feelings confused and wore her out. 'You are like a tin of mixed biscuits,' Iris Tree once told her. 'Your parents were Huntley and Palmer.' Yet, all her life, she remained a giver not a receiver and so uniquely herself that every look, every word, every gesture was unlike that of any other person.

Always an elusive subject for the camera, no photograph catches the sparkling colour, the impetuosity and dynamism of her physical personality, or conveys much idea of the impression she created on others. At first sight there seemed something childish about her – rather chubby round cheeks, and clear eyes, so false-innocent, but full of light. To strangers or casual acquaintances she was most easily recognizable by her thick, light-brown hair, tinged with gold, and worn short and perfectly straight, like a Florentine page-boy's. But perhaps her most striking features were her smooth milk-white skin, her hands which had a peculiar independent character of their own, and a pair of large, intensely blue eyes, rather sunk in their sockets, and carrying an unforgettably tragic look which would light up with quick mischievous amusement.

In the course of this week-end at Asheham, Lytton and Carrington went off one afternoon for a walk along the woods near by, and Lytton, being momentarily drawn to Carrington's boyish figure, suddenly

[1] Several members of the Bloomsbury Group were to have reason to be grateful to Barbara Bagenal, as she later became. With great devotion she nursed Saxon Sydney-Turner through his declining years, and, after the death of Vanessa Bell in 1961, looked after Clive Bell, whose life she certainly helped to prolong.

stopped and embraced her. Astonished, she broke away; and later that same day complained bitterly to Barbara Hiles that 'that horrid old man with a beard kissed me!' Her friend tried to reassure her that his advances would probably proceed no further, but she naïvely refused to understand what was implied until the giggling Barbara spelt out the word H-O-M-O-S-E-X-U-A-L. 'What's that?' she answered. And no amount of explanation seemed able to mitigate the fierce resentment which had welled up in her. Planning to pay him out at the first possible opportunity, she tiptoed very early the next morning into Lytton's bedroom, taking with her a pair of scissors with which she intended to snip off his beard while he slept. It was to be one of those simple, devastating practical jokes of which she was so fond – a fitting revenge for his horrible audacity. But the plan misfired. As she leant over him, Lytton suddenly, quietly, opened his eyes and looked at her. The effect was instantaneous. She seemed to become hypnotized, and fell, there and then and for the rest of her life, violently in love with him.

To understand the nature of Carrington's all-consuming attachment to Lytton, to define the poignant centripetal role she was to occupy in his future career, and to explain the complicated emotional entanglements in which Lytton became enmeshed, some short account of Carrington's previous history is essential. One of five children, she was the daughter of a retired Indian railway engineer who had married a governess. She loved her father, but detested her mother who still retained all the tutorial, bullying mannerisms of the governess, and who demanded from her children an endless, fussy attention. Carrington responded passionately to the English countryside in which she was brought up, but disliked her schooling at Bedford – a town much favoured by ex-colonels for its cheap education, and which retained some of the puritanism of Bunyan – and hated her home, which was entirely saturated by her mother's odious presence. Her parents she once likened to those of H. G. Wells's Anne Veronica. They were commonplace and material: she was a *new woman* striving to be liberated. 'It's just like being in a birdcage here,' she told Mark Gertler, 'one can see everything which one would love to enjoy and yet one cannot. My father is in another cage also, which my mother put him in, and he is too old to even chirp or sing.'

With her sister, who was older than herself and who had escaped from their humdrum home into a humdrum marriage, Carrington preserved little contact. On the whole she was always far closer to her brothers, the rather conventionally-minded Noel, who later became a publisher with the Oxford University Press and an editor of *Country Life*,[1] Sam, a pretty hopeless character who looked after dogs, and whom in later life she never mentioned except as a joke, and Edmund, her 'sailor-brother' shortly to be killed during the battle of the Somme.[2] Soon hardened and forced into independence by the rough-and-tumble world of these brothers, she reacted strongly against the callow, filial sentimentality ceaselessly exacted of her, and came increasingly to feel that she ought to have been born a boy. Her correspondence is full of disgusted complaints at her loathsome, vulgar, inefficient femininity. 'How I hate being a girl!' she exclaimed in an early letter to Mark Gertler. And in another: 'Today I have been suffering agonies because I am a woman. All this makes me so angry, and I despise myself so much.' As she grew up, this feeling of revulsion began to assert itself in various practical ways. She became an ardent supporter of women's emancipation. For many years, too, she kept intact an unremitting virginity complex, and found, once this had eventually been overcome, that she could derive pleasure from loving several people, of both sexes, pretty well concurrently. Not being strongly sexed, however, she never regarded her unpredictable, sporadic love-making in the customary light of a series of stereotyped 'affairs': each relationship was something completely *sui generis*.

At school Carrington had been considered odd, rather dreamy, careless and in perpetual need of discipline. Her reports stated that she was no good at anything except drawing, and, since she also caused trouble at home, her mother packed her off to the Slade School of Fine Art, where she won a scholarship.[3] Once there, rejoicing in her new freedom,

[1] Noel Carrington is the author of *Design in Everyday Life* and *Popular Art in Britain*, and editor of *Mark Gertler: Selected Letters*. For several years he was editor of the Penguin series *Puffin Picture Books*, but in 1946 decided to change to farming in Berkshire, where he now lives.

[2] Carrington always spoke of her brother 'Teddy' as a sailor and gave many of her friends the definite impression that he had been drowned at sea. A year or so older than she was, E. A. Carrington had just finished his time at Cambridge when war was declared. With a group of rowing friends he had decided to volunteer for a minesweeper, and joined the Navy as an A.B. After about eighteen months the Admiralty for some reason broke up his unit. He then put in for a commission in the Wiltshire Regiment, where his eldest brother Sam had served as a regular officer some years before the war, and where Noel had been serving since 1914. After a short training course he was sent out to France in 1916 and posted missing early in the battle of the Somme. There are other references in Carrington's letters to Sam, wounded in August 1914, and to Noel, wounded in June 1915. But the loss of Teddy was a great blow and did much to confirm her in her pessimism and pacifism.

[3] There are at the Slade two fine life paintings by Carrington, one of which won her a first prize in 1912–13. She was also awarded second place in the Melvill Nettleship Prize for Figure Composition (1911–12), and, in her last year, a first prize for a painting from the cast. Visual art and perceptions played a vitally important part in her existence,

she cut her hair short and dropped the use of her feminine baptismal name Dora – 'a sentimental lower class English name' as she once described it to Noel (27 December 1916), which she hated and by which only her mother continued to call her. For the rest of her life, even after her marriage, she was known as Carrington, *tout court*.[1]

From the moment she left home, 'there was a constant struggle to avoid returning for holidays and to evade by some ruse maternal discipline and inquisition', her brother Noel remembers. Their mother never ceased to regret this independence and her own loss of control over her daughter. It was at the Slade that Carrington had first been introduced by C. R. W. Nevinson[2] to the talented painter Mark Gertler. The son of devout, impoverished, Jewish parents, Gertler had spent a miserable childhood in the slums of Whitechapel. From his earliest years he had been determined to become an artist. In the autumn of 1908 he was sent to the Slade by the Jewish Educational Aid Society, acting on the advice of William Rothenstein. Like Carrington, he wrestled with an inability to adapt himself to Slade standards, and stood out from the uniform heap of students, among whom he soon gained a considerable reputation.

Gertler was immediately attracted to Carrington. With her short honey-coloured hair, now shaped pudding-basin fashion, her big blue forget-me-not eyes, delicate pale complexion, shy and diffident manner, she appeared to him as fragile and sublime as a piece of priceless First Period Worcester china. Her superior middle-class birth, emphasized by a rather mincing precise accent and punctuated between sentences by a little gasp, enhanced her distinctive feminine appeal – so utterly unlike the run-of-the-mill Jewesses, shop-girls and models with whom Gertler had previously carried on casual love-affairs. He was captivated by her air of simplicity, her extraordinary childlike innocence, her passionate love of beauty, her generous trustfulness and odd, unexpected impulses.

---

[1] After the suppression of her baptismal name, Carrington attempted to find a substitute, signing some of her letters 'Doric' or 'Kunak'. But none of these inventions lasted for long. It was only very secretly that Lytton eventually called her 'Mopsa'.

[2] C. R. W. Nevinson (1889–1946), later a member of the London Group and the New English Art Club. His most memorable paintings, with their semi-cubist technique, record the sufferings of the First World War, in which he was an official artist. As a student he was in love with Carrington; after she left him for Gertler he married Kathleen Knowlman, the daughter of a businessman. In 1937 he published an autobiography, *Paint and Prejudice*, which reveals something of his despondent sense of the world's ill-will towards him.

---

making up for much of what was otherwise unhappiness. She enjoyed visual experiences, for instance, during the course of an ordinary walk, that most people would never appreciate or even be aware of.

But appearances and early impressions were deceptive. She herself was not deeply in love with him. According to D. H. Lawrence, a close friend of Gertler's, who took Carrington as the prototype of Ethel Cane in his short story 'None of That', she was incapable of real love.[1] 'She was always hating men, hating all active maleness in a man. She wanted passive maleness.' Lawrence's explanation of Carrington's virginity complex, based mainly on what he had heard about her relationship with Gertler and subsequently with Lytton, was that what she chiefly desired was not love, but power. 'She could send out of her body a repelling energy,' he wrote, 'to compel people to submit to her will.' In Lawrence's view, Carrington was searching round for some epoch-making man to act as a fitting instrument for her evil and daemonic energy. By herself she could achieve nothing. Only when she had a group or a few real individuals, or just one man, could she 'start something', and make them all dance in a tragi-comedy round her, like marionettes. 'It was only in intimacy that she was unscrupulous and dauntless as a devil incarnate,' Lawrence wrote, giving her the standard paranoiac qualities of so many of his characters. 'In public, and in strange places, she was very uneasy, like one who has a bad conscience towards society, and is afraid of it. And for that reason she could never go without a man to stand between her and all the others.'

Although she did not passionately love Gertler, Carrington admired him and had what, to his chagrin, she termed 'an honest affection' for him. She wanted to value him as a brother, to be 'just friends'. 'I do not love you physically, that you know,' she wrote to him the same month as she met Lytton (November 1915), 'but I care for you far more than I do for any one else.'

But for Gertler this was not enough. Dark and handsome, he was, in fact, more physically attractive to Lytton than to Carrington – a state of affairs that really satisfied no one. There was indeed something striking and unforgettable about his presence – the shock of hair, the amazing vitality, the versatile gift for mimicry and extravagant humour, and the romantic excitement he communicated was given depth by a contrasting look of profound suffering in the eyes, 'the vivid eyes of genius and consumption'. Tempestuous and aggressive in his behaviour, he gave the impression of having schooled himself in the rudiments of polite society only through a most supreme effort of the will that might disintegrate at any second. He plunged into every

[1] Aldous Huxley also made some use – and to rather different ends – of Carrington's personality in his portrayal of Mary Bracegirdle in *Crome Yellow*. 'Pink and childish,' Huxley describes her. 'Her short hair, clipped like a page's, hung in a bell of elastic gold about her cheeks. She had large blue china eyes, whose expression was one of ingenuous and often puzzled earnestness.'

activity which took his fancy with sudden and unrestrained violence, and was an exacting friend, a demanding and jealous lover.

Undoubtedly Carrington felt excited by Gertler's wild personality. He held her spellbound with the ardent, impulsive flow of talk that poured from his lips. His eager response to the movement and colour of life found an immediate echo in her own heart and filled her with elation. Chaotic and newly alive, he seemed composed of elements which knew no tradition, which were as far removed from her own dull background as it was possible to imagine.

In time their friendship developed into a fierce, intimate struggle of wills in which Carrington proved herself to be by far the more subtle and intransigent of the two. A vein of high and unconscious comedy ran through their sad, harrowing relationship. Gertler impatiently declared his total love, and urged her without delay to become his mistress or his wife. She, finding herself unable to speak of such matters in any but the most oblique terms, reassured him that he was the mainland from which she made expeditions across the seas to remote islands, but to which she would always return. And when, growing tired and puzzled at these vague metaphorical evasions, he tried to cross-question her more precisely as to the date on which he might expect to be accepted as her lover, she would murmur 'next summer' or 'next winter', depending upon whether it was autumn or spring. Hope sprang eternal in Gertler's breast. Yet whenever the season appointed duly arrived, Carrington would slide off once more into evasions. He was the mainland . . . Finally, when Gertler's cries of anguish rose to fever pitch, she felt obliged to inform him that he was not ready yet for her 'corporeal body'.

He had almost despaired of ever winning her love, when, out of the blue, she would send him a parcel of spotted ties or a jar of honey together with a letter stating her determination in the future to be less selfish, to make him happier. And so he would be encouraged to take up the struggle once more. Her repeated exhortations to him to be happy, bewildered and depressed Gertler. What could she mean? What was she implying? He could never make her out. Her enchanting, elusive, enigmatic diffidence defied his mastery. He felt tantalized by her superior coolness. When she smiled, he imagined she was mocking him and stood amazed at the strange emotional dependence he felt upon everything she thought and did. But what exactly she was thinking and what she would do next he could never tell. It was hopeless. He had almost decided to give her up when, suddenly, yielding to his demands, she did go to bed with him – once. His predicament now seemed even worse than before. Still, somehow, she eluded him; still he had not really possessed her. She loved him – she swore she did – but the contact of his body 'made me inside feel ashamed, unclean. Can I help it? I wish to God I could. Do not think I rejoice in being sexless, and am happy over this. It gives me pain also.'

There was no deliberate intention on Carrington's part of torturing Gertler. On the contrary, she liked him immensely – but not in the way he wanted. Her independent nature could not submit to his bullying advances. Toughened by her fight to break away from the web of meaningless family gentility, she held this hard-won freedom very dear. From the experiences of her childhood, too, she had learnt never to abandon herself completely for any length of time to a single emotion; and it was this defensive measure which accounted for her inconsistencies, her minor deceptions, her aptitude for broken engagements, and which gave her ascendancy over the highly vulnerable enthusiasms of Gertler. Although, therefore, she was drawn to his exuberant personality, she sensed, through that part of her which remained detached from all she did and felt, that he represented a menace to her liberty. Consequently she was determined that their valuable friendship should evolve only as a blending of individual freedoms.

Yet, at a certain level of intercourse, the two of them were deeply incompatible. Neither was prepared or even able to forgo his or her own aims. Gertler, in particular, bitterly resented the inexplicable hold that this sturdy doll-faced girl could exercise over him. 'If only you could give yourself up in love,' D. H. Lawrence counselled him (20 January 1916), 'she would be much happier. You always want to dominate her, which is no good. One must learn to relinquish oneself, not to bother about oneself, but to love the other person. You hold too closely to yourself for her to be free to love you.'[1] Advice of this sort, always more pleasant to give than to receive, Gertler considered he could only hope to follow once he and Carrington were regular lovers. And when she point-blank refused this, he tried to talk himself out of his infatuation. She was, he reasoned, perfectly true to type; impulsive without being sensual, kind without being affectionate, with all the raw red passion for life decorously bred out of her. He was bewitched by this type simply because he was unused to it. She was the *lady* and he the East End boy. To take her seriously just because he was suffering an uncharacteristic set-back would be to make an utter fool of himself. So he reasoned. But

---

[1] Gertler was almost certainly D. H. Lawrence's model for the sculptor Loerke in *Women in Love*, and the original of the painter Gombauld in Aldous Huxley's *Crome Yellow* – 'a black-haired young corsair of thirty, with flashing teeth and luminous large dark eyes'.

G*

his eloquence, so efficacious in making others prisoners, had not the power to release him from his own captivity. For still she seemed to him like no other woman in the world, and without her life was 'awful and black'.

A one-time admirer of Nietzsche, Gertler held an opinion of women in general that followed superficially that of the German philosopher. An artist such as himself, he believed, needed women as he needed food. They were useful, perhaps even essential to him when he had time to spare for them. If one could not do without them, then one must dominate them – that, in any case, was what they liked. Carrington's apparent self-sufficiency wounded his vanity and contradicted his Nietzschean beliefs. In spite of himself, he had started to feel subservient to her; and this he could not tolerate – especially since her insidious influence disrupted the process of his art and corroded his creative faculties.

Carrington, on the other hand, believed that art derived from and was a distillation of personal experience. Gertler must be made to accept her at her own estimate, instead of treating her as a mere embryo to be incubated in a man's passion, hatched out into a common sluttish mistress or submissive dowdy wife and helpmate. Realizing that if she surrendered herself to his desires she might also have to relinquish her hold over him, she refused to comply with his authority. His crude insensibility, his trick of plunging into intimate life without waiting for the natural ripening of intimacy, his rough and tyrannical rages repelled her and roused her own fighting qualities, so that she gathered up all her forces to resist him. By the late autumn of 1915, when Carrington first encountered Lytton, their arduous affair seemed to have reached a deadlock from which neither side could advance or retreat.

But it was not to be so.

When Carrington returned from Asheham, she wrote to Gertler describing something of her visit, but saying nothing of the feelings over Lytton which had sprung up in her. 'I have just come back from spending three days on the Lewes downs with the Clive Bells, Duncan, Mrs. Hutchinson and Lytton Strachey. God knows why they asked me!! It was much happier than I expected. The house was right in the middle of huge wild downs, four miles from Lewes, and surrounded by a high hill on both sides with trees. We lived in the kitchen for meals, as there weren'T any servants, so I helped Vanessa cook. Lytton is rather curious.'

Gertler himself had met Lytton a year earlier at one of Ottoline's parties. At that time Lytton seems to have cherished some modest hopes that the young painter might succeed Henry Lamb as the artist in his life. He put himself out to be kind and gallant to Gertler, pressing on him copies of Virgil's Pastorals *Tristram Shandy*, *Hamlet*, the poems of Thomas Hardy, Keats's letters and the novels of Dostoievsky. Gertler, flattered by these educational attentions, read hard and widely. He did more: responding with invitations to tea, going off for walks with Lytton in Kensington Gardens, staying at The Lacket and Belsize Park Gardens. Often they were uphill work, these poems and tea-parties. Yet he was genuinely very taken with Lytton and, being grateful for his kindness, slightly in awe of his urbanity, always remained on his best behaviour. On one occasion Lytton sent him some of his own poems and a typescript of 'Ermyntrude and Esmeralda'. These pieces were not exactly to Gertler's taste, but he replied with commendable diplomacy: '"Ermyntrude and Esmeralda" I thought extremely amusing. But the poems I thought were fine. I wonder if you have any more work you could let me read? I should like to.'

What author could resist such an invitation? More poems quickly followed – interspersed with volumes of Shelley – and these helped to establish Lytton in Gertler's mind as a man of enlightened sexual views and serious artistic intent. It was now, in the late winter of 1915, that a plot of astonishing craftiness occurred to him. His estimate of Lytton's character had suggested a subtle and peculiar scheme for breaking down Carrington's resistance. He had tried, on his own behalf, every trick in the book: he had left her for three months at a time; he had bombarded her with his extremest attentions; he had spoken openly and honestly of his love for her; he had lied to her; he had lost his temper; he had reasoned; he had pleaded – all in vain. The odd conclusion to which his hysterical thoughts now impelled him, was that Carrington did not sufficiently esteem him as a painter. If his talent and the significance of his work could be authoritatively impressed upon her by a third, impartial being, then, he seems to have reasoned, the complicated knot of her sexual reserve might at long last be unravelled. After all, what girl would not give herself freely to a genius, to a superman?

The proper person to be entrusted with this vicarious task, Gertler decided, must undoubtedly be Lytton. He was the perfect catalyst. For it appeared from certain casual questions and comments which Carrington had let fall about him since her week-end at Asheham, that she shared Gertler's own respect for Lytton's culture and intelligence. The more he thought about it the more this scheme recommended itself to him from every conceivable aspect. Lytton, he felt sure, regarded him highly as a painter. And besides, although he very evidently believed in sexual licence and might well convert the impressionable Carrington to these incontinent beliefs, he would obviously have no interest in replacing Gertler himself in her affections. The plan seemed completely foolproof.

In pursuance of this plan, Gertler therefore saw to it that, while in London, Lytton and Carrington came regularly in contact with each other, tactfully absenting himself from these meetings so that his own artistic virtues and accomplishments might be fully eulogized without inhibition or embarrassment.

The result produced by these circumspect tactics was decisive. Carrington's infatuation for Lytton, which might in less propitious circumstances have wasted away into nothing, gained enormously in strength and purpose. Part of January 1916 she spent painting his portrait, and her diary entries for this month show the awe and veneration in which she already held him. 'I would love to explore your mind behind your finely skinned forehead,' she wrote on 5 January. 'You seem so wise and so very coldly old. Yet in spite of this what a peace to be with you, and how happy I was to-day.'

Her happiness in his company redoubled every time they met. She could not contain it, and soon she determined somehow to make herself indispensable to him – without at the same time relinquishing Gertler's friendship. The obstacles in her way must have appeared almost insurmountable. The anticipated hostility of the terrifying Bloomsberries, of her formidable mother, and, worst of all, of Gertler himself – all of whom must consequently be kept in ignorance of her devotion to Lytton for as long as possible – would have sufficiently deterred most women. Not so Carrington. For her they acted less as a cause for despair than a spur to renewed endeavour. An even more discouraging problem with which she had to contend was Lytton's brand of avuncular lassitude, so kindly and oh! so apathetic. She quailed before his giraffe-like aloofness, and so frightened of him was she that she would seldom even risk a telephone call, since he sounded 'so very frigid and severe on that instrument'. How then could she seduce him? Often he exasperated her by his silence, his bland unresponsiveness. But though she sometimes felt like bullying him out of this passivity, she never actually dared to do so for fear of alienating him altogether.

For Lytton's own feelings towards Carrington were more mixed, changing as their relationship progressed. At times he felt flattered by her adoration; and at other times it irritated and alarmed him. He admired her zest for life, but her total lack of education and intellectuality bored him dreadfully. He could make her feel her ignorance most acutely, and her apprehension before him was so great that she scarcely dared to open her mouth in his presence. Nevertheless, in some moods, Lytton derived a good deal of enjoyment from instructing this raw and eager recruit in the delights of English literature – lessons which she very willingly absorbed and then liked to pass on to the still waiting, still vainly attentive Gertler, who thus received a double quota of prose and poetry.

Lytton's liaison with Carrington was more or less platonic, and the one or two attempts which were made later on to extend their relationship on to a physical plane were not successful. There seems little doubt that, on her account rather than his, Lytton regretted this failure to make Carrington his mistress. As Samuel Butler has written of a similar predicament:

> *A man will yield for pity if he can,*
> *But if the flesh rebels what can he do?*

About this incompatibility there was little enough, of course, Lytton could do, and his slight sense of guilt really derived from another failure on his part. Though at first Carrington liked to recognize in her protracted insecurity a safeguard to her independence, in time her uppermost desire became to marry Lytton, to look after him as his wife. But since they never married, their unorthodox relationship was always very volatile. Lytton's rather flimsy sexual attraction to her did endure for a time, but his association with the other sex was always of a humdrum or filial kind. That image of the ideal which most men seek in women, appeared in a masculine form to Lytton, whose youthful hero-worship – a result of his adolescent feeling of ostracism – did not dissipate itself in more natural emotions as he grew up. Girls, who had no place at school and very little in the university, consequently did not fill any place in his imagination except in a domestic setting. Carrington therefore found herself being unconsciously manœuvred into a maternal role, in time succeeding Ottoline as the chief confidante in Lytton's emotional life, instead of becoming the chief object of his love. It was not ideally what she would have wished – more than ever now she hated her womanhood and poignantly regretted not having been born a boy – but since it preserved her nearness to him, she willingly accepted the part.

This, then, was the capacity in which she set about making herself absolutely indispensable to him. Her extraordinary success can be measured in terms of the very deep and enduring affection for her which sprang up in Lytton. In the last year of his life, he wrote to her expressing his gratitude with a moving humility that hints at the sense of inadequacy he felt in matters where she was concerned. 'Your behaviour to me is indeed miraculous,' he told her (May 1931), '– how you put up with my petulance and vagueness I hardly know. Existence without you would be altogether impossible.'

The kind of selfless love which he, in all his romances, had never quite attained, she succeeded in lavishing upon him without even trying. She almost lost her own identity, caring for him as other people care for themselves. When he was with her, she was alive; when he was away for a week-end, a day, she ceased to exist; and when he died, she ended her life.

Carrington's devotion is not easy to account for by any rough-and-ready, common-sense standards, especially since, as Sir Roy Harrod put it, 'Lytton Strachey had not much to offer women by way of ordinary masculine blandishment'. Those few who knew of her attachment to him were incredulous. When Arthur Waley asked her what on earth there could be about Lytton to appeal to her, she exclaimed lyrically: 'Oh, it's his *knees*!' – an explanation which left Waley more dumbfounded than ever. This answer, however, does, very obliquely, indicate a certain similarity between her and Lytton. The fantastic, slightly disconcerting sense of humour which they shared was an expression of their peculiar, half-audacious, and highly sensitive non-conformity. In some respects they were the same type of person, emotional to a degree, yet awkward, giving the superficial impression of being cold and remote, insular and egotistical. Carrington seems to have felt that she had discovered in Lytton a father-substitute with whom she could establish an intimate relationship free from the pernicious presence of her mother, which had so effectively destroyed her real father. Since her love for Lytton was never really consummated, she never met with the disillusionment common to such cases, the acute neurotic tension and recoil symptoms of fear. Instead, her attachment grew stronger until it came to infect every particle of her being. Thus, it would seem that both Lytton and Carrington were in search of some place of rapport away from their homes, where they might settle down with a parent-substitute – a mother to one, a father to the other – both pursuing their separate sexual lives free from any parent-fixation.

A somewhat scatterbrained and less sympathetic interpretation of their attachment has been put forward by Percy Wyndham Lewis, who diagnosed it simply as a father–daughter association, which Lytton embarked on in order to assert his revolutionary spirit of pseudo-manhood, and Carrington to establish, rather belatedly, the parental dominance which had been absent from her childhood. In his novel, *The Apes of God*, this arch-enemy of Bloomsbury culture – or of the

'Pansy-clan' as he liked collectively to call its tribesmen – has given a maliciously distorted and hilarious caricature of Lytton under the name of Matthew Plunkett. The crane-like Plunkett walks with an affected anarchical gait, adopts mannerisms reminiscent of his father, puts on in front of strangers an owlish ceremony of regulation shyness, and articulates with two distinct voices, one a high-piping vixenish shriek, the other of a more fastidious percussion – 'a nasal stammer modelled upon the effects of severe catarrh'. Being a modern man much taken up with modern psychology, this hero conceives the intensely original idea of submitting himself to psycho-analytical treatment in the Zürich consulting-den of the Jewish Dr Frumpfsusan – an extravagant notion obviously suggested to Wyndham Lewis by the career of James Strachey, Freud's pupil and English-language translator. Plunkett's aim, expressed in Jungian terms, is to get himself extroverted so that he can overcome a 'virulent scale complex of psychical-inferiority'. Dr Frumpfsusan explains that he must falsify nature to his own personal advantage. 'Inferiority-feeling', he flatteringly suggests, 'may result from an actual superiority! The handicap of genius, isn't it?' He tells Plunkett that, for successful extroversion, he must seek to dominate the scene, that he should contrive to be a Gulliver in Lilliput. 'For that truly uppish self-feeling,' he concludes, '. . . you must *choose your friends small*! . . . believe me, *you cannot choose your lady friend too small. . . .*'

It was therefore on doctor's orders that Plunkett took up with Betty Blyth, his Carrington-like girl friend, a petite doll-woman. Of the magical puppet prescription, her preternaturally tiny figure was dwarfed by the fairy giant of this Bloomsbury legend, who, towering far above her, would strive to assume the swaggering, buccaneering manner of the more flamboyant extrovert. When she calls on him one afternoon, he solemnly and with portentous concentration caresses one of his dollie's flaxen curls with the extreme finger-tips of an extended tapering hand and arm, and feeling at last 'a distinct vibration, in the recalcitrant depths of his person', he swoops down and picks her up 'as though she had been a half-ton feather'. With some difficulty, his knees bent and trembling, he staggers against the wall and then into his bedroom, only to drop Betty on the floor at the sudden shock of seeing, stretched out fast asleep on his bed, his last year's boy friend.

The explanation of Lytton's attachment to Carrington implied in this farcical drama is ingeniously malevolent. The acquisition of an awed and submissive girl friend, like the growing of a beard, was meant to conceal his dandified homosexuality and to establish him as a man of open virility, like his father, whom he unconsciously mimics. But this theory, which might plausibly enough be made to account for certain psychological factors in Lytton's character, does not follow the biographical course of events in his relationship with Carrington, either in the manner in which this relationship started up or in the extraordinary fashion in which it later developed. The basic triangular pattern of Lytton's emotional life was not, at its centre, altered by his association with Carrington. But, on the periphery, it became immensely complicated by the introduction of unlooked-for inter-relationships which sprang up between lover and confessor, and which sucked in and fatally involved fourth and fifth and sixth parties who all contributed, from time to time, something real and unique to Lytton's life.

Wyndham Lewis does, however, spot Carrington's father-fixation, of which she herself was unaware. The mysterious peace and happiness she experienced in Lytton's company, she put down, reasonably enough, to the very different nature of their friendship from the stormy affair she was still carrying on with Gertler. Lytton made no demands upon her, and did not seek to interfere with her freedom. In contrast to the tortured and tempestuous Gertler, he was at all times gentle and courteous. With him she felt safe.

And she felt more positive emotions, too. At the prospect of spending some days with him at Garsington, she wrote to Lytton (20 April 1916) – 'mon chère grand-père' – confessing her 'incredible internal excitement'. Her letters to Gertler over this same spring period are less simple and consistent. Written in her childlike, illiterate, eloquent scrawl, freely illustrated with drawings not always relevant to the text, these letters are frequently undated and from their emotional content could be placed in almost any order. In one she suggests parting from Gertler at least temporarily 'as it nearly sends me mad with grief, at seeing you so miserable'. In another she urges him to read Keats. Yet another contains a lethal analysis of their incompatibility: 'You are too possessive, and I too free. That is why we could never live together.' But in a pencil note, written that May, she sounds a more optimistic chord. 'You will not love me in vain,' she promises him (16 May 1916), '– I shall not disappoint you in the end.'

Perhaps, at long last, Gertler thought, the plan was beginning to work. And so, containing his impatience, he waited on, wondering what would happen next.

The last ten days of May Lytton and Carrington spent together at Garsington during one of Ottoline's most strenuous and rowdy house-parties. Other guests included Philip Snowden[1] and his wife, H. W. Massingham, Bertrand Russell, Maynard Keynes and various young ladies either deaf or French. 'The Snowden couple were as provincial as one expected,' Lytton wrote to James (31 May 1916), '– she, poor woman, dreadfully plain and stiff, in stiff plain clothes, and he with a strong northern accent, but also a certain tinge of eminence. Quite too political and remote from any habit of civilized discussion to make it possible to talk to him – one just had to listen to anecdotes and observations (good or bad); but a nice good-natured cripple . . .'

Into this powerful anti-Cabinet conclave, during the Sunday afternoon torpor and while the peacocks were setting up their continuous shrieking about the garden, the prime minister and party arrived, just in time to rescue a servant maid from drowning. The atmosphere was more like a campaign in Flanders than an English country garden-party, but when the excitement had died down and tea was served, Lytton was able to observe at leisure Asquith's entourage. 'They *were* a scratch lot,' he reported to James. 'Lady Robert Cecil, stone deaf and smiling most sweetly at everything she didn't hear, a degraded Lady Meux (wife of Admiral Hedworth[2]) with a paroqueet accent, and poor old [Sir Matthew] Nathan, in walrus moustaches and an almost Uncle Trevor air of imbecile and louche benignity.'

But it was the prime minister himself who chiefly interested Lytton. Asquith seemed to have changed, grown redder and bulkier, since their last encounter in the summer of 1914. Then they had met at the height of the Ulster crisis; now they met again only a few days after the Irish Rebellion. 'I studied the Old Man with extreme vigour,' Lytton wrote to James, 'and really he is a corker. He seemed much larger than he did when I last saw him (just two years ago) – a fleshy, sanguine, wine-bibbing, medieval Abbot of a personage – a glutinous lecherous cynical old fellow – oogh! – You should have seen him making towards Carrington – cutting her off at an angle as she crossed the lawn. I've rarely seen anyone so obviously enjoying life; so obviously, I thought, *out* to enjoy it; almost, really, as if he'd deliberately decided that he *would*, and let all the rest go hang. Cynical, yes, it's hardly possible to

[1] Viscount Snowden (1864–1937), then member of Parliament for Blackburn and champion of the conscientious objector. Later he became chancellor of the exchequer (1924; 1929–31). He had been one of the chief founders of the Labour Party, and second in the Party only to Ramsay MacDonald.

[2] Sir Hedworth Meux (1856–1929) who, the previous year, had been made Admiral of the Fleet. In 1910 he married Mildred, the third daughter of the first Baron Alington, and widow of Viscount Chelsea (d. 1908), and a few months later changed his name from Lambton on coming into a large fortune under the will of his mother-in-law. On his death he left the very pleasant sum of £910,465. His widow later married Lord Charles Montagu.

doubt it; or perhaps one should say just "case-hardened'. Tiens! One looks at him, and thinks of the War. . . . And all the time, *perpetually*, a little pointed, fat tongue comes poking out, and licking those great chops, and then darting back again. That gives one a sense of the Artful Dodger – the happy Artful Dodger – more even than the rest. His private boudoir doings with Ottoline are curious – if one's to believe what one hears; also his attitude towards Pozzo struck me – he positively shied away from him ("Not much juice in *him*", he said in private to her lady-ship . . . so superficial we all thought it!). Then why, oh why, does he go about with a creature like Lady Meux? On the whole, one wants to stick a dagger in his ribs . . . and then, as well, one can't help rather liking him – I suppose because he does enjoy himself so much.'

Enjoyment was the keynote of his personality, Lytton afterwards reflected. A big, sanguine, jovial man, he had clearly just enjoyed a good lunch with several glasses of good red wine. 'There was a look of a Roman Emperor about him (one could imagine a wreath on his head),' Lytton wrote in his unpublished pen portrait of Asquith (2–6 May 1918), 'or a Renaissance Pope ("Well, let me enjoy the world, now that I am Vicar of Christ."). . . . Standing beside him on the lawn, in the brilliant sunshine, with the house behind us and the landscape below us, I reflected that since I had last seen him a change had come over the world, as well. It was disgusting; and yet, such was the extra-ordinary satisfaction of the man that, in spite of everything, one could not help feeling a kind of sympathetic geniality of one's own.'

In the calmer moments of his stay at Garsington, Lytton read Rim-baud and Verlaine. 'Then, too, I have been for some enormous walks,' he told James, '– "expeditions" – with, precisely, Carrington. One was to the town of Abingdon, a magical spot, with a town-hall by Wren perhaps – a land of lotus-eaters, where I longed to sink down for the rest of my life, in an incredible oblivion. . . . As for Carrington, she's a queer young thing. These modern women! What are they up to? They seem most highly dubious. Why is it? Is it because there's so much "in" them? Or so little? They perplex me. When I consider Bunny, or Peter (he's close by, at Magdalen) or even Gertler, I find nothing particularly obscure there, but when it comes to a creature with a cunt one seems to be immediately désorienté. Perhaps it's because cunts don't particularly appeal to one. I suppose that may be partly the explanation. But – oh, they coil, and coil; and, on the whole, they make me uneasy.'

Part of this unease was due to Carrington's idolatry of him. But he also felt some disquiet on behalf of Gertler who, in reply to one of his own letters earlier that month, had written back a despairing account of

himself. Apart from his other worries, it appeared that he was nearly
bankrupt. Something, Lytton decided, must be done. 'I've just heard
from Gertler, who says he's on the brink of ruin,' he wrote from
Garsington to Clive Bell (12 May 1916), '– has taken his last £2 out of
the bank, and will have nothing at all in another week. Do you think
anything can be done? I'm sure £10 would make a great difference to
him, and I thought perhaps you might be able to invest some such sum
in a minor picture or some drawings. Or perhaps you could whip up
somebody else. If you do anything, of course don't mention me, as his
remarks about his finances were quite incidental, with no idea of begging.'

On the same day Lytton wrote a somewhat stilted but kindly and
generous letter to Gertler himself. 'I have long wanted to possess a
work by you – so will you put aside for me either a drawing or some
other small piece, which is in your judgement the equivalent of the
enclosed [£10] – And I'll carry it off when I'm next in London. I only
wish I could get one of your large pictures – what idiots the rich are!
And how I loathe the thought of them swilling about in their motors
and their tens of thousands, when people like you are in difficulties.
What makes it so particularly monstrous is that the wants of artists are
so very moderate – just for the mere decencies of life. All the same,
though I'm very sorry that you're not even half as well off as an ordinary
Civil Servant, you may be sure that I don't pity you – because you *are*
an artist, and being that is worth more than all the balances at all the
banks in London.'

Carrington was delighted that her friends, especially Lytton, were
aiding the impoverished Gertler, and wrote enthusiastically to say how
happy and relieved she was to hear that he was at last selling some of his
pictures. Her letters from Garsington, being written on the spur of the
moment and not for the eyes of posterity, contain no references to the
prime minister or the other important personages, except Augustus
John who, she assures Gertler, had 'made no attempt on my virginity
last Tuesday' when they were alone together in a taxi. Her comments
on Lytton are deliberately unrevealing. He is *very* serious, she remarks,
but interesting when one gets to know him better. He has been reading
poetry to her. Otherwise, she prattles on about the countryside, about
'the wonderful blue flowers, and so many birds singing all day'. She
has been painting tulips, she writes, and instead of returning to meet
Gertler in London she will stay on longer at Garsington – 'you could
not but be happy if you were here now I think' – in order to paint more
tulips – 'such tulips I feel weak with excitement'. She has also swum in
the swimming-pool twice before breakfast. 'The children wear no

clothes and run over the grass. and stand in the tulips. thigh deep in yellow tulips. It has made me depressed for they are so beautiful and I wished for the impossible to be more like them. and I hated this bulk of a body which surrounds my spirit. and yet I feel so lovely! Are you happy now because I love you.'

But somehow Gertler was not happy. His next meeting with Carrington had been summarily postponed, and all he got instead were descriptions of flowers and birds. It was more than human patience could endure. Sometimes he thought that she must be deliberately teasing him. Moreover, he had begun to suspect that she was concealing something from him, and accused her of being too friendly with Gilbert Cannan – then busy writing *Mendel*, his novel built round the Gertler–Carrington love-affair. Carrington, with literal justice, repudiated this accusation. Once, before a room full of people, Cannan had given her a brotherly kiss on the cheek – like a handshake – when she was about to leave. Nothing more. 'I care so little for anything except making you happy that I will promise not to kiss anyone since it causes you pain,' she reassured Gertler. Really, she went on, the incident was not worthy of discussion – though she nevertheless saw in it the opportunity for delivering a homily on trust: 'But do you not see that you cast a cloud of doubt on our trust in each other, by thinking for one moment that anything else or anyone could interrupt it? we shall always live in one sense apart. But I feel always come back to each other. There is nothing, absolutely nothing which can affect us now.

'You must cease being miserable at once, and believe me. What do I care for anyone else?, and you know it —'

Gertler's jealous suspicions had acted as a warning to her, and after this burst of self-exoneration and moral stricture she veered hastily towards harmless, irrelevant topics. How lovely the weather was; how lovely Dorothy Brett was looking. She wished that she could share with Gertler her love of Rimbaud, but it was all too new and enthralling for her to speak about yet. Finally she fell back once again to marine allegory: 'It has felt like a lock on the river, with our two boats up against the lock. Now it is open, and we can rush so swiftly down the river. and you won'T be impatient If my little craft is not quite so fast and sticks in the reeds. The great and lovely thing is that we are on the same river.'

But Gertler's suspicions were only partly allayed.

5

UNREGARDED HOURS

At the beginning of June, Carrington reluctantly dragged herself away from Garsington to join Gertler as a fellow guest of St John and Mary Hutchinson at Eleanor. Lytton, meanwhile, stayed on, grateful for the sudden influx of peace. Since his ordeal before the tribunals his health had not been good and he had been forced to lead rather a hole-and-corner life at Garsington, 'like a sick dog', he described it to Gertler (10 May 1916), 'dragging about from cushion to cushion, or creeping out into the sunshine to lie there dreaming'. Now that the rag-time of house guests, bustle and excitement had died down, Garsington was converted into a perfect Home of Rest. Even Ottoline herself had departed, and Lytton was free to sit out alone in the kitchen garden, idling, reading, and writing letters. 'I feel as if I were gradually turning into a pear-tree on a South Wall,' he told Vanessa Bell (2 June 1916), 'and unless you come and pull me up by the – root, before long, I shall very likely be doomed for the rest of my life to furnish fruit for her ladyship's table.' Even so the prospect of struggling out into the world again, of facing train journeys and the buffetings of London, filled him with palpitation and alarm.

When, in the third week of June, he eventually did leave, it was not back to the horrors of London, but for a remote Suffolk farmhouse, Wissett Lodge, which Duncan Grant had temporarily rented in order to set himself and David Garnett up as official fruit farmers, thereby discharging their obligations under the National Service Act. The atmosphere of amiability and charm, bees and blackberries, exactly suited his mood, and he hesitated here until the end of the month, with Harry Norton as the other guest. 'Is it the secret of life or of . . . something else . . . I don't quite know what? . . . Oblivion? Stupor? Incurable looseness? – that they've discovered at Wissett?' he asked Virginia Woolf (28 July 1916). 'I loved it, and never wanted to go away.'

These summer days at Wissett rolled by very lazily, and he sucked in an added strength. Most of the time he spent reclining under the rambler roses and laurel bushes composing poetry, wandering from gooseberry-bushes to easels, listening to Norton on Prime Numbers, crouching over a wintery fire looking at old magazines, eating huge meals and sitting up into the early hours of each morning arguing about art. Their only adventure occurred one Sunday morning – the farmers' day off – when the four of them set out for a long walk towards the sea – not a very wise direction, as they discovered when an agitated corporal rushed up to them and nearly flung them all into a military gaol owing to their collective Germanic appearance and the incorrect Suffolk accent in which they answered his questions.[1] Apart from this episode, their life was unbrokenly smooth. 'Everything and everybody seems to be more or less overgrown with vegetation,' Lytton informed Ottoline (20 June 1916), 'thistles four feet high fill the flower garden, Duncan is covered with Virginia (or should it be Vanessa?) creeper, and Norton and I go about pulling up the weeds and peeping under the foliage. Norton is in very good spirits, having evolved a new theory of cubic roots.'

During their long evening talks, Lytton, in strictest confidence, told his friends something about Carrington. Their curiosity was understandably roused, and since Duncan Grant had been joined at Wissett by Vanessa Bell, Lytton was encouraged to invite Carrington down. But, on this occasion, she was unable to abandon Gertler, and a temporary lull settled over their triangular affair.

Lytton filled in this lull by writing an unpublished autobiographical essay[2] which was by way of being a new literary experiment, exposing to view a side of his character usually latent in his writing. Abandoning his familiar technique of a neatly integrated compression of material set in a prefabricated and well-rounded form, he deliberately employed a more diffuse style and consecutive, linear mode of composition, to describe in considerable detail the minutiae of a single ordinary day, Monday, 26 June, its hackneyed occurrences and the spontaneous self-observations called forth by them. Such a digressive and tangential manner does not really suit Lytton's pen, though he manages the exercise very cleverly. The experiment, however, also reveals a few minor disturbances in his emotional life – a slight breach with Ottoline, which, though quickly healed, sounded the overture to a wider, more permanent dissidence later to break out between them; an uneasiness with Vanessa Bell over their mutual attraction to Duncan Grant, and some hint of awkwardness with Duncan Grant over their mutual attraction to Vanessa Bell; a tremulous flirtation in the garden with David Garnett; and, arising from this last incident, a confession that although he was singularly fortunate in knowing so many friends, he could never be sure if any of them quite liked him.

[1] The German spy question used recurrently to cause Lytton some embarrassment, especially in the country. 'It is distinctly unfortunate being so noticeable a figure,' he complained to Vanessa Bell (6 August 1917). 'Ought I to shave my beard for the period of the war? But would even that lull the suspicions of the yokels?'

[2] Like 'Lancaster Gate', this autobiographical essay was intended for, and subsequently read to, the Memoir Club.

More interesting, perhaps, is the description of Lytton's ecstatic surrender to a mood of not unpleasurable melancholia, nourished by the enveloping stupor and oblivion of Wissett, and induced within him by a slight mental tiredness, a convalescent sense of egocentric good health. This mood took the form of a fanciful flirtation with the notion of death — a sentimental excess which is usually destroyed pretty effectively by a single uneven heartbeat. 'Restful death', as the young and full-of-life Shakespeare phrased it in his sonnets, is, of course, a fictional concept, signifying the wish for a temporary removal of the world's wearisome afflictions, and has little enough to do with the actual unavoidable journey from Sunshine to the Sunless Land. Lytton's nostalgic languor represented a delicious renunciation of the will, its frustrations and inanities, together with that detachment from the world and that mystical exaltation of the spirit for which a part of him was always longing.

'I thought of Death,' he wrote, 'of Keats and the Ode to the Nightingale, of "easeful Death" — "half in love with easeful Death" — and I was convinced, as I'd been in the train coming down from London that if Death would only come to me in a mood of serene happiness, he would be very welcome. I thought of suddenly dying, painlessly, where I lay. . . . The dazzling happiness, coming in flood after flood, over my soul, was so intense that it was like a religious conversion. And through it all there was an odd waft of melancholy — a kind of vibration of regret. A strange importance seemed to invest and involve into a unity the scene, the moment, my state of feeling.'

On leaving Wissett, Lytton returned to London where he was shortly to undergo the first of his regular six-monthly medical check-ups to confirm and prolong his absolute exemption from military service. Soon after his return, he called on Gertler at his studio in Rudall Crescent to choose and collect the drawing for which he had already paid. The description of this visit which he gives in a letter to Ottoline (3 July 1916) emphasizes the real lack of affinity existing between them, and points to a natural antagonism so far held in suspense by the illusory belief of each that the other might be of some personal value to him. Gertler had shown him his 'latest whirligig picture', Lytton wrote. 'Oh lord, oh lord have mercy upon us! It is a devastating affair isn't it? I felt that if I were to look at it for any length of time, I should be carried away suffering from shellshock. I admired it, of course, but as for *liking* it, one might as well think of liking a machine gun. But fortunately he does all that for himself — one needn't bother with one's appreciations. He said it reminded him of Bach — Well, well!'

While Lytton was staying at Belsize Park Gardens, Carrington came over one afternoon to tea and told him that, later in July, she had been invited down again to Garsington – this time with Gertler. Lytton himself was expecting to return there about the same time, and now promptly wrote to Ottoline confirming his visit. 'I want to get my Arnold life done,' he had told her earlier from Wissett (20 June 1916), 'and I think under your peaceful shades it might be accomplished.' His few days in London, though entertaining, had quickly tired him, and he was eager for the repose of the country once more. 'I am accumulating writing material,' he wrote (3 July 1916), '– and mean to be very industrious for the next month or so.'

A week later he arrived down at Garsington, where he was able, over a period of rather more than a fortnight, to do no work whatever. Presided over by an apoplectic Ottoline, her face almost entirely covered by peeling flakes of white chalk, tightly swathed in a stiff gown of peacock silk, her slender throat encased in baroque pearls, a continuous whirlpool of a party surged about him – numberless guests all spiralling round one another in the house, and overflowing into a cottage and the village inn. To make it worse, Lytton complained to Mary Hutchinson (10 July 1916), most of them – including Clifford Allen,[1] Eva Gore-Booth,[2] H. W. Nevinson[3] and Lady Constance Malleson[4] – were 'so damned political and revolutionary that I got quite sick of the conscientious objector and the thought of Ireland's wrongs'. But there were plenty of other, less political guests within the crowd, among them Evan Morgan,[5] 'a tall bright-coloured youth with a paroqueet nose, and an assured manner, and the general appearance of a refined

---

[1] Clifford Allen (1889–1939), created Lord Allen of Hurtwood in 1932. For his leadership of the resistance to military conscription he was several times put in prison and his health seriously weakened.

[2] Eva Gore-Booth, sister of the rebel Countess Markievicz, and noted for her nerve and dash riding to hounds. Her gazelle-like beauty enraptured W. B. Yeats, who commemorated her in a poem. A minor poet herself, she later lost her way amid the coils of philanthropic politics.

[3] H. W. Nevinson (1856–1941), journalist and essayist, who during the war won fame as the *Guardian*'s correspondent at the Western Front and particularly at the Dardanelles, where he was wounded. His three tomes of autobiography have been abridged into one volume, *Fire of Life* (1935), by Ellis Roberts. His son, by his first marriage, was the painter C. R. W. Nevinson.

[4] Lady Constance Malleson, actress and writer. Youngest daughter of the fifth Earl of Annesly, she had recently married Miles Malleson, the actor, from whom, in 1923, she obtained a divorce.

[5] Later Viscount Tredegar (1899–1949) who founded the Tredegar Memorial Lecture at the Royal Society of Literature, and who was at this time an undergraduate at Christ Church, Oxford.

old woman of high birth'; and, once again, the alluring, impassive
Katherine Mansfield – 'an odd satirical woman behind a regular mask of
a face . . . She was very difficult to get at; one felt it would take years of
patient burrowing, but that it might be worth while.'

'The week-end is over – true enough – but . . . the party still goes on,'
he lamented in another letter to Virginia Woolf (17 July 1916). 'Carrington and Brett are here (ever heard of *them*) and now, a few minutes
ago, Gertler (ever heard of *him*) turned up. The rag-time has begun
again. I have fled into the garden – but one might as well try to fly from
the Eye of the Lord.'

Lytton's disinclination to be drawn into this mixture of conviviality
and altercation, as expressed to Virginia Woolf, was partly a device for
concealing his growing attachment to Carrington. Yet it was also a
very authentic apprehension that he voiced. The Gertler–Carrington
situation struck him as gloomy and complicated, he confided to Mary
Hutchinson (23 July 1916), 'but complicated in a dull way. The poor
thing [Carrington] seems almost aux abois with Gertler for ever at her,
day in, day out – she talks of flying London, of burying herself in
Cornwall, or becoming a Cinema actress. I of course suggested that
she should live with me, which she luckily immediately refused – for
one thing, I couldn't have afforded it. And there she is for the present at
Garsington, with Mark gnashing his teeth in the background, and
Brett quite ineffectual, and her Ladyship worming and worming for
ever and ever, Amen.' But at the same time, Lytton noticed that
Carrington still rather admired Gertler, and he sympathized with him
over the virginity question – 'unless she's the most horrible liar'.

But whatever the truth, the whole situation was growing too hectic,
blowing up, he felt sure, into an incredible hurricane of an affair, and
he soon decided to fly beyond the garden, into the arms of Oliver and
Ray Strachey at their suburban haven at Durbins. 'I came here with the
notion of working,' he wrote from Garsington to Barbara Hiles (17
July 1916). 'Mon Dieu! There are now no intervals between the week-
ends – the flux and reflux is endless – and I sit quivering among a
surging mesh of pugs, peacocks, pianolas, and humans – if humans
they can be called – the inhabitants of this Circe's cave. I am now faced
not only with Carrington and Brett (more or less permanences now)
but Gertler, who . . . is at the present moment carolling a rag-time in
union with her Ladyship. I feel like an open boat in a choppy sea – but
thank goodness the harbour is in sight.'

His anchorage at Durbins was a complete contrast to Garsington.
Since Oliver only returned in the evenings from the Foreign Office to
play Bach at the piano, Lytton was left with his mother, Ray and his

sister Pippa, who all conspired to look after him and make him totally comfortable. The days were warm and sunny and he would sit out in the garden, now strewn with hollyhocks and lavender, working on his 'Dr. Arnold' and recruiting after the agitations of the previous weeks. This peaceful and regular routine suited him well and his work went ahead very successfully. The only interruptions were provided by the occasional brief appearances of middle-aged visitors. Among these was Ray Strachey's uncle, Logan Pearsall Smith, who, Lytton told Ottoline (21 August 1916), 'is really now *more* than middle-aged – senile, one's inclined to say, poor old fellow – doddering on with his anecdotes and literature, which, in spite of the efforts of a lifetime, remain alas! American. I was rather amused by his view of Vernon [Lee], "I think on the whole she's the best talker I know" – I gave paralysed assent, and then ventured to add, "But perhaps at times she tends to be slightly boring" . . . He wouldn't have it though. Well, well, de gustibus non est disputandum, which may be translated:

> *'Tastes differ: some like coffee, some like tea;*
> *And some are never bored by Vernon Lee.'*[1]

Another visitor to Roger Fry's house was Walter Raleigh, who also seems to have struck the rejuvenated Lytton as being senile, though very pleasant. For the first time Lytton was feeling some sense of superiority over his distinguished seniors. 'He was far less outré and bloodthirsty about the war than I'd expected – chiefly just childish; rather timid too, it seemed, on controversial questions; and really I liked him more than I ever had before.'

Virginia Woolf had invited him down to Asheham after leaving Guildford in mid-August, but he had to refuse this invitation 'as I have engaged myself to go [to] Wales then, with a small juvenile party' (28 July 1916). He would, he added, be at large again in September, when he hoped to visit Leonard and Virginia in Cornwall.

The journey to North Wales was occasioned by Nicholas Bagenal, who had just then come out of hospital after recovering from a wound in the hip. He was in love with his future wife, Barbara Hiles, who persuaded Lytton to act as chaperon during a fortnight's holiday they were to spend together at her father's cottage, before Nicholas returned to the front. In agreeing to this Lytton had inquired whether he in turn might be accompanied by Barbara's friend, Carrington. And so the juvenile

---

[1] Violet Paget (1856–1935), the lesbian bluestocking who wrote books on aesthetics, politics and Italian art under the pseudonym of 'Vernon Lee'. In later life she grew rather deaf and was obliged to resort to an ear trumpet which she employed only when talking herself. She was famous also for appearing in the first line of a poem by Browning: 'Who said "Vernon Lee"?' There is a recent biography of her by Peter Gunn (1965).

party was formed – 'though really', Lytton confessed to Mary Hutchinson, 'I sometimes begin to wonder what the diable I am doing in this galère of grandchildren'.

Difficulties and anxieties abounded. Lytton felt apprehensive over the inherent amenities of North Welsh cottages, and almost regretted that he had not chosen instead the known qualities of Asheham. Barbara, too, began to wonder whether she had done the right thing by including the finicky and censorious Lytton Strachey on such an out-of-the-way expedition. 'Oh Lytton I'm so excited and so afraid you will be unhappy, or bored,' she wrote to him (5 August 1916). In his reply he endeavoured to set her mind at ease, though because of his own doubts the note is a little forced and pessimism gleams clearly through. 'I pray for this weather to last,' he answered (8 August 1916). 'But if it doesn't, we can always shut the doors and windows, and cook and eat and cook and eat indefinitely. In the intervals we can hum tunes and recite ballads. But if it's fine we must scale the mountains with gazelle-like tread. . . . I'll bring some books.'

The chief difficulties, however, were provided by Carrington, whose fears outmatched the sum of Lytton's and Barbara's and possibly, too, those of the wounded Nicholas Bagenal. The invitation had originally been extended to her at the end of July, while she was still at Garsington, and her excitement was at once shaken up by doubts. 'How much do you all really want me to come?' she asked Lytton (30 July 1916). She was penniless and too 'proud' to accept money from another woman, namely her friend Barbara, who was almost as poverty-stricken as herself. On the other hand, considerations for Gertler do not seem to have strayed into her mind. After her lecture on trust, surely he would not dare to object. She therefore resolved to *walk* to North Wales, or possibly to bicycle there. But was it all going to be worth such a tremendous effort? How could she tell? 'It would be awful to walk so far,' she admitted to Lytton (30 July 1916), 'and then be met with the chilly eye of criticism.' But her prevailing fear was that, under adverse conditions such as they might well come up against in Wales, her tenuous attachment to Lytton could be subjected to new strains and stresses, might snap altogether. Well, she could only do her best. She was, so she assured him, assiduously reading her Donne, and in order to please him had begun to take lessons in French. The rest of her news was gossip in the Strachey manner. 'Ottoline insists on trying her best to get my state of virginity reduced, and made me practically share a bedroom with Norton!! And poor Brett got sent out four times in one morning with Bertie for long walks across remote fields by her Ladyship.'

Early in August, her famous and refurbished virginity still intact, Carrington went off to stay with her parents at Hurstbourne Tarrant. She was in a fiercely rebellious mood, vanishing out of the house during the day for long walks over the hills with a dog named Jasper, and at night sleeping out on the roof under the open sky. Her mother, so she complained to Gertler, 'was more awfull than ever', and her father more pitifully ill and old: 'I hate him for living as he does or rather I hate life for making him live,' she raged. 'It is so undignified an end like this.'

Meanwhile negotiations over the holiday were still progressing and growing daily more involved. Lytton had offered to pay for Carrington's travelling expenses, but, possibly from a sense of delicacy, did not write to her at her parents' home to tell her so. Instead he communicated with Barbara Hiles. 'I am rather rich just now, I find,' he lied (8 August 1916), 'so it would be absurd for her [Carrington] to go by foot, or worse, for lack of money.' This news was speedily relayed on to Carrington, but still she hesitated, until her mother, learning of her projected journey now for the first time, absolutely forbade it. Her mind was then very simply made up. She would go.

At last the complicated preliminaries were at an end, and it was arranged that at four o'clock on the afternoon of Saturday, 12 August, the four of them would converge and assemble on the platform of Llandudno Junction – Barbara and Nicholas having travelled from Westbury-on-Severn in Gloucestershire, Lytton from Guildford in Surrey, and Carrington from Andover in Hampshire.

On the day beforehand Lytton left Durbins for Belsize Park Gardens to prepare for his journey. Late that Friday afternoon, as he was wandering down the Haymarket, all at once he sensed, pervading the atmosphere, an extraordinary spirit of cheerfulness, of bonhomie. Puzzled, he glanced round. 'The streets were empty . . . and I was vaguely strolling, when, (without exaggeration) I became aware of a curious sensation of "bien-aise" in the air,' he later recounted, describing the incident. For a moment or two he was at a loss as how to account for this feeling. Then, 'looking round I saw a motor coming up the hill; it was open, and in it was Asquith, alone, with a look of radiant happiness upon his face – happiness which was indeed literally radiant, for I had actually felt it when my back was turned. He passed on without seeing me – he really looked too happy to see anything. I think there was a portmanteau in the car, and I suppose he was off somewhere for the week-end.'

As the prime minister, glowing with joy, floated off from this singular unperceived *rencontre*, away into the distance, like – the simile is Lytton's – a seraph in a heavenly ecstasy, the immanent euphoria flooding the

Haymarket drained away, and Lytton was left with a sense of amused and astonished envy. How the devil did the old boy manage it? He wished that he could feel one half so buoyant over his own week-end. The good-humoured incredulity he felt was all the more remarkable since he strongly disapproved of Asquith's conduct over the recent Roger Casement trial. 'Casement, I don't take much stock of, somehow or other,' he had written to Ottoline (3 July 1916), 'though I perceive the romantic bravery of the man; yes, I do perceive it, but the absence of Wisdom refrigerates me – and something sentimental and cheap in his phraseology too. I could have imagined some much grander speech. Of course I should be very glad if they didn't hang him, but I can't believe there's much chance of that – especially with Asquith prime minister. That old buffer has certainly been distinguishing himself lately. Is he a coward, or a fiend, or simply a dunderhead I wonder?'

Whichever he was, Asquith continued, off and on, to fascinate and perplex Lytton, and, whenever they met, to instil within him a humorous grudging amiability. If only *he* could derive so much pleasure from life!

The fortnight in Wales on which he now embarked turned out, however, to be far more pleasurable than he had dared hope. In place of the bleakness and absence of comfort he had so much dreaded, everything was perfectly civilized – beeswaxed parquet floors, spring mattresses, air cushions, delicious meals and 'an old hag to wash up'. The cottage itself, very small and sequestered, painted white outside and with a tiny garden filled with flowers, was perched half-way up one of the chain of mountains which on all sides shut them in, while along the flat valley directly below there ran a broad and shallow river – the sort of wild precipitous country that agreeably reminded Lytton of Rothiemurchus. 'I enjoyed the Welsh fortnight very much indeed,' he afterwards told David Garnett (2 September 1916). 'You can't think how kind they all were to me – and how wonderfully nice. Barbara managed the cottage, and the cooking with the greatest skill . . . Nick was really charming – his gaiety of spirits never ceased. It will be too horrible if he is forced back into that murderous whirlpool. As for Carrington – we seemed to see a great deal of each other. But this let me remark at once – my attitude throughout in relation to *all*, has been of immaculate chastity, whatever the conduct of others may have been.'

As always, and increasingly as time went on, Lytton loved to be surrounded by men and women younger than himself. The high spirits and energy of young people infected him in such a way that he seemed able to shrug off his own inhibiting 'antique spirit', as he used to call it. One half of him, he once told Ottoline, felt as if it had gone back ten years or twenty, while the other half, he was pretty sure, had moved forward by about the same amount; so the result was – 'me voici, a mixture of 18 and 52'.

Although a teenager for most of this time, when things went wrong he would rapidly revert to a quinquagenarian. The only serious drawback to their holiday was the weather. On the very day of their arrival at the railway station, an icy wind started up which persisted non-stop for the next two weeks. Every hour great bundles of cloud would come toppling down the mountains and envelop the cottage; and not a single day passed without some rain. But there were warm intervals, during which the party, released from their hideout, sprang up into the mountain fastnesses with maximum agility. They also made expeditions to Conway and Llandudno, where the three younger members bathed while Lytton, according to Carrington, 'wandered aimlessly gasing at beautiful faced youths. Which in truth there were but few of.' Inevitably on one of these excursions, he fell victim to a chill, which reduced him to bed for most of the second week. Carrington sat at his bedside painting his portrait as he lay there, and listening to him declaim Shakespeare's sonnets and the poems of John Donne.

One highlight of the holiday was a bottle of champagne. Nick withdrew the cork with a pop – and Lytton, flinging his arms wildly in the air, shrieked: 'God! What the war must be like!'

In the final week of August the party broke up and Lytton and Carrington went off together for a few days to Bath – 'a most charming town' he informed David Garnett (2 September 1916). 'How one bounds along those elegant streets, and whisks from Square to Circus and Circus to Crescent! One almost begins to feel that one's on high heels, and embroidery sprouts over one's waistcoat. And then – the infectious enthusiasm of my youthful companion . . . you smile; but you are mistaken.'

Something of this infectious enthusiasm and the manner in which they both swept through these days is conveyed by a letter which Carrington innocently sent off to Gertler. 'Yesterday we investigated the whole town,' she wrote to him (29 August 1916). 'Every house nearly! and sat for about two hours in a 2nd hand book shop. I discovered accidently an early Voltaire which gave Lytton great joy. as he had been looking for it a long time. After tea we walked through the city upon to a high hill because we had seen in one of the books on architecture, (that I studied all Sunday), a wonderful house. Called "Widcomb House". and indeed it was beautiful! – Fielding lived in this village also – We boldly asked the maid if we might go over the garden. She fetched after a long time an incrediably old lady. Who said we might. But seemed utterly bewildered why anyone should want to see her house! The garden with a deep valley very big with high trees, distant hills gave me strange emotions. It was a sad morbid place. and deadly quiet – Lytton read the Voltaire to me. an account of Frederick the Great, and Voltaire's relationship with his son.'

After a gay and highly diversified couple of days in Bath, Carrington regretfully parted from Lytton and returned to Andover. She had been with him for three consecutive weeks, had lived with his moodiness, his invalidism, and loved him more than ever. 'I did enjoy myself so much with you,' she wrote back to him, '– you do not know how happy I have been, everywhere, each day, so crowded with wonders . . . Dear Lytton. I have been so happy, incredibly happy.'

Lytton himself, his money and adventurous feelings still not wholly eliminated, had by this time journeyed on to Wells, a town quite as charming as Bath. 'What a pity it is that it should now be the fashion for clergymen to believe in Christianity,' he wrote to his mother (3 September 1916). 'I should have so enjoyed being Bishop of Bath and Wells!' For a week he lingered on at 6 St Andrew Street, 'sunk down into lodgings under the eaves of this somewhat démodé Cathedral'.

He had done little writing during these 'unregarded hours' of wandering; but a short poem which he now composed gives some clue as to how, at this stage in its development, he liked to see his semi-platonic, oddly romantic association with Carrington a wholeheartedly half-and-half affair, so far removed from her own primary involvement.

> *Who would love only roses among flowers?*
> *Or listen to no music save Mozart's?*
> *Then why not waste life's unregarded hours*
> *With fragile loves and secondary hearts?*
>
> *Ah! Exquisite the tulips and the lilies!*
> *The Schuberts and the Schumanns, how divine!*
> *Then kiss me, kiss me quickly, Amaryllis!*
> *And Laurie, mix your wantonness with mine!*

6

FRAGILE LOVES AND SECONDARY HEARTS

Something had gone wrong.

No longer could Gertler place any reliance on Lytton. As his unknowing champion in the tilts of love, he had proved himself totally inefficient. Gertler felt, also, a mounting irritation at the prolonged, inexplicable friendship that had grown up between the two of them. This juvenile party in Wales was the last straw. He was not jealous of Lytton – that would be absurd – but he felt he had been cheated.

For already strange and disturbing rumours had begun to percolate through Bloomsbury. Ottoline Morrell, indignant at the thought of losing Lytton to Carrington, whispered mischievous scandal in his ear, echoed by Dorothy Brett who, almost equally possessive, feared the loss of her 'virgin niece'.[1] At the same time, none of Carrington's letters did anything to clear up the mystery. With implacable irrelevance she wrote to Gertler of Andrew Marvell, of Shakespeare and of John Donne 'who excites me to such a pitch. that I can think of nothing else some days'; and, in a more esoteric style, of how wonderful and extra-ordinary it was to wear trousers and feel like a young and eager boy 'not tied – with female encumbrances, and hanging flesh'. She also described, ecstatically, the 'Cezannesque' Welsh landscape, and very plaintively, the pygmy inhabitants of Wales – 'the most vilely ugly human beings I have ever seen. The women gave one actual pain to look at, with their crooked teeth and red shining faces and bleary bulbeous brown eyes!' Most depressing of all she dwelt on her expansive upsurge of happiness – an undiscriminating happiness which seemed altogether to exclude Gertler. 'I am excited over everything lately. The fullness of life. So many people alive who one doesn't know, so many wonders past which one finds everyday, and then the things to come. oh the wonder of it all!'

Gertler had by now grown intolerably weary of this blithe cultural correspondence. On those matters about which he really wanted to know, she told him nothing. He chided her for her secrecy, and she replied by blaming his egotism. Abruptly he switched his attack to Lytton's character, singling out, with paradoxical logic, his homo-sexuality as the chief cause of complaint. But to his surprise Carrington rushed to his defence, saying that she had recently come to change her views on that subject, since 'one always has to put up with something. pain or discomfort. to get anything from any human beings. Some Trait in their character will always jar. But when one relizes it is there, a part of them, and a small part – it is worth while overlooking it. for any-

---

[1] 'How and why Carrington became so devoted to him [Lytton] I don't know,' Dorothy Brett told the author. 'Why she submerged her talent and whole life in him, a mystery. . . . Gertler's hopeless love for her, most of her friendships I think were partially discarded when she devoted herself to Lytton. . . . I know that Lytton at first was not too kind with Carrington's lack of literary knowledge. She pandered to his sex obscenities, I saw her, so I got an idea of it. I ought not to be prejudiced. I think Gertler and I could not help being prejudiced. It was so difficult to understand how she could be attracted.'

thing bigger and more valuable —' And in conclusion she added: 'Lytton sends you *his* love. you must like him because I do so very much.'

Ironically, so it seemed to Gertler, Carrington's views on heterosexuality still appeared unchanged, and on her return to Andover, his vexation and disappointment overflowed into a long despairing cry, a bitter tirade of pleas and recriminations. The letter he now wrote (4 September 1916) summarizes very powerfully all the agony of frustration that had welled up in him over the past months and years.

'God I ask only one thing of you – one little tiny prayer. Let me love and be loved. Create an inseparable bond between some being and myself. God, I am lonely – so lonely. I can't bear my loneliness. . . . Do you love me? Can you love? Is there nothing between us except my own fiery love? . . . Have you any concentrated passion at all? . . . You are impossible – impossible to love. You are so inconsistent too, God save me from this Hell that I have been living in for so long. Save me soon, I can't bear it much longer! Your body seems most beautiful to me. Most painfully I Long for it. . . . How can you bear to let your beauty pass by, when you know there is a man dying for it! Have you a Heart. There is only one period of Youth in our life time – Don't waste it! and me, Take me off the Rack of Torture soon. . . . You have had Lytton with you and he easily made up for my absence. He did well enough, Ugh! Ugh! Ugh! How I hate the coldness of life! It is not your fault Carrington Life is so arranged. Life has made you cold. You can't come close – you can't nestle. You are too weak! You say in your letter you are "a wild Beast never to be tamed". For me you are not wild enough, You are too spread out – You are not concentrated – That's what I hate about you! Your ego has never been surpassed! You are frightened – Frightened always, of soiling yourself! . . . you are not a "wild" Beast but frightened Beast and a timid Beast – Please don't flatter yourself. If you had known many men – had had many lovers then you could boast of this "Wildness" and this flightiness of your soul! But my poor Virgin, you have known *no* man yet. . . . I hate your Virginity!'

Although Gertler was right in supposing Carrington to be drifting away from him, the situation between them was not yet so abysmally bleak as, in his despair, he had imagined. Indirectly, Lytton's influence on her was having something of the effect that Gertler had originally looked for. The author-poets of 'Venus and Adonis', 'To his Coy Mistress', and 'The Extasie' were, in fact, accomplishing more by way of overcoming Carrington's virginity than all Gertler's impassioned exhortations. Even though Lytton was to mean incomparably more to

H

her than any other human being – perhaps already did so – his importance in her life in no way coincided with the part Gertler played, and in no way diminished her affection for him. As a fellow painter he could appreciate certain sides of her character far more intimately than any writer, so that, while she admitted to being 'incredibly happy' with Lytton in Wales, Carrington could still, with what she thought to be perfect honesty, write back to Gertler that 'the intimacy we got at lately makes other relationships with people strangely vacant, and dull'.

Another of Carrington's peculiarities, which to some extent strengthened Gertler's position, was that she could never bear to give anyone up. Gertler's torrid infatuation ministered to her vanity and sense of power, which were also responsible for her long-preserved virginity. After her return home to Hurstbourne Tarrant, she sent off copious letters to him, along with which went various tokens of her abiding affection – presents of flowers and plums, and all the more ordinary endearments. Even her allegorical effusiveness – 'We will always be twin souls, but separate souls. mounting together' – and her most irritating literary tutelage – 'My admiration grows daily for John Donne. (you must pronounce it like the verb "Done". as if his name was spelt Dunn. I have only Just mastered it. But it is correct.)' – were often oblique indications that she sincerely valued Gertler's friendship and wanted to share more with him.

About this time Carrington began to make arrangements to live in London, so that she might be nearer Lytton and farther away from her parents. Towards the end of September she moved into an apartment with Dorothy Brett, on the second floor of No. 3 Gower Street. Above them in the same building lived Middleton Murry and Katherine Mansfield; and below, Maynard Keynes, Gerald Shove and Sheppard, who had been taken on as a translator by the War Office. For several weeks prior to this move Carrington had been writing to Gertler saying how much she was looking forward to seeing him more frequently. But when they did meet, Gertler flew into a rage, and on leaving him Carrington wrote from Gower Street to tell him that 'I simply must be alone for a little while – do you mind. It is *not* that I am in any way angry with you . . . only I could not see you and think at the same time as I want to. – And in my distantness which you would interpret as coldness, we will disagree and possibly quarrell.' Always prone to feelings of guilt, she could not bear anyone to reproach her. Gertler's anger and jealousy, which had brought about so many of their temporary estrangements, were soon to lead to her token submission and, only then, when that failed, finally and regretfully, her complete renunciation of him.

There were, however, hidden reasons to account for her 'distantness' and her inability over these autumn and winter months to see quite as much of Gertler as she had promised. While in Wales, it had been decided that a country cottage should be rented for Lytton, where he could work consistently and in peace. Unless some such haven could be found, he feared that he might sink back again into aimless and un-productive wandering. Since he could not afford this kind of gracious retirement on his own, the scheme was to be promoted on something like a company basis – various of Lytton's Bloomsbury friends taking shares (that is, paying an annual sum of money) in return for which they might use the cottage (which would be inhabited and vicariously looked after by Lytton himself) as their own occasional country retreat. 'Have you heard of the scheme for a country cottage?' Lytton asked Maynard Keynes (14 September 1916). 'Would you be willing to join? Barbara has already found something that sounds as if it might be suitable. Oliver and Faith [Henderson] are going to take shares – also perhaps Saxon. I don't know about Harold. Oh, Carrington, too.'

Barbara Bagenal's find was an unfurnished house in Hemel Hemp-stead, at an annual rent of forty-eight pounds and with 'a loft for conscientious objectors'. When this fell through, the quest was vigorously taken up by Carrington. 'I boldly went into all the estate agents in Newbury yesterday, and enquired about houses,' she reported to Lytton at the beginning of her search (16 September 1916). '. . . I have maps of every square inch of the country now! And corres-pondence with every auctioneer in Newbury Marlborough, and Reading!' Sometimes accompanied by Barbara, she would bicycle all over the countryside, often travelling fifty miles in a day. But though unflagging, she was, as both Lytton and Barbara came to realize, a highly impractical house-hunter. Her notions of what would accord with Lytton's literary genius were so extremely grandiose that, as time went by, the scheme seemed to enter the realms of elevated fantasy. 'Our country cottage still floats high in the air,' Lytton commented to Ottoline (1 October 1916), '– a cottage in Spain.'

In the meantime, Lytton was obliged to carry on as best he could. From Wells he had gradually and with great indecision drifted back, via Park Cottage, Ledbury ('among my dowagers'), Garsington and Eleanor, to London, which 'I found horrible – stuffy and chilly at the same time, and packed full and flowing over, with inconceivably hideous monstrosities. They push one off the pavements in their crowds, they surge round every bus, they welter in the tubes – one dashes wildly for a taxi, but there are no taxis left. In the night it's *pitch* dark; one walks wedged in among the multitudes like a soldier in an army – one peers in vain for some vestiges of beauty – all in blackness – but one can't help hoping; then at last somebody strikes a match to light a cigarette – and a seething mass of antique Jewish faces is revealed. No! London is decidedly *not* a place to be in just now.'

Nevertheless, it was in London that Lytton was to remain fairly continuously over the next fifteen months. On arriving back at Belsize Park Gardens, he at once settled down to work, and by the last week of October he was able to announce that 'cet épouvantable Docteur Arnold est fini – praise be to God!' Almost immediately he began reading and making notes for 'The End of General Gordon', but progress, he informed Ottoline, was very slow.

The winter passed by uneventfully. While he was working, there was little time for anything else. His existence, however, was never so dire or solitary as he liked to make out. There were parties at Barbara's studio in Hampstead and at Augustus John's in Chelsea, dinners at the Café Royal with Keynes, teas with Carrington and Katherine Mansfield at Gower Street, luncheons and occasional theatres with Boris Anrep ('very fat and friendly') or with Sheppard 'and a party of young men'. He also took Carrington over to Hogarth House in Richmond to see Leonard and Virginia (shortly to set up their Hogarth Press, for which Carrington did woodcuts);[1] he paid several visits to the new Omega Club in Fitzroy Square, where he met Arnold Bennett and W. B. Yeats; and inspected the Bloomsbury decorations at No. 4 Berkeley Street, 'which I found extremely depressing. They're in a very small room at the top of the house, and consist of colossal figures plastered on the walls, like posters, but without the gaiety of posters.[2] In the middle of the room stood Margot [Asquith], very stiff and straight, in a very short black dress and a white veil.'

He was by now being mildly courted and entertained, too, by a retinue of hostesses, among them Dorelia John, Ethel Sands and Mary Hutchinson, of whom the last was soon to emerge as the second woman of his life, whose intermittent role was largely overshadowed by that of Carrington. 'She is indeed a wonderful creature,' Lytton wrote of her some years later to Roger Senhouse (21 September 1927), 'and I am delighted that you should have experienced the activity and enthusiasm of her affections. It is very rare to find such a spontaneous warmth, isn't

---

[1] The first publication of the Hogarth Press, *Two Stories* (1917) – now a collector's item – has four woodcuts by Carrington, for which she received the sum of fifteen shillings.

[2] The decorations at No. 4 Berkeley Street had been specially commissioned from Roger Fry, who made, as part of them, a large circular rug and some tables in inlaid wood.

it? Such a generous appreciation of life! – I can realise what a comfort a talk must have been to you.'

After a week-end at Asheham in November, Lytton succumbed to a series of winter illnesses which greatly slowed down his work, and he decided to convalesce over Christmas at Garsington, immune from the newspapers and other vulgarities of London. Ottoline herself was none too well that winter, and as a fellow sufferer Lytton would send her letters full of compassion and solicitous advice. To Virginia Woolf he at the same time (21 February 1917) wrote to say that 'Lady Omega Muddle' as he sometimes referred to the wretched woman, 'is now I think almost at the last gasp – infinitely old, ill, depressed, and bad-tempered – she is soon to sink into a nursing-home, where she will be fed on nuts, and allowed to receive visitors (in bed).'

He had now started again his occasional articles and reviews for the *New Statesman* and this added to his customary winter discontent, which he tried to assuage by reading and re-reading *Gargantua and Pantagruel*. 'Yes, Rabelais has surged over me altogether,' he assured Ottoline (6 February 1917). 'I read very little else. I find him far the best antidote yet discovered against the revolting mesquineries de ces jours. I read him in the tube, and he is a veritable buckler of defence, warding off those miserable visages, with their miserable newspapers. What an adorable giant, to drop into the arms of! And then the interest of the book, from so many points of view, is so great. I am glad I never really read it before; it is intoxicating to get a fresh enthusiasm when one's over eighty.'

By the end of March, he had begun to feel again something like his actual age – now thirty-seven. The weather brightened and grew warmer. Spring was in the air once more, and with its coming the old desires for all manner of exploits and adventures revived within him. With a sigh of relief he gave up his contributions to the *New Statesman*, and determined to press ahead with his serious writing. 'I have been dawdling horribly lately over reviews – and now I feel that I really must set to and seriously attack the General,' he told Ottoline, who had invited him again to Garsington (23 March 1917). 'I'm afraid it would be fatal to leave my stool until I've captured his first line of trenches.'

Meanwhile, Carrington's dual relationship with Lytton and Gertler had slowly been moving towards a crisis. To Gertler, at any rate, her inconsistency had never been more baffling. At times she was closer and more intimate with him than she had ever allowed herself to be in the past; and then, on the spur of the moment, she would turn sulky and cold. She praised him for his wonderful patience with her (January 1917); and raged at him for his impetuosity (January 1917). From a Lawrentian 'Wild Beast' she would suddenly dwindle into one of Katherine Mansfield's defenceless, petite heroines – 'so young and rather little against the bigger issues', as she described herself (November 1916) – and then, alarmingly, evolve back again into uncompromising savagery. She blamed Gertler for not talking to her seriously; she blamed herself for failing to build up 'a descent relationship between us'. She told him something about the poet 'Marloe', and that she was painting portraits of Lytton and of her friend, the strange, austere, intellectual Alix Sargant-Florence – already in love with James Strachey, whom she later married. For weeks she would see Gertler almost every day; then, without warning, she would vanish for more weeks still with Barbara Bagenal and Saxon Sydney-Turner (then impotently in love with Barbara) to Asheham, where, like children, they spent much of the time tobogganing on tea-trays across the Downs.

Her prolonged exhortations to Gertler to be happy, which run like a Greek Chorus through the pages of her letters, had become a means of salving her own conscience for the wretchedness which she seemed destined to inflict upon him. 'I want you to love people more,' she instructed him; then followed this up by throwing herself passionately at him, and, when in delight he responded, freezing into distant immobility. In the course of her many apologies to him during this period, she describes herself as 'possessed of a devil' which she was powerless to exorcize. She felt, she said, in a vile mood, nervy, and strangely contaminated within. 'You cannot think how I hate myself sometimes – often,' she confessed (January 1917). 'I will try and get this over soon and will come and see you then . . . I've no more to say to you now. Except do not be unhappy —'

There were several good reasons for Carrington's remorseless discontent this winter. First, she had been bitter and disgusted over the publication of Gilbert Cannan's *Mendel*. 'How angry I am over Gilbert's Book,' she had complained to Gertler (1 November 1916). 'Everywhere this confounded gossip, and servant-like curiosity Its ugly and so damned vulgar.' In the same letter she laments over the loss of her brother. 'I am losing hope rather of Teddy. Its beginning to depress me terribly sometimes.' But four months later, when it was officially confirmed that her brother was dead, she turned for support not to Gertler, but Lytton. 'You will not mind if I want to see you often,' she wrote to him (26 February 1917). 'For its wretched being alone and knowing how he went – without ever having been seen or loved. He had the independence of a child like Poppet,[1] all his joys contained inside himself – made by himself.'

Lytton's kindness to her at this time, his compassion and gentleness, was her one source of relief. Only with him did she feel content, free from pain. Her adoration of him deepened. Of course, she knew that there must always be precise limits to their relationship, but it was satisfaction enough simply to be with him whenever that was possible; and when it was not, to receive and memorize his marvellous letters. She thought that she understood him better than anyone. In his reply to her from Alderney Manor, where he was staying with Augustus and Dorelia John,[2] Lytton ruefully apologizes for his inability to do more for her. 'I fear I *am* at times a trifle – unsatisfactory,' he admits (8 March 1917). 'Is it age, sex, or cynicism? But perhaps it's really only appearance – of one sort or another. The fellow, as they say, (only they don't) is good at heart. I wish I could be of more avail – I often think that if the layer of flesh over my bones were a few inches thicker I might be. But that is another of the tiresome arrangements of the world. . . . Ma chère, I'm sure I do sympathise with your feelings of loneliness. I know what it is so horribly well myself.'

Lytton's understanding and compunction increased, to some extent, the tension within Carrington. For much of her incalculable moodiness these months had sprung from a sense of guilt – a feeling that she was betraying Gertler with her affection for Lytton. If only Gertler were in some ways more like Lytton! Somehow she could not reconcile her attachment to both of them. She shrank from making an unreal, cut-and-dried decision between them – they were so dissimilar she could not possibly consider them as rivals or even alternatives. During the latter part of 1916, in an attempt to form some honest, mutually satisfactory relationship with Gertler and banish all traces of

---

[1] Poppet John, the daughter of Augustus John. She married Professor Derek Jackson, who owned £900,000 worth of shares in the *News of the World*, was one of the world's leading authorities on spectroscopy, and afterwards married Pamela Mitford, Janetta Woolley, Princess Ratibor and Barbara Skelton, who herself has had four husbands – one of them being Mr George Weidenfeld, the publisher, and another Mr Cyril Connolly.

[2] In her memoirs, *Two Flamboyant Fathers* (1966), Nicolette Devas records that she used to meet Lytton and Carrington with the Johns 'at Fordingbridge and neighbouring gymkhanas. A gymkhana was an incongruous place to find the drooping, indoor plant aesthete, with his limp hair undignified in the wind. . . . If you saw Strachey in a wilting pose on the periphery of the coconut shies, or drifting across the field on his long frail legs, Dora Carrington was his shadow, a pace behind, at heel, devoted, worshipping. . . . We called her the "North Wind" for the way she poked her face into the wind; her long black [*sic*] hair, cut with a square fringe, swished out at the back in a dark pennant, while her black skirt, too, always seemed to be under the influence of the wind, blown against her gaunt figure.'

self-reproach, she permitted him to start having full sexual intercourse with her – but only infrequently. 'I do not love passionately everyday and night,' she explained to him (1 February 1917). 'It comes over me with sweeps, and then sometimes I find myself so detached from the world and everybody that I hate any intrusion mental or physical at these moments you get aggravated, and I admit with reason because I am not consistant with what I was previously. If you try to force me to be perpetually consistant, we shall quarrell. I will try, and make you happy. Since I want to, as you suffer so much I know by my beastliness, therefore do not get depressed.'

Four days later she again assured him: 'I am going to be less selfish, and make you happier.' For Gertler, she knew, was still far from happy. This unpredictable, piecemeal love-making had stimulated his sense of frustration. It was neither one thing nor the other. The quarrels between them grew more violent, and he repeatedly scorned her for trying to look like a boy – with her short hair, her lack of make-up and her fondness for wearing trousers.

Early in April, Carrington went down to stay at Lord's Wood, her friend Alix Sargant-Florence's home near Marlow – 'a very nice house', as she described it to Gertler, 'one of the best sort. with great comforts and a most beautiful bathroom you ever saw with coloured tiles.' The other guests were Lytton and James, Harry Norton and Maynard Keynes. It was a wholly agreeable party; the sun shone, Carrington, happily dressed in breeches, roamed the great woods and commons all round, read Plato 'and was very excited over it', and in the evening listened to James playing Bach and Beethoven at the pianola. Sometimes, too, they would all sit round reading plays – Vanbrugh's *The Relapse* and Shakespeare's *Troilus and Cressida* – 'which was great fun', Carrington wrote. 'Only I was so agitated when it came to my part that I could hardly enjoy it as much as I should.'

In his 'Collins' to Alix (10 April 1917), Lytton afterwards wrote: 'It was very sad coming away. I wish I could have stayed for ever, quaffing Chianti twice a day, gorging Périgord Pie, dreaming by the fire and perpetually putting off the Grande Expédition. But such things must end, though your noble hospitality made me feel as if I were an Adam wilfully taking my departure from the Garden of Eden.'

For Carrington, these few days at Lord's Wood produced a decisive effect. The last vestiges of her doubts were dispelled. She was certain now that, with Gertler, she could never experience such serenity, and that it would be largely withheld from her until she had told him everything – which would probably mean breaking with him altogether.

Only by such drastic measures might she purge herself of that poison-
ing sense of sinfulness which had so lowered and demoralized her
lately. On her last day at Marlow, therefore, she wrote two letters, one
to Gertler telling him something of her conclusions and arranging to
meet him on the following Monday afternoon, and the other to Lytton
– who had just left Marlow – asking to see him the evening of the same
day. On Sunday she travelled up by train to London, and the next
morning woke from a disquieting dream of her brother Teddy drowning at sea. After lunch she took a bus to Penn Studio, where she found
Gertler, very calm, but pale as a ghost. At first they both, rather
nervously, talked about his pictures – a copy of Cézanne he was then
painting and his Merry-Go-Round.[1] In the middle of their conversation
he turned and quietly asked her what exactly she intended doing in the
future, how she wanted to plan her life. She had been prepared for all
sorts of insane rages and titanic fits of anger, and his perfect control
disarmed her. 'I became more and more wretched and wept,' she
scrawled in her diary. 'It seemed like leaving the warm sun in the fields
and going into a dark cold wood surrounded by trees which were
strangers. I suddenly looked back at the long [time] we had had between
us of mixed emotions. But always warm because of his intense love and
now I had to leave it all and go away.'

At this moment, too, for the first time Gertler seems to have become
aware that Carrington really meant this meeting to signal the end
between them, their final good-bye; and he broke down and sobbed.
His tears were more terrible than any eloquence or melodrama and
made Carrington feel more and more hateful to herself. It was an
agonizing, hopeless scene, 'for he wanted to die and I thought how
much this love mattered to him,' she wrote, 'and yet in spite of its
greatness I could not keep it, and must leave. His loneliness was
awfull.'

Shortly afterwards they left the studio and had tea together in a
café, hardly speaking at all. He asked her in a subdued voice whether
she intended to go and live with Lytton as his wife or mistress, and she
told him that she did not.

'But he may love you,' Gertler protested.

'No, he will not,' she answered flatly.

This last denial, she sensed, made their separation easier for him to
accept. But he still begged her to go on seeing him as a friend, a brother,
though both of them knew that any such arrangement must be quite

---

[1] This famous picture – 'the best *modern* picture I have seen' (D. H. Lawrence) –
shown at the London Group Jubilee Exhibition, 'Fifty Years of British Art', at the Tate
Gallery in the summer of 1964, is now in the Ben Uri Gallery, London.

impractical. As the time came for them to part, they grew all at once embarrassed with each other, as with a stranger. Carrington felt as if she had already left for some distant country from where communication was impossible. 'How very much I cared for him suddenly came upon me,' she recorded. 'The unreality and coldness of Lytton . . . I left – frightfully ill – with a bad pain in my side.'

She then returned to her rooms, which she was now sharing with Alix Sargant-Florence, had a hot bath and dressed for the evening. Lytton was already downstairs having tea with Alix and her mother. Carrington joined them, but felt too ill to pay much attention to the conversation, though she observed with a mixture of fascination and contempt how, in the mêlée of this great emotional drama, Lytton 'sat there quite calmly quibbling and playing lightly with his words'. Later, the two of them went out to dinner, and Carrington was glad to prolong the conversation about other things – Lytton's many friends and illnesses. But soon, the weight of what was being left unspoken began to press upon her unbearably. The time they took over each separate course was appalling. Should she speak up now in the restaurant or wait until Lytton took her home? In her bewilderment she fell silent, but Lytton himself appeared totally unaware of any uneasiness.

After he had escorted her back to her flat, and they had settled down in front of the fire, he at last broached the subject burdening her mind. Briefly he asked her what she had wanted to tell him, and she tried to explain.

'I thought I had better tell Mark as it was so difficult going on,' she said.

'Tell him what?' Lytton politely inquired.

'That I wouldn't go on. So I just wrote and said it.'

'What did you say in your letter?'

Carrington hesitated. 'I thought you knew.'

'What do you mean?'

'I said I was in love with you. I hope you don't mind very much.'

'But aren't you being rather romantic?' Lytton asked. 'And are you certain?'

'There's nothing romantic about it,' she answered wryly.

'What did Mark say?'

'He was terribly upset.'

Lytton looked alarmed. 'Did he seem angry with *me*?'

'No, he didn't mention you.'

'But it's too incongruous,' he protested. 'I'm so old and diseased. I wish I were more able.'

'That doesn't matter.'

'What do you mean? What do you think we had better do about the physical side of things?'

'Oh, I don't mind about that.'

Lytton paused. 'That's rather bad,' he commented.

As their discussion progressed, Lytton again brought up their apparent incompatibility, especially their physical incompatibility. He was 'so very ancient' – wasn't she being rather too romantic, that is, rather too *unrealistic*? But Carrington firmly repeated that she knew what she was doing. 'I wish I were rich,' Lytton remarked at one stage, 'and then I could keep you as my mistress.' This angered Carrington, and she told him that no amount of money could alter the incompatibility he had mentioned; and to this he rather ruefully agreed. 'Then he sat on the floor,' Carrington wrote, 'and clasped my hands in his and let me kiss his mouth all emeshed in the brittle beard and my inside was as heavy as lead, as I knew how miserable I was going to be.'

Secretly Carrington hoped that he might stay the night with her, but after some further talk he got up and left. Alone, she was suddenly overpowered by a maundering chaos of sensations – 'the misery at parting and my hatred of myself for caring so much, and his callousness – He was so wise and just.'

A little later she wandered downstairs to Alix, and began talking with her, long into the night – of how to cope with her incontrovertible worship of Lytton, of how to arrange their lives together, of how to avoid the necessity for secrecy, for deception, anxiety and tribulation. Only now, after all the years with Gertler, did she know what it was to love – for the first and last time. It seemed incomprehensible that there should be this painful barrier between them: as if two mated birds on their peregrination were caught and forced to live apart in separate cages. How could they be set free? How?

And although no answer presented itself, she felt some relief at being able to discuss the problem with someone who comprehended so well. And as she talked on and on, later and later, it seemed as though in a little while a solution must be found, and then a new and wonderful life would begin. And it was clear to her that the end was nowhere yet in sight, and that the most tortuous and difficult part of it was only just beginning.

CHAPTER V

Tidmarsh

Suppose the kind gods said, 'Today
You're forty. True: But still rejoice!
Gifts we have got will smooth away
The ills of age. Come, take your choice!'

What should I answer? Well, you know
I'm modest – very. So no shower
Of endless gold I'd beg, nor show
Of proud-faced pomp, nor regal power.

No; ordinary things and good
I'd choose: friends, wise and kind and few;
A country house, a pretty wood
To walk in; books both old and new

To read; a life retired, apart,
Where leisure and repose might dwell
With industry; a little art;
Perhaps a little fame as well.

Lytton Strachey (1 March 1920)

I

DRAMA AND UNCERTAINTY

Carrington's decision in the spring of 1917 to abandon Gertler for Lytton redirected the entire course of her life. Yet, although ultimately so momentous, her resolution was anything but quickly conclusive. As if eager to extract the maximum melodrama from this strange emotional nexus, she arranged to have dinner with Gertler on the very day following their 'final' interview. They were to meet that Tuesday evening at the Eiffel Tower restaurant in Percy Street. Gertler turned up a few minutes late, and for a brief while after he had joined her they exchanged stiff pleasantries across the table. Then, suddenly, Carrington blurted out that the two of them had really better not see each other any more.

Gertler at once agreed, adding that he had come to the same conclusion himself. They fell silent. Then, not knowing what to say, she referred to her interview with Lytton the previous night.

'How did that go off?' Gertler asked, curious about Lytton's reaction.

'All right.'

'Then what did you do?'

'Went to my rooms,' Carrington replied; and added: 'I told Lytton then.'

'What did he say?'

'He was sorry.'

'Was that all he said?' Gertler laughed incredulously.

Carrington felt slightly indignant. 'Well it wasn't his fault. What more could he say?'

'Fancy just saying that. Nothing more?'

'No.'

'Good God! And he doesn't care?'

'No. I knew he didn't.'

This seemed to disquiet Gertler greatly. 'I never want to see you again,' he told her. 'So will you mind if I leave you directly after dinner?'

'No.'

The conversation up to this point had been subdued. But all at once Gertler exploded: 'To think that after all these years, in three months you should have a man like Strachey, twice your age, emaciated and old!'

There was a long silence following this outburst. Shortly afterwards Gertler got up and left, and Carrington walked back to Gower Street alone. From there, the last thing before going to bed, she wrote him a letter (14 April 1917):

'Thank you very much for treating it as you have – and for your very great love in the past few years I thank you. I shall never forget it.

'Would you mind not Telling anyone (except your friend Monty[1] and Kot[2] if you wish to) about it. anyway for the present. as it was too great a thing to let them know about, and jeer.

[1] Montague Shearman, barrister and connoisseur of pictures. He was one of Gertler's most loyal friends and patrons, often lending him his rooms in the Adelphi. An exhibition of Shearman's collection was held at the Redfern Gallery in 1940.

[2] Samuel Solomonovitch Kotelіansky, who, in 1910, had come to England on a scholarship from Kiev to do research in economics for three months, and stayed for life. Swarthy, with a pale sensitive face and fierce black glance, he was, as his friend D. H. Lawrence once said, 'a bit Jehovah-ish'. He made a career for himself as a fine translator of the works of Bunin, Chekhov, Gorky, Kuprin, Tolstoy and others, sometimes in collaboration with his friends Lawrence, Katherine Mansfield, Middleton Murry and Leonard Woolf, who used to render his strange English into their own prose style.

'I will return your EL GRECO very soon. and any other books, if I have them – I hope you will soon be happy again. and forgive, for causing you so much sorrow your

friend   carrington.'

This letter, evidently intended by Carrington at the time to be her very last word to Gertler, in fact turned out to be the prelude to a more intimate, if no happier, spell between the two of them. After only a fortnight they were seeing each other again, and exchanging a stream of letters. What appears to have happened was this: Gertler soon found himself unable to keep up his initial renunciation of Carrington. His sexual vanity had, understandably, been mortally offended by her preference for an ill-defined platonic union with Lytton. Moreover, he disapproved of their friendship, he told himself, on moral grounds. The very thought of it revolted him to the marrow of his bones. Sickened and excruciated as he was by jealousy, the latent antipathy he had always felt for Lytton now emptied itself into a violent protesting, poignant, half-incoherent letter he sent to Carrington.

'I am afraid that I cannot support you over your love for Lytton,' he declared. '. . . I do believe in *you*, but nothing on earth will make me believe in Lytton as a fit object for your love – The whole thing in fact is most disappointing to me, even nauseating. I am sorry Carrington, but nothing will ever make me change my mind . . . I hate the whole business . . . If you had com[e] and told me that you thought L.S. was a wonderful man and that you had an admiration for him, I should have tried to dissuade you because I do not think that he is, I think very much to the contrary in fact. But you came and told me that you *loved* him . . . You have by your love for that man poisoned my belief in love life and everything, you by that love turned everything I once believed in and thought beautiful into ridicule . . . for years I wanted – you only tortured me, then suddenly you gave your love to such a creature, and you yourself said that had he wanted your body you would without hesitation have given it to that emaciated withered being, I young and full of love, you refused it. Tell me Carrington what am I to think of life now, you say you are happy, yes you are *But I am not.* I long to fly to another Carrington where I shan't smell the stench that fills my nostrils constantly from the combination of your fresh young self with that half dead creature who is not even man enough to take your body – your beautiful body – But thank God he cannot, because if that happened, I should be sick all day.

'I do not believe in [the] L.S. kind – His atmosphere is as thin as his body – he is merely learned and scholarly but fundamentally empty . . . He will deaden you in time and that is what hurts me so, You are absolutely at his feet. You follow him about like a puppy, you have lost all self respect, I shudder to think of it . . . Why do you not at least control yourself a bit, must you be so Slavish and abject Surely there is in me also Something to Study, if only my Art, You sicken me with your devotion . . . Having told you this Please let us leave the subject *once and for always*, I cannot discuss it because it hurts me so, And Please dont be hard on [me] now because of my opinion Remember that I love you still . . . I never change my mind. And if you hate me now please don't give me up at once, as I couldn't bear it.'

Incalculable as ever, Carrington actually felt less like giving up Gertler just then than she had done for months. She had expected her anguished decision in favour of Lytton to simplify her state of mind and deliver her from the harrowing chaos of the winter. But in the last fortnight of April, which she described as a 'nightmare', her confusion was only aggravated by a terrifying sense of isolation. Never had she felt so alone, so cut off from the glow of ordinary human warmth. It was as if she had exiled herself to some bleak, uninhabited island, where no ships passed. The astringency and reticence of Lytton's character chilled her. At times she could get nowhere near him. Of course, he was unfailingly *kind* to her, but emotionally quite incapable of being demonstrative – especially when, as now, his affections were not greatly stimulated by sexual passion. His spidery stillness and riveting silences – only occasionally would he stir to unfold and reorganize his complicated angular limbs – unnerved and hypnotized her. He looked, as Frances Cornford once described him, 'like a new variation of *Homo Sapiens*, slightly Mephistophelian yet with human and lovely brown eyes'.

Although he did his best to aid Carrington, Lytton still thought she was being alarmingly unrealistic in her attitude towards him, and so as not to deceive her, he made no attempt to play a part which he felt he could not keep up. She had, he reasoned, better know the worst from the start, before it was absolutely too late. The misery and frustration engendered within her by this scrupulous attitude naturally made her more sympathetic to Gertler's similar bygone agonies over herself. By the end of April, less than two weeks after their series of final farewells, the two of them were back together on very much the same footing as before. They met frequently; he sent her flowers; she wrote (28 April 1917): 'I will try and make you happy. all I can. I have just been reading King Lear by Shakespear. I think it his best work.' In his relief at having her back again, Gertler was unusually tactful and undemanding, and she responded to him sympathetically: 'I wonder why I am agitated already in case you are not happy,' she wrote to him early in

May. '. . . I did so love our day at Hammersmith. you see how contradictory it all is. But I love seeing you so much more now.'

By an ironic, circuitous route, something of the ends that Gertler had
first sought through bringing Carrington and Lytton together had
actually come to pass. She had at last become his mistress, originally
out of a sense of guilt, and now in order to keep him close to her, so
that his companionship might provide consolation against the chaste
severity of her foredoomed life with Lytton. 'I am really certain I could
never live with you sexually day after day,' she told him. But the
occasional night, week-end, even week maybe, she might be able to
manage. Yet though, with qualifications, Gertler seemed to have attained
his long-held aim, he was still very far from satisfied with the state of
affairs. Seldom had Carrington appeared to him more tantalizing and
seductive. For really what she had done was to pass on to Gertler, in a
slightly variegated form, the elusiveness which, in Lytton, so tortured
and perplexed herself. In their most intimate contact, Carrington even
now seemed curiously remote from Gertler. And though she sometimes
complained of Lytton's 'cynical frigidity and discipline', he knew that
his own incendiary passion must play a miserable second fiddle
to Lytton's most casual whims, to all of which Carrington reacted
with such breathless and servile promptitude. It was infuriating. He
tried not to censure Carrington, but his loathing for Lytton grew
intense.

Clear evidence of the corrupt influence Lytton was exercising over
poor Carrington was presented to Gertler in the second week of May
when he was invited by her and Alix down to Lord's Wood – only to
find on his arrival there that Carrington was on the point of leaving for
a hastily convened country party with Lytton, Barbara Bagenal and
Saxon Sydney-Turner. The four of them were hurrying off to spend a
week at Chilling, Logan Pearsall Smith's house at Warsash on the
Hampshire coast, which Oliver and Ray Strachey were then renting.
On their way down by train, they stopped off for some hours at
Winchester, and went round to explore the city, the cathedral and
school. 'That's one of the few things Lytton is rather good at. Exploring,' Carrington explained to her brother Noel (15 May 1917). They
arrived at Warsash in the evening. Chilling, an old but modernized
farmhouse with a splendid view, on one side of sea and ships, and on
the other of the Sussex Weald as far as the South Downs and Chancton-
bury Ring, was, according to Carrington, 'quite the decentest place
you ever saw . . . it's quite in the country miles from any village or
houses. a very old Elizabethan Farm house black half timbered house –
with a huge garden and orchard behind. and only two wheatfields

separate it from the sea. and Marvellous little woods full of primroses and bluebells . . .'

To Gertler in particular she was at considerable pains to convey something of her idyllic, pastoral happiness. Chilling, she assured him, was one of 'the most lovely houses and places' she had ever beheld. 'It's Elizabethan, very old. in the fields with an orchard outside. and lambs. and nightingales at night. and an orchard behind the house with trees in blossom. Dear friend I am so happy because it is all very beautiful. . . . Did you enjoy staying with Alix!'

Almost every day, she went on, she bathed naked in the sea with Oliver and Barbara, while the antediluvian members of the party, Lytton and Saxon, observed them from the safety of the beach. Otherwise there was not a single human being to be spied – only aeroplanes and sea-planes in their squadrons swooping down low over the waves where they swam and then high up into the heavens. Lytton was still working intermittently at 'The End of General Gordon', and Carrington herself spent some of the time painting and doing woodcuts. At other times the two of them would go off together for long walks along the sea-shore, Lytton reciting Keats's poems, *Romeo and Juliet* ('which I thought very beautiful'), *Henry IV*, and 'also some Greek History'.

Gertler, stranded at Lord's Wood, was enraged by these provoking stories. Some day, somehow, he would avenge these wrongs done to him by Lytton. But so happy was Carrington that all her apprehensions for the future were dissolving away. A solution to her problems, indefinable as yet, had never seemed nearer. 'If only like a magician I could frizzle up my parents into ether,' she wrote to Lytton after returning to Hurstbourne Tarrant (26 May 1917), 'and waft them to some remote town, and then encase you in the old wall nut tree so you could never escape me . . .'

2

SUMMER MANŒUVRES

On his arrival back at Belsize Park Gardens, a tedious ordeal awaited Lytton. The Government was combing out all those who, for whatever reason, had up till then been exempted from military service, and he was required to re-establish his case once again from the start. This time he hired counsel to represent him, restated in three measured paragraphs his conscientious objections to the war, and arranged for Philip Morrell to appear for him as a character witness. When the hearing took place, however, his barrister would not allow Philip Morrell into the room – 'which I'm sure was a great mistake, as if he had appeared the Chairman would have recognised him, and seen that I was "well-connected", which, as it was, he didn't grasp'. The conscience part of the case was soon adjourned pending a medical re-examination by the army doctors, and a few days afterwards, Lytton appeared again at the White City, where he was shuttled about from doctor to doctor for about six hours – 'fortunately without any clothes on for most of the time'. Although greatly fearing that on this occasion he would be ordered off at the very least to scrub tables and floors, he was once more given what amounted to absolute exemption from all kinds of service. His medical grading was confirmed as C 4, he was relegated to the reserve, and ordered to reappear every six months for further check-ups.

To recover from this 'fearful business', he hurried down to Garsington over Whitsun, 'leaving poor General Gordon alone and neglected on my writing table'. Among the other people who turned up there during the holiday were Bertrand Russell, Sheppard and, more briefly, Asquith – this time with Margot – who, now deprived by Lloyd George of his premiership, looked 'a very diminished deflated figure'. But primarily he was absorbed by two other guests, Augustine Birrell and the poet Robert Graves, who together seemed to represent the very opposite poles of life. 'Old man Birrell – decidedly a Victorian product,' he wrote to Carrington (28 May 1917). 'Large and tall and oddly like Thackeray to look at – with spectacles and sharp big nose and a long upper lip that moves about and curls very expressively – white hair, of course, and also rather unexpectedly sensitive and even sometimes almost agitated fingers. Altogether, a most imposing facade! And there he sits, square and solid, talking in a loud deep voice – can you imagine it? – and being very entertaining for hour after hour – telling stories and interjecting reflections and all the rest of it – and all with the greatest gentility – taking up one's remarks most good-humouredly, and proceeding and embroidering with an impression of easy strength. Underneath – there really seems to be almost nothing. The ordinary respectabilities and virtues, no doubt, and a certain bookishness, gleaned from some rather narrow reading, and then – blank.'

Later in the same letter to Carrington, he passes on to a description of Robert Graves, then on sick-leave from the front. 'The fashion for facades has its drawbacks,' he remarks. 'For instance there is the youth Graves, with one lung shot away, keeping himself going on strychnine, and with strange concealed thoughts which only very occasionally poke up through his schoolboy jocularities. Terribly tragic I thought. I

found him (I need hardly say) attractive – tall and olive-brown com-
plexioned, with a broken nose and broken teeth (the result of boxing) –
dark hair and eyes.'

From this time on, whenever they were apart, Lytton would be
punctilious in dispatching to Carrington the long chatty and amusing
letters to which she always looked forward so eagerly. She would
write to him herself, tirelessly, on page after page of foolscap paper or
the roughly torn-out leaves of children's exercise books, half-illegible,
bewitching scribbles, overlaid with caricatures, telling him all she was
doing each day and of her deep love for him. 'Do you know everytime
I see you now I love you even more,' she wrote to him that summer.
And again: 'More beloved than any creature please come next week
again. I could kill you dead with my hugs to-day.' More than ever she
felt keenly her lack of formal education, knowledge and literary finesse.
'I wish I could write properly to you,' she exclaimed (June 1917), 'but
you know its almost too hard.' Resolutely she went on trying, wrestling
with the inarticulate sensations which congregated within her, imitat-
ing Lytton's phrases, copying his French *mots* and expletives which
somehow helped to fashion and enrich her own mongrel style, and
always begging him to send back just one more of his wonderful letters.
To these pleas Lytton responded nobly, his meticulous, anecdotal
communications, with their vertiginous avoidance of deep feeling,
contrasting strongly with Carrington's sprawling and unpunctuated
pastiche. Over the next fifteen years they built up between the two of
them an oddly fascinating correspondence, extraordinarily voluminous
considering how much time they spent in each other's company.

Lytton's side of this correspondence, carefully informal, carefully
light and dismissive in tone, smoothly and easily constructed, catches
some part of his charm and humour, but steers clear of other more
serious aspects of his character – in particular his rigorous seeking after
truth. Carrington's letters are completely different. For all their lack
of co-ordination, they form a kind of unconscious improvised poetry,
creating a life of their own where things flow in and out of each other
perpetually and where objects, events and persons are all touched with
vibrant personal meaning, threats or blessings, pleasure or pain. They
were, Gerald Brenan, another superb letter-writer, once told her, like a
'gesture, speech, walk, expression, seen through a medium of words;
like the rustling of leaves, the voices of birds, the arrangement of
natural forms. Education has not deadened in you this mode of expression, has not, as it has for nearly all of us, reduced speech and
writing to the level of a vulgar formula, through which we can barely
let our own natures be recognised. You have not got this horrible

stickiness of civilised people, that makes everything they come in contact with – clothes, opinions, manners, morals, relationships, adhere to them, however inappropriate these things may be to them, however little they may be able to absorb them. You have a kind of virginity about you.'

Carrington was especially anxious that those who knew of her attachment to Lytton should not pity her. She felt their sympathy to be undignified, and did everything to discourage it. 'You must not think I am unhappy,' she wrote to Barbara Bagenal at the end of May. 'For I am often very happy only it is just that I cannot bear sometimes not seeing him even for a day . . . If it is fine I am going for a jaunt to Cambridge with him, Barbara, I am so excited.'

At Cambridge, early in June, the two of them stayed with Harry Norton. Lytton piloted Carrington all round the colleges – 'I was rather excited over King's Chapel windows,' she told Noel (3 June 1917). 'But mostly over the architecture of Wren at Emmanuel, and also the Library Trinity' – took her to the Fitzwilliam Museum, and over to the Old Vicarage at Grantchester where Rupert Brooke had lived, and where they met Miles Malleson and his wife.

On their return to London, Lytton made another effort to press ahead with his work on General Gordon. But progress was still slow, and there were frequent interruptions – theatres, a performance of *Figaro* and, most interesting of all, a private view of Augustus John's drawings at the Alpine Club. Very characteristically, Lytton seems to have interested himself more in the spectators than the exhibits. 'Such a strange well-dressed and respectable crowd,' he exclaimed in a letter to Ottoline. 'The great man appeared in the middle of it, dressed in a neat but not gaudy Khaki suit, with his beard considerably trimmed, and altogether a decidedly colonial air. On the whole, I must say I prefer him en bohème.'

What distracted him most of all from 'The End of General Gordon' was the worrying condition of his mother. For some time Lady Strachey had been experiencing pain in her defective eye, and in July she was advised to undergo an operation to have it out. While she was in hospital, and subsequently during her convalescence at Durbins, Belsize Park Gardens was shut up, and Lytton went to stay for some days with Carrington at her new lodgings at No. 60 Frith Street, in Soho. 'Lytton has been living with me this last week here since Wed.,' she wrote to Barbara Bagenal. 'He went on Sat. evening to Durbins. So I am still so happy that I thought I would write to you. Just to inform you that I've never been so happy in my *life* before. Hurray . . . It was fun persuading Mrs. Reekes, my housekeeper That Lytton was my uncle. But I think the general uproar that went on in the early morning in his room Rather upset her belief in me!'

Once again, however, Carrington seems to have been deliberately oversimplifying her feelings so as to keep at bay the dreaded 'sympathy' of her friend. She resented Lytton's unmitigated coldness, and the obvious fact that he could leave her for days or weeks on end without a qualm. Perhaps, for all she knew, he let out a sigh of relief at their parting. His lack of passion, she wryly remarked to Gertler, kept one pleasantly cool in the hot weather. And in her sixteenth – but far from final – letter to him that July, she wrote: 'Lytton will be away for two months. So you will have no more reason to curse him or me. For you will have me every night you want to. What confessions we honest people make!' As a confession this was certainly outspoken, but, as it turned out, hardly accurate. For part at least of this time, she retreated back to Hurstbourne Tarrant, writing to Gertler on literary, artistic and botanical matters, then suddenly erupting with: 'What a mess I've made of your life for you!' Even in her deepest disappointment she would permit no one else to criticize Lytton, and when Gertler sought to fix on him the blame for her unhappiness, she lectured him sternly on what his proper attitude should be: 'When anyone runs Lytton down you ought rather to say. he must be better than we think since Carrington loves him. Do you not see that if you love me, you *must* believe in what I love, and not agree with the public who are stupid, and prejudiced in saying It is ill sorted and I am mislead.'

At Durbins, the atmosphere was more placid and subdued. Lady Strachey, 'attended by a pug-faced nurse', was still very weak after her operation, and, feeling depressed, needed a good deal of attention from everyone. 'Marjorie is my principal companion,' Lytton told Mary Hutchinson (24 July 1917), 'and we seem to get on very well – in the kind of way in which brothers and sisters do, when they're not in love with each other.' Over the summer Roger Fry's house provided a convenient sanatorium for Lady Strachey. Fry himself was away for most of the time, so that there was ample accommodation for her own friends and family to visit her, especially since she was so near London. Lytton, too, found it a suitable base for his purposes – the writing of General Gordon. 'For he is still around my neck, the old albatross!' he told Ottoline (14 August 1917). 'But he won't be much longer, I'm thankful to say.' By the third week of August it was evident that his mother was well on the mend, and he prepared to leave Durbins and join Leonard and Virginia Woolf at Asheham. 'I find myself plunged in the gulf of Gordon, from which it is impossible to emerge for 2 or 3 days,' he wrote to Virginia. 'Then I hope the crisis will be over –

though there'll still be some finishing paragraphs to be applied. Please expect me on Thursday.'

'The End of General Gordon' was completed later that month at Asheham, where he read it over to his friends. From Asheham he moved on to Charleston, a house not far off, in Sussex, which Clive and Vanessa Bell were then sharing with Duncan Grant and David Garnett. In the neighbourhood of Lewes, and beneath the northern slope of the South Downs, Charleston provided a permanent country home for these Bloomsbury non-combatants, where they could peaceably discharge their wartime obligations under the Military Service Act. It also gave the Bells' three children, Julian, Quentin and Angelica (later to marry David Garnett) a reasonably secure place outside London in which to live, and became Maynard Keynes's chief refuge during weekends until his marriage to the ballerina Lydia Lopokova some eight years later, when he set up house near by at Tilton.

On this, Lytton's first visit to Charleston, he read out the first two essays of *Eminent Victorians* – 'Cardinal Manning' and 'Florence Nightingale'. The response within this Bloomsbury sanctum varied enormously. Duncan Grant fell asleep and Vanessa Bell was rather critical, not of Lytton's treatment of his subjects, but of the prose style, which she thought too brim-full of clichés. Clive Bell was more generously appreciative, and David Garnett seemed highly impressed, realizing, as he later wrote, 'that Lytton's essays were designed to undermine the foundations on which the age that brought war about had been built'.

Garnett's eager absorption of Lytton's writing was a striking factor in the friendship between them which had ripened rapidly through these war years, and was slowly to decline during the 1920s. Their intimacy was closely bound up with Garnett's youthful attractiveness and every year that passed interposed a certain added distance between them, making their relationship more casual and uncomplicated. In a sense, Garnett was a genuine disciple of Lytton's. Though in no way homosexual, he looked up to him as something of an emotional and literary mentor. Yet Lytton could scarcely believe in this young and gifted man's admiration of him. 'Do you think that he likes me *really*?' he had once questioned Barbara Bagenal (17 July 1916). Though his rowdy spirits and Georgian athleticism were sometimes too excessive for Lytton's indoor tastes, yet Garnett's robust good looks, his un-abashed conceit, his unselfconscious manner, his matter-of-fact imagination and vivid response to the physical and materialistic side of living, coupled with a strain of modern sensibility, were of a type to which Lytton felt himself inevitably drawn. His fair hair, broad shoulders and the very blue eyes which seemed able to mesmerize women, were as alluring to Lytton as his soothing countrified manner. This was most immediately noticeable in the slow, puzzled way of speaking he adopted, which was often most potent at 'smoothing down my fretful quills with the softest hand – when the rest of the world seemed to be conspiring against me'. At once generous and self-assured, Garnett was an easy companion, shrewd and independent, and with a strong vein of humour which he exploited very entertainingly at the expense of the vagaries of his friends.

Lytton felt great affection for Garnett as a young man, showing him many acts of imaginative and practical kindness. When, for instance, he was alone in Paris during the winter of 1915, Lytton had sent him a Shetland cardigan which, on Garnett's own testimony, had probably saved him from pneumonia, and also dispatched to him a series of letters in the hope of cheering him up. 'Mon cher,' he wrote in one of these letters which contains the essence of a message that he had been propounding in several of his wartime literary essays, 'go to the end of your Rue de Beaune and look for the house at the corner, on the Quai where Voltaire died, at the age of 84, having conquered both the Rulers of this world, and of the next – and where (though the inscription doesn't say so, I think) he had lived fifty years before as a young poet. Consider that life and take courage.'

In his autobiography David Garnett has recorded that 'Lytton would often make devastating comments on people he did not like, but he had an astonishing patience and sympathy with those he did. He often had an intuitive understanding of what I was feeling.' In exchange for these telepathic confidences, Lytton felt safe in discussing with Garnett some of his own personal problems, which, for fear of ridicule, he could seldom disclose to other of his Bloomsbury friends. As the sympathetic repository of Lytton's troubles, Garnett had been one of the very first to hear about Carrington. What could possibly be the outcome of this astonishing affair? Lytton asked. But neither Garnett nor anyone else could yet tell.

Although Lytton had finished his draft of 'The End of General Gordon' shortly before arriving at Charleston, the revisions he needed to insert within the essay were extensive, and to his dismay he found that further work had still to be done. 'That terrible General isn't yet done with,' he complained to Pippa (23 August 1917). He had been joined at Charleston now by Carrington, and together the two of them planned to travel westwards, via Salisbury, to Devon and Cornwall, during which Lytton hoped to add the final touches to his fourth eminent Victorian.

They set out early in September and soon arrived in North Cornwall, putting up for three weeks with a Mrs Elford, at Beeny Farm, three miles from Boscastle.[1] With them went James Strachey and Noel Olivier, the young girl who had once figured as the ideal virginal heroine of Rupert Brooke's antiseptic fantasies. The accommodation, according to Lytton, was rather severe – 'a small and dirty farm-house, with an old lame hag and a couple of cats to look after us'. Carrington's description of their life at the farm, recorded in a letter she sent to her brother Noel, is more graphic, and shows the obvious influence of Lytton's way of looking at and expressing things. 'This remote house,' she calls the place, 'Kept by an old hag. daughter, son, and old ancient farmer. All rather ramshackle. and decayed . . . The sea is quite near. But unfortunately un-get-at-able as theres a precipace of grey stone some 400 feet in height . . .

'It's a bit rough, no hot water in the morning, or conveniences. Just vast quantities of food and cream and long walks along the top of the coast cliffs. Lytton's reading the tempest to me. and in the evenings Mottley's Dutch Republic and last night Gibbon on the Emperor Claudius who was no doubt about it a bad fellow.'

When not walking or reading aloud to Carrington, Lytton spent his time indoors working on his book. By the third week of September his revisions were complete, though he still feared that further amendments might prove necessary after he had read the recently published two-volume Life of *Sir Charles Dilke* by Stephen Gwynn and Gertrude Tuckwell, which was to provide him with a useful summary of events concerning Gordon's assignment in the Sudan.[2] 'I am glad to say that Gordon is at last finished,' he wrote to Pippa (27 September 1917). 'In spite of every effort, he is about half as long again as Florence N. I think the four will fill a good-sized book – but perhaps a very short one ought to be added. I'm afraid the Life of Dilke will contain information on the Gordon affair, and make alterations necessary, which will be a nuisance. I'm now reading Creighton's Life – have you read it? I thought he might do for number 5; but I find he's not sufficiently unlike Manning – though full of interest.

'The post-horsewoman approaches. Farewell! Give my love to Mama, and all the other Durbinians.'

While Lytton worked, read and wrote letters, Carrington would go

---

[1] This cottage had been recommended to James Strachey by a Quaker lady in the Society of Friends office where he was doing Work of National Importance: distributing milk to German wives.

[2] Part V of 'The End of General Gordon' owes something to Gwynn and Tuckwell's volumes.

off into the cornfields and paint landscapes, having with difficulty extracted from the authorities a permit to do her painting near the coast. When it was wet or cold, she would sit 'like a poached egg' in front of the wood fire, reading and penning her long, muddled letters. Sometimes she was stricken by loneliness and a perverse jealousy over the fact that Gertler seemed to be able to manage quite well without her – at least, he had hardly written and appeared to be rather too adequately looked after by Dorothy Brett and Lady Ottoline Morrell. 'I long to be back with you and Brett,' she wrote to him in her twenty-first letter of the month. 'Theres a confession! But when I was at Charleston it was so good to be with artists who talked about painting, and sometimes I feel strangely isolated having lost my companions. Do not leave me Mark.' She implored him to write more often to her to put her mind at rest. She was, she said, longing for his forgiveness, and promised that when she returned to London in October, they would at last be *true* friends. 'I have learnt so much now,' she told him. 'I am humbled like the man in the Psalms even unto the dust – and do not hate me for my cruelness. it was impossible I should have known what you felt.' She was full of joint schemes for her return. They would work together. Perhaps they might read history one to the other in Monty Shearman's flat? What about Sir Thomas Browne? And why shouldn't they teach each other French? After the war, too, they must certainly spend some time in Devon and Cornwall.

At the end of some ten days at Beeny, all four of them 'were about at the ends of our endurance what with flea bites and the horrors of a real pigsty of a farmyard', and they decided to move elsewhere. Wires were dispatched to various outlying farms, and after several refusals, acceptance was signalled back from a Mrs Box, an unknown woman living some thirty miles north of them at Home Farm, Welcombe, near Bude, on the Devon and Cornwall border. On Saturday, 20 September, they therefore set off for this new farmhouse with some trepidation. 'I imagined of course a new bungalow farm, with a methodist female with spectacles and no food to eat!!' Carrington wrote to Barbara Bagenal (21 September 1917). 'After a 14 mile drive from Bude in a motor car we arrived here. It's simply perfect. A big grass paddock and walled garden and, a small farmhouse. We have a room each, two sitting-rooms, an unlimited supply of food and cream, and big double beds.'

This luxury, the fine weather and beautiful country round about put everyone in the best of spirits, and they remained on there for three weeks, idle and contented. The farm was perched on the tip of a steep hill rising between two deeply-cut green valleys, one of which formed the frontier between Devon and Cornwall, and along both of which streams ran to sea beaches. It was surrounded by animals – four black and white cats, a collie dog, a big pink pig and two smaller black ones, all very well behaved and all of whom Carrington named after her friends. The country with its immense sea-cliffs and rocks, its inland woods and brooks was so vast and strangely foreign to the tamer traditional English landscape that she felt she was living in a different country. She would wander off for long walks with Lytton, paint by herself, bathe in the sea with Noel Olivier, or lie alone in one of the swift silver rivulets under the hot sun and let the water rush over her body, as cold as knife blades. How good it was simply to be alive! Like all the others she ate enormously; when indoors she would either study Tolstoy and Dostoievsky, or else paint the 'veille mère Box' in her kitchen, and most evenings she sat gazing in rapt attention at Lytton as he read aloud from Gibbon or from his own work. Never – not even at Chilling – had she been happier. She felt she could go on living here for the rest of her life – and wrote to Gertler to tell him so. Some of her letters at this time are ecstatic. 'Barbara I am so happy here,' she told her friend Barbara Bagenal (21 September 1917). 'Almost a headache everymorning because I get so tired and exhausted. Simply loving so hard! . . .

'The sea has yellow sands and big rocks and there are valleys such as you never saw with rivulets which flow down to the sea and green forests on the hills. It is surely one of the best places in England. I am painting old Mere Box who is 70, an amazing old Lady, who wears a pink bonnet and curious garments. Miss Box and her sister and brother keep the farm. I have swum in the sea twice with Noel. Today is so hot and the flies buzz round our heads. I like Noel very much, She is very gay and amusing. Lytton also finished his Essay on General Gordon and read it to us. I think it is very masterly.'

By the time Carrington arrived back at Andover later in October, she was once again sure that the solution to her problems was imminent, and that a permanently new and wonderful life was at any second about to start up. All her instincts told her so. Devon and Cornwall had been a radiant prelude to their lasting life of happiness together. It was the first anniversary of her brother Teddy's death, and her parents had seldom seemed more remote to her. Only Lytton could offer real comfort and consolation. Already, on their first evening apart, she was impatient to be back with him again, to be seated once more near his lean and benign figure, gaze up at those calm geometrically composed features, those soft eyes, and hear once more his voice – his jokes, his reading, the wit and pithiness of his conversation on which he bestowed all the charm of some musical design. It was no longer he but other people who seemed distant, odd and uninteresting. She missed him painfully, and in desolation her heart overflowed with gratitude. 'Oh its wretched having lost you,' she wrote. 'And not to have you tonight to talk to. Dearest Lytton I can never thank you enough for these weeks. I did not relize how happy I had been until this evening . . . If only you were here – and so many wishes – you have spoilt me for too long. and now I feel as if suddenly I had walked into a greenhouse in the winter . . . Forgive me for writing but I wanted you so badly – one is not left alone to cry – Dearest Lytton I love you so much.'

Such artless intensity stirred within Lytton faint tremors of his old apprehensions, and his reply, as so often, was guarded and apologetic to the point of formality. 'I'm very glad you enjoyed the summer and so did I – very much indeed,' he told her, 'but I fear I am too crabbèd. I wish, too, I could be more effectual in other ways; but I am old, debilitated, and floating. However, you know all this.'

3

THE MILL HOUSE

Carrington's determination to secure a country cottage where she and Lytton could live had never seriously wavered. During the summer and early autumn she had written to David Garnett and other select friends who already knew of her liaison with Lytton, asking them to search round for somewhere suitable. She herself bicycled everywhere, stopping pedestrians and other bicyclists in the streets to inquire if they knew of any empty farms or small houses. The vague plan which had been hatched a year before to rescue Lytton from Belsize Park Gardens was now fixed in all its details, and ready to be put into operation. Disturbed by his forlorn condition, his penury and precautionary way of life amid the fogs of London, Oliver Strachey, Harry Norton, Saxon Sydney-Turner and Maynard Keynes had all agreed to participate in a scheme whereby each of them, together with Lytton himself, was to put up twenty pounds a year in order to rent and maintain a decent country house. In its practical effects, this represented a subsidy to Lytton, who was to act nominally as caretaker and, with Carrington, live there permanently. The others would only occasionally make use of the place, which would thus become yet another of those pastoral Bloomsbury outposts, along with Asheham and Charleston Eleanor, and provide a welcome alternative to the crowded and baroque rusticity of Garsington.

This scheme, therefore, though chiefly to the advantage of Lytton and Carrington, seemed to suit everyone. Barbara Bagenal volunteered to act as a kind of treasurer, collecting contributions by quarterly instalments and paying off the rent.[1] Other non-contributing friends might, of course, be invited down by the caretakers whenever the shareholders (who naturally took priority) were not in residence. 'I find London more and more disagreeable to work in; and Carrington also wants to be in the country; so it appears on the whole a reasonable project,' Lytton explained to Clive Bell (6 November 1917). 'I shouldn't be able to face it alone; female companionship I think may make it tolerable – though certainly by no means romantic. I am under no illusions. But in the present miserable, chaotic, and suspended state of affairs, it seems to me the best that can be done. A little quiet work is really almost all that one can look forward to, just now.'

Carrington's parents were planning in the near future to move from Hurstbourne Tarrant to Cheltenham, and realizing that this might be the most propitious time to break free from them, she redoubled her house-hunting expeditions. To the surprise of everyone, she was almost immediately successful. In the third week of October, while bicycling along the Thames Valley, she came upon the Mill House, in the tiny village of Tidmarsh, about a mile due south of Pangbourne, in Berkshire. This discovery – later to be the subject of her most remarkable painting – overjoyed her, and she wrote off excitedly to Lytton to tell him all about it and give him the terms and conditions of the lease.

The Mill House had been built on to the end of a large weatherboarded water-mill, the mill stream of which was banked to a high level and bounded one side of the garden. Although the mill-wheel did not now work, the corn-chandler's warehouse above it was still in operation. The house itself, Carrington explained, was 'old fashioned' with gables and some lattice windows. Inside, though rather damp and in need of some renovation, it was nicely decorated, and contained modern fireplaces and 'new oakbeams'. There were three reception rooms, a kitchen, bathroom with hot and cold water, six bedrooms and a box room, all of which were fitted with electric light. The grounds belonging to it, on two sides of the house, extended over an acre and a half, and included a small orchard, a sunken Roman bath kept replenished by the gushing mill water, and a tennis or croquet lawn. It was near a church and a post office, took thirty-five minutes to reach by express train from Paddington, was being offered for three years' lease

---

[1] Once this scheme had been put into operation, Maynard Keynes every three months or so used to take Barbara Bagenal to the Café Royal and over lunch or dinner there go through the formality of checking her book-keeping.

at a rent of fifty-two pounds per annum and, Carrington concluded, 'sounds too good to be alright!'

To Lytton also it sounded ideal. In such a place he might make a real home for himself, a tranquil asylum set apart from the mad, war-weary atmosphere of London, where his friends could gather, and where they all might be happy. 'It's this wretched separation of everybody that makes one uncomfortable,' he told Clive Bell (6 November 1917). 'But my hope is that if the house at Tidmarsh comes into being, it may be possible by the summer to have some pleasant reunions in the old style, whether the war's going on or not.' Of course, he had not the least intention of turning his back on the pleasures of London and immuring himself without respite in agricultural retirement. Far from it. If he could have been content to live from hand to mouth, it would have been absurd ever to leave the metropolis. But he felt very strongly the urge to write, and for that 'un peu de recueillement' was essential. 'My notion is not to retire altogether,' he wrote to Clive Bell (4 December 1917), '– but for 2 or 3 weeks at a time; and to spend happy intervals gadding about among such people as are left.' By enjoying alternately the best of both worlds, he hoped to remain industrious without becoming bored, to achieve some real literary prestige without bankrupting his personal life.

All the same, though this was what they wanted, both Lytton and Carrington had some qualms about the Tidmarsh experiment. They feared the kind of prying, malicious gossip at which, privately, they themselves so excelled. Already there was some scandalous talk about them. 'My plans for the future are quite devoid of mystery,' Lytton assured Clive Bell. And after describing the project in some detail, he ended up a little peevishly: 'This rather dreary explanation will I hope satisfy you that all is above board. Please don't believe in the hidden hand.' In the next few months he was more than once called upon to provide this same dreary explanation, since rumour and conjecture were still rife. He experienced some difficulty, too, in breaking the news to his mother, mainly on the grounds, it seems, that he would be sharing the house with a young unmarried woman. Lady Strachey did not voice her disapproval of this state of affairs – that was not her way. But her distaste was heavily implicit in everything she did not say. 'A curious scene at Belsize Park,' Leonard Woolf reported to Lytton a few weeks after the Mill House had been taken (January 1918). 'V[irginia] and I at tea with her Ladyship. V. very innocently: "Well, Lady Strachey, and what do you think of Tidmarsh?" An awkward pause and some very indistinct remarks from her Ladyship. A pause. Then across the table to me: "What do *you* think of it all?" (She was referring to the general European situation, but I naturally thought she referred to Tidmarsh).'

The difficulties which confronted Carrington were more drastic and widespread. Back at Hurstbourne Tarrant she concocted a special story for her parents. Tidmarsh, she told them, was to be a new retreat for Slade artists – girls only – where they could put up cheaply and devote their time to painting; and this casual explanation appears for a time to have satisfied them, preoccupied as they were with their own plans. But to other people, whose opinions she cared about more, there was no such way out. The Bloomsberries at first disapproved of her, treating her coldly like a tactless intruder. By going off to live with Lytton she must have known, too, that she would antagonize some of her oldest friends – Dorothy Brett, for example, whose company she sadly missed. She was also certain, of course, to attract the rancour of Ottoline, who, much to Lytton's perplexity, showed the obverse of this rancour in a sudden flowering of her friendship with Gertler. 'What does it mean?' he asked Clive Bell (6 November 1917). 'I should have thought, a priori, that they would have found it impossible to have anything to do with each other. It's very strange. . . . Perhaps they're so wildly different, that neither has any notion of what the other's like, and so they're able to mix and mingle without any difficulty – though, I suppose, after all, their interweavings don't go much further than an after-lunch pianola romp.'

The most complex and pressing of all Carrington's worries, however, was the problem of Gertler himself. The many improbable schemes about which she had written to him from Cornwall – the history, the French, and Sir Thomas Browne – were now all forgotten, probably rather to his relief. On the surface, their friendship filtered on much as before – endless letters, the occasional dinner, cinema or bed – as if nothing had or was about to change. For Carrington simply could not bring herself to tell him that she was about to go off and live with Lytton. In fact she went out of her way to conceal the facts, so that Gertler still had no idea of what was happening.

As for Lytton himself, he still rather admired Gertler 'in a certain way'. He wanted to explain everything to him, so that they could all be friends together. Then they could invite him down to Tidmarsh in the summer. What could be more reasonable? Or more delightful? Carrington, however, soon managed to persuade him that such urbane behaviour was out of the question. She knew Gertler better than he did. He was too volatile, too wild for any sort of rational, civilized treatment. If either of them, on the spur of the moment, blurted out the truth, the shock might drive him to madness, to actual physical violence, maybe. He could be dangerous, she reminded Lytton, and with dangerous men discretion was the better part of common sense. Lytton was convinced. She must do, he said, what she thought best. He would not interfere. He could see that she thrived on dissimulation and intrigue and extracted a mischievous excitement from deceiving people like Gertler, but he was forced to acknowledge that, in order to avoid any foolish unpleasantness, it might be wise to follow her advice. Perhaps, under Ottoline's advances, Gertler would anyway soon lose interest. At all costs, violence and unnecessary pain should be avoided. 'It all rather alarms me,' he admitted to Carrington (9 December 1917). '. . . I find *him* very attractive – I really do like him – and would like to be friends with him; but the worst of it is that I can't feel any faith in him. . . . It's a nuisance to have to be on one's guard, when one doesn't in the least want to be. – And it's so silly – his way of going on – because there's no point in it. However I don't suppose it can be helped.'

Carrington's attitude was altogether different from Lytton's, and her tactics, designed to postpone rather than to eliminate trouble, were almost certain to lead to more violent repercussions later on. At first she merely tended to mislead Gertler, telling him, with partial truth, that her frequent absences from London that autumn were due to her parents' move from Hurstbourne Tarrant. But so many stories of her and Lytton had been buzzing round lately that Gertler – whom Carrington had again accused of trickery and lack of trust – was sceptical. And so, in her twenty-sixth letter of November, she boldly attempted to give the lie to his suspicions. 'No, I'm not going away with Lytton!' she stated. 'But my people are leaving Hampshire, and are going to live in a town, Cheltenham, So I've got to go home for a little while when they move to help them. and take away my goods and furniture. Then I'll be back again in London all the winter I expect.'

Within this basic misconception, once laid, it was child's play to plant the hard core of a lie. In her twenty-ninth letter of the month it is done, with a neat and logical inconsequence that seemed for the moment to carry perfect plausibility. 'Oliver Strachey has taken an old water Mill House near Reading, so I am going to let him keep all my furniture for me. Until I have a place in London of my own. Its such a nice Mill House. and it will be good to have a retreat – like you and Brett have Garsington.'

And there, in this dangerous condition, the matter temporarily rested.

Pending the final negotiations over Tidmarsh, Lytton's miserable, chaotic and suspended way of life was meanwhile jogging along much as before. Belsize Park Gardens had been opened up again, and his mother and various sisters reassembled there. The war went interminably on, his old friends seemed fewer and less accessible, he was reviewing once more for the *New Statesman*, the weather grew colder and altogether he felt pretty dejected. 'The amenities are getting so few and feeble, and the horrors steadily increase,' he complained to Clive Bell (20 October 1917). 'Last night was spent waiting in vain for a bombardment – a most gloomy proceeding; and I suppose one that must be looked forward to now as the usual thing.' His longing for the quiet and seclusion of Tidmarsh mounted daily, and to Mary Hutchinson – 'the only sympathetic person in London' – he confessed (31 October 1917): 'London fills me with disgust; and I am hoping to leave it for ever (minus a day).'

All the same, his life was neither stationary nor dull. He made off for a week to Oliver and Ray Strachey at Chilling, and for a week-end to Ottoline at Garsington. When he was unable to escape from town, there were plenty of social engagements to occupy him. He was seeing a good deal of company, chiefly of the Café Royal kind, and full of good-natured eccentricity. This swirl of conviviality culminated in a farewell party given by Augustus John, who was shortly off to France as a Canadian major. Lytton's new attitude of disapproval towards John appears to have been touched by a small element of unconscious envy. Certainly an unkind critic might point out that the more conventional position which he sees Augustus John as occupying was, in many respects, similar to one into which he himself would move a little later. 'Poor John!' he lamented to Clive Bell (4 December 1917). 'Did you by any chance go to that show of his at the Alpine Club? The impression produced by the reduplication of all that superficial and pointless facility was most painful. Naturally he has become the darling of the upper classes, and made £5000 out of his show. His appearance in Khaki is unfortunate – a dwindled creature, with clipped beard, pseudo-smart, and in fact altogether deplorable. All the same, late on Saturday night, there were moments when, in spite of everything . . . mais assez! —'

Other exhibitions to which he dragged himself in these final weeks of 1917 included a show at the Omega Club – about which he mercifully kept silent – and one of Max Beerbohm's caricatures at the Grosvenor Gallery in Mayfair. He had gone there with forebodings of tedium, feeling that he had already seen enough caricatures to last him a lifetime, 'but I was quite carried away', he told Clive Bell (4 December

1917). 'He [Max] has the most remarkable and seductive genius – and I should say about the smallest in the world.'

When not out and about enjoying what he called his 'smart life', he spent his days at Belsize Park Gardens meticulously going over, for the very last time, his completed manuscript of *Eminent Victorians*. Having discarded the idea of adding a short life of Mandell Creighton, he toyed briefly with the notion of writing on Watts – one of his original twelve candidates – but this also came to nothing. The preparation, research and composition of the book had extended over some five years, and its completion now neatly coincided with a distinct and significant landmark in his biography, something for which he had been vainly struggling ever since he left Cambridge – the final end to his family life in London. It was a fitting moment to conclude his work as a tetralogy. Besides, now that he read through, in their sequence, the finished version of these essays, he realized that, from an aesthetic point of view, no further additions were necessary. To add even one more paper would be a wasteful and ridiculous excess, a pointless squandering of his small store of preciously garnered creative energy. In their symmetry, their delicate balance of mood and tone – variations on a single unifying and cohesive theme, comprising, in the opinion of Sigmund Freud, a treatise against religion – he saw that this series of four biographical portraits corresponded, as they stood, to the four inter-related movements of an orchestral symphony, or perhaps more appropriately to the intimate pattern of a string quartet:

> 'Cardinal Manning' – *Allegro vivace*
> 'Florence Nightingale' – *Andante*
> 'Dr. Arnold' – *Scherzo*
> 'The End of General Gordon' – *Rondo*

His final corrections to *Eminent Victorians* were completed by the beginning of December, at the same time as the negotiations over his lease of the Mill House at Tidmarsh were settled. Carrington, accompanied by Barbara Bagenal, hurried down there at once to start on the job of making it reasonably habitable by Christmas, when Lytton and some of his guests were expected. With the aid of the local postmistress, they set to work, painting walls, staining the floors, creating carpets and arranging furniture, all in the most energetic fashion. Carrington was a devotee of Cobbett, and her furnishing as well as her housekeeping expressed both the comfort and the poetry of cottage and farmhouse life. 'Her very English sensibility, in love with the country and with all country things,' wrote Gerald Brenan, who visited Tidmarsh two years later and was enchanted by the unique, unsophisticated

I

atmosphere of the place, 'gave everything she touched a special and peculiar stamp.' In Lytton's bedroom, for instance – later called 'the Adam and Eve Room' – she had let herself go, painting on one wall the lifesize, naked figure of Adam, faced, on the opposite wall, by the naked Eve.

And she was happy preparing for her new life, happy as she had seldom been. 'I am so happy Because I truly Believe it will be good living here,' she wrote to Lytton. 'and you will be contented, almost – dearest Lytton, all my love to you.' Handicapped by his complicated shyness from expressing openly the gratitude he felt, Lytton sent back the kind of gossipy letters which he wrote so well and which he knew delighted her, full of his adventures, and his acid and amusing observations on the 'smart life' he was still leading – a tea party, for instance, with Ethel Sands 'in her très-soigné Vale Avenue residence. There she was in a black tea-gown . . . and a tiresomely elegant young female of the name of Enid Bagnold,[1] fresh from the Tombola Fair. It was all absurdly polite and futile, and punctuated by milk-and-water indecencies which made my heart sink in my boots, and made them rock with laughter.'

In the third week of December, Lytton left Hampstead and went down to join Carrington at the Mill House. It was extremely cold, and many of the rooms were still in a state of wild disorder. While continuous pandemonium sounded from within, outside everything lay quiet and motionless in the stationary grip of winter. Yet whenever the sun came out, what a blessing it was to be in the country! And how pleasing was the prospect of their life together here, once all was in proper trim and the warm weather had begun.

Meantime there were many temporary horrors to be endured. A letter which Lytton wrote to Virginia Woolf on 21 December describes very bleakly the rigours of settling in, and, probably on account of a sudden frost which burst all their pipes, arrived in so damp a condition that it was in places totally illegible. 'Here I am in considerable agony. Nature turned crusty, the "pipes" congealed, and it has been so cold that my nose (to say nothing of other parts) dripped in icicles. . . . My female companion keeps herself warm by unpacking, painting, pruning the creepers, knocking in the nails, etc. . . . I try to console myself with Queen Victoria's letters . . . I still have the notion that I may be able to work in this seclusion, when all the nails have finally been knocked in. Nous verrons.

[1] Enid Bagnold, the novelist and playwright, who had been Frank Harris's deputy on the magazine *Hearth and Home*, and whose first book, *A Diary without Dates*, had just been published. In 1920 she married Sir Roderick Jones.

'. . . Ah dearie, dearie me, I am nodding over the fire, and she's sow-ing an edge to the carpet with a diligence . . . Ah, la vie! it grows more remarkable every minute.'

Lytton and Carrington's first guests at Tidmarsh were Gerald and Fredegond Shove, who dropped in for a quick gay visit. Then, on Christmas Eve, Harry Norton arrived carrying with him in a neat satchel one large turkey and four bottles of claret. For the Christmas holiday itself James Strachey and Alix Sargant-Florence joined the party. 'I am gradually settling down (amid a good deal of loose paint and calico) to a regular rural existence,' Lytton informed Clive Bell on the last day of December, 'and before long I hope to be really involved in work.' Later that day he set off to Garsington for a New Year week-end party, and from there returned to London, where he had arranged to have an interview with Messrs Chatto and Windus about the proposed publication of his *Eminent Victorians*.

Left on her own, Carrington now knew something of the way in which the next fourteen years of her life with Lytton, at Tidmarsh and later at Ham Spray House, would turn out. There would have to be many sacrifices. Already she missed some of her young artist friends, and the particular trees and fields of her home. Seldom again would she have much time for serious painting. Instead she became an excellent gardener and an erratic if conscientious housekeeper. Though she usually had a maid to help her, she did most of the cooking herself – an art for which she had had no training and only a latent aptitude. She prepared large and delicious country meals for Lytton and his friends – home-made wines, game and raspberry jelly and good helpings of green vegetables from the garden; and teas of farm butter, honey in the comb, rich plum cakes baked in the oven, skilfully concocted marma-lades and fresh warm loaves of currant bread, all neatly laid out on the table with a pink lustre tea-service. But behind the scenes, in the kitchen, there was indescribable chaos, as if a bomb had exploded. It was a wonder that Lytton was not severely poisoned, though, possibly, of course, some of his later sicknesses may not have been psychosomatic in origin at all, but simply gastronomical. Several of their guests suffered acutely. Carrington's rabbit-pie, for example, though a very tasty and succulent dish, was sometimes lethal in its after-effects, and Diana Guinness (later Lady Mosley) told the author that after one devastating plateful 'I had to have the Doctor at 3 A.M. – thought I was dying – I had to stay on some more days and that was how I became so fond of Carrington.'

In her capacity as nurse to Lytton's many indispositions, she could at first be equally solicitous and alarming: Barbara Bagenal once preventing her in the nick of time from serving him, as a drink, half a tumbler of undiluted iodine. But she had set out to make herself absolutely indispensable to him, and gradually, detail by detail, she taught herself to be so. She was his housekeeper, his confidante, his go-between. Unable to give an order to a servant in his own home, he would tell Carrington when he wanted a cup of tea, and she would solemnly inform the maid. If he were by himself, he would go without. She enveloped him in a love and admiration which struck others as excessive, but which exactly suited him, since their union could never be a midnight, tête-à-tête affair, but was of an everyday and practical nature. Lytton needed not a mistress, as Gertler had done, but a companion to look after him and to understand him with that sensibility, that selfless tolerance and quickness of mind that neither Lady Strachey nor Ottoline had ever really possessed. Carrington was this perfectly sympathetic spirit; her artistic flair, lively and exceptional nature acted as the salt preserving their relationship from the alkaline coating of tedium.

Though they lived together for the rest of their lives, neither ever became warder to the other's captivity. By mutual consent, both retained something of their independence, even if Lytton's flights from Carrington's attentions sometimes bore the look of a schoolboy's guilty truancy. For she, it appeared, would very willingly have become his prisoner and hated his departures which, she nevertheless instinctively realized, acted as the safety-valve to their unconventional union. When left alone in the country, as in these first days of 1918, she was overcome by fear. The Mill House seemed full of strange noises, either rats or ghosts, and both equally terrifying.[1] At night she would hurry up to bed early, and listen, and long for sleep. These inexplicable night-sounds echoed the frightening insecurity which had always lurked soundlessly beneath the surface of her contentment. In spite of everything, she hardly ever felt confident that her life with Lytton would continue for very long, and secretly went on hoping that somehow he might one day ask her to marry him.

Yet with all her fears and uncertainties, it was a good life she enjoyed with him, materially and otherwise. She travelled widely and met many people. Towards Lytton's young men she felt no jealousy, and since they adored her, she basked in their playful attentions. These years at Tidmarsh were probably the happiest in both their lives. For her

---

[1] The corn storehouse next door was, of course, a regular breeding ground for rats. 'One morning I was awakened by yells from Lytton's room,' James Strachey remembered, 'and went in and found something moving inside the bottom of his bed – a rat, which I caught in a chamber pot.'

happiness was Lytton's happiness, and all her energies were orientated towards what they both wanted. She was certain, too, that though he might feel no sexual desire for her, yet she would be closer to him, and better for him, than anyone else could be. Never again would he be enfeebled by unnecessary illness or prostrated by secret misery and depleted vigour. She would see to it that he led a regular life supported at every turn by glasses of warm milk, reviving country walks, measured doses of quinine, Bemax and Sanatogen, and sensible clothes, and Extract of Malt, and Dr Gregory's rhubarb powder, and eucalyptus oil and all the other wholesome syrups, nourishing foods and cunning medicaments the world had to offer.

4

'TOUT EST POSSIBLE'

While Carrington was busy renovating and redecorating the Mill House, Lytton had been looking round for a suitable publisher for his book. Several years earlier, Geoffrey Whitworth, the art editor of Chatto and Windus, had asked Roger Fry to write for them a book on Post-Impressionism. Fry had declined, but added that his friend Clive Bell was then engaged in writing just such a work, and that he would ask him to submit it to them. In due course the book, entitled *Art*, arrived, was accepted, and became an immediate success. 'And how very strange to be published by Chatto and Windus!' Lytton had commented shortly before its appearance (9 November 1913). 'I thought they did nothing but bring out superannuated editions of Swinburne variegated with the Children's Theological Library and the Posthumous Essays of Lord de Tabley.'

But now, four years later, everyone was conspiring to urge the same strange publishers on himself – 'including Mr. Robert Nichols,[1] who hurried up to me the other evening, and assured me that they were just the people for my book, with its delicate ironical flavour, etc., etc. as if he had read it all years ago'. Clive Bell, soon to bring out his *Pot Boilers* (1918) with the same firm, had recently spoken to Whitworth and his associate Frank Swinnerton about the manuscript of *Eminent Victorians*. They at once expressed interest, and so early in December,

[1] Robert Nichols (1893–1944), the poet and dramatist, who was at this time working in the Ministry of Labour, having seen service on the Belgian-French front. His recently published book of poems *Ardours and Endurances* had been widely read and he was regarded by many as a sort of new Rupert Brooke.

after having arranged for it to be typed, Lytton decided to send them the completed text.

He was not confident about its acceptance. According to Raymond Mortimer, he felt that it was too strong meat, too savagely critical and outspoken, to be readily digested, and that he might have to wait several years for its publication, until public taste became more amenable. In any case, it would almost certainly have to be postponed until after the war was over. In a letter to Clive Bell (4 December 1917), however, he expresses his uncertainties rather differently: 'I fear it might not strike them as quite sufficiently advanced,' he wrote.

Whatever the exact reason for these doubts, he cannot have been prepared for his publishers' heady reaction. Whitworth read it first, then passed it on to Swinnerton, who, finding the typescript in its cover of crimson paper on his office desk one morning shortly before Christmas, began casually to turn its pages. 'They were so enchanting', he later wrote, 'that I continued, and when night fell I could not leave the book, but took it carefully home. . . . I had hardly taken the type-script up again after dinner when . . . there was an air raid by Germans. The whirring of aeroplanes overhead, the rattle of machine-gun fire, and finally the frightful thunder of a gun in the field at the bottom of our garden, would all have served to distract a mind less happily engaged; but as it was, with curtains closely drawn to prevent the escape of light, I consorted that evening with Cardinal Manning, Thomas Arnold, Florence Nightingale, and General Gordon. The nineteenth century had come alive again.'

Both Whitworth and Swinnerton were 'as excited before publica-tion as the world was after it', especially since, outside Cambridge circles, the name of Lytton Strachey was relatively unknown. Frank Swinnerton vaguely recalled his primer on French literature, but as yet knew nothing of its author. His enthusiastic acceptance of the book reached Lytton shortly before Christmas. He replied (30 December 1917) asking for fifty pounds to be paid to him on the day of publica-tion, as an advance against a royalty of 10 per cent of the published price – and bringing up the matter of illustrations – always a most significant and carefully chosen part of his biographies. 'I think the portraits would be an important feature of the book,' he wrote, 'but I do not know how to obtain photographic prints of them, nor can I engage to pay for their cost. The portraits I have in mind are to be found in books which are easily procurable: would you be able to obtain reproductions of these? I should add that I think there should be five portraits, and not four, as a portrait of Newman (there is a very suitable one in Wilfrid Ward's biography) seems to me indispensable.'[1]

To agree the terms of his contract, Lytton arranged to call at the offices of Chatto and Windus early in January. The impression which he created at this meeting was so very vivid that Swinnerton later recorded it in *The Georgian Literary Scene*. '[Lytton Strachey] was fairly tall, but his excessive thinness, almost emaciation, caused him to appear endless,' he remembered. 'He had a rather bulbous nose, the spectacles of a British Museum bookworm, a large and straggly dark brown beard (with a curious rufous tinge); no voice at all. He drooped if he stood upright, and sagged if he sat down. He seemed entirely without vitality; and most people would have mistaken him for an elderly professor of languages who was trying to remember some grammatical rule which he had forgotten all about. Sad merriment was in his eye, and about him a perpetual air of sickness and debility.'

Lytton was delighted by Swinnerton's and Whitworth's high estimate of his work. But in the ensuing months between the acceptance of his typescript and the publication of his book, he was recurrently plagued with doubts as to its merits. Perhaps the style was too richly adorned, the adjectives too thickly plastered on; perhaps the tone was over-emphatic; perhaps the characters would fail to 'convince'. To reassure himself he solicited his friends' favourable opinions. He sent a copy of 'The End of General Gordon' to Philip Morrell, who liked it, and another to Virginia Woolf, who thought it masterly – 'It's amazing how from all these complications, you contrive to reel off such a straight and dashing story,' she wrote back to him, 'and how you weave in every scrap – my God, *what* scraps – of interest to be had, like (you must pardon one metaphor) a snake insinuating himself through innumerable golden rings. . . . I don't see how the skill could be carried further.'

Wherever he went during this winter he would seize the opportunity to read aloud some pages from his book. Anxious even at this stage to iron out any minor flaws which were still undetected, always fond of reading before a sympathetic audience, he found that this was the perfect method for testing the flow and effectiveness of his rather conversational prose style. At Tidmarsh he read it to Carrington, and at Hampstead to some of his family. Over Easter he spent a few days at Asheham, where he again read some passages to Leonard and Virginia Woolf and his fellow guests, James Strachey and Noel Olivier; and early in April he went on to Charleston and, as a sequel to the Manning and Florence Nightingale essays which Clive and Vanessa Bell, David

---

[1] In the first edition of *Eminent Victorians* there were actually six illustrations, the last one being a photograph of Gladstone.

Garnett and Duncan Grant had heard the previous autumn, he read them those on Arnold and Gordon. On another occasion, visiting 'Jack' [St John] and Mary Hutchinson, he sat, a Shetland shawl draped round his shoulders, in an armchair close to the fire, and, though uncomfortably afflicted with shingles, delivered in a faint and plaintive voice several selected chapters. One of the other guests was Osbert Sitwell, who recalled that their hostess 'pressed her lively young daughter of seven to allow him to see her imitation of him. While the precocious mimic showed off, Lytton watched the child with a look of the utmost distaste, and when asked by the mother what he thought of the performance – one of real virtuosity – remarked in a high, clear, decisive voice, "I expect it's amusing, but it isn't at all *like*!"'

These first four months of 1918 were extremely busy ones for Lytton. 'My life passes almost entirely among proof sheets, which now flow in upon me daily,' he told Ottoline (3 March 1918). 'It is rather exciting, but also rather harassing. All sorts of tiresome details, and minor crises – about covers, illustrations, contracts, and so on – keep turning up; but my hope is that in about six weeks or so "Eminent Victorians" will burst upon an astonished world.' Between proof sheets he was contributing reviews to the periodical *War and Peace*, which Leonard Woolf was editing while the regular editor, Harold Wright, was away, and experimenting with another play.

Mainly because of this work, Lytton spent a good deal of his time in London, where he had recently joined the left-wing 1917 Club. This club, evolving from some discussions between Oliver Strachey and Leonard Woolf, had started up the previous December, taking the lease of No. 4 Gerrard Street in Soho, 'in those days the rather melancholy haunt of prostitutes daily from 2.30 onwards', Leonard Woolf narrates. Its membership, which later became largely theatrical, was then a curious mixture of the political and the literary and artistic. 'It's quite a comfortable and attractive place,' Lytton assured Carrington after his first entry there, '– very nice rooms, and tolerable furniture and tea and toast to be had.' Apart from these homely amenities, the club furnished him, in the domain of politics, with a ringside view of much that was going on, and an opportunity to study some of its more illustrious radical members, such as Ramsay MacDonald, the rather uneasy first president of the club.

While in London this winter Lytton took time off to attend Bertrand Russell's trial at Bow Street. This trial arose out of an article Russell had written for the N.C.F. weekly, *The Tribunal*, advocating acceptance of a recent peace offer made by Germany. As a result of it, he was sentenced to six months' imprisonment in Brixton jail. Lytton felt that the more the friends who showed themselves in court, the better for Russell, but their laughter at some of the prosecution's misdirected sallies and the amusing quotes from Russell's article may well have helped to stimulate the magistrate, Sir John Dickinson's, ferocity.[1] 'I have never encountered such a blast of vitriolic hatred,' Russell later commented on Dickinson. 'He would have had me hanged, drawn and quartered if he could.' And Lytton echoed this view in a description of the case he sent to Ottoline (3 March 1918). 'It was really infamous – much worse, I thought, than those other proceedings before the Lord Mayor – even more obviously unjust, gross and generally wicked and disgusting. The spectacle of a louse like Sir John Dickinson rating Bertie for immorality and sending him to prison! . . . James and I came away with our teeth chattering with fury. It makes one abandon hope that such monstrosities should occur, openly, and be accepted by very nearly everybody as a matter of course.'

At about the same time, Lytton had to face a smaller ordeal of his own. Later that March he was summoned to yet another medical examination, this time to be conducted by the civil authorities. He had no clear notion of what to expect, of what this change in the system might entail. The general outlook of the war was not good, and there was little reason to expect its end in a mere seven months' time. In view of the tiresome possibilities that might, even now, ensue, the prospect was a disturbing one. As it turned out, the result of this medical board was very satisfactory, and he was declared to be permanently and totally unfit for all forms of military service. 'It is a great relief,' he admitted to Ottoline (20 March 1918), 'and I can now relapse into writing and reading without that anxiety hanging over my head. The whole thing was infinitely better managed than before – far more civilised, and careful, and the doctors positively polite and even sympathetic. This comes of the military having nothing more to do with it.'

Though the cause of his many trips to London was mainly matters of business, there were still some opportunities for 'gadding and whirling'. One particular dinner-party, given by Mary Hutchinson, led to an alarming corollary – 'the unfortunate occurrence in the purlieus of Ravenscourt Park', as Lytton afterwards used to call it – which formed what in effect was the final scene in Carrington's tragi-comic affair with Gertler. The two of them had continued to correspond, and whenever she visited London – which was not very often – she would call in at Gertler's Hampstead studio and tell him about her lovely life in the

[1] Sir John Dickinson (1848–1933), who had taken his law degree at Trinity College, Cambridge, and who from 1913 to 1920 was Chief Metropolitan Police Magistrate, Bow Street.

1*

country, the birds and the trees, and how much better it was than living
in foggy old London. He would sit there, sullen and crumpled, as she
explained to him how much lighter and more alive everything seemed
in Berkshire. The people all had friendly faces, and one could walk
along the roads without those snorting buses and motors on every side,
and that mob of scurrying pedestrians. She loved the Mill House – and
so would he. She would ask him to stay there when the others, Oliver
and the rest, were away. Their friendship, she added, her tactlessness
swelling to a rhapsodic crescendo, had taken on a new freedom and
flexibility – 'like birds in the air meeting on a tree suddenly. conversing
without discord – and knowing that we can both fly off and again meeT
perhaps soon perhaps next summer and we can still go on where we
left off.'

Of the true nature of the Tidmarsh *ménage* Carrington still revealed
nothing. But such matters could not for ever be kept secret, and within
two short months Gertler had picked up all the stories of what was
going on. 'I know that you live with Lytton,' he fulminated (24
February 1918). His first reaction was explosive. On the evening of
14 February, after Jack and Mary Hutchinson's party in Hammersmith, Lytton and Carrington were walking off down the blacked-out
streets, when the dark figure of Gertler loomed from the shadows,
overtook them, and, with a cry of rage, launched a two-fisted attack
upon the astonished Lytton. Luckily various Bloomsbury pacifists
were not far off; and a number of professors and mathematicians
hurried forward, succeeded in separating the two pugilists and led the
panting Gertler off. 'Anything more cinematographic can hardly be
imagined,' Lytton told Clive Bell (18 February 1918), 'and on looking
back it wears all the appearance of a bad dream. All the same it was at
the time exceedingly painful, especially as a little more presence of
mind on my part might have prevented the situation; but it all came
about with a speed. Poor Mark! The provocation was certainly great,
and I was very sorry for him. However, as he was obviously drunk,
perhaps he was rather less conscious than one supposed. Characteristically, Maynard came to the rescue, and eventually led him off, and
pacified him, with amazing aplomb. Monty [Shearman] had already
tried and completely failed; Carrington had fled under the protection of
Sheppard, who kept on repeating, during the height of the crisis –
"Who *is* it? Who *is* it?" in a most pained voice; and Harry supported
my trembling form from the field. It was really an intervention of
Providence that they should all have come up at the psychological
moment, as Heaven knows what mightn't have happened.'

A week later Lytton was dining at the Eiffel Tower restaurant with

when Gertler again appeared, but this time, being sober
nt, he came up and apologized for his earlier assault: 'I
ry about the other night. Please forgive me.'
Lytton giggled and replied: 'It was nothing at all. Please don't worry
yourself about it.'

'I don't think', David Garnett later commented, 'that was what
Gertler wanted to be told.'

But if Lytton's polite diminution of this incident ludicrously
trivialized Gertler's emotional upheaval, Carrington's more inconsequential attitude seriously aggravated it. She felt responsible for the
whole wretched affair, and greatly upset by it. The haunting look of
loneliness and despair in his face, deepened by the tubercular ill-health
which was to keep him in and out of sanatoria for the rest of his life,
contributing eventually, in 1939, to his suicide, testified to the suffering
with which she had afflicted him. She saw this clearly, and was chafed
by guilt. Her lies, devious neglect and lack of foresight had very largely
been to blame. 'Please do not worry about last night,' she wrote to him
the following morning. 'I am only *very* sorry if I gave you the cause of
your distress. It was quite unintentional.' He must, she wrote in another
letter, make new friends in London. She cared very much that he still
loved her, and: 'Remember I care always very much for you. Just as
much as I used to. It is in no way changed – and if you know how much
I felt your Pains and griefs it would lessen them for you.'

But still it was the old story. At every crucial moment, Carrington's
letters to Gertler were bafflingly irrelevant, full of unconscious irony.
She appreciated that their relationship was entering a new phase, and
that if this new phase were to be at all harmonious, unpoisoned by the
misdeeds of the past, then she must straightway contradict the various
rumours which had percolated through to him from Dorothy Brett and
others. The truth was far less damaging, less injurious than these lies.
A full explanation was needed to clear the air, but she shied away from
all explanations. 'I think if we are going to be friends again,' she
announced, 'I had better be quite frank and tell you about what I do
down here. and Lytton, and everything. or else it won'T be real.' That
was what she told him: and that was all. It was an avowed Statement of
Intent which hung in the air unsupported by any revelation of truth,
but which, as it gently floated away into the distance, took on for her
the aspect of an important disclosure.

Carrington had no talent for frankness, and the pregnant weight of
all she failed to say seemed to Gertler to consolidate his most salacious
and horrible suspicions. Her silence was more potent than any deliberate provocation could have been. In his anger, he replied crudely

and bitterly to her letter, and this, in one way, wa
wanted, enabling her to transfer back on to him her una
of guilt. His loss of temper seemed to exonerate her from responsi
After all, she had endeavoured to make an alliance, and her attemp
had been scornfully flung back in her face. 'I hardly see the use of
corresponding when you are so antagonistic towards me,' she answered indignantly (28 February 1918).' When I said I wanted to tell
you more about my self, I did not mean to make that crude statement –
which I knew you already knew. . . . Evidently from your letter *we
think so very differently about relative values of everything now.* Yet it is
impossible for me not to care everytime I see you very much. This
letter is not bitter. only I feel rather tireD, and perhaps disappointed
about it. But *Don'T* write anymore, I would rather not start it again. . . .
There is not answer to this letter.'

But, of course, there was; and for another two years the unanswerable
answers and replies, inquiries, vindications, apologies, misunderstandings, concessions and rebuttals, trickled on, until eventually, sad and
exhausted, they passed on out of reach of each other's lives for good.

There was much more, besides Gertler, to occupy Carrington's time
and attention now. The four weeks immediately prior to the publication of *Eminent Victorians* Lytton spent at Tidmarsh. Life there was a
steady stream of visitors – Oliver Strachey, who sat for a portrait by
Carrington; James, who had abandoned his projected career in medicine
after three weeks as a medical student to become dramatic critic of the
Athenaeum;[1] Alix Sargant-Florence, reading Rabelais with the aid of
six dictionaries; Barbara Bagenal and her husband Nick, who would
sometimes stay to keep Carrington company while Lytton was away;
Middleton Murry, very gloomy over the prospects of his wife, Katherine
Mansfield's, health, and very excited over his own prospects as editor of
the *Athenaeum*; Saxon Sydney-Turner, quiet and scholarly, reading
Euripides; and Maynard Keynes, who, Lytton told Clive Bell (18
February 1918), looked 'very prosperous, but not very well, I thought,
and full of the L[loyd] G[eorge] crisis. He thought it possible that a
vote of censure might be moved in the House by infuriated back-bench
Tories, that the Govt. might then fall and be succeeded by a Law-
Asquith combination, including tout ce qu'il-y-a de plus respectable,
but not pacifist, though destined to make peace. I doubt it – and I

---

[1] James Strachey had caught influenza, and never returned to his medical studies.
Instead, at the invitation of Middleton Murry, he had become dramatic critic of the
Athenaeum for about a year. He was already interested in psychology and in 1920 went to
Vienna where he was psycho-analysed by Freud and became his pupil. Alix, his wife,
also went out to Vienna, and also became a psycho-analyst. She is the author of *The
Unconscious Motives of War* (1957).

doubt still more, if it did come off, whether it would be any good. To be caught in the clutches of a second Coalition, and a respectable one this time, seems to me a dismal fate. But it's difficult to believe that the Goat won't clamber over this fence as he has so many others.'

Another less pleasant and untroubled visit to the Mill House in these first months was made by David Garnett, who has given an interesting glimpse behind the scenes there. Carrington's aura of disarming innocence was offset by a mischievous addiction to cruelty. Her truly appalling practical jokes had little in common with the high-spirited, extrovert hoaxes staged by Horace Cole and Adrian Stephen. *Their* chief targets were the humourless representatives of officialdom – those colourless puppets who blindly carry out their pompous traditional routine and make themselves the most obvious and legitimate butts for teasing – and they derived their fun from the long elaborate preparation each joke required beforehand, from the ludicrous pantomime effect of their performance and from the resulting embarrassment caused to those with an over-developed sense of responsibility. Carrington's exploits were more private matters – and sometimes very cruel. Like many divided natures she possessed a heightened capacity for unhappiness, and her practical jokes were often a means of revenging herself upon life. At her most unambitious, she would stop short at sewing up people's pyjamas. But often her schemes were more subtle and individual than this. Her favourite victims came from among those two types of person who had, in the past, inflicted most pain upon her – motherly women and virile, sexually adventurous young men.

David Garnett fell perfectly under this second classification. And when, in the early summer of 1918, he had almost reached breaking-point over a desperate love-affair, the opportunity presented to Carrington for wickedly exploiting the situation seemed too good to miss. She therefore sent him an invitation, asking him to come and stay with her and Lytton for the week-end, and to this she added a postscript promising him that he should find there the person he most wanted to meet. The implication was obvious. In a turmoil of excitement Garnett caught a train to Reading, hastened along the last eight miles of his journey to Tidmarsh on foot, and arrived at the Mill House late at night. Carrington was at once fully in command of the situation. 'I knew you would come to-night,' she exclaimed as she made him sit down to eat. 'I was certain of it. Lytton wouldn't believe me.'

'Where is . . . my fellow guest?' Garnett inquired as soon as he decently could.

Carrington answered that she was upstairs.

'I picked up my rucksack and went upstairs,' Garnett records, 'and Carrington followed to show me my room.

'"Which is *her* room?" I asked, for it was torture to wait another moment. I must find out if I was there with her knowledge, even at her wish.

'Lytton had come out on to the landing and looked at me with surprise. "Why, who do you think is there?" he asked.

'I stepped forward to open the door but Carrington seized my arm. "Stop! You mustn't go in!" she exclaimed.

'"Well, who is it, then?" I asked, bewildered.

'"Mrs. Swanwick," tittered Lytton who was mystified by the whole affair. This was an idiotic joke, for Mrs Swanwick was an elderly feminist and socialist.

'I freed my arm from Carrington and was about to rush into the room when the door opened and a young man whom I had seen once before in my life stood in the doorway.

'"He must be her lover! That is why Carrington is trying to stop me going in!" flashed through my mind.

'But the young man was so incongruous a figure – so terribly unsuited for the part, that I realised that I must be slightly mad and I pulled myself together sufficiently to greet him civilly and then retire to bed.'

Blinded by his infatuation, it did not occur to Garnett until much later that he had been the victim of a carefully planned and singularly brutal practical joke. And since Carrington had told nothing of her scheme either to Lytton or to Marshall, the young man, the incident passed off without further mention and without impairing Garnett's friendship. Carrington was very warm and friendly with him all the rest of the week-end, probably repenting of what she had done.

When there were no guests to entertain or be entertained by, Carrington would vanish up into the attic, painting pictures which no one was allowed to see, or disappear outside to busy herself among the early potatoes and the hens,[1] while Lytton sat on downstairs writing or reading. He had already begun to compose his biographical essay 'Lady Hester Stanhope', and also, during the week of 2–5 May, his revealing and rather wicked pen portrait 'Mr. Asquith'. He had, for the first time, been reading Charles Greville's *Memoirs*, the full text of which he was later to edit, and the six volumes of the Goncourts' *Journals*, which Virginia Woolf had put him on to. These journals he found full of interest, though his opinions of them, as set out in two

---

[1] 'We are trying to grow vegetables – and hens,' Lytton wrote to Dorelia John (10 May 1918). 'Neither seem to come up with sufficient rapidity – damn them – and in the meantime living costs about £100 a minute.'

letters to Clive Bell, are rather mixed. 'There are many reported conversations of intelligent persons –Flaubert, Gautier, Sainte-Beuve, and
such,' he wrote on 16 April. 'They *are* intelligent, though their French-
ness is paramount over everything. So open-minded, you know, and
yet . . . Those singular clichés, which seem actually to be clichés of
thought, and in fact of life itself, more than of the verbal sort. "Ma
maîtresse" – "la Femme" – "pendant sa jeunesse" – "la Pédérastie",
etc. etc. – they occur on every other page, all mixed up with the freest
language and the wildest speculations. And then – "l'immortalité de
l'âme" (and this comes on at dessert, apparently) – it is certainly most
odd, and rather attractive too. Gautier was perhaps more sensible than
the rest – I hadn't before realised his eminence. And they are all extraordinarily aesthetic.' But three weeks later he again wrote to Clive
Bell: 'The Goncourts . . . I must say I don't like 'em. The Frenchifica-
tion is really really too much – the bugger-bub story, for instance –
too painfully Parisien – and then they're au fond such vulgar little
snobs. Jules has now died, I'm glad to say, but Edmond remains, a
most lugubrious figure in the siege of Paris. But of course the conversations, and the general impression of a very distinct and remarkable
atmosphere, are highly interesting, and one feels one must read it all.'

Among recently published books he was reading a new study of
Byron ('what a splendid subject he would be for a really modern and
artistic biography!') and Sidney Colvin's biography of Keats. In spite
of all the biographer's pomp and tepidity, the tragedy of Keats's short
life came through to Lytton as overwhelming. 'It seems to me one of
the most appalling stories known,' he declared. 'One of the worst
features of it is that one gathers that he had never once copulated. Is it
possible, though?' His comments on one other new book that spring
are also interesting. This was *Remnants*, Desmond MacCarthy's first
collection of articles from the *New Statesman*, *The New Witness*, *The
Eye Witness* and *The Speaker*, which Constable had just brought out.
'I suppose you've seen Remnants – a book in the best of taste,' he wrote
to Clive Bell (10 May 1918). 'But it's difficult not to think that the milk
has been standing a very long time, and that, though the cream is
excellent, there's not much of it. However, nowadays, it would be
absurd to complain of anything that is genuinely charming. His
Asquith doings fill me with astonishment. I can still hardly believe that
he likes those people or can think it worth while to flatter them. Perhaps
really he only finds them amusing to pass the time of day with – one
can *just* imagine that – and that it may be rather fun to meet the Lord
Chief Justice.'

Soon enough Lytton's own incursions into aristocratic society would give rise to a similar wonderment in his other Bloomsbury friends. But for the time being his unsophisticated country life glided contentedly on amid the congenial company and conversation of his friends. A new optimism and buoyancy was in the air. Many years before he had written to Maynard Keynes (27 February 1906): 'When I have a home of my own, I should write up "Hope" over the door.' Now that at last he had a home of his own, his motto, he told a friend, was to be: '*Tout est possible.*' There is something of this hopeful, adventurous spirit, expressed with a characteristic tongue-in-the-cheek style, in several of his letters. 'We have many projects,' he wrote to Clive Bell (16 April 1918) '– to build a fire-place, a book-case, a theatre, to learn Spanish, to attach the pump to the mill-wheel by a leather band, to buy 24 geese, to borrow a saddle from Farmer Davis and saddle the Blacksmith's pony with it and ride into Pangbourne, to write a drawing-room comedy, a classical tragedy in the style of Euripides, and the History of England during the War. But le temps s'en va, mon cher, and we are left idling in front of the fire.'

Happy in the tranquil seclusion of Tidmarsh, looked after and idolized by Carrington, surrounded by his books, visited by his friends – and visiting them – the six years during which Lytton lived at the Mill House included some of the most successful, exciting and generally satisfactory days of his career. In the spring of 1918 only three ingredients to his happiness were still missing: a new passionate love-affair; a little fame as a writer to soothe away the mortifications of his early years; and the necessary money to make this ideal way of life permanent. All these were to be granted him. Soon he would fall deeply in love once more; while fame and fortune were even now about to be showered on him in full by the publication of *Eminent Victorians*.

CHAPTER VI

Eminent Victorians

'*Eminent Victorians* is the work of a great anarch, a revolutionary text-book on bourgeois society written in the language through which the bourgeois ear could be lulled and beguiled, the Mandarin style.'

Cyril Connolly –
Enemies of Promise

'Much of the present interest in the nineteenth century is often written and spoken of as a reaction against Strachey; but I do not at all feel it so. . . .

'The views of history with which I grew up were almost entirely created by Victorians; and Strachey did not necessarily contradict them; he directed attention to a rather different Victorian field, and he also woke me up to the possibility of treating the Victorians themselves as interesting, problematical, extremely relevant to my own life and the general life I was born into.'

Humphry House –
All in Due Time

'Brethren,

The President has asked me to propose the toast of "Eminent Victorians". I shall be delighted to do so. But I feel one difficulty: I find it very hard to decide what an eminent Victorian is. . . . Definitions are curious things and I've never been able quite to understand their workings. . . . There was once an eminent Victorian called Mr W. G. Ward, who used to say "When I hear men called 'judicious' I suspect them; but when I hear them called 'judicious and venerable', I know they are scoundrels". Similarly when I hear people called "Victorians", I suspect them. But when I hear them called "Eminent Victorians" I write their lives. So an Eminent Victorian might be defined, on this principle, as the sort of person whose life would be likely to be written by Lytton Strachey. And perhaps that's as near as one can get.'

Lytton Strachey –
Speech to the Apostles, proposing *Eminent Victorians*

I

DEFINITIONS

While reviewing biographies and histories for the *Spectator*, Lytton had evolved the credo which he later aimed at putting into practice in *Eminent Victorians*. As early as 2 January 1909, he had set out those principles by which he would seek to be guided, in a review of Guglielmo Ferrero's *The Greatness and Decline of Rome*, some passages of which read almost like a first extended draft to his celebrated Preface nine years later:[1]

'When Livy said that he would have made Pompey win the battle of Pharsalia, if the turn of the sentence had required it, he was not talking utter nonsense, but simply expressing an important truth in a highly paradoxical way, – that the first duty of a great historian is to be an artist. The function of art in history is something much more profound than mere decoration; to regard it, as some writers persist in regarding it, as if it were the jam put around the pill of fact by cunning historians is to fall into a grievous error; a truer analogy would be to compare it to the process of fermentation which converts a raw mass of grape-juice into a subtle and splendid wine. Uninterpreted truth is as useless as buried gold; and art is the great interpreter. It alone can unify a vast multitude of facts into a significant whole, clarifying, accentuating, suppressing, and lighting up the dark places with the torch of the imagination. More than that, it can throw over the historian's materials the glamour of a personal revelation, and display before the reader great issues and catastrophes as they appear, not to his own short sight, but to the penetrating vision of the most soaring of human spirits. That is the crowning glory of the greatest history – that of Thucydides, for instance, or Tacitus, or Gibbon; it brings us into communion with an immense intelligence, and it achieves this result through the power of art. Indeed, every history worthy of the name is, in its own way, as personal as poetry, and its value ultimately depends upon the force and the quality of the character behind it.'

The Preface to *Eminent Victorians* is a distillation of the ideas expressed in this paragraph and elsewhere, and it raises two distinct questions: How valid is Lytton's definition of the historical biographer's task? And to what extent did his own work conform to the principles he had laid down?

---

[1] Lytton had put forward the same point of view at greater length in a paper that was written in answer to 'The Science of History', J. B. Bury's inaugural lecture as Regius Professor of Modern History at Cambridge in 1902. Lytton disputed Bury's contention that history was a science, arguing that the greatest historians were invariably artists.

For the sake of convenience, historical biography may be divided into two opposing, though not wholly incompatible, categories: the non-artistic or 'scientific', and the literary. Each is designed to communicate a rather different sort of truth, the first documentary and factual, the second personal and imaginative. Only perhaps in the lives of writers, with their cento of recorded incidents and interpretative literary criticism woven into a pattern, can these two schools of biography be harmoniously brought together. Since Lytton always chose men and women of action and affairs, he was faced with a more simple choice. His credo, figuratively expressed in several essays, is an able formulation of those canons of historical biography which govern the artistic approach. A biographer or historian, he believed, should command a certain attitude of mind, should possess a certain natural ability, and should employ a certain literary method. The attitude of mind he defined as a civilized detachment or freedom of spirit coupled with a personal point of view. The ability he diagnosed as a scholar's capacity for absorbing facts together with a novelist's or dramatist's gift for presenting them. The most effective method of communicating not the flat threadbare actuality of events, so abstract and impersonal, but the true living relationship which existed between writer and his subject, he analysed as a selection of salient and an omission of irrelevant or superfluous matter. This was the boiling-down process by which from rough grape-juice he distilled a potent spirit. The biographer should strive for a brevity which elucidated and simplified the impact of the past upon the sensitive retina of his mind, imbued, through the perspective of years, with an impartial, enlightened vision.

It is largely because of these views that Lytton has been dismissed by some professional historians as having nothing to contribute to their subject. His arbitrary and partly concealed method of selection, his flashy yet commonplace style – half-fictional and wholly superficial – emanated, in their belief, from a defective angle of approach. To the sober, pedagogic recorder of history, both his detachment and his point of view were unacceptable. The former, by severing the umbilical cord which joins a figure of historical importance to the background of his age, artificially disentangled him from the religious and political climate of the day, and permitted the biographer to apply modern, individual standards to bygone customs and ways of thinking. By such means were the great events of history distorted so as to resemble mere ephemeral exploits, often unplanned and inconsequential, and embodying not the dignity of human endeavour, the measured progress of civilization, but the abundant farce, imbecility and blackguardism of unrefined human nature. The latter further trivialized the study of history by reducing major historical and political problems to questions of primitive behaviour and eccentricity, to coincidence, to accident, and to a succession of puerile brawls, childish bigotries and petty crimes. Further, in the academic view, the literary historian was guilty of naïvely focusing his readers' attention on the graphic details of personality, and made no evaluation of the social and economic forces of life, thereby demonstrating his preference for artificial colouring and neatness over the proper utilization of complex data. His claim that history was an art suggested only a predilection for fantasy above sober authenticity, and in practice meant that a historian should be more interested in himself and in the smoothness of his story-telling than in his subject-matter. Finally, his credulous trust in 'psychology' acted only as a licence for squalid or romantic speculation – an occupation usually associated with lightweight historical novelists of the female kind.

Such, in brief, is the burden of the orthodox historian's complaint against the innovations outlined in the Preface to *Eminent Victorians*. In counteraction to these criticisms, Lytton, like Goethe, believed that history yielded up more of her secrets to the heightened intuition of the artist than to the over-diffident, over-earnest, humdrum and humourless investigations conducted by scientific minds. With the revived form of historical biography which he inaugurated, he sought to disrupt the impression left by conventional historians, who, eager to enter the spirit of the times they were studying, mimicked the generals and statesmen of the past, condoning and making acceptable the worst excesses of history. The bloated solemnity of 'serious' historical narrative, weighed down with the pompous importance of its material, dealt onerously with events rather than sensitively with people, and devoted endless dry-as-dust disquisitions to the problems of political necessity, strategic reason and economic cause as if they constituted self-sufficient entities, divorced from the everyday fears, desires and ambitions of mortal men.

In his Preface, Lytton asserts that the individual human being, as the spearhead of sensibility and the residence of consciousness, should no longer rank last in the hierarchy of human values. The business of the historian should not be wholesale and unreal, but must involve a re-creation of human life in perspective, which, by putting a fine edge on our own days, tells us more about the present than the present by itself can tell us. The historian therefore should neither abstain from judgement nor should he indulge in tedious vituperation, but satirize the follies of the past; he should not depict a panoramic but a telescopic view of the ages; he should not relinquish the interpretation of all events entirely to the reader, but seek to direct him as a judge in the summing-up of a trial. Nevertheless he should, if possible, avoid drawing out one single conclusion, necessarily narrow and polemical, and rest content with a complete effect of irony, intensified in places to the point of wonderment.

'It is not his business to be complimentary,' the Preface concludes; 'it is his business to lay bare the facts of the case, as he understands them. That is what I have aimed at in this book – to lay bare the facts of some cases, as I understand them, dispassionately, impartially, and without ulterior intentions. To quote the words of a Master – "Je n'impose rien; je ne propose rien: j'expose."'

The cogency and validity of Lytton's credo is attested by its power of provoking hostility from among the scientific school of historians and biographers, and, at the same time, by its ability to provide reasonable replies, either specifically stated or directly implied, to their arguments.

But an altogether different stricture on Lytton's concept of biography has come from another, surprising quarter. Harold Nicolson, in his Hogarth Lecture, *The Development of English Biography*, suggests that by adopting a point of view, the biographer inevitably imposes upon his material a personal thesis which is destructive of 'pure' biography. To illustrate this contention, he contrasts Lytton's method with that of Boswell and Lockhart, who held no thesis, but 'worked wholly on the inductive method'. Yet, for all the dissimilarity of their writing, it would appear that Lytton, quoting Voltaire, has only put forward a more streamlined technique of achieving, under different circumstances, roughly the same ends as Boswell and Lockhart, who, in Harold Nicolson's words, 'neither propounded nor implied a theory; they merely, with the requisite degree of taste and selection, furnish facts. Their facts, although extensive, were limited by the taste of their age.' Boswell and Lockhart's inductive method, moreover, was also in practice destructive of 'pure' biography. For although they paraded no ulterior intentions, they did harbour some ulterior, partly unconscious motives – as all human beings must. Boswell's personal attitude to Johnson, for instance, though not raised to a point of awareness or control where it could be crystallized into a thesis, nevertheless high-lighted a particular aspect of Johnson's character, and, by insisting on the Doctor's verbal ascendancy, tended to further the impression that he was a bigoted champion of the social conventions and the established order, obscuring his genuine individuality to a degree where, so Bernard Shaw claimed, 'Johnson' became an invention of Boswell's. Lockhart's loyalty to Scott, also, was at least equal to that of Boswell to

Johnson, and the love and admiration which flows uninterruptedly through his ten volumes of biography is recurrently expressed at the unjust expense of minor figures in the book.

Harold Nicolson's concept of 'pure' biography is thus idealistic, as, perhaps, too, is Lytton's theory of how to recreate artistically *and* objectively a man's life. Boswell's and Lockhart's personal feelings played like a warm, luminous glow about their subjects; Lytton's 'point of view' was a concentration of this radiance into a sharp beam of light focused from the side and back of the theatre upon the centrally staged personality. Harold Nicolson's criticism, ostensibly one of Lytton's *theory* of biography, in fact turns out to be an adverse verdict upon his own deductive concept of biography as evolved from Lytton's *actual performance* as a biographer. It is, by implication, an admonition of Lytton for not upholding his own theories. Both Boswell's and Lockhart's Lives could be said to contain a superabundance of dispensable material. Lytton, working solely from published sources, recommended paring this material down to a special elegant pattern, the design of which was to be arranged by the biographer's particular interest in and response to his subject. By these means one might offer, instead of a whole mine of information, simply the jewels extracted from that mine. Harold Nicolson decries a notion of biography that encouraged natural prejudice, and that sought to elaborate a preconception of character by slanting the materials subsequently consulted to fit in with an initial, ill-informed bias. The former method was genuinely artistic; the latter apocryphal – a form of higher journalism. In his Preface to *Eminent Victorians*, Lytton had propounded biography as an art; to what extent he practised biography as polemics may be seen from an examination of the four essays which follow this Preface.

2

PRELUDE

Eminent Victorians is Lytton's best full-length work. Though it does not maintain the uniform and soothing texture of *Landmarks in French Literature*, though it does not quite achieve the immaculate synthetic cohesion of *Queen Victoria*, though it does not perhaps conjure up the Victorian age as vividly as *Elizabeth and Essex* does the Elizabethan, yet it touches reality more closely than any of these. For the impact between Lytton and his biographical subjects was of greater urgency and took place at a more intense level of experience during the war years, and while he was still unknown, than at any other period of his career. His four eminent Victorians are not painted with the grandiloquent formality of sentimental portraiture, the falsity of which can be apprehended by an ordinary knowledge of human nature, but they are rendered with the acuteness of true caricature. They are not photographs in literature, and some of the lines of character in their make-up bear only misshapen resemblance to the originals. But seen as creatures of parody and extravagance, each one constructed round a few easily recognizable and strongly developed traits, they each convey the impression of an authentically lifelike countenance.

In *Landmarks in French Literature*, Lytton had treated his writers exclusively as pioneers or reactionaries to the historical aesthetic exposition of the book, and had appraised their emotional experience, transmuted into timeless literature, in terms of tendencies and schools. Now he claimed to be doing away with these trappings of prestige and the ephemeral whims of fashion, to be presenting individuals as interesting in their own right. 'Human beings are too important to be treated as mere symptoms of the past,' he wrote in his Preface. 'They have a value which is independent of any temporal processes – which is eternal, and must be felt for its own sake.' The widespread and collective reaction to *Eminent Victorians* when it came out belies this admirably strict individualistic approach. It is possible that Lytton, not gifted with any great depth of self-knowledge and holding the opinion that art must depend on consistency, really believed that his four sitters symbolized for him nothing beyond themselves. But the distortions which he manipulated on all four of them are consistent with the view that *Eminent Victorians* represents his greatest and most prolonged onslaught upon the evangelicalism that was the defining characteristic of Victorian culture, and which, in his view, had been indirectly responsible for the First World War. Once again the reader is given a dramatized conflict between the powers of light and darkness, corresponding to Lytton's own internal division. Extolling the virtues of reason, simplicity, moderation and tolerance – qualities which he himself possessed in a high degree – he shows us how, to a greater or lesser extent, his Victorian quartet sacrificed these attributes by becoming, as Lord Annan succinctly puts it, 'the dupes of two false moral systems: ecclesiastical Christianity and the religion of success'.

In order to disperse the sacrosanct myths which enveloped Cardinal Manning, Florence Nightingale, Doctor Arnold and General Gordon, he was compelled to marshal a good deal of his critical attention on them as non-representational beings. Yet in all four studies, the parallel

and basically unsubtle oversimplification resulting from his monochromatic biographical technique impoverishes the rich complexity
of human life. There is no latent sense of revelation in his writing, no
'tiny trigger movement releasing enormous spiritual forces', for his
thought is not emotion, but rationalization given a personal twist.

3

ALLEGRO VIVACE

'Cardinal Manning', the longest of the four essays in *Eminent Victorians*,
is also one of the most severe. The opening is skilfully handled. In a
few paragraphs the silhouette of Manning's intransigent, Tamberlaine-
like character is imperishably etched in – that of an ambitious schemer,
prone to illusions of romantic grandeur, a self-deceiver whose acid
inhumanity and morbid aloofness, bred of a puritan preoccupation with
hell, cuts him off from his fellow beings. On the very first page, in a
series of apparently searching questions, Lytton charts the course which
his essay will take, and lays bare his essential preoccupation with
Manning's character:

'What had happened? Had a dominating character imposed itself
upon a hostile environment? Or was the Nineteenth Century, after all,
not so hostile? Was there something in it, scientific and progressive as
it was, which went out to welcome the representative of ancient tradition and uncompromising faith? Had it, perhaps, a place in its heart for
such as Manning – a soft place, one might almost say? Or, on the other
hand, was it he who had been supple and yielding? he who had won by
art what he would never have won by force, and who had managed, so
to speak, to be one of the leaders of the procession less through merit
than through a superior faculty for gliding adroitly to the front rank?
And, in any case, by what odd chances, what shifts and struggles, what
combinations of circumstance and character, had this old man come to
be where he was?'

J. K. Johnstone likens this passage to the outline drawn by an architect upon the turf denoting where the building shall rise. 'He [Strachey]
has flourished the grand plan before us, and, with a few waves of the
hand, has indicated the proportions of the structure.' The questions
themselves are, of course, rhetorical; they have been carefully loaded,
they all point in a certain direction and the answers to them are already
implied both in the manner in which they are phrased and the order in
which they are placed. 'Such questions', Lytton commented, 'are easier

to ask than to answer.' And this may be because they are not genuine queries, but problems artificially posed above an already fixed solution. For the theme of 'Cardinal Manning', which delivers a foregone verdict to this inquest, is the indictment of an age which could permit an astute and ruthless opportunist, whose repressed sexual drive was sublimated into religious fanaticism, to gravitate naturally to a position of such high authority.

So as to make this indictment really convincing, Lytton felt that he needed to establish, without reservation, his view of Manning as a superstitious egotist, goaded by unlimited personal ambition, and skilled in the sophistry and dissimulation of ecclesiastical politics. His chief dramatic method of pressing home this interpretation was to contrast Manning's career with that of the saintly, lamb-like Newman. The antithesis between the two men is made complete.

'In Manning, so it appeared, the Middle Ages lived again,' Lytton wrote. 'The tall gaunt figure, with the face of smiling asceticism, the robes, and the biretta, as it passed in triumph from High Mass at the Oratory to philanthropic gatherings at Exeter Hall, from Strike Committees at the Docks to Mayfair drawing-rooms where fashionable ladies knelt to the Prince of the Church, certainly bore witness to a singular condition of affairs.'

This is the tone which Lytton resourcefully employs to turn Manning's superficially impressive mask of virtue round to something slightly improbable. By the introduction of a faintly incongruous detail or two – sometimes no more than the overblown reverberation of juxtaposed polysyllables – he gives it an added twist which effectively screws the whole picture up to an angle of absurdity.

The same rather incredulous note is struck in the description of Manning's perambulations about the countryside, where he is made to reveal as preposterous a silhouette as in the performance of his earnest and energetic antics about the towns. The following passage amusingly depicts his full and active life as a country clergyman, its attitude of mock-sympathy exposing just one facet of character – vanity.

'His slim, athletic figure was seen everywhere – in the streets of Chichester, or on the lawns of the neighbouring rectories, or galloping over the downs in breeches and gaiters, or cutting brilliant figures on the ice. He was an excellent judge of horse-flesh, and the pair of greys which drew his hooded phaeton so swiftly through the lanes were the admiration of the county. . . . He was a good talker, a sympathetic listener, a man who understood the difficult art of preserving all the vigour of a manly character and yet never giving offence.'

Manning was fundamentally a man of action – almost a 'blood' –

someone cut out for worldly success. Newman, whose prose style Lytton particularly admired, is seen as 'a child of the Romantic Revival, a creature of emotion and of memory, a dreamer whose secret spirit dwelt apart in delectable mountains, an artist whose subtle senses caught, like a shower in the sunshine, the impalpable rainbow of the immaterial world'. The Victorian era, Lytton infers, had more in common with the Middle Ages than with the Age of Romance. It was a retrogressive, anachronistic, barbaric epoch, that preferred the ascetic and pretentious Manning to the finer, simpler nature of Newman – which, to a large extent, it also perverted, driving him to misuse his poetic faculties in the purposeless pursuit of everlasting theological lucubrations. Newman possessed none of Manning's downright, matter-of-fact determinism, his natural grace or athletic prowess – fair virtues all. Instead, like Lytton himself, he was a quietist, of donnish and didactic temper, destined, despite great gifts, to remain for many years unaided, misunderstood, ignored.

'His delicate mind,' Lytton explained, 'with its refinements, its hesitations, its complexities – his soft, spectacled, Oxford manner, with its half-effeminate diffidence – such things were ill calculated to impress a throng of busy Cardinals and Bishops, whose days were spent amid the practical details of ecclesiastical organisation, the long-drawn involutions of papal diplomacy, and the delicious bickerings of personal intrigue.'

All biographers, however painstaking their research, however scrupulous their methods, inevitably fall into some errors of fact and of interpretation of fact. But Lytton's small deviations from the strictest documentary truth were seldom haphazard: they have a peculiar consistency which shows them more likely to have been calculated than accidental, and which partly invalidates his high-toned claim to write 'dispassionately, impartially, and without ulterior intentions'. Several pertinent facts in Manning's life are omitted and their implications ignored, while both his character and that of Newman are oversimplified in order to fit in better with Lytton's personal point of view, and enable him to present this point of view to his audience with maximum ease and lucidity.

As an exordium to Manning, the scheming and dogmatic papist, Lytton shows him as a young man at Oxford contemplating visions of a splendid political career that is all at once cut short by the sudden bankruptcy of his father. Still indulging his secular dreams, he enters the Colonial Office as a supernumerary clerk, but is soon persuaded to take orders by 'his Spiritual Mother', the pious Miss Bevan. She, Lytton deduces, played shrewdly on the aspiring nature of the young man by planting within him the vainglorious notion that his father's bank-ruptcy, so far from curtailing the scope of his own ambitions, was in reality an example of the mysterious way in which God moved, His chosen vessels to select. That their crucial conversation should have taken place 'one day, as they walked together in the shrubbery' adds a certain ambiguous spiciness to the story. *In the shrubbery!* The phrase is, of course, Lytton's own. In Purcell's biography of Manning, on which he relied for this scene, there is mention only of 'walks together'. The added detail, like some suggestive backstage setting, gives inter-pretative colour to the whole business of the conversion. It is a slight and subtle manipulation of the available evidence, but it cannot be counted as inaccuracy unless, that is, *any* paraphrase of an original source is to be judged as such.

When the offer of a Merton Fellowship seemed to depend upon the taking of orders, a full awareness dawned upon Manning that he might fulfil a more exalted destiny than that of Member of Parliament. Lytton's assumption of Manning's motives, by throwing into the shade one side of his character, makes his decision to become a priest wholly one of narrow, if long-sighted, expediency.

To expediency Lytton then adds callousness. In sharp contrast to Newman, 'a creature of emotion and of memory', we are shown Manning numbering his wife's premature death as among 'God's special mercies', since it fortuitously released him for service in the Roman Catholic Church. 'In after years,' he wrote, 'the memory of his wife seemed to be blotted from his mind; he never spoke of her; every letter, every record, of his married life he destroyed.'

This passage has come up for some adverse comments from later critics. Baron von Hügel subsequently recorded Manning's last words, uttered in the presence of Bishop Vaughan, which partly contradict or at least modify Lytton's assertion.

'This is what happened shortly before his death,' Bishop Vaughan told Baron von Hügel. 'I was by his bedside; he looked round to see that we were alone; he fumbled under his pillow for something; he drew out a battered little pocket-book full of a woman's fine hand-writing. He said: "For years you have been to me as a son, Herbert: I know not to whom else to leave this – I leave it to you. Into this little book my dearest wife wrote her prayers and meditations. Not a day has passed since her death on which I have not prayed from this book. All the good I may have done, all the good I may have been, I owe to her. Take precious care of it." He ceased speaking and soon afterwards un-consciousness came on.'

It seems unreasonable to criticize a man on his death-bed, but

Manning's nostalgia was really little more than sentimentality, in that he preserved only that part of his dead wife which chimed in with his own far-reaching career. Lytton, in his efforts to accentuate Manning's unsympathetic nature, his abnormal coldness and emotional castration, played down this sentimentality, which would in fact have added depth to his portrait. As it is, he just over-states his case, giving us not the direction of a judicial summing-up, but a prosecutor's more exclusive slant before a jury who must be treated, like all juries, as a mixed bag of impressionable incompetents.

All the major decisions which Manning made during his career, Lytton interprets as having arisen from an overweening desire for self-aggrandizement. He insinuates, for example, that Manning's repeated repudiations of Newman's Tract No. 90 were nothing more or less than a series of determined efforts to dissociate himself from a party which was being condemned by the authorities and passed over for ecclesiastical preferment. That he might have acted from a less un-savoury motive has been intimated by Arnold Lunn, who suggested that his 'practical genius and common sense forced him to adapt himself to the ruling spirit of the Church. He was a sound Anglican, and later a sound Roman Catholic. A sense of practical realities rather than time-serving prevents such men ploughing the lonely furrow of revolt.'

It may well be that Lytton's intuition here is sounder than Arnold Lunn's, and certainly more percipient than that of most latter-day Catholic apologists, but his theory of artistic uniformity forbade him from putting at his readers' disposal the evidence necessary for them to come to their own opinion or to reach a reasonable assessment of his, without detailed reference to the sources mentioned in the bibliography. One's initial doubts are sometimes raised, too, by his reluctance to concede that a man's motives may be mixed. One is aware that some factor is missing, and often unjustly leaps to the conclusion that certain passages have been falsified.

There are, also, some occasions when Manning would appear to have acted with more sincerity than Lytton liked to admit, since real sincerity would of course conflict with his pungent study of a relentless power-seeker flourishing in an age of humbug. He maintains, for instance, that Manning's rejections of immediate short-term success were actually shrewd political decisions attracting to them far greater if more distant advantages. Yet this view, without some additional explanation, does not always bear even cursory examination. It is impossible to detect any practical gain in Manning's refusal of the office of sub-almoner, a position which almost certainly involved the reversion of the mitre, let alone his final refusal to have his name put forward as pope, the supreme honour which would have served as the perfect apotheosis to Lytton's essay. As it is, this final act of 'self-sacrifice' gives the lie to Lytton's too straightforward, one-dimensional portrayal of Manning. His avowed objections to election – namely, the conviction that a foreign pope might, for political reasons, disrupt the vital reconciliation of Italy with the Holy See – Lytton does not deem worth mentioning. This was too impersonal, too irrelevant to his theme. At the same time he can put forward no explicit alternative reason for this refusal which is both plausible and in line with his central argument. Manning's reasons, he hints darkly, were unspecified, vague yet sinister. 'Thus it happened,' he wrote, 'that the Triple Tiara seemed to come, for a moment, within the grasp of the late Archdeacon of Chichester; and the cautious hand refrained.' Why? Of what was Manning afraid? Lytton had always claimed to illustrate rather than to explain, and he dismisses the episode in under a dozen lines as though it were not real – 'seemed to come' – hurrying on as if anxious to deflect attention from a possible stumbling-block to his main thesis.

But it is the account of Manning's conversion to Catholicism that has stimulated the greatest controversy. Several historians, objecting to Lytton's uncompromising portrait of a proud and worldly prelate, have centred their attack upon this crucial point, and have, between them, built up a formidable-looking case. At the age of forty-three Manning was already an archdeacon. His prospects of a brilliant career in his own Church were extremely bright, especially since he could count on the support of Gladstone, a close and admiring friend and the future dis-poser of the unendowed archbishopric of Canterbury. Before him he could see the fate of Newman, certainly an inauspicious precedent which appeared to signify that the Church of Rome had little enough to offer its late English converts. Yet he turned his back on an easy and swift advancement and chose to become instead a middle-aged neophyte at the base of a new and steeper ladder where he could reckon on noth-ing like the same chances of success.

'Nevertheless,' Lytton wrote, 'it is difficult to feel quite sure that Manning's plunge was as hazardous as it appeared. Certainly he was not a man who was likely to forget to look before he leaped, nor one who, if he happened to know that there was a mattress spread to receive him, would leap with less conviction. In the light of after-events, one would be glad to know what precisely passed at that mysterious interview of his with the Pope, three years before his conversion. It is at least possible that the authorities in Rome had their eye on Manning; they may well have felt that the Archdeacon of Chichester would be a great catch. What did Pio Nono say? It is easy to imagine the persuasive innocence of his Italian voice. "Ah, dear Signor Manning, why don't you come over to us? Do you suppose that we should not look after you?"'

The popular and widely accepted criticism of this passage is that Lytton has deliberately contrived a mystery where none existed and seasoned it with his own picturesque and facile fancy. As F. A. Simpson has pointed out in a now celebrated article, Manning did not preserve a guilty silence concerning his interview with the pope on 11 May 1848, though there is only a cryptic reference to it in his contemporary diary – 'At eleven had audience at the Vatican.' Apparently, then, Lytton concocts his hypothesis round the brevity of this entry, which, he assures us, is very significant. The one other scrap of information which has come down to us about Manning's papal audience, Lytton contends earlier in his essay, only serves to make the whole episode doubly remarkable.

'Precisely what passed on that occasion never transpired; all that is known is that His Holiness expressed considerable surprise on learning from the Archdeacon that the chalice was used in the Anglican Church in the administration of Communion. "What!" he exclaimed, "is the same chalice made use of by every one?" "I remember the pain I felt," said Manning, long afterwards, "at seeing how unknown we were to the Vicar of Jesus Christ. It made me feel our isolation."'

A pope so ignorant of the chief ceremonials of the Anglican Church was hardly likely, Lytton's detractors have argued, to be more conversant with its hierarchical values, or the subjective tendencies of its members – though such political and psychological knowledge must have been essential for him to conduct the sort of seduction scene which Lytton had envisaged. This passage, they therefore claim, is of great interest as exposing Lytton's inflexible bias, not only by virtue of its implied contradiction to the 'mysterious' implications which, ten pages later, he essayed to draw out of this audience, but also by its indirect revelation that, so far from being 'all that is known' about the audience, it is not even all that Lytton himself knew. One critic has likened the effect of these two separated passages to that of a time-bomb, planted on one page and set to explode with carefully calculated force at the beginning of the subsequent chapter. Yet the line between them is so faulty that if there is any explosion at all it is under the feet of Lytton himself rather than of Manning.

For the words of Pio Nono and of Manning have been taken from a journal which Manning later wrote up to repair the omissions of his contemporary diary, and which puts on record far more than the little that Lytton describes as 'all that is known' of this interview with the pope. As F. A. Simpson, the arch-detractor, has pointed out, Lytton 'omits also to tell us that the "Journal" itself was supplemented by a further verbal account of "what passed on that occasion" dictated by Manning to his biographer Purcell; and this though that account stared him in the face on the open printed page opposite the one from which he drew upon Purcell's extract from the "Journal". The single topic which Strachey elects to mention (presumably because he regarded it as the most comic) as the one thing known about the interview was, in fact, but one of half-a-dozen or more of subjects which Manning records as having been discussed at it, even after its primary purpose had been discharged. That purpose, too, Manning describes and Strachey suppresses. There was nothing in the least mysterious about it. During his visit to Rome, his fellow Harrovian, Sydney Herbert, had charged Manning with the task of getting translated into Italian, at the expense of the British Government, a pamphlet by Sir Charles Trevelyan on English activities in relief of the recent Irish famine: this translation he was to present in person to the Pope.'

Pio Nono's reading from the most important passages of this pamphlet – which Manning with typical competence had marked – in addition to the harmless exchange of civilities which followed, were fully set out in Purcell's Life of the cardinal which heads Lytton's brief bibliography, 'and on a page of that book which there is internal evidence to show must actually have lain open before his eyes'.

Much has been made of Simpson's sweeping exposé: too much.[1] 'I

---

[1] Some brief account of F. A. Simpson's career as a historian is perhaps relevant in this context. He was born in 1883, educated at Queen's College, Oxford, and brought to Trinity College, Cambridge, by G. M. Trevelyan. 'Our best living historian', as Clive Bell called him, he is the author of two books, *The Rise of Louis Napoleon* (1909) and *Louis Napoleon and the Recovery of France* (1923) – part of an originally planned but never completed tetralogy. In a special Note to the 1960 Impression of the third edition of *Louis Napoleon and the Recovery of France*, he wrote: 'When this volume was first published, unsigned condemnations of it from the same pen appeared in the two most authoritative journals in the language. And during the thirty years' silence on their part which followed, the author was given some reason to suppose that, in the interests of consistency, similar treatment would await any continuation of his work; continuation which the various consequences of disparagement so sponsored tended in any case to make difficult. In the last few years, however, their condemnation has in both journals been tardily, but most handsomely, retracted. Had this kindness come sooner, the present reissue might have been not of two volumes only, but of the four volumes originally designed. But glad though the author is to have lived long enough to receive it, he lacks strength now to rekindle a flame which he ought perhaps never to have suffered to be snuffed out.'

Commenting on the words 'given some reason to suppose', Mr Simpson told the author that some time after the original attack on his book, while he was staying with the Hammonds, Lawrence Hammond showed him a review article he had just written for *The Times Literary Supplement*, from which the editor had deleted at the last moment, in final proof, without consulting the writer, a laudatory reference to the Louis Napoleon books – treatment unique in Hammond's experience as a reviewer. From this fact, Mr know nothing about this matter,' wrote Frank Swinnerton as recently as 1963. 'I take the criticism from F. A. Simpson's *Spectator* article, which, if it is correct, explains why, for all his brilliance and amusingness, Strachey was not admired by men able to estimate the travesty of Victorian principles and manners.' *If it is correct.* Most critics have blandly assumed that it is so – written by an English Churchman and a distinguished historian, in a convincing manner which suggests that he has rigorously checked every strand of the material used by Lytton. But most critics, unlike Frank Swinnerton, have not admitted that they 'know nothing about this matter'. In fact, if one consults the relevant chapter in Purcell's biography and applies the same strict method of checking Simpson's account as he appeared to have applied to Lytton's,

---

Simpson adduced that *The Times Literary Supplement* deliberately intended to deal with volumes 3 and 4 as they had dealt with volume 2.

What in fact had happened was this. *Louis Napoleon and the Recovery of France* was finished in 1921 and scheduled to be published in 1922. But, being delayed at the printers' and the publishers', the book was eventually held back until the following year. In July 1922, Philip Guedalla's *The Second Empire* came out, this work not being referred to in the bibliography of Mr Simpson's volume. Such an omission may possibly have incensed Guedalla, that so-called Stracheyesque biographer (though one never personally admired by Lytton). In any event, Guedalla anonymously held up the book to ridicule in *The Times* on the morning of its publication, and followed up this attack by a slashing review in *The Times Literary Supplement* – 'simply a travesty of criticism', as Leonard Woolf later called it. Shorn in consequence of its sales and of other reviews the book survived perilously until it received the praise that was its due from Frank Swinnerton, J. L. Hammond and many other literary critics and historians. But although Simpson had already completed some portion of the succeeding two volumes, *Louis Napoleon and the Liberation of Italy* and *The Fall of Louis Napoleon,* he never recovered the momentum to finish his *magnum opus,* delay giving way to abandonment when, in 1940, the entire stock of the existing volumes was destroyed in circumstances which made immediate replacement impossible, and even eventual republication improbable.

Mr Simpson's own attack on Lytton Strachey's 'Cardinal Manning' was published in two forms during the year 1943 – first in the *Cambridge Review*, then in the *Spectator*. 'My Spectator article', he explained to the author (24 February 1966), 'was merely a condensed version, furnished at the request of its editor, of the original Cambridge one. And owing to war-time paper shortage he could only allow me just over a page of space. Hence it was far *too* condensed.' Most people, however, have only read the *Spectator* piece, which partly suppresses, for example, Mr Simpson's admiration for Lytton Strachey's prose style, and omits all mention of the particular occasion of his essay – Max Beerbohm's Rede Lecture.

In answer to the author's questions, Mr Simpson allowed that 'the most damning exposures of Purcell's inaccuracies were only published after Strachey's death, so that it was not his fault not to know about them. And Purcell himself was quite as much concerned to run Newman up – "the illustrious Oratorian" as he always called him – as to run Manning down. So there again Strachey was outpacing him. What however *was* very unworthy in him was an occasional lack of honesty in his use of an authority whose *own* lack of honesty he did not know enough about the subject to recognise.'

Mr Simpson also added that, so far as he could discover, the accuracy of *Queen Victoria* could not be faulted.

Lady Ottoline Morrell

Bertrand Russell, J. M. Keynes and Lytton Strachey at Garsington, about 1917

'MR. LYTTON STRACHEY, TRYING* TO SEE HER WITH LORD MELBOURNE'S EYES.
*– and contriving –
                  M.B. 1921'
(a caricature by Max Beerbohm drawn in November 1920 and published in *A Survey*, 1921)

In the country

one discovers that he is guilty of having indited a considerably mis-leading summary himself. The conclusion of his article is that Lytton, through deliberate wickedness and irresponsibility, misrepresented this vital conversation in all its essential details; that he invented out of nothing its sinister undertones and motives, by tampering with the evidence supplied by Purcell. There was, he explains, nothing under-hand about the interview with Pio Nono; its air of mystery was con-cocted by Lytton through unsubstantiated innuendo and the suppres-sion of published information. Having absorbed Simpson's account, one is prepared for something rather commonplace in Purcell. Nothing of the kind! It was Purcell himself who suggested some mystery, who declares that no one knew for sure what happened during Manning's visit to the Vatican in 1848, who pointedly comments that 'not a line, not a word, not a syllable beyond the mere record of the fact' was entered in Manning's diary, who contends that – despite Trevelyan's rather unimportant pamphlet – we do not know for certain why Manning was granted this interview. Nor can one see in what way it would really have been to Manning's benefit had Lytton quoted or paraphrased more of Purcell's account, which displays a greater sense of high politics than of spiritual holiness. Here is what Purcell writes – and that it is closer in tone to Lytton than to Simpson is surely obvious:

'Still more unaccountable is the utter absence of any record in his Diary of its writer's private audience with Pope Pius IX. Not a line, not a word, not a syllable beyond the mere record of the fact, and that in the baldest form: "Audience to-day at the Vatican". The Pope's name even is not mentioned; Newman's name was not indicated in the Diary further than by its initial letter. Even such scant recognition was denied to Pius IX – Pius IX with whom, and only a few weeks later, he was on terms of such close and intimate friendship. To a man of Archdeacon Manning's antecedents, not to speak of his position in the "sister Church", a private meeting, still more a long conversation with the Pope of Rome, could not but be an occasion or an occurrence of exceptional interest. Was the wise and cautious archdeacon afraid that, if once committed to paper, an account of his conversation with the Pope might somehow or other reach suspicious ears, and arouse perchance against him the clamours of a too susceptible Protestantism at home? On the other hand, it is just possible that the grave and reverend Archdeacon of Chichester was disappointed with the Pope's reception, and preferred to pass over in silence what perhaps appeared to him the flippant or ignorant allusions of Pius IX to the Anglican Church. The Pope, it seems, knew a great deal about Mr. Fry and the Quakers, but little or nothing about Archdeacon Manning's own creed,

K

and even less about Anglican worship. His Holiness expressed his
surprise on learning from the archdeacon that the chalice was used
in the Anglican Church in the administration of Communion.
"What!" exclaimed Pius IX, "is the same chalice made use of by
every one?"

'Such an amazed expression of surprise; such ignorance of Anglican
ritual and belief on the part of the Pope, unwitting of offence, may well
have fallen like a douche of cold water on the susceptible temper of a
high Anglican dignitary. Little wonder then, if such were the case, that
Pius IX's name is omitted from the Diary, and the archdeacon's
audience with the Pope reduced to a form so bald as almost to be
obscure.'

Unwitting of offence? Lytton, who seldom weighs up his evidence in
public, chose to take the pope's declared astonishment as a subtle
offence, implying – almost defining – the narrow limits of Manning's
Anglican prestige. If his instinct is right, then of course the objections
of those critics who claim that Pius IX's genuine ignorance of Anglican
ceremony indicates a similar ignorance of Anglican hierarchy – a
dubious enough point anyway – automatically falls to the ground. In
any event, there can be little doubt that Manning left the Vatican aware
of his lowered standing as an archdeacon, and that this feeling of inferiority and isolation may well have contributed towards his later
conversion – it would be peculiar if it had not done so. But where
Lytton may be said to err is in his imagined theatrical reconstruction of
the unknown scene. Writing, as he always did, from books – many of
them incredibly tedious – he was at pains to present his material not
just briefly, but dramatically, and in this case melodramatically. The
effect here is lamentable: 'It is easy to imagine the persuasive innocence
of his Italian voice. . . .' The words and gestures with which Lytton
supplies the pope are peculiarly stagy. Whatever happened, it is far
from easy to imagine it taking place quite like this.

For Lytton, then, the story which he uncovered between the lines of
Purcell's biography was childishly simple. When Manning succumbed
to the Church of Rome, he acted under the ungovernable impulse of
megalomania. Any man possessing just the ordinary, healthy appetite
for a little fame would have found satisfaction enough with high office
in the Anglican Church. Not so Manning. Ignoring the dictates of
uninspired common sense, he obeyed a deeper, intuitive call. He had,
so Lytton tells us, 'scented nobler quarry. To one of his temperament,
how was it possible, when once the choice was plainly put, to hesitate
for a moment between the respectable dignity of an English bishop,
harnessed by the secular power, with the Gorham judgment as a bit

between his teeth, and the illimitable pretensions of the humblest priest of Rome?'

That Manning went over to Rome, not because of secular ambition and a preoccupation with the supernatural, but for the more 'curious' or 'singular' reason that he believed the immortality of his soul depended upon his being admitted to the one true Church, the Church of Christ, is never seriously entertained by Lytton – even as a possibility that needed to be dismissed. For theological motives and spiritual struggles of this traditional sort held no reality for him, and he reduced them to a series of comically futile gymnastics in the void. They could, however, usefully serve his aesthetic ends. He deals leniently with the Oxford Movement in order to deck his sympathetic picture of Newman with an appropriate setting; while to achieve a parallel artistic effect, he gives a marvellously sarcastic account of the General Council of 1869 at Rome – a fitting frame for his astringent portrait of Manning.

Although these summaries are very adroit, and nowhere rely on invention, Lytton's ironic incomprehension of the genuine instinctive appeal which all such pullulating rites and ceremonies hold for certain natures, his hilarious indifference to the obscured and distorted emotional ideals of ecclesiastical Christianity, may be said in some measure to diminish the dramatic panoply that he was so anxious to unfurl. The necessary contrast is very cleverly made, but one senses that really he considered it all six of one and half a dozen of the other. To his mind, established religion was a farrago of fantastic superstitions, mercifully susceptible to comic and picturesque presentation. Manning's religiosity – whether Anglican or Roman Catholic – was little more than a perverted form of bigotry; while poor Newman's was a naïve and grotesque mental aberration which poisoned the clear springs of his poetical genius. At best, religious belief was inspired nonsense; at worst, dangerous, cruel and seductive humbug. 'He investigates the feelings of Newman or Keble as a naturalist might the contortions of an insect,' wrote Edmund Gosse, '. . . and in their presence, if he suppresses his laughter, it is solely to prevent his missing any detail precious to his curiosity.'

One of the pivots of Lytton's thesis is Manning's behaviour on the occasion when Newman's name was mentioned with regard to a cardinalate. Being fascinated by personalities rather than ideas, Lytton represents Manning's dubious actions as emanating simply from feelings of petty jealousy over Newman's fame and potential eminence. Yet the two men were neither quite so incompatible nor so resolutely fixed in enmity as he wished to make out. The facts suggest that while

Manning disliked Newman's theology and had no desire to see it sanctioned, even honoured, in Rome, he felt little animosity for Newman personally. Thus, although he did much to ensure that Newman would never attain great power in England, he spoke up for him several times in Rome, and, on one notable occasion, his warm defence successfully diverted the official censure which Newman's reply to Gladstone seemed likely to bring about. This ambivalent attitude, which eludes Lytton, puzzled Newman himself, who, prone to take everything personally, was unable to conceive that Manning could differentiate between his public influence – i.e. the theological concepts which he represented – and the effect of his individual personality. His bewilderment at this discrepancy is perfectly reflected in a letter he sent to Manning which Lytton quotes only as evidence of the insuperable breach between the two men. 'I can only repeat what I said when you last heard from me,' Newman wrote. 'I do not know whether I am on my head or my heels when I have active relations with you. In spite of my friendly feelings, this is the judgment of my intellect.'

Despite a clerical brother-in-law's unkind observation that Manning's apparent magnificence of forehead was attributable to the fact that he had no face, he does largely resemble the fierce and rapacious eagle to which Lytton compared him. 'We might well pause in contemplation before the terrible face that confronts us in the best known photograph of Manning,' wrote John Stewart Collis, 'with the senseless severity and fear and disapproval in the eyes, and the ghastly tension of the lips drawn tight as by a bit in restraint of all the natural man within.' The complementary miniature of the dove-like Newman, a bewildered victim whose innocent and ethereal spirit is crushed by the tyrannical compulsion of a scheming prelate, is a long way from the truth, and is supported mainly by excisions (sometimes concealed) in his quotations and by the running together of letters written years apart (as in the letter quoted above), all tending to make Newman appear milder and weaker than he really was. 'Anyone less like a dove than J.H.N.', commented Augustine Birrell, 'it would be hard to picture.' And Lytton himself later conceded the truth of this censure. 'Your criticism of the "eagle and dove" passage went home,' he wrote to Birrell (2 June 1918). 'It is certainly melodramatic, and I should like to alter it. I think perhaps my whole treatment of Newman is over-sentimentalised – to make a foil for the other Cardinal.' Most of Newman's biographers have corroborated this view, including Sean O'Faolain, who remarked that Newman 'had a devilish temper, passions so ungovernable as to unman him, and a tongue that could clip a hedge'. Newman's own Memoranda, too, are full of instances of his impatience and ill-temper, and he undoubtedly was, as Manning regretfully acknowledged after his death, 'a good hater'.

But, from the first, Lytton had a precise artistic end in view. He thought he needed a passive, sweet-tempered human sacrifice to emphasize more effectively Manning's blistering, pitiless inhumanity. One of the most fascinating modifications of biographical fact, skilfully engineered and introduced at a particularly telling moment in the narrative so as to lend colour and substance to his argument that Newman was eclipsed by the propaganda of Manning's confederates, is the scene in which a tearful Newman returns incognito to Littlemore, and being accidentally recognized, refuses all offers of consolation from the sympathetic curate:

'At about this time the Curate of Littlemore had a singular experience. As he was passing by the Church he noticed an old man, very poorly dressed in an old grey coat with the collar turned up, leaning over the lych gate, in floods of tears. He was apparently in great trouble, and his hat was pulled down over his eyes, as if he wished to hide his features. For a moment, however, he turned towards the Curate, who was suddenly struck by something familiar in the face. Could it be —? A photograph hung over the Curate's mantelpiece of the man who had made Littlemore famous by his sojourn there more than twenty years ago; he had never seen the original; but now, was it possible —? He looked again, and he could doubt no longer. It was Dr. Newman. He sprang forward, with proffers of assistance. Could he be of any use? "Oh no, no!" was the reply. "Oh no, no!" But the Curate felt that he could not turn away, and leave so eminent a character in such distress. "Was it not Dr. Newman he had the honour of addressing?" he asked, with all the respect and sympathy at his command. "Was there nothing that could be done?" But the old man hardly seemed to understand what was being said to him. "Oh no, no!" he repeated, with the tears streaming down his face, "Oh no, no!"'

This scene, which is presented as the climax of Newman's humiliation at the hands of Manning, is of especial interest for two reasons. As a piece of writing, the paragraph, for all its vividness, demonstrates clearly Lytton's inability to convey pathos. He overdoes it: Newman has to be in 'floods of tears' as well as 'in great trouble', after which the tears must again be pointed out 'streaming down his face' – a high-water mark never approached in the original account. Written without the implied nuances essential to catch and communicate that most fragile of emotions, this description is less moving than it should be and strikes one as being an apocryphal device, swamped by a chorus of loud questionings, heavy punctuation and superfluous gestures. One's suspicions that the episode is not wholly authentic are confirmed when one compares it with the source from which Lytton took it – an account written by Canon Irvine for Wilfrid Ward, who published it in his biography of Newman. From this it appears that Newman returned to Littlemore undisguised and accompanied by his Catholic friend, Father Ambrose St John. He did say 'Oh no, no!' not, as in Lytton's version of the story, in answer to the Curate's deferential inquiry as to whether he might have the honour of assisting the eniment Dr Newman, but in reply to the suggestion that he might visit a Mr Crawley. Finally he was prevailed upon to do so, 'and had a long chat with him. After that he went and saw several of the old people in the village.'

Out of this incident Lytton manufactured a fragment which appears to complete the pattern of his theme with the absolute perfection of a piece in a jigsaw puzzle. Yet, in one sense, this contrived drama goes some way to contradicting the very concept it was designed to uphold. For, realizing that a fight between an eagle and a dove makes a pretty feeble spectacle, Lytton transformed the dove into a tamer, more in-competent eagle itself. Newman was lachrymose by nature, and the tears he shed on this visit to his beloved retreat at Littlemore – his first return there after twenty-three years – were occasioned by the sight of his old home with all its sacred memories and its associations of old friends and companions, many of whom still remembered him with heart-warming vividness. So much is evident from a letter chronicling the visit that Newman wrote to Henry Wilberforce. This letter, in which Newman confesses that he had always hoped to see Littlemore again before he died, appears in Wilfrid Ward's biography directly above Canon Irvine's impressions. Lytton elected to overlook this and ascribe Newman's tears not to nostalgia – which would have been in keeping with 'a creature of emotion and of memory' – but to a sudden bitter regret over his 'wasted efforts, disappointed hopes, neglected possibilities, unappreciated powers', for so much of which Manning had been directly or indirectly responsible. But by so interpreting the 'flood of tears' as a violent, immature expression of frustration, Lytton obliquely attributes to Newman an aspiring nature hardly less keen than Manning's own.

Near the beginning of his essay, Lytton states that his interest in Manning depends mainly upon two considerations – 'the light which his career throws upon the spirit of his age, and the psychological problems suggested by his inner history'. The fact that he chose the 'eagle and dove' motif, and went, in John Raymond's words, 'bald-headed after it', shows that he was chiefly interested by Manning's inner history in so far as it illustrated certain abhorrent aspects of

Victorianism, particularly that fanaticism, intolerance and rigid adherence to a repressive code of behaviour which violated the amenities of civilized human intercourse. Had Lytton been really interested in Manning, not as a representative of a debased Victorian culture, but as an individual human being too important to be treated as a mere symptom of the past, his biographical motif must have been rather different. For a dramatic enough conflict lay to hand within the very character of Manning, torn all his life between an inborn fascination with the supernatural and a persistent susceptibility to worldly honour, precedence, and the society of great people. He was, as Lytton depicts him, allured by the promises of mundane glory; but he was also an honest and scrupulous man by and large, whose writings reveal little talent for self-pretence but rather a full and tormented awareness of the struggle between secular temptation and the fear of divine punishment that raged within him.

Even before putting pen to paper, Lytton's opinion of Manning, one feels, was irretrievably settled. 'Some of you may be shocked to hear', said Ralph Partridge in the course of a B.B.C. talk (8 October 1946), 'that Strachey had the plan of a book already formed in his head before reading up all the authorities on the subject.' But one is not shocked, since a certain preconception is detectable in the style and structure of his books. In the very first chapter of 'Cardinal Manning', for example, we are told a story of him outwitting a Harrow schoolmaster, which, by revealing the cunning and the opportunism he habitually displayed whenever his own interests were at stake, acts as an allegory of his whole character and career. Manning's dexterity of conduct was always more than equal to the task of outmanœuvring his earnest concern for the salvation of his soul. He was throughout a tremendous egotist, but about halfway in the essay Lytton seems to become all at once aware of Manning's divided nature. His eye by then was already well focused upon a predestined end, and he deliberately discounts his own valid observations:

'In such a situation [the death of Cardinal Wiseman] the voice of self-abnegation must needs grow still and small indeed. Yet it spoke on, for it was one of the paradoxes in Manning's soul that that voice was never silent. Whatever else he was, he was not unscrupulous. Rather, his scruples deepened with his desires; and he could satisfy his most exorbitant ambitions on a profundity of self-abasement. And so now he vowed to Heaven that he would *seek* nothing – no, not by the lifting of a finger or the speaking of a word. But, if something came to him —? He had vowed not to seek; he had not vowed not to take. Might it not be his plain duty to take? Might it not be the will of God?'

By these ingenious means did Lytton endeavour to iron out the paradox, to unify the concept of a prelate whose 'scruples deepened with his desires' with the picture of a Machiavellian self-seeker, unfettered by any deeply sincere religious considerations. His scruples are therefore shown mainly as the mute complaints of an outwitted conscience.

Some of the features of Lytton's essay stem from Edmund Purcell's interesting but haphazard and unhistorical biography of Manning. It was Purcell's two-volume, amorphous *Life* that Lytton brilliantly synthesized into a concentrated, coherent shape. Purcell was his chief source, and indeed, as Manning's most recent biographer (1962), Vincent Alan McClelland, has pointed out, 'remained the sole source of information concerning this "Eminent Victorian" until . . . the early 1920's'. For this reason it is useful briefly to compare the two works.

Purcell's *Life of Cardinal Manning* is, in short, the very antithesis of Lytton's essay. Purcell's aim was to further the glory of the pope, of Manning and – not least – of himself; Lytton's was to frame an indictment of those factors within institutional religion that fostered an elevated lack of humanity. Purcell's method of achieving his aim was to give the world all the available evidence, the unedited correspondence of the archbishop including those letters which Manning had intended to destroy; Lytton's method was to digest this evidence in private, to eliminate the random and discursive quality of Purcell's volumes, and filter off from them his personal point of view, sharpened to the needle precision of an icicle. The effect of Purcell's indiscreet panegyric was explosive, since it contained enough irrefutable disclosures to justify a verdict for the prosecution. The reader, reacting to the biographer's suppressed bias in favour of his subject, fixes his attention on the latent truth of the matter and hastens to his own most hostile conclusions. Lytton, on the other hand, not appreciating perhaps that the most lasting impression that a book can instil is produced by the illusion of a collaboration between the author and his audience, endeavoured to do all his reader's work for him. The result was, in some part, opposite to the one for which he had striven so hard. After the first shattering impact, the public has come to regard his interpretation as attractive fiction founded only casually on fact – which is very far from being the case. His style, with its moments of emphatic oversimplification and romantico-psychological innuendo, has tended to liberate exaggerated misgivings over his own Voltairian prejudice. This reaction accounts for the weaker explosion produced in some quarters by his 'Cardinal Manning' than that of Purcell's inartistic biography, 'packed with secret dynamite', as Professor Trevor-Roper described it, 'whose detonation, in 1896, had shattered the unnaturally smooth front of Popery in England'. Explaining the incongruous fact that some of Manning's followers actually welcomed Lytton's tirade, Trevor-Roper continues: 'Against the documentary revelations of Purcell the defenders of Manning were helpless, and it is instructive to look back at their agonised and desperate writings. Strachey, by his excessive zeal in converting unassailable facts into questionable judgements, supplied an unexpected defence. Manning's supporters could thenceforth discreetly forget the name of Purcell and complacently dismiss his revelations as being "only Lytton Strachey".'

But Lytton's heart does momentarily soften towards Manning in old age, and there is a note of genuine respect in his writing when he shows us the octogenarian cardinal addressing, with magical effect, the dock strikers at Bermondsey. In funereal prose, rich and slow, he also pays tribute to Manning's 'bold and tenacious spirit' which struggled step by step with approaching death.

The reason for this more lenient tone seems to have been twofold. First, by skilful use of quotation, he is able to indicate that now, for the first time, the lonely old man realized the futility of his worldly ambitions, the dismaying emptiness of self-regarding achievements – and he is grateful to Manning for providing him with such a fitting last scene. His imagination is touched, too, by another change in the cardinal, a metamorphosis which renders him far more sympathetic. 'Though his bodily strength gradually ebbed,' we are told, 'the vigour of his mind was undismayed.' Being of such a fragile physical constitution himself, Lytton responded to mental power, but was repelled by an abundance of animal energy where it was combined with physical ugliness in the young and middle-aged. It was this overplus of unattractive vitality that had helped to alienate him from Manning, and, too, from Florence Nightingale, whom he also likened to an eagle.

4

ANDANTE

Lytton's dislike of Florence Nightingale was tempered by three factors: first, her ready and percipient wit, which he complimented by borrowing without acknowledgement ('Yet her conception of God was certainly not orthodox. She felt towards Him as she might have felt towards a glorified sanitary engineer; and in some of her speculations she seems hardly to distinguish between the Deity and the Drains'); secondly,

K*

her health, which broke down, leaving her an invalid, after the ordeal at
Scutari, while she was still a comparatively young woman; and thirdly,
her practical efficiency, which he held in high esteem.

His general attitude towards Florence Nightingale was more divided
than his view of Manning, and this gives rise to some dislocation in the
thread of his second essay. She had, of course, been born into a similar
stratum of life to which it had pleased God to call Lytton himself, and
he sincerely admired the amazing persistency with which she fought to
cut herself free from its conventional shackles, to make her own way in
the world and live in independence. He approved of the intellectual side
of her temperament which found satisfaction in art and literature, and
of the passional side which found liberty in human love. But he abhorred
her moral and active self, which gained ascendancy over her more
amiable qualities. Like Manning, she turned her back on an assured
unambitious happiness, preferring the egotism of ruthless devotion to
duty, and just as he had consecrated himself to celibacy within the
Roman Catholic Church, so she denied her womanhood and suppressed her erotic life in a frigid indifference to human relationships.
Through her choice of career, Florence Nightingale developed that
side of her character which was in every respect opposed to Lytton's
own. 'She would think of nothing', he complained despairingly, 'but
how to satisfy that singular craving of hers to be *doing* something.'

In order to assert this barren drive for action, Lytton switches the
emphasis in Sir Edward Cook's narrative, bringing out far more
dramatically her morbid affection for sickness, her self-righteousness,
her sexless misdirected energy. The main driving force in her life,
however, may have been a little less spinsterish than he cares to admit.
It was the very improbability of happiness with the kind of person
considered eligible by Victorian society that fortified her zeal. She was
not led on by visions of active good, so much as running away from
sexual nightmares which she had no way of assuaging except through
unremitting work. This would seem to be the truth delicately hinted at
in the pages of Cook's biography.

As the very incarnation of nineteenth-century humanitarianism –
that movement which salved the conscience of Victorian England –
Florence Nightingale has been enshrined as a legendary figure, saintly
and self-sacrificing – the Lady with the Lamp. By exploding for ever
this romantic fable, Lytton struck directly at the popular mythology of
Victorian England. *His* Florence Nightingale is a woman no less
remarkable or romantic than the angelic vision of modest female virtue
which he now so brilliantly disintegrated, but far less agreeable, an
Amazon who embodied the paradoxical spirit of her age by becoming

transfigured into the symbol of humanitarianism through the total rejection of 'the most powerful and the profoundest of all the instincts of humanity' – in other words, the sexual instinct.

As in his study of Manning, Lytton first charts the area which his essay will cover by propounding a series of rhetorical questions: 'Ah! To do her duty in that state of life into which it had pleased God to call her! Assuredly she would not be behindhand in doing her duty; but unto what state of life *had* it pleased God to call her? That was the question. God's calls are many, and they are strange. Unto what state of life had it pleased Him to call Charlotte Corday, or Elizabeth of Hungary? What was that secret voice in her ear, if it was not a call? Why had she felt, from her earliest years, those mysterious promptings towards . . . she hardly knew what, but certainly towards something very different from anything around her? Why, as a child in the nursery, when her sister had shown a healthy pleasure in tearing her dolls to pieces, had *she* shown an almost morbid one in sewing them up again? Why was she driven now to minister to the poor in their cottages, to watch by sick-beds, to put her dog's wounded paw into elaborate splints as if it was a human being? Why was her head filled with queer imaginations of the country house at Embley turned, by some enchantment, into a hospital, with herself as matron moving about among the beds? Why was even her vision of heaven itself filled with suffering patients to whom she was being useful? So she dreamed and wondered, and, taking out her diary, she poured into it the agitations of her soul. And then the bell rang, and it was time to go and dress for dinner.'

There are two chief objections to this passage. The prognosis obscures rather than clarifies the real theme of the essay, which is an examination of how a true epic story became translated by the pressures of Victorian society into a mock epic. But worse than this is Lytton's hackneyed attempt to find some dark, psychological significance in the growing child's everyday activities. In his eagerness to stress this precocious obsession, he manipulates to his own ends a number of rather trivial facts. The dog, for example, did not belong to Florence Nightingale, but to an old shepherd; it was not a pet but an outdoor working dog; Florence did not put its 'wounded paw into elaborate splints as if it was a human being', but merely assisted the local parson in the ordinary first-aid that was administered. All tiny errors, but needless. Sir Edward Cook, from whose biography Lytton's statements were taken, also wrote that 'it has been recorded that she used to nurse and bandage the dolls which her elder sister damaged'. The chief authority for this story which Lytton characteristically dramatized, appears to have been a Mrs Sarah Tooley, whose popular *Life of Florence*

Nightingale written in 1904, he very wisely does not include in his bibliography. But, less wisely, he ignored, too, Cook's explicit warning about the doubtful authenticity of tales illustrating Florence's precocious interest in nursing; and his attempt to give a modern psychological veneer to his essay was not so great a novelty as some critics were led to believe.

'It is a natural temptation of biographers,' Cook had sensibly written, 'to give a formal unity to their subject by representing the child as in all things the father of the man; to date the vocation of their hero or heroine very early in life; to magnify some childish incident as prophetic of what is to come thereafter. Material is available for such treatment in the case of Florence Nightingale. . . . But these things are after all but trifles. Florence Nightingale is not the only little girl who has been fond of nursing sick dolls or mending them when broken. Other children have tended wounded animals.'

There are no enormities of perverted truth in Lytton's essay, but he did consistently embroider small details to reinforce his view of Florence Nightingale as a being possessed by the overmastering mania for healing mankind. This type of treatment – which divests her of a certain sense of humour – constitutes not so much, as John A. Garraty has claimed, a violation of his oath as a biographer, but rather a naïvety in believing that his 'new' psychological approach was much less romantic than the conventional panegyric against which he was reacting.

The second chapter of 'Florence Nightingale' covers the twenty months that she spent in the Crimea. Lytton's description of the inferno that raged there on her arrival, ten days after the battle of Balaclava, is excellent. He allows the dreadful facts to tell their own absorbing story without accompanying the scene with picturesque questions or theatrical dashes and dots, exclamations and semicolons. The result is that he succeeds in doing what he often found most difficult as a writer – conveying in simple terms his deeply felt emotional response to a situation. 'One feels', wrote Professor Humphry House, 'that his very finger-tips were sensitive to the practical tasks which Florence Nightingale had to do, and his nose to all the smells of Scutari; and yet the design and proportion and becoming brevity are kept.' The prose in which he describes the condition of the dying and wounded is sufficiently vibrant and compelling in itself to eradicate for ever the popular image of him as a heartless, cynical and insincere pacifist, whose preoccupations were pre-eminently frivolous. The impact of these passages comes from their order and restraint, but once or twice this control falters, and he seems for a moment to recollect his readers, and to interpose them as a barrier between himself and the events he is describing. At the very end of the following paragraphs, for example, his style degenerates from the truly eloquent to the more positively loquacious, as soon as he leaves off recording his own impressions at the calamity of administrative collapse, and turns his attention to the task of striking his audience with the full horror of such chaos.

'The principal doctor was lost in the imbecilities of a senile optimism. The wretched official whose business it was to provide for the wants of the hospital was tied fast hand and foot by red tape. A few of the younger doctors struggled valiantly, but what could they do? Unprepared, disorganised, with such help only as they could find among the miserable band of convalescent soldiers drafted off to tend their sick comrades, they were faced with disease, mutilation, and death in all their most appalling forms, crowded multitudinously about them in an ever increasing mass. They were like men in a shipwreck, fighting, not for safety, but for the next moment's bare existence – to gain, by yet another frenzied effort, some brief respite from the waters of destruction.

'In these surroundings, those who had been long inured to scenes of human suffering – surgeons with a world-wide knowledge of agonies, soldiers familiar with fields of carnage, missionaries with remembrances of famine and of plague – yet found a depth of horror which they had never known before. There were moments, there were places, in the Barrack Hospital at Scutari, where the strongest hand was struck with trembling, and the boldest eye would turn away its gaze.'

By and large Lytton selects his facts with imagination, and lucidly, forcefully presents them. The occasional excrescences of his prose are matched by a number of rather far-fetched claims, all of which tend to bring out more graphically Miss Nightingale's demonic personality. He glorifies this vision of a black and rapacious eagle with hooked bill and crooked talons, and gloats over her pitiless and irresistible spirit of philanthropy, her ruthless compassion. Under his pen her obstacles wax even more stupendous, her achievements even more astonishing. The smaller irritations which beset her are magnified in such a way that everyone will acknowledge her to have been 'overburdened by the strain of ceaseless work, bound down by the traditions of official routine'. The hospital orderlies, for instance, who assisted her, were not, as Lytton describes them, a 'miserable band of convalescent soldiers'. A good many of them were willing and able-bodied N.C.O.s who, as Florence herself complained, were often sent back to the front after they had been given the bare modicum of hospital training. Her frenzied zeal, too, is stressed beyond the limits of human endurance.

She did not, literally, as Lytton makes out, carry out 'the whole business of purveying to the hospitals', and he rather overplays, too, the job she actually did in reclothing the army in socks, boots, shirts, trousers and dressing-gowns. He also maintained that her report, privately printed and at the time of his writing virtually unobtainable, was 'to this day the leading authority on the medical administration of armies' – an exorbitant claim. In addition to all this, Lytton imbues her with a tenacity and strength of will that is little short of the miraculous: 'Her powers of resistance seemed incredible,' he wrote, 'but at last they were exhausted. She was attacked by fever, and for a moment came very near death. Yet she worked on; if she could not move, she could at least write; and write she did until her mind had left her; and after it had left her, in what seemed the delirious trance of death itself, she still wrote.' Although this account is not actually untrue, the impression which it produces is far in excess of the facts – 'two little bits of paper, perhaps not thirty words in all, were the origin of the passage', commented Rosalind Nash.

The problems which hampered Lytton in securing a complete synthesis through the steady development of a single psychological thread were more complex in 'Florence Nightingale' than in any of the other studies which make up *Eminent Victorians*. He felt a deep and awful admiration for her extraordinary achievement in ending the turmoil at Scutari, for her consummate art in circumventing the pernicious influences of departmental etiquette, and, too, her enlightenment in treating the other ranks as if they were human beings and not insentient brutes. He therefore sought to reconcile this admiration with the theme he had chosen, by so heightening her superhuman powers as to reveal the underlying seeds of inhumanity which the soil of Victorian England would later nourish into full flower. The idea was a good one, but needed all the delicacy of understatement and subtle implication if it was to come off. Unfortunately Lytton was too insistent, too hyperbolic in his handling of this theme. The result of his over-emphasis was to transform Florence Nightingale into a grotesque schizophrenic monster, a female Dr Jekyll and Mr Hyde, at one moment a saintly crusader in the cause of hygiene, at the next a satanic personality, resorting to sardonic grins, pantomime gestures and sudden fits of wild fury. Between these two Florence Nightingales, Lytton charts some latent consistency, by contrasting the prosaic, common-sense figure she cut before her assistants, with the gracious angel of mercy in which guise she appeared before the wounded soldiers. The apparent inconsistency in her character, then, is shown as being partly impressionistic, depending on the angle of vision, that of patient, opponent or helper.

Lytton might not care about Miss Nightingale as a person, but he did feel some respect for her. Like him, though in a totally different sphere, she possessed the gift for creating order out of rubble. His deference sprang naturally and eloquently from the point of view of the invalid, and echoed the adulation of those wounded and dying soldiers. But though honouring some aspects of her personality, he could not approve of what she later came to represent – the legendary humanitarian cut off from humankind. As with Manning, Lytton was not simply interested in his subject as an individual person, but in the interaction between her and the abhorrent age in which she lived. To stamp out the counterfeit fable of her as the sentimental Lady with the Lamp, he added to his realistic portrait another interpretation, founded on modern psychological theories:

'It was not by gentle sweetness and womanly self-abnegation that she had brought order out of chaos in the Scutari Hospitals, that, from her own resources, she had clothed the British Army, that she had spread her dominion over the serried and reluctant powers of the official world; it was by strict method, by stern discipline, by rigid attention to detail, by ceaseless labour, by the fixed determination of an indomitable will.'

Had Lytton been content to draw attention in this way to the relentless willpower which was indispensable to her success, his portrait would in no way have been controversial. But then, obliquely, he hints at her perverted sexual compulsion which he presents as being responsible for her actions. By sacrificing her erotic love to her desire for power – especially power over men – she turned herself into a neurotic, whose frustrated sexual instincts were kept at bay only by a force which had to expend itself often on needless trivialities. Unstable and psychotic, her outward manner of quietly persuasive charm concealed a nature burning and belligerent:

'Beneath her cool and calm demeanour lurked fierce and passionate fires. As she passed through the wards in her plain dress, so quiet, so unassuming, she struck the casual observer simply as the pattern of a perfect lady; but the keener eye perceived something more than that – the serenity of high deliberation in the scope of the capacious brow, the sign of power in the dominating curve of the thin nose, and the traces of a harsh and dangerous temper – something peevish, something mocking, and yet something precise – in the small and delicate mouth. There was humour in the face; but the curious watcher might wonder whether it was humour of a very pleasant kind; might ask himself, even as he heard the laughter and marked the jokes with which she cheered the spirits of her patients, what sort of sardonic merriment this same lady might not give vent to, in the privacy of her chamber.'

These disagreeable, sharply egotistical qualities are elaborated more fully in the following chapter. As he rightly pointed out, the popular Victorian myth of Florence Nightingale – 'that gentle vision of female virtue which first took shape before the adoring eyes of the sick soldiers at Scutari' – rested on some superficial knowledge of her activities in the Crimean War, and a total ignorance of the more than fifty years of her life after it, during the greater part of which she was working to the full extent of her remarkable powers. In her own political estimation, the Crimea was a mere episode – 'scarcely more than a useful stepping-stone in her career' – an adventure which had given her knowledge and whetted her taste for power. For, as Lytton ably illustrates, her need for power – as for work – had developed into an obsession, arising from the repression of her womanhood. Though her health had been shattered, she was ravenous for more action. Like Manning in the grip of a more emasculated megalomania, she could pay little heed to common sense, to the voice of reason and moderation. Despite a constant expectation of death, she would not rest. A merciless addiction to work, to the exercise of political power from behind the scenes, had become her only relaxation. 'The doctors protested in vain,' Lytton wrote, echoing their fruitless expostulations, 'in vain her family lamented and entreated, in vain her friends pointed out to her the madness of such a course. Madness? Mad – possessed – perhaps she was. A demoniac frenzy had seized upon her.'

Lytton traces the path of this demoniac frenzy, kindled by her super-natural energy, to a pitch of murderous inhumanity – chiefly through her relationship with Sidney Herbert. This relationship fascinated him, as did other associations between a man and a woman – Victoria and Albert, Elizabeth and Essex, the Empress Dowager and the Emperor of China – in which the dominant partner was the woman, whose stronger, more coarse-grained nature devoured the high-born, effeminate, less tenacious male. Lytton's treatment of Sidney Herbert is quite dissimilar to his handling of Miss Nightingale. While she was utterly repugnant to him, Sidney Herbert obviously attracted him sexually, and he depicts him as attractive in order to make Florence's cool attitude to him less sympathetic. But though he approved of Sidney Herbert's moderation, his candour and aristocratic gentleness, his imagination was not fired by such altruism and lack of ambition. The description he gives of Sidney Herbert's personality is almost embarrassingly flat and so sentimental that one has to remind oneself that the 'great anarch' is not being ironic. Yet certainly he isn't. What has happened is that his romanticism has taken over from his more intellectual self. As with the contrast between Manning and Newman, Lytton externalizes the cleavage within his own character, so that the caustic wit and sharpness of observation – products of his mind – are replaced by something more emotional and affected when he deals with Sidney Herbert:

'He was a man upon whom the good fairies seemed to have showered, as he lay in his cradle, all their most enviable goods. Well born, handsome, rich, the master of Wilton – one of those great country-houses, clothed with the glamour of a historic past, which are the peculiar glory of England – he possessed, besides all these advantages, so charming, so lively, so gentle a disposition that no one who had once come near him could ever be his enemy. He was, in fact, a man of whom it was difficult not to say that he was a perfect English gentleman.'

In his literary criticism, Lytton had favoured culinary metaphors and similes; in his biographical essays, he made great use of zoological images and gestures. His 'Florence Nightingale' bristles with these literary animals like some weird menagerie. Lord Panmure was a bison of sorts ('the hide was the hide of a Mexican buffalo, but the spirit was the spirit of an Alderney calf'); Dr Hall was 'a rough terrier of a man'; Florence Nightingale herself, after hatching out into an eagle during early life had metamorphosed into a tigress; and Sidney Herbert was a stag, 'a comely, gallant creature springing through the forest; but the forest is a dangerous place. One has the image of those wide eyes fascinated suddenly by something feline, something strong; there is a pause; and then the tigress has her claws in the quivering haunches; and then ——!'

The analogy is clear: Miss Nightingale killed Sidney Herbert. That force in her which had created order at Scutari, which was naturally intended to love and give life, had now been transformed in the swamps of Victorian England into a force that destroyed. 'It was', Lytton explained, 'her Demon that was responsible.' She lured the defenceless Sidney Herbert out into 'that tropical jungle of festooned obstructiveness, of intertwined irresponsibilities, of crouching prejudices, of abuses grown stiff and rigid with antiquity', and there he met his doom. The strain which she imposed upon him was too great. She spurred him on, deeper and deeper into that chaotic jungle until his health and spirit broke, and he no longer cared whether he lived or died. And then she suddenly sprang at him, chewed up and absorbed the last ounce of digestible matter, and spat out the remainder with disgust.

As so often when advancing an unconventional and new point of view, Lytton's eagerness to 'convince' led him to adopt rather questionable methods of persuasion. He suggests, for example, that Sidney

Herbert was not the only man who fell victim to Florence Nightingale's relentless and unheeding zeal. Arthur Clough – 'this earnest adolescent, with the weak ankles and the solemn face, [who] lived entirely with the highest ends in view' – also succumbed, at about the same time, he points out with a hilarity (some have said facetiousness) which, like much of the humour of Belloc, considerably lessens the seriousness of the charge he is making, worn out by his meticulous tying-up of brown paper parcels.[1] For similar reasons, Lytton stresses, too, her selfish unconcern with other people's personal, non-medical affairs, citing the passionate diatribe she hurled against her ageing and faithful Aunt Mai, who had at last decided to leave her for closer, more imperative duties with her own family.

But it is when dealing with Sidney Herbert's final illness, and his last interview with Florence Nightingale, that Lytton's methods become freer and more controversial. For in these pages he set out to show, in dramatic terms, not that she was simply driving willing horses too hard, but that she was possessed by a depraved Demon of destructive power:

'He [Sidney Herbert] was attacked by fainting-fits; and there were some days when he could only just keep himself going by gulps of brandy. . . . He could no longer hope; he could no longer desire; it was useless, all useless; it was utterly impossible. He had failed. The dreadful moment came when the truth was forced upon him: he would never be able to reform the War Office. But a yet more dreadful moment lay behind; he must go to Miss Nightingale and tell her that he was a failure, a beaten man.

'. . . and, alas! when she brought herself to realise at length what was indeed the fact and what there was no helping, it was not in mercy that

[1] There have been a number of objections to this passage, among them one from B. A. Clough, Arthur Clough's daughter, who defended her father on the grounds that he was a conventional man. More sensibly, Lady Ritchie also demurred at this description, and in a letter to her (5 December 1918) Lytton replied: 'I think it was very good of you to write, and I am proud to think that (with reservations!) you like my book. As to reservations – perhaps I am wrong about Clough – it is difficult to be certain; but I can only say that my remarks represent my genuine opinion. I did not, of course, attempt to tell the *whole* truth about him: he was an incidental figure, and it was impossible to do more than set down what appeared to me the salient features. You say that I "dwelt on puerilities"; it was precisely the puerilities about him that seemed to me so important and so remarkable. You say he was a "sincere man, who all his life tried to do his duty". Of course; no one would dream of denying it; and if I have said anything to give a contrary impression, I must have failed in my object. But I cannot think that he was a wise man, or a man to be held up as an example to future generations. In fact, he seems to me to embody a whole set of weaknesses which have been hitherto either ignored or treated as virtues, and against which it was one of the main purposes of my book to make a protest.' Among the many other letters he received was one from Max Beerbohm (28 July 1918), who wrote that 'I think my favourite passage in all the book is the Clough passage'.

she turned upon her old friend. "Beaten!" she exclaimed. "Can't you see that you've simply thrown away the game? And with all the winning cards in your hands! And so noble a game! Sidney Herbert beaten! And beaten by Ben Hawes! It is a worse disgrace . . .", her full rage burst out at last, ". . . a worse disgrace than the hospitals at Scutari."

'He dragged himself away from her, dragged himself back to Spa, hoping vainly for a return to health, and then, despairing, back again to England, to Wilton . . . and at Wilton he died.'

Rosalind Nash, whose mother was in Florence Nightingale's household and who was deputed by her family to advise with Sir Edward Cook when he was writing his official biography, has shown how Lytton contrived this theatrical last scene by ingeniously mixing two passages from Florence Nightingale's correspondence to other people. First-person drama and jigsaw symmetry are characteristically preferred by Lytton to the more indirect methods of presentation. But since all the evidence needed to stage such a scene was lacking, some gestures and décor had to be invented. There existed, for example, no documentary source to show that, in a tirade of indignant rage, Miss Nightingale openly taunted Sidney Herbert with having been beaten by Ben Hawes – 'a worse disgrace than the hospitals at Scutari'. Something like these words were written by her in a letter to Sir John McNeill: 'What strikes me in this great defeat more painfully even than the loss to the army is the triumph of the bureaucracy over the leaders – a political aristocracy who at least advocate higher principles. A Sidney Herbert beaten by a Ben Hawes is a greater humiliation really (as a matter of principles) than the disaster of Scutari.'

Although there is no record of Miss Nightingale having mentioned Scutari personally to Sidney Herbert, in a letter to Harriet Martineau she did recall that they spoke of Cavour: 'And I was too hard upon him. I told him that Cavour's death was a blow to European liberty, but that a greater blow was that Sidney Herbert should be beaten on his own ground by a bureaucracy. I told him that no man in my day had thrown away so noble a game with all the winning cards in his hands. And his angelic temper with me, at the same time that he felt what I said was true, I shall never forget. I wish people to know that what was done was done by a man struggling with death.'

From the wording of these two letters, it would seem that Lytton's intermingling of them was not unreasonable. But, in converting this correspondence into a directly witnessed incident, he leaves out all the implied compliment which lay behind Florence Nightingale's disapprobation. In Lytton's version of their last meeting, her attitude is shown as one of violent invective, the impulse of which is only contempt; and her stern encouragement is intensified into a rabid, truculent resentment – a very death-blow to Sidney Herbert. And in the death-scene itself, Lytton's fondness for visual melodrama is again vividly illustrated. Sir Edward Cook had noted that 'among his last articulate words were these: "Poor Florence! Poor Florence! Our joint work unfinished"'. Under Lytton's alchemy this is transmuted into: '. . . then, almost unconscious, his lips were seen to be moving. Those about him bent down. "Poor Florence! Poor Florence!" they just caught. ". . . Our joint work . . . unfinished . . . tried to do . . ." and they could hear no more.'

In his last two chapters, Lytton leads Florence Nightingale down a sharp decline, past her cumbersome flirtation with Platonic mysticism and into an abyss of bland and senile sentimentality. Possessing no great imagination, he tells us, she grew bored, lonely, miserable, unless perpetually diverted by external activity. Throughout most of the essay, her superabundant energy had been pitted against the correspondingly superabundant inertia and incompetence of the authorities. Their antagonism was the battery which continuously recharged her vitality. And when it dwindled, and she was driven to seek inspiration in the more abstract realms of philosophy and religion, her spirit began to crumble and disintegrate. Neither a creative artist nor yet a true scientist, she remained, like most men and women of action, simply an empiricist. 'She was a capable woman,' Lytton commented to his mother while working on this essay, 'but rather disagreeable in various ways – a complete egotist, and also very full of tiresome religiosity; and I don't think very intelligent. In spite of spending all her life in medical concerns, she never seems to have got a scientific grasp of things.' In her heyday she had deeply relished the joys of power, and now, by her rigorously enforced seclusion, involving almost an invisibility from the public, she preserved and amplified the Nightingale legend.

Yet Lytton, too, now that it suits his purpose, contributes to this legend. 'Lying on her sofa in the little upper room in South Street,' he wrote, 'she combined the intense vitality of a dominating woman of the world with the mysterious and romantic quality of a myth.' To underline this still dominating spirit of the invalid, her bossiness and her craving for that power which had altogether displaced the more natural sensuality to be found in such energetic natures, he makes great play with Dr Sutherland's loyalty to her, which he represents as the attachment of a slave to his omnipotent master. Dr Sutherland, 'an indefatigable disciple', devotes all his time to her service, and is seen shivering in his shoes whenever she throws him a contemptuous glance.

Lytton does not inform the reader that, so far from acting as her full-time lackey, he had his own position at the War Office, and had agreed to become her personal secretary only during such hours as he could spare from his leisure – which appear nevertheless to have been considerable. Nor, from the recollections of those who knew him personally, does he emerge as the poor, muddle-headed mouse of a man whom Lytton depicts. Undoubtedly, however, he was bullied by the cantankerous Miss Nightingale, and there were often irascible exchanges between them.

To emphasize the 'mysterious and romantic quality' of this legend, Lytton pictures Miss Nightingale, by her own admission a fanatical advocate of sun and fresh air, as lying in her 'shaded chamber', an unseen presence above, while downstairs there raged a loud hubbub of imploring dignitaries, all desperately appealing for a few moments' interview. 'Great statesmen and renowned generals were obliged to beg for audiences; admiring princesses from foreign countries found that they must see her at her own time, or not at all; and the ordinary mortal had no hope of ever getting beyond the downstairs sitting-room and Dr. Sutherland.'

Though the spirit of what Lytton describes is perfectly true, his practice of collating documentary evidence and presenting it as a theatrically produced state of affairs – something that the reader can *see* – leads him into trivial errors. For again his mischievous fancy embroiders upon the data supplied in Cook's biography – his only source-book for such information – to enhance the aura of mysterious divinity. Cook described the chamber as not shaded, but full of light. Facing south, its large windows were without curtains, while all the walls were painted white. To give dramatic contrast to her solitary, awesome, even godlike image upstairs, Lytton fills the downstairs rooms with a constant influx of clamouring nobility, whereas the facts appear to have been that visitors came only by appointment and were seldom kept waiting. On the other hand, it was true that many important people were always applying unsuccessfully for such appointments, so that Lytton's reconstruction, though it exaggerates Miss Nightingale's lack of consideration, is not wholly misleading.

In his final short chapter, Lytton sums up in two sentences the antipathy he felt towards his subject. 'The benevolence and public spirit of that long life', he wrote, 'had only been equalled by its acerbity. Her virtue had dwelt in hardness, and she had poured forth her unstinted usefulness with a bitter smile upon her lips.' But in these last years, he added, her acerbity curdled into a vague and amiable sentimentalism. And then only, once 'consciousness itself grew lost in a roseate haze, and melted into nothingness', was it deemed fitting to bestow upon her a public honour, the Order of Merit. This final revivification of the ancient myth, in all its ironic inappropriateness, makes a perfect ending to Lytton's study. 'You can feel reading the book that he [Lytton] is pleased that Miss Nightingale grew fat and that her brain softened,' Duff Cooper indignantly protested to Lady Diana Manners; but, he added, 'I have enjoyed it enormously.'

5

SCHERZO

'I have read only Flo and Tom,' Walter Raleigh wrote to Lytton early in May. '(It is you who have made me so familiar). Pass a person through your mind, with all the documents, and see what comes out. That seems to be your method. Also choose them, in the first place, because you dislike them.'

Commenting further on 'Florence Nightingale', Raleigh implies that, in contrast to the wholly ironic manner he adopted to Dr Arnold, Lytton's divided attitude is responsible for the rather inconsistent effect left by his essay:

'It's no use your jeering at those who romanticised the lady with the lamp,' he wrote. 'You are a far more incorrigible sinner. You're like Kipling, who sees God in a machine. I find myself wondering whether all those stout military mules who got caught in the machine were really such sinners . . .

'No one can condemn except on the basis of a creed. Your creed comes easy to me. But I don't quite follow its dealings with Flo. "By God," I keep on thinking excitedly, "Flo has got off." A judge of feminist leanings is it?

'It's queer. Of course the cruelty of a really hard-bitten good woman is asserted, in the Flo sketch, and proved. But it is justified; and it is not deeply felt. The death of S. Herbert and Clough is enjoyable. They die because Juggernaut is great; not because they are silly . . .'

Lytton's denunciation of Florence Nightingale's hardness was, it is true, partly offset by his admission that, had she been of a softer, more pliant nature, she would never have succeeded in ending the degradation at Scutari or in bringing about humane and sensible reforms at the War Office. But if there was some justification for *her* unamiable qualities, there could be practically none for those of Dr Arnold, since his reputation as an enlightened reformer, unlike hers, was very largely sham. And so while she is let off, and her legend gingered up with a fresh if rather bitter spice, he is exposed as an appalling and pretentious impostor, with scarcely any redeeming features. An extraordinary portent, the myth which swirled about his indistinct figure still lingered on in 1918, since no one read him or knew very much about him. Lytton's portrait, unrelieved by any touches of furtive admiration or tenderness, is the most caustic in his book. It is also perhaps the most amusing.

There seem to have been both personal and literary reasons for the great enmity which Lytton felt towards Arnold. The reforms which the headmaster of Rugby enforced had made him, however unintentionally, 'the founder of the worship of athletics and the worship of good form', in which philistine climate Lytton had spent some of his most miserable days. Many of Arnold's innovations were similar enough to those of Dr Reddie for Lytton to have felt personally bound up with them. E. F. Benson, for example, who went to Marlborough, one of the new schools to feel the influence of Arnold's reforms, underwent 'the methods of tutors . . . who by making their pupils chop dry faggots of wood, hoped to teach them what was the nature of the trees that once the wind made murmurous on the hillsides of Attica' – a description which would have had for Lytton a familiar ring. His response to Arnold was therefore more directly evolved from personal experience than that to his other subjects. Much of the antagonism which he felt is revealed in such an ambiguously worded sentence as: 'The Communion service he regarded as a direct and special counterpoise to that false communion and false companionship, which, as he often observed, was a great source of mischief in the school; and he bent himself down with glistening eyes, and trembling voice, and looks of paternal solicitude, in the administration of the elements.'

The study of Dr Arnold is monochromatic in a sense that none of the other essays in *Eminent Victorians* are, since Lytton does not dramatize his career by contrasting it with that of some opponent or with the implacable façade of an antiquated institution. Instead, he places Arnold alone on the stage, and makes him rush around with the inexplicable urgency of the white rabbit in *Alice in Wonderland*, a ridiculous clown of a man, full of almighty zeal and energy, towards whom he never varies his look of blank distaste.

As delineated by Lytton, the pompous commonplace Arnold shares almost all the vices of his fellow eminent Victorians, but practically none of their few compensating qualities. Like Manning, he is vain and ambitious – 'I believe that naturally I am one of the most ambitious men alive,' he once wrote – and, like Manning too, the religious element in his life, which theoretically discountenanced all worldly ambition, was modified at crucial moments to a point where the natural disharmony between ambition and religion nearly vanished altogether. But he owned none of Manning's picturesque majesty or stateliness, and without his tortuous sophistication, his romantic flair for success, he remained little more than an overblown, portentous functionary. His life, to an even greater degree than that of Florence Nightingale, presented a barren spectacle of continuous activity, of – to use Carlyle's words – 'unhasting, unresting diligence'. Partly owing to a resolute lack of imagination, *she* had succeeded on a vast scale; his lack of imagination limited him, despite his untiring industry, to a comparative failure, which may have accounted for that puzzled look which Lytton discerns on his blunt, honest face. Only towards the end of her life, when her tremendous powers were at last failing, did Florence Nightingale involve herself in the solitary and awful grandeur of her chamber in South Street – 'the unseen power above'. Dr Arnold, on the other hand, chose to confuse his identity with that of the Almighty when in the prime of life, ruling 'remotely, through his chosen instruments, from an inaccessible heaven'. Nor did he possess, like Gordon, any implicitly heroic or bizarre fabric in his character to atone for this mediocrity. Even his most sympathetic qualities – his love of family and his love of nature – were kept sternly in check so that they might never interfere with his overbearing awareness of the knowledge of good and evil, his grim, humourless air of authority.

Lytton's unrelenting antipathy was also prompted by the only source-book of any importance on Arnold – that pious biography by Dean Stanley, one of his favourite pupils, from whom, however, Arnold had withheld the secrets of literary composition. Unlike Purcell's *Life of Cardinal Manning*, this biography smoothed over anything of even the most faintly controversial nature and carefully excluded all personal information concerning its subject's private life, for fear of distressing Mrs Arnold and her children. In marked contrast to Cook's *Life of Florence Nightingale*, which Lytton considered to be an excellent book, Stanley's *Life and Correspondence of Dr. Arnold* was narrow in outlook, designed solely to embalm the memory of a dead man. It had been written by someone with a strong personal prejudice, conscious that he had a definite case to make. Although, chiefly through its correspondence, these two volumes contained enough material for their readers, if any, to piece together a fairly clear view of Arnold, it was not, in the modern Stracheyesque sense of the term, a biography at all, but an extended obituary notice, the final item of the undertaker's lugubrious business, calling for a wreath rather than a review.

Lytton's essay attempts to reanimate Arnold by opposing the traditional attitude as expressed in Stanley's *Life* and, more popularly, in the Rugby *Iliad*, Thomas Hughes's *Tom Brown's Schooldays*. Yet his exposition of Arnold's paltriness was neither so unjust nor so revolutionary as the general reception given to the essay assumed. Over seventy years earlier, in a [once celebrated] review of Stanley's *Life* – which Lytton himself did not know – Dr Martineau had written of Arnold as 'respectable in scholarship, insensible to art, undistinguished in philosophy, great in action, though his sphere was not large'. Later in this review, the Arian divine had gone on to propound a point of view almost identical to Lytton's own, marking the very same passages to assist him in the critical assessment of Arnold's character. This coincidence is startling only if one accepts the view that Lytton drew a hideously disproportionate caricature, almost unrecognizable as the Arnold who was never a man of plain simplicity, but of true and lasting greatness.

But 'Dr. Arnold' *is* a caricature, and most of the hostility directed against this essay, in failing to recognize this or in naming it as such solely by way of adverse comment, has been curiously misplaced.[1] In literature the caricature has as rightful and legitimate a place as in the visual arts. 'The caricature's first duty is to be expressive,' Lytton once wrote of Caran d'Ache. His own sketch of Arnold, which deliberately ignored a vast quantity of documentary material in Stanley's biography and which consequently draws in only the outlines of his character, is certainly that. Occasionally – as in his description of the death of Arnold – the excision and transposition of sentences from Stanley's book, made so as to achieve a more ludicrous effect, are a little unfair.

---

[1] Because it is the most hostile of the essays in *Eminent Victorians* many critics have assumed that 'Dr Arnold' must be the most unfair. 'It is in the essay on Dr Arnold that he has most laid himself open to counter-attack,' wrote R. A. Scott-James. 'It is a brilliant caricature, but it is the reverse of impartial and is only outwardly dispassionate. It is quite evident that he is at daggers drawn with his subject.' R. J. Campbell may be said to have spoken for Arnold's later biographers when, in the Preface to his book, he wrote: 'If I have not included Mr Lytton Strachey's essay on Arnold (in *Eminent Victorians*) with the above-mentioned authorities, it is because I am compelled to regard it as a caricature and not a true impression of the character and career of a truly great and good man.' Writing to Lady Diana Manners (7 and 8 July 1918), Duff Cooper complained that Strachey's sneering attitude was that of a pamphleteer rather than a historian. 'Arnold of course is a bit too much,' he concluded. And in a letter to Lytton (12 August 1918) G. M. Trevelyan also objected to this essay, but mainly it seems because he had married into the family and because Matthew Arnold had said some good things about his father. But, Trevelyan added, 'I read it [*Eminent Victorians*] at one long sitting in the train across North Italy with the most intense pleasure, approval and admiration. . . . You have got a real historical sense which few professional historians have and hardly any literary people who dabble in history. You have not only historical sense, as Carlyle and Belloc have – but *judgement* which they have not.'

He also limits rather too severely the scope of Arnold's sympathies and greatly exaggerates his deified remoteness as headmaster. But, in the main, his purpose was to demonstrate Arnold's mediocrity as an educational thinker and reformer – and this he very effectively did. According to Lionel Trilling, the fundamental untruth of Lytton's portrait is that it translated Arnold's seriousness into sedentariousness; the central truth of the portrait, Trilling maintains, is that it convincingly exposes Arnold's seriousness as earnestness. The missing humour in Arnold's attitude Lytton supplies himself from without, and it is this injection of comedy that reduces Arnold's stature, setting it in a truer perspective.

Dr Arnold is seen as a political figure, the most influential teacher of the Victorians. His target was not merely the public-school system, the cult of which had tended to stultify all upper-middle-class intelligence through three successive generations, which had set hard the mood of the Victorian age and unnaturally prolonged its insidious spirit well into the twentieth century, but the whole movement of orthodox Victorian liberalism. Arnold had often declared himself to be a liberal, and with this definition Lytton had no quarrel. Taking him as a proto-type, he sets out to show that nineteenth-century liberalism was not based on the principle of progress or enlightened reform, but rather on the variation of an old and debased routine.

When Arnold was appointed headmaster of Rugby in August 1828, Lytton tells us, there existed throughout the country a general feeling of dissatisfaction with the barbaric, rough-and-tumble method of schooling typified in Keate's régime at Eton – 'a system of anarchy tempered by despotism'. The time was ripe for improvements. Public opinion was strongly in favour of educational reform. Some desired a more genuinely liberal curriculum; others, among whom Dr Arnold was one, were convinced of the necessity for a higher moral tone. Though the majority of parents would undoubtedly have opposed profound changes for the better, Dr Arnold's great reputation and authority could hardly have been resisted. 'But how was he to achieve his end?' asked Lytton, framing what was really his chief indictment of Arnold. 'Was he to improve the character of his pupils by gradually spreading round them an atmosphere of cultivation and intelligence? By bringing them into close and friendly contact with civilised men, and even, perhaps, with civilised women? By introducing into the life of his school all that he could of the humane, enlightened, and pro-gressive elements in the life of the community? On the whole, he thought not.'

The opportunity for humanistic reform was missed. Far from

breaking up the conventional, moribund conception of education, devoted almost entirely to the teaching of classical philology, Arnold merely altered some aspects in the running of an already well-established monastic institution. By introducing morals and religion into the heathen climate of the public school, by discounting intellectual ability and devaluing companionship, he gave to the ancient scheme of things a new lease of life. 'He would treat the boys at Rugby as Jehovah had treated the Chosen People.' The centre of his educational system – again like Dr Reddie's – was the school chapel, from where, with high-pitched exhortations, he diligently strove to convert his pupils into brave and useful, truth-telling English and Christian gentlemen. He might have changed the principles of education through all the public schools of England; instead he just gave them a temporary face-lift which slightly altered their physiognomy, but left untouched the basic cranial structure. He might have founded a new scheme of cultural and scholastic instruction, but 'he threw the whole weight of his influence into the opposite scale, and the ancient system became more firmly established than ever'.

Lytton's analysis of the alterations which Arnold effected within the conventional public school, the ironic discrepancy between the aims that lay behind his new measures and the results they finally brought about, is essentially just and, though short, extraordinarily complete. His sketch of Arnold's character, which was of rather secondary importance to him and which he etched in only as a shadow to his public image, is rather less satisfactory. He alludes only briefly to Arnold's more engaging and tender qualities, and because they were always held in control, minimizes their strength, assuming that they were never very potent.

Despite his high seriousness, Arnold had never gone through the process of growing up. At the age of ten he was already as great a prig as during his headmastership. His moral philosophy was evolved not as the outcome of experience, but through a fear of the deep springs of emotion which he so successfully damped down. He embraced this philosophy with a desperate passion. 'When the spring and activity of youth is altogether unsanctified by anything pure and elevated in its desires,' he once wrote, 'it becomes a spectacle that is as dizzying and almost more morally distressing than the shouts and gambols of a set of lunatics.' This pronouncement, and many others regarding the natural evil of boys – their abundance of sin combined with so little sorrow, the absence within them of any proper, manly sense of degradation or guilt – was a disavowal of what was best in Arnold's own nature. That he felt the danger of boyish evil within himself is attested to by the power of such spectacles to move him, to make him almost lose faith in his whole system of education. His wanderlust, his nostalgic sense of family, his naturalist's love of the country – all his most endearing traits – were closely linked with the childhood years he spent at Cowes. He can be seen at his most relaxed not at Rugby, but among the moors of Westmorland during the holidays, a boyish, boisterous figure rambling about with his children and momentarily permitting himself to enjoy what he fearfully described as 'an almost awful happiness'.

In Lytton's pages we seldom catch a glimpse of Arnold in these off-duty moments. The headmaster's hardness is represented not as a protective shell covering a soft and sensitive flesh, but as a uniform texture which extended in the same coarse consistency throughout the length and breadth of his being. We are never allowed to consider whether Arnold might have compelled himself to be hard so as to suppress those intimations of 'awful happiness' which so terrified him, threatening to surge up and swamp that sense of moral evil by which he steadfastly lived. The humanity latent in his nature found expression in some of his letters and in certain aspects of his private life which are excluded from *Eminent Victorians*. The man to whom Lytton confines his attention is the Arnold who wrote to Stanley: 'My love for any place, or person, or institution, is exactly the measure of my desire to reform them.' The Arnold who does not appear in this essay possessed a concealed poetic sensibility that came to the surface in his appreciative description of Laleham, the beautiful scenery of which he happily felt no compulsion to alter, and may also be seen towards the close of his short life in that wish to rest in Grasmere churchyard, 'to lie under the yews which Wordsworth planted, and to have the Rotha with its deep and silent pools passing by'.

'Nowhere', Dr Arnold once remarked, 'is Satan's work more evidently manifest than in turning holy things to ridicule.' Such a statement well conveys his profound lack of humour, that deficiency which Lytton so pointedly succeeds in making good, to the indignation of Arnold's admirers, who saw in his irony only another example of the Devil's work against which they had been warned. But, with his muddle-headed logic, his transcendent self-confidence, his strenuous obsession with moral righteousness, Arnold readily lent himself to caricature. He asked for it. Lytton needed to invent or suppress no major facts in order to produce the preposterous impression he wanted. All he did was to direct his readers' attention towards Arnold's public career, decorating his narrative with cunningly edited extracts from his writings and recorded statements, and away from his underdeveloped but still extant sense of poetry. By this slight readjustment of emphasis Arnold is entirely dehumanized and made to appear as totally absurd.

Much has been made of the summary shortening of Arnold's legs, which serves to show the whole man as stunted. There appears to be no evidence in the sources listed at the end of Lytton's essay to support his statement that the headmaster's 'legs, perhaps, were shorter than they should have been'. In fact both Arnold and Lytton were about the same height, though the former looked shorter and the latter taller than was actually the case. But in all other respects Arnold was the antithesis of Lytton, and their physical dissimilarity (by the general laws of a logically conducted universe, it stood to reason) must have extended to their legs. Aesthetically, at any rate, this seemed inevitable. At the same time, Lytton did not believe, as has been asserted by later critics, that he had invented this detail. Although, subsequently, he could find no authority for it, he was sure, so he told Logan Pearsall Smith, that he had read the fact somewhere, or had been told it by someone.[1] This error and other discrepancies scrupulously investigated by the distinguished American scholar, George Kuppler Simson, are put in their proper perspective by another artist in biography, John Stewart Collis: 'I note that even the warm admirers of Lytton Strachey, including Max Beerbohm, are inclined to rebuke him for his essay on Arnold as being in too much of a vein of mockery. The assumption is that Dr. Arnold should not have been mocked. But how could any mockery be too much for such a man? The biographer knew what he was doing, what he was called upon to do. It is complained that he quoted things out of context and made them look bad. "It is very startling," said Arnold, looking round upon the boys at Rugby, "to see so much of sin combined with so little of sorrow." How do you make that remark look good? – and he did say it.'

[1] A contradictory story is given by Eddie Marsh in a letter to Christopher Hassall (May 1941). 'Have you read the articles on Virginia Woolf in Horizon?' he asked. 'W[illiam] Plomer annoys me by speaking of "the slightly bow-legged Rupert Brooke", which is pure invention, like Lytton Strachey's, who told me he had said that Dr Arnold's legs were too short because he thought they ought to have been.' After Vanessa Bell had read Lytton's essay, she suggested: 'Why not Mrs Humphry Ward following in her uncle's or whatever it was footsteps. It wouldn't be libellous to call her legs too short, would it?' And Lytton wrote to her on 10 July 1918: 'Something certainly ought to be done about Mrs Humphry Ward. Have you by any chance seen her reminiscences, which are now coming out in the Cornhill? Of an incredible vulgarity. Apparently she is furious about Eminent Victorians, and wrote to Asquith – "How *could* you praise that horrid book?" Lord Esher, also, has become my enemy. On the other hand I am supported by Lord Knutsford!'

6

RONDO

For two reasons 'The End of General Gordon' stands apart from the other essays in *Eminent Victorians*. First, there was no single, pre-eminent source-book on which Lytton could depend, and which controlled and restricted the shape of his essay. His other studies had been, in a sense, miniature corrective re-writings of official biographies: with Gordon his sources were far more diverse and more evenly matched in their importance, with the result that his theme is less over-simplified, its treatment freer and more liberal.

'I am inclined to rate the "Gordon" as your highest achievement, because the construction of that seems to me the most ingenious and monumental of all,' Max Beerbohm later wrote to him (7 July 1920). 'I don't say the others don't equal it in the adjustment of their beginnings to their endings – or rather, in the lack of beginnings and endings, as such. The serpent swallows its own tail every time admirably. My reason for plunging for the "Gordon" is my admiration for that to-and-fro method of narration towards the end: Khartoum–Downing Street, Downing Street–Khartoum; by which device of the steady pendulum we get all the tragic irony of the whole matter.'   ·

From the aesthetic point of view, this wider, more flexible treatment was entirely appropriate to his subject, since it enabled Lytton fully to display the crazy illogicality of Gordon – 'that extraordinary mixture of incompatibilities – follies and sublimities', as he described it to Ottoline Morrell (20 May 1918). From a Bloomsbury point of view – the point of view of significant form – this lack of a single, unifying principle, lucidly spun out, was disappointing; and the reaction of the critics to this particular essay has been the most widely divergent of all. One B.B.C. critic, for instance, complained that Lytton had been too lenient with Gordon in failing to allude to the homosexual strain in his nature; while, more recently, Judge Gerald Sparrow censured Lytton because 'with remarkably little evidence . . . [he] advanced the view of Gordon as a homosexual'. There is, in fact, only one specific reference to homosexuality in the essay, and that relates not to Gordon, but to Rimbaud in Africa having 'forgotten the agonised embraces of Verlaine'. Yet undoubtedly Lytton did feel for Gordon a certain amused affection. Attracted, in any case, to split personalities, he was charmed and fascinated in a unique way by his subject's extravagant personality, and drawn to probe deeper into his character. The prose itself is closer in tone to that of 'Dr. Arnold' in that it relies less on rather suspect scenic devices than on the compelling power of lucid and compressed exposition. 'The writing I thought more than usually unadorned,' Virginia Woolf commented (28 December 1917), 'and surely the most flawless example of the master's style in its maturity.' Though unadorned, the strain is of a higher mood. The tragic but exhilarating inevitability of Gordon's fate is cleverly built up to its final crescendo against an undertone of half-amused, almost filial tenderness, which leaves the impression that, unlike his Victorian counterparts, Gordon was a man more sinned against than sinning.

But even if Lytton felt no persistent enmity for him, the hero of Khartoum, with his boundless energies so misdirected by irrational religious beliefs, fitted perfectly into the scheme of *Eminent Victorians*. Behind the gentle soldier of God, he sought to reveal a half-inspired, half-crazy Englishman, with his romance and his fatalism, his brandy-bottle and his Bible. This was certainly a valid aim, but in places he again falls to the temptation of over-emphasis, and by his tamperings and deletions of evidence focuses a rather unnatural attention on the general's eccentricities at the expense of his saner, more balanced sensitivity. The portrait of Gordon which he wished to project is described in his essay on Li Hung-Chang as an 'irresponsible knight-errant whom his countrymen first laughed at and neglected, then killed and canonised – a figure straying through the perplexed industrialism of the nineteenth century like some lost "natural" from an earlier Age'. In so far as his interest in Gordon's character prevails over his itch to shock latter-day Victorian susceptibilities, Lytton's criticism is mainly percipient, poetic and ingeniously balanced. He succeeds in shadowing him forth as a nineteenth-century Don Quixote, a bemused and deluded crusader, simultaneously comic and heroic, as seen through the half-incredulous, half-admiring eyes of a cautious, common-sense Sancho Panza.

Though Lytton's attitude to Gordon may be said to have been divided, it did not lead to the type of dislocation that had marred his study of Florence Nightingale. The contradictions in his character are neatly blended into his mad quixotism and further the artistic ends of the essay. He saw Gordon as a light, gliding figure, with candid open blue eyes, by temperament unassuming, *farouche*, and like himself a misogynist, ill at ease in conventional society – 'his soul revolted against dinner-parties and stiff shirts; and the presence of ladies – especially of fashionable ladies – filled him with uneasiness'. But he significantly edits the entries in Gordon's *Journals* so as to paint him as a wild man, contemptuous not just of sophisticated parties but of all civilization. Somewhat like himself, too, Gordon was gifted with an

impish talent for satirical fancies and a fondness for romantic speculation. By nature he was not really a power-seeker but an adventurer, in
whom, however, the germ of extreme religiosity, spreading like an
incurable disease, had stilled the workings of his conscience. Under this
illness, his ambitions were inflated to fanatical proportions, so that he
interpreted his actions as being ordained by an inscrutable but absolute
Providence. The essential honesty and nobility of his spirit was thus
fatally contaminated by a transcendental selfishness, more insidious
than any ordinary desire for wealth or titles, since it was largely
irrational. As 'a man of energy and action, a lover of danger and the
audacities that defeat danger, a passionate creature, flowing over with
the self-assertiveness of independent judgment and the arbitrary
temper of command', Gordon appealed immensely to Lytton's romantic
imagination. But once those religious tendencies within him developed
into a fixed and dominating factor in his life, once he became a willing
instrument not of God but of the extreme imperialist section of the
British Government, once he began to indulge his secret passion for
fame, 'for the swaying of multitudes, and for that kind of enlarged and
intensified existence "where breath breathes most – even in the mouths
of men"', then his sense of humanity and truth were perverted no less
surely than those of Manning, Florence Nightingale or Dr Arnold, and
he saw himself, through the eyes of pride and hypocrisy, transfigured
as a god on earth.

The initial signs of this disintegration – Gordon's impulsiveness,
incoherence, and whirl of contradictory policies – exerted a spell over
Lytton's mind like some larger-than-life figure from the pages of
Dostoievsky. Just as he had placed himself in Manning's congregation,
had looked up at Florence Nightingale from the sick-beds at Scutari,
had described Arnold's headmastership from the viewpoint of one of
his pupils, so he presented an impressionistic sketch of Gordon as
witnessed from the ranks. The reverence that the soldiers felt for him is
echoed in Lytton's description: 'Walking at the head of his troops, with
nothing but a light cane in his hand, he seemed to pass through every
danger with the scatheless equanimity of a demi-God.'

But once his peculiar malady had taken a firmer hold upon him,
Lytton notes, the relationship between the general and his troops
underwent a grim change. A prey to violent outbursts of temper, broken
by periods of conscience-stricken generosity, he treated his subordinates
at Khartoum with stern contempt, while they regarded him, no longer
with admiration, but abject fear.

'Gordon's fatalism swells from his personal belief into the outer
circumstances of his life,' commented J. K. Johnstone, 'and into the

Ham Spray House

Francis Birrell, Lytton Strachey and Saxon Sydney-Turner

Stephen Tomlin and his wife Julia
(*née* Strachey)

David Garnett

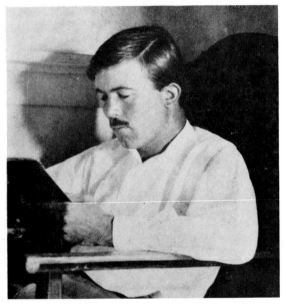

Gerald Brenan

Mark Gertler

very structure of the biography. In the first great adventure of his career, he leads an army against another religious fanatic, the Chinese Tien Wang, the Celestial King. Both Gordon and Tien Wang, Strachey tells us, turned to religion after experiencing an attack of illness – so Strachey points the similarity between them.'

At Khartoum, Gordon's last adventure, he again confronts a religious fanatic, the cruel Mohammedan divine, the Mahdi. Waiting for his strangely predestined end, he watches each day the splendid hawks that swooped and wheeled about the besieged palace. 'I often wonder', he reflected, 'whether they are destined to pick my eyes, for I fear I was not the best of sons.' This thought was prophetic, and fitted perfectly into the scheme of the essay, since Lytton represents Gordon's eyes as symbolizing all that is best and most innocent in his character, not fatally obscured by the cataract of atavistic superstition. After his death, Lytton recounts, Gordon's head was brought to the Mahdi as a trophy, and 'at last the two fanatics had indeed met face to face. The Mahdi ordered the head to be fixed between the branches of a tree in the public highway, and all who passed threw stones at it. The hawks of the desert swept and circled about it – those very hawks which the blue eyes had so often watched.'

Despite the sympathy which makes it the best of these four essays, 'The End of General Gordon' raised some of the loudest clamour against the author of *Eminent Victorians*. What right had a sickly scribbler to criticize the hero of Khartoum? people indignantly asked – this Strachey, this pacifist, who had never himself experienced the thirst and heat of the tropics or even been out under the pale English sun without a parasol? Whether his portraits of a prelate, a nurse and a schoolmaster had been worth painting, it was said, was an arguable question. Possibly they were. All were highly estimable professions, no doubt, but nevertheless a little dull – not the sort of thing to fire the ordinary man's imagination. But there could be absolutely no justification for discrediting a gallant British general. Soldiering, unlike religion and education, was no laughing matter: Strachey had gone too far.

The biography does contain several inaccuracies. In addition to his tampering with Gordon's *Journals*, Lytton makes no mention of a vital telegram from Sir Evelyn Baring which crossed with a telegram from the Government. He gives the somewhat erroneous impression that Gordon was produced from obscurity overnight by a sinisterly exploited journalistic stunt conducted by W. T. Stead. And he repeats a mistake originally made in a magazine article by G. W. Smalley, who confused two communications sent by Gordon – one in the spring, the

L

other in the autumn of 1885 – the latter, not the former, being the one
that Gladstone read in the *Dundee Advertiser*.

It was not however any of these lapses that stimulated the public
outcry against Lytton, but another mighty matter. People were outraged that, as Lord Elton wrote, 'a frail scholar in intellectual revolt
against his social and moral environment during the fourth year of a
war of which he bitterly disapproved ... contrived, in a characteristically
feline and unfounded innuendo, to convey the suggestion that Gordon
was a drunkard'. Critical opinion through the years has differed widely
over this controversial question. Some – among them Professor
Bonamy Dobrée – have maintained that Lytton's Gordon was never
intended to be a drunkard, but that like most men in hot climates he
sometimes resorted to brandy and soda as a necessary stimulant. Others,
including H. W. Nevinson, loudly asserted that Lytton had charged
Gordon 'with the drunken habit of continually tippling brandy and
soda'. And Alan Moorhead, who, with cautious reservations, was to
liken Gordon to the teetotal and married Field-Marshal Lord Mont-
gomery, saw in Lytton's version a 'pious toper . . . still brave, still
quixotically generous and kind, still an erratic sort of saint, but definitely
a little mad'.

There are only two main passages in which Lytton alludes to
Gordon's drinking habits. 'But the Holy Bible was not his only solace,'
he wrote in the first and most important of these. 'For now, under the
parching African sun, we catch glimpses, for the first time, of Gordon's
hand stretching out towards stimulants of a more material quality.
For months together, we are told, he would drink nothing but pure
water; and then ... water that was not so pure. In his fits of melancholy,
he would shut himself up in his tent for days at a time, with a hatchet
and a flag placed at the door to indicate that he was not to be disturbed
for any reason whatever; until at last the cloud would lift, the signals
would be removed, and the Governor would reappear, brisk and cheerful. During one of these retirements, there was a grave danger of a
native attack upon the camp. Colonel Long, the chief of staff, ventured,
after some hesitation, to ignore the flag and hatchet, and to enter the
forbidden tent. He found Gordon seated at a table, upon which were an
open Bible and an open bottle of brandy. Long explained the circumstances, but could obtain no answer beyond the abrupt words –
"You are commander of the camp" – and was obliged to retire, nonplussed, to deal with the situation as best he could. On the following
morning Gordon, cleanly shaven, and in the full-dress uniform of the
Royal Engineers, entered Long's hut with his usual tripping step,
exclaiming– "Old fellow, now don't be angry with me. I was very low

last night. Let's have a good breakfast – a little b. and s. Do you feel up to it?" And, with these veering moods and dangerous restoratives, there came an intensification of the queer and violent elements in the temper of the man.'

The second offending passage describes W. T. Stead's interview with Gordon at Southampton. 'Now when he was in the mood – after a little b. and s., especially – no one was more capable than Gordon, with his facile speech and his free-and-easy manners, of furnishing good copy for a journalist; and Mr. Stead made the most of his opportunity.'

Because it is endemic of the adverse criticism frequently levelled against Lytton's biographical writing as a whole, it is worth assembling the most stringent evidence that has been brought to refute Lytton's conjecture, and deciding what it is worth. To dispose of the second insinuation first: Miss Stead, who was present at Southampton, has contradicted outright Lytton's assertion that brandy and soda was drunk during Gordon's interview for the *Pall Mall Gazette*, by an explicit statement pointing out that no refreshments were served or consumed, and that her father never drank wine or spirits. But does that statement really invalidate Lytton's paragraph? It is unlikely that Lytton actually pictured to himself the Stead family in alcoholic conviviality with Gordon; or, alternatively, that he imagined them to be silent and scandalized spectators to Gordon's immoderate drinking. The whole point of his interpretation of Gordon's character is that he was describing a *secret* drinker. Nor did he insist that Gordon *always* drank to excess. The crucial words in this passage are '– *after* a *little* b. and s., especially –'. The implication is that Gordon, all too well aware of Stead's notorious teetotalism, may have taken anticipatory measures to offset the unrelieved dryness of their interview, the effects of which Stead, with his stoutly maintained ignorance of alcohol (inherited by his daughter), failed to detect. Of course there is no documentary material to support this supposition. Lytton did not proclaim it as an absolute authenticated fact, but, knowing Gordon's habits and judging from the fluency of his performance, he thought it possible that his tongue had been loosened by a little drink. That was all.

The first paragraph, in which Lytton depicts Gordon giving way to long drinking bouts under the influence of the African climate, being skilfully sewn together from several suspect and contradictory accounts, has been more difficult for Lytton's detractors to call in question. But by elaborate investigation, Dr Bernard Allen has shown, to his own satisfaction, that Lytton's reconstruction is totally false, an amalgam founded on demonstrably inaccurate or unreliable statements made by Sir Richard Burton and Colonel Chaillé-Long.

The germ of this drinking story had come from Sir Richard Burton, who could not have seen Gordon more than twice during his life, and who in all probability met him only once. After Gordon's death, he wrote in the columns of the *Academy* a review of the Khartoum Journals, in the course of which he gave instances of Gordon's peculiar changes of mind in matters of policy which he liked to ascribe to Divine guidance. 'And so in minor matters; for months he would drink nothing but water, and then prefer, very decidedly, water with whisky.' According to Dr Bernard Allen, it is clear that Burton's intention in this sentence was to comment merely on a trivial point, and not to bring a charge of intemperance in what, after all, was virtually an obituary notice. And to strengthen his argument, Dr Allen points to the inconsistency between water and whisky and brandy and soda. He also reports an interview he had with Hasan Ali, Gordon's servant, who was alive in 1931, and who bore obedient witness to Gordon's abstemiousness.

Lytton then, in Dr Allen's view, seized and dextrously twisted this extract from Burton to match it with two conflicting passages from two separate volumes of memoirs by Chaillé-Long. Blandly ignoring the considerable body of data which verified Gordon's sobriety, Lytton preferred the unconvincing picture given in these two books, though he must have known that Colonel Long did not scruple to bend facts to suit his own purpose. For Long cherished some outstanding grievances against Gordon, who had never thought highly of him, and who had been responsible for his humiliating withdrawal from Equatoria in 1875. Six years later, his sense of grievance had been further inflamed by the publication of Dr Birkbeck Hill's selection from Gordon's correspondence, which contained a number of uncomplimentary references to himself. By 1884, when Gordon was safely sealed off in Khartoum, he was ready to settle old scores. In a lecture delivered in Paris, he sarcastically described Gordon as a humbug who, to further his own ends, had resorted to bribery. This same year, his first book of memoirs, *The Three Prophets*, was published. The purpose of this book, which coincided well with Lytton's own theme, was to show that the religious fanaticism of Arabi Pasha, the Mahdi, and Gordon, had made them the tools of an unscrupulous, imperialistic Government in Britain. Lytton, who does not include this book in his bibliography, nevertheless found one extract of some value: 'In the short intervals of my stay in camp, going or returning from expeditions,' Long recorded, 'I had occasion to remark the singular habit which Gordon had of retiring to his hut, where he would remain, for days at a time, engaged in the perusal of his ever-present Bible and Prayer Book. When, in his retirement, his orders were that he should not be disturbed for any reason of service whatever; a hatchet and a flag were placed at his door as a sign that he was unapproachable.'

More than a quarter of a century later, in 1912, Long issued another volume of memoirs, *My Life in Four Continents*, which purported to give his travels and experiences in various parts of the world. Now in his seventies and, according to Dr Allen, still consumed by a spiteful hatred of Gordon, whose posthumous fame he took as an insult to himself, the old man decided to add fresh details to his original tale of prolonged ascetic seclusions with Bible and Prayer Book, converting them into bibulous orgies carried on under the mask of piety.

'A few days after my return to Lado,' he wrote, 'the camp was attacked in force one night. I had great difficulty in repelling the savage hordes, who, with lighted torches, were endeavouring to turn us out. Gordon was in his hut and gave no sign of coming out. It was during one of the oft-recurring periods when he shut himself up and placed a hatchet and a flag at the door as a sign that he was not to be disturbed, a seclusion which lasted from three to five days. I sent an officer to warn him of our danger but receiving no reply went myself. I entered abruptly and found him seated, very calmly at a table, on which were an open Bible and a bottle of cognac and sherry. I told him of the situation, to which he made abrupt answer "You are commander of the camp". Whereupon I hastily turned and left him, but not before I had posted an officer with a half-dozen men specially charged with Gordon's safety. The savages were finally driven away by a vigorous sortie. The next day Gordon entered my tent in the full-dress uniform of the Royal Engineers, and cleanly shaven. He came forward with a quick tripping step as was his habit, and said "Old fellow, now don't be angry with me. I was very low last night. Come and dine with me. We will have a glorious dinner.'

Sherry!

The earlier (1884) version of this episode had been followed by an invitation to a brandy and soda breakfast, not to an evening meal at all. But that was a minor discrepancy against the fact that no other contemporary or retrospective account of this time mentions a night attack by savages. There can be little doubt that Colonel Long was an erratic and unreliable witness, the factual mistakes being endorsed by his vain and phoney style of writing. But what about Dr Allen's own case for Gordon's sturdy temperance? All one can say is that the evidence of a faithful servant interrogated by an admirer of Gordon's, the mention of drinking even in a well-disposed, virtual obituary notice, and the minor inconsistencies which attest only to the tolerance of Gordon's alcoholic tastes, hardly provide very solid grounds for establishing him as a total abstainer.

The trouble, of course, is that secret drinking is not the sort of habit to be abundantly chronicled in academic sources, nor reliably substantiated by first-hand, unprejudiced witnesses. It was, however, even in fairly recent years a well-known rumour in the desert that on occasions Gordon drank immoderately. Moreover, testimonies which have subsequently come to light have tended to support Lytton rather than Dr Allen. For example, Lord Carnock is on record as having told his son, Harold Nicolson, that Gordon was definitely a drinker. And there is one especially relevant and vivid piece of evidence contained in a letter written many years later by Joseph Reinach (formerly Gambetta's secretary). This document was discovered among the Dilke papers, and has been quoted by Roy Jenkins in his *Sir Charles Dilke*:

'J'ai beaucoup connu Gordon,' Reinach wrote. 'J'ai fait sa connaissance en Janvier 1880 sur un bateau qui faisait le service entre Alexandrie et Naples. Nous passâmes plusieurs journées à Naples. Il me mena chez Ismail. Je le menai un soir au théâtre à San-Carlo. Il n'était pas allé au théâtre depuis vingt ans. On donnait un ballet Sardanapale, avec beaucoup de petites femmes à demi-nues. Il se scandalisa. "And you call that civilization!" me dit-il et il rentra à l'hôtel. Je l'y trouvais vers une heure du matin en déshabille, lisant la Bible et ayant vidé une demi bouteille de whisky. Il buvait terriblement de brandy. Plus tard, à Paris, il venait souvent me voir le matin. Et, au bout de cinq minutes, il demandait du *cognac*.[1]

'C'était un héros, à très courte vue comme beaucoup d'héros, un mystique qui se payait de phrases, et aussi, comment dirai-je? Un peu "un fumiste". Vous avez ce que nous appelons ainsi. Il s'amusait à étonner les gens. Il ne croyait pas tout ce qu'il disait. Dans les lettres de lui que j'ai conservées, il traitait volontiers Dizzie et ses amis de *Mountebanks*. Il était, lui-même, *Mountebank*. . . .'

On the balance of available evidence, it would seem that Gordon probably did drink. Lytton never suggested that he became a soak, a regular and fairly steady drinker. On such a scale and with such frequency, alcohol would soon have impaired his practical efficiency – and of this there was no real sign. Far more likely, since it fits in with what few facts we know and is in keeping with his neurotic temperament, was that Gordon drank to great excess occasionally, that he was a dipsomaniac, a nervous or manic-depressive drinker, who inter-

[1] Emphasis added.

spersed quick fits of potation with days and weeks of absolute abstemiousness.

Probably nothing like the volume of critical attention that has been aroused by this episode would have been forthcoming at all had there not been throughout England in 1918 a subconscious resentment against men like Gordon, prototypes, it was felt, of those who had been largely responsible for the Great War. The charge of drunkenness was confidently exaggerated and repeated, and Gordon was described as a dipsomaniac in magazine articles and in books. 'It was almost too good to be true,' wrote Esmé Wingfield-Stratford, 'that all and sundry should be conducted to Gordon's tent, that the flap should be stealthily drawn aside, and the Christian hero revealed, like Noah, blind to the world.'

In immediate reaction to the delighted publicity provoked by this most polemical item in Lytton's biography, various indignant denials were published in the Press by men who had known Gordon while in the desert. But this merely added to the general enjoyment. For who now could seriously listen to men with names like Chippendale, or Watson, or Rudolf Slatin Pasha – minor eminent Victorians themselves?

For the public, either Gordon must be an out-and-out, twenty-four-hour-a-day drunkard, or else Lytton was an irresponsible liar and a cheat; and they much preferred the former. In later years the pendulum of disbelief has swung too far in the opposite direction,[1] and even now, though more balanced and reasonable critical opinions are being aired, the bias is still set too far against Lytton. Professor Hugh Trevor-Roper, for instance, has written that this account of Gordon in the Sudan 'retiring into his tent "for days at a time" for secret communion with the Bible and the bottle is the richest flourish in his brilliant picture of that strange, unpredictable, complicated character. . . . The real object had not been the brandy-bottle but a prayer-book. Unfortunately, "brandy-bottle" is funnier than "prayer-book"; Strachey could not resist the final touch of absurdity; and his brilliant portrait of a crackpot crusader is, by that one dangerous detail, overdone.' But this criticism is inaccurate, and misses the point. Lytton did not invent the brandy-bottle. Trevor-Roper may have read *The Three Prophets* but must have overlooked *My Life in Four Continents* in which the open Bible and the bottle of cognac are placed on the same table. Lytton repeated the word "open" to increase the amusement, but he

---

[1] Anthony Nutting, Gordon's latest biographer (1966), who believes that Gordon's career was shaped by a death-wish possibly arising from the knowledge of his homosexuality, dismisses Lytton Strachey's 'charges of drunkenness' as a complete fabrication, though without examining all the evidence.

did not couple the brandy-bottle with the Bible simply because it was a funny combination of words and ideas. He believed that Gordon's addiction to religiosity and to alcohol sprang from the same epileptic source. In this way he could bring out Gordon's intoxicated, muddled, transcendentalist thinking which, allied to his thirst for fame, led inevitably to his self-destruction. As an interpretation of character, it is very similar in outline to Richard Burton's sketch, and is partly endorsed by Gordon himself, who in a lucid interval at Khartoum wrote: 'Either I must believe He does all things in mercy and love, or else I disbelieve His existence, there is no half way in the matter. What holes do I not put myself into! ... I believe ambition put me here in this ruin.'

'The End of General Gordon' is particularly rich in minor figures. 'One catches a vision of strange characters,' Lytton wrote, 'moved by mysterious impulses, interacting in queer complication, and hurrying at last – so it almost seems – like creatures in a puppet show to a pre-destined catastrophe. The characters, too, have a charm of their own: they are curiously English. What other nation on the face of the earth could have produced Mr. Gladstone and Sir Evelyn Baring and Lord Hartington and General Gordon?'

Gladstone, Sir Evelyn Baring and Lord Hartington, as they make their appearances in this essay, testify to Lytton's marvellous skill as a vocal and impressionistic writer. Of the three, Lord Hartington possesses by far the simplest and most straightforward nature, and Lytton's description of his solid, silent personality, seemingly proof against all quickening enthusiasms, and the ponderous and comic workings of his conscience which contributed so tantalizingly to Gordon's tragedy, is masterly – full of wit and imaginative humour, parodying, in its vocabulary and construction, Hartington's own voice and mannerisms. It is also a most affectionate likeness of Hartington, who occupies a role in the essay similar to that of Wiseman in 'Cardinal Manning' and Panmure in 'Florence Nightingale':

'Lord Hartington's conscience was of a piece with the rest of him ... it was a commonplace affair. Lord Hartington himself would have been disgusted by any mention of it. If he had been obliged, he would have alluded to it distantly; he would have muttered that it was a bore not to do the proper thing. He was usually bored – for one reason or another; but this particular form of boredom he found more intense than all the rest. He would take endless pains to avoid it. Of course, the whole thing was a nuisance – an obvious nuisance; and every one else must feel just as he did about it. And yet people seemed to have got it into their heads that he had some kind of special faculty in such matters –

that there was some peculiar value in his judgment on a question of right and wrong. He could not understand why it was; but whenever there was a dispute about cards in a club, it was brought to *him* to settle. It was most odd. But it was true. In public affairs, no less than in private, Lord Hartington's decisions carried an extraordinary weight. The feeling of his idle friends in high society was shared by the great mass of the English people; here was a man they could trust. For indeed he was built upon a pattern which was very dear to his countrymen. It was not simply that he was honest: it was that his honesty was an English honesty – an honesty which naturally belonged to one who, so it seemed to them, was the living image of what an Englishman should be. In Lord Hartington they saw, embodied and glorified, the very qualities which were nearest to their hearts – impartiality, solidity, common sense – the qualities by which they themselves longed to be distinguished, and by which, in their happier moments, they believed they were. If ever they began to have misgivings, there, at any rate, was the example of Lord Hartington to encourage them and guide them – Lord Hartington, who was never self-seeking, who was never excited, and who had no imagination at all. Everything they knew about him fitted into the picture, adding to their admiration and respect. His fondness for field sports gave them a feeling of security; and certainly there could be no nonsense about a man who confessed to two ambitions – to become Prime Minister and to win the Derby – and who put the second above the first. They loved him for his casualness – for his inexactness – for refusing to make life a cut-and-dried business – for ramming an official despatch of high importance into his coat-pocket, and finding it there, still unopened, at Newmarket, several days later. They loved him for his hatred of fine sentiments; they were delighted when they heard that at some function, on a florid speaker's avowing that "this was the proudest moment of his life", Lord Hartington had growled in an undertone "the proudest moment of *my* life, was when my pig won the prize at Skipton fair". Above all, they loved him for being dull. It was the greatest comfort – with Lord Hartington they could always be absolutely certain that he would never, in any circumstances, be either brilliant, or subtle, or surprising, or impassioned, or profound. As they sat, listening to his speeches, in which considerations of stolid plainness succeeded one another with complete flatness, they felt, involved and supported by the colossal tedium, that their confidence was finally assured. They looked up, and took their fill of the sturdy obvious presence. The inheritor of a splendid dukedom might almost have passed for a farm hand. Almost, but not quite. For an air, that was difficult to explain, of preponderating authority lurked in the solid

L*

figure; and the lordly breeding of the House of Cavendish was visible
in the large, long, bearded, unimpressionable face.

'One other characteristic – the necessary consequence, or indeed, it
might almost be said, the essential expression, of all the rest – completes
the portrait: Lord Hartington was slow. He was slow in movement,
slow in apprehension, slow in thought and the communication of
thought, slow to decide, and slow to act.'

Lord Hartington had left on his contemporaries a single, easily
recognizable impression. Gladstone, on the other hand, was a complex
and controversial personality, who impressed some as being the perfect
model of an upright man, and others as an utterly detestable humbug.
To employ the same sort of technique that he had used so successfully
on Lord Hartington was therefore impossible, and Lytton switched
apparently to a more analytical method. 'What, then,' he asks after
elaborately setting forth the contradictory passions of the man, 'was
the truth?' But that was not the question which he sought to answer.
His portrait of Gladstone is one of the finest passages in all his work;
but for all its lively imagery, its vividness and subtlety, its display of
controlled verbal pyrotechnics, it does nothing to reconcile the conflicting elements in Gladstone's character. Its purpose was to glorify
these splendid ambiguities, to heighten the enigma with those choice
rhetorical questions that indicate nothing so eloquently as his own
uncertainty of mind. But he does more than this. Lytton did not intend
to worry through to some analytical formula of truth; he did not wish
to 'explain', but to 'illustrate'. And so, in this passage, we are meant to
overhear Gladstone's own loquaciousness, 'the long, winding, intricate sentences, with their vast burden of subtle and complicated qualifications', which 'befogged the mind like clouds, and like clouds, too,
dropped thunderbolts'.

'What, then, was the truth? In the physical universe there are no
chimeras. But man is more various than nature; was Mr. Gladstone,
perhaps, a chimera of the spirit? Did his very essence lie in the confusion of incompatibles? His very essence? It eludes the hand that
seems to grasp it. One is baffled, as his political opponents were baffled
fifty years ago. The soft serpent coils harden into quick strength that
has vanished, leaving only emptiness and perplexity behind. . . . Could
it not then at least be said of him with certainty that his was a complex
character? But here also there was a contradiction. . . . His very egoism
was simple-minded: through all the labyrinth of his passions there ran
a single thread. But the centre of the labyrinth? Ah! the thread might
lead there, through those wandering mazes, at last. Only, with the last
corner turned, the last step taken, the explorer might find that he was

looking down into the gulf of a crater. The flame shot out on every side, scorching and brilliant; but in the midst there was a darkness.'

According to Professor Bonamy Dobrée, Lytton made no attempt to understand Gladstone and even ceased to think about him while putting together this intricate literary mosaic. 'The complicated rhythm, the bringing of the stress upon the right word, the modulated verbal sounds accumulating upon a finality of statement', all this virtuoso construction, Professor Dobrée explained, transforms the description into a poem. This is a not uncommon misconception of poetry, which fails to make that vital distinction between the mellifluous fluting of high sentiment, that pattern of elegant variations of word-play which describes or mimics something, and the lyrical compression which suggests far more than it actually states or defines, and in the lingering echoes of which there resides the seed of an emotional and timeless truth. As presented by Dobrée, Lytton's miniature conceals no such echoes. It is full of clever linguistic expertise, but has no living comprehension. Yet Dobrée's intended praise, in failing to catch Gladstone's voice in this passage, to overhear that complicated speech that formed the very fibre of his being, to draw the parallel between his brilliance and Lytton's vividness, his darkness and Lytton's emptiness and perplexity, unwittingly does less than justice to the writing. For Lytton did not forget Gladstone as a human being, but tried to show him as a man who, in the confusion of his conscience and his policy, was a kind of moral opportunist, not a humbug but a man greatly self-deceived.

By stressing Gladstone's equivocality and setting it in contrast to the fumbling slowness of Lord Hartington, Lytton made fast one knot in the tightrope stretching between the religious fanaticism of the Mahdi and the involved and deliberate passivity of the British Government – that tightrope on which Gordon found himself perilously stranded at Khartoum. Then he jerked the knot still tighter by twisting round Gladstone's baffling ambiguity and Lord Hartington's ponderous honesty, the bland irreproachability of Sir Evelyn Baring, a cool diplomat, 'cautious, measured, unimpeachably correct'.

The pages of *Eminent Victorians* certainly contain a few distortions of character – those worked on Newman and, to a much smaller extent, on Dr Sutherland, have already been noted. But there are others. Clough was dispossessed of what sense of humour he owned, together with his poetic sensibility, and shown as a ludicrous, post-office puppet. Lord Acton, who makes a brief appearance in 'Cardinal Manning', emerges, not as a miniaturist almost as acute as Lytton himself, but, as John Raymond puts it, 'ineffectual, meddling, opinionated, blinkered with scholarship, a huge purblind mammoth of erudition turning his great head this way and that in a pathetic attempt to snuff out priesthood and persecution'. Some have complained that Lord Granville was made too much of a nonentity;[1] others have observed that Julius Charles Hare was not the fanatical Low Churchman of Lytton's fancy, but a scholarly Broad Church latitudinarian. The occasional references, also, to Lord Wolseley are rather misleading, conveying a barely discernible figure of pygmy proportions, hurrying pointlessly hither and thither. And Odo Russell – 'poor Mr. Russell' – is portrayed as a political cipher, a fly buzzing ineffectually in Manning's spider's web of clinging diplomacy, whereas Russell's dispatches from Rome (published in 1962) reveal that he was playing a double game, and that Lytton's picture – reminiscent of Gregorovius's sketch of Manning at the time of the Council – totally discounts the power and perspicacity underlying the diplomat's suave manner.

But the most serious and controversial charge of misrepresenting a minor character concerns the portrait of Sir Evelyn Baring. 'You are hard on Cromer, and not quite convincing,' Walter Raleigh observed, and several other critics have agreed with him. In their opinion, Lytton had ignored the fact that Baring was a poor boy, was given a poor education and grew up almost completely self-made, and had cast him as a typically reserved public-school man, a character for which he felt there was a dramatic need in the essay. He wanted someone in the role of the odious, well-bred public official, whose inherent inability to understand the unorthodox Gordon would give added point to this humorous tragedy. Baring, to judge from his literary style, fitted this part pretty well, but to reinforce his characterization, Lytton seldom scrupled to ascribe to him the most damaging of motives. For example, after a fanciful description of his state of mind during his discussions over the necessity for an expedition to rescue Gordon, Lytton adds: 'From the end of April till the beginning of September – during the most momentous period of the whole crisis – he was engaged in London upon a financial conference, while his place was taken in Cairo by a substitute. With a characteristically convenient unobtrusiveness, Sir Evelyn Baring had vanished from the scene.' Lytton nowhere lets on

[1] In a letter to Maurice Baring, Lytton explained: 'I did not intend to convey that Lord Granville was a nonentity altogether – only that he was one as a Foreign Minister, and particularly with reference to our policy in Egypt. This I believe was so – though of course it is very difficult to disentangle the obscure complications of that Cabinet. Surely it is hardly correct to say that "Mr G. did not care a button about foreign affairs". My reading of the situation is that the two real forces in the Cabinet were Mr G. and Lord Hartington, pulling in opposite directions, and that Lord Granville, as you say, "vacillated" between them and was in effect alternately the tool of one and the other. That is why I described him as a nonentity.'

that in London Baring was far better placed than in Cairo to urge the need for preparing for an expedition. His summary condemnation of Baring on this matter draws attention to the absence in his bibliography of Bernard Holland's Life of Spencer Compton, eighth Duke of Devonshire, a book which showed clearly that Baring did agitate for an expedition, while Chamberlain was one of its opponents. This omission is all the more remarkable since Lytton owned this two-volume biography, and had marked several passages in it.[1] Similarly, none of Lytton's readers could have guessed that Baring in fact strongly backed Gordon's selection of Zobier as his successor in the Sudan, and that this recommendation was only upset by a majority of one at a scratch Cabinet meeting.

The controversial question of Baring's character was hotly disputed in the correspondence columns of *The Times Literary Supplement* shortly after the publication of *Eminent Victorians*. Lytton's old adversary, Sir Edmund Gosse, protested that this ill-natured caricature was hardly to be recognized as the man he had subsequently known as Lord Cromer. Far from being a colourless personality, cold and un-concerned, Baring was a copious talker, his conversation being generally stimulating and often delectable. 'It combined', wrote Gosse, 'warmth of feeling with vivacity of expression. Lord Cromer was accessible and responsive. He was a sober, but essentially an ardent patriot.'

Gosse also expressed himself as particularly anxious to check, before it was crystallized into accepted history, Lytton's calumnious statement that the East meant very little to Baring and that he took no interest in it. 'There was', he indignantly objected, 'nothing in which he took so much interest. It was seldom out of his mind; it furnished four-fifths of his conversation, in the course of which he never wearied of dwelling on minute points of difference between the Eastern and Western temperament. The most important of his later writings, his "Political and Literary Essays", is full of evidence of this preoccupation. "The Government of Subject Races", written in 1907, shows how deeply he meditated upon the problems of India. He knew India from 1872 to 1876, and again from 1880 to 1883; until the close of his life he was examining with peculiar care the intimate relation between religion and politics throughout Asia, and he watched with anxiety the high ex-plosives it produced. "Took no interest in the East" – prodigious.'

In a prompt reply, Lytton defended his portrait of Baring down to the

---

[1] Lytton, in fact, met Bernard Holland, who on 13 June 1918 wrote to him: 'I had not the opportunity last night of telling you that I had read your E.Vs. with much pleasure and admiration. I liked best the Gordon. I suspect that you found my life of the D. of D. useful for that because it is the best documented record of those curious episodes.'

last detail.[1] His letter, by its contrast, shows up Gosse's rather flatulent judgement, but indicates, too, his own immature romanticism over the mystique of the East – the sort of naïve attitude he was to ridicule in his essay 'A Diplomat: Li Hung-Chang'. It was hardly surprising, he pointed out, that the impression produced by Lord Cromer on Edmund Gosse in the private intercourse of friendship, and that produced on himself 'by a detached examination of Lord Cromer's published writings and public acts should be different'. In Lytton's opinion, since it was not always a man's friends who knew him best, the test Gosse applied to Cromer's character was superficial. His responsiveness and accessibility in the drawing-room in no way proved that his mind was 'not essentially secretive, cautious and diplomatic'. Garrulity on Eastern topics and how the Eastern temperament differed from the Western was not an unusual phenomenon among such men. 'We have all of us met gentlemen who "never weary" of drawing such comparisons,' he concluded, 'but their interest in the East remains problematical. To have denied that Lord Cromer took an interest in Eastern administrative questions – as Mr. Gosse seemed to suggest I did – would of course have been grotesque. But Eastern administrative questions are not the East. The signs of a true interest in the East – an interest resembling

---

[1] In a reply to Maurice Baring, who, besides objecting to this portrait of Lord Cromer in the columns of the *Spectator*, had sent a personal letter to Lytton, he wrote: 'My view of Lord Cromer is entirely based on the published material; and I can only say that I have tried honestly to set down the very strong impression of a personality, which it made upon my mind. *Your* view is a private one; and it seems to me that it does not necessarily contradict mine. It makes the character more complex than I had supposed – and for this reason I am particularly grateful for your letter; it shows that in private life Lord Cromer was very far from an official or a diplomat; but I cannot see that it affects my estimate of him as a public man. You say "his main characteristic was an outspokenness and directness and bluntness of speech mounting sometimes to brutality". It is interesting to know that this was the impression he produced in private conversation; but to argue from this that he was outspoken in his official dealings is surely impossible. To take a single instance, anything less outspoken, direct and blunt than his telegrams to the Government on the question of Gordon's appointment it would be difficult to imagine. I don't think I anywhere say in my book that he had a diplomatic *training*: but, writing of him as a public character, I judged that his cast of mind was eminently diplomatic, and nothing that you say in your letter appears to me to make this judgement untenable. Perhaps I may add, in my own justification, that, since my book has come out, I have found that my view of Lord Cromer is shared by a public man of great authority and experience.

'My error as to his "keeping up" his classics I admit and regret. But I'm sorry to say that, in face of some of the chapters in *Modern Egypt* I still find it very difficult to believe that he took any true interest in the East. As to his wishing to become an "institution", at any rate you must allow that in fact he did become one. I can't understand what posts, which you say he refused, could possibly have made him "far more of an institution" than he actually was.

'... I should be very sorry indeed if anything in my book suggested that I underrated either Lord Cromer's immense ability, or the extraordinary value of his work in Egypt. But this I think, can hardly be the case.'

even remotely a Du Perron or a Burton – are easily discernible; and so are those of the kind of temperament constitutionally incapable of possessing it. Such a matter, no doubt, must ultimately be decided by a personal judgement; and I can only say that whenever Lord Cromer touches upon the East in his writings he produces on my mind the effect of some musical authority who has a good working knowledge of counterpoint and orchestration, but whose musical outfit is unluckily incomplete in one particular – a feeling for music.'

That Lytton, unlike Gosse, would not have liked Cromer had they met, seems certain. He did not come up with this hostile interpretation simply to complete the design of his essay – though he did add certain dubious flourishes for artistic effect. When, as early as April 1907, Maynard Keynes wrote to him, 'I have been reading Cromer's Egyptian report – he seems a very intelligent man,' Lytton had at once demurred. 'I'm surprised to hear that you think Baring a clever man,' he replied. 'Oh! perhaps clever; but d'you only mean that? I thought you might mean great.' Yet it is ironic to note that Cromer's report on the Nile expedition in every way corroborates Lytton's own handling of that event, and that his summary of the situation, in the opinion of Professor George Kuppler Simson, 'could very well be the thesis of the whole of *Eminent Victorians*'.[1]

7

FINALE

'As you know I think your Cromer is wrong. But I like it, all the same,' Walter Raleigh had written. '. . . Nothing can make your book un-delightful.' Since 1918, this delight has infected a vast audience of readers. The book challenged the highest biographical standards. In his Preface, Lytton had advocated detachment as an artistic attitude of mind; a closer scrutiny reveals that his detachment was part of a

---

[1] 'In a word,' Cromer had written, 'the Nile expedition was sanctioned too late, and the reason why it was sanctioned too late was that Mr Gladstone would not accept simple evidence of a plain fact, which was patent to much less powerful intellects than his own. Posterity has yet to decide on the services which Mr Gladstone, during his long and brilliant career, rendered in other directions to the British nation, but it is improbable that the verdict of his contemporaries in respect to his conduct of the affairs of the Soudan will ever be reversed. That verdict has been distinctly unfavourable. "Les fautes de l'homme puissant", said an eminent Frenchman [Senancour], "sont des malheurs publics". Mr Gladstone's error of judgement in delaying too long the despatch of the Nile expedition left a stain on the reputation of England which it will be beyond the power of either the impartial historian or the partial apologist to efface.'

literary mannerism, skilfully employed so as to bring into sharper relief his irony and power of denigration. The historian, he had written, 'will row out over that great ocean of material, and lower down into it, here and there, a little bucket, which will bring up to the light of day some characteristic specimen, from those far depths, to be examined with a careful curiosity'. *Eminent Victorians* is apparently the haul from just such a voyage of random sampling. Lytton rowed out over the deep uncharted waters of the Victorian age, let down his buckets and drew to the surface four major samples of odd fish – and a host of smaller fry. These he transported back to the mainland to put on show in his well-highlighted aquarium. And the large public which came to the exhibition saw that a colossal, undreamed-of change had come over the assembled representatives of marine life. Robbed of their dull, awful surroundings in the mysterious depths of the ocean, rendered harmless inside their protective tanks, and somehow unnaturally distended by the shallow water that encased them, the aristocratic shark, the gorgeous octopus, the ravenous pike no longer appeared the formidable creatures of sea-legend. With their comic grimaces, their futile perambulating to and fro, their crazy retinue of dabs and polyps and squids, they presented a circus-spectacle, half-amusing, half-grotesque. Only the good-natured, uncompetitive sole, content to lie modestly in the sand, could still be seen to any real advantage. Some of the public were delighted by this ingenuity, others outraged by what they took to be wanton cruelty. And then, inevitably, there hurried along the ichthyologists with all their critical apparatus, measuring, inspecting, checking, and finding that the glass sheets of which Lytton had made his tanks were not, as he had claimed, perfectly even and clear, but contained here a subtle convex flaw, there a concave dent, blemishes which, though invisible to the naked eye, produced magnified distortions on the specimens swimming innocently behind them.

Though the reputation of *Eminent Victorians* was damaged, it was not, and never can be, fundamentally impaired. For, with its interpretative dramatic technique, it was a genuine pioneer work which has forged itself a permanent place in literary history, as the chief influence – and one that was more often beneficial than is generally admitted – in the field of serious biography this century.

Nevertheless, although Lytton's influence as a biographer has matched that of Plutarch and Boswell, *Eminent Victorians* occupies a curiously anomalous position in modern literature. For all its penetrating individuality, it lacked a certain sweep, a richness, because, in Virginia Woolf's opinion, the age was not behind him. Lytton 'has had to open our eyes before he made us see; he has had to search out and

sew together a very artful manner of speech; and the effort, beautifully
though it is concealed, has robbed his work of some of the force that
should have gone into it, and limited his scope'. The book's most
radiant virtue was its completeness, and it is this impeccable quality
that has dismayed some critics who have come to see it as something of
an isolated and transitional work. Its perfection, its smooth burnished
façade, was an end in itself.[1] It went as far as it was possible to go in a
certain direction, then stopped dead. There were no offshoots capable
of scattering, in other directions, some living seeds of development.
'There is not a line in it that gives it away, that allows one to penetrate
into the workshops where it was made,' wrote Gerald Brenan in a
letter to Lytton (10 April 1921). 'Is it possible that it came into existence
without any of those fevers of hope and despair and aridity and self-
disgust that other authors have to put up with? . . .

'. . . Books, even very great ones, ought to show signs of human
imperfection. Even Shakespeare does this – almost all artists have
respected the fondness we have for unevenness; they have been inspired and then to compensate they have been flat; why should you
almost alone abuse this good human instinct and maintain your book at
a high and even level, occasionally rising a little, but never at all sinking? I prefer Joyce to you: he does not taunt me, but leads me on,
points to very far horizons, and shows me a way that leads there. He
promises new discoveries, new methods, new beauties – you don't
promise anything. You just are. A vision, clear, complete, and yet
unattainable.

'. . . We are going I think to have a new age in English literature;
E.V. will then be on the border-line between new and old.'

[1] In a letter to Stephen Hudson (8 May 1925) Edwin Muir wrote: 'In [Lytton] Strachey,
because there is no *Sturm und Drang*, because he dislikes *Sturm und Drang* too much
even to overcome it, as the artist must, there is no joy. And on this plane of judgement I
may as well agree with you that Virginia Woolf is not a figure of sufficient importance to
warrant a difference of opinion between us. She does not face the problem, and it may be
that when I write my final essay in this series [*Transition*] I may have to put her down
along with Strachey and [David] Garnett among the forces which are imposing a premature and hardening limitation on contemporary literature – fencing it off into a small
perfection which is a denial of further progress.' (Published in *Encounter*, January 1966.)

PART II

'Whenever I think of old age I turn pale with horror – the rain, the loneliness, the regret – oh dear, let's turn away one's thoughts.'

Lytton Strachey to Duncan Grant (5 March 1906)

CHAPTER I

A Life Apart

At that, I'd stop. But then, suppose
The gods, still smiling, said 'Our store
Of pleasant things still overflows,
Look round; be bold; and choose some more.'

Hum! I should pause; reflect; then 'Yes!'
Methinks I'd cry, 'I see, I see,
What would fill up my happiness.
Give me a girl to dwell with me!

A girl with genial beauty dowered,
And health, and vigorous liberty,
By supreme Nature's self empowered
To live in loneliness and glee,

And clothe her fancies with fair form,
And paint her thoughts with vivid hue,
A girl within whose heart, so warm,
Love ever lingers – oh, so true!'

Lytton Strachey (1 March 1920)

I

SUCCESS!

Like Byron, Lytton awoke one morning to find himself famous. *Eminent Victorians* marked an epoch in biographical literature, and its immediate impact was tremendous. To the jaded palate of the younger generation, the merits of the book – its brevity, coherence and versimilitude, its reason and impertinency mixed – were as striking as its limitations have since become; and many could detect no faults in its entrancing pages. 'It might be described as the first book of the 'twenties,' wrote Cyril Connolly. '. . . He [Lytton] struck the note of ridicule which the whole war-weary generation wanted to hear, using the weapon of Bayle [*sic*], Voltaire and Gibbon on the creators of the Red Cross and the Public School System. It appeared to the post-war young people like the light at the end of a tunnel.'

Lytton was astonished by the long and laudatory reviews he read everywhere. He had scored a fine success, yet he felt somewhat uneasy at the lack of attacks. Even the Catholic Press seemed to be remarkably full of Christian charity. What could be the explanation for it all? 'I'm getting rather nervous,' he admitted to Ottoline Morrell (3 June 1918), '– the reviewers are so extraordinarily gushing that I think something must be wrong.' And in a letter to James (May 1918) he suggested: 'I fancy these good fellows [the reviewers] must think they're doing a politeness to the Editor of the Spectator.' Yet still the success rolled on, until it seemed at last as if he might also make some money from his writing. His name had become a household word; everyone was talking about the book – it was mentioned and quoted in leading articles, and before the end of the year had gone into seven impressions. 'So far it has all been sugar,' Lytton told Mary Hutchinson (30 May 1918), '... and I'm really rather disappointed that none of the Old Guard should have raised a protest. I did expect a *little* irritation. Is it possible that the poor dear creatures haven't a single kick left?'

He need not have worried. The custodians of popular mythology, the literary politicians, dons and bishops, were soon enough to denounce him as a bearded Mephistopheles, full of cunning and depravity, in sinister, hirsute league with such dangerous spirits as Bernard Shaw, Augustus John and D. H. Lawrence, together bent on destroying all that should be held sacred in society. This, of course, was exactly as it should have been. When the *Spectator* delivered its denunciation, he felt relieved; and he was encouraged, too, by Edmund Gosse's thundering fulminations in *The Times Literary Supplement*. 'As for Gosse,' he exclaimed, 'after having spent all his life saying disagreeable things about other people (his father included) – to turn round in self-righteous wrath, because someone criticises Lord Cromer!' Most heartening of all was another letter in the same paper from Mrs Humphry Ward, angrily defending her grandfather, Dr Arnold – 'What an old wretch! ... But it's a triumph to have drawn her.'

But for the most part, the reception given to his book was wonderfully favourable, and the few shrill notes of protest were drowned in a loud chorus of praise. 'I shall soon have to make a triumphal progress through the British Isles,' he announced to Ottoline; and he reassured Clive Bell (27 May 1918) that 'I remain calm even in the face of the praises of the Daily Telegraph and Mr. Asquith.'

The prestige and immediate sales of *Eminent Victorians* had been greatly boosted by Asquith when, in the course of his Romanes Lecture delivered at Oxford early that summer, he gave the book what Lytton called 'a most noble and high-flown puff'. The ex-prime minister was still a widely influential figure, and no better publicity could have been looked for than his flattering commendation. 'This must be circulated,' Lytton wrote off to Carrington (June 1918), 'and it's to be hoped and indeed presumed that every member of the great Liberal Party will buy a copy.' He had happened to be staying at Garsington on the Saturday when Asquith was delivering his speech, and drove over with Ottoline to hear it. 'It must be confessed that the lecture was a horribly dull one,' he afterwards told his mother (21 June 1918), '– but one can't be too severe after such a noble piece of advertisement. Apparently he was very enthusiastic about the book, talking about it to everyone. I didn't see him to speak to. The sight inside the Sheldonian was rather splendid – with red gowns – and Curzon (the Chancellor of the University) enthroned on a chair of state, in the highest pomp.'

It is possible that Asquith might not have spoken quite so warm-heartedly of 'Mr. Strachey's subtle and suggestive art'[1] had he known that, only a fortnight before, it had been applied no less trenchantly to himself, in putting together some reflections that arose from the publication of his *Occasional Addresses*:

'The fundamental material of Mr. Asquith I take to have been a middle-class, North-Country solidity, eminently respectable, almost nonconformist, moderate, cautious, humdrum, and with a not un-intelligent eye on the main chance. Then came the influence of Balliol and Jowett, which infused the timid Oxford culture and the timid Oxford worldliness into the virginal undistinguished mass. After that the Bar, with its training in agility of case-putting and its habit of pomposity. So far the development was ordinary enough; but the final influence brought with it some odd contradictions. The Margot set – rich, smart, showy, and self-indulgent – got hold of Mr. Asquith. The middle class legal Don became a *viveur* . . .

'His public career suggests a parallel with Walpole. But one gathers that under all Sir Robert's low-minded opportunism there was a certain grandeur, and that his actual capacity was supreme. In Asquith's case the inveterate lack of ideals and imagination seems really un-redeemed; when one has peeled off the brown-paper wrapping of phrases and compromises, one finds – just nothing at all. And as for his capacity, it was perhaps not much more than the skill of a parliamentary tactician. He could never deal with a serious difficulty. He mismanaged

[1] During the course of his Romanes Lecture, entitled 'Some Aspects of the Victorian Age', Asquith said: 'In a recently published volume – the most trenchant and brilliant series of biographical studies which I have read for a long time – Mr Lytton Strachey, under the modest title *Eminent Victorians*, has put on his canvas four figures (as unlike one another as any four people could be). . . . They are in less danger than ever of being forgotten, now that they have been re-created for the English readers of the future (not in a spirit of blind hero-worship) by Mr Strachey's subtle and suggestive art.'

Ireland; and, though it would be hardly fair to blame too severely his incompetence in the conduct of the war, his inability to cope with the internal situation was really inexcusable.'

Almost the only people from whom Lytton heard nothing after the appearance of *Eminent Victorians* were his publishers, who, in that quaint way publishers have, presumed that the author's interest in his work had automatically ceased on publication day. Perhaps they feared Lytton's continual pestering; if so, they had seriously misjudged his character. Chatto and Windus had brought the book out at the price of ten-and-sixpence, allowing Lytton 15 per cent of this on the first thousand copies sold, and 20 per cent thereafter. They had also undertaken to pay him fifty pounds, in advance of royalties, on 9 May. But the days went by, and still no money reached him. 'It's rather awkward,' he nervously admitted to Clive Bell on 27 May. 'Ought I to write to Geoffrey Whitworth? Perhaps if I'm patient it'll come all right – but perhaps not. I should be glad of your advice.' The following day a letter from Geoffrey Whitworth did turn up. It made no mention of the advance, but, almost regretfully, explained that *Eminent Victorians* was going so well that 'we are *being forced* to *think about* a reprint'. Meanwhile, Clive Bell very sensibly advised Lytton to bring up the matter of his advance without delay. He did so, and by return of post – exactly three weeks late – received a cheque with apologies.

After this false start, the relationship between Lytton and Chatto and Windus grew to be extraordinarily cordial.[1] They are always seeking out ways and means to pay him extra money (without any prompting from Lytton), always improving the mouth-watering clauses in his contracts, and subsequently breaking them for his increased benefit. They press him not to hurry with his next book; they offer to grapple with the tax authorities on his behalf; they invite him to witness the printing of his books[2] and send him innumerable dust jackets and alternative bindings from which he is asked to select his favourite;

[1] Most of the correspondence concerning Lytton's work was carried out by the senior partner at Chatto and Windus, Charles Prentice, who also designed all his books. Harold Raymond, who later became chairman of the firm, remembers Lytton calling there on several occasions. 'We found him a very considerate author to deal with,' he told the author (15 November 1966). 'We knew that he would hold decided views on many of the details of book publishing and we were careful to consult him on any matter on which we thought he would like to be consulted; and whenever we did, he would reply promptly and with sound sense.'

[2] On one occasion Lytton was invited to witness the printing and other machines in action. The performance was arranged in such a way that, at its conclusion, a first copy of his book would be magnificently produced and presented to him. As he stepped into the room, however, where all this was busily taking place, the machinery broke down and came to a halt. Nothing could start it up again, publishers and printers were overcome with confusion; but Lytton was probably rather relieved.

then out of the blue they write to congratulate him about nothing in particular, and urge him to submit all negotiations to the Society of Authors for his own protection. And Lytton, too, is extremely courteous. He invariably makes pressing inquiries after the health of the partners, apologizes for the slightest delay or for the legitimate corrections to proof copies; he recommends a friend of his to join the firm, and on one occasion tries unsuccessfully to rescue for them his *Landmarks in French Literature* from Williams and Norgate, which, in 1927, went bankrupt.

On 16 July, a third edition of *Eminent Victorians* was issued in Great Britain, making a total of three thousand copies in all. In November the American edition came out. In both countries the book sold steadily and well, and before long it was being translated into several European languages, including Swedish, German, French, Italian and Spanish.

Lytton was particularly anxious to have a good French translation and he consulted Dorothy Bussy about this. That summer Dorothy was in England, spending much of her time with André Gide, then living at Merton House in Cambridge as the guest of Harry Norton.[1] Gide had come over with Marc Allegret, carrying a letter of introduction to the Strachey family from Auguste Bréal. During his stay, he had seen something of Lytton and rather more of Dorothy, who was helping to improve his English, and who later translated many of his books. Cambridge, in the summer holidays, half-emptied of undergraduates and half-filled with wounded soldiers, was not at its best, and Gide passed much of his time reading and bicycling about the countryside. His opinion of Lytton as a biographer was qualified. He had been strongly advised to read *Eminent Victorians* by Arnold Bennett, and he began to do so that October. 'I can endure neither the flaccidity of his thought nor the amenity of his style,' he wrote of 'Cardinal Manning'. 'But this book nevertheless seems to me of great importance.' And again, in a letter to Dorothy Bussy: '*Eminent Victorians* lies on our sitting-room's table and is constantly "en lecture". . . . Yet I'm not at all sure this book may find in France many readers.'[2]

Very soon, for the first time in his life, Lytton was to become a person of independent means. During the final dozen years of his life, his average income, from all sources, must have been somewhere

---

[1] Gide had begun his stay at Grape House in Grantchester, but transferred to Merton House in order to be nearer Dorothy Bussy, then living at 27 Grange Road, Cambridge.

[2] On 29 September 1918, Gide wrote to Lytton: 'Un contretemps absurde fait que je n'ai reçu que trop tard votre aimable invitation, alors que déjà tout était décidé pour mon départ. Le plaisir que je me promettais, de vous revoir et Miss Carrington, était si vif que peu s'en fallut je me remisse mon voyage. . . . Du moins croyez la sincérité de mes regrets. Et pour me consoler, je vous lis.'

between two and three thousand pounds per annum. But success made little outward difference to his way of living. The first use to which he put his money was the repayment of past loans from Harry Norton and others, and the making of improvements to Tidmarsh – among them the fulfilment of an early Abbotsholme ambition, the building of an earth closet in the garden. Success suited him, emphasizing his natural modesty which had sometimes been distorted in the past by frustration and the malignant germs of envy, and making him as a companion more relaxed and kindly. At no time did he feel the urge to play the great man of letters, and though he made regular trips to London meeting many other celebrated literati, he never really overcame his natural shyness and was always happy to return to the seclusion of the Mill House. Although, therefore, his appearance was well-known to the public, his retiring and secretive personality remained hidden. People could judge only from what they saw, and their deductions were largely superficial, hardly more than beard-deep. Wyndham Lewis has given an imaginary and fanciful picture of him in his country cottage – a benevolent but rather inhuman old maid of a man, responding coquettishly to his few selected guests (of whom Wyndham Lewis was not one), and dragging his daddy-long-legs from room to room, languidly, like a sun-doped stalk. 'The big lips under his beard were dreamy and large and a little childlike, his big brown eyes were bovine but intelligent. He knew to what "tribe" he belonged, but probably did not practise the rites of the tribe. He liked watching.'

This frigid, impassive and essentially loveless public image is corrected by the intimate personal testimony of Carrington. 'I am glad at any rate the public does not share my feelings about your appearance and character!' she wrote to him that July, while on holiday with her brother Noel in Scotland. 'Since you are bored with praise of your creations, I will tell you that I think you are the most eminent, graceful person. The most worthy, learned and withal charming character. And I shall always love you in your entirety. You know Dear Lytton it has been rather amazing living with you For so long. Now that I am alone and think or ponder on or over it. Visions steal up – of those hot days when you wore your Fakire clothes – in the orchard – The one afternoon when I saw you in the baTH. – When I lay on your bed on Thursday And smelT your hair, and broke the crackling beard in my fingers.'

Both Carrington and Lytton were glad to have escaped from 'the buffeting of London'. After all the adversity, the turmoil and agitation of the past, their perplexed and tortured spirits could now find rest among the simple vegetable things they loved so well – the flowers and fields and trees. In their separate ways they were what Carrington termed 'particular-fastidious', disliking the *mélange* of living too closely against other people, yet always aware, as they grew older, of the dangers of becoming eccentric and old maidish. 'Mine is a "vita umbratilis"', as Cardinal Manning said,' Lytton told Clive Bell (27 May 1918), '– a life in the shade or a shady life, – whichever you prefer.' In the delicious summer heat, the Tidmarsh garden had burst out into a startling tropical refulgence, and Lytton would have been content, so he felt, to sit out there among the laburnums, lilacs, buttercups and apple-blossom, dressed in his Brahmin's robe (though with his mind not altogether Brahminical) serenely dreaming the hours away – would have been, that was, if only so many people were not still being slaughtered just round the corner. Would the war *never* end? But there was no purpose served by brooding over it – far better to return to his Sainte-Beuve.

One of the delights of living in a country cottage of one's own was the pleasure of inviting down one's friends. G. E. Moore came, and Lytton's sisters Pippa and Marjorie, his brother Oliver and a new girl friend, James who 'weeds with two fingers', and Noel Olivier avidly reading Havelock Ellis on sexual inversion, Clive Bell and Mary Hutchinson, and an odd inseparable trio made up of that 'vieillard ratatiné' Saxon Sydney-Turner, Nick and Barbara Bagenal – 'all are incredibly aged. Nick and Barbara (the one without a kidney, and the other with a child) totter and potter like an old couple in an alms-house; and Saxon is wonderfully young for eighty-seven'.

An interesting glimpse behind the scenes at the Mill House has been recorded by another guest there in the late summer of 1919, Gerald Brenan. The afternoon on which he arrived was heavily overcast. The trees and the grasses were steeped in a vivid green and the purplish clouds overhead threw the interior of the house into a dark and gloomy shade. 'Carrington, with her restless blue eyes and her golden-brown hair cut in a straight page-boy bob, came to the door,' Brenan later recalled, '. . . and I was shown in the sitting-room. At the farther end of it there was an extraordinary figure reclining in a deep armchair. At the first glance, before I had accustomed my eyes to the lack of light, I had the illusion – or rather, I should say, the image came into my mind – of a darkly bearded he-goat glaring at me from the bottom of a cave.[1] Then I saw that it was a man and took in gradually the long,

---

[1] In a letter to the author (14 September 1966), Gerald Brenan has emphasized that this passage records 'the first impression of a young man, just demobilised from the army, in a bad light, and that it reflects more on my *naïveté* than on him. As soon as I had got over my first shock, I felt his elegance and distinction.'

relaxed figure, the Greco-ish face, the brown sensitive eyes hidden beneath thick glasses, the large, coarse nose and ears, the fine, thin, blue-veined hands. Most extraordinary was the voice, which was both very low and in certain syllables very high-pitched, and which faded out at the end of the sentence, sometimes even without finishing it. I never attuned my ears to taking in everything that he said.'

But what struck Brenan more forcibly than anything else was the minute attention Carrington lavished upon this fabulous creature. 'Never have I seen anyone who was so waited on hand and foot as he was by her,' he wrote, 'or whose every word and gesture was received with such reverence. In a young woman who in all other respects was fiercely jealous of her independence, this was extraordinary.'

Over tea, Brenan was beset by a jarring assortment of impressions. With Lytton, 'elegant in his dark suit, gravely remote and fantastic, with something of the polished dilettante air of a sixteenth-century cardinal', he could not hit it off at all. He did not dislike him, but felt as though they were trying to communicate on altogether different wavelengths. And although Carrington, with her pre-Raphaelite clothes and her coaxing voice, blue eyes and honey-mouthed mischievous smile, attracted him physically, he did not take to her there and then, because he had heard that she had made cruel fun of his close friend John Hope-Johnstone, to whom he was very loyal.

So, by the time he left late that summer afternoon, he could have had no premonition that before long he was to be whirled up into the irregular mainstream of their two lives, and that for seven long years Carrington would be the leading person in his own life.

2

THE BEAU MONDE

Life at Tidmarsh, for all its expedience and amenity, did not in itself satisfy the whole either of Carrington's or Lytton's nature. Despite her unique bondage to Lytton, Carrington preserved some strange indissoluble particle of independence; and every so often she would take herself off for solitary expeditions to the sea, where, remembering her dead sailor-brother Teddy, she seemed to shed her neurotic worries and imbibe a fresh strength and resilience.

For Lytton, the Mill House was an ideal headquarters where he could rest between metropolitan adventures. After his success, he was being

taken up, much to his delight and slightly to his shame, by the aristocracy. 'The upper-classes rouse my curiosity, and for the present, I
think I shall proceed with my enquiries,' he confided to Carrington
(26 June 1918), who loved to hear his ironic descriptions of these
forays into the beau monde. And again: 'What I really need is the
Gentleman's Complete Guide to Society.'

In the weeks and months that followed – and increasingly as time
went on – he found himself a week-end guest at the country houses of
several brilliant society figures – of Lady Astor at Cliveden, of Lady
Desborough at Taplow Court, of Lady Horner at Mells Manor in
Somerset; and he was invited to luncheon- and dinner-parties by the
most celebrated London hostesses of the day – Lady Colefax and Lady
Cunard, Princess Bibesco and Lady d'Abernon, wife of the British
ambassador in Berlin. Society fascinated Lytton partly because it was an
hallucination. From a distance, it stood out as clear and well-defined –
formidable or absurd according to one's angle of vision. One read about
it in the newspapers as a homogeneous centripetal entity; and even on
its fringes, mesmerized by the whirl of self-flattery, the illusion of its
reality persisted. But penetrate into its glittering vortex, and it melted
away. It had existed only as a glow in one's mind; it was nothing. Yet
even a bright, well-conducted nothing was an escape from the self,
from the necessary solitude of the artist. Lytton hardly knew whether
to be pleased or disgusted at this new state of affairs, and his confusion
is implicit in many of his letters. 'I go next Saturday to the Duchess of
Marlborough's,' he wrote to Ottoline (7 July 1918), '– is it the beginning of the end? Personally I don't think you or Tolstoy need be
alarmed. In the first place, *they* won't like *me*; in the second place *I*
won't like *them*. You know I am not altogether uncritical! Curiosity is
what chiefly moves me. I want to see for myself. I met the D. of M. in
Maud's [Lady Cunard's] ante-room at Drury Lane, and thought her
(from a hasty inspection) more distinguished than the rest. Can you
give me any tips about her? Lady Randolph [Churchill] was also
there – an old war horse, sniffing the battle from afar.' Another member of this Drury Lane party was Margot Asquith who 'had the cheek'
to ask Lytton for a copy of his *Eminent Victorians*, and who invited him
round to tea so that he might make the presentation. Despite her
deplorable manners, he seems to have thought her a more valid
personality than he had at first supposed – less *exagérée* and 'even
faintly civilised'. But finally he decided that, like so many of these
society people, she was unsympathetic – rather like a creature in a play
instead of a real human being, someone to watch but never to make
friends with. Someone, also, to write home to Carrington about. 'Her

mauvais ton is remarkable,' he wrote (26 June 1918). 'There she sits in her box (cadged) thinks she's the very tip-top, the grande dame par excellence, and all the rest of it – and every other moment behaving like a kitchen-maid – giggling, looking round, and nudging Elizabeth [Asquith – Princess Bibesco]. As for music, of course it's never occurred to her that such a thing exists. Yet, as one looks at her small weather-beaten (perhaps one should say life-beaten) countenance, one wonders – there does seem a suggestion of something going on underneath.'

Lytton was a *succès fou* in London society; and in spite of his criticism, he was soon being afforded every opportunity to pursue his inquiries into this grand, artificial world of the upper classes. People who only half a dozen years earlier had wondered how on earth Lady Ottoline Morrell could put up with such a queer fish in her drawing-room, now began to entreat him to lunch or dine with them. In the second week of August he was invited down with Maynard Keynes to The Wharf, as house guests of the Asquiths. 'I'm not much looking forward to the outing,' he confessed to Clive Bell (10 August 1918), 'there is a certain frigidity in those altitudes.' But still, curiosity drew him on, and once he had turned up there he actually lapsed into enjoyment. Though not altogether uncritical, of course, he wanted them to like him; and to achieve this he was prepared to like them in return. His cynicism melted in the facile aura of their hospitality, to be replaced by warmer, more sentimental feelings. 'Maynard supported my tottering footsteps with great tact,' he reported to Ottoline (8 September 1918). 'Margot was extremely kind, and the Company (though not particularly brilliant) was entertaining. There were no great nobs. The Old Man was highly rubicund and domestic – also, I thought, a trifle sleepy. It was chiefly a family party – Violet,[1] Cys[2] and his wife, Anthony,[3] Elizabeth[4] – diversified by Lady Tree and one or two nonentities. Violet and I were very friendly. She certainly has changed enormously – so much more tolerant – at times almost humble, I thought, and even her appearance seems to have entirely altered, the angularity having disappeared, and something of the plenitude of the matron taken its place. . . . Am I a backslider? I don't think so, and she seemed to be almost intelligent. Even Elizabeth I got on better with (isn't it shocking?) and Margot's goodness of heart rather won me. But what I enjoyed best was the family side of the party – playing foolish letter-games after dinner with

[1] Violet Asquith, the daughter of H. H. Asquith by his first wife Helen (*née* Melland); later Lady Violet Bonham Carter, and later still Baroness Asquith.

[2] Cyril Asquith, the youngest of Margot's stepchildren.

[3] Anthony Asquith, usually known as 'Puffin' within the family; later a film producer.

[4] Elizabeth Asquith, Margot's daughter, who married Prince Antoine Bibesco.

the more frivolous (including the Old Man) while the serious persons –
Maynard, Margot, Elizabeth and Texeira de Mattos . . . gave themselves
over to Bridge. You see what I have sunk to! I even enjoyed going off
to Church on Sunday evening with Lady Tree – can you imagine the
spectacle. And Margot gave me a volume of her diary to read, which
was really very interesting, as it had a detailed account of the Cabinet-
making manoeuvres of 1906, and I sat up reading it till 2 o'clock in the
morning.'

His final comment on Asquith himself, too, is more nostalgic, and
shows a perceptible softening of his attitude of only four months earlier.
'From what I could see, it appeared to me almost incredible that he
should ever play a big part in politics again – the poor old fellow! The
worst of it is he'll hang on, and block everything. Though to be sure,
even if he did vanish, who could succeed him?'

After leaving The Wharf, Lytton raced straight on to yet another
country house party, this time at a sixteenth-century castle perched on
a rock off the Northumberland coast, the home of Edward Hudson, the
proprietor of *Country Life* – 'a pathetically dreary figure,' as Lytton
described him, '. . . a fish gliding underwater, and star-struck – looking
up with his adoring eyes through his own dreadful element. . . . A kind
of bourgeois gentilhomme also.' At the end of an alarming journey
undertaken in a tumble-down dog-cart, at sunset, across three miles of
desert sea-sand – partly in flood and dotted with sunken posts to indicate
the route – he arrived at this fortified rock, nervous, dishevelled and
weary, to find the rest of the house-party already assembled there,
attired in evening dress, and tucking into a banquet of lobster and
champagne. Lindisfarne, however, which had been converted into a
'dream castle' by Sir Edwin Lutyens, struck him as rather a poor affair,
except for its actual situation 'which is magnificent,' he told Mary
Hutchinson (7 September 1918), 'and the great foundations and massive
battlements, whence one has amazing prospects of sea, hills, other
castles etc. – extraordinarily romantic – on every side. But the building
itself is all timid Lutyens – very dark, with nowhere to sit, and nothing
but stone under, over and round you, which produces a distressing
effect – especially when hurrying downstairs late for dinner – to
slip would be instant death. No, not a comfortable place, by any
means.'

Predominant among the guests was Madame Suggia, the celebrated
'cellist, with whom Lytton at once made great friends.[1] She seemed to
possess the two principal qualities of which, among all women, he
stood in greatest awe – a real and unaffected talent, and superabundant

[1] Suggia afterwards confessed to being terrified by Lytton's formidable intellect.

physical vigour. 'She is very attractive,' he informed Mary Hutchinson, 'owing I think chiefly to (1) great simplicity – not a trace of the airs and graces of the "Diva" with a European reputation – no bother about playing or not playing – almost a boyishness at times; and (2) immense vitality – her high spirits enormous and almost unceasing – which of course is a great pleasure, particularly to a quiescent person like me. I suppose, besides this, that she's a flirt; but it is difficult to say, and there are so many grades of flirtation. Certainly she is full of temperament – of one kind or another; and there was one evening when she got tipsy – tiens! Her music was of course marvellous – and I got such masses of it! I used to go with her, her mother (a pitiable old remainder biscuit) and the accompanist, to her bedroom; she would then lock the door (to prevent the ingress of Hudson, I fancy) and practise – for hours – playing Bach suites one after the other, and every kind of miracle, with explanations and comments and repetitions, until one tottered down at last to lunch (for this used to happen in the morning) in a state of ecstasy. Then in the evening after dinner she gave her full dress performances. It was really all an extraordinary joy.'

The other guests were altogether less eminent and more eccentric. There was Lady Lewis, for instance, a cosmopolitan Jewess, who slightly distressed Lytton by talking for hours on end about his wonderful *Early Victorians*; and a couple of American Negroes, crude, amiable and inconceivably rich (he played a banjo, while she pored silently all week over Lytton's book, with results that were not communicated to him); then there was Suggia's mother – 'a subject in itself for a Balzac novel' – unable to speak a single word of any known language, perpetually neglected and perpetually smiling; and a Mr George Reeves, the attractive piano accompanist, who, together with Lytton, was forced by Hudson to go off on appalling fishing excursions in the early dawn. Of more authentic interest was William Heinemann, the publisher, pouring forth his eternal reminiscences of Whistler and Ibsen, and his elaborately old-world, improper stories which never failed to make Lytton shriek with laughter. 'I found him a fascinating figure,' he confided to Mary Hutchinson, '– one that one could contemplate for ever – so very very complete. A more absolute jew face couldn't be imagined – bald-headed, goggle-eyed, thick-lipped; a fat short figure, with small legs, and feet moving with the flat assured tread of the seasoned P. and O. traveller. A cigar, of course. And a voice hardly English – German r's; and all the time somehow, an element of the grotesque.' Last, and least of all, there was Mr and Mrs Fort: 'Mr. F. an ex-militaire with a voice like a megaphone and an infinite heartiness –

and a simplicity of behaviour. . . . One evening at dinner, after a good deal of champagne, carried away by exhilaration, he made a speech – a long, long speech, proposing the health of "our host" in heartfelt sentences – one sat gasping – the unimaginable farrago seemed to last interminably; and then, if you please, ce pauvre Hudson found himself replying, at equal length, and with an even wilder inconsequence. After that it was clear that the only thing to do was to get altogether drunk.'

After a week at this improbable castle, 'surrounded by cormorants and quicksands', Lytton made his escape and rejoined Carrington. His perambulations and adventures across Northumberland over the next ten days, 'with Carrington like a large woolly sheep trotting beside me', were disappointing, until the two of them came upon the beautiful village of Elsdon, where they put up for a week at The Bird and Bush Inn. Then they set off once more, travelling south through Durham and York to Gordon Square (for one night) and eventually, on 14 September, arriving back at Tidmarsh. For the next six weeks Lytton settled down here, spending his days very quietly and drinking infinite glasses of milk, brought to him by Carrington with precise regularity. 'To-morrow (or perhaps to-day) our calm is to be impinged upon by the arrival of —— and ——,' he wrote to David Garnett (24 September 1918). 'I think it very cheering to be with people who are thoroughly happy – for whatever reason.' Such a remark points to Lytton's refreshing new outlook on life, in complete contrast to those undergraduate and post-graduate days when the 'affectionateness' of the Bussys and 'couples in the road with their silly arms round their stupid waists' would irritate him by the unwitting emphasis they placed upon his own solitary condition.

One symptom of the past that still lingered on was a predisposition to sickness. Late this September, his summer dissipations suddenly subsided into 'a recurrent colic'; and he quickly took to his bed. His chief and most persistent complaint that autumn was shingles, which reduced him to 'a mere wraith – a ruined spectre . . . a state of de-liquescence'. Carrington somehow managed to step up her manifold and motherly attentions to meet the crisis, until eventually Lytton was able to tell Mary Hutchinson that 'the worst appears to be over. Becket's tonic (a mixture of blood and chloroform apparently) is working won-ders. And the infinite quietude here should be a solace for the soul. Me voici in bed, after breakfast, supported by pillows, and murmuring like Florence Nightingale "Too kind—too kind" to Carrington's ministra-tions.'

By the final week of October, he had recovered sufficiently to visit

M

Jack and Mary Hutchinson at the new house they had rented
in Robertsbridge. But Carrington was jealous of anyone else looking
after Lytton, fearing that they would do it very much more efficiently
than herself, and thereby diminish his absolute reliance on her. While he
was away in Sussex, she bombarded him with packages of shortbread,
bundles of flowers, and parcels of warmer and still warmer clothes; and
before he left Tidmarsh, she sent a characteristic letter, full of unresolved
contradictions of feeling, to Mary Hutchinson, telling her all about
Lytton's convalescence. 'I am sure you will be able to provide Lytton
with so many more comforts – Clive says you have four handmaids to
wait upon him! – Than he gets in this barbaric house. that I feel I
cannoT tell you of muCH. But I will go through his day 8.30 breakfast
in beD 2, eggs. toast, and jam *without pips* in it. If that is possible! –
11ock glass of hot milk with biscuiTs – LunCH His doctor recommends
his having rice or macaroni as vegetable with meaLs. and milk puddings
– Siesta in afternoon – tea at four ock – and so on till 10.30 when he
has a bowl of bread and milk before going to bed – and a glass of milk
with biscuits by his bedside incase he wakes up in the night – Lytton
adds that you will then be required to sleep in the next room and wake
at. one o'ck, two o'ck, five o'ck when he taps on the wall. and come in
to bath his arm or sympathise with his groanings! – I will send him
armed with his food booKs, and sugar BuT really his wants are few,
and as I said after this rude existence. and my appaling house management, and nursing. he is bound to be happy with you! . . . My constitution and appetite is that of an Ox, So nursing LyTTon hasn't exactly
impaired my health! He's been dreadfully disapointed aT not being
able to come to you sooner. BuT really to day for the firsT time he is
much better – I am really so happy. Mary, that he is going to stay with
you as I know you will care for him as noone else woulD . . . I feel so
moved, Mary, because you are so good to Lytton. and because Clive
was so charming. I can'T write proper letters like you written. BuT I
only want to thank you rather especially – for everything.

> with love
> yr
> affec
> carringTON

Lytton was still down at Robertsbridge on 11 November – Armistice
Day. When the news of peace came through, he found it at first
difficult to believe. After the long years of war, he could hardly recall
what peace was like. What did the papers write about, for instance,
when there was no war? Perhaps the weather made headlines. Carrington, who had gone up to London to see Barbara Bagenal, then in a

nursing home having her baby, expresses something of the same blank bewilderment in a letter to her brother Noel, written the next day from the 1917 Club. When the guns were fired at eleven o'clock, she explains, she had thought it must be some joke, or some elaborate new bombing device thought up by the Germans. 'But it soon turned out to be Peace. with a big P. instantly everyone in the city dashed out of offices and boarded the buses. It was interesting seeing how the different stratas of people took it Travelling from Hampstead. seeing first the slum girls, and coster people dancing. pathetic scenes of an elderly plumBer nailing up a single small Flag over the door. Then the scenes became wilder as one reached Campden Town and more and more frantic as one [approached] Trafalgar Square office boys and girls, officers, Majors, waacs all leaped on taxis, and army vans driving round the place waving Flags. In the Strand the uproar was appalling. I was to meet Monty Shearman in [the] Adelphi for lunCH, and it was almost impossible I found to get there! He then took me off to the Café Royal to meet some other rejoicing friends of his . . . then lunch aT the Eiffel Tower restaurant.'

Lytton himself came up to London to join in the orgy of patriotic euphoria. After a first stunned silence at the ill-omened booming maroons, the people had gone mad. The streets were crowded, and everywhere there was noise. In their immeasurable relief, the whole population of London seemed bent on bursting their throats in an effort to contribute to the general din. Motors hooted, handbells rang, police whistles shrilled – everyone felt the urge to do something ridiculous.

The evening was humid and rainy. Almost all Bloomsbury had assembled in Monty Shearman's flat in the Adelphi, where a large celebration party was being held. 'Everyone was THere,' Carrington wrote describing the scene to Noel, 'The halt, the sick and the lame. Even old Lytton [who] was on his deathbeD in Sussex rushed up, and joined in the merriment. . . . It was a great party. I Danced without sTopping for 3 hrs.' The rooms were packed with a familiar but constantly changing company – Clive Bell, Diaghileff and Massine, Roger Fry, Duncan Grant, Jack and Mary Hutchinson, Maynard Keynes, Lydia Lopokova, Ottoline Morrell, Osbert and Sacheverell Sitwell and, of all people, Mark Gertler. While Henry Mond, the chemicals manufacturer, strummed away on the piano, David Garnett paired off with Carrington and danced and danced with her amid the jostling crowd of guests. Lytton himself was also seen to dance, after his own irregular fashion. 'I remember the tall, flagging figure of my friend Lytton Strachey,' Osbert Sitwell wrote, 'with his rather narrow, angular beard, long, inquisitive nose, and air of someone pleasantly awakening from a trance, jigging about with an amiable debility. He was, I think, unused to dancing. Certainly he was both one of the most typical and one of the rarest persons in this assembly. His individual combination of kindness, selfishness, cleverness, shyness and sociability made him peculiarly unlike anyone else. As I watched him, I remember comparing him in my mind to a benevolent but rather irritable pelican.'

By late evening, the party had begun to lose some of its charm, and judging the conviviality to have grown excessive, Lytton prudently made his way back to Maynard Keynes's flat at 46 Gordon Square. There, over the next hour or two, the Bloomsbury Group soberly retired from the festivities to confirm themselves in their own opinions on the coming fate of the world.

Next morning, Lytton hurried back to Robertsbridge, where he stayed on a further two weeks. Carrington, meanwhile, remained up in London for several days before returning alone to Tidmarsh to paint and prepare the house for Lytton's homecoming. Though he was already held in great request by many of the London *salonnières*, Lytton passed most of the next four months of winter at the Mill House. Life was sometimes cold and damp, but never solitary. For Christmas James and Alix came down, and so did Harry Norton. 'We eat large chickens,' Lytton wrote to Ottoline (27 December 1918), 'which pretend to be turkeys not very effectively, and drink grocer's wine. Such is the force of convention.'

Immediately after Christmas, Carrington took off from Tidmarsh for Cheltenham to attend the funeral of her father, who had suddenly died the previous Saturday. It was for her a sad and even horrifying experience. 'Oh Mark I did suffer horribly,' she wrote to Mark Gertler (3 January 1919). 'It was ghastly to see a little yellow ghost. with a saint like marble face lyinG in a narrow coffin. Instead of that splendid old man in his wheelchair by the fire. And then thaT hard china faced sister – and my mother with her sentimental attitude – was almost more hurting.' She stayed on there a full week, a week of nightmare, becoming increasingly upset. So many new ideas and emotions shot through her every day, every hour. She had never felt death so cruelly before, and it sickened her by its awful indignity and ruthlessness. Her father had been so indestructibly large, so simple, so good-hearted – and now he was nothing. He had never altered his way of life to please conventions, and his big rough character compelled in her a sort of reverence. She felt guilty, now that it was too late, at not having fought for him more openly against the rest of the family. Her sister and her mother had never seemed so alien to her, so petty and female with their concern about their black dresses. She was glad once her father was actually buried away beneath the ground, for then the last connexion with her mother had been effaced for all time. Finally, unable to endure their company any longer, she travelled back to Tidmarsh, feeling tired and empty-headed. From this day on, Lytton was the only real family she would recognize; and his home would always be her home, even to death itself.

For the first ten weeks of the New Year, the two of them lived at the Mill House like a couple of hibernating animals. In refusing an invitation to go and stay with Leonard and Virginia Woolf, Lytton confessed (29 January 1919): 'I find London impossible . . . Later on, later on, when the snow has vanished . . . It is dreadfully dull down here, but healthy and for the moment there are fires.' He had changed into a complete St Anthony. And as for his friends in the smart set, he appeared to have abandoned them altogether – for the time being. 'The conditions of life seem hardly to be ameliorating,' he explained to Clive Bell (18 February 1919), 'and so I have decided definitely to give up the gay world, to become an anchoret, to read nothing but the various lives of the Prince Consort, to gaze out of [the] window at the snow, and to put another log on the fire.'

At the same time, through sheer *désœuvrement* it seemed, he had started work on a new book.

3

QUEEN VICTORIA AND OTHER ESSAYS

It was at Tidmarsh that Lytton's classic biography of Queen Victoria was originally conceived and brought to life. While moving into the Mill House in December 1917, he had already begun to 'console' himself with Victoria's letters. 'I am reading Victoria's diary, when a young maid,' he noted (11 December 1917), '– most absorbing, but not long enough.'

The first suggestion that he should make Victoria the subject of his next book had come from Walter Raleigh, shortly after the publication of *Eminent Victorians*. 'We want your method for some stately Victorians who have waited long for it,' he wrote on 13 May 1918. 'First the great Panjandrum – Victoria herself. This is obvious. How can an adjective have a meaning that is not dependent on the meaning of its substantive? . . . It's really wicked of you to leave those stout volumes alone, when you could put the gist of them within reach of us.'

Nevertheless, Lytton's initial idea, following the success of *Eminent Victorians*, was, he told Philip Morrell, to write a second series of pen-portraits, treating this time the scientists who had been among his original list of twelve candidates. Very soon, however, he relinquished this notion, though it was not until the end of this year that he seems finally to have made up his mind. Queen Victoria, he informed Clive Bell (28 December 1918), was 'an interesting subject, but an obscure one . . . It's very difficult to penetrate the various veils of discretion. The Prince Consort is a remarkable figure; but Sir Theodore Martin's life of him in five stupendous volumes is not to be recommended to the general public. Have you heard of Emily Cranford? There's a book by her on the queen which is not without merit – Irish and full of gossip about the forties – very disordered, but in parts distinctly good.[1] I'm beginning to think that most of the good books are overlooked. For instance the Private Life of Henry Maitland is surely highly interesting – but who mentions it? I found it the other day, quite by chance, and found it absorbing.'

By the New Year, Lytton had completed enough reading and research to feel reasonably certain that, as he phrased it to Chatto and Windus (3 January 1919), the subject of his next biography would be 'The Life of Her Late Majesty'. Writing the following day to his mother and sensing her displeasure at such a project, he is more diffident. 'I am beginning a serious study of Queen Victoria; but it's difficult to say as yet whether anything will come of it.' As he had probably expected, Lady Strachey was taken aback by this news, fearing that the venerable queen would come in for even rougher handling than her eminent subjects. 'I don't much fancy you taking up Queen Victoria to deal with,' she replied. 'She no doubt lays herself open to drastic treatment which is one reason I think it better left alone. She could not help being stupid, but she tried to do her duty, and considering the period she began in, her up-bringing, her early associations, and her position, this was a difficult matter and highly to her credit. She has won a place in public affection and a reputation in our history which it would be highly unpopular, and I think not quite fair, to attempt to bring down.

'What about Disraeli? He is near enough our own time to be topical, and too near to have been thoroughly dealt with as yet. His two reputations, the early one and the later which has developed into a

---

[1] Nevertheless this book is not listed in the bibliography or 'List of References in the Notes' at the end of Lytton's *Queen Victoria*.

legend, are quite contradictory, and until they have been welded together, are in my opinion equally false.'[1]

But Lytton was already determined to press on with this new book. All through the late summer, the autumn and winter months he had been reading copiously – biographies of Albert the Good, of Victoria herself and all manner of works on Victorian politics and history. His letters to Pippa sometimes contain lists of volumes for her to send down to him at the Mill House when he was unable to get up to London. Perhaps the most interesting of all the works he consulted was Sir Herbert Maxwell's two-volume edition of *The Creevey Papers*, on which he wrote a separate biographical essay. 'How can anyone read novels when there are Creevey Papers to be had – in which there is every variety of human, political, and historical interest, sur le vif – I don't understand,' he told Clive Bell (18 February 1919).

As with all Lytton's major works, the preparatory reading of books on his subject took up almost twice as long as the actual writing. Over the next two years he would stay up in London – at Belsize Park Gardens, or with his brother Oliver at 96 South Hill Park, or occasionally at the Savile Club – for weeks at a time, visiting the London Library and the British Museum Reading Room, and then returning to Tidmarsh with a few pages of notes in an exercise book and some sheets of foolscap devoted to quotations. At the Mill House, huge parcels of books would arrive regularly from booksellers and libraries, and be read through day after day – six or eight or ten hours reading a day. And at the end of each book, a dozen pencil entries on half a sheet of notepaper would represent all the salient material he had extracted. 'His critical faculty was so highly developed by the time he came to write biography that he rarely noted down a superfluous fact, and still more rarely had to return to a book once read for some fact he had previously rejected,' recorded Ralph Partridge (8 October 1946). 'Still, the reading to be done was immense; and he never skipped through books, and never trusted an index to pick out references to his subject. An outline of the book he intended to write was in his head before ever he began his course of reading, but not a word went on paper until the reading was finished. Then very likely he would take a holiday abroad before settling down to write.'

[1] In 1920 Lytton did in fact write an article on Disraeli for *Woman's Leader*. A review of Monypenny and Buckle's six-volume biography, 'Dizzy', as it was called, consists of little more than an elegant admission of perplexity. 'The absurd Jew-boy, who set out to conquer the world, reached his destination,' ran the opening sentence. And he had little to add to this statement, since, as he told Hesketh Pearson shortly after the publication of *Queen Victoria*, Disraeli's mummy-like inscrutability baffled him. 'I can't make him out,' he admitted; 'his character is so utterly contradictory.'

It was largely due to this intensive method of research that Lytton found such little time to concentrate on other writing. In the five years after the publication of *Eminent Victorians* he produced only eight essays for periodicals. Two of these, 'Dizzy' and 'Mr. Creevey', were direct offshoots from his *Queen Victoria*; two others (both written in the summer of 1918) were pacifist propaganda contributions to *War and Peace*; and the rest dealt with such old favourites as Shakespeare, Voltaire and Horace Walpole.

But there were other contributory reasons, too, to account for the small output over these years. The composition of *Queen Victoria* exhausted him, and he felt that while he was working on it he dare not squander the least drop of vital energy on unrelated articles. At the same time, he could seldom resist dashing off poems and plays, not for publication but for enjoyment and the enjoyment of his friends. Some weeks, for instance, of the summer of 1918 were given over to 'Quasheemaboo' or 'The Noble Savage', a drama which he composed for Madame Vandervelde and Jack Hutchinson to act in at a charity gala. 'The first performance is to be on July 1,' he informed his mother (5 June 1918). 'The plot of the play was suggested to me by you once – probably you've forgotten all about it – A wife who has become a successful actress without her husband knowing it. When she tells him he disbelieves her, whereupon she gets up a melodramatic scene, which completely takes him in – and then she rounds upon him. So if it's taken up, and performed on the Music Hall Stage and brings in millions, you shall have half the profits!' Though never professionally performed, it is a well-constructed and amusing farce, and contains some charming rhymed couplets – for example Captain Cutts's song:

> *Once in a way the sun is o'er us,*
> *Once in a way the sky stays blue,*
> *Bees are a-buzzing, and birds in chorus,*
> *Every rose is as sweet as you*
> *   – All summer delights in a single day*
> *   Once in a way, once in a way.*

> *Once in a way the twilight lingers,*
> *Once in a way the moon shines bright.*
> *Stars are lit by the angels' fingers,*
> *Kisses fall with the falling night.*

Over his published writings Lytton was strictly cautious in what he wrote, and for which paper he contributed. In the summer of 1918 he had been approached by J. C. Squire, then acting editor of the *New*

Statesman,[1] to write book reviews and articles for his paper. In refusing this offer, Lytton first objected to the rates of payment before coming to the primary reason why, at this time, he could not 'feel comfortable' in the columns of the *New Statesman*. 'Perhaps you won't mind my also saying that the idea of contributing to the New Statesman would be more pleasant to me if I could sympathise rather more with its war-policy. This, so far as I can make it out, seems to be a species of un-conscious jingoism. Your ideals are no doubt admirable but what you are really promoting is the policy of the knock-out blow – that is to say the wicked and impossible policy of the Northcliffe Press. That this is so is shown (to take one instance) in the tone of your remarks this week about Lord Lansdowne.[2] Whether you agree with him or not, you ought to be able to see that he is an honest man, and a man who is at any rate trying to use his reason. But evidently you see neither of these things, for you attack him in a style for which I can really only think of one epithet – blackguardly. It appears to me that the only possible explanation is that, whatever you may say, and whatever you may think, you are in fact a Northcliffian.

'I was very glad to hear that my book amused you – though I fear it may have seemed to you not quite Christian enough.'

Squire angrily repudiated these charges, but Lytton was obdurate. He did not contribute anything more to the *New Statesman* until, in 1931, under the new editorship of Kingsley Martin and as the amal-gamated *New Statesman and Nation*, the paper had completely changed its political policy.

By the year 1919, he had, in any case, begun to associate himself with

---

[1] Clifford Sharp, the regular editor of the *New Statesman*, had in 1917 been called up for military service, trained as an artillery officer and sent to Stockholm on an intelligence mission.

[2] In a letter to *The Daily Telegraph* on 29 November 1917 (a letter previously turned down by *The Times*), the veteran Lord Lansdowne had sought to counteract the internal propaganda of both Britain and Germany, which, he felt, was helping to prolong the war unnecessarily. 'What are we fighting for?' he asked. The answer, of course, was to defeat the Germans, not out of mere vindictiveness, but honourably and in such a way as to prevent another war in the future. He defined Britain's war aims with the aid of five guiding points. There was to be no annihilating knock-out blow; no imposition of an unwelcome form of government on the German people; no permanent economic sanctions after the war was over. Britain would work for international agreement on the 'freedom of the seas' question and help to set up a compulsory international pact to ensure peace. This letter provoked a hurricane of abuse from the Government and in the Press. North-cliffe, for example, endeavoured to discredit Lansdowne as a statesman, an Irish landlord, and an individual. But a minority of people applauded Lansdowne's courage and honesty. On 31 January 1918 he received a deputation led by the ex-Lord Chancellor, Lord Loreburn, who presented him with an address commending him for his initiative. Among the signatories were Noel Buxton, G. P. Gooch, Dean Inge, Gilbert Murray and Stanley Unwin.

M*

the *Athenaeum*, which had then reached a peculiar stage in its long and erratic history. 'It was about the end of 1828 that readers of periodical literature, and quidnuncs in those departments, began to report the appearance, in a Paper called the *Athenaeum*, of writings showing a superior brilliancy and height of aim.' So wrote Carlyle in *The Life of John Stirling*. But by the twentieth century, both brilliancy and height of aim had long since vanished, and as a monthly 'Journal of Reconstruction', the *Athenaeum* had barely survived the war. In 1919, however, it was given a drastic new lease of life when Arthur Rowntree purchased the paper and reconstituted it as a weekly 'Journal of English and Foreign Literature, Science, the Fine Arts, Music and the Drama'. By what F. A. Lea has described as 'a stroke of inspiration', Rowntree offered the editorship to Middleton Murry, then an undischarged bankrupt. The result was that during the two years that Murry reigned as editor, the paper lost almost ten thousand pounds. Its contributors over this period included a large number of men and women who were later to win leading positions in the literary world. The brilliance had been restored, but the aim was now so superior as to be right off target.

The letter which Murry wrote to Lytton (12 February 1919) rallying him to the *Athenaeum*'s happy band of regular contributors is very typical of him – almost a collector's item – showing how humility, a rather touching bewilderment, Himalayan earnestness and the dependence upon other people to make a name for him were so nicely muddled together in his character. 'I have been made editor of the new Athenaeum,' he announced, '– heaven knows what beneficent bee entered the bonnets of the owners – which is shortly to arise like the phoenix. I shall try to make it as good as I can. But to do that it is necessary that you should become a regular contributor. . . .

'But, my dear Lytton, it is your duty to the coming generation. I do think that a new Athenaeum is a great opportunity, and I know that unless you will join, we shall be unable to make the use of it which we ought to make. Therefore, though it will be a bother, and though the work will be no better paid than elsewhere, please be conscientious in your responsibilities and say you will.'

Although he thought little of Murry as a poet or creative writer, Lytton did feel that he should be proficient on a less exalted plane. Murry's obvious sincerity, his longing to be disinterested and his very evident seriousness impressed him, reducing the slight scepticism he felt at his lofty sense of purpose, out-topping common sense. In any event, there could be no doubt that he was infinitely preferable to

Squire, whom Virginia Woolf had very properly described as 'more repulsive than words can express, and malignant into the bargain' (26 May 1919). After inviting Murry down to Tidmarsh at the end of February, Lytton wrote to Clive Bell (3 March 1919): 'Talking of new papers, Murry was here for a night, to talk about the Athenaeum, the prospects of which sounded most hopeful. I think he ought to make a good job of it, with his extraordinary competence quâ journalist. I said I'll try and write a little for it – I should like to write a great deal, but I'm too slow, and then how does one put things? And perhaps on the whole books are more important than magazines.'

When Murry left Tidmarsh, he took with him 'Lady Hester Stanhope', and in the next six months Lytton found time to send him four further articles – one piece of dramatic criticism, 'Shakespeare at Cambridge', and three biographical essays. This last trio, together with 'Lady Hester Stanhope', provide a good index to his future development as an essayist, prefiguring his last series of minor compositions later assembled as *Portraits in Miniature and Other Essays*. They are fashioned after two distinct styles. In 'Voltaire' and 'Walpole's Letters' he was, of course, treating subjects for whom he felt a close affinity. Both had been his constant reading since Cambridge days, so much so that he had come to know each of their long-vanished faces as well as that of some living friend – 'one of those enigmatical friends about whom one is perpetually in doubt as to whether, in spite of everything, one *does* know them after all'. When he was not dealing with men who had much in common with his own character, he liked to amuse himself portraying the eccentrics, those grand, preposterous, inexplicable freaks of Nature, at once so intimidating and so delightful, whose extraordinary lives contrasted romantically with his own, and answered his inner sense of abnormality. 'Lady Hester Stanhope' and 'Mr. Creevey', both minor historical figures of extreme and triumphant unconventionality, fell into the second category. As with his 'Voltaire' and 'Walpole's Letters', the accent is placed firmly upon the biographical interest. Lytton is no longer so much taken up with public achievement as with the quirks of individual personality, which he gracefully sets off against the fat pastures of social and political high life.

A fortnight after 'Lady Hester Stanhope' had appeared, Lytton wrote to Ottoline (17 April 1919): 'I find the Athenaeum a great addition to existence. Don't you? It really, as they say, "supplies a long felt want".' But over the latter term of Murry's editorship, the paper began to lose some of its early momentum. Lytton's enthusiasm then cooled, and he contributed nothing further to its columns. 'The dear Athenaeum is much the best literary paper, it seems to me,' he told F. L. Lucas (27

June 1920), 'but lately one's rather felt it was in need of "new blood".
If you supply it, so much the better!'

The proprietors also felt the paper to be in need of 'new blood' in the
form of a new editor. Early in 1921, Murry resigned from his post, and
that February the *Athenaeum* merged with the *Nation*. Also financed by
the Rowntree family, the *Nation* had been founded in 1907, and was
skilfully edited by H. W. Massingham, the impress of whose personality was strongly marked upon every page. The paper's political
impact, however, was weak, and, mainly for this reason, it had not
expanded into a paying proposition. Moreover, a new body of ardent
Liberals, known as the Grasmere Group and numbering among its
members Sir William Beveridge, Philip Guedalla, Maynard Keynes,
Walter Layton, Ramsay Muir and E. D. Simon, seriously concerned
over the absence of a satisfactory Liberal weekly, had started discussions
with the Rowntree family, who were themselves growing restive under
the mounting loss of some thousands of pounds every year. As a result
of these talks, it was agreed that fresh money would be found to reduce
the burden upon the Rowntrees, if some marked radical alteration was
made in the political outlook of the paper. Massingham then resigned
as editor and Keynes was elected chairman of the new board. Ramsay
Muir and T. S. Eliot were at first proposed as editor and literary editor,
but eventually these posts were filled respectively by Hubert Henderson and Leonard Woolf. The first issue of what some critics have
regarded as a special pulpit for the Bloomsbury Group came out on
5 May 1923, and contained an appreciation by Lytton of Sarah Bernhardt. The literary section of the re-formed *Nation and Athenaeum* was
kept independent from the political policies in the main part of the
paper, and the freedom which Leonard Woolf allowed Lytton –
reminiscent of that in the *New Quarterly* and *Independent Review* –
exactly suited him. During the next five years he contributed eighteen
signed essays which were to comprise almost the whole of his sixth
published volume, *Portraits in Miniature*.

4

MEMOIR OF AN INFANTRY OFFICER

On the afternoon of 10 August 1918 there arrived at the Mill House a
visitor who was to enter very intimately into the lives of Carrington
and Lytton, affecting them both individually and in their relationship to
each other. This was Ralph Partridge, a wartime friend of Noel

Carrington. A large, powerfully built young man, with a high-coloured complexion and dancing light-blue eyes, he had left Oxford early in the war to join the army, in which he had greatly distinguished himself, being awarded a Military Cross and rising at the age of twenty-three to the rank of major, commanding a battalion. Noel Carrington had first introduced him to his sister at the beginning of July 1918. His irresistible zest for life, fascinating good looks and easy, open ways at once delighted her, and she immediately sent off a letter to Lytton reporting the discovery of this impetuous new personality. 'The young man Partridge has just come bacK from Italy – the one I was telling you about the other evening,' she wrote (4 July 1918). '. . . He adores the Italians and wanTs after the war to sail on a schooner to the Mediteranean Islands and ITaly; and trade in wine without takinG much money, and to dress like a brigand. I am so elated and happy. It is so good to find someone you can rush on and on with, quickly. He sang Italian songs to us on the platform and was in such gay spirits and used his hands gesticulatinG.'

This description sent through Lytton a flutter of curiosity and sentimental speculation. Of course, he was more than prepared to be disappointed; all the same he would like to interview this romantic-sounding creature for himself. 'The existence of Partridge sounds exciting,' he replied. 'Will he come down here, when you return, and sing Italian songs to us, and gesticulate, and let us dress him as a brigand? I hope so.'

And so, with Lytton's approval, it was agreed that Carrington should invite the young officer over to the Mill House. This visit, so eagerly awaited by both of them, was only a moderate success, and gave no hint of the strange role he was soon to play in that household. With fine and unabashed tactlessness, he started off almost at once on a heated argument about the war, claiming that all the carnage did not matter one jot, that he himself had no objection to being killed fairly and squarely by the enemy, and that all pacifists were skulkers and ought to be shot. Lytton, dismayed by this exhibition of bumptious arrogance, did not join in the discussion. After all, he reasoned, this major had come to see Carrington, not himself. But Carrington, angry that Lytton should have been exposed to such rudeness, fiercely and incoherently argued the virtues of 'passifism', and finally, in despair, led him off outdoors where his militaristic views might discharge themselves harmlessly into the open air.

Partridge himself seems to have remained obstinately unaware of his *faux pas*. 'I have been initiated into the Mill House,' he notified Noel Carrington the following week (17 August 1918), 'but as a great part of the μυστήρια took place on the river, I viewed the proceedings very favourably. Old man Strachey with the billowy beard and alternating basso-falsetto voice did not play a great part.' And in a letter to his friend Gerald Brenan, he described Carrington as 'a painting damsel and a great Bolshevik who would like to strike a blow for the Cause', while Lytton is dismissed as 'of a surety meet mirth for Olympus'. Partridge's name does not crop up in Lytton's correspondence this year at all, except cursorily in one letter to Clive Bell as 'some Major Partridge or other', a friend of Carrington's. But Carrington, for her part, communicated a rather lukewarm, disdainful account of him to her brother, in which she pays back some of the antipathy which he had so obviously directed towards her adored Lytton (12 August 1918): 'He isn't very interested in Books or poetry or painting,' she complained. '. . . He was surprised that Lytton had written that Book. as he said he didn't think he looked as if he could have. . . . Then he didn't see very much in the book except that the style was "rather good" – Then he was prejudiced against Lytton slightly for his beard and appearance. and confessed it.'

To all outward appearances, then, Ralph Partridge had absolutely nothing in common and no point of contact with the Tidmarsh régime. But beneath the clash of opinions and the contrast of personalities, at a more elemental level, the three of them had already begun to form that summer the basis of an odd triangular union which, despite many complicated strains and crises, would persist over the next thirteen years, until the death of two of them.

Immediately after the war was over, Ralph Partridge returned to Oxford, where he was supposed to be completing his law studies and from where he would bicycle over the twenty miles to Pangbourne for week-ends. He had fallen deeply in love with Carrington. And she responded to some extent, partly because he was a very attractive man and she was flattered by his attentions, and partly because, much to her joy and surprise, Lytton had now taken to him strongly.

It is not difficult to account for the warmth of Lytton's feelings. Although, in these happier, more successful years, he no longer thrived on scorn and disparagement as once he had done, it did not necessarily alienate him as it would most people. The initial disapproval he felt for Partridge's cocksure insensitivity gradually gave way before a susceptibility to his more potent charms. First and foremost of these was his vigorous, physical masculinity. Like Thoby Stephen's, like George Mallory's before him, his fine Herculean torso appeared to have been fashioned after the geometry of some mythical pagan deity. 'He seemed born to lead anything from a Polar expedition to an infantry assault,' recorded his friend Gerald Brenan. '. . . He was very sure of himself and did not easily submit to authority that he regarded as stupid or incompetent.' His hearty Rabelaisian laugh, his incredible blue eyes rolling wildly in their sockets like a Negro's, his rollicking high spirits, his formidable self-assurance supported by an enterprising efficiency in all practical matters, his lack of Christian feeling, all emphasized for Lytton this god-like aspect, inspiring him with a kind of hero-worship. There was, however, no question of any homosexual attachment between them, since Partridge was exclusively heterosexual. Indeed, his mind ran much on women, many of whom adored him; and he had many romantic conquests, especially among actresses and chorus-girls. He was, in fact, something of a sensualist and womanizer; yet Lytton seemed to like him all the more for this, for it was, after all, no more than a necessary part of his splendid masculine virility, and therefore to be admired.

Such were Ralph Partridge's more resplendent qualities; and had this been all, then Lytton's passion for him would have amounted to nothing new — just another item in the list of insignificant flirtations that would from time to time flare up and then die down again, like fireworks leaving no trace of their path in the skies. But this was not all. For already Lytton thought he could detect beneath the exterior beauty and bravado other traits which made him a far more complex and fascinating character than, say, George Mallory could ever have been. Despite his loud conventional opinions, he was really something of a rebel, and even in his casual remarks delivered in a half-jocular, half-ironic, stylized tone of voice, Lytton was able to observe the workings of a strong if undeveloped mind. His fierce and often uncontrolled emotions would lead to loves that were extraordinarily permanent, and dislikes that were stormy. Fond of conversation and discussion, he was far more aggressive in argument than he realized, but his outlook remained completely unsentimental and realistic. He had a tenacious memory and a passion for acquiring facts that made him a rewarding pupil.

Lytton soon set about trying to educate this young man, to develop his potentialities and instil into him some of his own tastes in literature and views on sexual ethics. The result was that, for all his determined individuality and disinclination to submit to authority, the burly, hot-headed man-of-the-world fell very largely under Lytton's sway. From a bluff and breezy extrovert, he slowly metamorphosed into an intelligent and cultivated man of letters, a sort of office boy-publisher for some time with the Hogarth Press, a *New Statesman* reviewer and finally an author. In time, he developed an almost feminine interest in people and states of mind, for which reason numerous people would confide in him and ask his advice. So fundamental was the change brought about in him by Lytton's tuition that people who knew him well only later in life could scarcely credit his earlier history. 'He was a very emotional man,' Gerald Brenan wrote, 'and whenever he held an opinion he held it passionately and liked to have it out with those who disagreed with him.' This characteristic at least never altered. During the First World War he had been in his element in the front line; twenty years later, as a conscientious objector, he was attacking militarism with the same emotional abandon that he had previously hurled against Lytton and other pacifists. This conversion was directly due to Lytton, who, as it were, made a new man out of him, only to find, once he had done so, that his infatuation for the ebullient and debonair army major he first met had partly faded away. Their association over a few years completely shifted its ground. The disdain which Partridge had spontaneously experienced for this pacifist and skulker with his billowy beard and his books, was replaced by a genuine admiration and devotion; while Lytton himself became extremely fond of this new disciple, who, on and off, was to act as his secretary.

There was one other unusual trait in Ralph Partridge's make-up which from early days appealed to Lytton, for whom it sanctified all the philistine errors of taste and judgement, and this was his utter lack of worldly ambition. Though naturally athletic, he was congenitally lazy – a curious mixture of indolence and vitality. At Oxford he had, in a leisurely way, taken up rowing, but when asked to row for the Varsity eight had declined to do so on the grounds that it interfered with a holiday he was planning. Later, when invited to represent Great Britain in the Olympic Games, he again refused since the training involved too much inconvenience and hard work. This kind of disinterestedness had in men always attracted Lytton, and he was charmed by such refreshing indifference to fame. What it must be to have the opportunity to turn one's back on such things! Lytton was deeply impressed, and for some time Partridge embodied a new vision of his ideal self. 'Lord!' he exclaimed on one occasion to Carrington (11 July 1919). 'Why am I not a rowing blue, with eyes to match, and 24? It's really dreadful not to be.'

On most evenings when the three of them were alone together at Tidmarsh, Lytton would read aloud to Carrington and Partridge – this being an important part in the curriculum of schooling his young friends. Carrington still found the greatest difficulty over the longer, more erudite literary words, but she had a feeling for poetry and came to absorb a good deal of it, particularly the Elizabethan song books. Meanwhile, Ralph, too, was gradually shedding his boorishness, and, with his natural intelligence, began picking up a fair education. But at this time, his attention was fixed less on the declaiming Lytton than on the rapt and enigmatic figure of Carrington. Predictably, she was still something of a mystery to him – yet all the more desirable for that. He was accustomed to quick, simple conquests over women, and to an equally precipitate loss of interest in them. Either that, or else they did not respond to him, and he did not like them. It was all cut-and-dried. But Carrington was quite different. His relationship with her baffled him. He found it impossible to understand her slavish attachment to Lytton, and although he could tell that she liked him and found him sexually attractive, he still felt her elude his reach, ever-appealing, impalpable, inexplicable. He tried everything he knew to make her his own property absolutely, but was never really satisfied. When the winter began to thaw and the warmer weather to spread through the country, he would appear in front of her stark naked and twist himself into provocative contortionist positions so that she could make sensational drawings of his strong, magnificently proportioned limbs. Carrington was touched and gratified by this artistic co-operation – he was a very thrilling partner for her, anatomically and in other more confusing ways. 'I've been drawing R.P. naked in the long grass in the orchard,' she told Lytton (May 1919) after one pastoral session. 'I confess I got rather a flux over his thighs, and legs so much so that I didn't do very good drawings.'

Throughout much of this winter Ralph had been trying to persuade Carrington to go off on a holiday with him. But she did not wish to leave Lytton, who, however, urged her to go. And so eventually, more for his sake than Ralph's, she went together with her brother Noel and Ralph's sister Dorothy. Nearly all her brief separations from Lytton were enforced in this peculiar way. 'I was never in all these 16 years happy when I was without him,' she wrote at the end of her life. 'It was only I knew he disliked me to be dependent that I forced myself to make other attachments.'

Towards the end of March, then, Carrington and Ralph, Noel and Dorothy, sailed away for a few weeks to Spain, leaving Lytton at Tidmarsh. The outcome of their trip, though it settled nothing, was to establish on a firmer basis their three-cornered relationship. Carrington's protracted absence brought home to Lytton just how much he had come to depend upon her in the ordinary but indecipherable business of running the household affairs. Without her help, he sometimes appeared hopelessly lost, comically, even wantonly so. 'This morning I visited the butcher's,' he wrote to James (7 April 1919), 'and stood for some hours among a group of hags and every sort of "joint" and horror. At last my turn came, and I asked if they had any mutton – of the butcher's wife. She said "Yes". I produced my coupon, on which she became rather mysterious, moved about, then brushed past me murmuring "wait a minute" in lurid tones. So I did. At last, on the departure of one of the hags, she said: "That was the food controller's wife." So I suppose we'd been committing some illegality, though what it can be I've no idea, as my principle is to understand nothing of such matters.'

To avoid the mysterious rules and rigours of 'shopping', Lytton decided to take himself off for a week to the Cove Hotel at West Lulworth, with its memories of Rupert Brooke, where he could be sure of being looked after properly. He expected to see James already installed there, but could find no sign of any brother and was obliged to 'sit solitaire, cheek by jowl with a quite silent (luckily) and half-witted military couple in a most higgledy-piggledy hotel', he complained to Ottoline (27 March 1919). '. . . There are splendid Downs going down into cliffs – all so pale and peaceful – into the sea, which yesterday was a Mediterranean blue. The sun was streaming down. I stretched myself full-length upon the grass, and basked. It seems incredible; and indeed I thought at the time there was some trickery about it – and so there was. As I was basking, an old seagull swooped past, and positively laughed in my face – a regular mocking jeering laugh – as much as to say "you wait" – and lo and behold in the night the weather completely changed, and now we are back in the old story of hurricanes and deluges – ugh! And to be penned in with the Major and Mrs. Major all day – oh! I shall struggle out and breast the elements, I think, what e'er betide.'

From West Lulworth, Lytton hurried on to Lyme Regis, where he caught up with James and Alix, spending Easter with them at a lodging-house in Sherborne Lane. 'Behold me basking in the sun,' he wrote to David Garnett (5 April 1919), 'on the Marine Parade, the sun sparkling below me, aged spinsters, discharged army youths etc. etc. floating round me.' Towards the end of the month he left this crowded, vacuous atmosphere and returned to the Mill House to rejoin Carrington and Ralph, now due to arrive back from Spain. He was grateful to have them back again, happy that life could proceed once more on its ordered, purposeful course. The last few weeks, though not wholly unpleasant, had seemed like a relapse into those aimless and nomadic days before the war.

By all accounts Carrington and Ralph had enjoyed a wonderful

holiday in Spain, walking up to thirty miles a day and travelling from
Cordova to Seville, from Toledo to Madrid. Though clouds of
anxiety over Lytton's solitary welfare had often thrown shadows across
her mind, Carrington became absorbed by the splendours of her
journey, marvelling with that extraordinary freshness and vitality of
hers at every new phenomenon she beheld – the paintings, the people,
buildings and mountains. 'I have seen sights one hardly dreamt of,' she
wrote excitedly to Gertler (30 April 1919). 'And people so beautiful
that one quivered to look at them – and then those El Grecos at
Madrid and Toledo – and yet one has to keep it all inside. I feel just
now so strong, and savage – But I see it will wear off in this cold
climate before many days.' Brown and plump and healthy, lit up by a
kind of Atlantic happiness, she seemed fonder now of Ralph than
ever, and fervently hoped that he and Lytton might continue to hit
it off together as they had begun to do late that winter. As for
Spain, it was a superb and dramatic country, so primitive and full of
startling colours. She longed somehow to convey all the pleasure
she had received to Lytton; he must certainly go there as soon as
possible, and she would show him round – with Ralph, too, of
course.

   As for Ralph, this gloriously happy vacation had helped to bring
about in his mind a major decision. He knew now that Carrington was
the only girl for him. Never had he felt like this about anyone. As soon
as he came down from Oxford, he must somehow persuade her to
marry him.

5

THE T. S. ELIOT FIASCO

The spring and summer months of 1919 once more drew Lytton forth
from his country hibernation, and soon he was caught up again in the
superior merry-go-round of London entertainments. 'My smart life
proceeds apace,' he informed Mary Hutchinson (15 May 1919). 'I find
it mainly simply comic, and distinctly exhausting. No pasturage for the
soul, I fear! Lady Cunard is rather a sport, with her frankly lower-class
bounce; she makes the rest of 'em look like the withered leaves of
Autumn, poor things. But she herself I fancy is really pathetic too. So
lost – so utterly lost! – She takes to me, she says, for the sake of that
dear nice Bernard Keynes, who's such an intimate friend of hers . . .
after lunch, Lady C. suddenly said she must go and fetch Princess

Bibesco (not Elizabeth – another) from the French Embassy opposite.[1] She dashed off to do so. Reappeared very quickly, with the Princess, and – who do you think? – George Moore. He looked too preposterous – like a white rabbit suddenly produced by a conjuror out of a hat. He was furious, of course, and went away at once. Apparently, he had told Maud [Lady Cunard] over and over again "I do not want to come" – but it was useless – he was carried off – propelled into Mrs [Saxton] Noble's arms, and then, out of Maud's clutch for a moment, vanished.'

Superficially, London was very agreeable to Lytton just now, and many of the letters he wrote over this period give amusing descriptions of his exploits there. 'To lunch with Lady Cunard to-day,' he announced to Carrington (16 May 1919), '– the prospect leaves me blasé . . . a blasé literary man I've become, I fear.' But for all the trivial delights and absurd social scenes he depicts, Lytton was never truly at home in this milieu. The glitter of it all would titillate his fancy for short stretches of time, during which his social apprehensions and his inherent boredom with society would seem to mix and cancel each other out. But beneath his open-eyed, ironic philandering with the *beau monde* there lay a hard centre of disapproval that occasionally makes itself apparent – however light-heartedly – in the retrospective accounts of parties he would send to his friends. In another letter to Carrington, written two days earlier, he describes a visit to Mrs Ava Astor, the wealthy widow of Colonel J. J. Astor, soon to marry Lord Ribblesdale. 'Yesterday I went (at my own suggestion) to tea with Mrs. Astor. For the first time my courage began to ooze. The immense size of that Grosvenor Square house – double doors flying open, a vast hall with a butler and two female footmen permanently established in it, vistas beyond of towering pilasters and a marble staircase and galleries – it struck awe into the heart. Then a door quite close at hand was swiftly opened, and I was projected into a large square room, in a distant corner of which, on a sofa, was a lady whom in my agitation I hardly recognised – the colour of hair seemed to have quite changed – and as I advanced three small dogs rushed out at me snapping. I at last reached the sofa and we had a long but not amorous tête-à-tête. The poor dear woman is terrified of Bolshevism – thinks Mr. Smillie[2] will lead the mob against her – and asks anxiously "Do you think they'll all go red?" I read her a lecture on

---

[1] Opposite Kent House. The Princess Bibesco Lytton referred to was probably Princess Marthe Bibesco, the friend of Proust and author of *Proust's Oriane* and *The Sphinx of Bagatelle*.

[2] Robert Smillie, president of the Miners' Federation of Great Britain (1912–21) who, in 1923, became Labour M.P. for Morpeth. A dour, granite-faced lowlander, he was said, by the few who knew him well, to be kind and intelligent, and was much admired by Oliver Strachey.

the unequality of wealth, and left her trembling to get ready for the Opera.'

One can detect in such a passage the unreconciled stages of Lytton's social attitude – the awe, the surprised amiability, the radical reproof. Society represented to him a direct challenge. When unknown and miserable long ago at Lancaster Gate, he had hated London for its vast anonymity, and the bland disregard it showed him. But now that it had begun to take notice of him, he wanted to assure himself that he was at least equal to its attentions. Determined not to be outfaced by the intimidating pomp and paraphernalia, he soon found, to his innocent wonderment, that many of the celebrated aristocratic per-sonalities framed by all this dazzling and ridiculous prestige were actually rather simple insensitive people. Like him they lived with bread, could feel want, taste grief, need friends, and lose their way among the thorns and dangers of this world. The armour of complacent inhumanity that they liked to put on was largely compounded of fear and a sense of unease, as if they had been inserted into the wrong planetary system. This was one of the main conclusions to which Lytton's inquiries among the upper classes had led him; and it made their unattractive aspects more understandable and more pitiable.

These fashionable circles, which only a year before were gravely pre-occupied with matters military and political, had recently turned their attention to the arts, and in particular the ballet. Early that summer, Diaghileff's company, with Picasso, Massine, Stravinsky and Ansermet, arrived in London to give their spectacular and triumphant performance of *La Boutique Fantasque*, *Le Tricorne* and *The Good-Humoured Ladies*. Immediately they were taken up once more by the best-known society hosts and hostesses. But Bloomsbury also shared in the festivities, and it was to introduce this odd confluence of artists, dancers and musicians into the more rough-and-tumble world of Upper Bohemia that Clive Bell and Maynard Keynes gave an informal supper-party for them at 46 Gordon Square. [1] Among the guests were Picasso, Derain, Lopokova and some forty young or youngish painters, writers and students. 'Maynard, Duncan Grant, our two maids and I waited on them,' Clive Bell later recalled. 'Picasso did not dress. We rigged up a couple of long

[1] Diaghileff had been taken up by London society (Lady Ripon, for example, and, of course, Ottoline) before the First World War. It is, however, a curious fact that Blooms-bury had not paid any attention to him until his reappearance after the war. This was because it was only during the war that Diaghileff became involved with Picasso and Derain. His earlier painters, such as Bakst, were despised by Bloomsbury, who took little interest in any elements other than painting. A feature of the return of Diaghileff was his new prima ballerina – Lopokova – eventually to marry Maynard Keynes.

tables: at the end of one we put Ansermet, at the end of the other Lytton Strachey, so that their beards might wag in unison.'

Most of the gatherings to which Lytton was asked were less intellectual and artistic affairs. During May he twice visited Garsington and found it on both occasions 'terribly trying'. In a letter to Virginia Woolf (27 May 1919), he wrote: 'I was often on the point of screaming from sheer despair, and the beauty of the surroundings only intensified the agony. Ott I really think is in the last stages – infinitely antique, racked in every joint, hobbling through the buttercups in cheap shoes with nails that run into her feet, every stile a crisis, and of an imbecility . . . She is rongée, too, by malevolence; every tea party in London to which she hasn't been invited is wormwood, wormwood.'

Another country house where his name regularly appears in the visitors' book was The Wharf. Twice that summer the Asquiths invited him over for week-ends, once in June, the second time in July. Here again the tedium was pretty extreme. Margot's friends now seemed to him a dreary lot, with the exception of Mrs George Keppel, who was the best of a large party, none of whom he knew. But the rich absurdity of his entrance there largely compensated for the dullness. 'My heart sank and sank – and sank still further on reaching this house, which is really a worse house than Charleston to arrive at,' he confided to Carrington (June 1919). 'No sign of Margot – only a faded group of completely unknown people. I lost my head – opened a door, and found myself projected into a twilight chamber, with four bridge players in the middle of it. Complete silence. Margot was one of them. At last, after a long time, in which nobody even looked in my direction, she said, "Oh, how d'you do?" – I fled – fled to the other house, where my bedroom is – opened another door, and there, at the end of the room, alone and dim, was the Old Man. He was as usual most cordial, and conducted me with incredible speed all round the garden, and then back again to the other house. He's a queer nervous old fellow, really.'

Altogether, it was 'one of those deplorable Wharf week-ends,' as he summarized it to Mary Hutchinson, 'after which one comes away, murmuring "never again, never again".' But a month later he was back there once more, though 'it's perhaps slightly better than the last time', he admitted to Carrington (17 July 1919). 'There's a middle-aged Scotch woman who plays chess with me while the others play bridge, and there are not quite so many absolute imbeciles. The "painters" are that creature Ranken[1] (a white haired pseudo Eddy) and a little sporting

---

[1] William Bruce Ellis Ranken (1881–1941), old Etonian, ex-Slade student, and for many years vice-president of the Royal Institution of Painters in Water Colours. He painted portraits, interiors, flower-pieces and landscapes, and was particularly known for

fellow – an ostler – called Mullings [*sic*], I gather, who, I also gather, paints race-horses for his living. . . .'

As a result of these excursions into society, among the overall second-rateness, Lytton was meeting a few people who stood out as being of some permanent interest in political and literary life. At a lunch given by Leonard and Virginia Woolf, he sat next to that curious couple, the Webbs, and, so Virginia noted in her diary, 'sported very gracefully'. She also commented: 'However one may abuse the Stracheys, their minds remain a source of joy to the end; so sparkling, definite and nimble. Need I add that I reserve the qualities I most admire for people who are not Stracheys?'

Another figure of portentous political significance whom Lytton encountered at this time was Lord Haldane[1], who, so he informed Ottoline (3 June 1919), was 'very satisfying – so incredibly urbane as to be almost a character in a French play – or as Mr. Asquith suggested an Abbé. In both of them I was struck by the fact of their talking of nothing but the past; what happened in August 1914 etc. seems to absorb them still. But really nowadays there are other things to think about.'

Several of his literary acquaintances were also out of the ordinary, including W. H. Davies, 'gnome and poet', and Aldous Huxley, who looked like 'a piece of seaweed', was 'incredibly cultured' and who 'produced a very long and quite pointless poem for me to read'. Though Lytton and Huxley were always friendly, their mutual sympathy seems to have been incomplete. 'I used to see Lytton Strachey quite frequently at Garsington, in London, at one or other of the centres of "Bloomsbury" sociability, and once or twice at his house in the country, when he was being looked after by poor Carrington and Partridge,' Huxley told the author. 'I always enjoyed his learning and his wit, but found his humanism rather too narrow for my taste.' On a number of occasions during this spring of 1919, the two of them would visit Osbert Sitwell, then a patient in a military hospital in London. To the eyes of the recumbent invalid, they made a startling and lugubrious couple, their 'silent elongated forms . . . drooping round the end of my bed like the allegorical statues of Melancholy and of a rather satyr-like

[1] The Rt Hon. Richard Burton Haldane, F.R.S., O.M., had been Secretary of State for War under Asquith from 1912 to 1915, and also, during the same period, Lord High Chancellor – a post which he regained in 1924, under the first brief Labour Government, having split off from the Liberals.

his portraits of British Royalty – including Queen Elizabeth (wife of George VI), Queen Mary and Princess Christian – and also for his interiors of Windsor Castle and Buckingham Palace. In 1936 he was one of four painters given facilities to paint the Coronation ceremony of King George VI in Westminster Abbey.

Father Time that mourn sometimes over a departed nobleman on an eighteenth-century tombstone. Lytton's debility prevented him from saying much, but what he did say he uttered in high, personal accents that floated to considerable distances, and the queer reasonableness, the unusual logic of what he said carried conviction.'

Another literary acquaintance for whom his feelings were peculiarly mixed was T. S. Eliot. They had first been introduced several years before, when Lytton appears to have registered a somewhat lukewarm response to the American poet. But after a second meeting at Garsington on 12 May 1919, he declared that 'he's greatly improved – far more self-assured, decidedly intelligent, and, so far as I could see, nice'. Two days later they met again in London, and Lytton reported to Carrington (14 May 1919): 'Poet Eliot had dinner with me on Monday – rather ill and rather American: altogether not quite gay enough for my taste. But by no means to be sniffed at.' At the same time, in a letter to Mary Hutchinson (15 May 1919), Lytton describes his friendship with Eliot as having reached a fluctuating stage. 'I do like him, though,' he added. 'He's changed a great deal since I last saw him – a long time ago. But the devitalisation I'm afraid may lead to disappointments.'[1]

These fears seemed well-founded. Invariably cautious, inhibited and formally polite, Eliot was an awkward person with whom to get on terms of intimacy. That month Lytton read *Prufrock and Other Poems*, which The Egoist Ltd had brought out in 1917, and although he was not altogether in tune with Eliot's profound obscurities and complicated states of mind, he sent him a letter which, he hoped, might advance their friendship. In his reply (1 June 1919) Eliot, with a characteristic blending of the precise and the nebulous, dwells on the processes of his writing. 'Whether one writes a piece of work well or not seems to me a matter of crystallisation – the good sentence, the good word, is only the final stage in the process. One can groan enough over the choice of a word, but there is something much more important to groan over first. It seems to me just the same in poetry – the words come easily enough, in comparison to the core of it – the *tone* – and nobody can help one in the least with that. Anything *I* have picked up about writing is due to having spent (as I once thought, wasted) a year

[1] A few days after their dinner together in London, Eliot wrote to Lytton (19 May 1919): 'Dear Strachey, I find that I am being sent on a tour of the provinces, by my bank, as soon as I can get off, and that I shall probably be gone some weeks. So unfortunately there is no possibility of my asking you to dine with me in the near future, as I should have liked you to have done. I only fear that when I am settled here [18 Cranford Mansions, W.1] again you will be buried away in the country. Perhaps you will keep me in touch with your movements, and perhaps you will even let me have your opinions and Reviews of anything of mine you see in print.'

absorbing the style of F. H. Bradley – the finest philosopher in English – "App.[earance] and Reality" is the Education Sentimentale of abstract thought.' Turning from his own writing to Lytton's letter, Eliot (who was then working for Lloyds Bank) comments: 'You are very – ingenuous – if you can conceive me conversing with rural deans in the cathedral close. I do not go to cathedral towns but to centres of industry. My thoughts are absorbed in questions more important than ever enters the heads of deans – as *why* it is cheaper to buy steel bars from America than from Middlesbrough, and the probable effect – the exchange difficulties with Poland – and the appreciation of the rupee. My evenings in Bridge. The effect is to make me regard London with disdain, and divide mankind into supermen, termites and wireworms. I am sojourning among the termites. At any rate that coheres. I feel sufficiently specialised, at present, to inspect or hear any ideas with impunity.'

Lytton described this letter as 'grim', and for some time he hesitated to communicate with Eliot again. 'I do intend to spur myself up though,' he assured Mary Hutchinson (17 July 1919), 'as I don't want to drop him. Only I fear it will take him a long time to become a letter writer.' Early in August, he opened up the correspondence once more, and Eliot answered saying how propitious it was that he had written just before he, Eliot, disappeared to central France, where no letters could reach him. 'I have not been away but in London, in my office or among my books or (several times) in bed,' he went on (6 August 1919), 'and have frequently imagined you sitting on the lawn at Pangbourne or in a garden, conducting your clinic of Queen Victoria with perfect concentration. . . . You have frightened me because I always expect you to be right, and because I know I shall never be able to retaliate upon your finely woven fabrics. I have lately read an article of yours on Voltaire which made me envious.' Ten days later he sent Lytton a postcard from the Dordogne, where, he was careful to point out, he had been walking the whole time and so had no address at all. London was extraordinarily difficult; very slowly one bled to death there. But wandering through the Corrèze he was happy and sunburnt, surrounded by 'melons, ceps, truffles, eggs, good wine and good cheese and cheerful people. It's a complete relief from London.'

In the months and years that followed, they met and corresponded only infrequently; and although Lytton made several overtures to a closer relationship, and although these were apparently welcomed by Eliot, there always persisted something rather reserved and diffident about their association, always something to hinder its further development.[1] While each of them, for politeness' sake, professed to admire the other's work, their reciprocal civilities never really carry great conviction, and they felt each other to be, if not wireworms, certainly not supermen.[2]

Bloomsbury had by this time tentatively taken up Eliot – the Hogarth Press in 1918 publishing his *Poems*, and four years later *The Waste Land* – but his dry, authoritarian manner still made him something of an enigma to them. 'When we first got to know Tom, we liked him very much,' remembered Leonard Woolf, 'but we were both a little afraid of him.' In the summer of 1922, various members of Bloomsbury set up the Eliot Fellowship Fund, a scheme which was designed to release Eliot from his work at the bank, which, they felt, was injuring his health and seriously interfering with his creative powers. A circular, which was distributed to all potential subscribers asking them to contribute at least five or ten pounds a year for a minimum term of five years in return for first editions of all Eliot's future volumes, expounded the scheme as follows:

'It is impossible that he [Eliot] should continue to produce good poetry unless he has more leisure than he can now hope to obtain, but his literary work is of far too high and original a quality to afford by itself a means of livelihood. For this reason it is proposed to raise a special Fellowship Fund to enable him to give up his post at the bank and devote his whole time to literary work. It is estimated that at least £300 a year for a period of not less than 5 years will be required, and it is hoped that many admirers of good literature will be glad to contribute to a fund which has for its aim the preserving of the talent of one of the most original and distinguished writers of our day.'

A committee, consisting of Ottoline Morrell, Leonard Woolf, Harry Norton and Richard Aldington, who acted as treasurer of the fund, was established in England to manage this project, and other committees in

---

[1] When, for example, Lytton wrote inviting him to spend a week-end with him at Tidmarsh, Eliot replied that he was delighted to hear from him and would love to have come (14 July 1920), 'but unfortunately I have some people motoring down for Saturday afternoon. Perhaps this is providential, as I ought to work Sunday on a book which is heavy on my conscience. How do you ever write a book? It seems to me a colossal task. *Perhaps* you will ask me again sometime?'

[2] Nevertheless, in a letter inviting Lytton to a small party at 38 Burleigh Mansions, Eliot wrote (10 December 1923): 'And once again – although I admire and enjoy your portraits in the Nation, it is to my interest to say that they are not *long* enough to do you justice. So – although you once refused – 2 years ago – please remember that I should like to lead off a number of the *Criterion* with you, up to 5000 or 8000 words. . . . I have thought that you ought to do MACAULAY – but anything from you would ensure the success of a number, besides the pleasure it would give me. Could you?' Lytton did not write his essay on Macaulay until 1927. Published in The *Nation and Athenaeum* (21 January 1928), it was 2,500 words long.

France and America were also formed to work in collaboration with the English group. But shortly after the circulars had been drafted Eliot gravely demurred, and a postscript had to be appended explaining that 'circumstances have arisen which make it necessary that Mr. Eliot should be allowed to use his own discretion as to continuing or relinquishing his present work at the bank'. Nevertheless, without imposing or implying any conditions on the reluctant beneficiary, the committee decided to go ahead with the plan as best it could, since it remained beyond dispute, even by Eliot himself, that 'any addition to his income would not only remove from him considerable anxiety which the expense of illness has brought upon him, but would make it possible for him to give more time to writing than he can now do'.

And so, in its amended form, the scheme was launched, quickly petered out and finally came to nothing. As one who shared his admiration for Donne – years before it was fashionable to admire him – Lytton naturally had some qualified respect for Eliot and was prepared to help him financially. But, hedged about by Eliot's own sombre caveats and qualifications, the Fellowship Fund struck him as being a rather ludicrous proposition, and he parodied the Bloomsbury circular in a mischievous letter to Leonard and Virginia Woolf (December 1922):

'THE LYTTON STRACHEY DONATION

'It has been known for some time to Mr. Lytton Strachey's friends that his income is in excess of his expenditure, and that he has a large balance at the bank. It is impossible, if his royalties continue to accumulate at the present rate, that he should be in a position to spend them entirely upon himself, without serious injury to his reputation among his more impecunious acquaintances. For this reason it is proposed that he should set aside the sum of £20,000 (twenty thousand pounds) to be known as the "Lytton Strachey Donation", the interest upon which shall be devoted to the support of such persons as the Committee shall think fit to select.

'All those in favour of this scheme are requested to communicate with Lady Ottoline Morrell, Garsington, Oxford, adding the sum which they themselves would wish to draw from the Donation annually. No sum less than £20 (twenty pounds) a year should be asked for, though demands for capital sums of £5000 (five thousand pounds) and upwards will be entertained.

'POSTSCRIPT

'Since the scheme in the accompanying circular was proposed it has come to the knowledge of the Committee that circumstances have arisen which make it impossible that Mr. Lytton Strachey should be prevented from using his own discretion as to the disposal of his ill-gotten gains. It is however certain that many persons would benefit even from such small sums as 5/– (five shillings) or 2/6 (two-and-sixpence), supposing that Mr. Strachey were willing to disburse them. Under these circumstances the Committee propose to continue the scheme in its present form, without, however, imposing upon Mr. Strachey any conditions as to how his money should be spent.'

It was through Eliot that the Hogarth Press was offered the un-completed manuscript of James Joyce's *Ulysses*. According to Leonard Woolf, he and Virginia decided to try and publish it in about 1919, but since no English printer was willing to risk prosecution, they were eventually forced to abandon the enterprise. Leonard refers to the novel as 'a remarkable piece of dynamite', but Virginia, as so often in her attitude to living writers, was more sceptical and malicious. When Lytton signified to her that he was willing to lend his support to their lame duck of an Eliot Fellowship Fund, she replied (24 August 1922): 'One hundred pounds did you say? You shall have a receipt. Cheque payable to Richard Aldington or O. Morrell as you prefer. My own contribution, five and sixpence, is given on condition he puts publicly to their proper use the first 200 pages of Ulysses. Never have I read such tosh. As for the first 2 Chapters we will let them pass, but the 3rd 4th 5th 6th – merely the scratching of pimples on the body of the bootboy at Claridges. Of course, genius *may* blaze out on page 652 but I have my doubts. And this is what Eliot worships, and there's Lytton Strachey paying £100 p.a. to Eliot's upkeep.'[1]

It may be that Virginia Woolf's scurrilous, semi-playful strictures were deliberately exaggerated to tune in with what she supposed Lytton's attitude to be. But it seems more probable that this criticism provided a vent to that jealous competitive spirit of hers, since Lytton, who always campaigned against censorship in any form, supported the free and unabridged publication of *Ulysses*. In any event, Virginia's sense of rivalry and lapse of sympathy did not prevent her from stirring up support for Eliot once again a few months later – this time over his appointment as literary editor of the *Nation and Athenaeum*. The chief strategist in putting over this plan was Maynard Keynes, who had met with great opposition from his fellow directors, none of whom had apparently heard of Eliot. The only way Keynes saw of ousting this opposition was to convince the directors that Eliot was well thought of

---

[1] It is significant to note that Lytton subscribed his hundred pounds some four months prior to writing the parody. In later years Eliot became a close friend of Dorothy and Janie Bussy.

by contemporary writers of the highest distinction – like Lytton Strachey – who would contribute to their paper should Eliot become its literary editor. It was Virginia who, on 23 February 1923, wrote Lytton a private and confidential letter recounting this state of affairs, and asking once more for his assistance. 'I have to approach you on a delicate matter – to wit, poor Tom,' she explained. '. . . As you are aware the Eliot fund business has proved a fiasco; and this certainly seems to be the only possible solution of the problem. In fact, the poor man is becoming (in his highly American way, which is tedious and longwinded to a degree) desperate. I think he will be forced to leave the Bank anyhow. So if you would write me a line giving some sort of promise that you would write, or at least would be more inclined to write for him than another we should all be very grateful.'

Lytton at once pledged his support directly to Keynes, who described the negotiated arrangement, with Eliot as assistant literary editor presumably under Leonard Woolf as 'poise and counterpoise', adding in a private note a fortnight later (9 March 1923): 'Pretty complete victory. Ramsay Muir[1] and Guedalla have committed suicide and Mrs Royde Smith[2] has been assassinated.' Yet, from the point of view of Eliot's appointment, this announcement of victory seems to have been premature, since, as Sir Roy Harrod rather disingenuously notes in his Life of Keynes: 'At first it was hoped to secure Mr. T. S. Eliot as Literary Editor, but he was not immediately available and the paper could not wait.'

Shortly afterwards, Eliot was appointed editor of the newly founded *Criterion*, a paper which, standing for Classicism in literature and religion, was almost totally alien to Lytton, Keynes and the Woolfs.

6

STRACHEY'S PROGRESS

Although, on and off, Lytton continued to work at the British Museum and the London Library during the spring and early summer months

[1] Ramsay Muir (1872–1941), historian and Liberal M.P. for Rochdale (1923–24). Chairman and president of the National Liberal Federation. Author of many books including *History of the British Commonwealth* (2 vols, 1920 and 1922).

[2] Naomi Gwladys Royde-Smith, prolific professional Welsh 'women's' novelist and eldest daughter of Michael Holroyd Smith. As editor of the *Weekly Westminster* – a paper that, in the pre-1914 days, enjoyed a great vogue – she had published a lot of Rupert Brooke's early verse. During the First World War she and Rose Macaulay had conducted a joint salon for writers and artists, founded on that of Julie de Lespinasse, about whom she wrote a biography. In 1926 she married Ernest Milton, the actor.

of 1919, his frequent rovings into the mansions of the great and wealthy had begun seriously to retard his progress on *Queen Victoria*. He remained so long up in town that it was rumoured that he had taken special lodgings near the Albert Memorial to keep in the right mood for his work.[1] The truth, however, was less whimsical. London, like a sticky spider's web, absorbed him; his wings were caught, and he fluttered, fluttered in vain. 'London continues to be very agreeable,' he admitted to Ottoline (30 May 1919), 'but I doubt whether I shall stay there much longer. A little work is really becoming necessary, and it's quite impossible to do a stroke in that charivari – I envy Harriet Martineau, whose autobiography I've been reading (rather an interesting book). She worked six hours a day writing political economy, and then every evening explored the beau monde. But in those days people were made of steel and india-rubber.'

It was not until the early part of July that Lytton succeeded in breaking free from the filigree of town life and retreating down to Tidmarsh. Here he was able to work with reasonable calm and concentration, the only respite being a week-end visit from E. M. Forster, with his 'curious triangular face, and a mind, somehow, exactly fitting'.

That month, Carrington had gone down with her brother Noel and a friend to Welcombe, next to the Box farm she and the others had been at in the summer of 1917 – 'a very good place for painting'. They were living in a remote little cottage, Westmill House. 'I do like small places like this where one can't spoil things,' she wrote to Mark Gertler, 'and the walls are white and one can sit with lovely still lives on the tables coloured jugs with flowers, bread Bottles of ink and tea-cups long after the meal is finished – and letters are written. outside the window one looks up a long valley with high Hills either side covered with trees, and Forests. behind the other way the cottage faces roaring sea. only a few minutes walk with huge crags, and cliffs. Fortunately there are [no] trippers here, so one can wear what one likes, and wander about the place without meeting stupid Fat Ladies with dogs.'

While she was away, Lytton, looked after by Boris and Helen

---

[1] On 1 March 1919, Lytton wrote to Vanessa Bell: 'By-the-bye, what is your view of the Albert Memorial as a work of art? It's not easy to consider it impartially– one's earliest memories are so intertwined with it – surely we must have met on those steps in long clothes? – but surely there's a coherence and conception about it not altogether negligible? – Compared, for instance, to the memorial to Victoria opposite Buckingham Palace, it certainly stands out. At any rate, it's not a thing one can easily forget.' Professor Quentin Bell comments on this letter that the Albert Memorial was 'the stock joke and aunt sally of the 1920s. Then a later generation Betjeman-wise in its day discovered or rediscovered it. Now the clever jokes at the A.M. are thought particularly "20sh" and are I fancy laid at Lytton's door. It's fascinating to find Lytton in 1919 coming so close in his judgements to the views of the post-Strachey epoch.'

Anrep's cook, pressed on with his biography. 'Now I am fairly in it, or should I say Her, immersed, pegging away daily, and quite, so far enjoying myself,' he told Mary Hutchinson (17 July 1919). In spite of this industry, he greatly disliked being left altogether alone, and in the fine summer evenings would sit out among the rambler roses in the mill-garden and dream wistfully of London, of Shaftesbury Avenue, the Soho streets, Soho Square, the little passage into the Charing Cross Road, and the Tottenham Court Road, along and along to the trees of Gordon Square – and so on endlessly. Every shop window, every paving stone, it seemed, he could call up before the mind's eye, especially when the light began to thicken, the street-lamps and illuminations to come on, though still weaker than the fading daylight, and all sorts of lovely creatures would flit from shadow to shadow across the roads. How he had hated London in the past: how the vision of it intoxicated him now in his quiet garden! 'I can hardly bear to think of it, I love it so much – to distraction.'

The result of this secluded, self-disciplined life was that he soon finished the first two chapters of Queen Victoria – 'Antecedents' and 'Childhood'. 'I have been absorbed by Victoria for the last month,' he informed his mother (19 August 1919), 'and have now written the opening part – as far as her accession. So far the variety of curious characters and circumstances keeps me going – the difficulty will be much greater, I expect, after the death of the Prince Consort.'

Before embarking on 'Lord Melbourne', Lytton took a brief respite. Following a week-end at Sybil Colefax's country house near Withyham in Sussex, he went on, at the end of August, to stay with Jack and Mary Hutchinson in West Wittering; and from here, early in September, he moved on to Charleston. 'Maynard, Clive, Duncan and Vanessa are here,' he wrote to Pippa on his arrival (2 September 1919). 'Work all day, and gossip all night is the regime, I gather.'

A few days later he returned to London, and spent three strenuous weeks dividing his time between the British Museum and Belsize Park Gardens, where the family were beginning to organize their move later in the year to a new home, 51 Gordon Square. Over these years, Gordon Square seems to have been largely taken over by the Blooms-bury Group and their friends. Duncan Grant and Vanessa Bell made good use of No. 37 for a time; James and Alix Strachey lived on the top floor of No. 41, where Lytton, Ralph Partridge and Carrington also had occasional rooms;[1] into the flat below them Lydia Lopokova had

[1] James Strachey and Alix Sargant-Florence had taken the whole of 41 Gordon Square in January 1919, and let off various bits of it at various times to various people. 'We began by living on the top two floors, before we were married,' James told the author. 'Then

moved during 1922, before her marriage to Maynard Keynes, when she transferred to No. 46; the ground-floor flat was occupied during one ballet season by Ernest Ansermet. No. 42 was in 1925 the home of Oliver Strachey and his daughter Julia. Near by, in Taviton Street, and subsequently Brunswick Square, lived Frances Marshall, David Garnett's sister-in-law, later to more into 41 Gordon Square and marry Ralph Partridge. No. 46, which had been taken by the Stephen family in 1904, was now the property of Maynard Keynes, who, during the war, shared it with Sheppard and Harry Norton – though Clive and Vanessa Bell and Duncan Grant still retained some accommodation in it. Adrian Stephen and his wife Karin, both psycho-analysts, inhabited No. 50, as did, for a very long time, Arthur Waley. And now, pure chance had decided that Lady Strachey and her daughters would dwell at No. 51. 'Very soon I foresee that the whole square will become a sort of college,' Lytton wrote to Virginia Woolf (28 September 1919). 'And the rencontres in the garden I shudder to think of. The business of packing, deciding what is to be sold, what sent to Tidmarsh, what given to the deserving poor etc. has been fearful, and is still proceeding, the brunt of it of course falling on the unfortunate Pippa. I am fit for very little more than wringing my hands. In the intervals I go to the British Museum, and try to dig up scandals about Queen Victoria. Altogether a distracting life, and the comble was reached in the small hours of Friday morning, when the policeman's wife who acts as caretaker gave birth to a baby just outside my bedroom door.'

His research work at this time, though it uncovered no scandals, was of particular advantage. With the help of Arthur Waley, then working in the Department of Prints and Drawings at the British Museum, and of H. A. L. Fisher, a trustee of the museum, he had been given leave to study the manuscript of the *Greville Memoirs*, the printed version of which had omitted many passages. Even if he did not come across anything very sensational, it was amusing to read through the old papers, and he was able to note down several points of value. On 9 October 1919, he wrote to H. A. L. Fisher: 'I have made a certain number of extracts from parts of the Memoirs that have not been published – dealing chiefly with Victoria's attitude towards the Tories in the first years of her reign. There are also a few other notes of minor

---

we took on the second floor and then for some time when we were rich, the first floor as well. There was even a very short period when we had the whole house, during which we gave a celebrated party with two hundred guests. Then by degrees we receded again till in our final period we had only the top three floors . . . Lydia [Lopokova] was on the ground floor and shook the whole house when she practised her entrechats.' In 1956, James and Alix Strachey gave up 41 Gordon Square and went to live near Marlow.

importance. I should be very glad to be able to refer to these in my book (I should not want to make long verbatim quotations) – and I think you will agree with me that there is really no reason at all why I shouldn't. Greville was very cross with the Queen for taking sides in politics – snubbing Wellington etc. – and it was natural that Reeve should refrain from publishing these passages while H.M. was alive. But now the conditions are different – and the attitude of Queen Victoria in 1840 (which, incidentally, she changed a few years later) is merely a matter of historical interest and Court politics of 80 years ago.'

Lytton went on to ask Fisher whether he would speak up for him at a meeting of the Trustees of the British Museum on 11 October, and Fisher, who completely shared Lytton's sensible views, agreed to do this. The result was that he was able to tell Lytton the following week that the Trustees had decided not to impose any restriction on his use of the *Memoirs*.

At the end of September, Lytton went back to the Mill House, where he stayed 'penned down' for the next six months, working hard at his book, and, in the intervals, arranging his library, which, having been brought down from Belsize Park Gardens, now covered the walls and floors of practically every room at Tidmarsh – while he sat in the midst of this confusion, happily cataloguing their titles in various coloured inks on a series of ruled cards. In this fashion the days succeeded one another in a most orderly manner, the sole excitements being an occasional week-end visitor, or an occasional new book. Among the latter were Daisy Ashford's *The Young Visiters* which was 'perfectly charming' and *La Porte Étroite* by Gide, which he thought 'decidedly remarkable'.[1] But most exciting of all were two books brought out that winter by his friends. The first of these was Virginia Woolf's new novel, *Night and Day*, which, he told Ottoline (15 November 1919), was a work not to read, but to re-read – 'there seemed so much in it that one could only just effleurer as one went along, and longed to return to. She [Virginia] was here last week, and appeared to be very well and cheerful, and of course more amusing than ever.' And to Pippa he wrote (13 November 1919): 'The visualisation of faces does make it difficult to judge of. But I think Mrs. Hilbery is a chef d'oeuvre.' The other highlight of these winter months was Keynes's polemical masterpiece, *The*

---

[1] Lytton also mentions at this time Ethel Smyth's reminiscences, *Impressions that Remained* ('extremely entertaining, not to say interesting. Curiously old-fashioned, too'), *The Education of Henry Adams* ('certainly very remarkable, though a trifle long'), Stephen Graham's *A Private in the Guards* which was enjoyable 'chiefly as a self-revelation, but also for accounts of things in the war', and Festing Jones's biography of Samuel Butler ('vol 2, after Miss Savage dies, decidedly falls off in interest, I think. *Her* letters are really excellent').

Economic Consequences of the Peace.[1] This book had been written by Keynes during the months of August and September down at Charleston, and he had read passages from it while Lytton was staying there. On his return to Tidmarsh a few weeks later, Lytton wrote to Keynes (4 October 1919): 'I seem to gather from the scant remarks in the newspapers, that your friend the President [Woodrow Wilson] has gone mad. Is it possible that it should be gradually borne in upon him what an appalling failure he was,[2] and that when at last he fully realised it his mind collapsed? Very dramatic, if so. But won't it make some of your remarks almost too cruel? – Especially if he should go and die.'

Although Keynes felt strongly that his sketch of Woodrow Wilson formed an essential part of his argument, and that, if the peace settlement was to be properly understood and the situation rectified, Wilson's character must be elucidated, he nevertheless did moderate some of his pages. The book was published in December, and on receiving a complimentary copy Lytton wrote back (16 December 1919): 'Your book arrived yesterday, and I swallowed it at a gulp. I think it is most successful. In the first place, extremely impressive; there is an air of authority about it which I think nobody could ignore. I was rather afraid at Charleston that it might appear too extreme, but I don't think this is at all the case. The slight softenings in the Clemenceau and Wilson bits seem to me distinct improvements, adding to the effect, rather than otherwise. Then the mass of information is delightful. I had never, for instance, had any definite idea as to what the Provisions of the Peace Treaty really were – it was impossible to gather from the newspapers, and the import of the Treaty itself would have been clearly incomprehensible – so that your exposé, apart from the argument, was most welcome; and of course this is only one of a great number of extraordinarily interesting sets of facts. As to the argument it is certainly most crushing, most terrible. I don't see how anyone can stand up against it. . . . One thing I doubted – and that was whether, on your own showing, even your proposed terms were not far too harsh. Is it conceivable that the Germany which you describe should be able to or in fact would pay 50 million a year for 30 years? To my mind

---

[1] This was the book that first made Keynes's name internationally famous. On publication it was smothered, to use Keynes's own words to Lytton (23 December 1919), 'in a deluge of approval; not a complaint, not a word of abuse, not a hint of criticism; letters from Cabinet Ministers by every post saying that they agree with every word of it, etc, etc. I expect a chit from the P.M. at any moment telling me how profoundly the book represents his views and how beautifully it is put. Will it be my duty to refuse the Legion of Honour at the hands of Clemenceau? Well, I suppose this is their best and safest line.'

[2] i.e. at the Paris Peace Conference, which Keynes attended as principal representative of the Treasury.

the ideal thing would be to abolish reparations altogether – but of course that is not practical politics – at any rate not just yet; perhaps in the end it will become so.'

Work on his own book was now advancing steadily. 'It is really very agreeable down here – what with one thing and another,' he told Mary Hutchinson (10 December 1919). 'Queen Victoria progresses with infinite slowness, but still moves.' Every morning, alone in his library, he would labour at it for about three hours, during which time he usually put down some three hundred words in ink, with hardly a correction. He composed, so he told Ralph Partridge, in his head, not sentences but entire paragraphs before committing them to paper – which may account for the extreme fluidity of his style. Nothing, except illness, was allowed to interfere with his work. 'Queen Victoria, poor lady, totters on step by step,' he reported on 9 December. 'As she's still in her youth, what will she be like in age at this rate? I can only hope that she may proceed in inverse fashion – growing speedier and speedier as she gets older, and finally fairly bundling into the grave.'

By the following spring he had completed the chapters on 'Lord Melbourne' and 'Marriage', and possibly the fifth chapter also – 'Lord Palmerston' – though this is not certain. At any rate, he felt that he had arrived at a convenient halting-place, and that, before setting to work on the final part of the biography, he would fortify himself with a few weeks' holiday abroad.

7

SOUTH FROM PANGBOURNE

'I am curiously happy just now,' Lytton wrote to Keynes on 16 December. This was for him what he described as a 'halcyon winter'. Not only was his writing going ahead very well, but the conditions of his life appeared more propitious than ever before. He was seeing a lot of Ralph Partridge. Sometimes he would brave the winter winds to go over and watch him row at Oxford; and often Ralph bicycled across to Tidmarsh for the week-end when they would read Elizabethan poetry together, and talk about literature, art, and all manner of complicated subjects. 'Lytton gets on so much better with him now,' Carrington confided to her brother Noel (12 December 1919). 'In fact they are great friends, and have long discussions on Einstein's theory whilst I darn the socks.'

It was an odd domestic communion, but one that suited Lytton admirably. For by now he had already fallen deeply in love with Ralph. Several times a week he would write to him, and these letters reveal both the intensity of his feeling and the teasing, affectionate manner in which he treated him. 'Clive and Mary are here – in great feather,' he wrote on 11 January 1920. 'We talk and talk and talk. I wished you had been here at dinner yesterday to enjoy the jugged hare with some wonderful jelly concocted by Carrington out of the remains of the Burgundy – delicious! – When are you coming back? Truth to tell, the Auld Mill Hoose is, as they say, "not itself" sans our Master Ralph. I see that if I had any sense I should have had you nailed up by the ear in the Tidmarsh pillory, so that you couldn't have escaped until everyone was quite tired of you. I warn you this is what you must expect when you return – it won't hurt *very* much, and will be an interesting experience. Imagine me sitting up in bed, in my muffetees. The wind howls, the rain pours, and the horror of Sunday covers the earth.'

Three weeks later he is writing to him again (3 February 1920): 'If you don't appear either tomorrow or Thursday, I shan't see you for a hundred years, it seems to me. My beard will be snowy white, and your ears will have grown so intolerably perky for want of pulling that they'll have to be clipped by the executioner. . . . I am feeling very cheerful and well. My dearest creature, don't bother too much about my health. The exhaustion that shatters is the kind that's caused by miserable baffled desires – in a black period of my life I was nearly killed by it; but now, dear, I am buoyed up and carried along by so much happiness! On this subject two generalisations have occurred to me. Generalisation no. 1. – The secret of happiness is to want neither too much nor too little.

'Generalisation no. 2. – No one can master this secret, under the age of 39.'

Sometimes Lytton felt tempted to ask too much from 'my sweet Ralph';[1] and then again, in reaction from this mood and especially when Carrington was not with them, he was overcome by anxiety lest Ralph should feel unnecessary disquiet, and he would hasten to reassure him – 'don't suspect darknesses, please'. Illness – any one of his 'quatre maladies mortelles' – could still swiftly deflate his high spirits. When Carrington and Ralph spent a few days together in Oxford, leaving him at Tidmarsh, the solitude closed in round him and he nearly burst into tears. 'My dear one,' he wrote on that occasion to Ralph (February 1920), 'I am feeling rather dejected and lonely, and feel that I must press your

---

[1] Partridge's actual Christian name was Reginald – Rex for short – but Lytton invented the name Ralph for him, and soon everyone was calling him by this.

hand before I go to my solitary couch. Carrington's too. . . . It seems so good when we're all three together that I grudge every minute that keeps us apart.'

From the first, then, it seemed as if an idyllic partnership had sprung up between the three of them. Carrington was delighted that her two men should have taken so well to each other. She was able now to play a still closer part in Lytton's emotional life. If she could attract the boy-friends whom he liked, then, she felt, her place with him was reasonably secure, her influence more indispensable. And Lytton did not resent Ralph's passion for Carrington – indeed their happiness seemed only to swell his own. For the time being, therefore, their three-cornered affair remained curiously unselfish, all of them adhering to the first of Lytton's generalizations – not to ask for too much or too little from it – so that each one derived added enjoyment from the pleasure of the other two. There appear to have been no real moments of awkwardness or misunderstanding between them – indeed they made fun of such possibilities. 'I send my fond love,' Lytton ended one of his letters to Ralph (February 1920), 'and all the kisses and etceteras that I didn't dare to send you by Carrington for fear of their being intercepted en route.'

The situation, however, could not stay poised for ever at this finely balanced point, which depended so much upon mutual tact, compromise and control. Ralph had been completely won over by Lytton's unwavering gentleness, his thoughtfulness, his alert and witty mind. He was charmed by him: but he was in love with Carrington. Towards the end of this winter, he started to put pressure on her to marry him. She strongly resisted, while Lytton, who wished everything to remain exactly as it was, looked on anxiously, wondering how things would turn out, but never attempting to influence either of them in any way.

Thus the first sinister shadow had been thrown across their strange relationship; but almost at once it was temporarily dissolved again when, that April, the three of them took off for six weeks' holiday together in Spain. They were to stop at all the places that Carrington and Ralph had visited the previous year – Carrington was insistent upon this; for only then could she share with Lytton in retrospect all her past experiences there, transmuting them from a meaningless confusion of pleasurable sights and sounds into something really memorable. In addition to this itinerary, they planned to spend a few days with Ralph's friend, Gerald Brenan, who, the previous autumn, had sailed from England with a hundred pounds in his pocket to set up house at the primitive and inaccessible mountain village of Yegen, in Andalusia. This was to be the highlight of their journey.

Full of the highest anticipations, they started out by boat towards the end of March, stopped off for a day at Corunna, and finally disembarked at Lisbon. From here they continued their journey through the night by train across the Spanish border to Seville, Lytton travelling first class, the other two third. 'At the best of times travelling in this country is hard,' he wrote to Mary Hutchinson (11 April 1920), 'all the train journeys last for twelve hours at a minimum, and the slowness of one's advances is heart-breaking. We had a fearful night coming out of Portugal – the 1st class carriage blocked with sucking babies and drunken commercial travellers – poor Ralph reduced to sleeping on the portmanteau in the corridor, etc. etc. But still, one does progress, and the sights one sees are worth the horrors.'

These horrors rapidly multiplied as they pressed on with their advance into the wilds of Spain. By the time they reached Seville, Lytton was already quite exhausted, but Ralph's strict, almost regimental schedule, which had unfortunately neglected to take account of his companion's lack of soldierly stamina, did not allow for many periods of rest. Soon he was hurrying the party on again, this time to Cordova – 'a most wonderful town', so Lytton informed Pippa (1 April 1920). Almost all the places he was to see were more spectacular than he had expected. But Cordova he loved best of all, describing it in a letter to Mary Hutchinson as 'oriental – a network of narrow narrow streets, and a very big and beautiful mosque, in the middle of which the astonishing Christians have stuck a huge rococo church – the effect is dizzying. One evening we went in after sunset, and found a mass in progress. A full orchestra was at work in the baroque building, a tenor was singing an aria by Mozart, and all round, dimly lighted by a lamp here and there, were the pillars and arches of the antique mosque, stretching away in every direction into far distant darkness. It was incredibly theatrical and romantic, and I felt like Uncle John, very very nearly a Roman Catholic.'

Ralph's time-table permitted them to linger on in Cordova three full days. Then they were up and off again, and after more agonizing hours of Spanish travelling, came to Granada, which, Lytton declared, was 'astounding – very high up, with immense snow mountains directly over it, and the Alhambra – huge dark red walls and towers – dominating the town. Before long, one observes picture-postcard elements in this, and the detail of the Alhambra is sheer Earl's Court, but the general grandeur of situation and outline remain.'

They arrived in Granada on 2 April, Lytton describing himself on a postcard to Virginia Woolf as 'very chirpy'. But his chirpiness did not long survive. As the party had fought their way onwards and upwards, so their difficulties and the complications of their trip had steadily mounted. After reaching Granada these tribulations came to a head. Every day there was some fresh crisis or disaster – and the victim of all these catastrophes was Lytton, who became more and more alarmed the further they left civilization behind. Already it seemed to him that he had been away from England for several years. 'I am breaking S[trachey] of his milksops,' Ralph had confidently predicted to Noel Carrington early on; but his optimism was ill-founded. At Granada Lytton suffered a serious relapse. The ruthless Spanish cuisine, with its emphasis on potato omelets, dried cod, and unrefined olive oil, played havoc with his delicate digestive system; he caught Spanish influenza; he nearly trod on a Spanish snake; he mislaid his pyjamas; he injured his knee and announced that he was liable to faint at any moment, though requiring no assistance to recover; and at all times he refused absolutely to exchange a word with any of the natives. Before embarking on this holiday, he had toyed for a while with the Spanish grammar, but not apparently to much practical avail. 'I began the study of the Spanish language last Thursday,' he had written to Ralph on 11 January, '– but I haven't quite completed it yet – there's still time for you to put on the finishing touches. . . . Te envio un baccio.' Such eloquence was confined to paper. And to England. On Spanish territory, nothing would induce him to order even a glass of water. Whenever he lost sight of his two companions he was seized with a sort of dumb panic and, in all matters of communication, relied on Ralph who, he admiringly wrote to his mother, 'can grapple with the Spanish language in a most talented way'.

Their nerves frayed by these set-backs, Carrington and Ralph had now begun to quarrel, and a trying emotional tangle quickly arose between them. Ralph, on whose shoulders the responsibility rested for every decision, complained with mounting exasperation that their holiday was rapidly turning into a fiasco. Carrington retorted that Ralph was insufferably dreary and stupid, that he might *look* very handsome and make a 'good bedding plant', but that he was 'not for use in the day time', and should consequently remain silent – except as interpreter. Outwardly it was a typical lovers' quarrel, but the underlying bone of contention was Lytton. Ralph felt at times that he was holding them back and spoiling their journey – which was less satisfactory than last year. Carrington seems to have felt that Ralph was using Spain like some open-air gymnasium, that he was incapable of enjoying the beauties of architecture and landscape in a relaxed and civilized manner.

At Granada their fortunes took a steep plunge. For it was here that they had arranged to join up with Gerald Brenan, who intended to escort them across Los Alpujarras – that wild tract of country between the Sierra Nevada and the hills which lie to the north of the Mediterranean – up to his small mountain cottage. Brenan, however, delayed by chronic mismanagement of his own affairs, failed to arrive on time, and so there was nothing for Lytton and the others to do but wait uncertainly in the Hotel de Paris, and in the meantime explore the town. They went to the mosque, to a bull-fight, and a concert. Carrington in a letter (undated) to her brother describes something of the unresolved stalemate in which they had landed up. 'Monday we spent trying to find Brenan who is due to meet us, and convey us over the hills to his cottage for a week. Lytton refuses to go until he has R.P.'s good word for his safety. which R.P. can't give until he sees Brenan. at present Lytton's rather ill I think with the slightly billious food of this hotel.'

Lytton himself uttered no complaints over Brenan's absence. The trip which he envisaged up vertical, zigzagging tracks and across the most primitive, out-of-the-way region of Spain, with all its incumbent trials and hardships, struck him as being the very height of folly. His spirit of adventure, so keen at the outset of their voyage, had been remorselessly worn away by never-ending mishaps, until by now he felt the strongest aversion to courting further and greater calamities. 'Partridge, the young man who is with me,' he told his mother (18 April 1920), 'has an eccentric friend who has taken up his abode in a remote village there (Los Alpujarras), and it was decided that we should go and see him.' Writing to Mary Hutchinson at about the same time, he felt able to express his feelings more explicitly, describing Brenan as 'an amiable lunatic . . . who has come to live here in pursuit of some Dostoievsky will o' the wisp or other, and whom Partridge had engaged himself to come and visit with solemn vows'. Despite the hideous prospect of this visit, he neither wanted to spoil it for the others nor to be left at Granada alone (or even with Carrington, in whose capabilities he had little confidence). With characteristic tenacity, he determined to accompany them all should Brenan turn up.

Not to be baulked by this reverse, Ralph had meanwhile dispatched an urgent telegram to his friend reminding him of their arrival in Granada and adding that, unless he contacted them, they would be leaving again in two days. This message brought Brenan, weak with influenza, scrambling down the mountains just in time to miss them – by half an hour – at their hotel, and barely in time to catch up with them at the bus station. The four of them then boarded a motor-bus and for several frantic hours bumped along a most appalling road until they reached Lanjaron, 'a small health resort in the hills'. Here they put up at an hotel, and began to discuss the next stage of their journey. The problem of transporting Lytton up to Yegen loomed large. He sat in a cane armchair drinking cognac, silent and bearded, and betraying no sign of enthusiasm for the various ways and means that were being debated. Finally, it was decided to engage a carriage for the following morning to carry them all to a village called Orgiva, where they would procure mules to transport them along the last few miles of their trek. Brenan, however, had forgotten about the floods that spring. All went well until they reached the Rio Grande, which was so swollen as to be virtually impassable. On arriving at the ford, the mules went in almost up to their girths amid the racing water, and Lytton drew back in alarm. The party then wearily retreated to the hotel, deciding to make a fresh start by another route early the following morning.

After this day's failure everyone's nerves were more than ever on edge, and the evening passed in general low spirits and an air of recrimination – Lytton gloomy but mutely resolute, Brenan harassed and ruffled, Carrington and Ralph full of reciprocal accusations. 'The conveyance of the great writer to my mountain village began to assume more and more the appearance of a difficult military operation,' Brenan afterwards recorded. 'Carrington, caught between two fires, became clumsily appeasing and only Lytton said nothing. As for myself, I never doubted my powers to go anywhere or do anything of a physical sort that I wished to, but under my friends' bombardment I felt my unfitness for assuming responsibility for other people.'

Next morning at nine o'clock they again set off. The day was very hot, and thirty miles of difficult and precipitous country lay before them, filling them all with the darkest forebodings. No sooner had they dismounted from the carriage and descended into the river valley, than Lytton, who was suffering by this time from piles, discovered that he could not ride on mule-back. Every half-mile or so the band of them would arrive at a river, he would perilously mount his animal, be agonizingly conveyed across, and then climb off again – all the while balancing an open sunshade high above his head. This procedure repeated itself with a monotonous frequency throughout the day, so tiring Lytton and so delaying their progress that at last they agreed unanimously to break their journey and put up for the night at the small village of Cádiar. But one look at the best bed available at the *posada*, and they quickly changed their minds and dragged themselves off again along the bed of the same river which they continued, as in a nightmare, to cross and recross on their mules, and so on and so on by narrow tracks, up and up into the hills until the day began to fade and the stars appeared in the sky.

N*

The last part of their march, straight up a mountainside of some two thousand five hundred feet, was undertaken in silent twilight. This dramatic ascent, along a steep path bordered by precipices, was made by Lytton sitting side-saddle. On reaching the top, Carrington and Brenan hurried ahead over the six miles that remained to give warning of the great man's arrival and see to it that a meal was prepared. Ralph and Lytton reached Yegen half an hour later – at about ten o'clock that night – having travelled a good twelve hours with only one halt in the middle of the day. 'Lytton and I certainly had mules,' Carrington wrote to Noel. 'But as we crossed a rapid torrent at least thirty times *on* the mules they were'nT altogether an unmixed joy! My God. I was never so glad to reach any place in my life as I was Gerald's cottage that night.' And in a letter to Mary Hutchinson, Lytton gave his comments on their adventure. 'Such a journey from Granada as you never saw, taking three days, beginning with a frantic motor-bus (the roads, ma chère, the roads!) and ending with a complete day on mule-back (Carrington on a donkey) winding up and up by the bed of a river, crossing and re-crossing, the water up to our beasts' bellies – oh it was a scene! – the sun scorching, the wind whistling, the rain drenching, at last the night coming on – Lady Hester wasn't in it: the emotional crises, too, of the strangest sort – until we arrived in pitch darkness and almost dead at our singular destination. . . . Well, I hardly guessed that I should ever live to be led to such a spot by the beaux yeux of a Major!'

But once there, Lytton began to feel that the expedition had almost, if not quite, been worthwhile. Brenan's cottage was magnificently placed, very high up, the hills all round being covered with fruit-trees and vegetation of every kind – olives, oranges, figs and vines, chestnuts and bright green poplars. To the north stood the towering snow-topped Sierra Nevada, far away to the south could be seen the blue glimmer of the Mediterranean, and all around were vast stretches of hill and rock and chasm – an extraordinary variety of landscape on an enormous scale, brilliantly coloured. 'Look at a map of Spain, and find Granada,' he instructed Mary Hutchinson (11 April 1920). 'Thence draw a line of 40 miles in a southwesterly direction, across the Sierra Nevada, and you will arrive – here. Yegen is a village among the mountains, high up with a view of the Mediterranean in the distance, and all round the most extraordinary Greco-esque formations of rocks and hills. Never have I seen a country on so vast a scale – wild, violent, spectacular – enormous mountains, desperate chasms – colours everywhere of deep orange and brilliant green – a wonderful place, but easier to get to with a finger in a map than in reality!'

Lytton passed most of his days at Yegen recovering from the fatiguing passage there and preparing himself for the terrors of the return journey. 'I am treated with the utmost consideration, of course,' he wrote, 'and I am enjoying myself greatly, but I shan't be sorry when this section of our trip is over, and we return to comparative civilization.' Only during the last day, cheered presumably by the prospect of leaving, did he relax completely and become almost lively. The others, however, were in high spirits, bathing and going off for picnics. Despite the general strain of their visit and her unflagging concern for Lytton's health, Carrington was especially happy during this week. She was attracted to Brenan and found him an enchanting companion.[1] 'He is such a charming person,' she wrote to Noel, 'very like Teddy in his good humour and charm. But oh so vague about distances, and any idea about time! We spent some of the best days there with him that I've ever spent in Spain.'

Soon they were on their way again, this time by another route, 'beginning with a mule journey', Lytton wrote to his mother, 'then going in a delightful diligence by a horse and a mule, then in a motor-bus over another incredibly horrible road to Almeria, which is on the coast, and where civilization begins again'. From here they travelled on by train to Toledo, where, in hot sunshine, Holy Week was being celebrated with a glittering religious festival. By a strange coincidence, Osbert Sitwell, recently risen from his sick-bed, was also visiting Toledo with his brother Sacheverell, and caught sight of Lytton and Carrington on the opposite side of a narrow street leading up to the Plaza from the Cathedral. Between them, like a slow-moving stream, passed the procession of worshippers, and it was not until half of it had filed by that the Sitwells beheld a phenomenon which, because of its startling incongruity, impressed them as being far more remarkable than any that had so far been exhibited – 'the lean, elongated form of Lytton Strachey, hieratic, a pagod as plainly belonging as did the effigies to a creation of its own. Well muffled, as usual, against the wind, and accompanied by his faithful friend and companion Carring-ton . . . who, with fair hair and plump, pale face, added a more practi-cal, but still indubitably English-esthetic note to the scene, he was

---

[1] 'Yes, we were none of us quite ourselves those few days at Yegen,' Gerald Brenan later wrote to Carrington (May 1920), '– not so gay nor so careless nor so witty as we generally count on being. Perhaps that's always the case. But you were admirable, you know, and so was Lytton . . . Lytton was so cheerful over that appalling endless journey! Ralph was gloomy at first – he had reason to be – and I, whilst we were at Yegen, felt angry about something – about what I don't know, for no doubt it all came from my feeling ill and overtired. But you have seen Yegen and will come back again. That's the main thing. Chiefly for Lytton's sake – because he may not want to repeat that journey of approach, I wish you had stayed at least another week.'

regarding the various giants and giantesses with a mute and some-what phlegmatic air of appreciation.'

Since Lytton did not at first notice his friends, partly concealed by the colourful throng jostling and scurrying between them, Osbert Sitwell was able to study him with some care, later recording his impressions in a volume of memoirs. 'His head', he recalled, 'was crowned with a wide-brimmed brown hat. He had by nature a narrow, long-shaped face, and his narrow, rather long beard, which extended it in similar fashion and showed itself to be chestnut-coloured in the sun, exaggerated this characteristic. . . . Humour and wit were very strongly marked in the quizzical expression of his face, and also, I think, a kind of genuine diffidence as well as a certain despair and, always, a new surprise at man's follies. . . . His long nose, the colour of his face and beard, his rather arched angular eyebrows, and his brown eyes, the sense of a cultured, scholarly man that permeated his entire outward aspect, all these characteristics and qualities were, though highly individual, essentially English. It is important to look the part one plays, and he gave consummately the impression of a man of letters, perhaps rather of one in the immediate past than in the present; a Victorian figure of eminence, possibly. Yet . . . it was an Elizabethan as well as a Victorian head that peered from aloft over the darker, more obviously excited people . . . as he stood there, thinly towering, impressive undoubtedly, but with an undeniable element of the grotesque both in his physique and in his presentation of himself, it was at him one looked, and not at anybody else.'

While Osbert Sitwell was forming these detailed impressions, Lytton suddenly caught sight of him and Sacheverell, and signalled to them with a look of amused and friendly recognition. At that moment, the two lines of spectators on either side of the road broke behind the procession, the Sitwells were whirled away in one direction and Lytton and Carrington were swept far out of sight in the other.

They did not meet again. Lytton's party were staying only forty-eight hours in Toledo, and the next day they had moved on to Madrid, 'which I think has little to recommend it besides the Prado', Lytton informed his mother, 'but that is a large exception'. They put up for several days here at the Hotel Terminus, 'rather a grand hotel above our means', as Carrington described it (26 April 1920), 'but its very enjoyable'. Almost every day they would visit the Prado to look at the Velasquez paintings 'and many other marvels'.

On 21 April, they left Madrid, travelling by train to Paris where they stayed at the Hôtel d'Orléans, in the rue Jacob, on the Left Bank of the Seine opposite the Louvre. Only an hour after arriving there on the morning of Friday 23, they ran into Nick and Barbara Bagenal, and all five of them went off 'very cheerily' to Versailles, where Nick and Barbara were taking a course in French literature. 'I was most delighted with Versailles,' Carrington wrote to Noel. 'It's beauty amazed me every moment. Lytton was of course in his element. And gave us a superB History of the French Kings and their intrigues.' In the sophisticated atmosphere of Paris, so familiar and so amenable, Lytton was at his best. The tribulations of the past weeks were quite forgotten and he became what Partridge termed 'an incalculable asset'. He took them to lunch at Foyot's, to a concert of classical quartets, to explore the bookshops, to see the pictures at the Louvre. He was animated, amusing, almost ebullient.

On the afternoon of Saturday 24, Ralph had to race back to England to see his mother, who had suddenly been taken ill. That evening Lytton wrote to him: 'My Angel, It was so miserable parting from you that I hardly knew what to do. After being with you for so long and so very very happily, it was dreadful to know that you had gone. But dearest we shall soon meet again – very soon after you get this – if not before! Paris is delightful – such a warm evening, and everything even more attractive under the night sky than the day one; but we miss you terribly – the little café where we dined again tonight seemed to have lost half its charm without the courier to order dinner and enjoy the wine with and to speculate over the whores. My dear one, I have enjoyed it all immensely, and how can I ever thank you enough for what you have done for me during these five weeks? It is indeed good to think of how many wonderful memories we have now between us – from the porpoises in the Bay of Biscay to the Fra Angelico in the Louvre!'

The following Tuesday Lytton and Carrington caught the Dieppe train, thankful to be returning at last to London and the Home Counties. They were met that same evening at the station by Ralph, and the three of them went off to have dinner together 'and to drink to the memory of the most glorious of holidays', as Lytton expressed it.

Such were the miraculous healing and inspiriting powers of love. But when, three years later, Leonard and Virginia Woolf were preparing to make a similar trip to Spain, and to visit Gerald Brenan, Lytton urgently warned them against such a plan. 'It's DEATH!' he shrilled. 'DEATH!'

. . . . .

8

THE END OF *QUEEN VICTORIA*

Shortly after their arrival back in England, the three of them went their separate ways – Ralph to row and complete his legal studies at Christ Church, Carrington into a London hospital for a minor operation on her nose, and Lytton down to the Mill House, where he was soon 'plunged in Queen Victoria'.

Since nearly all his research work had been finished before going on holiday, Lytton was to spend only a small part of the coming year in London. Whenever he did go up, he would usually stay at 41 or at 51 Gordon Square, where, late in 1928, he was given a self-contained, ground-floor flat. 'It would be hard to imagine a house more middle-class and more 19th century,' recorded the Italian critic Emilio Cecchi, who called on him there one summer evening. 'Victorian lithographs adorned the walls of the entrance hall, and the maid wore a crest of tulle; by the side of the twin pillars was to be found the classic tablet listing the various members of the family with the captions "In and Out".[1] . . . Such impressions were heightened within Strachey's studio; accentuated in fact to the point where they seemed to be prompted by a certain mischievousness. . . . It was as if one had stepped into a page of a Victorian novel. A Louis Philippe divan, a few books on a windowsill, a small desk, more lady-like than one would associate with an extremely successful author. Exceptionally, the desk bore a fair-sized Still Life of post-impressionist affiliation. Within the grate burned one of those ineffable anthracite fires which serve any purpose other than heating the room: one pace away you roast, at two paces your teeth chatter. The blue corkscrew candles, which stood on the marble fireplace, supported some prints which featured dandies of varying hues, beaus in their hats and patterned breeches, as well as blond beauties with wasp waists. Behind the muslin by the windows, the pale green of the trees of Gordon Square could be discerned in the setting sun.'[2]

The composition of *Queen Victoria* dominated the next eight months. Nevertheless, while Carrington was in hospital, he did allow himself

[1] When the author visited 51 Gordon Square in 1964 this tablet was still in position, with the word 'Out' slotted against those members of the family who were dead. The house has now been taken over by London University.

[2] Before 1928, whenever he stayed at 51 Gordon Square, Lytton would occupy Pernel's room on the second floor, while she was away in term-time at Newnham. Emilio Cecchi's published description of the flat at 51 Gordon Square, which Lytton moved into after his mother's death, must be read with extreme caution. According to James Strachey, it has 'every single detail incorrect, without exception'. It is also 'very silly indeed', serving only one purpose – 'to make fun of Lytton'.

several excursions away from the loneliness of Tidmarsh. One of the
first was a visit to Ottoline. 'As for me, I feel slightly melancholy, quite
worn out, from a long Garsington week-end,' he reported to David
Garnett (26 May 1920). 'Though her ladyship was affable and there was
almost enough to eat, it was none the less an exhausting business. Twice
we witnessed the "eights" at Oxford (poor Partridge rows in them) –
a horrid ceremony – crowds of dreadful women – mothers and sisters –
veritable harpies – gloating over the young men's tortures, in extreme
heat and extreme hideousness – so much effort wasted – so much pointless cruelty and vague stupidity everywhere.'

But if Oxford produced a lowering effect on his morale, Cambridge,
where he next went as the guest of Maynard Keynes, was full of
effervescence. He still believed London to be the most stimulating
place in which to stay, but its enormous human mechanism, churning
out a ceaseless round of work and amusement, soon palled, since it
served only to repress the peacetime spirit of rejuvenescence. In the
more sensitive, less anonymous atmosphere of Cambridge, the difference
between war and peace was, almost literally, the difference between
death and life. Once the war had ended, the place had gone through a
transformation as sudden and complete as that of a Roman spring. All
at once, after the icy season of sterility, the sap began to flow again, and
the exuberance of youth burst out. It was captivating – it was almost
incredible – to see college courts with caps and gowns in them, and
swishing boats tearing after one another on academic streams. Youthfulness was infectious, and it became possible to believe once more in the
New Age of Civilization.

'Life is more agreeable here than ever,' Keynes had assured him –
though lamenting that 'my bed is depressingly disengaged all this
month' – and he invited him over to King's, where he would meet Lord
Chalmers 'who has announced his intention of staying with me in
King's for the week-end of the 30th [May]. There will be room for you
too – unless you want to avoid him.' Lytton eagerly accepted, and
during the week-end wrote off an account of his visit to amuse the
convalescent Carrington. 'Lord Chalmers is a pussy-cat of an old buffer
with white hair and great urbanity – a plum on a wall, very far gone –
squashy, decidedly. He makes long elaborate speeches, likes dragging
in the eminent dead, and when he does so usually turns to me with a
slight bow and says – "a friend of Mr. Strachey's" – how Pozzo can
take such obvious absurdity at all seriously quite beats me. We had a
most pompous dinner yesterday in Hall, with the "Combination
Room" afterwards – the wine-bibbing dons assembled round a long
mahogany table, and drinking port, slowly, glass after glass (not very

good port, I thought). Then I went to Trinity, and talked for some hours with [F. L.] Lucas, who appeared to me decidedly fascinating – though exactly why I'm blessed if I know. The young, otherwise, seem to be rather in retirement, though Maynard promises me a luncheon with Spicer and Sebastian [W. J. H.] Sprott (he tells me a real person). . . . Cambridge is certainly a cosy, sympathetic spot after the grim grandeurs of Oxford – quite middle-class, which is always such a relief – at any rate for a day or two.'

By early June, Carrington had left the hospital and withdrawn down to the Mill House, racked by headaches, and feeling very sorry for herself. Lytton also hastened back to Tidmarsh in order to take care of her – 'so far I have induced her to keep in her bed', he told Ralph. 'With rest and feeding-up (if these can only be administered!) I think she ought to be all right again before long.'

In less than a fortnight she was back to normal and, with her usual energy, looking after Lytton, who was thus free once more to concentrate fully on his writing. These were uneventful, industrious months. Ralph, in his last term at Oxford and heavily occupied with his rowing and his reading, was scarcely able to see them, and so there was nothing for it but to work. 'It seems melancholy here without you,' Lytton confessed to him (9 June 1920). 'Truth to tell, I miss you very much.' Though he sometimes complained of laziness, his correspondence this summer shows that he was hard at work on his biography, which was giving him a lot of trouble. 'Queen Victoria proceeds at a fine rate,' he had reported on 19 May. But on 26 July he appears more gloomy: 'Victoria drops a lengthening chain, damn her. It is not easy to be sprightly with such a Majesty.' And three days later, he wrote in a similar vein to Ralph: 'I lead a life of complete regularity and painful industry here – piling page upon page – well! I hope somebody some day may be amused by it, but I feel damned uncertain.' On 14 August he told Mary Hutchinson: 'Up to the end of this month I must be here, struggling with Victoria, who's proving a tougher mouthful than even I had expected. I must masticate and masticate with a steady persistence – it's the only plan.'

By the beginning of September he had had enough of it, and on reaching another convenient halting-place, decided to recruit with a round of visits to his friends. 'I got at last perfectly paralysed by Victoria,' he admitted to James (September 1920). 'My brain spun round and round, and I thought I was going to sink into imbecility. So it became necessary to have a rest.'

He hurried down to stay with the Bells at Charleston, sending Carrington, in exchange for various parcels of sugar, gingerbread and clean clothes, a long and hilarious account of the domestic scene there, in particular a Bloomsbury Experiment with Time (4 September 1920). 'Typically, Maynard has insisted on . . . you'd never guess what: altering the time! So that the clocks are one hour in advance even of summer-time, with curious consequences. For one thing Jessie disapproves, won't have it, and has let the kitchen clock run down, so that the servants have *no* time. Then Clive is fitful on the subject, and insists upon always referring to the normal time; and altogether the confusion is extraordinary. How mad they all are! Maynard, though he sees what a rumpus it causes, persists. Vanessa is too feeble to put him down, and Clive is too tetchy to grin and bear it. The result is extremely Tchekhofesque. But luckily the atmosphere is entirely comic, instead of being fundamentally tragic as in Tchekhof. Everyone laughs and screams and passes on.'

From the topsy-turvy climate of Charleston, Lytton moved on to Monk's House, a cottage which Leonard and Virginia Woolf had recently taken after leaving Asheham, in the village of Rodmell, on the opposite bank of the river Ouse. Here, though the diet seemed extraordinary – jam and potatoes and bottled plums – the atmosphere was far quieter and more equable. 'This country seems to me the best in the world,' he wrote to Ralph (11 September 1920). 'I went for a perfect walk yesterday with Virginia. Oh, for a great farmhouse here, with many large panelled rooms and a walled garden, and barns, and horses for my two children, and a pianola, and multitudes of books, and a cellar of wine, and . . . but my imagination runs away with me. Well! Some day it may occur!'

After a week at Monk's House, he travelled on to Eleanor, Jack and Mary Hutchinson's home in West Wittering. 'The house is minute,' he informed Ralph (16 September 1920), 'with two children at the noisiest age ramping over it, and the tête-à-tête with Mary Hutch grows difficult as time goes on. The complete absence of sex-instinct is such a bore, unless there's a great deal of intellect to make up. When there's a slight flirtation – even an infinitesimally slight one, it makes such a difference!'

His autumn peregrination over, Lytton flew back at the end of the month to Tidmarsh to be confronted once more by *Queen Victoria*. 'Here I sit,' he wrote to Mary Hutchinson (4 October 1920), 'over the fire, trying to nerve myself for the coup de grâce on Victoria: but I hesitate . . . she quells me with her fishy eye.' He hoped to finish the book before Christmas, and longed to be free of it; but his hopes seemed doomed, the captivity endured, and on 11 November he admitted to Keynes: 'It seems to me still rather doubtful whether I shall kill Victoria or Victoria me.' The captivity, however, had its compensations. He was sending each chapter on to Ralph Partridge, who would type it out and correct the spelling. From one of his letters to Ralph (23 November 1920), it appears that he had to alter his description of the Prince Consort's death, and that this delayed him more than he had estimated. On 6 December, Geoffrey Whitworth of Chatto and Windus came down to Tidmarsh so that together they might plot and plan the book's publication. Lytton promised that his typescript would be completed early in the New Year, ready for Chatto's Spring List. He gauged the length to be around ninety thousand words – ten thousand words shorter than he had originally intended.[1] He and Whitworth also agreed the terms of the contract: seven hundred and fifty pounds in advance of royalties, which were set at 20 per cent of the published price on the first five thousand copies sold, and 25 per cent thereafter.

Arrangements for the American edition of *Queen Victoria* were more complicated and, in the long run, less satisfactory. Keynes, whose *The Economic Consequences of the Peace* had been recently brought out by Harcourt Brace, had persuaded Lytton to relinquish his own firm. On his advice, Lytton wrote to G. P. Putnam's, who had brought out *Eminent Victorians*, politely notifying them that they would not be handling his next book – a decision which gave rise to some consternation and bad feeling. At the same time Keynes opened up negotiations with Harcourt Brace, and after some exchanges of letters and telegrams, reported back to Lytton that he had secured an outright offer for the American rights amounting to seven thousand dollars – slightly over two thousand pounds – which could be safely invested to bring in something between one hundred and fifty and two hundred pounds a year for life. 'I hardly know what to advise,' he added (30 November 1920). 'But for you there seems a good deal of virtue in certainty. You would still have the whole of the English rights intact to gamble with. What shall I cable back?'

Lytton was rather doubtful whether this sum was really enough, especially since it was to include serial rights for a number of extracts in the *New Republic*.[2] Already from Putnam's he had received, on a

---

[1] Since Lytton's original estimate of one hundred thousand words held good until the early autumn of 1920, it seems likely that he had meant to deal with Victoria's old age at greater length, deciding on a more cursory treatment only while he was actually at work on the ninth chapter.

[2] On 27 January 1921, Lytton wrote to his brother James in Vienna: 'My state has been appalling – given over to Victoria for weeks and weeks without cessation – a fearful struggle, its horrors being increased by the "relaxing" cônditions at Tidmarsh – however it's now done – typed – and actually handed over to Chatto's. The relief is enormous; but the worst of it is that various crises are still pending. The American question is acute and complicated. Maynard has been acting as an intermediary with

20 per cent royalty basis, over seven hundred pounds from the immediate sales of *Eminent Victorians* – and here there had been no question of a serial. On the other hand he was impressed by what Keynes had said about the advantage of certainty on an outright sale, and so he asked his friend to demand on his behalf the sum of ten thousand dollars for all rights, or up to five thousand dollars excluding serial rights. Harcourt Brace cabled back that they were willing to make the ten-thousand-dollar payment, providing they were given the Canadian rights of the biography. Since Chatto and Windus generously agreed to this, the contract was then signed. And so, to everyone's satisfaction, was concluded a deal that over the years deprived Lytton and his literary executor of many thousands of pounds.

On 24 January, Lytton wrote to Geoffrey Whitworth telling him that the book was almost finished. There remained one more task, and that was rather peculiar. It consisted in fitting in the final paragraph, the famous death-bed scene of the queen, which was the very first paragraph he had written and towards which the rest of the book had been subtly manipulated.

Now at last he was a free man, and could roam the streets of London again. On 25 January, he came up to 51 Gordon Square, where he was to spend most of the next three months, 'leading a life of idleness and proof-reading'. His other reading included two books recently produced by his friends – Leonard Woolf's *Empire and Commerce in*

Harcourt, his American publisher, who, after some havering, offered 10,000 dollars for all the American rights complete. At that time this was worth nearly £3000 – and I thought it would do, and accepted. But since then the wretched dollar has sunk, so that it's now worth only about £2660. But still the contract has not been fixed. There are also various difficulties about the serialisations – in England and America and their dates. The Times (also via Pozzo) is being negotiated with, but nothing has been settled yet. In the meantime, Chatto has payed me £750, as advance royalties, payable in receipt of the MS. The arrangement is that I get 20% on the first 5000 copies, and 25% after that – viz. on the selling price of the book, which will probably be 15/-. So that the advance royalties covers the first 5000 copies. If I get £700 for the serial rights – which is conceivable – I may net something between 4 and 5,000 – which doesn't seem so bad – though I still shiver in my shoes over the American question which continues to hang in the wind. I suppose I shall have to invest it – which seems rather dull – and I daresay the best thing would be to buzz it all straight off. I wish to goodness you had been here to assist me in these terrific transactions. And as for the proof correcting, I shudder to think of it. C & W. say they'll have it out on April 7th. As for the work itself, I hope it's readable, and that it steers the correct course between discretion and indiscretion. I feel rather doubtful as to whether the presentment of her Majesty forms a consistent whole: the tone seems to shift so wildly – from tragedy to farce, from sentiment to cynicism: but let's hope it all forms up. It's almost impossible for me at the present moment to get an impartial view of it. The strain of such a long continuity has been extreme. I don't feel as if I should ever be able to face such a bulky affair again.'

Africa which he thought 'terrific'; and the *Œdipus Tyrannus* of Sophocles translated and expounded by Sheppard.[1] He did no work, bringing out between August 1919 and May 1923 only one essay – a very indifferent piece on Disraeli, which appeared in *Woman's Leader.* 'All is well,' he assured Carrington (24 February 1921), 'and the weather so marvellous that anything but idleness seems out of place.' He had been asked by the *Nation* to review Margot Asquith's auto-biography, but he so disliked it that he considered it prudent to refuse. A more fascinating volume, which had been sent to him by Hesketh Pearson, was Frank Harris's notorious Life of Oscar Wilde. 'It has a fair amount of rather new information,' he wrote to James (November 1920), 'though of course, it's not nearly detailed enough, and it isn't really *very* well done. However the story is a most remarkable one. The admirer is called Mr. Hesketh Pearson, and is apparently some sort of agent for Frank Harris in England. He sent me the book in order, as he said, to find out what the greatest English biographer thought of the greatest American one – a slightly double-edged compliment, I fear. But *is* F. H. American? Or what?' Pearson's letter, partly written in parody of Lytton's dramatic prose style, had declared that there was 'no dark and sinister motive' behind his action – an assurance which only served to alarm Lytton. 'I'm rather afraid he [Pearson] may want me to write some wretched review or puff,' he complained to Carrington (3 November 1920), 'so I shall tell him that I can't do that, but otherwise will graciously accept the book.'

Released from his long imprisonment at Tidmarsh, he now set his face towards a life of easy entertainment. He went down to Cambridge, met the new embryos and Apostles, and read a paper to the Heretics. Occasionally, too, he would return to the Mill House for a week-end, bringing with him one or two of these new undergraduate friends – Sebastian Sprott, F. L. Lucas, James H. Doggart – or some of his older associates – Roger Fry, Desmond MacCarthy, David Garnett. One of his pleasantest encounters over these months was with Max Beerbohm, who, the previous June, had sent him a letter executed after his most polished and whimsical manner – 'rather amusing and very elaborate', Lytton commented, 'but how to answer it, Christ alone knows. Of

---

[1] 'I am reading the Oedipus Tyrannus in a new edition that Sheppard has just brought out, with a translation (which is what I read – with an occasional puzzled glance at the other side of the page) and an elaborate and rather interesting commentary,' Lytton wrote to Ralph Partridge. 'In the entire list of the world's masterpieces, my fancy is to place it second, though I wish I could understand the Greek better than I do – and when I think of all the hours and years I spent learning the paradigms of the irregular verbs, and construing Thucydides!'

course completely for publication.[1] All very nice, in its way, when done by somebody else, but a bore, a dreadful bore, when one has to sit down oneself in cold blood, and compose.' Early in the spring, Max came to London to arrange for an exhibition of his drawings, and he asked Lytton whether he 'might professionally stare at him'. A few days later Lytton called round to see him at the Charing Cross Hotel. 'He rang me to ask me to go and see him, explaining that he drew a caricature of me, and wished to "verify his impressions"', Lytton afterwards wrote to James (14 April 1921). 'I went yesterday, and found him, very plump and whitehaired, drawn up to receive me. "Let us come out on to the balcony, where we shall have a view of the doomed city." He begged me to turn my profile towards him, and for a minute or two made some notes on the back of an envelope. He was infinitely polite and elaborate, and quite remote, so far as I could see, from humanity in all its forms. His caricatures are to be exhibited in three weeks – "if England still exists".'

[1] In which case it had better be published here. 'Dear Lytton Strachey, Some time in 1913, at this address, my wife and I acquired a young fox-terrier. We debated as to what to call him, and, as Henry James had just been having his 70th birthday, and as his books had given me more pleasure than those of any living man, I, rather priggishly perhaps, insisted that the dog should be known as James. But this was a name which Italian peasants, who are the only neighbours we have, of course would not be able to pronounce at all. So we were phonetic and called the name of the dog *Yah-mès*. And this did very well. By this name he was known far and wide – but not for long; for alas, he died of distemper. Now that we are re-established here, we haven't another dog; dogs aren't so necessary to one as they seem to be in England, and they have an odd and tactless way of making one feel that one *is* in England – perhaps because they don't gesticulate and don't speak one word of Italian and seem to expect to find rabbits among the olive-groves and to have bones of Welsh mutton thrown to them from the luncheon table. But the other day we were given a small kitten – charming in itself and somehow not distinctive of local colour. The old question arose: what shall we call it? Again I laid myself open to the charge of priggishness, perhaps. And again you will perhaps think I have taken a liberty. But – well, there it is: no book by a living man has given me so much pleasure – so much lasting pleasure in dipping and re-reading since I wrote to you – as your "Eminent Victorians". And the name of that kitten is, and the name of that cat will be: *Stré-chi* (or rather Stré-cci). I do hope you don't mind. I am sure you would be amused if you heard the passing-by peasants enticing it by your hardly recognisable name. We will re-christen it if you like.'
This letter was written from Villino Chiaro on 7 July 1920. Lytton, in his reply, expressed his sense of honour at this appellation, and two years later, in June 1922, Max took up the sequel to this story in another letter. 'The kitten of whom I told you last year is now a confirmed cat. He is much larger than he seemed likely to become, and is vigorous and vagrant, but not, I am sorry to say, either affectionate or intelligent. It is not known that he ever caught a mouse; he dislikes rain, but has no knowledge of how to avoid it if it falls; and if one caresses him he is very likely to scratch one. He is, however, very proud of his name, and sends his respectful regards to his Illustrissimo Eponymisto Inglese.'
In the course of this same letter Max refers to Lytton's essay 'Voltaire and Frederick the Great' as an 'abiding masterpiece', and adds: 'So is "Madame du Deffand".'

Max felt for Lytton a special sense of affinity that, in certain details, falsified his likeness. Though they were never very close friends, Max looked on him almost as a younger brother. For in an age that was busy vulgarizing and cheapening art, Lytton's good taste had remained uncontaminated. Max felt that he was to Lytton what Oscar Wilde had been to him. 'You are wonderful,' he had written to him after the publication of *Eminent Victorians* (28 July 1918). He saw Lytton not as a modern figure, but as a modified edition of himself, someone who had made further advances in the fastidious and refined craft of letters. 'He was no longer velveteen-jacketed,' Max noted with surprise when Lytton arrived at his hotel. 'He was dressed now in a worldlier manner, which, I told him, seemed to me less characteristic, and he willingly agreed that he should remain velveteen-jacketed in my drawing.' What Max, with his static and mannered ways, could not see was that Lytton had moved largely in step with the times. He was more eagerly up to date than Max allowed for or depicted in his caricatures. For Max himself, the earthquake of the war had opened up an abyss beneath his feet, cracking apart the formalized world of his youth. His pleasures – like Lytton's – were mainly those of travel and society. But during the last forty years of his life, spent in monotonous retirement at the unlovely town of Rapallo, he severely curtailed both these cultivated pastimes. For Lytton, on the other hand, London and the Continent had ceased to exist as places of entertainment only in the war years themselves. Now that peace was restored and he had money of his own to spend for the first time, he was able to indulge more fully these favourite recreations, emerging from his Home Counties hibernation, travelling and entering society as never before. The disorganized post-war world, which so horrified Max, enlivened him and at times even tempted him into believing that an age of peace and prosperity lay before mankind. The carnage, the philistinism, the reign of terror, stupidity and press dictatorship were over. Civilized people could again lead civilized lives, and meet civilized people in other countries. A few weeks after the publication of *Queen Victoria*, and a year since his energetic expedition to Spain, Lytton set off with Pippa from England to stay with the Berensons in Florence. A month of pleasurable relaxation and amusement lay ahead of him.

But, behind him, he had left a simmering volcano.

9

MOONS AND HONEYMOONS

During the closing months of 1920, while Lytton was putting the finishing touches to *Queen Victoria*, the emotional *sonate à trois* that was being played between Ralph, Carrington and himself, had slowly spiralled to a *sforzando*. Ralph, having come down from Oxford and failed to obtain a post as assistant to G. D. H. Cole, the Fabian economist and sociologist, had been engaged by Leonard Woolf to act as his secretary and compositor in the Hogarth Press. Minutely remunerated, such a job seemed hardly suitable for the burly and ebullient ex-major – 'I don't see Partridge setting up the type,' Lytton commented – but Ralph himself seemed well content. This job took him a step nearer marrying Carrington – indeed, he could see no reasonable obstacle to their immediate marriage. No obstacle, that was, except Carrington herself. For she still obstinately resisted his proposals, partly because, with her feminist ideals, she objected in principle to conventional marriage, and partly because she felt that Ralph, for all his affection for Lytton and his hastily assimilated education, did not really belong to her world. Few of her artistic friends and few of Lytton's at first liked him, though many came to do so later. Bloomsbury had been particularly sceptical about his role in the Tidmarsh régime, and resented his intrusions into Gordon Square. But despite all her opposition, Ralph was amazingly persistent, and Carrington began to fear that her own resolute stubbornness might soon alienate Lytton, ruining their life at Pangbourne together, which she loved so much. He had said nothing, of course. She would not expect him to. But she sensed his growing weariness and his disapproval of their fractious relations. As Ralph's exasperation mounted, so, in proportion, did her own anxiety.

'Lytton dear, do you know what comfort you are to me,' she wrote to him while he was staying down at Charleston that autumn. 'I feel as long as you live on this earth I can never mind anything.' Diagnosing at once the cause of her distress, Lytton answered with all his customary tenderness and concern, seeking to allay her fears. 'My dearest, I am sure that all is really well between us, which is the great thing. Some devil of embarrassment chokes me sometimes, and prevents my expressing what I feel. You have made me so happy during the last 3 years, and you have created Tidmarsh as no one else could have, and I seem hardly to have said thank you. But you must believe that I value you and your love more than I can ever say.'

Yet even now Carrington was not altogether reassured. If Ralph, becoming fed up with her uncompromising refusals, were to leave, then Lytton too, she suspected, might go. Either that, or, if his unfailing courtesy and sense of pity held him back, then he would certainly feel an involuntary resentment against her for driving away the man he loved. She therefore proposed a compromise. She would live with Ralph, on a more or less experimental basis, until Christmas. Since he had already begun working in London, this meant that the two of them must put up during the week-days at 41 Gordon Square[1] – a few yards from the Stracheys' house – going down together to Tidmarsh for week-ends. Though no one could tell at first what precisely this temporary plan would involve, all parties seemed reasonably well satisfied – in spite of the very considerable emotional complications. At least, for the time being, the worst crisis had, to everyone's relief, been postponed. 'On Fridays Carrington and the Major appear, departing again on Monday,' Lytton explained for the benefit of James (November 1920). 'How long the arrangement will last I haven't an idea. I rather fear that she may find it doesn't suit her – that the ménage at Gordon Square is too purely domestic – but I don't know. If it breaks up – but perhaps it's not much use in anticipating.' To prevent it breaking up he again tried to reassure Carrington: 'It seems to me that your trying the G. Square experiment is probably right,' he told her. 'But whatever happens you must rely on my affection.'

Nevertheless, Lytton did not believe that this emergency compact could succeed for very long. What would take its place, he had no idea – whether everything would collapse in ruins, or a new régime would arise, phoenix-like, from among the debris. Already, by the New Year, Carrington was feeling acutely miserable, shut in by the buildings of Bloomsbury, missing Lytton every day she was apart from him, longing for the open breathing country again, yet trying not to reveal her wretchedness to Ralph. But she was never adept at concealing her emotions. Ralph, well aware of her unhappiness, soon grew dissatisfied himself at their arrangement, and began urging her once more to marry him. Even though they were living together all the time now as man and wife, he still felt tantalized by her untouchable, uncontrollable passions, and convinced that only official wedlock could put an end to his torture. Marriage, he argued, would make no outward difference to *her* life – indeed, in some respects, such as travelling abroad with him, it would make things easier for her. But still she resisted. She was unwilling to change a proven beneficial state of life for another unknown one – however certain some people might be that it would make

---

[1] They took over the flat previously occupied by James and Alix Strachey, who that June had left for Vienna.

no difference. And what were the trivial difficulties of travelling abroad once a year to the permanent, inescapable ones of being attached to a brood of Partridges, with a mother and a father bird, for ever chirping at one? 'Oh dearie dearie I wish one never grew up,' she complained to Noel (11 May 1921), 'or else One could live in A land where conventions, and parents n'est existe pas.'

By May, they appeared to have reached a deadlock. The strain between them was very great. Then, suddenly infuriated beyond endurance by her childish evasions, Ralph threatened that if he did not marry her he would go off to Bolivia and become a sheep farmer. Was he bluffing, or had the moment of decision finally arrived? Carrington could not tell. He sounded serious, desperately serious. She did not know whether to laugh or cry. She did not know *what* to do.

It was just as the state of affairs had come to this crucial and explosive point, that Lytton chose to remove himself to Italy. He had punctiliously refrained from interfering in their drama, though its outcome would affect him profoundly, and now, by the same token, his letters to Carrington scrupulously omitted any reference to her drastic predicament with Ralph. Instead he wrote of visiting the Sitwells at Montegufoni, 'a truly outstanding place'; of Geoffrey Scott at the Villa Medici,[1] a superb eighteenth-century villa higher up in the hills; of Goldie Dickinson and Harry Norton whom he also saw. But chiefly his correspondence was taken up with descriptions of his host, Bernard Berenson, and his famous villa at Settignano, I Tatti. 'The house is just what I imagined – large – full of beautiful objects one can hardly look at, and comfort that somehow is really far less comfortable than Tidmarsh. A sister of Berenson's and her husband (poor American creatures) Lord and Lady Berwick, and some female secretaries (I gather) make up the party so far. His Lordship looks like an imbecile butler, and I should think was one. Lady B. is a sad pseudo-beauty....

[1] Immediately before the war Geoffrey Scott had been looking after the decorations and furniture of various new rooms at I Tatti, where he encountered and fell in love with Nicky Mariano, later Berenson's librarian and companion. Mary Berenson had planned that the two of them should marry, live together near by and act as her husband's helpers and advisers, but during the war Geoffrey Scott had married Lady Sybil Cutting (who later became the wife of Percy Lubbock). During his stay at I Tatti, Lytton saw something of Nicky Mariano, who remembers that Berenson urged him to take up Pius IX as his next subject, a suggestion by which he seemed to be tempted. 'I was by that time familiar enough with the intricacies of the English language to catch and appreciate the witty squeaks that interrupted Lytton Strachey's silences,' she records. 'One evening we had him to dinner at the Villino [Corbignano] and there in a small circle and feeling perhaps no necessity to be on his guard he talked freely and charmingly. His inquiries about our experiences at the end of the war were so full of delicate understanding that I wondered whether he had not more heart than his usual manner would have led one to suppose.'

There is a distinct air of civil war about, which is slightly unpleasant. Otherwise everything seems perfect.'

In another letter, a few days later, he writes: 'B.B. is a very interesting phenomenon. The mere fact that he has accumulated this wealth from having been a New York gutter-snipe is sufficiently astonishing; but besides that he has a most curious complicated temperament – very sensitive, very clever – even, I believe, with a strain of niceness somewhere or other, but desperately wrong – perhaps suffering from some dreadful complexes – and without a spark of naturalness or ordinary human enjoyment. And this has spread itself over the house, which is really remarkably depressing . . . one is struck chill by the atmosphere of a crypt. Oooh! – And so much of it, too – such a large corpse – so many long dead corridors, so many dead primitives, so many dead pieces of furniture, and flowers, and servants, such multitudes of dead books; and then, outside, a dead garden, with a dead view of a dead Tuscan landscape. . . .'

Back in England, the volcano had meanwhile started to erupt. Ralph's nerve had been the first to crack. Shortly after Lytton left for Florence, he suffered some sort of breakdown, threw himself at the feet of Leonard and Virginia Woolf and poured out his long accumulation of grievances and frustrations. They advised him to marry Carrington at once, or to put his threat into execution by leaving her and Lytton altogether. Virginia, with her love of stirring up trouble, and knowing only too well that everything she said would be remembered and repeated, interposed a few poisonous comments of her own. Lytton had told her, she said, that he did not intend to go down to Tidmarsh very much after he returned from Italy. He was nervous, she explained, that Carrington would feel some sort of claim on him if he continued living in the same house with her too long. It was a wonder to everyone, she added, how Lytton had put up with her even for three years. What on earth did they find to do when they were alone together? Possibly Ralph would be best out of it. Life in Bolivia was said to be very bracing.

Carrington, by this time, had returned to the Mill House, having been commissioned to paint the signboards of some public houses in Reading, where she would spend the days working.[1] It was here, after his discussion with the Woolfs, that Ralph now caught up with her. They met in a small workmen's café. The terrible deterioration in Ralph's appearance appalled Carrington. His mouth twitched; he

---

[1] 'What good news of the Greyhound!' Lytton wrote to her (6 July 1921). 'It will be splendid if you become Sign Painter in Ordinary to the Counties of Berks, Wilts and Hants! I am longing to see it in position.' She painted several other signboards in the neighbourhood, including that of John Fothergill's inn, the Spread Eagle at Thame.

looked dreadfully tired and ill, and seemed to have gone completely to pieces. Seeing him in this wretched, unbalanced state of mind, she felt fonder of him than ever she had done in his more swaggering, self-assertive moods. Their unhappiness and confusion intermingled, and they were closer to each other than at any other moment. But Carrington felt guilty, too. As with Gertler, she was the culprit. It was her selfishness that had so distracted and upset him, that had caused him such anguish and suffering.

Speaking in a flat, unnatural voice, without excitement, Ralph began by saying that he knew she was not in love with him, but he thought that her affections were nevertheless strong enough to make him happy. He could not go on any longer in the same uncertainty and pain. He would definitely leave the country if she would not marry him. He then repeated to her all that Virginia had told him. The effect of this on Carrington was like an electric shock. She had realized, of course, that Lytton was frightened of her becoming dependent on him, of her becoming, as she put it, 'a permanent limpet'. And she had known, too, all along, that she had nothing to hope from him, that marriage between them was out of the question. But Virginia's spiteful half-truths altered her way of looking at their relationship. Always, in future, she would feel a terror of being physically on Lytton's nerves, of revolting him. Therefore she decided, chiefly for Lytton's peace of mind, but also for Ralph's happiness, that she would have to surrender. That afternoon in the café she told Ralph that she would marry him. Even now, though, she shrank from the ultimate renunciation of her principles, hoping that, having agreed in theory to become Ralph's wife, she might somehow or other indefinitely defer putting it into practice.

And so, the final scene of their dramatic tragi-comedy was played out. Both of them were utterly exhausted, Ralph elated, Carrington soberly resigned, as they drove back that night to Tidmarsh. The next morning, Carrington sent off a long letter to Lytton, telling him everything that had happened. It was one of her most abandoned pieces of writing, a poignant and terrible document.

'All these years I have known that my life with you was limited. I could never hope for it to become permanent. After all Lytton, you are the only person who I have ever had an absorbing passion for. I shall never have another. I couldn't now – I had one of the most self abasing loves that a person can have. You could throw me into transports of happiness and dash me into deluges of tears and despair, all by a few words. But these aren't reproaches ... Of course these years at Tidmarsh when we were quite alone will always be the happiest I ever spent. And I've such a store of good things which I've saved up, that I feel I could never be lonely again now. Still its too much of a strain to be quite alone here waiting to see you or craning my nose and eyes out of the top window of 41 G.S. to see if you are coming down the Street. Then I know we'll be better friends, if you aren't haunted by the idea that I am sitting depressed in some corner of the world waiting for your footsteps . . .

'I saw the relief you felt at Ralph taking me away, so to speak, off your hands.

'I think he'll make me happier, than I shall be entirely by myself – and it certainly prevents me becoming morbid about you. And as Ralph said last night you'll never leave us, because in spite of our dullness nobody else loves you nearly as much as we do.

'So in the café in that vile city of Reading, I said I'd marry him. . . . After all I don't believe it will make much difference, and to see him. so happy is A rather delightful thing. I'd probably never marry anyone else, and I doubt if a kinder creature exists on this earTH . . .

'I cried last night Lytton, whilst he slept by my side sleeping happily – I cried to think of a savage cynical faTe which had made it impossible for my love ever to be used by you. You never knew, or never will know the very big and devastating love I had for you. How I adored every hair of your beard. How I devoured you whilst you read to me at night. How I loved the smell of your face in your sponge. The thin and ivory skin on your hands, your voice, and your hat when I saw it coming along the top of the garden wall from my window. Say you will remember it. That it wasnt all loST. and that you'll forgive me for this outburst, and always be my Friend. . . . Ralph is suCH a dear, I don't feel I'll ever regret marrying him. "Though I never will change my maiden name that I have kept so long," – so you mayn't ever call me anything but Carrington . . .

'You gave me a much longer life than I ever deserved or hoped for and I love you for it terribly. I only cried last night at realizing I never could have my moon – that sometimes I must pain you and often bore you. You who I would have given the world to have made happier than any person could be, to give you all you wanted . . .

'I see I've told you very little of what I feel. But I keep on crying, if I stop and think about you. Outside the sun is Baking they all chatter and laugh. It's cynical, this world in its opposites. Once you said to me, that Wednesday afternoon in the sitting Room, you love me as a Friend. Could you Tell it to me again ?'

The pathos of this extraordinary letter moved Lytton very deeply. It reached him in Florence on 20 May, and he wrote back immediately the same day so that Carrington's agony of mind should not be prolonged. He told her that Virginia, with characteristic neurotic malevolence, had lied about his feelings and intentions; that he thought her marriage to Ralph would be best for all of them. And he told her other things that made her as happy and grateful to him as the circumstances allowed. He came as near, in his reply, as his peculiar nature permitted to overcoming that 'devil of embarrassment' that choked the free expression of his feelings. All the pathos and tenderness of their relationship is conveyed in these two letters.

'But I hope that in any case you never doubted my love for you,' he wrote. 'Do you know how difficult I find it to express my feelings in letters or talk? It is sometimes terrible – and I don't understand why it should be so; and sometimes it seems to me that you underrate what I feel. You realise that I have varying moods, but my fundamental feelings you perhaps don't realise so well. Probably it is my fault. It is perhaps much easier to show one's peevishness than one's affection and admiration! Oh my dear, do you really want me to tell you that I "love you as a friend"? – But of course that is absurd, and you *do* know very well that I love you as something more than a friend, you angelic creature, whose goodness to me has made me happy for years, and whose presence in my life has been, and always will be, one of the most important things in it. Your letter made me cry, I feel a poor old miserable creature, and I may have brought more unhappiness to you than anything else. I only pray that it is not so, and that my love for you, even though it is not what you desire, may yet make our relationship a blessing to you – as it has been to me. Remember that I too have never had my moon! We are all helpless in these things – dreadfully helpless. I am lonely and I am all too truly growing old, and if there was a chance that your decision meant that I should somehow or other lose you, I don't think I could bear it. You and Ralph and our life at Tidmarsh are what I care for most in the world – almost (apart from my work and some few people) the *only* things I care for . . .

'. . . you seemed in your letter to suggest that my love for you has diminished as time has gone on: that is not so. I am sure that it has increased. It is true that the first excitement, which I always (and I suppose most people) have at the beginning of an affair, has gone off: but something much deeper has grown up instead.'

Carrington and Ralph were married on 21 May, at the registry office in St Pancras. Carrington described herself in the register book as an Artist (Painter) of Tidmarsh Mill House, Pangbourne; Ralph as a Private Secretary, living at 41 Gordon Square. The witnesses were Lytton's sister Marjorie, and a young friend, Alan MacIver. That evening the two of them left for Paris, journeying on the next day to

Venice where they spent their honeymoon, and where, for an 'enchanting week',[1] they were joined by Lytton and Pippa. At the end of May
they all returned to England.

To Lytton's mind, everything had turned out unexpectedly well. He
himself was delighted with the new system, which seemed to promise
just that mixture of emotional security and independence that best fitted
him. Ralph, too, seemed quite content, and so even did Carrington.
'Rex is happy,' she told her brother Noel, 'and that is the main thing.'
Her psychological reactions, however, were more complicated than
she yet knew, and because she had greatly valued her liberty, she bore
Ralph a secret resentment for its loss.

But, for the moment, the sun shone; and there was no trace of the
storm-clouds already massing beyond the horizon.

---

[1] 'I enjoyed Venice enormously,' Lytton wrote to Ottoline (29 June 1921). 'I think you
once told me it was the perfect place, and I quite agree with you. I had no idea it was so
splendid and enchanting, and I can hardly bear the thought that it is still going on in all
its fascination and that I am not in the middle of it. I want to rush back to the Piazza
without the delay of a moment. I want to sink into a Gondola and have myself wafted to
St George. Oh dear! The beauties – of all kinds! Why did I ever leave there?'

CHAPTER II

The Great Panjandrum

one of the most pathetic
sights however
is to see the ghost of queen
victoria going out every
evening with the ghost
of a sceptre in her hand
to find mr lytton strachey
and bean him it seems she beans
him and beans him and he
never knows it

Don Marquis –
'archy goes abroad' from *archy's life of mehitabel*

I

THE DEVELOPMENT OF A BIOGRAPHER

The change in tone and literary style between *Eminent Victorians* and
Queen Victoria gives some indication of the post-war development in
Lytton's character, and shows the greater refinement he brought to his
biographical method. His real originality and force are best seen in the
pages of *Eminent Victorians*. In *Queen Victoria*, the astringent, incisive
style has softened into a kindlier mood of mellow and affectionate
nostalgia. The pace is gentler, too, more explorative though less acute,
and the basis of the construction has shifted from a quartet of one-act
dramas to a single organic unit composed of a series of interconnected
chapter-scenes, more akin to a subjective novel.

Lytton's literary talent was naturally less reflective than dramatic.
The spectacle he had unrolled in *Eminent Victorians* was of a menagerie
of curious comedian creatures, born actors all of them, impelled towards
sinister conflicts and strange dooms, grappling now with one another,
now with the culminating fury of forces far greater than themselves, to
be swept at last to a common ruin. Their antics presented a vivid and

fascinating extravaganza, but were without much significance beyond
the cages in which they performed, from where, protected by stout
iron bars, Lytton coldly observed them, noting all the while that their
attitudinizing, their avowed purposes and ideals were but thin disguises
of the one reality of their animal life– the egotistical pursuit of satisfaction. This was Lytton's philosophy of a hostile world; and the illustration of it in his brilliantly amusing sketches of four people who all
shared one dominating quality – a sense of ambition, inflated beyond
reason by religious superstition, which took control of personal
relationships and destroyed humanity – accorded perfectly with the
spasm of disgust momentarily felt throughout England for an age
which had finally collapsed with the war.

In the Preface to *Eminent Victorians*, Lytton had asserted the importance of the individual; but the essays that followed exemplified only the
vanity and littleness of the self-important. The text for which his book
forms such a scintillating exposition is Isabella's speech in *Measure for
Measure*:

> *– but man, proud man!*
> *Dress'd in a little brief authority, –*
> *Most ignorant of what he's most assured,*
> *His glassy essence, – like an angry ape,*
> *Plays such fantastic tricks before high heaven*
> *As make the angels weep.*

Lytton's treatment of this central theme corresponds well with the
commentary he had written many years earlier in the Spectatorial review
of Guglielmo Ferrero's history, *The Greatness and Decline of Rome*.
'The greatest names seem to lose their lustre upon his pages; he shows
us the ignorance of the wise, the helplessness of the well-meaning; the
rest is darkness and fate.' It was not, however, after Signor Ferrero's
work that he sought to fashion his biography. His chief stylistic models
came from the great French biographical tradition – Fontenelle and
Condorcet. But his attitude as a biographer, so he once intimated to
Hesketh Pearson, was Johnsonian, and a foretaste of his writing might
be found in Johnson's *Lives of the Poets*. Among other critics, Clifford
Bower-Shore and André Maurois have attempted to develop this
parallel. Lytton, in his Preface, had written of 'those two fat volumes,
with which it is our custom to commemorate the dead – who does not
know them, with their ill-digested masses of material, their slipshod
style, their tone of tedious panegyric, their lamentable lack of selection,
of detachment, of design? They are as familiar as the cortège of the
undertaker, and wear the same air of funereal barbarism.' Here was a

definite and perhaps deliberate echo of two of Johnson's most celebrated pronouncements on the art of biography. 'Biography has often
been allotted to writers who seem very little acquainted with the nature
of their task, or very negligent about the performance,' Johnson wrote.
'They rarely afford any other account than might be collected from
public papers, but imagine themselves writing a life when they exhibit
a chronological series of actions or preferments; and so little regard the
manners of behaviour of their heroes, that more knowledge may be
gained of a man's real character by a short conversation with one of his
servants, than from a formal and studied narrative begun with his
pedigree and ended with his funeral.'

And in *The Rambler*, Johnson also wrote: 'There are many who think
it an act of piety to hide the faults or failings of their friends, even when
they can no longer suffer by their detection; we therefore see whole
ranks of characters adorned with uniform panegyric, and not to be
known from one another but by extrinsic and casual circumstances . . .
If we owe regard to the memory of the dead, there is yet more respect
to be paid to knowledge, to virtue, to truth.'

Had Lytton taken the precepts laid down by Johnson, and by himself in his Preface, to heart, then his four 'Lives' might more closely have
resembled Johnson's *Life of Savage*. But he was less troubled with
discriminating between what was sound and what was false in an
established reputation, than in enunciating his own humanitarian and
secular convictions. The superficiality of any close comparison between
Johnson and Lytton has been admirably expounded by Johnson's so-
called 'Stracheyesque' biographer, Hugh Kingsmill – though he tends to
belittle the concern which Lytton felt for mankind and to underestimate
the intended propaganda effect of his work. There existed in Johnson,
Kingsmill points out, a belief in absolute virtue combined with an
equally strong awareness of how far short of it even the best human
beings fall:

'Whether or not he [Johnson] had it consciously in mind, he was
directed in everything he wrote by the saying of Jesus: "None is good,
save one, that is God,"' explained Kingsmill. 'Strachey, on the other
hand, an epicurean sceptic who remarks in one of his essays that the
religious motive has quietly dropped out of the modern world, wrote
from the standpoint that no one at all is good, and that man's only
rational occupation is to observe from a distance the contention of
conflicting egotisms. To Strachey all mythologies were equally absurd,
whether they embodied the transient illusions of a particular epoch or
welled up out of the depths of the soul to illumine the mystery of life.
Looking at men from the outside, he interpreted their actions rationally,

o

like Swift in *Gulliver's Travels*, and therefore found no reason in them. To Johnson popular mythology was a distortion of Christian mythology, which contained for him the sole revelation of ultimate reality; it was an attempt to attribute perfection to imperfect beings, and so a means to retarding man's progress towards the divine. The difference in attitude between Johnson and Strachey was therefore fundamental; for Johnson felt with his whole being that life cannot be interpreted as a self-contained experience and that the relation of the individual to God underlies and conditions his relations to man. To mark a man's faults and failings was, for Johnson, to indicate where he had diverged from his true relation to God; for Strachey it was an agreeable intellectual pastime, which flattered his sense of superiority both to his subject and to the illusion-ridden mob.'

Though Johnson's prose, loosened by years of conversation, gradually grew more flexible, his basic attitude, compounded of a mixture of sympathy and severity, did not change. Lytton's biographical approach was evolved at a different level, and, since it constituted only indirectly an expression of his personal relation to life – being chiefly employed as a literary device to heighten the devastating effect of his irony – it soon shifted to accommodate a new literary position. There are fewer Johnsonian overtones in *Queen Victoria*: Lytton's later peacetime point of view could not be conveyed by the majestic Corinthian order of Johnson's style. For Johnson, with his distrust of the fictitious, was not an artist in the same sense as *Queen Victoria*, with its mandarin style so exactly suited to anecdote, is a work of art. Prior to 1918, there was perhaps no conscious art of biography in the language: there were biographer-artists, but no artist-biographers. Johnson believed that the value of a story depended upon its being true – 'A story is a picture either of an individual, or of human nature in general; if it be false it is a picture of nothing.' To Lytton, biographies were less rigorous and austere instruments of truth-telling than nicely proportioned entertainments, vehicles for the dissemination of certain aspects of the truth. To assist with this new and milder approach to his subject, which laid more stress on amusement than on propaganda, he adopted a more novel-like narrative, very un-Johnsonian.

In *Eminent Victorians*, Lytton had been exposing villains, and to stress their villainy masquerading as virtue, he had applied an apparatus of scientific detachment, a pretended non-personal method reminiscent to some degree of Gibbon, and lately assumed by Mr A. J. P. Taylor. In *Queen Victoria*, he came nearer to portraying a hero and heroine, and the artistic means by which he chose to represent them were of a quite different order. All pretence at a strictly impersonal attitude is now abandoned, and a more subjective spirit of romance is invoked. Lytton livens up his amiable portraits with just a hint of entertaining malice. His heroes were far from perfect, he is constantly reminding us. They had their full share of faults. Everything apparently conspires to a fair distribution of disqualifications. Yet the skill, of course, lies in apportioning the favoured characters with only the more diverting and endearing frailties, so that the untrained reader is led to believe, even against some of the evidence, that he has discovered for himself that Victoria was really quite a sweet little lady, and that the grossly underrated Albert possessed a considerable talent.

Lytton's gallery of villains, saddled with the more unappealing vices, were selected from among those whose robust constitutions, harnessed to an overriding lust for power, served to distinguish them clearly from himself. His heroes, now, were ordinary, homely, unexceptional people – 'the quiet little great', as Wyndham Lewis scathingly described them. 'At the head of that dazzling *élite* is usually some whimsical, half-apologetic, but very much sheltered and coddled projection of himself.' This, in the opinion of Wyndham Lewis, was the unobtrusive revolution that Lytton attempted to set in motion: the accepted heroes were villains, and the quietists heroes. But his actual influence which, as 'high priest of Gossip' extended beyond biography to political journalism, was one of partisanship. Between the 'good' and the 'bad' there was a great artistic gulf fixed. The former were to be enhaloed with an aura of charming sentimentalism; the latter subjected to a cool, clinical appraisal.

By seeking the man behind the nineteenth-century myth, Lytton had, in 1918, dealt a death-blow to the antiquated legend of the Victorian Age. But the substantive which Walter Raleigh had so eagerly awaited in no way matched up to the original adjective. For with the publication of *Queen Victoria*, Lytton inaugurated a new but no less legendary view of the queen – a whimsical, teasing, half-admiring, half-mocking view that found in Victoria a quaintly impressive symbol of a quaintly impressive age.

Nevertheless, *Queen Victoria* has claims to be considered a more mature work than *Eminent Victorians*. To a very large extent, Lytton relinquished his air of bland superiority; and the methods he used to convey a mellow and enfolding atmosphere were less arbitrary than those he had previously employed in uncovering a hidden core of diabolism. The scholarship is more thorough; the tone more finely controlled; and the writing no less lucid. His irony is lowered so that it flows like a sub-current flavouring the whole biography, and giving it its distinctive poise and harmony. In this sense, his prose style is more

subtle than in his earlier book, the extreme quietness and depth of both
the irony and wit being absorbed as a necessary part of the narrative,
rather than sitting as a gaudy embellishment upon it. 'You've discovered a new style which gives the essential and all pervading absurdity
of most human and all official life without losing anything of its pathos,'
Roger Fry wrote to him (18 April 1921). 'You're so kind and so
unsparing. It seems to me more nearly a true perspective than anyone's
yet found.'

The greater technical problems involved in *Queen Victoria* are also
triumphantly overcome. Harold Nicolson has enumerated these
difficulties and pointed to the craft and assiduity which Lytton needed
to master them with such fluency. 'The mass of his material was overwhelming. He was faced with eighty-one solid years, and each one of
those years was crowded with intricate and important events directly
relevant to his subject. He was faced with innumerable secondary
characters, most of whom were so interesting in themselves as to distract
attention from the central figure. He was faced with vast national
movements, with vital developments in imperial, foreign, and domestic
policy, with far-reaching changes in the industrial and social condition
of England, with intricate modifications in the constitution, with
obscure shapings in the national temperament, with all those hidden
forces which within those eighty years completely altered the structure
of the civilised world. To compress all these within three hundred
pages; to mould this vast material into a synthetic form; to convey not
merely unity of impression but a convincing sense of scientific reality;
to maintain throughout an attitude of detachment; to preserve the
exquisite poise and balance of sustained and gentle irony, and to secure
these objects with no apparent effort; to produce a book in which there
is no trace of artificiality or strain – this, in all certainty, is an achievement which required the very highest gifts of intellect and imagination.'
And so, because the foundations of research had been so diligently
prepared, the fact and fantasy so consistently interwoven and finely
shaped, the valid historical interpretation merged with such smooth
plausibility into a more fictional form of characterization, Lytton was
able legitimately to persuade his readers that a book which gives the
impression of a consummately written romantic novel was, in reality,
a serious and soundly evidenced work of history.

Another reason why, in the opinion of some critics, *Queen Victoria*
carries greater conviction than *Eminent Victorians*, is that the narrative
appears to have been more scrupulously put together. With the greater
choice of material at his disposal, there was no need for Lytton to
search after peculiar significance in trivial episodes, to manipulate

quotations or to present as accredited truth some evidence which had only dubious foundation in fact. Several apocryphal anecdotes and sayings are repudiated in footnotes; and when, for example, he recounts how Albert refused to open his door to Victoria so long as she demanded entrance as Queen of England, only consenting to admit her as his wife, Lytton, though not wishing to omit the story, describes it fairly and openly as 'ill-authenticated and perhaps mythical, yet summing up, as such stories often do, the central facts of the case'. At the same time, partly perhaps because of this greater scrupulousness, *Queen Victoria* remains a much less witty and irreverent book than *Eminent Victorians*.

It would have been almost impossible for Lytton to provide greater amusement at the expense of the Victorians, and the same crisp felicity of phrase is not to be found in the pages of *Queen Victoria*. In the first part of the biography, it is true, there are a few isolated flashes of his old and scintillating wit. His description of Baron Stockmar – 'Dyspeptic by constitution, melancholic by temperament, he could yet be lively on occasion, and was known as a wit in Coburg' – certainly has a Johnsonian ring to it. The miniature, too, of King William, is very vivid – 'a bursting, bubbling old gentleman, with quarter-deck gestures, round rolling eyes, and a head like a pineapple'. But in the main, such sallies as there are do not have the same rapier-like thrust as those in *Eminent Victorians*. When we read that the Baroness Lehzen 'had habits which betrayed her origin. Her passion for caraway seeds, for instance, was uncontrollable'; or when we learn of Albert that 'His Royal Highness's technical acquaintance with the processes of fresco-painting was incomplete', we are diverted, but realize that Lytton's irony has lost some of its cutting edge through being directed towards rather trivial targets. The arrow no longer has a poison head to it, only a rubber sucker to mark the place of impact. This change reminds us, too, how easily, in the spectrum of emotional attitudes, scepticism shades off into awe, since it is always haunting that perplexing borderline between the two.

As R. A. Scott-James observed, 'having grown up at twenty he [Strachey] had allowed something of the extremities of youth to master him at thirty-eight'. One feature of this alleged Immaturity Regained in *Eminent Victorians* was his obvious delight in the absurd names held by august divines, scholars and officials – Dowbiggin, Philpots, Wegg-Prosser, Gell, Burbridge, Walrond and Simpkinson. 'To allow such names to fall into the hands of Lytton Strachey,' commented Guy Boas, 'was to present an urchin with a water-pistol.' His satire, without the bitterness of Swift's, was largely a form of incredulously inverted romanticism. In *Queen Victoria*, this romanticism is no longer inverted, and is used not to sharpen his mockery – either deliberately through

satirizing the pretensions and hypocrisies of men or else, more indirectly, by exposing the drama of existence as a transitory, illusory
process made real to us only through habit – but to make it more playful,
more charming and innocuous. His intense preoccupation with religion,
the irrational duties and dogmas of which, he believed, induced a
blindness to real moral values, had fired his imagination. But this sharp,
intermittent beam of reality faded into an agreeable roseate glow, not
unattractive but less revealing, when he substituted for his quartet of
superstitious egotists, a single secular egocentric. *Eminent Victorians*,
for all its over-selection and over-simplification, has something of the
clean taste of truth; while the taste left by *Queen Victoria*, despite
several superior literary ingredients, is more cloying. For in one book
Lytton had ruthlessly laid bare the complacent credulity of the nineteenth century; and in the other he merely enshrined it with faint
dispraise.

2

VICTORIA AND ALBERT

The characters in *Queen Victoria* arrange themselves into three sharply
defined categories: there is the heroine and the hero; there are a procession of minor, mostly flamboyant, supporting figures; and there are
several off-stage, unsubstantial beings who appear to control from their
shadowy recesses the central machinations of the plot.

Towards Victoria herself, Lytton's feeling imperceptibly alters as his
story unfolds. The playful irony, the mixture of affection, amusement
and respect with which he regards her in the days of her youth, passes,
after the death of Albert, into a tender and more sentimental eulogy.
In 'Mr. Creevey', the essay published in 1919, he had written: 'Clio is
one of the most glorious of the Muses; but, as everyone knows, she
(like her sister Melpomene) suffers from a sad defect: she is apt to be
pompous. With her buskins, her robes, and her airs of importance she
is at times, indeed, almost intolerable. But fortunately the Fates have
provided a corrective. They have decreed that in her stately advances
she should be accompanied by certain apish, impish creatures, who run
round her tittering, pulling long noses, threatening to trip the good lady
up, and even sometimes whisking to one side the corner of her drapery,
and revealing her undergarments in a most indecorous manner.'
While writing the first part of *Queen Victoria*, Lytton saw his function
as to reveal the littleness underlying great events and to remind his

readers that the unlikely pageant of history was itself once everyday life. But as he proceeded, his attitude shifted slightly. The extent of this change may be gauged by comparing his early description of Victoria's coronation with his much later account of an official visit made to England by Napoleon III and the Empress Eugénie. In describing the first occasion, Lytton accompanies Clio, with appropriate gestures, as the young queen goes through her formal gyrations and the surrounding ceremonial works itself out, 'like some machine of gigantic complexity which was a little out of order'. The second passage is set in an entirely different key, and fuses together the historical and fabulous elements, being coated with a rather mawkish adulation, unmixed with irony, which he latterly reserves for the secondary characters such as Gilbert Scott.

There are, in fact, two Victorias whom Lytton elects to portray, the first of whom engages his intellectual attention, and the second to whom he responds emotionally. There is, of course, no reason to prevent one admiring some good qualities in a person whom one otherwise adversely criticizes. But it is perhaps a sign of his own split nature that these two simplified images seldom coincide. The result is that his Victoria loses something of the richness, the variety and irregularity of live portraiture – that organic complexity which an integrated portrait might have held.

In the closing two chapters of the book, this double image of Lytton's gives rise to a curious paradox. The final thirty pages contain a full inventory of Victoria's shortcomings – her imperialism, her religious obscurantism, her social reactionariness, her censorship of Greville, her nasty insistence on etiquette, her absence both of aesthetic taste and of any but the most unsubtle form of humour, her domineering character, above all her complacency, pride, egotism, her lack of sensitivity and of imagination. It is a formidable compilation; one made entertaining by anecdotes, well documented by reference notes, and apparently unanswerable. How, then, can it be that most readers have taken away from these last chapters a warm and sympathetic impression of the queen? How was it that G. M. Trevelyan could proclaim that Lytton Strachey had come to curse and stayed to bless Victoria – an opinion that is certainly untrue as describing Lytton's biographical intention or conscious attitude?

There would seem to be several factors that, taken together, might account for this anomaly. At no point in *Queen Victoria* is Lytton's disparagement of the queen so stringent as that of non-regal figures in *Eminent Victorians* or, for that matter, of the other non-regal figures in his Victoria biography, this being partly due to the fact that his subject was the grandmother of the reigning sovereign. Lytton goes out of his way to emphasize the reverence in which she was held by those closest to her and by the country as a whole. Her popularity was of a legendary kind. In many ways she did not merit such devotion. She was out of step with her epoch and she was sometimes insufferable to her family. Yet the extraordinary loyalty persisted, so that every limitation of character that Lytton points to only serves to increase our – and possibly his own – wonder at the spell of her personality. In this way is the force of his criticisms deflected and even turned to her advantage.

Lytton's tone, too, is largely responsible for his readers' reaction to these pages. He is more amused than censorious. Many of Victoria's failings are presented in a fundamentally sympathetic light. Her middle-class morals, for example, were really, we are led to believe, a distorted development of her very genuine family affection. Her passion for John Brown is, of course, laughable; but it does not take away from her intrinsic power, and it contributes to her humanity and to that most loved of English qualities – eccentricity. Her collecting instinct, which is described in terms of an obsessional neurosis, is seen to have its root in the fear of death, so that again our hearts are touched. Even her indefensible insistence upon changing the form of the verdict in cases of insanity is partly excused as being due to her memory of Albert's feelings on this subject.

The English, it is said, will warm to anyone, even a genius, providing he lives long enough. The most interesting thing about Victoria, however, is that, most emphatically, she was not a genius, not a great woman, not even in any way exceptional. What fascinated Lytton – and what is revealed by his skilled juxtaposition of incongruous facts – was her total mediocrity taken in conjunction with her grossly artificial position as Queen of England. That someone so commonplace should be elevated to the status of divinity aroused his sense of the dramatic and the absurd. At the same time, by appealing to the megalomania latent in all of us, such a theme gave him an almost certain best-seller. 'Just like ourselves,' middle-aged ladies from the circulating libraries could reflect with satisfaction after glancing through Lytton's flattering portrait of an essentially humdrum subject.

Yet it was not merely the accident of longevity that ameliorated Lytton's tone. It was the old queen's *lack of power*: 'Her desire to impose her will,' he wrote, 'vehement as it was, and unlimited by any principle, was yet checked by a certain shrewdness. She might oppose her Ministers with extraordinary violence; she might remain utterly impervious to arguments and supplications; the pertinacity of her resolution might seem to be unconquerable; but, at the very last moment of all, her obstinacy would give way. . . . By instinct she understood when the facts were too much for her, and to them she invariably yielded. After all, what else could she do?'

In the end therefore it is Victoria's sincerity and truthfulness that triumph. Lytton frames his picture of her old age with the abiding love of her people, and it is this love for a mother-figure that he most vividly evokes for his readers, a love which, rightly or wrongly, they felt that he too shared. He writes of her 'gentle benignity', her 'unforgettable charm', her 'impressiveness', of her writings which 'touched the heart of the public', and of 'those remarkable messages to the nation which, from time to time, she published in the newspapers' and in which 'her people found her very close to them indeed. They felt instinctively Victoria's irresistible sincerity, and they responded. And in truth it was an endearing trait.'

And so it is not in the vivid impulse of her youth, nor even in the full flower of her womanhood, but as an ageing and laborious widow, a grandiose matriarch, cloistered from the vulgar intrusions of the world, that Victoria grew mild and serene, and that her life, in Lytton's words, became 'lighted with a golden glory'. The young creature whom he depicts, with her 'ingenuous clarity, her sincerity, her simplicity, her quick affections and pious resolutions', and the adoring wife overcome by love of her husband, though both charming enough, are evidently less endearing to him than the little old lady with her white hair and plain mourning clothes.

Certainly the peculiar spell that Victoria came to exert over Lytton's readers sprang from the traits of protective motherhood which she extended not just over her own large family, but all her subjects. 'The Queen was hailed at once as the mother of her people,' he wrote in his penultimate chapter, 'and as the embodied symbol of their imperial greatness; and she responded to the double sentiment with all the ardour of her spirit. England and the people of England, she knew it, she felt it, were, in some wonderful and yet quite simple manner, *hers*. Exultation, affection, gratitude, a profound sense of obligation, an unbounded pride – such were her emotions; and, colouring and intensifying the rest, there was something else. At last, after so long, happiness – fragmentary, perhaps, and charged with gravity, but true and unmistakable none the less – had returned to her.'

Victoria's deepest happiness came, of course, from her marriage to Albert, which forms the central panel in the framework of Lytton's biography. Albert is introduced early on in the story, when he visits England with his brother Ernest. 'The Princes', Lytton observed,

o*

'shared her ecstasies and her italics between them; but it is clear enough where her secret preference lay. "Particularly Albert"! She was just seventeen; and deep was the impression left upon that budding organism by the young man's charm and goodness and accomplishments, and his large blue eyes and beautiful nose, and his sweet mouth and fine teeth.'

This first impression, however, was less deep than Lytton, for artistic effect, liked to make out. Victoria's emotions, though intense, were seldom very profound. Albert out of sight was Albert out of mind. As queen, she soon, as Lytton shows, fell under the influence of Lord Melbourne, viewing her uncle, King Leopold's, suggestion that Albert might make her a very suitable husband with the greatest repugnance. And when the time of Albert's next visit draw near, she confided to Melbourne that she 'had no great wish to see Albert, as the whole subject was an odious one'. Yet it was only when she did see him again, danced and talked with him that she was swept off her feet by a violent sexual infatuation that had been remotely fired on their previous meeting. In what R. A. Scott-James has called 'Ouida-esque language', Lytton describes the romantic upheaval that exploded within Victoria on again encountering Albert, and the proposal which followed a few days afterwards. But, characteristically, he does not bring to the surface her extraordinary self-absorption and lack of sensitivity in failing to appreciate that Albert's feelings were totally out of keeping with her own. A woman who could not sense this, could sense very little at all about other people.

'Albert arrived; and the whole structure of her existence crumbled into nothingness like a house of cards. He was beautiful – she gasped – she knew no more. Then, in a flash, a thousand mysteries were revealed to her; the past, the present, rushed upon her with a new significance; the delusions of years were abolished, and an extraordinary, an irresistible certitude leapt into being in the light of those blue eyes, the smile of that lovely mouth. The succeeding hours passed in a rapture ... She received him alone, and "after a few minutes I said to him that I thought he must be aware *why* I wished them to come here – and that it would make me *too happy* if he would consent to what I wished (to marry me)". Then "we embraced each other, and he was *so* kind, *so* affectionate". She said that she was quite unworthy of him, while he murmured that he would be very happy "Das Leben mit dir zu zubringen". They parted, and she felt "the happiest of human beings".'

Lytton tended to confer even on Victoria's more disagreeable traits the aura of a childlike simplicity; but his analysis of Albert's character does pierce some way below the surface, and, in portraying a man partially akin to himself, he reveals something of his own loneliness. Although, in the eyes of the queen, the prince was a mirror of manly beauty, Lytton explains, his constitution was not a strong one, and 'owing either to his peculiar upbringing or to a more fundamental idiosyncrasy he had a marked distaste for the opposite sex'. The prospect of his marriage to the adoring Victoria filled him with the deepest depression. But through the submissive sense of duty that had been instilled into him as a youth, he steadfastly buried his natural inclinations, the faint stirrings of personal ambition. Lytton told Hesketh Pearson that he had intended to suggest that Albert was homosexual – an interpretation of the Prince Consort's disposition likely to endorse the view that children of the British monarchy are, by tradition, immaculately conceived. This must be taken, however, as the key to several passages which Lytton devotes to Albert and which stress his foreign temperament, his sadness and isolation.

'A shy young foreigner, awkward in ladies' company, unexpansive and self-opinionated, it was improbable that, in any circumstances, he would have been a society success. . . . His features were regular, no doubt, but there was something smooth and smug about them; he was tall, but he was clumsily put together, and he walked with a slight slouch. Really, they thought, this youth was more like some kind of foreign tenor. . . . From the support and the solace of true companionship he was utterly cut off.'

Contrasting Albert's feelings for Victoria with her absolute and unconcealed devotion to him, Lytton wrote: 'He was not in love with her. Affection, gratitude, the natural reactions to the unqualified devotion of a lively young cousin who was also a queen – such feelings possessed him, but the ardours of reciprocal passion were not his. Though he found that he liked Victoria very much, what immediately interested him in his curious position was less her than himself.'

Like Lytton, Albert is seen as having the power of provoking in another an idolatry that in no way corresponds to his own innermost needs. Unlike Lytton, of course, he could not turn elsewhere for true companionship. This, then, was his 'curious position' to which Lytton returns in a later paragraph. 'The husband was not so happy as the wife,' he wrote. 'In spite of the great improvement in his situation, in spite of a growing family and the adoration of Victoria, Albert was still a stranger in a strange land, and the serenity of spiritual satisfaction was denied him. It was something, no doubt, to have dominated his immediate environment; but it was not enough; and, besides, in the very completeness of his success, there was a bitterness. Victoria idolised him; but it was understanding that he craved for, not idolatry; and how

much did Victoria, filled to the brim though she was with him, understand him? How much does the bucket understand the well? He was
lonely. He went to his organ and improvised with learned modulations
until the sounds, swelling and subsiding through elaborate cadences,
brought some solace to his heart. . . . Thus did he amuse himself; but
there was one distraction in which he did not indulge. He never flirted –
no, not with the prettiest ladies of the Court. . . . Throughout their
married life no rival female charms ever gave cause to Victoria for one
moment's pang of jealousy.'

Summing up the Prince Consort's career at the end of his short life,
Lytton again cautiously approaches the same theme, barely concealing,
in a commotion of vague verbal ambiguity, his real meaning. Albert,
he tells us, was sick at heart: 'For in spite of everything he had never
reached to happiness. His work, for which at last he came to crave with
an almost morbid appetite, was a solace and not a cure; the dragon of
his dissatisfaction devoured with dark relish that ever-growing tribute
of laborious days and nights; but it was hungry still. The causes of his
melancholy were hidden, mysterious, unanalysable perhaps – too
deeply rooted in the innermost recesses of his temperament for the eye
of reason to apprehend. . . . There was something that he wanted and
that he could never get. What was it? Some absolute, some ineffable
sympathy? Some extraordinary, some sublime success? Possibly, it
was a mixture of both. To dominate and be understood! To conquer,
by the same triumphant influence, the submission and the appreciation
of men – that would be worth while indeed! . . .

'But . . . Albert remained as foreign as before; and as the years passed
his dejection deepened.'

Unlike Lytton, Albert was never to find a favourable niche in life.
The father of a large family who did not care for women; a full-time
politician who was naturally indifferent to politics; the patron of the
sciences and arts who was neither a scientist nor an artist – the impulse
behind all these pursuits was of a vicarious or therapeutic kind. Lytton
responded very sympathetically to the loneliness of his exile, and to the
sincerity and warmth of his nature. He does not mock, as he might have
done in *Eminent Victorians*, when the dejected prince accepts his
engagement to Victoria as a test of his faith in the mysterious designs
of God. Indeed, he holds back from bringing out the mysticism and
religiosity latent in Albert's sense of duty, and poignantly revealed in
some of his letters – 'I am quite sure,' he wrote after his engagement in
a letter which Lytton does not quote, 'that Heaven has not given me
into evil hands.' Nor does Lytton deride the painstaking but often
trivial reforms which Albert effected within the royal household. His

portrait of the Prince Consort is moving, but incomplete, in that it fails to present the callousness that was the reverse side to his integrity. With adroitness and feeling, he shows us Albert's indifference to women as being the chief cause of his own unhappiness, but does not indicate how this misogynist bias could operate with inhumane intolerance upon others. On one occasion, for example, when Ernest, his brother from whom he had been inseparable before his marriage to Victoria, had a discreditable love-affair, Albert wrote him a violent, uncompromising letter – not mentioned by Lytton – in which he said that though he would never curse him or take away the love he owed him as a brother, he would leave him to perish in immorality.

Similarly, so as not to take away from the pathos of Albert's life, Lytton conceals that streak of arrogance and stupidity in the prince's nature which he sometimes failed to control – 'No tailor in England can make a coat,' he once announced; and, to a distinguished clergyman, he remarked that in England 'there is nothing to do but turn rogue or marry'. The prince's brother, in his memoirs, declared: 'Of mankind in general he [Albert] is contemptuous.' His attitude towards his own family, which Lytton hardly touches upon, was extremely interesting and not irrelevant. Sexually and intellectually bored with his wife, he seemed closer to the Princess Royal, his daughter, until she married Prince Frederick of Prussia, and left England to live in Germany. His grief at her departure was sharp, and it seems probable that her place as the closest woman in his life would have been taken by Princess Alice, had he lived longer – she never left his side during his last illness. But his attitude towards Bertie was inexcusable. He once confessed to Clarendon, rather indiscreetly, that the aggressive disciplinarian treatment of his eldest son which he and the queen meted out was a mistake. The disagreeable task of punishment, he added, always fell on him, and he had hesitated to resist this severity for fear of thwarting or exciting Victoria. Nevertheless, it is difficult to escape the conclusion that he vented on the Prince of Wales all his own disappointments and frustrations, having no other outlet for his long pent-up emotions. There was an element of cruelty in Albert's make-up. He needed an antagonist to spur him to his best efforts, and Victoria bored him with her tireless veneration. To some extent, Lytton exaggerated Albert's misery in the early days of their marriage. He was not unhappy then. Victoria's hero-worship of him – like Carrington's for Lytton himself – enveloped him very comfortably, and though it did not penetrate his being to any great depth, it does seem to have ministered pleasantly enough to his sense of vanity.

The peculiar fascination which this relationship between Victoria and Albert exerted over Lytton is clearly disclosed when he asks, 'was he the wife and she the husband?' and answers his own question: 'It almost seemed so.' For outward appearances belied the inner truth. Their marriage had begun as a struggle of angry wills. 'Victoria,' Lytton explains, 'no more than Albert, was in the habit of playing second fiddle. Her arbitrary temper flashed out. Her vitality, her obstinacy, her overweening sense of her own position, might well have beaten down before them his superiorities and his rights. But she fought at a disadvantage; she was, in very truth, no longer her own mistress; a profound preoccupation dominated her, seizing upon her inmost purposes for its own extraordinary ends. She was madly in love.' And so, Lytton wryly tells us: 'Time and the pressure of inevitable circumstances were for him; every day his predominance grew more assured – and every night.' The picture which Lytton now draws for us is of the queen's total capitulation before Albert – and beneath him. 'Victoria,' he writes, 'overcome by a new, an unimagined revelation, had surrendered her whole soul to her husband.' And a little later: 'Victoria fell more and more absolutely under his intellectual predominance,' until, 'with all the zeal of a convert,' she 'upheld now the standard of moral purity with an inflexibility surpassing, if that were possible, Albert's own'. In all things, like some topsy-turvy Duke of Plaza-toro, she followed from well in advance. When he felt disappointment, she exceeded him in mortification. When he seemed contented, she was ecstatic. He was, as she herself once wrote, 'my beloved lord and master'.

The development, skilfully traced by Lytton through his narrative, though true, does not perhaps constitute the whole truth. The account which Albert himself gave to the Duke of Wellington of his role as husband puts a very different emphasis on his relationship with Victoria. He considered it his duty, he said, to 'sink his *own individual* existence in that of his wife . . . – assume no separate responsibility before the public, but make his position entirely a part of hers – fill up every gap which, as a woman, she would naturally leave in the exercise of her regal functions – continually and anxiously watch every part of the public business, in order to be able to advise and assist her at any moment in any of the multifarious and difficult questions or duties brought before her, sometimes international, sometimes political, or social, or personal'.

So much for the Prince Consort's absolute predominance. From resembling a foreign tenor, he had changed during the course of his marriage, as Lytton observes, into an idealized butler. For a double process was at work. His victory over the queen's prepotent will was largely superficial and void. She had, it is true, changed; but change-ability was the very essence of her shallow being, since she possessed no special ambiance of her own, merely reflecting the light of those closest to her. Albert, on the other hand, by adapting himself body and soul to the part of the Prince Consort, had sacrificed almost everything that was original in his character, to become a cold caricature of a worthy man, a figure of bleached perfection, bowed down by domesticity, loneliness, misunderstanding and overwork.

What really pricked Lytton's curiosity was not so much Albert's apparent predominance as the underlying ascendancy of Victoria. Her superabundant energies suffocated the very breath out of him. It was hardly surprising that, lacking her inert tenacity, he should confess to setting no great store by his prolonged existence. 'I do not cling to life,' he once admitted to Victoria, '. . . I am sure, if I had a severe illness, I should give up at once, I should not struggle for life.' And so it proved to be.

Only when Lytton comes to see Victoria through the eyes of the declining Prince Consort does the sentimental haze enveloping her suddenly lift, and we are made to feel a real and positive repugnance. Albert's constitution was 'ill-adapted to meet a serious strain. He was easily upset; he constantly suffered from minor ailments. His appearance in itself was enough to indicate the infirmity of his physical powers . . . Beside Victoria, he presented a painful contrast. She, too, was stout, but it was with the plumpness of a vigorous matron; and an eager vitality was everywhere visible – in her energetic bearing, her protruding, inquiring glances, her small, fat, capable and commanding hands. If only, by some sympathetic magic, she could have conveyed into that portly, flabby figure, that desiccated and discouraged brain, a measure of the stamina and the self-assurance which were so pre-eminently hers!'

Although, owing to the subsequent publication of various papers, a few of Lytton's pages – such as the scene in which Bismarck is made to overawe the queen – have been proved to rest on false surmise, his portrait of Victoria has remained vividly in the public imagination, greatly influencing later biographies. But for those who do not share his habit of extolling her severe limitations as charming aspects of a quaint and whimsical personality, the clue to Victoria's character lies in her incredible unawareness of her husband's baleful submission to the mysterious fate that had decreed their marriage. She needed a man to whose father-like authority she could respond with constant love – a love preserved by constant challenge. To all else she was blind. It was enough for her that she was happy with Albert. That she represented for him the rigorous subordination in a virtuous life of the

desire for personal happiness to the arid claims of duty never consciously occurred to her. 'Very few', she wrote, 'can say with me that
their husband at the end of twenty-one years is *not* only full of the
friendship, kindness and affection which a truly happy marriage brings
with it, but the same tender love of the *very first days of our marriage.*'
This statement, in such striking contrast to the deepening gloom of
Albert's last years, Lytton does not quote. Nor does he quote the single
sentence in which, after Albert's death, Victoria came nearest to realizing that her husband's sombre calm had not concealed an exquisite
felicity equal to her own. 'His great soul', she wrote, 'is *now only*
enjoying that of which it *was* worthy.'

3

THE PRIME MINISTERS

Lytton devoted more than two-thirds of his biography to Victoria's
life before the death of Albert, leaving the remaining third to cover the
latter half of her career. The primary reason for this, it has been said,
was the smaller quantity of available information. 'The first forty-two
years of the Queen's life are illuminated by a great and varied quantity
of authentic information,' Lytton himself wrote. 'With Albert's death
a veil descends. Only occasionally, at fitful and disconnected intervals,
does it lift for a moment or two; a few main outlines, a few remarkable
details may be discerned; the rest is all conjecture and ambiguity. Thus,
though the Queen survived her great bereavement for almost as many
years as she had lived before it, the chronicle of those years can bear no
proportion to the tale of her earlier life. We must be content in our
ignorance with a brief and summary relation.' According to Raymond
Mortimer, the final volumes of Victoria's correspondence, which G. B.
Buckle brought out between 1928 and 1932, altered Lytton's view of
these later years: she was more robust, less gentle and droll than he had
envisaged. But, in any case, he did not wish to expand the last four
chapters of his book. The earlier chapters describe the long process by
which the character of the queen was formed; once that character had
crystallized, her actual life was of less significance to him. To amend
and enlarge this final section would have disrupted the biographical
pattern. For there seems little doubt that Lytton really welcomed the
darkness which descended over the last forty years of the queen's reign
as aiding his artistic purpose, which was to re-create his subject's intimate personality, her hidden or unconscious life. It was this aim that,

throughout the biography, guided his choice of material. The absence of detailed information about Victoria's widowhood legitimately opened the way to a more subjective interpretation of her temperament. Lytton regarded – as did Victoria – the death of Albert as the central turning-point in her history. 'She herself', he wrote, 'felt that her true life had ceased with her husband's, and that the remainder of her days upon earth was of a twilight nature – an epilogue to a drama that was done. Nor is it possible that her biographer should escape a similar impression.'

Critics who have complained that *Queen Victoria* omits too much of the nineteenth-century political scene have possibly failed to appreciate that the unity which Lytton brought to his book was achieved mainly by the process of seeing people and events through the eyes of Victoria herself. Though shrewd, she had little wisdom or imagination and none of the political genius of Elizabeth, with whom she has often been thoughtlessly compared. Her politics were more of the eighteenth century, and her interest in them was of a purely personal nature. She suspected political zeal and was repelled by political enthusiasm, her object being to maintain the vested interests of her family clan, at whatever expense to the British taxpayer. After Albert's death, she behaved like a widow who has been left in charge of a large estate, and means to exact the respect due to her from her less important neighbours. Her prime ministers she treated in the manner of family solicitors, whose duty it was to remain always vigilant in seeking out profitable investments for her spare moneys.

In these circumstances, it was inevitable that the professional historian should consider Lytton's treatment of nineteenth-century politics to have been sparse and inadequate. Only in order to estimate the developments which the Constitution underwent during Victoria's reign does he step aside from the main narrative of his story and allow some historical commentary. And here, by maintaining that the power of the Crown increased from 1840 until Albert's death, then steadily declined until, in 1901, it 'was weaker than at any other time in English history', he seemed to several constitutional historians to have entirely misunderstood the significance of the Reform Bill.

Lytton's portraits of individual politicians are deliberately uneven, since they are coloured almost completely by Victoria's own personal feelings towards each one of them. It was not their politics which impressed her, but their personalities. Lytton affects to see underlying her formal and official dealings with her prime ministers a more individual relationship, and he uses these minor political characters in such a way as to contribute directly to our more personal knowledge of

the queen's inner life, and of one aspect of this inner life especially –
her strong, subconscious sexuality. This he does not attempt to depict
in the rather scandalous, dubiously assertive manner of E. E. P.
Tisdall, but subtly, through suggestive metaphor and innuendo.

Lost in the large shadow of her mother's domination, Victoria's
early, formative years were likened by Lytton to those of a novice in a
convent. The Duchess of Kent never for a single day relaxed the pressure of her maternal vigilance. Her educational concepts were those of
Dr Arnold, and she saw to it that her daughter was drilled, with unyielding conformity, in the antique, endless duties of a Christian queen.
The whole household at Kensington was geared to the task of eradicating the minutest traces of ordinary human nature in the grown girl. An
antiseptic odour of sanctity enshrouded her, protecting her from the
contaminations of the outside world and from the disturbing presence
of the male sex. The justifiable horror which Lytton felt at this unnatural
process of incubating a human soul – a horror that may possibly have
gained something from his own incarceration within Lancaster Gate –
is very pronounced in the chapter which he devotes to Victoria's childhood: 'The child grew into the girl, the girl into the young woman; but
still she slept in her mother's bedroom; still she had no place allowed
her where she might sit or work by herself. An extraordinary watchfulness surrounded her every step . . . It was her misfortune that the mental
atmosphere which surrounded her during these years of adolescence
was almost entirely feminine . . . Henceforward female duty, female
elegance, female enthusiasm, hemmed her completely in; and her
spirit, amid the enclosing folds, was hardly reached by those two great
influences, without which no growing life can truly prosper – humour
and imagination.'

Schooled in the absolute virtues of simplicity, propriety and devotion,
she had received a training from which nothing had been omitted that
might help to ensure she ascended the Throne with the purest intentions,
the most just desires. Yet, as Lytton more than once hints, the female
domination to which she was subjected as a girl may itself have given
rise to an unforeseen reaction, namely, her eager dependence and
susceptibility in adult life to the influence of men – 'perhaps, after all,
to the discerning eye, the purity would not be absolute. The careful
searcher might detect, in the virgin soil, the first faint traces of an
unexpected vein.' Her unwearying love of dancing, her extreme
attraction towards handsome young men in uniform, were not the
qualities one looked for in a convent nun. 'The "illustrious Princess"
might perhaps, after all, have something within her which squared ill
with the easy vision of a well-conducted heroine in an edifying story-

book.' For all the care taken over her upbringing, for all the anxious, unceasing watchfulness which presided over her cloistered childhood and adolescence 'there was something deep within her which responded immediately and vehemently to natures that offered a romantic contrast with her own'.

This was the fundamental spring, bubbling incessantly below the hard, regal exterior of Victoria's personality, which Lytton sought to explore in describing her relations with a succession of politicians and other minor figures in the book. The romantic contrast between the queen, with her youth, her earnestness, and her endearing simplicity, and the absent-minded, sceptical, flippant old Lord Melbourne, her first prime minister, was certainly striking. Lytton obviously warmed to Melbourne, and he indulges his fondness beyond the strict artistic limits that controlled his other subsidiary portraits. We see Lord M. not only through the fascinated eyes of Victoria, but also with the admiring retrospective gaze of a biographer. The result is the most full and satisfying minor impressionistic study in the book. He does not seek to 'explain' Melbourne, but to exhibit him vividly before the reader. Consequently, Melbourne shares with so many of his other pen-portraits that standard Stracheyesque quality of being 'inexplicable'. Like most romantics, Lytton loved a mystery, and he uses all his knowledge of character to add a delicious confusion of colour to the accumulating incongruities he observes on the perimeter of his subjects' personalities, presenting them as supreme enigmas, ambiguous and contradictory, baffling all analysis. He possessed a wonderfully sharp eye for the externals of a personality, the gestures, tricks of speech, eccentric mannerisms, but he could seldom apprehend that directing principle, or complex of principles, that reconciles the apparently conflicting elements on the surface of any character. And without this clue, he is mystified. He throws up his hands in an elegant gesture of surrender, as if in the hope that the rhetorical grace of his movement will camouflage the fact that, theoretically, it is an admission of defeat.

Charles Greville once described Melbourne as 'a man with a capacity for loving without having anything in the world to love'. Victoria was enchanted by his sympathetic presence, his sophistication, his captivating masculine charm and exciting dissimilarity to herself. He soon became an integral part of her existence, and his undirected capacity for loving suddenly focused upon the young queen. In his description of Melbourne's response to Victoria's infatuation, Lytton picks out words and images which suggest the latent sexuality of their attachment: 'And so, cherished by the favour of a sovereign and warmed by the adoration of a girl, the autumn rose, in those autumn months of 1839, came to a wondrous blooming. The petals expanded, beautifully, for the last time. For the last time in this unlooked-for, this incongruous, this almost incredible intercourse, the old epicure tasted the exquisiteness of romance.'

Robert Peel, on the other hand, possessed none of Melbourne's sophisticated sex-appeal. Reserved by nature, he was easily embarrassed, particularly before women, in front of whom his manner would grow unpleasantly stiff and pompous. And so, since he made little positive impression on Victoria, he occupies little space in her biography.

After her marriage, Victoria – whose simple pleasures, Lytton tells us, were mostly physical – lost her 'bold and discontented' look, and her platonic infatuation for Lord Melbourne faded gently away. Completely obsessed by her husband, her response to any man was decided by his opinion alone. Her heart even softened towards the maladroit Peel; while the jaunty and volatile Palmerston, by whom she might otherwise have been attracted, repelled her during these years of her marriage precisely because he was the very antithesis of the Prince Consort, representing all that was most hostile to him in the spirit of England. Lytton, however, does briefly introduce the gaudy, gipsyish figure of Tsar Nicolas I of Russia into his narrative, in order to illustrate that, although contentedly married, Victoria was still naturally appreciative of any strikingly handsome man.

After Albert's death this power of appreciation gradually blossomed forth again more potently. In her own estimation, as Lytton makes clear, she was guided at all times by one principle – her deceased husband's approval. Yet whenever her strong sexual instinct was brought into play, Albert's hypothetical sanction seemed to have been taken for granted. The Prince Consort preferred Gladstone to Disraeli, yet because Gladstone, with 'his ceremonious phrases, his low bows, his punctilious correctitudes', behaved towards her not as if she were a human being but a cold, sacrosanct embodiment of venerable traditions, addressing her, so the story goes, more like a public meeting than a woman, she could never warm to him as a man. Disraeli's personality, so romantic and oriental, was in every respect the opposite of Gladstone's. Performing like some actor in his own exotic melodrama, and with himself as applauding audience, his flattery, his charm, his colourful and bewitching strain of charlatanism intoxicated the ageing queen. By treating her first and foremost as a woman and not as a symbol, he gave her back her self-confidence. Lytton passes swiftly over Gladstone as over Peel, and for similar reasons. But his portrait of Disraeli is almost as detailed as his Melbourne, though rather less satisfactory since, over him, he could not really see eye to eye with Victoria. His meta-phorical description of their relationship and of the swelling elation Disraeli aroused in her, deliberately makes use of imagery that recalls Victoria's friendship with Melbourne so many years before. 'After the long gloom of her bereavement, after the chill of the Gladstonian discipline, she expanded to the rays of Disraeli's devotion like a flower in the sun.'

To experience the sense of physical security for which she longed, Victoria needed to become filially dependent upon some man. But the extraordinary liberties which she permitted the Highland gillie, John Brown, would certainly never have been approved by Albert. That she obscurely sensed his mute protest from beyond the grave is suggested by the odd emotional spiritualism which she concocted – 'the gruff, kind, hairy Scotsman was, she felt, in some mysterious way, a legacy from the dead. She came to believe at last – or so it appeared – that the spirit of Albert was nearer when Brown was near.' Yet the truth of the matter was perhaps more mundane. The shade of Albert was receding in her mind. She never totally forgot him, but, as was natural, his loss became less terrible, her awareness of his overriding tastes and opinions more intermittent. Significantly, Munshi Abdul Karim, her Indian attendant who took the place of Brown after his death, was invested with no transcendental ties with the deceased Prince Consort.

Lytton constructed his *Queen Victoria* as a series of self-contained but inter-related chapter-essays. The chapters are neatly parcelled up round the principal men in Victoria's life, and sometimes by-pass the strict chronological sequence of historical events in a manner that can be misleading. The characters surrounding the queen appear and dis-appear as if they had no existence before or after the few paragraphs or pages where they are mentioned. In Chapter 4, 'Marriage', for example, we are shown Albert's ascent from a nonentity to a man of importance not only in his home life but in his position with the Government and the people of the country. We watch him gradually breaking down the antagonism and gaining the respect of the man in the street, and win-ning, too, the confidence of the ministers of state. Opposition dies away, and in the final section of this chapter his triumph is crowned by the Great Exhibition of 1851. But in the next chapter we learn with some sur-prise that Palmerston was Albert's bitterest opponent, and that since 1846 he had been foreign minister, continuing in this office until Novem-ber 1851. During these years there had been a constant struggle between the two of them. But it is only now, in Chapter 5, that we discover, for the first time, this major obstacle in the political advancement of Albert, which is the subject-matter of Chapter 4. This technique of parcelling chapters is most disconcerting in 'Mr. Gladstone and Lord Beaconsfield'. Both these men, well past middle age, who had for many years played important political roles, are only now introduced at this late stage into the story. The one intimation given to us that Disraeli was an eminent parliamentarian even in the time of the Prince Consort is that the prince once declared that he 'had not one single element of a gentleman in his composition'. Gladstone, Lytton tells us, 'had been the disciple of her revered Peel, and had won the approval of Albert'. By showing Victoria succumbing to the outrageous flatteries of Disraeli and regarding Gladstone with distrust and dislike, Lytton intended to illustrate how the queen's strong and unconscious sexuality overpowered her avowed determination to be governed by the doctrines and opinions of her late husband. What Lytton omits – and it is an omission which stems mainly from the structure of his biography – is that Disraeli in fact won Albert's qualified approval during his brief time of ministerial office before the Prince Consort's death, by his wholehearted support of Albert's crusade to strengthen England's military defences. Albert, who had a distinct strain of effeminacy in his character, had also sometimes taken a hesitating pleasure in conversing with the Leader of the Opposition, finding that Disraeli was more culti-vated and better read in English history than any other British states-man, and that his deferential attitude to the Throne was irreproachable.

4

UNSEEN POWERS

The third type of character in *Queen Victoria*, that collection of sinister and dimly-seen supers who lurk histrionically behind the scenes of power, contributes less to the reader's knowledge of facts than to the pervasive atmosphere and artistic design of the book. These mysterious, immaterial beings – the Duchess of Kent, Lehzen, Leopold and Stock-mar – are little more than stage props supporting the star performers in the cast. Lytton had devised them as the cog-wheels which made up the mechanical tricks of his trade, and any resemblance between them and actual human beings was coincidental. To some extent these artificial entities, and the parts they play, are products of his romantic and cynical conception of political intrigue and the struggle for power behind the scenes. But Lytton also uses them to great aesthetic effect. As latent supremacy passes from one to the other, so the kaleidoscope of the biography subtly shifts from one pattern to another.

The Duchess of Kent is seen as the first to exercise her hidden authority. 'Great forces and fierce antagonisms', Lytton wrote, 'seemed to be moving, obscurely, about the royal cradle.' As Victoria grows up, a battle for her allegiance develops between the child's mother and her governess, Baroness Lehzen. And it is Lehzen who finally emerges triumphant. Lytton describes her victory in highly charged, dramatic style. 'The pastor's daughter observed the ruin of her enemies. Discreet and victorious, she remained in possession of the field. More closely than ever did she cleave to the side of her mistress, her pupil, and her friend; and in the recesses of the palace her mysterious figure was at once invisible and omnipresent.'

During these first few years of her reign, Victoria is dominated by Lehzen, whom Lytton depicts as the real mistress of the royal household, responsible for the freezing etiquette that was permanently in control there. 'Over the whole of Victoria's private life the Baroness reigned supreme,' he informs us, 'and she had not the slightest intention of allowing that supremacy to be diminished by one iota. Since the accession, her power had greatly increased. Besides the undefined and enormous influence which she exercised through her management of the Queen's private correspondence, she was now the superintendent of the royal establishment and controlled the important office of Privy Purse.'

In international affairs it is Leopold, Victoria's uncle, who attempts to gain ascendancy over the young queen. For a while it looks as if he might be successful, but eventually his counsels, entreaties and creeping policies are overcome by Victoria's unyielding front. It is, however, Leopold's 'confidential agent', Baron Stockmar – a sort of Professor Moriarty controlling the destiny of kingdoms from his invisible lair – who at length carries all before him. If Victoria is Lehzen's pupil, Albert is the genie whom Stockmar calls out of his bottle to enact his every wish. After Albert and Victoria's marriage a kind of Punch and Judy show starts up, Stockmar and Lehzen violently activating the marionettes upon the stage until Punch-Albert-Stockmar is acclaimed the winner. Lehzen 'lost ground perceptibly', Lytton recorded. The prince, Stockmar's mouthpiece, is at first cautious. Then he waves a wand and the full annihilating power of his magic is at once omnipotent. 'He spoke, and Lehzen vanished for ever.'

And so the kaleidoscope shifts again. 'The tide of circumstance was flowing now with irresistible fullness towards a very different consummation.' It is hardly an exaggeration to say that, in Lytton's version, the queen and the Prince Consort were allowed to possess free will only within those limits ordained by the all-prescient baron. He is the good

fairy of the pantomime, working with all the tireless energy of disinterested devotion, cautious and wise, never acting under the spur of
personal ambition; while the royal couple are but two mandarin figures,
nodding their heads in assent or shaking them in denial as their master
pleases.

Lytton's reconstruction of Lehzen's great influence over the queen
was founded pre-eminently on romantic conjecture. His analysis of
Stockmar's character and the description he gives of the powerful role
the baron played in politics is adapted very largely from the mythical
version which Stockmar himself perpetuated in the self-hypnotic throes
of senile optimism. The passage in which Lytton conjures forth the
supernal baron is far-fetched in the extreme. 'The satisfaction of his
essential being lay in obscurity, in invisibility – in passing, unobserved,
through a hidden entrance, into the very central chamber of power,
and in sitting there, quietly, pulling the subtle strings that set the wheels
of the whole world in motion.' His trap-door exits and entrances to
and from these high places, Lytton later assures us, were of the utmost
political significance – so much so that, despite the most cunning discretion, a vague rumour of his power percolated through to the general
public. 'Stockmar's pupil had assuredly gone far and learnt well.
Stockmar's pupil! – precisely; the public, painfully aware of Albert's
predominance, had grown, too, uneasily conscious that Victoria's
master had a master of his own. Deep in the darkness the Baron
loomed. Another foreigner! Decidedly, there were elements in the
situation which went far to justify the popular alarm. A foreign Baron
controlled a foreign Prince, and the foreign Prince controlled the
Crown of England. And the Crown itself was creeping forward
ominously; and when, from under its shadow, the Baron and the
Prince had frowned, a great Minister, beloved of the people, had fallen.
Where was all this to end?'

In order to establish Stockmar from the very start as the Invisible
Man who exercised so prodigious a hold over the prince, the queen and
the whole of English politics, Lytton instances his peremptory dealings
with Melbourne. For with the extinction of Lord M. as an influence
over the queen – which Stockmar is made to engineer – came the final
emergence of his pupil, Albert. 'Stockmar, who had returned to
England, watched the departure of Lord Melbourne with satisfaction,'
Lytton wrote. 'If all went well, the Prince should now wield a supreme
political influence over Victoria. But would all go well? . . . He
[Melbourne] continued to write to the Queen as before; and two more
violent bombardments from the Baron were needed before he was
brought to reason. Then, gradually, his letters grew less and less

frequent, with fewer and fewer references to public concerns; at last, they were entirely innocuous. The Baron smiled; Lord M. had accepted the inevitable.'

So far from Albert having been a creation of Stockmar's, this Stockmar was an invention of Lytton's. His misconception of the baron's position – like part of his account of the queen's character in old age – follows the popular beliefs held at the time by the uninformed man in the street. The records, however, go some way to proving precisely the opposite of what Lytton attempted to foist on his readers as the hidden truth. Albert turned to Stockmar not for political guidance but for personal reasons – he felt more at home conversing with another foreigner. And Melbourne, too, seems to have taken little heed of the baron or his bombardments. When the political content of Lord M.'s letters to the queen eventually became less abundant, it had not been due to Stockmar's intervention, but to the new trust which Albert and Victoria had by then learnt to repose in Peel and the Tory Government. 'Stockmar's son,' E. F. Benson has sensibly pointed out in his own biography of Victoria, 'who compiled his Memoirs, seems to have been conscious of this, and very judiciously omits all mention of this signal defeat. The Queen and the Prince were very fond of the Baron, he had come to England with Uncle Leopold before either of them was born; Melbourne, Peel, Aberdeen and Palmerston in turn had the firmest belief in his integrity, and they liked a talk with the shrewd caustic old man, and he enjoyed it too; and then he went to his room and put down all the good advice he had given them. Sometimes they had agreed with him and then all was well; sometimes they thought otherwise, and then Stockmar recorded what a sad mess they had made through not listening to him. Whenever, as happened more than once, he interfered in political matters, we find that, as here, his schemings were singularly fruitless. The public misjudged him: his constant intimacy with the Prince led to the belief that he was a sinister foreign adviser, potent and mysterious, whereas he was an honest dyspeptic old gentleman, useful to him in many ways, with the harmless foible of thinking that he directed and controlled his old pupil. This conviction remained with him, and in 1855, shortly before he left England for good, he wrote of Albert and the Queen: "They have passed the point at which leading is required." But evidence that he had ever led them in their political dealings with the government is entirely lacking, and Albert had long ago assumed the position for which Melbourne himself had always considered him so admirably fit.'

The end of Lytton's Stockmar is heralded by the death of Albert. Deprived of his medium, his ventriloquist's dummy, the baron is suddenly made redundant. He is a magician without his magic wand. Having no further aesthetic function to perform in the biography, he feels the full force of this disaster. 'The Prince was his creation . . . The Baron, by his fireside at Coburg, suddenly saw the tremendous fabric of his creation crash down into sheer and irremediable ruin. Albert was gone, and he had lived in vain. Even his blackest hypochondria had never envisioned quite so miserable a catastrophe. Victoria wrote to him, visited him, tried to console him by declaring with passionate conviction that she would carry on her husband's work. He smiled a sad smile and looked into the fire. Then he murmured that he was going where Albert was – that he would not be long. He shrank into himself. His children clustered round him and did their best to comfort him, but it was useless: the Baron's heart was broken. He lingered for eighteen months, and then, with his pupil, explored the shadow and the dust.'

Then, for the last time, the kaleidoscopic pattern alters. Victoria, her being no longer animated to new life by the master puppet maker from behind the stage, can only go through all over again her old familiar tricks. Her friendship with Disraeli is a distorted mummery of her earlier love for Melbourne; her antagonism to Gladstone recalls her coldness towards Peel. With sedate majesty she enters into her second childhood.

The direction under which Baron Stockmar acts in *Queen Victoria* illustrates both the peculiar distinction and limitation of Lytton's book, as a perfect example of his biographical methods. Technically it is a dazzling *tour de force*. Despite a little tinsel in the extraneous ornament of its chapters, its excellence resides chiefly in the skilfully constructed architectural design. As a craftsman in biography, Lytton was second to none. 'He it was who first saw the possibilities of this new medium,' wrote Lord David Cecil. 'He it was who evolved the technical equipment for its expression. We may extend his building, but we must always construct on his foundations. He was the man who established the form.'

What shortcomings there are reside in the comparatively small amount of mental and emotional nourishment to be absorbed from his writing. In life, Lytton was habitually self-conscious and ill-at-ease with strangers and in matters of intense passion. Because he always bore his public in mind as a writer, this reserve of manner fastened on to his style, strangling the free, outward expansion and communication of feeling, drowning pathos in reverberating rhetoric. His emotions tended to turn inwards, curdle, and show fitfully in half-embarrassed spurts of sentimentality. The characters in his biographies are, perhaps more often than not, vividly painted pieces of cardboard, moved by a marvellous machinery of strings and pulleys within sharply defined margins, to give the illusion of life. Though memorable for this colour and dramatic décor, they are imbued with little real animation of their own, and leave the impression, for all the contrivances which have gone into their making, of being rather flat. Where he does feel a bond of direct and personal sympathy – as with Albert – his inclination to exaggerate and dramatize can sometimes oversimplify – for the sake of immediate entertainment – a really original interpretation of character.

The last, finely shaped paragraph in *Queen Victoria*, too well-known to be quoted, where Lytton makes the dying queen call up the shadows of her past, has been compared with James Joyce's stream of consciousness. For almost a decade this finale set a fashion for biographers who, if anxious to please their publishers, would indulge themselves in a last-minute orgy of plagiaristic retrospection[1] – a habit which Lytton himself wittily ridiculed in *Elizabeth and Essex*, in the last passage of which he makes Robert Cecil gaze prophetically into the future. Now that this fashion has long worked itself out, the real literary value of Lytton's evocation may be more accurately measured. We now have the eye-witness account left by Victoria's son-in-law, who watched the queen sinking like a three-decker ship, now rallying, now failing, and who heard the last coherent word she spoke – 'Bertie'. Lytton's imaginative peroration suffers by contrast with this account because it contains no suppressed humour and none of the pathos suggested by the utterance of that single name, with all the regret it implied and all she could no longer say. In the biography, the formal and gently scaled diminuendo of ordered imagery is softened by a tenderness that transforms this last scene into a charming, fairy-tale ending. Lytton, as producer and director, stands over the ebbing queen, receives, interprets her final thoughts and sensations, and confers on her his absolute blessing.

But the pathos of Victoria's death is everywhere mitigated by a feeling of admiration for Lytton's splendid artifice. Who, reading of Falstaff's death, thinks of William Shakespeare? And who, finishing *Queen Victoria*, does not think of Lytton Strachey and his biographical technique?

---

[1] But the most extraordinary piece of plagiarism is provided by Edith Sitwell's *Victoria of England*, in which, as Geoffrey Grigson rightly observed (*The Times Literary Supplement*, 11 February 1965, p. 107), the author looked up Lytton's quotations and merely extended them, modifying Lytton's accompanying comments, or sometimes paraphrasing them word for word, substituting a synonym for each in succession.

5

THE QUINTESSENCE OF STRACHEYISM

On both sides of the Atlantic, *Queen Victoria* was an instantaneous success, and has remained ever since Lytton's most popular work. Described by some as the quintessence of Stracheyism, and acclaimed by many as a classic, the book quickly established itself as a best-seller – four thousand copies of the first English edition of five thousand were sold within twenty-four hours – was awarded the James Tait Black Memorial Prize in 1922, and adapted by Walter Pritchard-Eaton for the stage. Most readers recognized that the biography represented a mainly flattering tribute to Victoria, and Lytton was deluged with letters of congratulation from prime ministers, colonels and clergymen. In academic circles the word went round that he had fallen in love with the queen. *The Times Literary Supplement* was loud in its thanksgiving, and a great sigh of relief went up from the universities – Sir Edmund Gosse much affected, Professor G. M. Trevelyan totally overcome, and all the dons astonished and delighted.[1]

Although Lytton was gratified by the large sales, he felt rather apprehensive over this fanfare of critical acclaim. It was all very well for Max Beerbohm to declare that he was the wittiest writer of the age,[2] but when he read reviews in the papers, written by second-rate critics whom he had long disparaged, stating that the dawning age had here bequeathed to posterity a model biography, his reactions were more mixed. To Hesketh Pearson, who asked him how it felt to be the author of a best-seller, he replied that it left him unmoved – 'indeed the success of my work is beginning to make me question its merit. Can a popular author be a good one?' Whenever he heard people say his

---

[1] 'On 6 May 1921 Trevelyan wrote to Lytton: 'Dear Strachey, I expect you are tired of hearing how good Queen V is. But I would like to say it to you. Much as I liked your last book, I think it beats it a lot. Did you ever meditate a book about Voltaire? "It would be such a nice change", as they say. Yours ever, G. M. Trevelyan.'

[2] 'Have you read Lytton Strachey's *Queen Victoria*? That I *am* a Stoic is proved by my having no jealousy of him at all, though his mind and his prose are so like mine and so exactly like what I should have loved mine to be. For sheer divine beauty of prose, and for clairvoyance of mind in dealing with past personages, and for wit, and for much else, nobody comes within a hundred miles of him. I was rather amazed and horrified that you did not seem to have quite realized what manner of book *Eminent Victorians* was. Pray tell me that you have been respectably bowled over by this other book.' (Max Beerbohm to Reggie Turner, 20 June 1921.) In a letter to another friend Max wrote: 'No! I am not nearly so witty as Chesterton for one. But certainly I have not prostituted and cheapened my wit as he has. How about Lytton Strachey? There's the wittiest mind of the age – and the virtue of it guarded even more strictly and puritanically than I have guarded the virtue of mine.'

treatment of the queen had been mature and discreet, he interpreted it as meaning that the book was tedious and flat. 'At any rate I feel that I ought to do something particularly outrageous for my next book,' he wrote to James (April 1921), 'in order to retrieve my reputation. It's alarming to be welcomed with open arms by Gosse, Jack Squire and the Times – though I suppose it's paying also.'

Even loftier honours seemed to be within his reach when he was suddenly summoned to Buckingham Palace for an audience, so he understood, with the king. As he waited to be ushered into the royal presence, the door silently opened, Lord Stamfordham entered carrying an open copy of *Queen Victoria*, in a quiet voice corrected its author on one minor point of *fact*, and departed as noiselessly as he had come in. Lytton was then free, he ascertained, to leave the Palace and return home.[1]

Some readers – a small minority – were disappointed. 'We're looking forward with the greatest excitement to the arrival of Queen Victoria,' James had written to his mother (9 March 1921). 'I wonder whether Lytton's read it to you yet, and whether it's very shocking. Will the whole family be involved in disgrace?' Other admirers, too, of *Eminent Victorians* must have expected that, in his subsequent portrait of the queen who had given her name to such a prudish and barbaric epoch,

---

[1] There are various versions of this story, the one above being told by Lytton himself to William Gerhardie, from whom the author heard it (see also *Resurrection* by William Gerhardie). In a letter to her brother Noel, Carrington wrote: 'The King accepted a copy. But his sec Lord Stanfordham wrote to Lytton "that his Majesty having read his book, there were a few points he would like to discuss would L.S. please call at Buckingham Palace at his earliest convenience". Lytton very wisely rang up to say he was just leaving for Italy. Evidently Lord S wasn't accustomed to S U C H treatment, for he was rather snooT Y Still Lytton mainTained, which was true that he was just off, and dashed down the receiver and ended the conversation.'

Lytton, too, referred to this episode in his correspondence with Mary Hutchinson (1 May 1921): 'Just back from Buckingham Palace and an hour's interview with Lord Stamfordham. His Majesty did not come up through a trap-door in the middle of it – as I'd rather expected he would. The poor old thing (a respectable maiden lady) was very amicable, though at moments pettish. The point of his remarks was very difficult to catch, but I rather gathered that the elder Princesses had insisted on "something being done", and that this was all they could think of. The world grows steadily more and more fantastic, I find . . .'

The response to *Queen Victoria* at Buckingham Palace seems to have been unequal. Miss Frances Stevenson (later Countess Lloyd George) notes in her diary (11 April 1921): 'Went down to Trent over Sunday after hectic week of unfruitful negotiations over coal strike. P[rince] of Wales came on Sunday with Mr Dudley Ward. We spoke of Strachey's life of Queen Victoria, which had just been published and the Prince said: "That must be the book the King was talking about this morning. He was very angry and got quite vehement over it". P of W had not seen the book, so we showed it to him and presently he was discovered in roars of laughter over the description of the Queen and John Brown.' See *The Decline and Fall of Lloyd George* by Lord Beaverbrook (1963), pp. 49–50.

with its outrageous fogs, its antimacassars and bed-bugs, Lytton would 'display his qualities of cold detachment, of sardonic scrutiny, and of a wit which had the sharpness, as well as the brightness, of a keenly polished dagger'. But, as Ivor Brown wrote, 'instead of being caustic he was genial; instead of writing in a mood of urbane detachment, he became, though still of course urbane, engaged and even affectionate. His book, with its closeness and cordiality of approach to its subject, surprised by the warmth of its tone. . . . So the cool and unsparing portrayer of Victorian notables was no longer the aloof scrutineer. Following the queen herself down the decades, he found himself at last engaged in a sentimental journey.'

Queen Victoria was dedicated to Virginia Woolf, who told Lytton that she considered it magnificent, 'an incredible gem, and a masterpiece of prose', even better on the whole than *Eminent Victorians*. After a party given to celebrate its publication and to congratulate Lytton, she confessed privately in her diary to a deepening jealousy of his success. Envy had so choked her appreciation of the book that she found herself unable to admit having finished it, and both she and Leonard later told Gerald Brenan that they considered it unreadable. Though he did not care for Lytton's flat spongy style, which gave him the sensation, he said, of treading on linoleum, Brenan very reasonably objected to this prejudiced opinion. But both Virginia and Leonard continued to pronounce decisively against the biography, while qualifying their verdict by speaking of Lytton's great subtlety of mind, his discrimination as a critic, and their personal attachment to him as friends. It was this personal consideration that prompted Virginia to send Lytton a letter on 17 April which was generous in its evidently unfelt praise. 'I've seldom enjoyed anything more,' she told him. 'I suppose the chief marvel is the way you spin the story perfectly straightforwardly, never a line slack, and yet contrive those wonderful little portraits, one after another, each exactly in its place, illuminating, without interruption or fuss or for a moment stopping, it seems, to go on talking simply. The effect is not merely satiric by any means. You seem to have reduced it to the last possible ounce, and yet to have kept all the meat and bone and guts. The great moments seem to me really moving. And the Queen herself comes out somehow surprising, solid and angular, and touching, though not exactly sympathetic. Amazing woman! My only criticism (and I'm not sure of its truth) is that occasionally I think one is a little conscious of being entertained. It's a little too luxurious reading – I mean, one is willing perhaps to take more pains than you allow.'

In spite of Virginia's observations to Gerald Brenan, such an appreciation does not read insincerely. Over ten years later, when

Lytton was dead, when she was famous as a novelist and there was no more cause for envy, Virginia composed a long essay on 'The Art of Biography'[1] in which she warmly commended *Queen Victoria* as 'a triumphant success', adding that it 'is a life which, very possibly, will do for the old Queen what Boswell did for the old dictionary maker. In time to come Lytton Strachey's Queen Victoria will be Queen Victoria, just as Boswell's Johnson is now Dr. Johnson. The other versions will fade and disappear. It was a prodigious feat . . .'

Another critic who at first condemned the book and later recanted was Arthur Quiller-Couch. The essay[2] in which he indicts Lytton for being 'smart and amusing' and contends that 'the book aims at showing up Albert the Good to ridicule' has often been quoted by critics who could not have known that several years later Quiller-Couch entirely reversed his opinion. 'When I first read the book,' he wrote to Lytton (15 September 1925), 'old and perhaps "impossible" loyalty raised certain bristles in me, and I spoke rather sharply about it in a lecture at Cambridge. Later on Dover Wilson staying here [The Haven, Fowey, Cornwall] with me, read my lecture, borrowed the book and read it in his bedroom, and informed me next morning that I had made a fool of myself. What is worse he convinced me.'

When, in 1926, Quiller-Couch brought out his *Oxford Book of English Prose*, he included lengthy extracts from Lytton's *Queen Victoria*, including the famous evocation of the queen's death. And this, in turn, led to a little-known criticism of the biography by T. S. Eliot. In an anonymous Front Article in *The Times Literary Supplement* (4 March 1926) reviewing the anthology, Eliot declared that there were two elements in the creative act of writing – the visual image and the emotions associated with this image. 'The image is there, stark, visible and real; to find the right words, the only right words, to body forth that image, becomes in the writer an actual passion. The image evokes the words; or if it fails, if to the visual memory there comes no corresponding emotive or expressive memory, then there is no art. A good writer must then be silent; and only the bad writer will accept the approximate expression – the first expression that comes into his head, which is usually a stale expression, for it is ever so much easier to remember phrases than to evoke words. These memorable phrases press invitingly round the would-be writer; they are the current coin and counters of verbal intercourse; and to refuse them, and to deal only in freshly minted coin, is possible only to a few autocrats. But these are

[1] 'The Art of Biography' was included in Virginia Woolf's posthumous volume *The Death of the Moth and Other Essays* (1942), and in Volume 4 of her *Collected Essays* (1967).

[2] Quiller-Couch's essay appears in his *Studies in Literature, Second Series* (1927).

the rulers of literature, the creators of style; and they should find a place in an anthology of best prose.'

To exemplify his argument, Eliot then analyses the differences between two selected pieces of prose – the final paragraph from *Queen Victoria* and a passage from Joyce not included in the anthology.[1] Lytton Strachey's writing is not altogether bad – it is not sufficiently bad to avert the reader's thoughts. Indeed, it has all the conditions of fine prose – wit, elegance, readability – but few of its essential qualities. When one compares it with the Joyce passage, one is immediately aware of a great difference – not the difference between two kinds of goodness, but between one quality and its opposite. Lytton Strachey's prose 'causes us less surprise: we are scarcely conscious of the kind of prose we are reading – apart from a certain ironic affectation; but we are, as a matter of fact, reading a prose densely packed with images and analogies, none of which we actually visualize. "Approaching end", "astonished grief", "grief sweeping over the country", "monstrous reversal", "the course of nature", "to take place", "vast majority", "an indissoluble part", "the scheme of things", "a scarcely possible thought", "divested of all thinking", "to glide into oblivion", "the secret chambers", "fading mind", "the shadows of the past", "to float before (her mind)", "the vanished visions", "through the cloud of years", – here in eighteen lines are eighteen images or analogies, not one of which is original, not one of which is freshly felt or sincerely evoked, and consequently not one of which evokes in the mind of the reader the definite image it actually portends. Now examine the second passage: there is not a single phrase which does not evoke – which does not force the mind to evoke – the image it expresses. Art, after all, is a question of effect; and does anyone give a second thought to the death of Queen Victoria as our author has described it? But merely to read of Stephen Dedalus walking on the beach is to have come into contact with the vibrating reflex of an actual experience.'

This is a powerful, but not unanswerable censure of Lytton's prose style. Eliot makes no allowances for the authentic and valid use of the stereotype, colloquial phrase; he evaluates the quality of imaginative writing too arbitrarily and exclusively by its visual impact; he contrasts

---

[1] The Joyce passage which Eliot uses runs as follows: 'The grainy sand had gone from under his feet. His boots trod again a damp crackling mast, razor-shells, squeaking pebbles, that on the unnumbered pebbles beats, wood sieved by the shipworm, lost Armada. Unwholesome sandflats waited to suck his treading shoes, breathing upward savage breath. He coasted them, walking warily. A porterbottle stood up, stogged to its waist, in the cakey sand dough. A sentinel: isle of dreadful thirst. Broken hoops on the shore; at the land a maze of dark cunning nets; further away chalk-scrawled backdoors and on the higher beach a drying line with two crucified shirts.'

Raymond Mortimer (standing), Frances Marshall and Dadie Rylands at Ham Spray

Ralph Partridge and Carrington about 1930

Lytton and Marjorie Strachey playing chess

Sebastian Sprott (holding Tiber the cat), Gerald Heard, E. M. Forster and Lytton Strachey
at Ham Spray

two passages which are not properly comparable; and he does not explain that, because the artistic effect of Lytton's style is cumulative, one of a gradually induced mood in which images are conjured up in the mind as if under a shallow hypnosis, one may not legitimately extract a single passage from its true context and expect it to perform adequately its original function. Lytton, however, on reading Eliot's criticism for himself, let the paper fall to the ground, sorrowfully telling his friend George Rylands that its strictures against himself as a 'would-be writer' were entirely justified, every one of them.

This capitulation shows very well Lytton's reaction to the success of his books. Though this success sat very well on him, his modesty and humility went almost too far. He had grown more mellow in his manner but he forfeited something of the sharp edge of his critical faculty. He was an easier companion, a less potent and original writer. He was also more easily approachable, and when an unknown admirer, Hesketh Pearson, wrote to him that April to express his gratitude and delight in *Queen Victoria* – 'not merely a Life of Victoria that happens to be a work of art, but a work of art that happens to be a Life of Victoria' – Lytton replied: 'You overwhelm me!' However, he added, 'I keep my head,' and he reassured his correspondent: 'But seriously you are very kind and I like your letter very much.' The following month he wrote again to invite Pearson to lunch at the Café Royal, going on to say that he would recognize him without difficulty: 'I am rather tall, with spectacles and a reddish beard.'

At first glance, Pearson noticed, the most striking thing about him was an intense and restless nervousness, which gave him a bashful, timid manner, not without grace, but emphasized by his thin wrists, his long, tremulous hands, tapering fingers and high-pitched quavering voice. Since his beard was not only red, but also long and square, there was, as he had promised, no difficulty over recognition. 'We shook hands, or rather I shook his hand and he winced. If I had glanced at it first I would not have shaken it with such vigour,' records Pearson. Altogether, his first impression was of some hirsute god, a dry edition of Father Neptune. 'Placid, wide-open eyes, perhaps a trifle owlish, stared at me through glasses that intensified their detached yet critical expression; and the beard gave a solemnity to the whole face, which was crowned by dark hair austerely brushed flat across the head with a side parting.' But this god-like aspect, mute and awe-inspiring, was shattered as soon as Lytton uttered his first sentence in a 'high-pitched tinny voice, which on certain notes cracked and became like a squeak'.

The general roar of conversation in the grill room where they lunched was so loud that Pearson had the utmost difficulty in hearing

P

what his host was saying, though again and again he raised his voice to its shrillest notes in response to Pearson's repeated 'What?' Because of this obstruction, Lytton soon appeared to grow discouraged and fell silent, while Pearson found himself monopolizing the talk solely in order to save his companion the annoyance of cracking his top chords. If Lytton had been hoping to encounter a pretty young lad with tastes sympathetic to his own, he was quickly disillusioned.[1] At one point in their lunch, Pearson leant right across the table and, cupping his hands, shouted out a scandalous story concerning Frank Harris in the Café Royal, which he hoped might amuse Lytton, but which considerably startled the fastidious old Bloomsbury gossip. 'He stroked his beard,' Pearson remembered, 'looked clean through me, and smiled with a sort of frightened frigidity.'

Lytton spoke with the greatest admiration of Gibbon and Sterne, but was less wholehearted in his approval when questioned by Pearson about contemporary writers. Most of Bernard Shaw's plays, he said, were already out of date, though Shaw himself remained a great joker. Of H. G. Wells he remarked: 'I stopped thinking about him when he became a thinker.' G. K. Chesterton was interesting only when he was not being Belloc; and as for Belloc himself, he dismissed him absolutely.

The conversation then switched to the Irish War of Liberation, which was then being waged. But Lytton did not expand. 'I prefer to discuss things about which I do not feel too strongly,' he explained. 'One must never confuse a people with its politicians. I love the English for all the qualities they have in common with Falstaff, not for the qualities they have in common with Cromwell.'

Questioned about his own work, he thought that he might write a play next. He would also like to write a study of Queen Elizabeth, a Life of Charles Darwin, a History of the World in a single, neat, easily portable volume. But none of these projects would occupy him yet for some time. 'It has taken me three solid years' work to write "Victoria",' and I am now suffering from mental prostration.' To recover from this weariness, he intended to devote himself over the next few months to the simpler intellectual and sensual pleasures of private life.

[1] After the publication of *Eminent Victorians* in 1918, Lytton had invited Lord David Cecil to lunch with him at the Café Royal, and with rather similar results. Cecil, then a schoolboy at Eton, had written a eulogistic review of *Eminent Victorians* in a school magazine. 'I hope you like Lord David C,' Lytton later wrote to Ottoline (26 October 1921). 'I thought him really very nice, but so young, so young . . . he made *me* feel positively in my *second* childhood!'

CHAPTER III

Eminent Edwardian

'The agitations are of course terrific. Do you think there is
no enD to love affaires. and one can never say "c'est fini"?'
Carrington to Alix Strachey (11 May 1925)

I

KISSING AND FISHING

The pleasures of private life seemed comfortably assured when Lytton returned from Venice in the early summer of 1921. The wedding of Carrington and Ralph had been rather alarming for the first moment or two, and, of course, on general principles, he objected to marriage. One saw such terrible examples of decent people caught like flies in the web of matrimony; one had experienced the horror that existed in most family life, and witnessed the persecution, cruelty and stupidity of that unreasonable institution. Was it surprising, then, if one disapproved of the whole paraphernalia? Besides, an artist, or any person with serious ambition, had to place his freedom and his art above everything else. Yet perhaps one ought not to hold such principles unless they could be scrapped when occasion demanded. People who did marry but who still remained individuals and did not quarrel among themselves, Lytton admired. In any case, this particular marriage, he now felt certain, would make little perceptible difference to their troika. Both husband and wife appeared perfectly satisfied, and the households at Tidmarsh and Gordon Square went on as of old. 'Private life continues to flow on very smoothly,' he assured James towards the end of May. 'The curious ménage or ménages work, I think, quite well. Ralph is really a charming creature, and seems quite content, and Carrington appears to be happy.'

Uncommitted to any serious literary composition, Lytton was no longer tied to the country but free to make regular forays into London society, obediently reporting back to his 'Angel Guardian' any item, however disappointing to himself, that might interest or amuse her.

'Last night [28 June 1921] the Sitwell dinner was dreadfully dull, and they took me off afterwards to an incredibly fearful function in Arnold Bennett's establishment. *He* was not there, but *she* was – oh my eye, what a woman! It was apparently some sort of Poetry Society. There was an address (very poor) on Rimbaud etc. by an imbecile Frog; then Edith Sitwell appeared, her nose longer than an ant-eater's, and read some of her absurd stuff; then Eliot – very sad and seedy – it made one weep; finally Mrs. Arnold Bennett recited, with waving arms and chanting voice, Baudelaire and Verlaine till everyone was ready to vomit. As a study in half-witted horror the whole thing was most interesting. The rooms were peculiarly disgusting, and the company very miscellaneous. . . . Why, oh why, does Eliot have any truck with such coagulations? I fear it indicates that there's something seriously wrong with him.'

And so, in literary idleness and social conviviality, the first few weeks of summer passed enjoyably by. But the pleasures of private life, though so palpably assured, were to be neither simple nor unclouded. Already, quite unknown to Lytton, the ground had been secretly prepared for every kind of ramification and intrigue. Over a year ago, when the three of them had gone out to Yegen, the first seeds of these impending complications had been planted. Although much taken up with Lytton's health at the time, and with the general strain of the visit, Carrington had felt greatly attracted to the village, the small house and its owner. Brenan, she reasoned, was a creature like herself – lawless, artistic and romantically cast adrift from the workaday world. He reminded her of her sailor-brother Teddy, and, according to David Garnett, she also spoke of him as a modern version of Trelawny's self-portrait in *The Adventures of a Younger Son*.[1] As soon as she returned to Tidmarsh, she had begun writing to Brenan regularly. 'On rereading these letters to-day,' Brenan told the author, 'I can see that she was making up to me. There were suggestions that if her life at Pangbourne broke down she would come out and join me. But I did not take this in then, partly because I was very innocent and partly because the problems of my own life were so great that I did not want to be tied up with a girl.' Yet even at this stage he certainly felt drawn to Carrington. When she had married Ralph, he wrote to congratulate her, but added half humorously: 'I am sorry for my own sake, because have love affairs I simply must, and whom shall I ever find as charming as you?'

[1] See David Garnett's *The Flowers of the Forest*, p. 242. But Brenan, in a letter to the author, comments: 'Carrington's comparison of me to Trelawny is meaningless because I am totally unlike him. Garnett was never a close friend of hers or of Lytton's, but if she really said this it can only have been because she knew nothing about Trelawny but his name.'

It was not until June 1921 that Brenan fully enters into the story, when his great-aunt, having adopted him as her heir, provided a little money for him to visit England. From his parents' house he bicycled over to the White Horse at Uffington, for a picnic with Carrington. Ralph was unable to join them because of his work at the Hogarth Press, and Lytton, who distrusted picnics, also stayed in London. Carrington and Gerald were therefore alone. It was possible that day to taste the full flavour of an English summer. The sun burnt the grass, made the air tremble around them, and sucked up the juices of the trees. Not a leaf moved, and everywhere above them the sky was a motionless dull purple. They laid out and ate their picnic on the pale crumbling slope of a hill, near a solitary haystack and a little misty wood. 'We talked and suddenly she put her arms round me and kissed me. I let her, but afterwards felt angry because I was Ralph's friend and because she meant nothing to me. . . .' The following week-end Gerald went to stay at Tidmarsh. He was determined that nothing more should come of this strange episode. 'Then as I sat in an armchair I saw her move across the window with the evening light behind her, and I knew I was in love. It was like the first attack of flu to a Pacific Islander – I was completely, totally under from the first moment. I had fallen for her in the same way in which she had fallen for Lytton, and just as violently. And she was in love with me.'

Of these sudden and startling developments Ralph Partridge suspected absolutely nothing. He had welcomed his friend's arrival in England with the greatest amusement and delight. 'He [Brenan] is the apotheosis of vagueness in man,' he reported to Noel Carrington (17 July 1921). 'He eats, moves and sleeps, entirely unaware of the natural laws which govern these processes. He will talk anyone into a coma and withal is always interesting. Also he may very likely write a good book before he breaks his neck day-dreaming.'

Once Gerald Brenan's week-end at Tidmarsh was over, he returned to London on his way back to Spain, while the other three left for a holiday in the Lake District. 'There is no need for me to tell you how fond I am of you,' he wrote to Carrington (29 July 1921), 'for you can see that every time I look at you – nor of what kind my affection is, for that I only vaguely know myself. There are moments when you appear so entirely, so tormentingly beautiful that I begin to lose my head a little . . . [you are] a creature so beautiful that it would be a sort of madness not to fall in love with you.' A few days later a telegram arrived from Carrington asking him to follow them. Without hesitation he put off his journey to Spain and set off northwards, joining them at Watendlath Farm, near Keswick in Cumberland. By this time, the party also included Marjorie Strachey, who had suddenly turned up 'in pitch darkness and a howling tempest . . . having lost a reticule containing £6', James and Alix, recently returned for a holiday from Vienna, much in love and busy translating Freud.[1] The seven of them led a crowded cottage life, herded together into the small back parlour of Farmer Wilson's sheep farm. 'I am sitting, as you may guess, rather comatose, in a small cottage apartment,' Lytton wrote to Virginia Woolf (23 August 1921), 'green mountains out of the window, the stuffed head of a very old female sheep over the window.'

For Gerald, this next fortnight sped by in a dream of surreptitious excitement. Everything that was beautiful and sad seemed crowded into these few days of his life. When the sun shone they would all clamber about over the stony hills, until Lytton's feet were covered with blisters and 'I can only wear silk socks and slippers in which I totter occasionally into the air'. After the first few days, however, the rain and cold were fairly continuous, and the two Strachey brothers would remain crouched over the fire – Lytton reading Beckford's *Biographical Memoirs of Extraordinary Painters*, and James, 'on an enormous air-cushion balanced upon a horsehair sofa', studying Dr Varendonck on the psychology of day-dreams. But whatever the weather, Ralph would go determinedly out to fish, without any cessation or luck, from morning until evening – he 'has caught two sardines so far' – and he was invariably accompanied by Carrington and Gerald, carrying fish-hooks and hard-boiled eggs wrapped up in newspaper. While Ralph sat, rod in hand, beside the river, the other two would kiss and cuddle behind a bank close by. Gerald was soon afflicted by a deepening sense of guilt about this deception. To such

---

[1] James Strachey was to become the translator and general editor of the Standard Edition of the *Complete Psychological Works of Sigmund Freud* (24 vols. Hogarth Press), in the preparation of which he was assisted by his wife Alix and by Anna Freud (Freud's youngest daughter). Started in 1946, it was officially completed twenty years later. Although James Strachey had begun to take an interest in psycho-analysis just before the First World War, it was not until he and his wife went to Vienna in 1920 to study under Freud that he took the subject up professionally. On 9 March 1921, he wrote to Lady Strachey that he and Alix were translating 'a series of Freud's "clinical" papers. There are to be five of them, each giving a detailed history of a specially interesting case and an account of the treatment. They were written at intervals during the last twenty years – the first in 1899 and the last quite recently – so that they give a very good idea of the development of his views. Altogether the book will probably be about 500 pages long. It is a great compliment to have been given it to do. And he thought of the plan on purpose to be of help to us in two different ways. First of all, it'll give us a specially intimate knowledge of his methods, as we are able to talk over with him any difficulties that occur to us in the course of the translation; and we now go on Sunday afternoons specially to discuss whatever problems we want to. In the second place, our appearance as official translators of his work into English will give us a great advertisement in psychological circles in England.'

wild things had passion led them. Beforehand, he had envisaged a kind of platonic attachment; he had thought he would be able to divert his affection for Carrington out of dangerous channels into some literary composition. But within a few hours of his arrival at Watendlath Farm, he knew that this was a mirage. Everything except for love was driven out of his head. He was like a man overwhelmed and drowned in the sea. That he should love his best friend's wife more than anyone else in the world became a fiendish torture. God knew how it had happened! Treachery to such a friend as Ralph seemed to him the blackest of crimes, intensely painful and discreditable. He blamed himself – and yet he could not give up loving Carrington. There was only one right course. He would go and explain to Ralph exactly what was happening. Surely, he urged, Ralph would understand that their relationship was, so they said, that of brother and sister. For in their desire not to be unfaithful to him they kept up the pretence of not being in love with each other, but simply very intimate friends. They would have been genuinely shocked to have heard their liaison referred to as 'an affair'. But Carrington, who knew Ralph better, would not agree to divulging anything. And so the kissing and the fishing continued, and there were several meetings in a barn. Carrington's happiness was stimulated by this exquisite concealment, while Gerald lived in a sort of romantic ecstasy, with few overt sexual feelings. He did not experience the least pang of jealousy, but on the contrary was infused with an increased affection for his friend. As for Ralph himself, he still suspected nothing, and felt pleased that Carrington and Gerald seemed so close. They were just like one another, he thought, vague, imaginative, hopelessly impractical.

The others, too, paid them little attention. 'The mysterious Brenan', as Lytton called him, was just Ralph's extraordinary friend. In one of his letters from Keswick to Mary Hutchinson, Lytton complains that the sole adventures in the vicinity appeared to be meteorological ones (25 August 1921), 'and – so far as I can see – there is precious little love-making'. The only sign from the Outer World, he informed Pippa (30 August 1921), 'has been a vision of Mr. Stephen McKenna trailing over the mountain-tops in company with a lady in magenta silk'. Altogether, he concluded, their holiday had turned out pretty uneventful.

On 2 September, the party broke up, and Gerald left for Spain. Haphazard, he planned to reunite with Carrington the following year. 'Oh, if I had never come back to England,' he lamented, 'if I never had, if I never had! I should then have been living an eventless life in Spain, calling myself happy. . . . I have lain awake sometime thinking that soon I shall see you no more for 8 months, and I feel absolutely sick at the thought. I do not want, as things are, to be with you any longer; but to be without you is horrible. It is like going out suddenly into complete darkness.' Still no one had detected the least sign of their unseen flirtation. But he and Carrington had placed a time-bomb beneath the Tidmarsh way of life – and who could tell when it would go off?

2

VIEWS AND REVIEWS

For the time being, at any rate, the bomb did not go off, and private life, on the surface, seemed smooth and unruffled. 'One wonders whether one has been quite wise in coming North,' Lytton had confided to Virginia Woolf from Watendlath Farm (23 August 1921). Now, in early September, he floated south again with considerable relief to the placid Downs and redbrick houses of Sussex. Amid these sympathetic regions he lingered on contentedly, staying with the Woolfs at Monk's House, with the Hutchinsons at Eleanor, and with the Bells at Charleston, where 'I read for the first time the (almost) complete account of Oscar's trials,' he told Carrington (September 1921). '. . . It is very interesting and depressing. One of the surprising features is that he very nearly got off. If he had, what would have happened I wonder? I fancy the history of English culture might have been quite different, if a juryman's stupidity had chanced to take another turn.'

There were plenty of other invitations to the country this autumn, among others from Ottoline, Henrietta Bingham and Lady Astor – who would invariably address him in her letters as 'Dear Author'. In town there were, of course, the Sitwells and the Bloomsberries, and various luncheon parties with Lady Colefax and Princess Bibesco. But by far the most rewarding of these social excursions were to Cambridge, where, as the guest of Maynard Keynes, he met the new and talented generation of post-war undergraduates, and grew absorbed once more by university and Apostolic affairs. Among those who soon became his special friends and whom he now began to invite back for week-ends to Tidmarsh were George ('Dadie') Rylands,[1] a charming, feline, fair-

---

[1] George Rylands (b. 1902) later became a Fellow, Dean, Bursar and lecturer at King's College. He is now a governor of the Old Vic, and chairman of the directors and trustees of the Arts Theatre, Cambridge. His best-known book is the Shakespeare anthology, *The Ages of Man* (1939). He is also director of the Long Playing recording of Shakespeare.

haired Etonian of great poise and elegance of dress, with a flair for stagecraft, then in his first year at King's and much under the influence of Sheppard; W. J. H. ('Sebastian') Sprott,[1] who had come up from Felsted to Clare College and was soon to be appointed as a demonstrator at the Psychological Laboratory at Cambridge; F. L. ('Peter') Lucas, later famous as a literary critic; the brilliant and precocious logician, Frank Ramsey, whose brother has become Archbishop of Canterbury; J. H. Doggart ('the Dog'), the celebrated eye-specialist; and the three eldest Penrose brothers, Alec, 'a complete womanizer', as Lytton once called him, Lionel, the geneticist, and Roland, the art critic and biographer of Picasso. 'He [Alec] is a man of character (rare nowadays), and determined to be aesthetic,' Lytton informed James (28 November 1921), 'but I rather fear with no very great turn that way . . . Lionel Penrose (younger brother) is at John's, and a complete flibberti-gibbet, but attractive in a childish way, and somehow, in spite of an absence of brain, quite suitable in the Society.'[2]

Towards the end of 1921, this life of recreation was mitigated by a little work on the preparation of his next book. Shortly after the publication of *Eminent Victorians*, Geoffrey Whitworth had suggested to him that he might bring out a volume of selected essays, as an interlude between his two major biographical works. 'Such a book would be sure of success,' Whitworth wrote (4 April 1919), 'even though it might be slight in bulk.' But already by that time Lytton was deep in *Queen Victoria*, and so the scheme was dropped. Now, after his biography had appeared, Lytton's mind did not immediately revert to this idea, which, in any case, he felt to be uneconomic. Significantly he did not mention it to Hesketh Pearson in May 1921, and wrote to Chatto and Windus that he was contemplating 'a follow-up volume on the Regency period'. He also discussed his various biographical projects with Virginia Woolf, in particular the 'History of the Reign of George IV', which she considered to be a magnificent subject for him. But there were difficulties. 'The worst of George IV,' Lytton announced one afternoon over tea at Verreys, 'is that no one mentions the facts I want. History must be written all over again. It's all morality.' 'And battles,' Virginia interposed.

While he was thus undecided, Chatto and Windus wrote to remind

---

[1] Since 1965, W. J. H. Sprott has been Emeritus Professor of Psychology at Nottingham University. He is the author of several books, including *Human Groups* (1958) and *Sociology at the Seven Dials* (1962).

[2] Lionel Penrose, F.R.S. (b. 1898), Galton Professor of Eugenics, University College, London, since 1945, and author of *The Influence of Heredity on Disease* (1934) and *The Biology of Mental Defect* (1949, 3rd edn 1963), who, as Lytton was soon to become aware, was one of the cleverest of his Cambridge friends.

him of Whitworth's original proposition for a volume of essays, this time making him a definite offer. He would receive an advance on royalties of seven hundred and fifty pounds, 20 per cent of the published price – twelve shillings and sixpence – on the first five thousand copies sold, and 25 per cent thereafter. These were handsome terms, and Lytton at once accepted. It seemed an easy method of making money. Seven hundred and fifty pounds was a 'fantastic sum' as an advance for such a production. Encouraged by this, he opened up bargaining with his American publishers, Harcourt Brace. 'I don't think you heard the end of my negotiations with Mr. Brace,' he reported to James (28 November 1921), '– they were perfectly hectic, and I spent days in which I alternated between the vast halls of the Hotel Cecil and the office of the Authors' Society, where poor Mr. Thring assisted me with his advice and exclamations. Mr. Brace was a very pale, worn out American, with the inevitable tortoises, and we had a high old time, struggling and bargaining in the strangest style. I made a gallant effort to recapture the copyright of Victoria, but I found that he wanted more for it than I was willing to give, and it ended by my agreeing to let him have my next book (on very good terms) and the offer of two others, in exchange for £1500 down. It was an extraordinary, prolonged and feverish battle, at the end of which Mr. Brace nearly dropped dead, as with shaking hand and ashy face he drew out his cheque-book. He had begun by offering £1200; but at the last moment I was able suddenly to raise my terms, and in a jiffy I had made £300. I can only hope that in some mysterious way I haven't been let in – but Mr. Thring supported my every movement.'

Once these arrangements had been settled, Lytton returned to Tidmarsh where, over the next two months, he busied himself gathering together a number of his fugitive essays, choosing those he liked best from the many reviews and articles he had written since his Cambridge days. Finally, he selected fourteen of these pieces, originally composed between 1904 and 1919, to make up this fourth volume. With the help of Ralph and Carrington, he passed each of them through a fine comb of textual emendation, making quite extensive alterations to the earlier ones such as 'Racine', for example, in which he rewrote no fewer than twenty-three passages. Some of the corrections he made were trivial – dealing merely with typographical errors and the rare grammatical slip. Others smoothed out awkward or redundant phrases which he had at first overlooked, but which stood out conspicuously when he read them aloud. 'Still others', records C. R. Sanders, who made a line-by-line comparison of the essays in the first and second versions, and documented all discrepancies, 'are motivated by the desire to convert journalistic articles and reviews into literary essays.' Footnotes were dropped or drastically reduced, adjectives were pruned, some new illustrative material and the occasional amusing comment was added, and the number of parallel constructions increased. Sometimes, also, he would alter a sentence so as to bring it in line with tastes he had more recently developed – 'We should not chide Tintoretto for not painting with the scrupulosity of De Hooghe' he changed to 'We should not impugn a Mozart quartet for not containing the orchestration of Wagner'. Apart from these amendments made necessary by the passing of time, there were a few other corrections deleting inaccuracies – 'David's Apotheosis of Homer', for example, was changed to 'Ingres's Apotheosis of Homer'. Some misquotations, too, were checked and rectified.

The most interesting revisions Lytton made were the improvements to his style. These were of two kinds: those which tightened up his prose, giving it more restraint, and those which indicated a desire to add greater force and emphasis to the original narrative. In the first category may be placed some over-long transitional passages that have either been trimmed and condensed, or thrown out altogether. Other paragraphs were also compressed, and dubious, over-bold opinions concerning living authors were toned down or occasionally qualified by the insertion of a 'perhaps'. A few long paragraphs were broken up so as to make for easier reading, but more often Lytton would fuse two paragraphs together so as to achieve an effect of greater weight. Similarly, several quotations only alluded to in the earlier text were now supplied in full, and in some cases, extra information has been given to bear out more convincingly the conclusions they were designed to support.

Since Lytton's prose style had matured early on, these revisions, though numerous, were mostly of a minor nature. A few reviewers, however, were to comment adversely on his writing. 'Here and there,' observed the critic of *The Times Literary Supplement*, 'the style falls into a mechanical vivacity: there are sentences that a more alert revision would have struck out.' Yet Lytton's revision, as has been demonstrated, was painstaking and minute. Any defects of the style are therefore organic rather than functional, for the style accurately mirrored the man.

By the end of January, Lytton had finished the preparations for this book – all but the title. First he had thought of calling it *Views and Reviews*, but rejected this after discovering that W. E. Henley had already used it. 'Help! Help!' he implored Pippa (31 January 1922). 'The title question is pressing, and I am almost desperate. What do you think of "Books and Brains" – with "French and English" added underneath on the title page? A mixture of pure literature and biography should be indicated. Other possibilities are "Men, Women and Words" – "Books and Characters". Send a p.c. if you or Lady S. have any suggestions.' Two days later he decided on *Books and Characters* – 'tame but harmless' he told Pippa – appending 'French & English' on the title page, as he had originally wanted to do.

To avoid the General Election, Chatto and Windus postponed the publication of *Books and Characters* until May, printing a first edition of five-and-a-half thousand copies. Most of the Press notices were favourable, notably *The Times*, whose reviewer praised Lytton's literary criticism rather at the expense of his biography. 'Mr. Lytton Strachey has cleared the honour of the nation. He has repaired past sacrileges by publishing the finest essay upon Racine which has ever been written in English. . . . Mr. Strachey's is perhaps the finest critical intelligence at work in English literature to-day.' Middleton Murry, who reviewed the book in the *Athenaeum*, was in complete agreement, proclaiming Lytton's critical work to be of the first order, and singling out for special praise his fine sense of justice. And Aldous Huxley, in the course of a generally appreciative notice, described him as 'a superlatively civilised Red Indian living apart from the vulgar world in an elegant park-like reservation', who rarely looked over the walls at the surrounding country. 'It seethes, he knows,' Huxley continued, 'with crowds of horribly colonial persons. Like the hosts of Midian, the innumerable "poor whites" prowl and prowl around, but the noble savage pays no attention to them.'

Although *Books and Characters* was naturally not a best-seller, it earned Lytton considerable prestige in the world of letters. The following year his *Landmarks in French Literature* was reprinted, and his growing eminence as a critic as well as a biographer was marked both by the award of the Benson Silver Medal[1] and by an invitation from the Royal Society of Literature to become a member of its Academic Committee. This last offer he rejected for reasons that are interesting biographically. After sending back a polite letter of refusal, disclaiming his 'election', he then asked Edmund Gosse, himself on the Academic Committee, to act as his interpreter *vis-à-vis* the Royal Society of Literature, whose members, he feared, might misjudge his sentiments if they had nothing but his official communiqué before them. He felt

---

[1] Under the endowment of A. C. Benson (1 May 1916) medals were to be awarded in respect of meritorious works in poetry, fiction, history, biography and belles-lettres. A selection committee was appointed each year by the Fellows of the Royal Society of Literature, who alone had the right to recommend recipients.

especially anxious in case they might think he was declining out of curmudgeonly or superior feelings, and he wanted to stress the fact that he felt sincerely the high and charming compliment that had been paid to him. 'It would be futile to argue the pros and cons of Academies and similar bodies in general,' he explained to Gosse (30 December 1922), 'and I realise that a good case may be made out for them; but so far as I am personally concerned I am convinced that I should really be out of place in one. This is as much a matter of instinct as of reason. Perhaps it is regrettable, but the fact remains that, as Saint-Simon said of himself: "Je ne suis pas un sujet académique" . . .

'. . . So I hope you will sympathise with me in my declining the honour and I am sure that if I am ever able to do any service to Literature, it will be as an entirely independent person and not as a member of a group.'

Lytton dedicated *Books and Characters* to Maynard Keynes, who, with Sebastian Sprott, came down to spend Christmas with him at Tidmarsh. Although Lytton had earned between seven and eight thousand pounds since the spring of 1918, he had up till now escaped paying any income tax.[1] 'The authorities here seem to have overlooked my existence,' he confided to Keynes (11 November 1921), 'and if this happy state of things could continue, so much the better.' But he knew that it could not, and he asked Keynes's advice as to whether he should be paid by his publishers *en bloc* or as the royalties came in. Keynes also furnished him with a 'detailed list of stocks of every kind, in which he insists that I shall put all I have. There is no choice but to submit, and face bankruptcy.'

During the rest of the winter Lytton languished uneasily at the Mill House, listening to Mozart on the gramophone, glancing listlessly through books sent to him from The Times Book Club, reading again Swift, Dante, Milton, Trollope and Keynes's *Treatise on Probability* (which Maynard had read to him over Christmas), spending hours turning over the pages of *The Dictionary of National Biography* ('one of the most useful books in existence, and the motto of which was: "No flowers by request"') and, when even this grew too exhausting, *Who's Who*. All this time he was waiting eagerly for the spring. '*My* state has long been quite deplorable,' he confessed to Virginia Woolf

---

[1] The accounts from Chatto and Windus show Lytton to have received by the end of March 1922 £4,867 2s 0d on the sales of his books in the British Empire, £1,105 11s 0d on sales in the U.S.A. (which does not include the outright sum of £1,500 from Harcourt Brace), and £99 in respect of French and Swedish rights. To this should be added a small amount from the continuing sales of *Landmarks in French Literature*, something from his contributions to the *Athenaeum*, etc., and possibly also an income from private investments.

(6 February 1922). 'I put it down to the Winter – the agony of thick underclothes, etc. etc.; but of course it may be sheer deliquescence of the brain. Anyhow, from whatever cause, I am sans eyes, sans teeth, sans prick, sans . . . but after that there can be no more sanses, – and on the whole I feel more like a fish gasping on a bank than anything else. It is terrible. I hope wildly that a change will come with the swallows . . .'

He had recently joined the Oriental Club, of which his father had been a prominent member,[1] and this new status, he felt, suited very well his condition of premature, winter senility. The place was like a luxurious mausoleum. 'Very ormolu,' Carrington noted in one of her letters to Noel. 'Full of old Indian Dug Outs.' And Lytton, in a letter to Virginia Woolf (6 February 1922), described it as 'a vast hideous building . . . filled with vast hideous Anglo-Indians, very old and very rich. One becomes 65, with an income of 5000 a year, directly one enters it. One is so stout one can hardly walk, and one's brain works with an extraordinary slowness. Just the place for me, you see, in my present condition. I pass almost unnoticed with my glazed eyes and white hair, as I sink into a leather chair heavily with a copy of the Field in hand. Excellent claret too – one of the best cellars in London, by Jove. You *must* come! I'll write again soon, if you can bear it.' But when he did write again, four days later, it was the same tale of cold and discontent. 'The horror of getting up is unparalleled, and I am filled with amazement every morning when I find that I have done it. To my mind there is clearly only one test of wealth, and that is – a fire in one's bedroom. Until one can have that at any and every moment, one is poor. Oh, for a housemaid at dawn!'

Towards the end of February, Carrington and Ralph left for Vienna to visit James Strachey and Alix, who was seriously ill with pleurisy, while Lytton, in order that he might be properly looked after, moved up to Gordon Square. 'Life here has been proceeding in its usual style of utter dullness punctuated by hectic frenzies,' he wrote to Carrington on his forty-second birthday. 'One of the latter occurred last night – a very absurd party at Lady Astor's to meet Mr. Balfour – a huge rout – 800 extremely mixed guests – Duchesses, Rothensteins, Prime Ministers, Stracheys (male and female) – never did you see such a sight! As it was pouring cats and dogs the scene of jostling taxis and motors in St. James's Square was terrific – it was practically full up. No one could get out it was so wet – for hours we sat ticking and cursing and occasionally edging an inch or two nearer the portals of bliss. To add to the confusion, various streams entered the Square by the side streets,

---

[1] There is in the Oriental Club a portrait of Sir Richard Strachey painted in about 1888 by Lowes Dickinson, the father of Goldie Dickinson.

and mingled with the cars. However the police and the good nature of the English lower classes saved the situation. If such a thing had happened in Paris it would have been simply Pandemonium. As it was, it was merely a great bore. The P.M. was leaving as we entered. Horror of horrors! The Rt. Hon. gentleman did *not recognise* Lytton Strachey! – though he bowed very politely – as did Mrs Lloyd George – an unparalleled frump. Mr. Balfour was very complimentary behind large demi-ghostly spectacles.'

Yet despite these hectic frenzies, the London scene, Lytton reported, was 'not very gay', and when Carrington and Ralph returned from Vienna, he went back to Tidmarsh contentedly enough. His own amorous adventures, and those of his closest friends, seemed to have become suspended, and though well and happy, he felt at times a little bored.

But the swallows were already on the horizon, and the climate was about to change.

3

MADNESS

Over the past six months, since Gerald Brenan sailed away to Spain, Carrington had been writing to him every few days; and he had replied. Although Ralph insisted on reading their correspondence, he still suspected nothing – principally because there were special, effusive postscripts attached to these letters which he was never shown. Now, at the beginning of April, they were all to meet again, Lytton and Carrington and Ralph and Gerald, at Norhurst, the house of Septimus Bollard and his wife Clare, in the Basses-Pyrénées. Norhurst faced west, was perfectly suited for the hot weather, and, to Ralph's great joy, overlooked a trout stream which ran just below. All around were deep valleys coated with the greenest grass, and everywhere grew bracken, tall and spreading itself into arches. Huge beech forests covered the headwaters of the streams, and above these, standing out against the blue sky, there pointed needle-sharp peaks of red and yellow rock. 'We are pretty high up among the hills,' Lytton wrote to Pippa (7 April 1922), '– a charming house full of the local furniture – armoires and cupboards innumerable – in a small village, with steep heights on every side. Everything seems quite nice, though not exciting. There is hope of fishing, when the streams, which are at present Niagaras, subside. The health, I think, should be greatly improved after about a fortnight of mountain existence. . . .'

'I am writing this in a basque bed, but now I shall have to get up and go downstairs and face the family. Le père de Madame (an Anglo–Indian planter, I gather) is rather distressing. He once went out to shoot Bustards in Nagpore, but never found any . . . However, Madame herself is very agreeable, and sings Italian songs very nicely after dinner.'

Clare, now married to a rather dull, diminutive, donnish husband with military idiosyncrasies,[1] was a voluptuous, highly sexed and unstable woman who had passed periods in an asylum. Dark and beautiful, though with some malformation which made hearing difficult, she was also rumoured to have been Derain's mistress and was herself a painter, whom Carrington had got to know at the Slade and to whom she now began to confide her secret feelings for Gerald. A late snow had fallen on the lilac blossom, and while Ralph resolutely fished below, and Lytton sat listening in silence to Professor Bollard as he recited from a book he was then composing on Elizabethan tragedy, Gerald, upstairs in the attic, would pose for Carrington. Probably because of physical feelings he was as yet quite unaware of, Ralph had taken a most violent dislike to Clare Bollard, and was persistently and gratuitously rude to her, so that the atmosphere at meals, when they were all obliged to congregate, became increasingly strained. Even more unaccountably, at least to Lytton, she began, in spite of this, to make up to Ralph. Then, to everyone's astonishment, on the very last day of their visit, Ralph and Clare fell into each other's arms with all the violence that had seemed to mark their previous incompatibility.

No sooner had this awkward situation been created than, the very next morning, Lytton, Ralph and Carrington packed up and departed, travelling, via Toulouse and Provence, back to England. They were hotly pursued across the Continent by the passionate Clare, and by Gerald, who waited only to collect a sleeping bag and the camping kit which he had been forced to abandon on his journey up from Yegen in the deep snow of the Roncesvalles Pass. Daily, the position seemed to grow more complicated and grave. During May, Gerald put up at Pangbourne, while Ralph proceeded openly to carry on his impetuous affair with Clare, adopting all the time a very aggressive and disparaging attitude to Carrington. For some weeks it looked as if the whole Tid-

---

[1] 'Bollard . . . has mildly literary and pedantic tastes. He is dull but harmless – I fear is writing a series of sixteenth-century lives in the style of Eminent Victorians. She is rather more interesting – perhaps a Saph – much attached to Carrington – but oh, not what might be called clever. She paints – à la Modigliani, etc. The place is pretty high up in the Pyrenees – a largish village with steep hills in every direction – snow to be seen in the distance. . . . I think I should be able to last out another 10 days or so. . . .' Lytton to James Strachey (9 April 1922).

marsh régime was about to crumble and disintegrate. Carrington, in despair, appealed to Lytton, who counselled patience, and in the meantime sent off to Professor Bollard a gift of some books on the Elizabethan dramatists. Up till this time, Gerald had kept his relations with Carrington confined to a more or less platonic level, out of a rather tarnished sense of loyalty to Ralph. But under these altered circumstances he now felt no further obligation to do so, and when Ralph and Clare went off for a few days together, he and Carrington – who, in any case, had never shared his scruples about making love – resolved to do the same.

Then the storm burst. While they were away together, Clare let out to Ralph that his best friend and his wife had fallen in love. She told him of the love-making that had taken place at Watendlath Farm, and that, in the Pyrenees, Gerald, Carrington and herself had hatched 'the Norhurst Plot' by which she should flirt with Ralph so as to leave Carrington and Gerald alone together. Ralph was thunderstruck. Being a very emotional and neurotic woman, Clare did not scruple to distort a few of the facts and put the most dramatic interpretation on others, and although Ralph believed her completely, she would no longer really mean anything to him after this. In an uncontrollable fury he rushed back to Tidmarsh. From his outraged reaction, it would seem that he considered it quite proper for him to have a love-affair with a married woman, but absolutely immoral for Carrington to take a lover. But there was more to it than this – there was the deception which burnt within him as a most wounding humiliation. For whereas he believed in complete openness at all times and about everything, Carrington cherished her secrecy closely and would even conceal small, quite unobjectionable matters to safeguard her privacy. The key to Ralph's character lay in his belief that marriage meant total trust, total communication. He had a passion for truth in love and friendship. So his unbridled frenzy on hearing Clare's news was caused less by questions of technical infidelity – though these became important – than by the dissimulation practised by his best friend and his recently married wife. This revelation of lies and deceit shattered him, and in a sense gave the death-blow to his marriage with Carrington, which no subsequent patchings-up could really resurrect.

After a furious argument with Carrington in the Mill House, Ralph dispatched a telegram to Gerald demanding to see him in London. When they met, he announced that unless Gerald could promise him that he had had no physical intercourse with Carrington, he, Ralph, would separate from her there and then and for ever. Gerald swore that he had not, for although his instinct was still to tell his friend the truth, he felt that he had no right, by doing so, to endanger Carrington's life with Lytton. Ralph, now somewhat at a loss, replied with stern uncertainty that he would have to consider what he would do, but that if he decided to go on living with Carrington, then Gerald must go back to Spain and give his word never to communicate with her again. Gerald promised. There was nothing else that he could do. The first person in Carrington's life was always Lytton, and Gerald himself could never hope to take Ralph's place with him. Also he was very poor, and for that reason any alternative arrangements would have been doubly impractical. And so, briefly and for the last time, Gerald returned to Tidmarsh to tell Carrington what had transpired at his interview with Ralph. Lytton, relieved that he did not mean to rock the boat and capsize them all, was especially kind,[1] and when Gerald had sailed again for Spain on 14 June, sent after him an affectionate and encouraging letter.

'Things are still unsettled here,' he wrote (15 June 1922), 'and the first necessity is to clear the atmosphere. Letters between you might seem ambiguous to Ralph, and all ambiguities just now are to be avoided.

'. . . I hope you will go on writing. From the little I've seen of your work, it seemed to me to differ *in kind* from everything else going about by writers of your generation. To my mind there is a streak of inspiration in it, which is very rare and very precious indeed.

'. . . Things have turned out unhappily; but never forget that, whatever happens, and in spite of all estrangements, you are loved by those you love best.

Yours ever affectionately,

Lytton Strachey'

Besides its accuracy in detecting the future author of *South from Granada*, *A Life of One's Own*, *Jack Robinson*,[2] *The Spanish Labyrinth* and other fine books, to be a writer of rare and original inspiration, this letter exhibits the compassion and the commiseration of someone who had himself suffered acutely in love-affairs, but who had never been embittered by his set-backs. It also illustrates just what Bloomsbury, at its best, meant by civilized behaviour in personal relations, and how difficult outsiders such as Ralph Partridge found this behaviour to accept. For Lytton, and a few others, laid great stress on such controlled and impeccable conduct, and their refusal to accede any rights or claims to jealousy was one of the rules they stood for most strongly – one that amounted, perhaps, to a real discovery in sophisticated, humane dealings

---

[1] 'I am very sorry for him [Brenan],' Lytton wrote to Ralph Partridge about this time. 'He has injured himself very badly, and his life at the best of times was not a particularly pleasant one.'

[2] Written under the pseudonym of George Beaton, and, in the opinion of David Garnett, a work equal to W. H. Hudson's *The Purple Land*.

with other people. Gerald greatly appreciated Lytton's friendship. 'Please forgive me the unhappiness I have caused to you as well as to others and do not think too badly of me,' he had written the night before his departure. 'And thank you for the kindness you have always shown me. It has been a great pleasure to me to have known you and to have caught a glimpse at Tidmarsh of people who cultivate a free, happy and civilised life. Now that I have lost my part in it, I see all its attractions.'

Everything that had happened over the past ten weeks appeared to Gerald to have been hideously grotesque. But though he certainly experienced some guilt and sense of responsibility for these tragic happenings, he was still convinced that they had been largely senseless and unnecessary. All his subsequent actions and his letters to Lytton make it clear that he did not change his feeling for Carrington or Ralph because of this crisis between them, and that, despite being extremely upset at having contributed to their unhappiness, he did not regret anything he had done.[1] 'But that, among reasonable people,' he wrote to Lytton from Spain (14 July 1922), 'I who am fond of Ralph, can be – O wonderful irony! Too fond of C, and that without being the cause of their seeing less of each other or of their affections diminishing,

[1] Gerald Brenan sent Carrington several long letters during the next few months via either Lytton or John Hope-Johnstone. On 11 June 1922 he declared: 'I have one request. When you are able to talk to Ralph about me, tell him what you know to be true, that my only treachery was to conceal from him my affection for you. That this affection did not begin suddenly but insensibly, that though I could not bear to end it by telling him, I tried to lead it into safe channels. That I hoped in the end, with time, seeing that my feelings are different from his and that I live so far off, to reveal it to him and that he would tolerate it. . . . My friendship with Ralph is at an end; that I accept, but what I cannot endure is that he should think it never existed. I was devoted to him as I have been, I think, to no other man; I do not believe I would willingly have injured him.'

In another letter, posted two days later, he added: 'Whatever I think of, my thoughts return to *you* and make me feel how much and how sweet a happiness I am deprived of. . . . You do not know how much I love you, how much I shall always love you. There is nothing about you which does not charm me or that could ever grate upon me; your face, your body, your character, your habits are perfect – not because they conform to any exterior standard of perfection but because they make up a unity of their own which is good and beautiful. Am I allowed to tell you that? I may fall in love, I may have other friendships and liaisons, but I shall not forget you, because my feelings for you neither exclude other affections nor can be excluded by them. What I feel for you I shall feel for no one else, and to you I shall always be different to what I am to other people. One part of me belongs unalienably to you, and when I am with you or when I am thinking of you everything else in me is obliterated.'

Some months later, when friendly relations between himself and Ralph had been resumed, Gerald Brenan wrote to Carrington from Yegen (15 September 1922): 'I have acted badly and foolishly, and you foolishly – but from now onwards let us be the only people to act sensibly, and with a view to the greatest possible happiness, for all concerned, in the future. Love. Gerald.'

and without my wishing for anything new for myself – that by these good and innocent means can be so great a source of unhappiness to all of us – is nothing less to me than madness, madness, horrible madness . . .'

4

THE AWKWARD STAGE

The task of reintroducing some sanity and spirit of affection into Tidmarsh during the next eighteen months fell predominantly on Lytton's shoulders. It was an arduous, extremely tricky exercise in patient diplomacy, and one that he played with the utmost tact. First of all he had to reconcile Ralph to Carrington – neither of whom would consent to see the other until he had engineered a satisfactory, face-saving peace settlement between them. He started off by assuring Carrington that he sympathized absolutely and completely with her feelings, and that, however things might turn out, he would never desert her. Nevertheless, he insisted that she must keep this confidence to herself, and for a while at least, look with extraordinary leniency and tolerance upon all Ralph's indiscretions. Ralph himself, having signified his willingness to return to the Mill House on certain conditions, had gone, pending Lytton's negotiations on his behalf, down to stay in Richmond. 'I think I was able to make her realise your feelings and point of view,' Lytton wrote to him there (June 1922). 'Of course, she was, and is, terribly upset. She said that you were essential to her – that Gerald was not at all – that this crisis had made her realise more than ever before the strength of her love for you. I explained your dread of a scene, reconciliations, etc., and said you wanted to sleep in the yellow room. She quite understood. I am sure that she loves you deeply. Be as gentle with her as you can when you come.

'We must try now to forget all those horrid details, and trust to the force of our fundamental affections to carry us through. At any rate, we know where we are now, which is a great thing.

'. . . As for me, my dear, I can't say how happy your decision to try going on here has made me. I suppose I *could* face life without you, just as I *could* face life with one of my hands cut off, but it would have been a dreadful blow . . .

'. . . My nerves are rather on the jump, and I am longing for your presence – the best restorative I know of! I sympathise with you so absolutely, so completely, my dear, dear love. Sometimes I feel as if I *was* inside you! Why can't I make you perfectly happy by waving some magic wand?

'Keep this letter to yourself.'

After the route had been paved for Ralph's difficult return, Lytton did all in his power to make life at Tidmarsh charming and delightful. He would invite over for week-ends the most interesting and amusing guests – some of his Cambridge friends whom Ralph liked and who adored Carrington, and other older luminaries such as E. M. Forster. He also bought a car. Since neither Carrington nor himself could run it, and since 'R.P. is a born driver', this naturally increased their joint dependence on Ralph together with his sense of responsibility towards them – though Lytton was quick to assure him that 'of course you know the little car belongs to you'. A little later in the year, when Ralph complained about his job at the Hogarth Press – his poor income and prospects – Lytton immediately stepped in and tried to argue his case with Virginia Woolf. 'There have been various conversations on the Hogarth question – with rather indeterminate results,' he reported to her (19 September 1922). 'I think the poor creature is really anxious to continue, but foresees difficulties. He is already brushing up his energies! On the whole I gather that he thinks less printing and more business might be a solution. Perhaps if some department in the business could be handed over in toto to him he would fling himself into it with more zest. But this is only a vague suggestion, and so please don't draw conclusions from it. I suppose he will write himself before long. The distance-from-London question is a very trying one.' After these tentative suggestions had led nowhere, and Ralph quitted the Hogarth Press, Lytton employed him as his secretary to answer his correspondence, deal with the income tax authorities, with publishers and editors, assist with proof-reading and other duties. And so, by these means, Ralph was gradually incorporated back into the Tidmarsh life. While his and Lytton's interdependence tightened, so, more obliquely but inevitably, would his feelings for Carrington slowly revive.

Outwardly, then, their triangular *ménage* continued much as before, and to those who did not know them very intimately, life at the Mill House appeared happy and serene. 'You have no idea what a perfect life we lead here,' Carrington wrote to Noel (25 July 1922). '3 Hives of Bees, 30 ducks, 30 chickens, a Forest of delicious raspberries, and peas, and a Roman Bath to bathe in out of doors. Annie who is a gay little girl of sixteen, exquisitely lovely, who cooks and housekeeps for us all and then Lytton who is a paragon of a friend, who buys new books for our delight. The new car is a great joy. We go lovely rides in it . . . Do you know we can sleep in the car, for the Front seat comes out and we can make it into a caravan (!). R. is a very perfect driver.'

But underneath this smooth surface of country contentment, the atmosphere remained critical. For Carrington, in particular, these summer months were miserable. Ralph still seemed completely hostile to her, and she felt that she had even lost Lytton's confidence because of her never-ending lies and subterfuges. Yet there was no alternative but to go on living at the Mill House where 'everything was completely awfull for me'. She felt strangely alone, and missed Gerald's letters and warm friendship 'more than I ever thought, in my wildest moments, I should, and when one mustn't talk of it, it keeps on tormenting my head. But I won't talk of him because it only makes me remember him more, then after all no one else can mind except me – only if I am grousy and sullen you [Lytton] mustn't think me altogether selfish. . . .'

Lytton went on calming and reassuring her, but for a time it seemed as if Ralph's love had been totally expunged by her deception. He was continuing his affair with Clare in the most brash and insensitive way. 'I can tell you it was pretty intolerable,' Carrington admitted in a secret letter to Gerald later in the year (19 October 1922). In order to retain Ralph's undivided affections, Clare was always stirring up his indignation against Carrington and Gerald, keeping alive the old embers of his humiliation and bitterness. Their affair was all the more tormenting for Carrington since – as if the ramifications of this story were as yet inadequate – she herself felt a strong sexual attraction towards Clare: 'It all follows,' she explained, 'from my lustful sapphism.' Yet despite this attraction, she now hated her, and was glad to see that Lytton, too, greatly disliked her, believing that it was impossible to include such a mischief-maker in their lives. Yet he still counselled patience, and advised Carrington not to try to coerce Ralph into giving her up. In time, he promised her, their affair would die a natural death.

Towards the end of June, Clare left England and went back to Norhurst with her new lover – Mark Gertler![1] Lytton, sensing that this might be a good opportunity for Ralph and Carrington to regain some of their lost harmony, and that this might more easily be achieved if he were not there looking on, left the same week for a fortnight in Venice. But before leaving, he summoned Barbara Bagenal down to Tidmarsh in order to keep Carrington company and see that she came to no harm.

[1] Mark Gertler hated Ralph Partridge, whom he used to call 'the Policeman', and it seems probable that he had urged Clare to go off with Ralph in order to stir up as much trouble as possible.

As a holiday companion, Lytton took with him his young Cambridge friend Sebastian Sprott, who, the previous year, had accompanied Keynes to Algeria and Tunisia. Together they journeyed in some style down to Venice and put up at the Casa Frollo in the Giudecca, a 'nice sort of broken-down place, which will just suit us', Lytton informed Pippa (22 June 1922). His own room looked out towards the Lido and on the day he arrived the weather was blue and a fresh breeze was entering the windows. Why, he wondered, did not he and all his friends live here permanently? The one drawback was a typically Venetian one – noise. 'An ice factory, if you please, is next door, and naturally chooses the hour of 3 a.m. for its most agitating operations – sounds of terrific collapses and crushes shake the earth, and I awake in terror of my life.' Otherwise there was little to complain about – everything was as beautiful as the previous year, when he had spent a week there with Ralph and Carrington on their honeymoon. 'Venice is very lovely – but oh dear! *not* so lovely by half as it was last year,' he wrote diplomatically to Carrington (July 1922). 'Such a difference does the mind make upon matter! Sebastian is really charming – most easy to get on with, most considerate, very gay, and interested in everything that occurs. . . . Of course he is young – also, somehow, not what you might call an "intimate" character – which has its advantages too. Nor is he passionate – but inclined if anything to be sentimental, though too clever to be so in a sickly style. His sentimentality is not directed towards me . . .'

Lytton's own sentimentality was directed towards a 'sublime' gondolier named Francesco, whom he had already taken to on his earlier stay there. 'Francesco carries one to the Piazzetta in about 10 minutes, according to wind and obstacles,' he wrote to Ralph (24 June 1922). 'He is exactly the same as ever. It was luck being able to have him . . . a few weeks after we went away last summer a new rule was made by which no one was allowed to hire a gondolier for more than a day at a time – except old clients – under which heading I mercifully come! Apparently Berenson last July tried to take Francesco as I did, with the result that a mob of enraged gondoliers collected booing and shouting, and he was nearly torn limb from limb. But *I* was at once recognised, and no mob assailed me . . . the rule was made by the degraded gondoliers, who found they were losing all their custom. It seems to me next year they'll do away with the blessed privileges of "old clients" as well – the pigs. . . . Sebastian enjoys everything very much, and keeps up a constant chatter of a mild kind, which just suits me at the present moment. I can't say he looks ultra respectable, with a collarless shirt, very décolleté, and the number of glad eyes he receives is alarming. However so far his *behaviour* has been all that could be desired.'

The news from Tidmarsh during these weeks was unsensational. But it did not sound as if Carrington and Ralph were drawing any closer. Lytton felt moments of great discouragement – 'a feeling that every-thing is too difficult and fearful – a feeling of the futility of life'. But such moods passed, and his letters were always trying to cement over these difficulties. To Carrington he is invariably cheerful, describing various social occasions, how, for example, he had called to have tea with some friends of Lady Colefax, 'Mr. and Mrs. Robinson, who have a grand palazzo with an immense garden rather far away facing the lagoon and the cemetery. It was a curious vision – the huge rooms filled with the richest furniture – marble courts, roses, fountains etc. and the two melancholy owners of it all – he a sad little nonentity, and she a large disappointed horse of a woman, grumbling incessantly, cursing Italy, the heat, the mosquitoes, the Church bells, complaining of every-thing you can think of that anyone could desire. . . . I am to dine tête-à-tête on Sunday. She is, with all her horror, slightly intriguing. One wonders how she can have got into such a state.'

Meanwhile, Lytton's correspondence with Ralph reveals more of his secret anxieties. Was he returning from Venice too early? he asks. Would it ease matters if he stayed at Gordon Square for ten days before coming down to Tidmarsh? Had Ralph already forgotten him? The uncertainty of the last months had greatly stimulated Lytton's feelings of affection. 'I hug you a hundred times and bite your ears. Don't you still realise what I feel for you? how profoundly I love you? . . . I wish I could talk to you now . . . I am always your own Lytton.'

Once back, he resumed the work of patching and repairing their broken relationships, trying everything he knew to dissipate the strained and uneasy atmosphere that still hung over the Mill House. Here was a man who detested violence and 'uncivilized' conduct, devoting months to mollifying and appeasing Ralph, just as a few years earlier he, who prided himself on refusing to speak to unintelligent people, had courted and borne with the company of an uneducated girl. By any standards this behaviour shows that he was much less of the blasé, squeamish intellectual that legend has painted him.

During the month of August he sublet Tidmarsh and with Carring-ton and Ralph set out on a five weeks' motor tour of Devon and Wales. This, he thought, might easily help in clearing the air. But from the very first, things did not go well. After the resplendent heat of Italy, the immoderately frigid climate, with snow, ice, sleet and hurricanes of rain, nearly killed Lytton, wearing him down to a mere shadow of his former shadowy self. 'I creep about on a broken wing, hélas!' he told Mary Hutchinson. And three weeks later he was able to report to Pippa that 'so far we have had exactly two fine days, and on one of them the motor broke down, so that we spent most of it in a garage'. They were constantly on the move from one dud and exorbitant hotel to another. 'I think my next work will be a fulmination on the Hotels of England,' Lytton groaned.

Throughout these misadventures, the Partridges had kept up a rather grim and bitter humour. In the third week of August, they took rooms for ten days at Solva, near St David's on the south-west coast of Wales. 'It is on the snout of Wales – a sea coast in the Cornwall style with rocks, coves, and islands, and would be perfect if there were any sun to see it in,' Lytton wrote to Pippa (18 August 1922). It was a relief to be settled at last in this pleasant and empty spot – for him, but not, perversely, for the Partridges. Now that there was no succession of calamities to distract them from their personal antagonisms, the tension mounted quickly; then exploded. All the time they had been driving through Devon and Wales, Carrington could sense that Ralph's thoughts were fixed far away on Clare, that he was completely obsessed by her life. At Solva, angry scenes broke out between them. Carrington declared that if he really cared for her, as he had maintained on returning to Tidmarsh, then he must see that it was becoming unbearable for her to go on living with him, knowing he was still friends with Clare. After all, she had sacrificed Gerald – why should he not give up Clare? Ralph retorted that he had no objection to her and Gerald being simply friends – and at once sat down and wrote off a letter to Gerald to tell him so. According to Ralph, Carrington had subtly imposed this law of non-communication upon herself so as to put him in the wrong with Clare. And so they argued about it and about, and as the days passed and the arguments went on, so the atmosphere between them showed signs of clearing, and, quite unintentionally, they grew fonder of each other.

On the first day of September, they left Wales and motored back homewards. That same day Clare Bollard came back with Gertler from Norhurst and Carrington, dreading another period of misery leading, perhaps, to an ultimate crisis, broke down. All that she most prized in life seemed to be slipping away from her. 'I love R very much,' she burst out in a letter to Gerald (19 October 1922). 'I suppose that when a person dies, or nearly leaves one for ever one becomes very aware of all one's feelings . . . I also love Lytton and I also love our life here. when I see other peoples lives' I see how good this is . . . I care enough for it to put a good Deal of energy into opposing any enemy who threatens it.' The crisis that she feared never materialized. By the end of October she and Ralph appeared to have arrived at some agreement. So long as Carrington herself did not resume relations with Gerald, Ralph promised not to see Clare. 'You say you mistrust Clare,' he told her, 'and think she is wicked. I tell you that I mistrust Gerald, and think, not from wickedness but from thoughtlessness and vagueness he may imperil my happiness.'

No one was more responsible for this new amnesty than Lytton. Carrington's life at Tidmarsh had been made endurable solely by his kindness, and that gentleness and understanding which he would always display when she most needed it. 'Lytton is still my Caesar, or whatever the expression is,' she exclaimed that autumn. 'Through all the scenes, the wretchednesses, he has been amazing. If it hadn't been for his friendship I should have rushed away. He makes one see that one ought never to let other people's meanesses wreck one.'

Ralph, too, had only stayed with Carrington during these awkward months because of his devotion and sense of loyalty to Lytton. That winter he gave up Clare altogether, and though he entered into some lighter affairs with women he met at London parties – with Marjorie Joad, among others – he grew in time to love Carrington again very deeply. But it was a different kind of love, less possessive and obsessive, one that would later admit all sorts of further complications for them both.

5

ON THE MOVE

'I am stiff – frozen stiff – a rigid icicle,' Lytton wrote to Virginia Woolf from Pembrokeshire (22 August 1922). 'I hang at this address for another week, and slowly melt southwards and eastwards – a weeping relic of what was once your old friend.'

He had made out an elaborate schedule for his September visitings. After a week-end with Sir Philip Sassoon at Trent[1] – 'rather boring,

[1] Sir Philip Sassoon (1888–1939), politician and connoisseur. He was Unionist M.P. for Hythe (1912–39), private secretary to Lord Haig (1915–18), under-secretary for air (1924–9, 1931–7) and first commissioner of works (1937–9). Despite this successful career, his gifts were, according to Osbert Sitwell, more those of an artist than a politician. He was a trustee of the National Gallery, the Tate Gallery and the Wallace Collection. His various houses, Trent Park, Port Lympe and New Barnet were renowned as centres of art and entertainment, always filled with politicians, painters, writers, professional golfers and airmen.

really' – he joined Clive and Vanessa Bell at Charleston, dividing the next week between them and the Woolfs at Monk's House. 'I'm enjoying myself here very much,' he wrote from Charleston to Mary Hutchinson (7 September 1922), 'it is positively hot enough to sit out of doors – I pretend to read, and really do nothing but chat. Clive and I go for vast walks over the downs, which have grown more beautiful than ever. Oh for a farmhouse at the foot of them, for my very own.'

The ugly complications of Tidmarsh now filled him with gloomy forebodings. In one sense he looked forward to the winter, which always seemed to bring with it a suspension of amorous adventures and entanglements. His spirit, so he confided to Mary Hutchinson (22 August 1922), had been almost broken by the perturbing events of the spring and summer. 'It would be indeed charming to see you again, and exchange confidences. But I hope you will lay in a good supply of wood, coal, mackintoshes, umbrellas and galoshes – rum punch for the evenings, too; followed, very likely, by glasses of porter in our bedrooms, warmed by red-hot pokers. I pray for Winter, when we shall be snug once more, and the sun will shine, and we will only *occasionally* shiver.'

After a short stay at Eleanor with the Hutchinsons, Lytton went off for a long, 'pretty grim' week-end to Garsington, the only other guests being W. J. Turner and his wife – 'a very small bird-like man with a desolating accent, a good deal to say for himself – but punctuated by strange hesitations – impediments – rather distressing; but really a nice little fellow, when one has got over the way in which he says "count"', he patronizingly wrote to Virginia Woolf (19 September 1922). 'Ott. was dreadfully dégringolée, her bladder has now gone the way of her wits – a melancholy dribble, and then, as she sits after dinner in the lamplight, her cheek-pouches drooping with peppermints, a cigarette between her false teeth, and vast spectacles on her painted nose, the effect produced is extremely agitating. I found I wanted to howl like an Irish wolf – but perhaps the result produced in you was different.'[1]

From Garsington he took himself off to the Manor House, Mells, to put up for some days with Lady Horner, 'my only other co-guest being Eddie [Marsh], who is quickly killing me with his dreadful self- and world-satisfaction. The house is a very charming one – the true country-house style, and the Horner famille seem a cut above the

[1] On the same day Lytton wrote to Ottoline herself: 'It was a great pleasure to see you and to have some talks – I only wish there could have been more of them. Needless to say that I enjoyed my week-end very much. It was delightful to find Philip in such good trim, and I liked making the acquaintance of Turner. I hope your health is really taking a turn for the better at last. What a disgusting arrangement one's body does become when its machinery goes out of order.'

ordinary run of the upper classes. Lady H. has heard of Beaumont and Fletcher, and Katherine A[squith][1] dabbles in theology.' The following week, he left for a brief visit to Berlin with James, who was attending a congress on psycho-analysis, with Sigmund Freud in the chair – 'it seems a good opportunity of being shown round'. Later, the two brothers visited Potsdam and Sansouci, and saw the Voltaire *Zimmer* prepared by Frederick the Great, its walls decorated with monkeys, and still with Voltaire's books on the shelves.

At last, early in October, he was compelled to retreat diffidently back again to Tidmarsh. To his deep relief, peace and happiness seemed to have been mercifully restored. In these improved circumstances, he was more than content to spend most of the winter there, returning some of the hospitality he had received during the autumn. 'The winter is too terrible,' he wrote with playful exaggeration to Maynard Keynes (28 November 1922). 'I can neither feel, think, nor write – I can only just breathe, read, and eat. I am impotent – my hair has turned perfectly white – my beard has fallen off . . .' But the winter, as he predicted, had brought with it a sweet cessation to all their painful emotional dramas. Over Christmas, Keynes and Lydia Lopokova came down to stay, and Lytton wrote a short playlet for Carrington and Ralph to perform for them. And so, quietly and harmlessly, the old year came to an end, with Tidmarsh, like a vessel which had weathered a menacing storm, limping slowly on its course.

The new year also opened quietly. During January and February, Lytton made only two expeditions away from the Mill House. The first of these was to Cambridge, where he attended a performance of *Oedipus Rex* given by the Marlowe Society. Among the audience were many of his new undergraduate friends – F. L. Lucas, Stewart Perowne and Dadie Rylands, who had already made something of a name for himself in *The Duchess of Malfi*, acting the part of the Duchess. Another spectator there was Cecil Beaton, who noted down the scene in his diary. 'During the interval, the audience rushed to the club room to shout and smoke. Lytton Strachey peered at everyone through thick glasses, looking like an owl in daylight. He is immensely tall, and could be even twice his height if he were not bent as a sloppy asparagus. His huge hands fall to his sides, completely limp. His sugar-loaf beard is thick and dark, worn long in the fashion of an arty undergraduate.'

His second excursion in these months was again to Ottoline's. 'Now I am off – est-il possible? – to Garsington,' he reported to James (February 1923). There seem to have been two chief reasons why he still consented to go there. Ottoline's invitations were frequent and

[1] Lady Horner's daughter, married to Raymond Asquith.

insistent, and despite his acid comments about her to others, Lytton remembered well her kindness to him in past, more discontented years, and he did not now want unnecessarily to hurt her. In her virulence, her disillusion, her life of crowded loneliness, she had grown much less sympathetic to him. Yet Garsington itself even now retained some afterglow of its old magical enchantment. Besides a core of the old Bloomsbury guard, there was usually an influx of clever, pink-and-white undergraduates from Oxford among the guests, and it was their presence which formed the most powerful inducement to Lytton. Among these younger men were Edward Sackville-West, David Cecil, L. P. Hartley, Lytton's cousin John Strachey, C. M. Bowra[1] and John Rothenstein. One hot Sunday afternoon, John Rothenstein records, 'I found myself with two companions, likewise Oxford undergraduates, in a house where none of us had been before, pausing at an open french window that gave upon a lawn, at the farther end of which a tea-party was in progress. We paused because the lawn was not so large that we could not discern among the tea-drinkers the figures of Lytton Strachey, Aldous Huxley and Duncan Grant, as well as that, so awe-inspiring upon a first encounter, of our hostess Lady Ottoline Morrell. At that moment this modest patch of grass seemed to us an alarmingly large area to cross beneath the gaze of so many august eyes. So it is that I can still picture the group: Lytton Strachey inert in a low chair, red-bearded head dropped forward, long hands drooping, finger-tips touching the grass; Aldous Huxley talking, with his face turned up towards the sun; Duncan Grant, pale-faced, with fine, untidy black hair, light eyes ready to be coaxed from their melancholy, and Lady Ottoline wearing a dress more suitable, one would have thought, for some splendid Victorian occasion, and an immense straw hat. . . . After listening to the discourse of Lytton Strachey and several others I vaguely apprehended that in this Oxfordshire village were assembled luminaries of a then to me almost unknown Cambridge world.'

Early in March, Lytton went up to Gordon Square to be with his mother, who was now on the point of going completely blind. 'I hope it will not be long before I get sight of you,' she had scrawled with a shaky and uncertain hand, in what was to be her very last letter to him (February 1923). '. . . I am not able to see what I write, but I hope you will be able to read. Ever, dearest, Your loving Mama.'

As the spring approached, Lytton again grew concerned over the

---

[1] C. M. Bowra, now Warden of Wadham College, Oxford, recalls that, on one occasion when Lytton was staying at Garsington, 'a party of Asquiths arrived and settled down to tea. Lady Ottoline left the room, and when she came back it was empty except for Strachey. She asked what had happened, and he said in his piping voice, "There's been a row." There had, about the war, and the Asquiths had retired in a dudgeon.'

status quo at Tidmarsh. Ralph and Carrington had jogged along on
friendly enough terms throughout the winter, but their new association
was not yet resilient enough, Lytton judged, to withstand any further
shocks or perils. To make life as pleasant and diverse as possible, he
arranged for them all to travel abroad extensively that year, hoping by
these means to circumnavigate the possible strains and tremors arising
from boredom or restlessness.

In the third week of March, therefore, the three of them set off from
England for a two months' holiday to the Mediterranean lands. After
one day spent in Marseilles, they travelled south to Tunis. Then, after a
tedious journey of eleven hours, they joined James and Alix at the
Établissement Thermal, a civilized hotel for invalids at Hammam-
Méskoutine, a tiny inaccessible village a few miles south-west of Bône,
where Alix was recovering from a serious attack of bronchitis. 'Apart
from the unfortunate circumstances, it is a pleasure to be here,' Lytton
wrote back to Pippa (27 March 1923). '. . . The hotel is almost by itself
in very beautiful country, with mountains all round, and masses of
vegetation, and wild flowers such as I have never seen before. Oranges,
lemons, palms, and bananas grow in the garden, and hoopoes hop from
bough to bough.' As for the Arabs, they seemed to Lytton highly
romantic in their white burnouses, but oh! so unapproachable! The other
inhabitants of their hotel were English couples, invalids all, who had
travelled there for the sake of the natural springs – 'extraordinary boiling hot affairs, which come bursting and bubbling out of the ground,
giving off steam, and literally too hot to put your finger in'.

No sooner had Lytton set foot in Algeria, than an extraordinary
change came over the northern African continent. Its climate altered.
While the Easter crowds in London sat out over their iced drinks in
Regent's Park, the Algerian population huddled and shivered round
their native fires. The weather was unprecedented, as it so often is, and
far worse than anything recalled even by the Oldest Biblical Inhabitant
– icy winds of the utmost penetration, sleet and cyclonic rain. Taken
unawares, Lytton quickly succumbed to a feverish cold, and while
Carrington and Ralph went off for a week to inspect Constantine and
Biskra, and James looked after Alix, Lytton nursed his sickness in
solitary confinement. But he was also working. On 12 April, he sent
off to Maynard Keynes his essay on 'Sarah Bernhardt' for the first
number of the newly reconstituted *Nation and Athenaeum*. 'She is *most*
suitable,' Keynes replied (27 April 1923). He had also dispatched to
him a review copy of Harold Nicolson's *Tennyson*, but at this Lytton
demurred. 'I'm sorry to say I can't face Lord Tennyson,' he wrote
back (16 April 1922). 'Harold N's book is so disgusting and stupid.'

Together with this, he declined to write on Winston Churchill's *The World Crisis 1911–1914*, which had come out that April and which Keynes had forwarded to him, on the grounds that he could add nothing to what H. M. Tomlinson had already written about it – unless his criticism was on technical lines, which he felt he was not up to managing. 'I had begun writing something before seeing Tomlinson – but that would hopelessly overlap; so I think the whole thing had better lapse.'

On the morning of Sunday, 15 April, all five of them left Hammam-Méskoutine for Tunis, then travelled on to Palermo, in Sicily, and after a week here pursued their journey north to Naples. 'We have been having a very enjoyable though rather exhausting time,' Lytton wrote to Keynes from Parker's Hotel (5 May 1923). 'I am now recruiting in this slightly dreadful place. The sun shines, the sea glitters, the trams ting-tang along – and this evening at 6.30 St. Januarius's blood will liquefy. But I fear that, like Cardinal Newman, I shan't "have time" to go and see the miracle.'

From Naples they went to Rome, and from Rome soon returned to London and to Pangbourne. 'I am back again,' Lytton announced to Keynes from Tidmarsh (28 May 1923), 'more or less alive, but furious at having been fool enough to exchange the heats of Rome for this fearful refrigerator.' The next week he again visited Garsington for what turned out to be the most disastrous week-end of all. At all costs, he felt that he must escape another such stay there. 'It has been even worse than I anticipated,' he complained to Carrington (3 June 1923). 'Appalling! A fatal error to have come, I see now only too clearly. The only other guest a miserable German doctor – a "psycho-analyst" of Freiburg – ready to discourse on every subject in broken English for hours.[1] The boredom has been indescribable. Most of the conversation is directed towards the dog, when the doctor is not holding forth. Imagine the ghastly meals. Then Philip at the pianola, then Philip reading out loud his articles in the Spectator, then Dr. Marten on mysticism – "it can be explained in a few sentences" – followed by an address for 40 minutes by the clock. After which Ottoline joins in. Horrible! horrible! . . . Julian [Morrell] has become a kind of young lady – plays Bach and cuddles the dogs all day. Mr. Ching came and played Bach. Pipsey is to play Bach after dinner. My brain totters.

[1] Dr Marten was one of the strangest characters Ottoline attracted to Garsington. 'Other friends of mine consulted him,' Robert Gathorne-Hardy records, 'and in later years we half suspected that he made experiments on English patients who had been so lately enemies of his country. With his practice he combined some superficial psychoanalysis. I asked Ottoline if he had found out anything peculiar about her. "I find," she droned with humorous solemnity, "that my brothers play an undue part in my life."'

Soon I shall be playing Bach myself . . . If there had been a telephone in the house, I really believe I should have rung you up and fled. I am tempted to start walking as it is.

'"Psycho-analysis" is a ludicrous fraud. Not only Ottoline has been cured at Freiburg. The Sackville-West youth was there to be cured of homosexuality. After 4 months and an expenditure of £200, he found he could just bear the thought of going to bed with a woman. No more. Several other wretched undergraduates have been through the same "treatment". They walk about haggard on the lawn, wondering whether they could bear the thought of a woman's private parts, and gazing at their little lovers, who run round and round with cameras, snapshotting Lytton Strachey. Query, what did Ott go to be cured of? Whatever it may have been, she is pronounced by all the youths to be "better – much better". Probably after playing Bach this evening, I shall hurry to Freiburg myself. I shall certainly be badly in need of some "treatment". But I admit that I would rather receive it at the hands of P. Ritchie than of the German doctor. I must go downstairs. He will explain to me the meaning of asceticism "in [a] few sentences" – and then Ottoline will join in. The bell rings. Terror and horror!'

Philip Ritchie, the eldest son of Lord Ritchie of Dundee, soon to embark on a legal career with the novelist C. H. B. Kitchen[1] in the chambers of Lytton's old friend, C. P. Sanger, was then still an Oxford undergraduate. Together with some of his friends, he had come over to tea that Sunday afternoon and 'was the one charming element', Lytton claimed. 'He told me shocking gossip about everyone, and in my gratitude I nearly flung my arms round his neck.'

Early on Monday morning, Lytton departed, lingered a little in Oxford having 'lunch with the Byam Shaw rosebud' and then hurried up to London for a sumptuous party at Philip Sassoon's. 'You never

[1] In his novel *Crime at Christmas* (1935), which is dedicated to Kenneth Ritchie, C. H. B. Kitchen wrote: 'It is my fate, in Bloomsbury, to be thought a Philistine, while in other circles I am regarded as a dilettante with too keen an aesthetic sense to be a responsible person.' This sentence, Mr Kitchen confirmed in a letter to the author (5 July 1965) 'has certainly an autobiographical overtone and largely sums up my social situation during the twenties. I was introduced to Bloomsbury by Philip Ritchie, who was a close friend of mine, and met most of the leading lights in that circle, but being in those days a tiresome mixture of shyness and conceit, I never felt sufficiently at home in it to form intimate contacts with its members. Strange to say, Virginia Woolf, the most formidable of them all, developed, I think, a slightly protective attitude towards me and it was thanks to her good offices that the Hogarth Press published my first two novels, *Streamers Waving* and *Mr Balcony*. I doubt if any other publishers would have considered them at that time.' Kitchen's reputation as a writer was made with his third book, *Death of My Aunt*, but Lytton, who liked his writing and who once, with his sister Marjorie, acted in a rather daring charade at a gathering in his house, preferred his first two novels and his fourth, *The Sensitive One* (1931), which he had in his personal library.

Roger Senhouse

James, Lytton and Pippa Strachey, Frances Marshall and Ralph Partridge at Ham Spray

Lytton Strachey instructing Carrington how to read Gibbon

End of Lytton's Augustus John period: Roger Fry, Clive Bell, Duncan Grant and
an unidentified guest look on as Vanessa Bell wields cutlery

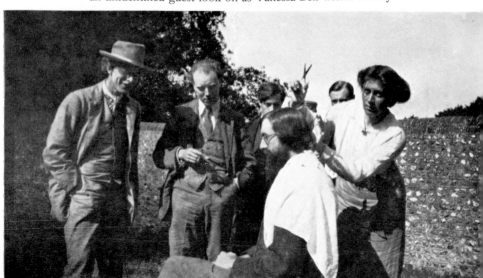

saw the like,' he told Carrington (June 1923). 'Winston [Churchill] was there, and I talked to him a good deal. Do you know, in spite of everything I couldn't help liking him. H. G. [Wells] says very much the same thing in "Men Like Gods"[1] – one somehow *can't* dislike the poor creature. He was delighted when I said I thought his book[2] very well done, and hardly seemed to mind when I added that I also thought it very wicked.'

As the warmer summer weather came in, Lytton's refrigerated spirit quickly thawed, and when Virginia Woolf encountered him at about this time, she observed that he seemed buoyant. The conversation between them turned to literature, and he declared, with an embracing, sunny optimism, that they had twenty years of creative work still before them. He himself had completely recovered by this time from the long period of prostration which followed his writing of *Queen Victoria*. 'I have pledged myself to write once a month for that fiend Maynard,' he also told Dadie Rylands (14 July 1923). Though he claimed to have been 'lured' into this 'perfectly mad occupation', it proved in fact to be a most rewarding one, and one that he enjoyed performing. Keynes, whom he had visited at King's early that June, had arranged for him to be paid forty pounds for each contribution – 'a splendid remuneration', Lytton acknowledged – and had also 'made a precarious arrangement with the *New Republic*' for each of these articles to appear in America, from where Lytton would receive almost as much again.

Now that he was writing regularly once more, there was less time available for social entertainments. He did not regret this, and turned down a number of invitations, especially Ottoline's, with positive relief. Life at Tidmarsh was calm and unclouded. During the whole of July, we hear of only a single week-end house party – with the Duchess of Marlborough at Blenheim, the potent architecture of which quite ravished him. 'Nobody was particularly interesting (except, perhaps, the Duchess),' he confided to Mary Hutchinson (11 July 1923), '– it was the house which was entrancing, and life-enhancing. I wish it were mine. It is enormous, but one would not feel it too big. The grounds are beautiful too, and there is a bridge over a lake which positively gives one an erection. Most of the guests played tennis all day and bridge all night, so that (apart from eating and drinking) they might as well have been at Putney.'

His work, however, did not prevent him from inviting his friends down to the Mill House. In the first two months of this summer there

---

[1] 'Have you read "Men like Gods"? In spite of its being Mr Wells, I can't help enjoying it.' (Lytton to Ottoline Morrell, 29 May 1923.)

[2] *The World Crisis 1911–1914.*

Q

was a long procession of such visitors – Pippa, Boris Anrep, J. H. Doggart, Frank Ramsey (twice), Sebastian Sprott, Dadie Rylands (who was soon to take Ralph Partridge's place in the Hogarth Press), and Stephen Tomlin, son of Lord Justice Tomlin, a brilliant and erratic sculptor, bisexual and deeply melancholic at times, yet perhaps the most acutely intellectual of all Lytton's younger friends.

So far there had been no sign of any friction between Carrington and Ralph, but Lytton did not intend to take any chances. His policy was still to keep them on the move. At the beginning of August he and Sebastian Sprott, together with Ralph, Carrington and Barbara Bagenal all crammed into the car and started out on an extensive motor tour of France. From Boulogne they drove first to Amiens, then on to Rouen and to Chartres, whose cathedral Lytton announced to be 'superior to any other I have seen'. From here they continued their journey south to Le Mans, then swept eastwards via Orléans to Dijon, where Sebastian Sprott left them to join up with a young friend at Basle. Lytton's destination was the Cistercian Abbaye de Pontigny, on the Yonne, where he had been invited to attend the annual '*Entretiens d'été*'. At these conferences, which used to last some ten days, writers and professors from a number of countries would assemble to discuss, *ad nauseam*, a few common moral or literary problems – some of intimidating erudition and obscurity. Lytton had been asked to come by André Gide, who was himself on *Le Comité provisoire des Entretiens d'été*, and who had written in his all but totally illegible hand to assure Lytton that they were anxiously awaiting 'votre présence à cette réunion "d'éminents" penseurs des pays divers, qui doit avoir lieu cet été – du 16 au 27 Août, à l'abbaye de Pontigny (celle-même où Thomas Becket trouvait asile). . . . J'aurais le plus grand plaisir à vous y voir et à vous presenter quelques amis qui ont un vif désir de faire votre connaissance.'

The original plan had been for Ralph to continue touring the country with Carrington and Barbara Bagenal while Lytton was stationed at this 'highbrow club' as he called it. But in response to an urgent wire telling him that his father was dying, he dashed back to England, depositing the two women at an inn near Vermonton, and promising to motor out again and collect them all at the end of the month.

Meanwhile Lytton was being introduced by Gide to his fellow *penseurs*,[1] in particular the strong French contingent which included Georges Raverat, Paul Desjardins, Charles du Bos (who was later to write a long critical essay on Lytton), Jacques Rivière, Roger Martin du

[1] Among the German contingent was Heinrich Mann, brother of Thomas, and then most as celebrated as a novelist.

Gard, Jean Schlumberger and Max Lazard. They were immediately
startled by his resemblance to the Henry Lamb portrait, which up till
then most of them had regarded as simply a caricature. 'On the first
day,' recalled André Maurois, 'we were alarmed by his tall, lanky
frame, his long beard, his immobility, his silence; but when he spoke,
in his "bleating falsetto" it was in delightful, economical epigrams.'

Lytton, too, was considerably startled by his experiences at Pontigny.
The sanitary arrangements at the Abbaye were 'crushing and inadequate'; his breakfast contained not a single egg; and his cold, bleak
bedroom turned out to be nothing more nor less than a monk's cell.
He felt melancholy, too, at being separated from Ralph, and at his own
'constant and immense difficulty in effecting any kind of communication with the natives'. Like a schoolboy pitchforked into a new school,
he was lonely and bewildered. Some of the older boys, though benevolent, were particularly aloof. 'Gide is hopelessly unapproachable,' he
told Carrington (26 August 1923). 'He gave a reading last night of one
of his own works – in a most extraordinary style – like a clergyman
intoning in a pulpit. It was enormously admired.' In a letter to Ralph
(25 August 1923) he explains that he is not really depressed, but overwhelmed by 'a sort of sentimental sunset Verlaine feeling'. He enjoys
'some secret love-affairs of course – confined, equally of course, to my
own breast'. One of these secret passions was for the young and austere
Blaise Desjardins – 'largish, pale, unhealthy, who sings very well – but
apparently particularly dislikes me, hélas!' And there were also some
pseudo-adventures in which he was the object of other people's admiration. 'La belle Américaine, with the short black hair, has already come
into my life – a slight bother – she is an "artist" – has asked me to sit to
her – has read my article on Racine, which she thinks wonderful –
gazes at me with slightly melancholy eyes, etc. etc. . . . I shall only, I
fear, turn out a disappointment. Her husband is an agreeable American-
speaking Frenchman. . . . I am beginning to wonder how we shall
weather through another week. Translation hardly seems to be a
subject adapted for 10 days of discussion! I only wish I were translated
myself, like Bottom. Sometimes I feel as if I *had* been! And my Titania?
– La Belle Américaine? Peut-être. Here she comes to do my portrait.'

Invariably the best part of each day was the morning, when he was
allowed to sit in the excellent library and, without superintendence,
read. But even then, owing to the lack of morning eggs, the exhaustion
was considerable. At moments, either from early faintness or the
soporific effect of the afternoon debates, everything at the old abbey
seemed like a dream. He listened to their discussions with an air of
politely scornful indulgence, never volunteering an interjection of his

own. 'The "entretiens" which occur every day from 2.30 to 4.30 (what a time to choose) are rather appalling,' he complained to Ralph. 'Almost perpetually dull – and then the constant worry of one's being expected to speak and never doing so. Up to now I have allowed exactly three words to issue from my mouth – in public; so that I am growing very unpopular. The fatigue is fearful.'

Some of the subjects were in themselves quite sufficient to start him yawning – 'LES HUMANITÉS, sont-elles irremplaçables pour former une Élite?' or 'Y a-t-il dans la Poésie d'un Peuple UN TRÉSOR RÉSERVÉ impénétrable aux Étrangers?' What could one say to questions such as these? During the long and heated conference on 'THE MEANING OF HONOUR', his boredom appeared to reach its summit, and lapping one of his gigantic grasshopper legs over the other, he shut his eyes and dropped off to sleep. 'And what in your opinion, Monsieur Strachey, is the most important thing in the world?' suddenly asked Paul Desjardins. There was a long and painful pause. Then from the slumbering beard there issued a tiny treble: '*Passion!*' This was one of his three words, and he uttered it with such suave and unexpected nonchalance that the solemn circle of intellectuals, relieved for an instant, broke into laughter. Pressed during another discussion on the subject of 'LES CONFESSIONS' to contribute something, he stood up, after an extended pause announced: 'Les confessions ne sont pas dans mon genre,' and sat down again. On another day, at the end of an exhaustive argument over the latest Gidean cult of whimsical behaviour and 'actes gratuits', his still small voice from the back of the hall was overheard inquiring plaintively: 'Est-ce qu'un acte gratuit est *toujours* désagréable?'

Predictably, most of the French *éminents penseurs* did not know what to make of this strange francophil in their midst. Perhaps he was too English to be interested in purely abstract problems; perhaps he was too frail to take a more active part in the proceedings; or possibly he felt their ideas were too unsubtle to hold any interest for him. 'Looking at him there,' André Maurois wrote, 'we had the impression of an almost infinite disdain, of a wilful abstraction, of a refusal . . . And yet . . . And yet sometimes, for one fleeting instant, a glance would flash behind his spectacles so vividly that we wondered if all this lassitude might not be the mask of a man really amused and keen, and more Britannic than any Briton.'

At the end of this month Ralph reappeared to rescue Lytton and motor them all back to England. They took this journey in leisurely stages, winding slowly up to Paris where 'anything more like Hell than the grands boulevards I've never seen,' Lytton commented in a letter to Dorothy Bussy (25 November 1923). 'We went to a revue – incredible. Nothing but very old and enormously fat and completely naked females walking about the stage. I was nearly sick. But the country towns were adorable. We had a most delightful tour back – via Vézelay and all sorts of lovely places – such a wonderful sense of civilization that at last one begins to disbelieve in the existence of M. Poincaré.'[1]

Back in England again, Lytton sped off for what was now his customary September trip to Charleston. The summer was almost over, and still no trouble had broken out between Carrington and Ralph. The last three months of this year they passed chiefly down at Tidmarsh, Lytton composing his *Nation and Athenaeum* essays. Occasionally, when the month's work was done, he would go up to spend a few days in Gordon Square, whirling among Bibescos, Cunards and Colefaxes. All this, however, was 'pure vapidity' and he preferred whenever practicable to visit Cambridge, which was always so 'delightfully hectic'. That Michaelmas term, he was able to make only one journey there, but this was 'perfect', he told Maynard Keynes (11 December 1923). 'So much sympathetic variety I never saw. I enjoyed myself deliriously – the only horror was going away. However, I was solaced in the train by finding myself sitting next to Sir A. Quiller-Couch, whom I was able to study out of the corner of my eye for an hour and twenty minutes. Could anything be more soothing?'

To Lytton's great satisfaction, his plan of extensive travel that year seemed to have preserved Carrington and Ralph's marriage perfectly intact. They had come through the summer wonderfully well – perhaps those wretched emotional disturbances were a thing of the past now. They had resumed marital relations, and Ralph was evidently finding it less and less necessary to see other girls. They had no quarrels, and they joked and laughed together like happy people. Then, that December, as if to demonstrate that all their difficulties were dead, and to flaunt the strength of the new intimacy which had sprung up between them, they went abroad again together – to visit Gerald Brenan at Yegen! Ralph now claimed that his attitude had completely changed. He was no longer consumed by any sense of bitterness, anger or humiliation – quite the reverse. In a letter from Spain (23 December 1923) he explained to Lytton that he had had a long, amicable chat with Gerald and that 'I feel no jealousy at all now seeing them together – it was only because I was certain it had passed that I came out – now they know that I know what happened in the past, the excitement has died away – I don't feel at all alarmed about it reviving, but that may be

---

[1] Raymond Poincaré (1860–1934) was then prime minister of France and minister of foreign affairs.

because I can't help my conviction that all nice people in the world are perfectly happy just as they are. I do hope it is true of you, dear, at least.'

Lytton, who had been worried over the possible repercussions arising out of this dangerous expedition, was overjoyed by this evident triumph of sweet reasonableness and sense. It seemed as if their troubles really were at an end, their mutual happiness cemented and assured. He lived quietly while they were away, inviting various friends down to stay – Philip Ritchie, Alec Penrose, Sebastian Sprott, Clive Bell and Mary Hutchinson – and early in January he went for three 'pleasant though exhausting' days to Paris. The future looked bright.

The early winter of 1924 was, however, a particularly severe one for Lytton's health. He was forced temporarily to abandon his work, and between February and June no essay of his came out in the *Nation and Athenaeum*. 'I am in rather a low state,' he told Pippa on 27 February. 'I was attacked by flu on my return here from London. When that went off lumbago supervened – not very badly – but it has been distinctly crushing and is still lingering about. The result is a general debility, as you may imagine.' A few days later he confided to Mary Hutchinson that 'I have been écrasé by disease – influenza, followed by lumbago. I am still very feeble, with pains in the back, and the weather is so fearful that recovery seems difficult.' Three weeks later he was still feverish. 'I'm sorry to say I'm still bedridden,' he scribbled in a faint and wobbly letter to Mary Hutchinson (20 March 1924). 'I can *just* get up for a little sometimes, but my feebleness is beyond anything you ever saw. . . . The wretched flu keeps coming back at intervals – in the form of a fever – so that I can't ever yet be sure that it's gone. But every attack is less bad than the last. A most unpleasant lingering malady!' By early April he was at last on the mend, and went down with his sister Pippa to convalesce at Lyme Regis. 'The Cobb is visited twice daily,' he dutifully reported back to Carrington, then deep in the novels of Jane Austen. 'Once there was a regular *Persuasion* accident – my hat flew off – I dashed after it – crashed to the ground – cut my trousers at the knee – but otherwise quite undamaged – except for the loss of dignity.'

At the end of a week's convalescence, Lytton returned 'more or less recovered' to Tidmarsh. But even now he was still not free to resume his *Nation and Athenaeum* articles. The Mill House, during the winters, had proved too damp for his health, and for some time he had been looking round for a new house. That winter Carrington came across one that seemed to please them all, and Lytton now decided to buy it. 'I believe I've bought Ham Spray for £2,300 – but it still totters,' he announced to James on 4 January. By the end of this month, the contract was signed, and the deal completed. Ham Spray House lay near the Downs between Newbury and Hungerford, and at this time had no drains or electric light, and was in need of a general overhaul. The builders started to put the place in some kind of order early in the spring, and while they were installing the sanitary and electrical fittings, Carrington would go over nearly every day to plan her decorations and the layout of the garden. 'We are beginning to be busy over our new house,' Lytton told Ottoline on 24 April. '. . . It is altogether rather agitating, and complete financial ruin stares me in the face. I suppose I shall have to write another masterpiece.' Even with some temporary help from a legacy which Ralph had received on his father's death, the move was turning out to be fearfully expensive, and even Carrington was forced to admit that they were 'on the rocks for d'argent'.

But she was in her element painting and decorating the rooms, staining the floors and doors. Ralph was always driving her and any of their guests from Tidmarsh that spring – Leonard and Virginia Woolf, Sebastian Sprott, Dadie Rylands, Maynard Keynes and others – over to the new house, and whenever possible they would be put to work on some job that needed doing. Lytton's letters are full of the bustle and activity of these months. 'We spent yesterday at our new house,' he wrote to David Garnett (23 May 1924), 'with various persons, among them Tommy [Stephen Tomlin] and Henrietta [Bingham] – I liked her more than before. She whitewashed amazingly and never said a word.'

There was always much to do; and when they left Tidmarsh on 15 July Ham Spray was still not really habitable. Lytton stayed away as much as possible during these first weeks, fleeing with Pippa for a fortnight to Brittany.[1] They were all extremely excited, but Lytton

[1] 'My darlings,' Lytton wrote from the Hôtel du Dauphin, Vannes, on 30 July 1924, '. . . Vannes is a very pleasant town largely old, with charming old houses, half-timbered, the wood painted in pale colours – grey, brown or pink – which has a very pretty effect. Unfortunately the modern frogs have built various atrocities all over it; but not enough to ruin the place. Our hotel looks over the chief square, in which the Breton boys tumble over each other in endless pleasure all day long. In the evening we sit outside the café, listening to the strains of a cultured trio as darkness falls. . . . At Le Mans, as we were going to our train, there were no porters at the station, so I took up my two green suitcases and proceeded to walk down the platform. Suddenly, without a word of warning, my back literally went crack – it was a fearful sensation – more terrifying than painful – as if something had broken inside. I tottered to a bench, and Pippa managed luckily to find a man who put the things into the train. When there I felt so shattered I thought I was going to faint. However, some food and brandy improved matters, and I was much better by the time we reached Rennes. . . . In the train between Le Mans and Rennes, as I lay pale and dim, a country youth with red hair, and, as they say, "the very picture of health", got in. I longed to be him, with a body which would do its work properly, and, well, an adequate mind. However, in the evening, at Rennes, feeling rather better, I perceived that the change, after all, would not have been a wise one.'

himself had been sorry to give up the Mill House, where, despite their difficulties, life on the whole had been so wonderfully happy. He was filled with a mixture of nostalgia and trepidation. 'Old age I suppose, but for whatever reason, the solid calmness of Tidmarsh exactly suits me,' he had written to Carrington during the negotiations for Ham Spray (1 January 1924). In later years, Tidmarsh was to retain a very special place in his memory. One night in July 1928, he almost wept as some music on a phonograph record recalled memories of his life there. 'Among others, there was a string quartet by Schubert, which brought back Tidmarsh to me with extraordinary vividness. I felt the loss of that regime very strongly, and in fact . . . nearly burst into tears. I hope and pray that our new grandeur . . . won't alter anything in any way – it would be wretched to lose our native simplicity!'

Lytton left Pippa at the Hôtel de Londres in Paris on 7 August, writing back to her the next day that his 'journey went off very successfully. . . . 'I found a perfect berth reserved in a cabin which I shared with a discreet Scotchman. England began directly I entered the large and spotless ship, everyone becoming instantly polite and sympathetic. The crossing was quite good, I had breakfast at Southampton, arrived at Newbury at 9.30, and was whisked back here in the car in time for a glass of milk and a biscuit.'

CHAPTER IV

Ham Spray House

'I lead a dog's life, between Queen Elizabeth's love affairs
and my own.'

Lytton Strachey to Dorothy Bussy (11 June 1927)

'What is love? 'Tis not hereafter – no; but it also isn't here-
tofore. Is it even here? Ah, well! – But the odd thing
is (among all the other oddities) that one occasionally
manages to enjoy oneself.'

Lytton Strachey to George Rylands (12 August 1927)

I

PAPER-GAMES AND PUSSY-CATS

Ham Spray was a pleasantly modernized country house of the Jane
Austen period, approached by a long straight avenue of lofty wych-
elms, and with a long veranda looking south up to the Newbury
Downs – a wonderful stretch of grand shapes and solitary expanses.
Less picturesque than Tidmarsh, it was also much larger; and though
its length and narrowness made it a difficult house to keep warm, free
from draughts and gusts, Lytton soon ensured a reasonable modicum
of comfort by introducing a number of improvements – central heating,
an 'electric light engine', a hot-water apparatus, the loft at the east end
converted into a studio for Carrington. At last, by his own definition,
he could count himself a wealthy man, being able to boast of an open
fireplace – beautifully adorned by Boris Anrep with the mosaic of a
reclining hermaphrodite figure – in his bedroom. According to Wogan
Philipps, the painter, he is also supposed to have fitted up an appliance
by which the wires of his bed under the mattress were electrically
heated, so that, lying in bed, he was agreeably grilled all night – one of
the many apocryphal stories that sprang up around him.

The study, in which Lytton now did all his writing, was also upstairs. Its walls were lined with French and English authors, mostly
of the eighteenth century, in their original editions; a large writing-desk
stood in the centre of the room, and, hanging over the mantelpiece so

Q*

that it dominated everything else, was a picture of Voltaire by Huber, showing him seated at a table, his hand raised in benediction above a group of friends. Here, during the mornings, Lytton would retire to work. He still never used a typewriter, disliked dictation, and wrote all his manuscripts out in a neat, flowing hand. In his most characteristic sitting-position at the desk, his body was completely relaxed so that the full force of his energy might be directed to the task before him. And since he constructed each sentence in his mind before putting pen to paper, he seldom needed to correct what he had written. On one occasion, some friends were discussing George Moore's extensive revisions to his novels, and one of them asked Lytton about his own amendments. 'I write very slowly, and in faultless sentences,' he replied. And this was hardly an exaggeration.

His daily routine at Ham Spray was simple and well-ordered. After breakfast he worked; after lunch he lay down; after tea he would usually go, stick in hand, for long walks over the Downs; and in the evening, after dinner, he either played piquet in the downstairs front drawing-room, or listened to music – usually Mozart, Beethoven or Haydn – on the ramshackle gramophone, or read out and discussed his manuscripts with Ralph and Carrington; all three of them, with Tiber the cat, seated round the fire.[1]

Under Carrington's hand, every room at Ham Spray was gradually transformed. She fashioned curious Victorian-style designs from coloured tinfoil paper, she decorated the doors and chimney-pieces, she hung pictures and made delicate paintings on glass and china. Upon the tiles, the plates, the cups and saucers, appeared passion-flowers, legs of mutton, fishes, abstract shapes and whole orchestras of cats playing 'cellos.[2] The atmosphere of Ham Spray, less characteristically individual than Tidmarsh, had something in common with Leonard and Virginia Woolf's new house in Tavistock Square, combining a certain austerity and restraint with some less definable feeling of epicurean ease. Besides Carrington's own decorations, there were also a few of Henry Lamb's drawings, and paintings and panels by Duncan Grant, Vanessa Bell and John Banting, executed mostly in thick browns and terracottas, rusty reds, eggshell blue or pale green. The walls of many of the rooms were embellished by 'Fanny Fletcher's Papers' – hand-blocked wallpapers made with carved potatoes and again in

[1] Besides Tiber (or Tiberius) there were at one time or another a number of other cats at Tidmarsh and Ham Spray, including Agrippa, Nero, Ptolemy and, christened by Carrington, Biddie.

[2] Lytton always encouraged Carrington with her painting and thought it important that she should be induced to show her pictures at various London Group exhibitions. But her shyness was inviolable and she would not be persuaded.

characteristic Bloomsbury shades, mauves, olives and cloudy yellows.

Though she employed a woman to deal with the housework, Carrington still did much of the cooking, which was unusual in those days. She was also passionately devoted to the garden and had made herself into a subtle and rather learned horticulturist, collecting and tending all sorts of rare plants to which she became personally attached – in particular a special lily-of-the-valley bed. She planted May trees and vines, and created an entire tulip garden. Now that all the quarrelling with Ralph had ceased, she seemed entirely happy and absorbed in 'my mole hole' as she called the new house. 'The loveliness of this country seems to make one permanently happy,' she wrote to her friend Barbara Bagenal, soon after moving there. 'I am indifferent almost to everything except looking at the downs, and wandering in the garden. There are so many things to do, in the end I do nothing but lie on a sofa like a cat and look at Bulb catalogues, think of gardening, think of painting, contemplate writing letters, talk to Lytton, read the newspapers and gaze eternally out at the downs.'

Once Ham Spray had been bought outright, and they had all moved in there, a deeper sense of security settled on Carrington. She felt more confident that, whatever disruptions might break in upon them from time to time, her life with Lytton could never be effaced. Everything that happened in the world beyond the circle of their home became of diminishing significance to her. She allowed her appearance to deteriorate, using no lip-stick or make-up, and growing rather unkempt and dumpy looking. 'It was as though she had been worn to the bone by life and love,' observed Nicolette Devas, 'eroded by her own cold North Wind.' But she was content. She never lost that quick intensity and wildness of her emotions. As she became more withdrawn, more preoccupied within herself and her immediate surroundings, so her sexual instincts grew more acutely lesbian, and in these later years, most of her closest friends were women. In particular she was at this time violently attracted to Henrietta Bingham, daughter of the United States ambassador at the Court of St James, a beautiful young girl with a perfect oval face, straight dark hair parted in the middle and long black eyelashes shading her brilliantly blue eyes. 'I dream of her six times a week dreams that even my intelligence is appalled by, and I write letters, and tear them up, continually,' Carrington confided to Alix Strachey (11 May 1925). Yet these unrequited fantasy passions do not seem to have caused her much really deep anguish, '– in fact,' she declared, 'I have seldom felt more self-possessed, and at peace with my lower self'. Spiritually she considered herself to be composed and tranquil as never before, and her past life now appeared infinitely muddled compared with the quietly flowing river of the present. Perhaps this was merely an illusion, perhaps merely the outcome of middle age, she reflected. Even so, it was 'rather a relief!' 'One of the comforts of being over thirty, I find, is at last to know what one feels, and only do the things one wants to do!' she wrote to Mark Gertler (7 October 1925). '. . . In reality I am very happy, I love the country, and house so passionately that I find nothing outside it seems to affect me very much. I do more painting than I used to, and now I have a fine studio here.'

The artistic, simple, yet sophisticated atmosphere that saturated their home, formed the best and most sympathetic expression of Carrington's and Lytton's strange life together. They made an eccentric but endearing couple. 'I have the memory of them both in their pleasant, large room at evening half-shadow,' their friend Iris Tree wrote to the author. 'Books, paintings, the sweep of the Downs through the windows, an ancient gibbet on high hill tops, the garden overlooked by a weeping Ilex tree, roses outside and in. And Carrington, rose-cheeked, pouring tea, laughing upwards from under her thatch of hair, licking her lips with a delicate greediness for delicious things and topics. Lytton wrapped in a shawl, purring with delicate malice and enjoyment of thoughts succinctly worded, his hands stretched out transparent to the flames in the firelight.' In the near-by village of Ham, Lytton was looked up to with a peculiar mixture of awe, affection and amusement. Because of his beard he was called 'God'; but he would often descend from his heights, and sit out on the village green surrounded by the village lads, dealing out forbidden cigarettes to them.

Though Lytton's oldest friends were to remember him best in the romantic setting of the Mill House, most people retrospectively picture him at Ham Spray. The eight years he lived here were less secluded than those at Tidmarsh, and the new régime was certainly grander. No longer did it appear to be quite the 'life retired, apart' which he had eulogized on his fortieth birthday. He entertained more, and his guests were more varied. During the daytime his personality might appear frail and apathetic as before, and he could still freeze a party with the depth-charge of his dreadful, destructive silence. But later on in the day he always seemed to wake up, delighting in the company of his young companions, and often playing the fool, putting his beard in his mouth, feigning extreme senility and acting up with fantastic high-spirits. In summer there were badminton matches on a converted tennis court, or gentle games of bowls on the lawn; and indoors, unexpectedly fierce ping-pong contests. For the evening's entertainment, he would sometimes produce one-act farcical playlets for his guests to perform, in which all the men were women, and all the women men, and the ingenious plots hurried the actors into a bewildering, hermaphroditic confusion. The fun of these pieces cannot be recaptured on paper, though there is an occasional neatly inverted epigram which comes over well.

> That proverb more than once you have been told
> Which says that all that glitters is not gold.
> True: but I think this proverb even fitter –
> Gold's always gold, although it may not glitter.[1]

Equally successful were the amateur film shows that they would sometimes prepare. David Garnett remembers a particularly imaginative one produced by Carrington and Stephen Tomlin and filmed by Bernard Penrose. 'The setting was Dr. Turner's private lunatic asylum, where the inmates were experimented upon and reduced to the condition of animals, the subject being Saxon Sydney-Turner's sinister attempts to experiment upon the innocent heroine who was played by Rachel MacCarthy,[2] wearing a daisy chain. The scene of Saxon, as Dr. Turner, peering round the bathroom door at her, had a macabre quality which I have never seen achieved in any other film. My sister-in-law Frances also achieved a success as a human quadruped lunatic wearing riding-boots on her arms.'

A glow encompassed the life at Ham Spray, a bright phosphorescence of spiritual and physical well-being; but it was never an entirely happy home, for the luminous layer of sophisticated 'native simplicity' covered over and partly concealed an area of much personal disappointment and secret regret. Some visitors there sensed this undercurrent of unhappiness beneath the attractive veneer, and to one of them, the novelist Rosamond Lehmann, Lytton confessed in an agonized voice that he would willingly surrender all his literary talent and success for the gift of physical beauty. But though he might never be handsome himself, he could at least surround himself with good-looking companions, and absorb pleasure from their beauty. As he grew older he gathered round him at Ham Spray many young men and women whose company he relished partly for their aesthetic appeal – he loved diffidently to touch their bare arms, to pinch their cheeks, to run his fingers through their hair – and partly from the satisfaction he derived from instructing and enlightening youth. The critical severity

---

[1] From 'A Castle in Spain', acted at Ham Spray one Christmas.

[2] Rachel MacCarthy was the daughter of Desmond MacCarthy. She later married Lord David Cecil, and wrote a long library novel, *Theresa's Choice* (1958).

of his mind would melt away before these young people, and, transported on the rosy clouds of sentimental speculation, he would endow
them with all sorts of fine imaginary qualities and potentialities. And
just as he found youth irresistible, so young people responded to his
enthusiasm, and adored him. In particular they loved his eager
generosity, his unembarrassed zest for fun and enjoyment. 'Is there
any reason why we should be bored *all* afternoon?' he once asked his
seventeen-year-old nephew Richard, then on holiday from Rugby
and supposed to be working at some dull holiday task. 'Let's go to the
theatre!' he added, and took the youngster off to just the kind of show
that would appeal most to a schoolboy, and which he very obviously
enjoyed too. But he could not always hit it off with adolescents, who
still found his appearance and sometimes his manner, too, formidable
and perplexing. The first steps to any intimacy were painfully difficult
for him, and he approached them with an hysterical bashfulness. Another nephew, the artist John Strachey, remembers him 'suddenly
showing me an 18th century French print of a young woman having an
enema, accompanying this gesture with a terrifying giggle. I daresay
that he was trying to get on some sort of terms with me. Unfortunately
the attempt was a failure and I became more scared than ever.'

As a host, Lytton was, in E. M. Forster's words, 'urbane and delightful', but his behaviour towards those of whom he disapproved could
still be deadly. Raymond Mortimer records that 'he possessed an
astonishing power of establishing intimacy. Of persons whom he took
against (sometimes on very inadequate grounds) he could be intolerant
to the point of rudeness, but he was one of the most warmly affectionate
men I have known. It was a great delight to arrive at his Wiltshire
home. . . . He had a particular taste and gift for nonsense, and when
playing some paper-game in the evening, would throw across at one an
improvised quatrain about a friend or a pussy-cat. . . . The mention of
some writer or politician would suddenly reveal, behind the wit and the
warmth, an unpardoning sense of right and wrong. The brisk assurance
of his indignation would have astonished those who thought to dismiss
him as an elegant trifler.'

As time went on, he filled Ham Spray with his rare personality.
There was a fine library, good food and wine, comfort but not luxury,
and always endless talk. Lytton regarded conversation as the pleasantest
occupation in life, 'and indeed,' Lionel Penrose commented, 'with the
Stracheys this ideal could be realised'. This talk revolved mostly round
literature and the arts, and their literary and artistic friends. He had a
gift for making the past actual as he spoke, and his knowledge never
smothered conversation, but nourished it. Friendship brought out the

best in Lytton, and he gradually built up at Ham Spray a private world of his own. His conversation had the merit of discovering hidden excellences in others, a quality to which Virginia Woolf paid tribute when, after Lytton's death, she remarked to Clive Bell: 'Don't you feel there are things one would like to say and never will say now?'

Though inclined to be malicious about people who were not present, Lytton was often extraordinarily warm-hearted towards those he liked, speaking to them about their own subjects and winning their confidence. 'Gradually he must have come to know his friends' secret thoughts about most things, including themselves,' wrote Clive Bell. 'Yet there was seldom anything tense in a conversation with Lytton; it drifted hither and thither in that pleasant atmosphere, gay, truthful (cynical if you will – the terms are interchangeable almost), amusingly and amusedly censorious. Lytton brought a literary and historical flavour into his talk so that, if the past were discussed sometimes as though it were the present, the perplexities and misfortunes of his contemporaries were treated often as though they came from the pages of Saint-Simon or Horace Walpole.'

Because of this outspokenness, his strong moral opinions and his refusal to ingratiate himself with those whose temperaments he found objectionable, he was not liked by everyone. His passion for ribald joking, schoolboy puns and charades embarrassed some, and strangers sometimes found him quite impossible to get on with. He could be markedly inconsistent and disobliging. Stephen Spender, who used to be taken over to Ham Spray by Wogan Philipps and his wife Rosamond Lehmann, certainly thought him the most astonishing of the Bloomsbury Group. 'He combined strikingly their gaiety with their intermittent chilliness,' Spender later recorded. 'Sometimes he would play childish games such as "Up Jenkins", which we played one Christmas. Often he would gossip brilliantly and maliciously. At times there was something insidious about his giggling manner; at times he would sit in his chair without saying a word.'

With more malevolence, Harold Nicolson used to speak of him as a bearded and bitchy old woman, rude rather than witty in society, injecting with his unnaturally treble voice jets of stinging poison into otherwise convivial gatherings.[1] Sir Herbert Read remembers him as 'rather a wistful, querulous figure'. And George Santayana, too, remarked abruptly: 'I am not an admirer of Strachey. I knew him.'

But none of these, in fact, knew him very well. Almost always the

---

[1] Harold Nicolson's wife, Vita Sackville-West, was also antipathetic towards Lytton. On 3 August 1938, she wrote to her husband from Sissinghurst: 'The drooping Lytton must have done its [Bloomsbury's] cause a great deal of harm. I hated Lytton.'

people who shunned him he wanted to shun him. Many of those who expressed really strong antipathy towards him had, it turns out, hardly ever met him. T. E. Lawrence, for example – whom Lytton himself considered a 'tawdry' character and a second-rate writer – appears to have based his aversion solely on a study of Lamb's portrait.[1] Most extraordinary of all is the inspired virulence of Wyndham Lewis, who encountered him casually once or twice in the entire course of their lives, but who nursed an obsessional hatred of him for over forty years. On 22 July 1926, he sent Lytton a letter that provides an almost perfect documentary specimen of the suspicious, paranoiac disease which afflicted him. 'Dear Strachey,' he wrote from 33 Ossington Street, Bayswater. 'It is a very long time since I saw you. I should very much like to see you soon, to discuss two or three literary matters with you.' He went on to suggest that they should meet 'incognito, or rather unobserved', in an unfrequented part of the town, for dinner, 'say at the Great Eastern Hotel Restaurant, called I believe the Great Eastern Restaurant; or for tea in some obscure tea-shop – say near the Law Courts in Covent Garden Market'; and that provisionally they should not divulge their arrangements. There is no record of Lytton having kept this rendezvous, nor of Wyndham Lewis ever going down to Ham Spray; but almost thirty years later – having carefully scrutinized Lytton's physiognomy with his hostile caricaturist's eye (this undoubtedly being one of the literary matters he referred to in his letter) – he published a novel, *Self-Condemned* (1954), in which the character of Cedric Furber, a rich, lonely bachelor in his forties, strict and fussy and old maidish, is founded on Lytton. The description he gives of this heavily bearded idiot-child living down at his country home is a brilliantly perverse and distorted view of what he took to be Lytton's disintegrating futility:

'Certainly Mr. Furber's mask most successfully suggested a distinct, and possibly a new zoological species. . . . A long shapeless black beard . . . stretched downwards from the base of his nose, and threw the onus of expression upon the eyes. . . .

'While he was with this queer creature René always felt that he was

---

[1] In a letter to Robert Graves dated 1 October 1927, T. E. Lawrence compared Lytton Strachey unfavourably with Bernard Shaw. 'It's hardly fair to bracket him [Shaw] with Lytton Strachey,' Lawrence wrote. 'The only portrait which I've seen of him, lately, (deliberate portrait) was that one of William Archer prefixed to three of Archer's plays: and it was direct and wholesome. Strachey is never direct: and not, I think, in himself wholesome. But I don't know him, and my memory of his books tangles itself with my memory of Henry Lamb's marvellous portrait of an outraged wet mackerel of a man, dropped like an old cloak into a basket-chair. If the portrait meant anything it meant that Lytton Strachey was no good.' See *T. E. Lawrence : Letters to his Biographers. Robert Graves and Liddell Hart.*

engaged in field work as an amateur naturalist. It was like being a bird-watcher, and Mr. Furber a great dreary owl. . . . Was he a soft, good-natured, "impish", old shit? No: he was not susceptible of a worldly classification after that manner. One cannot speak of an owl as a shit, for instance.'

Stephen Spender, on his visits to Ham Spray, noted that Lytton was 'delicate and hypochondriacal'. But his health responded well to this new environment; in his letters questions of illness began to take second place to financial topics, and a fall in the barometer was as nothing compared to a fall in the rubber market. 'Unfortunately, I am never sick now,' he complained to Virginia Woolf (11 September 1925), '– only sterile – every Monday, and all other days of the week.'

His manner, too, grew generally gayer and more placid than in earlier times. On hot days in the summer, he would arm himself with a green and white parasol or an enormous wopsical sun-hat, and descend from the safety of the veranda, manipulating his elongated joints as he stepped across the lawn with the slow, calculated elegance of some spectacular and precise secretary bird. Then he would subside into a deck-chair, a crumpled, ageless figure, his long, lanky legs tightly pressed together, his knees on a level with his head, his diaphanous hands resting on his baggy trousers; and he would begin to talk. He seemed, in all he now did, quietly, radiantly, joyful. There existed a flagrant contrast between his extreme physical passivity, and the frantic, delighted extravagance of his gestures. His immobility and stillness were apt suddenly to be disrupted by the most lavish gesticulations when he repudiated some enormity or hailed some audacity that pleased him. Lady Pansy Lamb, who married Henry Lamb in 1928 and met Lytton at Ham Spray for the first time during the previous year, was amazed to find him so happy and amusing after the stories she had heard of his perpetual invalidism and melancholy before the war. Other of his new friends were unable to believe that he had passed through such a prolonged black period. To his niece, the novelist Julia Strachey, he was 'the most vivid personality I have ever seen'; to Noël Coward 'a fascinating person. I liked and admired him enormously.'

In all the tributes of his friends, two qualities stand out as exceptional: his generosity and kindness. He set no value on money, and his success as a biographer meant above all added opportunities to share pleasures with his friends. Without shedding any of his mischievousness, he continued to grow gentler, more serene. He also regained something of the romantic imperialism of his Cambridge and *Spectator* days. David Cecil recalls him in his last years speaking with mild affection of the British Raj. And in a high indignant voice and with long grave face he exclaimed to Frederick Laws: 'When I read Dr. Renier's book *The English – Are They Human?* I felt just like the British lion. I waved my tail and I roared!'

On the surface his religious opinions also appeared to some to have eased slightly, though this was probably not true in fact. Wogan Philipps, a devout atheist, felt disappointed, however, that he did not rigorously rule out all hope of another life. The world, he said, was so extraordinary that no one could deny the possibility of some kind of personal survival. In fact he considered that Christianity, which throughout history had been such a bitter enemy of humanitarianism, was now largely a spent force: it was no longer omnipotent, controversial or even interesting. He had helped to fight the good fight against it, but now the war was over, the victory assured; and perhaps, for that very reason, militant and dogmatic atheists were out of date. 'One may say what one likes (more or less) on religion now,' he wrote to his nephew Richard (5 May 1926), 'but perhaps that is because no one's very much interested in it. There are other, more intimate subjects, which can't be mentioned – or only in the most recondite fashion.'

Elizabeth and Essex and all but six of the essays which make up *Portraits in Miniature* were composed by Lytton while living at Ham Spray. Much of his research, especially for the former, had of course to be done in London, and when working at the British Museum he would stay up in his rooms at 51 Gordon Square. While the younger members and second generation of Bloomsbury – later to be headed socially by Angelica Bell[1] – gave late-night parties at the studio in Fitzroy Street,[2] the old Bloomsbury Group re-formed round 52 Tavistock Square, where Leonard and Virginia Woolf lived on the top two floors above the Hogarth Press. Lytton was very seldom drawn into the rowdy Fitzroy Street parties, but he quite often turned up at the more sedate after-dinner gatherings held in Tavistock Square, and whenever he was expected, Virginia Woolf would add to her invitation cards by way of an inducement the words: *Lytton Strachey is coming.* Roger Fry, Duncan Grant, Maynard Keynes and Lytton himself were the great aces of these evenings, and, more occasionally, Desmond MacCarthy and E. M. Forster. Sometimes they would all assemble at

[1] Angelica Bell, the painter, and daughter of Vanessa Bell, who became the second wife of David Garnett.

[2] No. 8 Fitzroy Street, a studio once occupied by Whistler and by Sickert, into which Duncan Grant had moved after the war. Not all the parties here, at Taviton Street, or at 46 Gordon Square were confined to Bloomsbury and Cambridge alone. David Garnett remembers seeing Picasso talking to Douglas Fairbanks senior at one gathering; and at another, everyone formed an enormous circle, while, at the centre, two particular guests were left to introduce themselves – Lytton and the film actress Mary Pickford.

Vanessa Bell's house – congregations usually not exceeding six or seven in number, one or two of whom had been invited from the younger generation. No drinks were provided except coffee, and although the arrangements were quite informal, the unspoken purpose of these meetings was to conduct good conversation. The mellow, harmonious effect of these late-night conversaziones was of a well-practised orchestra, its members all seeming to share a very similar attitude to life, and displaying a pleasure in their friends' performances indistinguishable from their own.

Lytton's entertaining while in London was most often done at his clubs. John Lehmann, who had been introduced to him by Dadie Rylands, and who saw him fairly regularly during these later years, has told how he would meet him at his rooms in Gordon Square, or at the Athenaeum,[1] and encourage him to recount many fond and naughty stories of Leonard Woolf. 'I was in a glow of pleasure and amusement,' he wrote of their visits to the Athenaeum, 'as Lytton, in his high, thin but authoritative voice ordered an excellent wine and we settled down to a long discussion about the past of Bloomsbury and Lytton's Cambridge days, about poetry (which Lytton wrote copiously, though modestly and in secret), or modern French literature, in which he sadly found all the vices of German literature and very few of the great traditional French virtues. I also visited him at Ham Spray, and explored endlessly in his library while he worked, and afterwards would go for walks with him, during which we renewed our discussion – or rather I renewed my eager questioning and he his judicious and witty answers to the ever-unsatisfied disciple.'

Lytton was always thankful when, his researches over, he could return again to the serenity and comfort of Ham Spray. He had created there an environment exactly moulded to his tastes and temperament, and in these sympathetic surroundings, his shy personality, which was never completely liberated in his writings, could convey itself most memorably to his friends. 'One remembered afterwards his doubts and hesitations, his refusals to dogmatize, his flights of fantasy, his high, whispering voice fading out in the middle of a sentence, and forgot the very definite and well-ordered mind that lay underneath,' Gerald Brenan wrote. '. . . One observed a number of discordant features – a feminine sensibility, a delight in the absurd, a taste for exaggeration and melodrama, a very mature judgement, and then some lack of human

---

[1] In the first volume of his autobiography, *The Whispering Gallery* (1955), John Lehmann refers to the Athenaeum as being Lytton's club. In fact Lytton was only elected to the Athenaeum, under Rule 2, in 1931, just before his death. He never had the opportunity of using this club, and the Athenaeum allowed his executors off his entrance fee.

substance, some hereditary thinness in the blood that at times gave people who met him an odd feeling in the spine. He seemed almost indecently lacking in ordinariness.'

His tall, lean body, the great tawny beard and high voice, the charming and impudent smile that would flit across his narrow face to greet some subtly barbed observation, the soft and steady gravity of the eyes, witty yet serious, brooding behind his tortoiseshell spectacles, all went to make up a unique physical personality that infiltrated every fibre of the house with its odd, congenial presence. Perhaps the most vivid evocation of him there has been given by another visitor, F. L. Lucas. 'That tall red-bearded figure,' he recalled, 'with the exquisite hands, delicate yet looking so young for his age, who walked the fields of Ham Spray, had a foreign touch about his appearance, as of a Russian landowner; or like some pictured Jehovah, terrifying to strangers, who would yet relax at any moment into an amused Epicurean Zeus.'

2

ATTACHMENT

When Lytton returned with Pippa from France early in August, the renovations to Ham Spray had greatly advanced, and he decided to risk moving in. But there was still plenty of work to be done, and it was not until the autumn that he felt safe in reporting to Ottoline (8 November 1924) that 'we are established here pretty solidly now, and it seems a very satisfactory place – surrounded by all that is most romantic'. Except for one trip over to Garsington at the beginning of the summer – for the sake of the tulips and the undergraduates that flourished so abundantly there in that season – movement had been impossible. But by the start of the winter, the old régime seemed to be properly reasserting itself again around the new environment. Lytton was beginning to work regularly at his essays for the *Nation and Athenaeum*; and he resumed once more the familiar series of visitations[1] – to Mells, to Eleanor, to Garsington again and to Clare College, where, as the guest of Sebastian Sprott, he encountered another Victorian biographer, Hector Bolitho. 'There were so many people in a small room, packed tight as asparagus in a bunch,' recorded Bolitho who had

---

[1] 'Lytton came back from Lady Horner's on Wednesday,' Ralph Partridge wrote to Frances Marshall (19 September 1924). 'He had been to see Longleat with Mr [Stephen] McKenna and Lord Hugh Cecil, and had to lend them 2/6 to tip the housekeeper. He began a flirtation with McKenna, and the French governess fell in love with him and writes him admiring letters. . . .'

driven over to meet him, 'so I escaped to the kitchen with my drink, and a book. I had seen Lytton Strachey in the bedlam, looking like a bewildered owl released into a cage of parrots. He also wished to escape, for I looked up from my book and saw him at the door. He whispered, "Is this the kitchen?" I glanced at the stove and sink and answered, "Yes". He said, "I suppose they cook things here", and then vanished.'[1]

Bedlam of one kind or another had never really suited him, and least of all now. His journeys to London these days were always 'enthralling, but also wrecking'; and he seldom felt happy there for very long.

He was by now greatly lionized, but the vulgarity, rowdiness and sociality there quickly wore him out, and he would hurry back with evident relief to the haven of Ham Spray. For Ham Spray was unique: a most perfect and amenable vehicle for leading the contented life. Yet already, by the summer of 1925, his existence there with Carrington and Ralph had become subject to many subtle new strains and aberrations. Unlike the single crisis at Tidmarsh, there were no dramatic scenes, no sudden revelations, no exploding storms of passion and repression. Everything was quiet; quiet, open and uneasy. Outwardly, Carrington and Ralph had regained their love and affection for each other, while Lytton himself, so Carrington told Alix (11 May 1925) 'grows more and more benign, and charming, which means I suppose one is on the brink of some unseen volcanoe'.

Yet it was not an unseen volcano that was at work within Ham Spray, but an interior change in the chemistry of their lives together. Much developed since the pioneer days of 'the Tidmarsh experiment', and now removed to a modern well-equipped laboratory, their central nucleus had grown strangely unstable, had started to expand and attract into its field other particles that adhered and quickly built up a molecular structure of dangerous complexity.

They were not bored with one another, the three of them; but they seemed to have explored every logarithmic variation of mutual develop-ment, and now looked outside their small triple relationship for fulfil-ment and excitement. Each one wanted to promote that part of his or her emotional life that was kept separate from the other two, so as to achieve happiness without disarranging the triangular union they all prized so highly. But their independent passions and adventures *did*

---

[1] Bolitho continues: 'I thought this affected and odd until many years later when I found a paragraph in Frank Swinnerton's *The Georgian Literary Scene* in which he wrote of the "shuddering hand" with which Strachey "drew a curtain between himself and current vulgarity", and of his knowing, and wishing to know, "nothing at all", of whatever happens in the every-day houses of modern England.'

affect this union, demonstrating how intimately, how illogically, how vulnerably, their total lives were inter-connected. Tidmarsh had provided an unorthodox common ground for their oddly assorted personalities and divergent tastes. Ham Spray should be an arena where, jointly and individually, they might sport and enjoy themselves, indulge their appetites and express their feelings without endangering each other. They were determined that the sensitive domestic cell that enclosed them so delightfully there should not imperil or limit their private pursuits; they did not think these private pursuits should interfere with the happiness of anyone else.

Ralph Partridge was the first to fret against what he felt to be the restrictive influence of Ham Spray. His devotion to Carrington and Lytton never really faltered or diminished, but he knew that the two of them could never satisfy his whole nature, and, feeling hemmed in by their demanding practical reliance on him, he was sometimes caustic over their shortcomings, their lack of self-sufficiency. This irritation had been greatly aggravated when, towards the end of 1923, he had met a beautiful, dark-haired young woman, and gradually fallen deeply in love with her. Frances Marshall was the sister-in-law of David Garnett, very lively and intelligent, and utterly unlike the superficial type of pretty girl with whom he had been carrying on brief meaningless affairs during the last year. Though 'one of the prettiest girls one could find anywhere', she possessed a good educated mind, had read philosophy at Cambridge, and now worked in Francis Birrell and David Garnett's bookshop in Taviton Street, Bloomsbury. It was here that she had first encountered Ralph when he was travelling books for the Hogarth Press, and soon she was responding to his affection. But she would not permit his advances to proceed too far – a precaution that earned his respect for her and deepened his fondness. As he had begun to fall in love, so his retrospective attitude to Gerald Brenan started to soften; and it was indirectly due to Frances Marshall's influence over him that he had taken Carrington out to Yegen. They had been determined to eradicate once and for ever the bitterness that had divided them all; and they succeeded in doing even better than this. On arriving there, they had learnt that Gerald was intending, with his great-aunt's help, to return to England in the spring, and Ralph had magnanimously given his blessing to his friend then carrying on a full affair with Carrington. This having been settled to everyone's agreement, he had felt at liberty to pursue Frances Marshall, who came to meet them in Paris that January on their way back to Tidmarsh. Lytton, worried that this encounter might lead to trouble, had also hurried out there, and the four of them spent an enjoyable few days without any trace of friction.

The new molecule was to have Lytton at its centre, Ralph and Carrington revolving round him, and Gerald and Frances spinning in a wider orbit around the three of them. But in the months that followed, Lytton, incapacitated by persistent illness, had been unable to steer their overloaded craft, calm and unharmed, through the increasingly complicated shoals and reefs. Ralph's letters to Frances over the last months at Tidmarsh had revealed very clearly his gloom and vexation, prompted by the undying sense of responsibility he felt towards both Carrington and Lytton. He was baulked by the surrounding vagaries and infirmities. 'I'm restless and uneasy without you,' he confessed to Frances that spring. '. . . It's partly because I can't get absorbed directly into the current of this life – it's not very absorbing on a squelching day like this – you seem to have attached most of my interest in anything. . . . I feel silent before Lytton, and Carrington has an awful headache and stays in bed where I can only look after her and not talk to her.'

Then Lytton himself was struck down. For weeks he lay in his bedroom, with a bandage round his head, groaning, and looking like a wounded soldier. Carrington, in despair, had been worn out by her infinite duties round and around his bed, and Ralph, who tried to help, felt smothered by the sickly atmosphere. 'There have been lugubrious doings here,' he told Frances (8 March 1924). '. . . Pippa has come down for the week-end and we talk of diseases the whole time. Apparently Lytton used to get ill like this at the age of five and from then onwards – it is only in the last ten years that he's been free of disease. We now anticipate he will go back to this earlier condition, if we do not make still gloomier prophecies. It takes two people really to look after him, and a doctor, and we never stir out as it's too gloomy going for solitary walks. You *will* come down next weekend whatever happens, won't you? It's a grey sort of house to come to, but I do want you, if you can bear it. . . . What a bloody curse illness is – it ties everyone up for nothing. I'm not really depressed, only cross . . .'

But long after Lytton recovered, Ralph remained far from content. His thoughts had invariably been focused elsewhere; he could never get interested in the people or the conversations, or become re-immersed in the goings-on at the Mill House. 'I'm like a lost soul without you,' he had lamented to Frances (22 June 1924). 'I can't do anything but talk to Carrington about you.' Tidmarsh had appeared lifeless and empty, and he had felt sadly isolated from everything that happened there – as if he were watching all that went on beside him through the reverse end of a telescope. It was impossible, unnatural, for him to bisect his life into two water-tight compartments. He could not do it.

But although Ralph had experienced few difficulties over introducing Frances's name, often rather tactlessly, into their discussions at Tidmarsh, he had been assailed by uncharacteristic qualms about inviting her down there, and whenever doing so had given as his excuse the fact that she would be helping Carrington with the move to Ham Spray. He had been as eager as a schoolboy for them all to get on well together, but knew in his bones that probably they would not. And as it turned out, Frances's visits were not really a success. Both Lytton and Carrington could not help but regard her as a potential danger to their way of life. Besides, she was not really their type of person – emotionally too well-balanced and unneurotic for Carrington, and imaginatively too prosaic and unfanciful for Lytton. But they had been kind to her, over-kind perhaps, and tried to conceal their slight antipathy, hoping that Ralph's feelings for her would soon pass. Lytton's attitude towards her was at all times impeccable, while Carrington, who could not camouflage her prejudices so well, had gone out of her way to stress her friendship and excuse her occasional uncontrollable lapses. 'It is very charming of you, you know, to come and help me (us) at Ham Spray,' she had written to her about this time, 'and you must forgive my crabbidness which is only the reaction to this commotion of a move. Really I am the soul of friendliness! My love. C.'

But by the time they were ready to transfer to the new house, the state of affairs had given no signs of improving, and they had left Tidmarsh with sharply differentiated reactions that did not augur well for this fresh chapter in their lives. 'I feel completely out of it all,' Ralph had written to Frances (17 July 1924). '. . . I'm not intoxicated with delight to be off, or harrowed by regrets. I'm merely uprooted like a tree, and waiting to grow some more roots. Carrington has tears in her eyes very often but I'm not moved like that in the very least. . . . I feel uneasy because I'm engaged on something that you can't really share with me, it's such a waste of time and an irritation to the nerves. I *shall* be glad when I get back into the world again.' For Carrington the world was Lytton, Tidmarsh or Ham Spray; but for Ralph it was London and Frances. He saw the shell of the Mill House, utterly dreary and inert, and he saw the debris of uninhabited Ham Spray – and his heart sank. What odds did it make? Both, to him, were dried-up husks of houses, and he had little enough place in either of them. His exposed and tender roots sought not this stony ground, but the fertile soil of London.

·   ·   ·   ·   ·

Ralph had counted on their suppressed troubles being greatly alleviated, and some amicable sense of balance restored, by the arrival of Gerald Brenan, without whom their inter-dependent community was, so far, lop-sided. Gerald reached London towards the end of May 1924, taking a flat lent to him by Roger Fry in Fitzroy Street, next to Sickert's old studio. Almost at once the new régime was put into operation. Carrington would travel up every second week-end, or else Gerald would go down to Ham Spray, and for a short time took rooms near by at Shalbourne. But the experiment did not work out as Ralph had planned. Next to Lytton, Carrington had loved Gerald better than anyone because, while he stayed in Spain, he shared with Lytton one quality that was always irresistible to her – inaccessibility. But after Gerald landed in England, her passion for him began to lessen. He had belonged to her daydream world, and now, rather inconveniently, he had materialized as a living entity. To try and preserve the illusion of his veiled elusiveness, she made herself obstructive, out of reach, and saw much less of him than he had obviously bargained for. She had so little time, she would explain. There was her painting, and her life with Lytton; and when she did come up to London, she had many other friends to see – Henrietta Bingham, for instance, who has 'killed my desires for less jeunes garcons pretty completely'.

For Gerald, on the other hand, there was only work – a biography of St Teresa – which was going badly, and Carrington herself. During the fortnightly week-ends that they spent together in Fitzroy Street, Ralph would occasionally drop in to spend the night with them, and together the three of them would try and hit on some verbal solution to their problems. 'I was so miserable when I left you,' Ralph wrote to Frances after one such visit (4 July 1924), '. . . I went to Fitzroy Street. Carrington and Gerald in their respective beds, grunting with sleep – gloomy mutterings between us and then an uneasy tossing night of it. . . . I had a long talk with C. – but *not* about you this time, about Gerald and her and me. A sad talk that, too, because she thinks she ought not to go on seeing him like this; he doesn't settle down or try to find new friends while he thinks he is going to see her. They have decided not to meet again for a month. I hardly come into it, as it is between themselves they have decided this. Only it makes me melancholy that relations are so difficult between people who are fond of each other. That Gerald can't be happy unless he has too little of Carrington or too much for him to stand. My darling, I can't bear the spectre of unhappiness that one sees stalking about.'

So the confusion thickened, and the opportunities for unhappiness rapidly multiplied. Every tension set up in any part of the molecule, between any two of its atoms, would affect each and all of them. Carrington, with that peculiarly possessive yet independent nature of hers, would not give up Gerald, who had fallen more deeply in love with her than ever. She was still leading a full married life with Ralph; but it was perfectly natural for her to love several people, men and women, at the same time, and wish to enjoy sexual intercourse with all of them; though, as she was not strongly sexed, not very often. She also particularly wanted to see Gerald for another reason – to talk to him about Ralph! Now that everything was being conducted openly, the discussions between them all rolled and meandered on without end. Carrington, however, shrank from burdening Lytton with her worries. She knew how much he appreciated serenity, and so she confided in Gerald – in the same manner as Ralph confided in her – selecting the one person whom these confidences would hurt most. She was troubled, she told him, about Frances's growing influence over Ralph. Her own jealousy of Frances, though suppressed, was causing her to fall in love with her husband all over again. As even her affair with Gertler had shown, she never willingly gave up anyone, and as she sensed Ralph moving slowly away from her, so her emotions over him were freshly aroused. This was hardly encouraging news for Gerald, who had, in any case, been presented with many opportunities for remarking her renewed preference for Ralph over himself. Then she was worried, too, she went on to explain, about Lytton's attitude. If Ralph were to leave Ham Spray and go off and live with Frances, how would Lytton respond? Would he stay on with her, or might he even now leave?

This last fear, at least, seemed largely unwarranted. For Lytton also had not been inactive during these months and to add to the complications at Ham Spray now felt that he, too, was falling in love again. The person to have awakened these emotions in him was Philip Ritchie, the young Oxford undergraduate whom he had first met and liked so well at Garsington. Each time he saw him after that, Lytton's admiration grew, until he pronounced Ritchie to be 'one of the nicest people in the world'. He was not a handsome boy – some might have described him as ugly – but he had a peculiarly inverted kind of charm which his irregular features helped to bring out. He was gauche, but his manner was consistently individual and endearing; he was absolutely unsentimental, but noticeably warm-hearted; he was lively company, intelligent and unpretentious; and, when Lytton got to know him, he was being pursued by Princess Bibesco – a state of affairs with which he unconvincingly pretended to be bored to death, but which gratified his social if not his sexual tastes, and ministered to a mild and comical sense of persecution which he ingeniously adapted as a conversational ploy. It was not difficult for Lytton to see in him a younger, perhaps a superior version of himself, and his feelings of amiability soon deepened into love. 'I assure you he's a great rarity,' he wrote to Carrington (17 October 1924). 'It's true he's not immediately attractive to look at, and that he probably has no taste in pictures; but he's intellectual (a good point); and he's sensual (also good); and he gives not the slightest value to anything but what is really valuable (very good indeed).'

While on one of his visits to Garsington, Lytton had been introduced by Ritchie to his closest friend, another Oxford young man called Roger Senhouse, a romantic creature of extremely good looks, 'with a melting smile and dark grey eyes'. The two of them, Ritchie and Senhouse, were practically inseparable, and Lytton soon formed with them both a very intimate triangular friendship.

And so, quite early on, the new molecule formed round Ham Spray. By the spring of 1925, Philip Ritchie and Roger Senhouse had become almost permanent week-enders there, while Gerald Brenan and Frances Marshall would also come down once or twice a month. The outer structure of this molecule, for the time being, remained firm, but within it there raged a ceaseless pushing, pulling, quivering, throbbing commotion. Part of this activity was set up by Stephen Tomlin, who, though not as yet sucked into its circumference, spiralled around the outer rim emitting shock waves to which each of the atoms would react differently but always with an electric sensitivity. A frequent visitor to Ham Spray, he was devoted to Lytton, whom he came to regard as something of a substitute for his aloof and magisterial father. Lytton returned this affection; but Ralph, who thought him a born trouble-maker, distrusted and disliked him, while Carrington's emotions were more mixed because of his being, like herself, unhappily infatuated with the enigmatic Henrietta Bingham.

These anomalies churned up a constant air of pending and indefinable crisis, a calm but perpetual expectation of the unexpected. The position seemed to change almost hourly. One day, for example, Gerald and Carrington were pronounced to be getting on much better; twenty-four hours later, out of the blue, Gerald wrote to announce that he was not going to see Carrington again for at least two years – then, the following week-end, he turned up as usual without explanation. Occasionally, too, Ralph might suspect Frances of favouring some rival to himself, and ventilate his ill-humour on Lytton's friends. Meanwhile Lytton himself, caught in a 'semi-embrace' with Philip Ritchie, would wander off to deliberate as to whether in fact he was really in love after all, and if so, with whom. Carrington responded violently to every shift, especially when she and Lytton were apart, now appearing ecstatic and open-hearted, now solitary, fearful.

And over everything, like a balm, there flowed a river of conversation. From Friday night to Sunday night they swapped a mixture of analysis, gossip, scandal and advice; and from Monday back to Friday again they continued the exchanges on page after page of writing-paper. These colloquies, passionate and amused, would leap from general propositions to private speculation and back again with startling rapidity. As they sat in the garden, paced the veranda or pursued one another round the ping-pong table, the talk of psycho-analysis and masturbation, of jealousy, inquisitiveness, the prevalence of homosexuality, the peculiarities of their friends' love-affairs, sped on and on, suspended only occasionally by some universally recognized *pièce de résistance* – a recitation by Lytton, for example, from Stendhal's *Psychologie de l'Amour*, or a charade by Sheppard giving an imitation of poor Ottoline pretending to be as *petite* as Lydia Lopokova, or a performance by Marjorie Strachey singing nursery rhymes, hymns and traditional songs in a way that, without altering the words, made them sound extraordinarily obscene.

These cabarets and conversations often helped to relax the underlying tension, reducing the magnitude of their problems and temporarily dissolving their perplexities into laughter. Yet the spectre of a pervading unhappiness still stalked the rooms and grounds of Ham Spray, and Lytton was occasionally glad to escape for a week-end elsewhere. Early in 1925 he made the first of several attendances at David Garnett's new Cranium Club,[1] at the opening meeting of which his name had been proposed and 'carried by acclamation'. Here many of the younger Bloomsberries would meet once a month and, according to Carrington, 'try and discuss Einstein but actually sing "Rendel my son" at the Piano'. Early in March, too, he went to stay for the very last time at Garsington, which Ottoline was then preparing to leave on her return, a little later that year, to London. He had also planned a trip to Sicily in April with Carrington, but an attack of neuritis supervened, putting him against Sicily and in favour of the convalescent airs of Lyme Regis. Here he retired with Sebastian Sprott, while Carrington set off with Ralph, Frances and Harry Norton's sister[2] for a walking tour of Provence. 'We saw Arles, Nîmes and the Pont du Gard, Saint Remy, Carvillon and Tarascon,' she recorded afterwards. 'I climbed a

---

[1] The Cranium Club was named after Thomas Love Peacock's Mr Cranium in *Headlong Hall*, who personifies the cult of phrenology.

[2] J. E. Norton, the Gibbon scholar and author of *A Bibliography of the Works of Edward Gibbon* (1940).

mountain 2,500 feet high, and walked 20 miles the same day, I came back with no voice, a sore throat, and completely exhausted. But I think in spite of the exhaustion, it set one up rather. Spiritually I feel very composed and tranquil. . . . In Paris I completely collapsed to an Exquisite Spanish actress Raquel Mellor. Fortunately she is inaccessible.'

Lytton, also recovering his composure and tranquillity in Lyme Regis, was enjoying a more sedentary holiday. He and Sebastian Sprott would play piquet, read the trial of Leopold and Loeb, sometimes brave the remorseless east wind, and sit up talking late into the night – Lytton dreading to go to bed since he had brought his hot-water bottle without its stopper. 'There seems to be hardly another soul here,' he reported to Pippa (29 March 1925), '– except the town crier; and the Cobb is desolate.' Yet there were advantages to be gained from this solitude. He had been 'run down', he decided, but now he felt brisker and began to shed 'that dreary state of feebleness and incompetence, physical, mental, and moral, which at times seemed almost more exasperating than a downright disease'.

Another advantage was that, once separated from Carrington and Ralph, he was better able to indicate those feelings that he was constitutionally incapable of showing face to face – feelings which, even now, they might be tempted to overlook. 'Among other things I've felt a certain inability to express my feelings properly,' he admitted in a letter to Ralph (3 April 1925), '– I don't know why – and I've been afraid you may have thought, or dimly imagined, that they might have changed in some way – owing to Philip, perhaps, or other things. But it is not in the least so. All I feel for you is exactly the same, only strengthened by the passage of time; and it would be useless for me to try to say how much you and Carrington are to me. I can hardly imagine how I would exist without you both. Perhaps all this is unnecessary, and merely the result of the depression and fear of low vitality. But in any case you will understand.'

Love, that convenient monosyllable, was what Lytton hinted at – though he could not bring himself to write it down. But another, less rhapsodic term defines his attitude far more precisely – *attachment*. They were attached to one another by many ties of understanding, mutual affection, need. Ralph had become an essential part of Ham Spray. And though Lytton might from time to time wish to escape from its enervations, he cherished his home, and wanted above all to pursue his ideal way of life there, now being threatened by the bombardment of so many exterior forces. In Gerald Brenan and Frances Marshall he saw two particularly dangerous and disruptive influences; but he recognized their right to enter into the life there along with Philip Ritchie and Roger Senhouse. If the present unwieldy molecule, its atoms dedicated to eternal motion, could be held together by the gravitational pull of his own love and affection, then he could be counted on to do all in his power to preserve its equilibrium.

But he feared for the future. How long could their 'singular amatory arrangements' continue? How long could this vibrating level of intensity persist without rending asunder the whole perilous architecture of their lives? If he could himself be happy, then perhaps he might spread the bond of that happiness to the others, and entangle them in a magic web of harmony and stability. More than this he could do nothing but watch and wait as the entire structure shook, twisted and jerked in a restless, unending inner ferment.

3

THE MONKEY AND THE GOOSE

After Lytton's fame and prestige had been enlarged by *Queen Victoria*, he was frequently approached by publishers and academics asking him to perform various commissions. These, unless they were to help some friend, he very rarely accepted. Thus, although he did contribute an Introduction to George Rylands's anthology *Words and Poetry* (1928), he refused to provide Introductions to Paul Valéry's *Le Serpent*, to C. K. Scott Moncrieff's translation of Proust's *A la Recherche du Temps Perdu*, and, at the invitation of Richard Aldington, to a new translation of *La Vie Privée du Maréchal, Duc de Richelieu*. He also turned down the suggestion that, for the fee of a thousand pounds, he should reduce the six-volume Monypenny and Buckle Life of Disraeli to a two-volume edition.

One proposal, however, which did appeal to him came from his old Cambridge acquaintance, John Dover Wilson, who since 1921 had been at work on the now celebrated *New Shakespeare*. His co-editor, Arthur Quiller-Couch, had been forced to resign his post early on owing to ill-health, and in 1928 Dover Wilson received the consent of the Cambridge University Press to invite Lytton to write the Introductions to these volumes. 'He seemed quite attracted by the proposition,' Professor Dover Wilson told the author, 'and came, complete with the famous red beard which I had not yet seen, to discuss the matter over a cup of tea with me at King's College in the Strand where I was then Professor of Education.' After their conversation and a talk with

S. C. Roberts, Lytton accepted this offer, on the stipulation that the Cambridge University Press should allow Chatto and Windus to reprint his contributions. But this the publishers refused to do, and the agreement had to be called off.

His old university, Liverpool, had also been sounding him out as to whether he would like to succeed Oliver Elton in the Chair of English Literature there. Again he declined. He had not been happy at Liverpool; he seldom got on well with dons and academics; and he had always been careful to avoid the fate of those great scholars of the eighteenth century who 'sat bent nearly double, surrounded by four circles of folios, living to edit Hesychius and confound Dr. Hody, and dying at last with a stomach full of sand'. His voice, too, still presented a handicap and virtually debarred him from taking up any appointment that involved public lecturing. When in 1928 J. R. Ackerly had invited him up to Savoy Hill to record for sound radio a number of his essays, it had failed him altogether. 'I was filled with such feelings of guilt and remorse over my behaviour in the broadcasting', he wrote apologizing to Ackerly after the disastrous audition, 'that I lapsed into what I fear was churlish silence. Forgive me.'

The possible failure of his voice worried him also in connexion with one of the few offers he did accept over these years. This was an invitation from the vice-chancellor of Cambridge, A. C. Seward, to deliver the Leslie Stephen Lecture in June 1925. He had at once consented; then, as his qualms grew, wrote again asking whether, to amplify his thin falsetto, he might make use of a loudspeaker. The vice-chancellor's reply was discouraging. 'We have no loudspeaker and from what I have heard of the use of the instrument in London I feel rather shy of suggesting an installation of one here.' Lytton's doubts now redoubled alarmingly. Would anyone be able to hear him? He should never have agreed to it. Towards the end of May, he developed a sore throat, diagnosed by his doctor as being tonsillitis, and by James as a mere hysteria formation aimed at his lecture. But his aim, if it were the latter, had been over-eager, for by early June he had completely recovered, and there was no alternative but to go through with the ordeal.

When the day arrived, Lytton delivered his lecture with great character and attack, displaying not the least sign of nervousness. He knew exactly what he wanted to say, and how to say it. For the choice of subject and the actual composition of the lecture were comparatively easy matters. He had selected Alexander Pope. His deep and lasting admiration for the poetry of Pope dated from his earliest Cambridge days. Often in the years since then he had thought of writing about him, and in fact had treated him briefly in several of his essays. The fullest and most comprehensive statement of his attitude to Pope, the man, was set forth in a Spectatorial review (20 November 1909) of George Paston's *Mr. Pope: His Life and Times*. From this article it appears that Lytton considered Pope's notoriously perverted temper and crooked habit of mind to be simply manifestations of that sickly condition which had twisted his body and made one long disease of his whole life. 'He was,' Lytton explained, 'in modern parlance, a névrosé. Abnormally sensitive to stimuli, his frail organization responded frantically to the slightest outward touch. If you looked at him he would spit poison, and he would wind himself into an endless mesh-work of intrigues and suspicions if you did not. But it was not only in malignity and contortions that Pope's sensitiveness showed itself; throughout his life he gave proof of a tenderness which was something more than a merely selfish susceptibility, and of a power of affection as unmistakable as his power of hate. In spite of hysterical bickerings and downright quarrels, his relations with the Blounts were animated by a sincere and generous friendship; with all his egoism and vanity, he never lost his profound admiration for the only one of his contemporaries who was as great a writer as himself – Swift; and his devotion to his mother forms one of the most touching episodes in the whole history of letters.'

Lytton saw Pope's career as the battleground for discordant emotions, the intensity of which was the intensity of disease. Here was territory well known to him. There was much of Pope in Lytton's style and point of view. The first care in their writing was for sound. Bathos, with its sudden comic descent from the sublime to the absurd, was a favourite device they had in common. A certain discrepancy, too, between mind and emotion shows itself in the juxtaposition of studiously compressed passages making use of the shortest, plainest words, and passages of less expressive ornament in the rococo fashion. Lytton's comments upon the ultimate, artificial simplicity of Pope's early Pastorals call to mind the sort of literary criticism that in recent times has been applied to his own prose style: 'Everything is obvious. The diction is a mass of *clichés*; the epithets are the most commonplace possible; the herds low, the brooks murmur, the flocks pant and remove, the retreats are green, and the flowers blush. The rhythm is that of a rocking-horse; and the sentiment is mere sugar.'

Coleridge has observed that the personal satires of Pope lack the judicial tone so effectively assumed by Dryden. Lytton, on the other hand, preferred Pope to Dryden because, he tells us, the great genius of the latter 'with all his strength and all his brilliance, lacked one quality without which no mastery of the couplet could be complete – the elegance of perfect finish'. This preference for Pope's finer technical merit, formal beauty and decorative polish betrays something of that feminine taste which Lytton shared with his subject. To his way of thinking, Dryden's verse exhibited a comparatively mundane turn of mind. Yet *The Dunciad*, modelled on Dryden's *Mac Flecknoe*, altogether lacks that largeness and geniality of that satire. Dryden's invective has little of the refined delicacy of Pope's and practically none of its malice. He sweeps forward with the undiscriminating fury of an avalanche, while the feline and meticulous Pope hits unerringly at the same sensitive spot again and again.

Both in his early Spectatorial essay and in the Leslie Stephen Lecture, Lytton expresses astonishment at the miraculous manner in which Pope had fitted the language of passion into the smooth, ordered, conventional eighteenth-century couplet. Here, he reasoned, lay absolute proof of the poet's supreme genius. How had he achieved the apparently impossible? His dextrous handling of words and rhythms increasingly absorbed Lytton – 'those fine shades', as he had enviously described them, 'and delicate gradations of sound and expression of which the secret is only known to the true artist'. This was the secret, the mysterious process of blending unstinted passion with cool detachment into a perfect literary form, that, sixteen years later, drew him back to the subject of Pope.

In his five-thousand-word address, Lytton made no effort to rewrite Pope's biography, to provide a critical conspectus of his poetry or to sum up the full nature of his genius. Brief, emphatic, teeming with vivacious imagery and scintillating comment, the lecture was designed primarily to be heard rather than read. Its main theme involved an examination of Pope's very unheroic malignity and of the heroic couplet in which he gave that malignity its undying expression. Although, therefore, the lecture was more detailed and scholarly, it had little of the breadth or balance of his earlier review, ignoring, as it did, that explosive split in Pope's nature, which is frequently reflected in those extraordinary antitheses of his couplets.

Lytton did not primarily concern himself with the disorders of the poet, but with the exquisite structural order of his poetry. It is true that, in the opening part of the lecture, he does introduce Pope to his audience as perhaps the most representative of all eighteenth-century writers; but the picture is still essentially a literary one. Consequently, in this pen-and-ink world, he experiences no discomfort, only an appreciative delight at the agonies of Pope's victims; and he communicates no human feeling for the morbidly sensitive poet always throwing stones at others from within his own glass house. 'To us,' he declared, 'after two

R

centuries, the agonies suffered by the victims of Pope's naughtiness are a matter of indifference; the fate of Pope's own soul leaves us cold.' Similarly his picture of the eighteenth century as the most civilized that our history has known, is a literary as opposed to a general evocation. By emphasizing this particular aspect of the age, he can bring out more clearly Pope's gratifying ascendancy over the upper classes – a supreme example of the high respect literature then commanded. The immense success of Pope's translation of Homer, he writes, 'was a sign of the times. Homer's reputation was enormous: was he not the father of poetry? The literary snobbery of the age was profoundly impressed by that. Yes, it was snobbery, no doubt; but surely it was a noble snobbery which put Homer so very high in the table of precedence – probably immediately after the Archbishop of Canterbury.' Quite so. Yet the eighteenth century was not solely the era of the sophisticated Walpole and the genteel Chesterfield, but also of Jonathan Wild and Jack Sheppard and, before the magisterial work of Fielding, a reign of unsurpassed cut-throat terror by night throughout London. For outside the polite world of the upper classes, it is easy to forget that, during the mid-eighteenth century, England was a wild and uncivilized land.

In his Spectatorial review, Lytton had been careful to point out that Pope possessed 'a power of affection as unmistakable as his power of hate'. His Leslie Stephen Lecture deals only with Pope's malicious side. There is more than one probable explanation for this. Although Pope did on occasions express his tenderness and affection in verse – the lovely lines to Gray, 'The Epistle of Sappho to Phaon', and his 'Universal Prayer' are all fine examples – his feelings, as Lytton rightly observed in 'English Letter Writers', 'were far more easily roused into expression by dislike than by affection. Scorn, hatred, malice, rage – these were the emotions which, with Pope, boiled over almost naturally into fervent language; it is through its mastery of all the shades of these emotions that his verse has gained its immortality.' And so, since his lecture is not really concerned with Pope as a love or metaphysical poet, Lytton conveys the impression that he was a monster of malignity, and ignores to the point of contradiction that amiable side of his temperament underlined by Johnson's statement that 'in the duties of friendship he [Pope] was zealous and constant; those who loved him once, continued their kindness'. In earlier years, when he felt more closely akin to Pope in his bitterness and sickly sensitivity, Lytton had been anxious to provide a sympathetic interpretation of this malice, to uncover the frustrated generosity and love which it often concealed. But now that he was happier and better in health, he does not identify himself with Pope so readily. He is more of a spectator relishing, and urging others to relish, the rapier thrusts so excellently driven home, and interspersing his cries of appreciation with a more learned discourse on the art of fencing.

By depicting Pope as a fiendish monkey, he created for himself something of an artificial problem. 'What does seem strange,' he admits, 'is that Pope's contemporaries should have borne with him as they did.' His victims included some of the most powerful and elevated people in the land. In France, the fate which Voltaire had suffered on far less provocation illustrated that 'such a portent as Pope would never have been tolerated on the other side of the Channel. The monkey would have been whipped into silence and good manners in double quick time.' Lytton's explanation – that Pope relied on his legal and physical vulnerability to escape prosecution – contributes ingeniously both to the conception of an unscrupulous monster-poet and an enlightened eighteenth century. Yet it was more often his manner than the meat of what he wrote that earned him respect. In his *Essay on Man*, the comfortable philosophy of which was borrowed from Leibniz, he exalts himself into the chair of wisdom in order to tell us all much that is common knowledge, and much that was unknown even to himself. His satires were so patently cruel that, to some extent, they defeated their own immediate and practical aims. Their very infamy may have served to shield the libeller, for there is little evidence to show that anyone thought less of a man for having come under Pope's lash. 'The Great', as the aristocracy were called, would seem to have spared him less from sportsmanlike or liberal eighteenth-century principles than from a sense of their unassailable superiority. Moreover, many of them must have appreciated that Pope's attacks were, in some sense, a form of back-handed compliment to themselves. His scorn of 'the Great', Johnson sagely remarked, 'is repeated too often to be real; no man thinks much of that which he despises'.

It is almost certainly true, however, as Lytton points out, that Lady Mary Wortley Montagu and Lord Hervey, by publishing a lampoon in retaliation against Pope in which they emulated his style and substance, betrayed, not the contempt that they so boldly asserted, but a profound admiration of his powers. Yet surely, too, it is an exaggeration to claim that *all* Hervey's imitations were 'quite ineffective', 'inept and suicidal'. When, for instance, Pope had written:

> *Yes, I am proud, and must be proud to see*
> *Those not afraid of God afraid of me . . .*

Hervey had scored an undoubted point in his reply:

> *. . . the great honour of that boast is such,*
> *That hornets and mad dogs may boast as much.*

The second part of his lecture Lytton devoted to pure literary criticism. After repudiating the strictures levelled against Pope by the Victorian critics – Matthew Arnold and Macaulay – he conducts a skilful analysis of Pope's metrical technique, rapidly tracing the birth and evolution of the heroic couplet, from its accidental practice by the Elizabethans up to its apotheosis at the hands of Pope, where it constitutes, so he maintains – in answer to the well-known objection of Arnold – Pope's 'poetic criticism of life'. This idea, which had first occurred to him many years back on one of his visits to Saltsjöbaden, is faultlessly argued and expounded. We see how, for instance, a learned accumulation of certain accents and quantities will produce a smooth impression of polish and lucidity; or how a regular alternation of accented and unaccented syllables can give an effect, so well-ordered and scrupulously exact, of wonderful solidity and force.

To complement this analytical inquiry into the machinery of Pope's verse, Lytton then adds a brief section of impressionistic criticism, which is intended to convey more directly the passionate spirit of his poetry. Surprisingly, perhaps, this is rather less faultless. So as to illustrate that Pope could write with sensuous beauty as well as biting wit, he quotes the line

> *Die of a rose in aromatic pain.*

'If that is not sensuously beautiful,' he asks, 'what is?' But though the line might be called elegant, or witty, or even perfect in its peculiar manner, it is surely not a good example of *sensuous* beauty. Again, to show that Pope could call up a vision of nature as vibrant as Wordsworth, he unfortunately *misquotes* a famous couplet from *The Dunciad*. Then, in order to demonstrate that Pope could 'compose with his eye on the object' he instances those celebrated lines on the spider from the *Essay on Man*:

> *The spider's touch, how exquisitely fine!*
> *Feels at each thread, and lives along the line.*

But since these two lines were stolen almost without alteration from Sir John Davies, they could be advanced with equal weight as evidence in support of the very opposite of Lytton's contention.

For Lytton, the qualities of art – now as in his undergraduate days – were as mysterious as those of the magic ring in the Arabian romances which, in the twinkling of an eye, made beautiful everything it touched.

'The secret springs of art', he had written in a Spectatorial essay on Spenser, 'cannot be sounded with a footrule.' But this, to some extent, is what he had set out to do in his lecture. The mystery, therefore, remained inviolate; and it is almost with exaltation that he finally confesses the secret which first drew him to the poetry of Pope to be as tantalizing as ever. The magical, unexplained fascination lived on. 'The essence of all art is the accomplishment of the impossible,' he declared. 'This cannot be done, we say; and it *is* done. What has happened? A magician has waved his wand . . .

'It is true: Pope *seems* to be actually screaming; but let us not mistake. It is only an appearance; actually, Pope is not screaming at all; for these are strange impossible screams, unknown to the world of fact – screams endowed with immortality. What has happened then? Pope has waved his wand. He has turned his screams into poetry, with the enchantment of the heroic couplet.'

Lytton's *Pope* was published in June 1925, sold well, and attracted an unusually wide press coverage for a Leslie Stephen Lecture. Although these reviews were highly favourable, the paper was generally considered to be provocative, and has since more than once been strongly attacked. There seem to be two main reasons for this hostility: a failure to understand the fairly narrow literary theme to which Lytton had tried – admittedly not with complete success – to confine himself; and secondly, despite the publication of *Queen Victoria*, a misconception that anything coming from his pen must be heartless and debunking. For both these reasons the main flow of adverse criticism has been directed only against Lytton's oversimplified view of Pope as a man, not as a poet. Professor George Sherburn incorporated the most extreme case against him in the pedagogic Introduction to his *Selections from Alexander Pope* (1929). Describing Lytton as 'the man who brilliantly ruined the art of biography', he goes on to dispute every opinion advanced in the first part of the lecture. Pope was no peevish or venomous invalid, but a man whose mind was warped into its satiristic mould by the grotesque abnormalities of the eighteenth century. The malignity displayed in some of his verse was thus not innate, as Lytton assumed, but the natural consequence of his reaction to the times. By portraying Pope as a fiendish monkey, Lytton had identified himself with that confederacy of dunces, Pope's victims, who alone of his contemporaries held such a view. Perhaps the less attractive qualities that Lytton attributed to him were in fact more attributable to the satirists of the twentieth century, since 'a satirist who hunts living game is not necessarily less sportsman-like than one who attacks the dead'.

Slightly more tenable is the rebuke uttered by Sir Edmund Gosse, who complained that Lytton had misled his listeners as to Pope's real personality and had ignored his leading characteristic as a writer – 'loyalty to the dignity of literature'. He was appalled to learn, Gosse continued, that when Lytton spoke of Pope as a fiendish monkey ladling out spoonfuls of boiling oil from an upstairs window upon the passers-by whom the wretch felt he had a grudge against, his Cambridge audience had been delighted, breaking out into laughter. 'If it had been my privilege to be present,' sombrely recorded Gosse, 'I must have buried my face in my hands.'

Gosse's censure of Lytton, inflated into a long article in the *Sunday Times* entitled 'Pope and Mr. Lytton Strachey', and later reproduced in a volume of essays, *Leaves and Fruit*, dedicated 'to Lytton Strachey with Affectionate Admiration', is interesting as a last chapter in the vexed relationship between the two biographers, the influence of whose work is closely allied in so many tomes of literary history. Neither really liked the other. Gosse, for his part, concealed his dislike under an array of fine mannerisms designed, quite probably, to promote 'the dignity of literature'. Lytton was less circumspect. On one occasion when something by Gosse was published with his name fatally misspelt as 'Edmund Goose', he immediately seized upon it and from then on would refer to him as 'Goose Gosse'. Both, in their dealings with the other, set up something of a double standard between, in Gosse's case, a public and a personal level of communication, and in Lytton's, between his personal attitude and his private reflections. At almost all times a polite façade was kept up between them. When Gosse asked Lytton whether he was an Edwardian, he at once replied: 'I am an Edmundian.' But whereas Gosse reserved his most truculent incivilities for letters to the Press, Lytton discharged his discourtesies into his private correspondence. In his essay on Beddoes, for example, he had referred without comment to Gosse's small edition of Beddoes's letters and credited him with throwing 'additional light upon one important circumstance'. But in a letter to one of his sisters (30 July 1907), he had written: 'I am writing an article on Beddoes for the Quarterly . . . Of course the wretched Gosse had managed to trail his slug's mind over the poor man, and has left a slimy track. I shudder to think what Beddoes would have said if he'd foreseen who his editor was to be.' And when Gosse's classic autobiography, *Father and Son*, was published Lytton observed (January 1908): 'Modern books don't seem to come to much. Mr. Gosse's, though, was amusing. . . . I'm sure you'd like *it*, though not *him* – he comes out of it rather worse than usual.'

Lytton certainly did not consider Gosse to be a fresh revolutionary spirit in the field of biography. Though influenced by French literature, his writing lacked, for all its suavity and ironic poise, a true aesthetic sensibility. No one as pompous as Gosse had any right to be so slapdash and inaccurate. He was, to Lytton's mind, a prolific journeyman of letters, not untalented, but too close in temper to the hidebound Victorian way of thinking.

Gosse, on the other hand, distrusted Lytton for precisely opposite reasons – the lengths to which he exploited his anti-Victorian bias. The criticism which he wrote of *Eminent Victorians*, incorporated into his essay 'The Agony of the Victorian Age', shows that his real objection was to that streak of raciness which ran through Lytton's work, his undignified cinematographic devices and air of decadence which appealed, in his view, to tastes rooted in cheapness and superficial thinking. He acknowledged Lytton to be clever, and allowed that he possessed gifts of a very unusual order. But he held that Lytton had *misused* these gifts. He abhorred what he termed his 'errors in discretion'. The irritating glibness which was sometimes present in his four deterrent portraits, his attitude of hovering superiority, his lack of both sympathy and conventional insight, his intermittent mood of venomous contempt, all these had led him to pass pages that were not simply unjust, but which exhibited the very worst of all literary vices – *impoliteness*.

Their exchange of letters in *The Times Literary Supplement* on the character of Lord Cromer had perfectly reflected their opposing personalities and literary modes. But Gosse had found the author of *Queen Victoria* far closer to his way of thinking. This book, he insisted, was 'a riper, a more finely balanced, a more reasonable study than its predecessors'. He was particularly gratified that Lytton now paid him the compliment, admittedly unintentional, of quoting a number of times from the brief and cautious monograph of the queen contributed anonymously by him to *The Quarterly Review* of April 1901.

Although Lytton's remarks about Gosse in conversation with his friends were almost always derogatory, several of the alterations which he made to the essays appearing in *Books and Characters* were designed to show Gosse in a fractionally less distasteful light. Lytton had sent Gosse a complimentary copy of this volume, but Gosse did not review it. Instead he answered Lytton in a friendly, conciliatory letter thanking him for his kindness and courtesy, and congratulating him on a very lively and pertinent collection. Now safely in his seventies, Gosse added that Lytton was 'the best writer under fifty'.

With his criticism of the Leslie Stephen Lecture, Gosse defined more precisely still his dual attitude towards Lytton. As a biographer, he felt him to be continually in danger of indulging in uncomplimentary and vulgar bad taste; as a literary critic, preferably limiting himself to questions of syntax and philology, he was excellent.

'Also it is said you are getting up a subscription to give Edmund Gosse gold sleevelinks on his 100th birthday,' Virginia Woolf mischievously wrote to Lytton in January 1926. But two years later, in only his eightieth year, Gosse died, and his powerful position as leading critic on the *Sunday Times* was taken over by Lytton's old friend and ally, Desmond MacCarthy.

4

A MODERATE SUCCESS

Although Lytton's Leslie Stephen Lecture gave rise to a terrific amount of agitation at Ham Spray, undoubtedly the most exciting event of this summer was the first public performance of his old 'Chinese concoction', *The Son of Heaven*. Since 1913, when this 'tragic melodrama' had initially been planned as a stage thriller in the hope of making him a quick fortune, Lytton had allowed it to remain idly in his desk. But now that he had won money and fame with his biographies, the theatre managements, which had been so enthusiastically unhelpful in the lean years, wanted to consider the play afresh. The right time to stage it, they declared, had finally arrived: the right time for them, that was, but not for Lytton. He could no longer take this juvenile pot-boiler with any seriousness – his only real concern, in any case, had been with the machinery of constructing a play. His interest revived briefly on learning that the Lord Chamberlain objected to certain passages, but when the Stage Society approached him with an offer to produce it, he turned them down. Harcourt Brace, however, determinedly set themselves up in America as agents for the play, and the impecunious Desmond MacCarthy confidently predicted that, once turned into a film, it would make Lytton a millionaire. Mrs Patrick Campbell, too, seems to have taken some interest in Lytton as a playwright, and on being assured by him that there was no suitable star part for her in *The Son of Heaven*, begged him to write another play especially for her, providing him as she spoke with a detailed description of her role in it. But Lytton stared at her with such a depth of silence and incredulity that for a second the thought crossed her mind that he might have died of a sudden stroke. 'Well, will you, Mr Strachey?' she at last urged him after a long pause, whereupon he turned and piped up in his tersest, most emphatic treble: '*No!*' But to another, more humble request he felt himself obliged to accede. This was to allow two public charity performances at the Scala Theatre, put on in order to raise funds for the London Society for Women's Service, of which his sister Pippa was the secretary.

The action of *The Son of Heaven*, which takes place in the Winter Palace of the Chinese imperial court at Peking during the Boxer Rising, is sustained by an orderly yet ingenious progression of dramatic surprises, enriched by some colourful palace intrigues and subterfuges, and a full array of oriental magnificence – an Empress who speaks like a later version of Elizabeth I, a diffident, sensitive Emperor, Princes, Ministers, Courtiers, amorous Generals, Manchus, mobs and bodyguards, and a masked executioner played in the Scala production by Ralph Partridge. These historical materials Lytton welded together with a nice dramatic licence, inventing episodes to fit in with the theatrical development.

The Scala production of *The Son of Heaven* has been described by K. R. Srinivasa Iyengar as 'a moderate success'. Considering the quality of the acting and the violent altercations which, right up to the opening night, were being furiously waged between the cast and the producer, even a moderate success seems remarkable. The leading part of the Empress Dowager, which Lytton had originally created for the comic actress Fanny Brough, was taken by Gertrude Kingston, at that time a very well-known performer of the old professional school – intelligent and efficient, but perhaps slightly ham.[1] The producer was Lytton's Cambridge friend, Alec Penrose, who, being *avant-garde* and much influenced by the work of Edward Gordon Craig, felt that the whole play should be presented as a kind of ballet. Inevitably these two principal figures took great exception to each other, and since neither was willing to concede anything, the result was an appalling clash of styles and a succession of ear-splitting rows. Gertrude Kingston thought the producer's theatrical notions amounted to so much new-fangled nonsense, and utterly disregarded all his instructions. He was furious, but powerless to do anything with her since she was obviously the mainspring of the whole affair. During rehearsals a crisis would break out every few days that would threaten to capsize the entire production, and Lytton, in his now familiar role as mediator and diplomat, would hurry up to London to sort things out.

[1] It was for Gertrude Kingston that Bernard Shaw had written his one-act piece of buffoonery *Great Catherine* (1913), a music-hall divertissement, set at the court of the Empress Catherine, that displays his generosity rather than his genius. As well as being an actress and founder of the Little Theatre in London, Gertrude Kingston devoted herself to giving conferences on Political Speaking, getting up illustrated books for children and painting in lacquer.

R*

These rehearsals were not made any easier for anyone by the rest of the cast, which was made up of young amateur actors from Cambridge and the neighbourhood of Gordon Square, and included three future academic professors. Many of them had little notion of how to act. Professor Geoffrey Webb[1] played the part of Wang Fu, a provincial official, and also a European soldier; Sheppard was got up as a Manchu; Professor Dennis Robertson[2] was Li, head eunuch in the palace, whose retinue of lesser eunuchs included Lytton's artist-nephew John Strachey. Lytton's niece, Julia, who took the part of Lady Ling, chief lady-in-waiting, dressed in Chinese court costume, with red lips like two aces of hearts set tip to tip, fluttered through her part very prettily, but Gerald Brenan, a palace guard, who only had to say 'Yes, your Majesty!' was so nervous on the first night that he said, 'No, your Majesty!'

Most of the actors had parts that were singularly ill-suited to their characters in actual life, and were obliged to play love-scenes opposite people to whom they felt a particular dislike. From the very first, then, there was much competition for certain roles, much bartering of parts, much carping and rivalry. At Ham Spray nothing but the play was talked of for several weeks. 'Do you want a super part?' Ralph asked Frances (25 May 1925). 'I am put down to be a Russian, a Boxer, an executioner and a Eunuch – fellow eunuchs are to be Adrian [Stephen] and Frankie [Birrell] and Mouldy [Webb]. Alec takes it all very seriously. Lytton tries hard not to show any interest but is unmistakably excited. . . . I anticipate a great deal of bother and very slight fun in the end.'

By 7 July, with only a few days to go, it looked as if the production might have to be called off. Alec Penrose had threatened to resign, and Gertrude Kingston was preparing to walk out unless he did so. 'There's a Pirandello plot going on in Lytton's play,' Ralph explained, '– the Empress together with the chief Eunuch are plotting against Bea Howe in real life as on the stage, and wish to turn her out together with Alec. Lytton was telephoned for and had to rush up yesterday afternoon to get at Dennis Robertson and the conspirators. There is ferment at 51 Gordon Square – Pippa and Ray at their wits' end, how to appease

[1] Geoffrey Webb (b. 1898), who had been at Magdalene College, was to become Slade Professor of Fine Art at Cambridge (1938–49) and a member of the Royal Fine Arts Commission (1948–62). Among his books are a biography of Sir Christopher Wren (1937), *Architecture in Britain: the Middle Ages* (1956), and an edition of the letters of Sir John Vanbrugh (1928).

[2] Sir Dennis Robertson (1890–1963), then a Fellow of Trinity College, Cambridge, afterwards Sir Ernest Cassel Professor of Economics in the University of London, adviser to the Treasury (1939–44) and president of the Royal Economic Society (1948–50). As a past president of the Cambridge Amateur Dramatic Club, he was the only really good performer in *The Son of Heaven*.

Gertrude and yet maintain Alec. Lytton went up swearing to maintain the constitution, but also in great sympathy with the rebellion.' Once again a crisis was averted, the actors and producer appeased; and the play was at last ready for production.

Perhaps the best features of the Scala version were the Incidental Music, composed by the young William Walton,[1] the vivid costumes and the sets – of the Throne Hall of Heavenly Purity in the Winter Palace, the palace garden and the courtyard in the palace precincts – designed by Duncan Grant rather after the style of a D'Oyly Carte *Mikado*. The general atmosphere was of a pleasant teashop, James Agate commented, 'and one reflected that Sir Arthur Sullivan would have turned the whole thing into a delightful entertainment'.[2] The programme cover, 'The Son of Heaven' executed in Chinese characters, was done in mauve and red by Vanessa Bell.

The worst feature, undoubtedly, was the mutilation of Lytton's text. Enormous cuts had been made, including some of the chief speeches, in such a way that the original faults of the play were glaringly paraded, its merits concealed. The handling of the scenes was still commendably expert, and the long monologues incorporated many clever devices to forestall boredom. But the smooth texture and development of the play had been seriously damaged by the excisions so that that warring duality which is at the centre of so much of Lytton's work was here crudely exposed. 'Mr. Strachey himself appears to have been in two minds about the mood of his play,' wrote the *Times* critic, and most of the other dramatic critics noticed two opposing strains within the drama. The first, a highly charged, rattling melodrama, reached its climax in the final act, amid a staccato profusion of tremendous moments. This romantic crescendo, strongly influenced by Elizabethan drama, alternated with a softer air of modern poetic tragi-comedy, somewhat after the style of Chekhov. Mixed with the dramatic plot were many jokes about eunuchs and Queen Victoria, and much splendid regal absurdity – the Empress Dowager, for instance, indulging a royal whim by bidding the guns cease fire on the enemy because they disturbed her picnic. But the realism and the romanticism were never properly fused together as they appear to be in Lytton's biographies and essays, where supreme technical dexterity keeps them in a state of invisible suspension.

[1] This music, Sir William Walton wrote to the author, 'has long ago disappeared. If I remember rightly, he [Lytton] was not very interested in "The Son of Heaven", in fact I suspect he was against it being put on at all.' The tympanist in the scratch orchestra was Constant Lambert, who later became famous as a conductor.

[2] Other critics have taken strong exception to this description of James Agate's, pointing out that the designs were more in the style of a Diaghileff-Picasso ballet.

Desmond MacCarthy also sensed some disunity in the fabric of the play, which he ascribed to a muddling of two inharmonious themes. The one realistic character, he observed, was the Empress Dowager, 'The Old Buddha', always vital but violently inconsistent, cautious yet courageous, shrewd though ignorant, regal and vacillating. Lytton had, in fact, built up her character from the biographical portrait by J. O. P. Bland,[1] and she was the only figure to come fully to life upon the stage. Beside her, the helpless young Emperor was a waxwork. Yet it was he who occupied the centre of the stage. MacCarthy explained: 'Mr. Lytton Strachey, I like to think with youthful, though certainly with mistaken diffidence, was not content with one rich theme, namely, the struggle of this ruthless, adroit, ill-informed old bundle of passions and patriotism against "foreign devils" without and palace intriguers within. He brought the Son of Heaven right to the front when he ought to have remained part of the background . . . The Old Buddha should dominate the play completely. Even if the second theme had been able to rival in interest the other, it would have only pulled the play out of its proper centre of gravity, for the secret of good play-writing is the elaboration of a single theme, not the ingenious dove-tailing of two.'

All the major London critics gave the play leading notices that were in the main favourable. St Loe Strachey, much reconciled to his cousin's work since *Queen Victoria*, described the occasion and the audience as highly distinguished, and in his *Spectator* review demanded that the play be transferred to the West End. But though Gertrude Kingston wanted to try and put it on in America, and Sybil Thorndike, who saw

---

[1] J. O. P. Bland (1863–1945), the writer on Chinese affairs, who had worked in China since 1883 and been a representative of the British and Chinese Corporation Ltd. As a journalist, he was correspondent successively in Shanghai and Peking (1897–1910) for *The Times*. Among his many works was *China under the Empress Dowager* which he wrote in 1910 with Sir Edmund Backhouse, and a biography of Li Hung-Chang (1917) which Lytton reviewed in *War and Peace* and which was of use to him in 'The End of General Gordon'. During the early 1920s, Lytton wrote to Bland asking whether, in his opinion, he ought to allow *The Son of Heaven* to be produced, and Bland, replying as though the Shavian revolution in the theatre had never taken place, advised against it, 'for the reason that you have a big reputation, and this play would, I fear, give the heathen cause to blaspheme. You have followed the historical course of events so precisely, and reproduced the chief actors in the Boxer Crisis in such a manner, as to necessitate, I think, accuracy in depicting them; and this is lacking. A Chinese Empress who talks of kissing (oh, la-la!) and of masked balls at court would never do! – and no Chinese woman would say the things Ta-hé says. The play, in fact, whilst interesting and picturesque, is to me unconvincing, because it lacks the correct oriental atmosphere, and the characters talk like Europeans – I've always thought the Pearl Concubine's [Ta-hé] tragic life would make a grand basis for a Puccini opera, and I once sent him a synopsis of a three-act scenario based on it – but as Pierre Loti's "Fille du Ciel" proved (I think) it doesn't lend itself to the purposes of a European dramatist. The only way it could be made effective for the English stage would be in the high-serious, tragic vein – like Masefield's "Faithful", only more so.'

it at the Scala, was 'enormously impressed' and eager to follow up her triumph as Shaw's St Joan by acting the 'very wonderful part of the "Old Buddha"',[1] nothing came of these plans during Lytton's lifetime.[2]

But twenty-four years later, in the spring of 1949, *The Son of Heaven* was revived for a run of three weeks at the New Lindsey Theatre, where it was produced by Vera Bowen, a sensitive and intelligent Russian producer and a close friend of Lydia Lopokova. By all accounts, this wholly professional presentation was far superior to the Scala version, more smoothly integrated, and, in the crucial scenes, very moving.[3]

5

A NEW EXPERIMENT

The opening performance of *The Son of Heaven*, a brilliant social occasion, took place on the evening of Sunday 12 July. But Lytton was not there. A few hours before the curtain went up, having successfully steered the company through their last turbulent scenes, he fled the country, travelling through the night to Innsbruck, where he was to link up with Sebastian Sprott. Together they had planned an extensive walking tour of the Dolomites. But on only the second or third day, loaded down by an enormous pack strapped across his narrow shoulders, Lytton subsided into a crumpled heap in the middle of an empty road between two precipitous cliff walls and sighed shrilly: 'I can't go on! I simply can't go on!' They then returned a few yards down the road to a café filled with noisy young German girls selling freshly picked bunches of edelweiss. But when they offered one to Lytton, he brushed it aside

[1] 'I wonder if you would allow me to read your play?' Sybil Thorndike inquired. 'There are not many such parts this year for women – men get all the tremendous parts – (except in the Greek plays) I want to play a Queen Elizabeth one of these times. I've read 8 different plays and have been offered them – Bernard Shaw says she's too successful for him to tackle with interest – I hope that somebody might do her.'

[2] Lytton's attitude to *The Son of Heaven* seems to have undergone some change after the Scala production. In a letter to Frances Marshall (9 August 1925), Ralph Partridge wrote: 'Lytton said he was struck by the highbrowness of all his dear friends, as shown about his play, the way they scorned anything that didn't aim at "the heights" of Art (though all writing for *Vogue* themselves); he wants to write another play now, but thinks they'll all be severe on him if he's not as lofty as Shakespeare, as serious as Ibsen.' When Gertrude Kingston tried to get the play performed in America, he wrote to her (14 July 1926): 'I really don't mind what cuts or alterations are made, if you approved of them. I have always thought that what was needed was a hero – a young, clean-limbed Englishman (or whatever they're called) in the English Embassy, who would rescue Ta-Hé at the critical moment, etc., etc. – but I don't see how that's to be added now.'

[3] In 1950 and 1951, *The Son of Heaven* was successfully transmitted by the B.B.C. several times on various home and overseas programmes in a version arranged by Mr Harold Bowen.

with a tired wave of his hand – 'Cotton wool,' he whispered. 'Just cotton wool.'

It was impossible, they soon decided, to get anywhere unless, every day, they were prepared to tramp tremendous distances – upwards of thirty miles – weighed down with their luggage. And so, the expedition quickly degenerated into a commonplace bus tour, which pleased neither of them. By the time they had arrived at Cortina, they were both heartily sick of buses. 'It's a most wearing method of travelling,' Lytton complained in a letter to Carrington, '– there are crises at every turn – one never knows whether one will get a seat – then one's packed in with countless Germans got up like escaped convicts – and finally the machine breaks down on the top of a mountain 10,000 feet high and 18 miles from anywhere. This is what happened to us. There we sat, as night fell, among the convicts, the rain thundering down on the canvas roof – horror on horror! However, we got in safe at last. . . . Sebastian is charming, and makes existence possible by his command of the German tongue.'

On Wednesday, 5 August, while Sebastian hurried on to Florence, Lytton set off by an early train for London, arriving back the following day. At the week-end he returned to Ham Spray. 'He seems very much the same,' Ralph admitted with disappointment (9 August 1925), 'rather worn by his journey from Munich, and very pleased to be back.' Carrington, who still minded his departures abroad dreadfully, was enraptured at seeing him again. While he was away, her life had been deprived of all colour. Now, though the disagreeable domestic drudgeries went on, she could take enjoyment once more in the pleasant things around her – 'a very hot sun all day, the exquisite beauty of the downs, Lytton's very supporting affection'. He was so kind to her, she told Ralph (20 September 1925). 'He has such finesse of tact that he responds very quickly to one's moods.'

While Ralph spent most of the early autumn book-binding and dreaming of Frances, and while Carrington cooked, painted and wrote long letters to Gerald, Lytton settled quietly down to catalogue his library. He did no writing, and the only new books which gave him pleasure were those of his friends, especially Keynes's brilliant memoir of Alfred Marshall.[1] The domestic scene appeared calmer, less tor-

---

[1] On 21 October 1924 Lytton wrote to Keynes: 'It was very kind of you to send me your Life of Marshall, which I have read with the greatest interest and admiration. It seems to me to be one of your best works, and I only regret that it should be buried in an addendum to the Economic Journal. I wish there were more such things – just the right length and esprit – written in English. What a world it opens up! What strange people were the married monks of the nineteenth century! By-the-bye you don't say – perhaps in the circumstances you couldn't – whether he used French letters. Or was he

mented than for many months. Philip Ritchie had disappeared to Monte Carlo and never wrote to him. 'I confess at the moment I am depressed,' he confided to Mary Hutchinson. 'Such a lull everywhere.' James and Alix came to stay, and E. M. Forster and J. R. Ackerly. Also Henry Lamb, who seemed rather 'faded', Carrington observed. 'He positively crouched, and begged for the crumbs that fell from Lytton's beard. Rather ironical . . . That he should now beg to be allowed to come over again, when 10 years ago *he* made Lytton cringe at a LooK.'

Another old friend to visit them this autumn was David Garnett, who brought with him a copy of his new novel, *The Sailor's Return*. 'I think it is a beautiful work of art,' Lytton wrote to Garnett after he had left (20 September 1925), '– most skilful in its conception and treatment. Your power of omission seems to me particularly remarkable. I only wish (personally) that the subject had been rather different – I am slightly rubbed the wrong way by simple domesticity, babies and rattles. However, of course, this is a mere idiosyncrasy and does not affect the real value of the book.' He also tried to read Aldous Huxley, but, he told Ottoline, '"Those Barren Leaves" fluttered from my hands before I had read more than four of them'. *The Tales of Genji*, translated by Arthur Waley, was faintly pleasurable – 'very beautiful in bits – Country wine, made by a lady of quality – Cowslip brandy'.

On 20 September, Lytton once again started off on his 'Autumn Manœuvres', missing out Monk's House this time, and going straight to Charleston. 'Clive, whose clothes are really too shabby even for me – sprouting bits of cloth at the shoulder-blade, – buttons hanging on threads from the trousers – is an indefatigible walker,' he wrote to Carrington (24 September 1925), '– out we go for hours over the downs. In the evenings we sit up till half past one chatting.'

The subject of almost all these chats was Maynard Keynes's sensational marriage to Lydia Lopokova. On 25 August, they had been married at a London registry office and gone off for a couple of weeks' honeymoon to Russia, where Maynard could meet Lydia's parents. Bloomsbury was 'shocked'. They had all been given plenty of opportunity to inspect Lydia, and few of them really approved of her. How could Maynard, Lytton wondered, have brought himself to marry

---

(or she) naturally sterile? That they should have no offspring seems to have been an essential part of their system of existence. I am alarmed, horrified, impressed – almost over-awed – by such a life. Mon dieu! how wildly different are one's own experiences! The emotions and embraces in which I found myself involved as I read your Memoir – what, oh what, would the subject of it have said of them? After all, he took what was really an easy road to Heaven. And did he get there?' In his answer Keynes said that he didn't think that Marshall 'used letters', but that he became sterile soon after marriage.

such 'a half-witted canary'? There was nothing to her. She bobbed and
flitted about the furniture, chirruping away to everyone, and failing
in every way to conceal her incomprehension of even the most coherent
English speech. It was a disaster! What ever could have possessed
Maynard? Why had he done it? they wondered. Of course some
people might cynically suggest that being able to show off a brilliant
ballerina as his wife would prove a great asset in his aspiring career.
But it was not this. He actually seemed to be in love with her – and she
with him. Extraordinary! Before long they would be taking marriage
to the ultimate absurdity by having children – but that, on second
thoughts, was *too* improbable. And so the idle and misinformed gossip
went on at Charleston late into the night.

Lytton shared some of these ridiculous misgivings. He was never
personally impolite or unsympathetic to Lydia or to Maynard himself
and would often invite them down to Ham Spray. The general hostility
to their marriage within Bloomsbury, however, was very obvious, and
nowhere more so than down at Charleston. For many years Maynard
had been part of a very close three-cornered relationship with Duncan
Grant and Vanessa Bell. Now he was transferring the centre of his
personal life away from them. They had no right, by Bloomsbury
ethics, to object; but they resented his departure and released their
emotional resentment in all sorts of petty ways. Maynard, for example,
laid claim to a certain picture by Duncan; Vanessa argued that it was
hers, and Duncan, called in to adjudicate, naturally supported her.
Passions rose high. Maynard, they maintained, didn't *need* the picture.
He had no aesthetic taste and he was, in any case, *far* too rich. Besides,
he had other pictures. So they planned to remove it with their other
belongings from 46 to 39 Gordon Square. But Maynard, foreseeing
what might happen, had screwed the picture to his bathroom wall and
so frustrated their plot. Vanessa was furious, but still determined not to
be outwitted. Appearing to be mollified, she invited Maynard for a
week-end to Charleston, and while he was on his way down, herself
travelled up to London armed with her old latchkey to No. 46 and a
screwdriver. She unscrewed the picture, carried it across to No. 39,
and then returned quietly to Charleston that afternoon without a word.
These were not actions that could easily be forgiven, and Maynard's
association with several of his old Bloomsbury friends was severely
compromised.

But not with Lytton, who, whatever his private convictions, invariably remained, so Lydia Lopokova told the author, 'very kindly
and amiable'. He had a chance to judge the new *ménage* when, after
leaving Charleston, he visited Tilton for a few days – and he did not

judge it very highly. 'The Keynes visit was rather lugubrious, somehow or other,' he told Carrington (29 September 1925). 'For one thing the house was so hideous. Then Lydia is a pathetic figure, to my mind – and so plain. Maynard is as engrossed as usual in his own concerns. He was very interesting on Russia and Wittgenstein; but there is a difficulty of some kind in one's intercourse with him – he seems rather far off. . . . Would you believe it? Not one drop of alcohol appeared. The Charlestonians declare that il gran Pozzo is now immensely rich – probably £10,000 a year. I can believe it – and water, water everywhere! Such is the result of wealth.'

Eleanor, where Lytton next went to stay with Mary Hutchinson, was much more congenial – appetizing food, claret of an evening, and entertaining literary gossip about T. S. Eliot, who 'is giving up the Criterion, and is to edit a newspaper – the Nursing Gazette'. Clive Bell turned up, now 'a martyr to the piles – is it the result of his pulling up his trousers so very, very high?' But best of all was the sudden reappearance of Philip Ritchie, whom Lytton carried off back with him to Ham Spray early in October.

The momentary lull here was now at an end: the brief summer amnesty within the household waned, and they began moodily to pitch and flounder towards a fresh crisis. While Lytton anxiously hovered, blowing hot and cold over Philip Ritchie and alternately cold and hot over his companion, Roger Senhouse, tension between the other semipermanent guests and incumbents at Ham Spray tightened to snapping point. There was no question of ill will, but they were all more touchy and suspicious, more dissatisfied than ever with the *status quo*. Their carping sensitivity seemed to be unilaterally reserved for giving voice to their own grievances, slights and misfortunes. Skilful at analysing the effect that others were capable of producing on them, they wholly discounted the effect they produced on others. When E. M. Forster, for example, in a querulous outburst to Gerald Brenan, complained that he did not intend to return to Ham Spray again because of Ralph Partridge's inattentive attitude, Ralph was genuinely astonished, and hastened to repair the breach.[1] Ought they all to take more interest in

---

[1] 'I had a long walk with Morgan [Forster] to the Gibbet and on to the top of Walbury Camp,' Ralph Partridge wrote to Frances Marshall (undated); 'there was a terrific wind and the country looked bleak but sympathetic. I could hardly manage to talk to Morgan, though I tried *earnestly* – that's the word. I like him for liking me, but I'm completely in the dark as to his real character. His language is so linked up with his mother and his aunts that it's like a dialect which I can't talk. I agreed that I'd behaved badly to him on his previous visits, and said that that made me inclined to have a grudge against him. We talked about friendship but not with conviction or much interest. He likes it without intimacy, I with, otherwise it seems to me almost too mild . . . he likes so much and I so little that it's hard to agree.'

outsiders? he asked. Did their behaviour in public do them credit? The question was quickly taken up, and became one for general and exclusive debate.

But the weakest link in the Ham Spray molecule appeared to be that connecting Carrington with Gerald Brenan. She was at her most perverse, unable to relinquish him, half-loving him, but terrified by the violence of his passions which her own perversity was doing so much to inflame. Her tormenting habits had driven him more wildly eccentric than ever. He was almost at the end of his tether. Vainly he tried to break his jealous obsession over her, to plunge himself into meaning-less activity. He seized upon Ralph, interrupted his book-binding, implored him to tutor him in ping-pong, made him practise three, four and five hours a day, then suddenly contracted tennis elbow and had to give it all up. Still he had not set down a word of his biography of St Teresa. Instead he would take down twenty books at a time from the shelves, read half a page here and there, put them back and then, half an hour later, return, take down the very same books again and go through an identical performance. Every day he wandered in distraction from room to room, and from book to book. After an hour spent indoors extolling the glory of the open English country which he alone appreciated, he would pass another hour walking in the fields describing the architectural beauties of Fitzroy Street and the ad-vantages of a grimy environment for the literary temperament. Either he treated everything with a terrible microscopic earnestness or with the utmost triviality, according to his mood. Testy and cantankerous for much of the time, he also started to worry about his health and to worry others about it. He was the soul of indiscretion among visitors, and when there was no one else to abuse, would launch upon long denunciations against the cat Tiber – its lack of character, its bad manners, its ugliness, its inexplicable habit of scratching him when he tormented it. One way and another he unsettled everyone, worked himself up into dizzy and terrific states – but even so could not shake off his obsession.

This rising tension soon produced some unlikely feuds and alliances between the colliding atoms. Lytton tried hard to be sympathetic to all but was heard on one occasion to declare that people in love should never live together, since they either drove each other mad or out of love. Gerald was certainly never out of love, and neither, wholly, was Carrington. Each, now, had made a particular ally of Ralph, monopolizing his time with his or her private confidences and complaints. To all these he would give ear with a sublime detachment, afterwards passing on any items of amusement to Frances. By taking all Gerald's more unpleasant utterances quite literally, Carrington buried herself into an even deeper state of bewilderment and guilt. How could she deal with him? He was so unreasonable, demanding at a moment's notice that she should drop whatever she was doing in order to see him whenever – and for whatever reason – he felt unhappy about her, which was almost every other day. Her head spun round in confusion.

As for Gerald, his old friendship with Ralph, which had up till then been poisoned by unreasonable jealousy over Ralph's past married life with Carrington, began to mend. The current appeared to go in reverse, and the two men grew increasingly fond of each other, bound together by all they had suffered over her. Gerald's despair reminded Ralph of his own position some three and a half years ago. 'He [Gerald] is far more bitter about her than I am,' he wrote to Frances. 'The wounds are fresh in him, but scars in me.' The convulsions of Gerald's passion at times shocked Ralph. He would pour out all his long accumulation of rage against her maddening ways – her broken promises, her indifference when pursued, her ardour when pursuing. Yet how dreary she made other, better-behaved women seem! It was dreadful to think that her bewitching charm should depend upon so much pain; her power to hurt was perhaps her greatest fascination. In a panic, Gerald begged Ralph to restrain his wife from taking any other lovers. But at the same time he affected to be contemptuous of more peaceful love-affairs, and for that very reason, Ralph feared, might abuse Frances.

It was, in fact, from this less tempestuous love-affair between Frances and Ralph that the real danger threatened. The crisis sprang upon them suddenly that autumn. In the middle of September, Frances and Ralph had gone off for a month's holiday in Spain, become lovers, and on their return decided that they wanted to spend their lives together.

But how could they extricate themselves from this intolerable, clinging web of human relationships? How? Taking advantage of a week-end trip by Lytton to F. L. Lucas's home in Cambridge, Ralph treated Carrington to a prolonged discourse about the problems involved and his thoughts on solving them. For many months now, so he informed her, they had seemed to be travelling on divergent courses. Left to themselves, they might easily exasperate each other beyond endurance. The truth was, he had discovered, that the two of them were incompatible. She always liked getting her own way, and that way had to be different from everyone else's; while he could not bear letting her have it without a protest, which was his attempt to get *his* own way. Neither of them, in his opinion, was very yielding to the claims of the other. When he felt drawn to her, she drew back; and when he drew himself in, she felt wounded by his apparent hardness. It was an impossible set-up. From this time onwards, therefore, they should be to each other as brother and sister, not husband and wife. He could not part from Frances, whom he loved, he went on to explain, but must take steps to put their liaison on a more permanent basis. Since Frances obviously could not come and live at Ham Spray, he must go up to London.

Carrington stood before him, awkward and miserable, her toes pointed inwards, like a schoolgirl being reprimanded by a headmaster. She begged him not to abandon his life at Ham Spray altogether. If a complete separation between them could be avoided – even if it meant only seeing each other at infrequent but regular intervals – then his new life with Frances would be much easier for her to accept. Much upset, and with great emotion, she emphasized again and again the difficulty she would have in keeping Lytton once he thought Ralph no longer took any interest in her and wanted to sever all connexions. But he unequivocally denied that this was his intention. He could not bear to abandon her and Lytton, while Frances, he added, fully respected his feelings over this. What then should be done? The time had come to admit Lytton into the secret, for much depended on how he would react to the news.

After he had returned from Cambridge, a long interview was staged between the three of them. Ralph, who had been dreading this ordeal, mechanically repeated all he had said before. Carrington, now that Lytton was beside her, 'was calmer but so sad'; while Lytton himself listened carefully to everything, but without any comment or the least sign of emotion. His position was an extremely tricky one. Although he was no longer in love with Ralph, he depended upon his physical resourcefulness and competence a good deal, and was desperately anxious that he should not leave Ham Spray. Ralph's practical efficiency was indispensable. Without him, Carrington and himself would be constantly exposed to all manner of disasters from fused lights to unlighted fires. It would be shipwreck! They had come to rely on his great ability for controlling situations, for knowing what to do at all times. 'But does Ralph *always* know what to do?' E. M. Forster had once queried. 'Yes,' Lytton replied. 'He has an instinct which tells him how other people are going to behave. He never does the wrong thing.' The present situation, however, was clearly beyond Ralph's control, and Lytton was inhibited from saying everything he wished by the presence of Carrington. His best tactics, he reasoned, might be to approach Frances, who should prove less intransigent than Ralph. To her, he felt that he could say anything he liked. He therefore announced, at the conclusion of Ralph's speech, that he would be going up next day to London, where he would discuss the matter with Frances. He hoped he might be able to clear up his own and the Ham Spray problem with her more easily, he added cryptically, than with the others.

The meeting between Lytton and Frances Marshall took place the following evening at the Oriental Club. Lytton at once made his own views clear. If Ralph were to go and live permanently in London with her, he said, then he could not guarantee staying indefinitely on at Ham Spray alone with Carrington. The Ham Spray molecule might disintegrate entirely, and Carrington would then be left desolate. To all this Frances answered that she had no wish to drive a wedge between Ralph, Carrington and Lytton, and that if Ralph did decide to come and live in London with her, she would not prevent him constantly revisiting them, and would like to do so herself.

Lytton then hurried back to Ham Spray. He could do no more. He told Ralph that Frances had been admirably forthright in explaining what she wanted, and the next move must lie with him. In a difficult quandary, whatever one did, he said, always turned out better than one imagined it would. But this, mainly for Carrington's sake, was the full extent of his encouragement. Without being unfair, he wanted to bring home to Ralph and Frances the full responsibility for any action they might take. He had explained to them the possible consequences: beyond that he would neither help nor hinder them. It was their own decision.

By December, Ralph had decided. As an experiment, he would take a flat with Frances in London; but the two of them would go down practically every week-end to Ham Spray, he always spending at least one day and night alone with Carrington and Lytton before Frances arrived. Early in 1926, they arranged with James and Alix Strachey to rent rooms in 41 Gordon Square. Lytton, Ralph told Frances, 'seems very pleased that we are going to 41 and did not say a single crabbing word except that if he had known they were so cheap he would have taken the rooms himself'.

In fact, Lytton was vastly relieved that the split had not been more drastic. Really, this solution was the best he could reasonably have expected: he would still see Ralph every week and the continuity of Ham Spray was safely ensured. Now that everything was agreed to, he intimated that, whatever had happened, he would never have deserted Carrington.

Carrington herself was rapturous. She was keeping Ham Spray; she was keeping Lytton; and she had not lost altogether her hold on Ralph. Her letters convey a rush of hysterical happiness and relief. The appalling winter days of suspense were drawing to an end. Spring was already in the air, with all its sense of wonder and renewed promise of joy to come. 'Today the hot sun,' she wrote to Ralph (13 February 1926), 'the innumerable birds singing, the flowers which suddenly have all come out made me so happy I couldn't work indoors. I had to run about in the garden and put down sods on the empty flower bed, but in reality running round the garden out of high spirits. Lytton came out and pretended to be an old gentleman tottering on the esplanade. . . . Lytton suddenly said last night as I was reading over the fire "A game – or have you gone up the spout?" For some reason it made me laugh today every time I thought of it.'

In March, while Ralph and Frances were preparing to move into their new flat, Lytton took Carrington away to the Green Bank Hotel at Falmouth. Here he hoped 'to recuperate after the flu, which has reduced me as usual to ashes', he told Mary Hutchinson (10 March 1926), '– however, I suppose, as usual, the Phoenix will re-arise, eventually. Carrington accompanies me, for a week; after that heaven knows what.'

On their return, Ralph had left Ham Spray for London, and the new experiment was ready to begin. The house felt strange without him. 'In another year I suppose and hope I shall be as indifferent as Alix is to people,' Carrington wrote to Ralph (30 March 1926). 'But you must see that although everything is for the best in the best of all possible worlds for you and F., if you chose to live one day in Lytton's life or mine you would realise the difference . . .'

6

ELIXIR NO. 145

'How long were the pauses between his books!' Desmond MacCarthy exclaimed in his essay, 'Lytton Strachey and the Art of Biography'. But Lytton thought constantly and deliberately about his literary future in these pauses. What should he do next? There was no lack of suggestions, or of his objections to them. When Siegfried Sassoon, for example, asked him why he did not write about Dickens, he weakly protested: 'But I should have to *read* him!' He still often contemplated a biography of Voltaire, and used to say that he put aside this project because the subject would have been too sympathetic to exercise all his critical faculties – though the real reason may well have lain in those rows and rows of correspondence and thousands of as-yet-unpublished letters.[1] He already knew so much about Voltaire that he was appalled

---

[1] Lytton had, in fact, read the whole of Voltaire's correspondence (or as much as had then been published) many years before in his mother's 'complete' edition.

by the prospect of what he would have to read and handle. He kept the chess-board of literary success in the corner of his study and would, so to speak, often stroll indolently over to it, amused at his own hesitation, and wonder which piece would be the best to move next – a queen, a bishop, or a knight? Or what about a little attack meanwhile with pawns against the public?

Since moving into Ham Spray, his output had been remarkably slight – only four *Nation and Athenaeum* essays and the Leslie Stephen Lecture. For several months he deliberated half-seriously over writing a Life of Christ. But since the spring of 1924, he seems actually to have written little else but love poems to Philip Ritchie. Then, in the spring of 1925, he decided that he would not, after all, go through with his biography of Christ. 'Quite a good book has just arrived – Le Mystère de Jésus, by Couchond,' he told Ralph (3 April 1925), '– it finally relegates the poor fellow to the region of myth, and seems to me to be the last nail in the coffin of my book. What a nuisance! I think I shall have to take definitely to the drama.'

Again he studied the chess-board; and it was not a stage drama that he finally fixed upon. For in October, a completely new idea came to him. He would compose, he thought, a book of love-affairs: Queen Elizabeth and the Earl of Essex; Voltaire and Madame du Châtelet; Byron and his half-sister; Mr and Mrs Browning; and lastly, if he had the courage, Verlaine and Rimbaud. Such a scheme would yield admirably to those principles of biography formulated by Dr Johnson in his *Lives of the Poets*. A biographer's first business was not to deal with those of a man's actions that had become part of history; the biographer ought to 'pass slightly over those performances and incidents which produce a vulgar greatness, to lead the thoughts into domestic privacies and to display the minute details of private life'. And this, precisely, was what Lytton had in mind to do. He was determined now to proceed with this project – in any case he needed, so Ralph told him, the extra money to pay his colossal super-tax. To demonstrate his determination, he started reading about Queen Elizabeth at once.

Two months later his plans had entirely changed. The story of Elizabeth and Robert Devereux, Earl of Essex, so absorbed him that he decided to devote a whole volume to it. He would follow up his portrait of one queen by this study of another. But it was going to be an altogether different sort of book, an experiment to transform biography from the solid craft and classical style of his *Victoria* into the more exciting, impalpable spheres of poetic drama – that elusive world that moved between fact and fiction, fantasy and reality, and that was the world of his own love-affairs.

Lytton began work on *Elizabeth and Essex* on the morning of 17 December. The following day, Carrington wrote to Ralph: 'He [Lytton] has written two pages of Queen Elizabeth. He says he has forgotten how to write and finds it almost impossible!' During the next month he would work at the book nearly every day. 'I have been having quite a tussle with the Virgin Queen,' he admitted to Ralph (6 January 1926), 'and am feeling at the moment perfectly exhausted.' Of all his major works, *Elizabeth and Essex* was to be the most ambitious, and none gave him so much difficulty or wore him out so completely. For over a year he had serious doubts as to whether he could pull it off at all. His stamina seemed more vulnerable than ever, and he often needed to interrupt his work with short recuperative holidays. Early in June, after several months' slow grinding labour, he took himself off with Pippa for a few days to Paris where 'the great, the exciting, the absorbing news was that – Cocteau had become a Roman Catholic', he afterwards wrote to Ottoline (10 June 1926). 'Compared with that the collapse of the franc was nothing.'

The following month, at the end of another short burst at *Elizabeth*, he travelled up to Hexham, in Northumberland, to spend a few days with the novelist Rosamond Lehmann and her first husband, Leslie Runciman. 'Mr. and Mrs. R. share the establishment with a young man called Wogan Philipps – quite nice – and then there was Dadie – and that was the party,' he wrote to Carrington (19 July 1926). 'Leslie is to me extremely attractive – in character, even, as well as appearance. But I don't suppose many would agree with this. He is pompous, moody, flies into tempers, and is not mentally entertaining by any means. Perhaps you would be bored by the poor fellow. But oh! he's so strong, and his difficulties are so curious – and his eyelashes . . . there's a childishness about him that – I daresay all grown-up people are childish in some way or other – I find endearing. Rosamond is a much brighter character . . . though not as good-looking – gay, enthusiastic, and full of fun. She and Dadie get on like a house on fire. Wogan lies vaguely and sympathetically at their feet. And dear Leslie makes a pompous remark, to which no attention is paid, looks divine, scowls, until I long to fling my arms round his neck.'[1]

On 18 July, he continued his journey northwards into Scotland, where he was to be awarded an honorary doctorate in Law by the University of Edinburgh. He stayed at 16 Moray Place as the guest of

[1] Walter Leslie Runciman (b. 1900), afterwards Viscount Runciman of Doxford, who became director-general of B.O.A.C. (1940–43), had his marriage to Rosamond Lehmann dissolved the following year (1927). In 1928, Wogan Philipps (afterwards Baron Milford), a communist, farmer and painter, became Rosamond Lehmann's second husband.

Sir Alfred Ewing.[1] Everything was gloomy beyond words, a terrible descent into a middle-class, unromantic purgatory after the lost paradise of jokes and fluttering eyelashes at Hexham. 'I shan't exchange a sensible word with a single soul till I depart,' he complained to Carrington. '. . . Sir Alfred is a pawky little Scotch body, his wife a very plain, unfortunate, high-minded individual, without a spark of humour. Lord Allenby – a large, stupid man – is my fellow guest in the house.[2] It was certainly very wise of me to refuse the dinner, which is going on at the present moment, and where they all are, poor creatures, drinking bad champagne and listening to facetious speeches. This is a fine 1800 house, in a beautiful circle, – but oh! the taste of its internal decorations! How deplorable are the well-off!'

Two days later, after a laureation address by the Dean of the Faculty of Law, Professor James Mackintosh, the honorary doctorates were formally awarded.[3] 'The musical chairs went off very quietly this morning,' Lytton wrote later that day to Rosamond Lehmann, '– since then there has been a lunch and garden party, and in a few minutes a dinner party begins. What is left of me will return to-morrow – to face Lady Astor – and her son Bobbie (who is not so bad). Nothing could be more complete than the contrast between this and Anick Cottage.'

By the end of the month he was back at Ham Spray and working again. The love-story of Elizabeth and Essex was already involving him far more emotionally than his *Queen Victoria*. He seemed implicated in it personally, and it kept prompting memories of those love-affairs of his youth and mingling with the fantasies that hovered over

[1] Sir Alfred Ewing (1855–1935), a distinguished scientist noted for his researches into magnetism, was principal and vice-chancellor of the University of Edinburgh (1916–29).

[2] Viscount Allenby (1861–1936) – formerly Field-Marshal Sir Edward Allenby and nicknamed 'the Bull' – was later made rector of the University of Edinburgh. On this occasion he was being awarded an honorary doctorate in Law. On 20 July 1926 Lytton wrote to Rosamond Lehmann: 'Lord Allenby was in the train with me, and is in the house with me now – a large, stupid man, whom one would like to stick pins into – but it would be useless – he would never feel them.'

[3] In this laureation address, Professor James Mackintosh referred to Lytton as 'an eminent Georgian who first made his mark in contemporary literature by his witty and subtle biographies of Eminent Victorians. The book was the outstanding literary triumph of the last year of the war; its acid analysis of character and its brilliant irony delighted a generation grown somewhat weary of the ideals and idols of its forerunner. Three years later his *Queen Victoria* made a still more favourable impression by its sympathetic and illuminating portraits of the revered Queen and the Prince Consort and its penetrating and suggestive criticism of the spirit of the time. Although he disclaims the role of historian, Mr Strachey has blazed a trail through the thicket of this crowded epoch for which every future explorer passing that way will have reason to thank him. He is eminently worthy of our Order of Merit in the department of letters, if only for restoring to the delectable but almost forgotten art of biography its proper style, proportion and attitude.'

his present infatuations – especially for Roger Senhouse. In the days
when he was occupied with this 'tragic history' as he called it, he
appeared, like a creative novelist, to enter the dim, visionary world,
neither wholly embodied nor disembodied, of his own imagination. At
moments, it was difficult for him to disentangle what was real from
unreal, what belonged to *Elizabeth and Essex* from what belonged to
himself. Sometimes his whole being was suffused with a thrill that
could hardly be defined. His senses grew faint. He was a poet – a
dramatic poet. And then another flood of feeling suddenly swept
upward and engulfed him: he was something more – he knew it. What
was it? Was he a woman? A queen? And for a second he might fancy
himself, in some half-conscious daydream, possessed of something of
that regal femininity – while before him stood the young and spirited
Essex! Then the feeling fled away, and all was vacancy and a sense of
effort. In the aftermath of these periods of strange spectral concupiscence, he would feel drained of all energy, bereft almost of any positive
identity, as if encased and floating in the bubble of some somnambulistic
trance. 'A kind of dreaminess has descended upon me,' he confided to
David Garnett (11 August 1926), '– only momentarily, I fancy – but
there it is – I drift and drift; very pleasant, though shocking for my
morale. . . . Circumstances have slightly changed, but hardly feelings, I
think. As for me, so far as I can see I have always been identically what
I was at the age of two. Rather monotonous for the rest of the world,
perhaps!'

During this autumn, he seldom passed more than two consecutive
weeks down at Ham Spray. For now that Ralph came down only at
week-ends – and almost always with Frances – and he was faced in the
weekdays with the solitary ordeal of *Elizabeth and Essex*, he welcomed
all the more the society of his friends. He needed their company to bring
back a stronger awareness of his own personality and reaffirm the
reality of the external world. The first of a long succession of invitations came from Edward Sackville-West (later Lord Sackville), whom
he visited at Knole for a few days at the end of August. 'Knole was
interesting – beautiful on the whole externally, with College-like courts
and charming gardens and park,' he afterwards told Roger Senhouse
(2 September 1926), 'but the inside was disappointing – too much
hole-and-corner Elizabethanism; one longed for the spaciness of the
18th Century; and the bad taste of countless generations of Sackvilles
littered it all up. Eddie, it seemed to me, continued the tradition in his
ladylike apartments. . . . We had quantities of music, both on piano and
gramophone – interrupted from time to time, rather characteristically
I thought, by – a cuckoo-clock! I found the self-centredness of

my host a little chilling; and am very glad not to be the heir of Knole.'

On his return to Ham Spray, he 'rather scandalously dropped Elizabeth for the moment', in order to write a semi-serious essay on Racine which set out to prove that Racine displayed homosexual tendencies,[1] and, more incredible still, a long poem about a mouse. On 20 September, when these two *œuvres* had been polished off, he again left home for his customary stay at Charleston. 'It has been most agreeable here, with Clive, Vanessa and Duncan as hosts and Tommy [Stephen Tomlin] as a fellow guest,' he wrote to Roger Senhouse (24 September 1926). 'As you may imagine in such company there has been no deficiency in conversation. We totter to bed at two o'clock in the morning, having ranged at large over the characters of our friends and the constitution of the universe, and still uncertain as to the value of representation in art.' From Charleston he went on, loaded down with books, to spend a few days at Philip Ritchie's home in Winchelsea, and from here hurried up to London and, with a 'very gay and amusing' Dadie Rylands, witnessed the opening night of *Easy Virtue*. This he appears to have enjoyed, though 'not so much as the Queen', he informed Roger Senhouse (2 October 1926), '– partly because our places were not nearly so good, but also for other reasons. Those crude oppositions between reprehensible respectability and magnanimous loose living always seem to me too simplified to be of much interest. "Easy Vice" it might just as well have been called – or perhaps "Easy Drama".'

His own work was very far from being easy drama. The very thought of re-immersing himself in the ghostly familiarity of Elizabethan England had become inexplicably loathsome to him, and since Ralph Partridge was in any case spending part of the autumn in Toulon, Lytton felt in no mood to hurry back to Ham Spray. He lingered amid a roundabout of sociality and entertainment for a few days and then veered off northwards to visit Sebastian Sprott, who had recently left Cambridge to take up the post of Lecturer in Psychology at University College, Nottingham. 'I arrived here[2] on Friday with R[oger],' he notified Mary Hutchinson (11 October 1926). '. . . Nottingham is the oddest, grimmest place in the world, but with a certain hideous grandeur – Enormously large.' And in a letter to Pippa sent the same

---

[1] This essay was accidentally destroyed shortly after Lytton had completed it. On 17 June 1927 he wrote to Topsy Lucas: 'My writings are not in luck just now. A MS on Racine, that I'd written (to prove he was homosexual – not *very* seriously) has just been burnt by a housemaid in London. The only copy too!'

[2] 29A, Chamber Street, Nottingham.

day, he described the town as being 'grim and vast in a way I had hardly expected. The Explanation of England, probably.' There was little to do except sit on the edge of the gas-fire reading Elizabethan books, or wander without purpose through the dismal streets where 'so far I've seen nothing either in the shops or out of them, to deserve more than passing attention'. Fellow lecturers of Sebastian's came to tea, but they seemed a melancholy crew, particularly Professor Weekley, Frieda Lawrence's ex-husband – 'a pompous old ape, "You keep a man-servant, Sprott?" and so on'.

At last, after a couple of days with F. L. Lucas and his wife 'Topsy' in Cambridge, he came to rest at Ham Spray. The year seemed to be hold-ing its breath before taking its final dive into winter, and he knew that he should now be bracing himself to do some hard work on *Elizabeth and Essex*. Yet he could not seem to settle down to it. A terrible lethargy encompassed him after even the smallest effort. 'It seems to me that the world has stopped going round,' he confessed, 'but I am too lazy to bother about it.'

By the end of the month he felt weaker still and, deciding that a few days by the sea might revive him, he journeyed down with Roger Senhouse to Brighton, promising that after this short vacation he would apply himself diligently to the book. But it was of little avail. On his return he still shrank from the mental torment of his *magnum opus*, and when, in the second week of November, Carrington went off to Paris to collect 'various plates and bird pictures', he rushed up for another fortnight in London, seeing all his old friends and going off with them to parties and theatres and concerts. This time, on his return to Ham Spray, he took to his bed. He was not properly ill, but had been reduced by constant headaches and a small steady temperature to a state of complete feebleness and dilapidation. He even gave up reading books on Elizabethan subjects, and turned instead to Emil Ludwig's *Life of the Kaiser* 'which is quite well done – interesting and fairly intelligent, though the translation might be better', to a new edition of *Les Fleurs du Mal* 'with a most interesting Preface by Valéry [who] . . . persists in maintaining that Poe is a genius of the front rank', to the letters of Walter Raleigh which had 'some good things in it' but were rather too 'provincial', and to Arnold Bennett's *Lord Raingo* – 'dis-tinctly neolithic; but, qua flint spearhead, quite well done'.

It was now exactly a year since he had embarked on *Elizabeth and Essex* and his progress was extremely discouraging. 'Nobody can be more disgusted by my delay than myself,' he admitted to Chatto and Windus (13 December 1926). 'I am in hopes that I may be able to finish something on Queen Elizabeth before very long – certainly in less than a year – I hope much less. . . . The Elizabeth book would be a very short one – dealing with her love-affair with Lord Essex at the end of her life. I should of course wish you to publish it if you liked the idea; but I feel rather doubtful about the whole thing.'

This loss of confidence lowered his spirits immeasurably. He dreaded the onset of winter at Ham Spray. 'Comfort and conversation – it is my ideal of existence,' he wrote to Topsy Lucas (21 October 1926), '. . . but to be sure the Comfort department is not all that it might be in this arctic region as the Winter draws on.' He had, so he believed, become 'run down' during the course of the year and now planned on a fort-night's holiday in Rome with Roger Senhouse – 'a short jaunt with a divine creature!' as he described it to David Garnett (21 December 1926). 'I believe the breezes of the Channel and the sunlight of Rome will set me up completely,' he confidently predicted (16 December 1926). Accordingly, on Wednesday, 22 December, the two of them set off from London to arrive forty-eight hours later under a blue sky and brilliant sun. They had booked a big double room in the Hotel Hassler, 'the best in Rome', as Lytton proclaimed it to be (2 January 1927), 'high up over the steps that go down to the Piazza di Spagna . . . so that everything is spread before us – St. Peter's dome and a hundred churches. . . . We live in the height of luxury – private bathroom, etc., for £1 each day, including food. R. is a perfect companion – appreciates everything, and is continuously charming to me. He says he is enjoying himself very much, and I think he is – certainly I am.'

Now that he was far removed from *Elizabeth and Essex*, Lytton was soon feeling wonderfully re-invigorated. The holiday went so well in fact that he began to fear some unforeseen traps and snags. Something, surely, *must* go wrong – a slight chill on the entrails at the very least. But no, the days sped blithely past, full of miraculous sunshine and unbroken happiness – it was really quite disturbing. 'Everything has equalled my wildest hopes,' he announced to Ralph (3 January 1927). '. . . We lounge in the Forum, pant grilling up to the Coliseum, sit toasting on the Pincio. – I hardly dare describe the generous heat. . . . On Friday we took our lunch with us and motored out into the Cam-pagna, and ate among ancient tombs on the Appian Way and the cypresses and pines with their spreading tops, drinking chianti in the blazing sun, while lizards crept out of the Roman masonry and flicked their green tails at us.' In the evenings they would return to 'this dowdy German Hassler, where old Morganatic English females crouch and creep', to play piquet and read Dante. They also went to 'a delightful Roman opera', and on one notable day Lytton was entertained as guest of honour at a luncheon given by Princess San Faustino, who treated him throughout the meal to an involved explanation of a scheme she had recently devised to assist the unemployed. This scheme evidently revolved round the cultivation of the soya bean, from which magic substance, the princess assured Lytton, everything from factories and cars to synthetic chocolates and bath salts could be manufactured. After working this idea up, as course followed course, to an excitable climax, she turned at the very end of the meal to her principal guest and appealed: 'Mr Strachey, what do you think of my scheme?' But he, in his highest, most discouraging key, only answered: 'I'm afraid I don't like beans.'

After the delights of Rome, Ham Spray presented a vista of snow and desolation. But Lytton quickly acclimatized himself, and was soon extolling the beauties of the surrounding country – the enormous Downs in their perpetual shadow, and the opalescent fields and trees. The weather seemed to be surpassing itself, positively showing off, as if 'to demonstrate that, after all, there's not much to choose between England and Italy'. While Carrington spent most of these days out of doors, snowballing with Ralph or riding her new 'flea-bitten mare' Belle, Lytton would sit for long hours in his study 'busy with Elizabeth'. 1926 had been an appallingly unproductive year. He was determined to take himself in hand and achieve something worthwhile before the end of the summer. Yet even in these near-ideal conditions, he still seized every reasonable opportunity to turn aside from *Elizabeth and Essex* to some less exacting theme. During the last part of January, he made a characteristic divergence to compose another portrait-in-miniature for the *Nation and Athenaeum* on a seventeenth-century Master of Trinity – 'The Life, Illness and Death of Dr. North'. 'It's rather comic,' he explained (31 January 1927), 'and will I hope have the additional merit of bringing me £40.'

But for the next few months he struggled assiduously with *Elizabeth*. 'I can only write nonsense to-day,' he confessed to Roger Senhouse on 7 February. 'I wish I could write Elizabeth as well. If only she could be reduced to nonsense – that would be perfect. The whole of Art lies there. To pulverize the material and remould it in the shape of one's own particular absurdity. What happiness to do that! I must try again.'

During the late winter and spring he wrote nothing else for publication, and the only literary distraction he permitted himself was to read a number of books whose topics were very far removed from his own. Dadie Rylands, 'to pamper my passion for Eton', had sent him M. R. James's reminiscences – 'a dim affair', he described it (26 January 1927), 'vapid little anecdotes and nothing more. Only remarkable as showing the extraordinary impress an institution can make on an adolescent mind. It's odd that the Provost of Eton should still be aged 16. A life without a jolt.' He also read Emil Ludwig's *Napoleon* – 'interesting though really second-rate'. But the books which chiefly occupied him were three modern novels by his friends. The first of these, chronologically, was David Garnett's *Go She Must!* which he considered to be 'beautifully written, and some of the descriptions exquisite – the whole thing, so far as I can see, wonderfully well done – only – it's almost impossible to read. At least so *I* find. There seems to be no interior tide flowing through it, to carry one along. But that may only be because of some personal disability on my part. I only know that I suffer agonies of boredom – and admiration – on every page.'

Rosamond Lehmann's first novel, *Dusty Answer*, he found more readable. 'It seemed to me to have decided merit,' he wrote (11 May 1927), 'and for a first novel remarkable. The disadvantage to my mind is that it is too romantic and charged with sunset sentiment. A youthful fault, I suppose. Not sufficiently "life-enhancing". But very well and carefully done – without horrors in taste (a rare thing nowadays) and really at moments moving.'[1]

By far the most original of all, however, was Virginia Woolf's *To the Lighthouse*, which he greatly preferred to her previous novel, *Mrs Dalloway*. 'But it really is a most extraordinary form of literature,' he expostulated to Roger Senhouse (11 May 1927). 'It is the lack of copulation – either actual or implied – that worries me. A marvellous and exquisite arabesque seems to be the result. I suppose there is some symbolism about the lighthouse etc. – but I can't guess what it is. With anyone else, the suggestion would be fairly obvious, but it won't fit into the sexless pattern by any manner of means.'

Over the first five months of the new year, Lytton very seldom left the countryside. But he was careful never to overtax his stamina, and would lay aside all work during the week-ends to build up fresh reserves of strength against the coming week, and to relax in the company of his friends. These were very numerous, for besides the almost permanent platoon of visitors to Ham Spray that winter, there were many other more occasional guests – Dadie Rylands 'reading Shakespeare with a violent cold in the nose', the 'very whimsical and charming' E. M.

[1] In conversation with Rosamond Lehmann, Lytton remarked on the gusto and forward sweep of *Dusty Answer*. But to Topsy Lucas, who may have felt envious of Rosamond Lehmann's success, he wrote (7 May 1927): 'I positively read it – every word. It seemed to me to have certain merits, and to escape certain horrors. But I found it lowering on the whole – which can't be a good sign. Only of course I am hopelessly inexpert in modern novels. I am now in the middle of Virginia's [*To the Lighthouse*] – which I like, so far, much better than Mrs Dalloway. It really is most unfortunate that she rules out copulation – not the ghost of it visible – so that her presentation of things becomes little more, it seems to me, than an arabesque – an exquisite arabesque, of course.'

Forster, James and Alix arguing 'on Dr. Freud and the Artist', Raymond Mortimer and Francis Birrell 'whirling like loquacious windmills', Julia Strachey 'so vague and amusing', John Lehmann who 'with quite a slight adjustment of his features might have been a great beauty', Pippa 'a most sympathetic character', and Saxon Sydney-Turner 'a crane-like figure, for ever smoking – pipe in hand on one leg – or else perched on the arm of a chair, reading Plotinus in the original', who typically succeeded in avoiding the cab sent to meet him at the station, and walked the whole way from Hungerford, bag in hand – 'the sort of thing he thoroughly relishes!'

Once in a while, too, there were more spectacular invasions by strangers. 'As I was returning from my walk in the afternoon,' Lytton narrated in one of his letters to Roger Senhouse (9 February 1927), 'an aeroplane was seen to be gyrating round the house. 3 times it circled about us, getting lower and lower every time. Intense excitement! The farm hands, various females, Olive[1] and her mother, all the cats, and myself, rushed towards it, and Carrington was left solitary in her bed, like Antony "whistling in the air". Finally the machine came down in a field exactly opposite the lodge gates at the end of the avenue. There I found it – a group of rustics lined up at a respectful distance. I took it upon myself to approach – but in a moment perceived that the adventure would end in a fizzle. No divine Icarus met my view. Only a too red and stolid officer together with a too pale and stolid mechanic. They had lost their way. I told them where they were, asked them to tea which they luckily refused, and off they went. It *might* have been so marvellous! – What surprised me was the singular smallness and compactness of the contraption – not nearly as big as a motor bus.'

Early in February, Lytton had told Roger Senhouse that 'my own work goes fairly well, though slowly'. As the month advanced, and the weather grew colder, so his work went less well and even more slowly. 'The rain descends in spasmodic bucketfuls, and life here proceeds on its accustomed course,' he reported glumly on 23 February. 'I sit with books and papers. Carrington wanders endlessly up and downstairs, dressed in bright scarlet pyjamas and a cerulean dressing-gown, the cats grow more and more intolerable.' In the cold, his ideas solidified and ran dry; he subsided into a restless, spiritual palsy and by mid-March his work slackened to a complete halt.

There was nothing for it, he decided, but to rush up to London and try to drown his inertia in a sea of parties. After his long abstinence,

[1] Olive Martin, who helped Carrington with the cooking and housework and remained at Ham Spray until her marriage in the 1930s.

the social scene came to him with a certain freshness. He had lunch with Lady Curzon and her daughter, dinner with Ethel Sands, tea with Lady Horner with whom he met 'old Haldane, as urbane as usual, talking of Newton and Einstein in such a style that it was impossible to make up one's mind whether he understood a word of what he was saying'. He saw a production of *No Gentleman* 'and was rather struck by Owen Nares's acting to my surprise', and attended a lecture delivered at the Queen's Hall by Roger Fry. 'The hall was completely full – about 1800 people – and the lecture lasted from 8 to 10.30! – It was full of interest of course, the best thing being a quotation from Michael Angelo on Flemish art – really brilliant – I'd no idea he was a wit.'

By the time he went back to Ham Spray, spring had begun, and with it there came a renewed keenness for work. It was delightful to be in the country once more. 'Wonderfully enough I have begun to work again with new vigour – such a mercy!' he exclaimed. Steadily, but at a gradually declining pace, he struggled on until Easter. 'I am still lazy,' he confessed to Roger Senhouse (17 April 1927), 'but feel that at any moment I may plunge into hectic work.' But by now the new vigour had ebbed away. After the oasis of the Easter holiday, his rate of progress across the desert of *Elizabeth and Essex* decelerated still further, and he began to feel the need increasingly to slip away from Ham Spray for brief interludes. At the end of May he visited Peter and Topsy Lucas at The Pavilion, their house at Cambridge, and on his return he wrote to them (6 July, 1927): 'I am trying to work. It is not very easy. Truth to tell, I am almost in complete despair.' For a time he even considered abandoning *Elizabeth* altogether and restarting 'my novel of the Judge'. Surely that would be more amusing to do? But perhaps that, too, was by this stage beyond his powers. He must take up *Elizabeth* once more; he must try again. But first there was another smaller oasis at Whitsun, and then a few days' spree in London – a meeting with Emil Ludwig, a hectic evening as guest of honour at the 1917 Club, dinner with Douglas Davidson and Dadie Rylands at Boulestin's, tea with Lady Lavery, and an amusing luncheon-party with Lady Aberconway where he encountered Osbert Sitwell, 'distinctly charming', and Somerset Maugham, 'a hang-dog personage, I thought ... with a wife. Perhaps it was because I've eschewed such things for so long that I was amused – the odd mixture of restraint and laisser-aller struck me freshly – but eventually it's just that that becomes such a bore.'

Once more the gaiety of London seemed to inject him with new energies. 'My state is I believe ameliorated,' he allowed (17 June 1927).

s

'I have written a fair amount, and hope to continue – a most unpleasant form of occupation in my opinion – but one simply has to!' In spite of his best efforts, it soon became obvious that he could never finish the book by the end of the summer. After more than eighteen months of laborious exertion at it, he had actually written only 25,000 words – barely over a third of what would be the final narrative. 'I am afraid I cannot give a very satisfactory report of Her Majesty,' he told Charles Prentice of Chatto and Windus (5 July 1927). 'It seems impossible that she should be finished off before October, and I hardly think it would be safe to think of publishing before Christmas – and perhaps really the Spring would be a more likely time.

'So far as I can judge the affair is nearly half-done, and should come to about 50,000 words; but I am extremely vague about this. My experience has always been that things grow longer and take more time than one expects beforehand.

'. . . Please do not expect too much! "Rather a dull production", *I* expect!'

For a further ten days he continued to 'crouch in my writing-room fiddling with Elizabeth'. Then, feeling the springs of inspiration to be drying up again, he dashed off to London for a dinner at Philip Sassoon's and a nautical party – 'several creatures I'd not seen before – a few flirtations – drink and comfort – a sensation of being quite at home as an Admiral – perfect contentment in fact,' he confided to Mary Hutchinson (15 July 1927). 'It was sad leaving London yesterday, but I have no money and must work.'

But this time the trick was not effective. Back at Ham Spray he experienced no renewal of vitality, but 'one of those fearful collapses [that] sometimes overtake me', as he described it in a letter to Dadie Rylands (18 July 1927). Jack and Mary Hutchinson came down for a few days, and so did Peter and Topsy Lucas, and there was much talk about the old subjects – Freud and Sainte-Beuve, love and Cambridge. Lytton's convalescence passed. But his will to write seemed to have been fatally impaired. 'I cannot work,' he wrote in despair to Topsy Lucas (27 July 1927), 'perhaps tomorrow I shall be able to – but I've been idle for days and days. It's a wretched state of affairs, but useless to talk about.'

Carrington now eloped for a fortnight to stay with James in Munich, and Sebastian Sprott, who came down to keep Lytton company, busied himself sorting out and arranging in a series of concertina files the enormous number of old letters which Lytton had preserved.[1] His

---

[1] The only letter of interest which seems to have been missing – and which the author has been unable to find elsewhere – was one sent to Lytton by Thomas Hardy.

industry – from which the present biographer has benefited – was 'quite unparalleled', Lytton remarked (8 August 1927). For weeks he laboured away 'with terrific diligence'. Lytton could seldom resist leaving his desk to bury himself in these sheaves of old correspondence, gliding back on a river of nostalgia past Ottoline's 'gigantic mountain', and 'an exquisite, though too small collection' from Virginia Woolf, past the vanished visions of Sheppard and Woolf, through the cloud of years to older and still older memories of Keynes and Dicker, Papa and Mama. 'Oh, such a plunge into the past! – and so many pasts! Hectic under-graduate days – absurdly melodramatic,' he exclaimed in a letter to Mary Hutchinson (27 July 1927). 'George Mallory later – rather sweet. A bundle from Rupert Brooke – nice, decidedly. Some vague Duncan letters – very amusing. The Bunny [David Garnett] budget. And so on – until the present seemed to fade into some kind of mirage, and unreality reigned. I'm afraid my biography will present a slightly shocking spectacle! In the middle of it all, as I was dreaming over a snapshot of George I'd forgotten all about – so alluring! – the door opened, and who should come in but – Henry! Yes – that ghost. But accompanied, this time, by a far from spectral entity – his Pansy – a gay, sturdy, light-haired, dark-eyed young lady – positively attractive! (Her brother, so Henry says, is no less so – oh! oh!). He seems set up – perhaps that will end happily – perhaps she will be able to quell his evil spirit. Though I fear she'll never make him a good painter. But that hardly matters, I suppose!'[1]

As well as being his secretary, Sebastian Sprott also had to act as a *garde-malade* until Carrington's return later in the month. These next six weeks were unspeakably wretched. Lytton's letters are full of indefinite symptoms, diagnoses, complaints. For no apparent medical reason, he told Ralph (3 August 1927), he was confined to his sick-bed suffering from 'one of those fits of lassitude with slightly swollen glands in the throat'. For ten days he continued to feel unaccountably 'wobbly', 'feeble', 'in a sad state'. It was a great nuisance. Gradually, through the second week of August, he began to mend. 'My health is apparently recovered,' he informed Dadie Rylands (12 August 1927), 'though I still feel a little chancelant – and when shall I ever again do any work? Sebastian toils away in the most exemplary manner. Order rises out of chaos. Correspondence after correspondence is sifted, arranged, and

[1] 'Dadie has been here, and now Henry Lamb and his Pansy are with us for 2 nights,' Lytton wrote to Roger Senhouse (4 September 1927). 'Rather lugubrious, though I like her – she is a sister of Longford's – perhaps you knew him at Oxford? – very pretty, strong and gay – but so young that it's difficult to discover what's inside her, and I hardly think that H.L., who seems to be surrounded with an aura of pale purple depression will do much to open her out.'

bound up. I feel when it's all finished the only thing left for me to do will be to sink into the grave – it's all so neat and final.'

He still felt very fragile and was writing 'but little at Elizabeth' (15 August 1927). Yet his only chance of getting the 'wretched thing' out of his way was to keep at it daily, adding line upon laborious line. He had been looking forward at the end of the month to a holiday in the Pyrenees with Peter Lucas and Sebastian Sprott, but now decided that he must cancel this. 'I know I ought to have written before, to lament and moan over these horrid circumstances,' he apologized to Peter Lucas (18 August 1927). 'I curse that woman – why didn't she fall victim to the knife of a Jesuit? Why wasn't the Armada victorious? I don't know how long I shall stay here now, or what will become of me. I am ill again – reduced to bed – the vaguest symptoms – exhaustion – idiocy. Dear me! – The Lord have mercy.'

This second bout of illness persisted right into September. 'The outlook is rather gloomy,' he admitted to Mary Hutchinson (26 August 1927). 'I don't know what is to happen – how I am to get well – how I am to finish Elizabeth . . . I am taking tonics. One of them is called "Elixir No. 145" – but I don't put much faith in it . . . The annoying thing is that I have no symptoms, except this eternal decrepitude which makes me feel a hopeless imbecile – et voilà tout.' In all his letters there is the same tone of irritation and perplexity. How stupid it was to be beset by such a crowd of imprecise infirmities! What was wrong with him? He could not tell. 'I am still low,' he told Topsy Lucas (27 August 1927). 'Heaven knows why – whether it's "nervous" or "physical" or what – but the fact remains that I drift in a state of half-wittedness. Most annoying. . . .'

His tall and bony frame had become increasingly subject to strange weaknesses. The lurid unreality of the past now seemed to enfold him, absorbing and dissipating his precious store of energy, leaving him pale and wan. Though his serious illnesses were few, a long succession of minor maladies, a host of morbid, unspecified diseases held Carrington in a state of alarmed suspense. Our knowledge, both of the laws of medicine and of the actual details of his disorders, is too limited to allow a reliable diagnosis as to their cause. In some respects, like nearly all the Stracheys, his constitution was very sound. Fundamentally he was strong – he would often walk his friends into the ground over ten or twelve miles – yet his curiously unstable temperament remained vulnerable to a multitude of abnormal agues and fevers. With the approach of middle age, the emotional excitements that assailed him scarcely diminished, and while he was at work on *Elizabeth and Essex* they may actually have increased. He complains often in his letters that 'my nerves seem so edgy and disordered'. Why? What could be the special cause of those acute nervous infirmities that so shook and humbled him? Possibly an explanation lay in the fact that, like Elizabeth herself, most of his ailments were of an hysterical origin, and that his probing into her odd, neurotic condition had aggravated his own kindred diseases. It seemed almost as if this original neurosis was posthumously contagious, that it had, in part, been passed on to him. In his peculiar, rarefied manner, Lytton was living more intensely within Elizabeth than in any of his previous subjects, and from the mixing of their thoughts and feelings he emerged tainted with some of Elizabeth's sexually warped characteristics. Certainly his prolonged study of her taut, audacious temperament – nourished as it was not by a healthy physique, but an immense will and highly-strung nervous system – emptied his own bodily resources as no other book had previously done.

As a consequence of this exhaustion, everything came to a standstill by the end of August. With immeasurable relief he turned away from *Elizabeth* to some of his old favourites – Montaigne's essays, the *Confessions* of Rousseau in a 'first edition [that] omits some vital passages owing to prudery', and Swift's poems – 'that man certainly had a dirty mind, in the literal meaning of the word. But no doubt if he liked one it would have been extremely exciting.' His investigations into sixteenth- and seventeenth-century England had greatly whetted his appetite for 'those singular punishments they went in for in those days'. Much of his correspondence over this period contains exultant descriptions of these practices, which thrilled his naturally ribald and prurient imagination,[1] and influenced his choice of reading – of an eighteenth-century French Penal Code, for instance, in which he observes that 'the punishment for blasphemy was curious. For the first time, offenders were fined; for the second, third and fourth times, more and heavier fines; for the fifth time the pillory; for the sixth time, the upper lip was cut off; for the seventh time, the lower lip cut off; "et si

---

[1] 'I must tell you a curious tale of the 17th century that I've just come upon – à propos of what I told you of the singular punishments they went in for in those days,' Lytton wrote to Dadie Rylands (8 September 1927). 'It was discovered by Archbishop Laud that the Headmaster of Westminster had written a letter to a Bishop in which he referred to "that little meddling hocus-pocus". The letter was found among the Bishop's papers, and Laud (rightly) flew to the conclusion that it referred to himself. He had the Headmaster arrested and taken before the Star Chamber, where he was condemned to be fined £5000, and . . . to have his ears nailed to the pillory at Westminster in the presence of his scholars! – Can you imagine a more marvellous half-holiday for the whole school? Only conceive of it! – But, most unfortunately, the Headmaster made off, and the sentence was never carried out, and the dear boys were disappointed. If one had lived in those gay days how careful one would have had to be! – even more so than now I fancy.'

par obstination et mauvaise coutume invétérée, ils continuent" . . . the tongue cut off. After that, the imagination of the law gives out. There is also a section on "Délits commis dans les Bois" . . .' His other reading included *The Rodiad*, 'a very amusing Regency poem (reprinted) on a highly shocking theme', and among the new books, Katherine Mansfield's *Journal* edited by Middleton Murry, which he described as 'quite shocking and incomprehensible. I see Murry lets out that it was written for publication – which no doubt explains a good deal. But why that foul-mouthed, virulent, brazen-faced broomstick of a creature should have got herself up as a pad of rose-scented cotton wool is beyond me.'

'I am, I think, rather better in health – feeling, at any rate at the moment more cheerful, and with a faint prospect of being able to do a little work,' he reported to Mary Hutchinson on 12 September. But it was not at *Elizabeth* that he planned to work – not just yet. Instead, during the next six weeks, he added to his collection two further portraits-in-miniature, on Carlyle and Gibbon – and contributed a long review of the second volume of Sidney Lee's *King Edward VII* to the *Daily Mail*.[1] He was by now feeling much stronger, his health and spirits 'positively bouncing upwards', he told Virginia Woolf (16 September 1927). In the third week of September he and Carrington visited Augustus and Dorelia John in their 'curious establishment on the other side of Salisbury. You never knew anything quite so singular,' he assured Dadie Rylands, '– so vague – so utterly lacking in amenities – so (every now and then) fascinating. There were two girls – two boys – some sort of governess – such silences and driftings! Dorelia herself is a most wonderful person. I am fondly attached to her – but she moves on an unfortunate plane.'

A few days later, on 20 September, he left Ham Spray again for a week at Charleston. Before setting off, he had been 'slightly dreading the prospect of the general dégringolade plus Angelica,' he confessed to Dadie Rylands.[2] But on his arrival there, he found the household pleasant and sympathetic. 'Clive is nice, as he invariably is when not feeling the need to show off,' he reported to Roger Senhouse (22 September 1927), '– Vanessa very superb – and Duncan of course charming as ever. There is a youth too, Julian, whom I haven't seen since he was quite a boy – he's now on the brink of going to Cam-

---

[1] 'A Frock-Coat Portrait of a Great King', *Daily Mail*, 11 October 1927, page 10. For this review Lytton was paid fifty pounds. It has not been reprinted in any of his collected volumes.

[2] But on 1 September 1927 Lytton had written to Vanessa Bell specially asking whether he might come down to Charleston because he had been suffering from 'a mild "nervous breakdown" – physical collapse, which, of course, opens the way to depression. . . . It has prevented my working, and I am now horribly behindhand with Queen Elizabeth.'

bridge. He's a very nice creature, was once most beautiful, but all now is ruined by a most unpleasant fatness. A Socialist – despises Art – so I'm told . . .[1] Inside the house is rather ramshackle – a regular farmhouse, not done up in any way – but very beautiful in parts, owing to the taste and skill of Duncan and Vanessa's decorations. They paint most of the day in a studio they have built at the back, but I haven't yet been allowed inside. Clive spends the mornings writing his Great Work on Civilization.[2] After dinner we gossip and play the gramophone.' One day while he was staying there, the Woolfs came over from Rodmell, and Virginia, 'looking very young and beautiful', declared that they must all write their memoirs, on an enormous scale, and have them published in volume after volume in ten years' time. Ottoline, it seemed, had stolen a march on them, and was already scribbling out hers at Chirk Castle – though they were sure to be nothing but stale milk, that noisome fluid which permeates, congeals and sours even the most intimate organs of the body.

Most mornings here, Lytton worked at his 'Carlyle'. But whenever the afternoons were fine, he and Clive Bell would set out on magnificent walks together along the top of Firle Beacon – the sea on one side and the Sussex Weald on the other – and along the foot of the Downs through Firle Park, 'which is very attractive with an eighteenth century big house in it, belonging to Lord Gage, whose ancestor got his peerage (so they say) for discovering the greengage,' he informed Roger Senhouse (23 September 1927). 'His present Lordship is a very dull young man, though, who will never discover anything.'

By the time he came to leave Charleston, Lytton was completely well again. But he was taking no chances, and decided to go off with Carrington for a week in Weymouth. 'I feel sure I shall like Weymouth,' he announced as soon as he had arrived there. The streets were full of rare beauty, and the whole town, he thought, was entirely

---

[1] 'Clive and Vanessa's boy, Julian is here,' Lytton wrote to Topsy Lucas from Charleston (23 September 1927), '– he goes to King's next term. Obviously very nice – fat and rather plain – socialistic I fancy, and rather ponderous, as the young are apt to be, at moments.' At Cambridge, Julian Bell became an Apostle, also turning his talents to poetry, womanizing and left-wing politics. Deeply attached to his mother, he was yet reacting against the liberal milk-and-water humanitarianism and the out-and-out pacifism of Bloomsbury, and tried to escape from the clash between his sense of loyalty and his unsqueamish instincts by taking, in 1935, the job of professor of English at the Chinese National University of Wuhan. Two years later, his problems still unresolved, he returned home, where Vanessa Bell was trying to secure for him the post of company director, at a hundred pounds a year, of a family business importing feathers from China. He himself was eager to fight in the Spanish Civil War, and so a compromise was reached whereby he drove an ambulance with the Loyalist Forces in Spain. He was killed on 18 July 1937 at Villanueva de la Canada, in the battle of Brunete.

[2] The revised edition of Clive Bell's *Civilization* was published in 1928.

without pretensions, 'hardly altered, one feels, from the dim days of old George III'. His gratitude at having finally escaped from those endless weeks of defatigation made him unusually easy to please. 'Weymouth seems distinctly simpatico,' he told Roger Senhouse (29 September 1927), '– faded, but with genuine fisher life of its own. The sea very mild.' Lytton, too, was exceptionally mild. Everything seemed to interest or amuse him. He bought a very large and heavy Kodak camera, and sauntered about snapping 'enormous photos' – of the wishing-well at Upwey, of 'an absurd statue of George III, with a sort of Piazza del Popolo effect behind it', and of the lighthouse at the end of Portland Bill, 'a desolate region, extremely suitable for convicts'. His beneficence embraced all he saw. Even the lodging house where he and Carrington were staying delighted him. 'Our landlord is the Mayor of Weymouth,' he boasted. '. . . Life in lodgings is really very fascinating, it seems to me. Everything is fixed – so unconnected with real existence – so comfortably hideous. I could go on here for weeks and weeks.'

He was also being highly entertained by the work of a young novelist he had come across – William Gerhardie. On the whole, he tended to feel nonplussed by the style of contemporary fiction. 'I don't know whether I'm hopelessly classical, or simply out of date, or an irredeemable purist, or what,' he wrote to Topsy Lucas (30 October 1927). '. . . There are so many modern writers I can't see the point of, whom so many other people like very much, that it looks to me as if there were certain qualities I'm impervious to.' Whenever the intelligence of an author outstripped his artistic talent, Lytton would feel out of step with his work, and he preferred to be lulled by a surfeit of aesthetic sensibility and expertise. In Gerhardie's novels, especially his Chekhovian masterpiece *The Polyglots*, sensibility and intellect were finely balanced, and the result he found 'really very amusing, in the Dickens-Dostoievsky-Douglas style'.

As for his own writing, it was going remarkably well. He had finished 'Carlyle', was half-way through 'Gibbon', and planned two more portraits-in-miniature, on Macaulay and Hume. But *Elizabeth and Essex*, which he had not looked at since the middle of August, still awaited him. Even in his buoyant holiday mood, he could not make light of this undiminished ordeal. Chatto and Windus were becoming increasingly anxious over the protracted delay. This pause separating his books had already lengthened far more than anyone expected: how much farther still was it to be extended? 'I have been unwell all this summer,' Lytton explained to Charles Prentice (4 October 1927), 'and the result is that Elizabeth is not nearly so far advanced as I had hoped. It is most annoying; but I seem to have recovered now.' Under these

improved conditions, he estimated that he might have a typescript
ready before the end of the winter, in which case the book could be
published some time in the late spring. He would be overjoyed finally
to have got rid of it.

For, over the past year, his life had been jolted by a series of numbing
emotional shocks. He had lived under a shadow of obsessive anxiety
which obscured his clear thinking and impeded his progress. But, this
autumn, these problems had begun to resolve themselves. The shadow
slowly lifted. As he was driven back from Weymouth to Ham Spray,
his prospects appeared brighter than for a long time. He was strangely
happy.

He was in love again.

7

TWO IN THE CAMPAGNA

Once Ralph Partridge set up flat with Frances Marshall in the spring of
1926, the cloud which had hung so low over Ham Spray quietly dissolved. Yet the sky was subtly altered. For almost two years, Lytton
had wavered in his affections between the two friends, Philip Ritchie
and Roger Senhouse, and wavering, had committed himself deeply to
neither. Of the two, Philip Ritchie seemed to be his favourite: his
endearing ugliness had suggested somehow a more tangible, various
and available being than the beautiful and romantic Senhouse. But for
all his charm, Ritchie had in some ways turned out to be a disappointment. It was impossible to get properly involved with someone who so
often disappeared abroad without any word of explanation, who never
wrote letters, and who seldom encouraged Lytton to the exclusion of
other admirers.

Circumstances, too, had favoured a sentimental attachment with
Senhouse. In August, the young man had come down to stay with him
at Hungerford for three or four crucial days. After he had left, Lytton
wrote excitedly to Mary Hutchinson (11 August 1926). 'Ma chère, I
have just had a most unexpected piece of good fortune – a free gift
from Providence. The other day I gave a slight push to a door which
I had longed to turn the handle of for about two years but hardly dared
even to touch. To my amazement, it opened; and I found myself in an
exquisite paradise. I am still in it, so to speak. Nothing more charming
could be imagined. Perhaps you will guess the initial of the door – if
so, you will see at once that this is an extremely confidential communication!'

S*

These few days marked the start of what was to be the very last of
Lytton's major love-affairs, one that, with all its attendant crises,
miscalculations, and moments of bitter disillusionment, persisted until
his death nearly six years later.

The personality of Roger Senhouse dominated these final years. The
world, of course, still believed Lytton to be an icy, passionless intellectual – a 'Bloomsbury' cut-out. Yet even in middle age, the very
opposite seemed to be the case. Nature had implanted within him an
amorousness so odd and irrepressible as to be always obvious and
sometimes even shocking to his friends. His susceptibility to Roger
Senhouse was plain for them to see – the handsome, elegant youth,
with his open manner, his boyish spirit, his words and looks of admiration, fascinated Lytton. The descendant of a long line of Senhouses of
Maryport in Cumberland, and recently come down from Magdalen
College, Oxford, to work for a large import-export firm at Hays
Wharf in the London Docks, Roger Senhouse exhibited a medley of
inherited traits and purely personal proclivities that, in their strange
juxtaposition, Lytton found peculiarly compelling. The melodious
accents of Eton sounded sweetly in his ears and aroused something of
that exaggerated loyalty which non-Etonians sometimes feel for the
old school. Also, Roger was a connoisseur of books – later to be the
first partner of Frederic Warburg in the firm of Secker and Warburg,
and a sensitive translator of Colette; he was unambitious yet adventurous, a creature of curious taste and fantasy. His invariable manner of gentle, unruffled calm concealed a nature of hectic and bewildering eccentricity. His powerful physique, steel-blue eyes and firm jaw, all
promised a certain decisiveness in action that was also wildly misleading; he was swept hither and thither by the breezes of his moods
and the accidents of circumstance. His spirit, so vague and wayward,
combining the cross-currents of learning and lasciviousness, lived and
moved in a superb uncertainty. Something about him – his dark-brown
hair, perhaps – reminded Lytton of George Underwood, the second of
his 'desperate passions' at Leamington College. There was, he concluded, a marked resemblance between his feelings for Roger and for
that freckled, red-haired schoolboy of over thirty years ago. Recently
he had noticed Underwood's name in an Army List and reflected that
by now he must be a senior officer of nearly fifty, with a wife and
family – bald, with a few tufts of fading ginger hair – a short, podgy,
good-natured figure, very popular in the mess. But when he glanced
across at Roger, the years peeled away and his vital forces flowed
again, bringing with them the feverish excitements and jealousies of
youth. To be away from the struggle and the drudgery of adult life,

away from the fame, complexity and division; to be back in the simple unchanging past, a boy again at Leamington; to escape irrevocably into the prolonged innocence of boyhood, and insignificance, and dreams! – That was love.

Lytton was now in his late forties, approaching fifty, while Roger was only in his early twenties – a dangerous concatenation of ages. Yet for the moment – it was the autumn of 1926 – all was smooth and well. There were long talks, long walks across the Berkshire Downs, and in the evening more talk and more laughter, and then there was music, until at last the rooms of Ham Spray were empty, and they were left, the two, playing cards together. When he was in London, Lytton would often drop in on Roger at his flat, and every week they exchanged affectionate letters. There was a tender, playful quality to their friendship. Lytton liked to compose for him special love-poems, and in a more flippant vein even addressed his envelopes in verse:

> *Deliver this to SENHOUSE (Roger)*
> *I prithee, postman debonair!*
> *He is the handsome upstairs lodger*
> *At number 14 BRUNSWICK SQUARE.*

In October, when the two of them had gone up to stay with Sebastian Sprott in Nottingham, Lytton wrote to Mary Hutchinson (11 October 1926). 'How to describe my happiness? It is simply shocking – that's all that can be said. Sebastian is charming, but ignorant.' There was, in these first few months, a particular reason for trying to preserve the secrecy of their affair. Neither of them knew what would be Philip Ritchie's reactions once he found out. They dreaded hurting him. After all, it was he who had first introduced them. And was not Lytton now working the very same trick that Maynard Keynes had pulled on him twenty years back with Duncan Grant? Not quite, perhaps, but it could be something very close to it.

The news, however, could not be withheld from Ritchie indefinitely, and once the two of them had decided to go off to Rome together in the new year, there was no choice but to tell him something. Even so, for all their sakes, they allowed him to know no more than was completely necessary. 'R[oger] has told P[hilip] about it – as vaguely as possible,' Lytton informed Mary Hutchinson (17 December 1926). 'P[hilip] was extremely charming and sympathetic, R[oger] says, and didn't bother with cross-examinations. Please, if he talks about it to you, don't know much more than the bare fact. The details are so harrowing – to him and everyone else. Don't even know anything about dates,

He's coming here tomorrow. Rather agitating! Really rather a singular, not to say shocking, situation.'

This fortnight in Rome sounded the topmost note to the early part of their relationship. Seldom had Lytton felt happier. His happiness was such that he could scarcely believe in it, that he seemed scarcely conscious from day to day. If only time could have stood still for a little and drawn out those halcyon weeks through vague ages of summer! But there is no respite for mortal creatures. Human relationships must either move or perish. After they had left the sun and blue skies of Italy, this sweet prologue to their friendship came to an end, and the first scene of the ensuing drama which developed between them opened against the wintry climate of England.

As his memories of George Underwood suggest, the quality of Lytton's love-affairs did not greatly alter throughout the course of his adult life. Spasmodically, Lytton did experience some degree of sexual attraction towards women – the plump and innocent Maria Nys, for example, Katherine Mansfield, Nina Hamnett and, of course, Carrington herself – but these moods were always short-lived, and his customary emotional attitude to the opposite sex was one of instinctive and incapacitating alarm. In any event, since the way to heterosexual happiness was blocked, he naturally returned for his most satisfactory love-affairs to the adolescent period of his life, so that the character of all his infatuations – with their common ingredient of awe-struck hero-worship – remained to a large extent permanent, static. Because the very core of his homosexual affection was imbedded in a sense of unsureness and was, in effect, a natural regression to the sunlit days of his youth, there could obviously be little real chance of a ripening development in these affairs, except in the realms of fantasy. Yet they were not all identical. With a common emotional pattern there was room for a surprising variation of feeling. The people he fell in love with were still, generally speaking, the type of men he would himself like to have been, or who possessed specific attributes in which he felt himself to be woefully deficient. But the attributes he admired were various, often contradictory, and fluctuating.

The evidence of his love-poems points to other changes in psychological emphasis. In those poems written at, or immediately after leaving Cambridge, his sad obsession and revulsion from the physical act of love-making accurately reflects the mood of this black period of his life. His later poetry, however, tends to divide lust from love, treating most manifestations of the former with a ribald wit and humour, and true passion as something chiefly phantasmagorical, not subject to the decay of physical deterioration or the anti-climax of fully indulged intercourse. Lust is no longer a 'guttural voice' that rhymes with 'dust' to signify the grave of man's nobler aspirations: it is something far less earnest and more thrilling. Very characteristic of the lighter vein in which he presents erotic themes are some lines of verse which he sent to Roger Senhouse in the summer of 1929.

> *How odd the fate of pretty boys!*
> *Who, if they dare to taste the joys*
> *That so enchanted Classic minds,*
> *Get whipped upon their neat behinds;*
> *Yet should they fail to construe well*
> *The lines that of those raptures tell*
> *– It's very odd, you must confess –*
> *Their neat behinds get whipped no less.*

This verse, of course, is written primarily to provoke sexual amusement and appetite, not to express a disgusted aversion from concupiscence. They are the lines of a happier, freer and more pleasure-loving man. For Lytton the physical world always existed. But he needed sexual stimulation not so much to arouse and then gratify desire between himself and another man, but to pacify those awful pangs of prurient yearning which had so often in the past made a dungeon of his isolation. Once this need had been met, he was released from the cage of his corporeal passions into the misty and impalpable region of the spirit where love alone dwelt. And it is this delirious universe of ecstatic self-oblivion that his later love-poems celebrate. Happiness was a narcotic, inducing symptoms which were the very obverse of that nausea summoned up in Lytton by the actual, unromantic, strenuous processes of love-making – a nausea that combined something of the relish and exigency of hypochondria. In 'The Haschish', which he composed before the outbreak of the war, he pictures himself liberated from what he again describes as 'this wrong world', and admitted into a disembodied phantom world, not encumbered by the bonds of logic and reason, but strangely ambiguous, inconsequential, rapturous.[1] Here he can find the happy ending to man's laborious terrestrial journey, his promised peace. Despite many lines that seem to imply the occult and immortal nature of this dreamlike realm, the seance is not imbued with any real mystical glow, and consists

---

[1] James Strachey has urged that there was never any question of Lytton actually being a hashish eater. In those days, in England, hashish was not so much a drug (*Cannabis Indica*) as a purely literary substance – from the *Arabian Nights* (though later celebrated in France in more realistic fashion by Rabelais and Baudelaire). Lytton, in any case, was 'far too respectable ever to *dream* of going in for that sort of thing', and would have disapproved of the journalistic existence the drug now enjoys.

principally of a shedding of mundane egotism and vanity. He does not seek through love to discover any state of heightened awareness, or any awakening into a new vibrant dimension of life, but to attain a condition of gently melting unconsciousness, an ineffable ebbing away from the reach of a muddled, ugly world. For this reason, the most touching lines of the poem are those in which Lytton expresses his intense longing for self-forgetfulness, for a deliverance from out of the cocoon of his sick body and the hateful London life that walled him in, a life of pain and tribulation.

> *Oh, let me dream and let me know no more*
> *The sun's harsh sight and life's discordant roar;*
> *Let me eclipse my being in a swoon,*
> *And lingering through a long penumbral noon,*
> *Feel like a ghost a soft Elysian balm,*
> *A universe of amaranthine calm,*
> *Devoid of thought, forgetful of desire.*
> *And quiet as joined hearts which still suspire*
> *Love's ultimate tenderness, while faint bliss*
> *With pale mandragora drowns the accomplished kiss,*
> *So shall I find, inextricably sweet . . .*
> *– Looks that are felt, and lusts as light as air,*
> *And curious embraces like September flowers*
> *Vanishing down interminable hours,*
> *And love's last kiss, exquisitely withdrawn,*
> *And copulations dimmer than the dawn.*
> *Who now shall fret?*

It is only when chloroformed and emasculated in this way that the passions of lust and love could unite to the complete satisfaction of Lytton's fastidious nature. The entranced and guiltless vision he evokes becomes highly conventional, taking on the classical poetic diction of later Victorian sentiment, as soon as he tries to conjure forth a more palpable picture of homosexual bliss, and sees the

> *forms of golden boys*
> *Embraced seraphically in far lands*
> *By languid lovers, linking marvellous hands*
> *With early Virgins crowned with quiet wreaths*
> *Of lily, frailer than the air that breathes*
> *The memory of Sappho all day long*
> *Through Lesbian shades of fragmentary song . . .*

As he had grown older, so his health had become more robust, his temperament less squeamish. Already in 'Happiness', written while he was at work on *Eminent Victorians*, there is a definite regeneration of energy. As in 'The Haschish', the sensations of joy and multitudinous gladness are described as if they have been provoked by some drug – not an aphrodisiac, but an anodyne or opiate inducing drowsiness. An insidious music haunts his inward ear with harmonies that leave behind them a timeless, imperceptible refrain quivering in the air. The pre-war feeling of listlessness between these celestial crescendos to his romances is now replaced by something stronger and more resilient. Sometimes, Lytton explains, the ruthlessness of our fate seems to relent, and our destiny shines before us, marvellous and benign. Such inspiriting glimpses into the future, he implies, are bestowed upon those who have mastered their impatience, and whose senses are no longer drenched with elemental desire, either for lust or power. They are

> *oftenest known*
> *To those in whom the waiting soul has grown*
> *A little weary, and whose deep desires*
> *(As in black coal sleep unextinguished fires)*
> *All joy's rich possibilities ignore*
> *And, not despairing, not expect no more.*

He had reached the stage of expecting no more from love when Roger Senhouse suddenly and wonderfully re-ignited these unextinguished fires. The new flame burnt brightly, erratically, almost without control, giving out a rather different light from earlier conflagrations. During his Cambridge days, Lytton had, in schoolboy fashion, associated sex with excrement and been much obsessed by the idea of sodomy. Among his post-Cambridge writings, however, can be traced the development of more sophisticated sexual deviations, and the suggestion that he could become erotically aroused by other parts of the body, especially the ears. There are a few references to ears in the Duncan Grant correspondence, and, a little later, a curious pleasure in contemplating 'the strange divine ears, so large and lascivious – oh!' of George Mallory. But it is not until his infatuation for Ralph Partridge that ears crop up regularly in his letters, and by the time he is writing to Roger Senhouse, they seem to have taken on a magical, lickerish significance. He is always threatening to tweak or pinch Roger's ears for some slight misdemeanour, or slice off one or possibly both as punishment for some imagined crime; and he describes with horrified delight the mutilations to ears practised in the sixteenth and seventeenth centuries.

Such fetishes were an offshoot of the rich fantasy life to which, for the first time, he now seems to have abandoned himself. In his affair with Duncan Grant he had tried to force a reality out of his day-dreams by assuming, almost literally, the form and personality of the man he loved. With Henry Lamb, he had resorted to moods of sexual infantilism only in moments of crisis or reconciliation, so that fantasy and actuality had run alongside in a makeshift partnership that was bound eventually to break apart. With Ralph Partridge he had not attempted to transmute himself in an imaginative way, but to alter the object of his love so that they might be closer in everyday life – with the result that, once he had partly succeeded in this conversion, his initial amorousness was watered down into more ordinary amiability. But in the company of Roger Senhouse, he stepped into a wish-fulfilment world where both of them could adopt fictitious identities and play out vicarious roles. It was a more imaginative method of escaping from his own limited personality, of merging more intimately with his loved one – a method that was evolved out of Roger Senhouse's fanciful and capricious nature. Together they would pretend they were David and Absalom, Nero and his slave, a member of Pop (The Eton Society) and his fag, a parent and child – the invention was inexhaustible, the variety endless. And it was Lytton who took the lead. In a revulsion from tame and arid intellectuality, he would call for a flight back to nature. 'Why can't we return to our primeval forest, and swing from the boughs entranced in happiness?' he demanded (13 March 1927). 'We should live on three nuts a day, and sleep together, far up, in the middle of some marvellous palm. Never to touch the ground, Roger – how divine! Wouldn't that alone be worth all the intellect of humanity?' At other times he would visualize some more cosy domestic scene to act as a refuge from his present self. 'Won't you take me on as your servant instead of Peel?' he begged (December 1926). 'I have always longed for such a job. To have no will of one's own, no importance, no responsibility, hardly even a soul – how very satisfying it would be. If I shaved off my beard nobody would recognise me. "Disappearance of a well-known Author" – and it would be delightful.'

For Lytton, the knowledge that he could be drawn away from his single, pallid environment and absorbed into a multitude of imaginary-historical scenes and forms and places was an extraordinary boon that added to his love-life a wholly unexplored and enchanted territory, into which he might be liberated almost at will. Gradually, by means of certain aberrant experiments, he learnt how to rise above the murk and haze of the passing day into this magically illumined, fugitive wonderland. The aesthetic tastes which he and Roger shared – especially for literature and music – became invested with strange sexual properties. Books and their bindings began to haunt Lytton's dreams. 'One's feelings towards certain books certainly approach the libidinous, as Dr. Freud would say,' he observed. In Rome, during their fortnight of intense happiness together, they had read Dante, and afterwards Lytton discovered that simply by touching this book with lingering hands he could conjure up a wonderful sensuality. To trail his finger-tips over the delicious morocco bindings sent through him a shiver of delirious, throbbing excitement – 'for which I am sure Dante would have reserved a particularly ingenious circle of Hell – If only such a vice could have occurred to him.' Even reading together from a French first edition that had belonged to the 'Grand Dauphin' – the eldest son of Louis XIV – transported Lytton. No longer was he a middle-aged, twentieth-century author, but the heir apparent to the French throne; and there beside him sat – not a handsome, Etonian bibliophil – but the king himself! It was an experience too improbable for the most exaggerated novel. 'I fear I am almost too happy when I am with you,' Lytton confessed to Roger (February 1930). '. . . Oh dear, the intricacy and intensity of existence reduces me to a shadow. Every moment is peculiar beyond words.'

Music, too, could work the same strange spell between them, dissolving the walls of this too solid world, softening Lytton's heart, unlearning his mind, and stirring, with trembling compression, his whole being until it seemed to float, weightless and unsubstantial, like the airs that crept so softly upon the harp-strings and filled the silence of the spheres with their legendary echoes. He had always loved music, but this special sensitivity was quite in excess of anything he had felt before. Music *really was* the food of love, and all of heaven that we had on earth. It seemed to breathe voluptuous visions into the warm air, making him giddy with expectation, whispering unheard-of joys to his weary spirit, whirling him round and round and drenching his senses with an imaginary relish, sharp and sweet. Mozart he preferred. Bach was too religious. And as for Vaughan Williams, 'I have an instinctive feeling that he must be South Kensington – but I expect that's only because I once knew his female relatives'. Almost always he liked to hear string music. Such harmonies as those of the Beethoven Last Quartets lay in immortal souls, and it was only when he was uplifted beyond the muddy vesture of decay which ordinarily encloses us that he could become sensible to their full beauty and power. For it was to the fleeting strains of fine music that lust and affection could melt into one, a pale and tender union, assimilating all other passions. What was that shuddering sensation that swept through his body as he listened? It was almost as if he and Roger were the instruments themselves – the violin, its very strings and bow, with its exquisite taut movement, rhythmically back and forwards, in and out, so subtly potent, so ravishing.

Such experiences were beyond the range of words, but when, at the end of the first chapter in *Elizabeth and Essex*, he describes the highest point of rapture in the queen's love-affair with her courtier, it is with a musical metaphor that he awkwardly tries to evoke it. 'When two consciousnesses come to a certain nearness the impetus of their inter-actions, growing ever intenser and intenser, leads on to an unescapable climax. The crescendo must rise to its topmost note; and only then is the preordained solution of the theme made manifest.'

Less psychological, and more successful as literature, is a poem he composed for Roger Senhouse in the late winter of 1926, conveying something of the exaltation that invested their sessions of reading and music together.

> *Then such delight the enchanted spirit knows*
> *As when in June on a red-bosomed rose*
> *A golden rosebud leans an amorous chin;*
> *Or when all's hushed – breath's held – the strings begin!*
> *And with an answering harmony there flows*
> *O'er the rapt bass a thrilling violin.*

The rapture which Lytton felt he had discovered with Roger could not be perfectly fitted into the rest of his life. It was unique and in-divisible, neither wholly a part of Ham Spray nor any part at all of the Strachey household at 51 Gordon Square. In March 1927, therefore, he decided to take extra rooms somewhere else in London, which would be useful for the sort of entertaining that could not very well involve his mother and sisters, and could not properly be conducted at Hunger-ford without setting aside an entire week-end. After a consultation with James, he committed himself to renting a flat in 41 Gordon Square – the very house that Ralph and Frances had gone to a year earlier! Here he hoped to be able to see Roger more easily, and repay the hospitality of their mutual friends – Mary Hutchinson, Dadie Rylands, Raymond Mortimer and others.

This spring, Lytton stood at the very top of happy hours. Before Rome he had never really been able to credit his good fortune – his 'free gift from Providence'. But then the lure of unprogressive satis-factions had entrapped them both, engulfing Lytton in an air of indulgent and delusive ease. A seal seemed to have been set on his happiness. The fleeting hour stood still so that tomorrow always promised a miraculous renewal of today – what could be more natural, then, than to plan for the future? But when he wrote off to Roger telling of his new rooms, the reply was vacillating, indecisive. For so caught up had Lytton become with images from his make-believe world that he had mis-construed the facts. He expected to see his own sentiments exactly mirrored back to him by Roger. What he actually saw was something far more blurred, more formless and diffuse. 'It's really rather a wonder-ful combination of things we seem to have discovered, or perhaps invented,' Lytton had written to him. But Roger was not so sure. He felt frightened of being shifted into a false and untenable position, where his own bland affection would fail in opposition to such heady passion. By consenting to go to Rome with Lytton – who had paid for every-thing – he found himself bound by something more than airy friend-ship or flirtation, by the ties of gratitude for a very real benefit. All these further plans might tie him tighter still. So he began to struggle and seek refuge in dissimulation.

Lytton was at once bewildered and hurt. Roger's apparent in-consistency and lack of concentration gave him the feeling of trying to make an impression on cotton wool. What could be the explanation? He was uncertain of how to treat the situation in which he found him-self. On an impulse, while in London, he telephoned him 'feeling like a detected murderer'. But to his surprise Roger sounded extremely friendly, and they arranged to go to *Così Fan Tutte* together. The reconciliation was delicious, but even so Lytton remained puzzled. 'I feel a good deal happier, though rather alarmed,' he told Mary Hutchinson (25 March 1927), '– I don't quite know why – please support me!'

Although Lytton could not have known it until a day or two later, there were good reasons for this alarm, and much need, during the next weeks and months, for the support of his friends. Even as the two of them sat listening to Mozart that evening, a letter was in the post on its way to Ham Spray which set out many of Roger's apprehensions. Where were these flights of fantasy, these adventures of mind and imagination, leading them? he nervously inquired. Lytton would contrive roles and situations which were so gripping, so enjoyable, that he, Roger, was completely swept up by them. They were so amusing, too, and since they gave Lytton such evident pleasure, pleasurable to him also. But reality kept breaking through, plunging Lytton down a terrifying abyss. It was these sudden dizzying descents, when the knowledge, born of disaster to all his aspirations, would come to him that fiction is not fact, the image not the substance, earth not a timeless paradise – it was these agonizing, heart-sinking moments of transition that terrified Roger. He did not himself experience this dreadful recoil, for he had not the same craving for make-believe, but he saw their effect on Lytton and was sucked into the complicated passage of emotions. Although not fully understanding what was going on, he still felt lost, nervous, upset, and in some degree responsible for the anguish that played so horribly upon Lytton's spirit. What should he do? Their physical needs and inclinations proclaimed themselves as being so very different. It was all right when Carrington was there, and it was not so bad when Lytton came up to London, at which times Roger would, in some degree, take Carrington's place. But he was apprehensive about going down to Ham Spray alone. Quite literally, he feared that Lytton might go mad. There seemed to be no culmination to his feelings. That strange wild passion that inflamed his being burnt within him to a white-hot intensity, but, discovering nothing to ignite, devoured itself. In his excitement, he would urge Roger to more and more extravagant measures, would grow extraordinarily worked up: yet the pressure could find no exterior release. Even in his most extreme states, he was somehow still inhibited. Roger knew, of course, that Lytton's attitude towards him was not one of simple sexual desire. Their relationship was rather one of limitless sympathy, or empathy – and he was frightened of anything that might impair it. Most of all he dreaded paining Lytton, who was at all times very vulnerable and hypersensitive, who remembered everything one happened to say and gave it an unmeant significance.

'Lytton, I cannot bear to wound you in any way at all,' he wrote, '– it has an instantaneous effect upon me – and yet I am continually finding myself upon the point of doing so by some inconsiderate word or action, and if I hurt you and see that I have, I feel a sense of shame that makes me nervous. I want always to feel entirely open, straightforward and undisguised in front of you, but I discover too often that I have cloaked my proper feelings, and that I am falling into a part that is not true to my nature. . . . You are, Lytton, so overwhelmingly charming and considerate to me that I am quite at a loss to know how to reciprocate it, for were I to mention at any time dissatisfaction with what was taking place, I know the pains you would devote to amend it. . . . I know you say that you get all that satisfies you from things as they have existed for the last months, but I who keep watch, as it were, can only realise that what I have loosely termed "things" might be so very much better.'

The effect of this letter upon Lytton was unexampled. A blackness and a void closed in upon him, and the blood drained from his head. He could not conceal his agitation. 'I am in almost complete despair,' he lamented to Mary Hutchinson (1 May 1927). 'All is shattered!' He read only one meaning into Roger's hesitant words: that he did not feel for him what Lytton had taken for granted he felt – that he did not love him. And he had been so certain of this love, too! Just when happiness seemed within his grasp, when he had practically been able to see with Roger's eyes, adopt his will, set their two hearts beating in unison, and catch the very warmth from his soul, the good moment had fled. Where was the thread now? He was falling, falling into a blind desolation, while Roger, like a thistle ball, floated onwards and upwards, far beyond his reach, wherever light winds blew. The old trick! – and he had been taken in by it once again. Where did the persistent fault lie? Had he really forced Roger out of his true nature, or was he simply being irresponsible? Surely it must be irresponsibility, that delinquent, frivolous, incalculable irresponsibility which lay at the very root of his fatal charm. 'Yes, Roger's charm. But what pray is charm, I should like to know?' Lytton ruefully inquired of Mary Hutchinson. His character was so fluid and indefinable, so deceptively soluble that it appeared to take colour from whatever it touched. From day to day, he was never the same person – now tender and affectionate, now politely offhand as if faintly embarrassed to find himself the idol of an ageing invalid. No wonder Lytton had been misled!

The next four-and-a-half months were overhung with hideous uncertainty. Lytton's thoughts rushed round, confused and crowded, from disappointment to regret, from rage to repentance with brief flashes of false and febrile exhilaration. Unreasonable jealousies obsessed and agonized his brain. Like someone deranged, he was driven by a harrowing restlessness hither and thither. Kindness and company were what he sought, to numb the shock and to distract his mind from morbid, endlessly rotating preoccupations. He could not bear to be left alone, but hurried from Carrington to Mary Hutchinson and Topsy Lucas, from Dadie Rylands to Stephen Tomlin, frantically drinking in their words of comfort and reassurance.

In these friends, at least, he was fortunate. All that friends can do in such circumstances, they did. 'I am surrounded by infinite kindness and devotion,' he wrote to Dadie Rylands (18 July 1927), 'but how can I not sometimes feel lonely?' At Ham Spray a new orientation of human affairs was spinning into place, and involving all the complexity that had by now become *de rigueur* in that ambiguous household. In reaction from his disappointed passion for Roger, Lytton turned momentarily back to Ralph Partridge. Memories of their old intimacy– 'so intensely romantic and moving – rushed back upon me, and I felt strangely upset,' he confided to Mary Hutchinson (9 August 1927). 'There he was, downstairs, the same person, really, I couldn't help feeling; but six years or seven had gone – and where were we now? – I longed to say something – but it was impossible to do more than murmur some vague word or two, and he returned to London.'

Throughout this summer, Lytton tried to ease the heartache by a few light flirtations with young men. 'Yes, love is tiresome,' he admitted to Topsy Lucas (27 July 1927), 'but life goes on, and things do happen – quite fresh and exciting – even though one is chucked by some R[oger] or other.' The most abiding consolation and companionship, however, came from his other two friends, Dadie Rylands and Stephen Tomlin. The latter, for a brief spell, occupied a uniquely bipartite position in the Ham Spray régime. After months of mutually inflicted torture, Carrington and Gerald had temporarily split up, and Tomlin at once stepped into Gerald's place upon the stage. Being completely bisexual, it seemed that he ought to have been nicely suited to perform a sort of virtuoso solo *pas de deux*, and for a time he did just this. But his influence between Lytton and Carrington was never a very stable one, for though equally attractive to both, his personality was far too moody, too brightly painted, too brittle and volatile – like that of a lunatic putting on an inspired charade of normality. Besides – and this was later to be of tragic importance – Ralph strongly, if rather illogically, objected to his having a love-affair with Carrington. The relationship between the two men had always been rather variable. Ralph admired his outstanding intelligence and legalistic pleasure in argument. But he considered him to be essentially dishonest and corrupt, someone more likely to destroy than to create happiness – and he feared what this influence, acting upon Carrington, might lead to. At the end of July, however, their tenuous affair lapsed when Tomlin was married off to Julia Strachey. 'I am leading a decidedly queer life,' Lytton apprised Mary Hutchinson (19 July 1927). 'Both T[ommy] and D[adie] are devoted to me – and I to them; they please me in every way – though, to be sure, the ways are diffierent! . . . My relation with T[ommy] is exciting – there is strength there – and a mind – a remarkable character; – but there is a lull in the proceedings, for he is to be married on Thursday (I believe). There is also a lull with D[adie], who has gone to Cambridge – a delightful, gay affair that one. So you see altogether I have plenty to think about in my seclusion. . . . Was there ever such a world? Such lives? Such peculiarities?'

Despite these moments of freshness and excitement, his seclusion this summer was generally 'dank and cheerless'. For once he could find no escape from his troubles within his work, for imbedded in the story of *Elizabeth and Essex* he saw much that poignantly reflected back his own tragic history. This may largely have been the cause of his painfully slow progress at the book. He had been unhappily in love before, yet managed to carry on steadily with his writing because it afforded him relief, even forgetfulness, from his emotional problems. But *Elizabeth and Essex* only exacerbated this pain and worry. In his letters there are several detached sentences that could apply with equal aptness to his own love-affair or to Elizabeth's, and he passes from his lack of success with the biography to his failure in love in an abrupt way that clearly suggests some connexion. 'I feel as if I were in the middle of a very bad Channel crossing,' he wrote to Topsy Lucas (9 June 1927). 'I know that there is a high probability that I shall get to the other side, but I can't feel it – I can only feel a complication of dreadful disturbances. But of course there are mitigated moments. As for my friends, their kindness is almost divine. R[oger] is extremely suspicious and possesses what I can only call a female capacity for detecting anything tendentious in a conversation, so I beg you to be highly discreet. Please be kind to him, and give him self-confidence – it is what he needs. I assure you he is a most adorable creature, and I shall be devoted to him in saecula saeculorum.'

The withdrawal of Roger's radiant presence gradually became insupportable to Lytton. There was no satisfaction anywhere. At the end of June, Philip Ritchie came down to stay with him at Ham Spray in order to recruit after an attack of tonsillitis, and a momentary calmness fell upon Lytton. But soon all was gloom and hesitation once more. The estrangement between him and Roger was never complete. At all times the outward forms of affection and respect were maintained, and sometimes they appeared as close to each other as ever – disagreement vanished, the gloom lifted, hope returned. But Lytton could never tell how things would turn out from one meeting to the next. 'As for my young man, whom I went to on leaving you,' he wrote to Mary Hutchinson (15 July 1927), '– he was unexpectedly delightful – really most coming on – the villain!'

For a while, there did seem some detectable pattern to Roger's behaviour – or so Lytton believed. The farther apart from each other they were, the more affectionate he appeared – a highly unsatisfactory arrangement. 'I think of R[oger] still – no doubt too much – I wish I didn't,' Lytton confessed to Mary Hutchinson (27 July 1927). 'Things must take their course and it seems unlikely that I shall see him again before the autumn. There must no doubt be something tiresome about me, when seen very near at hand; but his reactions have I think been a trifle extreme.'

Whatever the attitude Lytton adopted in order to protect himself,

Roger would counter with a fresh surprise. His actions were quite unpremeditated, quite unpredictable, uncomprehending, incomprehensible. He was psychotic, neurotic, erratic, erotic. In desperation, Lytton even tried to interest him in another of his friends – at least there would be some certainty, some rest, in losing him altogether. But it was no use. His mood of philosophic fatalism lasted about a week before it was wrenched apart by a totally unforeseen visit from Roger to Ham Spray. By a strange coincidence, the day of his arrival marked an exact year since the visit on which Lytton first 'found myself in an exquisite paradise' – and Roger now 'kept the anniversary by sleeping, for the first time, by himself', Lytton told Mary Hutchinson (9 August 1927). 'However, such coincidences are ridiculous. . . . He looked far from well – pale and puffy – no beauty that I could see – really almost someone different. So dreadfully fat! – All went well, he was most amiable. I behaved with the highest propriety, he seemed to enjoy himself, and positively on going away gave me an entirely unsolicited kiss. A queer creature, certainly. Decidedly charming. . . . We spent a happy hour comparing Rabelais in the original with Urquhart's translation. He picked wild flowers and branches from shrubs on our morning walk – more flowers in the garden – and went back with a huge armful – to my mind a sympathetic thing to do, and what no one else I know (except Carrington) would dream of doing. Aren't things strangely – exasperatingly – mixed? What does one want? What does anyone want? – Really? Ah! – so little – and so much! –'

The search for this lost, complicated quality of love jolted him up and down a tortuous and exhausting switchback of emotions. 'The Lytton-clock needs winding up,' he wrote to Dadie Rylands (15 August 1927). 'The hands remain immovable in mid-career, and Ham Spray is the Realm of Chastity.' After receiving from Roger a 'desolating pale grey epistle', he rushed up to see him in London, where he was 'all tender solicitude'. But by this time Lytton felt apathetic – a victim resigned, almost insensible to his punishment. Their relationship had become totally inexplicable to him – though 'I suppose Time will make all things clear'. Early in September, Roger left for a holiday in Germany, dispatching back to Lytton a stream of postcards and long letters that 'positively sent his love!' But what, after all, was love? The contradiction of Lytton's state of mind grew more extreme than ever. Difficulties, dangers, griefs there might be in their singular friendship, but now absence momentarily made all things clearer. A feeling of vast relief spread over him after Roger had left – at least he could enjoy some peace for the next two or three weeks. But even this proved untrue. All too soon he started to wonder what Roger was doing, whether he himself occupied any place in his thoughts and emotions. Life was dull, colourless, almost non-existent without him. 'Do you think of me sometime?' he asked, '. . . are you beginning to forget that I exist? As for me, I can hardly believe that I do – exist I mean.'

This disturbed and uncertain frame of mind might have been prolonged indefinitely, had not, that September, a catalytic tragedy struck at them both. After an unexpected relapse from his tonsillitis, Philip Ritchie suddenly died. For his friends, the news came as a complete shock. 'I had imagined him well and possibly in Scotland,' Lytton wrote to Dadie Rylands (15 September 1927). '. . . It is crushing and miserable. Carrington too feels it terribly – she is infinitely sweet and good. Roger is not back yet . . . I feel very troubled about him. Fate has been unkind to him, certainly. I wish to be with him and comfort him, but it is an added irony that he may feel unable now to make use of my devotion.'[1]

Yet the real irony was that, even in this tragic adversity, Roger could not abandon his capacity for surprising Lytton. Far from being unable to make use of Lytton's devotion, he relied upon it absolutely. The death of Philip Ritchie wiped out at a blow all the previous months of estrangement and cruel suspense. Unhappiness might endure for a spell, but joy quickly superseded it. The two of them met as soon as Roger arrived back in London. He was in a wretched state, full of morbid self-reproaches, which Lytton tried to dispel by showing him how irrelevant and disproportionate they were. 'It is such a great mercy, Dadie,' he afterwards wrote to George Rylands (21 September 1927), 'the cloud that was between us has gone away, and it was possible for me to do all I could to console him and show him my affection quite naturally; and he was perfectly charming and affectionate.'

For the next two weeks, while Lytton was away at Charleston and Weymouth, they corresponded practically every day. They had never been closer. They were held together by the deepest ties of affection, and sorrow had given a new fibrous strength to this connexion. 'But you know, my dearest,' Lytton had written to Roger before returning from Weymouth that October, 'it is impossible not to feel an undercurrent of sadness – more than before; about Philip; and about more general things – the dangers and difficulties of all human life– the miserable pain of separations and misunderstandings – the wicked power of mere accident over happiness and goodness – I know you feel

---

[1] 'Philip died after an operation for taking out his tonsils,' James told the author. 'I remember it all very well. On the night that he went into the nursing-home he dined with me and Carrington at Boulestin's. His death was a complete surprise; but it ought not to have been – he was a soaker, and habitual drinkers have bad livers after operations.'

all this and as for me, when I reflect upon these things, I can't help crying, and then Roger, I sink into our love which comes like the divine resolution of a discord, and all is well.'

8

TOGETHER

'All is well', sounded a cheerful refrain to many of Lytton's letters over the following six months of the winter. 'It is delightful to find oneself down here again,' he wrote from Ham Spray to Topsy Lucas (29 January 1928), 'in freedom and comparative comfort, in spite of the incredible barbarity of the weather. Roger continues to be perfectly charming, and I am curiously happy.' Because of this contentment, because he again felt confident of Roger's devotion, health and spirits flowed back into his capricious organism, and his life became productive and well-balanced once more. 'All is well now between Roger and me,' he notified Dadie Rylands (15 October 1927). 'I am feeling so very happy about it. He is perfectly charming – and I have complete confidence in his affection. In all ways, too, I am much calmer. It is the greatest relief . . . thank you for all your sympathy, and kindness during that miserable time.'

Roger spent much of his available time at Ham Spray this winter, and he and Lytton made two trips to Brighton before the end of the year. Since Lytton's work was 'terribly behindhand', his visits to London and elsewhere, he told Ottoline (4 October 1927), 'will have to be more truncated than usual'. Even so, he found time to spend a couple of 'altogether perfect' week-ends with Peter and Topsy Lucas, to go and watch Dadie Rylands play Volumnia in a Cambridge production of *Coriolanus*, and make a number of dashes up to London to see Desmond MacCarthy, Sybil Colefax, Cynthia Asquith and the 'charming boy' Rex Whistler,[1] 'rather à la Philip IV of Spain in appearance – "maussade" perhaps is the word: but he seemed serious and unconceited'.

Back at Ham Spray, he would either 'sit mewed up, struggling with Gibbon', or 'sit reading the whole of Hume's History as mum as a

---

[1] Rex Whistler (1905–44), the English artist who, with great linear resourcefulness and wit, specialized in the rendering of eighteenth-century life in the rococo style. A versatile painter, he is particularly known for his book illustrations, murals (including 'The Pursuit of Rare Meats' at the refreshment room in the Tate Gallery) and designs for the theatre and ballet. But he also produced textiles, bookplates, china, carpets and even luggage labels for Imperial Airways. There is a biography of him by his brother, the poet and designer Laurence Whistler.

mouse'. By 2 November he had finished Gibbon and 'am pegging away at Macaulay', he told Roger, '– Hume, you see, left to the last – and hope to dispatch him (mac) before Friday'. A week later he reported: 'I plod on with Hume'; and three days later still he wrote to Dadie: 'I have been working like ten cart-horses lately, and have now finished all four of those bloody historians. A great relief! – And now once more I find myself face to face with that moblèd queen.'

His diligence over these weeks was impervious to all temptations, among them a most strange eruption of unexpected visitors from the expensive classes, including Osbert Sitwell, Christabel Aberconway, Siegfried Sassoon and Stephen Tennant, all of them entirely occupied with 'dressing up'. Lytton described the scene in a letter to Roger (27 October 1927). 'The night before they had all dressed up as nuns, that morning they had all dressed up as shepherds and shepherdesses, in the evening they were all going to dress up as – God knows what – but they begged and implored me to return with them and share their raptures. When dressed up they are filmed – and the next week-end, I suppose, the film is exhibited. Can you imagine anything more "perfectly divine"? One would have expected them to come in a vast Daimler, but not at all – a small two seater (open) with a dickey behind was their vehicle – they came very late, having lost their way on the Downs, and I shudder to think of the horrors of their return journey. Strange creatures – with just a few feathers where brains should be. Though no doubt Siegfried is rather different.'

In the last week of November, Lytton finally restarted work on *Elizabeth and Essex*. Earlier that month he had met his American publisher, Donald Brace, in London, and told him that it now seemed unlikely that he could finish the book before March. Brace in any case wanted the British publication delayed until the autumn. 'He said that this would make it much easier to prepare the way for the American sale,' Lytton explained to Charles Prentice (6 November 1927), 'which apparently is necessarily a long business – partly because of the size of the country – but also, I cannot help thinking, because of the slowness of the wits of its inhabitants.'

For the next three months he laboured steadily and with hardly an interruption at *Elizabeth* 'who marches forward with infinite slowness'. Frances Marshall, who, with Ralph, still came down to Ham Spray most week-ends, notes in her journal at this time that Lytton was constantly 'busy writing'. She also communicates something of the peculiar happiness which then irradiated the whole house – Carrington invariably charming, Lytton amiable and animated, discussing Wittgenstein, logic, the difference between *a priori* and empirical knowledge, or the theory that literary genius and children were incompatible; then joking until everyone burst out with laughter; playing chess, paper-games and drawing competitions; reading 'two little Gerhardie volumes', *Futility* and *Donna Quixote*,[1] T. S. Eliot on Shakespeare – 'interesting remarks, but not quite enough' – and Peter Lucas's edition of Webster in four stupendous volumes, a most noble work of astonishing erudition, though 'in some ways a juvenile book'.

One entry in Frances Marshall's journal catches very sympathetically the wonder and contentment of these winter days. 'Arrived at Hamspray with the black kitten. Roger Senhouse the only visitor. Lytton seems very much in love with him. Philip's death seems in some way to have brought them together. The effect on Lytton is to make him very gay and charming. Walked in the fields while Carrington galloped about on Belle. In the evening we let off some fireworks – an exquisite display of pink and green fountains under the pampas grass.' This same day (12 November 1927) Lytton wrote to Dadie Rylands: 'He [Roger] gives me so much happiness that I hardly know what to do about it. I sometimes feel inclined to stand on my head, and do cart-wheels all down the Downs. Do you think that would be a good plan?'

Over Christmas, Stephen and Julia Tomlin came down, with Frances and Ralph, and they were shortly joined by James. A Christmas tree was reared in the back room for the 'petit peuple' from the village who held a boisterous party round it – while, a little way off, like a beneficent shadow, Lytton moved among his books. Over night a heavy fall of snow filled the ditches and lanes with immense drifts and extraordinary shapes, like giant mushrooms, columns and sand-dunes. A brilliant sun shone in the white fields and trees, and a transparent blue sky extended from horizon to horizon, without a cloud. The horses in the farmyard cantered about jumping imaginary obstacles in their efforts to keep warm. Within Ham Spray, too, every psychological cloud seemed to have evaporated. 'Lytton, who had an assignation with Roger, was anxious to get away in spite of all difficulties,' recorded Frances Marshall (28 December 1927), 'and a procession set out to walk in to Hungerford. Lytton in a fur coat and waders, R[alph] in top boots, a ruck-sack and a crimson hat trimmed with monkey fur, James with his head entirely enveloped in a scarf, we must have looked a bizarre collection. The scene was fantastically beautiful; after Inkpen

---

[1] *Futility*, William Gerhardie's first novel on Russian themes, sponsored by Katherine Mansfield and later to be taken up and praised by Edith Wharton, Arnold Bennett and numerous other writers, was published in 1922. 'Why was there no shouting,' afterwards inquired H. G. Wells, '– shouting to reach the suburbs and the county towns?' *Donna Quixote* (1927) is a play by William Gerhardie, of which the first act is a farce, the second a comedy and the third a tragedy.

the roads were full to the top with snow; the blue sky brought out curious pink lights in it and deep blue shadows, cottages were grotesquely hung with post-card icicles, and the snow was marbled all over with ripplemarks made by the wind. At Hungerford the world seemed suddenly ordinary again; people stepped into the train wearing bowler hats, and gaped to see a troupe of Bulgarian peasants, headed evidently by their Prime Minister in his fur coat.'

The new year opened with undimmed radiance. 'Good Queen Bess' slowly trundled forward; Roger's charm, in its unaccountable fashion, continued unabated, while alongside it ran Lytton's own curious happiness. On the week-end of 11 February, the two of them made a lightning trip to France, crossing the Channel in a gale and terrific thunderstorm from Tilbury to Dunkirk, and hurrying on to Paris where they were to meet Norman Douglas. This meeting was the outcome of almost five years' intermittent correspondence between the two writers. Lytton, who had read practically nothing of Douglas's work before 1923, was first introduced to it that year by Carrington – a passionate admirer of all his novels and travel books. At first his enthusiasm was lukewarm, falling a good way short of hers. But two years later his opinion had risen appreciably, and he confided to Ottoline (16 February 1925) that Norman Douglas 'seems to me an attractive figure. I've become a great admirer of all his works; though I hardly dare say so, owing to the scoffs of the cultured.'

Under pressure from Carrington, he had opened up the correspondence between them in October 1923, writing to say how much he had admired and enjoyed *Siren Land* (1911), *Old Calabria* (1915), *South Wind* (1917), *Alone*[1] (1921) and *Together*, which had come out earlier that year.[2] This letter soon led the way to a long sequence of those reciprocal civilities to which authors are so poignantly and comically prone. 'I value your opinion more highly than that of any English writer,' Douglas eulogistically answered (9 November 1923). 'In

---

[1] 'I have a special love of *Alone*. How did you manage to fill it with that romantic beauty? The variety of moods in it is indeed extraordinary; and yet the totality of the impression is completely preserved,' Lytton wrote to Norman Douglas. 'I am delighted to hear you like *Alone*!' Douglas replied. 'So do I. What you discover in it to please you is no doubt the result of that ridiculous war, driving me into myself. I really felt *alone*, surrounded by a legion of imbeciles hacking each other in pieces. An exhilarating sensation; and one that has not quite faded away. May it never do so.'

[2] 'We are reading a new novel by Norman Douglas in the evenings,' Carrington wrote to Dorelia John (10 February 1928). 'Tell me, have you got it? It's rather Greek, and very lecherous. I've been doing some designs for some rooms at Cambridge. Panels for doors. I think I shall go over there and paint them soon. Its a Hideous gothic room in Kings, belonging to a sweet canary Don called. Rylands. So I'm doing Hideous Gothic pictures of roman emperor heads, and Greek urns to make a nice job of it.'

these decidedly lean years it is the fatness of your kine that is so particularly striking. Your books are so full; there is so much of so many things in them – so much experience, so much learning, so much art, so much humour, so much philosophy, and so much proof that there is so much, so very much, more underneath, that is unexpressed ... in fact for me, your opinion is a thing apart from that of others, even as your writings belong to a category by themselves ... do let me thank you for the real pleasure – joy, I should say – which I have derived from your books. A thing of art, unquestionably.'

By the end of this year they had already exchanged photographs – 'his [Douglas's] photograph seems to me much more prepossessing than I had expected', Lytton commented in a letter to Dorothy Bussy (25 November 1923). 'I had imagined something large, Scotch, and coarse.' Douglas had also sent Lytton the revised edition of *Siren Land* and Lytton had responded with 'a charming letter of thanks and appreciation', lamenting only the absence of a map.[1] Not to be outmatched in the offering of courtesy and literary garlands, Douglas straightway dispatched back 'a very nice letter' of his own. 'I wish you would write a biography of Heliogabalus, for example, drawn from new sources discovered yourself during a recent visit to Egypt,' he wrote (3 December 1923). 'Come here, and we'll do it together. Or the private journal of the Emperor Claudius.'

The heady compliments and mild whimsy trickled amicably on throughout the next year and, in February 1925, Douglas forwarded Lytton four copies of his privately printed brochure *D. H. Lawrence and Maurice Magnus. A plea for better manners*,[2] a theme nicely in harmony with the tone of their own correspondence. 'I hope you will not dislike it,' he wrote (4 February 1925). 'It is the first thing I have

[1] A revised edition of *Siren Land*, Norman Douglas's first serious book, was published by Martin Secker this winter. 'As for Siren Land,' Douglas wrote to Lytton (9 November 1923), 'seven of its twenty chapters were cut out by the publisher as being "too remote from human interests". *Without consulting me*, he also pulped the entire edition save what had already been sold, which is an infamous proceeding, as one would gladly have bought a copy or two to give to friends. It cannot be helped; one is in the hands of these brigands. Secker has now brought out a new one; the copies reached me last night and I am sending you *one* right away. You will find it stodgy in places, and precious, and unintelligible here and there; but it testifies to an appalling industry.'

[2] This pamphlet was written in 1924 as a reply to D. H. Lawrence's Introduction to *Memoirs of the Foreign Legion* by Maurice Magnus. Lytton forwarded one of his copies to Ottoline Morrell. 'I think it may amuse you,' he wrote (11 February 1925), 'even if you haven't read the book à propos to which it is written; for years I've thought that some such protest was wanted; and N.D., it seems to me, has done it effectively, in his own particular style. But I doubt whether "friend Lawrence" will see the error of his ways.' In the *New Statesman* (20 February 1926) Lawrence, 'weary of being slandered', defended himself against Douglas's charges.

written since October 1923, so you see you are not the only person afflicted with the complaint of non-productivity. . . . I heard a rumour that William Beckford, Esquire, might soon be engaging your attention. That would be wonderful. You are the only person who could handle that proposition. A lovely subject!'

Throughout this time the two of them had never met, though there had been several tentative arrangements to do so. 'Now come here if you can,' Douglas wrote from Italy on 25 September 1927. 'Florence is taboo for me also, at present. I am living at Prato and only go in for an afternoon now and then, thickly veiled and wearing blue glasses and a carroty beard. This will last, I daresay, till after Christmas. But there is no reason why you shouldn't come to the neighbourhood, anyhow.' When eventually they did come face to face some four months later, the suggestion had again come from Douglas. 'Now just think if you can't run (or fly) over to Paris for a week-end,' he urged Lytton (31 January 1928). 'I have to go there about the 10th, and have some 58 teeth pulled out, and 63 new ones put in, and I am sure you are the very person to hold my hand. Besides we can go to Pruniers in the intervals. Nancy Cunard is there: I hope you like her?[1] So do come along.'

After so much epistolary warmth, Lytton felt rather nervous of actually encountering Douglas man to man, and was glad to have Roger Senhouse with him. The week-end was, he confessed beforehand to Dadie Rylands (9 February 1928), 'a truly frantic project. . . . I am excited and terrified, as you may imagine. Good God! The crossing! The cold! The streets of Paris! And – most serious of all – Norman Douglas! Will he be charming, vulgar, too talkative, too vague, or what? – Perhaps a womanizer after all! Who knows? And what, oh what, shall I say? How *am* I to carry it off? A silent owl in an ivy bush. I shall beg Roger to wear a false beard, and shave mine off, so that we may change parts. And I'll let you know the upshot.' These preliminary fears were soon whipped to a frenzy by a series of last-minute calamities, as Carrington recounted to Dorelia John (10 February 1928). 'There is great agitation as his [Lytton's] drawers, and vests haven'T come back from the wash and the wind roars so fiercely that he is terrified all the ships will sink. But I expect it will be great fun boozing at Foyots.'

Before Lytton set off for Paris, Douglas had written to ask whethei he could put him on to someone who might help him collect 'the obscenest and most blasphemous Limericks (university or Stock

---

[1] After World War I, Nancy Cunard had gone to live permanently in France, set up her own Hours Press at Réanville and published (1928–31) some twenty volumes of contemporary authors. A journalist for the *Manchester Guardian*, a wide traveller and a poetess, she later wrote her memories of Norman Douglas and some reminiscences of George Moore.

Exchange?)', since he wished to make a full anthology 'for scholarly purposes of course', which would be privately printed some day 'with copious notes'. It was in this capacity, as adviser on limericks filthy and profane, that Roger Senhouse travelled out with Lytton.[1]

Their meeting, despite Lytton's apprehensions, was remarkably successful. After the rough passage, Lytton arrived feeling like 'a mere piece of wet brown paper', and now dreading more than ever their *rencontre*. Douglas, however, turned out to be most sympathetic, speaking with a memorable and amusing pseudo-Scotch accent and behaving not at all in the bohemian, florid manner that his letters had somehow suggested. He seemed to understand at once Lytton's aversion to 'those trailing café parties', and brushed it all aside, declaring that he, too, did not care for them. Then, so that Lytton should have an opportunity to rest and recover, they arranged to meet at Foyot's for dinner. That evening, Douglas arrived, very punctually, wearing a sombre black coat. But as soon as they started to discuss the limerick anthology, there was no black coat on his conversation. 'N.D. was rather older than I expected,' Lytton afterwards narrated in a letter to Mary Hutchinson (22 February 1928), '– not flamboyant (as I had rather feared) – in fact rather the opposite – very neat – something (as Roger said) of a schoolmasterish effect in *appearance* – one of those odd benevolent unexpectedly broad-minded schoolmasters one sometimes comes across. Superb in restaurants, ordering food, and so on. A curious, very marked accent – partly Scotch, perhaps, partly – I don't know what – distinctly fascinating. The talk was mainly on a certain subject. Roger played up admirably, quite admirably, and made everything go much more easily than would otherwise have been the case.

---

[1] Roger Senhouse, as it turned out, was of no practical use to Douglas over the limerick book. On 30 July 1928, Douglas wrote to Lytton from the Abruzzi mountains, where he had fled with 'two youngsters', asking whether 'our young friend' could be induced to send him some limericks. 'I should be ever so glad, as the book is under weigh (? way) and I want as much variety as possible.' On 12 September 1928, he again wrote: 'I have *finished* the limerick book. It will shortly be printed and bound, and a copy shall go to you. So you needn't bother the poor Roger (appropriate name).' A little later that year one hundred and fifty copies of *Some Limericks* were privately printed in Florence for subscribers only. They were all signed, bound in handsome amber-coloured canvas, and sold at five and even ten guineas each – after which all sorts of other private editions have been brought out. Douglas planned two sequels – *More Limericks* and *Last Limericks* – but because the police court in Florence, stirred up, it was commonly believed, by the British Home Office, threatened to take criminal proceedings, he judged it wiser to publish no further limericks. As to *Some Limericks*, Nancy Cunard has commented: 'They have to be seen to be believed, rollicking, scatological and dire, as they are, in their schoolboy mirth, stockbroker or Army-wit, and all of them frightfully funny. But not so funny as the learned note that accompanies each (and its variants), where the author (or collator) examines them closely, often in a pseudo-scientific manner. . . . The Index is a gem in itself.' (*Grand Man*, pp. 286–7.)

He seemed to be not particularly literary – which was slightly disturbing; and I think just a trifle too old – I mean belonging to a generation almost too distant for really intimate approach – a touch of Sickert – but perhaps I'm wrong. . . . A slight effect you know of having been not very well treated by life. He's been very unlucky with publishers, and has made hardly anything out of his books. One would like to surround him with every kind of comfort and admiration and innumerable boys of 14½.' In the course of their conversation Douglas said he might be coming to England that summer, and Lytton at once replied that he would give him a party at Boulestin's. 'I hope you will come to Ham Spray, too,' he added. 'Oh, shoorly, shoorly,' was the answer.

The following day, Lytton and Roger went over to the Hôtel d'Isly in the rue Jacob, where Douglas was staying with Victor and Nancy Cunard. 'Their relations were not very easy to disentangle,' Lytton reported. 'Christian names reigned – and they were all three living in the same hotel. N.D. insisted on coming to the station to see me off – insisted on paying for every meal – and eventually tried to tip the porter!'

The more Lytton thought of Douglas on his arrival back in England, the more he felt that there was something pathetic about him. He was a kind man, and he lived in want. It was particularly abominable that his books should have brought him so little reward. In return for his hospitality over the week-end, he immediately tried to interest Chatto and Windus in Douglas's work, especially his novel on religion, *In the Beginning*, a limited edition of which had been privately printed in Florence the previous year. 'Of course I don't know in the least whether such a thing would be possible for you,' he admitted to Charles Prentice (15 February 1928), '(nor did I say anything to him about it), but the suggestion seemed worth making, and I hope you won't mind my doing so. I feel he is exactly the sort of writer your firm would like to be connected with, and that he on his side would benefit greatly if this could happen. In my opinion he is a most distinguished person, and it's a scandal that his last three books should produce no more than £12 a year in royalties.' As a result of this letter, Chatto and Windus became Douglas's publishers, bringing out *In the Beginning* later that year, and subsequently a number of his other books, including his autobiography, reprints of his earlier works, and *An Almanac* (1945), a volume of Douglas's favourite passages from the whole corpus of his work.

For several days after this Paris excursion, Lytton lay in his bed recovering. From now on, he decided, until *Elizabeth and Essex* was finally off his hands, he must go nowhere. Determinedly he refused all

T

invitations – including one to a Birth Control Ball and another to a
charity performance of a play said to be dictated from the Other World
by Oscar Wilde. 'I feel I must stick to this wretched grindstone, or all
will be lost,' he explained to Mary Hutchinson (22 February 1928). 'Its
serpentine prolongation is getting past a joke.' He had reached the
thirteenth chapter, and all was proceeding well. 'I am getting on with
old Bess as fast as I can expect,' he had informed Roger (20 February
1928). A fortnight later, he wrote: 'Here I am all alone – it is wonderfully peaceful – a faint mist hangs about – but so far I have managed to
keep it out of my head. The Bess crisis is pretty serious – a regular death-
grapple![1] But I hope the worst will be over by the end of the week. . . .
Bemax supports me.' By the end of the week, the worst did indeed seem
to be over. 'I am beginning to see light through the Elizabethan jungle,'
he told Charles Prentice (13 March 1928), 'and so far as I can calculate,
the length of the book will be somewhere round about 75,000 words.
This is distinctly longer than I had originally expected; but I gathered
from what you said that a bigger work would if anything be an
advantage from your point of view. I think I still have about 10,000
words to write, and this with luck I should accomplish in about a
month.'

After two-and-a-half years of intermittent struggle, he was within
sight of the long-prepared last paragraph of his book. An uncharacteristic fit of impatience now seized hold of him. Every day he
worked longer and longer hours – until, suddenly, his stamina gave
way. Depression and a series of terrible headaches racked him, and for
a fortnight he was unable to write anything. With her customary
devotion, Carrington nursed him through this illness, and by Easter he
felt well enough to go and stay with Dadie Rylands at his home in
Tockington, near Bristol. Here, to assist in his recuperation, he would
read aloud each morning from the plays of Molière; and after tea he
permitted himself to do just a little work, arriving back at Ham Spray
with four closely written sheets of paper – another chapter done!

Very slowly the narrative edged forward, until once again there came
a death-crisis. 'At the moment I am almost dead with exhaustion from
this fearful tussle with the Old Hag,' he told Roger (19 April 1928), 'and

---

[1] Lytton uses this same phrase in a letter (3 March 1928) to Lumsden Barkway, who
had written to him on his forty-eighth birthday. 'I am in the death-grapple with a vile
book on Queen Elizabeth, and dare not relax my grip. It was delightful and astonishing
of you to remember my birthday. Yes – I am 48 – it seems absurd, and I should suggest
that there must be a mistake of twenty years in my birth certificate, if it were not that
you would arise as a witness against me! . . . The odd thing is that my hair refuses to
give any evidence – so far as I can see – it remains preposterously brown. But I always
felt I was a kind of Samson – *all* my strength is in my hair! . . .'

I think tomorrow I shall have to take a complete rest.' Finally, on the very last day of the month, the agony came to an end. 'I am glad to be able to tell you that my book is finished,' he announced triumphantly to Charles Prentice, 'and the last bit is being typed now.'[1]

The next week he travelled up to London and called on Prentice to deliver the completed typescript and to discuss its probable date of publication and the title. It was the first Thursday in May. When at last he left the office, late that afternoon, all the details had been agreed. The sun shone in the streets as he stepped out jauntily on his way back to Bloomsbury. He was a free man again.

9

END OF AN ERA

Elizabeth and Essex utterly prostrated Lytton – far more so than *Queen Victoria* had done seven years earlier. 'It was a terribly exhausting book to write,' he confessed to Ottoline (29 November 1928) '– I don't know why – I was sadly depressed most of the time.' He was to live for almost four years more, but over much of this final period the pulses of creative work seemed to have grown feeble, while over his love-life the clouds of weariness and suspense were perpetually forming and dissolving again. After *Elizabeth and Essex*, he published only four new essays – besides compiling a number of the notes to *The Greville Memoirs*. To some of those nearest him, it appeared occasionally as if the inner spring had lost its elasticity, and the mechanism continued to act by the mere force of momentum. 'I had not realised what a weight Elizabeth had been on me – especially for the last few months,' he confided to Roger (25 May 1928). '– and the relief of getting rid of it – of really being mentally free again – is very great. My spirits are beginning to bounce about again as they ought.' Once, during the last, hardest months of his work, he had told Topsy Lucas (30 October 1927) that he wished 'I never had even to pretend to do any work – I believe I should whirl round in a perpetual circle of pleasure'. For the remaining two thirds of the year there was no further need either to work or to pretend to work, and he was at liberty to revolve to his heart's content in a smooth ellipse of travel and sheer indolence. He had become, like George IV, an artistic idler. There was nothing whatever to do – and he was just the man to do it. Laziness, he told Lumsden Barkway, was

---

[1] The typing was done by Ethel Christian's of Southampton Street, to whom Lytton would send batches of his manuscript at intervals.

'an accomplishment which I have thoroughly mastered! I could give you lessons in the art.'

But now came over him the absolute necessity to move. A few days after having relinquished the typescript, he and Carrington set off on a four-week tour of Provence, spending the first ten days at Aix – 'a truly delightful place – utterly dim – with house after house of extraordinary beauty'. They put up at the Hôtel Nègre-Coste, and each day, in architectural ecstasies over the house fronts and doorways, they would wander through the fascinating streets, or explore the antique shops where they bought, among other items of furniture for Ham Spray, a large chest-of-drawers – 'Oh dear, oh dear! The gigantic packages!' One morning they motored over to Cassis to have lunch with Duncan Grant and Vanessa Bell in their small house 'La Bergère'. 'They seemed very cheerful, but wouldn't show us any pictures,' Lytton remarked in a letter to Roger (17 May 1928). 'Rather a singular ménage.'

From the first all went well. Already 'that horrid feeling of exhaustion has passed away', he wrote to Dadie Rylands. Aix was definitely a town to come to again. Carrington was behaving like an angel. 'We have enjoyed Aix enormously. C. has been a charming and infinitely accommodating travelling-companion. Luckily her propensity for wild-cat actions has calmed down, so it's all been plain sailing.'

On 18 May they left and were driven – 'by a perfect driver who steered his course with complete aplomb round all the precipices' – through Les Beaux, to Arles, where they met Brian Howard,[1] apparently sent out there to write an article on the great gathering of gipsies at Saintes-Maries. 'He cottoned on to Lytton,' Carrington wrote to Ralph (20 May 1928), 'but mercifully we were just starting off in our automobile, so we were spared his company. I can't imagine anything more awful than having that chattering mouldy crow (a better name) at meals . . . Of course I should love to go to the great concourse of gypsies next Thursday at Santa Maria. Where they offer a sort of Fête to their patron saint, Saint Sara, but Lytton I can see *dreads* the gypsie world, so I don't feel I can ask to go = They say the gypsies allow nobody to their revly rites in the cathedral, and *tear* Foreigners limb from limb, if they are discovered at the ceremony. When Lytton asked Brian Howard if he would mind (being torn to pieces), He replied in a décrepid voice, – "well – I suppose it might have its fascination and attractions". He hopes to secret himself in the Cathedral and take some

[1] Wit, poet, critic and friend of the famous, Brian Howard dazzled Eton, Oxford and London during the 'twenties and 'thirties by his exotic manner of living and of conversation. In the opinion of Evelyn Waugh, who pilloried him as Anthony Blanche in *Brideshead Revisited* and Ambrose Silk in *Put Out More Flags*, he was 'mad, bad and dangerous to know'. He committed suicide in 1958.

photographs by the help of an introduction from "Country Life" to the Archbishop. He seemed very dim and had never taken a photograph before.'

After two grey days in the Hôtel Forum, spent – Baedeker in one hand, Kodak in the other – driving to the tombs, along the bank of the Rhône and amid the suburbs of the town, they hurried on to Nîmes, where the buzz and gaiety was extraordinary after the decayed droning of Arles. They arrived at the Hôtel du Cheval Blanc, where 'there are no men servants – only females. Except one very old walrus waiter. Lytton was rather agitated when he found himself having his trunks carried by a female!' In spite of being extremely tired, they went out at once to inspect the theatre and the arena. 'Very remarkable both,' Lytton noted in a letter to Roger, 'but the latter seemed oddly small after the Coliseum . . . the central space seemed too constricted to hold any crucified miscreants at all comfortably – hardly room for a lion to turn round in – and besides rows of neat green garden chairs were ranged about in preparation for some horrid concert business to-morrow.'[1]

The last stage of their holiday took them, via Pont du Gard, to Avignon. For days they had been journeying against a bitter, incessant wind that cut to the bone. But now a sultry and oppressive heat settled over the country, reducing Lytton to a wraith. He and Carrington battled up through this motionless weather to Paris where, to their dismay, the heat was even more torrid. After booking into the Hôtel Foyot, Lytton crept out, half dead with giddiness, to try and get a little air under the trees in the Luxembourg Gardens. But it was no use. After an hour he limped back again and subsided on to his bed where, for the next four days, he was fed by relays of food from the restaurant.

---

[1] Carrington, in a letter to Ralph (21 May 1928), gives a fuller description of their adventures: 'Lytton's impatience to see everything the moment he arrives, is always extraordinary! Inside the arena we found a curious Bull fight going on. A young bull entered the arena to the sound of Buggells; and about a dozen young men – not drest up – just in shirts, and cotton trousers started darting from side to side, in front of the Bull. At last one braver than the rest, (very attractive with light red shoes . . .) rushed up to the Bull and seized a red cocKade off its head between its horns, and got away with it. Then they all tried to touch the Bull's horns. It was a curious game. I found it difficult to believe there was any danger. The Bull seemed so bewildered, and slow, like a very poorly cross old widow, having to play "Touch" with a gang of little scaramouches.'

When this performance was over, they went off to have a large tea in the Boulevard Hugo, and Carrington 'ate so many cakes I felt almost ill'. After which they walked to the gardens which were 'crowded with all the nobility of nîmes in their grandest clothes', and Lytton climbed the Hill of Pines to look at the monument at its summit – 'all monuments look their best about 5 o'clock, I've noticed' – and finally, before retiring to their hotel, the two of them sat by one of the lakes, listening to the evening music from the Pavillon, and sipping vermouth – 'It was a BosKy scene.'

Much as he enjoyed travelling, Lytton was always happy to return home. He longed passionately now for the soothing grey English skies, the mild and gentle – the inevitable – English rain, confident that once he had quitted the artificial hot-house of Paris and set foot once more 'on the soil of Old England, I shall be well again'. Yet the prospect of further arduous travel made him shrink back in alarm, and eventually it was Ralph, driving a large new Sunbeam which Lytton had just bought, who came out to rescue him.

It was a relief to be back amid the cool and quiet of Ham Spray. For a few days he pondered over whether he might compose a complex idyllic poem about Eton – 'a mixture of Tennyson and T. S. Eliot' – but decided against this once the proof sheets of *Elizabeth and Essex* arrived – unexpectedly early – from Chatto and Windus. With meticulous care he read through these three times – besides having them checked separately by Goldie Dickinson and Roger Senhouse – and it was at this stage that he inserted the Essex poem at the end of Chapter VII. There was also the endless enmeshment of making the index, fussing over illustrations and preparing a special, limited, American edition of the book – 'I spend my days signing my name at 4 guineas a signature for the Americans.'

All this, of course, did not occupy his full time, and he had more opportunity than usual for reading. 'I've been reading a great many books,' he told Roger (19 September 1928). 'Rather an amusing one by Robert Graves and . . . [Laura Riding] called a pamphlet against Anthologies[1] – ditto by Laurence Houseman, called the Duke of Flamborough, another (not quite so amusing) by Evelyn Waugh called Decline and Fall.' Other books which he added to the modern section of his library were Kenneth Clark's *Gothic Revival*, which he described as 'full of interest and very well done, considering the extreme difficulty of the subject. A great deal of new information – and an extraordinary account of Pugin'; Christopher Hollis's biography of Dr Johnson – 'pretty trifling, it seems to me. But what can one expect from a Roman Catholic'; W. P. Ker's *Form and Style in Poetry* – 'full of learning and sense'; Siegfried Sassoon's anonymously published *Memoirs of a Fox-Hunting Man* – 'good, to my surprise. Positively written by a gentleman, among other things!'; and Edwin Muir's *The Modern Novel* – 'excellent, really to my mind better than E. M. F[orster]'s [*Aspects of the Novel*]. But I imagine few will agree with me.'

---

[1] In the previous year Robert Graves (b. 1895) and Laura Riding (b. 1901) had collaborated to produce *A Survey of Modernist Poetry*. Later, they went together to Majorca, where they operated the Seizen Press until the Spanish Civil War forced them to leave the country.

Among contemporary novels that he was reading were two that have become particularly well-known – Aldous Huxley's *Point Counter Point* and D. H. Lawrence's *Lady Chatterley's Lover*, neither of which he greatly liked. 'I have bought – I hardly know why – *Point Counter Point*, and am making a heroic effort to read every word of it,' he wrote to Topsy Lucas (7 October 1928). 'So far it seems to me worthy but not at all interesting. Is this my fault?' By the time he had finished the book, he felt more certain that the fault must principally lie with the author. It was, he told Dadie Rylands, 'a bad book, in my opinion. The man can't write; his views are rotten; and the total result of his work is a feeling of devitalisation and gloom.'

About *Lady Chatterley's Lover*, his feelings were more mixed. 'In many ways I liked it,' he wrote to Roger (23 October 1928), '– the ordinary Lawrenceisms were less in evidence – and it was excellent to attack that subject frontally. But I complain of a sad lack of artistic intention – of creative powers thrown away – of an obsession with moralising. To say nothing of a barbaric, anti-civilization outlook, which I disapprove of.' He had been persuaded to read Lawrence's novel in the first place by Norman Douglas, who also wrote asking him for his opinion of it (30 July 1928), adding that 'I liked it on the whole'. After finishing it, Lytton set out his reactions in much the same words as he used to Roger Senhouse, drawing from Douglas some approving qualifications (12 September 1928). 'As to Lawrence (D.H.) – you are perfectly right,' he answered. 'He writes too quickly; a perfect diarrhoea, or rather cholera; besides he can't control his impulses. Lady Chatterley is better than I expected.'

On 3 August, Lytton finished correcting his proofs, sent them back to the publishers, and the following day started out with Roger Senhouse for a short Scandinavian holiday. At the end of 'a highly successful journey' they arrived in Copenhagen, whose charming eighteenth-century houses in the rococo style reminded Lytton of Aix. The main square, with its four miniature palaces at each corner and its green bronze statue of a toy king on horseback which stood at the centre, especially delighted him. 'We have had all sorts of meals in all sorts of restaurants – have spent hours in second-hand bookshops, with no result – have walked through endless streets and gardens – and so far have seen no sights,' he wrote to Carrington (8 August 1928). '. . . The inhabitants are pleasant, but oh! so lacking in temperament! Duty seems to guide their steps, and duty alone.'

On their very last day in Copenhagen, Raymond Mortimer appeared, having arrived the night before from Berlin and put up in the Phoenix Hotel where they were staying. 'We spent the day with him,' Lytton told Carrington (14 August 1928), 'he was in rather a flutter what with one thing and another – not in his best mood – talked of Venice and those delightful things one went about in there – those charming motor-boats – etc. etc. so that I nearly shrieked. However he was mainly pathetic – and it seemed cruel to leave him alone in that strange city . . .'

At the end of the week, Lytton and Roger moved on to Stockholm. Even though the fearsome medicinal halls at Saltsjöbaden, to which Lytton paid a brief nostalgic visit, appeared totally unchanged from when he had been a patient there eighteen years ago, Stockholm itself had altered. It had grown in size, was more evidently a capital city, yet still retained its charm. 'There is a great deal of water in every direction – broad limbs of the Baltic permeating between the streets – so that there really *is* some resemblance to Venice,' he wrote to Carrington (14 August 1928). 'The blueness of the water in this northern light is often attractive, and there are quantities of white steam ferry boats moving about, which adds to the gaiety of the scene. The best building to my mind is the royal palace, which stands on the central island of the town – a large severe square pale brown 18th century structure, dominating the scene. Then, slightly remote, on a broad piece of water, is the new Town Hall[1] – distinctly striking – very big – and of an effective bigness, built in dark red brick, with one very high tower at the junction of two wings – one (facing the water) longer than the other. . . . The worst of it is, however, that in spite of a certain grandeur of conception, there is no real greatness of feeling about it. It is ex-tremely clever and well thought out, but the detail is positively bad – in bad taste, and sometimes actually facetious – and there is no coherency of style – classical, gothic, oriental, byzantine, modern Viennese, etc. etc., so that one has no sense of security or repose. It is a pity, as the site is so good, and the hulk *is* impressive – which is certainly some-thing; but the more I looked the more certain I became that it was infinitely far from real goodness. One longs for some of the severity of Kennedy – and more still for the splendour of Bramante.'

The days sped by all too quickly and soon they were returning. Back at Ham Spray, a desperate band of workmen, under Carrington's leadership, was making alterations to the house. Every hour their activities grew more frenzied, leaping upward in a dreadful crescendo of noise and confusion. 'No peace, no repose on this earth I plainly see,' Lytton grumbled (30 August 1928). 'One rushes out of doors to escape from the eternal maelstrom only to find oneself set upon by ten million wasps, who, having demolished every particle of fruit in the

---

[1] This celebrated Town Hall was built between 1911 and 1923 after drawings made by R. Östberg.

garden, now begin to devour human beings.' While the pandemonium lasted, Lytton fled up to London where he continued to lead 'a shockingly lazy life. But,' he added to Topsy Lucas, 'I find it very good for my health, which is something.' There were lunches at the Ivy, dinners at Boulestin's, long conversations in the Oriental Club – strawberries – asparagus – cider cup. And there were copious parties. At Argyll House, one of his fellow guests was A. J. Balfour. 'I like watching him,' Lytton told Roger Senhouse, '– the perfection of his manners – the curious dimness – the wickedness one catches glimpses of underneath. But of course any communication of ideas is totally out of the question. One might as well talk to the man in the moon.'

In Bloomsbury, he went to the evening gatherings of the 'Woolves' and Bells, Duncan and Maynard, and special literary afternoons, with tea, given by Ottoline at her new house in Gower Street. This was the last and dingiest phase in her career as patroness of the arts, and not even the presence of W. B. Yeats – 'with grey coat-tails and wide-ribboned pince-nez that recalled an old fashioned American politician' – could quite dispel the atmosphere of mediocrity. On Lytton's first visit there, the guests included Aldous Huxley and the Irish poet and chatterbox James Stephens, 'a little gnome-like Irishman,' he described him to Roger Senhouse (9 November 1928), 'with a touch of the nautical, quite nice, but gassing away thirteen to the dozen with endless theories and generalisations. One of those essentially frivolous minds that mask themselves under a grand apparatus of earnestness and high-mindedness. On and on he went – inveighing against "destructive criticism" (that tedious old story), pointing out that no one could write about love, but only about sex, lamenting that there were no epics, etc., etc. Aldous didn't say much – he was very agreeable as usual. I enjoy his company, partly because (I can't help it) I somehow feel so definitely his superior! A question of astral bodies, or auras, I think. "Son génie étonné tremble devant le mien" – or something of that sort. Do you believe in those magnetic influences? I almost do – how otherwise to account for the mysterious aversions, engouements, dominations etc. that seem to have no reasonable explanation? Ethel Sands filled up gaps with her appreciative shiny teeth, and Pipsey interrupted and floundered as usual. . . . I was suddenly asked to give my opinion upon some long-winded dictum of Mr. J.S's on medieval clothes – the differences between the sexes – beauty of women – love – and all the rest of it. I was rather at a loss and could only shriek. "Armour! I'm in favour of armour!" . . . Mr. J.S. condemned me, of course, as destructive.'

Lytton's second visit to Gower Street went off rather better, except

T*

for a painful circumstance at the beginning. 'I made a pompous entry –
late – everyone sitting round at the table – a general remuement, etc.
and some slightly dazed looks,' he wrote to Senhouse (8 January 1929).
'I didn't know why, but on at last taking my seat found that *all* my
front buttons were undone, from top to bottom. . . . There was also
cet éternal Stephens, Max [Beerbohm] himself was most quiet – like a
great round pussy-cat. He was snowed under by the Irishman, though.'

At week-ends, he liked to go down to Cambridge, staying either
with Dadie Rylands or in Maynard Keynes's rooms, where each young
man was more enchanting than the last, and the chief topics of conversation seem to have been the wireless, Bernard Shaw and God. 'I felt
sorry at coming away – they all seemed so charming,' he remarked
after one of his visits (23 October 1928), 'but no doubt after a week the
iron would enter into one's soul.' Occasionally he would go off to
compare the subtle nuances of rural Bloomsbury at Charleston or
Tilton, and once he went to a 'slightly alarming' house-party at
Rushbrook Hall, near Bury St Edmunds, a large, very handsome redbrick Tudor building, with a moat, converted into a Queen Anne
Renaissance style – the seat of Lord Islington.[1] He had been invited
there out of the blue, and thinking that if he refused, it would mean
that he had lapsed into a permanent hermit, accepted – only to regret
his decision the minute he arrived, convinced that a permanent hermit
was what he really ought to be. The sight of a small neatly prepared
bridge-table, as he passed through an enormous sitting-room on the
long march to his bedroom, confirmed his very worst fears. All the old
sensations returned; his exasperation at the elegant vapidity of the
upper classes, made more acute by the difficulty of putting his finger on
the actual spot of degradation – perhaps, after all, it was something
wrong with the glands. How could he shine in such company? 'I had
envisioned some sort of crowd, into which one could disappear,' he
wrote to Topsy Lucas (7 October 1928), '– but there are only 2 other
guests – Lord Hugh Cecil and Evan Charteris.[2] The conversation is
ceaseless, impossible to join. Lord I. is a country gentleman of about

[1] Sir John Poynder Dickson-Poynder (1866–1936), politician and administrator, who
had been governor of New Zealand (1910–12) and was created first Baron Islington
(1910). Among his later appointments had been under-secretary of state for the colonies
(1914–15), parliamentary under-secretary for India (1915–18) and chairman of the
National Savings Committee (1920–26). In 1926 he had officially retired.

[2] Sir Evan Charteris (1864–1940), the barrister and biographer, who later became
chairman of the trustees of the National Portrait Gallery (1928–40), chairman of the
Tate Gallery (1934–40) and a trustee of the National Gallery (1932–9). Among his
books are a biography of John Sargent (1927) and *The Life and Letters of Sir Edmund
Gosse* (1931).

60. Lady I. an ex-beauty, a brilliant mimic (oh dear!) and a feather-head. Evan C. is a middle-aged man about town – mild, pungent, dull and amusing. Lord Hugh – you can imagine – a very unreal figure with all the regulation Cecil charm. During a long discussion last night on the pros and cons of capital punishment, his view was that there was only one objection to it – that (as at present arranged) it involved a voluntary executioner. Medievalism itself! —'

Down at Ham Spray, there were the usual stream of visitors – E. M. Forster, Raymond Mortimer and Francis Birrell, Lytton's niece Janie Bussy, Gerald Heard,[1] who delighted everyone by his 'unexpected intensity', Arthur Waley, 'admirable, triumphant, talking away like anything and rather less remote than usual', Saxon Sydney-Turner, who strolled about 'looking very shrewd and nervous, amiable and ill, and reading Isocrates in the original', the ebullient Boris Anrep, who 'bubbled along in a perpetual fountain of amusement', and another friend who told 'an absurd story of Reginald Piebus in Paris . . . that solemn handsome personnage. He confessed that his one pleasure was whipping women, but he didn't know how to manage it – could G. tell him what to do, and where to go? G. handed him over to one of his numerous friends, who had every renseignement at his finger tips. R.P. announced that he had only 4 hours – had to leave Paris after that. They sat in a café discussing every possibility. R.P. could not quite make up his mind what he would like best. The friend described a certain lieu, where the naked ladies entered the room on all fours, pecking grain from the floor like chickens, while the customers lashed their behinds. R.P. was struck by this . . . and yet . . . did not after all feel *quite* sure that it was exactly what he wanted. And so it went on, until at last the four hours were up, and he went back to England. The poor fellow's debauches are always of this nature.'

[1] Gerald Heard (b. 1899) was at this time the author of *Narcissus: An Anatomy of Clothes*, a book which attempted to work out historically the connexion between architecture and costume. Later, as H. F. Heard, he gained fame as the writer of mystery stories, and, as Gerald Heard, the author of studies in theological and scientific subjects. In 1937 he was to leave England for America where he became a close friend of Christopher Isherwood and Aldous Huxley, who portrayed him as the mystic William Propter in *After Many a Summer* and, possibly, Bruno Rontini in *Time Must Have a Stop*. Bishop Barkway, in a letter to the author (20 May 1963), writes of 'a side of his [Lytton's] nature which he kept tightly concealed from others, but it is characteristic of the many conversations he had of the deepest of all mysteries. Once in the "Backs" he confided to me how much he was attracted to the oriental point of view. It was then a foreshadowing of the interest in the Indian religions such as is manifested by Gerald Heard and others like him in this time.' But Gerald Heard has recorded that 'L.S. never said anything to my knowledge re Oriental Religions. He did once suggest he would write a Life of Christ but in a Queen Victoria key, and one did suggest it wouldn't be a successful composition.'

The year, which had opened in such a brilliant glow of happiness, ended sadly. Early in December, Lady Strachey, now in her eighty-ninth year, developed bronchitis. There was little hope of a recovery. Almost to the last she had retained her extraordinary zest for life. But gradually, though the vigour of her mind was as phenomenal as always, it had seemed to withdraw from the contemporary world and focus itself ever more distantly on the past. She could not clearly remember what had happened the day before, but incidents from her London life of over fifty years back lived vividly in her imagination – Browning's indignation at being called 'Robert' by a troop of unknown and unintroduced American women; Tennyson reciting his poetry in a surging, monotonous voice; the night Salvini lost his shaven wig in the middle of Alfieri's *Samsone*; George du Maurier singing French songs with a meticulous accent in his tiny, mosquito voice; the quiet and serious manner of George Eliot and Carlyle's Homeric shouts of laughter. And farther back, and more vivid yet, her mind retraced the incredible voyage out to India – the water-spouts, the flying fish, the albatrosses wheeling overhead, the tremendous storms, the unearthly sea calms, and her mother playing the cottage piano on board the *Trafalgar*. Those far-off days in India were more real and dear to her than ever – there was Lord Lytton, the viceroy, in his blue silk dressing-gown, and Lord Roberts mending her sewing-machine; she could re-experience the excitement of the amateur theatricals in Calcutta, and remember the time she chased a leopard with a croquet mallet.

Blindness had been a great deprivation, seeming to emphasize her natural remoteness from post-war England, the emptiness of her declining years. Old age was an uneven patchwork of bright memories – visions from the dead and the black surface of her present antiquity. 'It is like looking out on a garden once filled with life in all its variety and emotion,' she wrote at the close of her memoirs, 'children frolicking, youth in all its vigorous activity, lovers meeting in the shade, friends eagerly discussing every aspect of humanity, exquisite music rising and falling, artists at work on the heavenly beauty around them; and now all has vanished, nothing is left but a space, empty of all but graves, among which wander a few time-worn figures; while the faint echoes of once familiar sounds, reaching the ear, tell us of a new-crowded space outside our ken.'

This autumn, her strength was already beginning to fail. She was subject to alarming fits of fainting, and had grown too frail to walk more than a few steps without assistance. Leonard and Virginia Woolf, strolling along the pavement of Gordon Square one November day, happened to glance up at her window, and saw her blind and silent figure sitting on the balcony, with Pippa close behind. They waved up, and on being told of their gesture, she leant forward and opened her arms in an unforgettable signal of affection, a vast maternal benediction.

It was the last they saw of her. Death came fairly peacefully. For two weeks she lay in bed, fitfully conscious, looked after night and day by Pippa. Lytton visited her often, and tried to take some of the strain off his sister. 'I have been rather numbed and exhausted with this wretched business,' he admitted to Roger Senhouse on 14 December, 'and at the same time emotionally perturbed and chaotic.' Each day she grew a little weaker, a little more sequestered and forlorn, though she had curious bursts of energy almost to the end. On the afternoon of Friday, 15 December, she died, quite quietly, in her sleep. Although her death had been expected (and, being so very old, it was not possible in any case that she could live much longer), her loss was a great sadness to Lytton. He felt the shock deeply. 'It is impossible to escape the grief, though one has discounted it so long,' he wrote to Topsy Lucas (21 December 1928). 'The prospects of old age are indeed miserable. Yet some manage to keep a hold on life till the last moment – and then vanish suddenly; but they are the lucky few.'

CHAPTER V

Elizabeth and Strachey

'The natural pleasure of reading it is enormous. You seem, on the whole, to imagine yourself as Elizabeth, but I see from the pictures that it is Essex whom you have got up as yourself. But I expect you have managed to get the best of both worlds.'

Maynard Keynes to Lytton Strachey (3 December 1928)

'Isn't it possible that without experience certain minds can build up these edifices out of their sensibilities and their dramatic power. There *is* something (as they say) "hot-house" about the quality of his [Richardson's] sensuality – as if he had not really fully known what enjoyment was. But, in any case, the dramatic process remains inexplicable. Perhaps it is really the distinguishing faculty of Man – the creature who can imagine someone else.'

Lytton Strachey to Dorothy Bussy (3 January 1930)

I

STYLE AND ANALYSIS

Elizabeth and Essex has been called Lytton's only work of fiction – a description that is unfair both to the book itself and to the Victorian biographies. In form, in planning, and partly in its illustrations, it bears an interesting resemblance to Virginia Woolf's *Orlando* (the experiences of whose hero with the same queen are those of Essex himself); but the structure of this tragic history is nearer to that of a five-act play than a novel. The long meditations attributed to the main characters have their origin in the monologues of Elizabethan drama, where the protagonist often occupies the stage alone, delivering in rhetorical poetry the passions and perplexities which divide his soul. The use, too, throughout this narrative, of omens to Essex's final disaster – such as the tempest which his expedition against Ferrol encounters – are Senecan theatrical devices of the sort to which Shakespeare was particularly addicted.

Wherever possible, Lytton treats his readers as direct onlookers. He avoids all formulated interpretation of action, and even his purely informative passages are cast in visual terms. So far as is practical, he transforms every source – letters, diaries and documentary eye-witness accounts – into pictorial illustration. 'Howard was Lord Admiral, but Essex was an Earl; which was the higher? When a joint letter to the Queen was brought for their signature, Essex, snatching a pen, got in his name at the top, so that Howard was obliged to follow with his underneath. But he bided his time – until his rival's back was turned; then, with a pen-knife, he cut out the offending signature; and in that strange condition the missive reached Elizabeth.' In another instance, he brings in word for word a letter from Essex to Elizabeth in such a way that the reader is given the impression that he is actually watching Essex writing, since Lytton interrupts the text several times: 'as he wrote, he grew warmer'; and 'now he could hold himself in no longer'; and again 'the whole heat of his indignation was flaring out'.

The great visual scenes which Lytton unfolds are neatly framed by theatrical entrances and exits. He writes at times as if he is giving stage directions to a group of actors. In the scene, for example, where Elizabeth makes her speech to an assembly called by the Speaker of the House of Commons, he uses her exact words and at the same time provides us with instructions as to how they should effectively be spoken: 'There was a pause; and then the high voice rang out'; and 'She stopped, and told them to stand up, as she had more to say to them'; and 'Pausing again for a moment, she continued in a deeper tone'. In conclusion, at the end of Chapter XVI, he writes: 'She straightened herself with a final effort; her eyes glared; there was a sound of trumpets; and, turning from them in her sweeping draperies – erect and terrible – she walked out.' There are many other passages, too, where he gives his characters this stage director's advice which takes the place of ordinary biographical description. When Essex has just been appointed Lord Deputy of Ireland at a Council meeting, Lytton handles the exit in a single sentence: 'With elongated strides and flashing glances he [Essex] left the room in triumph; and so – with shuffling gait and looks of mild urbanity – did Robert Cecil.' Exeunt, and the curtain falls.

Elizabeth and Essex is Lytton's *Antony and Cleopatra*. 'There is only one thing which could have blinded a man in Antony's position so completely as we now know he actually was blinded,' he had written in one of his *Spectator* reviews (2 January 1909), 'and that thing is passion.' Passion is the overriding theme of *Elizabeth and Essex*. Essex was a typical Court favourite, and in Lytton's pages his sensuous temperament and genius for friendship are brought out in a manner that helps to emphasize his similarity to Antony. Like Antony he leaves and returns to his Queen; and like Antony he dies a violent death. Elizabeth is no Cleopatra; but each in her own way was 'a lass unparallel'd' – the Queen of England's infinite variations of temper forming an obvious dramatic equivalent to the 'infinite variety' of the Queen of Egypt. In Sir Robert Cecil, the master-mind of the piece, who performs a function in the biography analogous to that of Baron Stockmar in *Queen Victoria*, there is a close approximation to the calculating Octavius. Shakespeare closes *Antony and Cleopatra* with the triumph of Octavius; Lytton, in the carefully weighed passage with which *Elizabeth and Essex* ends, employs another device borrowed from the Elizabethan stage, picturing Cecil brooding over the destiny of England and the future of his own house. With some qualifications, the comparison may be extended. Essex's loyal friends, Sir Christopher Blount, Henry Cuffe, Lord Southampton and Sir Charles Travers, who shared his shattered fortunes, may be likened to Shakespeare's Eros and Scarus. But Lytton is tempted to simplify his characters so as to transpose them into more striking phenomena. Hence, Francis Bacon is painted a blacker villain than Enobarbus, and Sir Walter Raleigh an infinitely more sinister and capable being than Lepidus.

Elizabeth and Essex was largely a calculated biographical experiment, incorporating much autobiographical interest. Unlike *Queen Victoria*, the story is not compactly arranged around the main regal figure, but carried along in a looser episodic form. The difference in construction, narration and mood between this book and his earlier ones underlines the full flexibility of Lytton's style. It has been said that his writing is indebted to, among many others, La Bruyère, Anatole France, Gibbon, Sainte-Beuve, Saint-Simon, Walter Pater and Voltaire. But although his prose was certainly a composite affair, it was also highly personal. Very characteristic, in all his biographies, is his use of indirect speech which serves to recount the facts as seen from the viewpoint of the characters themselves, which enables him to interpret the secret thoughts of these characters, and to impersonate their tricks of speech. There are many examples of this technique in *Elizabeth and Essex*. 'The Attorney-Generalship fell vacant, and Essex immediately declared that Francis Bacon must have the post,' he writes at one point. Then, slipping into Essex's own reflections, he proceeds directly on: 'He was young and had not yet risen far in his profession – but what of that? He deserved something even greater; the Queen might appoint whom she would, and, if Essex had any influence, the right man, for once, should be given preferment.'

In these soliloquies, Lytton withdraws completely and conceals himself behind his characters, who present their own, often one-sided view of a situation or verdict on another person. A good instance of this occurs in the passage where Elizabeth – thinking back over her whole relationship with Essex – deliberates about his pardon. Lytton passes from an introductory statement of fact to the 'stream of consciousness' without any verbal conjunction (elsewhere, to make the connexion outwardly visible, he often uses a dash or colon); but in the word 'actually' we at once begin to hear the indignant tone of the Queen's inner voice.

'The animosity which for so long had been fluctuating within her now flared up in triumph and rushed out upon the author of her agony and her disgrace. He had betrayed her in every possible way – mentally, emotionally, materially – as a Queen and as a woman – before the world and in the sweetest privacies of the heart. And he had actually imagined that he could elude the doom that waited on such iniquity – had dreamed of standing up against her – had mistaken the hesitations of her strength for the weaknesses of a subservient character. He would have a sad awakening! He would find that she was indeed the daughter of a father who had known how to rule a kingdom and how to punish the perfidy of those he had loved the most. Yes, indeed . . .'

With its marvellous dash, its changes of pace and colour, its chorus of rhetorical questions, its quickly mixed metaphors and dying falls, the narrative throws out a fine sheen of excitement, of hurtling activity. The punctuated rhythm of the shorter sentences, cleverly disposed among his more elaborate constructions, tightens up very effectively the tension wherever the event-plot quickens. Yet for all these skilful and entertaining literary devices, the impact of the writing is frequently pale and thin. It is all speed and ease and slotted-in arrangements; the texture is too shiny, too impoverished of more tough and solid matter. Lytton insists upon the importance of passion with all the urgency of a man who has never experienced it full-bloodedly in life, and whose loss naturally communicates itself, with debilitating effects, to his own prose. He uncurls his phosphorescent day-dreams about a no-man's-land that floats between two actual worlds, one dead, one powerless to be born. It was as though, with a shiver of delight, he imagined that he had lived in Elizabethan England himself, or rather that his ghost even now flitted to and fro among these gorgeous characters. He was more than half in love with all of them, and could never quite shake the gossamer of this fantasy out of his mind. Consequently the atmosphere he evokes is strangely impalpable rather than passionate. For it is in the sound and complexion as well as in the stated opinions of a writer's work that one must look for a true revelation of his temperament. Balzac, whose vitality and physical potency, though set in a filial groove, have never seriously been doubted, preached a monastic chastity as an essential part of the creative work to which he devoted himself, and offset his robust nature with themes of severe and obsessive idealism. But the earthy and profane sweep of his *Comédie Humaine* is as unmistakable as is the giddy, bloodless hysteria that underlies all the hints and exaggerations of Lytton's pages. 'Incapable of creation in life or in literature,' T. R. Barnes cruelly commented in *Scrutiny*, 'his [Strachey's] writings were a substitute for both.' The implication of these words is, of course, unjust. Lytton was never impotent. But whenever his sexual desires approached boiling-point, they began to change from a more solid corporeal substance into something metaphysical, a vapour, a mist. It is this immaterial quality that one can detect, like the smell of an ether, about his style.

Probably the most noticeable feature of Lytton's prose style is his regular employment of the stereotyped phrase. Many critics have carped unduly at this aspect of his writing, for the most obvious combination of words is not necessarily the hallmark of inferior prose or second-hand thinking. By making use of a very simple vocabulary and humdrum, colloquial epithets, Lytton was sometimes able to summon forth a feeling of personal intimacy that could never have been beguiled by more recondite methods. 'Platitudes', he once wrote, 'are, after all, the current coin of artists, critics and philosophers; without them all commerce of the mind would come to a standstill; and a great debt is owing to those who, like Macaulay, have the faculty of minting fresh and clean platitudes in inexhaustible abundance.' Neither Lytton nor Macaulay were perhaps deeply original thinkers. But they shared one compensating gift – the power of expressing more ordinary thoughts in the most striking manner, so that there are few paradoxes so brilliant or pleasing as their vivid commonplaces.

'To be brief,' wrote George Santayana, 'is almost a condition of being inspired.' In Lytton's tightly drawn pages, the neat conversational clichés fit perfectly, like old gems made new and luminous by their improved setting. But in his weakest and most flamboyant strain, overloaded with picturesque adjectives and adverbs, he seems to be unsuccessfully trying to avoid the banal. This failure may in part be the penalty he paid for trying to reproduce in English the chaste and abstract vocabulary of the French. But if style ultimately reveals the man, then the flat and simulated passion of these more high-flown, ambitious passages only shows how oddly his desire outran his performance.

In his Rede Lecture, Max Beerbohm has drawn particular attention to the great pliability of Lytton's style, which accorded so well with every variation of his theme. Each character was accorded a special rhythm and refrain. In *Queen Victoria* this technique had shifted subtly so as to bring the reader into the very presence of a succession of widely disparate premiers. 'Note the mellow and leisurely beauty of the cadences,' Beerbohm wrote, 'in which he writes of Lord Melbourne – "the autumn rose", as he called him. Note the sharp brisk straight-forward buoyancy of the writing whenever Lord Palmerston appears; and the elaborate Oriental richness of manner when Mr. Disraeli is on the scene.' A more personal change of manner took place when Lytton left the Mother Empress for the Virgin Queen. Her heterogeneous nature called for altogether different treatment – a new construction, of course, and a new combination of tones. The comedy becomes less farcical, the story is flavoured less strongly with his characteristic light and lambent mockery. The gentle aura of sentimentalism splits sharply into two patches of light – the one brilliant, golden, romantic; the other rancid, yellow, and perverted. 'We are aware,' wrote Edmund Wilson in what was mainly a very favourable article on Strachey's writings, 'for the first time disagreeably of the high-voiced old Bloomsbury gossip gloating over the scandals of the past as he ferreted them out in his library. Strachey's curious catty malice, his enjoyment of the discomfiture of his characters is most unpleasantly in evidence in *Elizabeth and Essex*.'[1]

[1] Edmund Wilson definitely preferred Lytton's Victorian essays and biographies. 'Lytton Strachey's chief mission, of course, was to take down once for all the pretensions of the Victorian Age to moral superiority,' he declared (21 September 1932). '. . . *Eliza-beth and Essex* seems to me the least satisfactory of Strachey's books. His art, so tight and so calculated, so much influenced by the French, was ill-suited to the Elizabethan Age. . . . His study of Queen Elizabeth in the light of modern psychology brings her character into sharper focus, but the effect of it is slightly disgusting; it marks so definitely the final surrender of Elizabethan to Bloomsbury England. . . . Certainly one of the best English writers of his period, he makes us feel sharply the contrast between Shakespeare's England and his. Shakespeare is expansive and untidy and close to the spoken language. Lytton Strachey, whose first-published work was a history of French literature, is so far from being any of these things that one of his chief feats consists in having managed to achieve in English some of the effects of the French.' In Edmund Wilson's opinion, the real force and audacity of Lytton Strachey's work are therefore seen best earlier in his career. 'The harshness of *Eminent Victorians* without Strachey's wide learning and bitter feeling, the intimate method of *Queen Victoria* without his insight into character, had the effect of cheapening history, something Strachey never did – for, though he was venomous about the Victorians, he did not make them any the less formidable. He had none of the modern vice of cockiness; he maintained a rare attitude of humility, of astonishment and admiration, before the unpredictable spectacle of life, which he was always finding "amazing" and "incredible". But neither the Americans nor the English have ever, since *Eminent Victorians* appeared, been able to feel quite the same about the legends that had dominated their pasts. Something had been punctured for good.'

Elsewhere, Edmund Wilson credits Strachey with making biography in England 'a

Both biographies were love stories, but love stories of a very different order. In his treatment of Victoria's strong sexuality, Lytton had been decorously unobtrusive. In dealing with Elizabeth's sexual make-up, he adopted a far more salacious and erotic tone, full of suggestive allusion and innuendo. In the opinion of one reverend gentleman – who belongs to a body of men especially well-suited to nosing out such matters – he also showed himself in this last biography 'preoccupied with the sexual organs to a degree that seems almost pathological'. This is a great exaggeration. But undoubtedly there is some libidinous imagery in *Elizabeth and Essex*, and several dark passages that contain sly and vibrant animal overtones. When endeavouring, for example, to probe the mystery of Elizabeth's virginity, Lytton wrote:

'Though, at the centre of her being, desire had turned to repulsion, it had not vanished altogether; on the contrary, the compensating forces of nature had redoubled its vigour elsewhere. Though the precious citadel itself was never to be violated, there were surrounding territories, there were outworks and bastions over which exciting battles might be fought, and which might even, at moments, be allowed to fall into the bold hands of an assailant.'

In the process of showing how the profound psychological disturbances of Elizabeth's childhood had made normal sexual intercourse impossible for her, Lytton invented on the queen's behalf an early traumatic experience carrying the most precocious and sinister implications. 'Manhood', he wrote, '– the fascinating, detestable entity, which had first come upon her concealed in yellow magnificence in her father's lap – manhood was overthrown at last, and in the person of that traitor it should be rooted out. Literally, perhaps . . . she knew well enough the punishment for high treason.'

The punishment for treason included castration – a barbarity that terrified and obsessed Lytton. Later on in the book, while evoking the soft, insidious atmosphere of Ireland at the time of Essex's expedition against Tyrone, he again hints at this awful, absorbing topic. 'What state of society was this,' he asks, 'where chiefs jostled with gypsies, where ragged women lay all day long laughing in the hedgerows, where ragged men gambled away among each other their very rags, their very fore-

form of literary art' (2 January 1924), compares his work very favourably with that of Harold Nicolson and Philip Guedalla, who both tried to copy and tended to misapply his methods (June 1925), describes *Portraits in Miniature* as 'one of Strachey's real triumphs', and praises very highly his Leslie Stephen Lecture (16 September 1925): 'One is persuaded that Mr Strachey has made out the strongest possible case for Pope and has appreciated certain aspects of his genius as they have never yet perhaps been appreciated.'

locks, their very . . . parts more precious still, where wizards flew on whirlwinds, and rats were rhymed into dissolution?'

If fetishism is to be explained in terms of a fear of castration, then it is not perhaps surprising that Lytton, whose erotic attention was partly directed towards the ears, should have experienced this fear. There are almost as many references to the mutilation of ears as to castration itself. At the end of Chapter V, for instance, he tells the story of Mr Booth, one of Anthony Bacon's dependants, 'who, poor man, had suddenly found himself condemned by the Court of Chancery to a heavy fine, to imprisonment, and to have his ears cut off'. This brutal tale is intended, ostensibly, to illustrate the fearful caprice and cruelty of the happy-go-lucky world of Elizabethan England. After two pages given over to recounting the sordid, ridiculous intrigue that was carried on around this sentence, Lytton concludes: 'Then there is darkness; in low things as in high the ambiguous age remains true to its character; and, while we search in vain to solve the mystery of great men's souls and the strange desires of Princes, the fate of Mr. Booth's ears also remains for ever concealed from us.'

It is difficult to see what this story really adds to the vivid picture of Elizabethanism – its canting inconsistency, its savagery, its alluring mystification – that Lytton etches in so racily during the course of his second chapter – one passage of which brings together both castration and the cutting off of ears, and castigates religion as the ultimate killjoy:

'Who can reconstruct those iron-nerved beings who passed with rapture from some divine madrigal sung to a lute by a bewitching boy in a tavern to the spectacle of mauled dogs tearing a bear to pieces? Iron-nerved? Perhaps; yet the flaunting man of fashion, whose codpiece proclaimed an astonishing virility, was he not also, with his flowing hair and his jewelled ears, effeminate? And the curious society which loved such fantasies and delicacies – how readily would it turn and rend a random victim with hideous cruelty! A change of fortune – a spy's word – and those same ears might be sliced off, to the laughter of the crowd, in the pillory; or, if ambition or religion made a darker embroilment, a more ghastly mutilation – amid a welter of moral platitudes fit only for the nursery and dying confessions in marvellous English – might diversify a traitor's end.'

This preoccupation with sexual themes and deviations is decked out with certain Freudian overtones. Significantly, Lytton dedicated his book to James and Alix Strachey, who were by this time pupils of Freud and who were to produce the standard English translation of all Freud's works. Despite his war-time tuition, Lytton did not read

German at all proficiently, and until well into the 1920s Freud's writings were available in English only in extremely indifferent – and even incorrect – translations. Lytton had read a very few of these, and to begin with, was mainly sceptical as to their value. None of his character sketches in *Eminent Victorians* were influenced in the slightest by Freud, and nor was the portrait of Queen Victoria. The great psychological influence on his earlier work had been Dostoievsky – who, of course, reveals a lot of the same material as Freud, and whom Freud himself regarded as the greatest of all novelists.

But ever since 1922, when James had published his translation of Freud's *Group Psychology and the Analysis of the Ego*, this position had altered considerably. By 1926, Lytton had learnt a good deal about psycho-analysis and psychology from talks with James and Alix. And he accepted pretty completely the interpretation that they – and especially Alix – gave him, in some detail, as to what seemed the probable underlying attitude of Elizabeth to the execution of Essex. His account of this in the later part of the book (as well as in some earlier passages preparing for it) is purely psycho-analytic. He is obviously riding a Freudian thesis, and riding it hard, as the references to sexuality – the reverend gentleman indignantly notes that the narrative contains at least eleven direct or indirect allusions to the sexual organs – attest. Freud's discovery that unconscious processes, among them infant sexuality and the adult operations of the sex instinct, permeate all human thought and action, was especially appealing to Lytton. He was attracted to a way of thought that seemed to encourage freedom from superstitious restraints in human relationships and to confirm his own fervently maintained ideals. Even though he was at first sceptical of their truth, Freud's brilliant probings into human nature gave immediate support to his general moral unorthodoxy. 'It also provided him with a scientific method whereby he could rationally cope with certain previously ignored facts of life,' commented Professor Martin Kallich, '– and so, sharpening his mind, made more acute his psychological insight.'

The use to which Lytton put his psycho-analytical knowledge was partly an aesthetic one. He was able more freely to exploit his own twofold nature, from which, unconsciously, arose the literary emphasis he placed on ambiguity and dualism; and he was able to savour the enigma of Elizabeth's personality with several unsqueamish reflections. Like himself, Elizabeth commanded no great powers of self-analysis. She found it impossible to predict her own impulses or to explain the peculiar motives that lay behind her decisions. Throughout the biography, Lytton stresses this element of fluctuating uncertainty which

counts for so much in directing hither and thither the tragic course of
the story. But he relies on Freudian principles to suggest that, in the
primitive depths of her and Essex's unconscious, their tragedy was
inevitable; that, given the facts of their backgrounds, it was preordained. In bringing out this contrast between the different levels of
consciousness, Lytton produces a composite pattern that is once again
on Shakespearian lines:

> There's a divinity that shapes our ends,
> Rough-hew them how we will.

Lytton harboured in his nature a streak of almost superstitious
fatalism, which forms part of the texture of much of his writing. This
new employment of Freudian theses was partly romantic, a method of
connecting up a general pattern of predestination at the expense of
isolated character analysis, something systematic rather than intuitive.
For example, he subtly implements Freud's theories concerning father–
daughter relationships when, in describing Elizabeth's feelings on
sending Essex to his death, he imagines, rising within her being, the
spirit of her father, who had had his own wives executed:

'Yes, indeed, she felt her father's spirit within her; and an extraordinary passion moved the obscure profundities of her being, as she
condemned her lover to her mother's death. In all that had happened
there was a dark inevitability, a ghastly satisfaction; her father's destiny,
by some intimate dispensation, was repeated in hers; it was supremely
fitting that Robert Devereux should follow Anne Boleyn to the block.
Her father! . . . but in a still remoter depth there were still stranger
stirrings. There was a difference as well as a likeness; after all, she was
no man, but a woman; and was this, perhaps, not a repetition but a
revenge? After all the long years of her life-time, and in this appalling
consummation, was it her murdered mother who had finally emerged?
The wheel had come full circle.'

Lytton was far too sensitive and professional a writer to substitute
acquired erudition for private insight or to allow his prose to be eroded
by the lifeless terminology, the standardized clinical vocabulary of
psycho-analysis. Yet in some parts of *Elizabeth and Essex*, where he
attempts a rather ambitious, uncontrolled analysis, his style does
deteriorate. The most outstanding example of this is the passage, already
quoted in the previous chapter, which appears at the end of the opening
chapter of *Elizabeth and Essex*, foreshadowing the lovers' inescapable
fate. In these turgid sentences, with their involved, almost meaningless
accent upon some twin predestination, Lytton's style, by surpassing the
effective limits of hyperbole, seems to have run completely to seed.

But the real deteriorating force at work in *Elizabeth and Essex* would appear to have been his own physical weakness, mental and emotional weariness. Signs of this enfeeblement are freely discernible in these pages. There are, of course, passages which eloquently show off his verbal artistry – the description, for instance, of Elizabeth's vacillating disposition, which he likened to a ship: 'Such was her nature – to float, when it was calm, in a sea of indecisions, and, when the wind rose, to tack hectically from side to side.' And there are a few ironical flashes, such as the portrait he paints of King Philip, the spider of the Escorial 'spinning cobwebs out of dreams', who is troubled on his death-bed by one thought: 'Had he been remiss in the burning of heretics? He had burnt many, no doubt; but he might have burnt more.' Around these oases stretch flat and sandy deserts of dry words, colourless transitions, weak puns. 'On the whole, it seemed certain that with a little good management the prosecution would be able to blacken the conduct and character of the prisoners in a way which would carry conviction – in every sense of the word.' 'The state of affairs in Ireland was not quite so bad as it might have been.' 'They [the Spanish ambassadors] had come into contact with those forces in the Queen's mind which proved, incidentally, fatal to themselves, and brought her, in the end, her enormous triumph.' Such blurred and unscanned sentences as these lack the incisiveness and bite of the Lytton who wrote *Eminent Victorians*.

Critics have put forward two main reasons for the comparative failure of *Elizabeth and Essex* as measured against *Queen Victoria*. Lytton's temperament was, they have suggested, too wildly incompatible with the Elizabethan Age; and, because of the overall lack of information relating to this age, he was forced to adopt an inadequate biographical technique. Such opinions cannot be accepted without qualification. Perhaps significantly, it has always been literary critics and not historical commentators who have pointed to the alleged dearth of material. About Victoria all was known; about Elizabeth very little. And so, Virginia Woolf deduced, everything seemed to lend itself to a fresh artistic combination which gave the biographer freedom to invent, yet guided his invention with the signposts of some fact. 'Nevertheless,' she continued, 'the combination proved unworkable; fact and fiction refused to mix. Elizabeth never became real in the sense that Queen Victoria had been real, yet she never became fictitious in the sense that Cleopatra or Falstaff is fictitious. The reason would seem to be that very little was known – he was urged to invent; yet something was known – his invention was checked.' J. K. Johnstone, who also found something weightless and incomplete in Lytton's biography, attributes this lack of substance, like Virginia Woolf, to the paucity of historical data: 'The main cause of Strachey's difficulties in *Elizabeth and Essex* is a lack of intimate information,' he wrote. 'He is unable to take us into the minds of his characters as often as he does in *Queen Victoria*; and when he does reveal their inner lives, the revelation is not always convincing . . . Bacon's character is revealed to posterity more fully, thanks especially to his essays and his letters, than the character of any other of the Elizabethans with whom Strachey is concerned, and the letter in which he warned Essex may still be read, and is quoted from by Strachey. There can be little doubt that *Elizabeth and Essex* would have been more successful if Strachey had had more material of this sort at his disposal.'

In striking contrast to this statement, G. B. Harrison, in the Commentary which appears at the end of his *Robert Devereux, Earl of Essex*, has written: 'A complete bibliography of materials for the life of Essex would include every major source for the last twenty years of the reign of Elizabeth. There is so much material that between 1591 and 1601 it is possible to trace Essex's whereabouts almost for every day of his life.' In the book itself, Harrison gives the texts of numerous letters sent by Elizabeth and Cecil to Essex, and Essex's letters to the queen and her secretary.

A great many historians and biographers have written on Elizabeth, and the number and variety of anecdotes, of scandals involving personal relationships between the queen and her subjects which appear in their books would seem to suggest that the period was especially well documented. The Elizabethans were great correspondents, and the lives of both Elizabeth and Essex are remarkably fully, if not always intimately, recorded in the letters that passed between them. But although there was no great lack of original material in the Public Record Office, the Manuscript Department of the British Museum, and the stores of the Bodleian and other archives, Lytton confined his research entirely to published sources. An examination of his bibliography shows, too, that he has omitted at least five of the most important source-books for the life of Essex. The need, then, was perhaps less for invention than for imagination. From the start he had envisaged *Elizabeth and Essex* as a work of creative drama, not of historical exploration. Essex himself was a character of no great historical significance – he finds no place, for example, in G. M. Trevelyan's *History of England*. Moreover, Lytton did not have to cover a life span of over eighty years, crowded with complex political incident, as he had done in *Queen Victoria*. Instead, he limited himself to a period, comparatively placid, of about one sixth of that time. Essex's close association with the queen had lasted only a fairly short span of her long reign, and most of the issues of great

historical moment preceded his brief rise to power. He was nineteen
when first he began to assume a position of prominence, and just thirty-
four at the time of his execution. During those fifteen years, he was
away from England on a number of occasions and over the final twelve
months of his life saw Elizabeth only once – or possibly twice – since
he was first occupied with his ill-fated Irish command, and subsequently
in disgrace. There was, too, a certain monotonous repetition in their
highly-charged emotional relationship – a short period of unnatural
affinity; a quarrel (generally arising from some rash or incompetent
action on the part of Essex); a separation, during which Essex would
sulk and the queen rage; then a reconciliation accompanied by new and
greater favours. At each spin of the wheel, the violence of their discord
grew more intense, their alienation more bitter, and their reconciliation
harder to achieve. Using this classic pattern of mounting tragedy, Lytton
felt he could break free from the restricting conditions of orthodox
biography, and by a deft orchestration of this theme, produce a more
histrionic and sumptuous work of dramatic literature.

The film of nebulous, dream-like vacancy and soundlessness that
both Virginia Woolf and J. K. Johnstone discovered in *Elizabeth and
Essex* arose not so much from any hindrances inherent in the art of
biography, or from any absolute lack of day-to-day documentary
information, but more from the peculiar quality of Lytton's temperament and his romantic attitude towards the sixteenth century. It was not
at all the case, as has sometimes been suggested, that he was largely
ignorant of Elizabethan history. 'Underneath the sceptic and scholar',
wrote Cyril Connolly, 'flamed a passionate Elizabethan.' Yet, he was
still largely out of his element in those remote, half-barbarous times.
The Elizabethans, as no one can help feeling, found their inspiration in
the pulse and glow of reckless living; while it seems equally clear that
Lytton found his simply in the Elizabethans. Decked out in scarlet and
gold brocade, these imponderable, airy phantoms peopled a distant
fantasy world, lit up by exotic paradox and enigma, into whose outlandish and intemperate realms he might elope, away from his own so
shy and shrinking, tough and vaporous personality. The Utopian
contrast of these days gave him a wonderful inebriated release from the
coils of his mordant self-obsession, an illusory flight into that chimerical,
intoxicated, extramundane land that never seems quite real to the sober
reader. For Lytton preferred to feel that the spirit of Elizabethanism
belonged not to the actual world at all. 'In fact,' he declared in one of his
Spectator reviews, 'the Elizabethans when they were most themselves
turned their backs upon realism, and rushed towards the extraordinary,
the disordered, and the sublime, so that if one wished to sum up their

most essential qualities in a single word, "extravagant" would probably come nearest to the truth. Their extravagance was of course the extravagance of greatness; it was based on strength and knowledge and it was controlled by the high necessities of art.'

Yet because the realism of the epoch could never be totally expunged, the dream might in an instant swivel into nightmare. It was this mingling of allurement and revulsion, of palpitating horror and sentiment that made up the cataleptic fascination Elizabethanism held for Lytton.

As a work of passion and drama, *Elizabeth and Essex* has the agreeable period texture of finely twilled fustian: as a historical reconstruction, it is often stagy and unreal. Lytton skims lightly over those aspects of Elizabeth which make her unacceptable as the heroine of a great and tragic love-affair, and, so far as is possible, rejects any direct interpretation of sixteenth-century England that does not convey the impression of a varied landscape, flooded with the last blaze of evening light. It is a personal evocation of a never-never land, thrilling and unfathomable; a deliberate construction, by theatrical processes, of the inexplicable quality that formed, in his opinion, the essence of the finest art. 'With very few exceptions', he wrote, '– possibly with the single exception of Shakespeare – the creatures in it meet us without intimacy; they are exterior visions, which we know, but do not truly understand.' Lytton Strachey exploits this recognizable lack of understanding until it becomes part of the very fabric of the book. But it is because his characters are simply exterior visions that we are moved so little by their misfortunes, do not grieve at their deaths. They are no more to us than monumental silhouettes, the shadows of substantial beings who never appear. At best we may picture them as the figures in a game of chess, knights, bishops, pawns and the all-powerful queen, ivory pieces whose carved beauty we may admire, whose movements will engage our interest, but for whom we can feel nothing personal. Nor can we become very emotionally caught up by the game itself, for it is not being carried on between two ordinary mortals, but vast and unrealizable super-beings:

> *'Tis all a Chequer board of Nights and Days*
> *Where Destiny with Man for Pieces plays:*
> *Hither and thither moves, and mates, and slays,*
> *And one by one back in the Closet lays.*

2

ESSEX AND ELIZABETH

By choosing *Elizabeth and Essex* as the subject for his book, Lytton may
vainly have hoped to escape the appalling exhaustion that had beset him
after *Queen Victoria*. His research was not so thorough, and he needed
to delve into far fewer books of reference. In any case, there were
artistic as well as practical advantages offered by such a theme. Everyone knew the legend of old Gloriana. But then, need he accept this
legend without certain subtle reservations, without some amplifications
appropriate to that most enigmatic of epochs? With his brand new
psycho-analysis to give him confidence, was he not entitled – was he
not, perhaps, even compelled – to inquire into that peculiar absorption
which bound together the bold, exquisitely boyish courtier and that
old and extraordinary regal creature? What could the secret of their
intimate and incongruous association be? From what exotic, bitter-
sweet essence had their weird, disturbing passion been so cunningly
distilled? Such questions, with their cloak of inscrutable mystery, were
tantalizing. Yet where it was injudicious to assert, was it not still
possible to suggest? Where one was unable to define, might one not,
by some unexpected juxtaposition of opposing syllables, catch a
reverberating echo of those remote, vital times, so oddly chromatic and
melodious?

So, in parody, may Lytton have reflected to himself. Yet there
existed other, deeper causes, more instructive and of greater psychological significance, to account for the compelling attraction he felt
towards the handsome Essex, the baffling Elizabeth, and their tempestuous affair – causes which, running between the lines of his
narrative, evince an extraordinary sense of tension and design.

The first two chapters act as Argument and Prologue to the main
story. In less than seven thousand words of rich, romantic prose, Lytton
parades the extravagant excitement and inconsistency of the age, his
baroque, metaphor-studded sentences sounding like a fanfare of
trumpets to set the mood and background of his tale. He also offers a
brief sketch of Essex and a longer, more involved analysis of the queen,
tracing their separate lives up to the early summer of 1587, when the
tragedy of their dual history may be said to have begun.

It was Essex's 'double nature' – that standard Stracheyesque quality –
which partly led Lytton to identify his own personality with that of the
glamorous courtier. As depicted in this book, the more latent side of the
earl's temperament – that of the pale and sorrowful scholar, incapable of

great thought or action, shivering in the agonies of ague, lying in darkness upon his bed and dreaming of happiness only in his obscurity from convivial society, from the loves and hates of ordinary people – bore a good enough resemblance to the conditions of Lytton's own student days. But Essex's more flamboyant qualities – reflected best, perhaps, in the early, breathless evocation of a 'handsome, charming youth, with his open manner, his boyish spirits, his words and looks of adoration, and his tall figure, and his exquisite hands, and the auburn hair on his head, that bent so gently downwards' – infatuated Lytton, and proclaimed a vision of himself as he often imagined he would like to have appeared before the world, the type of man he found irresistible – his own self, romantically idealized. In the contemplation of this literary general's physical transformation from sickly recluse to dashing man of action, Lytton seems himself to have experienced a kindred lifting of the spirit, and he clearly attributes some of his own feelings to Elizabeth, giving his biography an unusual emotional synthesis.

The short description of Essex which Lytton introduces into his opening chapter contains one particular passage that touches on this alluring duality: 'The youth loved hunting and all the sports of manhood; but he loved reading too. He could write correctly in Latin and beautifully in English; he might have been a scholar, had he not been so spirited a nobleman. As he grew up this double nature seemed to be reflected in his physical complexion. The blood flew through his veins in vigorous vitality; he ran and tilted with the sprightliest; and then suddenly health would ebb away from him, and the pale boy would lie for hours in his chamber, obscurely melancholy, with a Virgil in his hand.'

This picture of Essex at Trinity catches both the social and sexual appeal of the young man. Lytton was immediately anxious, however, to dispel the notion that, by choosing this young earl as his hero, he was simply displaying an esoteric prejudice. Essex's career, he maintained, illustrated an important social change brought about by the English Reformation. On the first page of his biography he tells us that in Essex, the outgoing social system – 'the spirit of the ancient feudalism' – flamed up for the last time. The old dispensation had met its inevitable doom when the Duke of Norfolk was beheaded. 'Yet', Lytton argues, 'the spirit of the ancient feudalism was not quite exhausted. Once more, before the reign was over, it flamed up, embodied in a single individual – Robert Devereux, Earl of Essex. The flame was glorious – radiant with the colours of antique knighthood and the flashing gallantries of the past; but no substance fed it; flaring wildly, it tossed to and fro in the wind; it was suddenly put out.'

Historically, this image has little enough meaning: its purpose was brilliantly ornamental. Lytton may have wished to blind his audience to his personal attitude towards Essex which would at best have been considered trivial, and to deepen and enlarge the temper of a Court squabble by making it symbolize the overthrow of one world by another. Along with the falling of Essex's head, we are invited to hear the fall of thousands of hearts and hopes for a lost way of life.

If Essex, the protagonist, was to represent the old doomed way of life, then Elizabeth, it followed, must embody the new. The crafty old queen, though bewitched by the earl's mercurial and seductive chivalry, nevertheless places her reliance on the new dry-eyed servants of absolutism, the Bacons and Cecils, in conflict with whom Essex is fated for destruction. The queen is, naturally enough, 'the supreme phenomenon of Elizabethanism'. But Elizabethanism, he eloquently explains, is a vague and equivocal cargo. 'It is, above all, the contradictions of the age that baffle our imagination and perplex our intelligence,' he states. And in a full paragraph containing eight rhetorical questions, he shows how 'the inconsistency of the Elizabethans exceeds the limits permitted to man'.

It follows that if Elizabeth is to symbolize the spirit of such an unaccountable age, she herself must be supremely, astonishingly, unaccountable. 'Under the serried complexities of her raiment', Lytton writes, '– the huge hoop, the stiff ruff, the swollen sleeves, the powdered pearls, the spreading, gilded gauzes – the form of the woman vanished, and men saw instead an image – magnificent, portentous, self-created – an image of regality, which yet, by a miracle, was actually alive. Posterity has suffered by a similar deceit of vision. The great Queen of its imagination, the lion-hearted heroine, who flung back the insolence of Spain and crushed the tyranny of Rome with splendid unhesitating gestures, no more resembles the Queen of fact than the clothed Elizabeth the naked one. But, after all, posterity is privileged. Let us draw nearer; we shall do no wrong now to that Majesty, if we look below the robes.'

The implication of this passage is that a rarer satisfaction is to be found in tracing the ambiguous convolutions of reality than in reposing upon the comfortable simplifications of romance. But the impressionistic language with which he lingeringly describes the queen's outward apparel indicates that, despite his zest for the guidance of that interior psycho-analysis which he will shortly introduce, he was still at heart an inveterate romantic, concerned largely with the theatrical fitness of things.

The long analysis which he then devotes to Elizabeth is full of percipient observations. He notes, for example, that she was flatly unromantic except about her own charms. 'Her clear-sightedness, so tremendous in her dealings with outward circumstances, stopped short when she turned her eyes within. There her vision grew artificial and confused.' Her political habit of vacillation – which is exalted into a genius for the policy of delay – was composed, he suggests, partly out of a deliberate means for gaining time and so prolonging peace, partly from an innate predisposition to hedge. This passion for postponement revealed both masculine and feminine traits inextricably fused together. After briefly describing the horrible circumstances in which her childhood and puberty were passed, Lytton then goes on to explain that the result of these early years upon the mature woman had been seriously to warp her sexual organization. Of a severely neurotic temperament, it was only her immense and brittle vitality that carried her through to her seventieth year, since she was never of a robust constitution, but fed ravenously off her will and nerves. This second chapter bristles with many arresting images. But they are never wholly co-ordinated so as to present a balanced study of character. Every time Lytton's diagnosis threatens to unravel the enigma of the queen's personality, he seems to pull himself up short, since, for aesthetic purposes, the queen must remain regally enigmatic, the emblem of a magnificently shrouded age.

His preference, too, for an unconscious, psychological explanation of Elizabeth's motives, especially of her virginity, though extremely acute, is sometimes indulged at the expense of some pertinent biographical and historical facts. 'The crude story of a physical malformation', he wrote, 'may well have had its origin in a subtler, and yet no less vital, fact. In such matters the mind is as potent as the body. A deeply seated repugnance to the crucial act of intercourse may produce, when the possibility of it approaches, a condition of hysterical convulsion, accompanied, in certain cases, by intense pain. Everything points to the conclusion that such – the result of the profound psychological disturbances of her childhood – was the state of Elizabeth.' That the horrors she suffered as a child could have caused her neurotic condition seems extremely probable. Yet other memories, too, of which Lytton nowhere takes account, may also have contributed to her fear of marriage and her aversion from sexual intercourse. Jane Seymour, the mother of Elizabeth's small half-brother, to whom she was greatly attached, had died in childbirth, as had Catherine Parr – then the wife of Thomas Seymour – with whom Elizabeth lived after her father's death. Death in childbirth was by no means uncommon in the sixteenth century. One of Alençon's confidential London agents once wrote to him: 'She

[Elizabeth] wants nothing in the world so much as you; there is no one in the world she would rather have near her if only, il se pouvait faire sans enfants.' In spite of what the doctors had said, 'il semble que par la disposition de son corps elle a peur de mourir.'

From this it seems at least possible that Elizabeth nursed a very natural, if extreme, fear of the dangers of childbirth. Lytton, intent upon furnishing a more intricate explanation for her virginity and ennobling her unhappy appetites with similitudes from Greek mythology, overlooked this simpler reason. By relying so heavily on a system of psycho-analytical theory to interpret Elizabeth's character, he produces, from the aesthetic point of view, a rather too insubstantial picture for so realistic and terrestrial a nature.

It is the purely descriptive passages which succeed best in this second chapter. Lytton portrays Elizabeth as a forceful, baroque personality, a larger-than-life being of resplendent courage. It may be that he deliberately withheld from attributing to her an abnormal but conscious apprehension of death, associated in particular with childbirth, because this might have disturbed the impact of such an otherwise superhuman figure. 'Deep in the recesses of her being,' he tells us, 'a terrific courage possessed her.' Elsewhere he alludes to her 'personal fearlessness', and declares that 'considerations of her own personal safety were of no weight with her'. Her courage was certainly spectacular – but was it so vastly unqualified as Lytton makes out? She did not fear anyone or anything she could see or understand. But the terrible dreams that harrowed her nights testify to a terror of the unknown. The almost insane ferocity, too, which she showed to anyone who, directly or indirectly, threatened her life or wounded her vanity suggests – as does her reluctance to set a regal precedent by executing Mary, Queen of Scots – that her early experiences had bred into her not just a repugnance for sexual intercourse, but also a dread of old age and of extinction.

Preoccupied with Elizabeth's sexual maladjustment, anxious to inject an extra zest into his love-story, Lytton spotlighted the thwarted, passional side of her being without ever indicating how a more predominant, hereditary strain had twisted and partially overshadowed her sensuality. The daughter of Henry VIII and Anne Boleyn, she ininherited not only a strong susceptibility to the opposite sex, but also a still stronger lust for power. Her high-arched nose, prominent cheek bones, firm mouth and watchful eyes all call attention to this prevailing bent handed down from her father, and greatly stimulated by the long sequence of dangers through which she passed between the ages of fourteen and twenty-five. Of all Lytton's subjects, Elizabeth was perhaps the most ruthlessly ambitious and determined. Yet she is not

Lytton *couchant*. (The mosaic fireplace is by Boris Anrep.)

Carrington and Lytton in the garden at Ham Spray

Ham Spray House about the time of Lytton's death: *above*, the little front sitting-room; *below*, the study

treated to the summary justice previously meted out to his eminent Victorians, since his relationship to the Virgin Queen was of an altogether more fantastic character. At first sight no two figures could be more dissimilar than the rather masculine Elizabeth and her effeminate biographer. But seen through the perspective of *Elizabeth and Essex*, their lives appear to run along parallel lines – sharing something of the same resilient tenacity, fluctuating nervous constitution, and personality bewildering even to their closest associates – until they meet at vanishing-point in their feelings for Essex. From the intellectual standpoint, both looked on him with an amused, sometimes infuriated scepticism; but both were powerless to resist for long the hypnotic emotional spell he cast about him.

Having in his two preliminary chapters painted a resplendent décor, Lytton then proceeds to plot the intersection of his two momentous lives in a style that is generally lean, sparse and fast-moving. For the most part Essex is rather an unanimated figure, but in one passage Lytton does adumbrate an excellent subject for his tragedy that he never quite succeeded in developing: 'The motives of the most ordinary mortal are never easy to disentangle, and Essex was far from ordinary. His mind was made up of extremes, and his temper was devoid of balance. He rushed from opposite to opposite; he allowed the strangest contradictories to take root together, and grow up side by side, in his heart. He loved and hated – he was a devoted servant and an angry rebel – all at once. For an impartial eye, it is impossible to trace in his conduct a determined intention of any kind. He was swept hither and thither by the gusts of his passions and the accidents of circumstance. He entertained treasonable thoughts, and at last treasonable projects; but fitfully, with intervals of romantic fidelity and noble remorse.'

As a man of action, Essex may have lain outside the range of Lytton's imagination, and, by projecting his own romantic dreams into the figure of this tragic hero, he made the portrait original but not wholly convincing. Essex was a born opportunist whose charm would have lost its potency had it been controlled by the prudence necessary to make the most of it. Though occasionally paying lip-service to the virtue of prudence, Lytton glories in Essex's most absurd and reckless feats of audacity. He recreates the earl's personality largely from his elevated epistolary flourishes. 'Never were his words more gorgeous and his rhythms more moving,' he writes of one of Essex's short letters to the queen, 'never were the notes of anguish, remonstrance, and devotion so romantically blended together.' Rather in the manner of Oscar Wilde, Lytton wanted to believe that a beautiful and ornate style must reflect physical good looks. Despite evidence to the contrary, he

U

pictured Essex as magnificently handsome, rejecting the portrait of him
at Trinity because it made him appear too cerebral. 'It is certainly very
fine,' he told Charles Prentice after having gone down to inspect the
portrait (3 August 1928), 'but I had not remembered how extremely
intellectual the face was.' Eventually, he chose from Woburn Abbey a
more idealized likeness which, in Keynes's view, bore some resemblance to Lytton himself.

Lytton also repeats the somewhat dubious legend of Essex's tremendous popularity throughout the country, without giving any of the
stories that might perhaps have accounted for it. At the end, when Essex
marches upon the City, the citizens' supposed devotion to him vanishes
so swiftly that 'not a creature joined him', a catastrophe which Lytton
represents as the triumph of patriotic loyalty to the queen over the
more personal hero-worship for Essex. Again, Lytton fails to reveal that
Essex was inordinately susceptible to mockery, and that he destroyed
Dr Lopez not out of misguided chauvinism, but from motives of
trivial revenge, since Lopez had made him appear ridiculous before the
queen and others at court.[1] The explanation which he offers for
Essex's merciless hounding of Lopez is one of his least plausible theories
put forward to uphold the ardent and capricious chivalry of this young
cavalier. Dr Lopez was palpably innocent, and his terrible fate shocked
and fascinated Lytton. One could understand professional politicians
and intellectuals such as the Bacons, Burghley or Sir Robert Cecil
cynically failing to recognize the rights of truth and justice, but never
Essex. 'Generous, strong, in the flush of manhood, is it possible that he
failed to realise that what he was doing was, to say the least of it,
unfair?' Lytton asked. 'Years afterwards, when Spain was no longer a
bugbear, his animosity against Dr. Lopez seemed only to be explicable
on the ground of some violent personal grudge. But in truth no such
explanation was necessary. The Earl's mind was above personalities;
but it was not above the excitement of political rivalry, the cruel
conventions of human justice, and the nobility of patriotism.'

In one of his *Spectator* reviews, Lytton wrote: 'Tragedy cannot
flourish without a little barbarism at its roots.' There is plenty of
barbarism in *Elizabeth and Essex* – the burning of heretics by King
Philip of Spain; the hideous hanging, castrating, drawing and quarter-
ing of Dr Lopez, and a number of vivid and terrible death scenes:

---

[1] The truth of the Lopez affair seems to have been that, very foolishly, Lopez chose to
double-cross Essex. He would receive information from foreign parts which he first gave
to the queen and Burghley, and subsequently to Essex. When Essex came bursting into
the palace with his information, he would be laughed at for bringing stale news. Moreover, if Bishop Goodman is to be believed, Lopez gossiped about Essex's private infirmities; and (so Goodman hints) let it be known that Essex was suffering from V.D.

Essex stretching out his scarlet-sleeved arms as the signal for his own execution; Elizabeth lying speechless on a cushioned floor, four days and four nights, with a finger in her mouth; Philip waiting in his gloomy mausoleum of a palace to be welcomed into heaven by the Trinity. These scenes of magnificent anguish and ghastly mutilation are described with many strokes of telling detail and act as a contributory means to a general artistic end – that of making our flesh creep. By such methods did Lytton hope to bring alive again that golden blend of idealism and savagery that was the nucleus of the English Renaissance. In this hope he has succeeded far better than most of the well-thought-of Elizabethan scholars such as J. E. Neale or Milton Waldman, from whose books one might infer that to have one's ears or hands chopped off under the reign of Elizabeth I would have hurt very much less than in the reign of her successor, Elizabeth II. The special virtue of Lytton's book is that he had a peculiar and uncanny insight into the atmosphere of the sixteenth century, highly personal and fantastic, combined with a special literary gift for delineating an era through its most representative personalities.

Against the violent and brutal mood of this age, Lytton sets the comparative humanity, the sensitivity, of his two mighty principals. Of Essex, he wrote with truth that 'there was no settled malignancy in his nature'. After leading the successful assault on Cadiz, Lytton tells us, Essex's 'humanity had put a speedy end to the excesses that were usual on such occasions. Priests and churches were spared; and three thousand nuns were transported to the mainland with the utmost politeness.' Yet Lytton steers away from the fact that Essex's humanity was a highly temperamental affair, depending entirely upon his uppermost feelings at the time. At Cadiz he had unquestionably been merciful to the enemy in the afterglow of his personal triumph. Much later, in Ireland, when his campaign against Tyrone was going badly and he felt miserable and unwell, he behaved – as Lytton fails to mention – with excessive brutality to his own soldiers, cashiering and imprisoning all the officers of a detachment of some hundreds of men which had shown cowardice in the field, executing a lieutenant, and having every tenth man in the rank and file put to death.

Lytton is equally charitable to Elizabeth in furthering the questionable theory of her unusual benevolence. 'Undoubtedly there was a touch of the sinister about her,' he conceded. 'One saw it in the movements of her extraordinarily long hands. But it was a touch and no more—just enough to remind one that there was Italian blood in her veins – the blood of the subtle and cruel Visconti. On the whole though she was infinitely subtle she was not cruel: she was almost human for her times and her occasional bursts of savagery were the results of fear or temper.' As an apologia, this seems a little disingenuous. A study of Anglo-Saxon history does not lead to the conclusion that the British have lagged very far behind the Italians in the practices of barbarity. Nor do most inhumane people indulge in acts of cruelty except as the result of fear or temper. Elizabeth's venom and resentment stemmed from her neurotic condition, in particular her fear of death and her overblown vanity, and they were often directed against relatively innocuous people. It was in one of these bursts of unwarranted cruelty that she ordered Stubbs's right hand and that of his publisher to be cut off because of a pamphlet which, although in itself an expression of loyalty, offended her *amour propre*. Public opinion in this instance was decidedly against her, though she herself deplored the fact that the law would not permit the hanging of them both. Neither can she be exonerated from all blame for the execution of hundreds of the poorer folk who took part in the Northern Rebellion. Although urged by her ministers to approve this act, she must have been fully aware of the injustice in which she acquiesced by allowing the wealthy leaders of the Rebellion to ransom their lives to her exchequer, while their destitute followers were being butchered. Moreover, in signing the death-warrant of Dr Lopez, her physician-in-chief and old acquaintance, she was impelled not even by fear or temper, but mainly by a passing wish to gratify Essex's immoderate self-conceit. She herself was never properly convinced of the Doctor's guilt, yet her supposed humanity did not deter her from sanctioning the full rigours of the law. Lytton, however, concludes his chapter on the Lopez episode on a mild and whimsical note: 'Elizabeth was merciful to the Doctor's widow. She allowed her to keep the goods and chattels of the deceased, forfeited by his attainder – with one exception. She took possession of King Philip's ring. She slipped it – who knows with what ironical commiseration? – on to her finger; and there it stayed till her death.'

Lytton shows us that Elizabeth's infatuation for Essex arose, against her better judgement, from an insatiable craving for the devotion of young men, while he, though not immune to the very real aura of personal magnetism with which Elizabeth was able to invest herself, was impelled forward mainly by the dazzling prospects of power, prestige and the financial benefits accruing from such a relationship. This relationship is presented as being very similar in its underlying pattern to all the others in Lytton's writing. In every case the predominant partner is the woman, whose terrific overplus of vitality crushes the gilded butterfly male. Essex, Lytton recounts, 'was a man, with a man's power of insight and determination; he could lead if she would follow;

but Fate had reversed the rôles, and the natural master was a servant. Sometimes, perhaps, he could impose his will upon her – but after what an expenditure of energy, what a prolonged assertion of masculinity! A woman and a man! Yes, indeed, it was, too obvious! Why was he where he was? Why had he any influence whatever? It was not only obvious, it was ludicrous, it was disgusting: he satisfied the peculiar cravings of a virgin of sixty-three.'

In unfolding what, in places, almost amounts to an imaginary love-affair with himself, Lytton failed to explore and clarify the emotional changes that developed in Elizabeth's attitude to the young earl. Each was flattered, as Lytton brings out, during the early years of their friendship, by the other's attentions. Her preposterous vanity was gratified; his search for high renown was given direction. But while Elizabeth's affection for Essex deepened with time, the turbulent though platonic affair which she carried on with him never came so near to shaking her virginal resolution as had her previous liaison with his stepfather, Robert Dudley, Earl of Leicester. The reason for this, of course, may have lain partly with her greater age, partly with the more complex and mixed emotions which the warm and headstrong nature of the young man aroused in her. Her lust for flattery was voracious. At the age of sixty, with a red wig and a few blackened teeth, she could still relish Walter Raleigh picturing her with 'the gentle wind blowing her fair hair about her pure cheeks, like a nymph; sometimes sitting in the shade like a goddess; sometimes singing like an angel; sometimes playing like Orpheus'. Yet her shrewd sense of reality was never al-together extinguished. The highflown flattery of her court favourites was, she always knew, a tribute to her immense personality and power, not her charm. She was thus drawn to Essex partly because his insolence made her feel a woman, however much she resented it as a queen. When, on one occasion, she refused a request he made of her to appoint Sir George Carew as Lord Deputy of Ireland, he turned his back on her, and she boxed his ears. In fury he put his hand to his sword, but the Earl of Nottingham came between them, and he rushed from the room vowing that he would not have endured such an outrage even in front of Henry VIII. Lytton narrates this incident in full, but he omits Elizabeth's significant last remark: 'He would do well', she cried, 'to content himself with displeasing her on all occasions and despising her person so insolently, but he should beware of touching her sceptre.'

As a woman, Elizabeth's fondness for Essex generally overcame the mistrust she felt for him as a queen, and which she extended whole-heartedly to his adherents, of whom she disapproved both as a ruler and a woman, suspecting them as the potential agents of Essex's wild though unfocused ambitions, and disliking them as the personal friends of the man she loved. As for Essex himself, she treated him like a small boy who was habitually associating with the wrong company. Her affection for him was composed out of a mixture of maternal feeling and starved desire, the former predominating. These sentiments had less in common with the infatuation of an elderly mistress for her young lover – which Lytton describes – and more, as G. B. Harrison has observed, with 'the jealous love of a widow towards her only son'. In his presence she seems to have experienced some warm and bitter consolation for the terrible loneliness of her position as Queen of England. 'Towards her ministers or servants,' Harrison continued, 'she felt annoyance or approval, Essex roused in her passion, of admiration which might rise into ecstasy or of anger which might swell into hate. Moreover beneath the ceremonies and trappings of royalty she was a very lonely childless woman whom no one loved for her own sake: perhaps Robin might.'

Ever since her girlhood, Elizabeth had been fond of children, and there is ample evidence to suggest that she felt her own childless condition keenly. At the birth of James she is said to have exclaimed: 'The Queen of Scots is lighter of a fair son and I am but barren stock.' Unable to conceal from herself all that she had sacrificed to the desire for political power and the need for safety, she would erupt into insane fury whenever one of her maids-of-honour became pregnant. With men she was less violent, on the whole, than with women. But her obsessive resentment of others marrying was notorious. Pembroke and Southampton were both imprisoned; Catherine Gregg and the Earl of Hertford were sent to the Tower; and Walter Raleigh and Bess Throgmorton were similarly dealt with, though in their case Elizabeth could not plead the excuse that their offspring would stand in the line of succession. It is hardly surprising that Leicester and Essex should have smarted under her fury, since she regarded their marriages as acts of personal infidelity to herself.

It is not uncommon for a man or woman whose deepest drive has been for power, to establish a dominant parental relationship with the opposite sex. Elizabeth enjoyed thwarting Essex in order to provoke highly emotional scenes that led to even more highly charged reconciliations, more dangerous each time, and more delicious. Tossing him about on a violent sea of passion, she would play with him like a cat with a mouse, enjoying having her own sensations tickled by Essex's beauty, while his impetuosity and contrariness added spice to the contact. She abused him for trivialities, but tolerated his more foolish actions as an indulgent mother would the sweet follies of a pampered child. Alternately caressing and chastising him, she employed a kind of primitive Pavlovian system to unhinge Essex's already unstable character, and was herself the principal architect of his final disgrace. Responsive to his charm, she held no high opinion of his capabilities or achievements. While she was with him she could not deny his wishes for long, but would experience a contemptuous reaction against her own weakness once he had departed. In long vitriolic letters she visited on him her displeasure with herself. And in this alternating response, one can see the warring of those two great forces in her nature, with her desire for power gradually displacing her need for love. During the last rebellion, her uncharacteristic behaviour shows the growing supremacy of her will over her imagination. She was calm and undisturbed amid the rising clamour which went up from Essex House, unable to acknowledge any acute danger emanating from the incompetent, boyish earl. It is even possible that Essex would not have paid for treason with his life, as Lytton points out, had it not been reported to Elizabeth that, in one of his outbursts, he had cried that the queen was an old woman, as crooked in mind as in carcass. This insult helped to harden her resolve when, in signing his death-warrant, she killed for ever her own sensual emotionalism, the dying convulsions of which fretted the surface of her being in a fit of hysterical laughter.

The mother-and-son relationship which stares out at us from the pages of *Elizabeth and Essex* was one which naturally interested Lytton, but which he did not sufficiently investigate or define. In one passage only does he appear to recognize this aspect of their love-affair. Describing the disciplinary tribunal that Elizabeth personally devised to punish Essex for his failure in Ireland, he wrote: 'There should be a fine show, and the miscreant should be lectured, very severely lectured, made to apologise, frightened a little, and then – let off. So she arranged it, and everyone fell in with her plans. Never was the cool paternalism of the Tudors so curiously displayed. Essex was a naughty boy, who had misbehaved, been sent to his room, and fed on bread and water; and now he was to be brought downstairs, and, after a good wigging, told he was not to be flogged after all.'

3

THE SERPENT, THE PYGMY AND THE FOX

Behind the two principal actors, the lesser characters are arranged so that they become engrafted into the main design of Lytton's Elizabethan tapestry. Some of these subsidiary figures stand out in the limelight; others are set in the shade. Among the latter, perhaps the most surprising is Robert Dudley, Earl of Leicester. Although Elizabeth's love-affair with Leicester lasted right up until his death, Lytton treats their relationship laconically and, presumably to make Essex a unique phenomenon in Elizabeth's life, subordinated his stepfather to a comparatively trifling role.

Of the other subordinates on Lytton's canvas, the most important are Francis Bacon, the serpent; Sir Robert Cecil, the pygmy; and Sir Walter Raleigh, the fox.

Bacon, the bad man of the tragedy, is brilliantly depicted. Lytton seemed to possess a specially penetrating insight into the workings of his mind. For though of a far more aggressive and amoral nature than himself, Bacon shared with Lytton some of the same tastes, proclivities and turns of mind. As an essayist, Bacon reigned as supreme master of the sententious style, which the great French writers had made their own. His aphorisms were worthy of La Rochefoucauld. His prose combined the use of resplendent colouring with a remarkable concentration of thought. But the very qualities that enabled him to write the most sublime prose brought about his own spiritual ruin. 'His imagination, with all its magnificence, was insufficient,' Lytton explained: 'it could not see into the heart of things. And among the rest his own heart was hidden from him. His psychological acuteness, fatally external, never revealed to him the nature of his own desires.'

Bacon's part in the condemnation of Essex, though regrettable, was amazingly clever. The pamphlet which he prepared to justify the execution of his former patron evokes this comment from Lytton. 'This result was achieved with the greatest skill and neatness; certain passages in the confessions were silently suppressed; but the manipulations of the evidence were reduced to a minimum and there was only one actually false statement of fact. . . . Yet such a beautiful economy – could it have arisen unbeknownst? Who can tell? The serpent glides off with his secret.'[1]

[1] 'No wonder Mr Strachey admires such handiwork,' commented the distinguished historian, G. B. Harrison, 'for these are his own methods.' Although Harrison imperfectly understood Lytton's attitude to Bacon, it is true that in his *Elizabeth and Essex*, by dovetailing fragments of letters and conversations, Lytton did practise a number of silent suppressions of the truth. For example, he represents Elizabeth's last speech to Parliament as far shorter and more striking than it actually was, by leaving out whole passages without indication, and by transposing the rhythms of what he does quote. The scene, as he depicts it, closes to the sound of trumpets, and the queen makes her exit with the words: 'And, though you have had and may have many mightier and wiser princes sitting in this seat, yet you never had nor shall have any love you better.' Elizabeth's own words were 'any that will be more careful and loving', after which she went on speaking for a further minute or so and finally gave directions that the whole delegation might come forward and kiss her hand. On scientific rather than aesthetic grounds, critics have also objected to Lytton's pretence of knowing what his characters were secretly thinking or

Lytton points to a central division in Bacon's character – a hiatus between his sensitivity and ruthlessness. Describing the part he played in the preliminary examination of Essex, Lytton wrote: 'He had no hesitations or doubts. Other minds might have been confused in such a circumstance; but he could discriminate with perfect clarity between the claims of the Earl and the claims of the Law. Private friendship and private benefits were one thing; the public duty of taking the part required of him by the State in bringing to justice a dangerous criminal was another.' With all his array of fine intellect, his underlying instinct – that melting-pot of primitive emotions and undeveloped thought – was faulty and distorted. Both as a literary artist and a politician this was his flaw, his fatal limitation. Lytton illustrates this very well. Bacon, like the Prince Consort, was no enigma to him. But to accentuate the treachery of his villain – the matchless observer with the callous 'viper-gaze' – he blew up his portrait to Machiavellian giant-propor-tions. Having picked up a remark from Harvey that Bacon had 'a delicate, lively hazel eye, like the eye of a viper', he quite simply made him into a viper. The most serious misjudgement that this process involved was the deprivation from Bacon of one idea he held very fast – loyalty to the Crown. Essex's rebellion horrified him as a monstrous breach in nature. He had tried his best to keep Essex straight. The letter he wrote after the Cadiz expedition contained the most brilliant diagnosis

feeling in certain situations – a notorious instance of this trait being his elaborate presentation of Elizabeth's state of mind just before the death of Essex.

Perhaps the most telling and significant indictment of Lytton Strachey as a serious historian on the evidence of this book, was contained in Professor G. B. Harrison's review in the *Spectator* (24 November 1928), entitled 'Elizabeth and Her Court'. This article, while it acknowledged the skill and vitality of Strachey's portrait of the queen, criticized his manipulations of historical data, which it referred to as 'privileges denied to the pedestrian scholar'. The piece, however, should be read with some caution, especially with regard to its remarks on Francis Bacon and on the appropriateness of the manner in which the narrative ends. For the published review was not, in fact, quite what Harrison wrote. The literary editor at that time, Celia Simpson (who later became the second wife of John Strachey, the politician and writer), finding the article less eulogistic than she desired, rewrote the first and last paragraphs herself – the latter originally being a parody of the final paragraph in *Elizabeth and Essex*: 'The Master biographer wrote on ... the enhancing of a great reputation.'

'I only discovered the changes when they sent me a proof which I had hastily to tinker in the office,' Professor Harrison told the author (6 January 1967). '... I was only a beginner at that time, and since this was my first invitation to review for the *Spectator*, I was too timid to make a proper protest.' Celia Simpson had evidently objected to the view, expressed with true academic sarcasm, that Lytton Strachey did not care enough for historical facts, an attitude 'disturbing to the creeping critic – the pedant – who cares for such things'. When Professor Harrison protested that Strachey's scholarship was deficient she retorted: 'Scholars exist to provide material for people like Strachey!'

Professor Harrison also confirmed that his own *Robert Devereux, Earl of Essex* 'was partly intended to answer *Elizabeth and Essex*, which was a fine scenario but not history'.

U*

of Essex's position, but one that Essex himself never heeded. In a sense, therefore, it was Essex who deserted his wise counsellor rather than the other way round. Lytton also suggests, at another point, that Bacon was always unfeeling, whereas he appears to have been extremely sensitive, even if unable to deploy this sensitivity into his outward manner or his style. He overplays, too, the predominance in his make-up of a prohibitively inhumane intellect, so as to contribute to the general atmosphere of predestination: 'The miserable end – it needs must colour our vision of the character and the life. But the end was implicit in the beginning – a necessary consequence of qualities that were innate.' And to strengthen the drama of this fatalistic mood he alludes, quite misleadingly, to the story of Bacon on Highgate Hill stuffing a dead fowl with snow, representing him not as a scientist experimenting with the technique of refrigeration, but as a King Lear – 'an old man, disgraced, shattered, alone'.

In the course of a *Spectator* review, 'Bacon as a Man of Letters', Lytton had written of him as being neither spiritual, like Pascal, nor fundamentally an artist, like Keats. He was more of a political sociologist, whose 'deepest interests were fixed upon the workings and welfare of human society'. The reptile that, to weird musical rhythms, slips and slithers across the stage of *Elizabeth and Essex* would scarcely be recognized in this Spectatorial figure. In a crucial passage of the book, which sets out Lytton's interpretation of Bacon's character as a man of action, and shows us the dramatic purpose which he is to serve, Lytton wrote:

'He was no striped frieze; he was shot silk. The detachment of speculation, the intensity of personal pride, the uneasiness of nervous sensibility, the urgency of ambition, the opulence of superb taste – these qualities, blending, twisting, flashing together, gave to his secret spirit the subtle and glittering superficies of a serpent. A serpent, indeed, might well have been his chosen emblem – the wise, sinuous, dangerous creature, offspring of mystery and the beautiful earth. The music sounds, and the great snake rises, and spreads its hood, and leans and hearkens, swaying in ecstasy; ... His mind might move with joy among altitudes and theories, but the variegated savour of temporal existence was no less dear to him – the splendours of high living – the intricacies of Court intrigue – the exquisiteness of pages – the lights reflected from small pieces of coloured glass. Like all the greatest spirits of the age, he was instinctively and profoundly an artist. . . . Intellect, not feeling, was the material out of which his gorgeous and pregnant sentences were made. Intellect! It was the common factor in all the variations of his spirit; it was the backbone of the wonderful snake.'

The Bacon of *Elizabeth and Essex* is determined to prove a rascal. The result is that as an agent in the movement of the drama he is superb, and his character is fastened together with an absorbing richness and complexity. But as a malefactor he is overcoloured, and transposed from life into the caricature of bad, conventional melodrama. 'It is the *Lion and the Snake*,'[1] Wyndham Lewis commented in a letter to Charles Prentice (27 November 1928), 'Essex as the embodiment of simple-minded chivalry and poor Bacon as the "Machiavel"! What a villain! One is almost inclined to believe after reading S[trachey]'s book, that he wrote Shakespeare's plays and did all the other things he is accused of.'

With his cousin, Robert Cecil, in mind, Bacon had once generalized: 'Deformed persons are commonly even with nature, for as nature hath done ill by them so they do by nature being for the most part void of natural affection and so they have their revenge on nature. Deformity stirreth in them and especially to watch and observe the weakness of others that they might have somewhat to repay. So that, upon the matter in a great wit deformity is an advantage in rising.'

Lytton presents Cecil's malformation less as a spur to his ascendancy than as the clue to a riddle. He can detect no inner spark within the man to account for his exemplary, expeditious toil: 'He sat at his table writing; and his presence was sweet and grave,' Lytton wrote. 'There was an urbanity upon his features, some kind of explanatory gentleness, which, when he spoke, was given life and meaning by his exquisite elocution. He was all mild reasonableness – or so it appeared, until he left his chair, stood up, and unexpectedly revealed the stunted discomfort of deformity. Then another impression came upon one – the uneasiness produced by an enigma: what could the combination of that beautifully explicit countenance with that shameful, crooked posture really betoken? He returned to the table . . . While he laboured, his inner spirit waited and watched. A discerning eye might have detected melancholy and resignation in that patient face. The spectacle of the world's ineptitude and brutality made him, not cynical – he was not aloof enough for that – but sad – was he not a creature of the world himself? He could do so little, so very little, to mend matters; . . . At a moment of crisis, a faint, a hardly perceptible impulsion might be given. It would be nothing but a touch, unbetrayed by the flutter of an

---

[1] W. K. Rose, in a footnote to his edition of *The Letters of Wyndham Lewis* (1963), p. 185, n. 6, comments: 'L[ewis] refers to his own *The Lion and the Fox* (London, 1927), in which he sees Othello as the simple-hearted, noble lion and Iago as the wily, vulgar "Machiavel".' For six years (1926–32) Lewis's publishers were Chatto and Windus, and he dealt, as did Lytton, with C. H. Prentice (d. 1949) who gave both writers his most responsive and unstinting support.

eyelid, as one sat at table, not from one's hand, which would continue writing, but from one's foot. One might hardly be aware of its existence oneself, and yet was it not, after all, by such minute, invisible movements that the world was governed for its good, and great men came into their own?'

This is an outline of the puzzling silhouette Robert Cecil casts across the pages of *Elizabeth and Essex* – a shadowy Master Mind, not entirely disembodied but attached to a hump; an Invisible Man suspended in an almost eternal state of purposeful inanimation; an assiduous quill-pusher bent double over his orderly accumulation of papers, and directing the momentous affairs of the nation with fractional gesticulations of his feet. Like the reticent and resourceful Baron Stockmar, Cecil is made to achieve the maximum political consequences with the very minimum of behind-the-scenes action. But whereas Stockmar had in reality been a political cipher, Cecil was a major influence, and it is all the more disappointing that he should have been cast for this historical masquerade in such a darkly theatrical part.

There can be no doubt that, as Lytton tells us, Cecil's administrative aptitude and knowledge of the work he was called upon to perform as secretary was unrivalled. In early youth he had been coached for the job by the ablest man in England, his father Lord Burghley. Yet there was a marked dissimilarity between father and son which Lytton does not bring out. While both were masters at political intrigue, there was always an element of altruistic greatness in Burghley's actions, which were prompted by some consideration of what he felt was best for Elizabeth and for England. The same tempered spirit of detachment had not been granted to his son. As the years advanced, so this lonely, shrunken being withdrew ever more remotely from his fellow men. His retirement, of which Lytton makes great play, does not seem to have derived from any inscrutable motive. From boyhood Cecil had been morbidly self-conscious of his grotesque deformity, and after Burghley's death he grew, under his impassive, rather mild manner, increasingly bitter and isolated. His driving-force became a personal grudge against humanity, and his actions appear to have been for the most part governed by the dual considerations of self-advancement and self-preservation.

Yet Cecil never seemed to harbour any particular malevolence towards Essex, in spite of what the young earl had said and written about him to the queen. His attitude was guided either by a determination not to leave himself vulnerable to a man who, up to the very last hour, might still be re-elevated to the royal favour, or by his understanding of what Essex meant and would always mean, wherever his impulsive nature led him, to the queen. It is even possible that he may have partly succumbed to the illimitable charm which Essex was able to exercise over his contemporaries.

A very real responsibility rested on Cecil at the time of Essex's rebellion, and Lytton credits him with a superhuman intelligence in dealing with this crisis. 'Essex could decide upon nothing; still wildly wavering, it is conceivable that, even now, he would have indefinitely postponed both projects and relapsed into his accustomed state of hectic impotence if something had not happened to propel him into action.

'That something bears all the marks of the gentle genius of Cecil. With unerring instinct the Secretary saw that the moment had now arrived at which it would be well to bring matters to an issue; and accordingly he did so. It was the faintest possible touch. On the morning of Saturday, February 7th, a messenger arrived from the Queen at Essex House, requiring the Earl to attend the Council. That was enough. To the conspirators it seemed obvious that this was an attempt to seize upon the Earl, and that, unless they acted immediately, all would be lost. Essex refused to move; he sent back a message that he was too ill to leave his bed; his friends crowded about him; and it was determined that the morrow should see the end of the Secretary's reign.'

Perhaps it was because he was asked to appear before the Council at the Lord Treasurer's house that Essex's apprehensions were so violently agitated. In fact, the Lord Treasurer was himself ill, and for this reason only was it proposed that the Council should assemble there. The summons was couched in moderate and reasonable words, merely requesting that Essex should state his grievances so that the Council might investigate them. There is no evidence nor solid reason to support Lytton's inference that this manœuvre was arranged by Cecil alone. Following previous biographers, whose number includes Robert Cecil's direct descendant Algernon Cecil, Lytton presumes that the secretary was absolute master of the situation from start to finish. Yet the actual precautions he took were minimal. The guard was doubled at Whitehall, and the Lord Mayor was warned of the danger. Trained bands had been collected together, but they were not brought to London. Obviously Cecil was not of the same opinion as Lytton as to Essex's great popularity. Had the earl been the people's hero, these precautionary measures could never have proved effective against a rebel army marching on the court. And if he had simply had the sense to rush the palace instead of that futile march into the City, he might well have won.

Lytton's Cecil is that most familiar of all his stock characters – a brilliant enigma. But Robert Cecil, the little man who diminished the scope of his undoubted talent by the meanness of his spirit, was surely of a more human origin. Nowhere, perhaps, is the unpleasant aspect of his personality more obviously exhibited than in his double-dealings with Walter Raleigh – which even seem to have caused himself some qualms of conscience. Cecil's undermining of Raleigh falls outside the main course of Lytton's prose drama, but he refers briefly to Cecil's fear, some time after Essex's execution, that 'the dashing incompetence of Essex would be replaced by Raleigh's sinister force' – though he then goes on to show that Cecil was by far the more sinister individual, while Raleigh remained 'utterly unsuspecting'.

Walter Raleigh, so versatile and contradictory a man that Fuller did not know whether he should be catalogued as a statesman, seaman, learned writer or what you will, presented Lytton with a figure who could be placed with equal authenticity at almost any part of his canvas. He seems to have appreciated that Raleigh was the antithesis of Essex in temperament, and since the latter symbolized 'the spirit of the ancient feudalism', the former is represented as 'the ominous prophet of Imperialism'. But Raleigh's character is never developed in *Elizabeth and Essex*. Lytton employs him in a purely decorative capacity, shrouding his personality from all clear view, possibly from the fear that, if given a more prominent part, he might steal the show from Essex. More handsome than his rival, well-born, a cool and courageous fighter, a student and fine poet, he combined more personal advantages than any other man at court. Possessing an imaginative relish for intrigue, though of too naïve a mind to manage his intrigues very successfully, and a delicate sensibility, he was nevertheless unable to liberate that warmth of feeling in others that Essex could call forth at will. He paraded his consummate brilliance in a manner that actively provoked hostility. Proud and arrogant he certainly was, as indeed were most men attracted to the court, but there was more, perhaps, of the open air adventurer in him than the power-seeker. Lytton, however, confines himself almost exclusively to this minor aspect of his personality. In the struggle for ascendancy behind the throne, Raleigh is depicted as Essex's principal rival, a lurking, ever-potential threat. In Chapter III he is introduced as 'a dangerous and magnificent man'. And in the following chapters there are constant references to him designed to build up in the reader's mind the vision of a dark and sinister force, menacing the career of Essex.

'Raleigh celebrated the occasion [his reinstatement to Elizabeth's favour] by having made for him a suit of silver armour; and so once more, superb and glittering, the dangerous man stood in the royal ante-chamber at Whitehall.'

'But more dangerous still was the odious Raleigh. Everyone knew that that man's ambitions had no scruples, that he respected no law, either human or divine.'

In portraying Raleigh in this manner, as the implacable enemy of Essex, Lytton was not advancing an objective historical judgement, but echoing Essex's own unbalanced opinion. 'What booteth it to swear the fox,' Essex had cried during his trial. Lytton does not quote this. But it is as a fox that Raleigh prowls about the scenery, a fine embellishment that agreeably tightens the suspense of the story, but resembles only slightly the extraordinary man who was his original.

4

MINORITY REPORT

Never had one of Lytton's books got off to such a mercurial start. How mixed the notices were in Britain – and how well it sold! Already the advance subscription sales topped twelve thousand, in addition to a further hundred of the special signed edition at four guineas, and a second impression of an extra ten thousand copies had to be hastily prepared before publication. 'It's being very successful,' Lytton wrote with amazed jubilation to Topsy Lucas (30 November 1928), 'and I gather from Prentice that the only difficulty is to get enough paper and binding material for the multitudes of editions that will have to be printed. However a good many copies will have to be sold to keep pace with my growing extravagance. Aubusson carpets, for instance – I am plunging wildly in that direction – egged on, of course, by Carrington.' By the first week in January, this pre-publication total had been doubled, and over thirty thousand copies were sold within four months.

In America, where seventy thousand copies were distributed in the first three weeks of December, the book made publishing history.[1]

[1] The manuscript of *Elizabeth and Essex* was in the hands of Harcourt Brace & Co. in May 1928, but, since it had been arranged that there should be a limited edition with the Crosby Gaige imprint as well as the trade edition, the making proceeded slowly, and, when it was found that trade dummies could not be ready for the summer visits of the travellers, the publishers boldly wiped the announcement completely off their autumn catalogue and set 1 December as their publishing date, the travellers making a special trip in November with orders for this one book. The risk was considerable, as the season might go bad, or the booksellers might already have overbought other titles and be disinclined to add any other large item to their purchased stock. As the autumn advanced, it was decided to make separate plates for the trade edition, and this was done under

Even the critics here were eulogistic. Lytton would lie in bed during the mornings and read the extraordinary comments and appreciations his publisher had forwarded to him – 'Essex as 16th Century Lounge Lizard' was one of the headlines. 'It's really rather amazing!' he exclaimed in a letter to Roger Senhouse (14 December 1928). 'The reviews they enclose are hectic. Certainly the Americans have their uses.' Much of this transatlantic furore had been whipped up during the autumn by the serialization of extracts in the *Ladies' Home Journal*, for which he was paid the then record price of thirty thousand dollars (between six and seven thousand pounds). 'The version they print of *Elizabeth and Essex* is extraordinarily mutilated,' Lytton had commented to Charles Prentice (21 September 1928). 'I suppose some abbreviation had to be made, but the result is frightful – rather like an execution for High Treason.' Nevertheless it was this tasteless hors-d'œuvre that had so colossally stimulated the sales. On New Year's Day, William Harcourt, the president of Lytton's American publishing firm, wrote to congratulate him on his 'wild success'. A week later he was writing again: the demand flowed on unchecked and the situation had become 'unprecedented'. 'For three weeks,' Harcourt added, 'your book was being manufactured *night and day.*' Ninety thousand copies had now been printed – 'but doubtless they'll be gone in a minute or two'.

Lytton's contract had been based on his agreement for *Queen Victoria*, and on 1 May, six months after publication day, he received his first cheque from his two publishers, amounting, after his advance on royalties had been deducted, to some ten thousand pounds. 'I have made incredibly huge sums out of E & E,' he told Dorothy Bussy (February 1929), '– chiefly owing to America where the sales have been

Donald Brace's direction at the plant of Quinn and Boden. An edition of 30,000 was printed, and an advance of 15,000 was in hand when shipments began. The first review which added a strong impulse to the sales was in the *New York Times* of 2 December. The publishers were on edge to see what the first re-orders would be. They did not have long to wait. And when the telegrams began to pour in, no moment was lost in putting another edition on the press. In the first week after publication 17,000 copies had been added to the original 15,000, most of these on re-orders by telegraph. In the next six working days 25,000 more copies were sent out, and up to Christmas Day a total of 70,000 copies had been shipped. Not once had the book been reported out of stock. Two big presses and one small one were used, and with every revolution of these three presses one complete book was printed. When, on the week-end of 8 December, it was realized that the 15,000 in hand would shortly be wiped out, these presses and the bindery ran day and night from Saturday to Monday. Following the first edition of 30,000, editions of 10,000, 22,000, 10,000 and 15,000 were in rapid succession sent through the machines. And still the demand went on into the new year. This was a record for the quick production and distribution of a big non-fiction book – a quarter of a million dollars, worth of one biography sold in three weeks.

unparallelled – but unfortunately my extravagance has kept pace with them, so that I am very low at the moment, almost in tears, with anticipations of complete ruin hovering over my head.'

Elizabeth and Essex was not what the public had generally expected, but they found it grand entertainment. In France, Italy, Germany and Sweden translations were soon being brought out, and also in Spain, where the translation rights fetched just fifteen pounds – 'a deplorable result of the Armada'. In Germany, the playwright Ferdinand Bruckner made a stage version of the book which was adapted for the English stage by Ashley Dukes. In America, a film was later made of the book.[1] In England, Henry Ayliff attempted another stage adaptation and the poet Louis MacNiece a radio version. Later still, the text of the book contributed substantially to the libretto which William Plomer wrote for Benjamin Britten's opera *Gloriana*. The idea for this was Britten's. 'He had a special liking for *Elizabeth and Essex*,' William Plomer told the author, 'and a strong interest in the character and fate of Essex, and had for some time seen the story as a possible theme for an opera. . . . Like Britten, I was impressed on re-reading the book, by its dramatic qualities, its vividness, and Strachey's sense of character and situation.'

But despite all the excitement it aroused, and the incredible number of impressions and editions it rapidly went through, *Elizabeth and Essex* was never to establish itself as the classic that *Queen Victoria* had become or to exert anything like the same revolutionary effect as *Eminent Victorians*. Reviewing the Malone Society's reprint of *King Lear* in the *Spectator*, Lytton had once observed that 'the greatest works of art appear to demand, like Kings in a procession, a train of noble fore-runners to prepare the way; and genius only reaches its highest mani-festation when it has, so to speak, a ready-made mould to flow into'. Lytton's fresh and brilliant Victorian biographies constructed an entirely new mould, and have secured a permanent place in literary history, owing largely to the new tradition that they founded. But *Elizabeth and Essex* founded no such tradition. It was an original but abortive experiment, leading up a cul-de-sac where the procession quickly came to a standstill.

Many critics have objected to the guesswork on which so much of the narrative seemed to be based. They carped at its questionable taste, its spicy modernity and the resonant, semi-flamboyant style – the phrases turning in upon themselves – which, though it might be said to harmonize with the Elizabethan pageant it described, had been indulged to the detriment of Lytton's quick and sardonic genius. Compared with

[1] The American film was planned and to some extent paid for in advance but, in the manner of films, never completed.

Queen Victoria it was, as George Dangerfield put it, 'an exquisite failure'.

Upon professional historians the book would appear to have had little influence. J. E. Neale, whose *Queen Elizabeth* (1934) is considered a standard modern biography, makes no mention of it, and ascribes to the behaviour of the queen one massive parliamentary motive. The fall of Essex had not been due to the temperamental reprisal of an insulted woman, but was a measure taken by Elizabeth to quench the political ambition of a subject. But if Lytton's Freudian theories won little support from academic scholars, his book has received some surprising, little-known tributes from among them. Conyers Read in his book *The Tudors* concedes that 'there are some brilliant glimpses of her [Elizabeth] and her court' in *Elizabeth and Essex*. J. B. Black, whose *The Reign of Elizabeth 1558–1603* is included in the Oxford History of England series, calls Lytton's work a 'penetrating and suggestive study'. And A. L. Rowse declared that the book was a fine evocation of the sixteenth-century scene. 'He [Strachey] had a penetrating sense of motive; in my own opinion, he succeeded in unravelling the extraordinary complex web of Elizabeth's feelings about Essex, to a degree that was not even clear to herself, certainly not to Essex, and perhaps only to Cecil. His sympathy all through with the point of view of Cecil, in that brilliant and insufficiently appreciated book, is evident.'

Among literary critics there have also been several remarkably interesting and distinguished exceptions to the majority verdict. E. M. Forster, for example, while admitting that the book did contain inaccuracies, pronounced it to be 'in other ways his greatest work'. Desmond MacCarthy believed it to be undervalued because the intellectual readers had judged the book by wholly inappropriate standards – they 'wanted him to do the same thing over and over again, they wanted to go on enjoying his irony playing round historical figures, hitherto beyond the reach of irreverence and above suspicion'. Norman Douglas wrote to say it was 'so artful and sound and pleasing. I don't know how it could have been better done. Ripe! The cumulative touches are most effective.' And Logan Pearsall Smith, in a letter to Lytton, described the book as 'masterly', though in another letter to Mrs Berenson he wrote: 'Lytton must look to his laurels – his Queen Elizabeth, the judicious feel, won't add to his reputation – it is to my mind melodrama rather than history, and he has made no use of his real gift – his exquisite sense, like that of Voltaire or Gibbon, of human absurdity, of the unbelievable grotesqueness of men's actions and beliefs on this planet. It is a rare and shining gift and should not be laid under a bushel.'

For many weeks following the publication, Lytton was submerged by readers' letters – warm congratulations, queries, advice and stiff correctitudes. 'I am deluged by E & E correspondence,' he complained to Dadie Rylands (29 November 1928), 'it's perfectly fearful, and I foresee will continue for weeks. Quite futile.' Of all these letters, two – both praising *Elizabeth and Essex* as his greatest accomplishment and testifying, one to its historical the other to its psychological authenticity – are still of particular value. The first of these came from G. M. Trevelyan (25 November 1928):

Dear Strachey,

I have just finished Elizabeth. We have not waited 7 years in vain, and your long hesitations over a subject have been rewarded by a success as great as crowned Elizabeth's long hesitations in her happier years. She is much subtler and a much greater subject than Victoria and one more completely suited to your genius. The idea of telling the tale of her and of her age not by full biography but by this particular episode was most happy.

It is much your greatest work. And its success bears out my theory as against your own – or what used to be your view. You used to tell me that your strength was satire and satire alone, so you must choose people whom you did not much like in order to satirize them. I thought the argument bad then, and now the time gives proof of it. Your best book has been written about people to whom you are spiritually akin – far more akin than to the Victorians. And it is not a piece of satire but a piece of life.

Yours ever truly
G. M. Trevelyan

A month later, Lytton received a congratulatory letter from Sigmund Freud, written from Vienna on Christmas Day. He had sent Freud a complimentary copy of his book, and in the course of a long courteous reply, transcribed in his odd, almost totally illegible Gothic hand, Freud answered:

'I am acquainted with all your earlier publications, and have read them with great enjoyment.[1] But the enjoyment was essentially an aesthetic one. This time you have moved me deeply, for you yourself have reached greater depths. You are aware of what other historians so easily overlook – that it is impossible to understand the past with certainty, because we cannot divine men's motives and the essence of their minds and so cannot interpret their actions. Our psychological

---

[1] In a letter to his brother James (15 February 1922), Lytton wrote: 'I was delighted to hear of the Doctor's [Freud's] approval of Eminent Victorians, and I agree with his preference of it to Q.V.'

analysis does not suffice even with those who are near us in space and time, unless we can make them the object of years of the closest investigation, and even then it breaks down before the incompleteness of our knowledge and the clumsiness of our synthesis. So that with regard to the people of past times we are in the same position as with dreams to which we have been given no associations – and only a layman could expect us to interpret such dreams as those. As a historian, then, you show that you are steeped in the spirit of psycho-analysis. And, with reservations such as these, you have approached one of the most remarkable figures in your country's history, you have known how to trace back her character to the impressions of her childhood, you have touched upon her most hidden motives with equal boldness and discretion, and it is very possible that you have succeeded in making a correct reconstruction of what actually occurred.'

CHAPTER VI

Another World

'Human life in its last stages is certainly a miserable affair.
And yet we are horrified when Death comes to put an end
to it.'

Lytton Strachey to Carrington (19 November 1931)

I

THE LOST GIRL

He was rich, but impenetrably exhausted. Of striving with *Elizabeth
and Essex* there had seemed no end; and prolonged study had amassed a
great weariness of the flesh. For the next six months a low fever and the
universal presence of unhappiness sat upon his enfeebled spirit, reducing him on and off 'to bed and ashes'. He was seldom acutely miserable,
but often during this period his life appeared to have become simply a
long process of getting tired. He felt tired of himself, tired of sustained
composition, tired above all of tears and laughter.[1]

Ham Spray, that season, rang to the sound of tears and laughter.
Roger Senhouse came and Roger Senhouse went, very much as usual –
'sweetness and vagueness incarnate'. And very much as usual Lytton's
dubitations multiplied, were deliciously melted away, and returned
again in greater numbers. 'I feel it's my métier to accept his [Roger's]
peculiarities and peccadilloes,' he stoically remarked to Topsy Lucas
(14 July 1929).

The other eruptions at Ham Spray he accustomed himself to treat
with equal stoicism. The new living experiment which he had helped to
inaugurate in the spring of 1926, with Frances and Ralph spending the

---

[1] Although it did not manifest itself openly until the last four months of his life and
was not, even then, recognized for what it was, the disease which finally killed Lytton
must, according to present-day medical knowledge, in all probability have affected his
health in various indirect ways (such as pernicious anaemia) for something like two years
before his death. It was this, combined probably with a change-of-life period and in
addition to the normal mental prostration which followed the writing of a full-length
book, that seems to have so influenced these years.

weekdays away together in Gordon Square, was not turning out as he
had hoped. Increasingly he found it impossible to see Ralph except in
the company of Frances. Every time Ralph came down to Hungerford
he brought her; and at the end of their stay there they would leave
together. Lytton did not dislike Frances, but he could not easily get on
with her, and nor could Carrington. The two women had never been
real friends. Frances, it is true, felt a deep admiration for Carrington,
never thought her tiresome, and spoke of her as a unique person,
unlike anyone else in the world. But the most that Carrington felt
for Frances was a genuine gratitude for having accepted so readily
Ralph's links with Ham Spray. Their outward manner was usually
polite, complimentary, apologetic, lukewarm. They strove to outdo
each other in diffident civilities, for neither wished to feel indebted to
the other. Carrington's reactions were also complicated by a lesbian
attraction for Frances, her feelings shot through with sudden rushes
of tenderness, moments of despair. They were therefore not simply
rivals for Ralph's love, but two people who, because of odd quirks of
circumstance, found the independent lines of their happiness joined
and knotted together in a way that no one could unravel. They
kept their distance, not wanting to tamper too boldly with this knot
for fear of damaging themselves. Somehow it all seemed beyond
them.

The situation was particularly awkward for Carrington. She never
complained to Lytton about this latest arrangement, in case it should
alter for something worse. But he could sense from her fretful, nervous
manner, and from the recognition in it of his own secret reactions, the
inner discomposure that was troubling her. Both of them resented
Frances's habitual presence which fanned the embers of their fading
emotions in the most painful and involuntary way. The atmosphere
between the four of them at week-ends had consequently become forced
and uneasy, heavy with a weight of unspoken feeling that all Ralph's
parades of jocular friendliness could not dispel.

Eventually, in the autumn of 1928, Lytton decided to try and remedy
this ticklish state of affairs. His approach was characteristically reasonable. After one particularly grim and silent week-end, he wrote to
Ralph (6 November 1928) a long, tactful, undemanding letter: 'My
dearest, I am writing this without telling Carrington, and perhaps you
may think it best not to show it to Frances, but of course you must do
just as you like. I have felt for some time rather uneasy about F. – but
have been unable to bring myself to say anything. What worries me is
her coming down here with you so much, and staying for so much of
the time you are here, so that we see so little of you alone. It is not

quite what I had expected would happen – and I think not exactly what you intended either. I am afraid you may suppose that this indicates some hostility on my part towards F.; but this is far from being the case. Can you believe this? I hope so. I hope you will trust that I am telling the truth, and believe in my affection for you, which is something I cannot describe or express. I feel it too deeply for that. I know that this must be painful to you, but it seems better that I should tell you what is in my mind than that I should continue indefinitely with a slight consciousness of a difficulty not cleared up between us. Perhaps it can't be cleared up – but at any rate I think it's better open than secret. I don't want to force you into anything unwillingly. If you feel that you can do nothing – then it can't be helped. If you feel that you cannot answer this either by writing or in talk, do not do so, I will say nothing more about it, and all will be well between us. But conceivably it might be possible for you to suggest to F. that it would be better if she came down rather less often – and if that could be managed the situation would be very greatly eased. It is for you to judge what you can do. I trust your judgement. I only feel that you may perhaps have allowed things to drift from an unwillingness to take an unpleasant step. I don't know. And please do not do anything under a sense of "pressure" from me. I press for nothing. I only ask whether perhaps it may be possible, without too much pain, to make me happier.'

It was practically impossible for Ralph to turn his back on such a modest appeal, so diffidently – so effectively – expressed. The two of them met the following week on neutral territory – 37 Gordon Square – to disentangle the problem. And, as a result of their discussion, circumstances did grow a little less congested down at Ham Spray, though the atmosphere there was never entirely cleared.

No sooner, however, had the tension in one part of the molecule relaxed slightly, than, dramatically, it tightened up elsewhere. The weakest link in its structure had long been that securing Carrington to Gerald Brenan. After their temporary break-up, when Stephen Tomlin had briefly become Carrington's lover, there was a final attempt at reconciliation in 1928. But by then their relationship had already grown explosive. Gerald's inability to affect Carrington permanently and profoundly was an endless exasperation to him. She seemed by her very character to be armour-plated against his emotional assaults. And although his rushes of bitterness and anger had made her frightened of seeing him, she still could not countenance the thought of giving him up. It was the old problem. They seemed, therefore, to have reached a stalemate, since, for the sake of his own peace of mind, neither could leave the other in peace.

The end came over a ludicrously trivial incident involving a bundle of old ties. Carrington, going through Lytton's clothes one day, had come across the ties in his wardrobe. He no longer wanted them – she did not want to throw them out. Then a brainwave had occurred to her – a solution that would please everyone. She liked making parcels – firm, neat, satisfactory objects. And she liked to delegate certain articles to certain particular people – it ministered to some peculiar sense of order and justice in her. She therefore wrapped up the bundle of Lytton's used ties and sent it off to Gerald. Being hardly able to afford a tie himself, he was sure, she reasoned, to be overjoyed by this gift.

But Gerald was outraged. To be handed Lytton's cast-off clothes symbolized cruelly, even cynically, the second-hand place he had for so long occupied in Carrington's affections. She took no account of his own tastes, his individuality. He and Lytton had practically nothing in common with each other, yet he was obliged continuously to live under Lytton's shadow, to rely upon his constant beneficence and hospitality, to listen to stories about him when he was not present and now, as the final indignity, to walk about dressed up in his old clothes. It was the last straw. His anger flared out, and Carrington, terrified and bewildered by this vitriolic reaction to her present, tried vainly to reason with him. He was finding, she said, a quarrel in a straw. There was nothing at stake. But for him honour was at stake. The incident had all at once clarified matters, the clouds parted and he saw everything in a hard perspective. Their love-affair had led nowhere, could never do so. He reproached her scathingly. They parted and did not see each other again until after Gerald's marriage to the American poetess, Gamel Woolsey, in 1930. 'She [Carrington] could not bear anyone to reproach her because she was all too prone to feel guilty,' Gerald Brenan explained to the author, 'and that was how I lost her.'

Over the last four years of her life, that is from 1928 to 1932, Carrington kept a sort of random, unco-ordinated diary – spasmodic and disjunctive entries in no particular sequence, sometimes undated, ranging from brief notes to fierce, unchecked outpourings that ramble repetitiously on over the scrawled unpunctuated pages, full of ravening pathos, tiresomeness, deep despair – on the stiff beige-coloured cover of which she inked in, with her child's hand, a title: *D. C. Partridge: HER BOOK*. This unique volume records with shocking and melancholy vividness the vast disorganization of her life, the unlocated muddled agitations that so upset her peace of mind.

These last years were seldom calm, seldom happy. Her days, especially when Lytton was absent from Ham Spray, were often long and dismal, racked by headaches and ill thoughts of death; and at night she was plagued by hideous dreams – dreams of decapitation and dripping blood, of young boys being drowned on rafts, of making violent lesbian love to girls. Her solitary and promiscuous nature, like that of a cat, with its awkward quirk of virginal integrity, refused to be at ease with other people, with 'bouncy groups', yet dreaded isolation from humanity. Whenever Lytton left her side, she felt the draught, and like an anxious mother she feared for his safety and for her own. Lytton, who appreciated much of what she was silently feeling, would try to reason away these apprehensions, minimize her terrors. 'What absolute despair can seize one without warning or apparent cause,' she wrote at one point in her diary. 'Lytton maintains it is the adrenalin glands not working.'

Lytton's nearness brought some order and cohesion to her chaotic, incomplete existence. Otherwise she could only find serenity and meaning in her painting, and here infrequently. Every year since 1918 she had made a resolution to paint more, but every year her human relationships had complicated this resolve. Sometimes she could not bear the thought of anyone touching her, of even coming close to her – yet she needed desperately to love people. All her passions and affections were attempts to recreate some childish situation. If Lytton may be said to have represented to her a father, then the affairs she entered into with young men were chiefly endeavours to find a substitute for her dead brother Teddy. Her love for Gerald Brenan had long been one attempt to replace him – but as she got to know Gerald better so he had filled the part less and less convincingly. He was too articulate, too much, unblinkingly, himself. But now after he had left, she took up with someone else who was better fitted by character to approach her ideal. This was Piers Noxall, nicknamed Snipe. Like Teddy, Snipe was rather a rough, unintelligent, mute man, who in spite of a large income had lived some time as an ordinary seaman before the mast, and in this capacity travelled the clipper route from China in one of the last of the wind-jammers. To look at he was generally considered attractive, having a square muscular body and a brick-red face. But in all forms of communication he was severely limited, clumsy, by Bloomsbury standards, and an imbecile. In the opinion of Stephen Tomlin he had little feeling or consideration for other people, and apart from ships his only tastes were for drink and making love to girls.

It might seem surprising that a woman of Carrington's individuality should have allowed herself to become deeply involved with such a shallow and conventional person. In fact Snipe's slow, incurious nature, his self-centredness, seems to have been especially pleasing to her. She was better able to recapture the lost, yearning sensations she had experienced for her rugged and reserved brother. To be with him had all the advantages of being alone. There was an uncomplicated morning light that played about their love, casual and blameless. 'His [Snipe's] remoteness just suits me,' she recorded in *HER BOOK*. 'For I feel I am not being "observed" all the time, that No reactions are expected. That whatever happens is alright. a moon shining in the window across the beD. – In the morning seeing a tousled face lying beside me. and then embraces, and more Love. But the sky is light, it has to come to an end and reality must return.'

Fleetingly this reality did return, and the man she had thought so beautiful would appear an irretrievably dull and monstrous fellow. One episode in the love-affair, which probably took place early in 1929, catches brilliantly the beat of her mixed sensations – the desire, in-difference, excitement, anxiety, disillusion, obsession.

'A short love affair. Then a month of thinking about little else. a weekend to Cornwall. The pleasure of leaving London invisibly in the rain, like a ghost, curious how little interest anyone takes in one's movements. The tedium of the journey and the slowness of trains. and then a sudden panic as usual. "I am too old, it is ridiculous. Probably it is all a mistake". at Exeter the car outside and thens later on the Plat-form. And my misgivings returned. as I felt it would all be a delusion. One of my own day dreams which had No relation in anybody else's head. at Oakhampton. the disappointment because the bedroom wasn'T exactly as I had imagined. I had "seen" a big tester bed, a large low room with Dark maghogany furniture, and burning fire . . . Instead a neat spare room in my Mother's style with No fireplace and every-thing white and polished. I felt Nothing can survive this. But curiously enough, it did. In the cinema he held my hand. and I teased him . . . I lay in bed, and read Tristram Shandy, while he drank in the bar. When I said it doesn'T matter tonight He never questioned, or enquired. Not very much curiosity. Yet that is probably the main attraction. Perhaps the most beautiful moment with a shirt in dark close fitting trousers and a brass belt. Do men know the beauty of their appearances as exactly as females do?'

Over the next two years her obsession became fiercer, mounting into a violent passion that was all the more unrestrained for being so meagrely reciprocated. She was ten years older than Snipe, and always painfully aware that their attachment could not last for long. Each day was important. After they had become lovers, she went about with him constantly, ordered his ship's stores and fittings down at Polperro where he lived, and generally managed his affairs. But all this time she had to put up with other, younger and quite vulgar mistresses, who made remarks about her worn appearance and her age – remarks that were inevitably repeated back to her.

In 1930, Snipe made her pregnant. Her horror and disgust at the process of childbearing had always been overwhelming. She used to maintain that only by Lytton could she endure to give birth to a child. And so she arranged to have the pregnancy terminated. Lytton himself did not conceal his disapproval of this affair. Though he had made little point of contact with either Frances Marshall or Gerald Brenan, he was always perfectly tolerant of Ralph's and Carrington's friends, and never jealous of their attachments to younger men and women. In the past he had made an exception only of that *femme fatale*, Clare. But now, not unreasonably, he found himself objecting to Snipe's stupidity, his egotism and callousness. He feared what the outcome of so unchecked and ill-chosen a passion upon Carrington's happiness might be. Yet what could he do? For over a dozen years she had been making persistent sacrifices for his welfare, had sought and willingly endured privations. No one so self-willed and independent as she was could, for so long, have immolated herself to another person without many unconscious longings for liberty. Had he therefore the right to complain now these secret longings were taking a form inconvenient to himself? On the whole he thought not. Yet inconvenient this state of affairs certainly was for Lytton. He had to tolerate frequent visits by Snipe to Ham Spray. And on one occasion Carrington brought him to the house when he was suffering from jaundice, nursing him there for a whole month while Lytton crept noiselessly about in the next room. On any previous occasion such an event would have been unthinkable.

Then, in 1931, after the abortion, Snipe left her altogether to get married; and it seemed to Carrington that with him had gone her last connexions with youth and beauty. In some ways she was relieved. She had been attacked by pangs of remorse at neglecting Lytton on certain occasions in favour of her lover. But now that this last adventure was over, now that she was less restless and her 'lusts had run dry', she would start to make it up to him. By the summer of 1931 she was already painting more and looking forward with deeper contentment to a serene and happy life with Lytton among the rooms and gardens she had created for them both at Ham Spray.

2

PORRIDGE AND SEALING-WAX

'It is really shocking, I am becoming a nature-lover and observer – fatal!' Lytton had exclaimed to Roger Senhouse early that winter (12 November 1928). 'The intellect fades in proportion.' The most potent attraction holding him down at Ham Spray was the climate of irreproachable, almost compulsory idleness that hung about there. In the aftermath of *Elizabeth and Essex*, idleness had become the chief refuge of his fading intellect. Of course there were always plenty of improbable schemes in the air for a new *magnum opus*. On one occasion he spent three hours discussing with Francis Greenslet the suggestion that he might try his hand at a historical biography of Julius Caesar – 'immaculately dressed, curled up into a double knot, in a big armchair, presenting his views on Caesar as a man, lover, historian, general and emperor' – but it all came to nothing. Robert Nichols vainly urged him to tackle Louis XIII – 'one of the most extraordinary beings who have ever lived'. Peter Davies, the publisher, offered him a contract to write a short book on Edward VII, but this Lytton refused on the grounds that his Life, without such details as could only be touched upon after the death of certain people still living, would not be of sufficient value. As an antidote to the huge but dubious success of *Elizabeth and Essex*, he then considered writing a biography of more limited appeal, on General Booth perhaps, or even Benjamin Jowett. And he also toyed for a while with the idea of a book on George Washington, from which he was apparently dissuaded by the voluminous mass of material that was unhappily written 'in that almost incomprehensible and quite intolerable language – American'.

Throughout the year he published only two pieces, one of them, a review of Walter Raleigh's *Discoveries of Guiana*, being his final contribution to the *Nation and Athenaeum*. Hubert Henderson was then preparing to give up his editorship of the paper on being appointed, together with Keynes, to the staff of the Economic Advisory Council. There was talk of a new Bloomsbury weekly to take its place – which Lytton proposed should be called the *W.C.1.* – and from this time on he switched his allegiance to Desmond MacCarthy's newly formed *Life and Letters*.

MacCarthy had first approached Lytton that March asking him to write something for this periodical, and Lytton replied giving him as his choice of subject either *King Lear* or Bishop Creighton. MacCarthy selected the latter, and Lytton set to work early in April, describing himself in a letter to Roger Senhouse (9 April 1929) as 'in rather a state, as . . . I am now faced with the necessity of writing the affair out of my head apparently, as the blessed London Library, deaf to my frenzied shrieks, has refused to send me any books'. But the crisis quickly evaporated, and in another letter to Roger a fortnight later he was able to report almost as an afterthought: 'Oh! I've finished Creighton, to my great relief.'

To *Life and Letters* Lytton was also to contribute his essay on Froude (originally entitled 'One of the Victorians'), this being the last of his series 'Six English Historians', and 'Madame de Lieven', the last but one of his portraits in miniature. His final essay did not come out until April 1931 – only a month before its reappearance in the collected volume, *Portraits in Miniature and Other Essays* – and was printed in the amalgamated *New Statesman and Nation*, which had recently come under the editorship of Kingsley Martin, for whom Lytton had promised to write regularly.

In this final period of his life, Lytton was the most unprolific of authors. But he was still infected by an inveterate and incurable itch to read. He seemed to be reading constantly, and almost always had a book in his hand. Every time he travelled up to London, he would scour The Times Book Club, finding there that spring only Hugh Kingsmill's *Matthew Arnold* and I. A. Richards's manual of his laboratory methods of literary study, *Practical Criticism*, which he thought 'fascinating'. Soon he returned again to his old favourites, to Chesterfield, to Virgil, to Moore's *Principia Ethica* – 'such pleasant reading' – and out-topping all, Gibbon. 'My laziness is becoming more scandalous than ever,' he happily informed Roger (13 September 1929). 'I do nothing but read Gibbon – first in the quarto – then in Bury's edition.' The dearth of contemporary literature, he complained to Topsy Lucas, was 'serious'. But later that year three new books did manage to win his favour. The first of these was Richard Aldington's celebrated war novel, *Death of a Hero*. 'I've got Death of a Hero from the Times, and am quite enjoying it so far,' he told Roger (14 October 1929). 'I like the brightness of the fellow, rather to my surprise. But I really don't understand why he should have deliberately made such an ass of himself on the "comradeship" question. Most unnecessary!'

His admiration for Virginia Woolf's *A Room of One's Own* was unqualified, and in a letter to Dorothy Bussy he described it as 'a masterpiece'. Also a masterpiece was Richard Hughes's first novel, *A High Wind in Jamaica*, about which he wrote to many of his friends, including Norman Douglas, in terms of the very highest praise. 'My chief conversation will be, now and henceforward, on the subject of a

High Wind,' he notified Roger Senhouse (1 October 1929), 'insisting
that everyone should read it who hasn't and that everyone should admire
it who has.' Eighteen months later, Lytton met Hughes briefly one
afternoon at Ham Spray. 'Yesterday there was an incursion in the
shape of Richard Hughes, who arrived with Faith Henderson, with
whom he was staying,' he notes in a letter to Roger (5 May 1931).
'Slightly sinister, we thought – but perhaps only timid under a mask.'
To Richard Hughes's eyes, it was Lytton who appeared sinister, while
he himself seems to have been rather apprehensive over their encounter.
'My first impression was of the extraordinary beauty of the inside of the
house,' he wrote to the author, '– a beauty based on little original
architectural distinction. Lytton, I think, spent most of his time deep in
a chair – he was certainly ill at the time – but I was too frightened of
him to look at him closely: my general impression, however, was that
he looked as if he had been designed as the perfect *objet d'art* to go with
the background of the house.' Characteristically, Lytton did not mention his admiration for *A High Wind in Jamaica*, and Hughes never
suspected it. 'How cock-a-hoop I should have been at the time had I
known it!'

If he was still idle, at least he was not solitary. The blue weather
continued to fasten him down at Ham Spray, where he was visited for
a time by Pippa, who, after the torturous weeks of nursing Lady
Strachey, had come down to Hungerford to rest. Lytton and Pippa
had been appointed joint-executors and trustees of their mother's will,
a long and complicated document containing two codicils, under
which Lytton himself was left two thousand pounds, minus any sum
which he had received from her during her lifetime.[1] Later this year,
Lytton arranged with Pippa to move back into 51 Gordon Square,
taking over the ground floor which he converted into a self-contained
flat. On 13 June, he also made what was to prove his own last will, in
which he bequeathed ten thousand pounds together with all his pictures
and drawings to Carrington, and a further one thousand pounds to
Ralph, the residue of the property – with the exception of the books
given to Roger – being left to his brother James, whom he also
appointed his executor.

Slowly, as the days lengthened and grew warmer, Lytton's round of
idleness became more strenuous. It was impossible to enjoy his leisure
thoroughly unless there was plenty to do. He went up to London to

---

[1] Lady Strachey's estate had been valued at £36,810 11s 8d. Twenty years earlier Sir
Richard Strachey had left only £6,470 16s 8d – possibly because he had made over
some of his capital to his wife. Lady Strachey had also, in the meantime, inherited the
estate of her sister Elinor (Lady Colvile).

watch Edith Evans act in Reginald Berkeley's *The Lady with the Lamp*, a play about Florence Nightingale which 'seemed to me entirely based on E.V. except for some foolish frills added by the good gentleman', and to lunch, unsuccessfully, with Lady Cunard who 'talked the whole time, so that Max [Beerbohm] was never once allowed to open his mouth. Idiocy! Idiocy!'[1] Then, with Roger as his guest and companion, he hurried down to Cambridge to see Dadie Rylands's production of *King Lear*, and retired, after the prostration of several days' unintermittent hospitality, to stay with Rosamond Lehmann and Wogan Philipps ('Ros and Wog') at the Old Rectory Farm at Kidlington, near Oxford – 'a slightly invalidish ménage . . . very early hours – gentle talk – a dreadful little dog etc.'

The weeks slipped by as in a recurring dream. While Carrington went to France and Ralph dealt with his publishers and managed his finances, Lytton returned to King's – 'such sunshine – such crowds of young gents – such benignity', was invited to still more lunches, more enormous tea-parties and, once again, retreated for a period of recuperation to Ros and Wog. Soon he recovered, then, like a spent taper, went out again. He seemed to have caught an everlasting cold and lost his voice most irrecoverably – 'at present it takes the form of a frog in the throat. Croak! Croak! Most tiresome!' There was nothing for it but to hibernate within Ham Spray and be nursed by Carrington. 'I am dreadfully lazy,' he wrote from his bed to Ralph (2 May 1929), 'and do nothing but dip into Voltaire.' After a month's convalescence, his fell disease subsided, he felt 'almost like a human being again' and well enough to go off for 'a perfect week-end with Roger' to Bath. They stayed together at the Pulteney Hotel, in Laura Place – 'a perfect spot – and quite a sympathetic établissement,' he told Carrington (3 June 1929), 'with a lift boy no less sympathetic, who at last said to me (in a broad West Country accent) "Excuse me, zurr, bout are you the zelebrated author?" . . . We inspected all the favourite sights – including Prof. Saintsbury at No. 1. the Crescent – his white hair and skullcap were visible as usual through the window.'[2]

---

[1] 'That blasted woman wouldn't let Max open his mouth once – a ceaseless stream of pointless babble, really too maddening! In a few asides edged in between her blitherings, he seemed charming – but of course resigned.' (Lytton to Mary Hutchinson, 2 March 1929.)

[2] George Saintsbury (1845–1933), historian and literary essayist, friend of Mandell Creighton and noted especially for his writings on French literature. On retiring from his post as Regius Professor of Rhetoric and English Literature at the University of Edinburgh, he had gone, in 1916, to live at 1 Royal Crescent, Bath, where, among several other works, his *Scrap Books* and *Notes on a Cellar Book* were written – the latter leading to the foundation of the Saintsbury Club. He was an adulator rather than a critic, a romantic with high Tory prejudices and a slightly snobbish fastidiousness. His attitude

Early the next month, Lytton, Carrington, Ralph and Sebastian Sprott set off for a fortnight's holiday in the flat, phlegmatic land of Holland. It was a peculiar and not very successful trip. On board ship the four of them huddled together cheerlessly drinking gin and watching their Dutch and German fellow passengers who sat, for six hours at a stretch, in long rows of deck-chairs, moving only twice a day for heavy meals, and otherwise just staring stonily at the horizon as it tilted gently above one rail and then slipped gently below it, in an endless ding-dong fashion.

They arrived at Rotterdam, examined the zoo in the morning and the museum in the afternoon, then journeyed on to The Hague. Most of their thirty-six hours here were spent looking at the Van Goghs, and visiting the Municipal Museum 'with twenty rooms containing every sort of broken pot and dug-up coin, and the Prison with instruments of torture and engravings of prisoners being castrated by the mob', Ralph wrote to Frances Marshall (3 July 1929). 'Apart from the sights, Lytton rushed into a bookshop and found it was exactly like Maggs, so grand that it was quite out of the question to buy anything except a novel by H. G. Wells.' That night was Gala Night, and Lytton sought to entertain his party at the Royale Restaurant, where a deafening band of Ruritanian Jews scraped the strings of their instruments and ogled the guests, while two impassive Dutch couples danced interminably, and immense quantities of food were served. The tone of all four of them was still curiously sombre, and, hoping for a rapid uplift in their spirits, they left next day for Leyden, which Nancy Cunard had told Lytton was 'wonderful' – though exactly in what way she had not specified: *'just wonderful'*. But once again they were disappointed, and quickly made their way to Amsterdam, where they remained a week, 'looking at cheeses'.

Their mood continued generally irritable and cheerless. 'I have been rather maddened by the sporadic behaviour of the party,' Ralph burst out in one of his letters to Frances (4 July 1929), '. . . all are piano, piano, I don't know why. Perhaps we are all very old indeed, or perhaps we are growing a little Dutch.' Ralph himself was anything but piano, bubbling over with small grievances, disgruntled, quick to quarrel. Each member of the party seemed buried in his own distant thoughts, yet slightly resentful of what Ralph termed the 'selfish egotism of the others' which made no attempt to dig him up into the daylight of the immediate present. He himself was severely missing

---

to criticism and biography in general may be adduced from one sentence: 'Let us also once more rejoice in, and thank God for, the fact that we know nothing about Homer, and practically nothing about Shakespeare.'

Bust of Lytton Strachey by Stephen Tomlin, 1929 (*The Tate Gallery*)

Portrait of Lytton Strachey by Carrington

Lytton and
Carrington near
Llandudno, 1916.
('As for Carrington –
we seemed to
see a great deal
of each other. But . . .')

Frances, wondering why he had consented to come on this dull and purposeless journey; Sebastian, though pleasant, was unfathomable, unforthcoming; Carrington tiresome and wayward, her thoughts reeling back across the sea to the absent Snipe; while Lytton, lonely and fastidious, concerned over Roger, contributed to the unfestive spirit his most alarming silences. Their holiday was thus strangely uneasy and unreal. A pall of apathy seemed to have settled on them, choking their normally acute faculties. They behaved listlessly, like hollow men, leaning together. Much of what they were now seeing for the first time appeared irrelevant to their feelings, or else oddly misplaced, like scenery erected by accident for the wrong drama. For the most part, their reactions to Rotterdam, The Hague, Leyden, Amsterdam were numb. Beside each one moved the unseen presence of another, a loved-one, whose company he kept more closely than that of his companions: so that the four of them appeared to travel among a world of spectres, feeling themselves the shadows of a dream, unable to make fresh contact with the foreign sights and sounds that slowly passed them by.

In a letter to Mary Hutchinson written from Amsterdam (4 July 1929), Lytton, more charitable and understanding than Ralph, conveys something of this miasma, of the painless, bewildering shadow that fell between his actions and his preoccupations. 'Have you ever been to this hydroptic country?' he queried. 'My days pass pleasantly enough, though amid the discomforture of travelling and the dubious recollections of love. I have *three* companions! – Rather a multitude; but they are very charming, and I have no right to feel lonely – none at all – and yet – it is idiotic – I keep imagining what it might be with – almost saying to myself, if only —— were here! Almost, because I'm really not quite so silly as all that, and enjoy everything – pictures, houses, canals, even barges, just as they come. It makes an odd mixture of impressions. The few days before I left England were curiously filled with experiences, and they are as much present with me as the beautiful seventeenth-century doors and windows – so solid, so rich – that line the waterways, and the Rembrandts and De Hooghes in the picture galleries, and the delicious dinners at a pound a head that one stumbles into quite accidentally, having intended simply to have a snack at an A.B.C. . . . but it is true that I am troubled about Roger – in an unexpected way. It is not easy to know one's own mind – not easy to balance instinct and reason – not easy to be sensible and in love. Do not mistake me, though – I am *not* unhappy – only speculative, a little dubitative, faintly uneasy, perhaps. I wake up at three o'clock in the morning and lie awake for an hour, trying drowsily to disentangle the puzzle of my mind and heart – and then sink to sleep again, having

x

accomplished nothing and not in the least put out. I wish I could write poetry; but the mould seems to be lacking into which to pour the curious fluid – melted silver? porridge? gilded sealing-wax? – of my emotions. I have found no solution in these antique masterpieces – another world! another world! With them everything is fixed and definite and remote; but with me there is nothing but hazard, intensity, and interrogation.'

Lytton returned from Holland the following week to find that Roger had abruptly left with a friend for the south of France. Days passed in silence and speculation. A week-end, on which they had planned to go away together to the country, came and went – and still there was no news. Lytton, quite in the dark, did not know what to feel – anger, jealousy, fear, indifference. 'I am in rather a state about R., as you may imagine,' he confessed to Mary Hutchinson (25 July 1929). 'The possibilities are so various – the poor thing may be ill – or the wretch may be dreaming – or the little devil may have sailed for Greece in Mr B's yacht. In any case there's nothing to be done, but twiddle one's thumbs, and seek such consolations as are available.'

These consolations, however delightful, could not dispel for long the nagging hazard, intensity and interrogation of his mood. What could have happened? A few days later, a letter at last arrived from Cannes, written in Roger's most cramped style, and answering practically none of Lytton's queries. He had come down for a 'rest', Roger explained, had stayed on an extra ten days or so 'through weakness', but regretted it now, and would be back in England on the same day as his letter. Lytton immediately rang up Brunswick Square – but there was no Roger. Next day there arrived a further letter, which mentioned that he had been obliged to postpone his return because of – constipation! 'Surely, surely, something better might have been thought of as an excuse for another week in the South of France,' Lytton complained to Dadie Rylands (29 July 1929), '– but such are our friend's strange fancies. I . . . have grown inert – cannot really bother any more . . . I shall twiddle my thumbs like an aged Barbary Ape.'

Uncertainties now crowned themselves assured, and all further speculation became futile. Roger was so irresponsible that one could not take anything he did very seriously. Even so, until these mysteries could be elucidated, Lytton knew that he must go on living in a state of suspense. Though he still could not hope to unravel the puzzle of his own mind, he determined to let things pass, to act sensibly even in love, and shake off the heartache by involving himself in some literary work – *The Greville Memoirs*, perhaps, which he had for long been putting off. To his friends who visited him at Ham Spray that August he seemed 'rather low and flat', but 'this does not mean that I am depressed or worried – quite the reverse', he assured Dadie Rylands (2 August 1929). 'I feel extremely cheerful, and seem to have emerged on to some upper plateau from which I can contemplate all the eventualities with equanimity. It is something of a miracle, and a great relief.'

This state of calmness and euphoria was not perhaps a very natural condition. But while it lasted, he was happy, and more than happy, to turn back to his work, and absorb himself, at last, in *The Greville Memoirs*.

3

AMBITIONS

There is a passage in one of Lytton's letters to Roger Senhouse that is crucial to the full understanding of his character. 'Do you know how ambitious I am?' he asked (16 January 1929). 'Don't breathe a word of this to anyone, but I long to do some good to the world – to make people happier – to help to dissipate this atrocious fog of superstition that hangs over us and compresses our breathing and poisons our lives. – But it can't be done in a minute.'

Lytton was not wholly an observer, nor a participant, but a sufferer of life. His gentleness and generosity prevented these sufferings from turning sour within him, so that, for the most part, his cynicism stopped short at common sense. He wished to infiltrate his humanitarian principles, subtly, through literature, into the bloodstream of the people, and in such a way that they accepted it all quite naturally, if need be, without at first realizing what it was to which they were agreeing. He wanted to seduce his readers to tolerance through laughter and sheer entertainment. Never keen on scoring quick debating points, he sought to write in a way that would contribute to an eventual change in our ethical and sexual *mores* – a change that couldn't 'be done in a minute', but would unobtrusively permeate the more flexible minds of young people. Unlike most professional moralists and reformers, his general theories were not held at the expense of private conduct, but represented an extension of it. His humanitarianism was not, therefore, an assumed ethical attitude, to be worn and taken off again like a coat, and always cut to fashion, but a normal, instinctive expression of his kindness. Twice in the 1920s, for example, he had anonymously helped out Desmond MacCarthy with gifts of money. His support of many *avant-garde* and philanthropic causes, from birth control to the relief of war victims, came from the same desire to prevent avoidable suffering and, more aggressively, to obliterate those misguided forces that caused this suffering. This was the real success he had been striving for.

Eminent Victorians had, of course, been his fiercest and most influential piece of polemics, dissipating the atrocious fog of Victorian sentiment and exposing much of its sham folklore. But he was never a propagandist in the political or revolutionary sense. He admitted to being 'left wing', yet repudiated any description of himself as a socialist. He had no wish to regulate personal behaviour or add further restrictive actions to the natural obstacles that must always prevent mankind from reaching its dreams of enjoyment. Since Cambridge, he had largely been out of step with the established order. The incursive post-war tendency to interfere with the private life of the individual was due, both directly and more obliquely, to the Great War itself, which had subordinated the individual entirely to the State – that is nearly fifty million persons to a few thousands. In the ensuing years of peace, this desire to regulate others still persisted, though its expression varied in each country according to the traditions of that country and to its good or bad fortune in the war. In America, where the war fever had been most virulent and the losses of men smallest, and where the dragooning of vast masses of fellow citizens had come as a new experience, the cessation of conscription had left a want which was supplied by the enforcement of prohibition. In Italy, Germany and Russia autocracies were formed, the unconscious aim of which was to recover in another war the national prestige lost in the Great War. France alone left its citizens in peace, for France, unlike America or Britain, knew conscription before the war, and unlike Italy, Germany and Russia, emerged from the war with its prestige enhanced.

The position in Britain during the 1920s was peculiar. The country had suffered very grievously during the years of hostilities, and was further safeguarded from the lunacy of American prohibition by a certain balance in the national character. Yet State interference with the individual had for many the charm of novelty. The Defence of the Realm Act lingered on, vexing the ordinary man and encouraging empty and energetic busybodies to plan more penetrating attacks on the individual. It was this type of governmental officiousness that particularly exasperated Lytton.

One example was the Oscar Levy affair. Dr Levy, a distinguished philosopher, scholar and man of letters, had left England in 1914 and returned again in 1920 on business, staying on because of ill-health. After a few months he was threatened with deportation under the

Aliens Restriction Act – a law that was due to expire at the end of 1921. In the early autumn of that year, Lytton had joined the Semitic Bloomsbury Committee which was making protests against his expulsion, and signed a petition to Lloyd George pointing out that Dr Levy had relinquished his German citizenship and had nowhere to go. 'The police expulsion of so eminent a man,' this petition concluded, 'is surely a grave reflection on English civilization.'

By this time all sorts of rumours were being broadcast – that Levy was connected with espionage during the war, that he was in counterintelligence or the secret service. The Government confirmed or denied nothing, though granting a short delay of the deportation order for him to recover his health and for them to re-examine his statements. But Lytton was not optimistic. He disliked joining movements and committees, much preferring to work for what he believed by himself. The secret springs of his ambition were not nourished by belonging to anonymous, dry groups of improvers. He thirsted after an effective dual role as poet and reformer. But one had to be effective, and collectivism bred collectivism. As so often amid the pitched battles between light and darkness, he felt ill-at-ease among his allies, his foul-weather friends. 'I have become involved in the great pro-Dr-Oscar-Levy movement,' he reported to Ralph (5 October 1921). '. . . I was summoned this afternoon to the headquarters of the movement at 34 Gordon Square, one of the principal props of which turned out to be Mr. [David] Bomberg, painter. . . . Another Jew welcomed me, and I rather gathered that I too was a Jew – which made me uneasy. At last I tore myself away, but I am in dread of being pursued for the rest of my life by this strange collection. As for poor Dr Oscar Levy I can't believe that with such supporters his chances are very good.'

And so it turned out. On 25 October, Dr Levy left England for France, the French Consulate having given him permission to enter the country and stay there without time limit. Once again French civilization had shown itself to be superior to the English.

One of the chief dangers to the liberty of the individual was the rising popularity of autocratic controls. Autocracies, whether they were called Fascism, Bolshevism or Puritanism, claimed that they subordinated the selfish, prurient desires of the individual to the service of the community. To Lytton's mind, they in fact subordinated these individual desires to the passion for power of a few emotional misfits with enormous vigour and no internal resources. He objected to autocracy for much the same reason as he had objected to militarism. For all autocracies, however excellent the ideals with which they started, inevitably move towards war, partly because war is the simplest and most comprehensive expression of power, and partly because the suppression of the man-in-the-street cannot continue for ever. If the State must add artificial restrictions to those restrictions on enjoyment inherent in the nature of things, then the pressure of unsatisfied desire must eventually be eased, and war is the most effective way to ease it – removing fear of unemployment and modifying, in the near neighbourhood of death, the severe tenor of private and public opinion.

In Britain, the most threatening form of autocracy was Puritanism. In the field of literature and the arts, this Puritanism took the form of a prudish censorship exercised by those substantial citizens who permanently seemed to fear that society would at any moment flounder into a quagmire of vicious iniquity, but for some swift and drastic steps designed to restore to the community a proper, biblical sense of sin. All through his career as a literary critic, Lytton waged a continuous offensive against the expurgated text. In reviewing the first four volumes of Mrs Paget Toynbee's sixteen-volume edition of Horace Walpole's letters, he complained vehemently against certain omissions. 'The *jeune fille* is certainly not an adequate reason, and, even if she were, the *jeune fille* does not read Walpole. Whoever does read him must feel that these constant omissions are so many blots upon perfection, and distressing relics of an age of barbarous prudery.'

Some fifteen years later, in 1919, Lytton reviewed Paget Toynbee's two-volume *Supplement to the Letters of Horace Walpole*, and protested with even greater vigour at the numerous passages dropped on the score of propriety. 'Surely,' he exclaimed, 'in a work of such serious intention and such monumental proportions the publication of the *whole* of the original material was not only justifiable, but demanded by the nature of the case.' Paget Toynbee was quick to defend his policy in the correspondence columns of the *Athenaeum*. Great care and forethought, he assured his readers, had been taken over his responsibilities as editor. Improprieties would be too mild a word with which to describe the excised passages, which might be compared 'to the grossest of the avowals contained in the unexpurgated editions of Rousseau's Confessions'. In any event, the manuscripts had been deposited under sealed cover in the Bodleian 'where they will be available to any future editor of the letters at the discretion of the Delegates of the Clarendon Press'.

The following week Lytton returned to the attack in a letter that stated his views with uncompromising allegorical force. 'If a surgeon were charged with having made an unnecessary amputation,' he pointed out, 'and were to answer that after all the limb was still in existence, carefully preserved, under a sealed cover, and that, if need arose, it might be sewn on again by another surgeon, at a future date, the patient's friends would hardly feel that the reply was reassuring.' After expressing wonder at the type of literary man who would, presumably, wish to see Rousseau's *Confessions* reproduced only in a hideously truncated version, Lytton passed to the general problem of personal censorship: 'It is, moreover, extremely hard to see what good purpose is served by the deletion of passages which, in the opinion of individual editors, are indecent. . . . Literature is inundated with improprieties and grossnesses of every kind; the mischief – if mischief it be – has been done already. It is too late to be prudish: Catullus, Rabelais, and a hundred others stare us in the face; the horse is gone, and no locking of the stable door will bring him back again.'

When, in 1926, Paget Toynbee brought out a further supplementary volume of Walpole's letters, there were again expurgated pages. 'The editor', complained Lytton, 'is still unable to resist meddling with the text. The complete edition is incomplete, after all. Apparently, we should blush too much were we to read the whole of Walpole's letters; those privileges have been reserved for Dr. Toynbee alone. It was impossible not to hope that, after so prolonged tête-à-tête with his author, he would relent at last; perhaps, in this latest volume at any rate – but no! the powers of editorship must be asserted to the bitter end; and the fatal row of asterisks and the fatal note, "passage omitted" occur, more than once, to exacerbate the reader. Surely it would have been kinder not to reveal the fact that any deletion had been made. Then one could have read on, innocent and undisturbed. As it is, when one's irritation has subsided, one's imagination, one's shocking imagination, begins to work. The question must be asked: do these explicit suppressions really serve the interests of the highest morality? Dr. Toynbee reminds one of the man who . . .[1] But enough; for, after all, it is not the fly but the ointment that claims our attention.'

Lytton, however, was continually spotting this fly in the ointment, and grew increasingly vexed by it. Not only Walpole's correspondence, but Blake's poems, Pepys's Diary and Boswell's letters had been mutilated by earnest professors who claimed at the same time to be rehabilitating the author's original text. 'When', Lytton demanded, 'will this silly and barbarous prudery come to an end?'

In one particular instance he saw an opportunity for defeating such prudery. *The Greville Memoirs* is not listed among the four bibliographies of *Eminent Victorians*, but on 6 November 1917, while still at work on 'The End of General Gordon', Lytton had written to Clive Bell: 'I spend most of my time reading Greville's Memoirs (do you

[1] Passage omitted [Lytton's footnote].

know them?) – very dry, and as they are dry – just the kind of book
that pleases me. He was a slow-going medium member of the governing
classes of those days – the days of Sir Robert Peel and Lord Melbourne
– and he writes with a restraint and a distinction.'

When Lytton had come to compare the complete manuscript in the
British Museum with the Silver Library edition – which he included
among the 'Works Referred to in the Notes' at the end of *Queen Victoria*
– he had been disgusted to discover just how badly tampered with even
the fullest published version was. He drew attention to this state of affairs
both by a preliminary note in *Queen Victoria* acknowledging his in-
debtedness to the Trustees of the British Museum for their permission
to make use of certain unpublished passages from the memoirs, and in
the text of the biography itself, where he tells of Victoria's indignation
at seeing the contents of the abridged version that came out during her
reign. Two years later, in 1923, Lytton published his essay 'Charles
Greville' in the *Nation and Athenaeum*, stating his opinion that
Greville's diary was good enough 'to make him certainly famous and
possibly immortal'. Throughout this essay, which gave the background
history of the diary, he very sensibly resisted the temptation to exaggerate its merits in the hope of securing immediate publication, comparing it, unfavourably, with Saint-Simon. Very many of its pages, he
explained, were rather metallic in style – a reflection of one side of
Greville's nature – and in political matters, its information was not
always reliable. Yet, he added, it was of extreme value, since the sheer
quantity of Greville's knowledge was enormous, and it was first-hand.
'He was not exactly a gossip, nor a busybody; he was an extremely
inquisitive person, in whom, somehow or other, it seemed natural for
everybody to confide. Thus the broad current of London life flows
through his ample pages, and, as one turns them over, one glides
swiftly into the curiously distant world of eighty years ago. A large
leisureliness descends upon one, and a sense that there is plenty of
room, and an atmosphere of extraordinary moderation. Reason and
instinct, fixity and change, aristocracy and democracy – all these are
there, but unaccountably interwoven into a circumambient compromise
– a wonderful arrangement of half-lights . . . So Greville unrolls his
long panorama; then pauses for a little, to expatiate in detail on some
particular figure in it. His portraits, with their sobriety of tone and
precision of outline, resemble very fine engravings, and will prove,
perhaps, the most enduring portions of his book.'

After defining the special merits of the diary – in particular its
obituary portraits, its impressive spaciousness, and its faculty, typical
of all the best diaries, for providing a panoramic view of past events so

that the reader can still live through them with some of the thrill of actual experience – Lytton went on to present a summary of the brighter incidents in Greville's own life. This was the sort of thing at which he always excelled, and here he admirably succeeds in whetting the reader's appetite for the full, unexpurgated version. 'Perhaps', he modestly suggested, 'the time has now come when a really complete edition of the whole work might be produced with advantage; for the years have smoothed down what was agitating and personal half a century ago into harmless history. When the book first appeared, it seemed – even with Reeve's tactful excisions – outrageous. The later Victorians were shocked. . . . To turn from their horrified comments to the Greville Memoirs themselves is almost disappointing. In those essentially sober pages the envenomed wretch of the Victorian imagination is nowhere to be found.'

The outcome of Lytton's plea was ironically inconsistent with his hopes. Quite unknown to him at this time, a copy of the diaries made by a clerk employed by the original editor, Henry Reeve, had found its way, after the death of Reeve's widow, to the United States. Shortly after the appearance of Lytton's essay in the American magazine *New Republic*, this unabridged manuscript fell under the notice of P. W. Wilson, formerly a writer on the *Daily News* and a Liberal member of Parliament, who, in 1927, brought out in two volumes a collection of extracts from it, containing some information that had never hitherto been printed. This publication gave rise to an even more anomalous and untidy situation than before. The manuscript diary, which filled ninety-one small quarto books bound in red morocco, had originally been published in three instalments, totalling eight volumes altogether, in 1874, 1885 and 1887. Reeve had silently made excisions of three kinds – 'scandalous stories, which might give pain to persons then living; observations upon the writer's private affairs; and reflections upon the character and conduct of Queen Victoria'. P. W. Wilson's compilation, while apparently supplying these omissions, contained only a series of rearranged fragments from the diary, and provided no means of distinguishing the new material from the old. The result was that the public were still without a satisfactory, unbowdlerized text.

In a letter to *The Times* on 12 November 1927, Lytton proposed that, in order to resolve 'this curious state of affairs', a full and accurate edition of the diaries should at once be prepared. 'The old version,' he wrote, 'purporting to be complete, has been shown to be mutilated; and the new publication, though it divulges some suppressed passages, bears little resemblance to the original work. Two conclusions suggest themselves:

x*

(1) It can no longer serve any useful purpose to put obstacles in the way of public access to the original manuscript in the British Museum;

(2) The time has now come when the Greville Memoirs should be published in their entirety, with all the editorial care which a document of such historical and literary importance deserves.'

The following day, Lytton received a wire from Allen & Unwin, the publishers, asking him to edit a complete version of the memoirs. The task commended itself to him on several grounds. He was already well familiar with the social and political world between 1814 and 1860, having studied it in great detail for his *Queen Victoria* (for which, of course, he had consulted the diary in manuscript), and he was therefore exceptionally well qualified to act as editor. The job, too, would come as a relief from the rigours of *Elizabeth and Essex*. His editorial duties, though exacting, were sure to be more congenial than any further original composition on a large scale. He might look forward to many absorbing, civilized hours of methodical occupation – work that would bring with it a curious comfort of its own.

It seemed now as if he were within reach of achieving the end for which he had been campaigning ever since 1921. But after a month of indecisive negotiations, the Trustees of the British Museum at length washed their hands of the whole business. Greville's niece, Lady Strafford, then aged ninety-seven, would probably institute proceedings, they informed Lytton, were any uncorrupted narrative brought out. In these circumstances they could not be a party to his scheme. 'What a world!' Lytton exclaimed to Carrington in exasperation.

For the time being there was nothing more to be done, and his negotiations with Allen & Unwin lapsed. Then, the following summer, Lady Strafford died. Almost immediately Lytton applied again to the Trustees, who, this time, opposed no obstacles. Work began late in August. 'It is very agreeable here,' Lytton wrote to Carrington from London (11 September 1928). 'The weather is most soothing – and so is the work in the British Museum. We have been so far most industrious. I enjoy it very much and R[alph] is an excellent work-companion. The only question is whether I shall ever be able to give it up. It seems to me an ideal way of spending the hours – and we can hardly bear to tear ourselves away from the beloved MS at a $\frac{1}{4}$ to 5, which is closing time.'

Another aspect of this state of affairs is given by Frances Marshall. In her diary entry for 15 September she wanly noted: 'R[alph] has now become to all intents a business man, going to the British Museum every day until 5, and as he lunches at present with Lytton I don't see him from morning till evening, which is the strangest sensation.' The very next week, however, Frances herself was to change into a business woman, joining the others at work in the manuscript department. 'R[alph] and I are both now working on the Greville MSS in the British Museum,' she wrote (21 September 1928). 'It becomes more fascinating each day.'

Lytton's plan was that Ralph and Frances should transcribe the missing and disputed pages of the memoirs, and that every so often Ralph should come down to Ham Spray bringing with him the material they had prepared, which he would then annotate. 'I have been working with Ralph nearly every day at the British Museum,' he told Roger Senhouse (19 September 1928). 'Now Frances takes my place in the afternoons, and before long she will altogether I think. It is very pleasant work. Various amusing details keep turning up, sometimes in a childishly easy cipher.'

Presently, as he had predicted, Lytton ceased going to the British Museum almost entirely, Frances taking over from him in the mornings also. This arrangement, besides freeing Lytton so that he might compose occasional essays, enabled him and Carrington to see rather more of Ralph by himself, and so helped to ease the feeling of tension at Ham Spray. Already, by the end of January, the three of them had made considerable headway. Ralph 'brought an enormous quantity of Greville MSS', Lytton wrote to Roger Senhouse from Ham Spray (2 February 1929), 'and I see that the moment is rapidly approaching when I shall have to plunge into that ocean in good earnest'.

Even so, he judged, this moment had not yet properly arrived. First there was the problem of interesting some publishers. 'I am beginning to fear that I may have some trouble with the publishers about printing *everything* – which is what I want to do,' Lytton confided to Roger Senhouse (19 September 1928). Although no publisher could deny that it was a very interesting work and of great historical importance, there was little sensational appeal in such a book, and the sale could hardly be large. On the other hand, Lytton reasoned, all the public libraries and educational institutions would have to possess it, and his edition – if it did contain *everything* – would never be replaced. It would provide the complete text, together, of course, with an introduction, explanatory notes, and an elaborate index. Altogether, it was to be a most comprehensive and scholarly enterprise, one that should sell, if not widely at least steadily. But Lytton still doubted whether these arguments, appealing more to literary prestige than solid commercial interests, could be properly effective with any publisher. The firm which stood most to gain was Heinemann, having been responsible for bringing out the English edition of P. W. Wilson's two piecemeal volumes. Early this year, Ralph called at the Heinemann offices and persuaded them to agree, in principle, to bringing out the full text.[1] A few months later, Harcourt Brace wrote to Lytton inquiring whether they might publish the American edition. 'It is very interesting to hear that your firm contemplates the publication of the new and complete Greville,' Lytton replied to Donald Brace (24 October 1929). '. . . no doubt it would be a serious undertaking; I think it will take about ten large volumes; probably it would bring you more glory than profit! From my point of view, nothing would please me better than that you should undertake it. Our relations have been so pleasant that I would welcome any extension of them, and there is the minor point that a republication of the introduction would be facilitated . . . It is really the size of the affair that is the vital point – both from the point of view of the publisher and from that of the reader, who will not buy it unless he is a serious student: the plums of scandal and surprise – and there *are* some – are too few and far between to allure anyone else.'

Once these tentative agreements had been fixed, Lytton finally settled down to work. From the summer of 1929, despite a few 'sad interruptions', he devoted a regular part of his time to *The Greville Memoirs*, and his correspondence over the next two years carry intermittent remarks about 'getting down to' and 'continuing to grovel in Greville'.

[1] The firm of Heinemann did not eventually publish these volumes. P. W. Wilson's version of the diaries had been so ill received that the publishers felt obliged to offer to undertake a complete edition of the text, which, they agreed, should be entrusted to Lytton Strachey. When Lytton died, the negotiations fell through. What happened then has been described to the author by Mr Roger Fulford. 'Some time after my first book was published – which was in 1933 – I was approached by Mr James Strachey to know if I would complete the book and, if need be, find another publisher. Mr Thomas Balston, who had been responsible for the publication of my first book and was at that time the active mind in Duckworth's, agreed that his firm would publish it, and it may well have been that he suggested my name to Mr James Strachey. Plans with Duckworth advanced and, owing to the cost of production, we contemplated doing it in the old-fashioned way with subscribers' copies. When Mr Balston left Duckworth (I think in 1934) that firm declined to complete the project. Mr Balston most generously put me in touch with Mr Daniel Macmillan and Macmillans agreed to publish it, and carried out their undertaking. The cost of the finished book and the numbers printed were nothing to do with me. It is obvious that the commercial hazards at that time were very great and, if Macmillan's book was expensive, at least it was published.

'Part of the explanation for the high price which this book fetches in the second hand market is that it was beautifully produced by the Cambridge University Press. Mr and Mrs Ralph Partridge behaved with great generosity; they had done a great deal of work on the text and on the footnotes, this was neither acknowledged financially nor on the title page of the finished book.'

Mr Balston writes that 'I am still very proud of my small part in its production, and of having immediately realised how very great its importance would be to the many historians who would be working on that period in the next fifty years or so . . . I am also glad that I thought it so important that I sent it to the C[ambridge] U[niversity] P[ress], then with Walter Lewis as their typographer the best printers in England, and of course, very expensive.'

This year, too, saw the publication of *Leaves from the Greville Diary*, a potted version in one volume, with an agreeable introduction by Lytton's old friend, Philip Morrell. This book, by drawing attention to the need for a complete and authoritative edition, acted as a spur to Lytton and his team. In 1930, Lytton arranged with Gabriel Wells of New York for the American manuscripts to be transferred back to England and placed in the Bodleian Library at Oxford. By the time of his death, early in 1932, all the passages omitted from Reeve's edition, including those in cipher and those scratched out with a pen, had been transcribed from the original manuscripts. 'The latest and best edition by Reeve,' Roger Fulford tells us, 'that in the Silver Library published by Messrs Longmans in 1888, had been collated with the manuscripts and his frequent liberties with the text corrected. The notes are almost all Mr. Strachey's – though here and there it has been found possible to add to them in the light of information published since his death.'

After Lytton's death, the work was carried on by Ralph and Frances, who collaborated in the thankless and monumental task of preparing a full index volume, and Roger Fulford contributed a Preface to the edition. Eventually, in 1938, seventy-eight years after Greville had concluded the last page of these diaries, they were given to the public in their entirety. Yet not even then was this definitive edition to be easily accessible, costing fifteen guineas and being limited to only six hundred and thirty copies – of which six hundred were for sale. 'When so much labour and learning have been expended upon this edition,' Raymond Mortimer commented, 'it is deplorable that the ordinary reader should still be obliged to use the old mutilated text.' And he went on to express astonishment that Macmillan, the publishers, 'should have condescended to this method of publication, against which Lytton Strachey himself would certainly have been the first to protest'.

In attacking censorship and celebrating sex in literature among contemporary authors, whose work had not yet subsided into harmless history, Lytton was equally forthright. He identified himself, for instance, with that faction opposing the prosecution of Radcliffe Hall's lesbian novel, *The Well of Loneliness*, though he does not seem to have thought very highly of the book's merits. And when, in March 1930, Gilbert Murray wrote a letter to the *Nation and Athenaeum* deploring the cult of obscenity in modern writing, which, he claimed, had a peculiar power for destroying the higher imaginative values in its vicinity, Lytton at once replied, calling up in evidence to refute this statement two classical writers, Rabelais and Swift. 'Both in "Pantagruel" and in "Gulliver" it is obviously this very element [obscenity] which acts as a stimulus to the authors' most profound observations and

most astonishing flights.' The issue in dispute was never sociological –
a fear that the behaviour of the characters in a book might be imitated
by the book's readers – but purely literary. And in so far as obscenity
could be defined as plain speaking on distasteful or embarrassing
topics, then obviously Lytton's defence was unimpeachable. But, more
controversially, he also condoned the use of salacious passages introduced into the narrative simply to arouse or excite by their quality of
unmixed salaciousness – passages which, so far from fitting in to the
overall aesthetic tone, might be entirely alien to it. For he believed that
this kind of excitement or amusement constituted in itself a total
aesthetic effect, and that one's artistic susceptibilities could never be so
jaded as to become incapable of enjoying the subtler pleasures of the
imagination. Did *Lady Chatterley's Lover*, *Ulysses* or even *Elizabeth
and Essex* spoil one for *Pride and Prejudice*, *Cranford* or *Barchester
Towers*? The notion seemed to him ridiculous.

Yet Lytton vastly preferred Jane Austen's well-ordered reticence to
what he considered to be the uncontrolled, inverted prudery of D. H.
Lawrence. His opinion of Lawrence had not altered much since they
had encountered each other at Brett's studio during the war. He saw
him as a kind of Puritan standing on his head, an evangelist of sexual
obsession, a confused mind allied to a disordered temperament, one
who wrote in bouts of happiness but more often in despair. 'Above all,
the fact is that I cannot abide prophets,' he told Emilio Cecchi. Yet in
the past he had petitioned against the suppression of *The Rainbow*, and
now, most unwillingly, found himself supporting Lawrence once again.
On 14 June 1929, an exhibition of Lawrence's pictures, organized by
Philip and Dorothy Trotter, had opened at the Warren Gallery in
Maddox Street, London. For three weeks this exhibition had continued,
then suddenly, after some thirteen thousand people had already been to
the gallery, the police swooped down and carried off thirteen of the
pictures, which, preparatory to having them burnt, they stored away in
a cellar of the Marlborough Street Police Court. 'I suppose you heard
about the police raid on Lawrence's pictures at the Warren Gallery?'
Lytton wrote to Roger (15 July 1929). 'I saw Dorothy and her spouse
at Boulestin's one evening, and heard her account of it. The police
appear to have been singularly idiotic, but D. herself, it seems to me,
was almost equally so. They were on the point of seizing a drawing by
Blake of Adam and Eve as obscene, and she was silly enough to tell
them it was by him, and so make a cheap score; but if she had only let
them do it, there couldn't have been a better exposé of their methods.
Next day I had lunch with Mary [Hutchinson] and she showed me the
book of reproductions from his pictures. They are wretched things –

no drawing or composition so far as I could see – and in fact no point –
not even that of indecency; there were some pricks visible, but not a
single erection, which one naturally supposed would have caused the
rumpus.'

To make sure that he was not being unfair to Lawrence, Lytton
shortly afterwards went round to the Warren Gallery with Geoffrey
Scott. But his low opinion was only confirmed by what he saw, he dismissed the exhibits as 'poor' and declared that in his view the whole
show had been a mistake. 'At least you think the pictures respectable?'
queried Scott in the context of the impending trial. 'Much too respectable!' Lytton answered.

Respectability, or the absence of it, however, was not the real issue.
It was a question of law. Immediately after the police seizure, Philip and
Dorothy Trotter had started to get up a petition, but sensed, as Philip
Trotter wrote, 'a winter wind from Bloomsbury in the dudgeon of
Lytton Strachey and the silence of Roger Fry'. This petition, which
they asked Lytton publicly to support, was embodied in the following
formula:

'Since many pictures of admittedly great artistic value contain
details which might be condemned as 'harmful to the morals of those
who are unstable or immature', we protest in principle against the
destruction of pictures on that ground. The burning of a book does not
necessarily destroy it, and condemned books have sometimes taken their
places among the classics, but the burning of a picture is irreparable.'

The Trotters were careful to emphasize that they were not inviting
Lytton's judgement about Lawrence's ability as a painter. The matter
went far beyond the question of the merits of any individual artist's
talent. They were seeking to change a law that, as it stood, permitted
an anonymous informer, spurred on by the sensationalist section of the
press, to put into action the machinery by which a serious painter's
work was placed in peril of total destruction. After a brief hesitation,
Lytton signed, to help 'protect contemporary art from the grave menace
implied in the terms of the summons issued in regard to Mr. Lawrence's
work'. Probably to his relief, however, this issue was never pressed,
since at the trial St John Hutchinson, acting on Lawrence's instructions,
offered to withdraw the offending pictures and assured the court that
they would not be shown again.

Because of its special wording and the wider purpose implied by this
petition Lytton felt his course of action to be reasonably straightforward. His moral and aesthetic principles had not been brought into
open conflict with one another, but were able to operate in an uneasy
partnership. He longed amicably to reform the world, and could not

logically ignore any chance that was presented to him to help bring this about through ordinary legal processes. But the amelioration that really interested him was less a matter of laws than of the attitudes to which these laws were meant to give social expression. What he in fact sought, to appease his secret ambitions, was not simply a civilian reformation, but a spiritual renaissance, not just a precedent in the Statute Book, but a place in literature.

4

'DEAREST DADIE . . .'

51, Gordon Square. July 29, 1929.

'Dearest Dadie,

'My drive to London I enjoyed very much. . . . I arrived at exactly the right moment at the Oriental, where I found Ralph. He was *most* helpful, and completely set me up (at any rate for the time being) and I think all may be well in that direction. . . . I went round to Bernard Street, and chatted with Helen [Anrep], whom I found as usual very stimulating. *Her* Roger [Fry] is in a gloomy place in France, drinking water like urine and surrounded by scenery so hideous that even he can't paint it – but his health is steadily improving . . .'

Ham Spray House. August 2, 1929.

'I am occupied most of the day sitting to Tommy [Stephen Tomlin] – luckily I am allowed to read. We go for a long walk after tea and I must say I enjoy his conversation very much – Ralph, Frances, and James arrived to-day – Julia [Tomlin] is also here . . .'

Ham Spray House. August 9, 1929.

'The prodigal [Roger Senhouse] returned on Monday, and I have had a letter in his most winning style, so I am feeling for the moment very happy, and wish at any rate for the time being to pass an act of oblivion. He comes to-morrow for the night. . . . I sit all day to Tommy who is creating what appears to me a highly impressive, repulsive, and sinister object.[1] Perhaps it is the pure truth. Otherwise, we argue up hill and down dale (literally as well as metaphorically).'

[1] Stephen Tomlin's bust of Lytton's head may now be seen at the Tate Gallery. After it was finished, Lytton gave a sherry party at 51 Gordon Square so that his friends could inspect it. 'It seemed to me very successful,' he wrote of the sculpture to David Garnett (3 November 1929).

Union Club, Carlton House Terrace. August 16, 1929.
'Stephen Tennant and Siegfried Sassoon have just been having dinner with me here – accidentally. The former asked after you. Extremely beautiful – but frail beyond imagination. S.S. seems to be his garde malade. . . . I'm off to Lady Horner's to-morrow till Tuesday – it won't be very exciting. I fear the sick-room atmosphere that always pervades that sort of society.'

Salt Mill House,[1] Fishbourne, Chichester. August 29, 1929.
'It's charming down here – on the very edge of Chichester harbour, whose waters creep and gurgle at the bottom of a lawn mown by countless guinea-pigs. A strange, romantic, flat country, with a cathedral spire in the distance. Mary [Hutchinson] is delightful, and Jack [St John Hutchinson] mostly away, failing to get off homicidal motorists at country-town police courts. . . . No adventures – except with the local doctor, to whom I went in a panic over crabs. A young, a positively non-hearty, an almost good-looking individual. Some dim excitement, during the examination, as you may imagine. Then – "are you any relation to Mr. *Lytton* Strachey?" – "I *am* Mr. Lytton Strachey". – "Oh! Indeed!" Mutual blushes – a climax clearly approaching – it came in the shape of – "I am to be married on the 16th". For the rest, no crabs.'

Charleston, Firle, Lewes, Sussex. September 19, 1929.
'The inevitable dolce far niente reigns. It is as beautiful as ever. One walks, one talks, one drinks, one thinks, one writes idiotic letters.'

Royal Albion Hotel, Brighton. October 12, 1929.
'This hotel seems to be quite unchanged – the same rooms, the same food, the same appalling band after dinner – and so life floats away . . .'

Ham Spray House. November 4, 1929.
'It was rather amusing – I took [E] Morgan [Forster] and Carrington – a lovely drive. When we got there [Stephen Tennant's house], we found . . . no Siegfried, but Arthur Waley, Willie Walton and Rex Whistler. We had lunch on the lawn, in such blazing sun that our host was given an excuse for sending for a yellow parasol for himself and a series of gigantic plaited straw hats for his guests. We were filmed almost the whole time by a footman (a dark young man in spectacles). We inspected the aviary – very charming, with the most wonderful

[1] The Salt Mill House was 'a small abode, owned by an Admiral', which the Hutchinsons had taken for the summer.

parrots floating from perch to perch and eventually from shoulder to shoulder. Finally we went indoors, and in a darkened chamber were shown various films of the past, worked by the footman, who also turned on a gramophone with suitable records. Stephen was extremely amiable, though his lips were rather too magenta for my taste; Arthur was positively gay; Morgan shone as required; W.W. said absolutely nothing; and I, sitting next to Rex Whistler, couldn't make up my mind whether I was attracted or repelled by his ugly but lust-provoking face . . . Morgan was charming at the week-end – full of accounts of Africa from bottom to top. He read two stories to C. and me – improper – quite amusing – but there always seems to be a trace of Weybridge in his style, whatever the subject may be.'

Extract from Frances Marshall's Journal – December 3, 1929.
'At the weekend there were only Lytton, R[alph], C[arrington] and I and it was spent very quietly. R. went for walks with Lytton and I worked at my Plutarch in the back room. On Sunday Snipe turned up after lunch, but his Bentley soon carried him away, and then came Mozart and Beethoven quartets on the wireless and after dinner Lytton reading Hamlet aloud to us. That was very enjoyable. He read with obvious excitement in a trembling fiery voice, his eyes piercing, and making pouncing movements with his long right hand.'

Ham Spray House. December 23, 1929.
'How I wish you were coming to Little Kidlington for Christmas! . . . The drear months are now beginning, and we shall all of us have to give each other the support, love, lust, etc. that we can. There can be no doubt about that. In the meantime an immense cargo of wood absolutely wringing wet has entered this house, and every fire is quite black and cold, with a faint singing note added. Oh dear, oh dear! Where are the heats of next July?

all my love
Lytton'

5

MISADVENTURES

Early in April 1930, Lytton left England for a holiday in Rome with Dadie Rylands.
Ever since Carrington's thoughts became taken up with Snipe, Dadie had stepped forward as the principal confidant of Lytton's heart. Whenever the love and lust he desired from Roger were being with-

held, it was Dadie who chiefly provided the support he so badly needed. Exquisitely sympathetic to all Lytton's varying bouts of ill-fortune, Dadie was none the less critical of the weakness that would again and again lead Lytton back into those secret, unbridgeable lands of ecstasy, where he, Dadie, could not follow. Irritably he complained of the absurd and dismal pattern into which Lytton's relations with Roger seemed to have drifted. And Lytton, obliged to defend his conduct, would reply with just the lightest hint of reproof (20 November 1929): 'People must gang their ain gait . . . And I also feel that it's specially my business to understand and make allowances for that peculiarly sweet creature. So you see . . .'

But Dadie could not be expected to see. During the drear spiritless months of winter, he was very close to Lytton. Then, once the heats of July had returned, and Lytton was again very much happier, their friendship sagged a little with the indefinable weight of guilt. There were moments when Lytton felt slightly ashamed of having to confess that, for the time being, he had no further absurd or dismal indiscretions to unburden. He suspected that Dadie was envious of the undivided love which he and Roger shared. Intermittently that summer, the vision of Roger spread across the whole horizon, obliterating all other friends. 'To me our relations have always been among the greatest blessings of my life,' he wrote to Roger (30 July 1930), '– that I have never doubted. The truth is I'm gorged with good fortune, and really if I can't be extremely happy it's a scandal.'

The early winter and spring of this year were overloaded with scandalous, lacklustre moods, holed by brief emotional crises, and pitched into the troughs of a sad desolation. His vitality reached its very lowest ebb. 'I am at the moment sunk in sloth,' he admitted to Topsy Lucas (2 January 1930), 'which I believe is very good for the health, though perhaps not very good for the morals. So I shall say no more.' The effects of even an attack of 'collywobbles' or 'a wuzzle buzzle of a cold' upon him were now so devastating that he felt it essential to watch over his every symptom with the greatest caution, and he went about carrying a small pouncet box loaded to the brim with an assortment of coloured tablets which he would slip into his mouth at the conclusion of every meal. He was also feeling the cold more. According to reports in the London Press, he had been advised one winter by a friend to wear a body-belt, and this advice he followed with the utmost satisfaction. But when the milder weather had arrived he had felt unable to discard his comforter, and so kept it on all through the summer. When the next winter came and the weather turned colder, something had to be done to meet the emergency, and what Lytton did was to wear two body-belts. Again the summer came and again it was too tepid for the shedding of clothes. All through this second summer Lytton wore two belts. And so, as the seasons alternated, this process had gone on.

Whatever the small element of truth in this story, Lytton undoubtedly suffered most acutely this winter, and being unable to wait for the far-off heats of July, decided to break out of his freezing hibernation and escape for a few weeks to Rome. This idea immediately brought him to life. The perturbations over clothes and hotels were tremendous. Roger, after prolonged indecision, came to the conclusion that he could go, and then that he could not. At last Lytton invited Dadie, 'a charming and conscientious companion', to accompany him. They booked in at the Hotel Hassler and New York – where Lytton had previously taken Roger – Dadie carrying with him a portable edition of Shakespeare, and Lytton some novels of Trollope and most of Proust's *A la Recherche du Temps Perdu*. As it turned out, once they had done the *Times* crossword each day, there was little opportunity for reading. When the sun shone, they would march off on long sightseeing expeditions. 'The beauty of everything is very great,' Lytton wrote to Carrington (13 April 1930), 'but it is a rigorous vigorous life one has to lead – so difficult ever to dream in Italy – and the Italians, one gathers, do nothing else! I don't understand it.'

Mostly the weather was too wet for sightseeing, and they were thrown back on social life, which proceeded in a kind of caricature of the London scene – 'upper-class vagueness and unreality, American frenzy, intellectual sodomy etc. etc.', as Lytton described it all in a letter to Ralph (19 April 1930). 'It is rather amusing, but it would be much nicer to lie under a tomb in the Campagna, or linger among the cypresses of Tivoli.' They seemed doomed to a life of 'cosmopolitan bohemianism'. One afternoon the two of them went to have tea with an old countess who inquired whether Dadie was Lytton's son; another day they encountered Lady d'Abernon who, 'poor soul, appeared out of space, and disappeared again after a slightly painful interchange of civilities'; they dined at the British Embassy with Maurice Baring; they met Beverley Nichols one evening and his American millionaire companion, Warren Curry, both of whom 'after wandering in despair over Europe and Africa, now openly quarrel standing in the street outside hotels'.[1]

[1] This description is a very typical piece of Stracheyesque extravaganza and has, Beverley Nichols assures the author, 'little basis in fact. It is true that I knew a young American called Warren Curry who came over to England to study for a short while and stay with me. But we certainly never wandered "in despair over Europe and Africa". We never went near Africa, and our only excursion abroad was a brief trip to Rome where, far from quarrelling, we had a very enjoyable week-end.'

The climax to their social life took the form of 'a particularly mad lunch party at Lord Berners'.[1] A desperate antique hag (by marriage an Italian Princess), dressed in flowing widow's weeds, and giving vent to a flowing stream of very dimly veiled indecencies, kept the table in a twitter.'

On his return to England, Lytton hurried down to Ham Spray and quickly recommenced work on *The Greville Memoirs*. 'I've been managing to get through quite a lot of work – and it's a pleasant soothing occupation,' he informed Roger after he had been back some three weeks (16 May 1930). Otherwise he was reading David Cecil's biography of Cowper, *The Stricken Deer*, Hugh Kingsmill's anthology *Invective and Abuse*, a copy of which he sent to Roger because it would be excellent, he thought, to read in tube trains on his way to work, and F. L. Lucas's long historical novel *Cécile*, which he described as 'a leisurely affair. After 198 pages (and the pages are large) the heroine reaches Paris. Fifty pages later she goes to an At Home. On page 287 she is kissed by an Englishman. So you see the excitement's breathless. I've now reached page 309 – and am feeling rather wan. An old gentleman has died in the country; what *can* happen next? But perhaps you've read it and know. If so, for goodness sake don't tell me and ruin the whole effect. I rather suspect that the cat has kittens on page 512 – I can hardly refrain from looking to see.'

Almost all May he stayed down at Ham Spray since (11 May 1931) 'I feel as if I *must* stick to Greville for this month and get it done (more or less) . . . [and] in order to read in peace'. At week-ends he was visited by relays of relatives and friends – the Bussys, the James Stracheys, the Tomlins, the Guinnesses, the Lambs, the MacCarthys, Sheppard, Norton and Doggart, Clive Bell 'who chirps away with swinging legs which reveal a strange span of drawers below the knee, as ever', and Boris Anrep who never ceased to pace the rooms like a maniac, exhausting and amazing everyone with the fertility of his ideas, playing boisterous games of chess, plotting Lytton's future career in all its distant details, and then going off on long descriptions of the enormous fishes he had seen off the coast of Brittany, some round as footballs, others rhomboid, and one with a cruel triangular mouth which, if you wedged a brick into it, gave a crack! – and spat it out as powder.

Once he had finished off this next section of *The Greville Memoirs*, Lytton abandoned himself for the rest of the summer to a varied social

[1] Sir Gerald Tyrwhitt-Wilson, fifth baronet and fourteenth Baron Berners (1883–1950), musician, artist and author, whose ballet music 'Luna Park' was this year being performed in C. B. Cochran's revue. He had been honorary attaché in Rome (1911–19) and after the war often stayed at 3 Foro Romano, his house overlooking the Forum.

life. Living for much of this time at his flat in 51 Gordon Square, he would turn up occasionally at select and fashionable dinner-parties, or at Boulestin's, or The Ivy or Bellometti's in Soho Square. William Plomer, meeting him in Tavistock Square for the first time, has etched a vivid profile of what he must have looked like in this last phase of his life. The beard and spectacles, Plomer observed, made him appear older than his real age of fifty. 'Although he was lanky and Edward Lear was rotund, I imagine that Lear's beard and spectacles may also have seemed to create a certain distance between himself and others. About Strachey's eyelids, as he looked out through the windows of his spectacles over the quickset hedge of his beard, there was a suggestion of world-weariness: he had in fact just two more years to live. To me he did not seem like a man in early middle-age, and although his beard made him look older than he was, I did not think of him in terms of a sum of years but as an intelligence alert and busy behind the appendage of hair and the glass outworks. A glint came into his eyes, the brain was on the move as swiftly as a bat, with something of the radar-like sensitivity of a bat, and when he spoke it was sometimes in the voice of a bat.'

This strange Byzantine spectacle had puffed up around the shy and kindly personality of Lytton the clouds of a prodigious and awesome reputation. He was more than ever in demand at London social events. To these he submitted with a characteristic mixture of enthusiasm and malice, curiosity and goodwill. 'I've been plunging in the oddest manner among the Upper Classes,' he reported to Dadie Rylands (8 July 1930). Among the very oddest of these functions was an unconventional tea-party given by the Duchess of Marlborough, the purpose of which was to assemble the most eminent living writers in the land and record photographic groups to correspond to Conversation Pieces. If these proved sufficiently exciting, it was planned that paintings should be made of them. A most miscellaneous crowd assembled in the gilded salons of Carlton House Terrace – including Harold Nicolson, David Garnett, Raymond Mortimer, Francis Birrell and Augustine who 'seems extraordinarily vigorous, and in fact younger than anyone else'. While the duke, who absolutely forbade the use of a spiked tripod on his parquet floor, or of flashlight bulbs in case their smoke discoloured the ceiling, argued to a position of stalemate with an American photographer, the writers interminably waited in their formal group. 'The exhaustion was terrific,' Lytton complained, 'the idiocy intense. Oh dear, oh dear, oh dear!'

London society swirled and bubbled about him this year more crazily than ever before, and his attitude of boredom and amusement is nicely conveyed in a letter he wrote to Carrington (28 May 1930) after a dinner-party at the London home of Bryan and Diana Guinness. 'I had quite an interesting time last night, though I started off in a fit of depression to No 10 Buckingham Street. On the way I fell in with the endless stream of motors going to the "Court", each filled with a sad bevy of débutantes – and an occasional redcoat. A considerable crowd lined the Mall, gaping at this very dull spectacle. I found again a large party – about 18 – with Eddie Marsh, but not Lady Cunard – again sat next to Diana [Cooper]. Once more Harold Acton figured – I feel myself falling under his sway little by little. At last, after a rather dreary dinner, we reached Rutland Gate, where, as I'd feared, Pa and Ma Redesdale[1] were in evidence. However, it was really a pleasant and a very young party – everyone looked very nice and behaved very well, it seemed to me – such good, gentle, natural manners – no stiffness – no blatancy – more like a large family party than anything else. The effect was rather like a choice flower-bed – each tulip standing separately, elegant and gay – but a ghostly notice glimmered – "Please do not pick".'

His criticism, though often severe and ironical, is never ill-tempered. Its purpose was to amuse people rather than to ease some interior pain. For the old corrosion had lost its bite, envy and bitterness had been washed away. Throughout all his experiences, however, Lytton never seemed to lose that youthful capacity of attracting to himself the most ludicrous and embarrassing situations. One misadventure that summer concerned his trousers and a firm of invisible menders. Discovering early one morning that there was a disastrous rent in his trousers, he put on a large ulster overcoat and made his way to an invisible-mending shop near Piccadilly. On arriving there he surveyed the young person behind the counter and asked in his high-pitched voice: 'Can you mend trousers?' On being reassured, he turned round, and, after considerable commotion beneath the ulster, produced the trousers. But upon examination it was decided that the tear was too severe to be invisibly mended and would have to be tacked. Lytton said he would return that afternoon. He then walked off and lunched at the Oriental, still clad in the ulster, his legs lapped tightly one over the other. After lunch he returned and there was a similar pantomime with the ulster. Then, safely trousered once more, he strode off back to Gordon Square.

Another, scarcely less preposterous incident took place early that

[1] The parents of the celebrated Mitford sisters, Diana, Jessica, Unity and Nancy who, in her novel *The Pursuit of Love*, caricatured her father as the crazy and uncontrolled Uncle Matthew, a man who 'knew no middle course, he either loved or hated, and generally, it must be said, he hated'.

June. 'I had a curious adventure at the National Gallery where I went yesterday to see the Duveen room – a decidedly twilight effect: but spacing out the Italian pictures produces on the whole a fair effect,' Lytton told Carrington (10 June 1930). 'There was a black-haired tart marching round in india-rubber boots, and longing to be picked up. We both lingered in the strangest manner in front of various master-pieces – wandering from room to room. Then on looking round I perceived a more attractive tart – fair-haired this time – bright yellow and thick hair – a pink face – and plenty of vitality. So I transferred my attentions, and began to move in his direction when on looking more closely I observed that it was the Prince of Wales – no doubt at all – a Custodian bowing and scraping, and Philip Sassoon also in attendance. I then became terrified that the latter would see me, and insist on performing an introduction, so I fled – perhaps foolishly – perhaps it might have been the beginning of a really entertaining affair. And by that time the poor black-haired tart had entirely disappeared. Perhaps he was the ex-king of Portugal.'

To recover from excitements such as these, he fled down to stay with Dadie at King's where everything should have been delightful, and he could enjoy himself greatly in the company of Goldie Dickinson, Gerald Heard – now literary editor of the *Realist*[1] – and Steven Runciman, whose *The Emperor Romanus Lecapenus* he had recently read and much admired.[2] Poetic fields, gay gilded scenes and shining prospects encompassed him; but very soon the pace of life in Cam-bridge, with its river-parties and dinners, theatres and young men, had grown almost as hectic as that of London. Fearing to be reduced to a mere wraith, he hurried on for a few days to Taplow Court, a large mansion in the French château style, set high amid green lawns over-looking the sparkling reaches of the Thames – the home of Lady Desborough, perhaps the most celebrated and brilliant hostess of the

[1] For the period of a year Gerald Heard edited what he describes as 'a monthly effort which, backed by a number of writers and scientists, was to advocate Scientific Humanism. It called itself the *Realist*, but as it had no money backing, its title was as ill-chosen as its history was brief.'

[2] 'I used to see him [Lytton] quite often from the time that I first went up as an undergraduate to Cambridge in the autumn of 1921,' Sir Steven Runciman told the author (3 July 1965). 'He was always immensely kind and friendly; but I was horribly shy in those days and must have been very unrewarding company. He really much pre-ferred my brother, who was not a striving intellectual as I (alas) was, but was remarkably good-looking – and was much flattered by Lytton's friendliness, though embarrassed by what his rowing friends might think of it.

'My most vivid memory of him is at a dinner-party given by Maynard Keynes in, I suppose, 1924, W. J. H. Sprott and myself being the other guests. I thought then, – rightly, – that I was unlikely ever again to listen to such brilliance of talk. But I have to admit that, brilliant as Lytton was, Maynard was the more brilliant.'

age. The names of the guests staying with her over the previous
week-end would appear on Monday mornings in *The Times*; a long list
of statesmen, diplomats, proconsuls, fashionable beauties, terminated
generally with one or two men of learning or letters. Lytton, however,
does not appear to have been very impressed by this distinguished
clientele which included, on that occasion, 'a knot of dowagers and
[J. M.] Barrie. Also Lord D[avid] Cecil, who struck me as being too
much at home among the female antiques. Desmond was there too – a
comfort; but I came away feeling pretty ashy. Lord Desborough[1]
himself was really the best of the crew – a huge old rock of an athlete –
almost completely gaga – I spent the whole of Sunday afternoon with
him tête-à-tête. He showed me his unpublished books – "The History
of the Thames" – "The History of the Oar" etc., etc.. He confessed he
had read the whole of Shakespeare. – "And, you know, there is some
pretty stiff stuff in him"!'

A visit to Ireland a few weeks later gave him the opportunity for
several more social misadventures, and comments upon them. He had
been invited by Bryan and Diana Guinness to Knockmaroon, in
Castleknock, a large comfortable house on the farther side from
Dublin of the enormous Phoenix Park. In preparation for this holiday,
he had purchased a very splendid and aggressive suit of orange tweeds,
and happily attired in these he travelled by a luxurious first-class train
over the smooth obedient sea to Kingstown, where, 'owing to the
incompetence of the idle rich', there was no one to meet him. He was
then obliged to board another, uncomfortable train to Dublin, and
next a lawless taxi which 'wandered for hours in the purlieus of the
various Maroons and Knocks – the rain all the time pouring cats and
dogs'. At an advanced hour of the evening he arrived, to be met with
looks of faint horror from the large assembly of guests. 'Oh dear me!'
he exclaimed in a letter to Roger (9 August 1930). 'My new tweeds
were far too loud, and, when I burst in rather unexpectedly, quite
horrified (I could clearly see) Lady de Vesci – but no matter, she left for
England almost at once (whether in consequence of my tweeds or for
some other reason) accompanied – this I regretted – by her son (or so I
gathered) Lord Rosse,[2] a foolish young man, but not unattractive.'

[1] Lord Desborough, the father of Julian Grenfell the poet, was one of the most
esteemed all-round sportsmen of his generation. He swam the Niagara pool, slaughtered
a hundred stags in a single season, played cricket for Harrow and ran the three-mile for
Cambridge, ascended the Matterhorn three times by three alternative routes and fenced
in the Olympic Games.

[2] Now a pro-chancellor of Trinity College, Dublin. Much of his work has been
associated with the National Trust; but perhaps his main achievements were as vice-
chancellor of Trinity College, in which capacity he is still remembered by his friends as
having borne the heat and burden of the day of the library appeal, etc.

The company, which rapidly diminished the longer Lytton stayed on (until, after ten days, there seemed to him to be no one else there) included Nancy Mitford, the sister of Diana Guinness and 'amusing', whom he made 'shriek with laughter all the time and [think] how adorable' he was, Henry Yorke[1] and his wife ('rather nice, I think') and a 'pretty but non-existent' Peregrine Willoughby. Besides these, of course, there were the 'little Guinnesses', his hosts. 'He is so small . . . as to be almost invisible; but she is I suspect more interesting, but probably too young to provide any real sustenance.' Dominating this company, looked up to by all and evidently enjoying everything tremendously was Henry Lamb, who had come with his 'very agreeable' wife, Pansy. The change that had taken place in him was extraordinary. 'Henry will obviously be my great support in this gathering,' Lytton wrote to Carrington (9 August 1930). '. . . [He] is a great success. They all adore him, and he is evidently quite happy. A strange unlooked-for transformation. Great play was made of his having hired an evening rig-out for the ball – 7/6 the night. . . . How curious to be thrown together with Henry after all these years, and in Ireland, too, where such a fearful crisis was once enacted between us.'

'Everything is pretty much as I'd expected,' Lytton soon decided. Even so, he informed Mary Hutchinson (9 August 1930) 'the grass doesn't grow under one's feet at Knockmaroon.' In rapid succession he was whisked off to a ball at the Viceregal Lodge, assisted along a mountain-climbing expedition, escorted round the Dublin National Gallery and taken to the Abbey Theatre, 'where Diana G. grew so restive over the brogue and the boredom that she swept out in the middle of the performance with the whole party at her heels'. Some aspects of this drawing-room life, in particular its mixture of decorum and impropriety, did come as a surprise to him. 'The state of civilization here is curious,' he reported to Roger, '– something new to me. An odd betwixt-and-between-ism. The indecency question, for instance – certain jokes are permissible, in fact frequent – but oh! there are limitations. And I must say I am always for the absolute. And the young men invariably leap to their feet when a young woman enters the room.'

On his return to Ham Spray, Lytton began to write again. 'A sudden

---

[1] Henry Green, the novelist, who had already published both *Blindness* and *Living*. Mr Yorke remembers (1967) Lytton as being extremely well dressed, 'as bright as a button', invariably courteous, amiable: 'a real charmer'. In particular he was struck by the fact that Lytton always listened very attentively to what everyone said, would encourage them to speak, then, when they had finished, gently utter just two or three words that might completely deflate them. His technique was superb. Yet people did not feel aggrieved; for there was always more humour than malevolence in his remarks.

inspiration has come upon me,' he confided to Roger (2 September 1930), 'and I am dashing off an article on Froude ... Quite a pleasure to be working again! A sudden influx of energy!' He completed this essay on 4 September, though it was not until December that it appeared in *Life and Letters*. Meanwhile, he tried his hand at a 'sadistic story' and then, his zeal still not abated, the long essay on Madame de Lieven which 'absorbs me'. This burst of creative industry, after months of semi-idleness, astonished him. 'I only wish I could send you some of my own bouncing strength,' he told Roger (23 September 1930), '– I never thought in days gone by that I should have any to spare for other people.'

He had energy to spare, too, for somersaulting once more through the endless hoops of social entertainment. He visited Charleston to stay with the Bells, went down to Brighton for some days with Roger, and in company with Dadie Rylands, Rosamond Lehmann and Wogan Philipps completed a fortnight's motor tour of the French cathedral towns – Saint-Malo, Trébeurden, Brest, Douarnenez, Nantes, Poitiers and Bourges. Back in London, he attended the opening production of the Camargo Ballet Society which, he assured Lydia Keynes (26 October 1930), was admirable.

Among the authors whom he met for the first time this autumn were Caradoc Evans, the short-story writer from Wales, the young Italian novelist, Alberto Moravia, and the English poet and critic, Stephen Spender. 'Such a scene last night at the Ivy when Caradoc Evans, rather the worse for drink, apostrophised me in Anglo-Welsh for ¾ of an hour,' he told Roger (23 September 1930). 'But I daresay that name conveys even less to you than it does to me. "Truly to God" was one of his favourite phrases – "Truly to God, Mr. Strachey, you can write English – English – you know what I mean – you *know* – yes, Mr. Strachey, English, truly to God!" It was only ended by his mistress, a vast highly coloured woman in the Spanish style, taking the whole party in her car to this house [51 Gordon Square] – where I cleverly escaped, without letting the others in. So you see one does have a certain sort of adventure even in this deserted London.'

His encounter with Alberto Moravia, whose *Gli Indifferenti* had recently been brought out in Italy, was a far more sober and fastidious affair, and took place in 'that palace of faded grimness', the Reform Club, to which they had both been invited by E. M. Forster. 'E.M.F. assured me that he [Moravia] really was good-looking,' he related to Roger (15 November 1930), '– however (knowing the peculiarity of his taste) I wasn't surprised to find a human weasel awaiting me under the yellow-ochre Ionic columns of the central hall. Otherwise he wasn't so bad, as foreigners go. He's apparently written a novel that is so shocking that even Beryl de Zoete refuses to translate it. "I deescra-eeb nékeed weemin" was his explanation. (Rather a disappointing one!).'[1]

It was at Ipsden Manor, some forty miles from Hungerford, near Wallingford, where he had been invited for a Christmas Eve lunch by 'Ros and Wog', that Lytton first met Stephen Spender 'whom I liked very much' he afterwards confided to Roger (27 December 1930). The young poet's red cheeks, blue eyes and romantic expression delighted him, and he described him as 'a gay, vague lively creature – youthful and full of talk. Has written a homosexual novel, which he fears will not be published. Thinks of living in Germany with a German boy, but hasn't yet found a German boy to live with. Writes poems after lunch, and reads them aloud to Rosamond.' On the Boxing Day, 'Ros and Wog' and Stephen Spender motored over to Ham Spray for dinner, at which the other guests were Clive and Vanessa Bell, Carrington's brother Noel, Ralph and Frances. 'It was a curious little party, but I enjoyed it,' Lytton wrote. 'Got some talk with S.S. who was very amusing and nice. Then we played Up Jenkins – rather a fearful game. Then the wireless was turned on, and dancing took place – Clive tottering round with Frances, Wogan gyrating like a top with Carrington – and for a moment with me! . . . The latest scandal is that the Woolves (aided and abetted by Dadie, of all people) are trying to lure John Lehmann to join the Hogarth Press, and put all his capital as well as to devote his working hours to doing up parcels in the basement. And the large ape is seriously tempted.'[2]

A few days later, on 29 December, Lytton took Pippa down to Weymouth for the New Year. They put up at the Gloucester Hotel, a large edifice, reconverted from the palace of George III. Outside, an appalling storm raged for a week, perpetually dashing the rain and wind against the windows. The heated rooms were heaped full of derelict inhabitants, mostly, so far as Lytton could detect, retired and aged greengrocers and their more retired and aged wives. 'Pippa and I sit side by side in our sitting-room and shall continue to do so, as far as I can see, for the next week,' he wrote to Carrington (30 December 1930). 'I suppose one day we may struggle out through the blizzard as far as the circulating library, but I doubt it. Everything appears the same. The royal bathing-machines are still drawn up on the beach;

---

[1] *Gli Indifferenti* was not translated and published in England until 1935, when it appeared under the title *The Time of Indifference*. Alberto Moravia's regular English-language translator is Lytton's old friend Angus Davidson.

[2] A full account of how John Lehmann joined the Hogarth Press and of his subsequent career there as a publisher is given in the first volume of his autobiography, *The Whispering Gallery* (1955).

the statue of George III rises still between the lion and the unicorn; the motor-bicycles still whirl up and down the parade after dinner.'

In the second week of January, after a few days at Gordon Square, Lytton returned to Ham Spray, feeling unaccountably happy and light-headed. A new book of his was shortly to be published, and he busied himself making the final corrections to his typescript.

He had just one more year to live.

6

PORTRAITS IN MINIATURE

By 1931, Lytton had reached a much-envied yet not altogether enviable stage in his career. It was almost impossible for him to increase his reputation, and extremely difficult for him to maintain it. There are two stages in the career of every successful author which may be labelled crucial. The one occurs when his work has been so long before the public that reviewers have grown tired of pointing out its merits, while inferior imitators – of whom Lytton had very many – have made them sick of his methods; and the other, when he first emerges from being the idol of a small group to become the property of the big common world.

In Lytton's case, these two stages had followed close upon one another. Nothing cools so much the ardour of early admirers as hearing their applause amplified by others. When *Elizabeth and Essex* appeared, not a few of his most fervid devotees declared themselves disappointed. It was after this book, which contained some of the most original pages he had ever written, that, for the first time, the question was seriously debated as to whether, after all, he was a first-rate writer. A Renaissance subject had not stimulated Lytton's gift for ironic description, for diminishing the stature of his heroes. And there was another reason why this exciting and, in places, beautiful biography was not, in 1931, well looked upon by the critics. It had sold. In thousands, in tens and hundreds of thousands, it had sold. The time was therefore ripe for a steep critical recoil from Lytton's work. But his next book, a collection of eighteen essays, partly forestalled this reaction. For one thing, it seemed too slight a volume on which to launch such a major reaction. It was his least important and most amusing book. And so, though there was a rather sour taste in some of the notices, antagonistic reviewers were content to tell their readers of the limited appeal of Lytton's subjects – a gathering of forgotten eccentrics, most of them, about whom these brief sketches could only serve as footnotes to history.

The vignettes which make up *Portraits in Miniature* had begun coming out in the *Nation and Athenaeum* during the autumn of 1923. On 22 February 1927 Lytton wrote to Charles Prentice: 'I find that I have now written ten of the short biographical studies which I have been contributing to the "Nation" for the last few years. Whitworth at one time suggested publishing them, and it now occurs to me that if I added two more this might be done . . . The quality of the whole seems to me satisfactory; and as to the quantity, it is possible that a small volume of such things makes a better authentic whole – less monotonous and emphatic – than a big one.' But Prentice feared that a book of this kind might then interfere with the sales of *Elizabeth and Essex*, which he expected to bring out at Christmas. Then, several months after the biography had been published, Prentice suggested that he might bring out a little booklet entitled *Six English Historians*. Lytton, however, considered this a 'horrid' idea, and eventually a compromise was reached in the form of a volume containing in its first section the twelve biographical papers originally suggested by Lytton in 1927, followed by a separate section devoted to the six historians, and collectively entitled *Portraits in Miniature and Other Essays*.[1]

From the end of November, Lytton was 'plunged into the literary business' of preparing this book. Unlike *Books and Characters*, these essays needed few emendations, and his chief business seems to have been, with the aid of *Roget's Thesaurus*, weeding out the 'deliciousnesses' and 'indefatigables' which were peppered over the pages, and inserting various fancy blooms in their place. By the end of January he had finished these corrections, and two months later received the proofs 'which looked rather nice'. It was only a very small work, he warned Roger (20 March 1931). 'I think of writing a book moulded on Malinovsky,[2] called "the Sexual Life of the English", it would be a remarkable work, but no doubt would have to be published in New Guinea. In the meantime "Portraits in Miniature" is progressing in its tamer fashion. I've corrected the proofs, and now only have to settle which is the least repellent of the specimen covers for binding.'

---

[1] Earlier titles which Lytton considered include *Little Lives* and *Six Historians, and Other Essays*. To Dadie Rylands he wrote (26 November 1930): 'I have at last decided to bring out a book of Collected Monstrosities in the spring – and have to write some to collect. At the best it will be a tiny wisp of an affair. "Jewels five words long" might be a good title – culled from your favourite poet.'

[2] Bronislaw Malinovsky (1884–1942), the Anglo-Polish anthropologist, whose *The Sexual Life of Savages in North-Western Melanesia* had just been published.

Portraits in Miniature and Other Essays was published that May simultaneously in two editions – a limited one of two hundred and sixty copies (of which two hundred and fifty were for sale) signed by Lytton and costing two guineas; and an ordinary one priced at six shillings, of which eight thousand copies were sold in Britain within the first eight weeks. The volume was dedicated, 'with gratitude and admiration', to Max Beerbohm, and, as always, the dedication was exactly appropriate. Lytton's miniatures were painted with a precise delicacy and lightness of touch that is nicely comparable to Max's subtle and ironic art. Max himself was delighted by this compliment. 'I feel immensely proud that you should dedicate a book to me,' he replied with characteristic over-modesty (21 March 1931) to Lytton's letter asking for his permission. 'Much older though I am than you, my admiration for your prose, since first I knew it, has had the fresh wild hot quality that belongs rather to a very young man's feeling for the work of a great congenial veteran. I have always felt, and shall always feel, such a duffer and fumbler in comparison with you. But I shall be better able to disguise this feeling when my eye shall have seen my name in your book.'

As an epigraph to this collection, Lytton quoted Horace:

> *Est brevitate opus, ut currat sententia, neu se*
> *Impediat verbis lassas onerantibus aures.*

The eighteen studies which follow are all constructed with the terseness and artistic control that Horace declared necessary for effective satire. The miniature essay is one of the most difficult of literary techniques. The usual compromise between form and matter is either to leave it empty or to chatter for two thousand words or so about a series of haphazard points, and then stop. But for Lytton, this was the perfect vehicle for his talent. His writing is never vacuous; nor does he wearisomely over-elaborate his tiny subjects. With the greatest tact and craft he compresses within each cameo a serried mass of biographical facts that merge into an immaculate unity of design. Though the pace apparently remains unhurried, almost leisurely at times, the manner is invariably crisp and cool, the effect of each story, in its few brilliant pages, taut and absorbing. He uses two principal methods of construction. Either, as in the first piece, 'Sir John Harington', he telescopes into ten minutes reading the whole biography of his subject; or – as in 'The Président de Brosses' – he takes as his *motif* a dramatic quarrel and groups round this everything else of significance. The focus is always upon small matters, but within the narrow limits prescribed by this form, his treatment, despite its surface impression of ease and simplicity, manages to suggest far more than it actually states.

These miniature essays present the most natural expression of one side of Lytton's personality. Like A. E. Housman, he 'is content to reign over a tiny kingdom', behind whose frontiers he can display his most characteristic mannerisms. Peculiarity is one of the themes that he constantly exploits. He accentuates the amusing, the extraordinary and the trifling. He makes use of eccentric situations and grotesque physical circumstances in a way that achieves striking effects but sometimes lacks the creative intensity that really penetrates through the habits and appearances of men to the human truth within.

The first section of *Portraits in Miniature* contains a dozen papers on obscure pedants, antiquaries, scientists, sectaries, biographers and other oddities. Lytton delights in bringing out the weird contrasts and paradoxes thrown up by the careers of such men, and eagerly welcomes any departure from conformity. In particular he excels in academic satire. His accounts of 'The Life, Illness, and Death of Dr. North' and 'The Sad Story of Dr. Colbatch' are small masterpieces of historical burlesque. With much literary malice, there was no spite or malevolence in his art. It is the comic spirit that is triumphant. He stares at the human farce with unblinking, imperturbable amazement, and crystallizes his astonished observations in short, pungent sentences that are all the more effective for their tranquil understatement. Sometimes he finds no need for comment of his own at all, as for example, when he quotes Dr North's remark: 'Of all the Beasts of the Field, God Almighty thought Woman the fittest Companion for Man.'

In very many of these essays there is a tone of real geniality and friendliness. The very excess and remoteness of his subjects' abnormality robs Lytton of his anti-religious zeal. Poor Lodowick Muggleton, that tiny prophetic solipsist, crazy rather than eccentric, an incomprehensible priest without craft or congregation, he sees not as a frenzied oppressor of mankind but a victim of the world's strains and tribulations, badgered by the small persecutions of authority, condemned to the pillory at the age of sixty-eight when 'he was badly mauled, for it so happened that the crowd was hostile and pelted the old man with stones'. And at the end, his narrative is suffused with tenderness, and he can find words of ironic praise for the diminishing band of Muggleton's followers. His capital letters draw attention to a real if amused charity and graciousness of spirit. 'Two hundred and fifty Muggletonians followed him to the grave, and their faith has been handed down, unimpaired through the generations, from that day to this. Still, in the very spot where their founder was born, the chosen few meet together to celebrate the two festivals of their religion – the Great Holiday, on the anniversary of the delivery of the Word to Reeve, and the Little Holiday, on the day of Muggleton's final release from prison.

I do believe in God alone,
Likewise in Reeve and Muggleton.

So they have sung for more than two hundred years. . . . It is an exclusive faith, certainly; and yet, somehow or other, it disarms criticism. Even though one may not be of the elect oneself, one cannot but wish it well; one would be sorry if the time ever came when there were no more Muggletonians. Besides, one is happy to learn that with the passage of years they have grown more gentle. Their terrible offensive weapon – which, in early days, they wielded so frequently – has fallen into desuetude: no longer do they pass sentence of eternal damnation. The dreaded doom was pronounced for the last time on a Swedenborgian, with great effect, in the middle of the nineteenth century.'

At first sight these miscellaneous papers, on all sorts of unusual people, seem to possess no particular adhesive unity. One is entertained so much by the stories and squabbles that it is only afterwards that one becomes aware of a thread which runs through all of them – a line tracing, from the Elizabethan to the Victorian age, the evolution of modern society. The career of Sir John Harington reflects perfectly the alternating whimsicality and danger mixed with impropriety that characterized Elizabethan times. That of Muggleton exhibits the un-paralleled self-assertiveness which the human mind attained about the year 1650, when the disintegration of religious authority reached its culminating point. 'If one were asked to choose a date for the beginning of the modern world,' Lytton wrote, 'probably July 15, 1662, would be best to fix upon. For on that day the Royal Society was founded, and the place of Science in civilization became a definite and recognized thing.' The lives of John Aubrey and Dr North are both advanced to bear out this contention. Dr North, a member of the old dispensation, whose ideas were rapidly becoming obsolete, is depicted as an almost pathologically inadequate Master of Trinity. Aubrey, on the other hand, he represents as belonging partly to the old world, partly to the new. 'His insatiable passion for singular odds and ends had a meaning in it,' Lytton explains; 'he was groping towards a scientific ordering of phenomena; but the twilight of his age was too confusing, and he could rarely distinguish between a fact and a fantasy. He was clever enough to understand the Newtonian system, but he was not clever enough to understand that a horoscope was an absurdity; and so, in his crowded curiosity-shop of a brain, astronomy and astrology both found a place, and were given equal values.'

Unwinding this central thread, Lytton next reconstructs the argument that flared up between Congreve and Jeremy Collier and which he presents as being symptomatic of an age in which the mysterious requirements of dogmatic theology obscured all discussion of ethics and aesthetics. By introducing Macaulay's later version of this affair, Lytton also touches upon certain changes in attitude and style brought about by the Industrial Revolution. In 'Madame de Sévigné's Cousin' we are shown the first signs of putrefaction, the *rigor mortis* of the great epoch of Louis XIV; while 'The Sad Story of Dr. Colbatch' illustrates very well the terrifying and preposterous academic life carried on during the early years of the eighteenth century, 'agitated, violent and full of extremes. Everything about it was on the grand scale. Erudition was gigantic, controversies were frenzied, careers were punctuated by brutal triumphs, wild temerities, and dreadful mortifications.'

In the following essay, 'The Président de Brosses', Lytton takes us across to eighteenth-century France. The theme of this study is a quarrel about firewood. First, in a few charming sentences, Lytton reminds us of a 'sometimes forgotten feature of the world as it used to be before the age of trains and telephones'. In those days there were provincial capitals, 'centres of local civilization'. The Président de Brosses was the great man of Dijon, the capital of Burgundy. Brosses' ambition, we are told, was to become a member of the French Academy, one of 'the forty immortals'. After Voltaire had settled at Ferney, he bought from the Président the neighbouring estate of Tournay. But he was not pleased with his bargain, since the cut firewood on it had already been sold to a peasant called Charlot Baudy. Voltaire, a shivery old mortal by this time, used a good deal of fuel, but he was outraged when a bill for 281 francs for wood from off his own estate was presented to him by Baudy. A prolonged and absurd argument broke out, in the telling of which we get to hear about the character of the Président, and come to understand how Voltaire's virulent vindictiveness, and the ferocious energy he flung into this trivial episode, implied a microscopic concentration upon everything connected with himself, and a feverish sense of its utmost importance. We also learn, almost incidentally, something of the relations of the provincial way of life to the central life of France in the mid-eighteenth century.

In each miniature, Lytton transforms his sitter into one of those characters in comedy who is there neither to instruct us nor to exalt us, but simply to amuse. But he also blends each character with some sympathetically glimpsed aspect of the age in which he lived. 'The Abbé

Morellet', for instance, is an essay designed to elucidate the meaning of Talleyrand's remark that only those who had lived in France before the Revolution had really experienced *la douceur de vivre*. Mary Berry, the friend of Horace Walpole and Thackeray, provides a curious transition-scene bridging the eighteenth century and the Victorian age. And the story of 'Madame de Lieven', the last of the Portraits in Miniature, symbolizes for Lytton the final capitulation under Victoria of the magnificent aristocratic qualities that he had so greatly admired in their full bloom in the sixteenth century. He begins: 'Aristocrats (no doubt) still exist; but they are shorn beings, for whom the wind is not tempered – powerless, out of place, and slightly ridiculous. For about a hundred years it has been so . . . Madame de Lieven was one of the supreme examples of the final period. Her manners were of the genuinely terrific kind. Surrounded by them, isolated as with an antiseptic spray, she swept on triumphantly, to survive untouched – so it seemed – amid an atmosphere alive with the microbes of bourgeois disintegration. So it seemed – for in fact something strange eventually happened.' This strange something was a liaison with Monsieur Guizot, the living epitome of all that was most middle-class. 'The crash came on June 24, 1837', wrote Lytton, '– the date is significant: it was four days after the accession of Queen Victoria.' Yet after the death of the prince, her husband, Madame de Lieven did not marry Guizot. 'Was this the last resistance of the aristocrat?' Lytton asks. 'Or was it perhaps, in reality, the final proof that Madame de Lieven was an aristocrat no longer?'

Preferring his specimens dried and pinned, Lytton approached no nearer to the contemporary world. Since the 1830s the aristocracy had been virtually dead, the last barricade swept away. For this, and for other reasons, *Portraits in Miniature* is the obverse of *Eminent Victorians* – a work of elegant sentiment rather than virulent propaganda. The men he examines are mostly very far from being thought of as eminent. Inhabitants of a dwindling civilization, their prestige and influence, such as they were, had disappeared with them, not lingering on to vex the twentieth century. Their butterfly careers colourfully illustrate the waywardness of the human spirit, the frustrated offshoots and cul-de-sacs of ambition. And since their reputations have lapsed, their faiths decayed, their arguments been buried in the dust, they may be treated with a disinterested amusement, an irony that is lenient, not vindictive. Like some of the minor characters in *Eminent Victorians* – Newman and Sidney Herbert – like Albert or even Essex, the men appear to be more fragile beings than the women in the book: they seem crazier, more vulnerable. Mainly they are eccentric little gentlemen, with a tendency to gossip, and some esoteric talent distorted by a variety of social and biological disturbances. It was their queerness that fascinated Lytton, and we seldom see them so vividly as when, in the course of their mincing gait, they trip over the train of some great lady.

As in all his books, it is the conflict between the power-loving masculine side and the submissive feminine side of his characters that exercises Lytton's imagination most strongly. And it is usually the men who are most submissive and effeminate. The women belong to that special matriarchal type, virile and substantial, that held him in such awe: Mary Berry, for example, whose fate was the very reverse of Madame du Deffand's, the emotional tragedy coming at the beginning of a long life instead of at the end. 'And yet, in the structure of their minds, the two were curiously similar,' Lytton noted. 'Both were remarkable for reason and good sense, for a certain intellectual probity, for a disillusioned view of things, and for great strength of will. Between these two stern women, the figure of Horace Walpole makes a strange appearance – a creature all vanity, elegance, insinuation, and finesse – by far the most feminine of the three.'

It was the *stamina*, the tremendous frustrated potency of these women, that Lytton enshrined. Like their prototype, Lady Strachey, they all lived to a great age – Lady Hester Stanhope and Madame de Lieven, the two youngest, died at sixty-five; Queen Elizabeth and Madame du Deffand at seventy or more; Queen Victoria at eighty-two; Mary Berry at eighty-nine: Florence Nightingale at ninety. Of these, only Florence Nightingale survived into the Edwardian age, and her terrific energies alone broke out of the social and diplomatic spheres traditionally assigned to women. She was the eagle, and the rest were swans. For in the days before 1850, the great world was still a small and immaculate place, and women were debarred from major roles in life. There was nothing that Mary Berry could not bring about in her drawing-room, Lytton tells us, but 'her masculine mind exercised itself over higher things . . . Had she been a man, she would not have shone as a writer, but as a political thinker or an administrator; and a man she should have been; with her massive, practical intelligence, she was born too early to be a successful woman. She felt this bitterly. Conscious of high powers, she declaimed against the miserable estate of women, which prevented her from using them. She might have been a towering leader, in thought or action; as it was, she was insignificant. So she said – "insignificant!" – repeating the word over and over again. "And nobody," she added, "ever suffered insignificance more unwillingly than myself".'

It was a similar story with Madame de Lieven, who, as an ambassadress, 'was endowed with social talents of the highest order', whose passion was for high diplomacy, who had a finger in every political pie, but whose actual influence, as Lytton demonstrates, was negligible. She might be 'the terror of the embassies', yet the force of her personality was magnificently irrelevant to serious embassy affairs. Her influence was confined to society. And it is principally as society hostesses that Lytton depicts and venerates this prepotent breed of women, within their *salons* brilliantly enhancing and intensifying the charm of life. They were the sort of imperious super-females whom he had searched for in vain in his own age; for compared with them, Lady Desborough and the Duchess of Marlborough, Lady Astor and Lady Cunard, poor dear old Ottoline and all the rest of that sorry crew were only pale imitations, 'shorn beings, for whom the wind is not tempered – powerless, out of place, and slightly ridiculous'.

In his paper on John Aubrey, Lytton had declared: 'A biography should either be as long as Boswell's or as short as Aubrey's. The method of enormous and elaborate accretion which produced the *Life of Johnson* is excellent, no doubt; but, failing that, let us have no half-measures; let us have the pure essentials – a vivid image, on a page or two, without explanations, transitions, commentaries, or padding.' Lytton's miniatures are themselves almost of Aubreyan length and split-second focus. He did in a polished form what Aubrey had done sketchily, giving the essential lines of a life, a character, in a few swift pictures and penetrating phrases. But, as works of art, the historians, which make up the last third of the book, are less perfect, for it was impossible to deal adequately with these great and complex men by employing such a small-scale technique. His tendency to presume that the most absurd statements a man utters are the most revealing, is excellent for a preposterous oddity like Muggleton, but it is less suitable for a Macaulay. He has space to exhibit only one facet of each historian – the detachment of Hume, the balance of Gibbon, the philistinism of Macaulay, the morality of Carlyle, the provincial protestantism of his disciple Froude, and, finally, the ever-dry, patient, sober scholarship of Mandell Creighton. The effect of this one-dimensional treatment is, in some instances, to caricature and, unwittingly, to distort the true likeness of his subjects.

Lytton's special aptitude for judging historians by their peculiarities and literary style, though interesting, is sometimes too restrictive. As if in acknowledgement of this, he adds some of the commentary and explanation specifically excluded by him from among the pure essentials of the Aubreyan technique, which he then attempts to offset by an exaggerated lightness of touch. The five-hundred-word satirical account he gives in 'Froude' of the quarrel between Professor Freeman and Mr

Horace Round is as amusing as any of the other agitated academic disputes in the first section of the book. It harmonizes well with the mood and tone of these earlier pieces; but it is a disproportionate digression in a miniature essay on the historian, and, strictly speaking, an aesthetic blemish.

'Mr. Horace Round, a "burrower into wormholes" living in Brighton, suddenly emerged from the parchments among which he spent his life deliciously gnawing at the pedigrees of the proudest families in England, and in a series of articles fell upon Freeman with astonishing force . . . The effect of these articles on Freeman was alarming; his blood boiled, but he positively made no reply. For years the attacks continued, and for years the professor was dumb. Fulminating rejoinders rushed into his brain, only to be whisked away again – they were not quite fulminating enough. The most devastating article of all was written, was set up in proof, but was not yet published . . . Freeman was aghast at this last impertinence; but still he nursed his wrath. Like King Lear, he would do such things – what they were yet he knew not – but they should be the terrors of the earth. At last, silent and purple, he gathered his female attendants about him, and left England for an infuriated holiday. There was an ominous pause; and then the fell news reached Brighton. The professor had gone pop in Spain.'

No other passage in the whole of *Portraits in Miniature* so animated the feelings of the reviewers. Lytton, it was considered, this time had really gone too far. The culminating sentence of this dreadful description of Freeman's death was heartless – it was worse: it was *bad taste*. Lytton himself could hardly have felt more pleased by this outraged response. Recently he had come to fear that he might be fossilizing from the original lively saboteur of *Eminent Victorians* into a respectable literary institution. Even the latest attacks on his works had treated him almost as an established classic. One reviewer had already suggested that he should be awarded the Nobel Prize for Literature. Soon, if he did not take precautions, he would solidify into a well-loved, grand old man of letters. To avoid this fate, he particularly wanted to offend the successors of men like Freeman, his modern counterparts among the academic historians of the 1930s. And here he seems to have been reasonably successful. Shortly after 'Froude' appeared in *Life and Letters*, he wrote off happily to Roger (17 December 1930): 'Virginia had just met Lord Esher who had told her that *he* had just met George Trevelyan, who was foaming at the mouth with rage. – "Really! I should never have believed that a writer of L.S.'s standing would use an expression like that – went pop!" So some effect has been produced, which is something.'

These six essays on English historians enable Lytton to expound his doctrine that history, like biography, should be an art. With their literary rather than historical emphasis, the essays are particularly original for the relationship they suggest between Lytton himself and his subjects. With Hume, whom he greatly admired, he shared both inferior health and an inner restlessness of spirit – disruptive influences which were regulated in such a way that they never damaged the clarity and elegance of the writing. But by claiming for Hume the historical detachment that he, as a literary manner, liked to assume himself, he muddled the philosopher with the historian. So far from being 'absolutely free from temporal considerations', Hume's history, as Desmond MacCarthy has pointed out, is an easy, lucid and entirely Tory pamphlet.

Lytton's style, in any case, had more in common with that of Gibbon. For both of them, physically ill-equipped to command a life of action, style became a form of power. But, as with Hume, Lytton over-plays a single aspect of Gibbon's attitude – in this case, an imperturbable balance – to the point of biographical inaccuracy. Blandly he presents us with an *insouciant* Gibbon who totally neglected his fatal disease, whereas the truth appears to be that he lived in terror of it. Lytton himself seems to echo this doubtful *insouciance*. Obviously feeling the medical diagnosis to be inappropriate for a light magazine essay, he is unspecific as to the nature of the disease, merely drawing our attention to the ano-pubic region of the body – 'a protuberance in the lower part of his person'.

Between Froude and himself there were several isolated points of connexion, mixed with some feeling of antipathy. Whereas he was over-protected by his mother, Froude had been bullied by the old patriarchal figure of Mr Froude, whom he never ceased to admire, though his admiration might, at its source, be rather ambiguous. This sketch of Froude's life reads like the biography of Queen Victoria in miniature, especially in his unconscious search for a father-substitute to satisfy his craving for authority. There was much in Froude's career to stir Lytton's sympathy. There existed some parallel in their ill, overgrown, miserable schooldays and their subsequent need for a simplifying parental relationship. There was some affinity, too, in their writing. Lytton's exposition of Elizabeth's political policy in *Elizabeth and Essex* had closely resembled Froude's own conclusion. Lytton's opinion of Froude was more complex than that of the other historians, and makes for a finely proportioned evaluation of his work. He notes the use of narrative drama sometimes raised into melodrama, of a romantic strain, and the bias which gives a spice to his prose, 'a cheap spice –

bought, one feels, at the Co-operative Stores'. And in his concluding estimate of Froude's work, he writes: 'A certain narrowness of thought and feeling: that may be forgiven, if it is expressed in a style of sufficient mastery. Froude was an able, a brilliant writer, copious and vivid, with a picturesque imagination and a fine command of narrative . . . the extraordinary succession of events assumes, as it flows through his pages, the thrilling lineaments of a great story, upon whose issue the most *blasé* reader is forced to hang entranced. Yet the supreme quality of style seems to be lacking . . . Perhaps, after all, it is the intellect and the emotion that are at fault here too; perhaps when one is hoping for genius, it is only talent – only immense talent – that one finds.'

What Lytton found it hard to forgive was Froude's adoption of Carlyle as a second father. His naïve and submissive acceptance of the crude Puritan dogmas propounded by that keeper of the Victorian conscience encouraged his worst qualities for a historian – insensitivity, distortion and an over-emphasis upon the momentousness of human action. Towards Hume and Gibbon, Lytton had extended a profound, unmixed sympathy, relishing the similarity he discovered between himself and them. Towards Carlyle and Macaulay, whose likeness to himself was less gratifying, he was correspondingly less sympathetic. For this reason, he was at pains, when dealing with the first pair, to stress one primary quality that distinguished his own style; while, with the latter two, he brings out characteristics – moral dogma and philistinism – that were clearly absent from his own writing. By these means did he align himself with the former and dissociate himself more remotely from the others.

As the embodiment of biblical Victorian fervour, whose egotism marred his poetic genius, Carlyle exasperated Lytton, and his inspired bravura sentence on 'that most peculiar age' – the star passage of Georgian condemnation of the Victorian jungle – is uncharacteristic of the rest of this volume, belonging, more fittingly, to *Eminent Victorians*. Abandoning his customary tone of persiflage for the rhetoric of satire, he scales up a crescendo of righteous irony. It was, he tell us, 'an age of barbarism and prudery, of nobility and cheapness, of satisfaction and desperation; an age in which everything was discovered and nothing known; an age in which all the outlines were tremendous and all the details sordid; when gas-jets struggled feebly through the circum-ambient fog, when the hour of dinner might be at any moment between two and six, when the doses of rhubarb were periodic and gigantic, when pet dogs threw themselves out of upper storey windows, when cooks reeled drunk in areas, when one sat for hours with one's feet in dirty straw dragged along the street by horses, when an antimacassar was on every chair, and the baths were minute tin circles, and the beds were full of bugs and disasters.'

The philistinism of Macaulay is made more ruthless to Lytton by his apparent inability to experience love. The barrenness of Macaulay's prose style conveys only too well the absence in his make-up of any intense physical emotion, just as the loss of identity implicit in Lytton's love-affairs makes itself felt in the thinness, the lack of tangible expansive warmth in his more romantic passages. 'And it is noticeable,' Lytton points out, 'how far more effective he [Macaulay] is in his treatment of those whom he dislikes than of those whom he admires . . . Macaulay's inability to make his hero live – his refusal to make any attempt to illuminate the mysteries of that most obscure and singular character – epitomises all that is weakest in his work.' How well Lytton understood the mechanism of Macaulay's writing, for it involved a technique substantially similar to his own. Both of them excelled at vivid characterization and story-telling. 'History', Lytton wrote, 'is primarily a narrative, and in power of narration no one has ever surpassed Macaulay. In that he is a genius. When it comes to telling a story, his faults disappear or change into virtues. Narrowness becomes clarity, and crudity turns into force. The rhetoric of the style, from being the ornament of platitude, becomes the servant of excitement. Every word is valuable: there is no hesitation, no confusion, and no waste . . . Unsatisfying characters, superficial descriptions, jejune reflections, are seen to be no longer of importance in themselves – they are merely stages in the development of the narrative. They are part of the pattern – the enthralling, ever-shifting pattern of the perfect kaleidoscope.'

As the most obscure and pedagogic of these 'Six English Historians', Mandell Creighton, the last of them, might have been better placed in the first section of the book, alongside 'The Sad Story of Dr. Colbatch' and 'The Life, Illness, and Death of Dr. North'. In the manner of these earlier miniatures, Lytton uses Creighton's personality and career to illustrate some peculiar social facet of the times – in this case the dual Anglican tradition of scholarship and administrative energy, of which Creighton was the last exponent of a long line stretching from Whitgift to Jowett. Lytton respected Creighton's gift for the clear exposition of complicated political transactions and the intricate movements of thought with which they were connected, and also his refusal to be stampeded by popular contemporary sentiment. But he could not warm to him. A supremely conventional man and an anaemic personality, Creighton was without humour, and his writing without romance. Yet, as Lytton knew well, there are no greater figures of fun than people lacking in humour. The unmoved, unamazed moderation with which Creighton dissected the worst atrocities of the Inquisition was laughably incongruous. And then, what an antiquated figure he cut, this Bishop of London, with his glinting gold spectacles, his dapper episcopal gaiters, his grizzled beard and bald forehead, gravely examining the novels of Mrs Humphry Ward and setting the teacups tinkling in Fulham with his academic paradoxes. Everything human and endearing within him had been suppressed. He was an abstract entity. Dryness was his chief quality as a historian, dryness and sobriety. Yet, in the conduct of his incombustible life, there was one faint spark of that preposterous eighteenth-century world of learning so well represented by that other reverend scholar, Dr Colbatch. Lytton hints at this resemblance between the two men by employing in his studies of them an identical technique, repeating at the very end of his monograph the previous topmost note of ridicule, the most absurd single utterance, now made more absurd still for being re-quoted out of context, shrill, insistent, bewildered – 'Arrogat, my Lord!' and 'Where's my black bag?'

Lytton was a master of beginnings and endings. *Portraits in Miniature* enabled him to exploit to the full his skill in the description of death-beds. Never did an author arrange so anxiously for the demise of his characters, or see to it that their last moments should be so typical. Where the original living portrait has been slightly distorted, then, for consistency, slight nuances have to be added to these death-bed scenes. Gibbon, for example: 'Life seemed as charming as usual,' Lytton wrote. 'Next morning, getting out of bed for a necessary moment, "Je suis plus adroit," he said with his odd smile to his French valet. Back in bed again, he muttered something more, a little incoherently, lay back among the pillows, dozed, half-woke, dozed again, and became unconscious – for ever.' Lord Sheffield's statement, on which Lytton based this description, is: 'At about half-past eight, he got out of bed, and got into bed again without assistance, better than usual.' The small differences – the addition of an 'odd smile', the omission of the words 'better than usual', serve to suggest a man still philosophically happy, well-co-ordinated, self-sufficient. His end is an orderly, peaceful descent into unconsciousness. We are not told that he was frightened of being left alone, that after returning to his bed he twice implored his servant to stay with him, for such details disturbed the impression of impervious sang-froid. The dying man is a form of aesthetic decoration. Yet Lytton is far from unfeeling, and he describes the last days of Hume – which in many essentials would closely resemble his own slow death – in words that carry a restrained expression of the pathos of human destiny: 'In 1776, when Hume was sixty-five, an internal complaint, to which he had long been subject, completely undermined his health, and recovery became impossible. For many months he knew he was dying, but his mode of life remained unaltered, and, while he gradually grew weaker, his cheerfulness continued unabated. With ease, with gaiety, with the simplicity of perfect taste, he gently welcomed the inevitable. This wonderful equanimity lasted till the very end.'

Perhaps the most acute criticism of *Portraits in Miniature*, and in particular of Lytton's handling of the death scene, has come from Carrington. In the summer of 1931, *The Week-End Review* ran a competition for the best profile of Lytton Strachey – done in his own manner. After briefly reminding its readers of the group of essays entitled 'Six English Historians', the preamble went on: 'Let us suppose that to these a seventh is added – that of Mr. Strachey himself.' Signing herself 'Mopsa', Carrington submitted an imaginary death scene of Lytton, easily winning the prize in a contest that the organizer, Dyneley Hussey, described as having inspired competitors to the best efforts he had ever seen in the course of his experience as a judge. 'If Mopsa be thought cruel,' he wrote, '– and I was in two minds whether on that score she might not have to be ruled out – the victim is, after all, only getting as good as he gives.' Carrington's almost unknown parody, with its quoted *mots*, its contrived suspense, its characteristic turns and twists of phrasing, its jokes, cryptic insinuations and, above all, its flippant, 'thrown-away' moment of extinction, is a wickedly apt mimic of Lytton's style, of the affectations and peculiarities of his personality. Not a word is out of place. It is a perfect caricature, composed with the loving malice of someone who had become utterly immersed in his life, but was moved at times by a fierce, unconscious drive to escape from him.

'Crouching under the ilex tree in his chaise longue, remote, aloof, self-occupied and mysteriously contented, lay the venerable biographer. Muffled in a sealskin coat (for although it was July he felt the cold) he knitted with elongated fingers a coatee for his favourite cat, Tiberius. He was in his 99th year. He did not know it was his last day on earth.

'A constable called for a subscription to local sport. "Trop tard, trop tard; mes jeux sont finis." He gazed at the distant downs; he did not mind – not mind in the very least the thought that this was probably his last summer; after all, summers were now infinitely cold and dismal. One might as well be a mole. He did not particularly care that he was no longer the greatest biographer, or that the Countess no longer – or did he? Had he been a woman he would not have shone as a writer, but as a dissipated mistress of infinite intrigues.

'But – lying on the grass lay a loose button, a particularly revolting specimen; it was an intolerable, an unspeakable catastrophe. He stooped from his chaise longue to pick it up, murmuring to his cat "Mais quelle horreur!" for once stooped too far – and passed away for ever.'

This, the least practical of Carrington's jokes, was to rebound upon herself with tragic consequences, throwing her neurotic temperament fatally out of equilibrium. Some six months afterwards, when Lytton actually died, she became convinced that somehow she had helped to kill him. The unconscious motives behind this parody came to the surface as a fantastic, tormented sense of guilt that assisted in her own pitiable self-destruction – a haunting belief that her fictitious obituary notice had been responsible for Lytton's untimely death.

7

STRACHEY'S FINAL PERIOD

Death was much in Lytton's thoughts over these last few years. The necrology of those who had been close to him makes melancholy reading. Apart from Philip Ritchie and Lady Strachey, whose deaths had affected him most sombrely of all, many of his best and most admired friends had died. Several of them were Apostles.

How fast has brother followed brother,
From Sunshine to the sunless land.

In the spring of 1922, he had gone to the cremation service of one of the eldest and most eminent brothers – Walter Raleigh. Lytton had not seen his uncle Raleigh for two or three years, but the occasion prompted many memories of the old days at Liverpool and Cambridge, and filled him with a sad nostalgia.

The previous year, one of the most brilliant undergraduates, Michael Davies, was drowned bathing at Oxford in almost exactly the same circumstances as his uncle, Lytton's old Trinity friend, Theodore Llewelyn Davies. The pointless annihilation of such a promising young man greatly upset Lytton, bringing back something of the discouraged sense of futility that had overpowered him during the holocaust of the war. 'Michael Davies's death was a dreadful tragedy,' he wrote to Ottoline (29 June 1921). 'He was a charming creature – and what is rarer, an intelligent one. Last year he seemed to me to be the only young man at Oxford or Cambridge with real brains, and I am sure if he had lived he would have been one of the remarkable people of his generation. The uselessness of things is hideous and intolerable.'

Lytton's objection to death was not one simply of humanitarian sentiment. It had something in common with the idea behind Shaw's *Back to Methuselah*. Expectation, not experience, controlled human behaviour. It followed that men and women would only work for a happier world if they could look forward to a longer span of life in which to enjoy it themselves. Above all, it was the purposelessness of death, its indiscriminate desecration and sterility that riled Lytton. The brevity of our lives was such that the thinking few did not have sufficient time to cultivate science, to improve their intellect to its furthest point, or to produce the noble works of creation of which they were capable. Death had incalculably slowed down the advance of civilization, and robbed mankind of untold masterpieces. When Jane Harrison, the classical anthropologist, died in the spring of 1928 aged seventy-seven, Lytton mourned not just the demise of an old friend, but the deprivation to the whole world of a fine talent, a talent that ought to have been permitted to conceive still further ideas, and to continue with her invaluable teaching. 'I've been feeling rather sad about Jane Harrison's death,' he told Roger (18 April 1928). 'She was such a charming rare person – very affectionate and appreciative, very grand, and very amusing. Her humour was unique . . . I had not realised that she was quite as old as 77. What a wretched waste it seems that all that richness of experience and personality should be completely abolished! – Why, one wonders, shouldn't it have gone on and on? – Well! there will never be anyone at all like her again.'

How unreasonable was even the extinction of an old person when his faculties were still intact! One short period of waking past, and we slept for ever – the arrangement seemed ridiculous; it irritated him. There were, in any case, so very few people of genuine talent that the death of any one of them seemed to diminish him personally, for he was involved in mankind. Geoffrey Scott, for instance, who died in August 1929, he had never particularly liked. But he respected his intelligence and felt that the loss to English scholarship was considerable – especially in view of the fact that his work on the multi-volume *Private Papers of James Boswell from Malahide Castle in the Collection of Lt-Colonel Ralph Hayward Isham* had not been completed. Justifiably, Lytton feared that the Boswell papers would be exported from Europe to some tinkering or pottering old transatlantic professor – a dismal fate. 'One doesn't see who can grapple with them,' he wrote to Roger (18 August 1929). 'I only hope they won't be handed over to some wretched American.'

The most serious and fundamental shock of these years was the sudden death of that precocious mathematical logician and philosopher, Frank Ramsey. He had been suffering from an undiagnosed disease of the liver, had entered hospital for an operation, but never recovered. The loss to Cambridge was immense. He was just twenty-six years old, perhaps the most brilliant man of his generation, and the main body of his work as yet hardly begun. Already, like Moore at the turn of the century, he had revived the Society, acting as a tremendous stimulus on his contemporaries and starting up a new, vintage, Apostolic era. He was the same stamp of man as Moore, with the same unassuming, natural manner about him, the same good-natured, unselfseeking character, illuminated by an air of divine vocation. 'I am terribly distressed about Frank,' Lytton wrote to Dadie Rylands (19 January 1930), who had also known him well. 'It is truly tragic. He was one of the few faultless people, with a heavenly simplicity and modesty, which gave a beauty to his genius such as I have never known in anyone else. He had all the charm of childhood, and yet one never doubted for a moment when one was with him that one was in the presence of a very great mind. The last time I spoke to him was – do you remember? – when we met him coming out of the Provost's Lodge, and he told us, with those delightful fits of laughter, about the cat that came into his lecture room. I am miserable – miserable – to think that I shall never be able to make him laugh again, never hear him again at the Society, never again be able to say to myself, after reflecting on the degradation of humanity – "Well, after all, there is Frank". The loss to your generation is agonising to think of – and the world will never know what has happened – what a light has gone out. I always thought there was something of Newton about him – the ease and majesty of the thought – the gentleness of the temperament – and suppose Newton had died at – how old was he? – twenty-six? – I am afraid Richard [Braithwaite][1] will be particularly upset – will you please give him my love?'

The following month, another pre-eminent Apostle had collapsed and died after a short illness – Lytton's friend, C. P. Sanger. He had belonged to that class of men, aspiring yet unambitious, whom Lytton most unenviously admired. Like Ramsey, like Moore, and very few

[1] In 1931, Professor Richard Braithwaite (b. 1900), at that time University Lecturer in Moral Science (now Knightsbridge Professor of Moral Philosophy at Cambridge), edited and introduced a volume of Frank Ramsey's posthumous papers entitled *The Foundations of Mathematics* – 'mostly quite incomprehensible', Lytton claimed (7 October 1931), 'and even those recommended (by Braithwaite in his introduction) to the "general reader" seem to me alarmingly obscure. I'm glad to see that G. E. Moore (in a preface) confesses that (owing no doubt to his stupidity) he can make neither head nor tail of them. One *can* see an extraordinary eminence, though, showing through the fog.'

others, he had combined great talent with natural modesty, and in his qualities of sincerity, of humour and humility, he fulfilled the highest ideals of the Apostles. Sanger was one of the most penetrating intellects and one of the most truly noble characters, Lytton once declared, he had ever encountered. His kindness in the far-off days at Trinity had been a wonderful benefit for a young man, and their friendship ever since had remained a cherished possession. He was one of those men whose extraordinarily great attributes were never, because of their very greatness, properly appreciated by the world at large. For some days beforehand, Lytton had realized that the end was probably inevitable. 'A nervous breakdown was the apparent cause,' he explained to Roger (11 February 1930). 'I fear it was the result of a long process of over-work, underfeeding, and general discomfort – a wretched business. He had an astonishing intellect; but accompanied by such modesty that the world in general hadn't any idea of his very great distinction. And he was so absolutely unworldly that the world's inattention was nothing to him. I knew him ever since Cambridge days, when he constantly came for week-ends for the Apostles' meetings – and then in London, when, at first, they lived in a little set of rooms at Charing Cross – and afterwards by a curious chance, Philip [Ritchie] became an added link between us. How he loved Philip, and how often he used to talk to me about him, with mild expostulations over his illnesses! – And so all that is over now, and I shall never go to New Square again.'

The deaths of these friends prompted within Lytton many bitter-sweet memories over the past, and these were given a new twist and impetus by Sebastian Sprott, who had again come down to Ham Spray to arrange and file away the last of Lytton's vast bundles of correspond-ence. As before, Lytton could not resist dipping into these papers, though they aroused in him a whole range of complicated sensations. Why, he wondered, should it sometimes depress him so much to go through old letters? Perhaps there was some false illusion attached to it, like the putting on of a pair of distorting spectacles, some hallucina-tion that persuaded one to view distant episodes as other than they were.

For assuredly the past seemed more exciting than the present. Otto-line had written him a letter that April which recalled many incidents now long closed and half-forgotten. He seldom saw Ottoline these days – just occasionally in Gower Street, where she presided as the faded relic of a great hostess. In her prime, she had been a splendid figure, he remembered; but disaster seemed to have spread over her relationships like a winter blight. Even in her best days she had possessed no self-knowledge and no control over her vigorous contradictory instincts.

She referred in her letter to the ashes and poisonous vapours scattered on what might have been too good; yet the ashes and vapours, alas, had been of her own making. Lytton experienced some uneasiness over answering this letter. After all, one could not get milk when the udder had run dry. Clearly a certain amount of sentiment was called for, and a little sincerity, too – but how tactfully to provide it? After ten days' hesitation, he replied in what was to be the last long communication to pass between them, kind, partly truthful, agreeably clouded with metaphor, the conclusion to a long friendship, now obsolete. 'For me,' he wrote (18 April 1931), 'getting to know you was a wonderful experience – ah! those days at Peppard – those evenings in Bedford Square! I cannot help surmising that if H[enry] L[amb] had been a *little* different – things would have been *very* different, but perhaps that is an impossible notion. Perhaps we are all so deeply what we are that the slightest shift is out of the question. I don't think I want to go back. It was thrilling, enchanting, devastating, all at once – one was in a special (a very special) train, tearing along at breakneck speed – where? – one could only dimly guess – one might be off the rails – at any moment. Once is enough! . . . I have been astonishingly happy now for a long time – if only life were a good deal longer – and the sunshine less precarious!'

Yet it was sometimes less the sunshine than the sunless land that had begun to preoccupy Lytton. When a number of one's contemporaries and people from a younger generation die, one's mind automatically considers the possibility of one's own death. Something of the sober, practical mood of Lytton's thoughts at this time may be glimpsed from an entry made by Carrington in *D. C. Partridge: HER BOOK*, dated 20 March 1931. 'At tea Lytton said to me. "Remember all the bird Books and flower Books are yours". I said "Why". "Well, after I am dead it would be important". Then I said, and "all my pictures, and objects are yours". and he said "Really?" almost as if he didn't believe me. I said "but if you died first —" but I felt suddenly serious, and gloomy, and Lytton noticing the change, like a wind sweeping across the lawn through the laurels, changed the conversation.'

But the interior dialogue persisted. He did not expect to die, and looked forward like most of his family to a long life. Yet there were other reasons, besides the deaths of his friends, to account for these vague forebodings. Throughout 1931 he was almost perpetually ill. These illnesses did not in themselves appear to be very serious, but they seldom left him in peace and their cumulative effect was very enfeebling. Of course, he had been familiar with sickness all his life. But in the past, it seems probable that part at least of his bad health had been self-induced. Now, when, unknown to himself, he was in the clutch of an insidious and lethal disease, his condition appeared, paradoxically, less real to him. The sensation was very odd. As if anaesthetized, he felt that his physical awareness of things was being painfully wrenched apart from his emotional or spiritual consciousness, as though he had become strangely suspended, almost stationary as in a dream, between two orbits of existence, swimming lightly between them while all the other solid entities of the universe rushed about him on their well-co-ordinated courses. It was not so much a vivid pain that attacked him as the blurred, invading presence of some internal discomfort that he could not precisely define or locate, and which made all movement unpleasant, and sitting or bending curiously difficult. At first his physician, Dr Starkey Smith, diagnosed internal piles and prescribed some suppositories. Later, changing his diagnosis, he arranged for Lytton to be attended by a professional masseuse and treated with an ultra-violet lamp. The wandering symptoms came and went, and came again in a more complicated form, accompanied by headaches, a slight temperature and a buzzing in the ears that made him slightly deaf. 'I feel inclined to retire into a monastery,' he concluded after four months of these disorders (31 April 1931), 'but on second thoughts that couldn't be much good really – a nunnery, possibly . . .'.

In his letters, Lytton invariably makes light of his illness, is invariably eager to detect and report the least symptom of a recovery. He admits that he feels weak, describes his condition as 'tiresome', but, always hopeful of a quick improvement, predicts that, within a few days, he will be brisker again. Yet the truth is that this long series of attacks had bankrupted his physical resources so that he found it more and more difficult to sustain a period of resuscitation. Occasionally he comes near to admitting this deficiency and its darker implications: 'I suppose I am gradually recovering,' he wrote to Roger (26 January 1931), 'but there are still moments when I feel as if I were at the bottom of a well with only the dimmest chance of getting out.'

Rather uncharacteristically, too, perhaps because he no longer had any unconscious control over his ailments, Lytton was frightened of appearing fussy and over-tedious to his friends. Especially he feared, through seeming a liability, to incur the disapproval of Roger Senhouse, whom he nevertheless issued with regular hebdomadal bulletins of his progress – often in the form of optimistic pronouncements which had to be quickly corrected by disappointing statements of fact. 'As for my health,' he wrote on 20 March 1931, the same day as his recorded conversation with Carrington, 'it's now becoming the Grand Bore of Christendom, and I fear to refer to it. However, I'll just remark that

I'm perhaps rather better – but not yet right. I feel quite well – and then seem to sink back into a buzzing ineptitude.'

Because of his invalidism, Lytton was restricted for most of this year to an unusually subdued mode of life down at Ham Spray. He seemed to exist in something of a trance, incorporeal and fairly contented, supersensible to the familiar yet ever-changing surroundings, from which he took his mood. Winter gave way to spring with its lovely pale afternoon colours spreading across the Downs, its friendly unemphatic shapes, its gently falling rain and bright watery sunbursts; and spring soon merged into summer, turning the trees into a lush and tropical green, and the field in front of the house to a brilliant yellow, up to the eyes in buttercups. In the long twilight evenings, he would wander off, sometimes alone, sometimes with Carrington or one or more of his house guests – Saxon Sydney-Turner, Raymond Mortimer and Francis Birrell, Virginia Woolf, David Garnett or Clive Bell – for walks across the country, to gaze over the calm crepuscular landscape and reflect upon how English it all was and how admirably it suited him. While his multiplying ailments continued to nag and gnaw at him, he turned increasingly to exterior comforts, to the company of his oldest friends, to the soothing solitude of Nature. He was reading Keats, 'who is perfect', and whose poetry always seemed to heighten his awareness of the slumbering mystery of the vegetable world, making him feel at one with it. 'C. and I are left alone in this vague garden with its weeds and roses – ah! one draws a long breath, and looks out dreamily at the dreaming downs,' he wrote to Roger on 29 June. 'Last night, just after sunset, an extraordinary light, as of some vast motor car appeared behind the trees on the top of the downs – a blaze between the trunks – we gazed – and then realised that it was the moon, that was just there – it moved rapidly upwards and sideways – a surprising and romantic spectacle, until at last it was balanced – a golden circle on the edge of the hill.'

They were unexciting but seldom boring, these first seven months. 'Life trundles along here in the quietest style,' he told Roger (17 April 1931), '– the question of the next book to read is the only pebble that ruffles the surface of the pond. Yesterday there was an event though – 2 visitors by aeroplane – viz. Dorelia and Kaspar John. The latter took C. up for a turn – she adored it; but *I* refrained – the attraction, somehow or other, was not sufficient.' After her flight, Carrington again tried to coax Lytton into going up, but he seemed not at all keen, and Caspar John felt that he must be cursing him under his breath. Mentally and physically he recoiled from Carrington's entreaties to 'have a go'. 'No,' he said. 'It is too violent – too alarming – too positive – too demanding an experience for me to contemplate.' Carrington replied that she knew him well enough to tell him that it would be none of these things, and Caspar chipped in to say that he would certainly deal gently with one of so gentle a nature. Dorelia then asked him how, in the future, he would be able to discipline Carrington if he wilted where she had braved, and the argument continued until they had reached, what was for Lytton, the safety of the house. The dreaded two-seater aeroplane was now out of sight in the field beyond the trees, and with renewed confidence he rounded on his tormentors, and in high-pitched words declared that he was the wrong *shape* for flying and that his beard presented a hazard that was likely to foul the controls. Exhausted, he coiled himself down into an armchair. There was no more to be said, and so ended the story of his non-flight with a future admiral of the fleet.

Most social events now appeared to him as lacking in attraction, and he had little wish to meet new people. When he stayed up in Gordon Square among the Bloomsbury crowd he had 'to clench my teeth in preparation for the infernal boredom of the next few weeks'. He went down to King's, by affinity, though not by topography, an extension of Bloomsbury, and although there was certainly no diminution of social life, 'it's the social life of a preparatory school to my mind'. With Alan Searle – 'my Bronzino Boy' as he used to call him – he visited Oswald Balfour[1] at the White House, in Thorpe-le-Soken, Essex, but was not sorry to leave after two nights. The Bronzino had behaved very tiresomely, to his mind, getting himself bitten in the stomach by their host's bulldogs, and then collapsing into hysterics; an intolerable Dickensian charwoman called Mrs Scroggins had appeared and bearded Lytton from morning to night with tales of village politics; and the rest of the house guests seemed sorry figures all of them, a melancholy, painful crew – Nature's second fiddles. Towards Oswald Balfour himself, the first violin, Lytton did not feel the least attraction at all 'except physically in a very odious way. The English upper class characteristic of going in for character as opposed to mind is annoying,' he commented to Roger (4 July 1931), 'even when it crops up in such queer (in every sense of the word) surroundings.'

It was a relief after paltry adventures such as this to return from the queerness and the bulldogs of the White House to the cats and queerness of Ham Spray, where the only complication was a certain hesitation over what book to read. George Trevelyan's *Queen Anne* was 'very

---

[1] Lieutenant-Colonel Oswald Balfour, who had been military secretary to the governor-general of Canada (1920–23) and who, before his death in 1953, became a prominent industrialist, chairman and director of several steel companies.

good and instructive', and the ex-prime minister A. J. Balfour's *Chapters of Autobiography* he thought 'very well done in its way – that is the way that tells you nothing of any real interest – curiously 18th century, in fact – so clear and limited. But the silly fellow was a Christian, and that I cannot forgive.' Philip Guedalla's Life of Wellington, *The Duke*, he could not finish – 'after going through the Peninsular War and Waterloo, I've given up,' he told Roger (7 October 1931), '– the way of writing is too tiresome and the mentality too thin to make 500 gigantic pages endurable. Queen V[ictoria]'s letters are much better in every way – so full of incident and feeling, and so idiotically to the point.'[1]

Among recent fiction, there was a new novel by Somerset Maugham – to whom he had once been introduced by Alan Searle – the notorious *Cakes and Ale*. This book, he explained to Dorothy Bussy (November 1930) 'is causing some excitement here as it contains a most envenomed portrait of Hugh Walpole, who is out of his mind with agitation and horror. It is a very amusing book, apart from that – based obviously on Hardy's history (more or less) – only marred, to my mind, by some curious lack of distinction.' In other contemporary novels he could, as usual, find little merit. 'I don't know what to read,' he complained to Roger (27 June 1931), '– except perhaps Mr. Gerhardi.'[2]

Eventually, for want of anything better, he fell back on Proust, determined finally to get to the end of his great *roman à clef*. Everyone had urged him to read it – in particular Clive Bell – but oh! the effort required to restart that heavy, shapeless monstrosity, with its labyrinthine analyses, its endless subjective digressions, its infinitely protracted involutions of prose. In the second volume of his fine biography of Proust, Mr George Painter has listed Lytton's name among the earliest admirers of Proust's work in Britain. Certainly the Bloomsbury Group as a whole appear to have taken him up, convinced that, since he dissected life at a different angle from his predecessors, he would alter our attitude to life. But Lytton could never really be termed a Proustian.[3] For him, books

---

[1] Lytton, in fact, had never thought well of Guedalla's work. Professor John Dover Wilson, in a letter to the author (18 May 1964), recounts that when, in about 1926, 'I saw him [Lytton] off at King's, I said, "There's a lecture going on in the Hall as you go by. You might like to go and listen, incognito." "What!" he said. "In this beard?" The lecturer, I replied, was also a famous figure, Philip Guedalla. "One of my imitators?" was his comment.'

[2] *Pending Heaven*, William Gerhardie's fourth novel, about two men treading the donkey-round of paradise deferred, their literary friendship strained to breaking-point by rivalry in love, had been published a few weeks beforehand.

[3] But he liked Proust more than Joyce. In a letter to his brother James (7 May 1922) he had written: 'My only serious occupation is the reading of Proust, and that I do find a pretty strenuous business. As for Ulysses, I *will not* look at it, *no*, N O.'

were like friends, and reading an extension of companionship – a way of expanding beyond the circumference of time and place the circle of one's kindred acquaintances. For Proust, on the other hand, art was the only purpose and justification of life. Worldly pleasures caused the kind of ailment provoked by the ingestion of abject nourishment; at best friendship, which was always a simulation, could throw up fresh material to be distilled off into his life's work; at worst, by wasting valuable time, it represented a sacrifice of reality – that sole reality that was his novel. The precious, egocentric austerity of this vocational spirit was quite foreign to Lytton, who strove to combine the truth of his writing with some extraneous entertainment, and so, by adding to the sense and gaiety of nations, enrich our *savoir vivre*. Proust gave no quarter to entertainment for entertainment's sake. *A La Recherche du Temps Perdu* is not a book to read, but to re-read – yet Lytton could hardly read it at all. Had literature, even fine literature, he wondered, got to be so dull? What, in any case, was this subtle quality of unreadability which Proust possessed in such an astonishing degree? No wonder he had felt himself unable to provide an Introduction to C. K. Scott-Moncrieff's matchless translation of *Swann's Way*. And so he grimly struggled on, boredom clogging admiration on every magnificent, laborious page. Then, with a sigh of relief, he turned to other more amiable books – Diderot's letters, and the verses of that 'supreme poet' Burns. 'I now spend all my spare time reading Burns,' he had told Dadie Rylands (26 November 1930), '– an unfashionable occupation, no doubt; but personally I prefer him to T. S. Eliot. I was led on to this by the new life of him, by a woman called [Catherine] Carswell[1] – not at all badly done and full of interest.'

Because of the dearth of new reading matter, he soon came back to some of his old favourites, in particular to the sixteenth century. 'So here I am in my solitude,' he wrote from Ham Spray to Roger (12 May 1931), 'buried in books – chiefly about old atheists – such strange stories are told of them! The Elizabethans grow more and more peculiar. In Norwich, about 1580, a unitarian was burnt alive, but as a preliminary had his ears cut off! – Because he had said things about the Queen as well as about Christ! Then there was a superb Dutch Inquisitor, about 1500, who suddenly had a revulsion, and declared in public that Christianity was idiocy, Christ a scoundrel, immortality a delusion, and that there was no God. He was imprisoned for 10 years, and then,

---

[1] 'I still go on with Burns. Do you?' Lytton asked Dadie Rylands (28 December 1930). 'There is an essay on him by Walter Raleigh in "Some Authors" which is worth reading, and contains a superb quotation from one of Keats's letters. It reminded me of what one sometimes forgets – that Keats was far the most delightful person who ever existed.'

as he was unrepentant, burnt alive. Perhaps on the whole we live in better times, but it's difficult to calculate.'

Possibly some compromise, he thought, between the sixteenth and twentieth century would have suited him best. And this, in a sense, was what he evolved. For the fantasies which these old stories gave rise to in his mind acted as a makeweight in his emotional life, a deviation through which he sought to make up for the satisfaction he had failed to extract within his own person and from his own times. They were the excitements of a man partly and permanently disappointed in his aspirations of forming an actual, ideal intimacy. For some years the sado-masochistic imagery of this make-believe, taken largely from the randy and savage days of Elizabeth, and framed in total contrast to his kindly, gentle behaviour in practice, had not altered very much. But the fantasies persisted and grew in strength while the relationship upon which they had been constructed dwindled, and from acting as a stimulation of love, they were becoming a substitute for it. By this time he had known Roger for seven years – perhaps too long, since his capacity for being surprised by him, for some months on the wane, seemed finally to have been exhausted. Roger's dogged unpredictability no longer enlivened him; he expected it, and it wearied him. Tenderness and great affection certainly he still felt, but the gross adulation he had directed towards him had too often in the past dispersed itself into the empty spaces left by Roger's elusiveness; and the spell of vacuity had ceased to bewilder and entrance him. Even Roger's virtues could be singularly exasperating. Always unmercenary, he never bartered affection for gifts. Naturally, Lytton did not want this; but there is no doubt that he would have liked to barricade him round with presents. Besides, he enjoyed spending money on him, taking him to places that he knew beforehand he would like and watching his pleasure. He did not ask for gratitude, but resented Roger's vague distaste for accepting too much. After one reconciliation, for instance, Lytton had offered to buy him a Citroën car – but Roger simply did not want it. Lytton's fears, too, of six months ago were now being realized. Earlier in the year, Roger had been 'simply angelic' about his illnesses. But gradually his attitude seemed to change, becoming more casual and indefinite. 'My mood lately has been a new one for me,' Lytton wrote to him on 18 August. 'I've had the feeling that our relationship was coming to a dead end – or perhaps just fading away.'

From the fatigue and disillusion of love he escaped back into writing again. To abstract his mind from these 'dim and helpless' reflections over Roger, he began 'a thing on Othello' which was 'fiendishly difficult to do, as it's all solid argument – and is perhaps rather mad; but

I shall try to finish it'. 'Othello', which was never finished but appeared in its uncompleted form in the posthumous volume, *Characters and Commentaries*, was planned as the first of a series of essays upon some of Shakespeare's plays. Perhaps because of his failing strength, it is a sadly disappointing piece of work, inferior by far to his 'Shakespeare's Final Period'. After many years he had returned from biography to literary criticism as a refuge from his life, with the result that there is little sense of human reality in this essay. It is literary criticism written to an inanimate formula, an inorganic thing, which suffers from the method of coming to premature aesthetic conclusions, and arguing in odds and ends afterwards, often ingeniously, to fit in with them.

The 'solid argument' of 'Othello' has at its centre the concept of dramatic necessity. Shakespeare, as we know, went for his plot to the seventh story in the third decade of Cinthio's *Hecatommithi*. But was it not possible, Lytton asks, that he also deliberately submitted himself to the Greek theatrical influence? Cinthio's story was bleak and colourless; the salient features of *Othello* were its passion and strong characterization. The reason for this difference, Lytton suggests, may have been due to Shakespeare having studied Sophocles. Ignoring the fiery and intensely personal love-poem which runs through this play, its power released by a deep longing for some ideal unflawed beauty, and confining himself absolutely to its constructive principles, Lytton then draws a parallel between the basic scheme of *Othello* and that of *Œdipus Tyrannus*. The dramatic requirements for Œdipus' situation were, he explains, naturally not identical with those needed for the different plan of Shakespeare's tragedy. But he makes his comparison by noting how the incidental similarity and contrast between the two principal characters, Œdipus and Othello, stem automatically from the theatrical demands of each play. From this hypothesis, Lytton proceeds to follow his examination backwards in finer detail, conducting a post-mortem on the dead carcass of the plays at the expense of the still-living spirit. That critical literature has not lost much through this dehydrated paper remaining unfinished, may be judged from such flashes as: 'At one of the supreme moments of Othello's tragedy ... Shakespeare puts into his mouth the astonishing lines about the Propontic and the Euxine. What manner of man is this? We need no telling: it is the mariner, whose mind, in the stress of an emotional crisis, goes naturally to the sea.'

In his comments both upon Othello and Iago, Lytton treats the play as a theme on which Shakespeare worked from the outside. He shows no sense of the internal, emotional necessity which at that moment in Shakespeare's life made him attempt an imaginative solution to the conflict between his belief in virtue and his experience of human nature, and he makes use of Shakespeare's drama of jealousy and passion to distract himself from the lassitude and vain expectations of his own love-life. But why *Othello*? At first sight the choice of such a play seems entirely inappropriate. But Lytton's instinct and knowledge of Shakespeare were not at fault. Recently, in a more optimistic and invigorated mood, he had wanted to write an essay on *King Lear*. Now he rejected that supreme masterpiece of concentrated, agonizing reality for a tragedy that, although a triumph of dramatic technique, is peopled not by human beings, but by creations of stagecraft, untouched by the fresh winds of heaven and unaffected by the common things of earth. Since Lytton wanted to forget the presence of actual people, he buried himself in the world of these magnificent phantoms, whose energy was simply that of their master-manipulator. Like some of his own biographical portraits, these men were too over-simplified for reality: Othello is too noble, Iago too evil.

Iago, especially, has been the great stumbling-block of literary critics, and it is when examining Iago's character that the inadequacy of Lytton's methods is most obvious. In Cinthio's story, Lytton reminds us, Iago was governed by a very real and powerful motive in that he, as well as Othello, loved Desdemona. Why then did Shakespeare discard this plausible motive and reduce the impulse behind Iago's treachery merely to the love of evil for its own sake? The answer, Lytton claims, lay once again in the play's dramatic requirements. To depict two characters in love with the same woman would have thrown out the artistic balance of the piece. Shakespeare, therefore, must have re-adjusted the regulation plot for one reason alone – to complete the structural effect of his story:

'Othello is to be deluded into believing that Desdemona is faithless; he is to kill her; and then he is to discover that his belief was false. This is the situation, the horror of which is to be intensified in every possible way: the tragedy must be enormous and unrelieved. But there is one eventuality which might, in some degree at any rate, mitigate the atrocity of the story. If Iago had been led to cause this disaster by his love for Desdemona, in that very fact would lie some sort of comfort, the tragedy would have been brought about by a motive not only comprehensible but in a sense sympathetic; the hero's passion and the villain's would be the same. Let it be granted, then, that the completeness of the tragedy would suffer if its origin lay in Iago's love for Desdemona; therefore let that motive be excluded from Iago's mind. The question immediately presents itself – in that case, for what reason are we to suppose that Iago acted as he did? The whole story depends upon his plot, which forms the machinery of the action; yet, if the

Desdemona impulsion is eliminated, what motive for his plot can there be? Shakespeare supplied the answer to this question with one of the very greatest strokes of his genius. By an overwhelming effort of creation he summoned out of the darkness a psychological portent that was exactly fitted to the requirements of the tragic situation with which he was dealing, and endowed it with reality. He determined that Iago should have no motive at all . . . This triumphant invention of the motivelessness of Iago has been dwelt upon by innumerable commentators; but none, so far as I know, has pointed out the purpose of it, and the dramatic necessity which gave it birth . . .'

From one of Lytton's letters to Dadie Rylands, it appears that not long before embarking on this paper, he had been studying Professor G. Wilson Knight's recently published *The Wheel of Fire*, the first volume of that tetralogy which would, with the blessing of T. S. Eliot, inaugurate a new school of Shakespearian study. There is no evidence to show that this work had specifically influenced what he wrote. But, following Wilson Knight's general principles of Shakespeare interpretation, he avoids any attempt to criticize, that is to detect or point out faults, but assuming the works of Shakespeare to be of a transcendent order, he deduces that *Othello* must be perfect. Under this idealistic gaze, apparent blemishes melt away, and necessity takes their place. For Wilson Knight, it was the necessity of poetic vision; for Lytton, it is the aesthetic necessity of dramatic form. His essay is therefore in the nature of a reconstruction rather than a criticism, and follows the general tradition of Coleridge, who speaks of Iago's 'motiveless malignity', and elsewhere confesses that where he and Shakespeare are out of sympathy, it is he himself who must be in the wrong.

The disadvantages of the pure deductive approach – that it tends to substitute the play for actual life and reduce the poetry to a question of linguistics, sound and design, a question of style divorced from our personal emotions and experiences – can perhaps best be demonstrated by comparing the above passage from Lytton's essay with an equivalent passage from Hugh Kingsmill's *The Return of William Shakespeare*, a work of highly individual judgement which had come out in 1929, but which Lytton does not seem to have read. '*Othello*', Kingsmill explains, 'expresses the struggle between two opposing forces in Shakespeare himself, not, like *Lear*, the conflict between the complete man and the nature of things. Neither of the two principal characters, therefore, is a whole human being. Othello is almost exclusively passion seeking an ideal satisfaction, Iago almost exclusively the intellect disintegrating passion by exposing its roots in sensuality. . . . As for Iago, I cannot see him at all. You will remember that, at the end, Othello looks at Iago's feet to see if he is hoofed like a devil; a touch which, in the equally passionate atmosphere of *Lear*, would seem unnatural if directed against Edmund.'

Within this criticism, the tragedy of Othello reflects, not just a matchless exercise in play-making, but, in a simplified and over-idealized form, the tragedy of a Shakespeare who was attempting to isolate and destroy his perception of evil with which virtue and beauty are entangled on earth, and to re-establish virtue and beauty in immaculate perfection as realizable within human experience. That Iago was not the enemy of this ideal, but some defect inherent in life itself, could only become clearer to Shakespeare after he had revenged himself on Iago and expiated his remorse in Othello – a development which has taken place in the ensuing *King Lear* and *Macbeth*.

The symbolic value which Kingsmill attaches to Othello and Iago saves one from forcing some kind of actual plausibility into Iago's motives, or from concocting some ingenious schematic reason to account for his abysmal spirit of evil. At the same time, it resolves the discrepancy between Othello, the sober, elderly general, and the Othello who strikes Desdemona in front of the Venetian envoy, Lodovico. While Othello embodies Shakespeare's generous, re-awakened idealism, the function of Iago, like that of Philip Francis in Lytton's dissertation on Warren Hastings, is to force the unqualified idealist 'to see life from the opposite standpoint, which explains every action in terms of lust or self-interest; and he so far succeeds that, while the agony of Othello is not the mere rage of sensual jealousy, neither is it to be characterised as simply, in Coleridge's phrase, "the solemn agony" of a disillusioned idealist, but as the medley of both these passions which Shakespeare himself experienced.'

By constantly bringing his sense of the man Shakespeare before our view, Kingsmill – like Johnson in his Preface and Notes, like Hazlitt, Walter Raleigh, Peter Quennell and a few others – is able to show us the extraordinary generic quality of his mind. This intuitive, personal angle of criticism, though sometimes blurred by self-identification and emotional prejudice, can make us understand Shakespeare's vivid power of communication with all other minds, in ages past and present. He is like us, and he is like others too, having within himself the roots of every faculty and feeling. But Lytton's 'Othello' neglects this quality; it lies outside the scope of his examination. He presents *Othello* as a flawless dramatic pattern created, not by a man like us, but by some automaton, some tragedy-computer which has been fed with the ingredients of a simple plot and a vast store of knowledge relating to the machinery of the Greek Theatre. And that is all.

8

FAREWELL TO FRANCE

The unreality of 'Othello' was partly a consequence of Lytton's dis-
pirited mood this summer – itself the result of steadily worsening
health and a worried antipathy arising from his relationship with
Roger Senhouse. The essay was written with his last reserves of strength,
and they were exhausted before he could finish it.

A less arduous flight from reality, he seems to have felt, would be to
leave England for a while, and travel gently abroad. He had been invited
by Raymond Mortimer to join him, Francis Birrell and Clive Bell in
Venice, but decided instead to go off by himself on a 'little perambula-
tion' round France. He wanted to cut adrift from people, from common
sense. He was tired: tired of humanity, tired of real life, tired, in fact, of
everything except poetry and poetical dreams. Solitude alone could
relieve his weariness – solitude, plenty of comfort, good food, and
travel from one palliative place to another. He wished to console his
spirit with beauty, to be uncomplicated, uninvolved. For the time being,
his problems seemed too intricate and universal to unburden upon any
confidant. Carrington, in any case, had parted only recently from Snipe
and was too full of her own guilt-ridden worries to be overloaded with
his. And Dadie Rylands could never be trusted as a brother-confessor
with matters that concerned Roger. And so, for the first time since
1902, Lytton resorted to keeping a diary. 'A Fortnight in France', as he
labelled the exercise book to which, each night, he committed his
reflections and the impressions of his journey, is one of the best and
most unselfconscious of his autobiographical pieces, and before the end
of September, when he returned to England, it had helped to purge
much of his temporary distaste for life.

He started out for Paris on 3 September, arriving at the Hôtel
Berkeley, in the Avenue Matignon, later that day. After many weeks of
strangely febrile tension, he could at last take a long breath, rest on his
oars, pause and look round. More than once that summer, his visionary
existence had seemed more real than the physical world around him.
He was drowsy with a nervous, highly-strung defatigation that seemed
to recall and to include all the bodily and love-sickness of the past.
Nostalgia soothed and confused him with mixed feelings – a distant
reminder of that brief interlude in Paris some twenty-five years ago
with Duncan Grant, up those forty-two soaring flights of stairs in the
Hôtel de l'Univers et du Portugal, and other visits, the most recent
and most vivid of them with Roger. He was alone this time, but not

lonely. Places, not people, exercised the forefront of his mind. By the time he returned to his hotel that night, satisfaction and sleepiness blanketed all other sensations.

'I am sleepy after the journey and the excitement of Paris,' he wrote on the first page of his diary late that night, '– after the hideous examination of so many horrid people – after the doubts and alarms which will even still attack me about my luggage and the non-appearance of porters – after the enormous lunch in the train – after several chapters of Lord Salisbury – after the Lord knows what besides. . . . After the decidedly dreary and by no means cheap dinner at the restaurant here, I struggled out to a glass of coffee at the Rond Point . . . and then, not very conscious, strolled down the Champs-Elysées towards the Place de la Concorde, in the darkness. Lights in the distance caught my eye, and then I remembered the new illuminations. I went on, beginning to be excited, and soon came to the really magical scene: the enormous place – the surrounding statues – the twin palaces on the north side – and in the middle the astonishing spectacle of the obelisk, a brilliant luminous white, with black hieroglyphics, clear as if drawn by ink all over it. A move to the right revealed the Madeleine; and then, looking back, I saw the Arc de Triomphe, brightly lighted, with the avenue of lamps leading to it. A most exhilarating affair! It was warm, the innumerable motors buzzed, the strollers were many and – so it seemed – sympathetic.'

The next day, after a visit to the Louvre and lunch at Foyot's, he left Paris by train for Rheims – literally 'a godforsaken city'. He was dismayed at seeing the large areas of the original town that had been hopelessly wiped out by the war, including, of course, the cathedral. 'Naturally with the cathedral banished God goes,' he observed; 'but what's more serious is that nearly everything else has gone as well. I had imagined a few neat German bombs had blown up the sacred building and that that was all. Far from it – the whole town was wrecked. A patched-up remnant is all that remains – the patches dated 1920. Miserable!'

The next morning it was drizzling with rain, and Lytton set off with overcoat and umbrella to explore the town more thoroughly. 'The Cathedral, what with pre-war restorations, war destructions, and post-war restorations, presents a deplorable spectacle,' he noted down in his diary. 'I doubt whether even in its palmiest days it was anything very much – except, probably, for the glass. I tottered away from it to lose myself in dreary streets, jumping sky-high at one moment before the startled gaze of an elderly inhabitant – an attack of the Strachey twist.'

Like a true hypochondriac, he scrutinized, half-relished and pencilled

down his spasms and convulsions with sensuous care. All his adult life
he had dreamed of breaking out from the prison of his wretched body,
to which his ailments acted as the pin-pricks of an unwelcome reminder.
And recently, in the last months, these dreams had begun to obtrude
over reality, so that he felt himself to be moving along two unconnected
planes of existence – one, the familiar yet oddly remote part of Lytton
Strachey; the other, vacuous and undefined, just beyond the gross
envelope of his physical being. It was as if these attacks of the
'Strachey twist' were the literal, premature straining of his spirit to
wriggle free from the dying carcass in which it was incarcerated. And
because this escape was partly successful, he could look upon himself
now more objectively, from the outside, no longer overwhelmed by
the humiliation and remorse of youth. Still pre-occupied with his
appearance, he had learnt to accept it with resignation, with humour,
and with a kind of shocked detachment that made it appear as if he were
regarding someone else. Even the inexorable advance of middle age did
not affect him so sharply as once he thought it must. Passing down the
rue St-Honoré one day, he inspected his own image mirrored back to
him in a shop-window, philosophically, like some sophisticated
woman *d'un certain âge* before her dressing-table. 'I saw for the first
time,' he recorded, 'how completely gray my hair was over my temples.
So that has come at last! I was beginning to think it never would. Do I
feel like it? Perhaps I do a little – a very little. A certain sense of
detachment declares itself amid the agitations that continue to strew
my path.'

This, then, was the consolation of a middle age he had once so
dreaded. A numbness had spread over his being, cushioning him from
the awful heartache and the pain that only a short time ago could
plummet him into such terrifying despair. It was an agreeable change.
Buoyed up by a curious composure in the region of the heart, he felt
that he could never again be much upset by romantic trials. The india-
rubber ball, having been bounced up against a brick wall an infinity
of times, had finally sunk quietly to the floor. At any rate, thank heaven,
he seemed to have achieved some kind of detachment about Roger. As
on a previous occasion some two years back, Roger had gone off with
his friends to the Riviera in preference to travelling with Lytton. But
'I hardly feel as if I *could* now be shattered by him as I was,' Lytton
reflected. '. . . I am really calm – that dreadful abysmal sensation in the
pit of the stomach is absent. What a relief! Whether this means that I
am out of love or not I can't pretend to say. I hope it means that my
feelings are at least more rational. The inexpressible charm of his
presence, the sweetness of his temper, his beautiful affectionateness–

why should these things make it difficult for me to accept the facts that
he must be allowed to have his own tastes, and that his tastes happen not
to be what I would have wished?'

Every renunciation should be followed by regret; and it was this
placid absence of regret that perplexed Lytton. Could it be maturity?
Could his chloroformed fading away of awareness be what was termed
'the prime of life'? Thoughts of age led him unavoidably back to
thoughts of death. Maybe death itself was merely an extension of this
agreeable anaesthesia that had invaded him. But what, in that case, was
his attitude to death? Dying, perhaps, would be, as people said, like
leaving a party, and it must all depend on what party one was leaving.
'If one's in love with life,' he wrote, 'to leave it will be as terrible as the
dreadful moment when one has to leave one's beloved one – an agony,
long foreseen – almost impossibly fearful – and yet it inevitably comes.
And really it is a kind of death whenever the beloved object goes;
which is why sleeping together is such a peculiar solace – death is
avoided – one loses consciousness deliciously alive.'

Then again this mild, inebriated mood would shift, and he felt that
his half-alive composure could not possibly survive his re-crossing of
the Channel. He was not ready yet to return to England. His antipathy
to life in general had centred upon the English. One had only to see
them here, in Rheims, among the French – their shapeless features,
their desiccated self-conscious expressions, their idiotic little clipped
moustaches . . . but enough! Presently he would be working himself
up into a rage. And no doubt the French, too, were just as bad in their
own way. One evening at a restaurant in Rheims, he noticed a sober,
white-haired, rather indigent Englishman at the next table, undoubtedly
an admirable example of the race. A schoolmaster, perhaps, – no, a
cashier – with his unfortunate wife. Quiet, dim, but able to speak to the
waiter with complete efficiency. Lytton envied him – except that he
had made that fatal mistake of a wife. How did one speak to waiters?
One of the main problems of existence, he sometimes thought.

On his last day in Rheims, the weather cleared, and having strolled
through the Musée, with its remarkable tapestries from the cathedral
and its multitude of odds and ends, he went to look at some of the
champagne cellars. 'The Musée, anyhow, was better than Mumm's
cellars,' he decided, 'with their pointless miles of bottles, heaven knows
how many kilometres underground. In the middle of the endless
avenues, half-a-dozen slaves – sweet creatures – sat bottling and cork-
ing. Impossible to speak to them, as the odious cripple who was showing me round gave no possible opportunity for any such thing. All I
could do, as I vanished down one of the avenues, was to wave my hand

to them – and I'm glad to say they waved back.' After this, he rose to the surface of the world again, had tea on the pavement and watched the people. It was Sunday, a free day, and the streets were crowded with pedestrians, many of them hurrying off to the Musée. Why? It was impossible to discover. 'Is it snobbery or sex that drives people to look at works of art, for which, in reality they care nothing at all? A pathetic business – also a paradoxical one. The aesthetic instinct – such an intimate rarity – and making such a tremendous to-do!'

On Monday 7 September, he caught a train at Rheims station, stopped off at Châlons for an hour or two to inspect the cathedral, and then travelled on to Nancy, 'a perfect town', like a miniature rococo Bath, laid out with the most enchanting squares, all sorts of vistas, a triumphal arch or two, the most lovely gilded iron-work done by a resident bearing the propitious name of Lamour, and a delightful little park called the Pépinière, completely in the French style – regular alleys of charming trees, amateurish lawns, neat flowerbeds, a fountain, some statues. Yet, in the first hours after arriving there in the rain, his heart had shown a tendency to sink. The Grand-Hôtel in the Place Stanislas, where he had booked in, was moribund. Nothing worked; the lift never moved; the hot water was cold; even the door-key dropped to pieces. But he resolved to stay on for a few days. Perhaps tomorrow would be fine, and he might linger and loiter all over the place – in that glorious rococo square, under those triumphal arches, along the alleys in the Pépinière – and sip vermouth on the cobble-stones, and dream of Voltaire.

And so it turned out. The time slipped by very agreeably in eating, idling and walking. The only out-of-the-way episode took place over dinner on his first evening. It was one of those trivial incidents that set off Lytton's powers of acute and humorous observation in their best vein, and indicated a slowly reawakening interest in his fellow beings, still struggling with his general distaste. 'The table next to me was reserved for one,' he narrated that night in his diary. 'Presently the guest arrived – one of those thin-lipped intellectual epicures, who correspond exactly to some of our friends who interest themselves in art. Enjoyment the one thing that is *not* present. With my neighbour, the severity and pedantry of taste was carried to its most ascetic pitch. He ate his melon like a scrupulous rabbit, and then, in flawless French, entered into elaborate and distressed dissertations with the waiters. "Où est le maître d'hôtel?" etc. The French in fact was so flawless that I decided that he must be an Englishman. The clothes seemed certainly English. No decoration in the button hole. The only slightly suspicious object – and this really ought to have decided me – was a rather effeminate wrist watch. But I came to the conclusion that he must be some distinguished member of the Civil Service – one of those infinitely cultivated and embittered eunuchs who, one must suppose, govern the country, and perhaps afford the most satisfactory explanation of its present plight. But really the wrist watch ought to have shown me that I was wrong. However, at last I determined, coûte que coûte, to satisfy my curiosity. After a great deal of complicated manoeuvring of orders and counter-orders, he ate a fig. I also had figs; but before eating mine, I turned to him and said, in the most off-hand and idiomatic English style possible – "Are these all right?" I calculated that if he'd been French he would have been quite at sea. As it was, there was a moment's hesitation, and he answered, with the precise politeness that one expected. "They're excellent." The question seemed solved, and I ate my fig, which, as a matter of fact was not very good. But then doubts suddenly assailed me. Giving way to the instinct of the moment, I very rashly said– "May I ask you another question? Are you an Englishman who speaks French very well, or a Frenchman who speaks English very well?" A faint – a very faint smile – appeared (for the first and last time) and he answered "I'm Italian". This completely ruined me. The eventuality had never occurred to me; and I saw at once that he belonged to that dreariest of classes, the cosmopolitan, that he was doubtless merely a diplomat. At the same time – naturally, given his status – not the remotest sign of unbending: he coldly continued with his cigar. I had got into an impossible position – was being tacitly told that I was a tiresome intruder – and all I could do was to depart in silence as soon as I could and with whatever dim dignity I could muster.'

Three days later, Lytton went for the night to Strasbourg – a most engaging German mediaeval city, far better to be in, while it rained, than Nancy. The contrast between eighteenth-century France and mediaeval Germany was very striking. 'I'd no idea how thoroughly teutonic this town was,' he noted, 'everyone speaks German in the streets – everybody is German – the place is simply German – and how the French managed to get up such a hullabaloo about it I can't understand.'

After walking about the streets for about two hours, he was glad to get back to the Hôtel de la Maison Rouge and have a bath before dinner. What a blessing it was to be able to afford such comforts! Of course it meant as a rule, in those days of inflation, paying twelve shillings a day for one's room, instead of about eight shillings; but even so, it was well worth it. Whether these luxuries would be available very much longer remained to be seen. The inter-war depression in

England and the world at large made it seem doubtful. Following the Wall Street crash of October 1929, the blizzard of a financial crisis had sprung up from the west. That September, Britain abandoned the Gold Standard and prohibited the export of gold from the country. Unemployment rose; poverty and dissatisfaction grew; a split developed within the Government and a General Election was imminent. To avoid a slump the second Ramsay MacDonald administration had instigated what Keynes described as 'a policy of Bedlam', and public confidence in Britain's stability quickly diminished. How much longer, then, could expensive pleasures such as Lytton was treating himself to, be maintained? Surely not for long. 'All the more reason to snatch at them while one can,' he decided, '– to plunge into a hot bath immediately, before the revolution comes and all the water's permanently cold!'

The following day, he journeyed back to Nancy, and was quite pleased to get his old room again in the Grand-Hôtel, from where he could look out at the fountains and cupids and gilding of the Place Stanislas. If only, instead of motors, there had been a few elaborate and enormous coaches floundering about! But an old revolution had done for them. During this, his second three-day visit, Lytton explored the remoter and more unfashionable quarters of the town. The dingy outskirts, the smelly and decayed streets reminded him strongly of the slums of Liverpool. Yes, another revolution would, regretfully, have to come. 'France, with all her gold, seems pretty poverty-stricken,' he commented. 'The beggars here are such as I've rarely seen – they look as if they'd all sat to their fellow townsman Callot – visions of utter horror and degradation. The soldiers are uncouth rustics with red noses and (about half of them) spectacles – which doesn't seem quite the thing.'

One morning in Nancy, as he was sitting outside a café drinking a glass of grenadine and seltzer, 'my mind pleasantly blank', a passing motor slowed down and a woman, slightly fashionable in appearance and slightly familiar, too, looked in his direction, then seemed to whisper his name to her male companion. 'The motor stopped, and I automatically got up, thinking it might be Diana Cooper, but – such is my vagueness for faces – not at all sure.' Only after she had introduced her companion as Dr Rudolph Kommer – that spherical, remorselessly shaved, enigmatic 'dearest friend' – did Lytton's hesitation disappear. 'The truth was that she was looking younger,' he observed, 'more cheerful, and less like the Madonna than usual.[1] They got up and

---

[1] Lady Diana Cooper had played the role of the Madonna in Max Reinhardt's famous New York production of *The Miracle* in 1924.

insisted on my moving with them to the Café Stanislas – more expensive. There we sat for some time.' After Duff Cooper's return to London in August to be made under-secretary of state for war, Diana Cooper explained to Lytton, she had stayed on in Venice with Laura Corrigan at the marvellous Palazzo Mocenigo, enjoying the wild and festive season there and meeting many younger people who, as she put it, frolicked her along with them. Now 'she was driving back to London – with this ghastly-looking dago – an odd couple, but somehow or other not in the least compromising. But why?' Lytton questioned. 'Perhaps he was paying . . . She was very agreeable; but I had, as I always do with her, the sensation of struggling vainly to show off that I'm not a fool – mysterious, because really her own comments are very far from being out of the ordinary. K[ommer] (or C) was polite. They admired Nancy; but it was too early for lunch and they had to hurry on to catch the boat to-morrow (September 12) at Calais. They went to their car, and I then observed that there was another member of the party – a kind of chauffeur, who sat in the Dicky behind. He grinned a great deal – rather tendentiously I thought; perhaps he was K (or C's) man – in every sense – and I daresay the brightest of the three.'

Two days later, Lytton returned to Paris, putting up this time at the Hôtel Foyot. On his second day here, he wandered off to the Musée de L'Orangerie in the Tuileries, to look at an exhibition of portraits by Degas. 'The pictures were fascinating,' he wrote that evening in his diary, 'so exquisite, witty, and serious; and there were admirable sculptured studies too, in bronze. Then a stroll down the Tuileries Gardens – how supremely enjoyable it all was! My old dread and dislike of Paris melted into nothing in the shining sun. A rainbow in the fountain – the long alley beyond – the magnificent Louvre closing in the distance – nothing but radiance and exhilaration.'

The truth was that Paris had become for him a city of nostalgia, of le temps retrouvé. He went once again into the lovely Luxembourg gardens, in the brilliant morning light. The trees were beginning to turn, and he remembered that time – almost exactly twenty years ago (but at the very end of September 1911) – when he had strolled along these same happy, well-ordered avenues after his visit to Henry Lamb in Brittany, following a night journey through Nantes, and felt an extraordinary current of vitality and excitement push through him. This morning he was happy, though less excitedly so. As he walked on, he remembered, too, another curious visit, not so long ago, with Carrington, in the intense heat, when, half-dead with exhaustion, he had crept out to try and get a little air under the trees, but, not succeeding, had then limped back again to that same Hôtel Foyot where he remained in bed until Ralph came and rescued them.

Carrington and Ralph. For two weeks now he had been cut off from them both without a word of news. Meeting two old friends, Peter Morris and the artist and illustrator John Banting, in a Paris street one afternoon, he suddenly realized how he had come to miss England, and all the pleasures of Ham Spray. What kind of life had he been leading this last fortnight? A visionary one certainly, subjective and evanescent. The complete absence of letters had produced a strange vacuum round him. Yet it had been a fine relaxation, stimulating his appetite again for the rigours and complexities of human relationships, for work, and all that made up life itself. He longed to be back in England. Carrington, Ralph, Ham Spray – it would be delightful! And when the winter came, perhaps they could all set up somewhere in Africa or southern Spain. The torture of the English climate was getting past a joke now that he was over fifty, nearly fifty-two. After all, whatever happened, life could hardly be more dilatory or expensive than it was, oscillating between Hungerford and London.

And so he prepared to return home, took a final farewell of his beloved France, and made the last entry in his diary. 'Well, I must pack, and tell them to get my bill ready. I wish I was like K (or C) and had a man! But even that would impinge upon my freedom – which has been so absolute. And now it's dwindling, dwindling. The flèche d'or awaits me. I must get in and roll off – to what? – London, Ham Spray, the London Library, the Oriental, notions of work, notions of Love, R[oger], and, in short, ordinary life!'

9

THE FINAL SILENCE

For a further two months after his return to England, Lytton was able to sample the pleasures of ordinary life. There were few notions of work, but plenty of social junketings. He dined with Somerset Maugham, and with Lady Cunard, Desmond MacCarthy and Noël Coward. He met William Gerhardie and Victor Cazalet at a party given by Syrie Maugham in the King's Road,[1] and Charlie Chaplin at one of

---

[1] Syrie Maugham, daughter of Dr Thomas Barnardo the celebrated physician and philanthropist, was one of the most fashionable interior decorators of her day. In 1927 she had been divorced from Somerset Maugham, who was her second husband, her first being Sir Henry Welcome, a noted American scientist. William Gerhardie, who remembers

Ottoline's Gower Street receptions. In the country he saw 'Ros and Wog' and a good deal of the 'little Guinnesses' at Biddesden, their large country house near Andover.[1] That September, Diana Guinness had given birth to her second son and Lytton bravely went over to visit her while she was still in bed at 10 Buckingham Street. 'In those days one did not put a foot to the ground for 3 weeks after the birth,' she wrote to the author. 'I told the nurse to take the baby to her room "because Mr. Strachey can't abide babies". However, when Lytton and I were in the midst of our chatting she came in with the child in her arms and insisted on holding it practically under poor Lytton's nose. He said politely: "What a lot of hair!" To which she replied in a rather scornful way: "Oh, that will all come off." Lytton gave a faint shriek: "Is it a wig?"'

His well-known nervousness with infants had on this occasion been aggravated by the doleful sick-bed atmosphere. 'Poor dear Lytton. He had an absolute horror of sickness,' Alan Searle remarked, 'but he used to come and visit me in a nursing home when I was recovering from an operation, and used to bring me bunches of dead flowers – it had evidently taken him days to get up the courage to come.'[2]

He himself had fallen ill about this time with what was apparently just a winter fever, and despite feeling unusually 'low and dim' he could not believe it to be anything exceptional. The cure, really, was more shattering than the disease, and 'no doubt in a day or two I shall be all right again'. Before very long he did seem better, and was greatly cheered at having made everything up with Roger. The following

---

[1] Biddesden has a window painted by Carrington which depicts a girl peeling an apple. This was done by her in September 1931 as a surprise for Diana Guinness when she returned from London after having her baby.

[2] In a letter to the author (29 January 1963) Mr Searle also wrote: 'Lytton was an old friend of mine. I introduced him to Mr Maugham . . . I can tell you that Maugham and Strachey liked each other very much. We used to talk about him a great deal to his sister Madame Bussy. . . . On one occasion I gave him a number of letters that had passed between Queen Victoria and the Iron Duke, and in return he gave me a silver tea caddy that had belonged to Samuel Butler.'

---

this party, writes to the author that 'I asked Cazalet, since he knew everybody, to introduce me to the most glamorous débutante present. He confessed that as she was rumoured to be engaged to a royal duke, and was highly sought after, he must seek an appropriate moment; meanwhile fobbing me off with Lytton Strachey. When Strachey was in the heat of relating his experience of driving in a taxi into the courtyard of Buckingham Palace, and the anti-climax of being fobbed off with the king's secretary Lord Stamfordham, Cazalet came back to say that the débutante was now available, and Strachey was left mournfully alone. I never saw him again. . . . As for poor Cazalet, he crashed to death in an aeroplane accident (suspected of political sabotage) in his capacity of dispenser of affectionate reassurance to the Polish wartime leader, General Sikorski, sitting beside him.'

month, the two of them went down for a happy week-end together to Brighton, staying this time at the Bedford Hotel since 'it seemed to me rather unadventurous not to try something new'.

At the beginning of November, Aldous Huxley and his wife Maria came down to spend a week-end with him at Ham Spray. 'The Huxley visit went off quite well,' he reported to Roger (7 November 1931). 'For one thing the weather was really perfection, and they were evidently out to be agreeable – especially Maria, who hasn't quite got over her early Ottoline bringing-up. Aldous is certainly a very nice person – but his conversation tends to be almost perpetually on high levels with a slightly exhausting effect.'

This exhaustion, which came over him very easily now, he put down to 'too much wit and too little humour perhaps'. Even so, despite feeling drained of all energy, he was suffering from a restless sense of impatience – 'one of the worst cares of life!' He had little wish to work, but an overpowering urge to enjoy himself, and he rushed up to the idle and idyllic whirl of London. Dining with Clive Bell one evening shortly after arriving in Gordon Square, he complained of feeling off colour, and left early, saying that they must meet again soon when he was well. The following Friday they dined once more. This time he appeared to be better, and Clive Bell 'enjoyed one of those evenings which Lytton contrived to turn into works of art'. The next day, Saturday, accompanied by Pippa and some other relatives, he travelled down by train to Ham Spray. At Paddington he discovered by chance that Clive Bell was journeying to Wiltshire in the same coach. 'He came to see me in my compartment,' Clive Bell recorded, 'where I was alone, and we had some talk, mostly about my tussle with the Commissioners of Inland Revenue, who, as usual, were behaving disagreeably. At Reading he rejoined his party. At Hungerford I watched him walk along the platform on his way out. That was the last time I saw Lytton.'

Several of his other friends, too, were never to see him again. Shortly after his return to Ham Spray, he retreated up to his bed with what appeared to be a bad attack of gastric influenza. On 4 December, in one of his very last letters, he wrote to Roger: 'I'm sorry to say I'm still sadly pulverised – have been for some days in bed – now creep about, but in an enfeebled semi-miserable condition. I cannot feel that I'm really on the mend yet. A sudden reversion to a state of affairs that I thought had gone about 15 years ago! . . . This is a gloomy recital, I fear! – In a way particularly annoying because there doesn't seem to be anything serious the matter. Only an eternal lack of equilibrium inside. Hélas! Luckily there are a lot of books to read.'

The books with which he lightened these hours included Margaret

Kennedy's novel *Return I Dare Not* – 'mediocre' – Somerset Maugham's *The Painted Veil* – 'class II, division I' – Burns's Letters to Mrs Agnes Maclehose – 'an amusing, curious book, published in the '40's' – and Leonard Woolf's first volume of *After the Deluge* – 'on Civilization, History, Humanity, Life etc. . . I find it quite readable'. Virginia, too, had recently sent him a copy of her latest novel, *The Waves*, but he shrank from immersing himself in it. 'It's perfectly fearful,' he admitted to Topsy Lucas (4 November 1931). 'I shudder and shiver – and cannot take the plunge. *Any* book lying about I seize up as an excuse for putting it off – so at the moment I'm in the middle of Lucien Leuwen (Stendhal) – said by the French to be one of *the* masterpieces . . . well, well! —'

During the last week of November and the first two weeks of December, there were days when he seemed to start a recovery, but the general drift was downwards, and soon he was hardly able to read anything more. The attacks of diarrhoea, to which he had always been prone, became much more severe and unremitting. Although his pulse stayed remarkably steady between 100 and 120, his temperature fluctuated wildly, sometimes soaring to 104, and then tumbling down again to 96 within the space of a single day. He was able to retain practically no food, and, for week after remorseless week, could only be fed on what Carrington termed 'sparrow's food' – rusks, mashes, Benger's Food and tumblers of brandy. He lost weight and strength rapidly. For almost two months the appalling struggle went on, bringing into play all the visceral toughness of Lytton's character, his iron determination. Though no one allowed himself to consider the likelihood, he was in fact already dying, and with the help of too many physicians – at one time or another four specialists, two general practitioners and three nurses. Dr Elinor Rendel, Lytton's niece, who was not officially called in, pronounced his case to be one of typhoid, due to the 'deep well water' at Ham Spray. But his regular consultant from Hungerford, Dr Starkey Smith, appeared more doubtful. There was, he assured everyone, no cause for alarm. Nevertheless he admitted the possibility of Lytton's illness being either a bad attack of colitis or one of four groups of paratyphoid.

Meanwhile the only treatment that Lytton could be given was a strict diet and constant nursing. A trinity of professional nurses moved into the house and took it in turns to look after him. One was named Mooney, another McCabe, and the third, who had St Vitus's Dance and was as deaf as a post, Philipps. Lytton, however, made up nicknames for all three of them: Clytemnestra; Old Mother Hubbard; Mousie. Pippa had also come down to join Carrington and Ralph at Ham Spray, and the routine of a long illness now set in. The Bear Hotel at Hungerford was packed with Stracheys – Oliver, Marjorie, Pernel and many others. Frances Marshall went to live close by at Ham post office, and soon friends were coming down almost every day from London.

The brunt of the prolonged and sickening anxiety fell on Ralph, Carrington, Pippa, and James, who was there regularly over these weeks. Ralph attended to the electric light, the water supply, the fetching and carrying from Hungerford or Newbury. Carrington, who could only respond to the situation emotionally, was also, in a sense, a patient, and it was with her that Ralph felt he had to deal. Every minute she was eaten up by a terrifying dread. She would not stir beyond the garden, and avoided seeing all callers. At nights, she hardly slept at all, or if she dozed off, woke every few minutes from ghastly nightmares. 'I feel nothing as bad can happen again,' she told Mary Hutchinson. By day she would sit at Lytton's bedside, sponging his face with syringa scent or eau-de-Cologne. Whenever she left his room she would burst into tears, then fling herself into the running of the house, the cooking, even painting. Enormous glass-pictures found themselves hastily brought into the world. For hours on end Ralph, who was none too controlled himself, would talk to her and attempt to restrain her from rushing into needless panics. Pippa, much calmer than Carrington, alternated with her at Lytton's bedside, and it was she whom he probably liked to see most. As he sank deeper and deeper into his illness, his mind reverted, like Queen Victoria's, to scenes from his childhood, and these he was best able to communicate to his sister, who had nursed him through several early illnesses. She adored Lytton, and never betrayed her grief or thought of herself. Her screeching laugh, too, seemed to cheer him. Once, when his temperature had reached 104, Ralph entered the bedroom to find him weakly but coherently discussing with her the merits of McTaggart's philosophy. James, also, was a great support. Admirable in all emergencies, less alarmist than Ralph yet unexcelled by anyone except possibly Carrington in his devotion to Lytton, he sat reading detective stories by the fire when there was nothing practical to be done. His pink unruffled presence reassured Carrington. 'James is such a truthful *exact* person,' she noted, 'that I believe everything he says and Looks.'

On 9 December, the eminent bacteriologist and Physician-Extraordinary to George V, Sir Maurice Cassidy – 'very grand specialist, bluff, 50, toothe-moustache', as Carrington described him – took over the case. He was called in by Starkey Smith, who had been with him at medical school and who knew him personally. After driving down from London, he examined Lytton with great thoroughness, concluded that he was suffering from ulcerative colitis – adding that his heart, lungs and pulse were all satisfactory – and carried off with him two samples of blood. His cheerful matter-of-fact manner inspired everyone with fresh confidence. The following night, his report came through via Starkey Smith: the samples had shown nothing. At various stages over the next week he examined six more blood cultures, but they, too, proved negative. Nevertheless, he felt convinced that Lytton was suffering from some sort of enteric fever. On 17 December, Ralph took him further samples to be analysed – but with the same result. By now Cassidy's optimism had begun to ebb, and the state of affairs seemed more inexplicable and more grave than at practically any other time. On the advice of Lionel Penrose, the family also consulted Leonard Dudgeon, professor of pathology at the University of London, superintendent of the Louis Jenner Clinical Laboratory at St Thomas's Hospital, and reputed to be about the best diagnostician in the country. After the most elaborate examination, he definitely confirmed the ulcerative colitis verdict. Throughout these weeks, this diagnosis was on the whole maintained, though, round about Christmas, the possibility of paratyphoid was admitted, and everyone in the house was instructed to be very scrupulous over all forms of hygiene.

Meanwhile, Lytton continued to get steadily worse. The real danger which Cassidy and the other doctors feared was the risk of perforation, which is constantly present in enteric. The worst of this condition was that it might go on for months. It had no curve and no crisis; the danger period might be almost as lengthy as the sickness itself. The critical stage gave no warning usually of its approach, Cassidy declared, and could occur at any time, day or night, regardless of temperature or pulse or any haemorrhages. An immediate emergency operation would then become essential. Plans for this operation had already been made. If Lytton were to collapse entirely and his temperature sink well below normal, Ralph was to telephone Starkey Smith, who had instructions to summon John Ryle, the surgeon at Guy's Hospital specializing in gastro-intestinal illnesses, down to Ham Spray at once. The operation would then be performed in Lytton's bedroom. At some moment an injection of blood would be needed, not a transfusion, and Ralph was shown how to provide this. Since no anti-toxins and scarcely any treatment were then known for this complaint, nothing more could be done.

The house was submerged in ponderous gloom. Carrington and Ralph, Pippa and James were obliged to conduct an entirely defensive campaign. The continual strain reminded Ralph of the worst days of the war. 'I feel back in the trenches myself,' he wrote to Frances (13

December 1931), 'there are the same orders for the day to carry out, telephone messages from headquarters, visits from the Colonel and Staff, N.C.O.'s to question and tell to carry on with what they do infinitely better than you could, and at the back of one's mind the anxiety at night, the possibility of something unexpected being sprung upon one. I sleep as lightly as a feather. During the dark hours I breathe with only the top half of the lungs, and when I see daylight I take a deep breath and eat a hearty breakfast.'

It remained to be seen whether Lytton, with all his tenacity, could withstand the double strain of prolonged high fever and low diet. For a further week his tough constitution held out. He knew that a great deal depended upon his own efforts, and so long as there was hope of recovery he concentrated every particle of his strength and will-power upon this objective. But each day his symptoms remained unaltered or grew worse, and his strength slowly declined. He knew about the possibility of enteric, from which his cousin, Sir Arthur Strachey, had died, nursed by Pippa out in India, and the question of whether the struggle was worth continuing, of whether recovery was at all possible, must have occurred to him. The crisis came, very alarmingly, on Christmas Eve. His condition sank swiftly and he appeared to be dying. Cassidy, Ryle and an anaesthetist were sent for from London, but everyone had by this time given up hope. Everyone except Carrington. 'I simply wouldn't believe that he could be defeated,' she said, 'and I still can't.'

Then, when it appeared almost impossible that he should do so, he rallied. The doctors now decided to administer injections of a new serum. Lytton was told that if he could maintain the fight a little longer, there was every hope of his fever subsiding. He did his best. He took up the fight once more. Miraculously, by the evening he had grown a little better, and over the next few dangerous days he somehow managed to hold his own.

At the end of the year he was still maintaining this advantage, and having once escaped death so narrowly, his fight for life fired all his friends with a new spirit of hope. Describing the new year celebrations at Ipsden, Rosamond Lehmann wrote to her brother John: 'That evening was the first for a week when the feeling of being in a bad dream lifted a bit – as we had just heard that a miracle had happened and Lytton pulled round after being given up by everybody. I now feel he will live, though the danger is still acute. The bottom would fall out of the world for us if Ham Spray were no more.'

Incredibly, this slight improvement was sustained over a further fortnight. At all times Lytton was a model patient. Although always in

z*

discomfort and sometimes in pain, he never complained, but lay, day after day, without moving, eating everything he was given and swallowing his 'vile black medicines' without a murmur. His courage, constant high spirits and the undimmed clearness of his mind amazed the doctors. 'D'you know,' remarked Cassidy, 'I'd quite dote on that chap if I saw much of him.' He appreciated the awful strain his illness was imposing upon the others and strove to lighten it by his own wry and unfailing cheerfulness. He was too weak to speak very much, but towards Carrington he was especially careful to remain optimistic, always greeting her with some joke. At night he had to be given sleeping draughts and these, he claimed, induced a whole series of amusing dreams. 'I've spent the whole night skipping,' he told her one morning, 'so curious. I didn't know I could skip. It was rather delightful.'

He thought about literature all the time, not so much about people. He talked of Shelley's youth; and with deep satisfaction, he would recite lines of poetry:

Lorsque le grand Byron avait quitté Ravenne . . .

It was the music of such lines, like a river of sound, noble and slow-moving, that soothed him. But sometimes, as with Villon's unanswerable refrain, with its despairing intimations of mortality, the lines that came into his mind would have a poignant aptness to his own predicament.

Mais où sont les neiges d'antan?

He tried, also, to compose poems of his own. 'But it's so difficult, 'he sighed. 'Poetry is so very difficult.'

'Don't think about poetry,' Pippa advised him, 'it's too tiring. Think of nice simple solid things – think about teapots and chairs.'

'But I don't *know* anything about teapots and chairs.'

'Well,' replied Pippa, 'think of people playing croquet, moving quietly about on a summer lawn.'

Lytton seemed pleased. 'Ah yes, that's nice.' Then a pause. 'But I don't remember *any* reference to croquet in French literature.'

Once, in the early hours of the morning, when he was alone with the night-nurse, Clytemnestra or Old Mother Hubbard – stupid women, whose stupidity vexed him – he began trying under his breath to compose a new poem.

'Don't you weary yourself, Mr Strachey,' she commanded. '*I'll* write all the poetry that has to be written.'

There was a long silence. Then the puzzled nurse overheard two whispered words, incomprehensible to anyone who did not recognize the slang of thirty years before: 'My hat!'

The poems of these last two months Lytton transcribed, very faintly in pencil, into a small exercise book. For the most part they celebrate and expound the nature of his agnosticism, his fastidious epicurean appetite for life, his resignation to the mysterious inevitability of death, and his acceptance of things as they are – calm, incurious, inexplicable:

> *Let me not know the wherefore and the how.*
> *No question let me ask, no answer find;*
> *I deeper taste the blessed here and now*
> *Bereft of speculation, with eyes blind.*
> *What need to seek or see?*
> *It is enough to be.*
>
> *In absolute quiescence let me rest,*
> *From all the world, from mine own self, apart;*
> *I closer hold the illimitable best,*
> *Still as the final silence, with calm heart.*
> *What need to strive or move?*
> *It is enough to love.*

Love was his real religion, and he could only envisage and worship a god who would sanctify those loves which had formed the deepest and most enduring passions of his life. A puritan, Old Testament God he could neither believe in nor understand. If God was anything, God was love – actual love as he had experienced it. Another of these poems, cast in the simple and traditional mould of a prayer, is really a hymn to sexual passion and love, addressed to a personal, officially unknown god.

> *Lord, in Thy strength and sweetness,*
> *Be ever by my side*
> *Close as the foot to fleetness*
> *The bridegroom and the bride.*
>
> *Through sickness and through sadness*
> *Still let me see Thy face;*
> *Bestow upon my gladness*
> *Thy consummating grace;*
>
> *Fill with a golden clearness*
> *My crowded hours of light;*
> *And hallow with Thy nearness*
> *My most abandoned night!*

With its unexpected last line, this poem acts as a satirical mockery of the orthodox Christian concept of a God of platonic love. Yet the

agnosticism he proclaims is swept aside by the intensity of his feeling in
these final poems, especially in the last one of all.

> *Insensibly I turn, I glide*
> *A little nearer to Thy side . . .*
> *At last! Ah, Lord, the joy, the peace,*
> *The triumph and the sweet release,*
> *When, after all the wandering pain,*
> *The separation, long and vain,*
> *Into the field, the sea, the sun,*
> *Thy culminating hands, I come!*

The days passed: the position remained the same. On 6 January,
Pernel Strachey wrote from the Bear Inn at Hungerford to Lumsden
Barkway: 'We are still very anxious about Lytton though on the whole
he is better than in the Christmas week when things were almost
desperate. . . . It is really a question of whether his strength can hold out
against the high temperature – but the consultant who saw him on
Sunday after a fortnight's interval was pleased with his condition in
spite of his weakness and thought him better than when he saw him
last. But we cannot feel anything but great anxiety while he is like this.
His mind has been absolutely clear all through and his calmness most
wonderful.'

While he lay motionless in his bedroom, willing himself to live a little
longer, a little longer, letters of condolence from his friends poured in,
and these were read out to him by Pippa and Carrington. The last one
which he was able to read for himself came from Virginia Woolf. To her
friend Vita Sackville-West, she now wrote: 'I should mind it to the
end of my days if he died, but they think he may get through now. Like
all the Stracheys he has a fund of Anglo-Indian tenacity, besides which
remains perfectly calm, collected and cheerful and likes to argue about
truth and beauty – you must admit that this is admirable.'

The newspapers, too, were taking a great interest in his illness, and
Ham Spray was besieged by reporters' telephone calls until, through an
arrangement which combined the Strachey administrative common
sense with their odd quirk of humour, inventive and unreliable reports
were made up each day and issued to all newspapers through the Ham
village post office.

By the second week of January, another celebrated specialist had
been called in on the recommendation of Ottoline Morrell. This was
Sir Arthur Hurst, 'a weird little man', Carrington told the Guinnesses.
'I feel great confidence in his queer excited manner, and he looks
extremely intelligent.' Hurst, who inclined to Cassidy and Dudgeon's

original diagnosis though admitting the possibility of paratyphoid, recommended certain variations in Lytton's treatment, and said he had seen similar cases recover. And by 15 January, it actually did appear as if Lytton was getting better. Hurst confirmed this improvement. But by now Lytton had shrunk to such a shadow of himself that to those who were visiting him for the first time since November and who saw the extraordinary fragility of his appearance, worn down by weeks of illness, it seemed scarcely possible that he could ever get well again.[1] His weakness was so great that he seemed barely conscious at all; he could seldom speak, though occasionally he would murmur something about Malaga, where he wanted to go later that winter with Carrington and Ralph. The doctors, however, since they believed the ulcers to be abating, still gave every hope – if only Lytton could hold out. He tried; but the last frail fabric of stamina was already leaving him.

Three days later, his condition began to deteriorate once more. By this stage his friends and family did not know what to believe. The doctors' wavering bulletins and diagnoses filled them with uncertainty. Following the various symptoms, hour by hour, they lived on an endless switchback of alternating hope and despair. Whether there was any real chance of a cure or not, they could not tell. One new anxiety had been added to the previous ones. They had discovered from a paper Carrington had written, intended to be opened only upon her death, that should Lytton die, she meant to follow him. Ralph had not the least doubt that she was set on this course, and if allowed to, would kill herself. Who, that knew her, could doubt the violence of even the least of her desires or her absolute determination, in spite of all obstacles, to carry them out? Ralph felt certain, however, that she would choose certain ways of suicide and reject others – those, for example, which were disfiguring. James openly accused her of planning suicide, and she denied it. But her denial meant nothing. They secretly searched her studio and took away a medicine that was poisonous.

On the afternoon of Wednesday, 20 January, while Carrington was

---

[1] Visitors to Ham Spray over the final weeks of Lytton's illness were generally discouraged. Lytton himself was usually too weak to see them, and Carrington had not the heart to speak to anyone. Since everything possible was being done for him, callers or guests, however close to him, could be of no practical help and might even increase the strain within the house. Roger Senhouse, for example, did not go down at all – though this was partly because his brother-in-law was also fatally ill at the time. He exchanged many letters with Carrington, however, asking for news and trying to distract her from worrying. After Lytton's death, Carrington, who was especially fond of Roger, wrote to him: 'Darling. Nothing can be said to make anything better. But I wanted to tell you, that Lytton loved you so much always, and talked so often to me of all the happiness he had with you. You altered his Life more than anyone, and it was marvellous that his last evening with you was so completely happy. . . . Your loving Carrington.'

bathing his face, Lytton suddenly whispered: 'I always wanted to marry Carrington, and I never did.' It was not true; but he could not have said anything more moving or consoling to her. Later he fell asleep for an hour, his mouth open, and she watched him, as she had done so often, with terror in her heart, thinking that if he died, she could not live. At a quarter to three, she observed a change in his face. 'I suddenly noticed his breathing was different although he did not wake up, and I thought of the Goya painting of a dead man with the high light in the cheeK bones.' She ran out and called the nurse, who at once asked her to telephone Dr Starkey Smith and find out how much strychnine Lytton might be administered. After telephoning, Carrington rushed back and held his arm while the nurse injected thirty grains. Presently his breathing became less short, and Carrington ran off to tell James and Pippa. When Lytton regained consciousness, Pippa told him that the doctor would soon be calling again. 'I shall be delighted to see him,' he said weakly. 'But I'm afraid I shan't be able to do much socially.'

That afternoon, for the first time, Carrington gave up hope. 'It became clear to me that he could Not live,' she scrawled in *HER BOOK*. Dr Starkey Smith arrived shortly afterwards and gave him another injection. 'I saw from his face he had no hope,' Carrington noted. 'He slept without any discomfort or pain. a Hatred for nurse Philipps came on me. I cannot remember anything now except watching Lytton's pale face, and his close shut eyes lying on the Pillows. and Pippa standing by his bed.'

At four o'clock, Ralph returned from a late picnic with Gerald Brenan, whom Carrington had specially invited over to tea, saying she wished to see him. Hardly were the two of them at the door when James came out. There had been a fresh crisis, he told them, and Lytton was sinking fast. Ralph hurried in, and Gerald drove to the post office to send off telegrams, since James did not want to use the telephone in the house for fear of being overheard by Carrington. Then he motored back, went in, and sat waiting in the drawing-room. Presently he heard Carrington's low and musical voice, more exquisitely modulated, more caressing than ever. They had not met since Gerald had gone back to live in Spain. He did not feel able to look at her, but she came up behind him and took his hand.

It had been decided, in the event of a crisis occurring, to send for Stephen Tomlin. This was Ralph's idea, who was eager to mobilize anyone who might help to ensure Carrington's safety. They had got in touch with him and he was standing by. While Tommy was in the house, it was felt, she would not attempt to take her own life. It was a cruel but subtle expedient, for its success depended upon the fact of his already being so unbalanced and neurotic, so prone himself to suicide. shattered by his brother Garrow having been killed flying only the previous month, the failure of his own marriage to Julia Strachey and by all the supports in his life tottering, that Carrington's sense of responsibility would be aroused, and that she would pull herself together to attend to him. In addition to this, of course, there would be the shock of Lytton's death. Stephen Tomlin's principal relations with other people contained always a strong element of dependence. Lytton was not merely one of his closest friends; he relied, in some almost filial way, upon his existence. Carrington would have to control herself and him.

Stephen Tomlin having been sent for, Gerald drove off to Hungerford station in Ralph's car to meet him. 'He stepped out of the train looking more than usually undecided and pale and we set off in silence for Ham Spray,' Gerald Brenan recorded in his diary. 'But D.C., though apparently glad to see him, would not hear of him staying there and declared she could not understand why he had come.' So the two of them went back to the Bear Inn at Hungerford, where they sat up late, talking. 'When at last we went upstairs to bed, he asked if he might sleep in my room, since he could not face the idea of sleeping alone,' Brenan continued. 'I consented and then, instead of lying down in the other bed, to my embarrassment he got into mine and like a child that is afraid of the dark and cannot bear to be separated from others, burst into tears. It was impossible not to be touched by his misery and I regretted that I was not a young woman so as to be able to console him more effectively.'

At Ham Spray that night special watches were arranged by Lytton's bedside. Pippa was to remain there till midnight; Carrington, it was planned, would replace her until three o'clock; Ralph would then relieve her and carry on for the next three hours, until James took over for the last three. At three o'clock Carrington passed James on the landing on her way to Lytton's bedroom. Neither of them had slept. During the early part of her vigil, Carrington had asked Nurse Mooney whether there was any chance of Lytton living. She seemed surprised at the idea. 'Oh no – I don't think so now,' she said. Carrington leant over the bed and gave Lytton a kiss on his forehead: it was damp and cold. Ralph, also unable to sleep, came in with a cup of tea, and sat down by the fire. Carrington went over and kissed him too, told him she was going to her bedroom and asked him not to wake her, since, after weeks of her 'non-sleeping disease', she was worn out. James, she noticed, had gone downstairs to the front room. She walked quickly along the passage and down the back stairs.

It was half-past three. The house was very quiet, and outside the moon shone in the yard through the elm trees and across the barns. She walked over to the garage. The door was stuck fast open, and she could hardly move it. Every jerk seemed to shriek through the still night air. At last she scraped both doors closed. She got into the car, and accidentally touched the horn. 'My heart stood still, for I felt R[alph] must have heard As the laundry window was open. I stood in the yard watching for a light to go on in the passage. after some time I crept back again, and made every preparation all Ready that I could start up the car directly the milking engin started in the Farm yard.'

Then she waited, feeling very cold in her dressing-gown. Outside there was not a sound. Her plan was to stay there until half-past four, at which time every morning the farmers started up the milking-machine, the noise of which would drown the humming of the car engine. Half-past four came by the car clock, and still nobody stirred. Then she remembered it ran ten minutes fast. She went outside again and continued patiently to wait, her resolution unfaltering. At half-past five she suddenly heard sounds from across the yard, and movements in the milking-shed. She ran back to the garage, shut the door once more, and a few moments after the milking-machine had started up, switched on the car engine.

'I was terrified by the noise once it nearly stopped so I had to turn on the petrol more. There seemed no smell. I got in the back of the car and lay down, and listened to the thud of the engin below me, and the noise of the milking-machine puffing away outside. at last I smelt it was beginning to get rather thick. I turned on the light inside the car and looked at the clock only 10 minutes had gone. However Ralph would probably not come exactly at 6 ock. The windows of the car looked foggy, and a bit misty. I turned out the light again, and lay down. gradually I felt rather sleepy. and then the buzzing noise grew fainter, and further off. Rather like fainTing I remember thinking . . . I thought of Lytton, and was glad to think I shouldn'T know any more. Then I remember a sort of dream which faded away.'

Shortly before six o'clock there was yet another serious crisis in Lytton's condition. Thinking that this time he must be dying, they sent for Carrington, and when they could not find her in her bedroom, searched the house. Going out to the garage, Ralph saw her lying behind the exhaust pipe of the car, the engine still running. She was unconscious. He carried her up to her room and immediately summoned Dr Starkey Smith. Had he found her ten minutes later, she would have been dead.

The doctor gave her an injection: there was a terrible buzzing in her ears, she woke up, saw Dr Starkey Smith still holding her arm with the syringe, and cried out: 'No! No! Go away!' pushing his hand off, until he seemed to vanish 'like a cheshire cat'. Then she looked up and saw her bedroom window. It was daylight. 'I felt angry at being back after being in a very happy dream. Sorry to be awake again a Buzzing in my ears and something wrong with my eyes. I couldn'T see my hands or focus on anything.' Ralph was there. He held her in his arms, and kissed her, and said: 'How could you do it?' It had never occurred to him that she would attempt anything with Lytton still alive. She would wish, he thought, at all costs to be there at the last moment, and that was why, when Lytton was apparently on the point of death, he had gone in search of her. She had solemnly promised him not to try anything. But she must have been aware that, the moment Lytton died, she would be closely guarded, and that Stephen Tomlin, waiting a few miles away with Gerald Brenan, would be brought into the house. By some obscure train of feeling, she had hoped, through the offer of her own life, to rescue Lytton's. 'It is ironical,' she scribbled in HER BOOK, 'that Lytton by that early attack at 6 'ock saved my life, when I gave my life for his. he should give it back.'

But Lytton was not dead. Although everyone had tried to keep from him the gravity of his illness, he was not deceived. He accepted the idea of extinction with a quizzical and diminutive humour, very typical of him. 'If this is dying,' he remarked quietly, just before falling into unconsciousness, 'then I don't think much of it.'

Early that morning, Stephen Tomlin was urgently called to the house. Other friends and relatives arrived, their cars crunching backwards and forwards on the gravel. The fine frosty weather that had gone on without a break since Christmas still lasted. It was intensely still – the sort of weather Lytton had always loved. A soft golden mist lay over the green meadows and enfolded the elm trees. The sunlight, sprinkling through their branches, seemed to linger and delay, before touching the walls of the house, and streaming through the windows. It was impossible for those who waited not to contrast this beauty with Lytton dying, or to wonder what result might follow for the three, bound together in precarious balance, whom he left behind.

At midday, Carrington got up and went into Lytton's room. He was still sleeping, breathing very deeply and fast. Pippa sat near his bed. 'I went up and sat in a chair, and watched him,' Carrington wrote. '"So this is death" I kept on saying to myself. The two nurses moved about behind the screen. Ralph came, and sat on the floor I felt completely calm. His face was very pale like ivory. Everything seemed to be transfixed. The pale face of nurse MacCabe standing by his bed in her white clothes, Pippa watching with those sweet brown eyes all tear stained, her face mottled. The noise of the electric light machine outside. I sat there thinking of all the other mornings in Lytton's room. . . . It seemed as if time had lost all its properties. as if everything was marked by Lytton's breathing Not by the Ticks of the clock. Suddenly I felt very sicK, and ran out to my bedroom, and was violently sicK into the chamber Pot. . . . I went back to Lytton's room, and sat in the chair. about 1.30 Lytton grew worse, and his breathing became shorter. I stood holding Pippa round the waist. Lytton never opened his eyes. I could Not cry . . . sometimes his breathing almost stopt. But then he breathed again fainter. suddenly he breathed no more and nurse MacC. put her hand on his heart under the clothes and felt it. I looked at his face it was pale as ivory. I went forward and Kissed his eyes, and his forehead. They were cold.'

Epilogue

He first deceased, she for a little tried
To live without him, liked it NOT, and died.[1]

Final entry in *D. C. Partridge: HER BOOK*

A post-mortem, carried out at James's insistence on the afternoon Lytton died, revealed that his stomach was practically eaten up by cancer. A malignant growth had formed, completely blocking the intestine and actually making a perforation (through which food must have been passing) into the colon. From the first, he had had not the slightest chance of recovery. His body was left for a day lying on the bed. Carrington placed on his head a crown of evergreens which she had picked in the garden. He looked incredibly tired and frail, the lines of awful fatigue and infirmity frozen deeply into his face. The next day the body was removed for cremation at Golders Green,[2] and a bronze plate commemorating him was later placed in the Strachey Chapel, at the church of St Andrew, Chew Magna, in Somerset.

Meanwhile, at Ham Spray, the routine of life went on much as usual. James and Pippa having left for London, there were now, briefly, five of them staying there – Carrington, Ralph, Frances Marshall, Stephen Tomlin and Gerald Brenan. The main function of the last-named, it seemed, was to lend support to the others – to go for long walks with Ralph and to sit up late talking to Stephen Tomlin. Frances Marshall found relief to her feelings in running the house. It seemed surprising, after all that had happened, that there should still remain in these people assembled here the ordinary needs for eating, conversation, sleep. Carrington alone did not leave her room. She stayed in bed, where she would pass most of the day and night in tears. Even with the strongest sleeping draughts, she scarcely slept. The long nights which never

[1] 'Upon the death of Sir Albert Morton's wife' by Sir Henry Wotton.

[2] Apart from the functionaries, the only people present at the cremation were James Strachey and Saxon Sydney-Turner, who insisted on coming. 'There was, of course, no ceremonial of any kind,' James told the author.

seemed to end, and the days which ended all too soon, prostrated her
with grief and weariness. Tormented by hideous nightmares about
Lytton and 'terribly deformed faces cut in half', she felt each morning
as if he had died afresh: and each day his loss was harder to bear. 'I am
hot facing things,' she admitted to Rosamond Lehmann, 'I can't for a
bit . . . I find it difficult to go on with ordinary life, and I almost hate
anybody else who can . . . although I know it's unreasonable to expect
the world to stand still.'

Ralph was in and out of her room all the time. Stephen Tomlin, too,
saw her a good deal, and it was he who appeared to be the most successful in halting her from making another immediate attempt to destroy
herself. 'He persuaded me that after a serious operation, or fever, a
man's mind would not be in a good state to decide on such an important
STEP,' she wrote in *HER BOOK*. '– I agreed – So I will defere
my decision for a month or two until the result of the operation is less
acute.'

To Stephen Tomlin, also, she liked to read poetry, some of the
verses she and Lytton had shared, and especially from a favourite
Elizabethan anthology he had once given her. One short poem in this
volume, 'Misery' by Thomas Howell, she had heavily marked, turning
down the page on which it was printed.

> *Corpse, clad with carefulness:*
> *Heart, heaped with heaviness:*
> *Purse, poor and penniless:*
> *Back, bare in bitterness:*
> *O get my grave in readiness,*
> *Fain would I die to end this stress.*

On the second day after Lytton's death, Carrington asked to see
Gerald. 'I had been somewhat dreading this,' he wrote in his diary,
'for – besides the pain of seeing her in such distress – I guessed beforehand that our past estrangement, present uneasy terms and above all
the fact that in the past it was Lytton who had really come between us,
must at present make any real communication impossible. Besides we
now belonged to different countries and had no common language: she
was excessively unhappy and I was the opposite: she must feel chiefly
hate where I felt chiefly guilt, and no pretence could conceal this.

'I sat in the chair by her bed: and she began to question me about my
life, about our cottage, about Gamel; her tone was not unkind nor even
insincere, but so remote, indicating such a gulf between us, that it was
clear that no natural form of conversation was possible. I asked her
about her plans – she answered vaguely. It seemed to me that she was

cut off not merely from myself but from everyone, and that for the time being neither sympathy nor pity were acceptable.'

She wanted to suffer. Into the random, hysterical pages of *D. C. Partridge: HER BOOK*, she poured out her agonized emotions, not so that she could unburden herself of them, but so they might be set down, and reproduced in such a way that she should never permit herself to forget even the very least of them. The whole structure of her unstable life had depended on Lytton, and his disappearance took away all meaning, all purpose. 'Oh darling Lytton you are dead,' she scrawled, 'and I can tell you nothing.' The house, the fields and trees they had known and loved together meant nothing to her alone. She could not rouse herself to care about anything, could not apply her mind to anything but the living past. 'He [Lytton] was, and this is why he was everything to me, the only person to whom I never needed to lie, Because he never expected me to be anything different to what I was. and he was never curious if I did not tell him things. . . . No one will ever know the utter happiness of our life together. The absurd and fantastic jokes at meals and on our walks, over our friends – and his marvellous descriptions, and then all his thoughts he shared with me.'

Pain was the only link she still preserved with Lytton, and she could not bear the thought that she might get over her pain. To this natural affliction was added remorse – remorse imposed upon herself as a punishment for having (as she thought of it) neglected him over the last year or two for Snipe Noxall. Yet even had there been no Snipe, there must necessarily have been guilt. The result of the autopsy, which showed that Lytton's condition, even if properly diagnosed, was inoperable, had come as some slight relief to her. But guilt was threaded into her personality. Had she not felt a premonition that Lytton might die after writing that parody death-scene for *The Week-End Review*? She blamed herself, not for overt acts, but secret thoughts; for moments of depression or bitterness, and hours spent needlessly away from him in the company of others.

On all these accounts, it appeared doubtful whether she could be persuaded to continue living. Stephen Tomlin had made her promise to attempt nothing for a month or two, and he and the others hoped that, if she could be got through a few months after that, there would be many things that might help to attach her to life. But the foundation was gone, nothing could really mitigate that, and for years to come there would always be moments of depression when she might easily decide to end it. The one essential was never to allow her to be at Ham Spray by herself. Arrangements were therefore made by which she would always be surrounded by friends. When Gerald Brenan left, Julia

Tomlin came down, and the vigilant, compassionate supervision of her life went on.

Up in her bedroom Carrington would scribble out innumerable letters in a quivering, shapeless handwriting, to her friends – Barbara Bagenal, Diana Guinness, Rosamond Lehmann, Mary Hutchinson, Dorelia John and others. Many of these friends were helpful; others were less so. The unresolved problems of this desperate transitional period at Ham Spray gave plenty of scope for those who liked to find some roundabout vent for the hostile feelings which death arouses in almost everyone. A few, showing great injustice and a complete misconception of the true state of affairs, sought to blame Frances Marshall, declaring that 'but for her everything would be different'. The majority tried to insist that Carrington should at once sell Ham Spray and 'make a fresh start' elsewhere. They did not understand that, in her eyes, this would be almost tantamount to killing Lytton a second time; they could not sense the cold and melancholy consolation that the house afforded her. 'I have a longing to immesh myself in his [Lytton's] relics,' she confided in *HER BOOK*, 'that craving for death which I know he disapproved of, and would have disliked. If I could sit here alone just holding his clothes in my arms on the sofa with that handkerchief over my face I would get comfort, but I know these feelings are bad.'

Practically the only people whose company did not jar on her during these first weeks were Dorelia John, and Stephen and Julia Tomlin. Even Ralph's presence distracted her. 'No death,' he had written to Charles Prentice (11 February 1932), 'has ever hurt me more than his.' His grief and despondency, which at times were almost too much for him to bear, only made Carrington worse. He was ready to give up his entire time to her, for his position – a subject for much ambiguous rumour and concern to others – was to himself perfectly well-defined. He considered himself married to Frances in all except name, yet loved Carrington, no less deeply, as a sister. 'I cared for Carrington in a way I've never cared for anybody and I know I could never care again,' he told Rosamond Lehmann (March 1932), 'she was an obsession to me – once she got into anybody's blood she was ineradicable.' Carrington herself, though certainly jealous of Frances, probably did not want Ralph, with all the inconveniences this would entail for her, back as a husband. As for Frances, she was ready to do almost anything that would best fit in with the situation. She would not give up Ralph, but she was prepared to continue sharing him with Carrington, and to allow them, if necessary, to go on a long holiday together.

Progressively this situation grew worse. The atmosphere at Ham

Spray, brittle, full of tension, after the departure of Gerald Brenan became steadily more explosive. Ralph's very natural and unavoidable suspicions vexed Carrington, and his anxieties helped to inflame hers. Consequently his own presence by no means acted as a reliable guarantee against another suicide attempt, and it was therefore imperative that the Tomlins – or Stephen Tomlin alone – should remain in the house. Ralph was the only person who could arrange this, but he had come greatly to resent the superior power of persuasion that Carrington's former lover was exercising over her. His old irritation broke out, and he could hardly bring himself to speak to him. Stephen Tomlin's attitude, too, was not especially mollifying; and Carrington's daemon could not, even at this time of abject misery, resist playing on the bad feeling between the two of them. Nervy and irritable, Ralph's aggressiveness discharged itself daily on Stephen Tomlin who, in February, returned with Julia to London.

Any precipitate crisis that might have resulted from their departure was staved off by an invitation from Dorelia John, asking Carrington to go and spend some days at Fryern Court. It had been planned that Dorelia should afterwards come back to Ham Spray, taking the Tomlins' place there for a time. But Augustus John fell ill and she had to cancel this visit. However, she arranged with Carrington that they should all three go off on a holiday to France in the middle of March.

On her return from Fryern Court, Carrington seemed rather better. She was, it appeared, pulling herself together. In the kitchen garden at Ham Spray she made a bonfire, dropping on to it a miscellaneous collection of Lytton's personal belongings, clothes, pyjamas, and lastly his spectacles – without which no one ever saw him – and watching them vanish in the curling smoke. Her immense activity in tidying the house, in arranging books and papers, reassured everyone. The piece of waste ground under the ilex-tree and the Portugal laurels was cleared out, new trees planted, a seat put up facing the Downs. Desmond MacCarthy came down to see her, and tried to interest her in the publication of Lytton's unpublished essays and letters; and this, though premature, was a good plan. She started to read through these miscellaneous writings, and to connect Lytton's memory with the future.

Yet, inwardly, she still pined for him as before. Five weeks had passed since his death, and the period of immunity she had promised Stephen Tomlin was almost up. Still she could see no hope for the future; her existence was empty, bleak. 'Every hour some habit we had together comes back and I miss you,' she wrote to Lytton in *HER BOOK*, '– at night I dream of you in the day you are wiTH me —. I read over and over again our favourite poems but there is no one to talk about their beauty now. No use now devising surprises to please you. You were more dear to me every year – What is the use of "adventures" now without you to tell them to? It is all wrong, there is no sense in a life without you.' The good days were past, the sun had gone out, and before her stretched an eternity of dull blank skies. Lytton had been 'more completely all my life than it is possible for any person to be'. She was unfit to go on living. Nothing and no one could keep her. She was not young enough to start afresh – besides what was there to start? She had no one – not even Ralph. She was alone. Soon she would be thirty-nine. Old age, which she had always dreaded, lay before her – wrinkles, hollow cheeks, disease, feebleness, decay – things far more horrifying than death. From her Elizabethan anthology she cut out two of the beautiful stanzas which Chidiock Tichborne had written in the Tower before his execution, and pasted them into *HER BOOK*.

> *My prime of youth is but a frost of cares;*
> *My feast of joy is but a dish of pain;*
> *My crop of corn is but a field of tares;*
> *And all my good is but vain hope of gain;*
> *My life is fled, and yet I saw no sun;*
> *And now I live, and now my life is done.*

> *The spring is past, and yet it has not sprung;*
> *The fruit is dead, and yet the leaves be green;*
> *My youth is gone, and yet I am but young;*
> *I saw the world, and yet I was not seen;*
> *My thread is cut, and yet it is not spun;*
> *And now I live, and now my life is done.*[1]

On the last day of February, Carrington and Ralph, Frances Marshall and David Garnett, went over to visit some friends living not far off.

---

[1] Chidiock Tichborne (1558?–86) had joined the Babington conspirators and agreed at a meeting held in St Giles's-in-the-Fields in June 1586 to be one of six to whom the deed of killing Queen Elizabeth was specially allotted. He was seized in St John's Wood on 14 August and lodged in the Tower. At his trial on 13 and 14 September he pleaded guilty. Six days later he suffered the full penalty of the law, being disembowelled before life was extinct. But his final speech and noble demeanour before being hanged moved many to compassion, as did the pathetic letter he wrote to his wife Agnes on 19 September. In addition to the two beautiful stanzas which Carrington pasted into *HER BOOK*, there is a third one:

> *I sought my death and found it in my womb,*
> *I look'd for life and saw it was a shade,*
> *I trod the earth and knew it was my tomb,*
> *And now I die, and now I was but made;*
> *My glass is full, and now my glass is run*
> *And now I live, and now my life is done.*

While there, Carrington asked if she might borrow a gun to shoot the rabbits that were destroying her garden. Ralph was present at the time and heard her make this request, but his powers of vigilance were at an end, and he wearily accepted at face value her explanation. For six weeks, in an agony of mind night and day, he had been plotting and devising schemes to fasten her to life. The signs of improvement he thought he detected in her recently had encouraged him to relax too far. A week after this, Carrington demanded that she be left alone at Ham Spray. Ralph remonstrated with her, begged her to let him stay by her side. But she insisted, reassuring him that she was much better. In any case, she would be off with the Johns in a few days, she pointed out. Her calm and reasonable manner allayed his suspicions, and he left for London.

It may be that Ralph's actions over this final week or two – his renewed antipathy to Stephen Tomlin, his extraordinary and very untypical negligence over the gun and now his weakness in giving way to Carrington's dangerous demands – were guided by unconscious motives. Things could not go on for ever as they were. Undoubtedly, at some level, he must have longed for almost any end to these weeks of anguish, any solution to his entangled domestic and emotional problems. Carrington's manner had not, in fact, altogether taken him in. In a letter to Gerald Brenan early that March, he wrote that, while welcoming the visible signs of her improvement, he still did not trust her. She had some secret up her sleeve, he believed. And he had noticed also that she was giving away too many of her possessions.

Nevertheless, he left. And since Olive, the cook, was away with flu, for the first time since Lytton's death Carrington was alone in Ham Spray. On Thursday, 10 March, Leonard and Virginia Woolf came down to see her. Though the day itself was sparkling and sunny, the interior of the house felt bitterly cold. Carrington gave them tea, and talked a lot of Lytton, his ways, his friends. There was a look of dead pain in her great blue eyes, and she seemed, as Virginia said, 'helpless, deserted, like some small animal left'. At first she appeared calm, but there came a moment when she kissed Virginia, and burst into tears. Just before they left, Virginia asked her to come and see them in a few days, and Carrington replied: 'Yes, I will come, or not.'

Next morning she woke – as she always did now – very early, made herself a cup of tea and ate an apple. When the post came, she opened her letters and read *The Times*, which was later found crumpled up in her cupboard. Then she put on Lytton's yellow silk dressing-gown, which no one had ever known her to wear before, and took up the gun. It was nearly eight o'clock. She moved towards the window and saw, walking on the lawn below, two partridges – it would have been like her to find a joke, a bitter pun, in shooting not one of them, but herself.

She had thought out her preparations carefully. First she removed her favourite rug so that it should not be spoilt by the blood, and laid down another inferior rug in its place in such a way that it might appear that she had slipped on it. Next she turned and stood with her back to the window, facing a tall mirror in which she could see her position. Then she placed the butt of the gun on the floor and the barrel against her side. Finally she pulled the trigger.

Nothing happened.

She had forgotten to release the safety-catch. Now she did so, but this must have put her aim out, for when she pulled the trigger a second time, the gun was not pointed correctly, and the shot, though taking away part of her side, missed her heart.

The gardener had heard the noise, and coming under her window, caught what he thought was the sound of groans. He hurried to the foot of the stairs and she called out to him, said that she had slipped on the mat and asked him at once to fetch the woman who lived in the lodge at the end of the drive, and to summon the doctor. When the woman came, she repeated to her the same story and told her to telephone Ralph. To Dr Starkey Smith, she again said the same thing, and, since she was in acute pain, he injected morphia. He seemed upset – he had known her for several years – so she sent him down to get the key of the cellar and help himself to a drink. She also apologized for giving so much trouble. Although he could not examine her properly for fear of increasing the flow of blood, he saw that she was probably too seriously injured to recover.

Ralph had been to a party the night before, had slept heavily and late in his rooms at Great James Street, and was awakened by the telephone message giving him this news. David Garnett, who was sleeping up-stairs at the Nonesuch Office, luckily had his car, and drove him and Frances down. They arrived about 11 o'clock, and found Carrington lying on the floor of her bedroom where she had fallen, still conscious and, in spite of the morphia, in pain. She told them that she hated life, that she wished to die – but even this she had bungled. Then on seeing how distraught Ralph was, she changed her story, claimed that it had all been an accident, and promised him that she would try, for his sake, to live.

Partly because of these conflicting stories, there was some question in her friends' minds later on as to whether this act had been premeditated from the first. In Frances Marshall's opinion, she had never wavered.

'Nothing,' she wrote to Rosamond Lehmann, 'I do believe, would have shaken her determination.' Certainly, since Lytton died, she had been obsessed by death. Like a prisoner who earns remission through good conduct, her pretended amelioration had been a manner put on to earn for herself the opportunity she needed. No doubt, having made her preparations, the knowledge that she could do away with herself at almost any moment acted as some sort of reserve of strength. Yet there were also signs – unfinished letters, a diary filled up ahead with future appointments and so on – which seemed to indicate that she was half ready to go on living. These, however, were inconclusive. Perhaps suicide can only be premeditated up to a certain point, and Carrington did not definitely make up her mind until the last minute. Perhaps, too, since she was not an accomplished actress, she really was beginning to get over the worst of Lytton's death, and was driven to kill herself by some fear of gradually weakening intentions. Ralph was coming down to join her that evening; and the following week she was due to go off to the South of France with Augustus and Dorelia John. This day, then, was her very last opportunity. There was, too, some element of spite in her action, a wish to show those friends who had tried so diligently to nurse her back to life that they meant absolutely nothing to her. No possibility of anything resembling recompense existed for her on the wide, wide earth, since she could no longer talk with Lytton; since of all the scenes around her, of all her favourite pursuits, of whatever delighted her ear, her eye, and her understanding, his society was the vivifying soul.

As the pain increased, the doctor again injected morphia. Towards midday she became unconscious, and at a quarter-past two, she died. 'I went into the room and saw her dead,' David Garnett wrote. 'There was a very proud expression on her face.'

Presently David Garnett left and Gerald Brenan arrived to find Ralph 'scarcely able to control his feelings or speak coherently'. Alix Strachey, Carrington's oldest friend, had also come down by train and was the greatest support imaginable to the other three.

Carrington had left a letter for Ralph in which she said that she hoped he would marry Frances and have children. A long list of presents she wished given to her friends followed, and instructions that her ashes were to be buried under the Portugal laurels, with Lytton's close by, she hoped, under the ilex. Her activity in the garden, which a month ago had so heartened everyone, had therefore been the preparation for her grave. She also set aside one hundred pounds for Stephen Tomlin to design her tombstone, but Ralph suppressed this altogether, perhaps because he saw the disadvantages, so near to the house, of any monument. This letter was not produced at the inquest, held on Monday, 14 March, which found her death to have been due to a 'gun shot wound in the left side caused through accidentally slipping when holding a loaded gun in her hand'. There was no post-mortem.

Ralph and Frances, Alix Strachey and Gerald Brenan stayed on at Ham Spray until the inquest was over. 'Before they took her away, I saw her,' Gerald Brenan recorded in his diary, '– or rather the terrible changes wrought in her by death. The same hard frost, the same icy weather prevailed as when Lytton had died, seven weeks before. As I lay awake in his room – for they had put me to sleep in his bed – I could hear the rooks calling all through the night among the frozen trees. It was not possible, even by walking into the next room where her body lay, to understand it.'

Select Bibliography

There is a helpful Chronological Check List of Lytton Strachey's books and published essays at the end of Professor C. R. Sanders's *Lytton Strachey: His Mind and Art* (1957). Most of the information on which the present work is based has been taken from unpublished material, the sources of which are indicated in the text. The following miscellaneous and special studies, however, have proved useful.

Allen, B. M.: *General Gordon*. London: Duckworth, 1935.
—— *Gordon and the Sudan*. London: Macmillan, 1931.
Altick, Richard A.: *Lives and Letters*. New York: Knopf, 1965.
Annan, Noël: *Leslie Stephen: his thought and character in relation to his times*. London: MacGibbon and Kee, 1951.
Beaton, Cecil: *The Wandering Years*. London: Weidenfeld and Nicolson, 1962.
Beaverbrook, Lord: *The Decline and Fall of Lloyd George*. London: Collins, 1963.
Beddington-Behrens, Sir Edward: *Look Back – Look Forward*. London: Macmillan, 1963.
Beerbohm, Max: *Lytton Strachey* (The Rede Lecture). Cambridge University Press, 1943.
—— *Letters to Reggie Turner*, edited by Rupert Hart-Davis. London: Hart-Davis, 1964.
Bell, Clive: *Euphrosyne* (anonymously edited). Cambridge: Elijah Johnson, 1905.
—— *Old Friends: Personal Recollections*. London: Chatto and Windus, 1956.
Bell, Julian: *Essays, Poems and Letters*, edited by Quentin Bell (with contributions by J. M. Keynes, David Garnett, Charles Mauron, C. Day Lewis and E. M. Forster). London: Hogarth Press, 1938.
Bennett, Arnold: *Journals*, vol. 2, *1911–1921*; vol. 3, *1921–1928*, edited by Newman Flower. London: Cassell, 1932, 1933.
Benson, E. F.: *As We Are*. London: Longmans, 1932.

Birrell, Augustine: *More Obiter Dicta*. London: Heinemann, 1924.

Bloomfield, Paul: *Uncommon People: A Study of England's Élite*. London: Hamish Hamilton, 1955.

Boas, Guy: *Lytton Strachey* (An English Association Pamphlet). London: 1935.

Bolitho, Hector: *My Restless Years*. London: Max Parrish, 1962.

Bower-Shore, Clifford: *Lytton Strachey: An Essay*. London: Fenland Press, 1933.

Bradford, Gamaliel: *The Journal of Gamaliel Bradford, 1918–1931*, edited by Van Wyck Brooks. Boston, Mass.: Houghton Mifflin, 1933.

—— *The Letters of Gamaliel Bradford, 1918–1931*, edited by Van Wyck Brooks. Boston, Mass.: Houghton Mifflin, 1934.

Brenan, Gerald: *South from Grenada*. London: Hamish Hamilton, 1959.

—— *A Life of One's Own*. London: Hamish Hamilton, 1962.

Britt, Albert: *The Great Biographers*. New York: McGraw-Hill, 1936.

Brookfield, Frances M. : *The Cambridge 'Apostles'*. London: Pitman, 1906.

Campbell, Roy: *Light on a Dark Horse: An Autobiography 1901–1935*. London: Hollis and Carter, 1951.

Campos, Christophe: *The View of France from Arnold to Bloomsbury*. Oxford University Press, 1965.

Cannan, Gilbert: *Mendel: A Story of Youth*. London: T. Fisher Unwin, 1916.

Carver, George: *Alms for Oblivion*. Milwaukee: Bruce Publications, 1916.

Cecchi, Emilio: *Scrittori Inglesi e Americani*, revised edition. Milan: Mondadori, 1947.

Cecil, Lord David: *Max*. London: Constable, 1964.

Clemens, Cyril: *Lytton Strachey* (International Mark Twain Society, Biographical Series, No. 11). Webster Groves, Mo., 1942.

Clifford, James L. (ed.): *Biography as an Art: Selected Criticism, 1560–1960*. Oxford University Press, 1962.

Connolly, Cyril: *Enemies of Promise*, revised edition. London: Routledge and Kegan Paul, 1949.

Cooper, Lady Diana: *The Rainbow Comes and Goes*. London: Hart-Davis, 1958.

Dalton, Hugh: *Call Back Yesterday: Memoirs 1887–1931*. London: Muller, 1953.

Devas, Nicolette: *Two Flamboyant Fathers*. London: Collins, 1966.

Dobrée, Bonamy: 'Lytton Strachey', in *Post Victorians* edited by W. R. Inge. London: Nicholson and Watson, 1933.

Du Bos, Charles: *Approximations*. Deuxième Série. Paris: Editions G. Crès et Cie, 1927.

Dyson, A. E.: *The Crazy Fabric*. London: Macmillan, 1965.

Edel, Leon: *Literary Biography*, revised edition. London: Hart-Davis, 1959.

Elton, Lord: *General Gordon*. London: Collins, 1954.

Epstein, Jacob: *Let there be Sculpture*. London: Michael Joseph, 1940.

Forster, E. M.: *Goldsworthy Lowes Dickinson*. London: Edward Arnold, 1934.

—— *Abinger Harvest*. London: Edward Arnold, 1936.

—— *Two Cheers for Democracy*. London: Edward Arnold, 1951.

Fry, Roger: *Duncan Grant*. London: Leonard and Virginia Woolf, 1930.

Garnett, David: *The Flowers of the Forest*. London: Chatto and Windus, 1955.

—— *The Familiar Faces*. London: Chatto and Windus, 1962.

Garraty, John A.: *The Nature of Biography*. London: Cape, 1957.

Gerhardie, William: *Memoirs of a Polyglot*. London: Duckworth, 1931.

—— *Resurrection*. London: Cassell, 1935.

Gertler, Mark: *Selected Letters*, edited by Noel Carrington, and with an Introduction by Quentin Bell. London: Hart-Davis, 1965.

Glenavy, Beatrice: *Today We Will Only Gossip*. London: Constable, 1964.

Goldring Douglas: *The Nineteen Twenties*. London: Nicholson and Watson, 1945.

Gordon, George: *The Lives of Authors*. London: Chatto and Windus, 1950.

Gosse, Sir Edmund: *Some Diversions of a Man of Letters*. London: Heinemann, 1919.

—— *More Books on the Table*. London: Heinemann, 1923.

—— *Leaves and Fruit*. London: Heinemann, 1927.

Grant, Patrick: *The Good Old Days*. London: Thames and Hudson, 1956.

Graves, Robert: *Goodbye to all That*. London: Cape, 1929.

Guiguet, Jean: *Virginia Woolf* (translated by Jean Stewart). London: Hogarth Press, 1965.

Hamnett, Nina: *Laughing Torso*. London: Constable, 1932.

Harrod, Roy: *The Life of John Maynard Keynes*. London: Macmillan, 1951.

Hassall, Christopher: *Rupert Brooke: A Biography*. London: Faber, 1964.

House, Humphry: *All in Due Time*. London: Hart-Davis, 1955.

Huxley, Aldous: *Crome Yellow*. London: Chatto and Windus, 1921.

—— *On the Margin*. London: Chatto and Windus, 1923.

Iyengar, K. R. Srinivasa: *Lytton Strachey: A Critical Study*. London: Chatto and Windus, 1939.

John, Augustus: *Chiaroscuro: Fragments of Autobiography*. London: Cape, 1952.

Johnson, Edgar: *One Mighty Torrent*. New York: Stackpole Sons, 1937.

Johnstone, J. K.: *The Bloomsbury Group*. London: Secker and Warburg, 1954.

Kallich, Martin: *The Psychological Milieu of Lytton Strachey*. New Haven, Conn.: Yale University Press, 1961.

Kendall, Paul Murray: *The Art of Biography*. London: Allen and Unwin, 1965.

Keynes, John Maynard: *Essays in Biography*. London: Macmillan, 1933.

—— *Two Memoirs*, with an Introduction by David Garnett. London: Hart-Davis, 1949.

Kingsmill, Hugh: *The Table of Truth*. London: Jarrolds, 1932.

—— *The Progress of a Biographer*. London: Methuen, 1949.

Köntges, Günther: *Die Sprache in der Biographie Lytton Stracheys*. Marburg: Hermann Bauer, 1938.

Lawrence, D. H.: 'None of That', in vol. 3 of *The Complete Short Stories* (Phoenix Edition). London: Heinemann, 1955.

—— *Women in Love*. London: Martin Secker, 1920.

—— *Selected Letters*, edited by Aldous Huxley. London: Heinemann, 1932.

—— *Collected Letters*, 2 vols., edited by Harry T. Moore. London: Heinemann, 1962.

Lea, F. A.: *The Life of John Middleton Murry*. London: Methuen, 1959.

Lehmann, John: *The Whispering Gallery*. London: Longmans, 1955.

—— *I am My Brother*. London: Longmans, 1960.

Leslie, Seymour: *The Jerome Connexion*. London: John Murray, 1964.

Lewis, Percy Wyndham: *The Apes of God*. London: Nash and Grayson, 1930.

—— *Self-Condemned*. London: Methuen, 1954.

Lunn, Sir Arnold: *Roman Converts*. London: Chapman and Hall, 1924.

MacCarthy, Sir Desmond: *Memories*. London: MacGibbon and Kee, 1953.

Mais, S. P. B.: *Some Modern Authors*. London: Grant Richards, 1923.

Martin, Kingsley: *Father Figures: A Volume of Autobiography*. London: Hutchinson, 1966.

Marwick, Arthur: *Clifford Allen: The Open Conspirator.* Edinburgh: Oliver and Boyd, 1964.

Maurois, André: *Aspects of Biography.* Cambridge University Press, 1929.

—— *Poets and Prophets.* London: Cassell, 1936.

Mirsky, Prince D. S.: *The Intelligentsia of Great Britain.* London: Gollancz, 1935.

Moore, G. E.: *Principia Ethica.* Cambridge University Press, 1903.

—— *Ethics.* London: Williams and Norgate, 1911.

Moore, Harry T.: *The Intelligent Heart: The Story of D. H. Lawrence.* London: Heinemann, 1955.

Morrell, Lady Ottoline: *Ottoline: The Early Memoirs of Lady Ottoline Morrell 1873–1915;* edited and with an introduction by Robert Gathorne Hardy. London: Faber, 1963.

Mortimer, Raymond: *Channel Packet.* London: Hogarth Press, 1948.

—— *Duncan Grant.* Harmondsworth: Penguin, 1948.

Muir, Edwin: *Transition.* London: Hogarth Press, 1926.

Nathan, Monique: *Virginia Woolf* (translated by Herma Briffault). New York: Grove Press, 1961.

Nehls, Edward: *D. H. Lawrence: A Composite Biography.* 3 vols. Madison, Wis.: University of Wisconsin Press, 1957–59.

Nicolson, Sir Harold: *Tennyson.* London: Constable, 1923.

—— *Some People.* London: Constable, 1927.

—— *The Development of English Biography.* London: Hogarth Press, 1933.

Olivia (pseudonym of Dorothy Bussy): *Olivia.* London: Hogarth Press, 1949.

Oman, Charles: *On the Writing of History.* London: Methuen, 1939.

Pearson, Hesketh: *Modern Men and Mummers.* London: Allen and Unwin, 1921.

—— *Ventilations.* Philadelphia, Pa.: Lippincott, 1930.

—— *Thinking it Over.* London: Hamish Hamilton, 1938.

—— 'About Biography' (The Tredegar Memorial Lecture, 1955); included in *Essays by Divers Hands, Being the Transactions of the Royal Society of Literature,* vol. xxix, 1958.

Pippett, Aileen: *The Moth and the Star: A Biography of Virginia Woolf.* Boston, Mass.: Little, Brown, 1955.

Plomer, William: *At Home.* London: Cape, 1958.

Quennell, Peter: *The Singular Preference.* London: Collins, 1952.

—— *The Sign of the Fish.* London: Collins, 1960.

Quiller-Couch, Sir Arthur: *Studies in Literature.* Second Series. Cambridge University Press, 1927.

Raleigh, Sir Walter: *Letters 1879–1922*, edited by Lady Raleigh. London: Methuen, 1926.

Rantavaara, Irma: *Virginia Woolf and Bloomsbury*. Helsinki: Annales Academiae Scientiarum Fennicae, Series B, tom. 82, 1, 1953.

Raymond, John: *England's on the Anvil*. London: Collins, 1958.

Reddie, Cecil: *Abbotsholme 1889–1899, or, Ten Years' Work in an Educational Laboratory*. London: G. Allen, 1900.

Robertson, Graham: *Letters from Graham Robertson*, edited by Kerrison Preston. London: Hamish Hamilton, 1953.

Roosevelt, Eleanor: *This is My Story*. London: Hutchinson, 1937.

Rothenstein, John: *Modern English Painters*, 2 vols. London: Eyre and Spottiswoode, 1952, 1956.

—— *Summer's Lease*. London: Hamish Hamilton, 1965.

Rothenstein, William: *Men and Memories*, 2 vols. London: Faber, 1931, 1932.

Russell, Bertrand: *Portraits from Memory*. London: Allen and Unwin, 1956.

—— *The Autobiography of Bertrand Russell 1872–1913*. London: Allen and Unwin, 1967.

Rutherston, Albert: *Contemporary British Artists: Henry Lamb*. London: Benn, 1924.

Sanders, Charles Richard: *The Strachey Family 1558–1932*. Durham, N.C.: Duke University Press, 1953.

—— *Lytton Strachey: His Mind and Art*. New Haven, Conn.: Yale University Press, 1957.

Sassoon, Siegfried: *Siegfried's Journey*. London: Faber, 1945.

Scott-James, R. A.: *Lytton Strachey* (Writers and their Work, No. 65). London: Longmans, 1955.

Sherburn, George: *Selections from Alexander Pope*. New York: Thomas Nelson and Sons, 1929.

Simson, George Kuppler: 'Lytton Strachey's Use of his Sources in *Eminent Victorians*': a thesis submitted to the Faculty of the Graduate School of the University of Minnesota (unpublished), 1963.

Sitwell, Edith: *Taken Care Of*. London: Hutchinson, 1965.

Sitwell, Sir Osbert: *Laughter in the Next Room*. London: Macmillan, 1949.

Spender, Stephen: *World within World*. London: Hamish Hamilton, 1951.

Squire, Sir John: *Books Reviewed*. London: Hodder and Stoughton, 1922.

Stansky, Peter, and Abrahams, William: *Journey to the Frontier: Julian*

Bell and John Cornford: their lives and the 1930s. London: Constable, 1966.

Stein, Gertrude: *The Autobiography of Alice B. Toklas*. London: John Lane, 1933.

Stephen, Adrian: *The 'Dreadnought' Hoax*. London: Leonard and Virginia Woolf, 1936.

Stone, Wilfrid: *The Cave and the Mountain*. A Study of E. M. Forster. Oxford University Press, 1966.

Strachey, Julia: *Cheerful Weather for the Wedding*. London: Leonard and Virginia Woolf, 1932.

Strachey, Lytton: *Landmarks in French Literature*. London: Williams and Norgate, 1912.

—— *Eminent Victorians*. London: Chatto and Windus, 1918.

—— *Queen Victoria*. London: Chatto and Windus, 1921.

—— *Books and Characters: French and English*. London: Chatto and Windus, 1922.

—— *Pope* (The Leslie Stephen Lecture). London: Cambridge University Press, 1925.

—— *Elizabeth and Essex: A Tragic History*. London: Chatto and Windus, 1928.

—— *Portraits in Miniature and Other Essays*. London: Chatto and Windus, 1931.

—— *Characters and Commentaries* (with a preface by James Strachey). London: Chatto and Windus, 1933.

—— *Spectatorial Essays* (with a preface by James Strachey). London: Chatto and Windus, 1964.

> This volume contains thirty-five of the essay-reviews that Lytton wrote for the *Spectator*, less than half of his total contributions to that paper. The essays in *Books and Characters*, *Portraits in Miniature* and *Characters and Commentaries* have been regrouped into two volumes in the Chatto and Windus Uniform Edition of the Collected Works of Lytton Strachey: *Biographical Essays* and *Literary Essays*, both first published in 1948.

Strachey, Lytton, and Fulford, Roger (editors): *The Greville Memoirs*, 8 vols. (Joint editors: Ralph and Frances Partridge.) London: Macmillan, 1937–38.

Strachey, Lytton, and Woolf, Virginia: *Virginia Woolf and Lytton Strachey: Letters*. London: Chatto and Windus, 1956.

> This volume has several cuts, deletions of names, and omissions of whole letters. The present biographer has had access to the full correspondence.

Strachey, St Loe: *The Adventure of Living*. London: Nelson, 1922.

Swinnerton, Frank: *The Georgian Literary Scene*. London: Dent, 1938; rev. ed. 1951.

—— *Figures in the Foreground: Literary Reminiscences 1917–40*. London: Hutchinson, 1963.

Thurston, Marjorie: 'The Development of Lytton Strachey's Biographical Method': a dissertation submitted to the Graduate Faculty of the University of Chicago (unpublished), 1929.

Toklas, Alice B.: *What is Remembered*. London: Michael Joseph, 1963.

Trevelyan, G. M.: *Autobiography and Other Essays*. London: Longmans, 1949.

Trevor-Roper, Hugh: *Historical Essays*. London: Macmillan, 1957.

Trilling, Lionel: *E. M. Forster: A Study*. London: Hogarth Press, 1944.

Unwin, Sir Stanley: *The Truth about a Publisher*. London: Allen and Unwin, 1960.

Warburg, Frederic: *An Occupation for Gentlemen*. London: Hutchinson, 1959.

Webb, Beatrice: *My Apprenticeship*. London: Longmans, 1926.

—— *Our Partnership*. London: Longmans, 1948.

Wilson, Edmund: *Axel's Castle: A Study in the Imaginative Literature of 1870–1930*. New York: Charles Scribner's Sons, 1931.

—— *The Shores of Light: A Literary Chronicle of the Twenties and Thirties*. London: W. H. Allen, 1952.

Wood, Alan: *Bertrand Russell: The Passionate Sceptic*. London: Allen and Unwin, 1957.

Woolf, Leonard: *Sowing: An Autobiography of the Years 1880–1904*. London: Hogarth Press, 1961.

—— *Beginning Again: An Autobiography of the Years 1911–1918*. London: Hogarth Press, 1964.

—— *Downhill All the Way: An Autobiography of the Years 1919–1939*. London: Hogarth Press, 1967.

Woolf, Virginia: *The Voyage Out*. London: Duckworth, 1915.

—— *Jacob's Room*. London: Hogarth Press, 1922.

—— *The Waves*. London: Hogarth Press, 1931.

—— *A Writer's Diary*. London: Hogarth Press, 1953.

—— *Roger Fry*. London: Hogarth Press, 1940.

—— *The Death of the Moth and Other Essays*. London: Hogarth Press, 1942.

—— *Granite and Rainbow*. London: Hogarth Press, 1958.

Young, G. M.: *Victorian England: Portrait of an Age*. Oxford University Press, 1960.

Index

AA*